Psychology

third edition

Mike Cardwell
Liz Clark
Claire Meldrum

Collins

An imprint of
HarperCollins*Publishers*

Published by Collins
An imprint of HarperCollins*Publishers*
77–85 Fulham Palace Road
Hammersmith
London W6 8JB

Browse the complete Collins catalogue at
www.collinseducation.com

Psychology for A Level first published 1996
Second edition published 2000
This edition first published 2004

Reprint 10 9 8 7 6 5 4 3 2

ISBN-13 978 0 00 717043 2
ISBN-10 0 00 717043 2

Mike Cardwell, Liz Clark and Claire Meldrum assert their
moral rights to be identified as the authors of this work.

British Cataloguing in Publication Data.
A cataloguing record for this publication is available from
the British Library.

Commissioned by Thomas Allain-Chapman
Project managed and edited by Sarah Clarke and
    Hugh Hillyard-Parker
Cover design/internal design template by Blue Pig Design,
    Essex
Typesetting by Hugh Hillyard-Parker and Liz Gordon
Illustrations by Mike Parsons, Barking Dog Art (Units 1 to 8)
    and Oxford Designers and Illustrators (Units 9 to 32)
Picture research by Suzanne Williams and Thelma Gilbert
Index compiled by Fiona Barr and Christine Boylan
Photo treatment by Pip Blakemore, Design Study, Norfolk
Production by Sarah Robinson and Hilary Quantrill
Printed and bound by Printing Express, Hong Kong

You might also like to visit:

www.harpercollins.co.uk
The book lover's website

Acknowledgements

From planning to execution, this book has taken much
patience to produce. Acknowledging the part played by all
those people that have selflessly allowed us the space to
work and provided the vital practical and emotional support
over those long months never seems sufficient, but here goes.

Mike Cardwell would like to thank Denise for putting up
with the grumpy old man who sits in the study night after
night. She is, as one colleague put it, quite clearly a saint.
Ultimately, it is the achievements of our children that make us
most proud, and Chris, a fine photographer, and Alex, now a
psychologist in her own right, do that in abundance.

Liz Clark would like to thank Charley for his loving support
and considerable patience throughout, particularly when
everything has taken me at least three times longer than
predicted – 'I promise it's nearly finished' has been a
constant refrain over the last five months! My parents and all
the rest of my family also deserve a special mention for being
so understanding about the impact of this project on family
time that can never be regained.

As always, *Claire Meldrum* thanks Stuart for his unstinting
support and encouragement and, of course, the preparation
of food and pouring of wine so essential to keep the spirits
up during such a project. Thanks are also due to her
colleague, Vivien Kitteringham, for constructive comments
about the previous edition of the book and to the students at
Notre Dame High School in Norwich whose frank remarks
about 'boring books with no colour' certainly help
concentrate the mind!

The editors would also like to thank the staff at Collins,
particularly Sarah Clarke who has lived, breathed and,
probably also, dreamed about this textbook for as long as she
can remember. Sarah always manages to come up with ever
more creative solutions to all those seemingly impossible
challenges that we throw at her. Also, Thomas Allain-
Chapman for his support, guidance and wise counsel.

Finally, we simply cannot believe our continuing good fortune
that Hugh Hillyard-Parker, who is responsible for the book's
editorial production, is still working with us on this third
edition. Any lesser mortal would have given up years ago, but
Hugh continues to live up to his reputation of achieving the
unachievable, and while everyone around him becomes
increasingly stressed and bad tempered, he calmly delivers
nicely designed page after page after page... solving a host of
problems along the way.

We are indebted to you all.

Mike Cardwell, Liz Clark and Claire Meldrum
April 2004

Contents >> Psychology third edition

PSYCHOLOGY FOR AS-LEVEL

PSYCHOLOGY FOR A2-LEVEL

Note: the second, smaller numbers in this list are the equivalent page
numbers of units and topics in Collins *Psychology for A2-level.*

Mike Cardwell is Senior Lecturer in Psychology at Bath Spa University College, where he teaches courses in social psychology, and a Senior Examiner for a major awarding body. Mike is an experienced author, an Editor of the journal *Psychology Review*, and a regular contributor to student conferences. Away from all this he avidly follows the fortunes of his hometown football teams, Premier League Liverpool, and Marine of the Unibond League.

Although a psychologist at heart, *Liz Clark* has worked in nurse education since 1985. She is currently Head of Distance Learning (DL) at the Royal College of Nursing, where she is responsible for developing and delivering DL courses for qualified nurses, in addition to developing bite-sized chunks of online learning. Her experience of creating highly accessible, interactive learning resources influenced the original ideas and vision behind the first edition of this book.

Claire Meldrum teaches part-time at Notre Dame High School, Norwich. She has over 20 years of experience teaching psychology on A-level, degree, and 'Access to Higher Education' courses. She has also been an A-level psychology examiner and has written *Instant Revision AS Psychology* and been a co-author on *Do Brilliantly AS Psychology*. Claire also acts as a consultant for the National Extension College and, when time and weather allow, she enjoys gardening, the theatre and cinema.

Roger Cocks is a Senior Lecturer in psychology at University College Worcester. He is a Chartered Educational Psychologist and his specialist teaching areas are abnormal psychology, learning theory and perception. He has an interest in teaching using new technology and has contributed to the development of supplementary CD-ROM resources for well-known psychology textbooks. His interests include squash, swimming, tennis and golf with a little gardening on the side.

Graham Davies is a lecturer at Eastbourne College of Arts and Technology and has been Senior Examiner and Principal Moderator for a major awarding body. He remains one of the team of Regional Coursework Advisers. Graham has written various journal articles and has been a speaker at a number of psychology conferences. He is an Honorary Life Member and former Chair of the Association for the Teaching of Psychology, for whom he edited the journal *Teaching Psychology* for some years.

Cara Flanagan is a Senior Examiner for a major awarding body and a freelance academic author, having written extensively for psychology A-level. Her books include the Letts' *A-level Revision Guides* and *Psychology AS and A2: The Complete Companion* written with Mike Cardwell. She contributes regularly to *Psychology Review* and speaks at many student conferences and teacher courses.

Simon Green is Head of the School of Psychology at Birkbeck College, University of London. He is a Senior Examiner for a major awarding body. He is the author of *Principles of Biopsychology* and a contributor to several other psychology books. Simon has also written articles for a number of journals, including the *Psychology Review*. His main interest is finding better ways of managing stress.

Paul Humphreys is Senior Lecturer in Psychology at University College Worcester. His research interests include social relationships, sexualities, psychology and the media, and (ab)normality. He is a Senior Examiner for the new A2 examination for a major awarding body. Paul is the author of several books and has Honorary Life Membership of the Association for the Teaching of Psychology for his services to psychology. Paul also has Chartered Psychologist status with the British Psychological Society.

Pamela Prentice is Programme Manager for Humanities at Filton College, Bristol. She teaches A-level psychology and counselling up to HND level, and is an experienced A-level examiner and moderator. She served five years on the committee for the ATP and two years on the BPS committee for the Division for Teachers and Researchers in Psychology. Her background, prior to teaching, was as a Counselling Psychologist with the NHS. She has written a number of articles for *Psychology Review*.

Jane Willson is Director of Studies for the A-level programme at City College, Norwich. She has many years' teaching experience in schools and FE colleges and currently teaches psychology at A-level, access and degree level. She is a senior team leader for one of the major examining boards in psychology A-level and has written chapters for several psychology text books.

Alison Wadeley is Senior Lecturer in Psychology at Bath Spa University College. She taught psychology GCSE, AS- and A-level psychology for 20 years and has many years' experience as an examiner for a major awarding body. Alison has published a number of textbooks and revision guides ranging from GCSE to undergraduate-level psychology. She is a commissioning co-editor for *Psychology Review* to which she also contributes regular articles.

Lance Workman is Principal Lecturer in Psychology at Bath Spa University College. His research interests include the evolution of cerebral lateralization and its relationship to human emotion and language and development in animals. He is also interested in clinical issues and supervises postgraduate research on brain injury, depression and autism. Lance regularly works in the media appearing on radio, television and in national newspapers explaining and discussing psychological principles. He also co-authored *Evolutionary Psychology* (2004) with Will Reader.

WHAT IS PSYCHOLOGY?

<< Psychology, like all other sciences, can be misapplied. But, rightly used, psychology can make an immense contribution to human happiness .>> (Rex and Margaret Knight 1959, p. 264)

Psychology is the scientific study of behaviour and mental processes (the mind), and psychologists are interested in every aspect of behaviour and every type of mental process.

You may have come across the comment that 'psychology is just common sense'. Be assured, it is much more than that! Of course, sometimes psychology reinforces what people call 'common sense' or 'gut feelings' (intuitions). For example, most people believe that children who are raised in warm, loving families are best placed to be warm and loving parents in their turn. Psychologists carrying out research in this area have confirmed this 'common sense' view. However, psychological research sometimes produces results that are not what you would expect. That is, the findings are what are called 'counterintuitive'. Who, for example, would have predicted that during a memory experiment, 65 per cent of participants would obey a stranger who asked them to give electric shocks of 450 volts to a mild-mannered man who had earlier complained of heart trouble? Certainly, none of the people (including psychologists) whom the researcher, Stanley Milgram, asked before he carried out his research! Common sense predicted that the vast majority of people would refuse to give anything but the mildest shocks, but common sense was wrong. Milgram's research is discussed in detail in Unit 5, on pp. 171–5.

The important point to remember is that psychology bases its claims on research evidence, not guesses or mere anecdotes. Of course, the quality of the evidence offered by psychologists varies and one of the things you will be better able to do by the end of your AS course is evaluate (judge) just how convincing the evidence being offered is.

Note, also, that so-called common sense may be neither sensible nor consistent. Common sense proverbs often contradict each other. If 'many hands make light work', why also may 'too many cooks spoil the broth'? If common sense says 'absence makes the heart grow fonder', how do we reconcile this with 'out of sight out of mind'?

THE GOALS OF PSYCHOLOGY

Sometimes myths masquerade as common sense and one important goal of psychology is to clarify what is myth and what is reality. Take the common sense adage 'spare the rod and spoil the child'. Psychological research has played a significant role in demolishing the myth that only by using regular punishments could parents raise well-behaved children or teachers instil diligence in their pupils. Owing to the research of psychologists such as Skinner (Unit 4, p. 134), we know that rewarding desirable behaviour is more important for learning than punishing what is undesirable.

In order to distinguish myth from reality and to understand human behaviour better, psychology sets out to describe, explain, predict, and (where appropriate) change or control behaviour.

- *Describing behaviour* – The first step to understanding behaviour is to describe it accurately. For example, if we wish to find out whether boys are more physically aggressive than girls, we must first describe exactly what we mean by 'physical aggression'. Once we have a precise definition, we can begin to observe whether there is any difference in levels of physical aggression between boys and girls.

- *Explaining behaviour* – The next step in understanding behaviour is to explain why it occurs, that is, to understand what causes it. Psychologists often start with a theory (hypothesis) about an observed behaviour and then test to see if there is evidence to support their theory. For example, our hypothesis could be: 'Boys are more physically aggressive than girls because boys are rewarded more often than girls for physically aggressive behaviour.' To test this, we might carry out an observation study in a school to see if boys do indeed receive more reinforcement than girls for their aggressive acts.

- *Predicting behaviour* – After describing and explaining a behaviour, psychologists will often try to predict when that behaviour is likely to occur. For example, we know that lacking a sense of control is associated with so-called stress symptoms such as migraine and gastric ulcers. We might predict, therefore, that people whose work is monotonous, repetitive and regulated by others will be more likely to have high rates of absenteeism than people whose job allows them some freedom to organize their work. Unit 3 looks in more detail at causes of stress.

- *Changing/controlling behaviour* – Under certain circumstances it may be desirable to modify behaviour. Take, for example, the case of someone who suffers from a life-threatening eating disorder, such as anorexia nervosa. Although some treatments for this condition are controversial, there are therapists who work with anorexic people to help them overcome their disorder and adopt healthier eating behaviours. See Unit 4 for more information on eating disorders.

APPROACHES IN PSYCHOLOGY: HOW PSYCHOLOGISTS TRY TO ACHIEVE THEIR GOALS

People have always been interested in how the mind works and what causes behaviour. The roots of modern psychology go back to the ancient Greek philosophers of the 4th and 5th centuries BC. However, it was only towards the end of the nineteenth century that psychology became established as a branch of knowledge (discipline) in its own right when Wilhelm Wundt (1832–1920) began the first experimental psychology laboratory in the University of Leipzig in Germany. Since then, many different approaches (perspectives) have been developed in psychology. Some of the most important current approaches are:

- *Psychoanalysis* – This approach developed from the work of Sigmund Freud (1856–1939). The term 'psychoanalysis' relates to both the theory that much of our behaviour is motivated by unconscious thoughts, and to the therapy that Freud developed for treating neurotic conditions. In the course of treating psychiatric patients, Freud became convinced that adult problems often have their origins in early experiences, particularly those that occur during the first five years of a person's life. To help people gain access to the unconscious mind, Freud developed a number of psychoanalytic techniques, including dream interpretation and free association. By these means, he sought to uncover unconscious conflicts, help people understand their causes and come to terms with their problems. You will read all about Freud's work and ideas in Unit 4 (see pp. 130–3).

- *Behaviourism* – Behaviourism dates from 1913 when John Watson (1878–1958) stated that psychologists should concentrate on observable behaviour instead of mental processes. However, its roots stretch back to the Russian physiologist, Ivan Pavlov (1849–1936), famous for his work in conditioning animals (see Unit 4, p. 133). Behaviourism had a profound effect on psychology for about 50 years and some of its basic ideas remain important in contemporary psychology. For example, one important legacy from the behaviourist approach is the scientific concept of an 'operational definition', a precise statement of how a concept (such as aggression – see above) is measured. You will learn more about the importance of operational definitions when you come to Unit 7 (p. 225).

- *Social learning theory* – In the 1960s social learning theorists such as Bandura demonstrated that sometimes learning was possible without the need for reinforcement (being rewarded for a behaviour). All that was needed was the chance to observe the behaviour of others. This observational learning was called imitation or modelling.

- *The cognitive approach* – Cognitive psychology concentrates on the mental processes that people use to acquire, store, retrieve and use the knowledge they have about the world. This approach arose as a reaction against the narrow view taken by behaviourists, which concentrated solely on observable behaviour and neglected complex activities like perceiving, remembering and planning. In Unit 1, you will come across the cognitive approach in the study of human memory.

- **The physiological (biological) approach –** Physiological psychologists believe that to describe and explain human behaviour and experience we need to look closely at human biology. For example, how do different areas of the brain contribute to behaviours? In Unit 3, you can read about the physiological response to stress, while Unit 4 discusses the biochemical explanations for eating disorders.

- **The evolutionary approach –** The evolutionary approach also emphasizes the importance of biological factors. Its starting point is Darwin's theory of evolution: that processes of natural selection have shaped human behaviour and experience. According to evolutionary psychology, individuals should act to maximize their own and their relatives' chances of reproducing (called 'inclusive fitness'). While this approach has become popular in recent years, many people criticize it.

USING THE BOOK

This book aims to provide a detailed coverage of all aspects of the AS- and A-level psychology courses offered by the Assessment and Qualifications Alliance (AQA), Specification A.

Since the first edition of *Psychology for A-Level* in 2000 there have been some modifications to the AS- and A-level specification. This new edition matches the revised specification and introduces a number of new features, as well as a full-colour design with many new pictures and illustrations.

As before, the contributing authors are all teachers and/or examiners of psychology, and so have a clear understanding of the needs of students. Our aim is to make the study of psychology informative and fun, and to prepare you thoroughly for the exams that you will take at the end of this part of your course.

Key features

The book provides the usual features you would expect to find in any textbook. There is an *Index*, a comprehensive list of *References* and a *Glossary*, which includes specification and exam terms. The additional features within each unit make it easy to use and to relate to the requirements of the AQA specifications. These include the following:

- A *Preview* at the start of each unit and a *Unit summary* at the end to enable you to check quickly the topics covered.

- *Getting you thinking...* provides a way in to new topics, designed to help you engage with new ideas before getting to grips more closely with the technical issues or terms involved.

- *Key terms* and *Key concepts* that you may need to define or explain are listed and boxed at the start of each topic. These should prove extremely useful when you are preparing for your exam.

- *Activities*, within each topic, help you test your knowledge, apply psychological findings, carry out practical exercises and discuss ethical implications.

- *Key research* within topics is clearly laid out in highlighted form (it is always set against a green panel). For the AS-level units (1 to 5), *Key studies* are clearly laid out in the form that will help you tackle those AQA questions that ask you to describe aims,

procedures, findings, conclusions and criticisms of research (so-called 'APFCC' questions). Many of the key studies feature an AO2 check 'magnifying glass' which is designed to help you consider how to evaluate criticisms of studies when answering AO1+AO2 questions.

- Frequent *diagrams*, *tables* and *pictures* help make the psychological material even more accessible.

- A *Check your understanding* feature at the end of each topic will help you review what you have just read and help you pinpoint any areas of the topic you need to revisit.

- *Expert interviews* – A number of distinguished psychologists have provided us with their own views about some of the important areas within psychology. Who better to comment on the effects of stress on the immune system, for example, than the leading researcher in the field, Professor Janice Kiecolt-Glaser? The interviews in Units 1 to 7 are specifically aimed at helping you deal with the demands of the 18-mark questions in your AS psychology exam.

- At the end of each topic, we have included a *Revision summary* that is focused on the exact requirements of exam questions appropriate to that topic area.

There are other features specific to the AS-level and A2-level units:

- In Units 1 to 7, for certain topics, *An eye on the exam* provides an examiner's commentary on key issues when answering questions in this area.

- Unit 8, *Preparing for the AS examination*, has been expanded to include focused advice on answering the different styles of exam questions, together with a full sample exam paper with answers and examiner comments.

- In Units 9 to 21, you will find *AO2 Commentary* and *Evaluation* panels. A unique feature of this textbook, they have been introduced in the light of teaching and examining experience. These sections clearly highlight material that might be used as the basis of AO2 commentary on a particular topic, helping you to develop your own commentary and evaluation skills, revise effectively and gain maximum marks in the exam.

- *Example exam questions* feature at the end of each topic at A2-level, with examiner's guidance and tips on issues to concentrate on when answering questions in this area.
- Unit 32 *Preparing for the A2 examination* has been fully expanded to give advice on answering the different styles of question, with a focus on how to approach the AO2 answers. A sample answer is also included and discussed.

The specifications and the exams

The AQA (A) A-level course is organised into six modules, which mysteriously change their name to units when we deal with their assessment. Thus, you will be taught a *module* on Cognitive and Developmental Psychology, but examined on a *unit* of the same topics – simple really! In this book we tend to refer to 'AQA modules' (to avoid confusion with the textbook units). The AS-level course consists of three modules and a further three A2 modules make up the full A-level course.

The specification entries are very carefully worded and questions will reflect that wording. We have endeavoured to use the same wording as the specification wherever possible to make it easier for you to track your route through each topic. It is worth remembering that when questions are set, the question-setter will attempt to sample (eventually) all areas of the specification. It is, therefore, unwise to leave out any areas – even small ones – simply because they do not appeal to you.

The exams will test your knowledge and understanding (known as 'Assessment Objective 1' or simply AO1), and your analysis and evaluation (known as AO2) skills, together with your ability to design, conduct and report (in the Research Methods and Coursework sections, and known as AO3). As we stress in the exam guidance units (Units 8 and 32), AO2 questions are really quite different from AO1 questions and require you to engage 'critically' with the subject material in the topic areas.

Several entries on the AQA specification are preceded by the words 'including' or 'e.g.'. The word 'including' indicates prescribed material on which questions may be asked, but the use of 'e.g.' is merely illustrative of appropriate subject material. We have covered all prescribed material in this book and have endeavoured to cover all the examples mentioned in the specification as well.

AQA (A) AS specification and examination

Units 1 to 8 are designed specifically for the AQA, AS-level psychology course (Specification A) and their contents correspond very closely to the specification. Before you use this book as part of your study programme, we recommend that you look closely at the specification and information about the exams provided by AQA. You can obtain this either direct from AQA or by downloading it from their website (details on the right).

The AS-level specification is designed to be midway between the skills required for GCSE and the full A-level (A2), and to take account of the target age (17+) of the majority of students who will be taking this exam.

You will learn about the five core areas of psychology and about research methods. Each of these core areas is represented by a topic that will give you a good introduction to that area of psychology. The five core areas and their related topics are as follows:

- *Cognitive Psychology* – Human memory
- *Developmental Psychology* – Attachments in development
- *Physiological Psychology* – Stress
- *Individual Differences* – Abnormality
- *Social Psychology* – Social influence.

Each area also contains a 'critical issue', which represents either a key application of an area (e.g. eyewitness testimony in memory) or something that has special relevance to a particular topic area (e.g. ethical issues in social influence). The specific issues surrounding the assessment of these topics and critical issues are covered in Unit 8, but it is worth emphasizing a few points here.

- The five core areas above, together with Research Methods, are grouped together in three modules, each of which is worth one-third of the total marks:
  - *Module 1:* Cognitive and Developmental Psychology
  - *Module 2:* Physiological Psychology and Individual Differences
  - *Module 3:* Social Psychology and Research Methods.
- All areas of this specification are compulsory – this means that you must cover everything in Units 1 to 8. The specification entries are very carefully worded and questions will tend to reflect that wording. We have endeavoured to use the same wording as the specification, wherever possible, to make it easier for you to track your route through each topic. When questions are set, the question-setter will attempt to sample (eventually) all areas of the specification. Therefore, it is unwise to leave out areas, even small ones, simply because they do not appeal to you.
- There is some choice of questions in the AS-level exam, but there will not necessarily be a question on everything that appears in the AQA specification. There will, of course, be two questions on every area (i.e. Cognitive, Developmental, Physiological, and so on), so a good proportion of the specification will be covered in every exam.

The AQA (A) A2 specification

The A2 part of the specification (Modules 4 to 6) allows you to focus on topics in more depth, to make links between different perspectives, approaches and methodologies, and to put your studies into practice by completing your own psychological investigation. The A2 modules are summarized below, but you need to read

Unit 32 to find detailed guidance on the Assessment of Modules 4 and 5, and Unit 30 for coursework.

Module 4 allows you to specialize in some of the areas of psychology you sampled in the AS part of the course. Assessment takes the form of three essays from at least two different sections. This means you will need to study a minimum of two of the following:

- Social Psychology
- Physiological Psychology
- Cognitive Psychology
- Developmental Psychology
- Comparative Psychology.

Module 5 is worth slightly more as a proportion of your total A-level than the other modules. Here, in addition to studying *Individual differences* in more depth than at AS-level, you will look at important *Issues and debates* in psychology. You will also be asked to apply different theoretical and/or methodological *approaches* to a situation or case study provided in the exam.

Module 6 is a coursework module that gives you the chance to conduct your own psychological study. The investigation needs to be carefully planned using a Project brief, then carried out and reported on in a maximum of 2,000 words. Unit 30 contains advice and guidelines to help you with this part of the course.

By examining theories, concepts and research studies in this book, you should acquire an understanding of the different perspectives and methods used by psychologists and gain some insight into the ethical and cultural issues that concern people working in psychology today.

Feedback from readers is enormously helpful and, as a result of previous comments, we supplied a Resource Pack for teachers to accompany the previous edition of *Psychology*. An updated Resource Pack will also be available to accompany this new edition. Do, please, let us know, care of the Publisher, what you think of the book, and we shall pay close attention to it when we come to write the next edition of *Psychology*.

Mike Cardwell
Liz Clark
Claire Meldrum

AQA
Stag Hill House
Guildford GU2 5XJ
www.aqa.org.uk

Text permissions

The following permission to reproduce material is gratefully acknowledged. Numbers in brackets refer to pages:

Fig. 1.1 (10) – Dept of Psychology, Temple University, Philadelphia
Graph (14), activity (33), diagrams (35) – Academic Press Ltd
Table 2.1 (45) – Random House
Table 2.2 (49) – *Child Development*
Table 3.1 (89) – Elsevier
Tables 4.1 & 4.2 (124 & 131) – John Wiley & Sons Ltd
Fig. 4.4 (135) – American Medical Association
Bridget Jones's Diary (139) – Macmillan, London
Anorexia case study (141) – W.W.Norton & Co
Bulimia case study (142) – W.H.Freeman & Co
Fig 5.2 (104) – Carnegie Press
Interview extract (169) – *New York Times*
Table 5.2 (173) – The American Psychology Association
Zimbardo interview (187) & Table 5.3 (188–9) – Blackwell Publishers
Table (203) – American Psychological Association
Fig. 7.1 (222) – Allyn & Bacon
Fig 7.2 (222) – Holt, Rinehart & Winston
Table 7.5 (223) & Fig. 7.3 (224) – Blackwell Publishers
Graph A (231) – *Social Trends*
Diary extract (233) – Academic Press
Table 10.1 (308) – Penguin Books Ltd
Table 10.2 (314) – John Wiley; extract from Close Relationships by Kelley *et al.* © 1983 by W.H. Freeman & Company. Used with permission
Table 11.1 (355) – © 1968 by the American Psychological Association. Adapted with permission
Fig. 11.6 (354) – Simon and Schuster
Table 11.2 (357) – Blackwell Publishers
Key Research (359) – Reproduced with permission from the *British Journal of Psychology* © The British Psychological Society
Fig. 13.2 (412) – Allyn & Bacon
Key Research (424) – *The Times*
Fig. 15.5 (467) – Kahnemann (1973)
Fig. 16.3 (489) – Scientific American Inc.
Fig. 16.7 (496) – Palmer (1975)
Key Research (503) – Harcourt Brace and Co Ltd
Fig. 16.16 (507) – Scientific American Inc.
Fig. 16.20 (513) – Deregowski (1972)
Getting You Thinking (519) – Braine (1971); McNeil (1966); Brown and Hanlon (1970)
Fig. 17.1 (522) – The American Psychological Association
Table 18.6 (569) – Child Development
Fig. 18.6 (577) – Gleitman (1991)
Table 18.8 (579) – American Psychological Association © 1983. Adapted with permission
Fig. 19.3 (600) – Kohlberg (1966) cited in Hetherington and Parke (1993, p.547)
Fig. 20.1 (623) – Sterling Lord
Table 20.2 (626) – Simon and Schuster
Table 20.3 (641) – Macmillan (Kübler-Ross) With permission from OMEGA, *Journal of Death and Dying*, 1(1), pp.23-8; Baywood Publishing Co. Inc. © 1970 (Fulton); Tavistock Publications Ltd (Murray Parkes)
Fig. 23.2 (706) – Smith (1984)
Key Research (731) – Science
Table 24.3 (733) – © 1988 Routledge
Getting You Thinking (789) – BBC News Report, 29 June 2002
Coloured box (795) – *The Independent*, 4 October 1994
Fig. 26.1 (803) – Phillip Allan Publisher Ltd *Journal of Rational-Emotive and Cognitive-Behaviour Therapy*
Fig. 27.2 (839) – *New Scientist*
Coloured box (853) – © Toby Andrew, *The Independent*, 23 January 1996
Table 30.2 (902) – Davies (1994)
Coloured box (903) – ATP (1992)
Appendix 3 (929) – With permission of the McGraw-Hill Companies
Appendix 4 (932) – © 1963 R.A. Fisher and F. Yates. Reprinted by permission of Pearson Education Ltd
Appendix 5 (933) – Reprinted with permission from the Journal of the American Statistical Association ©1965 by the American Statistical Association. All rights reserved
Appendix 7 (933) – Reprinted with permission from the Journal of the American Statistical Association ©1972 by the American Statistical Association. All rights reserved

Whilst every effort has been made to contact the copyright holders, this has not proved possible in every case.

Photographs

The publishers would like to thank the following for permission to reproduce photographs. Page numbers are in brackets and are followed, where necessary, by T (top), B (bottom), C (centre), L (left) or R (right). SPL = Science Photo Library.

Front cover: Getty Images

Inside: Topham (3); Ann Ronan Picture Library (4); Ronald Grant Archive (5); Bubbles/C.Rout (20); Popperfoto (25T); Topham/PA (25B); Popperfoto/Reuter (26T); D.Levenson/Rex Features (26C); Corbis (32); Kobal Collection (34); Shout Pictures (37); Bubbles/Granata (43); Sally Greenhill (44,46); S.Boness/Panos Pictures (49); G.Pirozzi/Panos Pictures (51); Sally Greenhill (52); SPL (53,54); Bubbles/D.Hager (55); Mary Evans Picture Library (58); Bubbles/L.Thurstun (59); G.Tompkinson/SPL (61); R.Young/Rex Features (62); Corbis (65); Sally Greenhill (67); Bubbles/L.Thurstun (68); Bubbles/I.West (70); Bubbles/C.Rout (77L); R.Tang/Rex Features (77C); R.Judges/Rex Features (77R); Corbis (80); The Natural History Museum, London (81L); Topham/The Image Works (81R); PA Photos (88L); Alamy/C.Osborne (88C); Sally Greenhill (88R); R.Gardner/Rex Features (92); Sam Greenhill (93L); Shout Pictures (93R); Alan Edwards Sports Photography (97L); Sally Greenhill (97R); J.O'Brien/Photofusion (98); SPL/D.Plummer (103L); SPL/M.Fermariello (103R); SPL/D.Campione (104); Education Photos/John Walmsley (107); Rex Features (115L); G.Norman/Rex Features (115R); Hulton Getty (117T); Corbis (117B); Kobal Collection (118); Bubbles/J.Woodcock (120L); Topham/PA (120C); Andrew Cooney (120R); Popperfoto (124); SPL/W.McIntyre (129); P.Brooker/Rex Features (132T); SPL/BSIP Laurent/Pioffet (132B); Kobal Collection (133); Sally Greenhill (134); Bubbles/P.Cutler (139TL); Kobal Collection (139TR); Rex Features (139B); Sally Greenhill (140); Corbis (142); CosmoGIRL! (145); emap elan Network Ltd/J17 (145); H Bauer Publishing/Blush (145); M.Campbell/Photofusion (155T); G.Glover/Photofusion (155B); Rex Features (156); Lambert/Hulton Archive (161L); Hulton Getty (161R); Philip Zimbardo (163); Hulton Archive (164L); Topham/PressNet (164R); Kobal Collection (165); Hulton Archive (169L); Popperfoto/Reuter (169R); Hulton Getty (170); Alexandra Milgram (171,172); Shout Pictures (176 all); Popperfoto (178 both); Alexandra Milgram (181); Corbis/T.Stewart (183); Alexandra Milgram (185); Philip Zimbardo (186); Sally Greenhill (195T); Isopress/Rex Features (195C); Bubbles/J.Woodcock (195B); Alexandra Milgram (197); Ardea/C.Haagner (199); M.Towski/DMI/Rex Features (203); Oxford Scientific Films/S.Osolinski (206); Sally Greenhill (208); Corbis/Jim Cummins (209); Rebellion (215); Corbis/T.&D.A.McCarthy (229); Topham Picturepoint (235); Roger Scruton (246); Education Photos/John Walmsley (249). Corbis/T.Nebbia (271L); Corbis/R.Gomez (271R); PA Photos/P.Jordan (273); Bubbles Photo Library/A.Hampton (285); Corbis/D.Turnley (291); Corbis/K.Dannemiller (293); Action-Plus/N.Tingle (297); Corbis/W.Gottlieb (299); Alamy/M.Campbell (305R); Getty Images/D.Cody (305L); PA Photos/EPA (307); Alamy/Image State (309); Alamy/R.Chapple (320); Alamy/A.Vitale (326); Corbis/R.Kaestner (327); Corbis/P.M.Fisher (329); Getty Images/V.Kasala (331); Rex Features/DCY (339T); Corbis/T.Fadek (339B); Rex Features (340); Corbis/P.Turnley (344); Rex Features (347); PA Photos/EPA/A.Krusberg (364); Photofusion/C.Leahy (368); Getty Images/Studio MPM (375L); Corbis/D.Tardif (375R); SPL/Montreal Neuro Institute/McGill University/CNRI (382); Don and Rae Cousins, by kind permission (387); Alamy/B de Wilde (403L); Corbis/P.Thompson (403R); SPL/BSIP Laurent/Laeticia (405); Photofusion/R.Pilkington (414); Corbis/P.A.Souders (420); Alamy/Comstock (429L); Corbis (429R); Corbis (434); Getty Images/D.Madison (440); Corbis/R.Morsch (445); Corbis/P.Matthew/Sygma (455L); Getty Images/M.Salmeron (455R); Rex Features/P.Wilson (465); Getty Images/A.Errington (487); Corbis/P.A.Souders (518); SPL/B.Seitz (525); Bubbles Photo Library/ L.J.Thurstun (551L); Bubbles Photo Library/F.Rombout (551R); Bubbles Photo Library/Ian West (558); Getty Images/C.Tokerud (563); Corbis/N.Shaefer (567); Alamy/D.Young-Wolff (569); Getty Images/Studio MPM (587T); Alamy/Brand X (587B); Photofusion/M.Friend (599); Alamy/S.Voss (602); Bubbles Photo Library/F.Rombout (619L); Photofusion/P.Baldesare (619R); Magnum Photos/Patrick Zachmann (640); Corbis/O.Franken (642); NHPA/T.Kitchin & V.Hurst (647L); Getty Images/E.Pearle (647R); FLPA/M.B.Withers (654); Oxford Scientic Films (660); FLPA/R.Thompson (666); Punchstock (675L); NHPA/A.Williams (675R); NHPA/J.Carmichael Jr. (678); NHPA/N.J.Dennis (868); FLPA/R.Wilmhurst (695); Rex Features/SIPA (701); Corbis/C.Swift (702); Getty Images/T.Bean (713); FLPA/T.Whittaker (721); Corbis/D.Turnley (753L); Rex Features/SIPA (753R); Punchstock (761); Photofusion/P.Solloway (774); Getty Images/R.Lockyer (789L); SPL/C.Bach (789R); Alexandra Milgram (814L); SPL (814R); Zefa (934)

Psychology
FOR AS-LEVEL

UNIT 1

HUMAN Memory

PREVIEW

After you have read this unit, you should be able to:

>> discuss research into the nature and structure of memory

>> explain the differences between short-term and long-term memory

>> understand the processes of encoding, capacity and duration

>> explain different models of memory, including the multi-store, the working memory and the levels of processing models, and discuss research into these models

>> explain why people forget from both short-term and long-term memory

>> discuss research into emotional factors that affect forgetting, including flashbulb memories and repression

>> discuss research into eyewitness testimony.

INTRODUCTION

Memory is studied within the branch of psychology known as cognitive psychology. This research field focuses on the mental processes humans use to acquire, store, retrieve and apply their knowledge about the world. Cognitive psychologists have investigated a wide range of topics including perception, attention, imagery, language, problem-solving, reasoning and decision-making. In this unit, we look at memory, central to *all* cognitive processes because we use it whenever we need to maintain information over time.

In the first topic in the unit, we will look at the structure of memory and the way that it is divided into short-term and long-term stores. We will also discuss some important models of memory, i.e. explanations of how memory works.

As we know from experience, our memories can sometimes let us down, and cognitive psychologists have also been interested in the mechanisms involved in forgetting. In Topic 2, we will look at the reasons why people sometimes fail to retrieve information.

Psychologists are increasingly turning their attention to more everyday aspects of memory. In the final topic in this unit, we will look at one such practical application, namely research into eyewitness testimony.

Jane
Willson

GETTING YOU THINKING...

On the right is a description of the case of Clive Wearing – a man with a particularly profound case of amnesia (based on Baddeley 1997).

Imagine for a moment what would happen if you woke up one morning to find that you had completely lost your memory. To help you think about this, try to answer the following questions:

1 What do you normally do in a day that you would no longer be able to do because of your memory loss? Consider, for example, when you need to know your name, your age and where you live. Write a list of up to ten things.

2 What would you be unable to do if you could not recognize your friends or members of your family?

3 What experiences would you miss if you could not remember TV programmes or articles in newspapers?

4 If you were unable to recall what you were thinking about just moments ago, how would you plan your day?

After contracting a viral infection called encephalitis, Clive Wearing, a highly talented musician and broadcaster, was left with extensive brain damage, causing major memory disruption. He is still able to talk, read and write, and can still sight-read music and play quite complex piano pieces. In all other respects, however, his memory is dramatically impaired. For example, he has no recollection of his wedding, pictured below.

KEY TERMS

Memory: the mental processes involved in registering, storing and retrieving information.

Capacity: the amount of information that can be stored in memory at any particular time.

Duration: the length of time that information can be kept in memory.

Encoding: changing sensory input into a form or code to be processed by the memory system.

Short-term memory (STM): a limited capacity system for storing information for short periods.

Long-term memory (LTM): an unlimited capacity system for storing information for long periods.

Multi-store model of memory: an explanation of memory as a flow of information through a series of stages in a fixed sequence. The best-known model of this type was proposed by Atkinson and Shiffrin.

Working memory: a model of memory formulated by Baddeley and Hitch to replace the concept of short-term memory. It proposes a multi-component, flexible system concerned with active processing and storage of short-term information.

Levels of processing: a theory of memory put forward by Craik and Lockhart, that the amount of information retained in LTM depends on how deeply it is processed during learning.

As your answers to the questions in 'Getting you thinking...' will have highlighted, you would be virtually helpless without your memory. In fact, we take memory so much for granted that it can be hard to imagine the impact of its loss on our daily lives.

Psychologists have learned a great deal from the study of people such as Clive Wearing who suffer from loss of memory (amnesia) after brain damage. More details of the effects of amnesia on Clive's life are described in the panel below.

Clive Wearing's case demonstrates that memory is crucial to our wellbeing and everyday functioning. It also demonstrates the enormous complexity of human memory. The fact that Clive continues to be able to talk, walk, play music, read and write in spite of huge impairments in his memory for personal history and general knowledge suggests that memory is not a unitary system.

Even more disturbing is Clive Wearing's apparent inability to lay down new memories. Clive is convinced that he has only just woken up and keeps a diary in which he records this obsessive thought. There are pages of closely written text, in which he gives the date and time followed by the statement, "I have just regained consciousness" or "I'm conscious for the first time". Whenever his wife visits, he greets her effusively as if he has not seen her for ages. If she leaves the room for a couple of minutes, the emotional greeting is repeated and this can happen time and time again.

ACTIVITY

Why can't Clive Wearing remember?

Clive Wearing's case raises a number of questions for cognitive psychologists. This activity will help you to explore some of them.

Why is Clive unable to recall a visit from his wife just two minutes earlier? One possible explanation is that her visit never actually registered in his brain and so no memory trace is laid down. Try to think of two other explanations. You may find it helpful at this point to read the definition of 'memory' (see Key terms on p. 3).

An answer to this question is proposed at the end of the unit (see p. 38)

Clive Wearing's 'living hell'

Clive Wearing's memory for past events in his life is hazy although he can recall certain key highlights with prompting. His visual memory is impaired: for example, he is unable to recognize pictures of his old Cambridge college, where he had spent four years of his life and which he had visited many times in subsequent years. His general knowledge is also reduced and he has no idea who wrote the play *Romeo and Juliet*. Nor can he recall anything about the sixteenth-century composer Orlando Lassus, in spite of having written a book about him.

Years after the onset of the illness that caused Clive's memory loss, he is still trapped in an eternal present – he cannot use the past to anticipate the future. He is unable to enjoy books or television because he cannot follow the thread, and he does not read newspapers because he has no context within which to embed the news stories. He cannot go out alone because he immediately becomes lost and is unable to tell anyone who finds him where he is going or where he has come from. Clive himself has described his situation as "Hell on earth. It's like being dead".

Clive Wearing can play the music of Orlando Lassus, but cannot recall any details of the composer's life, despite having been an authority on him.

THE NATURE AND STRUCTURE OF MEMORY

Several theories of memory are based on the assumption that there are three kinds of memory:

- sensory memory
- short-term memory
- long-term memory.

We shall consider each of these in turn, but note that this distinction is no longer accepted by all memory researchers. It is most associated with structural models such as the one proposed by Atkinson and Shiffrin (1968), discussed on p. 13.

Sensory memory

Sensory memory is a storage system that holds information in a relatively unprocessed form for fractions of a second after the physical stimulus is no longer available. Baddeley (1988) suggested that one function of this kind of storage is to allow information from successive eye-fixations to last for a long enough time to be integrated and so to give continuity to our visual environment. For example, if you watch a film, your conscious experience is of a continuous visual scene in which all of the action appears to be moving

smoothly. In fact, the film is actually being presented as a rapid series of frozen images interspersed by fleeting moments of darkness. In order to make sense of it, your sensory store has to hold the information from one frame of film until the next is presented. Such everyday examples seem to suggest that we are capable of storing visual images for very brief periods. It is assumed that we have separate sensory stores for all the senses, but it is the visual sensory store (iconic memory) which has attracted most research.

Memory researchers, however, have focused their interest more on short-term and long-term memory.

SHORT-TERM MEMORY

Short-term memory (STM) is a system for storing information for brief periods of time. Some researchers (e.g. Atkinson and Shiffrin 1968) see STM simply as a temporary storage depot for incoming information, whereas others (e.g. Baddeley 1986) prefer to use the term 'working memory' to indicate its dynamic, flexible aspects. We shall return to this difference of opinion when we consider various models of memory later in this topic. For the moment, we will look at specific aspects related to the nature of STM:

- capacity
- duration
- encoding.

The capacity of short-term memory

Please try the next activity before you read any further.

ACTIVITY

How much can you hold in your short-term memory?

Work out the following sums in your head.

1 5 × 7 =   2 53 × 7 =   3 53 × 78 =

You probably found problem **1** extremely easy and that problem **2** was also possible. Problem **3**, however, is much more of a challenge: it will have stretched the limits of your STM by requiring you to carry too much information at once. It can feel quite frustrating as you struggle to hold on to relevant bits of information while manipulating others.

This exercise indicates that STM has a limited capacity, that is, we can only hold a small number of items at any one time. One way of assessing how much your STM can hold – its capacity – is by finding out how many digits you can repeat in correct order immediately after hearing them. This is known as your immediate digit span. This technique, which has frequently been used in psychological studies of memory, usually involves reading out a list of random digits and requiring the participant to repeat them back in the correct order. The sequences usually begin with about three digits and steadily increase in length until it becomes impossible to recall them in serial order. Over a number of trials, the sequence length at which the participant is correct 50 per cent of the time is defined as their digit span. Most people have a digit span of "seven, plus or minus two" (Miller 1956). This has been called Miller's magic number seven. Miller claimed that this finding holds good for lists of digits, letters, words or larger chunks of information.

According to Miller, 'chunking' occurs when we combine individual letters or numbers into a larger meaningful unit. For example, the digits 9, 3, 7, 1 would represent four separate items to most people, but would form a single chunk for you if they happened to be your bank PIN number.

Factors affecting capacity

- *Influence of long-term memory* – There are some difficulties in using immediate digit span as a measure of STM capacity. One problem is that it is difficult to exclude the influence of long-term memory. For example, Bower and Winzenz (1969) found that digit strings that are repeated within a series of immediate memory span trials become progressively easier for participants to recall. This indicates that information stored in LTM is helping to increase STM capacity temporarily.
- *Reading aloud* – If participants read the digits aloud before attempting to recall them, performance is better than when they simply read them subvocally to themselves.
- *Rhythmic grouping* – Performance also improves if the numbers are grouped together rhythmically. This is probably why we tend to divide up telephone numbers into rhythmic groups rather than reciting the whole string of numbers in a monotone.

KEY STUDY >> CAPACITY OF STM

study of immediate memory span by Baddeley *et al.* (1975)

Aim >>

To see whether people could remember more short words than long words in a serial recall test, and so to demonstrate that pronunciation time, rather than the number of items to be recalled, determines the capacity of short-term memory.

Procedures >>

- The reading speed of the participants was measured.
- Participants were then presented with sets of five words on a screen.
- The words were taken from one of two sets: a set of one-syllable words (e.g. *harm, wit, sum*) or a set of polysyllabic words (e.g. *opportunity, aluminium, university*)
- Participants were asked to write down the five words in serial order immediately after presentation. They recalled several lists of both short and long words.

Findings >>

- Participants could recall considerably more short words than long words.
- They were able to recall as many words as they were able to articulate in about 2 seconds.
- There was a strong positive correlation between reading speed and memory span.

Conclusions >>

- Immediate memory span represents the number of items of whatever length that can be articulated in approximately 2 seconds.

Criticisms >>

- It might simply be that short words are easier to recall than long words because they are more familiar to us.
- This was a laboratory experiment using lists of unconnected words and did not reflect everyday use of STM.
- Miller was not able to account for the findings of research which showed that immediate span depends on the nature of the stimulus, i.e. the kinds of words and the language in which they are spoken. This study can explain such findings.

Baddeley and colleagues responded to this criticism in later versions of the study and showed clearly the importance of pronunciation time over familiarity.

● *Pronunciation time* – Some more recent researchers have found that pronunciation time may be a more important indicator of STM capacity than Miller's digit span. Schweickert and Boruff (1986) tested immediate memory span for a number of different types of stimulus, such as letters, colours, shapes and nonsense words. They found that people consistently remembered as many items as they were able to pronounce in approximately 1.5 to 2 seconds. Naveh-Benjamin and Ayres (1986) have tested immediate memory span for speakers of various world languages. They found, for example, that the digit span for native English speakers is considerably greater than for Arabic speakers. The only explanation for this finding is that Arabic numbers take longer to pronounce than English numbers. These results confirmed earlier findings in a classic experiment by Baddeley *et al.* (1975) (see key study, *Capacity of STM,* on p. 6).

The duration of short-term memory

However capacity is measured, it seems clear that STM is only able to hold a few items at any one time. It is also the case that, by its very nature, STM has a brief duration. STM is a temporary store and anything we need to remember for longer needs to be transferred to LTM. The first attempts to measure the duration of STM used an experimental method known as the Brown-Peterson technique. The key study, *Duration of STM,* below, explains how Peterson and Peterson used the technique in this experiment.

Factors affecting duration

● *Rehearsal* – The key point about findings based on the Brown-Peterson technique is that items disappear from STM only when rehearsal is prevented. New items can only take their place if existing items move on – either to LTM or because

KEY STUDY >> DURATION OF STM

study of duration by Peterson and Peterson (1959)

Aim >>
To test how long STM lasts when rehearsal is prevented.

Procedures >>
● Participants (Ps) were briefly shown a consonant trigram (i.e. three letters such as CPW or NGV).
● Participants were asked to count backwards in threes from a specified number to stop them thinking about the letters.
● After intervals of 3, 6, 9, 12, 15 or 18 seconds, participants were asked to recall the original trigram.
● The procedure was repeated several times using different trigrams.

Findings >>
● Participants were able to recall 80 per cent of trigrams after a 3-second interval.
● Progressively fewer trigrams were recalled as the time intervals lengthened.
● After 18 seconds, fewer than 10 per cent of the trigrams were recalled correctly.

Conclusions >>
● If rehearsal is prevented, information vanishes rapidly from STM.
● Therefore, decay is the mechanism for forgetting in short-term memory.

Criticisms >>
● Trigrams are rather artificial things to remember and may not reflect everyday memory.
● It is possible, however, that interference from the counting task (not merely decay) caused the poor recall.

AO2 check Note that the experimental method used in this study allows us to see the (causal) effect of time passing (independent variable) on recall (dependent variable).

they are forgotten. If we want to remember something for a short period of time, we tend to repeat it to ourselves, as for example when we look up a number in the phone book and need to hold it in our memory for long enough to dial it accurately. This repetition serves as a method of continually re-inserting the information into STM and thereby strengthening the memory. Without rehearsal, the duration of STM is very brief.

● *Deliberate intention to recall* – Sebrechts *et al.* (1989) briefly presented participants with lists of three common English nouns and then gave them an unexpected, serial recall test. Correct recall of the items fell to 1 per cent after only 4 seconds. Studies such as these demonstrate that information can vanish from STM in a matter of a few seconds if people are not making a conscious effort to retain it.

● *Amount of information to be retained* – Murdock (1961) presented participants with either a single three-letter word such as *cat* or three unrelated words such as *hat, pen, lid*. He then followed the same procedure as in the Brown-Peterson technique. The forgetting curve for the three unrelated words was the same as for the consonant trigrams in the Peterson and Peterson study. However, the single, three-letter word (which could be processed as one chunk) was remarkably resistant to forgetting and accurate recall level was still at 90 per cent after 18 seconds. This shows that, as in Miller's digit span, the important factor is the number of chunks to be remembered rather than the number of individual items, i.e. letters.

Encoding in short-term memory

A further question about the nature of STM concerns coding. When information arrives at the sensory registration stage, it is still in its raw form or original 'modality'. For example, information presented visually is still in the visual modality. Psychologists have been interested in the question of what happens to such information when it reaches the STM. Does it stay in its original modality or is it recoded in some way?

There are various ways in which we can encode stimulus inputs. Imagine looking at the word 'glove'. This could be stored as a visual representation so that you form a visual image of either the printed word itself or a pictorial image of an actual glove. You could form an acoustic representation by saying the written word aloud or under your breath – this has the effect of converting the written word into a verbal or speech code. Alternatively, you could form a semantic representation, which depends on your knowledge about the meaning of the word. You might, for example, think about circumstances in which you need to wear gloves or a specific pair of gloves that you own.

It is not possible simply to ask people what codes they are using because memory processes are often unconscious. Much of the evidence about coding comes from studies into so-called substitution errors. These occur when people confuse one item for another. If, for example, they confuse letters, which *sound* alike, it indicates that acoustic coding is being used. If, however, letters that *look* similar are confused, it indicates that visual coding is being used. (See key study, *Encoding in short-term memory*.)

Factors affecting encoding

● *The sound of words* – Conrad's study suggests that short-term memory relies heavily on acoustic coding. Other researchers thought that the type of stimulus to be remembered might affect the way it is encoded. Baddeley (1966), for example, wondered whether Conrad's results were dependent on using consonants as his stimulus material. After all, they

A stimulus input can be encoded visually as a word or picture (left), acoustically (middle) or semantically (right). Can you work out how you process stimuli?

study of acoustic confusion by Conrad (1964)

Aim >>

To find out whether people use acoustic coding in STM, even when information is presented visually.

Procedures >>

- Participants were shown a random sequence of six consonants projected in rapid succession onto a screen.
- Strings of consonants were either acoustically similar (e.g. P, C, V, T, B, D) or acoustically dissimilar (e.g. L, Z, F, X, H, W).
- Participants were asked to write down the letters in the same order as they appeared.
- Letters were presented too rapidly for the participants to keep up, so they had to rely on memory.
- Conrad carefully noted the errors made by participants.

Findings >>

- The majority of the errors involved the substitution of a similar-sounding letter (e.g. B for D, or S for X).
- Participants found that it was more difficult to recall strings of acoustically similar letters in the correct order than acoustically dissimilar letters, even though they were presented visually.

Conclusions >>

- Items are stored in STM in some form of acoustic code.
- Even if consonants are presented visually, they are recoded into acoustic form in order to be stored in STM.

Other studies have shown that acoustic coding is not exclusively used in STM. When steps are taken to prevent acoustic coding, visual coding may be substituted (see the study by Brandimonte *et al.* (1992) on the next page).

---

tend to be more similar in sound than in any other characteristic, such as visual form or meaning. Baddeley set about testing this idea by presenting participants with words rather than consonants and comparing the effect of acoustic similarity with similarity of meaning (semantic similarity). He presented participants with sequences of five short words that were acoustically similar (e.g. *man, mad, mat, map, can, cat, cap*). He noted how well they were recalled compared with a sequence of short, acoustically dissimilar words (e.g. *pen, day, few, sup, cow, pit, bar, hot*) and a sequence of short, semantically similar words (e.g. *big, large, wide, high, great, tall, long, broad*). Baddeley found that words with similar sounds were much harder to recall than words which did not sound alike. Similarity of meaning had only a very slight detrimental effect on performance. Baddeley's study in fact supported Conrad and he, too, concluded that short-term memory relies more on the sound of words than on their meaning. Interestingly, he found that the effects of sound similarity disappeared when he tested participants' long-term learning (see key study, *Encoding in STM and LTM*, on p. 12). This suggests that a major factor affecting encoding is whether the items are being stored in STM or LTM.

ACTIVITY

Conrad on acoustic confusion

Reread the description of the study of acoustic confusion that Conrad undertook in 1964 (see key study, above). Then answer the following questions:

1. What type of research did Conrad use to study encoding in short-term memory?

2. Does this type of research allow Conrad to conclude that there is a causal relationship between the nature of the stimuli and accuracy of participants' recall?

3. Note down one important criticism of this study that limits the usefulness of the findings.

Answers are given on p. 38.

- *Other ways of encoding* – It seems likely that acoustic coding is the preferred method of encoding in STM, but there are several studies that show that other modes of representation are also possible (see the panel on p. 10).

An interesting study by Brandimonte *et al.* (1992) demonstrates not only that visual coding can be used in STM, but that, under certain circumstances, it is a superior method. Participants were presented with six line drawings of familiar objects, such as the one shown in Fig. 1.1, and were asked to memorize them in order.

Participants were then asked to form a mental image of each one in turn and to subtract a specified part of the drawing as shown. They were then asked to name the resulting image; for example, the left-hand picture is a wrapped sweet, but it becomes a fish when the right-hand section of the image is removed. Participants were able to name on average 2.7 of the six items.

Another group of participants was given the same tasks to do except that they were prevented from articulating during the learning stage. While they were being shown the original pictures, they were

asked to repeat the meaningless chant "la-la-la-...". This prevented them from converting the pictorial image into a verbal code, as they would have done under normal circumstances. They were actually more successful when it came to identifying the subtracted image and were able to name 3.8 items correctly. Because they were using visual coding, they found it easier to subtract a part from the visual image than the first set of participants who had coded the original stimulus in verbal form.

This study shows that the nature of the task may affect the type of coding used. If prevented from using acoustic coding, visual coding may be substituted. There is also some evidence that items in STM can be coded in terms of their meaning, so it seems reasonable to conclude that acoustic coding is generally the preferred, rather than the exclusive, method of representation.

Line drawing　　*Subtracted part*　　*Remaining part*

Figure 1.1 >>
Sample of the line drawings used by Brandimonte and colleagues

LONG-TERM MEMORY

Long-term memory (LTM) holds a vast quantity of information, which can be stored for long periods of time. The information kept here is diverse and wide-ranging, and includes all of our personal memories, our general knowledge and our beliefs about the world. It also includes plans for the future and is where all our knowledge about skills and expertise is deposited. LTM is not a passive store of information, but a dynamic system that constantly revises and modifies stored knowledge in the light of new information. LTM is a much larger, more complex memory system than STM, from which it differs in terms of such factors as capacity, duration and simple encoding. It seems likely that LTM is not a single store, but a number of different systems with slightly different functions.

Capacity of long-term memory

It is not possible to quantify the exact capacity of LTM, but most psychologists would agree that there is no upper limit – we are always capable of more learning. The huge capacity of LTM requires a highly organized structure, otherwise items would be difficult to retrieve. Many researchers have suggested that LTM is divided into a number of different memory systems. This would

explain why Clive Wearing (the case study described on pp. 3–4) can remember some things from his LTM but not others.

Duration of long-term memory

The duration of the memory trace in LTM is considerably longer than in STM and can last almost a whole lifetime. Bahrick suggested the term 'permastore' to refer to memory held for a very long time (see key study, *Duration of long-term memory*, on the next page).

Factors that affect duration of LTM

● *Childhood amnesia* – Try to jot down some of your earliest memories. You may have some quite vivid memories, but it is unlikely that you can accurately remember many events from before your third birthday. If you can, it is probably because you have been told about these events by your family or have seen them recorded in photos. The most likely explanation for this so-called childhood amnesia is that very young children are incapable of laying down well-organized and integrated memories, and so these are not available for later recall.

Aim >>

To establish the existence of very long-term memory (VLTM), and to see whether there was any difference between recognition and recall.

Procedures >>

- Investigators tracked down the graduates from a particular high school in America over a 50-year period.
- 392 graduates were shown photographs from their high-school yearbook.
- For each photo, participants were given a group of names and asked to select the name that matched the person in the photo (recognition group).
- Another group of participants was simply asked to name the people in the photos without being given a list of possible names (recall group).

Findings >>

- In the name-matching condition, participants were 90 per cent correct even 14 years after graduation.
- After 25 years, these participants were 80 per cent accurate; after 34 years, 75 per cent accurate and, even after 47 years, 60 per cent accurate.
- The second group who had to identify the photos without any name cues were not quite as successful. They were 60 per cent accurate after seven years, but the level of accuracy had dropped to less than 20 per cent after 47 years.

Conclusions >>

- People can remember certain types of information for almost a lifetime.
- The accuracy of very long-term memory is better when measured by recognition tests than by recall tests.

Criticisms >>

- Unlike many memory experiments, this study used meaningful stimulus material (high-school yearbooks) and tested people for memories from their own lives.
- It is unclear whether the drop-off in accuracy after 47 years reflects the limits of duration or a more general decline in memory with age.

Aim >>

To explore the effects of acoustic and semantic coding in STM and LTM.

Procedures >>

- In the STM study, participants were asked, immediately after presentation, to recall, in serial order, a list of five words taken from a pool of words in the following categories:
  - acoustically similar words (e.g. *man, mad, map*)
  - acoustically dissimilar words (e.g. *pen, day, few*)
  - semantically similar words (e.g. *great, big, large*)
  - semantically dissimilar words (e.g. *hot, old, late*).
- In the LTM study, each list of words was extended to ten and recall was tested after an interval of 20 minutes.

Findings >>

- Words with similar sounds were much harder to recall using STM than words with dissimilar sounds.
- Similarity of meaning had only a very slight detrimental effect on STM.
- When participants were recalling from LTM, recall was much worse for semantically similar words than for semantically dissimilar words.
- Recall from LTM was the same for acoustically similar and acoustically dissimilar words.

Conclusions >>

- STM relies heavily on acoustic coding.
- LTM primarily makes use of semantic coding.

Criticisms >>

- The use of the experimental method allows a causal link to be drawn between type of coding used in STM and LTM and the accuracy of recall.
- The conclusions of this study may not reflect the complexity of encoding. Evidence from other studies shows that, in certain circumstances, both STM and LTM can use other forms of coding.

- *How duration is measured* – Another factor that seems to be important in measuring the duration of LTM is the method used to tap into memory. As you can see from Bahrick's study, people are much better at remembering information from long ago if they are tested by recognition, rather than by free recall.

- *Thorough learning* – It also seems that people are more likely to hold material in permastore if they learned it very well in the first place and if they continued to learn about related material in the interval. Bahrick and Hall (1991) tested long-term memory for algebra and geometry. They found that people who had only taken maths up to high-school level showed a steady decline in the accuracy of their recall over the years, whereas students who had taken a higher maths course at college showed remarkably high levels of accuracy as much as 55 years later.

Encoding in long-term memory

As far as coding is concerned, there is some evidence that the meaning of the stimulus is often the main factor here. In other words, semantic coding is important (see key study, *Encoding in STM and LTM*, above).

Factors affecting encoding in LTM

It is clear from our own experience that material can be represented in other ways as well. Our ability to recognize sounds such as police sirens and telephones ringing shows that we can store material in an acoustic form. We can also easily bring to mind pictorial images of people or places, which suggests some visual coding in LTM. It seems that the type of stimulus material can affect the way we encode in LTM.

MODELS OF MEMORY

The multi-store model of memory

A number of memory theorists have proposed that the memory system is divided into three stores as outlined in the previous section. Atkinson and Shiffrin (1968) proposed a typical model of this type. Their model arose from the information-processing approach where memory is characterized as a flow of information through a system. The system is divided into a set of stages and information passes through each stage in a fixed sequence. There are capacity and duration limitations at each stage, and transfer between stages may require recoding. Models based on information processing are represented in the form of flow charts, such as the one illustrated in Fig. 1.2.

Atkinson and Shiffrin proposed that external stimuli from the environment first enter sensory memory where they can be registered for very brief periods of time before decaying or being passed on to the short-term store. STM contains only the small amount of information that is actually in active use at any one time. Information is encoded at this stage in terms of its sounds. Atkinson and Shiffrin believed that memory traces in STM are fragile and can be lost within about 30 seconds unless they are repeated (rehearsed). Material that is rehearsed is passed on to the long-term store where it can remain for a lifetime, although loss is possible from this store through decay or interference. Coding in LTM is assumed to be in terms of meaning, i.e. semantic.

In addition to describing the structural features of the memory system, Atkinson and Shiffrin also proposed various control processes, which are strategies used by individuals to manipulate the information flowing through the system. One of the most important of these is rehearsal that allows information to be recycled within STM and passed on into LTM.

In evaluating the multi-store model of memory, the key points are as follows:

- The multi-store model has stimulated considerable research, but it is too simplistic to explain the whole memory system.

- A crucial aspect of the multi-store model is that it distinguishes between short-term and long-term stores, which suggests that LTM and STM operate differently in terms of capacity, duration and encoding. Evidence in support of the distinction between STM and LTM comes from case studies of people with brain damage that gives rise to memory impairment (see panel below).

The distinction between LTM and STM

Milner (1966) reported on a young man referred to as H.M., who was left with severe memory impairment after brain surgery. He was able to talk normally and to recall accurately events and people from his life before surgery, and his immediate digit span was within normal limits. He was, however, unable to retain any new information and could not lay down new memories in LTM. When told of the death of his favourite uncle, he reacted with considerable distress. Later, he frequently asked about his uncle and, on each occasion, reacted again with the level of grief appropriate to hearing the news for the first time. Cases such as these and that of Clive Wearing (see p. 3) lend support to the multi-store model by pointing to a clear distinction between LTM and STM.

Figure 1.2 >> *Summary of the Atkinson and Shiffrin (1968) model of memory*

There are, however, problems with the model of Atkinson and Shiffrin. The model is too simple and inflexible, and fails to take account of factors such as the strategies people employ to remember things. It also places emphasis on the *amount* of information that can be processed rather than its nature. Some things are simply easier to remember than others, perhaps because they are more interesting, more distinctive, funnier, etc. The multi-store model cannot account for this.

It is also criticized for focusing on the structure of the memory system at the expense of adequately explaining the processes involved. For example, visual stimuli registering in sensory memory must be changed to an acoustic code for access to STM. In order to translate the pattern of the letter 'M' into the sound 'em', the individual needs to access knowledge about letter shapes and sounds that is stored in LTM. This means that information from LTM must flow backwards through the system to the recoding stage prior to STM. This suggests that the flow of information through the system is interactive rather than strictly sequential as Atkinson and Shiffrin suggested.

The suggestion that rote rehearsal is the only means of transfer from STM into LTM has also been criticized. This criticism will be considered in more detail in the discussion of alternative models of memory, such as the levels of processing approach on p. 16.

Similarly, another model – the working memory model of Baddeley and Hitch (1974) – casts doubt on the assumption of Atkinson and Shiffrin that STM is a unitary store with a severely limited capacity.

ACTIVITY

Evidence for separate stores

Look back at the section under the heading 'The multi-store model of memory', and note that in the multi-store model of memory, short-term memory and long-term memory are viewed as two separate, distinct stores.

Glanzer and Cunitz (1966) conducted the following experiment to see if they could find evidence for these separate stores. Participants were presented with a list of words one at a time. They were asked to recall the words and could do so in any order (this is known as *free recall*).

● Half of the participants recalled the words immediately after they had memorized them (the *immediate recall* condition).

● The other half of the participants counted backwards for 30 seconds before they recalled the words (the *recall after distraction* condition).

The results are shown in the graph on the right.

Now answer the following questions:

1 In the immediate recall condition, which words were remembered best?

2 Why do you think this happens?

3 In the recall after distraction condition, which words are remembered best?

4 What is the main difference in the recall performance of the two groups?

5 What is a possible explanation of the difference in the way that the two groups performed?

6 Do these results provide evidence that supports or challenges the multi-store model of memory?

Answers to these questions are given on p. 38

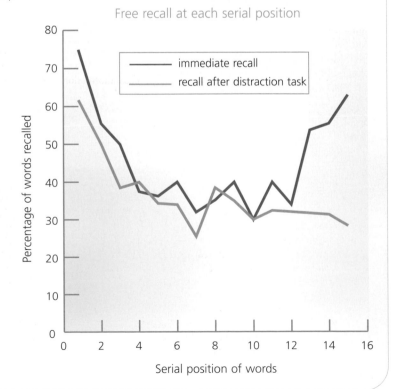

Free recall at each serial position

— immediate recall
— recall after distraction task

Percentage of words recalled

Serial position of words

The working memory model

One of the criticisms of the multi-store model is that it is too simplistic and assumes that STM and LTM act as unitary stores. It seems much more likely that both memory systems are divided into separate components that have different functions. The first people to explore the notion of a multi-component short-term store were Baddeley and Hitch (1974). They conducted a dual-task study in which participants were given digit strings to rehearse while, at the same time, carrying out verbal reasoning tasks similar to those in the activity on the right. Try the activity now.

Imagine trying to do these reasoning tasks and simultaneously rehearsing a string of digits – you probably think that this would be very difficult if not impossible. However, the participants in the study were able to recall six-digit strings and perform accurately on the reasoning task. This finding is not compatible with Atkinson and Shiffrin's view of a short-term store that can hold only a small amount of information. Instead, it suggests that STM, or working memory as Baddeley and Hitch prefer to call it, consists of several different components that can work independently of one another and so handle more than one task at a time.

Baddeley and Hitch concluded on the basis of this and other studies that STM is a flexible and complex system that consists of a central control mechanism assisted by a number of slave systems. The model has been modified slightly in the light of experimental studies and is shown in simple form in Fig. 1.3.

ACTIVITY

Verbal reasoning task

Read the following list of ten short statements and decide for each one, as quickly and as accurately as you can, whether it is true or false.

1	B is followed by A	BA
2	A does not follow B	BA
3	A is not preceded by B	BA
4	A is not followed by B	BA
5	B follows A	AB
6	B is preceded by A	BA
7	A does not precede B	BA
8	B is not preceded by A	BA
9	B is followed by A	AB
10	A follows B	AB

Baddeley (1997) suggested that you can get a good idea about how working memory operates by carrying out the task in the Activity on p. 16. Try it for yourself.

Figure 1.3 >> *The working memory model*
Source: Cohen et al. (1993)

Central executive

The central executive is the most important component in the model and is responsible for monitoring and coordinating the operation of the slave systems. It is flexible in that it can process information from any modality and also has some storage capacity, although this is very limited. It seems to play a major role in attention, planning and in synthesizing information, not only from the slave systems but also from LTM.

Phonological loop

The phonological loop stores a limited number of sounds for brief periods and can be thought of as an inner ear. It is thought to consist of two components. One component is the phonological store (inner ear) that allows acoustically coded items to be stored for a brief period. The other component is the articulatory control system (the inner voice) that allows subvocal repetition of the items stored in the phonological store.

Visuo-spatial scratchpad

The visuo-spatial scratchpad stores visual and spatial information and can be thought of as an inner eye. Like the phonological loop, it has limited capacity, but the limits of the two systems are independent. In other words, it is possible, for example, to rehearse a set of digits in the phonological loop while simultaneously making decisions about the spatial layout of a set of letters in the visuo-spatial scratchpad.

How working memory operates

Work out how many windows there are in your home. When you have finished, make a note of how you did it and then discuss your answer a friend or fellow student. Did you use similar strategies?

If you are like most people, you will have formed a mental image of your home and counted the windows either by imagining the outside of the house or by walking through the house room by room. The image will be set up and manipulated in your visuo-spatial scratchpad and the tally of windows will be held in the phonological loop as you count them subvocally. The whole operation will be supervised by the central executive, which will allocate the tasks and recognize when the final total has been reached.

In evaluating the working memory model, the key points are as follows:

- The working memory model appears to have a number of advantages over the concept of STM as outlined in the multi-store model. It effectively accounts for our ability to store information briefly, while at the same time actively processing the material.

- There is a considerable body of empirical research that seems to support the existence of the phonological loop slave system. For example, Baddeley *et al.* (1975) conducted a series of studies that investigated the word-length effect (see key study on p. 6). If participants were prevented from rehearsing the words subvocally by repeating an irrelevant sound such as "la-la-la..." (articulatory suppression), the word-length effect disappeared (i.e. short words were recalled no better than long words). It is assumed that the articulatory suppression task fills the phonological loop and, therefore, takes away the advantage of rehearsal. Since *some* words could be recalled, it is likely that the central executive takes over the recall task.

- The visuo-spatial store has not been investigated in the same depth as the phonological store, but there is experimental evidence that supports its existence. For example, Baddeley *et al.* (1973) gave participants a simple tracking task that involved holding a pointer in contact with a moving spot of light. At the same time, participants were asked to perform an imagery task. Participants were required to imagine the block capital letter 'F' and then, starting at the bottom left hand corner, were to classify each angle as a 'yes' if it included the bottom or top line of the letter and as a 'no' if it did not.

Participants found it very difficult to track the spot of light and accurately classify the angles in the letter imagery task. However, they were perfectly capable of carrying out the tracking task in conjunction with a verbal task. This suggests that the tracking and letter imagery tasks were competing for the limited resources of the visuo-spatial scratchpad, whereas the tracking task and the verbal task were making use of the separate components of the visuo-spatial scratchpad and the phonological loop respectively.

- The working memory model has proved influential and is still being developed and expanded. The main weakness, however, is that the component we know least about (the central executive) is the most important. It has a limited capacity, but no one has been able to quantify it experimentally. Richardson (1984) argues that there are problems in specifying the precise functioning of the central executive. He believes that the terminology is vague and can be used to explain any kind of results. In other words, it can give rise to a circular argument. For example, if we give participants an articulatory suppression task and this affects performance, we assume the phonological loop is normally utilized in the task, but if performance is not affected, we assume the central executive is normally utilized in the task, rather than the phonological loop. Hence, it is difficult to falsify the model.

Levels of processing

The working memory model has been much more effective than the multi-store model in explaining the active nature of short-term memory processing. However, it does not consider the effects of differential processing on long-term retention of information. An important approach which looked specifically at this aspect was put forward by Craik and Lockhart (1972). They rejected the idea of separate memory structures put forward by Atkinson and Shiffrin, believing instead that stimulus inputs go through a variety of processing operations. According to them, processing varies in terms of depth.

- *Shallow processing* – the first stages of processing are shallow and involve recognizing the stimulus in terms of its physical appearance, e.g. the shape of the letters a word is written in.

- *Deep processing* – the deepest level of processing involves coding the input in terms of its meaning.

- Rehearsing material simply by rote repetition is called *maintenance rehearsal* and is regarded as shallow processing. It is distinguished from *elaborative rehearsal*, in which links are made to semantic associations.

- The assumption of the model is that shallow processing will give rise to weak, short-term retention, whereas deep processing will ensure strong, lasting retention. This central assumption has been tested in numerous studies, such as Hyde and Jenkins' study (1973) (see the panel on the right).

An evaluation of the levels of processing approach brings out the following points:

- The levels of processing approach was influential when it was first formulated and researchers in the field welcomed its emphasis on mental processes rather than on rigid structures.

- However, it soon became clear that the model was descriptive rather than explanatory. A major problem is circularity, i.e. there is no independent definition of depth. The model predicts that deep processing will lead to better retention – researchers then conclude that, because retention is better after certain orienting tasks, they must, by definition, involve deep processing. In the Hyde and Jenkins study, for example, the orienting task that gave rise to the lowest level of recall was the sentence frame task. Hyde and Jenkins assumed that the poor recall reflected shallow processing and yet, on the face of it, judgements about sentence frames would appear to require semantic analysis and, thus, deep processing.

- Other researchers have questioned the idea that depth of processing alone is responsible for retention. For example, Tyler *et al.* (1979) gave participants two sets of anagrams to solve. Some were easy (such as *doctro*), and others were more difficult (such as *ocdrto*). In a subsequent, unexpected recall task, participants remembered more of the difficult than the easy anagrams despite processing levels being the same. Tyler and colleagues suggested that retention was influenced by the amount of processing *effort* rather than depth. Craik and Lockhart (1986) have since suggested that other factors such as elaboration and distinctiveness are also important in determining the rate of retention and this idea has been supported by research. For example, Hunt and Elliott (1980) found that people recalled words with distinctive sequences of tall and short letter sequences better than words with less distinctive arrangements of letters.

Hyde and Jenkins' study (1973)

Hyde and Jenkins presented lists of 24 words auditorily and asked different groups of participants to perform one of the following so-called orienting tasks:

- rating the words for pleasantness
- estimating the frequency with which each word is used in the English language
- detecting the occurrence of the letters 'e' and 'g' in any of the words
- deciding the part of speech appropriate to each word (e.g. noun, adjective)
- deciding whether the words fitted into a particular sentence frame.

Half the participants were told in advance that they would be expected to recall the words (intentional learning group) and the other half were not (incidental learning group). In addition, there was a control group which was required simply to learn the words without doing any of the orienting tasks. After testing all the participants for recall of the original word list, Hyde and Jenkins found that there were minimal differences in the number of items correctly recalled between the intentional learning groups and the incidental learning groups.

This finding is predicted by Craik and Lockhart because they believe that retention is simply a by-product of processing and so intention to learn is unnecessary for learning to occur. In addition, it was found that recall was significantly better for words which had been analysed semantically (i.e. rated for pleasantness or for frequency) than words which had been rated more superficially (i.e. detecting 'e' and 'g'). This is also in line with the theory because semantic analysis is assumed to be a deeper level of processing than structural analysis.

ACTIVITY

Expert interview

1 What two problems does Phil Beaman identify concerning the multi-store model of memory as an adequate explanation of human memory?

2 Why does he think that the working memory model offers a better explanation?

3 Why does remembering where you heard a voice or recalling touch pose problems for the working memory model?

Working *memory*

Dr Philip Beaman is a Lecturer in Psychology at the University of Reading. His PhD research undertaken at Cardiff University on the effects of noise on human cognitive performance was followed by a postdoctoral research fellowship at the Medical Research Council's Cognitive Development Unit, University College London. His current research interests are auditory attention and memory, particularly the distracting effects of unwanted noise, short-term or 'working' memory, and the effects of memory limitations on problem-solving and reasoning.

Q What was wrong with the multi-store model as a representation of human memory?

A In the model, any information not passed on to long-term memory is lost within about 30 seconds. Information can be held in short-term memory (or passed on to long-term memory) only by repeating it to yourself (rehearsal). However, in many studies of individuals with brain-damage, a patient may have obvious difficulty with short-term recall but no real problems when their longer-term memory is tested. You have also probably learned information 'all in one go', without repeating it to yourself. If all information had to be encoded first in short-term memory and could only be passed on to long-term memory by rehearsal, none of this should be possible.

Philip Beaman

Q In what way does working memory offer a better account of memory?

A Working memory acknowledges the complexity of memory and suggests that memory is used for something rather than existing just as an object of study for psychologists. Working memory aims to provide an explanation for the type of memory consulted on a daily basis to support everyday tasks, for example carrying out the sort of simple verbal reasoning and comprehension necessary to follow complicated conversations and arguments, keeping track of the locations of objects in a room without needing to continually look for them, and so on.

Q Are there any problems with the current view of working memory?

A Maintaining that such-and-such a subsystem of working memory model is involved in a particular task isn't, by itself, much of an explanation. This is a particular problem with the central executive component. Suggesting that a particular activity (e.g. planning) is 'governed by' the central executive is not very helpful without a clearer idea of how the central executive works. The visuo-spatial sketchpad and phonological loop are much better worked-out components of working memory, but it is still not clear how information from these systems might be coordinated, or what happens to information that could be coded in both systems (e.g. the spatial location of a voice) or neither (e.g. the memory of a touch).

Check your understanding of the nature and structure of memory by answering these questions. Try to do this from memory at first. You can check your answers by looking back through Topic 1.

1   What do you understand by the following terms:
    (a) short-term memory (b) long-term memory?

2   List three differences between STM and LTM.

3   According to Miller, how does 'chunking' increase the capacity of STM?

4   Identify two factors that affect the duration of STM.

5   Outline the procedures and findings of the Peterson and Peterson study of duration in STM.

6   What is the preferred method of encoding in (a) STM (b) LTM?

7   Outline the findings of the study by Bahrick *et al.* (1975) into very long-term memory. Identify one criticism of this study.

8   Outline the main features of the working memory model.

9   Outline findings of research investigating the levels of processing model.

10 To what extent does the multi-store model explain how memory works?

REVISION SUMMARY

Having covered this topic you should be able to:

✓ define 'short-term memory', 'long-term memory', 'capacity', 'duration' and 'encoding'

✓ explain the differences between STM and LTM

✓ discuss research into aspects of STM and LTM

✓ describe the multi-store model and evaluate research that has investigated this model

✓ describe working memory and evaluate research that has investigated this model

✓ describe levels of processing and evaluate research that has investigated this approach

✓ describe the aims, procedures, findings, conclusions and criticisms for a key study in duration in STM, duration in LTM, capacity in STM, encoding in STM and encoding in LTM.

Working either on your own or in a small group, write down three lists:

1 some examples of the types of things that you regularly forget, such as people's names or where you put something important, such as your keys, purse or wallet)

2 the main reasons why you forget these things

3 techniques you have used to try to improve your memory – which ones have been the most successful and which the least successful?

Forgetting: the loss of the ability to recall or recognize something previously learned.

Displacement: items currently in STM are pushed out to make room for incoming new ones.

Decay: the memory trace fades away with time so that the memory is no longer available.

Interference: memory traces are disrupted or obscured by other information.

Retrieval failure: items stored in LTM cannot be accessed because no suitable retrieval cues are available.

Flashbulb memory: a vivid, long-lasting memory of a highly significant event accompanied by recollection of details such as where we heard the news and what we were doing at the time.

Repression: an unconscious process in which a distressing memory or impulse is excluded from conscious awareness.

FORGETTING IN SHORT-TERM MEMORY

To understand how the memory system works, it is important to look at some of the reasons why we lose information – in other words, how we forget. The way we forget seems to differ depending on whether the information is in STM or LTM.

Displacement in STM

We have already considered the view that the capacity of STM is limited to approximately seven chunks of information (see Miller's magic number seven, p. 5). If this were the case, a possible mechanism for forgetting from STM could be displacement. In other words, material currently circulating in STM which has been insufficiently processed to pass on to LTM, will be pushed out or displaced by new, incoming information. Waugh and Norman (1965) investigated this idea using the serial probe technique. They presented a set of

digits followed by the repetition of one of those digits (the probe). Participants then have to recall the digit that followed the probe in the original list. Waugh and Norman found that recall was good if the probe came towards the end of the 16-digit list, but poor for items at the beginning of the list. This is consistent with the notion of displacement because digits at the end of the list would still be available in STM whereas digits at the beginning of the list would seem to have been displaced by the ones that came later.

Displacement may not be the only explanation. Shallice (1967) found that a faster rate of presentation of the digits produced better recall, which suggests that time may be an important factor in forgetting. With the faster presentation rate, earlier digits had less time to disappear from memory. In practice, it has been difficult to isolate the effects of displacement from decay.

Decay in STM

According to decay theory, information is forgotten because of the passage of time rather than because of the displacement of the memory trace. It is thought that some kind of structural change occurs in the brain when a memory is laid down. Hebb (1949) believed that, as a result of excitation of the nerve cells, a brief memory trace is laid down. At this stage of the process, which corresponds to STM, the trace is very fragile and likely to be disrupted. With repeated neural activity (e.g. brought about by rehearsal), a permanent structural change comes about and the memory is transferred to LTM where it is no longer likely to decay.

Studies based on the Brown-Peterson technique discussed on p. 7 seem to provide support for the decay theory of forgetting in STM. You will recall that forgetting of consonant trigrams was rapid when rehearsal was prevented. This finding was initially interpreted as evidence that the memory trace for the trigram becomes increasingly faded and decayed as time elapses. However, it is notable that participants generally have little trouble recalling the trigrams on the first couple of trials. Problems seem to set in only as the number of trials increases, suggesting that earlier trigrams may be interfering with later ones. Try the activity below before you read any further.

You probably found that the first triplet of words was accurately recalled, but that it was harder to recall the subsequent triplets. However, you should have noticed that recall improved again when you got to column 5 (*dog, goat, pig*). This seems to be because items from a *new* category give you the opportunity to start afresh and avoid confusion with earlier items. This kind of evidence suggests that forgetting can be explained in terms of interference rather than decay.

It is difficult to test decay theory without introducing confounding factors such as interference, but Reitman (1974) proposed a technique which she hoped would be as pure a measure as possible. Participants were given a task that intervened between learning and recall, which not only prevented rehearsal but also offered no opportunity for interfering with learning. She showed participants lists of five words for two seconds and then, for a further 15 seconds, asked them to listen out for a faint tone presented over earphones. She reasoned that this tone detection task would require effort and attention, but not involve any new learning. Under these conditions, recall of the five words declined by about 24 per cent over the 15-second period. She concluded that this decline in performance could be explained by decay. However, it is of course impossible to guarantee that no new information entered STM during the 15-second delay.

STM is clearly a fragile store from which information can be easily and quickly lost. The precise mechanism of forgetting is unclear, but it seems likely that interference, displacement and decay all have a role to play.

discussed on p. 7

ACTIVITY

Interference or decay?

Cover up the lists of words below with a piece of paper and uncover them, from left to right, as you work through the exercise. Under each list of words is a number. Looking away from the lists, count backwards in threes from this number for 10 seconds and then, without looking back, try to write down the three words in the list. Carry on until you have completed all eight lists. When you have finished, write down how many words you recorded correctly for each list.

banana	apple	cherry	apricot	dog	cat	sheep	daisy
peach	grape	lemon	melon	goat	cow	horse.	rose
plum	orange	pear	lime	pig	fox	mouse	tulip
327	519	128	385	729	610	486	923

FORGETTING IN LONG-TERM MEMORY

Decay in LTM

We have already seen that memories transferred to the long-term store are relatively stable and long lasting. It is, however, only too obvious from our own experience that we often fail to remember things. Trace decay was discussed above as a method of forgetting in STM, but some psychologists have also argued that material can be lost from LTM in the form of decay through disuse. The idea here is that knowledge or skills that have not been used for a long time will eventually fade away. However, skills that require motor memory, such as riding a bicycle or swimming, do not seem to be forgotten, even after long periods without practice. This lack of forgetting does not, however, seem to be true of all skills.

McKenna and Glendon (1985) studied 215 shop and office workers who had volunteered to learn the skills of cardiac resuscitation. Various measures of performance were tested over a three-month to three-year period after completion of training. Performance dropped sharply on all measures after only three months and declined to extremely low levels after three years. Baddeley (1999) suggests that riding a bike involves a continuous skill where each action provides the cue for the next action. Such skills appear to require little maintenance to be retained. Skills such as resuscitation, however, are much more complex and require accurate knowledge as well as motor skill. According to Baddeley, these need frequent refreshing if they are to be maintained.

There is evidence to suggest that certain verbal memories are remarkably resistant to long-term decay. Bahrick and Phelps (1987), in a long-term study of American college graduates, found that they showed rapid forgetting of Spanish vocabulary over the first three or four years after graduation, but then showed remarkably little further decline over the following 30 to 50 years.

All these findings suggest that, even where time plays a part in forgetting, it cannot be the only factor. It seems likely that we forget because other, similar memories get in the way.

Interference in LTM

There are problems in separating out the effects of time and interference, but Baddeley and Hitch (1977) conducted a study in which they attempted to avoid these difficulties.

Baddeley and Hitch asked rugby players to recall the names of teams they had played against during the previous season. Because of illness, other commitments, etc., some of the players had been unable to play in all the fixtures. This meant that, for some players 'two games back' meant two weeks ago, whereas for others 'two games back' meant four or five weeks ago. In other words, over the same period of time, some players had taken part in more games than others. This allowed Baddeley and Hitch to find out whether forgetting depended on elapsed time or the number of intervening games. The findings clearly showed that the mere passage of time was not the factor that determined how well team names could be recalled. The critical factor was the number of games played during that time period. In other words, forgetting appeared to be due to interference rather than trace decay.

If interference is the major cause of forgetting in LTM, it should be the case that people will remember things over time provided no interfering material intervenes. It is clearly difficult to create a situation where human participants are isolated after learning with no opportunity for any intervening new learning. Instead, researchers have turned their attention to looking at the effects of different types of interfering material on recall. McGeoch and MacDonald (1931) conducted a classic study into interference (see right).

McGeoch and MacDonald's study of interference (1931)

McGeoch and MacDonald asked participants to learn and relearn lists of adjectives and then compared their performance on recall tests after delays during which they carried out unrelated tasks.

Findings:

● Forgetting was least when participants simply had to rest during the interval between learning and recall.

● Forgetting rates increased when participants were required to learn unrelated material, such as nonsense syllables in the interval.

● Rates were even higher when other adjectives were learned in the interval. Rates were at their highest when the adjectives to be learned were similar in meaning to the original list.

Conclusion:

This study demonstrates that forgetting increases as a function of the similarity of the interfering material.

Types of interference

A distinction has been made between two types of interference:

● *Retroactive interference* – when new information interferes with old information. For example, if you move house and change telephone number, you will soon find that the new number supersedes the old.

● *Proactive interference* – when an old memory trace disrupts new information. You may, for example, suddenly find yourself dialling your old number even though you have not used it for months.

Retroactive interference was widely studied up until the 1960s, but has attracted less attention since then. Such studies typically made use of the technique of paired-associates in which a word is associated with one word on list A (e.g. *apple – fish*) and with a completely different word on list B (e.g. *apple – shoe*). Participants are required to learn list A and then to learn list B. When given the stimulus *apple* and asked to recall its paired associate from list A, participants frequently suffer from retroactive interference – in other words, they recall the paired associate from list B.

Proactive interference was studied by Underwood (1957). He noted that students who had learned a list of nonsense syllables showed a greater rate of forgetting when tested after 24 hours than would be expected. Given that these students had not been required to learn any more nonsense syllables in the intervening period, Underwood decided that retroactive interference was not causing the forgetting. Instead, he realized that this group of students had taken part in a number of his earlier memory experiments and so concluded that the interference causing their forgetting was proactive. He confirmed this suspicion by gathering data about the number of previous studies completed by the students and found that, the more lists of nonsense syllables they had learned earlier, the more likely they were to forget a new list over a 24-hour period.

There seems to be little doubt that interference between memory traces can cause forgetting. Recall can be impaired both from prior learning (proactive interference) and from later learning (retroactive interference) and, in both cases, the greater the similarity of the interfering material, the greater the interference. However, much of the evidence for interference theory has come from artificial laboratory experiments which have little relevance to everyday situations. There is also experimental evidence that demonstrates that interference cannot be a complete explanation of forgetting (see panel below).

Tulving's study of free recall (1966)

Tulving gave lists of words to participants and then tested their free recall. One group was given one presentation of the words followed by a single recall test. These participants were then re-presented with the list and tested again. A second group was given the list of words and then tested on three separate occasions without any further presentation of the list. A striking finding was that participants in this group recalled, on average, about 50 per cent of the words on each of the three tests, but that the words differed on each trial. Tulving concluded that all the words were still available in memory but not always readily accessible. This finding is difficult to reconcile with interference theory. How could a word that had been lost through interference on trial 1 suddenly become available again on trial 3? Studies such as these made psychologists think that forgetting can occur as a result of problems at the retrieval stage.

Retrieval failure in LTM

According to retrieval failure theory, forgetting occurs because the correct retrieval cues are not available. We are all familiar with the feeling that we know something, but just cannot bring it to mind – the name of an actor in an old film on TV, for example.

Brown (1991) has reviewed 25 years of research into the so-called 'tip-of-the-tongue' phenomenon, and reported that people can generally correctly recall the first letter of the target name or word between 50 and 70 per cent of the time. They also seem to be fairly accurate at identifying the correct number of syllables in the word.

Tulving has conducted much of the research into retrieval cues. For example, Tulving and Osler (1968) presented participants with lists of words, each of which was paired with a weakly associated cue word, e.g. *city – dirty*. Participants were then tested either for free recall (i.e. required to recall the first word of the pair without any prompt) or were cued with the associated word, e.g. given the word *dirty*. Cued recall consistently produced better performance than free recall. To counteract the argument that any semantically associated word might have elicited the target, Tulving and Osler gave some participants weak, semantic associates that had not been the original cue words, e.g. *busy*. Such cues did not facilitate recall and so Tulving and Osler (1968, p. 593) reached the following conclusion: "Specific retrieval cues facilitate recall if, and only if, the information about them is stored at the same time as the information about the membership of the word in a given list."

While Tulving has continued to stress the importance of cues at the memory encoding stage, he later (1983) acknowledged that cues not present at the time of learning can be helpful under certain circumstances.

Context-dependent retrieval

While it is clearly important how we encode material at the time of learning, psychologists have also been interested in the effects of the learning environment on recall (see the panel describing Smith's study). Smith's findings obviously have practical applications and raise

Learning environment and recall

Smith (1970) gave participants a list of 80 words to learn while sitting in a distinctive basement room. The following day, he tested some participants in the same basement room and others in a fifth-floor room with completely different furnishings and atmosphere. Average recall for the basement group was 18 items, but for those in the fifth-floor room, recall averaged 12 items. A third group were tested in the upstairs room, but first instructed to imagine themselves back in the basement room. These students recalled an average of 17 items.

the question of whether students will perform better in exams if they are tested in their original lecture rooms.

In general, it has been found that environmental differences need to be substantial before any significant difference in recall performance can be demonstrated. It has also been shown that simply imagining the original environmental setting can be helpful.

State-dependent retrieval

There is some evidence that the internal environment (i.e. physiological state or mood) might also affect retrieval. Goodwin *et al.* (1969) found that heavy drinkers who learn things in a drunken state are more likely to recall them in a similar state. Eich (1980) has shown this effect with a range of other drugs, including marijuana.

Although there is less conclusive evidence that mood affects retrieval, a review of research studies into mood dependence (Ucros 1989) found a moderately strong relationship between mood at the learning and retrieval stage. She also found that mood-dependence was more likely if the stimulus material was about real life rather than artificially constructed material, and that adults were more likely to demonstrate mood dependence than children.

THE ROLE OF EMOTIONAL FACTORS IN FORGETTING

Psychologists have often ignored the role of emotion in human cognitive processes, but it seems likely that the way we feel has an impact on the way we remember things. There is some evidence that memory is better for material that fits a person's current mood. For example, depressed people tend to recall more unhappy memories than non-depressed people do. Clark and Teasdale (1982) investigated people whose depression fluctuated through the 24-hour cycle and found that they were consistently less likely to recall happy memories during their sad phases than during their relatively neutral phases.

Flashbulb memories

One particular type of memory that seems to be influenced by emotion has been called a flashbulb memory. This is a particularly vivid, detailed and long-lasting memory of the circumstances surrounding a momentous event. The event is usually highly significant and emotional, and is often somewhat unexpected. It can be personal or something that provokes worldwide interest, such as the assassination of President Kennedy in 1963 or the death of Princess Diana in 1997. According to Brown and Kulik (1977),

September 11th – a flashbulb memory?

1 What time of day was it and where were you when you first heard about the terrorist attacks on the World Trade Center in New York on 11 September 2001?

2 Who told you the news?

3 What were you doing at the time?

4 Who else was with you at the time?

5 How did you react and how did you feel when you heard the news?

6 If others were with you at the time, how did they react?

7 Did you pay particular attention to the news bulletins as the details of the series of terrorist attacks in the United States on the morning of September 11th unfolded?

8 For many people, the recollection of hearing about the terrorist attacks on September 11th can be described as a 'flashbulb memory', because it is a vivid, relatively permanent record of the circumstances in which they heard the news. Can you think of any other incident(s) about which you have an equally vivid memory?

Ask an older person this same question and note down their answer.

who first described this type of memory, the event must be surprising and have real consequences for the person's life. They believed that such an emotional event triggers a neural mechanism that causes the details to be imprinted on the memory. They believed that this is a special type of memory because of the detail and accuracy with which the event is remembered and the fact that the structural form of the memory is always so similar. They found that six kinds of information were most likely to be recalled about the moment when the news of the event was first heard. People remember:

● where they were
● what they were doing
● the person who gave them the news
● what they felt about it
● what others felt about it
● what happened in the immediate aftermath.

Research on flashbulb memories

Conway *et al.* (1994) found that 86 per cent of British undergraduate students had vivid and accurate memories of the unexpected resignation of Margaret Thatcher as prime minister in 1990, even after 11 months. This compared with only 29 per cent of non-British students. Conway claimed that this event met the criteria for a flashbulb memory for British people: somewhat unexpected, highly significant and arousing deep emotions.

Not all psychologists agree that flashbulb memories are special (see key study, *Flashbulb memory*). Neisser (1982), for example, believes that the enduring nature of such memories results from frequent rehearsal and reworking after the event, rather than from neural activity at the time. As far as the uniformity of the memories is concerned, Neisser believes that this is caused simply by our using the common conventions of storytelling. In other words, when we recount important events, we do so by using conventional storytelling techniques. Neisser also argued that flashbulb memories are subject to the same types of inaccuracy and forgetting as any other memories. It is difficult to check the accuracy of so-called flashbulb memories.

A flashbulb memory ...

Where were you and what were you doing when you found out that Princess Diana had died after her car crashed in a Paris subway?

KEY STUDY >> FLASHBULB MEMORY

a study by McCloskey *et al.* (1988)

Aim >>

To test the accuracy of flashbulb memory.

Procedures >>

- People were interviewed a few days after the explosion of the American space shuttle *Challenger* in 1986 about their memories surrounding the event.
- The same people were interviewed again after nine months.

Findings >>

- There were inaccuracies in the memories.
- There were discrepancies between what was recalled shortly after the accident and what was remembered nine months later.

Conclusions >>

- So-called flashbulb memories are subject to the same types of inaccuracy and forgetting as other memories.
- Therefore, so-called flashbulb memories are not special memories but are products of ordinary memory mechanisms.

Criticisms >>

- This was not an artificial, laboratory study. People were asked to recall a real event that they had witnessed on TV or heard about through the media.
- Conway and colleagues reject the idea that flashbulb memories are simply stronger versions of ordinary memories. They have claimed that the Challenger accident did not meet the criteria for flashbulb memories.

For example, Neisser was sure that he had been listening to a baseball match on the radio when he heard about the Japanese bombing of Pearl Harbor (during World War II). However, when he checked this, he discovered, much to his surprise, that this was impossible as the bombing happened outside the baseball season.

Weaver (1993) found that American college students had no more vivid memories about the decision of the US president George Bush to bomb Iraq in 1991 than they had of a trivial event, such as meeting a friend. Conway (1995) has criticized such studies by pointing out that such an event (i.e. the bombing of Iraq) did not meet the criteria for a flashbulb memory. He believes that it was neither unexpected nor likely to have immediate consequences for the students concerned.

As you can see, the evidence is mixed and it is still unclear whether flashbulb memories represent a particular type of memory, or whether they are substantially similar to most memories for events.

Repression

According to Freud (1915), repression (or motivated forgetting) is an unconscious process, which ensures that threatening, or anxiety-provoking memories are kept from conscious awareness. Freud formulated his ideas on repression in the course of treating patients with neurotic disorders and he gave examples in his case studies. It has proved more difficult to demonstrate the existence of repression in the laboratory although a number of attempts have been made (see Key study, *Emotional factors in forgetting*).

KEY STUDY >> EMOTIONAL FACTORS IN FORGETTING

a study of repression by Levinger and Clark (1961)

Aim >>

To investigate the retrieval of associations to words that were emotionally charged, compared with the retrieval of associations to neutral words.

Procedures >>

- The time taken to produce associations was recorded.
- Immediately after the word associations had been generated, the participants were given the original cue words and were asked to recall their associated words.

Findings >>

- Participants took longer to provide free associations to the negatively charged words compared with the neutral words.
- Compared with the neutral words, the negatively charged words produced higher galvanic skin responses (GSR) in the participants.
- Participants found it more difficult to recall their associations for the negatively charged words compared with the neutral words.

Conclusions >>

- Repression led to the emotionally negatively charged words being more difficult to recall. This may have arisen from the arousal these words produced (as shown by the GSR data).
- Results, therefore, support Freud's theory that repression (of anxiety-provoking responses) causes forgetting.

Criticisms >>

- More recent evidence challenges these findings. Bradley and Baddeley (1990) ran a similar experiment using 32 student participants and found that when words were recalled after 28 days, the emotional associations were better recalled than the neutral associations. This does not support the repression hypothesis since emotional words actually became more memorable over time.
- Holmes (1990) has reviewed a number of studies of repression and forgetting, and concludes that there is no convincing experimental support for repression causing forgetting.

Although laboratory studies have not produced clear-cut support for the repression hypothesis, there is some evidence that real-life experiences of pain are forgotten more easily than those associated with pleasure.

Memory for pain

Robinson *et al.* (1980), in a study on the effectiveness of three different types of painkillers, asked women to rate the pain they had experienced during childbirth. They rated the pain at the time of the birth, after 24 hours, after five days and, again, after three months. Although the levels of pain experienced varied depending on the type of analgesic used, all three groups of women demonstrated that the memory of the pain faded considerably over time.

However, it could be argued that the pain of childbirth is not typical. Hunter *et al.* (1979), for example, found no decline in pain ratings over time when patients were asked to assess painful procedures such as sampling spinal fluid.

Recovered memories

Recently, research interest has focused on repressed memories associated with child sexual abuse. This is a controversial area because memories of abuse

'recovered' in psychotherapy can lead to great distress and, in some cases, to prosecutions years after the alleged events. The controversy revolves around the issue of whether these recovered memories are genuine. The main problem with establishing the validity of the claims is that there is usually no independent, objective, corroborative evidence. There is sadly no doubt that cases of child abuse do occur and it may well be that memories of abuse are repressed. Williams (1992), for example, found that 38 per cent of a group of African-American women who were known to have suffered abuse some years before, had repressed memories of the abuse. However, it also seems clear that some of these so-called repressed memories are false memories.

Loftus (1997) has conducted an extensive review of studies. These indicated that even psychologically healthy individuals can be made to alter their memory for events on the basis of false suggestions. As Baddeley (1999, p. 143) has written about reports of recovered memories:

<< It is important to exercise great caution in interpreting such reports, particularly when they become part of a legal process which is likely to be costly both financially and emotionally to patients and their families. >>

CHECK YOUR UNDERSTANDING

Check your understanding of the nature and structure of forgetting by answering these questions. Try to do this from memory at first. You can check your answers by looking back through Topic 2.

1 What do you understand by the term 'forgetting'?

2 Outline two ways of forgetting from STM.

3 Explain how the serial probe technique used by Waugh and Norman supported the idea of displacement in STM.

4 Outline the findings of Reitman's study of decay in STM. Explain how she tried to rule out the effects of interference in her study.

5 What is the difference between retroactive and proactive interference?

6 Give two criticisms of interference theory as an explanation of forgetting in LTM.

7 Outline the findings of research into retrieval failure.

8 Explain what is meant by the term 'flashbulb memory'.

9 Explain why Conway criticized previous research into flashbulb memories.

10 To what extent does the theory of repression explain forgetting from LTM.

or, in this case, an eye on the clock!

One of the most important skills in answering examination questions *effectively* is to get your time management right. You can apply a simple formula when answering a typical AS question.

30 marks = 30 minutes

Simple? Well, almost. The problem is that this same 30 minutes includes many other things that have to be accomplished within the same time period. For example, you have to *choose* which question you are going to attempt, *plan* your response, and do anything else you have to do along the way (*including* taking a breather between questions).

The first two parts of each question constitute the **AO1** component (see pp. 247–8). These are worth 6 marks each, and should take you about 5 minutes each to answer. The 'tricky' part of each question is the (c) part, as this inevitably has a number of different things that have to be dealt with in the time available. A typical part (c) for this area of the specification is as follows:

<< Give a brief account of, and evaluate attempts to explain forgetting in long-term memory. >>

(18 marks)

● 18 marks = 18 minutes, but you will need to *choose* carefully and *plan* your answer before embarking on your response to the question above. That effectively gives you about 15 minutes writing time for this part of the question, or about 300 words.

● There is a split in the marks awarded for all part (c) questions. **AO1** (the descriptive part of the question) is worth **6 marks**, and **AO2** (the evaluative component) is worth **12 marks**.

● '*Give a brief account of ....*' indicates the **AO1** component and requires a brief précis of at least *two* explanations of forgetting in long-term memory. Given the ratio of AO1 to AO2 is one-third to two-thirds, that's **5 minutes** on the AO1 content or about $2\frac{1}{2}$ minutes (or 50 words) on each of the two explanations – such as retrieval failure (see p. 24) and interference (see p. 22).

● As the AO2 or *evaluation* component of this question should be two-thirds of the time available, that allows you **5 minutes** (or 100 words) to evaluate retrieval failure and **5 minutes** to evaluate interference.

There are many advantages in good time management of AS psychology questions. Time spent planning and arranging your response in advance means that you organize everything in such a way as to maximize your marks, and – let's face it – tackling small tasks (such as a 50-word description or 100-word evaluation) is far less intimidating than a 300-word 'mini-essay'.

REVISION SUMMARY

Having covered this topic, you should be able to:

✓ define 'forgetting', 'displacement', 'decay', 'interference', 'retrieval failure', 'flashbulb memory' and 'repression'

✓ explain the processes of decay and displacement from STM

✓ explain the processes of interference and retrieval failure in LTM

✓ describe and evaluate research that has been carried out into the role of emotional factors in forgetting

✓ describe the aims, procedures, findings, conclusions and criticisms for a key study in the areas of flashbulb memories and emotional factors in forgetting (repression).

Unit 1 // Human memory

GETTING YOU THINKING...

Without looking anything up, try to do the following three tasks.

1 Draw a picture of a 10p coin.

2 Write down the name of the person shown on the back of a new £5 note. Write down the words written at the top of the front of a note of any denomination (i.e. £5, £10, £20 or £50).

3 List the three main colours on the front cover of this textbook. Draw a picture or write a brief description of the front cover of this textbook.

You may be surprised how difficult it is to remember exactly what a 10p coin looks like without having one in front of you. If you compare your drawing with a real coin, you will probably find a number of inaccuracies. In everyday life, you do not need to remember every detail, as long as you are able to recognize coins so that you can use them appropriately. Similarly, you may not have remembered that Elizabeth Fry is shown on the back of a £5 note or that the words "Bank of England – I promise to pay the bearer on demand the sum of 5 pounds" are written on the front. And even though you use this textbook regularly, you may not be able to recall either the colour or the detail of the front cover. In other words, there are many areas of everyday memory where we don't need exact recall. However, in certain instances, such as taking exams or giving testimony about a crime, accuracy is vitally important.

In 1978, Neisser wrote a paper called *Memory: what are the important questions?* He criticized contemporary psychologists for concentrating almost exclusively on theoretical concepts and ignoring practical issues about memory. One exception to this was the work of Bartlett (1932) described below, but his ideas had little influence at the time. Since Neisser's challenge there has been a growing interest in practical, applied aspects of memory. One particular area of interest is eyewitness testimony.

KEY TERMS

Eyewitness testimony: an area of memory research that investigates the accuracy of memory following an accident, crime or other significant event, and the types of errors that are commonly made in such situations.

Reconstructive memory: a term usually associated with Bartlett which refers to a memory distorted by the individual's prior knowledge and expectations

Inaccurate eyewitness testimony can have very serious consequences leading to wrongful convictions and, in some cases in the US, to the death penalty (Loftus and Ketcham 1991). For example, Rattner (1988) reviewed 205 cases of wrongful arrest and found that, in 52 per cent of cases, this was due to mistaken eyewitness testimony. Psychologists have been interested in investigating some of the reasons why eyewitness testimony can be unreliable, and some of the ways that accuracy might be improved.

AS Cognitive Psychology

RECONSTRUCTIVE MEMORY

One possible reason why people recall events inaccurately is that memory is distorted or reconstructed by the individual's prior knowledge and expectations. Bartlett (1932) carried out the pioneering work on reconstructive memory. He argued that we do not record memories passively, as we would if we were taking a photo. He believed that we need to make what he called 'effort after meaning' in order to make more sense of the event. So, instead of storing an exact replica of the initial stimulus, we weave it with elements of our existing knowledge and experience to form a reconstructed memory (see Key study, *Reconstructive memory*).

Bartlett carried out a number of other studies to investigate how people recall things such as stories, pictures and faces. For example, he presented line drawings, such as those in Fig. 1.4, and then asked his participants to draw them from memory.

Although not asked to do so, participants spontaneously gave a label to the drawing; for example, they variously named the second picture 'pickaxe', 'turf-cutter', 'shovel', and their subsequent reproduction reflected this label, so that the final drawing was a distortion of the original.

Figure 1.4 >> *Figures used by Bartlett to study memory for drawings*
Source: Bartlett (1932)

KEY STUDY >> RECONSTRUCTIVE MEMORY

a study by Bartlett (1932)

Aim >>
To investigate the effects of unfamiliarity on the recall of a folk story.

Procedures >>
- English participants heard an unfamiliar North American folk tale called 'The War of the Ghosts'. The story contained words and ideas that would not have appeared in a conventional Western story.
- After 20 hours, participants were asked to recall as much of the story as possible.
- Hereafter, participants were asked to retell the story many more times.

Findings >>
- The recalled story was distorted in a number of ways. Participants retold the story using language and narrative techniques that were influenced by their own cultural and literary background. Specifically, Bartlett found the following differences: rationalizations, omissions, changes in the order, alterations in importance and distortions of emotions.
- Distortions became even more pronounced over time, so that it increasingly resembled an ordinary English story.

Conclusions >>
- Memory for the folk tale continued being reconstructed over time and became less like the original story.
- The reconstruction made the story more coherent and so more easily remembered by the participants.

Criticisms >>
- This was an important study that drew attention to the way our schemas influence how we store memories.
- The study has been criticized for being poorly designed and controlled. For example, Gauld and Stephenson (1967), in semi-replications of Bartlett's story studies, found that errors were significantly reduced where participants were given explicit instructions that highlighted the importance of accurate recall.

SCHEMAS

According to Bartlett, we store memories in terms of our past experience or schemas. Schemas are knowledge packages which are built up through experience of the world and which can aid the interpretation of new information. Imagine, for example, that you are going for a meal in a restaurant. Through past experience, you will already be familiar with the kinds of things you would expect to see in a restaurant (for example, tables, chairs, waiters, menus, other customers) – in other words, you will have a restaurant schema.

Bartlett's ideas were regarded as rather vague and his studies were seen to lack experimental rigour by his contemporaries. It is certainly true that his experiments were poorly designed in some ways and that his instructions to participants were rather vague. However, in the 1970s, there was a revival of interest in the idea of schemas and their effects on memory. Cohen (1993) has suggested five ways in which schemas might lead to reconstructive memory.

1 We tend to ignore aspects of a scene that do not fit the currently activated schema.

2 We can store the central features of an event without having to store the exact details (e.g. the gist of a conversation rather than the exact words).

3 We can make sense of what we have seen by 'filling in' missing information (e.g. we see someone running and a bus pulling away from a bus stop, and assume that the person was running for the bus).

4 We distort memories for events to fit in with prior expectations (e.g. we might 'remember' that a bank robber wore a stocking mask, whereas he had actually worn a cap).

5 We may use schemas to provide the basis for a correct guess (e.g. if we cannot recall exactly what we had for breakfast last Tuesday, our schema for weekday breakfast supplies 'cereal' and this has a good chance of being correct).

This means that schemas are usually useful to us because they make our experiences more predictable and use our attentional resources efficiently. However, research has shown that schemas may also lead to distortions in memory.

Research findings on schemas

Brewer and Treyens (1981) investigated the effects of schemas on visual memory by asking their 30 participants, one at a time, to wait in a room for 35 seconds. The room was designed to look like an office and contained 61 objects. Some objects were compatible with an office schema, such as a desk, calendar and typewriter (this was 1981!), but a few items were included which were incompatible, such as a skull, a brick and a pair of pliers. In a subsequent, unexpected recall test, participants were most likely to recall typical office items, i.e. items with high schema

expectancy. They were less successful at recalling the incompatible items such as the brick, but eight participants recalled the really bizarre item – the skull. Most of the errors in recall were substitutions, i.e. participants tended to recall falsely the presence of objects such as books, pens and a telephone, which would have high schema expectancy but which were not actually present on this occasion. Other errors involved wrong placement of items, e.g. a note pad was 'remembered' as being on the desk (where it might be in an office schema) instead of being on the seat of a chair (as it was in reality). These findings suggest that participants were using schemas to ensure rapid encoding of the visual information available to them during their 35-second wait. At the retrieval stage, recall was influenced by the schema so that typical items were recalled, even if they were not actually present. The Brewer and Treyens experiment showed that people can sometimes falsely remember objects that did not exist. List's shoplifting scenarios (see below) give another example of how schemas influence what is recalled.

List's shoplifting scenarios (1986)

List asked people to rate various events in terms of their probability in a shop-lifting scenario. She then compiled a video showing eight different shoplifting acts, each of which incorporated some of the events rated as high probability and some rated as low probability. She showed this video to a new set of people and, one week later, tested their recall. She found that they were more likely to recall high- rather than low-probability events and that, if they made inclusion errors of events that had not actually occurred in the video, they were more likely to be high-probability events.

Evaluation of Bartlett's research

- Bartlett has been criticized for his choice of material in his studies of reconstructive memory. He used folk tales that he assumed would be less meaningful to people of other cultures, but he had no objective measure of meaningfulness.

- Later studies have provided support for some of Bartlett's ideas by using more rigorous methods. Bransford and Johnson (1972), for example, constructed some prose passages that would be difficult to understand in the absence of context. They then compared recall performance between a group of participants who had been supplied with contextual information and a group who had not received this additional information. You can try one of their studies for yourself in the activity (right).

- You probably found the task in the activity quite difficult because the passage was hard to understand – in other words, you lacked an appropriate schema and so could not relate the passage to stored information. However, if you now turn to p. 38 and look at Fig. 1.5, then read the passage again, it will probably make sense. Bransford and Johnson found that recall was significantly better for the group given the picture than for the group that simply read the passage.

- There seems little doubt that we do use stored knowledge and past experience to make sense of new information, and that memories for events can be distorted (reconstructed) because of this. This

ACTIVITY

Activity (based on Bransford and Johnson 1972)

Read the following passage through once at normal reading speed. Then cover it up and write down as many points from the passage as you can remember.

>> If the balloons popped, the sound wouldn't be able to carry since then everything would be too far away from the correct floor. A closed window would also prevent the sound from carrying, since most buildings tend to be well insulated. Since the whole operation depends on the steady flow of electricity, a break in the middle of the wire would also cause problems. Of course, the fellow could shout but the human voice is not loud enough to carry that far. An additional problem is that the string could break on the instrument. Then there would be no accompaniment to the message. It is clear that the best situation would involve less distance. Then there would be fewer potential problems. With face-to-face contact, the least number of things could go wrong. >>

may well account for some instances of inaccurate eyewitness testimony. However, schema theories have been criticized on several counts (Cohen 1993). The main problems are that a schema is rather a vague concept and schema theory offers no explanation as to how the schemas are acquired in the first place.

LOFTUS' RESEARCH INTO EYEWITNESS TESTIMONY

Jurors place considerable importance on the evidence provided by eyewitnesses. Baddeley (1997) has reported that 74 per cent of suspects were convicted in 300 cases where eyewitness identification was the only evidence against them. However, numerous research studies have identified several problems with eyewitness testimony. One of the leading researchers in this field is Elizabeth Loftus.

Misleading post-event information

We have already seen that schemas (i.e. prior knowledge) can affect the way we remember events. Elizabeth Loftus has been primarily interested in the effects on memory of information provided *after* the event. She and her colleagues have carried out many studies that show that memory for events can be changed or supplemented by later information. They used the experimental method which has the advantage of the controlled environment of the laboratory, but which uses stimulus material that mimics real-life situations. In a typical experiment, participants are first shown a film or series of slides depicting an event such as a car accident. In the interval between viewing the slides and being tested for recall, participants are provided with information which either conflicts or is consistent with the original witnessed event.

For example, Loftus (1975) showed 150 participants a film depicting a car accident. After the showing, participants were divided into two groups and each group was asked ten questions about what they had seen.

- Group 1 was asked questions which were entirely consistent with the original film, e.g. "How fast was the white sports car going when it passed the 'Stop' sign?"

- Group 2 was given the same questions with the exception of one – "How fast was the white sports car going when it passed the barn when travelling along the country road?" This question was misleading because there was no barn in the film.

After one week, the participants were all asked a further ten questions and, for both groups, the final question was: "Did you see a barn?" Loftus found the following:

- Only 2.7 per cent of the participants in Group 1 gave the incorrect answer "Yes".

- On the other hand, 17.3 per cent of those in Group 2 (i.e. those given the misleading question) answered "Yes".

Loftus concluded that for those in Group 2, the non-existent barn had been added to the original memory representation of the event at the question stage so that it was now recalled as being part of the original event (see key study, *Eyewitness testimony*, opposite, for another example).

Other factors that affect eyewitness testimony

- *Leading questions* – Loftus and Palmer (1974) showed participants a film of a car accident and then asked them: "How fast were the cars going when they hit each other?" All participants were asked the same type of question except that the word 'hit' was variously replaced with 'smashed', 'collided', 'bumped', or 'contacted'. It was found that the word used affected speed estimation – 'smashed' produced the highest estimate (40.8 miles per hour) and 'contacted' produced the lowest estimate. A week later, when people were asked if they had seen any broken glass, those in the 'smashed' group were consistently more likely to answer 'Yes' (wrongly).

  In a similar study, in which film footage of a car accident was shown, participants were asked either "Did you see *a* broken headlight?" or "Did you see *the* broken headlight?" People who had seen a version of the film in which there really was a broken headlight were equally likely to answer 'Yes' to either of the questions. However, people who had seen a version with no broken headlight were more than twice as likely to recall one when asked about 'the' rather than 'a' broken headlight.

- *Anxiety of the witness* – Loftus (1979) reported a study where participants were exposed to one of two situations:

  1 They overheard a low-key discussion in a laboratory about an equipment failure. A person

then emerged from the laboratory holding a pen and with grease on his hands.

  2 They overheard a heated and hostile exchange between people in the laboratory. After the sound of breaking glass and crashing chairs, a man emerged from the laboratory holding a paper knife covered in blood.

  Participants were then given 50 photos and asked to identify the person who had come out of the laboratory.

  1 Those who had witnessed the man holding the pen accurately identified the person 49 per cent of the time, whereas

  2 Those who had witnessed the man with the bloodstained letter-opener were successful only 33 per cent of the time.

  This finding has come to be known as the 'weapon focus', whereby the witness concentrates on the weapon (in this case, the bloodstained paper knife) and this distracts attention from the appearance of the perpetrator. Loftus concluded that the fear or anxiety induced by the sight of a weapon narrows the focus of attention and gives rise to very accurate recall of the central details of the scene, but diminishes accurate recall of peripheral details.

- *Consequences* – Findings from laboratory studies have not always been supported by evidence from real life. It is possible that participants in experiments are less accurate than genuine witnesses because they know inaccuracies will not lead to serious consequences. Foster *et al.* (1994) tested this possibility in a study where participants were shown a video of a bank robbery and subsequently asked to identify the robber in an identity parade. One group of participants were led to believe that the robbery was a real event and that their responses would influence the trial, while the second group assumed that it was a simulation. Identification of the robber was more accurate for the first group, suggesting that the consequence of identifying someone is an important factor for witnesses.

How would you approach the task of choosing a suspect from an identity parade if you knew your choice could make all the difference in getting someone convicted?

a study of the effects of misleading information on accurate recall
by Loftus *et al.* (1978)

Aim >>

To see whether participants would recall an event inaccurately if they were fed misleading questions.

Procedures >>

- Participants were divided into two groups.
- Both groups were shown a set of slides depicting events leading up to a car accident.
- The sets of slides were identical except for one slide: for one group, this slide depicted a red car stopping at a junction with a 'Yield' (Give Way) sign; the other group saw the same car stopping at a junction with a 'Stop' sign.
- After the slide presentation, both groups were given a set of 20 questions. For half the participants in each group, this set included the question "Did another car pass the red one while it was stopped at the 'Stop' sign?", while for the other half, the critical question was "Did another car pass the red one while it was stopped at the 'Yield' sign?" (i.e. half the participants received a misleading question and half received a question that was consistent with what they had actually seen).

- After 20 minutes, the participants were given 15 pairs of slides to look at and had to pick from each pair the slide that had been included in the original set (a recognition test). The critical pair consisted of one slide showing the car stopped at the 'Yield' sign and the other slide showing the car stopped at the 'Stop' sign.

Findings >>

- 75 per cent of participants who had received consistent questions picked the correct slide, as opposed to 41 per cent who had been given the misleading question.
- When the recognition test was delayed for a week, accuracy in the misled group fell to 20 per cent.

Conclusions >>

- Loftus and her colleagues concluded that the misleading question had served to delete the correct information from memory and replace it with false information.
- The effect of misleading questions becomes more pronounced over time.

Criticisms >>

- The conclusions of this study have been supported by other studies. For example, Loftus and Loftus (1980) found that accuracy in the misled group did not increase even when they were offered money for picking the correct slide.
- Although the results of this study are significant, it is important to note that by no means everyone in the misled group was inaccurate in the recognition task.
- Participants were simply shown static slides. We cannot conclude that memory would be affected by misleading questions in a real-life situation.

● *Method of testing witnesses* – Loftus often used forced-choice tests (e.g. picking one of two slides), but this may give a false picture. Koriat and Goldsmith (1996) have shown that witness accuracy can be dramatically increased if tests do not rely on forced-choice format and if witnesses are allowed to give no answer if they feel unsure. It also seems to be the case that witnesses are able to produce far more accurate memories for events if they are given the appropriate cues. The Cognitive Interview technique, for example (see p. 37) seems to elicit memories that are more accurate and richer in details than other types of questioning.

So far we have looked at factors that seem to increase witness fallibility, but under some circumstances, recall seems less susceptible to error.

● *Witnessing real-life events* – For example, Christianson and Hubinette (1993) questioned 110 witnesses who had, between them, witnessed a total of 22 genuine, as opposed to staged, bank robberies. Some of these witnesses had been onlookers who happened to be in the banks at the time, whereas others were bank employees who had been directly threatened in the robberies. Victims were more accurate in their recall and remembered more details about what the robbers wore, their behaviour and the weapon used, than people who had been bystanders. This superior recall continued to be evident, even after a 15-month interval. Christianson and Hubinette concluded that people are good at remembering highly stressful events if they occur in real life rather than in the artificial surroundings of the laboratory.

● *Blatantly incorrect misinformation* – People are generally not misled by information if it is blatantly incorrect. Loftus (1979) showed participants a set of slides that depicted the theft of a large, red purse from a handbag. In an immediate recall test, 98 per cent of the participants correctly remembered the colour of the purse. They were then asked to read

an account of the incident allegedly written by a professor of psychology (this was designed to lend weight to the accuracy of the account). One of these accounts contained errors relating to unimportant items in the slide sequence, e.g. the wrong colour was given for items that were not central to the action. The other account contained, in addition to these minor errors, the more glaring statement that the purse was brown. In a second recall test, all but two of the participants resisted this blatantly wrong information and again correctly recalled that the purse was red. This suggests that memory for information that is particularly noticeable and salient at the time is less subject to distortion than memory for peripheral details. In other words, people can ignore new information under certain circumstances and so maintain their original memory representation intact.

What happens to the original memory?

Loftus believes that, in the light of misleading information, the original memory is deleted and replaced by the new, false memory. Other researchers have disputed this and claim that the original memory trace is still available, even though it has been obscured by new information. Bekerian and Bowers (1983) replicated the study by Loftus *et al.* (1978) in which a car is shown stopping at either a 'Stop' or a 'Yield' sign (see key study, *Eyewitness testimony*, on p. 35). In the recognition phase of the study, the participants were presented with the pairs of slides in chronological order, i.e. the order in which they were first shown (unlike the Loftus study where presentation was random). Under these circumstances, recall of the misled participants was almost exactly as accurate as of the control group. Bekerian and Bowers concluded that the original memory representation had not been lost for these participants. Looking at the slides in the correct sequence provided enough cues to reactivate the original memory in spite of the post-event misleading information. However, other researchers have failed to replicate this result, so it remains unclear whether the original memory trace is destroyed or obscured.

Evaluation of Loftus' research

● Loftus and her colleagues have made an important contribution to our understanding of the fallibility of eyewitness testimony. It seems clear from her research that memory for events can be fundamentally altered in the light of misleading post-event information. This has important implications for the way in which the police question witnesses and also in the courts.

● However, her studies have been criticized for artificiality. In real life, events that might have to be recalled later in a court of law, often take place unexpectedly and in an atmosphere of tension. It is difficult to reproduce such conditions in the

ACTIVITY

Assessing Christianson and Hubinette's research

1 What do you think is the main strength of the study that Christianson and Hubinette undertook in 1993?

2 Why is it sometimes important for researchers such as Christianson and Hubinette to study recall after a long period of time (e.g. after a 15-month interval), rather than just gather data over short periods of time, as tends to be the case in much laboratory-based memory research?

laboratory for various practical and ethical reasons, and it is quite possible that eyewitnesses remember real events rather differently from staged events (e.g. see Christianson and Hubinette above).

● She has also been criticized for her method of testing recall. People are much more accurate if they are asked questions in a logical order and if they are not forced to answer if unsure. The success of the Cognitive Interview technique has demonstrated that the type of questioning has a huge effect on witness accuracy (see below).

Accounts from eyewitnesses are often fallible and incomplete

THE COGNITIVE INTERVIEW

In view of the finding that accounts from eyewitnesses are often fallible and incomplete, psychologists have attempted to develop memory retrieval techniques aimed at eliciting more accurate information. One example is the Cognitive Interview Schedule that was developed by Geiselman *et al.* (1985) and designed to be used by police investigators. The interview technique is based on four instructions:

● *To recreate the context of the original incident* – This does not involve revisiting the scene of the crime, but trying to recall an image of the setting including details such as the weather, the lighting, distinctive smells, any people nearby and what you were feeling at the time.

● *To report every detail* – You are required to report back any information about the event you can remember, even if it does not seem to you to have a bearing on the crime.

● *To recall the event in different orders* – You are encouraged to describe the event in reverse order, or to start with an aspect of the scene which seems most memorable and work backwards or forwards from that point.

● *To change perspectives* – You are asked to *try* to describe the incident from the perspective of other people who were present at the time.

Geiselman and colleagues tested the effectiveness of the Cognitive Interview Schedule by comparing it with standard police interviewing techniques. They showed police training videos of violent crimes to a group of 89 students. About 48 hours later, the students were interviewed individually by American law enforcement officers (detectives, CIA investigators and private investigators). The interviewers had either been trained in standard police interviewing techniques or in the new Cognitive Interview Schedule. Each interview was taped and analysed for accuracy of recall. Results were recorded as:

● the number of correct items recalled

● the number of errors – this category was subdivided into incorrect items (number of items incorrectly recalled, e.g. the assailant was wearing a brown coat instead of a black one) and confabulated items (number of items described, but not actually shown on the video).

As you can see, people recalled considerably more items in the Cognitive than in the Standard interview, although error rates were very similar. The interviewees in this study were undergraduate students who watched videotapes and so the study could be criticized for artificiality. However, Fisher *et al.* (1989) later trained a group of detectives in Florida in the use of the Cognitive Interview and then assessed their performance when interviewing genuine witnesses to crimes. When their performance was compared to pretraining levels, it was found that the information gain was as much as 47 per cent.

There have since been a number of studies that have investigated the effectiveness of the Cognitive Interview Schedule. Bekerian and Dennett (1993) have reviewed 27 such studies and found in all cases that the Cognitive Interview approach has provided more accurate information than other interview procedures.

Average number of items recalled in Cognitive and Standard Interviews

	Cognitive	Standard
>> Correct items	41.15	29.4
>> Incorrect items	7.3	6.1
>> Confabulated items	0.7	0.4

Source: Based on Geiselman (1988)

Use the information provided by
Elizabeth Loftus in the interview on
the next page to outline:

1 why our memories are not always
reliable

2 which factors are likely to improve
the accuracy of eyewitness
testimony.

WEBSITES

www.faculty.washington.edu/eloftus
To find out more about the work of Elizabeth Loftus.

www.faculty.washington.edu/chudler.stm0.html
For an interactive test on short-term memory.

ANSWERS TO ACTIVITIES

Activity, p. 4

Another possible explanation for Clive Wearing's
inability to remember is that the memory trace is laid
down, but fades away very quickly.

The third possibility is that the memory trace is laid
down, but cannot be retrieved. The answer is not clear,
but it is important to recognize that a normally
functioning memory system must be capable of:

● registering information

● storing information over time

● retrieving information when required.

Activity, p. 9

1 Conrad used the experimental method to study
encoding in STM.

2 A well-designed experiment allows a researcher to
draw conclusions about the cause-and-effect
relationship between the independent variable and
the dependent variable. Conrad concluded that the
nature of the stimuli (i.e. whether or not they
sounded similar) affected the accuracy of
participants' recall.

3 A laboratory study using artificial stimuli does not
necessarily reflect everyday memory, so this study
may be criticized for lacking ecological validity.

Activity, p. 14

1 The first and last words on the list are
remembered best.

2 Where there are too many words for them all to be
remembered, the primacy effect results in the first
words being recalled and the recency effect results
in the last words being recalled. According to
Glanzer and Cunitz, the primacy effect occurs
because words remembered from the beginning of
the list have already been stored in LTM, while the

words at the end of the list are still in STM and so
are also easily recalled. The words in the middle of
the list are displaced from STM memory but have
not yet had a chance to be stored in LTM.

3 Words at the beginning of the list.

4 There is no recency effect for the 'distraction' group
(but note that both groups show the primacy effect).

5 By introducing a distraction task before the
participants recall the words, Glanzer and Cunitz
show that information in STM is easily disrupted
while information in LTM is not affected. Therefore,
they claim, STM and LTM are two separate stores.

6 As interpreted by Glanzer and Cunitz, these results
support the multi-store model. However, other
researchers have suggested that recency effects can
be explained differently. For example, Crowder
(1993) proposed that recency effects occur because
the most recent items are simply the most
distinctive, not because they are held in a separate
STM store.

Activity, p. 33

Figure 1.5 >>
*Visual source for
activity on p. 33*

Eyewitness *testimony*

Elizabeth Loftus is Distinguished Professor of Psychology at University of California, Irvine. Professor Loftus's research has focused on human memory, eyewitness testimony and courtroom procedure. She has served as an expert witness or consultant in hundreds of cases, including the trial of former White House adviser, Oliver North, the trial of police officers accused in the Rodney King beating case, and the Michael Jackson case. Professor Loftus is the author of 20 books and over 250 scientific articles. Her fourth book, Eyewitness Testimony, *won a National Media Award from the American Psychology Foundation.*

Q **Eyewitness testimony is sometimes referred to as the 'most damning' of all evidence. It is based on memory, which is not a foolproof system. Why isn't it?**

A Human memory is far from perfect. Forgetfulness is a fact of life. One of the most obvious reasons for poor memory is that the information was never stored in the first place. We look at one part of a crime and fail even to notice other parts or details. But even if we are careful observers and take in a relatively accurate picture of what we have seen, it does not stay intact in memory. Other forces begin to corrode the original experience. With the passage of time, or with the introduction of interfering or contradictory facts, our memories can change, often without our conscious awareness. We can then come to believe in memories for details or events that never happened.

Elizabeth Loftus

Q **If psychological research has shown that eyewitness memory is sometimes unreliable, what are some of the situations where it is particularly unreliable?**

A Eyewitness memory can be mistaken because of things that go wrong at the time of the event itself. For example, poor lighting or extremely high stress or fright. Memory can also be mistaken because of things that go wrong after the event is over. For example, one witness is exposed to the mistaken recollection of another witness, or the witness is questioned in a biased way, or the test of memory is unfair in some way, and leads the witness to say the wrong thing.

Q **Are there some situations where eyewitness memory is likely to be more accurate?**

A Many factors are known to make eyewitness memory unreliable, such as poor lighting, brief exposure to the crime details, and long passage of time between the crime and the witness's memory report. Conversely, the absence of these factors would lead to more accurate eyewitness memory: good lighting, extended exposure to crime details, and a short passage of time between the crime and the memory report.

Other situations that lead to better eyewitness memory include:

- when the witness is close to the crime, rather than viewing from a distance
- when the witness and the criminal suspect are of the same race, rather than a different race
- when the witness is sober, rather than under the influence of alcohol or drugs
- when the witness is interviewed in a neutral manner, rather than in a biased or suggestive manner.

Check your understanding of eyewitness testimony by answering these questions. Try to do this from memory at first. You can check your answers by looking back through Topic 3.

1   What do you understand by the terms 'eyewitness testimony' and 'reconstructive memory'?

2   Why do you think that eyewitness testimony research is important?

3   Outline some of the ways participants changed the details in the 'War of the Ghosts' study.

4   What did Bartlett mean by the term 'schema'? Give three ways in which schemas might produced reconstructive memories, according to Cohen.

5   Explain why people sometimes falsely remember objects and events that did not exist in the original event.

6   Give two criticisms of the study by Loftus *et al.* (1978) that used the 'Yield' and 'Stop' signs.

7   Briefly outline two factors that affect the accuracy of eyewitness testimony.

8   Explain why the study by Christianson and Hubinette (1993) was different from studies carried out by Loftus.

9   What is meant by the 'Cognitive Interview'? Why do you think that it improves accuracy of recall?

10 To what extent has psychological research supported the idea that eyewitness testimony is largely unreliable?

REVISION SUMMARY

Having covered this topic you should be able to:

✓ define the terms 'eyewitness testimony' and 'reconstructive memory'

✓ describe the aims, procedures, findings, conclusions and criticisms for a key study in the areas of eyewitness testimony and reconstructive memory

✓ describe and evaluate findings from a range of research in the areas of eyewitness testimony and reconstructive memory.

UNIT SUMMARY

Topic 1: Short-term and long-term memory

● **Short-term** and **long-term memory** (STM and LTM) are two types of memory store.

● STM and LTM differ in terms of capacity, duration and encoding:
  – **Capacity** of STM is limited, but is infinite in LTM.
  – **Duration** of STM is limited to a few seconds, but can last up to a lifetime in LTM.
  – **Encoding** in STM is primarily acoustic, but is primarily semantic in LTM.

● The **multi-store model** of memory, first proposed by **Atkinson and Shiffrin** in 1968, distinguishes between STM and LTM. It was the first information-processing model of memory and was very influential. However, it was criticized for being too simplistic and inflexible.

● **Baddeley and Hitch** (1974) believed that STM operated more like a **working memory** and proposed that it consisted of a flexible and complex system of components under the control of a central executive. This model has been supported in many experimental studies. Its major weakness, however, is the lack of evidence about the precise role and functioning of the central executive.

● In the **levels of processing model**, **Craik and Lockhart** (1972) believed that the crucial factor in laying down new memories is the amount and depth of processing they receive. This model has received experimental support, but is criticized because it is descriptive rather than explanatory.

Topic 2: Forgetting

● We are generally good at retrieving information stored in memory, but we do sometimes forget. There are several **explanations** for **forgetting**.

● Decay and displacement seem to be the main forgetting mechanisms in STM:

  – **Decay** occurs when the memory trace simply fades away over time because of lack of rehearsal.

  – **Displacement** occurs because of the limited capacity of STM – new items can only find a place in STM if existing items are pushed out.

● Retrieval failure and interference account for much of the forgetting from LTM.

  – **Retrieval** failure occurs when the correct cues are unavailable.

  – **Interference** occurs when memory traces are obscured by other memories. In retroactive interference, new information interferes with old, and in proactive interference, old information interferes with new.

● **Cognitive theories** often fail to take account of **emotional factors**, but it seems possible that we forget some things because they are too painful to recall. **Freud** called this kind of forgetting **repression** or **motivated forgetting**, and suggested that we push threatening memories out of our conscious awareness. There is some research evidence to support this view, but it is difficult to demonstrate unconscious processes experimentally.

● **Flashbulb memories** have been a particular area of interest. These are memories associated with important events in our lives which appear to be remembered with enormous clarity and accuracy. However, some psychologists, such as **Neisser**, reject the idea that flashbulb memories are special in any way. They believe that they are subject to the same kinds of distortion and forgetting as other memories for events.

Topic 3: Eyewitness testimony

● One important application of memory research is **eyewitness testimony**. People are often able to recall events accurately and in detail, but eyewitness testimony can be fallible. Given the potentially serious consequences of inaccurate testimony, psychologists have sought to understand why people remember inaccurately and to find ways of improving their recall.

● One important factor is a tendency to distort or reconstruct memories. **Bartlett** introduced the concept of **reconstructive memory** to explain how we store memories in terms of our past knowledge and experience (**schemas**), which influence us when we come to recall the memory. Bartlett's research has been criticized for lack of experimental rigour, but the concept of schemas continues to be important.

● **Elizabeth Loftus**, one of the most influential researchers into eyewitness testimony, has been particularly concerned with the effects of misleading information provided after the event. Her studies, showing that testimony can be distorted by post-event information and by leading questions, have serious implications for the legal system.

Answering exam questions on Human memory

For sample examination questions and answers on Human memory, together with examiner comments on the answers, see pp. 251–2.

Unit 1 // Human memory

UNIT 2

ATTACHMENTS IN
Development

PREVIEW

After you have read this unit, you should be able to:

>> describe the development and variety of attachments, including individual and cross-cultural variations

>> explain how such attachments form (e.g. learning theory and Bowlby's theory of attachment)

>> distinguish between and discuss separation, deprivation and privation

>> describe the effects of being separated from one's attachment figure and being deprived of emotional care at this time, and the effects of having formed no attachments at all (privation)

>> discuss the critical issue of day care and how it may affect children's cognitive and social development.

INTRODUCTION

When you become attached to someone, it means you have formed a special bond or relationship with that person, and they with you. Relationships and attachments are important throughout people's lives, but they have a special importance during infancy. In Topic 1, we will look at the sequence of the development of attachments, and at how development varies from one individual to another. We will then consider explanations of *why* an infant becomes attached, and why they become attached to one particular person rather than another. (Psychologists generally use the term 'infant' to refer to children of less than 2 years; the term 'child' is used to refer to anyone between the age of 2 and adolescence.)

If attachments are so important, then this would lead you to expect that a loss of attachments would have negative consequences for an individual. In the second topic, we will consider the short- and long-term effects of separation on development. Furthermore, we will consider the different effects of loss of attachment (deprivation) and lack of attachment (privation).

Does this psychological research have any relevance to 'real life'? It most definitely has. People are very concerned about the effects of separation when parents go out to work and their children are placed in day care. Does this harm the cognitive and social development of their children? The final topic in this unit considers this critical issue.

Cara
Flanagan

GETTING YOU THINKING...

In psychology the term 'attachment' is used to describe a special kind of relationship between two people. Attachments are a special kind of affectional bond. According to Mary Ainsworth (1989), an affectional bond is a "relatively long-enduring tie in which the partner is important as a unique individual ... [and where there] is a

desire to maintain closeness to the partner". Bearing this in mind, do the following activities:

1 Make a list of the people with whom you have an affectional bond.

2 Now select from your list any people with whom your relationship would be better described as an attachment.

3 Make a list of the attachment behaviours that you and the other person use. These are the behaviours that psychologists could use to infer the existence of an attachment.

Now work in a small group to discuss the following:

4 If an attachment is designed to maintain proximity to another person, what attachment behaviours are commonly used by:

(a) *infants* – to maintain closeness to their parents or to those who care for them?

(b) *school-aged children* – to maintain closeness to their parents or to those who care for them?

(c) *adults* – to maintain closeness to their parents or to those who cared for them?

KEY TERMS

Attachment: a strong emotional and reciprocal bond between two people, especially between an infant and its caregiver(s). Attachments serve to maintain proximity between infant and caregiver because each experiences distress when separated. The attachment relationship also serves as a basis for subsequent emotional development.

Secure attachment: the optimal form of attachment, associated with healthy emotional and social development. Securely attached infants feel content to explore a strange environment using their caregiver as a safe base. They show some distress when left by their caregiver, but are relatively easily comforted and show joy at reunion. Securely attached children are more likely to show stranger anxiety than insecurely attached children.

Insecure attachment: a less optimal form of attachment, at least in Western culture. Insecurely attached children show disturbed behaviour during separation and reunion. One type of insecure attachment is called resistance-insecure. Children who are resistant-insecure are distressed on separation and resist reunion with their caregiver. A second type, avoidant-insecure, are indifferent at separation and avoid contact on reunion. Insecurely attached children tend to have less successful relationships with peers, lovers and their own children later in life.

Cross-cultural variation: variations between people of different cultures. A culture is a set of beliefs and customs that bind a group of people together, such as child-rearing practices. These practices may influence the kind of attachments, so that people from different cultural groups have different kinds of attachments with their children. These differences tell us something about the effects of child-rearing practices on attachment.

THE DEVELOPMENT OF ATTACHMENTS

Attachment is a strong emotional tie that develops over time between an infant and their primary caregiver(s) – the person(s) to whom they are most strongly attached. It is a reciprocal tie because each partner is attached to the other. Maurer and Maurer (1989) suggested that attachments "are welded in the heat of interactions". In other words, attachments depend on interaction between two people rather than their simply being together. Maccoby (1980) identified four characteristic effects of this tie:

● seeking proximity, especially at times of stress

● distress on separation

● pleasure when reunited

● general orientation of behaviour towards the primary caregiver.

Schaffer and Emerson (1964) conducted a classic study of the development of attachments in order to investigate the way infant behaviours change over time. Specifically, Schaffer and Emerson wanted to find out how old infants were when they first became attached, who they became attached to and how strong these attachments were. Schaffer and Emerson also wanted to search for any individual differences between infants in their attachment behaviours. They studied 60 infants from a mainly working-class area of Glasgow. The infants were observed every four weeks until they were 1 year old and then again at 18 months. At the start of the investigation, the youngest participant was 5 weeks and the oldest 23 weeks.

Observations were conducted in the children's homes. Schaffer and Emerson used two measures to determine the strength of attachment. One was separation anxiety

– the distress shown by the infant when separated from their main caregiver. This is regarded as a sign of attachment because infants only show such distress when separated from certain people. Schaffer and Emerson asked the mothers about situations where separation protest was shown, and to whom these protests were directed. This meant that they could rate the strength of attachment at each monthly visit. They asked the mothers to consider seven everyday situations, i.e. where the infant was:

1 left alone in a room

2 left with other people

3 left in their pram outside the house

4 left in their pram outside the shops

5 left in their cot at night

6 put down after being held by an adult

7 passed by while sitting in a cot or chair.

The second measure of attachment was stranger anxiety. Very young infants show no anxiety when they are left with a stranger but, at a certain age, this stranger anxiety starts. Schaffer and Emerson regarded this as another sign of the onset of attachment. Schaffer and Emerson measured stranger anxiety by approaching the infant at the start of every visit and noting at what point the infant started to whimper, thus displaying anxiety.

Schaffer and Emerson's findings were as follows.

● **Age of first attachment** – Half of the children showed their first specific attachment (i.e. displayed separation anxiety with respect to one primary caregiver) between 6 and 8 months. Fear of strangers occurred about a month later in all the children.

● **Attachment figures** – Soon after one main attachment was formed, the infants also became attached to other people. By 18 months very few (13 per cent) were attached to only one person. One third of the infants had five or more attachments, such as their father, grandparent or older sibling. In 65 per cent of the children, the first specific attachment was to the mother. In a further 30 per cent the mother was the first joint object of attachment. Fathers were rarely the first sole object of attachment (3 per cent), but 27 per cent of them were the joint first object.

● **Strength of attachment** – This peaked in the first month after attachment behaviour first appeared. However, there were large individual differences. Schaffer and Emerson observed that intensely attached infants had mothers who responded quickly to their demands (high responsiveness) and offered the child the most interaction. Infants who were weakly attached had mothers who failed to interact.

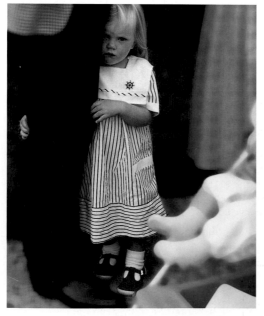

Seeking proximity in times of stress a sign of attachment. Who do you turn to when you are anxious?

- *Time spent with infant* – In 39 per cent of the cases, the person who usually fed, bathed and changed the child was *not* the child's primary attachment object. In other words, many of the mothers were not the individuals who performed these tasks, yet the mother did tend to be the main attachment object.

The three main conclusions are these:

- Specific attachments appear to be formed first around the age of 7 months.
- Multiple attachments develop soon afterwards.
- Attachments seemed to be formed to individuals who were prepared to play, be responsive and interact socially with the child, rather than simply with those who were most often present.

The sequence of development

Schaffer and Emerson's account indicates a sequence of development: infants display separation anxiety first with respect to one primary caregiver, and soon afterwards they show separation anxiety from other caregivers. Stranger anxiety appears to be a developmental stage. Such stage accounts are common in developmental psychology as a means of outlining the *typical* ages when infants and children achieve certain milestones – physical or psychological. Sometimes the word 'phases' is used instead to suggest that there are no clear distinctions between one stage and another.

John Bowlby (1969) proposed a four-phase framework for viewing the changes that take place in attachment behaviour over time. The information in Table 2.1 is based on this account.

An evaluation of Bowlby's phase account

More recent research suggests that some aspects of this phase account are not entirely accurate. Very young infants appear to be far more social than was once thought. They recognize their caregivers at an earlier age and interact far more with other people. For example, Bushnell *et al.* (1989) found that infants who were less than 24 hours old looked longer at their mother than at another woman.

Table 2.1 >> Phases in the development of attachment

Age	Phase	Description
>> 0–2 months	**Pre-attachments** (indiscriminate social responsiveness)	Infants produce similar responses to all objects, whether they are animate or inanimate. Towards the end of this period, infants are beginning to show a greater preference for social stimuli, such as a smiling face, and to be more content when they are with people.
>> 2–6 months	**Attachment-in-the-making** (recognition of familiar people)	Infants become more social. They prefer human company and can distinguish between familiar and unfamiliar people. However, they are still relatively easily comforted by anyone and do not yet show anxiety with strangers. The most distinctive feature of this phase is their general sociability (enjoyment of being with people).
>> Around 6 months	**Specific attachments** (separation protest and stranger anxiety)	Infants begin to show a distinctly different sort of protest when one particular person puts them down (separation protest). Equally, they show especial joy at reunion with that person and are most comforted by this person. They are said to have formed a specific attachment. Around the same time, the infant also begins to display stranger anxiety, an uneasiness with strangers.
		Soon after the main attachment is formed, the infant also develops a wider circle of attachments depending on how many consistent relationships they have. Nevertheless, according to Bowlby, the primary attachment bond remains special (called monotropy).
>> 2 years onwards	**Goal-corrected partnership**	Relationships become more two-sided. The infant learns to predict and understand the mother figure's behaviour, which means that the mother's behaviour can be consciously controlled. The mother figure has been doing this all along. In this enduring phase, individuals in a relationship can adjust their behaviour to the others' needs, the beginning of a real partnership adjusted according to each individual's needs.

Source: based on Bowlby (1969)

Camras *et al.* (1991) found that, by about 3 months, infants are beginning to smile more at familiar than unfamiliar people, suggesting that they are relatively discriminating in their social interactions, even at that early age.

As regards the appearance of separation anxiety, there appears to be close agreement, according to a recent review of research evidence by Schaffer (1998). This may be explained in terms of general mental or cognitive development. Around the same age that the first specific attachments form (at about 6 months), there are other aspects of development that are also changing. Perhaps most important is the infant's sense of object permanence – the knowledge that things that are out of sight actually still exist. It was Piaget (1954) who introduced the concept that younger infants lose interest in things that disappear (you can demonstrate this yourself by trying to play the game of peek-a-boo with a very young infant – they are simply not interested). Once infants have acquired a sense of object permanence, they are also aware that when their caregiver leaves the room, the caregiver continues to exist. They continue to watch for the caregiver's return rather than instantly turning their attention to something else.

We should also consider physical development. It is no accident that the time when specific attachments develop in human infants is also the time when they first become mobile.

Interestingly, Ainsworth (1967) reported that Ugandan babies expressed stranger anxiety at the slightly earlier age of 6 months *and* that their motor development was more advanced.

Therefore, we can conclude that there is support for the view that a certain kind of attachment appears around this age of 6 months – the kind of attachment where an infant expresses separation anxiety. However, other evidence is less supportive of the phase theory. Infants are much more social at an earlier age than was once thought and the attachment process begins from the moment of birth, if not before that.

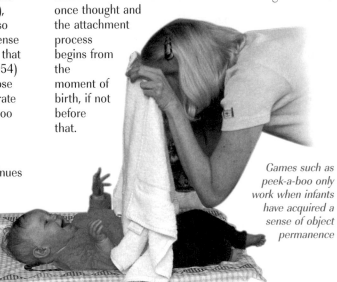

Games such as peek-a-boo only work when infants have acquired a sense of object permanence

VARIETY OF ATTACHMENTS: INDIVIDUAL DIFFERENCES

We will now move from the topic of the development of attachments to the topic of individual differences, i.e. the ways that attachment varies from one individual to another, and from one culture to another.

Secure and insecure attachment

One way to distinguish between individual infants is in terms of the *quality* of the attachment bond between them and their mother figure or primary caregiver. Schaffer and Emerson (see p. 44) found that some infants were more strongly attached to their primary caregiver than others. This was shown by the extent of their anxiety when separated from their caregiver.

Mary Ainsworth, who worked with Bowlby in the 1950s, sought to develop a reliable method of measuring quality of attachment using a procedure called the Strange Situation, which is described in the panel on the right and in the key study on p. 47.

The main reason for having a method of classifying attachment is to be able to measure the effects of attachment on later behaviour – the long-term consequences of early attachment. Bowlby claimed that early attachment is important for healthy psychological development. In order to test this belief we need some

The Strange Situation

What happens in the Strange Situation:

1 Mother and child are introduced to the room.

2 Mother and child are left alone and the child can investigate the toys.

3 A stranger enters the room and talks with the mother. The stranger gradually approaches the infant with a toy.

4 Mother leaves the child alone with the stranger, and the stranger interacts with the child.

5 Mother returns to greet and comfort the child.

6 The child is left on its own.

7 The stranger returns and tries to engage with the child.

8 Mother returns, greets and picks up the child. The stranger leaves inconspicuously.

measuring secure and insecure attachment by Ainsworth & Bell (1970)

Aim >>

To produce a method for assessing quality of attachment by placing an infant in a situation of mild stress (to encourage the infant to seek comfort) and of novelty (to encourage exploration behaviour). Both comfort-seeking and exploration behaviour are indicators of the quality of attachment.

Procedures >>

- About 100 middle-class American infants and their mothers took part in this study.
- A method of controlled observation was developed. This involved observing infants with their mothers during a set of predetermined activities (this is known as the Strange Situation – see the box on p. 46 for a description). All the sessions, except the first one, took three minutes.
- Observers recorded the infants' and mothers' behaviours, especially noting the following:
  - separation anxiety: the unease the infant showed when left by the caregiver
  - the infant's willingness to explore
  - stranger anxiety: the infant's response to the presence of a stranger
  - reunion behaviour: the way the caregiver was greeted on return.

Findings >>

The observational record led Ainsworth and Bell to classify the infants into three broad groups:

- *Type B: Securely attached* (66 per cent) – One group of infants tended to explore the unfamiliar room; they were subdued when their mother left and greeted her positively when she returned. The infants showed moderate avoidance of the stranger, although were friendly when the mother was present. The mothers were described as sensitive.
- *Type A: Avoidant-insecure* (22 per cent) – A second group did not orientate to their mother while investigating the toys and room; they did not seem concerned by her absence and showed little interest in her when she returned. These infants also avoided the stranger, but not as strongly as they avoided the mother on her return. It was observed that these mothers sometimes ignored their infants.
- *Type C: Resistant-insecure* (12 per cent) – A third group showed intense distress, particularly when their mother was absent, but they rejected her when she returned. These infants showed ambivalent behaviour towards the stranger, similar to the pattern of resistance and interest shown to the mother on her return. These mothers appeared to behave ambivalently towards their infants.

Conclusions >>

- This study shows that there are significant individual differences between infants.
- It also shows that most American children are securely attached.
- There appears to be a distinct association between the mothers' behaviour and the infants' attachment type, which suggests that mothers' behaviour may be important in determining attachment type.

Criticisms >>

- It would be unreasonable to make generalizations about all infant behaviour on the basis of this sample. The study and its findings are restricted to middle-class American infants, i.e. are culturally biased.
- In another study, Main and Cassidy (1988) identified a further group of children; this classification group is referred to as disorganized (type D). These children show inconsistent behaviour, confusion and indecision. They also tend to freeze or show stereotyped behaviours such as rocking.

AO2 check

One of the major concerns with any study is the extent to which it is *valid,* i.e. that the findings of the study are legitimate or real. A study that is based on a particular group of people (in this case, middle-class American infants) can only really tell us about how *this* particular group of people behaves. This is called *population validity*.

Unit 2 // Attachments in development

reliable and valid measure of early attachment. Any form of measurement (such as a ruler) should be reliable or consistent. It should also be valid – it should be measuring something that is real.

In general, studies have found that for a particular child the Strange Situation Classification (SSC) is usually the same at different ages (i.e. it is reliable). For example, a study conducted in Germany found 78 per cent of the children were classified in the same way at the ages of 1 and 6 (Wartner et al. 1994). When differences occur, these are often associated with changes in the form of care, such as changes in family structure (Melhuish 1993).

On the other hand, there are studies that challenge the meaning or validity of the SSC. For example, it has been found that infants behave differently depending on whom they are with. For example, they may be classified as having a secure attachment to their mother and an avoidant relationship with their father (Lamb 1977). This suggests that what is being measured is particular attachments rather than a general attachment type. For example, if infants are securely attached to their mother but appear insecurely attached to their father, then what are we to conclude about these infants' attachment type? This leads us to conclude that the Strange Situation only measures particular relationships and not some general characteristic of the child.

Van IJzendoorn et al. (1992) discussed this multiple caregiver paradox: the idea that infants have qualitatively different relationships with different caregivers (mother, father and perhaps a professional caregiver). They found that the best predictor of later development was a kind of aggregate of all the child's attachments – by considering a kind of average of all the child's attachments. This suggests the Strange Situation measurement is valid, but that attachment type must be derived from a consideration of more than just one attachment relationship.

One important question about attachment types is whether they are *caused* by the primary caregiver's behaviour or something else. Why are some children securely attached whereas others are not? Ainsworth and Bell supposed that secure attachments were the result of mothers being sensitive to their children's needs. Isabella et al. (1989) supported this in a study that found that mothers and infants who tended to be responsive to each other at 1 month were more likely at 12 months to have a secure relationship. Those who had a more one-sided pattern of interaction tended to have insecure relationships. If you recall, Schaffer and Emerson (1964) produced similar findings. Ainsworth et al. (1974) called this the caregiver sensitivity hypothesis, that attachment depends on the warm and loving responsiveness of the caregiver.

There is an alternative explanation. Some infants may form secure attachments because they are born more friendly. This is called the temperament hypothesis

(Kagan 1982). Certain innate personality or temperamental characteristics might account for behaviour in the Strange Situation, rather than it being the result of the caregiver's sensitivity. (The term *innate* refers to any behaviour that is inherited.) It may be that some children are innately more vulnerable to stress, so each child will respond differently according to their innate temperament. Research has found, for example, that newborns who showed signs of behavioural instability (e.g. tremors or shaking) were less likely to become securely attached to their mother than were newborns who did not (Belsky and Rovine 1987). Thus, there is a possibility that infant temperament, rather than caregiver sensitivity, contributes to the form of attachment and to later behaviour.

Evaluation of the Strange Situation technique

The importance of the Strange Situation as a research tool is that it enables us to assess whether or not children are securely attached and how attachment type relates to later behaviours. We have already considered some evidence about the reliability and validity of the SSC, including the question of ecological validity (do these findings apply to settings beyond the laboratory?) and population validity (do these findings apply to societies other than middle-class Americans?). In the next section we will consider the validity of the Strange Situation in relation to research conducted in different cultural settings.

Cross-cultural variations in attachment

Most psychological research has been conducted in the USA, which means that most psychological theories are based on this group of people and assume that all other people the world over will be similar. In the last few decades, psychologists have come to recognize that this is a narrow view of human behaviour. To redress the balance, psychologists endeavour to look at studies conducted in different cultural settings to see whether their theories are universal (apply to all people because they concern innate behaviours) or are culture-bound (apply only to the culture in which the research took place because the behaviour is related to cultural practices).

An increasing number of studies have measured attachment behaviours in cultural settings outside middle-class America. Strictly speaking, these are not cross-cultural studies as they do not always explicitly make comparisons between two or more different cultures. However, this comparison is implicit in many of the studies, as is demonstrated by their conclusions about cultural variation. Note that culture is not a group of people, but is the beliefs and customs that a group of people shares, such as its child-rearing practices. A subculture is a group within a society that shares many practices with the dominant culture but also has some special, different characteristics.

Research on secure and insecure attachment

Researchers in many different countries have used the Strange Situation to investigate secure and insecure attachment. The results of 32 such studies undertaken in eight different countries have been summarized (this is called a *meta-analysis*) by Van IJzendoorn and Kroonenberg (1988), as shown in Table 2.2.

Bee (1999) also points out that the most striking finding of the data that Van IJzendoorn and Kroonenberg (1988) bring together is that there is considerable consistency across cultures. She concludes that it is likely that the same caregiver–infant interactions contribute to secure and insecure attachments in all cultures. However, the universal nature of caregiver–infant interactions may be cultural rather than innate. Van IJzendoorn and Kroonenberg observe that the similarity between countries may well be due to the increasing effects of the mass media (i.e. nurture rather than nature).

The finding of consistency across cultures is in direct contrast to the conclusions drawn by Takahashi (below) and others such as Grossmann and Grossmann (1991), who studied German infants and found that these infants were more likely to be classified as insecurely attached. This may be related to the German cultural norm of keeping some interpersonal distance between parents and children. As a result, infants do not engage in proximity-seeking behaviours in the Strange Situation and thus *appear* to be insecurely attached. It may not

be reasonable to make comparisons between different countries/cultures because it appears likely that the Strange Situation may not mean the same thing in different cultures. This means the findings from Van IJzendoorn and Kroonenberg lack validity.

Another limitation of the data presented in Table 2.2 is that, although it tells us how many studies were included from each country, it does not include the number of infants involved in each study. You need, therefore, to be cautious about interpreting these figures because in many cases the sample sizes were fairly small. For example, there were only 36 infants in the single Chinese study.

Table 2.2 >> Cross-cultural differences in secure and insecure attachment

Country	No. of studies	Percentage of each attachment type (to the nearest whole number)		
		Secure	Avoidant	Resistant
>> West Germany	3	57	35	8
>> Great Britain	1	75	22	3
>> Netherlands	4	67	26	7
>> Sweden	1	74	22	4
>> Israel	2	64	7	29
>> Japan	2	68	5	27
>> China	1	50	25	25
>> United States	18	65	21	14
>> Overall average		65	21	14

Source: Van IJzendoorn and Kroonenberg (1988, pp. 150–1)

ACTIVITY

Criticizing Takahashi's study

Read the key study of Takahashi's work (1990) on p. 50, up to and including the list of Conclusions, but not the Criticisms. This is a study investigating whether it is appropriate to use the Strange Situation procedure with Japanese children. As you read it, think carefully about any criticisms that you can identify in relation to (a) ethical issues and (b) the sample used, and whether it would be reasonable to generalize the findings to all Japanese people.

Make a note of your answers to these two questions before reading the Criticisms given.

Unit 2 // Attachments in development

study of Japanese children by Takahashi (1990)

Aim >>

To consider whether it is appropriate to use the Strange Situation procedure with Japanese children. The key question is whether the Strange Situation is a valid procedure for cultures other than the original one, i.e. other than American, middle-class, white, home-reared infants and their mothers.

By making comparisons between the American and Japanese group, it may be possible to reveal the cultural assumptions on which the procedure is based.

Procedures >>

● The participants were 60 middle-class Japanese infants, aged 1 year, boys and girls, and their mothers. They were all raised at home.

● The infants and mothers were observed in the Strange Situation (as described on p. 46).

Findings >>

● 68 per cent of the infants were classified as securely attached, almost identical to the original American sample.

● There were no infants classified as avoidant-insecure.

● 32 per cent were classified as resistant-insecure.

● When the observational data were examined in more detail, differences emerged. The Japanese infants were much more disturbed after being left alone. In fact, the 'infant alone' step was stopped for 90 per cent of the participants because the infants were so distressed. If the infants had not become so distressed, many more of them (possibly more than 80 per cent) would have been classified as securely attached (the observation of distress led to an alternative classification).

Conclusions >>

● The findings suggest that there are cross-cultural variations in the way infants respond to separation and being left alone. This difference may be due to the fact that Japanese infants experience much less separation, for example they generally sleep with their parents until over 2 years of age, are carried around on their mothers' backs and bathe with parents. Japanese infants are almost never left alone. This means that, for them, the Strange Situation was more than mildly stressful, and thus the behaviours observed were reactions to extreme stress – not the original aim of the Strange Situation.

● The findings also highlight a second cross-cultural variation – the total lack of avoidant behaviour in this sample. This can also be explained in cultural terms. Japanese children are taught that such behaviour is impolite and they would be actively discouraged from displaying it.

● The final conclusion must be that the Strange Situation does not have the same meaning for the Japanese as it does for American participants and therefore is not a valid form of assessment for that culture.

Criticisms >>

● Research with children, especially with infants, needs to be especially careful in terms of potential psychological harm to participants, which is an important ethical issue.

● Takahashi's study was carried out on a limited sample of only middle-class, home-reared infants (as was the original study by Ainsworth and Bell). It may therefore not be reasonable to generalize these findings to all Japanese people, although the results do demonstrate that there are important cultural or subcultural differences in attachment.

A common means of criticizing any study is to consider ethical issues and guidelines, but you must be clear about *why* any particular study infringes ethical guidelines (considered fully in Unit 5). One of these guidelines is that participants should be protected as far as possible from psychological harm. Takahashi showed sensitivity by stopping those observations where infants became too distressed. However, the study itself was not stopped, even though it became obvious that extreme distress was likely.

When using any kind of psychological assessment, it is important to be cautious about attributing what is measured (in this case the type of attachment) to the individual. There might be something about the test situation that makes some of these infants *appear to be* insecurely attached.

Research on monotropy and multiple attachments

Bowlby (1969) claimed that infants need one special attachment relationship, which is qualitatively different from all others, in order to develop an internal working model and emotional maturity. He used the term monotropy, which literally means 'being raised by one person', to describe this special relationship which is at the top of the hierarchy of all other relationships. The internal working model is a mental model of the world that enables individuals to predict, control and manipulate their environment. Individuals have many such models or schemas (a concept you should be familiar with from your study of cognitive psychology). Some schemas are concerned with the environment or world in general, while others are organismal and tell us about ourselves and our relationship with the world. One such organismal model is concerned with the relationship between oneself and one's primary caregiver, and Bowlby suggested that this model provides a basis for all other relationships.

There is considerable debate about whether this primary bond (monotropy) is universally true. In some cultures, children have equivalent relationships with many caregivers, and still develop into psychologically healthy adults. Thomas (1998) questions whether the tendency to form a single main attachment is actually good for healthy psychological development. It might be more desirable to have a network of attachments to sustain the needs of a growing infant who has a variety of demands for social and emotional interactions. Thomas claims that in Caribbean cultures, multiple

attachments are the rule. Even in Western European culture, infants do form several attachments and these are all beneficial, probably precisely because of their qualitative differences. For example, fathers' style of play is more often physically stimulating and unpredictable, whereas mothers are more likely to hold their infants, soothe them, attend to their needs and read them stories (Parke 1981).

On the other hand, in Schaffer and Emerson's study (1964), it was found that even though infants do form multiple attachments, they appear usually to have one primary attachment. Ainsworth (1967) studied members of the Ganda tribe of Uganda, where the pattern of childcare involved multiple carers, and concluded that the infants nevertheless formed one primary attachment. Tronick et al. (1992) studied the Efe (Pygmies from Zaire, Africa) who live in extended family groups. Infants and children are looked after by whoever is closest to hand. They are breastfed by different women, but usually sleep with their own mother. Tronick and colleagues found that by the age of 12 months, the infants still show a preference for their mothers, a single primary attachment.

A study by Fox (1977) looked at life in kibbutzim in Israel, where children spend most of their time with nurses called metapelets, but see their mothers for a few hours a day after work. When the children were placed in the Strange Situation, they protested equally when either mother or metapelet left, but were more comforted by their mothers at reunion. This would again suggest that, despite having multiple carers, the infants still had one special relationship. However, we should note that the metapelets changed fairly frequently. They also had to divide their attention among many children and had less interest in any one individual, which would explain why the children were usually less attached to their metapelet. On the other hand, the children slept communally, which might reduce their maternal attachments.

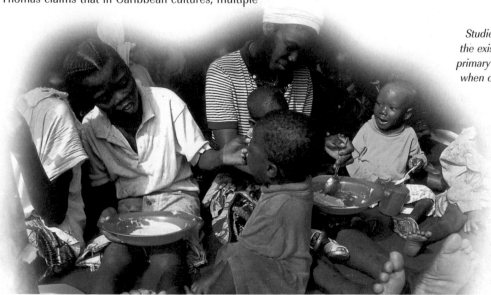

Studies in Africa found the existence of a single primary attachment even when childcare involved multiple carers

EXPLANATIONS OF ATTACHMENT

Why do infants become attached to one person rather than another? What is the purpose of attachment? We have already considered some answers to these questions. For instance, it appears that a child becomes attached to a sensitive caregiver (Ainsworth's caregiver sensitivity hypothesis). Here, we will focus on two explanations for who and why: learning theory and Bowlby's approach. Learning theory takes the view that attachment is a learned process (nurture), whereas Bowlby argued that attachment is an inherited behaviour (nature). These are examples of the 'nature–nurture' debate.

Learning theory

Learning theory is the view put forward by behaviourists to explain how all behaviour is acquired, using the principles of conditioning:

- *Classical conditioning* – Dogs salivate when they feed. Salivation is an unconditioned response (UR) to an unconditioned stimulus (US), in this case food. The stimulus (US) and response (UR) are innately linked. If a bell is rung every time food appears, the animal comes to associate bell and food so that the bell alone will produce the UR. The bell was a neutral stimulus (NS), but is now a conditioned stimulus (CS) and the salivation is now a conditioned response (CR). Thus the animal has learned a new stimulus–response link.

- *Operant conditioning* – An animal is placed in a cage where food will be delivered if it presses a lever. At first the animal presses the lever accidentally and is rewarded by receiving food. This reward increases the probability that the behaviour (lever pressing) will be repeated. The food or reward is reinforcing. If the lever press results in an electric shock, this will decrease the probability of the response being repeated. The shock acts as a punishment.

Classical conditioning

We can explain attachment in terms of the principles of classical conditioning. An infant is born with reflex responses. The stimulus of food produces a response of pleasure – an unconditioned stimulus and an unconditioned response respectively. The person providing the food (usually the mother) becomes associated with this pleasure and therefore becomes a conditioned stimulus. The food-giver then becomes a source of pleasure in herself, independent of whether or not food is supplied. This, according to learning theory, is the basis of the attachment bond.

Operant conditioning

Dollard and Miller (1950) proposed a further adaptation of the learning theory account of attachment, based in part on operant conditioning, but with the inclusion of a mental state (mental states are usually excluded from behaviourist accounts). Dollard and Miller suggested that the human infant, when hungry, feels uncomfortable and enters a drive state. The drive motivates the baby to find some way to lessen the discomfort of being hungry. Of course, in early infancy the baby can do little more than howl and it is up to other people to feed it. Being fed satisfies the infant's hunger and makes it feel comfortable again. This results in drive reduction, which is rewarding, and the child learns that food is a reward or primary reinforcer. The person who supplies the food, the mother, is associated with the food and becomes a secondary reinforcer. From then on, the infant seeks to be with this person because she is now a source of reward. The infant has thus become attached.

ACTIVITY

Learning theory and attachment

Learning theory predicts that an infant's attachment will be to the person who gives greatest pleasure or drive reduction. Look back to the description of the study that Schaffer and Emerson carried out in 1964 (see p. 44) and also at the classic research undertaken by Harlow and Harlow, investigating the formation of love in infant monkeys, described below on p. 53.

Does the evidence from these studies (a) confirm, or (b) contradict the predictions from learning theory? Explain the reasons for your answer.

AS Developmental Psychology

Perhaps the most famous study to show that attachment is not based on the supply of food was conducted by Harlow and Harlow on infant monkeys. The infant monkeys were placed in a cage with two wire mesh cylinders, each with a face. One cylinder was bare and provided the baby monkey with milk from a teat, while the other cylinder was covered with towelling (giving contact comfort). If food were the cause of attachment then one would expect the monkeys to cling to the bare cylinder that supplied the milk. In fact, the monkeys spent most of their time on the towelling-covered cylinder and would jump on to this cylinder when frightened, a characteristic of attachment behaviour. They also used the towelling-covered cylinder as a secure base for exploration, another characteristic of attachment behaviour. The study indicated that simply supplying food is not sufficient for the formation of attachment.

However, the towelling-covered 'mother' did not provide sufficient 'love' to enable healthy psychological development. In later life, the monkeys were either indifferent or abusive to other monkeys and had difficulty with mating and parenting. This shows that contact comfort is preferable to food comfort, but not sufficient for healthy development. Presumably, infants need a responsive carer.

In another experiment four young monkeys were raised on their own, without any 'mother'. They spent the first few months huddled together,

but gradually developed more independence and finally appeared to have suffered no ill-effects. This suggests that the infant–infant affectional bond can be just as effective as the mother–infant bond.

This work, which would now be considered unethical, was critical in demonstrating that neither feeding nor physical contact could explain attachment and healthy development.

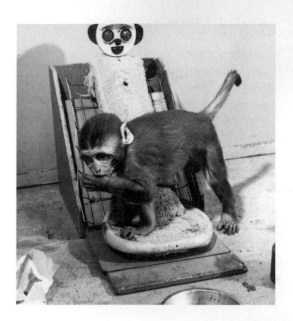

One of the monkeys in the Harlow and Harlow research, shown with the cloth-covered 'mother'

Evaluation of learning theory as an explanation of attachment

Clearly, learning theory predicts that an infant's attachment will be to the person who gives greatest pleasure or drive reduction, probably the person who feeds the infant. Schaffer and Emerson (1964) found that this was not always true. In their study, fewer than half of the infants had a primary attachment to the person who usually fed, bathed and changed them. Another piece of evidence against the role of reinforcement came from the classic research by Harlow and Harlow on the behaviour of rhesus monkeys (see above). This, again, showed that feeding was not the main source of reinforcement and, therefore, not the sole basis for attachment. However, Harlow and Harlow did find that contact comfort was a key source of reinforcement, but this was still not sufficient for healthy development. We should, of

course, be cautious about making any generalizations about human behaviour on the basis of research with rhesus monkeys.

Behaviourism is often criticized for being reductionist. This means it 'reduces' the complexities of human behaviour to over-simple ideas such as stimulus, response and reinforcement. It then uses these concepts as building blocks to explain complex human behaviours such as attachment. It may be that these behaviourist concepts are too simple to explain such a complex behaviour as attachment.

Bowlby's theory

John Bowlby (1969) proposed that attachment was important for survival. Infants are physically helpless and need adults to feed, care for and protect them; without such assistance they cannot survive. Therefore, it is likely that infants are born with an innate tendency to form an attachment that serves to increase their chances of survival. Since attachment is a reciprocal process, it is also likely that adults are innately programmed to become attached to their infants – otherwise they would not respond to their infant, and the attachment bond would not develop.

It is also likely that attachment has a long-term benefit in addition to the short-term benefit of ensuring food and safety. In the long term, it may be of fundamental importance for emotional relationships because it provides a template for relationships, as a result of the internal working model discussed earlier (see p. 51). These short- and long-term effects of attachment are similar to the effects of imprinting observed in some non-human animals (see below).

There are three important features of Bowlby's theory:

- Infants and carers are programmed to become attached.
- As attachment is a biological process, it takes place during a critical period of development or not at all.
- Attachment plays a role in later development – monotropy and the continuity hypothesis.

Innate programming

Bowlby suggested that attachment could be understood within the framework of evolutionary principles, that all psychological and physical characteristics are naturally selected. A characteristic is selected because it helps those individuals who possess it to survive and reproduce. This notion of selection is clearly a passive one: no one is doing the selecting – it is selective pressure. The essential principle is that any inherited behaviour that increases an individual's chances of survival and reproduction will be passed on to the next generation and thus continues to reappear in subsequent generations. It has been selected because of its usefulness.

The result is that infants are born programmed to become attached, and adults are also programmed to form this kind of relationship with their infants. Social releasers are necessary to ensure an interaction takes place. These are social behaviours that elicit a 'caregiving reaction from another, such as smiling, crying, cooing and simply looking appealing. Bowlby suggested that these behaviours are innate in infants (and other animals), and that the responses are innate in caregivers. They are critical in the process of forming attachments.

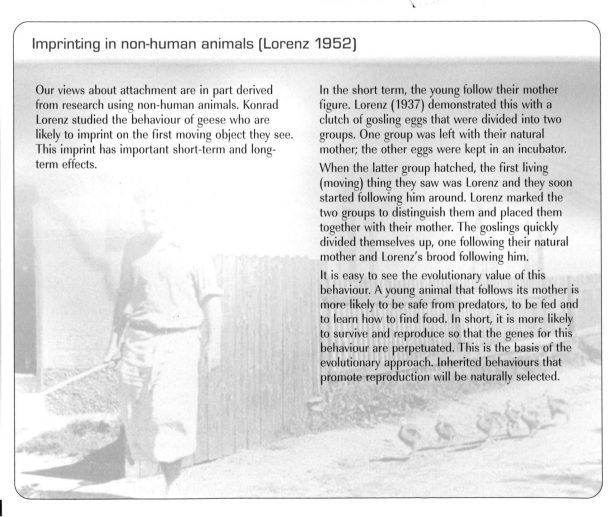

Imprinting in non-human animals (Lorenz 1952)

Our views about attachment are in part derived from research using non-human animals. Konrad Lorenz studied the behaviour of geese who are likely to imprint on the first moving object they see. This imprint has important short-term and long-term effects.

In the short term, the young follow their mother figure. Lorenz (1937) demonstrated this with a clutch of gosling eggs that were divided into two groups. One group was left with their natural mother; the other eggs were kept in an incubator.

When the latter group hatched, the first living (moving) thing they saw was Lorenz and they soon started following him around. Lorenz marked the two groups to distinguish them and placed them together with their mother. The goslings quickly divided themselves up, one following their natural mother and Lorenz's brood following him.

It is easy to see the evolutionary value of this behaviour. A young animal that follows its mother is more likely to be safe from predators, to be fed and to learn how to find food. In short, it is more likely to survive and reproduce so that the genes for this behaviour are perpetuated. This is the basis of the evolutionary approach. Inherited behaviours that promote reproduction will be naturally selected.

Social releasers

A social releaser is any behaviour that encourages a caregiver reaction from another person. Work with one other person to draw up a list of ten social releasers used by infants, children or individuals of any age. For each social releaser on your list, state whether you think that the behaviour is innate (I) or learned (L) and identify what response(s) you think it might elicit from a caregiver.

Do you think that the caregiver's responses to the social releasers are innate or learned? To what extent do you think caregivers differ in their responses to the same social releaser, and why?

A critical period

The concept of a critical period is a feature of biological characteristics. If development does not take place during a set developmental period, then it may not take place at all. For instance, in the development of the human embryo, the arms begin to develop between Day 24 and Day 26. Any interference with development at this critical stage will permanently affect the limbs' development. If attachment is innate and therefore biological, we would expect there to be a critical period for its development. Bowlby suggested that if a child does not form an attachment before the age of $2\frac{1}{2}$ years, then it would not be possible thereafter. We will consider the evidence for this in the section on deprivation and privation.

The continuity hypothesis

The argument behind the continuity hypothesis is that the relationship with one special attachment figure (monotropy) provides an infant with an internal working model of relationships (described on p. 51).

Secure children develop a positive working model of themselves, based on their feelings of security derived from having one sensitive, emotionally responsive and supportive primary caregiver (the caregiver sensitivity hypothesis). In contrast, avoidant children are assumed to have a primary caregiver who is rejecting, resulting in their having a working model of themselves as unacceptable and unworthy. Ambivalent children have a primary caregiver who is inconsistent; consequently, the children tend to have a negative self-image and exaggerate their emotional responses as a way to obtain attention. This continuity hypothesis provides one possible explanation of the fact that early patterns of attachment are related to later child characteristics.

Evaluation of Bowlby's theory

There are many studies that support Bowlby's theory, as shown in the summary of Bowlby's theory on p. 56. We will now consider evidence to support the continuity hypothesis. The Minnesota longitudinal study (Sroufe et al. 1999) has followed a cohort of children from the age of 12 months to adolescence. The children were rated throughout their childhood by teachers, trained observers and camp counsellors at special events arranged for the children. Those children who were rated as being securely attached in infancy were also later rated as being more popular, having more initiative, and being higher in social competence, self-confidence and self-esteem. In other words, social competence was associated with early attachment style, supporting Bowlby's views of continuity from infancy to adulthood in terms of social development.

McCarthy (1999) also used attachment data from infancy. A group of women were contacted who had been assessed in infancy as insecurely attached. The study recorded their attitudes and experiences of friendships and romantic relationships. Women previously classified as avoidant-insecure were more likely to have romantic problems, while those classified as resistant-insecure were more likely to have problems in friendships.

However, even though there are positive correlations between early experiences and later social experiences, you may remember that there is an alternative explanation to that of the internal working model – namely that some infants may simply be better than others at forming relationships, the temperament hypothesis (see p. 48). Children who are appealing to their parents are also likely to be appealing to other people and this can explain continuities.

A second study that investigated the continuity hypothesis perhaps offers some better support because it involved individual's attitudes. Hazan and Shaver (1987) printed a 'love quiz' in an American newspaper, collecting information from people about (1) their early attachment experiences and (2) their current romantic attitudes and experiences. They found that individuals who were securely attached as infants tended to have happy and lasting love relationships and to believe that love was enduring and about mutual trust. In contrast, insecure types found relationships less easy, were more likely to be divorced and felt that true love was rare. This supports Bowlby's concept of an internal working model because it assesses attitudes that must be generated from an internal working model.

A summary of Bowlby's theory

- Attachment is adaptive and innate: infants are born with a drive to become attached.
- They elicit caregiving through innate social releasers. Adults respond to social releasers.
- Bonds are formed with adults who respond most sensitively – e.g. Ainsworth's caregiver sensitivity hypothesis (see p. 48), and evidence from Harlow and Zimmerman (1959).
- This must occur during a critical period of development.
- Infants form one special relationship: monotropy – evidence from Schaffer and Emerson (1964).

- This leads to an internal working model (a schema) and the continuity hypothesis – evidence from Sroufe et al. (1999 and Hazan and Shaver (1987).

There are also flaws with the theory. For example, it does not explain why some children are able to cope with poor attachment experiences while others suffer long-term consequences, as we will see in the next topic on deprivation and privation.

One final point to note is that the evolutionary argument is a post-hoc (after the fact) assumption rather than proven fact. In other words, we are making the judgement by looking backwards and arguing that a specific behaviour must be adaptive because it persists. We cannot know this is true, but are assuming it is likely. It could be that the value of the behaviour is simply neutral rather than positive.

Despite the criticisms, Bowlby's theory continues to be the major theory of attachment, to generate a great deal of research (an important positive feature of any theory) and to have an enormous impact on the emotional care of young children.

✓ CHECK YOUR UNDERSTANDING

Check your understanding of the development and variety of attachments by answering these questions. Try to do this from memory at first. You can check your answers by looking back through this first topic.

1 Fill in the blank space: "Attachments depend on _____ between two people."

2 Briefly explain the term 'internal working model' as used by Bowlby with reference to attachments.

3 What exactly is a 'critical period'?

4 What does the term 'imprinting' mean?

5 Why is imprinting so important for a young animal?

6 How many stages did Schaffer and Emerson (1964) identify in the development of attachments?

7 Give two criticisms of Schaffer and Emerson's stage account of developments in attachments.

8 List four characteristics seen in an 'attached' infant.

9 What aspect of cognitive development coincides with a child showing separation anxiety?

10 List the steps in the Strange Situation procedure.

11 What are the three types of attachments that Mary Ainsworth identified?

12 Name the fourth type of attachment that Main and Cassidy identified in 1988 and list two of its features.

13 In which country have most Strange Situation studies been carried out?

14 Why is it difficult to show that a child's early attachment style (as measured by the Strange Situation procedure) affects the nature of their later relationships?

15 Define the term 'monotropy'.

16 Why might it be beneficial for infants to develop more than one attachment?

17 Name one study that supports the claim that infants tend to become primarily attached to one person even though several people may look after them.

18 According to learning theory, what two processes explain the development of attachment? Give one criticism of the learning theory explanation of attachment.

how good is an explanation?

When asked to evaluate an 'explanation' of attachment, you are being asked to do more than simply describe material that may be relevant to this subject area; you are being asked to *show* how this enhances, or even detracts from, the overall value of your chosen explanation. Examination questions always present you with a fairly challenging task in the final part of each question. These AO1 + AO2 questions (part (c) of each question) test your ability to work with the material you have learned in order to consider a particular issue in a more critical light.

In practical terms, these questions always have 6 marks available for descriptive content and 12 marks for analysis and evaluation, so it is important to get the balance right. For example, when asked to 'consider' an explanation of attachment, there is a temptation to spend much of the time available describing it and not enough doing the AO2 bit!

Take the learning theory explanation of attachment as an example. The task of answering an AO1 + AO2 question requires a brief descriptive response followed by a slightly more extended evaluative response – for example: *"Give a brief account of, and evaluate **one** explanation of attachment."*

● *Task 1* – Can you précis this theory in such a way that it illustrates how learning theory has been used to *explain* attachment (rather than just describing learning theory itself). Remember that this part of your response is only worth 6 marks, and so it does need to be brief. On p. 56, we have shown you the main points of Bowlby's explanation of attachment, but can you do the same for the learning theory explanation?

● *Task 2* – Is your evaluation *informed* (i.e. how much is there, and is it *relevant*?) and is it *effective* (i.e. have you done more than *identify* some critical points)? This is not always as easy as it sounds, so it pays to look carefully at the evaluation covered on the preceding pages.

Harlow and Harlow's study (p. 53) clearly casts doubt on the learning theory explanation of attachment, but why? This is where you need to show evidence of engaging with the material in order to construct a convincing critical argument. By adding a few well-chosen words or phrases (shown in bold below), it shows that *you* understand the significance of each piece of information you are using, within the wider context of the question you are answering. For example:

<< **Contrary to the claims made by the learning theory** explanation, it showed that feeding was not the main source of reinforcement and, therefore, not the sole basis for attachment. **However,** Harlow and Harlow did find that contact comfort was a key source of reinforcement, **but this was still not sufficient** for healthy development. We should, of course, be cautious about making any generalizations about human behaviour on the basis of research with rhesus monkeys, **as we cannot assume that the processes of attachment are exactly the same for each species.** >>

The secret of effective performance, then, is to choose your material carefully, make sure you are using it in an evaluative context, and elaborate each point sufficiently to give it impact.

REVISION SUMMARY

Having covered this topic you should be able to:

✔ define 'attachment', 'secure attachment', 'insecure attachment' and 'cross-cultural variations'

✔ describe research findings and conclusions related to the development of attachments

✔ describe phases in the development of attachment

✔ describe and evaluate research into individual differences in attachment, including secure and insecure attachment and cross-cultural variations

✔ describe the aims, procedures, findings, conclusions and criticisms for a key study in the areas of secure and insecure attachment and cross-cultural variations

✔ describe and evaluate two explanations of attachment.

GETTING YOU THINKING...

1 Read the following experiences of children being separated from people they love. What possible short-term and longer-term effects do you think the separation might have on the individuals concerned:

(a) a 1-year old going into hospital for a long period, part of it being spent in intensive care?

(b) 8-year-old twins who go off to boarding school for the first time – their older brother is already at the same school?

(c) two sisters, aged 12 and 15, who had always lived in Glasgow with their parents, being evacuated during the Second World War to a farm in a rural, English community?

2 Think back to some of your own experiences of being separated from people you love – either when you were younger or more recently. How did the separation make you feel? What things helped you to feel better?

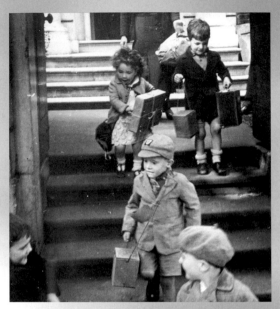

During World War II, thousands of children experienced the shock of separation from loved ones

DEPRIVATION AND SEPARATION

Around the time of the Second World War, a number of psychologists became interested in the negative effects of separation on the emotional development of children, leading eventually to a formal statement of the link between separation and emotional maladjustment – Bowlby's maternal deprivation hypothesis.

KEY TERMS

Deprivation: to have something taken away, such as food or warmth, i.e. a *loss*. In the context of attachment, deprivation refers to the loss of emotional care that results in the breaking of emotional bonds. A child is denied emotional care for a period of time. Bowlby's maternal deprivation hypothesis proposes that emotional deprivation disrupts the attachment process, which may harm emotional and social development.

Separation: to be physically set apart from something – in the context of attachment, to be physically apart from one's caregiver, especially one's mother figure. Separation does not inevitably result in deprivation. Substitute emotional care can be provided to avoid the disruption of emotional bonds.

Privation: a lack of the necessities of life. In the context of attachment, privation refers to a complete lack of emotional care, especially during the first few years of life. Such a lack of emotional care results in no attachments being formed. It has been proposed that this lack of early attachment results in permanent harm to emotional and social development.

Bowlby's maternal deprivation hypothesis

Some 20 years before the publication of his attachment theory, Bowlby proposed the maternal deprivation hypothesis (Bowlby 1953). This hypothesis was the forerunner of the attachment theory (described on pp. 54–6) and was considerably less complex (after all, it was called a hypothesis and not a theory).

The maternal deprivation hypothesis stated the belief that if an infant was unable to develop a "warm, intimate, and continuous relationship with his mother (or permanent mother-substitute)" (Bowlby 1953, p. 13), then the child would have difficulty forming relationships with other people and would be at risk of behavioural disorders.

There are three important things to note:

● The hypothesis focuses on the importance of a continuous relationship between a child and mother. Relationships that are discontinuous (i.e. where there are separations) become unstable and less predictable, which disrupts the development of the relationship.

● Bowlby suggested that the development of this continuous relationship must occur during a critical period. If a child experienced repeated separations before the age of $2\frac{1}{2}$ years, then it would be likely to become emotionally disturbed. Bowlby felt that there was a continuing risk of disturbance up to the age of 5. After that age children are better able to cope with separation.

● Bowlby did not suggest that the relationship had to be with the child's mother. The term 'maternal' was used to describe mothering from a mother 'or any mother-substitute'. He did believe that a child needed to form a relationship with one primary caregiver for healthy emotional development to take place (the concept of monotropy). This is most likely to be a child's mother, but does not have to be.

Note that there is no mention in this hypothesis of evolutionary principles, of adaptiveness, social releasers, internal working models and the continuity hypothesis. It is important to be able to distinguish between Bowlby's attachment theory and his maternal deprivation hypothesis.

The key contribution of this hypothesis was to identify the importance of emotional care in healthy emotional development. In the 1940s, it was a common belief that children simply needed a good standard of physical care and that emotions would look after themselves. Bowlby famously said "mother-love in infancy and childhood is as important for mental health as are vitamins and proteins for physical health" (Bowlby 1953, p. 240).

Research into the effects of deprivation

One source of evidence for Bowlby's maternal deprivation hypothesis was his own research, described in the key study, *The effects of deprivation*, on p. 60.

A number of studies conducted in the 1930s and 40s strongly influenced Bowlby's views and led to the development of his maternal deprivation hypothesis. For example, Spitz and Wolf (1946) studied 100 apparently normal children who became seriously depressed after staying in hospital. The children generally recovered well if the separation lasted less than three months. Longer separations were rarely associated with complete recovery.

Research into separation

There is often an interchangeable use of the words separation and deprivation. Bowlby believed that separation threatened the attachment relationship and led to emotional deprivation. However, research done by James and Joyce Robertson (Robertson and Robertson 1971) showed that separation need not lead to emotional deprivation. A mother and child may be separated but if substitute emotional care is provided, then deprivation may be avoided.

The Robertsons filmed various children under the age of 3 during short separations. One boy, John, spent nine days in a residential nursery. The staff had little time to attend to his personal needs. The film shows him being overwhelmed by the strange environment and, just as Harlows' monkeys clung to the cloth-covered mother when frightened, John clung to a teddy bear.

John progressively became more withdrawn and despairing, and when his mother came to collect him, he struggled to get away. He continued for months to show outbursts of anger towards his mother.

In contrast, several other children were filmed while they were cared for by Joyce Robertson, a foster mother, in her own home. She arranged for the children to visit their mothers in hospital and to bring things from home with them, thus maintaining emotional bonds with home during separation. These children ate and slept well while staying in foster care, and welcomed their parents at the end of their stay.

Did you have a favourite toy or 'cuddly' as a child that gave you comfort when you were anxious?

a study of 44 juvenile thieves by Bowlby (1944)

Aim >>

To test the maternal deprivation hypothesis, that is, to see whether frequent early separations were associated with a risk of behavioural disorders: in particular, a disorder termed 'affectionless psychopathy'. Bowlby used this term to describe individuals who have no sense of shame or guilt; they lack a social conscience. Is it possible that such individuals were more likely to have experienced a disrupted early childhood?

Procedures >>

- The participants in this study were 88 children ranging in age from 5 to 16 who had been referred to the child guidance clinic where Bowlby worked.
- Forty-four of the children had been referred to the clinic because of stealing (the 'thieves'). Bowlby identified 16 of these thieves as affectionless psychopaths (described above).
- The remaining 44 children in the study had not committed any crimes; they were emotionally maladjusted, but did not display antisocial behaviour. None of this control group were diagnosed as affectionless psychopaths.
- Bowlby interviewed the children and their families and was able to build up a record of their early life experiences.

Findings >>

- Bowlby found that a large number (86 per cent) of those thieves diagnosed as affectionless psychopaths had experienced "early and prolonged separations from their mothers".
- Only 17 per cent of the other thieves (the ones who weren't classed as affectionless psychopaths) had experienced such separations.
- Even fewer (4 per cent) of the control group ('non-thieves') had experienced frequent early separations.

Conclusions >>

- These findings suggest a link between early separations and later social and emotional maladjustment.
- In its most severe form, maternal deprivation appears to lead to affectionless psychopathy. In its less severe form it leads to antisocial behaviour (theft).
- These findings support the maternal deprivation hypothesis.

Criticisms >>

- The evidence is correlational, which means that we can only say that deprivation/separation and affectionless psychopathy are linked, not that one *caused* the other.
- The data on separation were collected retrospectively and may not be reliable. Parents may not have accurately recalled separations during infancy. They may have over- or under-estimated the frequency. In addition, how do we know whether these children experienced deprivation (the loss of emotional care) or whether they had good substitute emotional care during their separations?

AO2 check

This issue is a frequent problem in many developmental studies where it is difficult to manipulate an independent variable. Bowlby's study demonstrated a *link* between two variables: frequent early separations and emotional maladjustment. The maternal deprivation hypothesis proposed that the first *causes* the second, but the evidence cannot support this causal conclusion. It could be, for example, that children from unhappy homes are more prone to becoming ill. This leads them to spend more time in hospital and also leads to emotional maladjustment. In this case it would be the unhappy home that is the causal factor, not the separations. This is discussed further on p. 61, under Rutter's criticisms.

It would appear, from the Robertsons' research, that separation need not lead to deprivation as long as:

● separation is minimized
● substitute emotional care is provided.

This conclusion is supported by another early study by Skeels and Dye (1939). They compared the development of one group of orphans raised in a home for women who were mentally retarded (where the women there gave them attention) with a control group who remained in the original institution. After one and a half years, the IQs of the control group fell from an average of 87 to 61 points, whereas the average IQs rose in the group who were transferred to the home from 64 to 92 points. Skeels (1966) assessed the children 20 years later and claimed that the effects were still apparent. This was credited to the emotional care they received from the adults that reduced the emotional deprivation experienced in the institution.

Evaluation of Bowlby's maternal deprivation hypothesis

There are various issues to be considered. First, much of the evidence used to generate and support the maternal deprivation hypothesis came from studies of children in institutions where they were deprived *in many ways*. Therefore, it may not be maternal deprivation, but other forms of deprivation (e.g. physical deprivation) that affected subsequent development.

Second, not all research has found that deprivation leads to maladjustment. Another study by Bowlby *et al.* (1956) found no such ill effects. A group of children with tuberculosis was studied. They were under the age of 4 when they were first hospitalized. The nursing regimes tended to be strict and the care impersonal. Many of the children were visited weekly by their families, but this probably did little to prevent emotional deprivation (John in the Robertsons' study

was also visited regularly by his father). Information was obtained about these children when they were between 7 and 14 years old. Psychologists assessed them and their teachers were also interviewed. When the children who had TB were compared with a control group of children who had not been in hospital, it was found that there were no differences in terms of delinquency or problems in forming social relationships. Therefore, it would appear that deprivation does not inevitably have harmful effects. Bowlby and colleagues suggested that individual differences might be important. For example, children who are securely attached may cope better with deprivation.

Michael Rutter (1981) identified some further problems with the maternal deprivation hypothesis in a classic book entitled *Maternal Deprivation Revisited*. Rutter supported Bowlby's hypothesis in general, but felt refinements were needed. He claimed that:

● Bowlby confused cause and effect with an association (see p. 60). The fact that early separation and later maladjustment are linked does not mean that one caused the other. Rutter suggested that instead, it could be that some families are 'at risk' because of, for example, poor living conditions or unsettled interpersonal relationships. These factors might lead to both early separation and later maladjustment. Rutter (1976) interviewed over 2,000 boys and their families on the Isle of Wight and found that delinquency was most common in cases where boys had experienced separations due to discord in their families. This supports Rutter's hypothesis that it is family discord, rather than separation on its own, that causes delinquency and emotional maladjustment.

● Bowlby did not distinguish between different kinds of deprivation. An infant or child can be deprived of a caregiver's presence, meaning that the child had formed attachment bonds, but these were now disrupted; or the child can suffer from privation,

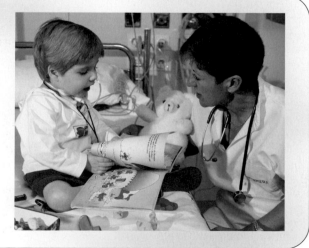

ACTIVITY

Putting it into practice

Imagine that you are a psychologist and have been invited to advise a unit where sick children are being cared for. The senior management team wants to know what they should do to improve children's experiences while staying in hospital, particularly with regard to their separation from parents.

1 Discuss in a small group what advice, based on sound psychological research, you could offer them.

2 Note down three pieces of advice that you would give and the research on which each recommendation is based.

which is the lack of ever having any attachments. It may be privation rather than deprivation that has permanent and irreversible effects.

Before moving on to consider privation as distinct from deprivation, there is one final point to make. Bowlby's maternal deprivation hypothesis was developed in the early 1950s. He later went on to formulate the more positive attachment theory (described on p. 54). This theory focuses on the benefits of attachment rather than the consequences of deprivation. The maternal

deprivation hypothesis also had an enormous impact on the way we treat children. For example, it changed the treatment of children in hospitals. In 1950, parents were discouraged from visiting their children because it was thought to cause too much distress to them; today, parents are encouraged to stay overnight when their children are in hospital because it is recognized that this prevents emotional deprivation and promotes quicker recovery through reduced anxiety. (This may be one of the measures you thought of in response to the activity at the bottom of p. 61.)

PRIVATION

Rutter suggested it might make better sense to look at privation (lack of attachments) rather than deprivation (loss of attachments). Bowlby's hypothesis may be refined as the maternal privation hypothesis and again tested to see if it is correct. There are three main lines of evidence regarding privation:

● longitudinal studies of children in institutional care

● case histories of children raised in extreme isolation

● studies of reactive attachment disorder, a category of mental disorder attributed to a lack of early attachments.

Longitudinal studies of children in institutional care

One way to study privation is to consider the effects of institutionalization in situations where infants have never had the opportunity to form any attachments. One early study showed that children living in orphanages did improve dramatically in terms of intellectual development when they were given greater emotional attention (Skeels and Dye 1939, described on p. 61). Barbara Tizard and colleagues conducted a larger-scale study of institutionalized infants over a period of 16 years. This is described in the key study, *The effects of privation*, opposite.

One of the consequences of psychological research into the effects of institutionalization has been to reduce greatly the extent to which children are placed in such care. As a result, it has not been possible to replicate such studies until recently, when a natural opportunity for further study presented itself. In Romania, many children were placed in orphanages from birth and experienced considerable deprivation. Rutter *et al.* (1998) studied 111 Romanian orphans adopted in the UK before the age of 2. On arrival, these children were physically undersized, but by the age of 4 they had caught up spectacularly to age-related

milestones. However, age at adoption was negatively correlated with attainment of developmental milestones. In other words, the later the children were adopted, the slower their progress. This suggests that the longer children experience emotional deprivation, the longer it will take for them to recover – but that recovery is possible.

An earlier study by Quinton *et al.* (1985) found the reverse. The researchers followed a group of ex-institutional women (reared in institutions). These women had extreme difficulties when they became parents, for example their children were more frequently in care and the women were less sensitive, less supportive and less warm with their children than a control group of non-institutionalized women who were also observed. However, it may *not* be early privation that explains their lack of parenting abilities. It may be more simply that they had inadequate models for how to parent and this made them less able to cope as mothers. This is supported by further data from Quinton and colleagues, who found that those institutionalized women who had had positive school experiences in childhood and favourable psychosocial circumstances in adulthood functioned as well as the comparison group. This again suggests that continuing poor experiences are associated with poor recovery, but that recovery is possible when a child has improved care during childhood.

a study of ex-institutional children by Hodges and Tizard (1989)

Aim >>

To investigate the effects of early privation on subsequent social and emotional development, and to test the maternal deprivation (or privation) hypothesis. The study aimed to follow the same children over a long period of time (a longitudinal study) to collect reliable information linking early experiences to later outcomes for the same individuals.

Procedures >>

- This longitudinal study was a natural experiment. The independent variable (attachment experiences) varied naturally. The participants were 65 children who had been placed in an institution when they were less than 4 months old. There was an explicit policy in the institution against caregivers forming attachments with the children. This would suggest that the children experienced early privation.
- By the age of 4, 24 of the institutionalized children had been adopted, 15 had returned to their natural homes, and the rest remained in the institution.
- Assessment at ages 8 and 16 involved interviewing those children who were adopted and those who had returned to their original homes. Their parents, their teachers and their peers were also interviewed. Data were also obtained about a control group of 'normal' peers.

Findings >>

- There were some differences between the adopted and 'restored' children. The adopted children generally had close attachments to their parents and good family relationships, whereas this was much less true for the restored children.
- However, there were similarities in the behaviour of the adopted and restored children *outside* the family. For example, both groups were more likely to seek adult attention and approval than the control children, and both groups were less successful in peer relationships.

Conclusions >>

- There is evidence that does *not* support the maternal deprivation hypothesis. The two ex-institution groups, adopted and restored, differed *within* their family relationships. The restored children often returned to the same difficult circumstances that had precipitated the need for care in the first place, and to parents who may have felt ambivalent about them. In contrast, adopted children went to homes where the parents had very much wanted a child. This shows that recovery is possible given the right circumstances.
- There is evidence that *does* support the maternal deprivation hypothesis. *Outside* the family environment it would appear that early privation did have an effect on subsequent social development. Clarke and Clarke (1979) put forward a transactional model to explain the findings. It may be that the adopted children in Hodges and Tizard's studies got on well within their families because the families made special efforts to love them, whereas they did not experience this outside the home and thus were unable to form relationships as easily or well.

Criticisms >>

- Random allocation of participants to experimental groups is used to ensure that the participant groups in an experiment are equivalent. In Hodges and Tizard's study, there may have been important differences between the two groups – the adopted and the restored group – *besides* the independent variable. It is possible, for example, that the children selected for adoption were the more attractive and socially able children. The children's temperament thus becomes a confounding variable in this study – confounding because it acts as another independent variable. This means that we cannot infer a causal relationship between the effects of early privation on later social and emotional development from this study.
- Attrition is a common problem in longitudinal research. Inevitably, some participants are no longer available or willing to take part in the study as the years pass by. It is possible that a certain kind of individual is more likely to drop out from the study – for example, those who are less highly motivated or, in the case of Hodges and Tizard's study, those who were less well adjusted. This leaves the study with a biased sample. If a study sample is biased, the researchers have to be very careful about what conclusions they can draw and it is not appropriate to generalize the findings.

Children raised in extreme isolation

Case histories of children who have been raised in isolated and deprived circumstances demonstrate two things:

● Some children never recover from early privation.

● Other children show remarkable recovery.

Two case histories of isolation are described in the panel on the right. Read these now, before continuing with the text below

Why did Genie fail to recover while the other children seemed to be more resilient? It may be due to the length of time in isolation. Genie was 13, which may be beyond the age of recovery, whereas the others were much younger. It may be because of the actual experiences in isolation. The Czech twins had each other, although Genie's mother claimed to have had a relationship with her daughter (Rymer 1993). It may be related to some unique characteristic of the individual – Genie's father had locked her up because he thought she was retarded. It may be related to subsequent care – the Czech twins were cared for by a pair of loving sisters, whereas there is uncertainty about the quality of the foster care that Genie received because there were continuing wrangles about who should look after her. Also, she was later fostered by a family where she was abused.

These questions highlight some of the problems with the case history approach. The evidence is also retrospective, so we cannot be sure about the actual conditions the children endured; nor is it possible to make generalizations about human behaviour on the basis of individuals who may have unique characteristics. Nevertheless, we might cautiously conclude from these case histories that recovery from privation does seem possible when good emotional care is offered at a sufficiently young age.

Studies of reactive attachment disorder

Some children who experience early disruptions in the attachment process *do* appear *unable* to recover. These are children who are diagnosed with reactive attachment disorder. The symptoms are: lack of ability to give and receive affection, cruelty to others especially pets, abnormalities in eye contact and speech patterns, lying and stealing, lack of long-term friends, and extreme control problems (Parker and Forrest 1993). It is suggested that the cause of the disorder is a lack of primary attachments due to early maternal rejection and separation. For example, one typical case history described a young boy whose mother had not wanted him and offered him for adoption. This was followed by a series of foster homes until he was finally adopted at age 18 months. However, he appeared unable to accept the affection that his adopted parents tried to give him and, as an older child, engaged in lying, stealing, sending death threats and going into wild rages (Flanagan 1996).

Two cases of isolation

● The first case involves Czechoslovakian, male, identical twins whose mother died after giving birth (Koluchová 1976). The children went to a children's home for 11 months, then spent six months with their aunt, and next went to stay with their father and stepmother. The father was of low intelligence and the stepmother was exceptionally cruel. The boys were never allowed out of the house and were kept in either a small, unheated closet or in a cellar. When discovered at 7 years, the children could hardly walk, had acute rickets, were very fearful and their spontaneous speech was very poor. After placement in a hospital and then a foster home, excellent gains were made. The children are now adults and appear well adjusted and cognitively able (Clarke, personal communication).

● Genie, the second case, was found when she was 13 years old (Curtiss 1977). Her history was one of isolation, severe neglect and physical restraint. She was kept strapped to a child's potty in a bare room. Her father punished her if she made any sound. On discovery aged 13, her appearance was of a 6- or 7-year-old child. Curtiss described her as "unsocialized, primitive, and hardly human"; she made virtually no sounds and was hardly able to walk. Genie never achieved good social adjustment or language despite intervention and being placed with a foster family.

Maternal rejection can occur even when the mother remains present, as in the case of primary rejectors (Jones et al. 1987). These tend to be middle-class women who have had an unwanted child, a difficult pregnancy, and/or experienced early separation from their infant due to problems at the time of birth. The mothers may well have good relationships with other offspring and are able to offer a good standard of physical care. Rejection starts from the time of birth and the mother–infant relationship never recovers. Gradually, the guilt and lack of empathy that the mother feels turns into anger and later, as the child grows up, a period of stress or naughtiness may result in excessive punishment and abuse.

However, it is possible that the reason for the initial breakdown between caregiver and child was some aspect of the child's temperament, and this has continued to affect other attempts to form relationships.

Maternal *deprivation*

Penelope Leach is a research psychologist specializing in child development. Best known as the author of Your Baby and Child *(Penguin Books 1997) and as a passionate advocate for children and parents, she is a Fellow of the British Psychological Society, and an Honorary Senior Research Fellow in the Leopold Muller Centre of Child and Family Mental Health at the Royal Free and University College Medical School, where she is currently Co-Director of the UK's largest programme of research into the effects of various kinds and combinations of care on children's development in the first five years.*

Q Is Bowlby's view of the importance of the bond between mother and child justified?

A Yes, indeed, and his recognition of the nature of that bond – for which he coined the term 'primary attachment' – did the world a great and lasting service. Many earlier observers had noted that infants seek to get close and stay close to their mothers and had assumed that this was entirely in order to assure themselves of food and warmth; a clear case of cupboard love. Bowlby realized that it was not only physical requirements babies sought from their mothers, but also comfort and closeness for their own sake. Babies are born primed to 'attach themselves' to an adult – usually, though not necessarily or invariably the birth mother – because without adult care they cannot survive. But the survival that is at stake is emotional as well as physical. Bowlby came to see the bond between mother and child as the primary love relationship in every individual's life.

Penelope Leach

Q Are children more vulnerable to absence of that bond or to its disruption?

A The first. This first love relationship is irreplaceably important. It is through it that babies learn about themselves, other people and the world; experience emotions and learn to cope with them. And it is through this baby-love that they will become capable of more grown-up kinds of love; capable, one far-distant day, of giving children of their own the kind of devotion they now need for

themselves. Loss of a primary attachment figure is always a tragedy, but as long as babies have had such a relationship with at least one special person who loves them and whom they love, they will be able to make good use of secondary attachments to other special people.

Q Is there evidence to suggest that deprivation or disruption of attachment has long-term effects?

A Those orphanage babies used to be described as suffering (and even dying) of 'maternal deprivation', but we now see what they were missing in terms of an active and interactive relationship rather than passive dependency, and we can see that lesser degrees of deprivation matter too. Babies are liable not to develop as fast or as far as their innate drive and their potential for personality allow if:

● they receive adequate physical care but little emotional response (as sometimes happens if a mother is very depressed)

● they are looked after by a succession of caretakers who either never make themselves special to each baby or form a special relationship, which is then broken because they leave. The development of babies who are suddenly separated from parenting-people is always put at risk.

But as long as babies *do* have at least one special person who loves them and whom they love, they can make excellent use of other special people too. A baby's capacity for love is not rationed, any more than an adult's is. The reverse is true. Love creates love.

Expert interview

In the interview on p. 65, research psychologist Penelope Leach gives her views on the importance of the attachment process. For this activity, take the following statements from the interview and find evidence from elsewhere in this unit that gives research support to these views.

<< Loss of a primary attachment figure is always a tragedy, but as long as babies have had such a relationship with at least one special person who loves them and whom they love, they will be able to make good use of secondary attachments to other special people. >>

<< Babies are liable not to develop as fast or as far as their innate drive and their potential for personality allow if they are looked after by a succession of caretakers who either never make themselves special to each baby or form a special relationship, which is then broken because they leave. >>

✓ CHECK YOUR UNDERSTANDING

Check your understanding of deprivation and privation by answering these questions. Try to do this from memory at first. You can check your answers by looking back through Topic 2.

1 Define the terms 'deprivation' and 'privation'.

2 What did Bowlby's maternal deprivation (1953) hypothesis predict?

3 List the three most important elements of Bowlby's maternal deprivation hypothesis.

4 What are the three main conclusions from Bowlby's (1944) study of 44 juvenile thieves?

5 Give two criticisms of this study of juvenile thieves.

6 The Robertsons' research suggests that separation need not lead to deprivation. What two elements do they claim are important in avoiding deprivation becoming a consequence of separation?

7 Although Rutter (1981) broadly supported Bowlby's maternal deprivation hypothesis, he did feel that certain refinements were necessary. List the two main refinements that Rutter proposed in his classic book *Maternal Deprivation Revisited* and explain why these refinements are important.

8 Name the researcher who studied the Czech twin boys who were discovered at the age of 7 after years of neglect and abuse.

REVISION SUMMARY

Having covered this topic you should be able to:

✓ define 'deprivation', 'separation' and 'privation', and explain the differences between these terms

✓ describe and evaluate the maternal deprivation hypothesis

✓ describe research findings and conclusions related to the effects of deprivation

✓ describe research findings and conclusions related to the effects of separation

✓ describe research findings and conclusions related to the effects of privation

✓ describe the aims, procedures, findings, conclusions and criticisms for a key study on the effects of deprivation and on the effects of privation

✓ consider the reversibility of early deprivation and/or privation.

Topic 3 >> Critical issue: Day care

GETTING YOU THINKING...

Consider the following statement:

<< Day care jeopardizes the development of children. >>

Think carefully about this statement and decide whether or not you agree with it. Make a note of your decision.

If possible, arrange to discuss or debate this statement with a group of other students studying psychology. If you arrange a formal debate, divide the group into two smaller groups, one to prepare arguments in support of the statement, and the other to prepare arguments opposing it.

Present each side of the debate in turn, allowing an opportunity for questions.

At the end of the debate, take a vote to see what support exists for either side of the argument about the effects of day care. Then consider the following questions:

- Did you change your views as a result of hearing other people's views?
- How many people (and what percentage) supported the statement before the debate?
- How many people (and what percentage) supported the statement after the debate?

KEY TERMS

Day care: a form of care for infants and children, offered by someone other than close family, taking place outside the home. Children spend part or all of the day in care, but return home at night. This is distinct from a residential nursery, where children are looked after for a short spell, such as a week, and sleep there as well. Day care also differs from institutional care, which refers to long-term, 24-hour care.

Cognitive development: the changes that take place throughout one's life with respect to mental abilities, including memory, perception, language and intelligence. Attachment promotes cognitive development because it offers a secure base for exploration and increases opportunities for stimulation. Deprivation may therefore harm cognitive development.

Social development: the changes that take place throughout one's life with respect to social behaviour, such as relationships with friends and family, popularity, ability to negotiate with peers, friendliness and aggressiveness. Attachment promotes social development because it provides an internal working model for conducting relationships. Separation may therefore harm social development.

Some of the research looked at so far in this unit may seem rather dated. This is because psychology has moved on from the issue of how deprivation and privation affect children, to focus on how we can improve situations where children are experiencing separation, deprivation and privation. The care of adopted children is one area of concern; another relevant issue is the effects on children of day care.

We almost take it for granted that local communities should be equipped with good preschool day-care

facilities. However, psychologists have not always promoted this idea. One of the major issues raised by Bowlby's (1953) maternal deprivation hypothesis was the potentially detrimental effect of day care. If separations from the child's main caregiver are harmful, especially before the age of 2, then shouldn't we stop mothers (or primary caregivers) going out to work? Although Bowlby did not actually suggest that women should stay at home to look after their children, this was the message taken from his work (Holmes 1993).

EFFECTS OF DAY CARE ON COGNITIVE DEVELOPMENT

Cognitive development concerns the growth of a child's mental abilities. There are several factors that would lead us to expect that separation (i.e. disruption of attachment bonds) might cause delays in cognitive development:

- **A secure base for exploration** is important for cognitive development. Bowlby's theory of attachment proposed that a key purpose of attachment is the provision of a secure base. Children who are insecure are less able to explore their world confidently and this may hinder their cognitive development. This is supported by research. For example, Hazen and Durrett (1982) found that securely attached young children were more independent explorers of their environment and were also more innovative in their approach to problem-solving.

- **Stimulation** is important for cognitive development. Greenough et al. (1987) found that rats reared in an enriched environment had larger brains, neurons with more connections and were smarter than rats reared in an impoverished environment. It is possible that children in day care receive less stimulation. For example, Bryant et al. (1980) found that childminders tended to reward quiet behaviour, thereby encouraging passivity and understimulation. On the other hand, day care may provide a more stimulating environment, especially for children from disadvantaged backgrounds.

The negative effects

The research described above provides support for the view that day care has negative effects on cognitive development. This is confirmed by a survey conducted by Russell (1999) of the findings of about 100 studies of day care. Russell concluded that, overall, the effects of day care were negative rather than positive. The studies surveyed were conducted between 1957 and 1995. It is possible that the *quality* of day care has improved considerably in this time; studies that look at poor-quality day care may well find negative effects, as we will see.

However, research continues to indicate a link between poor cognitive development and day care. For example, Ruhm (2000) found that preschool children had lower reading and maths skills if they spent time before the age of 3 in day care.

The positive effects

Not all research has found that day care has negative effects on cognitive development. In fact, some studies have indicated that there are actually *beneficial* effects for cognitive development. Such beneficial effects are found in situations where the quality of care is high. They are also found in situations where enrichment programmes linked to day care are provided for disadvantaged preschool children.

High quality of care

One of the reasons that day care may be detrimental is lack of stimulation, therefore it stands to reason that where day care is stimulating (high quality), it may actually be beneficial. Campbell et al. (2001) conducted a 20-year follow-up study of children who had been in day care. They found that those children who attended high-quality day care scored significantly higher on reading and maths tests. A study by Andersson (1992) in Sweden, a country that provides high-quality day care, found that school performance (at age 8 and age 13) was highest in those children who entered day care before the age of 1. School performance was lowest for those who did not have any day care. Such findings suggest that high-quality day care is beneficial.

Studies have found that attending high-quality day care can improve children's later performance at school. How does this tie in with your own experience?

Perhaps the most impressive evidence comes from an ongoing study being conducted in America by the National Institute of Child Health and Human Development. This study has followed over 1,300 children from birth through childhood (the cohort is currently nearing the end of primary school). Reports are published at regular intervals. In 1997, NICHD reported that the higher the quality of child care in the first three years of life, the greater the child's language abilities at 15, 24, and 36 months, and also the better the child's performance on the Bayley Scales of Infant Development (a measure of cognitive development) at age 2, and the more school readiness the child showed at age 3. High-quality care included frequent interactions between carers and children, referring to such things as how often caregivers spoke to children, asked them questions and responded to their vocalizations.

EFFECTS OF DAY CARE ON SOCIAL DEVELOPMENT

Social development concerns the growth of a child's abilities to interact with others and behave in a prosocial manner. There are several factors that might lead us to expect that separation might affect social development:

- Secure attachment is claimed to be of prime importance for emotional and social development. If separation affects the security of a child's attachment by disrupting their continuous relationship with a caregiver, then we would expect to see differences in terms of social and emotional development in those children placed in day care.

- On the other hand, the opportunities for social interaction that occur in day care might promote social development. For example, children in day care are more likely to have to learn negotiation skills.

The negative effects

An early study, Belsky and Rovine (1988) found that children who spent more than 20 hours per week in day care were more insecurely attached (as assessed in the Strange Situation) than home-cared children. This has led many people to conclude that day care is harmful. Recent findings from the NICHD (2001) support this. They found that those children who spent more than 10 hours per week in day care were more aggressive when they reached school age, both at home and in school. Such aggressiveness may be due to insecure attachment.

The lack of negative effects

Clarke-Stewart et al. (1994) investigated the relationship between time spent in day care and quality of attachment in 150 American children. They found that 15-month-old children who experienced high-intensity childcare (30 hours or more a week from age 3 months) were equally distressed when separated from their mothers in the Strange Situation as low-intensity children (less than 10 hours a week). The NICHD study in 1997 showed that infants with extensive day-care experience did not differ from infants without day care in terms of the distress they exhibited during separations from their mothers in the Strange Situation. The findings of these studies suggest that the day-care experience had no negative effects on attachment.

The positive effects

There is evidence to show that children who attend day care are more sociable and popular when they attend school. For example, Clarke-Stewart and colleagues also found that children who had attended day care coped better in social situations in their first year at school and were better able to negotiate with peers.

Enrichment programmes, such as Headstart, have also been assessed in terms of their benefits for social development. Schweinhart et al. (1993) found that children who took part in the High/Scope Perry Preschool Project had lower delinquency rates in adolescence and were less likely to have a criminal record when young adults than a control group who did not take part in the project.

FACTORS WHICH AFFECT THE EXPERIENCE OF DAY CARE

When considering the research findings, we have already noted that the quality of care is important in determining whether or not day care has positive or negative effects. We have also seen that time spent in day care may be significant (NICHD findings on aggression), but that it may not always be a significant factor (Clarke-Stewart and colleagues found no difference). A third factor apart from quality of care and time spent in day care, may be the child's age. In Andersson's study, children in day care before the age of 1 actually did *better* in terms of school achievement.

There are many other factors. One is individual difference. Pennebaker et al. (1981) reported that shy children find the day-care situation quite threatening and are likely to find it a less beneficial experience. Another possible factor is the quality of experiences at home. Securely attached children may respond differently to day care than insecurely attached children. Egeland and Hiester (1995) found an interesting interaction effect. They looked at about 70 children, half of whom entered day care before the age of 1, while the rest remained at home with their mothers. All the children came from impoverished backgrounds. Security of attachment was assessed around the age of 1 and again at 3. Day care appeared to have a negative effect for secure children, but had a positive influence for insecure children. However, we might be able to explain this in terms of the fact that insecurely attached children *needed* compensatory care, and therefore benefited from day care, whereas the securely attached children did not require this extra attention and separation from good-quality care was detrimental.

Such variations as those discussed above make it very difficult to make any definitive statements about day care in general.

SO DOES DAY CARE HARM CHILDREN'S DEVELOPMENT?

There is evidence that day care can have harmful effects. For example, Ruhm produced evidence of lower school performance in children who had been in day care. This may be due to less willingness to explore or to a lack of stimulation. In terms of social development, Belsky and Rovine found that children who spent more time in day care were more insecurely attached, and we have seen previously (see Sroufe and colleagues, p. 55) that insecure children are less popular. The NICHD study found that day care children were more aggressive when older.

There is also evidence that no harm is done. For example, Clarke-Stewart found no evidence of attachment differences between children cared for at home or in day care. Harvey reached a similar conclusion (see the panel below).

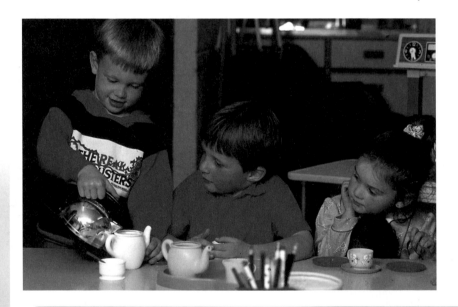

There is evidence of day care having beneficial effects on children's development, in terms of sociability and negotiating skills, for example. What is your view about the benefits and drawbacks of day care? Would you choose it for your children?

<< Children are not harmed by working moms >>

<< A study (Harvey 1999) evaluating the development and health of more than 6,000 youngsters suggests that children of women who work outside the home suffer no permanent harm because of their mother's absence.

Harvey's study came to a different conclusion than some earlier studies of the same group of children. The new work examined the children at a later age, 12 years old. This suggests that problems detected in children of working mothers at age 3 and 4 may have gone away by the time the children were 12.

Fundamentally, said Harvey, the study suggests issues exist in raising children that are more important than outside employment of the mother. These include the quality of the parent–child relationship and the quality of the child's day-care arrangement, she said. 'The message should be that being at home during the early years, or being employed during those years, are both good choices,' Harvey said. 'Both can result in healthy, well-developed children.' >>

Source: Adapted from the *Beloit Daily News,* 1 March 1999

And there is evidence of day care actually having beneficial effects. Andersson found improved school performance from children placed in day care at a very young age. Enrichment programmes have had moderate success for both cognitive and social development. Clarke-Stewart found that day-care children were more sociable and better able to negotiate with peers, and Schweinhart and colleagues found lower delinquency as a result of an enrichment programme.

One important question to ask is why the research findings are so inconsistent? The simple answer is that it is a complex issue – as we have seen there are many factors that influence a child's cognitive and social development, such as different attachment experiences, different kinds of day care and different temperaments. This means one factor (being in day care) is not likely to have consistent effects.

USING RESEARCH FINDINGS TO IMPROVE DAY CARE

Studies of day care tend to focus on the question of whether it is harmful or not. It may be more productive to consider the question: "What factors contribute to good day care?"

Schaffer (1998) suggests that consistency and quality of care are important. The question of consistency, according to Schaffer, is an organizational matter. A day-care centre needs to find some way of ensuring minimal turnover of staff, and to arrange that each child is assigned to one specific individual who is more or less constantly available and feels responsible for that child. It may also be important to establish consistent routines and physical environments.

It is probably more difficult to define quality, although Schaffer suggests that it can be expressed in terms of:

● the amount of *verbal interaction* between caregiver and child, which should ideally be one to one as far as possible – Tizard (1979) found evidence that, irrespective of social class, the conversations between mother and child were more complex than between nursery teacher and child

● having *sufficient stimulation*, such as suitable toys, books and other play things

● giving *sensitive emotional care* – the NICHD study found that about 23 per cent of infant care providers gave 'highly sensitive' infant care, while 50 per cent of them provided only 'moderately sensitive' care, and 20 per cent were 'emotionally detached' from the infants under their care.

One study (Howes *et al.* 1998) considered the value of a programme designed to improve the quality of caregiver interactions. A number of caregivers were involved in in-service training to increase their sensitivity. Six months after training, Howes and colleagues found that the children (aged around 2) became more secure and the caregivers were rated as more sensitive after training. There was a control group of caregivers who received no training. The attachment of the children in their care and their own sensitivity remained unchanged. The results of this study suggest that a modest intervention programme that is directed at improving caregiving practices can improve the attachment security of the children in day care.

ACTIVITY

Reviewing your ideas

Before carrying out this activity, read the interview with Jay Belsky on the next page.

Think back to the statement that you considered at the beginning of Topic 3 that *Day care jeopardizes development.*

Now that you have read about some of the research that has been carried out into the effects of day care, and have heard the views of Jay Belsky, are there any additional conditions that you would wish to highlight when discussing this statement?

In particular, think about:

1 the effects of day care on cognitive development

2 the effects of day care on social development

3 the effects of the quality of the day care on development

4 whether some children are more vulnerable to the effects of day care than others.

Effects of *day care*

Jay Belsky is Director of the Institute for the Study of Children, Families and Social Issues and Professor of Psychology at Birkbeck College, University of London. Professor Belsky is an internationally recognized expert in the field of child development and family studies. Amongst other things, he is involved in a multi-million dollar investigation in the USA of the effects of early childcare on children's development to the age of 11. He is also involved a long-standing longitudinal study of 1,000 young adults in New Zealand who have been studied intensively since the age of 3. He served as a consultant to former US Vice-President Gore on the issue of work and families.

Q **Research seems pretty inconclusive about whether day care has any significant effects on children's development. Is this a fair statement?**

A Not really. Evidence indicates that the more time that children spend in day care across their infant, toddler, and preschool years (combined), the more likely they are to behave in aggressive and disobedient ways as 4– to 8-year olds. Starting day care on a full-time basis in the first year may be especially risky in this regard. The evidence also indicates that children who experience better-quality day care tend to benefit, especially in terms of their cognitive and language development, when compared to those who experience poorer-quality care. The degree to which caregivers are attentive, responsive, affectionate, and stimulating defines the extent to which day care is of high or low quality.

Jay Belsky

Q **Why would poor-quality day care have such negative effects on a child's subsequent development?**

A When children are not caringly attended to and regularly stimulated, they find it difficult to develop the secure and positive sense of self that comes from being loved and attentively cared for, and which fuels so much of development. After all, knowing that one is loved and cared for fosters self-confidence and curiosity, both of which stimulate learning. Poor-quality care also directly undermines intellectual and language development by not providing children with the kind of stimulation they need to learn about the world and how to communicate with others. And if children's language and knowledge are not developed, then it is difficult for them to succeed in school. And failure in school feeds back to further undermine one's sense of self-esteem.

Q **Is there evidence to suggest that some children are especially vulnerable whereas others are more resistant to these effects?**

A There has been repeated indication that boys may be more vulnerable to the adverse effects of poor quality or to too much day care than girls. But such findings do not emerge in relevant studies either all the time or even most of the time, so it is difficult to conclude with certainty that boys are more at risk to the effects of poor day-care experiences. There is also some evidence that infants and young children who are highly negatively emotional may benefit more from exposure to good childrearing and be more adversely affected by poor childrearing than other infants. Although strong conclusions are premature, it is reasonable to treat as a working hypothesis that boys and highly negative infants/toddlers may be more vulnerable to poor day-care experiences than other children.

Check your understanding of the critical issue of day care by answering these questions. Try to do this from memory at first. You can check your answers by looking back through Topic 3.

1 Define 'day care'.

2 Give two reasons that are sometimes given for why day care involving separation from a parent might be thought to delay cognitive development.

3 What conclusions can you draw from Andersson's (1992) study undertaken in Sweden and also from the ongoing study by the National Institute of Child Health and Human Development in the USA?

4 Give two possible reasons why day care involving separation from a parent might be thought to delay social development.

5 Which of the following statements are true and which are false?"

   (a) "Opportunities for social interaction such as negotiation skills that occur in day-care situations may serve to promote children's social development."

   (b) "All research undertaken to date has found that day care has negative effects on cognitive development."

   (c) "Intervention programmes designed to reverse the effects of social disadvantage by providing intensive preschool education through day-care programmes failed to boost cognitive development or tackle the cycle of failure."

   (d) "One of the reasons that day care may be detrimental is lack of stimulation; therefore, it stands to reason that where day care is stimulating, it may actually be beneficial."

   (e) "Schweinhart and colleagues found that children who took part in the High/Scope Perry Preschool Project had similar delinquency rates in adolescence and were just as likely to have a criminal record when young adults than a control group who did not take part in the project."

6 What five factors may affect the experience of day care?

7 Why do the factors that you listed above in response to Question 6 make it difficult to make any definitive statements about day care?

8 Cite (name) one study that found day care does harm to children's development, one that found no evidence of harm, and one that reported evidence of day care having beneficial effects.

9 List at least four ways in which research findings can be used to improve day care.

10 Explain briefly why the single factor of being in day care or not being in day care has generated inconsistent research findings.

REVISION SUMMARY

Having covered this topic you should be able to:

✓ define 'day care', 'cognitive development' and 'social development'

✓ describe research findings and conclusions related to the effects of day care on cognitive development, including why day care might harm or benefit cognitive development

✓ describe research findings and conclusions related to the effects of day care on social development, including why day care might harm or benefit social development

✓ consider whether day care has harmful effects on the development of children

✓ describe how research can be applied to improving day care.

Topic 1: The development and variety of attachments

- **Attachment** is a strong emotional and reciprocal bond between two people, especially between an infant and its caregiver(s).

- Infants become attached to **one person first**, followed soon by **multiple attachments**. Strength of attachment varies between individual infants and appears to be related to responsiveness rather than time spent with a caregiver.

- **Bowlby** proposed **four phases of development**: pre-attachment, attachment in the making, specific attachments and goal-corrected partnership.

- Research into secure/insecure attachment is based on the **Strange Situation** classification.

- **Ainsworth and Bell** found that infants could be classified as **secure** (Type B), **avoidant–insecure** (Type A) or **resistant–insecure** (Type C). Type B was the most common group. A further group (Type D) has been identified.

- Further research shows that the Strange Situation is **reliable**, but may not be **valid**. Classifications vary from attachment figure to attachment figure (multiple caregiver paradox), but this can be resolved by taking an aggregate of attachment relationships.

- The **caregiver sensitivity hypothesis** proposes that sensitivity in caregiver interactions is a key feature of secure attachment. The **temperament hypothesis** suggests infants' innate temperament explains their behaviour in the Strange Situation.

- **Cross-cultural research** tests the validity of the Strange Situation and may indicate which aspects of attachment behaviour are innate and which due to cultural practices.

- **Takahashi** found that Japanese infants were much more distressed when left alone in the Strange Situation, which distorted the classification of the participants. Further research by **Van IJzendoorn and Kroonenberg** found similar rates of secure and insecure attachments in different countries.

- Advantages have been claimed for both **monotropy** and **multiple attachments**. There is evidence that infants do form one primary attachment in many cultures.

- Learning theory suggests that attachments form through **classical conditioning** (associating food with the person doing the feeding) and **operant conditioning** (food is the primary reinforcer, and the person supplying the food is the secondary reinforcer).

- Criticisms come from research by **Schaffer and Emerson** and from **Harlow and Harlow**, indicating that infants are not most attached to the person who feeds them.

- **Social releasers** encourage adult responses, and sensitive responses (caregiver sensitivity hypothesis) lead to the formation of attachments during a critical period. One special relationship (monotropy) leads to the formation of an internal working model and continuity in later relationships (the continuity hypothesis).

- However, correlations do not demonstrate a cause. Further criticisms are drawn from studies of deprivation and privation, and lack of evidence for evolutionary theory.

Topic 2: Deprivation and privation

- **Deprivation** refers to the loss of emotional contact with a primary caregiver.

- The **maternal deprivation hypothesis** states that healthy emotional development depends on having a warm, continuous relationship with a mother (or mother-substitute) before the age of $2\frac{1}{2}$ years.

- **Bowlby** found that young thieves were more likely to have experienced separations than children who were disturbed but not antisocial.

- Further research found that **hospitalized** children could recover if separations were for less than three months (**Spitz and Wolf**).

- **Separation** is a physical disconnection between child and caregiver that may, but need not, result in deprivation. The **Robertsons**, and **Skeels and Dye** demonstrated the benefits of emotional care during periods of separation.

- **Rutter** suggested that negative effects are not due to separations but to other intervening variables, and that privation rather than deprivation may be more important.

- **Privation** refers to the lack of contact with a primary caregiver. Privation is not the opposite of deprivation.

- **Hodges and Tizard** found that the **adopted children** appeared to recover (not supporting the maternal deprivation hypothesis). However, both groups had difficulties outside the home, which does support the maternal deprivation hypothesis.

- Further research into institutional care indicates that recovery is possible (**Rutter and colleagues**) although not all evidence supports this (**Quinton and colleagues**).

- Case histories suggest that recovery is possible if good subsequent care is provided at a young enough age. However, such studies are highly flawed. Studies of **reactive attachment disorder** indicate that sometimes recovery is not possible.

- There is evidence for and against the view that deprivation/privation is irreversible. All studies have problems related to methodology and/or explanations for the findings, which makes the data difficult to interpret.

Topic 3: Critical issue – Day care

- **Day care** is care that takes place outside the home, by someone other than close family, and does not involve overnight care.

- Day care may affect **cognitive development** because disruption of attachment bonds affects the secure base for exploration and reduces opportunities for stimulation.

- Studies indicate a link between poor school performance and preschool day care, e.g. the survey by **Russell**, and studies by **Hazen and Durrett**, **Bryant and colleagues** and **Ruhm**.

- Studies of **high-quality** day care show that day care can have beneficial effects. **Enrichment programmes** such as Headstart have been found to have small but significant long-term effects on the cognitive development of disadvantaged children.

- Day care may affect **social development** because it affects the continuity of the infant–caregiver relationship.

- Some research points to **negative effects**: less security of attachment (**Belsky and Rovine**) and increased aggressiveness (**NICHD study**).

- Some research has found **no negative effects**, e.g. **Clarke-Stewart and colleagues**.

- Some research has found **positive effects** in terms of better social abilities (**Clarke-Stewart and colleagues**) and less delinquency (**Schweinhart and colleagues**).

- Many factors affect a child's experiences of day care, including **time spent** and **quality** of day care, age, **temperamental** differences and **attachment** experiences at home.

- Research can be used to improve day care. Consistency and quality of care are important. Caregivers can receive training to improve quality.

Answering exam questions on Attachments in development

For sample examination questions and answers on Attachments in development, together with examiner comments on the answers, see pp. 253–5.

3
UNIT

Stress

PREVIEW

After you have read this unit, you should be able to:

>> explain stress as a bodily response, including the physiological systems underlying the stress-response

>> discuss research into the links between stress and physical illness, and the effects of stress on the immune system

>> discuss research into the sources of stress, such as life changes and workplace stressors

>> understand individual differences in reactions to stress, including factors such as personality, culture and gender

>> discuss methods of managing the negative effects of stress, including the strengths and weaknesses of physical and psychological approaches

>> understand the central role of 'control' in the ways that stress is perceived.

INTRODUCTION

Stress is a common topic of conversation nowadays. For instance, we often hear people say: "I'm feeling really stressed at the moment." Stress is believed to account for high levels of anxiety and depression, for increased vulnerability to colds and flu, and for heart attacks and strokes (damage to the brain's blood supply). Every week in papers and magazines, there are articles on how to cope with the high levels of modern-day stress, while thousands of professional and amateur psychologists make a living out of helping people to manage stress and its consequences.

You will notice that stress is generally referred to in a negative way. Yet, Hans Selye, one of the pioneering researchers into stress, pointed out that stress can also be associated with positive as well as negative experiences. To distinguish between the two, he referred to 'eustress' and 'distress', where eustress is the amount of stress needed for an active, healthy life. However, when levels of stress increase and exceed a person's ability to cope, it becomes potentially harmful; this is distress. The focus of this unit will be on the negative experiences associated with stress that is maladaptive.

In this unit, we shall look at the background to modern stress research, and evaluate the evidence for links between stress, and psychological and physical disorders. We shall see that some common assumptions about the effects of stress are well founded, but that some are not supported by experimental evidence. Topic 1 looks at stress as a bodily response, while in Topic 2 you will explore different sources of stress.

We shall also see how successful methods of coping with stress have to take into account the causes of stress and the physiological mechanisms of the stress-response. Stress management is the focus of Topic 3.

Simon Green

GETTING YOU THINKING...

1 Look at the three photos above. Do any of these photos show something that you typically find stressful?

2 List some of the other causes of stress (i.e. stressors) that you experience in your life.

3 Compare your list with the lists of one or two other people in your class. Alternatively, ask one or two of your friends to tell you about their list of stressors. Are there many differences between the stressors identified?

KEY TERMS

Cardiovascular disorder: any disorder of the cardiovascular system, e.g. high blood pressure, coronary heart disease (heart attack) or stroke. (The cardiovascular system consists of the heart and the blood vessels. It is responsible for distributing oxygen and nutrients to the body's organs.)

General Adaptation Syndrome (GAS): a model, described by Hans Selye, of how the body reacts during stressful situations. There are three stages: (a) alarm stage when an arousal response is activated, (b) resistance stage when the body is apparently coping with the stressor, (c) exhaustion stage – if stress continues for too long, it can lead to physical symptoms such as a stomach ulcer or heart attack.

Immune system: the system that protects the body against infection; a network of cells and chemicals that seek out and destroy invading particles.

Stress: can be defined in three ways: (a) as a response or reaction to something in the environment, (b) as a stimulus or stressor, i.e. a feature of the environment that produces a stress-response, (c) as a lack of fit between the perceived demands of the environment and the perceived ability to cope with those demands; this transactional model of stress is the most popular among psychologists.

Stressor: any stimulus in the environment that produces the stress-response, as described by Selye – for example, life events (such as dealing with death and bereavement or the breakdown of a long-term relationship) or events associated with the workplace (such as workload, conflict between home and work, keeping up with changes or lack of career prospects).

MODELS OF STRESS

Before we look at the bodily responses involved in stress, we have to be clear about what we mean by stress. The term, as we use it today, was first used by the American physiologist, Walter Cannon, in 1914. However, it was the experimental work of Hans Selye in the 1930s that really introduced the topic into the scientific and psychological world. After studying the reactions of rats to the stress of repeated daily injections, Selye proposed that in animals and humans, the body responds to a range of psychological and physical stressors with the same pattern of physiological activation. He called this pattern the General Adaptation Syndrome (Selye 1956), and suggested that it could in some circumstances lead to harmful changes in the body. This was the beginning of the modern study of stress.

The transactional model of stress

The transactional model of stress is the most popular approach to studying stress today. This model proposes that stress is a lack of fit between the perceived demands of the environment and the perceived ability to cope with those demands.

Selye had a stimulus view of stress, whereby any stimulus that produced the physical signs of the stress-response was defined as a stressor. The transactional approach argues that the key to defining the degree of stress experienced by an individual lies in their perception of themselves and their world. It defines a state of stress as a mismatch between the demands we perceive the world is making on us and our perceived strategies for coping with those demands, i.e. our coping strategies.

Some people overestimate the demands of exams, and underestimate their preparations. They will be highly stressed, even though, objectively, they should not be and will do extremely well. Others underestimate the

ACTIVITY

The transactional model and your stressors

Look back at the list of stressors you wrote in response to the questions in 'Getting you thinking...' on p. 81. For each stressor you noted, write down how the transactional model of stress would help to explain why it causes you stress.

demands of the examination and overestimate their preparations; they will do badly, but at least they will not be stressed when they fail. The key features are how people perceive and evaluate demands, and coping abilities. The important development, then, compared with Selye's original ideas is the introduction of a central cognitive element. This allows us to emphasize and explain the role of individual differences in how people perceive and react to stressful situations. It also means that we can use cognitive strategies to help people cope with stress, as we shall see later.

Before considering Selye's General Adaptation Syndrome (GAS), however, we need to look at some physiology in order to understand the stress-response.

The body's response to stressors

There are two main ways in which our body responds to stress, and both involve the adrenal gland.

We have two adrenal glands, lying just above the kidneys. Each adrenal gland is made up of two distinct sections – the adrenal cortex and the adrenal medulla. These two sections release different sets of hormones into the bloodstream (see Fig. 3.1) and are controlled by two different pathways.

The transactional model emphasizes the role of individual differences in how people perceive and react to stressful situations. What is stressful to one person may not be so for another person.

The hypothalamic–pituitary–adrenal cortex pathway

This is under the control of the hypothalamus and the pituitary gland. The hypothalamus is a small structure at the base of the brain, while the pituitary lies in the skull cavity just below the hypothalamus (to which it is connected by the infundibulum). The pituitary has been called the master gland of the body because it releases a number of hormones into the bloodstream, which in turn control many vital body functions. One of these hormones is the adrenocorticotrophic hormone (ACTH), which travels to the adrenal cortex and stimulates the release of hormones called corticosteroids into the bloodstream. There are a large number of corticosteroids which have a range of effects on the body and are a vital part of the stress-response. The hypothalamic–pituitary–adrenal cortex pathway (HPAC) is activated when higher brain centres evaluate a situation as stressful and instruct the hypothalamus to stimulate the release of ACTH from the pituitary.

Figure 3.1 ≫ *Physiology of the stress-response*

The hypothalamic–autonomic nervous system–adrenal medulla pathway

The control of this part of the adrenal gland is very different. The autonomic nervous system (ANS) is a network of nerve pathways running from centres in the lower parts of the brain (the brainstem) out to the organs of the body such as the heart, digestive system, the circulatory (blood) system and various glands, including the adrenal medulla. The ANS centres in the brainstem are in turn controlled by higher brain structures, especially the hypothalamus. The role of the ANS is to maintain the normal functioning of bodily systems in response to demands. When you run, you need more energy and oxygen supplied to the muscles, so our energy reserves (fats and carbohydrates) have to be converted into sugars and fatty acids in the bloodstream, and our heart rate and blood pressure have to increase. All this is carried out by the ANS without our conscious control.

To help it carry out its functions, the ANS has two subdivisions – the sympathetic and the parasympathetic. Each has nerve pathways running to the internal organs of the body.

● When the *sympathetic* subdivision is activated, we see a pattern of bodily arousal: heart rate and blood pressure increase; fats and carbohydrates are mobilized; activity in the digestive tract slows down – this pattern is known as 'sympathetic arousal'.

● When the *parasympathetic* subdivision is activated, this leads to the opposite picture: heart rate and blood pressure return to normal and digestion speeds up – a pattern of calm and bodily relaxation.

The adrenal medulla is controlled by the ANS, and activation of the sympathetic branch stimulates it to release the hormones adrenaline and noradrenaline into the bloodstream (in the USA these are called epinephrine and norepinephrine). Adrenaline is well known as an arousal hormone, and noradrenaline has similar effects. Together they reinforce the pattern of sympathetic activation, stimulating heart rate and blood pressure, and further mobilizing energy reserves.

So, in stressful situations, the hypothalamus activates both the HPAC and the hypothalamic–ANS–adrenal medulla pathways.

Activating the body's stress-response

Selye identified the activation of these two pathways – the HPAC and the hypothalamic–ANS–adrenal medulla – as the main components of the body's response to stressors. He also began the debate about why they should be activated under these conditions.

The key to this is to understand that the two systems, when aroused, prepare the body for energy expenditure. Corticosteroids, adrenaline and noradrenaline mobilize energy reserves and sustain blood flow and heart rate to get oxygen to the muscles. They do this under normal circumstances to supply our daily energy needs, but in stressful situations we also have to consider the role of higher brain centres.

Normally, the hypothalamus and the ANS function perfectly well without our conscious involvement, making sure that the body's physiological systems function within normal limits. However, we do need the higher centres when things happen in the world around us to which we have to respond quickly.

To our ancestors, the appearance of a sabre-toothed tiger on the horizon was a signal to run for their lives. Or, if they were hunting, the appearance of a suitable target was a signal to chase. Either way, the reaction was due to higher brain centres in the cortex and limbic system perceiving and evaluating the situation as either threatening or attractive. But to run in any direction needs energy. So, to make sure the energy was available, the higher centres would communicate with the hypothalamus and the ANS, and would stimulate a pattern of bodily arousal; ACTH would be released from the pituitary, leading to the secretion of corticosteroids from the adrenal cortex, and sympathetic ANS arousal would lead to the secretion of adrenaline and noradrenaline from the adrenal medulla. When the emergency was over, the systems would return to their normal level of functioning.

Hans Selye

Cannon (1914) called this pattern of bodily arousal the 'flight or fight' response. Selye's experimental studies showed that it was also central to the stress-response he observed in rats. Later, he proposed that any physical or psychological stressor activated the two pathways. Selye developed a model, the General Adaptation Syndrome (GAS), which explained the short-term effects of exposure to stressors, but also accounted for stress-related illnesses such as gastric ulcers.

The General Adaptation Syndrome

The GAS (Selye 1956) has three stages (see Fig. 3.2):

- In the first *alarm* stage, the presence of a stressful event is registered; this can be a threat from outside or a physical stressor, such as injury or illness affecting the body. The hypothalamus–pituitary system secretes a surge of ACTH which, in turn, releases corticosteroids from the adrenal cortex, while sympathetic ANS activation leads to increased adrenaline and noradrenaline secretion from the adrenal medulla. The body is prepared for energy expenditure, i.e. to respond to the perceived threat.

- In the second stage of *resistance*, the body's stress-response is fully activated and is apparently coping with the stressor, and so from the outside, things seem to be back under control.

- However, if the stressor is long lasting or chronic, the body enters the third stage of GAS, the stage of *exhaustion*. Selye felt that hormone reserves were depleted, and it is at this point that stress-related conditions such as raised blood pressure, ulcers, depression and anxiety may develop as stress systems become exhausted.

In evaluating the GAS, the key points are as follows:

- **Experimental support** – The GAS was the first systematic attempt based on experimental data to describe the body's responses to stress. Selye was the first to emphasize the central role of the HPAC and the hypothalamic–ANS–adrenal medulla pathways.

- **Use of non-human animals** – All Selye's early work was carried out on rats, using physical stressors. There are differences in physiology between rats and humans; humans respond mostly to psychological stressors and rely more on cognitive processes, making it difficult to generalize his research findings to people. However, Selye did use human participants in his later work.

- **Individual differences** – The GAS ignores individual differences, such as Type A behaviour (discussed on p. 95) and gender. It assumes we all respond in the same way to stressors, but we now know that personality and gender can significantly affect reactions to stress (see pp. 97–8).

The body systems underpinning the stress-response are responsible for providing energy resources whenever we need them. Most of the threats facing our ancestors

Figure 3.2 >> *The three stages of Selye's General Adaptation Syndrome*

AS Physiological Psychology

were external (e.g. large predators and other people), and for that reason a physical response that enabled them to expend energy and either fight the threat or take flight was appropriate (adaptive). It was a highly effective mechanism for survival, and this is still the case if we find ourselves in an extreme situation that requires an immediate physical response. However, our world today is very different; while physical threat and violence are still too common, they are not part of most people's daily experience. For the most part, the daily concerns we have are dominated by psychological stress involving such things as our relationships, careers, the future of the environment, pressures to be successful. Unfortunately, worrying about a big telephone bill or what we look like can trigger the same stress-response as running away from a large predator. Our stress-response is geared to providing the resources we need for physical action (such as fighting or running away) and therefore provides energy that has nowhere to go. If a psychological stressor is long lasting and the physical response to it occurs over long periods, then damaging effects of stress can occur, as we shall see in the next section. Now try the following activity.

ACTIVITY

How do you feel when you experience stress?

1 Think back to the last time that you felt stressed because you were in a frightening situation – perhaps you were walking home along an unlit street late at night? How did you feel? What happened to your heart rate? How did your mouth feel? How did your stomach feel? How did you deal with this situation?

2 Now think of the last time you were stressed because you were struggling to finish some homework by the deadline for handing it in, or you had to give a presentation, but hadn't had enough time to prepare properly. Again, how did you feel and how did you react? What are the possible signs of stress that others might notice in you (e.g. moodiness, irritability)?

3 Were there any similarities in the way that you felt about each of these situations? Did you deal with each of these in similar or in different ways?

For our ancestors most stressors were physical. Nowadays, stressors are more often psychological – and yet the stress-response prepares us for fight or flight

STRESS AND PHYSICAL ILLNESS

The last phase of Selye's GAS is the stage of exhaustion. Selye thought that the constant outpouring of stress hormones eventually depleted our stores, so that a literal state of 'exhaustion' occurred. It was this that led to stress-related illness. Nowadays, the view has changed; it is the hormones themselves that are believed to be responsible for the negative effects of stressful situations. The two main reasons for this change in view are that:

● hormone supplies are rarely exhausted – even under the most severe pressure

● we now know far more about the widespread effects of these hormones on the body.

Stress-related activation of the HPAC pathway and the sympathetic branch of the ANS leads to the increased secretion of corticosteroids, adrenaline and noradrenaline. Heart rate and blood pressure increase and energy reserves are mobilized in the form of fatty acids and glucose in the bloodstream. We will look at some of the possible harmful effects of this energy mobilization below, but another important feature of the body's stress-response is that, besides activating some systems, it shuts down others. Blood supply is prioritized, increasing to heart and skeletal muscles and the brain, whilst decreasing to systems that are of no immediate use, such as the digestive tract.

Our immune system is also inhibited in stressful situations. The immune system is an immensely complex system of cells and chemicals that protects the body from infection by viruses and bacteria, and helps to repair tissue damage. During stress, however, everything is geared to escape, so protection and tissue-repair can wait until the emergency is over.

So the picture is one in which the body's systems are totally directed to survival in the face of threat. As long as the threat is short lived, this is an excellent survival strategy. However, if the threat is long lasting, the combination of maximum activation of the stress-response arousal pathways and the shutting down of non-essential systems can lead to problems.

Stress-related illness

Many illnesses are believed to be related to stress, including the following cardiovascular disorders:

- *hypertension* – raised blood pressure due to the furring up of the cardiovascular system
- *atherosclerosis* through raised blood pressure wearing away the blood-vessel lining, scarring of blood vessels that act as a collection point for fatty acids and glucose circulating in the bloodstream, and the formation and deposit of plaques that slowly block blood vessels
- *stroke* caused by plaques blocking the tiny blood vessels in the brain
- *raised blood pressure*, which can also cause a brain haemorrhage (the breaking of a blood vessel and bleeding into brain tissue)
- *coronary heart disease* (heart attack) caused by damage to the functioning of the heart, which is responsible for pumping blood around the body.

Other illnesses related to stress include migraine, asthma, gastric ulcers and eczema.

All of these conditions can have other causes besides chronic (long-lasting) stress. Heart disease and hypertension may have a genetic component and are certainly linked to diet. Often, it may be a case of stress interacting with these other factors to make the situation worse.

Furthermore, while chronic stress may not lead to obvious illness (such as a heart attack, flu or stomach ulcers), it can damage the body, making these conditions more likely to occur. There are many stages of deterioration between a healthy heart and blood supply and an actual heart attack or stroke.

We can divide the possible ways in which stress can damage the body into four simple categories:

- direct mechanical effects (atherosclerosis)
- energy mobilization (hypertension, atherosclerosis, brain haemhorrhage, stroke)
- suppression of the immune system
- other effects.

Direct mechanical effects

The body's stress-response increases heart rate, pumping blood around the body at faster speeds and at a higher pressure. At particular points in the cardiovascular system, notably where blood vessels branch, this increased mechanical pressure can simply wear away the blood-vessel lining, resulting in atherosclerosis. Like any hydraulic system, increased pressure leads to increased damage and a shorter life.

Energy mobilization

Nowadays, most of our stress comes from psychological sources, such as life events and the workplace. Physical activity is rarely the coping response to psychological stress. However, the core of stress-induced arousal is the effect of corticosteroids, adrenaline and noradrenaline in releasing stored carbohydrates and fats from their storage cells into the bloodstream in the form of glucose and free fatty acids. These are then transported to the muscles and brain cells that need them as a source of energy. If they are not burnt up in energy expenditure, the body's systems will try to restore balance by reabsorbing the excess levels back into storage cells when the current emergency passes.

If the stress is chronic, reabsorption cannot cope, so high levels of glucose and free fatty acids remain in the bloodstream, where they contribute to the 'furring up' of the cardiovascular system. This can lead to hypertension and atherosclerosis.

Suppression of the immune system

The immune system is our main defence against infection by foreign agents. It is an immensely complicated network of cells and chemicals throughout the body that functions to seek out and destroy invading particles. Any agent that stimulates an immune response is called an antigen. Familiar antigens are bacteria, viruses and fungi (such as moulds and yeasts). Sometimes particles that are normally harmless, such as dust and pollen, cause an overreaction of the immune system, and this is the basis of allergies.

Key players in our immune system are the white blood cells, which are manufactured in the bone marrow and circulate in the bloodstream. The two types of white blood cell are lymphocytes and phagocytes, and these provide three different mechanisms of immunity:

- *Non-specific immunity* – phagocytes surround and ingest foreign particles wherever they encounter them.
- *Cell-based immunity* – lymphocytes called T cells (because they mature in the thymus gland) seek out and destroy any cells recognized as foreign (e.g. in transplanted tissues) and also cells infected with antigens such as viruses and bacteria. Closely related to T cells are NK (natural killer) cells, which also seek out and destroy antigens.
- *Antibody-based immunity* – another class of lymphocytes called B cells (because they mature in the bone marrow) destroy invading agents while they are still in the bloodstream and before they enter the body's tissues. They do this by producing large proteins called antibodies which attach themselves to the virus or bacteria, slowing them down and making it easier for other immune cells such as the phagocytes to destroy them.

The immune system is complex and stress-response hormones can affect it directly. For example, high levels of corticosteroids can shrink the thymus gland, preventing the growth of T cells. The immune system is also more sensitive to stress than was originally thought. Even short-lasting life events such as brief marital strife can cause suppression of the immune system (immunosuppression), while long-term life stress causes parallel long-term reductions in immune function (Willis *et al.* 1987). On the other hand, exercise, diet and social support can improve immune function, and as a self-regulating system, it will also recover from suppression if the stressful situation is resolved (Sapolsky 1994).

Short-term immunosuppression is not dangerous, but chronic (long-lasting) suppression leaves the body vulnerable to infection and disease. The best current example is AIDS, which leaves the sufferer vulnerable to a host of possible illnesses. So we would expect chronic stress to lead to more frequent illnesses and infections. We will look at the experimental evidence in the next section.

Other effects

The stress hormones, such as corticosteroids, adrenaline and noradrenaline, have many complex effects on the body. Apart from energy mobilization and immunosuppression, they also affect many hormones released by the pituitary gland. Earlier, we referred to the role of the pituitary as a master gland, secreting many hormones, which in turn control a variety of bodily functions. Secretion of many of these hormones is disrupted by the stress-response, leading to various problems.

The pituitary controls sexual and reproductive functions. In males, testosterone production declines during the stress-response, leading to problems with erections and sexual desire. In females, menstrual cycles can be disrupted and sexual desire reduced. Pituitary release of growth hormone is inhibited, potentially affecting growth and repair of bone structure. There is a rare condition known as 'stress dwarfism', in which children suffering extreme chronic stress through deprivation or abuse fail to grow normally.

Another aspect of the body's stress-response is a loss of pain sensitivity (stress-induced analgesia). During emergencies, the release of brain neurotransmitters called enkephalins and endorphins is increased. These control our pain sensitivity, and it makes sense for this to be reduced in situations such as a battle, when people suffering severe injury only realize it when the conflict has subsided.

Complete the next activity before reading on.

ACTIVITY

How stress can indirectly affect your health and wellbeing

As we have seen, chronic stress can lead *directly* to physical illness, such as heart disease or weakening of the immune system. Sometimes, however, stress may cause physical illness *indirectly*, by altering the way a person behaves, which could in turn damage their health.

In what ways might a stressed person behave that could later increase the risk of damage to their physical health?

To help you to start thinking about this, consider the following three 'stressful' scenarios:

1 A student studying for an exam in a subject that they find quite difficult.

2 A person who has just broken up with their girl/boyfriend after several years of being together.

3 Someone who is caring for a relative who is terminally ill.

In the last activity, you identified a range of behaviours that might result from being in a stressful situation and could indirectly affect a person's health in the longer term. These probably included smoking, drinking excess alcohol, drug abuse or neglecting oneself by eating a poor diet over a period of time, making it more likely that the person will suffer from illnesses such as colds and coughs. Later in the unit we will be considering a range of techniques that can help to reduce the negative effects of stress.

RESEARCH INTO STRESS AND PHYSICAL ILLNESS

Many studies have investigated the effects of stress on:

- physical illness (including cardiovascular disorders)
- the immune system.

The key studies described below are two of the best known. See also the Western Collaborative Group Study undertaken by Friedman and Rosenman (1974), described on p. 95, for a study of the relationship between stress and cardiovascular disorders.

KEY STUDY >> STRESS AND PHYSICAL ILLNESS

the 'executive monkey' study by Brady et al. (1958)

Aim >>

To investigate whether the stress of receiving electric shocks would lead to stress-related illness in monkeys, and whether this would interact with the degree of control over the shocks.

Procedures >>

- Monkeys received electric shocks to their feet at 20-second intervals for periods of six hours at a time, with six hours' rest in between.
- The electric foot shocks were not signalled.
- Monkeys were run in pairs, with one in each pair – the so-called 'executive' monkey – able to press a lever to postpone shocks for 20 seconds.
- The other monkey in the pair could not press the lever, but received all the foot shocks that were delivered (this second monkey in the pair was the 'yoked' animal).

Findings >>

- Not all shocks could be avoided on this schedule.
- After 23 days the 'executive' monkeys began to die of gastric ulceration.
- The yoked control monkeys, who received shocks but could not try to avoid them, remained healthy.

Conclusions >>

- Brady concluded that the shocks themselves were not severely stressful as the yoked monkeys showed little gastric ulceration; the critical factor was the stress associated with trying to avoid the shocks.
- Having *control* was the stressful element in this study, causing gastric ulceration in the 'executive' monkeys.

Criticisms >>

- Brady used monkeys, so there is a problem of generalizing his results to humans. Monkeys have a different physiology to humans and may respond to stress in different ways. However, Brady did show that trying to cope with stressors is highly stressful for monkeys.
- Brady also chose monkeys who were the most active bar-pressers as the executives; as a group, they were more active generally than the yoked control group, and this may have made them more sensitive to the stress of the footshocks. This means that the experiment was poorly controlled, as both groups should have been made up of monkeys that were equally active.

A02 check — Stressing monkeys (or any animals) until they die or become severely ill is highly unethical and would not be permitted today. All researchers are now obliged to follow clear ethical guidelines (see Unit 5), which ensure that such a study could not be carried out again.

AS Physiological Psychology

KEY STUDY >> STRESS AND THE IMMUNE SYSTEM

a study into the functioning of the immune system by Kiecolt-Glaser *et al.* (1984)

Aim >>

To investigate whether the stress of important examinations has an effect on the functioning of the immune system.

Procedures >>

- This was a natural experiment using 75 medical students.
- Blood samples were taken: (a) one month before their final examinations (relatively low stress), and (b) during the examinations (high stress).
- Immune function was assessed by measuring NK cell activity in the blood samples.
- The students were also given questionnaires to assess psychological variables such as life events and loneliness.

Findings >>

- NK cell activity was significantly reduced in the second blood sample, taken during their final examinations, compared with the first sample (taken one month before their final examinations).
- NK cell activity was most reduced in participants who also reported high levels of life events and loneliness.

Conclusions >>

- Examination stress reduces immune function, potentially leaving the individual vulnerable to illness and infections.
- Immune function is also affected by psychological variables such as the stress of life events and feelings of loneliness. These long-term stressors may make individuals more vulnerable to the added effect of short-term stressors such as examinations.

Criticisms >>

- This was essentially a correlational study, so a strong conclusion about a cause-and-effect relationship cannot be drawn.
- It was a natural experiment using a natural source of stress and therefore had reasonable ecological validity, but students may be a special group and generalizations should be made with caution.

AO2 check

However, the results are in line with other studies linking stress to reduced immune function. Kiecolt-Glaser's research group has carried out many other studies on stress and the immune system. They have shown that immune function is significantly reduced in highly stressed groups such as carers for patients with Alzheimer's disease (dementia) (Kiecolt-Glaser *et al.* 1991) and women going through divorce proceedings (Kiecolt-Glaser *et al.* 1987). Even short periods of marital conflict have been known to lead to immunosupression, with women showing a greater and longer-lasting reduction than men (Kiecolt-Glaser *et al.* 1998).

ACTIVITY

Expert interview

Read the 'Expert interview' with Janice Kiecolt-Glaser on p. 86. As you read it, pay particular attention to:

1 the effects of short-term stress on the immune system

2 the immunological consequences of personal relationships

3 any evidence of gender differences.

Stress and the *immune system*

Janice Kiecolt-Glaser is Professor of Psychiatry and Psychology in The Ohio State University College of Medicine. Working in the area of psychoneuroimmunology, she has written more than 160 articles, chapters and books, most in collaboration with Dr Ronald Glaser. Their studies have shown the important health consequences of stress, including slower wound-healing and impaired vaccine-responses in older adults. In addition, their work has focused on the ways in which personal relationships influence immune and endocrine function, and health.

Q Would the reductions you see in immune function always make people more vulnerable to infection and illness, or would it only be in chronic states, such as caring for Alzheimer's patients? Are the changes associated with *short-term* stressors (such as examinations, marital arguments) unlikely to increase vulnerability to illness?

A Even short-term, predictable and relatively benign stressors can increase vulnerability to illness. For example, dental students participated in a study in which small standardized wounds made three days before a major test healed on average 40 per cent more slowly than those made during the summer vacation; indeed, no student healed as rapidly during exams as during the vacation. Similarly, medical students who were more stressed took longer to produce a protective antibody response following hepatitis B vaccination than students who were less stressed, suggesting that the stressed students would also be slower to develop an antibody response to other pathogens. Theoretically, therefore, they could be at greater risk of developing more severe illness.

Q Have you noticed any characteristics in your participant groups that seem to protect people against the effects of stress on the immune system?

A Individuals who have stronger close personal relationships are less likely to show adverse

Janice Kiecolt-Glaser

immunological consequences when stressed. For example, when we followed students through exams, we found that lonelier students had lower NK cell activity than students who were not as lonely. Additionally, students who reported lower social support experienced a weaker immune response following hepatitis B vaccination than those with greater support. Spouse caregivers of dementia sufferers who reported lower levels of social support showed the greatest and most uniformly negative changes in immune function one year later. Lower marital satisfaction was also associated with poorer immune function.

Q Have you noticed any consistent gender differences in your studies? If so, how do you explain them?

A In our studies the most consistent gender differences occurred in response to marital conflict. The relationships between adverse hormonal and immunological changes, and negative or hostile behaviors, were stronger for women than for men, and women's physiological changes following marital conflict showed greater persistence than men's.

Arguments with the spouse are more upsetting to women than men, and wives demonstrate more detailed and vivid memories of marital disagreements than their husbands. Women reminisce more frequently about important relationship events, and spend more time thinking about their marital relationships than men – all reasons to expect that women would show greater responsivity.

Suppression of the immune system need not necessarily lead to illness and disease if immune function remains within the normal range. Even if it is not, you still have to be exposed to an infectious agent for illness to develop. Cohen *et al.* (1993) demonstrated this in a classic study. Participants filled in questionnaires on negative life events, how stressed they felt, and the degree of negative emotions (depression and hostility) they felt. These scores were combined into a stress index. The participants were then exposed to low doses of the common cold virus. 82 per cent of the 394 participants became infected with the cold virus, and infection was highly correlated with their stress index score, i.e. the higher their score, the more likely they were to become infected. Although this was a correlational study, it strongly suggests that high levels of stress reduce immune function and make a person more vulnerable to viral infection.

Research evidence suggests that there is a relationship between stress and physical illnesses, and in some cases this comes about through immunosuppression. Findings on life events and workplace stress are also relevant to this area; some of these studies are reviewed in the next topic.

CHECK YOUR UNDERSTANDING

Check your understanding of stress as a bodily response by answering these questions. Try to do this from memory at first. You can check your answers by looking back through Topic 1.

1 What are (a) stressors (b) a stress-response? Who did the earliest systematic studies of the stress-response?

2 Describe the transactional model of stress.

3 Outline the two main pathways of the body's stress-response.

4 Outline the three stages of Selye's General Adaptation Syndrome (GAS) to show how chronic stress may lead to illness.

5 What does the body's immune system do and what is immunosuppression?

6 Describe one important confounding variable in Brady and colleagues' 'executive' monkey study.

7 How did Kiecolt-Glaser and colleagues measure activity of the immune system?

8 Outline one strength and one limitation of Kiecolt-Glaser and colleagues' work.

9 How did Cohen and colleagues measure the stress levels of their participants and how did they test immune function?

10 Outline one strength and one limitation of Cohen and colleagues' study.

REVISION SUMMARY

Having covered this topic you should be able to:

✓ define the following terms: 'cardiovascular disorders', 'General Adaptation Syndrome', 'immune system', 'stress' and 'stressor'

✓ describe at least two ways in which the body responds to stress – these should include the two main pathways of the body's stress-response

✓ describe and evaluate the General Adaptation Syndrome

✓ outline the effects of stress on the body, including physiological arousal and immunosuppression

✓ describe and evaluate research into stress and cardiovascular disorders

✓ describe and evaluate research into stress and the immune system

✓ describe the aims, procedures, findings, conclusions and criticisms for a key study investigating stress and physical illness, and a key study investigating the effects of stress on the immune system.

GETTING YOU THINKING...

In 1967, Holmes and Rahe published a scale called the Social Readjustment Rating Scale (SRRS), reproduced in Table 3.1 opposite. This scale consists of a list of 43 major life events that were perceived as being potentially stressful because they forced people to make substantial psychological readjustments. Each life event in the list is allocated a point value to reflect the relative amount of change it requires. This is known as the Life Change Unit (LCU).

1 Look at the three photographs below. Why do you think that Holmes and Rahe included each of the events illustrated in their scale?

2 Why do you think that each event was allocated the rating it was?

Outstanding personal achievement is ranked 25 in the SRRS, with a LCU of 28.

Taking a holiday is rated 41, with a LCU of 13.

Marriage is ranked 7, with a LCU of 50.

Life changes: major life events, such as marriage, divorce, moving house and having a baby, that are scored according to their psychological impact within the Social Readjustment Rating Scale (SRRS) and used to investigate the relationship between life changes and stress-related health breakdown.

Control (psychological): the sense that we can anticipate events that occur in our environment – a feeling that we can accomplish things and are not at the mercy of forces beyond our control.

Workplace stressor: any stimulus in the workplace environment that produces the stress-response, such as work overload or role ambiguity.

RESEARCH INTO SOURCES OF STRESS

As we saw in Topic 1, the common definition of stress views it as rooted in the demands that we perceive in our environment compared with our perceived ability to cope with those demands; therefore, we can describe many sources of stress. We make many demands on ourselves – am I happy enough, rich enough, do I look okay, will I meet this deadline? Other people also make demands on us – get this job done, make me happier, earn more money, be my friend. We get stuck in traffic jams or break down on the motorway; friends and relations have accidents, become ill or even die; we all have illnesses and accidents. Whether these situations are regarded as stressful depends on our coping abilities, but some of them are almost certain to be.

Experimental approaches to the study of stress need to define and, if possible, quantify the amount of stress in people's lives, so that reliable links can be made to physical and psychological disorders. The problem is that the sources of stress are so varied that many different approaches have been developed to assess stress. We will look at some of the most popular ones.

The Social Readjustment Rating Scale (SRRS)

This scale, developed by Thomas Holmes and Richard Rahe in 1967, is also known as the Holmes–Rahe Life Events Rating Scale. Together with some later variations, the SRRS has been the most widely used of all methods for assessing life stress.

Inevitably, things happen in life that force us to make psychological adjustments. The more we have to adjust, the more stressful the event is. Holmes and Rahe made a list of major life events, based on their experience as clinicians. They then asked hundreds of men and women, of a variety of ages and backgrounds, to rate the events in terms of the amount of readjustment they would require, i.e. their psychological impact. The death of a spouse came out top, and was given an arbitrary value of 100. Other events were given ratings relative to this ranking, so that redundancy, for instance, came out as 47, a house move as 20, and holidays as 13.

Table 3.1 >> The Social Readjustment Rating Scale (SRRS)

	Life event	LCU		Life event	LCU
1	Death of spouse	100	22	Change in responsibilities at work	29
2	Divorce	73	23	Son or daughter leaving home	29
3	Marital separation	65	24	Trouble with in-laws	29
4	Jail term	63	25	Outstanding personal achievement	28
5	Death of close family member	63	26	Wife begins or stops work	26
6	Personal injury or illness	53	27	Begin or end school	26
7	Marriage	50	28	Change in living conditions	25
8	Fired at work	47	29	Revision of personal habits	24
9	Marital reconciliation	45	30	Trouble with boss	23
10	Retirement	45	31	Change in work hours or conditions	20
11	Change in health of family member	44	32	Change in residence	20
12	Pregnancy	40	33	Change in schools	20
13	Sex difficulties	39	34	Change in recreation	19
14	Gain new family member	39	35	Change in church activities	19
15	Business readjustment	39	36	Change in social activities	18
16	Change in financial status	38	37	Mortgage or loan less than US$10,000	17
17	Death of close friend	37	38	Change in sleeping habits	16
18	Change to different line of work	36	39	Change in number of family get-togethers	15
19	Change in number of arguments with spouse	35	40	Change in eating habits	15
20	Mortgage over US$10,000	31	41	Vacation	13
21	Foreclosure of mortgage or loan	30	42	Christmas	12
			43	Minor violation of the law	11

Source: Holmes and Rahe (1967)

Once the scale was constructed, it was simply a matter of asking participants to check off any of the 43 life events they had experienced over a given period – usually two years, but sometimes less. The researcher then totalled their score and used it as an index of that person's life stress. Using studies that were both retrospective (asking people with possible stress-related illnesses to look back at the previous two years) and prospective (assessing life stress and then observing participants over the following months), Holmes and Rahe proposed that a score of 150 or more increased the chances of stress-related health breakdown by 30 per cent, while a score of over 300 increased the odds by 50 per cent.

KEY STUDY >> LIFE CHANGES AND STRESS

a study by Rahe *et al.* into life changes as a source of stress (1970)

Aim >>
To investigate whether scores on the Holmes and Rahe Social Readjustment Rating Scale (SRRS) were correlated with the subsequent onset of illness.

Procedures >>
- 2,500 male American sailors were given the SRRS to assess how many life events they had experienced in the previous six months.
- The total score on the SRRS was recorded for each participant.
- Then over the following six-month tour of duty, detailed records were kept of each sailor's health status.
- The recorded number of Life Change Units were correlated with the sailors' illness scores.

Findings >>
- There was a positive correlation of +0.118 between Life Change scores and illness scores.
- Although the positive correlation was small (a perfect positive correlation would be +1.00), it did indicate that there was a meaningful relationship between Life Change Units and health (this is often referred to as a statistically significant correlation).
- As Life Change Units increased, so did the frequency of illness.

Conclusions >>
- The researchers concluded that as Life Change Units were positively correlated with illness scores, experiencing life events increased the chances of stress-related health breakdown.
- As the correlation was not perfect, life events cannot be the only factor in contributing to illness.

Criticisms >>

- The study does not take into account individual differences in reactions to stress.
- A correlation does not imply causality nor the direction of any effect; depression or anxiety may not be caused by life events, since depressed or anxious people may bring about life events such as separation or divorce.
- The sample was restricted to male US Navy personnel; therefore it was ethnocentric (Americans only) and androcentric (males only). This reduces the validity of the study and makes it difficult to generalize to other populations.

On the positive side, these findings support other research that suggests that life-event scores do have a low but significant association with stress-related health breakdown.

AS Physiological Psychology

Evaluation of the SRRS

Many studies have been done on the link between life events and health breakdown using the SRRS. Although significant correlations are often found, they tend, like the study undertaken by Rahe and colleagues outlined earlier, to be relatively small (the highest is about 0.30). This suggests a relationship between stress and health, but not a strong one. However, it also became clear that there were problems with the scale:

- *Individual differences* – The scale values for different events are arbitrary and will certainly vary from person to person. Some people really dislike holidays or Christmas, and would have them near the top of their list of stressors, rather than at the bottom. Others might find marital separation a relief from a highly dysfunctional relationship. The stress of taking out a large mortgage depends on your income. Each of us could devise a personal rating scale since the stress of an event depends upon our individual perception of it.

- *Causality* – The relationship between SRRS score and health is correlational and so tells us nothing about causality. Depression or chronic physical illness may lead to life problems rather than being caused by them.

- *Positive life events* – Some life events are positive. People getting married probably see it as a positive change, while 'change in financial state' can clearly be positive or negative. The SRRS does not distinguish positive from negative because the model assumes that any life change is stressful, without evidence to support such an assumption.

- *Self-report* – Self-report of life events can be surprisingly unreliable. Raphael *et al.* (1991) asked participants to fill out a life-events scale for the previous year, and then repeated the exercise every month for another year. As time passed, the agreement on life events between the later reports and the first declined significantly.

However, despite these criticisms, the SRRS was a major step in stress research for two main reasons:

- It was the first detailed attempt to quantify levels of stress in people's lives.
- Its use confirmed that life events can lead to health breakdown.

Life Experiences Survey

In the years following the introduction of the SRRS, refinements were made to life-event scales to try and overcome the criticisms outlined above. A popular version is the Life Experiences Survey (LES) (Sarason *et al.* 1978). Based on the SRRS, the LES has 57 items, but these can be rated in terms of their positive or negative impact on a seven-point scale (highly negative, –3, through neutral, 0, to highly positive, +3). This allows for individual differences in the perception of

events to be taken into account. There are also specialized sections that can be used for particular groups of people, such as students. The LES produces scores for positive change, negative change and total change. As you might expect, health problems correlate more highly with negative life-change scores, than with positive or total change.

One general problem with any life-event approach is that it concentrates on events that are by their very nature unusual. In any given study, 10 to 30 per cent of participants may experience none of the scale items, while still not being free of stress. This is because incidents we would not count as major events – the everyday hassles of life – can also be a source of considerable stress. These are everyday occurrences such as worrying about friendships, losing the car keys, concerns over appearance (weight, hair loss, skin condition), keeping up with college courses and minor health problems. For most people, these have more daily impact than items included in scales such as the SRRS or LES.

Hassles scale

Table 3.2 >> Examples of hassles and uplifts

Examples of hassles
>> Concerns about weight
>> Health of a family member
>> Rising prices of certain goods
>> Home maintenance
>> Too many things to do
>> Misplacing or losing things
>> Physical appearance

Examples of uplifts
>> Relating well to your spouse/partner/lover
>> Relating well to friends
>> Completing a task
>> Feeling healthy
>> Getting enough sleep
>> Eating out
>> Visiting, phoning or writing to someone

Household chores are a hassle for many people

To assess these very real sources of stress, Lazarus and colleagues devised the Hassles Scale (Kanner *et al.* 1981). The original form had 117 items, although versions can be constructed for subgroups, such as students (e.g. unfriendly classmates, boring teachers). Since they thought that positive events in life could reduce the impact of daily hassles, the group also introduced an Uplifts Scale, with 135 items that cheer people up; items include getting on well with your partner and feeling healthy. See Table 3.2 for some examples taken from the Hassles and Uplifts Scales.

Research shows that scores on the Hassles Scale can correlate with levels of depression, anxiety and health problems. DeLongis *et al.* (1982) compared Hassles scores with Life Events, and found that although both correlated significantly with health status, the association for Hassles scores was greater. No statistical relationship was found between Uplift scores and health outcomes.

In the final topic of this unit, we shall see that various factors can help protect us against the negative effects of stress. Recent variations of the life-event approach to stress include some assessment of these factors along with the life-event scale. For example, Moos and

Swindle (1990) propose eight areas of common life stressors:

- illness and other medical problems
- home and local environment (items such as safety and traffic)
- family finance
- relationship with partner
- children
- extended family
- work (discussed in the next part of this topic)
- relationships outside the family.

These areas are assessed using their Life Stressors and Social Resources Inventory, which also incorporates measures of factors that may help cope with life stressors. These include social support networks and financial state.

In evaluating research using life events scales and hassles/uplifts scales, the following points are important:

- Research using scales of major life events and daily hassles supports the idea that there are many sources of stress in life, and that they can affect physical and psychological health.
- Correlations are not huge, but are often significant. This means that in a general sense, the stress in each of our lives can potentially affect our health and how we operate from day to day.

There are also situations where stress-related problems can have more direct effects, and this brings us to the area of applied stress research.

Workplace stressors: research findings

Through its effects on psychological and physical health, stress can affect performance at work, whatever your job. All jobs involve a certain amount of stress, but there is a growing interest in work conditions that increase stress. Companies have an interest in maintaining productivity and performance, which are both affected by stress-related illness. The study of workplace stress is an area of occupational psychology and is one of the fastest growing fields of psychology.

Different types of work bring different stressors. Which of these would you find more stressful?

Sources of stress in the workplace depend on the type of work or enterprise. An assembly-line worker in a car factory has different problems from a middle-rank manager in a City bank. A fire fighter has different problems again. There are, however, some sources of stress that apply to most workers:

● *Physical environment* – Space, temperature, lighting and arrangement of an office (open plan or separate rooms) can all affect the individual. Physical stressors make work more difficult and more energy has to be expended to overcome them. The increased arousal can also lead to frustration, and many studies have shown that increased temperature (e.g. Halpern 1995) and exposure to intense noise (e.g. Evans *et al.* 1998) can lead to stress and aggression.

● *Work overload* – We seem to be moving to a culture in which long hours at work are seen as a mark of esteem, at the cost of both the individual and social structures. Overload is frequently reported as one of the most stressful aspects of the workplace (Dewe 1992). A key element in this is the impact long hours have on family life (the home–work interface).

● *Lack of control* – In many organizations, other people often determine workload and work patterns. Both animal studies (for example, the work on learned helplessness by Seligman (1975), see p. 109) and work with humans (e.g. Marmot *et al.* 1991, see p. 94) show that a perceived lack of control increases the stress-response and contributes to depression and illness.

● *Role ambiguity* – This occurs when the requirements for a particular work role are unclear or poorly defined, and is a major factor contributing to work-related stress. This sometimes results either from having no clear guidelines separating one role from another, or ones that are contradictory. Role ambiguity will also contribute to other sources of workplace stress, such as relations with co-workers and lack of control.

ACTIVITY

Categorizing workplace stressors

Four possible sources of workplace stressor are listed on the left. Spend a few minutes talking with your teachers, parents, relations and any friends with full-time jobs about what they find most stressful in their work. Include both men and women in your sample. Make a note of their answers.

When you have gathered all their responses, put each response into one of the four categories on the left. If there are answers that do not seem to fit any of the categories, try to think of a new descriptive category (for instance, home–work interface, career progression, job insecurity).

How many categories did you need to accommodate all the responses? Which category or categories had the highest number of responses? Why do you think this is?

Sources of stress are highly significant to the individual concerned, but they also affect the organization. Stress can lead to physical and psychological consequences, which, in turn, affect productivity, through decreased motivation at work and time off with health problems. In the USA, and increasingly in companies in the UK, occupational psychologists are brought in to identify sources of stress in the workplace and to advise on methods of reducing them. By assessing the organizational structure and interviewing employees at all levels of the hierarchy, they try to pinpoint key problems and identify solutions. These can involve changes in methods of communication or the physical arrangement of workplaces, or the introduction of different work schedules or management structures.

The key study on the following page (*Stress in the workplace*) describes one study of work stressors and the possible link with work-related illness.

KEY STUDY >> STRESS IN THE WORKPLACE

a study by Johansson *et al.* (1978) into work stressors and stress-related illness

Aim >>

To investigate whether work stressors such as repetitiveness, machine-regulated pace of work and high levels of responsibility increase stress-related physiological arousal and stress-related illness.

Procedures >>

● The researchers identified a high-risk group of 14 'finishers' in a Swedish sawmill. Their job was to finish off the wood at the last stage of processing timber. The work was machine-paced, isolated, very repetitive yet highly skilled, and the finishers' productivity determined the wage rates for the entire factory.

● The 14 'finishers' were compared with a low-risk group of 10 cleaners, whose work was more varied, largely self-paced, and allowed more socializing with other workers.

● Levels of stress-related hormones (adrenaline and noradrenaline) in the urine were measured on work days and on rest days.

● Records were kept of stress-related illness and absenteeism.

Findings >>

● The high-risk group of 14 finishers secreted more stress hormones (adrenaline and noradrenaline) on work days than on rest days, and higher levels than the control group.

● The high-risk group of finishers also showed significantly higher levels of stress-related illness such as headaches and higher levels of absenteeism than the low-risk group of cleaners.

Conclusions >>

● A combination of work stressors – especially repetitiveness, machine-pacing of work and high levels of responsibility – lead to chronic (long-term) physiological arousal. This in turn leads to stress-related illness and absenteeism.

● If employers want to reduce illness and absenteeism in their workforce, they need to find ways of reducing these work stressors, for example by introducing variety into employees' work and by allowing them to experience some sense of control over the pace of their work.

Criticisms >>

● Some important variables, such as individual differences, are not controlled in this study; it may be that certain people who are vulnerable to stress (e.g. those exhibiting Type A behaviour – see opposite) are attracted to high-risk demanding jobs, such as finishing in a sawmill.

● In addition, the study does not identify which of the various work stressors may be the most stressful. The high-risk group was exposed to low levels of control through repetitive machine-paced work, physical isolation and high levels of responsibility. To separate out the effects of these different factors, a more controlled experimental study would have to be carried out, but this would be at the expense of ecological validity.

Many other studies have been carried out on stress in the workplace. For example, Marmot *et al.* (1991) carried out a three-year longitudinal study of over 3,000 civil servants, measuring job control and stress-related illness. They found that people with low job control (i.e. type and amount of work decided by others) were four times more likely to die of a heart attack than those with high job control (i.e. more independence in deciding the type and amount of work). Job control and illness were negatively correlated: as job control decreased, the chances of stress-related illness increased. This was supported by a review of research that concluded that a combination of high job demands and low control is associated with an increased chance of heart disease (Van der Doef and Maes 1998).

As mentioned earlier, research on stress can be affected by individual differences. For example, not all workers with high scores on life event scales or jobs with low control and high demands become ill. The study of these individual differences is an important area of stress research and we will look at this area of study next.

INDIVIDUAL RESPONSES TO STRESS

Personality and Type A behaviour

From the early 1960s, Friedman and Rosenman (1974) studied the behaviour of patients suffering from coronary heart disease (CHD), and proposed that a particular behaviour pattern was associated with increased vulnerability to this stress-related illness. This pattern is known as the 'Type A behaviour pattern' and is characterized by constant time-pressure (always being in a hurry), doing several tasks at once, being intensely competitive in work and social situations, and being easily frustrated by the efforts of others. The frequency with which this pattern is observed has led to it often being referred to as the Type A personality (see Table 3.3 and the key study below – this key study is also relevant to the debate about the relationship between stress and physical illness).

> ### Table 3.3 >> Type A behaviour pattern
>
> **Time pressure**
> >> working against the clock
> >> doing several things at once
> >> irritation and impatience with others
> >> unhappy doing nothing
>
> **Competitiveness**
> >> always plays to win at games and at work
> >> achievement measured as material productivity
>
> **Anger**
> >> self-critical
> >> hostile to the outside world
> >> anger often directed inwards

KEY STUDY >> STRESS & CARDIOVASCULAR DISORDERS

the Western Collaborative Group Study by Friedman and Rosenman (1974)

Aim >>
To investigate links between the Type A behaviour pattern and cardiovascular (heart) disease.

Procedures >>
- Using structured interviews (see p. 209), 3,200 California men, aged 39 to 59, were categorized as either Type A, Type X (balanced between Type A and Type B) or Type B (the opposite of Type A, i.e. more relaxed and not showing Type A characteristics of time pressure, competitiveness and anger).
- This large sample was followed up for $8\frac{1}{2}$ years to assess their lifestyle and health outcomes.

Findings >>
- By the end of the study, 257 men in the sample had developed coronary heart disease (CHD), of which 70 per cent were from the Type A group – twice the rate of heart disease found in the Type B group.
- This difference in the incidence of CHD between the two groups was independent of lifestyle factors, such as smoking and obesity, that are known to increase the chances of heart disease.

Conclusions >>
- The Type A behaviour pattern increases vulnerability to heart disease.
- Behaviour modification programmes to reduce Type A behaviour should result in a reduced risk of heart disease.

Criticisms >>
- Although some aspects of lifestyle were controlled for, there may have been other variables that could have affected vulnerability to heart disease, such as elements of hardiness (see p. 96).
- This was not an experimental study, so cause and effect cannot be assumed; other studies have failed to show a relationship between Type A behaviour and heart disease.

AO2 check

An example of a study that did not show a relationship between Type A behaviour and heart disease is the large-scale, seven-year longitudinal study involving 12,000 men carried out by Shekelle *et al.* in 1985.

In evaluating Type A behaviour, the key points are:

● **Lack of consistent research support** – Since the original work by Friedman and Rosenman (1974), many studies have looked at the relationship between Type A behaviour and CHD. Some of these have been retrospective (looking at the previous behaviour of patients with CHD) and some prospective (measuring Type A behaviour using questionnaires and then following participants' health outcomes over months or years). Significant correlations have been found, but these are never very high, and many negative findings have been reported. Even the value of the Type A concept has been questioned (Evans 1990).

● **The role of hostility** – To try to make some sense of this, the behaviour pattern has been more closely analysed, and it turns out that a critical personality variable is hostility. When high levels of hostility are combined with high levels of Type A behaviour, correlations with CHD are significantly increased (Matthews and Haynes 1986). Particularly vulnerable are individuals who repress high levels of hostility rather than express it (although that may be better for the rest of us, of course!).

● **Type A and hardiness** – Despite the fact that Type A behaviour seems to be a risk for stress-related illness, many Type A individuals survive quite happily with their pressured and competitive lives. In the third topic of this unit, which looks at stress-management techniques, we will see that one of the key factors in managing stress is a strong sense of commitment, control and challenge. These are key elements of Kobasa's hardy personality (discussed below), which, she proposes, is resistant to the damaging effects of stress. There is no reason why Type A people should not also show high levels of commitment and control; in fact, they would be expected to. They are high achievers and so must be very committed, and they like to do everything themselves, as they do not believe anyone else can do it as well, i.e. they have a strong sense of control.

● **Protective factors** – So, along with factors which make them vulnerable, such as haste, time pressure, doing too many things at once and hostility, the Type A person may also score highly on protective factors such as control and commitment. There are also other less specific elements that have been shown to protect against stress, such as physical exercise and social support – these may also help the Type A person avoid the negative effects of stress.

Hardy personality

According to Kobasa (Kobasa and Maddi 1977), the concept of hardiness (or the hardy personality) is central to understanding why some people are vulnerable to stress and some resistant. Hardiness includes a range of personality factors that, if present,

provide defences against the negative effects of stress. These factors are:

● **Control** – This is the belief that you have control over what happens in your life, rather than attributing control to outside influences. It is similar to locus of control, discussed later, and attributional style, which is the tendency to attribute causes either to yourself (dispositional attribution) or to external factors over which you have no control (situational attribution).

● **Commitment** – This is a sense of involvement in the world around you, including people as well as jobs and careers. The world is seen as something to engage with, rather than to stand apart from. It includes a strong sense of purpose in your activities.

● **Challenge** – Life changes are seen as challenges to be overcome or as opportunities, rather than as threats and stressors. Life is not about comfort and security, but change and growth.

Kobasa has presented evidence that people who have high scores on scales measuring hardiness are significantly less likely to suffer stress-related physical and psychological disorders than those with low hardiness scores. In theory, their positive approach means that life events are not seen as stressful, but as challenges and opportunities that can be overcome. This leads to less activation of the stress-response and its negative consequences.

Kobasa's studies of personality and stress have identified other factors involved in coping with stress and have implications for stress management. Using previous work suggesting that physical exercise and social support also protected against stress-related illness, Kobasa et al. (1985) rated participants on the presence or absence of the three factors:

● hardiness

● social support

● regular exercise.

In this prospective study, Kobasa and colleagues then followed the participants and assessed the severity of any subsequent psychological problems (depression and anxiety) or physical illnesses.

Results showed clearly that participants with no protective factors had higher scores on severity of illness scales than any other group. In addition, the presence of one, two or all three protective factors was associated with steadily decreasing illness scores. This implied that the factors acted additively in improving resistance to stress. Of the three, hardiness seemed to have the greatest impact.

In evaluating hardiness and the hardy personality, the key points are:

● **Participants** – Much of Kobasa's work has been carried out with male, white-collar workers, and so the findings may not be generalizable to other groups. Stressors and coping responses differ between men and women, for example.

- **Components of personality** – Control, commitment and challenge have never been very clearly defined, so control, for instance, may be an important part of commitment and challenge, rather than being separate from them. This would mean that Kobasa is only looking at the role of control in protection against stress rather than a full 'personality type'.

Gender

Although sources of stress may vary between males and females – especially if the female takes most responsibility for home and children – there is no evidence that the levels of stress each experience are any different. There is some evidence that physiological reactions to stressors (the stress-response) may distinguish the two groups.

ACTIVITY

Gender differences in coping with stress

It is commonly believed that men and women deal with stress in different ways. Either on your own or in a small group, ask at least 20 of your peers who are not studying psychology how they tend to deal with stressful situations.

1 What gender differences, if any, did you find to support this belief?

2 Are men more or less likely than women to use social support (such as talking through things with someone else) to help them cope with stressful situations?

3 What other ways of dealing with stress did the people in your sample use?

Evidence for gender differences includes the following:

- **Physiological reactivity** – Frankenhaeuser et al. (1976) measured levels of the stress hormone adrenaline in boys and girls taking an examination. The boys showed a much more rapid increase in hormone levels, which took longer to return to normal after the examination. The girls' increase was slower and smaller, and returned to baseline more quickly. Interestingly, performance in the examination was roughly the same for the two groups and so were levels of reported (subjective) anxiety and stress.

- **Support for Frankenhaeuser** – Similar results were reported by Stoney et al. (1990) who found that women showed smaller rises in blood pressure due to stressful tasks than did men. Possible explanations for these findings might be that:
  - the hypothalamus-pituitary and ANS stress pathways are more reactive in men than in women
  - men and women vary in their attitude to the test, and this psychological difference influences the stress-response; for instance, men may be more competitive and 'aroused' during the test, leading to more sustained physiological arousal.

- **Gender differences in coping** – On the whole, men show more stress-related physiological arousal than women across a range of psychological and physical stressors (Vogele et al. 1997), even though both genders report similar levels of subjective stress. This means that men should be more vulnerable to stress-induced illness but, as we shall see, other factors influence responses to stress and vulnerability to illness. Physical exercise and social support are important 'buffers' against stress-induced illness, and you can argue that these vary between the genders. Men take more physical exercise, while women make more use of social support networks, so predictions as to who should show more vulnerability to stress are very difficult.

Does your own experience support the idea that men and women make use of different buffers against stress?

One simple conclusion reached by Frankenhaeuser is that women live longer on average because they show less stress-related physiological arousal than men. One exception she found was that women in occupations traditionally regarded as 'male', such as engineering students and bus drivers, show a male-pattern physiological response to stress. Of course, we do not know if this was produced by the role or that they were attracted to such occupations because of their physiological make-up.

Look back at the expert interview with Janice Kiecolt-Glaser on p. 86 to remind yourself of what she has to say about gender differences.

See 'An eye on the exam', opposite, for an evaluation of the effects of gender.

Culture

Stress is found in all communities, but the sources can vary a great deal depending on the sort of society. In the developing world, we do not worry so much about finding food and water day by day, while people in developing countries spend less time worrying about which primary school to choose or why they haven't been promoted. However, all of these different sources of stress conform to the basic idea that stress exists when the perceived demands on you outweigh your perceived ability to cope.

Several studies have looked at different ethnic groups in Western societies and how they cope with common stressors.

- *Cultural differences in social support* – Social support is an important protective factor against stress, and there are clear ethnic variations in how it is used. Kim and McKenry (1998) looked at social support networks in a range of ethnic groups in America. They found that African-Americans, Asian-Americans and Hispanics all used parents and children for social support more than Caucasian (White) Americans did. African-Americans were more likely to be members of religious organizations, while Asian-Americans and Caucasians took more part in recreational groups. Such cultural variations in social networks have clear implications for coping with stress.

For instance, compared to White Americans, African-American and Asian-American carers for Alzheimer's patients report more belief in filial (children's) duty to parents, use faith and religion as part of their coping strategy, and report lower levels of depression and stress related to caring (Connell and Gibson 1997). Their lower levels of stress could be linked to the cultural differences in attitudes to social and family life, and their religious networks.

- *Other cultural differences* – One of the difficulties in assessing cultural variations in relation to stress and responses to stress is that cultures vary along many other dimensions that can affect health. Heart disease, hypertension and depression, for instance, can be affected by your genetic inheritance, diet, general lifestyle and social organization. To isolate effects of stress is therefore virtually impossible. As an example, Weg (1983) studied the Abkarsian people of Georgia (formerly part of the USSR), who have a high percentage of individuals living beyond 100 (400 per 100,000, compared to 3 per 100,000 in the UK). Factors that emerged as important were:

  - genetic inheritance
  - high levels of social support
  - physically active lifestyles of work and recreation
  - diet high in fruit and vegetables, low in meat
  - no alcohol or smoking
  - low reported stress levels.

It is impossible to decide which of these factors is most important. Regardless of which culture you study, health outcomes are a complicated mix of inheritance, lifestyle, social networks and stress. Sources of stress and methods of coping will vary between cultures, but stress-related problems will still depend on available coping strategies versus the demands being made on the individual.

See 'An eye on the exam', opposite, for an evaluation of the effects of culture.

individual differences and stress

The preceding sections dealt with two of the most important factors that modify the experience of stress for an individual – gender and culture. However, this raises two important questions concerning the *nature* of such individual differences. First, *why* are there gender differences in stress reactions? Second, is cultural diversity itself a stressor? The following material constitutes AO2 *commentary* in these two areas (see pp. 247–8 for an explanation of different types of question).

Gender differences – an adaptive response to stress?

In humans and animals, biological and behavioural responses have evolved that allow the individual to maximize their chances of survival when confronted with a stressor. Traditionally, it has been adaptive for males to deal with a threat using a 'fight-or-flight' response. However, although this fight-or-flight response may be advantageous for the survival of the individual male, it puts defenceless offspring at a significantly greater risk of being harmed. Compared to males, females make a greater investment in offspring, initially in pregnancy and then in supporting them to maturity. This greater maternal investment should result in the selection of female stress-responses that do not jeopardize the safety of offspring in times of threat, and maximize the chances that they will survive. Taylor *et al.* (2000) believe that this should favour the development of biological mechanisms that *inhibit* the fight-or-flight response and shift the female's attention when faced with a threat to tending to the young (i.e. showing attachment behaviour) and seeking the company of other females as a defensive network against external threats.

Taylor and colleagues claim that high sympathetic nervous system activation (which is targeted primarily at the cardiovascular system, thereby optimizing physical performance) and high cortisol responses are characteristic biological components of the *male* stress-response. In contrast, neurophysiological mechanisms within the female brain inhibit the fight-or-flight response, and instead promote attachment behaviour – Taylor and colleagues refer to this as the 'tend-and-befriend' response to stress. It is entirely possible, therefore, that these differences also apply to the non-life-threatening stressors of daily life, and could play a role in the fact that men are more likely than women to die of cardiovascular disorders.

Cultural diversity – is diversity itself a stressor?

What we understand about the ways in which stress affects members of different cultures and, indeed, different groups within the same culture, is relatively limited. It is difficult to separate out the very different experiences of individuals within those cultures and pinpoint exactly how the experience of stress may differ for those individuals. It is possible, for example, that cultural diversity itself is a major stressor for members of minority ethnic groups within a majority culture. However, traditional stress scales (such as the SRRS developed and used by Holmes and Rahe) focus on mainstream stressors, such as divorce, bereavement and debt, and fail to address the specific situations that may affect some groups more than others. Such specific stressors might include economic marginality, unemployment and discrimination.

The major stressors for many members of minority ethnic groups are precisely those associated with their diversity and their consequent experiences of discrimination. Research is beginning to show evidence of a dual identity among diverse populations. Members of an minority ethnic group sometimes maintain two identities – one for work and the other for 'real life'. This allows them, as part of their stress management strategy, to maintain a positive self-image in their 'real world' when they believe they are subject to intolerable stress and discrimination in the workplace (Kelly-Radford 1999).

Check your understanding of the sources of stress by answering these questions. Try to do this from memory at first. You can check your answers by looking back through Topic 2.

1   What is the name of the rating scale devised by Holmes and Rahe in 1967 to investigate life stress? How many life events were on this scale and which was was given the highest score of 100?

2   Outline two criticisms of the Holmes and Rahe scale and its use.

3   Describe one difference between the Holmes and Rahe scale and Sarason's Life Experiences Survey.

4   What term is used to describe incidents that we would not call major life events, but which nevertheless can be a source of stress?

5   Why were the Hassles and Uplifts scales introduced?

6   Outline the procedures and findings of one study of stress in the workplace.

7   How did Johansson et al. (1978) measure levels of stress in their study of Swedish sawmill workers?

8   Describe two or more sources of stress in the workplace.

9   Describe the main characteristics of the Type A behaviour pattern.

10 Which characteristic of the Type A pattern seems to be especially important in increasing vulnerability to stress?

11 Of people with Type A behaviour pattern, why might some be less vulnerable to stress-related illness than others?

12 Outline some research findings that demonstrate gender differences in reactions to stress.

13 Describe two factors that might lead to gender differences in reactions to stress.

14 Describe one way in which cultural variations may affect reactions to stress.

15 Why is it difficult to investigate cross-cultural differences in the relationship between stress and illness?

REVISION SUMMARY

Having covered this topic you should be able to:

✓ define the following terms: 'life changes', 'control (psychological)' and 'workplace stressor'

✓ describe and evaluate research into life changes as a source of stress

✓ describe the aims, procedures, findings, conclusions and criticisms of a key study into life changes as a source of stress

✓ describe and evaluate research into workplace stressors

✓ describe the aims, procedures, findings, conclusions and criticisms of a key study into life changes and stress, and a key study into workplace stressors

✓ discuss the role played by personality, gender and culture in modifying the effects of stressors.

Look back to the questions in 'Getting you thinking...' on p. 77. For each of the stressors you noted there, think about how you try to cope with that particular source of stress. Create a table, using the format shown below. List each stressor, and next to it, record the ways of coping that you have found particularly successful. Then list any coping methods that have been less successful. Which ways of trying to cope with stress are better than others ?

Perceived stressors	Successful ways of coping	Unsuccessful ways of coping

Stress management: methods of managing the negative effects of stress. These include (a) the use of drugs and biofeedback (b) the use of relaxation and meditation (c) cognitive and behavioural training (d) the use of exercise and social support networks.

Physiological approaches to stress management: the use of drugs and biofeedback to target directly the stress-response systems themselves.

Psychological approaches to stress management: this includes (a) general psychological approaches such as the use of techniques of relaxation and meditation to reduce bodily arousal associated with stress (b) specific psychological approaches, such as cognitive and behavioural training, to help people control specific stressors in their lives.

The public considers stress to be one of the most prevalent 'diseases' of the past 20 years. It is also seen as fundamental to the way we live; as the pace of life increases, so, inevitably, does the stress of keeping up. In parallel with the increase in research into the negative effects of stress, such as psychological and physical disorders, so an industry has grown up devoted to methods of managing stress. These are by now many and varied, but can be divided into four major categories:

- *Physiological approaches* – The use of drugs and biofeedback to target directly the stress-response systems themselves.
- *General psychological approaches* – The use of techniques of relaxation and meditation to reduce the bodily arousal associated with stress.
- *Specific psychological approaches* – For example, cognitive and behavioural training to help people control specific stressors in their lives.
- *Aspects of lifestyle* – For example, exercise and social support.

PHYSIOLOGICAL APPROACHES TO STRESS MANAGEMENT

Drugs

The most commonly used drugs to combat stress are the benzodiazepine (BZ) anti-anxiety agents and beta-blockers. BZs, such as librium (chlordiazepoxide) and valium (diazepam), are the most prescribed drugs for psychological disorders and can be very effective against states of stress and anxiety. They appear to act by reducing activity of the brain neurotransmitter serotonin and reducing central (brain) arousal. Beta-blockers, such as inderal, do not enter the brain, but directly reduce activity in pathways of the sympathetic nervous system around the body. As sympathetic arousal is a key feature of stressful states, they can be very effective against symptoms such as raised heart rate and blood pressure. (They have also been used when bodily arousal can reduce performance in groups such as musicians and snooker players.)

When evaluating the use of drugs, there are important drawbacks to note associated with their use:

- *Dependency* – Long-term use of BZs especially can lead to psychological and physical dependency. A proportion of people trying to come off BZs will experience a physical withdrawal syndrome, with symptoms such as increased anxiety, tremors and headaches. BZs should only be prescribed for short periods of a week or so, to help cope with short-term stress. Dependency is far less of a problem with beta-blockers as they do not have a significant effect on central brain mechanisms.

- *Side effects* – All drugs have side effects; BZs can cause drowsiness and affect memory.

- *Only targeting symptoms* – Drugs treat symptoms, not causes. Many stressors are essentially psychological, so while they may help in the short term, drugs may prevent the real cause of stress being addressed. They are best used to manage acute (short-lived) stressors, such as the initial shock of a bereavement or examinations (although see side effects, above). They are most effective when psychological coping techniques are employed at the same time.

However, drugs are also a vital part of the armoury against the harmful effects of stress:

- *Speed and effectiveness* – Drugs can work quickly, rapidly reducing dangerous symptoms such as raised blood pressure (beta-blockers) or reducing disabling levels of stress-related anxiety (BZs).

- *Availability* – Drugs can be prescribed immediately. In addition, the range of treatments available is increasing rapidly, with newer agents such as angiotensin-converting enzyme inhibitors (ACE-inhibitors, e.g. Captopril) providing a variety of ways of tackling the symptoms of stress.

Biofeedback

This technique involves recording the activity of the physiological systems of the body's stress-response, such as heart rate, blood pressure or tension in the neck muscles that can lead to stress-induced headaches (see Fig. 3.3 below). Recording is usually made via electrodes on the skin leading to a hand-held monitor that the person holds.

People are encouraged to try various strategies to reduce the physiological readings. These can be muscle relaxation or meditation, or even altering their posture. The aim is to find a strategy to reduce, for instance, blood pressure consistently, and then to transfer the strategy to the world outside the laboratory and to practise it regularly.

In evaluating biofeedback, the key points are these:

- *Effectiveness* – Biofeedback can be very successful for some individuals, especially children (Attanasio *et al.* 1985) who enjoy the technological aspects in controlling, for instance, migraine headaches.

- *Role of relaxation* – Biofeedback is often found to be no more effective than muscle relaxation procedures without biofeedback (Masters *et al.* 1987). This suggests that feedback on symptoms such as blood pressure is not a vital part of the procedure, but that training in relaxation techniques is.

- *Expense* – This is related to effectiveness, as biofeedback is expensive in terms of equipment and time. If relaxation is the important feature, then the cost of the equipment could be avoided and training time would be much reduced.

Figure 3.3 ≫ *Biofeedback: outline of the procedure*

Different approaches to stress management

GENERAL PSYCHOLOGICAL APPROACHES TO STRESS MANAGEMENT

Progressive muscle relaxation

Although we all think we know how to relax, effective relaxation has, in practice, to be learned. Rather than simply thinking about nice things, progressive muscle relaxation is – strange as it may sound – an active approach to reducing bodily arousal. A standard procedure would be to train clients consciously to clench and unclench muscles, to get them used to the sensations of tension and relaxation. Whole-body relaxation would begin with the muscles of the toes, tensing and then relaxing them, and then working up through the legs, body, arms, shoulders and head (facial muscles).

Eventually, the client understands the sensations well enough to use progressive muscle relaxation in everyday life as a method to reduce bodily arousal. During relaxation, stress-response mechanisms are inactive, heart rate and blood pressure fall, and the parasympathetic subdivision of the autonomic nervous system is activated (see p. 79).

The activity on the right encourages you to experience the effects of progressive muscle relaxation for yourself.

An evaluation of these techniques would focus on the following points:

- *Effectiveness* – If practised regularly, relaxation techniques are effective in reducing stress, but are not effective in all situations because of space and time constraints (see the next point).
- *Practicality* – These techniques take time and space. If you are stuck in a traffic jam or in the middle of an examination, full progressive relaxation is inconvenient, if not impossible. However, the

ACTIVITY

Relaxation techniques

It is easier to focus on your studies when you are feeling relaxed. If you find this or any other unit difficult to take in, it may be because you are feeling stressed and so find it hard to concentrate. If you are feeling stressed, then take a few minutes out to practise a relaxation technique.

The progressive muscle relaxation technique is most effective if you lie on the floor. Tense each of the areas in turn, starting with your toes and ending with your facial muscles. For each area, tense your muscles as hard as you can and count to five. Then relax the muscles, counting to five before moving on.

By the end of the process, a lot of the tension in your body will have disappeared and you should feel much more relaxed as your heart rate and blood pressure reduce. Try it for yourself and use this technique whenever you are feeling stressed.

training also involves cognitive strategies to help relaxation, such as imagining yourself in pleasant, non-arousing surroundings, taking deep breaths, and consciously telling yourself to relax. Relaxation of some muscle groups is usually possible. Taking two minutes to run through a learned procedure like this can pay dividends in many stressful situations.

- *Targeting symptoms* – Relaxation techniques address bodily or physiological arousal by reducing activation of stress-response systems. This is undoubtedly beneficial, but long-lasting severe stressors need more than non-specific relaxation; their source has to be identified and targeted, usually via cognitive and behavioural strategies. Relaxation can still remain as an important component of stress management, but long-term adjustment requires more focused intervention as well.

Meditation

Meditation is similar to progressive muscle relaxation in that the aim is to reduce bodily arousal and to achieve a state of transcendental calm. This is achieved through sitting quietly and repeating your mantra – a single sound or word – while breathing deeply and regularly. The aim is to empty your mind of distracting and arousing thoughts. Like muscle relaxation, it can be used to combat stressful situations with a state of calm, thus preventing activation of the stress-response systems (Lichstein 1988). With your mantra readily available it may be more 'portable', but otherwise has the same problem of not addressing the source of long-term stressors. With practice, though, it gives the individual confidence in coping with short-term stress, and can be an important accessory to other methods of stress management.

In evaluating the use of meditation, the following factors are important:

- *Effectiveness* – Meditation can be used to reduce the physiological arousal associated with stress, and can do so very effectively. It is especially effective if incorporated as a part of your lifestyle and performed regularly. It can also be used to combat immediate stressful situations, such as examinations, because it can be done anywhere, and even a short period of meditation can reduce arousal.

  - *Targeting symptoms* – With severe, long-term stressors, such as a poor marriage or problems at work, meditation does not provide a solution but only temporary respite. For this type of problem, strategies have to address the cognitive element of the stress-response using specific psychological techniques.

SPECIFIC PSYCHOLOGICAL APPROACHES TO STRESS MANAGEMENT

At the beginning of this unit we discussed the definition of stress. The trigger in stressful situations, according to the definition, is the perceived gap between the demands being made on you and the coping responses you have available. So, a straightforward approach to stress management would be either to reduce the perceived demands or to improve your coping abilities or, preferably, both. Cognitive–behavioural approaches aim to do this by encouraging clients to perceive and evaluate stressful situations accurately (often we overestimate the demands being made on us), and to improve coping skills and techniques through training and practice.

Meichenbaum's Stress-Inoculation Training

Meichenbaum's (Meichenbaum and Cameron 1983) approach has three phases:

- *Conceptualization* – This is the main cognitive element. Clients are encouraged to relive stressful situations and to analyse various features. What was actually stressful about it? How did they attempt to cope? Why wasn't it successful? If many situations are stressful, do they have elements in common, such as the presence of strangers or the knowledge that performance is being assessed, as in exams and tests? These discussions can be individual or take place in groups, where the sharing of experience can help achieve a greater understanding of the nature of stress and the client's reactions to it. Clients are able to reach a more realistic understanding of the demands being made on them.

- **Skills training and practice** – Once the key elements of the stressful situations have been identified, clients can be taught specific and non-specific strategies for coping with them. The relaxation techniques described earlier help them to cope with the initial arousing effects of stress. Training in particular skills then helps reduce the specific demands. For instance, if examinations are the problem, knowing the syllabus in detail and developing simple strategies for learning, revision and time allocation can help to reduce stress. Relaxation techniques can be used in the examination room to keep arousal under control. Mock examinations can be taken to practise stress management. As another example, many people find social interactions stressful. Surprisingly, perhaps, social skills such as body posture, eye contact and conversational give-and-take can be taught relatively easily and practised in a therapeutic setting. Again, general relaxation techniques can help to limit stress-induced arousal.

- **Real-life application** – The final stage is for the client to go out into the real world and to put the training to the test. Contact with the therapist is maintained, and follow-up sessions and further training are provided if necessary. The reinforcement of successful coping with examinations or social interactions then becomes self-sustaining.

In evaluating Meichenbaum's approach, the key factors are as follows:

- **Targeting symptoms and causes** – Meichenbaum's programme is directed at both ends of the stress problem, i.e. sources of stress and coping strategies. By reviewing the coping methods they have used in the past, clients can gain a clearer understanding of their strengths and weaknesses. By acquiring new skills and techniques, they reduce the gap between demands and coping resources, and gain more confidence in their ability to handle previously stressful situations.

- **Effectiveness** – The combination of cognitive therapy (i.e. thinking about situations in the past and using cognitive strategies as part of a general relaxation technique) and behavioural therapy (i.e. training in new skills) makes stress-inoculation training a powerful method of stress management. However, few controlled studies of its effectiveness have been carried out, although Meichenbaum has reported some encouraging results (Meichenbaum and Turk 1982).

- **Practicality** – It takes time, application and money. Clients have to go through a rigorous programme over a long period, analysing their responses to stress and learning new techniques. This requires high levels of motivation and commitment, so it is not a quick-and-easy fix.

- **Difficulties** – There is evidence that the way we cope with life's stressors can reflect basic aspects of our personality, possibly innate or acquired during early experience. Examples include locus of control, (discussed later in this topic on p. 108). Any technique aimed at improving stress management may be acting against habits that are well established, even if they are not very effective. Changing cognitions and behaviour will always be difficult.

Increasing hardiness

Kobasa's belief that hardiness (see p. 96) is an important element in stress management led her to propose ways in which it could be increased. As with stress-inoculation training, the procedure has three aspects, the first two of which are quite similar to the first stage of stress-inoculation training:

- *Focusing* – Clients are trained and encouraged to spot signs of stress, such as muscle tension, increases in heart rate and anxiety. This allows them to recognize stressful situations and thereby to identify sources of stress.

- *Reliving stressful encounters* – Clients analyse recent stressful situations in terms of how they were actually resolved, ways in which they could have turned out better, and ways in which they could have turned out worse. This gives them insight into their current coping strategies and how they may be more effective than they imagine.

- *Self-improvement* – Central to hardiness is the belief that you can cope with life's challenges. Often, however, we are faced with stressors that cannot be easily managed. It is important, then, to recognize and to take on challenges that we *can* cope with. In this way we confirm that we still have control over some events in our lives. It is this sense of personal control and effectiveness that is fundamental to stress management. So, an essential

part of hardiness training is to begin with challenges the client can cope with before moving on to more complex problems.

In evaluating Kobasa's concept of hardiness, note the following key points:

- *Theoretical issues* – The concept of hardiness itself has been criticized. The relative importance of the three factors – control, commitment, challenge – is unclear, although there is evidence for the role of control and commitment in reducing responses to stressors. As we shall see, the importance of control in stress management cannot be exaggerated, and the concept of hardiness overlaps substantially with issues of personal control.

- *Generalizability* – Kobasa's studies usually involve white, middle-class businessmen, so the results cannot reliably be generalized to women or to different classes and cultures.

- *Effectiveness and practicality* – There are few systematic studies of the effectiveness of hardiness training. As with stress-inoculation training, it is lengthy, and requires commitment and motivation. It would never be a rapid solution to stress management problems. It also has the problem of addressing basic aspects of personality and learned habits of coping that are notoriously difficult to modify.

ASPECTS OF LIFESTYLE AND STRESS MANAGEMENT

Exercise

Earlier in this unit we reviewed the physiological mechanisms of the stress-response, and the role of these systems in mobilizing energy reserves and increasing heart rate and blood pressure. Many of the damaging effects of stress are linked to energy mobilization in situations where physical action is not appropriate or possible, leading to high levels of glucose and free fatty acids floating around in the bloodstream. These can then contribute to the 'furring up' of the arteries (atherosclerosis).

If the stress is short lived, our physiological systems will restore normal blood levels by storing excess glucose and fats. If stress is long lasting (chronic), then the constant energy mobilization overwhelms our body's capacity to cope, and disease can result. Physical exercise is one way of dealing with stress-related arousal and removing excess glucose and fats. It also has significant psychological effects, and so could be seen as both a physiological and a psychological method of stress management.

When evaluating exercise, there are two key points:

- *Effectiveness* – Correlational studies, where levels of fitness and exercise are recorded, along with frequency of stress-related disorders, such as depression and high blood pressure, consistently show that exercise is associated with lower levels of depression and a lower incidence of hypertension (raised blood pressure) (Holmes 1993). But causality is a problem; perhaps depression leads to people taking less exercise, rather than vice versa?

- *Supporting evidence* – Luckily, many studies have used prospective designs. Jennings *et al.* (1986), for instance, had participants undergo physical training programmes. Separate groups followed programmes of either less than their normal physical activity, the same level as normal, above-normal levels, or far-greater-than-normal levels. Results showed clearly that regular exercise at above-normal or far-above-normal levels produced significant reductions in heart rate and blood pressure.

Social support

Although it is easy to make the assumption that having a wide network of friends and relations must make life less stressful, it is more challenging to provide convincing experimental evidence to support this claim. In their extensive work, Brown and Harris (1978) demonstrated that loneliness and social isolation were factors in causing depression in women with young children. This can be related to the idea that social support protects against the psychological effects of stress. Before looking at more recent evidence, we should first examine what social support can mean.

There are various categories of social support:

- *Emotional support* – This can provide comfort and reassurance, and, by raising the person's sense of self-esteem and self-worth, help them feel able to cope with the situation.

- *Practical support* – Friends and support groups can help in practical ways, for example by lending money or helping sort out affairs after bereavement.

- *Advice* – Friends, and especially special interest support groups, can be a source of information and advice, commenting on possible coping strategies and suggesting others. They will often have met the particular situation before and can help the individual learn from their experience.

The mechanisms underlying the protective effects of social support are unclear. Talking with other people can help the cognitive evaluation of stress-induced demands and give reassurance that friends are around who will help with coping. However, work with monkeys shows strongly that isolation is very stressful, and that the simple physical closeness of others directly reduces physiological arousal. One could speculate that with humans, we have a combination of help at the cognitive and practical level, along with a more primitive need to be close to other people. The evidence suggests that hugging children is both reassuring and stress reducing. Before reading on, try the activity at the bottom of the page.

When evaluating social support, there are several factors to take into account:

- *Effectiveness (research support)* – Most studies are correlational, assessing levels of social support through questionnaires and correlating these scores with levels of stress-induced disorder. Evidence consistently shows a significant association. Social support was used by both male and female students in reducing the effects of stress (Weinstein 2002). In the workplace, job-related stress is reduced in organizations with high levels of support from co-workers (Constable and Russell 1986).

ACTIVITY

Your experience of social support

Using the three headings – emotional support, practical support, advice – make a list of all the people you think provide you with these kinds of social support.

1 How many different names appear in your lists? This provides an indication of your perceived social support network.

2 Do some names appear in more than one of your lists? If so, why is this?

3 When do you make the greatest use of these three types of social support?

4 Which people do you, in turn, offer social support to?

6 Think of some examples where social relationships can actually harm an individual's health or increase feelings of being stressed (e.g. by providing a bad example).

When you have completed this activity, you should have an idea of the size and composition of your own social support network. Some people are very happy and feel well supported by a relatively small number of social contacts, so please don't worry if your network seems rather small; quality of support is just as important as quantity.

More direct studies have demonstrated lower levels of cardiovascular activity (heart rate and blood pressure) during difficult tasks when a friendly companion is present (Kamarck *et al.* 1998), indicating less stress-induced arousal. Even recovery from heart disease is faster when a patient has high levels of social support (Kulik and Mahler 1989). Prevention of relapse and survival rates in cancer patients are helped by high levels of social support (De Boer *et al.* 1999)

- **Effectiveness (animal studies)** – The most convincing findings are from studies of monkeys. Some species, such as the cynomolgus monkey, are highly social animals with complex networks of relationships. If they are kept in isolation, heart rates and blood pressure immediately increase, while chronic (long-lasting) isolation leads to atherosclerosis and heart disease. When isolated animals are returned to the colony, they increase their rate of affiliative (friendly) behaviours over pre-isolation levels, as though they are compensating for the lack of social contact (Watson *et al.* 1998).

- **Gender differences** – It is clear that the level of social support varies. For example, one study found that men seem to have larger networks, but women seem to use them more effectively (Ratcliffe-Crain and Baum 1990). This has been related to the more severe effects of bereavement stress in men than women (Stroebe *et al.* 1999). On the other hand, Weinstein (2002) reported that female undergraduates had larger networks and used them more than male undergraduates did.

- **Types of network** – Whether people receive social support depends on the nature of the networks they have with other people. Social networks vary in their quantity and quality; for example, they differ in terms of the size of the network, the frequency of contact, the composition (who makes up the network) and the closeness of individual relationships within the network. These can vary with gender, age and the stage of one's life or career. It should also be remembered that the various types of social support (see above) could be provided by a small number of very close relationships.

CONTROL

The concept of control is central to stress and stress management. When there is a gap between perceived demands and perceived coping resources, we define it as a state of stress, but it is also a situation of being out of control. The Meichenbaum and Kobasa approaches to stress management both directly address ways of increasing the feeling of being in control. Analyses of how people try to impose control reveal that several different types of control exist:

- **Informational** – Your train stops unexpectedly on the way to an important meeting. Informational control is finding out what the problem is and how long the delay is likely to be.

- **Decisional** – Before you travel, there are alternatives, such as car, train or bus. Even if the decision turns out badly, you have control at that stage.

- **Behavioural** – Is there any direct action you can take? If the train stops in a station and you know the problem is serious, are there alternative forms of transport you can take, such as a bus or taxi?

- **Cognitive** – This refers to the use of cognitive relaxation techniques (as described earlier) to reduce the stress-induced arousal directly. Think about the meeting itself: is it absolutely critical that you be there? Will it really matter if you are late?

- **Retrospective** – This means thinking about the stressful situation after it is resolved. How did you cope, was it effective, what would you do differently next time, e.g. leave more time, not travel by train? Explaining how things happened and how they

could be avoided in the future are important aspects of control.

When described in this straightforward manner, stress management appears simple. Unfortunately, in real life it can be hard to act so rationally, especially when it goes against aspects of one's personality.

Individual differences: locus of control

The concept of locus of control (Rotter 1966) refers to individual differences in how we see the world and our ability to control what happens to us. There are two extremes:

- **Internal locus of control** – People attribute events that happen to them to sources within themselves; they are responsible. This can be misplaced because some events are clearly out of our control. For instance, if the train breaks down, a strong internal locus of control would lead to the assumption that the situation was a result of your choice of travelling by train. On the positive side, a strong internal locus of control is associated with the belief that you can control much of your life and succeed in difficult or stressful situations. People with a strong internal locus tend to cope well with stressful situations, showing less physiological arousal. They would be more likely to take behavioural control.

- **External locus of control** – The person with an external locus of control attributes events in their lives to outside agencies and factors. They have a sense that 'things happen to them' and are largely uncontrollable. Luck or fate are important factors.

As you would expect, people who sense they have little control over life events confront stressful situations with a more passive or fatalistic attitude, when a more active strategy is usually better for stress management. They suffer more stress-related illness and are less active in coping (Kamen and Seligman 1989).

Most people are not located at the extremes, but can often be characterized as more internal or more external. Locus of control questionnaires are commonly used in stress research, as locus of control relates to how we cope and how we react to stress, and one of the aims of stress-management training is to internalize the sense of control. However, as a fundamental part of personality, locus of control is hard to modify. It emerges during development, probably as a mixture of inherited factors and early social experience.

Research on the role of control

Many experimental studies have examined levels of control and reactions to stress.

- *Learned helplessness* – The work of Seligman (1975) on learned helplessness is probably the best known. He demonstrated that rats that were given inescapable foot shocks failed to learn to escape from avoidable foot shocks on a later test. He called this 'learned helplessness'. It can also be demonstrated in humans. Using loud noise as a stressor, Hiroto and Seligman (1975) found that participants exposed to uncontrollable loud bursts of noise performed poorly on a later task in which the noise was controllable. They had learned from their earlier experience that they could not control the noise, so did not even try. Seligman suggests that the experience of life as uncontrollable is stressful and an important factor in the development of stress-related disorders such as depression.

- *Personal control* – The important role of control is also supported in a study that has much greater ecological validity. Langer and Rodin (1976) carried out a study in a nursing home for older people. On one floor, residents were given some control over their lives, such as arranging their rooms, and deciding when to have visitors or go to watch films. On another floor, the residents had all these decisions made for them, as is often the case in many nursing homes. After a year and a half, over 90 per cent of the group who had been given greater control were rated by the nurses as having improved; the older people themselves also stated that they were more active and much happier. On the other hand, 70 per cent of the group without control were rated as less active and generally worse than before the study began.

- *Illusion of control* – Other research shows that even the illusion of active coping can reduce stress. Rats that were given repeated and uncontrollable foot shocks developed gastric (stomach) ulcers. However, when rats were given a lever to press, even though pressing it had *no* effect on the number of shocks, they developed far fewer ulcers (Sapolsky 1994). A similar effect has been found in people exposed to uncontrollable loud noises. Glass and Singer (1972) reported that a group that was given a button to press, which had no effect on the frequency of noises, still showed a smaller activation of the stress-response than a group simply exposed to the loud noise. This can also be seen in everyday life. People tend to be far more stressed by air travel than by car travel, even though statistically you are much safer when travelling by air. One explanation may be that we have no control when flying, whereas the car is far more under our control.

ACTIVITY

Expert interview

In the 'Expert interview' on p. 110, Dr Rob Briner, a psychologist specializing in organizational psychology, tells us his views on stress and whether stress management techniques can help reduce the bad feelings that can be associated with stress.

As you read his answers to the three questions, think carefully about:

1 whether you agree with what he is saying

2 what evidence from Unit 3 you would cite either to support or challenge a particular idea.

ACTIVITY

Research studies

This final activity should help you to check your understanding of some of the research in this unit. Select a study on each of the following topics:

- individual differences in modifying the effects of stressors

- stress management

- the role of control in perception of stress.

For each study complete a table like the ones that have been developed for key studies (see, for example, p. 84), using the following headings:

- Topic
- Aim
- Procedures
- Main findings
- Main conclusions
- Some criticisms

Expert interview >> Rob Briner

Stress *management*

Dr Rob Briner is Senior Lecturer in Organizational Psychology at Birkbeck College, University of London, and is a self-proclaimed sceptic when it comes to the subject of stress and stress management. His research has led him to become increasingly convinced that the 'stress' concept is not only limited, but also unhelpful, in trying to understand the links between work and wellbeing.

Q **Stress is bad for us and needs to be managed, yes?**

A Maybe. The answer depends on two things: what you mean by stress and what the research shows about the effects of stress. What researchers and lay people mean by stress is wide, varied and confusing. It sometimes means something 'out there' – a situation or experience that makes us feel bad. Sometimes it refers to something inside, something we experience – a feeling such as fear, anger, tiredness, sadness or frustration. There certainly is some evidence that some of the experiences or feelings we label 'stress' can be bad for us. However, this evidence is not as strong as most people imagine. Also, some of the things we label 'stress' may also be good for us or at least not harmful.

Rob Briner

Q **Has research shown one psychological method of stress management to be more effective than others in dealing with the negative effects of stress?**

A There are many so-called stress management techniques and a booming stress management industry. However, in most cases there is no or little evidence to support these techniques. Some have been shown to make some people feel better, such as counselling and relaxation. But in claiming this, we return to the problem: what does stress mean anyway? What may be effective in dealing with feelings of fear may not be effective in dealing with anger, yet both these things can be described as 'stress'. Just as it is not possible to have one best way of treating all illnesses (as it depends on the illness), it is not possible to have one best way of managing stress because it depends on what we mean by stress.

Q **Are there any dangers in developing a culture of stress management rather than dealing more constructively with the sources of stress?**

A In general, yes, because prevention is certainly better than cure. But before we can treat the sources of stress, we need much more evidence about what kinds of situations are psychologically harmful to people, how they cause harm and the nature of that harm. Some researchers have argued that believing that 'stress' is bad for us and makes us ill, together with the general hype around 'stress', is harmful. For example, people may ignore the real causes of their illness, blame it on 'stress', and fail to seek medical care. Also, people may get quite worried that being 'stressed' is going to make them ill when there is only limited evidence to support this.

Check your understanding of stress management by answering these questions. Try to do this from memory at first. You can check your answers by looking back through Topic 3.

1 Describe one physiological approach to stress management.

2 Outline one strength and one weakness of the approach to stress management that you described in Question 1.

3 Explain the principle underlying biofeedback.

4 Describe one psychological approach to stress management.

5 Outline one strength and one weakness of the approach you described in Question 4.

6 Name and outline the three phases of stress-inoculation training.

7 Describe the three components of the hardy personality.

8 What procedures did Kobasa recommend to improve hardiness?

9 Outline two criticisms of Kobasa's concept of hardiness.

11 Why does physical exercise help in coping with the effects of stress?

11 Name three types of social support and describe how each might help in coping with stress.

12 Outline three ways in which we might try to impose control in a stressful situation.

13 What is 'locus of control'? Describe what it means for a person to have an internal locus of control.

14 Why is it difficult to change a person's locus of control?

15 Outline findings from two studies concerned with levels of control and reactions to stress.

REVISION SUMMARY

Having covered this topic, you should be able to:

✓ define the following terms: 'stress management', 'physiological approaches to stress management' and 'psychological approaches to stress management'

✓ describe physiological approaches to stress management, such as the use of drugs and biofeedback

✓ describe psychological approaches to stress management, such as stress-inoculation and increasing hardiness

✓ evaluate the strengths and weaknesses of methods of stress management

✓ discuss the role of control in relation to stress.

Topic 1: Stress as a bodily response

● A state of stress exists when there is a mismatch between the **perceived demands** (**stressors**) on us and our **perceived coping strategies**.

● Stressors lead to activation of the bodily **stress-response**. This involves the **autonomic nervous system** (ANS) and the **hypothalamus–pituitary gland** link, both acting on the **adrenal gland** to release different sets of hormones that control many vital bodily functions.

● **Selye's General Adaptation Syndrome** (GAS) has three stages: **activation** of stress-response, **resistance** (apparent coping with stressors), and **exhaustion** (through long-term or chronic stress), when stress-related conditions may develop.

● The **relationship between stress and physical illness** involves various mechanisms. Increased heart rate affects the **cardiovascular** system, by wearing away blood vessel linings. **Corticosteroids, adrenaline** and **noradrenaline** release stored carbohydrates and fats into the bloodstream, which, if not expended or reabsorbed, remain in the bloodstream leading to **hypertension** and **atherosclerosis** (blocking of blood vessels). Stress hormones also suppress the **immune system**, which can – especially if long term or chronic (**immunosuppression**) – leave the body vulnerable to infection and disease.

Topic 2: Sources of stress

● Research into sources of stress has produced several life-event scales, the most widely used being **Holmes and Rahe's Social Readjustment Rating Scale** (SRRS). This scores **major life events** and **life changes** according to their psychological impact, proposing that higher scores on the SRRS increase the chances of stress-related health breakdown.

● Other scales, such as the **Hassles scale**, deal with minor, everyday stressors, which correlate significantly with health status.

● Research into **workplace stressors** includes studies of workplace **relationships**, the **physical environment**, **work overload** and **role ambiguity**. Workplace stress significantly affects not only individuals, but also organizations and productivity.

● **Individual differences** have been shown to relate to vulnerability to stress. **Friedman and Rosenman's** (1974) **Type A behaviour** pattern showed some correlations with increased vulnerability to stress-related illness, but Type A people may also score highly on protective factors such as control and commitment.

● Research into **gender differences** reveals that men show more stress-related physiological arousal than women, and that sources of stress may vary between genders. However, both genders report similar levels of subjective stress.

● **Social support** is an important protective factor against stress, and there appear to be clear cultural and ethnic variations in how it is used. However, **cultures** vary along many dimensions that affect health – such as genetic inheritance, lifestyle and diet – and in the range of stressors experienced. Therefore, assessing cultural variations to stress can be difficult.

Topic 3: Stress management

● **Physiological approaches** to **managing the negative effects of stress** include **drugs**, such as benzodiazepines (BZ) and beta-blockers. While drugs can be effective in reducing states and symptoms of stress, they can also lead to dependency, have side effects and may prevent the real causes of stress being detected. **Biofeedback** involves recording the body's physiological systems, e.g. blood pressure, and then finding strategies to reduce the readings.

- General **psychological approaches**, such as **relaxation** and **meditation** are used to reduce the bodily arousal associated with stress. Specific psychological approaches, such as **Michenbaum's Stress-Inoculation Training** uses **cognitive–behavioural** techniques to encourage clients to relive, analyse and evaluate stressful situations more accurately. They are then taught specific and non-specific strategies for coping, which should become self-sustaining.

- **Kobasa**'s concept of **hardiness** centres on personality factors that provide defences against the negative effects of stress. These include: belief that we have **control** over our lives, **commitment** to engaging in the world around us, and seeing life changes as **challenges** rather than threats or stressors. Kobasa proposed increasing hardiness by focusing on recognizing signs of stress, reliving stressful encounters, and self-improvement, especially by taking on challenges that we can cope with.

- **Physical exercise** (to keep the cardiovascular system in shape) and using social support networks effectively are both thought to help protect against the damaging effects of stress.

- The concept of **control** is central to stress and stress management. The gap between perceived demands and perceived coping resources produces a state of stress, but also a feeling of being 'out of control'. Several different types of control exist, such as informational, decisional and behavioural. Improving the sense of being in control is an important part of cognitive approaches.

- **Internal locus of control** refers to people who attribute events that happen to them to sources within themselves. They generally cope well with stressful situations, showing less physical arousal. **External locus of control** refers to people who attribute events in their lives to outside forces. They generally suffer more stress-related illness and cope less well.

- There are **strengths and weaknesses in stress-control methods**. The difficulties include: trying to change fundamental aspects of personality, the time, commitment and money needed to follow these methods through, the few controlled studies of their effectiveness and the generalization of results across gender and cultures.

Answering exam questions on Stress

For sample examination questions and answers on Stress, together with examiner comments on the answers, see pp. 255–7.

WEBSITES

www.about.com/

A searchable site that covers (among other things) a wide range of sites about stress and stress management.

www.mentalhealth.net/

A starting point for searching the web for topics related to stress, stress management and other areas of mental health.

http://agency.osha.eu.int/publications/reports/203/en/stress.pdf

A comprehensive report on work-related stress for the European Agency for Safety and Health at Work. It includes an excellent review of the concept of stress, measuring stress, and evidence linking stress with illness, besides covering workplace stressors.

Unit 3 // Stress

4
UNIT

Abnormality

PREVIEW

After you have read this unit, you should be able to:

>> describe attempts to define psychological abnormality

>> explain the limitations associated with attempts to define abnormality, including cultural relativism

>> discuss the assumptions made by biological and psychological models of abnormality with regard to the causes and treatment of abnormality

>> describe the clinical characteristics of anorexia nervosa and bulimia nervosa

>> explain eating disorders in terms of biological and psychological models of abnormality, and discuss research studies on which such explanations are based.

INTRODUCTION

Abnormal psychology, or 'psychopathology', is the field of psychological study that deals with mental, emotional and behavioural problems. It involves research into the classification, causation, diagnosis, prevention and treatment of psychological disorders. The range of disorders classified under this term is huge, but some well-known examples are phobias, clinical depression, eating disorders and schizophrenia.

It is difficult to define precisely what is meant by the term 'abnormality', as there is no single characteristic that applies to all instances of abnormal behaviour. Therefore, people have to make judgements about whether or not a particular behaviour is abnormal. Judgements are often influenced by social and cultural factors, and so people from different backgrounds may disagree. However, there is general agreement about certain key components of abnormal behaviour and, in Topic 1, we shall look at some of the ways these have been used in attempts to definite abnormality. Whilst most of these definitions have some practical value, we shall also consider their limitations in terms of operational or ethical difficulties. We need also to be aware that judgements about labelling human behaviour as 'normal' or 'abnormal' cannot be made in absolute terms but only within the context of a given culture (called cultural relativism).

A model of abnormality offers a complete and coherent explanation for the origins of abnormal behaviour and psychological functioning according to its own perspective. Each model leads to quite different ideas about how to treat mental disorders or psychological problems. In Topic 2, we shall consider the biological model and a number of psychological models of abnormality.

The critical issue for consideration in this unit is eating disorders and in Topic 3, we shall look at two major examples of this category of disorder: anorexia nervosa and bulimia nervosa.

Pamela
Prentice

Jane
Willson

GETTING YOU THINKING...

1 Look at the photos on the right. How many people do you know who dress (or don't dress!) in a similar way to the people shown in these two photos? How would you explain their behaviour?

Would you consider people who behave and dress in these ways to be abnormal or even psychologically disordered?

2 Read the descriptions below. Which of the behaviours described do you consider normal and which abnormal? How do you decide what is normal and what is abnormal?

A "Sian always puts things off until the last minute. She's always late with assignments and now she's in danger of being thrown off the course."

B "Ashok has gone to pieces since splitting up with his girlfriend two months ago. He sleeps all the time now and never wants to do anything. He often misses classes and today he told me that he couldn't see the point of going on."

C "Pete's really nervous. He hates standing up in class to read out anything – he gets all shaky. Now he's started turning down all invitations to go out. People will stop asking him soon."

D "Katie has this weird habit – she says it's really important to chew an even number of times when eating. No one talks to her at mealtimes any more because she's so busy counting that she doesn't pay any attention."

KEY TERMS

Psychological abnormality: behaviours and psychological functioning that are considered different from normal behaviour within a given society.

Statistical infrequency: in psychopathology, this term is used for behaviour that occurs rarely within the general population.

Deviation from social norms: behaviour that violates the implicit and explicit rules and moral standards of a given society.

Failure to function adequately: an assessment of an individual whose disability prevents them from pursuing normal activities and goals (e.g. alcohol addiction preventing normal performance at work or interfering with social activities).

Deviation from ideal mental health: behaviour that does not meet the six criteria relating to mental health or optimal living first proposed by Jahoda (1958).

Cultural relativism: the idea that judgements about definitions of human behaviour (e.g. abnormal behaviour) cannot be made in absolute terms but only within the context of a given culture.

In the first topic of this unit, we look at four definitions of abnormality, along with their limitations. These are:

1 statistical infrequency

2 deviation from social norms

3 deviation from ideal mental health

4 a failure to function adequately.

STATISTICAL INFREQUENCY

Using this definition, it is assumed that most people do not stray very far from the norm or average. Hence, any behaviour that is statistically infrequent is regarded as abnormal.

People who adopt the statistical approach measure specific characteristics and assess how such characteristics are distributed in the general population. One way of showing population distribution is by means of a normal distribution curve, which is bell shaped and has certain mathematical properties. It tells us, for instance, that for a given characteristic most people score around the middle.

It also tells us the percentage of the population that falls within a certain spread of scores. The spread is measured by a statistic called the standard deviation. Mathematicians have calculated that approximately 68 per cent of the population fall between one standard deviation either side of the mean, and approximately 95 per cent fall within two standard deviations either side of the mean. It follows that scores outside this range are very unusual, that is, only 2.5 per cent fall below it and 2.5 per cent score above it. A physical example of this would be, for instance, height or foot size. Shoe manufacturers will take this into account when deciding how many of each shoe size to produce. They know, for example, that 95 per cent of a given population of adult females placed into a normal distribution curve, would take a shoe size of between 3 and 9. Therefore, manufacturers produce very few adult female shoes below or above these sizes

and people requiring them would probably need to find a specialist or have their shoes made to measure.

In terms of psychological attributes, it is assumed that personality traits and behaviour can also be measured and assessed in terms of population distribution. The assumption is that individuals are 'normal' if they do not deviate too far from the average on a particular trait or behaviour pattern – see Fig. 4.1, which illustrates how IQ (intelligence quotient) scores are normally distributed within the population.

Limitations of the statistical infrequency definition

To define abnormality in terms of statistical frequency seems to be common sense. However, there are several problems associated with this approach.

● *Which characteristics to choose* – The statistical infrequency approach simply provides a method for measuring abnormality. It does not suggest which characteristics might be related to abnormal behaviour. According to the statistical frequency approach, behaviour is deemed abnormal if it is at *either* end of the normal distribution. For example, both very low scores and very high scores on an anxiety scale would be seen as psychologically abnormal. However, this is not always the case. Consider the example of IQ given above. One criterion for mental retardation, a psychological disorder, is an IQ score of 70 or under. As Fig. 4.1 shows, approximately 2.5 per cent of the population fall into this category. However, it is equally rare to have an IQ score of over 130, but exceptionally high intelligence is not classified as a psychological disorder. This raises the issue of desirability. Some behaviours are statistically rare, but would not be classified as psychologically abnormal because they are seen as desirable (for example, high levels of heroism or exceptional artistic ability).

Figure 4.1 >>
The normal distribution pattern of IQ scores

68.26% of all scores

95.44% of all scores

99.74% of all scores

55 70 85 100 115 130 145

IQ scores

Mozart (below) was giving keyboard recitals at the age of 5. Serena and Venus Williams (at foot of page) dominated women's tennis in the early 2000s. Are these examples of abnormality?

● *Where to draw the line* – Another difficulty with the statistical approach is deciding where the cut-off point is for defining abnormality. There is no agreed point on a scale at which behaviour is classified as abnormal and, in any case, it is unlikely that abnormal states can be categorized in such black-and-white terms. For example, there are degrees of severity in disorders such as depression or anxiety.

● *Common disorders* – Problems such as depression or anxiety are classified as psychological disorders because they adversely affect normal functioning. However, in purely statistical terms, they are not particularly unusual. Angst (1992), for example, has found that one in 20 Americans is severely depressed and that there is a one-in-ten chance of having a serious depressive episode at least once in your lifetime. A large-scale survey undertaken across 48 states in the USA and reported by Kessler *et al.* (1994) found that 48 per cent of the people in their survey had suffered from at least one psychological disorder at some point in their lives.

● *Misleading statistics* – Statistical infrequency may be a useful definition of abnormality in general terms, but it falls short when applied to mental disorders. It is only possible to determine mental-disorder statistics for those who have been diagnosed by a clinician. This may not necessarily reflect the true occurrence of any given mental disorder because many people suffer from mental disorders but do not seek professional help.

Females are more likely than males to consult their doctor for anxiety problems, whereas males are more likely to bottle up their anxiety, or try to deal with it in physical ways, such as vigorous sporting activity. Some people believe that in industrialized societies men are taught from an early age to distance themselves from their emotions. This socialization creates masculine stereotypes that alienate men from seeking help for psychological problems. Therefore, statistical data may be more a reflection of male and female socialization than a true reflection of real differences between men and women for any given mental disorder.

● *Cultural issues* – Mental disorders appear to be statistically infrequent in some ethnic groups, but this may simply reflect a reluctance to seek professional help, owing to cultural beliefs. In India, for example, mentally ill people are cursed and looked down on. Rack (1982) points out that in China, mental illness also carries a great stigma. The Chinese are, therefore, careful to diagnose only those whose behaviour is indisputably psychotic (i.e. where thinking and emotion are so impaired that the individual is out of contact with reality).

Depression, a frequently diagnosed disorder in Western culture, appears to be absent in Asian cultures. A general explanation for this has been that Asian people tend to live within extended families with ready access to social support. However, Rack (1982) claims that depression is equally common among Asians, but that Asians consult their doctor only for physical problems and rarely with 'emotional' distress. They do not see this as the responsibility of the doctor and instead sort it out within the family. Therefore, statistical infrequency merely reflects the statistical likelihood of seeking professional help, rather than an indication of whether a particular mental disorder is really present or absent in a particular culture.

A further example of this is found with Puerto Ricans, who generally react to stressful situations with severe heart palpitations, fainting and seizures, but this is regarded as a quite normal reaction in their culture (Guarnaccia *et al.* 1990).

DEVIATION FROM SOCIAL NORMS

Every society sets up rules for behaviour based on a set of moral standards. Some of these rules are explicit and to violate them can mean breaking the law, such as stealing, arson and driving on the wrong side of the road. Others rules are implicit and agreed as a matter of convention within a particular society, such as not standing too close to someone in a face-to-face conversation, dressing according to a particular code or sitting silently during a play at the theatre. These rules (codes) of conduct, whether implicit or explicit, become established as social norms and people who violate these norms are regarded as deviant or abnormal. For example, inappropriate affect (emotion) is often found in people with schizophrenia, e.g. laughing when told that someone has died or crying when watching a comedy show. Similarly, people with phobias often demonstrate bizarre behaviour when trying to escape their feared object.

At a practical, everyday level, deviation from social norms can be a useful way to identify mental problems. We learn what to expect from individuals and, if their behaviour drastically deviates from this, then we become concerned on their behalf. This may be vital in securing appropriate help because, for example, people with clinical depression are often unable to motivate themselves to seek assistance. However, there are several limitations associated with this approach.

Limitations of the deviation from social norms definition

● *Eccentric or abnormal?* – Deviance from social norms does not always indicate psychological abnormality. We tend to make judgements about whether behaviours that deviate from the norm are merely eccentric or whether they are abnormal in a pathological sense. Running naked across a rugby pitch, or taking part in a marathon dressed as a giant rabbit may be regarded as strange or idiosyncratic, but we would not necessarily assume that the person is mentally disturbed. However, if someone is walking down the street talking out loud to an invisible person, or if someone insists that Martians have taken over their brain, then we would be more likely to suspect a mental disorder. Thus, only particular kinds of 'abnormal' behaviour tend to be regarded as pathological.

ACTIVITY

Eccentric or abnormal?

Look back at the two photographs on p. 115. What do these two photos tell us about the limitations of using deviation from social norms as a means of identifying psychological abnormality?

● *The role of context* – Much of our behaviour is context-specific and, out of context, may seem bizarre. For example, what would you think if you were walking through the park and someone sitting on a bench suddenly jumped up and started singing and dancing? You would probably think them rather odd. But if you then saw a film crew, you would contextualize the scene, assume the person was an actor and perhaps stay around to watch.

● *Change with the times* – Beliefs about abnormality and social norms of morally acceptable behaviour change over time, so what is regarded as deviant by one generation may be perfectly acceptable to the next. Consider the changes that have taken place in society's attitudes towards unmarried mothers and towards homosexuality (see p. 124 for more information).

● *Abnormal or criminal?* – The behaviour of people who violate *legal* norms is usually regarded as criminal and the behaviour is rarely attributed to underlying psychological disorder. Would you consider someone convicted for fraud, for example, to be psychologically disordered? There are, however, types of behaviour that are generally regarded as unacceptable, such as rape and mass murder, where it is difficult to accept that such violation of others could possibly be normal. In such cases, there is a tendency to regard the perpetrators of the crimes as abnormal and their extreme antisocial behaviour as inherent in their personality. Otherwise, if they, as people, were regarded as 'normal' and merely their *behaviour* as 'abnormal', then the inference would be that anyone could be a potential rapist or mass murderer. This is too unsettling a notion for most people to contemplate. On the other hand, studies in social psychology have shown that, in certain circumstances, so-called 'normal' people can behave in violent and antisocial ways. A prime example is football hooliganism.

Abnormal or just criminal?

- *Cultural issues* – In Western societies, there is a common assumption that the behaviour of the White population is the norm and that any deviation from this by another ethnic group indicates psychological abnormality.

In certain cultures with rigid political or social structures, using deviation from social norms as a means of classifying abnormality can be a form of social control. For example, political dissidents in Russia used to be seen as abnormal because they did not toe the party line; they were diagnosed as insane and often detained in mental asylums. In Japan, a diagnosis of insanity has been used as a threat to ensure a strong work ethic. According to Cohen (1988), because of Japan's drive for industrial

success, 'loony-bins' are required for those who are unwilling to conform to the demands of industry. Therefore, in order to instill the appropriate terror, the 'bins' must be sufficiently unattractive. Conditions in Japanese mental hospitals are similar to the old Victorian asylums in the UK, being overcrowded, dirty and often brutal places.

Social norms vary: what is abnormal in one culture, may be acceptable in another. For example, walking around nude in public may be considered normal in some cultures and talking to an invisible person is considered normal in certain African and Indian cultures following a bereavement (where people believe it is possible to remain in contact briefly with a lost loved one).

DEVIATION FROM IDEAL MENTAL HEALTH

The notion of ideal mental health was first put forward by Jahoda in 1958. It turns the traditional notion of abnormality on its head, by looking at positives, rather than negatives – the notion of mental *health* rather than mental *illness*. Jahoda identified six major criteria for optimal living which, she believed, promoted psychological health and wellbeing. Anyone unable to show these qualities would be vulnerable to mental disorder.

Jahoda's six criteria are as follows:

1 *Positive attitudes towards the self* – This means having a positive self-concept and a sense of identity. Jahoda suggested that a mentally healthy attitude towards the self included self-respect, self-confidence, self-reliance and self-acceptance; the person has learned to live with themselves, accepting both their limitations and their possibilities. What is important here, is to view oneself realistically and objectively. Unfortunately, many people develop a negative self-concept or low

self-esteem because of the way they have been treated by others and perhaps made to feel small and unimportant. Jahoda claimed that to be mentally healthy, a person must know who they are and like what they see.

2 *Self-actualization of one's potential* – This idea was proposed by Abraham Maslow (1968), who suggested that we all have potential in certain directions (for example, intellectual, artistic, athletic) and that we constantly strive to fulfil this potential. mental-health problems occur when we are prevented from fulfilling our true potential.

3 *Resistance to stress* – Jahoda called this the ability to tolerate anxiety without disintegration. The mentally healthy person will have developed good coping strategies for dealing with stressful situations. Indeed, it does seem that those people who are more vulnerable to stress and anxiety are more likely to develop psychological problems. A great deal of research has been undertaken to identify effective coping strategies to reduce stress (see Topic 3 in Unit 3, starting on p. 101).

4 *Personal autonomy* – This means that the person is reliant on their own inner resources and can remain relatively stable even in the face of hard knocks, frustrations and deprivations. This is because autonomous people are not dependent upon other people. They are self-contained and depend upon their own resources. Jahoda describes personal autonomy as an ability to make our own decisions on the basis of what is right for ourselves, rather than to satisfy others.

5 *Accurate perception of reality* – This means seeing oneself and the world around one in realistic terms, rather than through either 'rose-tinted glasses' or in an overly pessimistic manner. Indeed, if someone continually distorts reality, then they are not really living in the real world and their views

and behaviours are bound to appear abnormal to others. If someone only ever sees the best in people then this may endear them to others, but it also leaves them vulnerable to those who may take advantage. Conversely, someone who is overly morbid and pessimistic is a likely candidate to develop a depressive disorder and would not endear themselves to others very easily.

6 *Adapting to the environment* – This means being competent in all areas of life: at work, in personal relationships and in leisure activities. It also involves being flexible rather than rigid, being able to adapt and adjust to change. Someone who is fixed in old ways of thinking and behaving may appear abnormal to younger people and to those who have been able to adjust to a changing environment.

Limitations of the deviation from ideal mental health definition

This is a refreshing approach in that it focuses on positive aspects of life rather than negative ones, but meeting all six criteria appears to be quite demanding. Most people are likely to fall short of 'ideal mental health'. Specific limitations include the following:

● *The difficulty of self-actualizing* – Unfortunately, in reality, very few people achieve their full potential in life, which may be because of their own particular environment or through some failing within themselves. It would seem, then, that if self-actualization is a criterion for ideal mental health, most of us would be regarded as mentally unhealthy.

● *Possible benefits of stress* – As far as resistance to stress is concerned, some people actually work more efficiently in moderately stressful situations. For example, many actors say that they give their best performances when they experience a certain amount of anxiety.

● *Cultural issues* – The idea of mental health is culture-bound and Jahoda's ideas are based on Western ideals of self-fulfilment and individuality. Seeking to fulfil your own potential, for example, may be seen as a prime goal in life within some cultures but not in others. In some cultures, elders in the family plan the person's future out for them. This planning might include such things as arranged marriages, which are common in Asian cultures. It may, therefore, be regarded as 'abnormal' to pursue your own goals if they are in conflict with those of your culture. The pursuit of self-actualization or personal happiness is, perhaps, a privilege for those living in an affluent, industrialized society, where people are freed from the need to pursue the basic necessities for survival.

Similarly, with regard to personal autonomy, there is an overwhelming sense of duty to others in many cultures; it would not be regarded as 'normal' to put your own wishes before those of others.

Perceptions of reality differ over time (remember people once thought the world was flat) and also differ between cultures. For example, seeing or hearing someone who has died would be considered normal in some cultures, but regarded as psychotic hallucinations in other cultures.

Parenthood, winning awards, achieving feats of physical endurance (in 2003, Andrew Cooney became the youngest man to walk to the South Pole) – these are all self-actualizing experiences. But how many people do you know who have reached full self-actualization? If we don't, does that make us 'mentally unhealthy'?

FAILURE TO FUNCTION ADEQUATELY

People with psychological disorders often experience considerable suffering and distress, as well as a general inability to cope with their everyday activities, such as being unable to go to work or take part in social activities. Such dysfunction is so common that it is taken into account when making a diagnosis of an individual with psychological problems. There are diagnostic manuals available to doctors when they are trying to identify particular mental disorders. One of the most widely used is the Diagnostic and Statistical Manual of Mental Disorders (American Psychiatric Association 1994), which requires doctors to assess

people on various psychological and physical measures. One of these measures is called the Global Assessment of Functioning Scale (GAF), shown in Fig. 4.2. This is an important part of the overall assessment, although a poor score on its own would not be seen as an indication of a psychological disorder.

The failure to function adequately view of abnormality carries certain implications. If someone's behaviour appears strange or 'abnormal' to others, then provided they are not harming themselves or others, and provided their behaviour is not dysfunctional, such as preventing them from carrying on their daily lives,

Figure 4.2 >> *Global Assessment of Functioning (GAF) Scale*

Consider psychological, social and occupational functioning on a hypothetical continuum of mental health–illness. Do not include impairment in functioning due to physical (or environmental) limitations.

Code (Note: Intermediate codes can be used when appropriate e.g. 45, 68, 72.)

Code	
100	Superior functioning in a wide range of activities. Life's problems never seem to get out of hand. Is sought out by others because of his or her many positive qualities. No symptoms
90	Absent or minimal symptoms (e.g. mild anxiety before an exam), good functioning in all areas, interested and involved in a wide range of activities, socially effective, generally satisfied with life, no more than everyday problems or concerns (e.g. an occasional argument with family members)
80	If symptoms are present, they are transient and expectable reactions to psychosocial stressors (e.g. difficulty concentrating after family argument); no more than slight impairment in social, occupational, or school functioning (e.g. temporarily falling behind in school work)
70	Some mild symptoms (e.g. depressed mood and mild insomnia) OR some difficulty in social, occupational, or school functioning (e.g. occasional truancy, or theft within the household), but generally functioning pretty well, has some meaningful interpersonal relationships.
60	Moderate symptoms (e.g. flat effect and circumstantial speech, occasional panic attacks) OR moderate difficulty in social, occupational, or school functioning (e.g. few friends, conflicts with peers or co-workers).
50	Serious symptoms (e.g. suicidal ideation, severe obsessional rituals, frequent shoplifting) OR any serious impairment in social, occupational or school functioning (e.g. no friends, unable to keep a job).
40	Some impairment in reality testing or communication (e.g. speech is at all times illogical, obscure or irrelevant) OR major impairment in several areas, such as work or school, family relations, judgement, thinking or mood (e.g. depressed man avoids friends, neglects family and cannot work).
30	Behaviour is considerable influenced by delusions or hallucinations OR serious impairment in communication or judgement (e.g. sometimes incoherent, acts grossly inappropriately, suicidal preoccupation) OR inability to function in almost all areas (e.g. stays in bed all day, no job, home).
20	Some danger of hurting self or others (e.g. suicide attempts without clear expectation of death, frequently violent, manic excitement) OR occasionally fails to maintain minimal personal hygiene (e.g. smears faeces) OR gross impairment in communication (e.g. largely incoherent or mute).
10	Persistent danger of severely hurting self or others (e.g. recurrent violence) OR persistent inability to maintain minimal personal hygiene OR serious suicidal act with clear expectation of death.
0	Inadequate information.

then no intervention is required. A failure to function adequately does, however, mean that someone with a psychological problem that falls outside the criteria for a serious mental disorder should still be given appropriate professional help if their problem is causing a dysfunction in their daily living. Unfortunately though, NHS provision (in the UK) is not always available for people with less severe psychological problems and there are generally long waiting lists for treatment.

Limitations of the failure to function adequately definition

Using the criterion of failure to function adequately as a definition of abnormality may be the most humane way of addressing psychological problems and mental disorders, as it is left to the person (or others close to them) to decide whether they need or wish to seek help. However, there are problems with this approach:

- *Not the whole picture* – This is not a true definition of 'abnormality'. Rather it is a way of determining the extent of a person's problems and the likelihood that they might need professional help. Comer (2000) points out that psychological abnormality is not necessarily indicated by dysfunction alone. For example, some people protest against social injustice by depriving themselves of necessities, such as food. It is when abnormal behaviour interferes with daily functioning, such that people lose the ability to work or the motivation to care for themselves properly, that the behaviour becomes is viewed as abnormal.

- *Exceptions to the rule* – A student experiencing anxiety and distress about a forthcoming exam may behave uncharacteristically, even inadequately, but this would not necessarily be regarded as abnormal behaviour. Conversely, *sociopaths* (people with antisocial personalities) might exhibit violent or aggressive behaviour, but be unlikely to experience personal suffering, distress or any general dysfunction, because of their amoral attitudes.

- *Cultural issues* – It may be that the inability to cope with the demands of daily living is the cause rather than the outcome of mental disorder. It might explain why statistics show a higher incidence of psychological problems among people from minority ethnic groups, owing to the exploitation, deprivation and harassment they often experience. Cochrane and Sashidharan (1995) point out that racism and prejudice have a significant impact upon psychological wellbeing. Migration from developing to developed Western countries also means that the first generation of migrants is likely to be exposed to economic uncertainty, substandard housing and harsh working conditions. These have mental-health implications for new immigrants, but their problems may mistakenly be attributed to ethnicity.

Is he 'failing to function adequately'?

CULTURAL RELATIVISM

We have looked at some of the limitations of attempts to define abnormality and found that a major problem with all of them is the fact that they are culturally specific. In other words, it is impossible to provide a clear definition of abnormality that applies to the whole of humankind because each culture has a different set of norms and expectations. It may be inappropriate for a member of one cultural group to make judgements about the behaviour of a member of another, and doctors involved in diagnosing mental disorder need to be aware of this. The implication of culture and its relationship to diagnosis is set out in DSM-IV:

<< Diagnostic assessment can be especially challenging when a clinician from one ethnic or cultural group uses the DSM-IV classification to evaluate an individual from a different ethnic or cultural group. A clinician, who is unfamiliar with the nuances of an individual's cultural frame of reference, may incorrectly judge as psychopathology those normal variations in behaviour, belief, or experience that are particular to the individual's culture. For example, certain religious practices or beliefs (e.g. hearing or seeing a deceased relative during bereavement) may be misdiagnosed as manifestations of a psychotic disorder. >>

Subculture

There can be groups of people within a wider culture that have their own particular set of norms and beliefs; these people are said to have a distinctive subculture. For example, ethnic groups within the UK, such as African-Caribbeans, while conforming to many of the norms of the wider society, often have their own particular behaviour patterns that may make them vulnerable to misunderstanding. For instance, in Britain, Black (African-Caribbean) immigrants are between two to seven times more likely to be diagnosed with schizophrenia than White people (Cochrane 1977). There are many factors that might account for this difference, but one possible reason is that cultural variations in communication style (i.e. that deviate from White social norms) may lead to mistaken diagnosis. In a broad interpretation of the term 'subculture', it is interesting to look at gender and social class issues. These are discussed in the two panels below.

Social class issues

Research has indicated that the higher prevalence of severe mental disorders in socially disadvantaged groups is largely due to their exposure to more stressful life experiences, compared with those in more advantaged social groups. The first large-scale survey to support this hypothesis was the Midtown Manhattan Study (Srole *et al.* 1961). The study found the lowest levels of psychiatric impairment in the upper classes, slightly more in the middle classes and the highest levels in the lower classes. These findings were supported in a British study (Cochrane and Stopes-Roe 1980), which also found that lower social status was associated with higher risk of psychological problems.

A major study by Brown and Harris (1978) found a high incidence of depression among working-class housewives in Camberwell, London. The main vulnerability factors they identified were long-term periods of adverse circumstances, together with the cumulative effect of short-term life events, combined with factors such as lack of paid employment. In addition, while the middle and upper classes have more 'positive' life experiences to offset the 'negative', those in the lower classes have less control over their environment.

Cochrane (1995a) points out that people living in high-rise flats are more prone to psychological problems than those in traditional accommodation. This may be because they have poorer relationships with their neighbours – an important factor in mental health, as neighbours are a potential source of social support. Of course, as Cochrane points out, neighbours can also be a source of irritation and even fear. Halpern (1995) claims that if a neighbourhood becomes labelled as a dumping ground for 'problem families', then people who did not originally experience problems may develop adverse reactions which may affect their mental health.

The *social drift* hypothesis offers another explanation for the higher incidence of serious mental disorder in lower socio-economic groups: the early onset of a major mental disorder, such as schizophrenia, might reduce the chances of establishing a career and the person may then subsequently 'drift' down the socio-economic scale. This suggests that social class is largely a consequence of, rather than a contributory factor in, mental disorder. Support for this is found in cases where the initial onset of schizophrenia has occurred later in life. It has been noted that many such individuals had previously had good careers. The higher incidence of schizophrenia in poor areas could reflect the number of people who move to those areas after the onset of their illness, because it is all they can afford (Cochrane 1983).

Gender issues

Other studies have examined reasons why certain psychological problems appear to be more prevalent in men or women. Howell (1981) points out that women's experience in British culture predisposes them to depression and therefore clinicians are diagnosing a situation rather than a person. Cochrane (1995b) explains that depression can be related to the long-term effects of child abuse and also to gender-role socialization, which produces increased female vulnerability. He points out the adverse effects on women of power relationships and sex discrimination. Despite the vast amount of evidence that relates women's depression to sociocultural factors, some clinicians continue to ignore environmental circumstances that may contribute to depressive symptoms. Johnstone (1989) believes this also applies to men. Unemployed men have a high rate of psychiatric breakdown. Johnstone explains that by labelling the problem as a mental disorder, not only does the person have the stigma of a psychiatric label, but the problem is seen only in individual terms, rather than in the wider political and social context. Furthermore, Bennett (1995) believes that the socialization of men in industrialized societies has created masculine stereotypes that alienate men from seeking help for psychological problems.

Cultural change

Attitudes, values and beliefs can change over time within a given culture and this will affect judgements about abnormal behaviour. Two examples serve to illustrate this:

- Until as recently as the early years of the twentieth century, unmarried women in the UK who became pregnant were sometimes sent to mental institutions. In many cases the babies were taken away for adoption. Some of these women were in their early teens when they became pregnant and remained in mental institutions for the rest of their lives.

- In recent centuries, homosexuality has been regarded as a deviation from social norms. In the UK, homosexual acts were criminal offences, even among consenting adults, until 1967. In the USA until 1973, the American Psychiatric Association classified homosexuality as a mental disorder.

Culture-bound syndromes

Certain psychological disorders appear to be universal and are found in cultures all over the world. However, there are a few disorders that seem to occur only within certain societies. These are called *culture-bound syndromes* (see Table 4.1). The actual symptoms described in Table 4.1 would be recognized in most cultures, but it is the unique grouping of symptoms (known as a syndrome) that marks these disorders out as culture-bound. Note that bulimia nervosa is included because, so far, it has only been observed in Western cultures.

An example of cultural change: in 2002, Alex Cannel and Ian Burford became first same-sex couple to sign the London Partnerships Register set up by the Greater London Authority.

ACTIVITY

Expert interview

Read the expert interview given by Ray Cochrane on p. 125 and answer the following questions:

1 What two examples does Ray Cochrane give to show how cultural factors may influence whether or not we class a behaviour as abnormal?

2 What are the two main dangers of ignoring culture when we define mental illness?

3 To what extent is it "impossible to escape entirely the blinkers of one's own culture when assessing abnormality"?

Table 4.1 >> Culture-bound syndromes

Diagnosis	Country/Culture	Characteristics
>> *Latah*	Malaysia, Indonesia, Bantu in Africa	Exaggerated response to a minor stimulus; tendency to mimic people nearby in speech and gesture; only occurs in females.
>> *Behainin*	Bali	Abdominal pain, headache, ringing in the ears, impaired vision, screaming, weeping and convulsions; exhaustion follows episode and individual (usually female) has no memory of what happened.
>> *Taijin-kyofusho*	Japan and some other Asian countries	Occurs mainly in males; anxiety, fear of rejection, fear of eye contact, blushing, worry about body odour.
>> *Bulimia nervosa*	North America and Western Europe	Food bingeing, self-induced vomiting; may occur alongside depression and substance abuse.
>> *Tabanka*	Trinidad	Depression in men abandoned by their wives; high rate of suicide.

Source: Based on Geiselman (1988)

Cultural *relativism*

Ray Cochrane is Professor of Psychology at the University of Birmingham. His main interest is in the mental health of immigrants and ethnic minorities in Britain. He has also undertaken research into the delivery of mental-health care, particularly into how services relate to the needs of black and ethnic minorities.

Q **In what ways do cultural factors compromise traditional definitions of abnormality?**

A It is easy to forget that both the definition of what constitutes mental illness and the diagnostic schemes used to categorize patterns of symptoms were developed from within the European cultural tradition (largely in France, Germany, the USA and the UK). The operational definition of what is pathological behaviour is very strongly influenced by the culture within which the observer is embedded. So, for example, in contemporary Northern European culture, building a shrine to a dead relative in one's house and leaving food and gifts beside it each night would be seen as abnormal, whereas in another culture this might be seen as perfectly appropriate, normal behaviour.

Even where there might be a cross-cultural consensus that a particular behaviour is 'abnormal', there might be sharp cultural differences in explaining why it occurred. While there might be wide agreement that seeing visions and talking aloud to someone who is not present is very unusual, this could be attributed to either madness or extreme holiness depending on the culture in which it occurred.

Q **What are the dangers of ignoring cultural issues when attempting to define abnormality?**

A There are two main dangers of ignoring culture when defining mental illness. First, when scientists, anthropologists and doctors from Europe and North America have gone looking for evidence of mental illness in other cultures, they have taken their own definitions with them and seen the culture they are exploring through Western European eyes. In most instances, there are no objective tests for the existence of mental illness. This can lead to great mistakes being made. Sometimes, it has resulted in conclusions being drawn that a particular cultural group do not have experience of a disorder – depression was believed to be rare in black Africans right up until the 1960s because it was not manifested in the same way as in Europe. On other occasions, people whose behaviour contravenes Western Europeans' social norms have been defined as mentally ill even though their behaviour was compatible with local standards.

The second danger is based on the same set of misconceptions, but is much more acute in multicultural Britain today. This is the danger of misdiagnosing someone from a non-European background as having a particular mental illness when they in fact do not, or overlooking serious mental-health problems because they are expressed differently from the way they are in the local tradition. Misdiagnosis has been used to account for the much higher rate of diagnosed schizophrenia in Britain's Black (African-Caribbean) population than in the White population. The most plausible version of this hypothesis is that some Black people display symptoms (such as hallucinations) which would be indicative of schizophrenia in a White person but which are in fact the result of a different mental-health problem in people from the West Indies. Being 'misdiagnosed' as suffering from schizophrenia means that they are unduly stigmatized and receive totally inappropriate treatment.

Ray Cochrane

Q **Does this mean that such attempts to define 'abnormality' are doomed to failure?**

A It would be tempting to throw up one's hands in despair and agree that a universal definition of abnormality that is appropriate in all cultures is impossible. Realistically, though, we have to get on with dealing with people in distress and accept that, whatever their shortcomings, the current Western concepts of mental health and illness, and Western medicine are dominant worldwide. In certain areas, the situation is not that problematic – a syndrome that we call 'schizophrenia' is recognized in almost all cultures and is almost always considered to be abnormal and undesirable. The World Health Organization has also established through a very carefully devised programme of research that the incidence of schizophrenia is similar in most cultures. For other forms of 'mental illness' the situation is less clear cut. It has not been possible to establish that depression, or the neuroses, as defined in the West, are recognised in other cultures either as specific syndromes or as resulting from an illness.

That said, with the gradual evolution of diagnostic systems such as ICD-10 and DSM-IV, cultural factors have increasingly been taken into account, and certainly in the UK the training of all mental-health workers now includes substantial consideration of the issues discussed here. While it might not be possible to escape entirely the blinkers of one's own culture when assessing abnormality, greater awareness that one is blinkered does help.

Check your understanding of definitions of abnormality by answering these questions. Try to do this from memory at first. You can check your answers by looking back through Topic 1.

1   What do you understand by the term 'statistical infrequency'?

2   Give one limitation of this definition of abnormality.

3   What is meant by the term 'social norm' and give one example of a social norm from your own culture.

4   Give an example of a social norm that has changed over time.

5   Explain how the use of the social norm definition of abnormality can be used as a form of social control.

6   Describe the cultural issues raised by the deviation from mental health definition.

7   Describe the six criteria identified by Jahoda as being necessary for optimal living.

8   Why is the failure to function adequately definition of abnormality a humane way of defining abnormality?

9   Give two limitations of this definition of abnormality.

10   "It is impossible to define abnormality for all humankind." To what extent is this statement true?

REVISION SUMMARY

Having covered this topic, you should be able to:

✓ define the terms: 'statistical infrequency', 'deviation from social norms', 'failure to function adequately', and 'deviation from ideal mental health'

✓ describe the way in which each of these terms has been used to define abnormality

✓ explain the limitations associated with each of these attempts at definition

✓ explain how cultural relativism affects the definition of abnormality.

GETTING YOU THINKING...

Read the brief descriptions of the following terms, given in the 'Key terms' box below:

- the medical (or biological) model
- the psychodynamic model
- the behavioural model
- the cognitive model.

Now read the six cases below and decide which model is being used to determine the treatment described.

1 Rebecca has a spider phobia and is no longer able to stay in the house alone with her young daughter whilst her partner goes to work every day. She is being treated by systematic desensitization. This is teaching her to relax and confront her fear of spiders in a relaxed setting, so that she learns to associate a feeling of calm with the presence of a spider.

2 Lynda has been diagnosed as suffering from schizophrenia. She regularly takes the drug chlorpromazine that helps to keep her severe symptoms in check and enables her to live with her family and keep her job.

3 Rational-emotive therapy is being used to treat Karl's panic attacks. In his twice-weekly session with the therapist, Karl is being helped to recognize the irrational assumptions that he has about his life and change these into more positive views of himself and his situation.

4 Bill suffers from severe depression that has not improved with the drugs that he was prescribed. He has recently been admitted to hospital for electroconvulsive therapy (ECT) which involves passing an electric current through the brain.

5 Tom suffers from severe headaches that have no physical cause but leave him unable to get out of bed or go to work. His therapist encourages him to free associate on dreams and early childhood memories by letting his mind wander and saying aloud whatever comes into his mind. This may bring uncomfortable desires or repressed thoughts into conscious awareness. The therapist interprets his words, dreams and behaviour. This helps him to make sense of, and come to terms with, his experience and to work through repressed thoughts.

6 Lou is keen to give up smoking and is being treated by aversion therapy: a drug that induces sickness is given to her so that she learns to associate unpleasant feelings with cigarettes and stops smoking.

KEY TERMS

Model: a term that is used synonymously with theory. In psychopathology, it refers to an explanation of the causes of psychological disorders.

Medical model (or Biological model): a view of abnormality that sees mental disorders as being caused by abnormal physiological processes such as genetic and biochemical factors. Abnormality according to this model is seen as an illness or disease.

Psychodynamic model: a view that abnormal behaviour is caused by underlying psychological forces of which the individual is probably unaware.

Behavioural model: a view that abnormal behaviours are maladaptive, learned responses in the environment which can be replaced by more adaptive behaviours.

Cognitive model: a view that stresses the role of cognitive problems (such as illogical or irrational thought processes) in abnormal functioning.

BIOLOGICAL/MEDICAL MODEL

Models of abnormality are conceptual models, each offering a different explanation for the origins of mental disorders. Which particular conceptual model is adopted is important because it will influence the type of research that is conducted and also the methods of treatment adopted. We will start by looking at the biological/medical model.

Basic assumptions of the medical model

The medical model has dominated the field of mental health for the past 200 years. It is a biological approach that regards abnormality of mental functioning as an illness or disease. Mental disorders are thought to be related to the physical structure and functioning of the brain. Some mental disorders are thought to have an organic basis, for example, poisoning due to alcohol or drug abuse that results in anatomical deterioration. Disorders where a clear organic cause has not been identified have been traditionally referred to as 'functional disorders'. However, people who adopt the medical model believe that research will eventually show that all mental disorders have an underlying physical cause.

Advocates of the medical model are psychiatrists who are medically qualified practitioners specializing in mental disorders. They approach psychological abnormality in the same way that they would investigate physical illness: by classifying disorders, seeking the underlying cause, developing appropriate treatments and devising methods of prevention.

They consider four possible causal factors that sometimes overlap:

- *Brain damage* – Abnormal behaviour may occur if the structure of the brain is damaged in some way. Once disease or brain damage has caused mental deterioration, there is, unfortunately, little that can be done to stop it. A good example of this is Alzheimer's disease, a type of dementia caused by the malformation and loss of cells in a number of areas of the nervous system.

- *Infection* – We are familiar with the idea of bacteria or viruses causing physical illness such as flu or meningitis. It seems, though, that infection can also give rise to mental illness. Syphilis, for example, was identified in the nineteenth century as the cause of deterioration in specific regions of the brain resulting in symptoms of a mental illness known as 'general paresis'. The symptoms of this disorder were:

  – delusions of grandeur, such as believing that you are God

  – delusions of persecution, believing that everyone is plotting against you

  – other bizarre, irrational behaviours, which now come under the general heading of psychosis.

  This disease is now rarely seen, as the use of antibiotics in the treatment of syphilis prevents subsequent brain damage occurring.

- *Biochemistry* – During the twentieth century, the medical profession has increasingly learned more about the role played by biochemistry in mental disorders.

  Neurotransmitters, which are the chemicals that transmit nerve impulses from one nerve cell to the next, are thought to be out of balance in the nervous systems of individuals with certain psychological disorders. For example, schizophrenia has been associated with an excess of the neurotransmitter dopamine, and depression has been associated with decreased availability of serotonin.

  Hormones, which are chemical messengers released by the endocrine system (see pp. 78–9), have also been implicated in the origins of some mental disorders. For example, people with depression are often found to have higher than normal levels of the hormone cortisol. The reasons why these chemical changes take place are not yet clear, but they may be due to infections, life stress or a genetic defect.

- *Genes* – Important new genetic research has highlighted the possibility that some people may be genetically at risk of developing a mental disorder, but so far the only strong evidence relates to conditions such as schizophrenia and bipolar depression (a disorder characterized by alternating periods of depression and mania). It has been demonstrated, for example, that a first-degree relative (e.g. son, daughter) has a 10 per cent chance of developing schizophrenia. This is far in excess of the 1 per cent risk to the normal population. In order to investigate genetic links, researchers do family studies to see whether particular disorders run through families. These studies can be difficult to interpret because the similarity of family members might simply reflect their shared environment rather than their shared biology. Some physical disorders, such as muscular dystrophy, appear to arise from defects in single genes. It seems unlikely that this is the case for mental disorders such as schizophrenia. In disorders such as this, it is more likely that there are defects in several genes. The Human Genome Project, which aims to determine the sequence of all human DNA, will provide the means to establish genetic linkage in psychiatric disorders.

Advances in genetic research raise ethical and practical concerns about the consequences of trying to engineer a better society by genetic means.

Treatment and the biological/medical model

Since mental problems are viewed in this model as physical illnesses, then physical treatments are regarded as the most appropriate. These physical interventions fall into three main categories:

- *Drug therapy (chemotherapy)* is the main treatment and is based on the assumption that chemical imbalance is at the root of the problem. Drugs for mental disorders range from minor tranquillizers (for anxiety disorders), to antidepressants (for depressive disorders), through to major tranquillizers (for severe psychotic disorders such as schizophrenia). These drugs have been found to be effective in relieving the symptoms of mental disorders in many, but not all, people. However, they also have side effects that may be considered worse than the original symptoms of the disorder. The fact that chemotherapy is effective in reducing symptoms of mental disorders is regarded as sufficient evidence to support the theory that chemical imbalance is the cause of the problem. Indeed, it is now known that some chemicals can affect the functioning of particular neurotransmitters, producing the symptoms of certain mental disorders. However, some psychologists disagree, believing the chemical imbalance to be the effect, rather than the cause, of mental problems.

- *Electro-convulsive therapy (ECT)* involves passing a high current through the brain for approximately half a second. This induces convulsions that last for approximately one minute. Patients are anaesthetized before the treatment and recall nothing about it once they come round from the anaesthetic. It is now used mainly for people with severe depression and can be an effective short-term treatment. However, approximately 60 per cent of patients will become depressed again within a year. It is not clear exactly how ECT works, but it may increase the availability of certain neurotransmitters in the brain.

- *Psychosurgery (brain surgery)* is the most invasive form of biological therapy because it involves removal of brain tissue and the effects are irreversible. This method is rarely used now and is only offered as a last resort.

Evaluation of the biological/medical model

- *No blame* – A diagnosis of mental 'illness' implies that the person is in no way responsible for the abnormality of functioning and as such is not to blame. The concept of 'no blame' is generally thought to be more humane and likely to elicit a much more sympathetic response from others.

- *Stigma* – However, Szasz (1972), pointed out that even more than physical illness, mental illness is something that people fear – largely because it is something they do not understand. In general, people do not know how to respond to someone diagnosed as mentally ill. There may also be fears that the person's behaviour might be unpredictable and potentially dangerous. Therefore, sympathy is more likely to give way to avoidance of the person, which in turn leads to the person feeling shunned.

- *Research* – A huge amount of research has been carried out within the framework of the medical model and this has greatly increased our understanding of the possible biological factors underpinning psychological disorders. However, much of the evidence is inconclusive and findings can be difficult to interpret. For example, in family studies, it is difficult to disentangle the effects of genetics from the effects of environment. It can also be difficult to establish cause and effect. For example, raised levels of dopamine may be a *consequence* rather than a *cause* of schizophrenia.

- *Use of drugs* – Many psychologists criticize psychiatry for focusing its attention primarily on symptoms and for assuming that relieving symptoms with drugs cures the problem. Unfortunately, in many cases where the drug treatment is ceased, the symptoms recur, suggesting that drugs are not addressing the true cause of the problem.

A patient receiving ECT

- *Relinquishing responsibility* – Another criticism of the medical model is that people are encouraged to become patients, handing over responsibility for their 'wellness' to professionals, and so not feel responsible for their own recovery.

- *Treatment success* – Some successful treatments have arisen from the medical model that have helped people with psychological disorders. However, many treatments have been criticized as being unethical or ineffective. Prescribed treatment may not be appropriate and yet there is an expectation that patients will comply with medication, despite the fact

that, as the British National Formulary (an index of pharmaceutical drugs and preparations) indicates, most medication carries side effects and often long-term dependency upon the drugs.

- *Reductionist* – The biological explanation of abnormality is criticized for being reductionist. This means that it attempts to explain phenomena by breaking them down to the most fundamental level, that is, it explains abnormal behaviour in terms of the activity of brain cells. It seems, however, much more likely that psychological disorders are caused by the interaction of many factors.

PSYCHODYNAMIC MODEL

Basic assumptions

Freud and others developed the psychodynamic model in the latter part of the nineteenth century through clinical work with mentally disordered patients. Freud believed that problems arose directly from the dynamics of the personality (*psyche*), rather than from physical causes. According to Freud, the psyche consists of three interrelated systems:

- *Id* – the unconscious, insatiable set of instincts with which people are born. The id is pleasure-orientated and completely selfish.

- *Ego* – the conscious, rational part of the psyche that has to arbitrate between the demands of the id and the demands of the superego, the last part of the psyche to develop.

- *Superego* – the moral part of the personality concerned with right and wrong. The superego develops through the process of socialization when people learn the moral standards and expectations of their culture.

The id and the superego, therefore, are in direct conflict and need to be managed in a rational way. The well-adjusted person develops a strong ego that is

able to cope with the demands of each by allowing both the id and the superego expression at appropriate times. If, however, the ego is weakened, then either the id or the superego, whichever is the stronger, may dominate the personality. If id impulses emerge unchecked, then they are expressed in destructiveness and immorality, which may result in conduct disorders in childhood and psychopathic (dangerously abnormal) behaviour in adulthood. A too-powerful superego rigidly restricts the id to such an extent that the person will be deprived of even socially acceptable pleasures. According to Freud this would create neurosis, which could be expressed in the symptoms of anxiety disorders, such as phobias and obsessions. Psychological disturbance, therefore, results from the inability of the ego to manage conflict within the psyche. Freud maintained that these internal conflicts occur at an unconscious level, so that we are unaware of their influence.

Although psychical conflict can occur at any time in our life, it is most marked in early childhood because the ego is not developed fully enough to mediate between the id and the superego. Nor is it developed fully enough to deal with external events, such as maternal absences, parental shortcomings or competition with siblings. Traumatic or confusing events in childhood, therefore, are pushed into the unconscious – a process which Freud called repression – because they are too painful for the ego to bear or because the child hasn't developed sufficient knowledge of the world to make sense of the event (A. Freud 1936). Distressing feelings around traumatic events do not disappear, however, simply because they are repressed. They find expression in dreams and irrational behaviour, and may eventually erupt and express themselves in psychological disorders.

Defence mechanisms

In order to balance the demands of the id and superego, the ego employs defence mechanisms (see Table 4.2). These distort or deny reality and are essential ways of protecting the ego from distress and allowing the person to cope with life. They have a powerful, yet unconscious, influence upon our behaviour, and everyone uses them. Freud said that they are perfectly natural and normal, and offer a way of satisfying the demands of the id without upsetting the superego. Whilst useful for protecting the ego, however, they do not offer a long-term solution to problems, and if defence mechanisms are adopted too frequently, or get out of proportion, they themselves can create psychological problems of their own.

According to Freud, the behaviour of all people is to some extent 'abnormal', in that none of us is free from the dynamic conflicts caused by our unconscious drives and repressed memories. Therefore it is perfectly 'normal' to experience anxiety. Abnormality is, therefore, both inevitable and beyond our conscious control. Now try the next activity at the top of p. 132.

Table 4.2 >> Defence mechanisms

Mechanism	How it works
>> **Repression**	Prevents unacceptable desires, motivations or emotions from becoming conscious. Repression does not mean that you consciously cover up guilty secrets; it means that you make them unconscious so that you are not even aware of them. The repressed drives do not disappear; they remain in the unconscious where they influence behaviour in ways that we are unaware of, and may cause emotional difficulties. *Example:* A person who is normally placid acts in a violent way towards someone else and subsequently has no recollection of this.
>> **Projection**	When people's own unacceptable faults or wishes are attributed to someone else. In the extreme, this defence mechanism can become paranoia. *Example:* Accusing someone else of being angry, secretive or thoughtless, when it is actually you who are feeling angry or being secretive or thoughtless.
>> **Denial**	People sometimes refuse to believe events or to admit they are experiencing certain emotions that provoke anxiety. *Example:* An alcoholic may deny that they are dependent on alcohol.
>> **Regression**	Sometimes people respond to anxiety by behaving in childish ways, such as adults who resort to stamping or kicking, which they may have found effective as children. People may also regress to an earlier type of behaviour when they suffer a traumatic experience. *Example:* A 9-year-old child whose parents are getting divorced may revert to thumb-sucking or bed-wetting.
>> **Displacement**	Diverting emotions onto someone else because the emotions cannot be expressed to the person concerned or because accepting faults in ourselves will cause anxiety. *Examples:* A child who feels angry towards their parents may resort to bullying a younger or weaker child at school. A student who fails an exam may blame the teacher.
>> **Sublimation**	Diverting emotions onto something else (rather than someone else). This is the socially acceptable form of displacement, and a defence mechanism that is encouraged in our society. *Example:* Playing a vigorous sport as an expression of aggressive drives.

Source: Based on Geiselman (1988)

Using defence mechanisms

1 In what way can hard physical activity be a form of sublimation?

2 Spend a few minutes identifying:
   — times when you might have used defence mechanisms
   — occasions when others might have used defence mechanisms with you.

Note down all the examples you can think of.

When you have done this, try to provide additional examples for any of the six defence mechanisms from Table 4.2 that you have not included in your examples.

Is this an example of sublimation?

Treatment and the psychodynamic model

Freud was instrumental in changing ways of thinking about people who are mentally ill, by pointing out that physical symptoms could have psychological causes. He developed a method of treatment for psychological distress, known as psychoanalysis, which is often called the 'talking cure'. From this, many other psychodynamic therapies have evolved. These therapies seek to uncover unconscious psychodynamic processes in order to facilitate insight into the conflicts and anxieties that are the underlying causes of abnormal behaviour. The belief is that if someone can better understand what happened in the past and what is going on at an unconscious level within their psyche, then they can better deal, at a conscious level, with situations that are happening in their life now.

According to psychodynamic theory, the unconscious is revealed in dreams; therefore, one of the techniques of psychoanalysis is the analysis of dreams. Another technique is free association, in which clients are encouraged to let their thoughts wander and say whatever comes into their heads. The idea is that such uncensored thoughts will reveal underlying conflicts and uncomfortable or unfulfilled wishes. The analyst is then able to offer an interpretation of the client's behaviour and make the thoughts that had been repressed available to the client's conscious mind.

Evaluation of the psychodynamic model

● *Validity* – Freudian theory has been enormously influential and was the first model to establish talking therapy as an acceptable form of treatment in mainstream mental-health practice. However, the psychodynamic model has proved difficult to test scientifically, which has led some theorists to claim that the theory is lacking in validity. However, Kline (1988) claims that a theory is not invalidated because it cannot be tested scientifically; it merely means that no one has yet found a way to do it.

- *Defence mechanisms* – These have been difficult to demonstrate experimentally, but there appears to be some support from everyday experience. Although early traumatic experiences may not necessarily emerge in adulthood as psychological problems, research indicates that many people with psychological problems do recollect having experienced emotional trauma in childhood. However, It is important to understand that retrospective data (i.e. information gathered from clients years after the event) may be unreliable.
- *Determinism* – The psychodynamic model claims that abnormal behaviour results from unconscious psychic conflict related to innate, biological drives. The model also claims that early relationships with parents are important to psychological development. For these reasons it has been claimed that the theory is deterministic, that is, individuals are portrayed as having very little conscious involvement in their own personality development. The implicit assumption is that people are not to blame for their own abnormal behaviour, but may be partially responsible for the development of abnormal behaviour in their offspring. This may prove a heavy burden for parents who feel they have 'done their best' and, according to the model, may also be grappling with their own inner emotional conflicts.
- *Cost and efficacy* – Critics of classical psychoanalysis, such as Eysenck (1967), have suggested that the treatment is costly, time-consuming and ineffective.
- *Relevance* – Some critics have suggested that the theory is culture-bound and that it has little relevance for modern times.

BEHAVIOURAL MODEL

Basic assumptions

This model focuses on the behaviour of an individual in order to explain psychological problems. Advocates of the behavioural model would not use the term 'mental disorder' or 'mental illness', since they have no interest in mental structures, only in overt behaviour. They claim that abnormal behaviour is quite simply learned in the same way as most other behaviour. The behavioural model explains the emergence of specific, maladaptive or dysfunctional behaviours, such as phobias, anxiety, depression and eating disorders, through the processes of classical conditioning, operant conditioning and social learning.

Classical conditioning

The theory of classical conditioning (Pavlov 1927) explains how behaviour is learned through stimulus–response associations. An event in the environment (stimulus) results in a physiological reaction (response) in the individual. The event and the reaction are then forged into an association. Phobias (pathological fears of objects or situations) are thought to develop in this way. For example, a person may climb to the top of a high building and, when looking down (environmental stimulus), experience nausea and dizziness (physio-logical response). This association may then develop into a fear of heights so strong that it becomes a phobia and the person will then be so afraid of heights that they will avoid all situations involving them.

In classical conditioning, it is not the object, nor the situation, which is the cause of the fear but the conditioned response to the object or situation. For example, it is the response of feeling sick and dizzy when looking down from a high building that causes the fear of heights, not the height itself. What is important is that the person must have first experienced a fearful reaction to the situation or event so extreme that they will avoid it (or anything similar) at all costs in the future. This may be fine if the person can avoid being in high places, but will be dysfunctional if the person works in a tall office block, for example, or has a job that involves airline travel. In such cases, the person would either have to seek alternative employment or seek help from a therapist to overcome the phobia. In a classic study, Watson and Rayner (1920) conditioned a young boy to fear white rats in order to illustrate how phobias are the consequence of learned behaviour (see panel on next page).

Are height phobias caused by classical conditioning?

'Little Albert' study by Watson and Rayner (1920)

Watson and Rayner attempted to show how a phobia could be conditioned. With his parents' consent, they conducted an experiment on an 11-month-old child – known as Little Albert. Albert was first introduced to a tame white rat and showed no fear. During the experiment, each time Albert reached out to touch the rat the experimenters made a loud noise by striking two metal bars together. The noise startled Albert and soon he became afraid to touch the white rat. In this classic study, Watson and Rayner showed that an association had been formed between touching the white rat and fear of the noise. This conditioned fear then became generalized to other stimuli that resembled the white rat, such as other fluffy animals and objects such as cotton wool. Unfortunately, Little Albert's parents became concerned and withdrew him from the experiment before the experimenters had the opportunity to try and countercondition him. This experience raises ethical issues around the use of humans in such experiments.

ACTIVITY

Counterconditioning

Can you think of a way in which Little Albert could have been counterconditioned? The clue lies in the way in which he was originally conditioned.

Operant conditioning

In his theory of operant conditioning, Skinner (1974) explained how our behaviour is influenced by the consequences of our actions. We learn at an early age, for example, which of our actions are rewarded and which are punished. Conduct disorders and antisocial personality disorders have been explained in operant conditioning terms. If childhood aggression is rewarded, then that behaviour is likely to be repeated and reinforced again and again. However, behaviours that may appear maladaptive to others may be functional or adaptive for the individual. For example, anxiety or depression might gain a reward in the form of attention and concern from others.

Social learning

According to social learning theory (Bandura 1973), a child learns antisocial behaviour by observing and copying violent behaviour in others. A study of monkeys by Mineka et al. (1984) showed how a phobia could be developed through observation alone. Monkeys raised by parents who had a fear of snakes did not automatically acquire this fear themselves, and so Mineka concluded that the fear was not genetically inherited. Those monkeys, however, who had the opportunity to observe their parents showing fearful reactions to real and toy snakes did acquire an intense and persistent fear themselves.

Treatment and the behavioural model

If maladaptive or dysfunctional behaviours have been learned through classical and operant conditioning, it should be possible to change them through the same processes. Behavioural therapy, therefore, takes a practical, problem-solving approach. The therapist's role is to identify maladaptive learning and then to educate the person into more adaptive learning strategies.

Does comforting simply reinforce children's anxious behaviour?

- *Therapies based on classical conditioning* – These therapies aim to replace a maladaptive response such as fear with a healthier one. The main techniques are:
  - systematic desensitization, where clients are taught relaxation techniques and are then gradually exposed to feared objects or situations until the fear diminishes
  - aversion therapy, where the therapist tries to get rid of undesirable behaviour, such as alcoholism, by presenting unpleasant stimuli to the client at the same time as the desired object, for example, giving an electric shock while simultaneously offering alcohol.

- *Therapies based on operant conditioning* – These therapies are based on the assumption that maladaptive behaviour can be reshaped through a system of rewards and punishments, known as behaviour modification. One such method is token economy – this is a procedure that is often used in institutions such as prisons or mental hospitals to discourage antisocial behaviour. Tokens, used to reward any instances of desired behaviour, can be collected and then exchanged for privileges.

Evaluation of the behavioural model

- *Focus on behaviour* – The behavioural model overcomes the ethical issue raised by the medical model of labelling someone as 'ill' or 'abnormal'. Instead, the model concentrates on behaviour and whether it is 'adaptive' or 'maladaptive'.

- *Individual and cultural differences* – The model allows individual and cultural differences to be taken into account. Provided the behaviour is presenting no problems to the individual or to other people, then there is no reason to regard the behaviour as a mental disorder. It is the behavioural model that led to the definition of abnormality previously outlined as a 'failure to function adequately' (see p. 121).

- *Underlying causes* – Those who support the psychodynamic model, however, claim that the behavioural model focuses only on symptoms and ignores the causes of abnormal behaviour. They claim that symptoms are merely the tip of the iceberg – the outward expression of deeper underlying emotional problems. Whenever symptoms are treated without any attempt to ascertain the deeper underlying problems, then the problem will only manifest itself in another way, through different symptoms. This is known as symptom substitution. Behaviourists reject this criticism, however, and claim that we need not look beyond behavioural symptoms because the symptoms are the disorder. Thus, there is nothing to be gained by searching for internal causes, either psychological or physical. Behaviourists point to the success of behavioural therapies in treating certain disorders. Others note that the effects of such treatments are not always long lasting

- *Ethical issues* – Some critics claim that behavioural therapies are dehumanizing and unethical. For example, token economy systems and aversion therapy have sometimes been imposed on people without their consent.

- *Reductionism* – Behavioural theory is accused of being reductionist and simplistic because it seeks to explain human behaviour in very narrow terms, that is, that all behaviour is learned through the processes of conditioning.

COGNITIVE MODEL

Basic assumptions

The cognitive model assumes that emotional problems can be attributed directly to distortions in our thinking processes (cognitions). These take the form of negative thoughts, irrational beliefs and illogical errors, such as polarized (black and white) thinking and overgeneralization. These maladaptive thoughts, it is claimed, usually take place automatically and without full awareness.

This approach to understanding abnormality was founded by Albert Ellis (1962) and Aaron Beck (1963), who thought that the weakness of the behavioural model was that it did not take mental processes into account. The rationale behind the cognitive model is that the thinking (cognition) processes that occur between a stimulus and a response are responsible for the feeling component of the response.

Ellis (1962) maintained that everyone's thoughts are rational at times and irrational at other times. Psychological problems occur only if people engage in faulty thinking to the extent that it becomes maladaptive for themselves and others around them (see Fig. 4.3).

According to Ellis, when we *think* rationally, we *behave* rationally, and as a consequence we are happy, competent and effective. When we think irrationally, however, the result can be psychological disturbance, because people become habituated to their disturbed thoughts. Ellis observed that irrational thinking is often revealed in the language that people use, in particular the use of words such as 'should', 'ought' and 'must'.

Examples of irrational thinking that Ellis claimed could lead to psychological problems:

- "I ought to be good for my parents."
- "David should be nice to me."
- "I must do well in all my A levels."

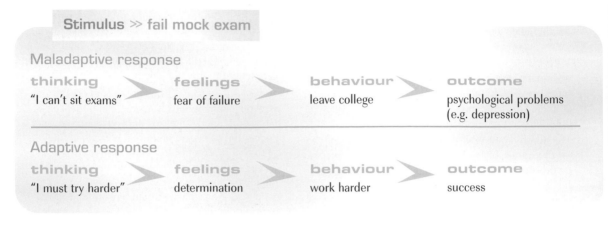

Stimulus >> fail mock exam

Maladaptive response

| **thinking** | **feelings** | **behaviour** | **outcome** |
| "I can't sit exams" | fear of failure | leave college | psychological problems (e.g. depression) |

Adaptive response

| **thinking** | **feelings** | **behaviour** | **outcome** |
| "I must try harder" | determination | work harder | success |

Figure 4.3 >> *Rationale behind cognitive theory*

Ellis also claimed that some people tend to exaggerate or 'catastrophize' events. For example: "I must be an awful person because Mary ignored me when I spoke to her this morning." They tend to fail to consider rational alternatives, for example that Mary was perhaps engrossed in thought, or was feeling ill, or may be a moody type of person.

Beck, who also believed that negative thoughts underlie mental disorder, was particularly interested in finding out why people become depressed. He found that depressed people tend to draw illogical conclusions when they evaluate themselves. Such negative thoughts lead to negative feelings, which, in turn, can result in depression. Beck identified three forms of negative thinking that he called the cognitive triad and that he thought were typical of those suffering from depression (see Fig. 4.4).

Treatment and the cognitive model

● Cognitive therapy is aimed at encouraging people to examine the beliefs and expectations underlying their unhappiness and to replace irrational, negative thoughts with a more positive, adaptive pattern of thinking. Therapists and clients work together to set new goals for the clients in order that more realistic and rational beliefs are incorporated into their ways of thinking.

Negative views about the future (e.g. "I'll never be any good at anything")

Negative views about the world (e.g. "Everyone is against me")

Negative views about oneself (e.g. "I'm worthless and inadequate")

Figure 4.4 >> *The cognitive triad that leads to depression (Beck 1963)*

- Ellis developed Rational-Emotive Behaviour Therapy (REBT) based on his theoretical model of how psychological problems emerge. He claimed that REBT helps people to 'cure' themselves in an elegant way because they become less disturbed and less anxious, and they maintain this over a long period, or even permanently. The ultimate aim is that REBT should be incorporated into a person's way of life, in order to overcome procrastination and eradicate self-defeating thoughts.

- Beck's cognitive therapy is used mainly with people with depression. It is aimed at training clients to monitor situations where they make negative assumptions, and to encourage them to challenge these distorted thoughts and to take part in activities that will help them to see that such assumptions are unfounded.

- Cognitive therapies are becoming more and more popular and diverse in their applications. For example, they are increasingly being applied in stress management, as well as with marital and family problems, and in educational settings. They are also being applied to eating disorders, which will be considered later on in this unit.

Evaluation of the cognitive model

- The cognitive approach offers a 'model for living' which promotes psychological wellbeing and avoids the stigma of 'mental illness'.

- Research has shown that many people suffering from mental disorders do exhibit thought patterns associated with maladaptive functioning. For example, Gustafson (1992) found that maladaptive thinking processes were displayed by many people with psychological disorders such as anxiety, depression and sexual disorders.

- A criticism of the model is that it does not attempt to examine the origins of irrational thinking, nor does the treatment address these origins. Beck (1991) has pointed out that, although cognitive processes are involved in many psychological disorders, they may well be a consequence rather than a cause of their problems.

- The cognitive model has also been criticized because it suggests that everyone should be self-sufficient. Indeed, Ellis himself had little sympathy with those suffering from depression, regarding it as an 'indulgence' of self-defeating thoughts. A belief in self-sufficiency lays the blame for psychological problems firmly with the individual, rather than with the social environment. Consequently, attention may be drawn away from the need to improve social conditions that have a significant effect on the quality of life.

- The cognitive model also ignores the possibility that some so-called irrational thoughts might actually be true and therefore rational.

✓ CHECK YOUR UNDERSTANDING

Check your understanding of models of abnormality by answering these questions. Try to do this from memory at first. You can check your answers by looking back through Topic 2.

1 What is an alternative name for the medical model?

2 What are the four possible causal factors according to the medical model?

3 What are the three main categories of treatment suggested by the medical model?

4 Give one strength and one weakness of the medical model of abnormality.

5 Give a brief description of the process of repression.

6 Explain what is meant by the term 'defence mechanisms'.

7 Give a brief description of psychodynamic therapy.

8 What is meant by (a) classical conditioning (b) operant conditioning?

9 Give one strength and one weakness of the behavioural model of abnormality.

10 Outline the basic assumptions of the cognitive model of abnormality.

biological and psychological models of abnormality

We have just finished a fairly extensive coverage of four different models of abnormality. You will now have a good understanding of where each of these models stands on the causes and treatments of abnormal behaviour. However, as the title of this panel suggests, it is always wise to keep a careful eye on the examination. Let's review what the specification dictates for this subsection.

<< Assumptions made by biological (medical) and psychological (including psychodynamic, behavioural and cognitive) models of abnormality in terms of their views on the causes and treatment of abnormality. >>

Now let's look at some possible examination questions for this area (note, this is not meant to be an exhaustive list):

1 Outline the biological (psychodynamic, behavioural, cognitive...) model with respect to the causes of abnormality.

(6 marks)

2 Outline the biological (psychodynamic, behavioural, cognitive...) model with respect to the treatment of abnormality.

(6 marks)

3 Give two criticisms of the biological (psychodynamic, behavioural, cognitive...) model of abnormality. (3 + 3 marks)

4 Outline and evaluate the biological (psychodynamic, behavioural, cognitive...) model of abnormality. (18 marks)

What does this tell us? Although you may know a great deal about a particular model, in an examination you will only ever get the chance to offer a précis of that model. Can you, for example, describe Freud's psychodynamic theory (as it applies to an understanding of the causes of abnormality) in just 100 or so words? A well-prepared student thinks ahead and can fit what they know to what is required in the exam. Look again at the questions and think what is actually required in response to each.

1 requires a précis (approximately 100 to 120 words) of one of these four models concerning the **causes** of abnormality (you will, of course, need to be able to do this for all four models)

2 requires a précis (approximately 100 to 120 words) of one of these four models concerning the **treatment** of abnormality

3 requires a short description of **two** criticisms (approximately 50 to 60 words each) of one of these four models – remember these can be positive as well as negative

4 requires a précis (approximately 100 to 120 words) of one of these four models concerning the causes and/or treatment of abnormality **together with** a longer (200 to 250 words) evaluation of that model.

Performing well in an examination is only partly to do with having a good understanding of the material. It is also important to have good editorial skills, knowing what to leave out as much as what to put in. Practising these skills will pay off when you have to do it for real.

REVISION SUMMARY

Having covered this topic, you should be able to:

✓ define what is meant by the following models of abnormality:

– the medical (biological) model

– the psychodynamic model

– the behavioural model

– the cognitive model

✓ explain the assumptions of these models in terms of causes of abnormality

✓ explain the assumptions of these models in terms of the treatment of abnormality.

GETTING YOU THINKING...

Tuesday 3 January

9st 4 (terrifying slide into obesity –
why? why?), alcohol units 6 (excellent),
cigarettes 23 (v.g.), calories 2472.

9 a.m. Ugh. Cannot face thought of
going back to work. Only thing that
makes it tolerable is thought of
seeing Daniel again, but even that is
inadvisable since am fat, have spot on
chin, and desire only to sit on cushion
eating chocolate...

Extract and photo from Bridget Jones's Diary

Look carefully at the images portrayed above.

1 What do they tell us about our attitudes to eating and body image in the Western world at the beginning of the 21st century?

2 Why do you think that the incidence of eating disorders is rising among young women and also among young men?

KEY TERMS

Eating disorder: a condition where there is serious disruption of healthy eating habits or appetite.

Anorexia nervosa: an eating disorder characterized by the pursuit of extreme thinness and by an extreme loss of weight.

Bulimia nervosa: an eating disorder characterized by secret binge eating followed by vomiting, misuse of laxatives, diuretics, excessive exercise, etc., in order to lose weight.

Unit 4 // Abnormality

ANOREXIA NERVOSA

This topic looks at two subtypes of eating disorder – anorexia nervosa and bulimia nervosa. You will consider a number of explanations for the cause of eating disorders. Each explanation has its origins in one of the models of abnormality already outlined in this unit.

What is anorexia?

The term anorexia nervosa means literally a nervous loss of appetite. However, this is slightly misleading because people with anorexia usually have normal appetites and may often be very hungry, but will nevertheless behave as if they have lost their appetite – see the panel below for the characteristics of anorexia nervosa. Ninety per cent of cases of anorexia occur in females, usually between the ages of 13 and 18, and it is rarely diagnosed before puberty. The American Psychiatric Association (1994) states that anorexia occurs in 0.5 to 1.0 per cent of females in late adolescence and early adulthood. In the UK, surveys indicate that around 1 per cent of schoolgirls and female university students suffer from anorexia (Gelder *et al.* 1998). Although still low by comparison, cases of eating disorders in males are becoming more frequent. Currently in the UK, figures for men are between 5 and 10 per cent of those diagnosed with anorexia nervosa.

The course and outcome of anorexia are variable:

- Around 20 per cent of anorexics have one single episode with full recovery.
- Around 60 per cent follow an episodic pattern of weight gain and relapse over a number of years.
- The remaining 20 per cent continue to be severely affected and, in many cases, hospitalization is required to restore weight and fluid balance.

Studies with weight-recovered anorexics have found significantly reduced grey matter in the brain, which affects cognitive functioning. This brain damage is irreversible. For some people with anorexia, it is a chronic unremitting course until death. The mortality rate of those admitted to hospital is over 10 per cent, with deaths occurring from starvation, suicide or organ malfunction. See the box on p. 141 for a case study of a girl with anorexia nervosa.

Clinical characteristics of anorexia nervosa

- *Refusal to maintain expected body weight* – Body weight is below 85 per cent of normal for one's height and age. Even though the person is underweight, there is an intense fear of gaining weight or becoming fat. Food intake is restricted to around 600 to 800 calories or less per day, with an avoidance of any food regarded as fattening.

- *Cessation of menstruation* – This is an early sign in females and, in about 40 per cent of cases, precedes obvious weight loss.

- *Ritualistic behaviour* – Food is often cut up into small pieces and eaten in a ritualistic way.

- *Preoccupation with food* – Anorexics like reading cookery books and preparing food for others, and often work in environments involved with food.

- *Body perception* – People with anorexia have a distorted body image and tend to believe themselves to be overweight or deny that they are seriously underweight.

- *Mood disturbance* – People with anorexia often show signs of depression, anxiety, mood swings and irritability.

- *Denial* – People with anorexia often deny the seriousness of their abnormally low weight.

- *Physical effects of starvation* – Apart from the huge weight loss which is the central feature of anorexia, there are other consequences of starvation, including dry skin, brittle nails, fine hair growth over the body, but thinning hair on the scalp.

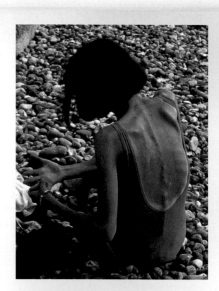

Frieda had always been a shy, sensitive girl who gave little cause for concern at her home or in school. She was bright and did well academically, although she had few friends. In early adolescence she had been somewhat overweight and had been teased by her family. She reacted to this teasing by withdrawing and becoming very touchy. Her parents had to become very careful about what they said. If offended, Frieda would throw a tantrum and march off to her room. This was hardly the behaviour they expected from a bright and sensitive 15-year-old.

Frieda began dieting. Initially, her family was pleased, but gradually her parents sensed that all was not well. Mealtimes became battle times. Frieda hardly ate at all. Under pressure, she would take her meals to her room, and later, having said that she had eaten everything, her mother would find food hidden away untouched. When her mother found her deliberately inducing vomiting after a meal, she insisted they go to the family doctor. He found that Frieda had stopped menstruating a few months earlier. Not fooled by the loose, floppy clothes that Frieda was wearing, he insisted upon carrying out a full physical examination. Her emaciated body told him as much as he needed to know and he arranged for Frieda's immediate hospitalization.

Source: Adapted from Rosenhan and Seligman (1984)

BULIMIA NERVOSA

Bulimia nervosa was named as a condition distinct from anorexia nervosa only in 1979. Its clinical characteristics are outlined in the panel below. It is diagnosed in around 1 to 2 per cent of women aged between 16 and 40 (Gelder *et al.* 1998). Ninety per cent of cases are female, with bulimia being very uncommon in men.

Bulimia frequently follows on from months or years of anorexia. It differs from anorexia, however, in a number of ways:

- Bulimia is more common in the UK than anorexia.
- Bulimia tends to occur in older people (most sufferers are in their 20s) compared with anorexia.
- There is some evidence that people with bulimia are more likely than anorexia sufferers to engage in self-destructive or antisocial behaviours, such as drug/alcohol abuse, deliberate self-harm or shoplifting.
- Nearly all those with bulimia nervosa are within 10 per cent of their normal body weight.
- People with bulimia nervosa are not likely to die from starvation. However, their continual purging has long-term effects on their physical health.

Clinical characteristics of bulimia nervosa

- *Normal or above normal weight*
- *Binge eating* – There are recurrent episodes of uncontrollable overeating. These is usually precipitated by stress and accompanied by a loss of control.
- *Compensatory behaviour* – Binge eating is accompanied by feelings of guilt and disgust, followed by an extreme need to control body weight; in order to compensate for overeating, the person then engages in purging. This involves behaviours such as self-induced vomiting, misuse of laxatives, diuretics, enemas, medications, excessive exercise or fasting.
- *Physical effects of purging* – an increased risk of urinary infections and kidney disease and a tendency to develop epileptic fits. Repeated vomiting can cause the erosion of enamel on the teeth.
- *Body perception* – Unlike those with anorexia, the bulimic person is usually within the normal weight range. However, as with anorexia, this is accompanied by a disturbance in self-perception of body weight, size or shape.
- *Mood disturbance* – Depression is common and people sometimes feel suicidal after bingeing.
- *Awareness* – Denial is unusual in people with bulimia nervosa; they usually recognize that they need help.

ACTIVITY

What causes eating disorders

Consider the following statement:

<< Psychological processes cause eating disorders.>>

Discuss this statement with a friend. Note down any ideas that you have that support this statement and also any arguments against such a statement. On balance do you think that this statement is true?

We shall return to reconsider this statement later in the unit, once you have looked at the available evidence.

Bulimia nervosa – a case study

Extracts from an account given by a married woman who suffers from bulimia nervosa. Her husband has left home for work and she is on her own:

≪ I float to the refrigerator knowing exactly what is there. I begin with last night's brownies. I always begin with the sweets. At first I try to make it look like nothing is missing but my appetite is huge … I know there is half a bag of cookies in the bathroom, thrown out the night before and I polish them off immediately. I take some milk so that my vomiting will be smoother. I get out six pieces of bread and toast one side, turn them over and load with butter … I take all six pieces on a plate to the television and go back for a bowl of cereal and a banana to have along with them. Before the last toast is finished, I am preparing the next batch of six more pieces. Maybe another brownie or five and a couple of bowlfuls of ice cream, yogurt or cottage cheese. My stomach is stretched into a huge ball below my ribcage. I know I'll have to go into the bathroom soon, but I want to postpone it. I am in never-never land. I am waiting, feeling the pressure, pacing the floor in and out of the rooms. Time is passing. It is getting to be time.

I finally make the turn into the bathroom. I brace my feet, pull my hair back and stick my finger down my throat, stroking twice and get a huge pile of food. Three times, four and another pile of food. I can see everything coming back. I am glad to see those brownies because they are SO fattening. The rhythm of the emptying is broken and my head is beginning to hurt. I stand up feeling dizzy, empty and weak. The whole episode has taken about an hour. ≫

Source: Adapted from Comer (2000)

BIOLOGICAL EXPLANATIONS OF EATING DISORDERS

Biological explanations of eating disorders fall into two categories:

- genetic inheritance
- biochemical dysfunction of neurotransmitters in the brain.

A biochemical dysfunction or imbalance may have been genetically inherited or may be due to other causes.

Genetic explanation for eating disorders

As yet, genetic science has been unable to identify genes for specific behaviours, such as those associated with eating disorders. Research is based, therefore, on examining whether a particular disorder runs in families. The American Psychiatric Association (1994) reports that there is an increased risk of eating disorders among first-degree biological relatives of those diagnosed (parents, children and siblings), with a number of studies showing a much higher prevalence rate than in the general population. However, since relatives usually share the same environment, this does not necessarily support a genetic cause, as the behaviour may have been learned from other family members.

Twin studies provide more reliable evidence. The nature of this research is to compare monozygotic (MZ) twins with dizygotic (DZ) twins. MZ twins have identical genes, whereas DZ twins are no more alike genetically than any other siblings. Therefore, environmental factors could be largely eliminated if a significantly higher concordance rate were found among MZ twins compared with DZ twins. Concordance means that both twins have the same disorder.

Both Holland *et al.* (1984) and Kendler *et al.* (1991) claim to have found evidence in support of a genetic basis for anorexia and bulimia nervosa respectively (see the following two key studies).

KEY STUDY >> ANOREXIA NERVOSA

a study of 34 pairs of twins and one set of triplets by Holland *et al.* (1984)

Aim >>

To investigate whether there is a genetic basis for anorexia by studying identical (MZ) and non-identical (DZ) twins where at least one twin in each pair suffered from anorexia.

Procedures >>

- Participants were: 30 female twin pairs (16 MZ and 14 DZ pairs), four male twin pairs, and one set of male triplets.
- The twins and triplets were selected because one of the twins (and one of the triplets) had been diagnosed as suffering from anorexia nervosa.
- Data were collected on the other twin and triplets to check for concordance.

Findings >>

- High concordance rates were found for monozygotic female twins – 55 per cent compared to 7 per cent for dizygotic female pairs.
- Five of the non-anorexic female co-twins had either other psychiatric illnesses or minor eating disorders.
- None of the male co-twins (or triplets) had anorexia (i.e. they were discordant).
- The anorexic male twins tended to have been disadvantaged at birth and to be the less dominant of the pairs.

Conclusions >>

- Results support the view that there is some genetic basis for anorexia among females, since identical twins (who share the same genes) had 55 per cent concordance, while DZ (fraternal) twins (who share only half of their genes) showed only 7 per cent concordance.
- No conclusions can be drawn from the data from the male twins owing to small numbers.

Criticisms >>

- The higher concordance rates among identical twins may be caused by the similar ways in which they were treated by family and friends rather than by their genetic similarity.
- Holland and colleagues acknowledge that if genes do contribute to anorexia, their role is small.
- The sample size is very small and so is probably unrepresentative; other studies have not supported a genetic basis.

AO2 check

For example, Wade *et al.* (1998) studied both genetic and environmental risk factors in 325 female twins. They found a significant environmental influence in shaping women's attitudes towards weight, shape, eating and food, but little evidence of a genetic component.

KEY STUDY >> BULIMIA NERVOSA

a genetic epidemiology study of bulimia nervosa by Kendler et al. (1991)

Aim >>

To establish the prevalence (number of cases) of bulimia and to see whether there were genetic risk factors.

Procedures >>

- 2,163 female twins were given personal, structured, psychiatric interviews.
- The twins were assessed for psychiatric disorders.
- The risk factors for bulimia nervosa were recorded.

Findings >>

- The prevalence of bulimia nervosa was 2.8 per cent of those interviewed.
- Risk factors for bulimia included: being born after 1960; poor parental care; dieting and fluctuating weight; slim ideal body image; low self-esteem; feeling a lack of control over one's life.
- In identical (MZ) twins, concordance was 23 per cent.
- In non-identical (DZ) twins, concordance was 8.7 per cent.

Conclusions >>

- There are genetic risk factors involved in bulimia nervosa.
- There are also other important risk factors, for example relating to age and childhood experiences.

Criticisms >>

- Compared with many twin studies, this investigation involved quite a large number of participants.
- The higher concordance rates among identical twins may be caused by the similar ways in which they were treated by family and friends, rather than by their genetic similarity.
- People may not inherit a risk for bulimia (or anorexia), but rather a risk of developing an obsessional personality which makes them susceptible to eating disorders under certain circumstances.

There is clearly a significantly higher concordance in MZ twins compared with DZ twins in these studies, but, even with the Holland study reporting 55 per cent concordance, this still leaves 45 per cent of the MZ twins in their study who were discordant (that is, one twin had the disorder, but the other twin did not).

Hsu (1990) has suggested, on the other hand, that the genetic element may relate to personality traits such as emotional instability, which make the person more susceptible to stressful life events. These could manifest in an eating disorder or, alternatively, in some other mental disorder. In many cases of anorexia and bulimia, there is a family history of mood or personality disorders.

Biochemical explanations for eating disorders

- One view amongst the medical profession is that eating disorders may be associated with a biochemical imbalance. Research in the biological field has focused on the region of the brain known as the hypothalamus. Animals have been found to stop eating – and even to starve themselves to death – when the hypothalamus is damaged

  According to Keesey and Corbett (1983) the lateral hypothalamus (LH) and the ventromedial hypothalamus (VMH) work alongside each other to provide a 'weight thermostat'. When activated, the LH produces hunger and the VMH depresses hunger. If weight falls below the set point on the 'thermostat', the LH is activated; if weight rises above the set point, the VMH is activated. Once either the LH or the VMH is activated, the hypothalamus will send messages to areas of the brain responsible for thinking and behaviours that will satisfy whichever is activated (LH or VMH). A malfunction in this part of the hypothalamus offers a possible explanation for eating disorders, although there is as yet no conclusive evidence to support this.

● Amenorrhoea (loss of menstrual cycle) can occur *before* weight loss, which suggests a primary disorder of low endocrine levels, again associated with a hypothalamus dysfunction. Also, the endocrine levels of anorexics of around 19 years old are similar to those of a healthy 9-year-old. However, postmortems have not revealed damage to the hypothalamus, and eating disorders do not appear to be accounted for by any known physical disease.

● More recent research has focused on certain hormonal chemicals, including norepinephrine, dopamine and, most especially, low levels of serotonin, which has been found to be associated with binge eating. The most effective drug treatment for bulimia is serotonin-active antidepressant medication which decreases binge eating. In the light of such findings, Jimerson *et al.* (1997) conducted clinical tests comparing serotonin function in patients with bulimia and in healthy

controls. They found considerable differences and concluded that impaired serotonergic responsiveness may contribute to the onset, persistence or recurrence of abnormal eating patterns in people with bulimia nervosa. The problem with biochemical research is that it is difficult to differentiate between the cause and the effect, since the behavioural symptoms of anorexia and bulimia have a direct, and significant, adverse effect on the person's physiology, which, in turn, may affect their biochemistry. In simple terms, starvation may eventually cause an imbalance in biochemical functioning.

Evaluation of biological explanations

● Twin studies have provided some support for a genetic basis for eating disorders. However, most of the studies have used small samples, and it is difficult to disentangle the effects of a shared environment from a shared genetic make-up.

● Although many studies have demonstrated biochemical changes in individuals with eating disorders, it is not always easy to tell whether these changes are the cause or the consequence of the disorder.

PSYCHOLOGICAL MODELS OF EATING DISORDERS

Behavioural explanations

Advertising in teenage magazines and on television promotes the message that 'slim is beautiful'. It is not surprising, therefore, that so many people turn to diets with such frequency. This has led to the layperson's view of anorexia as 'slimming that got out of hand'.

Is it accurate to say that all teenage magazines promote the message 'slim is beautiful'?

Classical and operant conditioning

Classical conditioning incorporates the layperson's view, suggesting that slimming becomes a *habit*, just like any other habit, through stimulus-response mechanisms. The person first goes on a diet and after a while receives admiration from others, either for their endeavour or their new, slimmer appearance. In other words, they learn to associate being slim with feeling good about themselves. Operant conditioning comes into play as admiration from others further reinforces the dieting behaviour. Refusing to eat may also provide an additional reward in the form of attention gained from parents, and starving oneself can even be rewarding as an effective way of punishing parents.

Cross-cultural studies

Cross-cultural studies appear to support the behavioural explanation. It has been noted that anorexia and bulimia are more prevalent in industrialized societies, mainly Europe, USA, Canada, Australia, Japan, New Zealand and South Africa. In these societies, there is an abundance of food and yet, at the same time, being attractive is associated with being slim.

The American Psychiatric Association (1994) states that immigrants from cultures where these disorders are rare have been found to develop anorexia just as frequently as those born in industrialized societies, once these ideals of attractiveness are assimilated. A study by Nasser (1986) compared 50 Egyptian women in London universities with 60 Egyptian women in Cairo universities. Twelve per cent of those in London developed an eating disorder. None of those in Cairo did so. However, another study of Asian schoolgirls living in Bradford, found that concerns about weight and body shape were more commonly found among those girls who used Asian languages and wore Asian dress. It has been suggested that the more traditional Asian girls might be experiencing greater internal conflict about their identity as they grew up within two sets of cultural values (Mumford *et al.* 1991).

There are still very few studies conducted in non-industrialized countries, so it is quite difficult to provide adequate comparisons. The idea that pressures to be slim in Western cultures play a part in eating disorders is supported in studies conducted on groups of people for whom slimness is essential, such as gymnasts and ballet dancers. For example, Garner *et al.* (1987) found that in a group of 11- to 14-year-old ballet students, 25 per cent developed anorexia over the two-year period of their study. Other studies, such as that by Pike and Rodin (1991), have identified family pressures on daughters to be thin, particularly from mothers who are perfectionist, overly concerned with external appearance and who continually diet themselves.

In evaluating behavioural explanations for eating disorders, the following points are important:

- Operant conditioning techniques have been helpful in promoting weight gain in some people with anorexia.
- This model does not address the underlying problems of depression and loss of control apparent in people with eating disorders.
- The model has been more useful in explaining how eating disorders are maintained rather than in providing a comprehensive explanation of how they originate.

Cognitive explanation

This model focuses on the irrational beliefs that some people hold that they cannot be valued unless they have an ideal physical appearance. People with eating disorders often have a distorted body image and perceive themselves to be unattractive because they think they are fat.

A consistent pattern of distorted thinking among people with anorexia was found by Bemis-Vitousek and Orimoto (1993). They noted their cognitive convictions, which were consistent with the cognitive model of abnormality – for example, "I must lose more weight since I am not yet thin." They also found irrational attitudes about control – for example, "I must continue to lose weight so I can continue to be in control of my body" – yet at the same time, they were clearly not in control because they were losing weight to a dangerous degree. Fairburn *et al.* (1999) conducted an interview study comparing 169 people with eating disorders, 102 people with other psychiatric disorders and 204 healthy controls. They identified 'perfectionism' and 'negative self-evaluation' as high-risk factors for both anorexia and bulimia. What is not clear in the cognitive model, however, is where irrational beliefs come from in the first place.

An evaluation of the cognitive explanation for eating disorders would focus on the following points:

- This model, unlike the behavioural explanation, takes account of the way people with eating disorders think about their bodies.
- The model has suggested therapies designed to help people with eating disorders develop more realistic ways of thinking about themselves.
- The cognitive model explains how eating disorders are maintained, but does not really explain why the distorted self-image first occurs.

Psychodynamic explanations

- *Repressed sexual impulses* – Freud maintained that eating is a substitute for sexual expression and therefore, in psychoanalytic terms, anorexia could be viewed as the person's way of repressing sexual impulses. Hilde Bruch (1979) has been particularly influential in applying psychodynamic theory to anorexia. She suggested that anorexia is associated with psychosexual immaturity in a number of ways. One suggestion is that women have fantasies of oral impregnation and confuse fatness with pregnancy. They unconsciously believe that eating will lead to pregnancy and therefore starve themselves.

Another suggestion is that eating becomes equated with taking on an adult sexual role and that women who cannot face this starve themselves in order either to remain children or to regress to childhood. Bruch suggested that this provides a mutual reward for both mothers and daughters. The mother may become over-anxious about her daughter and therefore curtail her independence and thus retain her 'child'. For the daughter, her behaviour has secured a way of continuing to be dependent upon her mother.

● *Sexual abuse and gender socialization* – Eating disorders have been strongly related to early traumatic experiences, and psychotherapy studies indicate that a large proportion of patients report early experience of sexual abuse (see also a key study below by Wonderlich and colleagues).

ACTIVITY

Childhood sexual abuse and bulimia

Wonderlich *et al.* (1996) suggest that the psychological trauma associated with childhood sexual abuse is a risk factor for bulimia.
Do you think that childhood sexual abuse might place a person at risk of a later eating disorder? If so, why?

Compare your ideas with those given in the following text.

KEY STUDY >> CHILDHOOD ABUSE AND BULIMIA

a study by Wonderlich *et al.* (1996)

Aim >>

To see whether childhood sexual abuse is a significant factor for the development of bulimia in women.

Procedures >>

● A representative national sample of 1099 women in the United States was interviewed about:
  – their sexual experiences during childhood
  – whether they had shown bulimic behaviour at any time during their lives.
● Calculations were carried out to find out whether sexual abuse in childhood increased a woman's risk of developing bulimic behaviour (once age, ethnic group and parents' educational level had been controlled for).

Findings >>

● Those women who had experienced childhood sexual abuse were significantly more likely to develop bulimia nervosa than those who did not report having been abused.

Conclusions >>

● Childhood sexual abuse is associated with dissatisfaction about one's weight and body.
● Consequently, childhood sexual abuse is a risk factor for bulimia nervosa.

Criticisms >>

● The data for this study came from interviews with adults who were asked to recollect childhood experiences. Such data can be unreliable, as respondents are prone to errors of memory. If they suffer from an eating disorder, they may also try harder to recollect some cause from their past to explain their adult problems.
● However, later research by Wonderlich *et al.* (2000) using data from abused and non-abused girls between the ages of 10 and 15 confirmed these findings from the adult women; abused girls were more dissatisfied with their weight and used more dieting and purging behaviour.

A study conducted in an eating disorder clinic by McLelland *et al.* (1991) reported that 30 per cent of clients had a history of childhood sexual abuse. The suggestion is that such experiences are repressed into the unconscious and express themselves in adolescence and adulthood through the symptoms of anorexia or bulimia. Sexual abuse in childhood can lead to a rejection by victims of their own bodies; in adolescence this rejection can turn to disgust and an unconscious desire to destroy their bodies.

An interesting suggestion is that early traumatic experiences are repressed and then become expressed in later life in ways associated with gender socialization. Females are taught to be subservient and self-critical and so early trauma is turned inwards upon the self in the form of self-harm. Males, on the other hand, are taught to be dominant and outwardly expressive. Thus their early trauma is more likely to be directed outward in hostility towards others. This could explain why eating disorders are predominantly a female disorder and why most violent crimes are perpetrated by males. A study of anorexia and bulimia in males was conducted by Carlat *et al.* (1997) on 135 patients in Boston, USA from 1980 to 1994. They observed that 42 per cent of the bulimia group were either homosexual or bisexual, and 58 per cent of the anorexia group were identified as asexual. They concluded that sexual orientation was a major factor in male eating disorders.

Evaluation of the psychodynamic explanation:

- Although a number of studies have been carried out to investigate the psychodynamic explanations, it is difficult to obtain convincing empirical support.

- Not all people who have experienced childhood sexual abuse develop an eating disorder, and not all people with eating disorders report having been sexually abused as children.

Other psychological explanations

- *Individual identity* – Some psychologists suggest that eating disorders relate to family relationships, and in particular to an adolescent's struggle to gain a sense of individual identity. In some family relationships, the parents exert such a strong level of control that children grow up without a sense of their own identity and, consequently, with low self-esteem. In adolescence, this control is maintained through roles within the family, such as the mother cooking the meals and the daughter dutifully eating them. This may form the arena in which the daughter struggles for her identity by refusing to eat.

- *Pressures to succeed* – Anorexia is much more prevalent in middle-class families, particularly among those whose parents have a professional background. It is also more prevalent in those

who go on to higher education. Consequently, it is suggested that family pressure to 'succeed' may be too great for some young people and may lead to psychological problems, such as depression and anorexia.

- *Negative self-evaluation* – The study by Fairburn *et al.* (1999), mentioned previously, also supports this explanation. They found that negative self-evaluation was identified as a high-risk factor for bulimia nervosa, along with parents who had high expectations for their daughters and yet had low contact with them. The prospective study by Button and colleagues also identified low self-esteem as a risk factor for eating disorders (see key study opposite). Further support comes from Joiner *et al.* (1997) who conducted a ten-year study from 1982 to 1992 on 459 females diagnosed with bulimia, aged 18 to 22 years at the beginning of the study. What they found to be the most significant factors sustaining the disorder over the ten-year span were a drive for thinness, maturity fears, perfectionism and interpersonal distrust.

A distorted body image may contribute to the development of anorexia

- *Family conflict* – Family systems theory implicates family factors in a quite different way. Minuchin *et al.* (1978) suggest that the development of anorexia serves the function of preventing a prospective study by Button *et al.* (1996)

Aim >>

To investigate the role of self-esteem as a cause of eating disorders (such as anorexia or bulimia nervosa).

Procedures >>

- Self-esteem was measured in 594 schoolgirls aged 11 to 12 years, using the Rosenberg Self-Esteem Scale.
- 400 girls were followed up at age 15 to 16. They completed a questionnaire about eating and other psychological problems.

Findings >>

- Those with low self-esteem at age 11 to 12 were more inclined to have low self-esteem at 15 to 16 years.
- Girls with low self-esteem at age 11 to 12 were significantly more at risk of eating disorders than those with higher self-esteem.
- Girls with low self-esteem at age 11 to 12 were more likely to display other problems at age 15 to 16 relating to health, family and school.

Conclusions >>

- Low self-esteem at age 11 to 12 is a significant risk factor for girls developing eating disorders later on.
- This study lends support to the argument that psychological factors play a part in eating disorders.
- It may be worth trying to enhance self-esteem in childhood and adolescence to help prevent eating disorders.

Criticisms >>

- This study relied on questionnaire data that may be unreliable and the sample was incomplete as some head teachers declined to let their pupils participate. This resulted in a biased sample: 60 per cent of girls' families were in social classes 1 and 2.
- We cannot be sure that the self-esteem measured at age 11 to 12 predated the onset of eating disorders. Early processes in eating disorders might have already started.

disagreements within the family. For example, it may be the adolescent's way of preventing a marriage break-up by diverting attention onto themselves. In so doing, the hope is that joint concern for the child will bring the parents back together. Other researchers have found that parents sometimes became more anxious and depressed if their anorexic child started to recover and gain weight. This finding fits in with the idea that anorexia may be a way of defusing family conflict.

Family relationships are thought to be a central feature in eating disorders, so much so that family therapy (based largely on family systems theory) is currently the most significant form of intervention for eating disorders.

ACTIVITY

The causes of eating disorders revisited

Think back to the following statement which you considered near the beginning of this topic:

<< Psychological processes cause eating disorders. >>

Now that you have read about the biological and psychological explanations of eating disorders, you should read the Expert interview by Gill Harris on p. 150. Write a short essay to answer the question:

<< To what extent can eating disorders be explained by biological factors? >>

Unit 4 // Abnormality

Eating *disorders*

Gill Harris is a Senior Lecturer In Psychology at the University of Birmingham, and a Consultant Clinical Psychologist at The Children's Hospital Birmingham. Her research interests are in feeding and eating disorders in children and adolescents. She also runs a clinical service at the Children's Hospital for children and adolescents with eating problems.

Q Can we explain eating disorders such as anorexia nervosa and bulimia nervosa purely from a biological perspective?

A We can't really say that eating disorders occur irrespective of cultural and psychological factors. Eating disorders are more prevalent in cultures where a slim body shape is seen as desirable, and where the media promotes images of thin bodies as the norm. Eating disorders are also more frequently observed in women rather than in men, where the drive for thinness is greater. Having said that, eating disorders are now being reported more frequently in homosexual men, perhaps in response to an increasing preoccupation with appearance in the male homosexual community.

The best explanation, especially for AN, is that there is a predisposition for the disorder, which is triggered by environment factors and cultural norms. The genetic predisposition shows itself in certain personality traits. Girls with AN tend to be obsessive-compulsive, high-achieving perfectionists. The need to achieve in a competitive society produces stress, the response to which is dietary restraint and the control of body shape to conform with desirable norms. Those with BN tend to be more impulsive, and show more self-harming behaviour, and this might lead to the binge–purge cycle when dietary restraint cannot be maintained.

Q But could the family environment act as the trigger?

A It has been argued that the drive to succeed comes from the family of those girls who develop AN, and it is the family environment and not a genetic predisposition that triggers dietary restraint as a response to stress. Family members have been implicated in the development of eating disorders since the disorders were first recorded (Gull 1874). However, much of this work has been carried out with families after the eating

Gill Harris

disorder has developed, and the effect of caring for an adolescent who is trying to starve herself has not been taken into account. It has also been suggested that early negative experience affects core beliefs about self that are then resistant to change (Young 1994), and that it is these core beliefs that give rise to the personality profiles typically associated with the disorders.

Q Could EDs be a 'normal' reaction to dieting triggered by socio-cultural factors?

A EDs are most frequently seen in girls as they come into their pubertal growth spurt, so might it be that the disorders are just a normal biological response to dieting? Many people choose to diet or fast, for many reasons, and most of them do not develop eating disorders. For dancers and gymnasts (who have the highest incidence of EDs), there is emphasis on a slim body and low calorie intake, so do they react to stress by inhibiting signals of hunger?

There is no one pattern of eating in response to stress: some people eat less and some people eat more. This variation is possibly determined by sensitivity to stress hormones. But the differential response to stress may explain why some people can inhibit eating completely and go on to develop AN, and others to develop BN.

The normal response, if you do try to inhibit food intake, is for gut hormones to act to make you eat again, and to eat sufficient food to compensate for the calories that you have missed out. Binge eating is therefore an evolutionary determined response to periods of fasting. Those with AN are more able to inhibit signals as a response to stress and find that eating restraint improves their mood and lowers stress. Those with BN are not able to inhibit eating, and respond to this incomplete control with vomiting and purging, which in turn reduces stress.

This model does not explain, however, the extremes of binge eating seen in those with BN. It is therefore probably easier to explain AN rather than BN purely in terms of physiological factors.

AS Individual Differences

Check your understanding of eating disorders by answering these questions. Try to do this from memory at first. You can check your answers by looking back through Topic 3.

1   Identify three characteristics of anorexia nervosa.

2   What is meant by the term 'binge eating'?

3   Identify three characteristics of bulimia nervosa.

4   Give a brief description of the procedures and findings of the study by Holland *et al.* (1984) that investigated the genetic basis for anorexia.

5   Briefly outline the findings of research that has investigated biochemical factors in eating disorders.

6   Explain why cross-cultural studies lend support to the behavioural explanation of eating disorders.

7   Give one strength and one weakness of the cognitive explanation of eating disorders.

8   Give a brief explanation as to how anorexia nervosa can be linked to repressed sexual impulses.

9   What is meant by 'family systems theory'?

10   To what extent is it reasonable to claim that eating disorders are caused by psychological factors alone?

REVISION SUMMARY

Having covered this topic you should be able to:

✓ outline the clinical characteristics of 'anorexia nervosa' and 'bulimia nervosa'

✓ explain these eating disorders in terms of biological and psychological models of abnormality

✓ discuss research on which the various explanations have been based

✓ outline the aims, procedures, findings, conclusions and criticisms for one study each about a biological explanation of anorexia and of bulimia and one study each about a psychological explanation of anorexia and of bulimia.

Topic 1: Defining psychological abnormality

● There are various ways in which abnormality can be defined, including:

– behaviour that occurs infrequently (i.e. **statistical infrequency** definition)

– behaviour that deviates from accepted standards (i.e. **deviation from social norms** definition)

– behaviour that that lacks the elements needed for optimal living (i.e. **deviation from ideal mental health** definition)

– an inability to pursue normal activities and goals (i.e. **failure to function adequately** definition)

● These definitions offer a useful general guide for distinguishing forms of functioning that might be regarded as pathological. However, their use is limited because there are no universal definitions of 'normality' and 'abnormality'.

● All of these attempts at definitions, however, have limitations in terms of their relevance to people of **different cultures**.

Topic 2: Biological and psychological models of abnormality

● Biological (medical) and psychological (psychodynamic, behavioural and cognitive) models of abnormality are based on very different assumptions about the nature of human functioning, and the origins and causes of abnormality. Each model offers quite different **treatments** (or **therapeutic strategies**).

● The **biological (medical) model** claims that mental disorders should be viewed as disease or illness. This approach proposes four possible causes of mental illness: brain damage, infection, biochemical imbalance and genetic predisposition. Since mental problems are viewed as physical illnesses, it follows that they are best treated by physical means. These include: **drug treatments** (chemotherapy); **electro-convulsive therapy** (ECT) and **psychosurgery** (brain surgery).

● An advantage of the biological approach includes the increased knowledge gained from research into the possible biological factors underlying psychological disorders and the treatments that have resulted. However, disadvantages include side effects of and dependency upon drugs, as well as the stigma endured by those who have been medically diagnosed as abnormal.

● The **psychodynamic model** states that unconscious psychological forces cause abnormal behaviour. According to **Freud**, psychological disturbance occurs when the **ego** (the rational part of the psyche) fails to manage the conflict between the **id** (the insatiable set of instincts with which we are born) and the **superego** (the moral part of the psyche concerned with right and wrong). Such conflicts are most marked in early childhood when the ego is less developed. To balance the demands of the id and the superego, **defence mechanisms** (such as repression) are used, but these do not provide permanent solutions and may themselves create psychological problems. Treatments aim to uncover **unconscious psychological processes** in order to facilitate insight into the conflicts and anxieties causing the abnormal behaviour.

● The psychodynamic model has been influential but has also received much criticism. It is difficult to test scientifically and is accused of being deterministic. Critics also claim that treatments are often expensive, time-consuming and ineffective.

● The **behavioural model** views abnormal behaviours as maladaptive, learned responses, acquired through conditioning and social learning processes. If maladaptive behaviours are learned, then they can be replaced by other learned, adaptive behaviours. Main techniques include **systematic desensitization**, **aversion therapy** and the use of **token economies** to reward desired behaviour.

- The behavioural model avoids labelling a person as abnormal; it focuses upon behaviour (which is seen as changeable) rather than the person. However, the model is accused of ignoring the possible underlying causes of abnormal behaviour. Other criticisms are that it is reductionist and its treatments have sometimes been imposed on people without their consent.

- The **cognitive model** of abnormality assumes that emotional problems are caused by distortions in thinking processes, such as negative thoughts and irrational beliefs. According to **Ellis** we can become habituated to irrational thinking and then may tend to exaggerate the negative aspects of events. **Beck** identified the cognitive triad (three forms of negative thinking) that he claimed underlie depression: negative views about oneself, about the world and about the future. Cognitive therapy aims to help people examine their irrational thoughts and replace them with more **positive, adaptive ways of thinking**.

- One criticism of the cognitive model is that it does not address the origins of irrational thought processes. The model has been accused of underestimating the role of social conditions in the development and maintenance of psychological disorders because it places responsibility for psychological abnormality firmly within the individual.

Topic 3: Critical issue – eating disorders

- **Eating disorders**, such as **anorexia nervosa** and **bulimia nervosa**, have very serious consequences for physical health and so it is important to understand the causes of these disorders. Anorexia is characterised by the pursuit of extreme thinness and by an extreme loss of weight. Bulimia is characterised by secret binge eating followed by purging behaviours such as vomiting, misuse of laxatives and excessive exercise in order to lose weight.

- Research into **biological explanations** has found no links with disease. Biochemical dysfunction is more likely to be a consequence of the disorder, rather than the cause. Genetic links have been investigated by looking at concordance rates among family members including twins. Support for a genetic basis is considered weak and difficult to prove, because members of a family tend to share the same environment.

- **Behavioural explanations**: eating disorders originate when a person goes on a diet and is complimented (reinforced) for being slim. This results in the person associating thinness with feeling good about themselves. Operant conditioning has been helpful in promoting weight gain among some anorexia sufferers, but the approach fails to address the underlying problems of depression and loss of control.

- **Cognitive explanations** point to the irrational beliefs that some people hold that they will not be valued unless they achieve some ideal body shape. However, the approach does not explain how these irrational beliefs come about in the first place.

- **Psychodynamic explanations**: anorexia is viewed as a way of repressing sexual impulses or as a means by which women can remain children and so avoid adult responsibilities. Psychotherapy studies have also found that women who have experienced childhood sexual abuse are more likely to develop bulimia nervosa. However, data collected from recollections about childhood can be unreliable.

- Other psychological explanations for eating disorders include low self-esteem, struggling for a sense of identity, pressure to succeed and family conflict.

Answering exam questions on Abnormality

For sample examination questions and answers on Abnormality, together with examiner comments on the answers, see pp. 257–9.

5
UNIT

SOCIAL
Influence

PREVIEW

After you have read this unit, you should be able to:

>> explain why people yield to majority and minority influence, and discuss research in these areas

>> explain why people obey and how people might resist obedience

>> discuss research into obedience to authority and the issues of experimental and ecological validity associated with research in this area

>> discuss the ethical issues concerned with deception, informed consent and the protection of participants from psychological harm, particularly as these relate to research on social influence

>> discuss the ways in which psychologists try to deal with these ethical issues.

INTRODUCTION

Social influence is the process by which an individual's attitudes, beliefs or behaviours are modified by the presence or actions of others. Some forms of social influence, such as when a teacher insists that you hand in work on time, are obvious (though not always successful). Other types of social influence are more subtle, sometimes unintended and, on occasions, even unnoticed by those who are influenced.

In Topic 1, we will look at the topics of conformity (majority influence) and minority influence. Then, in Topic 2, we will explore the research studies of obedience, one of the most challenging and controversial topics in social psychology. Not only are the results of such studies unsettling, but the methods used by those who have researched this area (e.g. Stanley Milgram) have come in for much criticism. Consequently, in Topic 3, we will look at some of the ethical issues that have arisen in psychological investigations and particularly those that are evident in social influence research.

KEY TERMS

Social influence: the process by which a person's attitudes, beliefs or behaviours are modified by the presence or actions of others. There are two types of social influence that lead people to conform: normative social influence (based on our desire to be liked) and informational social influence (based on our desire to be right).

Conformity/majority influence: a form of social influence where people adopt the behaviours, attitudes and values of other members of a reference group.

Minority influence: a form of social influence where a persuasive minority exerts pressure to change the attitudes, beliefs or behaviours of the majority. Minorities are most influential when they appear consistent and principled.

Claire
Meldrum

GETTING YOU THINKING...

1 What do these photos tell us about conformity?

2 To what extent do you think that the people in the second photo are displaying anticonformity? To what extent are they actually conforming?

3 Do you think that the people in the second photo are more or less aware that they are conforming, compared with those in the top photo?

4 To what extent do *you* conform? What do you conform to?

CONFORMITY

Conformity is the process of yielding to majority influence and is defined by David Myers (1999) as "a change in behaviour or belief as a result of real or imagined group pressure". Zimbardo *et al.* (1995) defined it as a "tendency for people to adopt the behaviour, attitudes and values of other members of a reference group". You may find it easier to identify with Myers' definition because it focuses upon the kind of experience most of us have had at one time or another: the feeling that others are putting pressure on us to change our minds or behaviour. However, the Zimbardo definition proposes that when we are evaluating our status, we tend to go along with those people with

whom we compare ourselves (i.e. our reference groups). If you accept that the process of conformity can occur without your being aware of it, then you may prefer the wording of the Zimbardo definition.

Although most people think of themselves as autonomous individuals, they nevertheless tend to go along with (conform to) the social norms (rules and expectations) that their groups and societies have evolved. The social norms that indicate how we ought to behave may be explicit (such as a 'No Smoking' sign in a restaurant) or they may be implicit (such as the unspoken but well-understood norm in the UK of not standing too close to strangers).

The pressure to conform

1 Think of an occasion when you have felt under pressure to behave in a particular way because of group pressure. How did you behave? What was it about the situation that caused you to conform? In what kinds of situation do you feel under pressure to conform?

2 Was the group pressure to behave in a particular way *real* (i.e. those around you were actually telling you how you must behave) or was it *imagined* (i.e. you felt you ought to behave in a particular way in order to be seen to 'go along' with your friends, your family or a group of peers)?

3 How did it make you feel?

4 Are there situations in everyday life when it is perhaps desirable to conform, or is conforming behaviour inherently bad? What are the dangers, if any, of being overly conformist?

TYPES OF CONFORMITY

As long ago as 1958, Kelman identified three types of conformity (that is, three responses to social influence):

● *Compliance* – publicly conforming to the behaviour or views of others but privately maintaining one's own views. For example, if you are with a group of friends who support a particular football team, you might not reveal that you support a different one, even if asked directly.

● *Identification* – adopting the views or behaviour of a group both publicly and privately because you value membership of that group. However, the new attitudes and behaviours are often temporary and not maintained on leaving the group. For example, when young people move away from home to go to college, they may begin to question the lifestyles they had previously taken for granted. New students often enthusiastically adopt the dress and behaviour codes of their new student groups. However, on graduating and moving into employment, they often change the way they dress and behave again.

● *Internalization* – a conversion, or true change of private views to match those of the group. What distinguishes this type of conformity from identification is that the new attitudes and behaviours have become part of your value system; they are not dependent on the presence of the group. For example, a person searching for some greater meaning to life may be influenced to convert to a religious faith if the members of that faith seem able to provide the answers being searched for. A true conversion will survive even if the person loses contact with those who influenced them originally.

Resisting majority influence

There are occasions, however, when people appear not to conform. There are at least two ways of explaining their behaviour:

● *Independence* – being unresponsive to the norms of the group, such as a student who ignores the dress norms of her fellow students and dresses only to please herself. Note that sometimes this student might dress like her friends if their dress sense happened to coincide with hers. She is not reacting against their code; she is just unaffected by it and is, therefore, truly independent.

● *Anticonformity* – consistently opposing the norms of the group. Anticonforming behaviour is quite common, such as deliberately choosing to dress or wear your hair in a way that is different from others. It may seem paradoxical, but anticonformity is, in fact, a type of conformity as it is determined by the norms of the group; if the group favours long hair, anticonformists will wear theirs cut short; if the group decides that short hair is cool, anticonformists will wear theirs long.

Singer and DJ, Boy George – an example of independence or anticonformity?

ACTIVITY

Types of conformity and non-conformity

Look back at the two photos in 'Getting you thinking...' on p. 155. For each one, decide whether it is an example of compliance, identification, internalization, independence or anticonformity.

What about the singer and DJ Boy George, shown opposite? Make a note of your reasons.

WHY DO PEOPLE CONFORM?

According to Deutsch and Gerard (1955), there are two types of social influence that lead people to conform:

- *Normative social influence* – based on our desire to be liked. We conform because we think that others will approve of and accept us. The conformity that results from this desire to be liked is often called compliance, that is, publicly going along with the majority but privately holding to one's own views (see p. 156)

- *Informational social influence* – based on our desire to be right. We look to others whom we believe to be correct, to give us information about how to behave, particularly in novel or ambiguous situations. Informational social influence may be particularly strong when we move from one group to another. For example, young people moving from school to university might redefine themselves as students (no longer pupils) and look to other students to learn what are acceptable ways of behaving (the norms) in this new situation. Informational social influence can sometimes lead to a genuine and long-lasting change of belief or attitude, called internalization (see p. 156)

Deutsch and Gerard's explanation of conformity is called the dual process model because it offers two explanations as to why people yield to majority influence. It is sometimes criticized for implying that

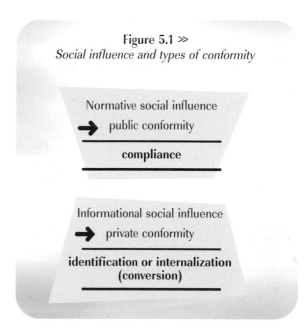

Figure 5.1 >>
Social influence and types of conformity

the two types of social influence are separate and independent. Instead, Insko *et al.* (1983) claimed that normative and informational influence often work together to affect levels of conformity.

ACTIVITY

Types and effectiveness of social influence attempts

1 Prepare two lists. In List A, write down at least two examples of situations where others have tried to influence your behaviour (e.g. parents trying to persuade you to stay in and work instead of going out with friends). For each example, note down the type of influence that was used (e.g. how your parent tried to persuade you). Which attempts were more successful and which ones were less successful or unsuccessful?

2 In List B, write down at least two examples of situations where those being influenced are unaware of what is happening. Under what circumstances do you feel that people might be influenced without realizing it?

3 Why do you think that some attempts at social influence succeed and others fail? Consider a range of factors, including: (a) the person(s) doing the influencing (b) the person who is being influenced (c) the circumstances that exist at the time.

4 When are people best able to resist attempts to influence their behaviour?

RESEARCH INTO CONFORMITY

Many psychologists have attempted to answer the question "Why do people conform?" by conducting research studies aimed at teasing out the different factors that cause people to yield to majority social influence.

Asch's original study (1951)

Asch (1951) wondered what would happen if participants were exposed to normative social influence in a group situation where there could be no doubt about the correct answer to a question. How many participants would conform to the group, deny the evidence of their own eyes and give the wrong answer when it was their turn?

Complete the activity on the right now.

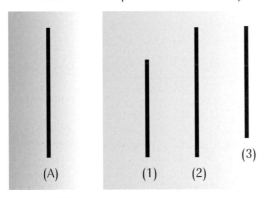

Figure 5.2 >> *A sample of the stimulus material used in Asch's experiments on conformity*

Standard line   *Comparison lines*

ACTIVITY

Identifying weaknesses of Asch's study of conformity

1 Read the key study, *Majority influence*, up to and including the Conclusions. Do not read the Criticisms. Note down any criticisms that you can identify in relation to:

   – the sample he studied

   – the time and place of the study.

2 Compare your thoughts with the criticisms at the end of the key study. When reading any research study, it is important to get into the habit of trying to identify any weaknesses. This will help you to develop your evaluation skills (referred to as AO2 skills – see p. 247).

The set-up in Asch's studies, in which a minority of one (answering last but one) faces pressure to conform to an otherwise unanimous majority

In addition to the specific criticisms made of Asch's study, he is also sometimes criticized for implying that conforming behaviour is 'bad' and that resisting (not yielding) to majority influence is somehow always good. Clearly, there are dangers involved if people are too conformist. Nevertheless, without widespread conformity, society could not function effectively. Conformity to prosocial norms, such as helping others in distress, is obviously highly desirable.

Extensions to Asch's research

In order to find out exactly which features of a situation made it more likely that someone would conform,

Asch varied some of the situational factors in his original study. He introduced the following changes and observed the effects:

● *A non-unanimous majority* – Asch found that levels of conformity dropped dramatically (to only 5 per cent) when just one other participant dissented from the majority and supported the naive participant. A majority of three with no other dissenters was more effective in producing conformity than a majority of eight with one other dissenter.

● *The size of the majority* – When the majority consisted of only two people, conformity responses in naive participants dropped to 12.8 per cent of their

study of conformity by Asch (1951)

Aim >>

To see if participants would yield (conform) to majority social influence and give incorrect answers in a situation where the correct answers were always obvious.

Procedures >>

- Seven male, student participants looked at two cards: the test card showed one vertical line; the other card showed three vertical lines of different length.
- The participants' task was to call out, in turn, which of the three lines was the same length as the test line. The correct answer was always obvious (see Fig. 5.2).
- All participants, except one, were accomplices of the experimenter. The genuine participant called out his answer last but one.
- Accomplices gave unanimous wrong answers on 12 of the 18 trials. These 12 trials were called the critical trials.
- In total, Asch used 50 male college students as naive, genuine participants in this first study.

Findings >>

- Participants conformed to the unanimous incorrect answer on 32 per cent of the critical trials. This might not strike you as a very high figure but remember that the correct answer was always obvious.
- 74 per cent of participants conformed at least once.
- 26 per cent of participants never conformed. Some of these 'independent' participants were confident in their judgements. More often, however, they experienced tension and doubt but managed to resist the pressure exerted by the unanimous majority.
- During post-experimental interviews, some conforming participants claimed to have actually *seen* the line identified by the majority as the correct answer. Others yielded because they could not bear to be in a minority of one and risk being ridiculed or excluded by the group. Most participants who had conformed, however, experienced a distortion of judgement: they thought that their perception of the lines must be inaccurate and for that reason they yielded to the majority view.

Conclusions >>

- Even in unambiguous situations, there may be strong group pressure to conform, especially if the group is a unanimous majority.
- However, after interviewing his participants, Asch concluded that people go along with the views of others for different reasons. Some people experience normative social influence and feel compelled to accept the mistaken majority's norms or standards of behaviour to avoid being rejected. Others experience informational pressures and doubt their own judgements – "Surely they can't all be wrong!"

Criticisms >>

- All the participants were male college students and so a very limited sample.
- The time and place when the research was carried out might have affected the findings. In the 1950s the USA was very conservative, involved in an anticommunist witchhunt against anyone who was thought to hold left-wing views (this became known as 'McCarthyism', named after the senator who spearheaded the witchhunt) and its educational institutions were more hierarchical than they are today.

AO2 check Since all the participants were male and college students, it might not be valid to generalize the findings to a wider population. The way to check this is to rerun the study using different types of participants. Do you think that male college students are typical, or more or less conformist than the general population?

total judgements. Optimum conformity effects (32 per cent of responses) were found with a majority of three. Increasing the size of the majority beyond three did not increase the levels of conformity found. Some psychologists have suggested that people may suspect collusion if the majority rises beyond three or four. When only one confederate (accomplice) was used, no conformity effects were found.

● *Losing a partner* – The naive participant started with a 'partner' who responded correctly to begin with but who 'deserted' to the majority in the middle of the procedure. This resulted in conformity levels of 28.5 per cent on critical judgements.

● *Gaining a partner* – When a participant who had started the procedure as a minority of one received a 'partner' part way through, this reduced conformity responses to 8.7 per cent.

● *The nature of the task* – The levels of conformity increased (see also Crutchfield's results in the next section) as tasks were made more difficult.

● *Mode of response* – When Asch asked his participants to write their answers rather than call them out loud, conformity levels dropped sharply. This illustrates the difference between public compliance (overtly adhering to social norms) and private acceptance (actually thinking as others do).

Table 5.1 >> Factors affecting conformity levels

Factors increasing conformity levels	Factors decreasing conformity levels
>> Unanimous majority	>> Non-unanimous majority
>> Difficult task	>> Majority of only two people
>> Being deserted by a partner who had previously given correct answers	>> Writing responses rather than calling them aloud (i.e. private rather than public responding)

FURTHER RESEARCH ON CONFORMITY

Although many criticisms have been made of Asch's findings (see key study on p. 159), one of the strengths of his work is the amount of subsequent research it generated.

When participants can't see each other

Crutchfield (1955) thought that the face-to-face arrangement of participants in the Asch procedure might be responsible for the levels of conformity found. Therefore, he arranged his participants in booths out of sight of each other, but all able to see the stimulus cards (see Fig. 5.3). This enabled him to collect data more economically by running several naive participants at the same time. Participants sat individually in booths with a row of switches and lights in front of them. They had to press the switch that corresponded to their judgement when their turn came to answer. They were told that the lights on the display panel showed the responses of the other participants. In fact, the experimenter controlled these lights and each participant saw an identical display. Despite the absence of an actual face-to-face group, Crutchfield found the following:

● Conformity levels were 30 per cent when using Asch's line comparison tasks.

● When the task was made more difficult, conformity increased.

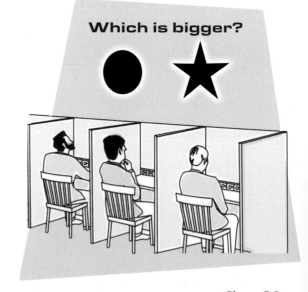

Figure 5.3 >>
Crutchfield's conformity-testing procedure: people sit in adjacent booths and answer questions shown on the wall in front of them after being told of other people's apparent responses

Research into individual differences

Crutchfield was also interested in individual differences and how these might affect conformity. He found that participants with high scores in intelligence and leadership ability displayed less conformity. However, there has been a lack of evidence subsequently to support any idea of a 'conforming personality'. Crutchfield's studies can also be criticized for their artificial setting. The findings do, however, support those of Asch, suggesting that conformity pressures operate on people other than students.

Furman and Duke (1988) looked at how lack of confidence might make people more likely to conform. They asked students to listen to two versions of each of ten musical excerpts. On their degree programme the students were majoring either in music or in another subject. Each student, on their own, selected a preferred version for each of the ten pairs. They were then individually tested in the presence of three confederates who unanimously stated a verbal preference from each pair of excerpts. Their findings were as follows:

- Music majors were not influenced to change their already stated preferences.
- However, the publicly stated preferences of non-music majors were significantly affected by the preferences of the confederates.

Research into historical and cultural contexts

Some observers have suggested that Asch's findings tell us more about the historical and cultural climate of the USA in 1951 than they do about fundamental psychological tendencies. Some more recent studies of conformity have failed to confirm Asch's findings:

- Perrin and Spencer (1980) replicated Asch's procedure, using 33 British students. They found only one conforming response in 396 trials. They concluded that cultural changes over 30 years had led to a reduction in the tendency of students to conform. Another factor that might have influenced the results is the type of students used. They were drawn from engineering, chemistry and mathematics courses, and it is possible that the knowledge and skills acquired in their courses had equipped them to resist conformity pressures during a task of this sort. Another study by Perrin and Spencer (1981) using youths on probation as participants and using probation officers as the confederates demonstrated levels of conformity similar to those found by Asch in 1952. The researchers concluded that where the perceived costs for people of not yielding were high, conformity effects would still be demonstrated.

- Nicholson *et al.* (1985) compared conformity levels in British and in American students using the Asch procedure. They found no significant differences between the two groups, suggesting some similarity in British and US student cultures, at least at that point in history. The students in 1985 were found to be significantly less conformist than their 1951 American counterparts but more conformist than the British students in 1981. Nicholson and colleagues have suggested that the experience of the Falklands War (when Britain went to war with Argentina over the occupancy of the Falkland Islands) might have contributed to group cohesiveness and, in turn, to a higher degree of conformity. (The war took place in 1982, between the collection of Perrin and Spencer's data and the collection of their own data.)

ACTIVITY

Conformity and war

Look at the two photos below: one of a woman buying food using government-issued ration coupons, the other of Londoners taking shelter in Picadilly Underground station during the London Blitz of the 1940s. Why might people be more likely to conform during times of war?

- Finally, Smith and Bond (1998) reviewed 31 studies of conformity conducted in different cultures using Asch's procedures. They concluded that people in collectivistic cultures show higher levels of conformity compared with those who live in individualistic cultures. In collectivistic cultures, people emphasize loyalty to the group and being concerned about the needs and interests of others. Group decision-making is preferred to individual decisions. In individualistic cultures, people are more concerned with their own and their family's self-interest, and individual initiatives are valued.

Zimbardo's prison simulation study (1973)

Philip Zimbardo and colleagues conducted one of the best-known and most controversial studies in psychology. They looked at how people conform to the expectations they have about social roles. He used a simulated prison set-up to see to what extent normal, well-balanced people would conform to new social roles. For example, Zimbardo wondered whether participants who were assigned the role of guards would act in a way that conformed to their stereotyped view of how prison guards should behave. (In a simulation, participants are asked to act (role-play) as though the simulation is real. Simulations are used to study behaviours to which psychologists would not normally have access.)

According to Zimbardo, his results demonstrate how easily people can come to behave in uncharacteristic ways when placed in new situations and given new roles. Another possible explanation is that the volunteers might have tried to be 'good subjects' and behaved in the ways they thought the researcher wanted (called demand characteristics).

Ethical issues in Zimbardo's prison study are discussed further on p. 186.

MINORITY SOCIAL INFLUENCE

Minority influence is a form of social influence where a persuasive minority exerts pressure to change the attitudes, beliefs or behaviours of the majority. If people simply went along with the majority all the time and minority viewpoints never prevailed, there would be no change, no innovation. There are, of course, many instances where small minorities – or even lone dissenters – have influenced majority opinion. Nemeth (1986) believes that even when minorities are wrong, their views can stimulate productive thinking. Small minority groups may be dismissed initially by the majority as eccentrics or extremists. However, under certain circumstances and over a period of time, these small groups or even individuals can eventually become very influential. The dissociation model (see p. 166) offers one explanation for the slowness of minority influence.

Moscovici's (1969) 'blue–green' slide study

Moscovici and colleagues carried out one of the best-known studies of minority influence and one that led to a great deal of subsequent research. They asked six participants to estimate the colour of 36 slides. All the slides were blue but adding filters varied their brightness (see key study, *Minority influence*, on p. 164). Clearly, consistency on the part of the minority is important. Although the levels of yielding found in the consistent condition are nothing like as high as those found by Asch in his studies of majority influence, they do indicate that minorities can exert some degree of influence, even when yielding is measured publicly and immediately after the influence attempts. Furthermore, minorities may be even more influential with the passage of time provided they adopt the appropriate style of behaviour.

ACTIVITY

The ethics of the study by Moscovici and colleagues

Reread the key study on p. 164, this time thinking about the ethics of the experiment. For example, how do you think that the participants might have felt when they were told about the true purpose of the study?

Behavioural styles of minorities

Following many investigations, Moscovici (1985) identified the behavioural styles that minorities must possess if they are to exert social influence on majorities:

- They must be consistent in their opposition to the majority. Consistency, according to Moscovici, comprises "resolution, certainty, clarity of definition, and coherence". Consistency is generally recognized as the single most important factor for a minority to be influential.
- They must not appear dogmatic by rigidly reiterating the same arguments. They need to demonstrate a degree of flexibility.

Others psychologists (e.g. Hogg and Vaughan 1998) have also claimed that minorities are more likely to be influential if they:

- appear to be acting from principle (not out of self-interest)
- are seen to have made sacrifices in order to maintain their position

AS Social Psychology

Stanford prison simulation study by Zimbardo *et al.* (1973)

Aim >>

To investigate how readily people would conform to new roles by observing how quickly people would adopt the roles of guard or prisoner in a role-playing exercise that simulated prison life. Zimbardo was interested in finding out whether the brutality reported among guards in American prisons was due to the sadistic personalities of the guards or had more to do with the prison environment.

Procedures >>

- Well-adjusted, healthy male volunteers were paid $15 a day to take part in a two-week simulation study of prison life.
- Volunteers were randomly allocated to the roles of prisoners or guards.
- Local police helped by 'arresting' nine prisoners at their homes, without warning. They were taken, blindfolded, to the 'prison' (actually the basement of Stanford University), stripped, sprayed with disinfectant, given smocks to wear and their prison number to memorize. From then on they were referred to by number only.
- There were three guards, who wore khaki uniforms, dark glasses and carried wooden batons.
- No physical aggression was permitted.

Findings >>

- The guards, who were permitted to devise most of the rules, harassed the prisoners and conformed to their perceived roles with such zeal that the study had to be discontinued after six days.
- Prisoners rebelled against the guards after only two days. Guards quelled the rebellion using fire extinguishers.
- Some prisoners became depressed and anxious; one prisoner had to be released after only one day. Two more prisoners had to be released on the fourth day.

Conclusions >>

- The 'prison environment' was an important factor in creating the guards' brutal behaviour (none of the participants who acted as guards had shown sadistic tendencies before the study).
- People will readily conform to the social roles they are expected to play, especially if the roles are as strongly stereotyped as those of prison guards.
- The roles that people play shape their attitudes and behaviour. If it took only six days to alter the behaviour of the participants in this study, then the roles we play in real life will have even more far-reaching effects.

Criticisms >>

- The study has received many ethical criticisms, including those about lack of fully informed consent by participants and the humiliation and distress experienced by those who acted as prisoners.
- Zimbardo was wrong to act as both prison-superintendent and chief researcher as this produced a conflict of roles whereby he lost sight of the harm being done to the participants.

Participants did not know, for example, that they would be arrested at home. Zimbardo thought, however, that withholding this type of procedural detail was justifiable given the nature of the study. Those acting as guards had to face up to the unpalatable fact that they had been willing to mistreat their prisoners. They, as well as the 'prisoners', might have suffered psychological harm. However, Zimbardo's follow-up interviews with participants found no lasting negative effects.

Unit 5 // Social Influence

experiment by Moscovici *et al.* (1969)

Aim >>

To see whether a consistent minority of participants could influence a majority to give an incorrect answer in a colour perception task.

Procedures >>

- 172 participants in total were involved. All had good eyesight.
- Six participants at a time were asked to estimate the colour of 36 slides.
- All the slides were blue, but of differing brightness.
- Two of the six participants were accomplices of the experimenter.
- There were **two conditions:**
  - **consistent:** the two accomplices called the slides green on all trials
  - **inconsistent:** the two accomplices called the slides green 24 times, and blue 12 times.

Findings >>

- Participants in the consistent condition yielded and called the slides green in 8.4 per cent of the trials.
- 32 per cent of participants in the consistent condition reported a green slide at least once.
- Participants in the inconsistent condition yielded and called the slides green in only 1.3 per cent of the trials.

Conclusions >>

- It is important that those in a minority behave consistently if they are to influence a majority to change its viewpoint.
- Individual members of a minority must maintain a consistent viewpoint and there needs to be agreement among the different members of the minority group.
- Inconsistent minorities lack any real influence on majorities. Their opinions are viewed as groundless.

Criticisms >>

- The artificiality of the laboratory setting is unlike real-life situations where minorities such as pressure groups exert their influence on the prevailing majority opinion.
- Later research, using similar procedures, found that consistency alone was not sufficient to ensure minority influence. Minorities must also avoid appearing rigidly inflexible.

A Suffragette march in the early 1900s (below) and a gay rights parade (right). How can these situations be seen as minority social influence?

- are seen as similar to the majority in terms of class, age and gender
- advocate views that are consistent with current social trends (e.g. as our society becomes more concerned with environmental issues, so the views of certain minority groups, once derided, attract a wider audience and become more persuasive).

Clark's (1994) *Twelve Angry Men* study

Clark carried out an unusual experiment to see what aspects of minority influence had the greatest effects on an individual's views. He asked 270 college students to role-play the part of jurors and read a summary of a court case presented in the film *Twelve Angry Men*. The students, who were unfamiliar with the film, had to decide whether or not the accused was guilty.

Clark gave his participants a summary of a murder case and of the jury's discussions about key pieces of evidence. The persuasiveness of the arguments and the views of the jury were manipulated. The participants were asked their views about the guilt of the defendant at various stages. Clark found that participants were most persuaded when they heard consistent persuasive arguments from the minority jury members and when they learned that more than one juror had defected

from the majority position. He concluded that it was a combination of convincing arguments and a shift by other majority members that resulted in the minority exerting the greatest influence.

In the film, Twelve Angry Men, *Henry Fonda played a member of a jury in the trial of a young man accused of stabbing his father to death. At the start, Fonda's character alone held to the belief that the man was innocent. Gradually, by sticking to his guns, he persuaded his fellow jurors to re-examine the evidence. Eventually he succeeded in persuading the other jurors to change their minds and the innocent young man was found not guilty.*

ACTIVITY

Do minorities really exert influence on jury decision-making?

Read the accounts of the Tanford and Penrod experiment, and the Chicago Jury Project. Then answer the following questions:

1 To what extent do these studies reflect the outcome of *Twelve Angry Men*?

2 Do these laboratory studies of juries' behaviour resemble what happens in real juries?

The Chicago Jury Project (Kalven and Zeisel 1966) interviewed jurors and used tape recordings of actual jury deliberations. Although the real juries studied in this project differed in some respects from the experimental juries used by Tanford and Penrod, there were similar findings concerning the lack of influence by minority jurors. In only 5 per cent of the cases did an initial minority prevail and then only if the minority began with at least three members of the jury.

This does not mean that an articulate and determined person who holds a minority viewpoint can never persuade others to change their minds. However, the dramatic example of the Henry Fonda character in the film *Twelve Angry Men*, in which one courageous, lone juror sways the majority by his intelligent questioning, is almost absent from the historical record.

Tanford and Penrod (1986) designed an experiment where six-person juries watched videotapes of a trial being re-enacted. The jurors voted immediately after the trial before any discussion, and then after they had talked about it. Results showed that after the discussion:

- The view first held by the majority always prevailed if initially only one person disagreed. This evidence is similar to the results that Asch found when he investigated majority influence. Therefore, it would appear from this study that when people are discussing serious issues, it is majorities, not minorities, that are influential.
- In only 7 per cent of cases did an initial minority of more than one manage to persuade the majority to change its verdict.

WHY DO PEOPLE YIELD TO MINORITY INFLUENCE?

The following explanations have been proposed for minority influence.

Consistency

There are two types of consistency:

● *intra-individual* – where a person maintains a consistent position over time
● *inter-individual* – where there is agreement among members of the minority group.

If members of a minority fail to demonstrate either of these forms of consistency, the majority is unlikely to pay them much attention. However, a consistent minority punctures any illusion of unanimity among the majority and so it becomes easier for majority members to express any doubts they may have.

The snowball effect

The term 'snowball effect' (Van Avermaet 1996) is used to describe what sometimes happens in minority influence. Once a few members of the majority start to move towards the minority position, then the influence of the minority begins to gather momentum as more people gradually pay attention to the potential correctness of the minority view. Recall what Clark (1994) found in his jury study: once a few people had begun to defect from the majority viewpoint, the student participants were increasingly influenced by the minority arguments to find the defendant not guilty.

Group membership

According to Hogg and Vaughan (1998), we are most likely to be influenced by those we perceive to be like us (called our in-group). For example, the attitudes of straight men towards gay men are more likely to become more liberal if other straight men (the in-group) express liberal attitudes than if only gay men (the out-group) express such attitudes. However, even within an in-group, minority influence works slowly. The dissociation model provides one reason for this.

The dissociation model

Mugny and Perez (1991) propose that minority groups influence majority group members through a process called social cryptoamnesia, meaning that minority ideas are assimilated into the majority viewpoint without those in the majority remembering where the ideas came from. In other words, the content and the source become dissociated. According to this model, minority ideas are so strongly associated with their source that to adopt the message risks assuming the negative identity of the source. If, on the other hand, the ideas can be dissociated from their source, the majority can resist overt identification with an out-group while still drawing inspiration from their ideas.

This may account for why the conversion effect (outlined by Moscovici) generated by minority groups is often delayed. The process of assimilating ideas is slow because initially they have been resisted vigorously, purely because of their source. Over time, the ideas become detached from their source and begin to reappear in the individual's mind as their own.

The dissociation model does not lend itself to experimental testing, but it does provide an appealing explanation as to how dominant ideas or trends within a culture (*zeitgeists*) can be launched by minority groups despite the strong resistance they encounter from majority positions.

Differences between majority and minority social influence

Different processes

According to Moscovici (1980) majorities and minorities achieve influence through different processes. Majority influence, he claimed, involves public compliance (rather than private acceptance) where the person is more concerned with how they appear in front of others than with the issue itself. The majority, therefore, exerts normative social influence (as seen in Asch's experiments) to exact compliance from the minority.

By contrast, minorities use informational social influence to persuade those in the majority to change their views. Minorities are aiming for conversion rather than compliance. They hope that by focusing on the issue, the majority will come to examine the arguments proposed by the minority. In turn, this may start the process of conversion whereby, at least in private, attitudes genuinely begin to shift.

Instant vs delayed effects

Majority social influence may produce instant effects where people conform rather than appear foolish or risk rejection. However, there is no such risk in the case of minority influence. After all, who cares what a small minority thinks and, furthermore, minorities are often ridiculed for their unpopular positions. In fact, many people holding mainstream views would wish to avoid being associated with oddball minorities (see 'The dissociation model', left). Nevertheless, by using informational social influence, a consistent minority may plant the seed of doubt in the mind of someone holding a majority viewpoint. Over time, that doubt may lead to a change of view, albeit delayed, especially if others from the majority are seen to be wavering or converting to the minority position.

Minority *influence*

Charlan Nemeth is a Professor of Psychology at the University of California at Berkeley and received her PhD in Social Psychology at Cornell University. Professor Nemeth has written and spoken extensively on the positive contribution of dissent within groups and its role in creativity. These research interests have many applied aspects, including jury deliberations, innovation in organizations, and the value of diversity.

Q What do you consider to be the main lessons learned from minority influence research?

A First, I think the research shows us that people holding minority viewpoints are not just passive recipients of influence. Their choices are not simply to conform or to be independent (or to be silent). They can actively promote a differing viewpoint and they can prevail. The important ingredient is that they need to be consistent in their position. If they capitulate to the majority, they tend not to exert influence. Second, we need to realize that, even with consistency and commitment, minority views do not often prevail. And - regardless of whether they prevail or not - the person holding the minority (dissenting) viewpoint is often disliked, seen as incompetent and rejected. Third - and I think this is the most important lesson from my own work over the past 25 years - we profit from minority views. Even when they are wrong and even though we find them to be incompetent or even immoral, exposure to dissenting minority views stimulates us to be better decision-makers and more creative in our thought. We search for more information on all sides of the issue; we consider more alternatives in our problem-solving and decision-making; and our thinking is even more creative. Thus, we should learn to "welcome and not fear the voices of dissent".

Charlan Nemeth

Q Is minority influence potentially more powerful than majority influence?

A Yes, but not in terms of direct influence, but rather in terms of indirect influence and the stimulation of thought. Majorities have much more power when it comes to 'winning'. Many people will adopt the majority opinion because they assume that the majority is right and, further, they don't want to incur the rejection that maintaining a minority viewpoint brings. Thus, you will find that people will conform to error, even on issues that have an objectively clear and correct answer, when a majority takes that erroneous position. This is far less likely when we are faced with a minority viewpoint. However, the minority's power comes from our reflection on

the issue after the confrontation. Sometimes, we change our opinions to that held by the minority - but we do it in private, or later, or on related topics. Often, we think differently about the issue as a result of exposure to that minority view and, in general, we think more broadly, more deeply and come up with better judgements and decisions.

Q How successfully do the insights from minority influence research extend beyond the laboratory?

A I will give you two examples, as these are areas in which I have taught and published related work. One is the law, especially trial by jury. As you know, juries are lay people who decide on conviction as a group. The important issue here is NOT who wins (the majority or the minority position) but, rather, how do we best achieve the 'truth'. How do we serve the aims of justice? Given that minority viewpoints stimulate better decision-making (but are often not given credit for such stimulation and, in fact, are derided), they need to be protected. We have substantial research showing that a requirement of unanimity (rather than some form of majority rule) provides some protection. It increases the likelihood that the minority views will be expressed and maintained and, further, it increases the perception of justice.

A second example, one that I teach executives in Business Schools, is that flexibility and innovation are indispensable elements in a global economy and that, in this context, dissent should be protected and valued. Many times, executives would rather learn how to get power and keep it, how to get their employees to do their bidding and 'like it'. If they want people to implement their ideas, that is fine. However, if they want an organization which anticipates changes in products or the marketplace, if they want one that is flexible and able to innovate, they must harness the power of dissenting views for the stimulation of thought that this provides.

And finally, perhaps the best application of all is the value of dissent for democracies. As John Stuart Mill noted, diversity, variety and choice, the allowance of refutation and the airing of differing views are great strengths of democracies. They serve as a safeguard against tyranny but, importantly, they serve the detection of truth and the vitality of our beliefs.

Expert interview: Charlan Nemeth

This activity aims to boost your all-important AO2 evaluative skills. Using the material from the Charlan Nemeth interview on p. 167 and other material on minority influence, complete the following sentences. Using lead-in phrases such as these will help you to focus on what is AO2 material and will make your intentions explicit to the examiner.

- "Nemeth believes a particular important lesson from minority influence research is ..."
- "Minority influence has the potential to be more powerful than majority influence because ..."
- "However, studies of jury decision-making ..."
- "An important application of minority influence research is ..."
- "This is particularly important because ..."

✓ CHECK YOUR UNDERSTANDING

Check your understanding of conformity and minority influence by answering these questions. Try to do this from memory at first. You can check your answers by looking back through Topic 1.

1 What do you understand by the terms: 'social influence', 'conformity' and 'minority influence'?

2 Give two reasons why people conform.

3 Explain the difference between compliance, identification and internalization.

4 Give the main findings and the main conclusions of Asch's study of conformity.

5 How did the results found by Perrin and Spencer in Britain in 1981 differ from those found by Asch in 1951? What explanation did Perrin and Spencer offer for this?

6 In what ways did the participants in Zimbardo's prison simulation study demonstrate conformity?

7 Give two explanations for people yielding to minority influence.

8 Outline the procedures and conclusions of one study of minority influence.

9 Outline two differences between minority and majority influence.

10 To what extent does research on conformity tell us anything about conformity in the real world?

REVISION SUMMARY

Having covered this topic, you should be able to:

✓ define 'social influence', 'conformity' and 'minority influence'

✓ explain why people yield to majority influence

✓ explain why people yield to minority influence

✓ describe and evaluate the research that has been carried out into majority and minority influence

✓ describe the aims, procedures, findings, conclusions and criticisms of a key study in the areas of majority and minority influence

✓ outline differences between majority and minority influence.

GETTING YOU THINKING...

A guard supervises inmates of a Nazi concentration camp during World War II

A lone Chinese student protester faces up to tanks in Tianenman Square, Beijing, 1989

During the Vietnam War, American soldiers rounded up hundreds of women, children and old men from My Lai village – and were ordered them to kill them. Mike Wallace from CBS News interviewed one of the soldiers, reported in *The New York Times*, 25 November 1969:

Q: *How many people did you round up?*

A: Well, there was about 40, 50 people that we gathered in the center of the village...

Q: *What kind of people – men, women, children?*

A: Men, women, children.

Q: *Babies?*

A: Babies. And we huddled them up. We made them squat down and Lieutenant Calley came over and said, "You know what to do with them don't you?" And I said yes. So I took it for granted that he just wanted us to watch them. And he left, and came back about 10 or 15 minutes later and said, "How come you ain't killed them yet?" And I told him that I didn't think you wanted us to kill them, that you just wanted us to guard them. He said, "No, I want them dead." So – ...

Q: *And you killed how many? At that time?*

A: Well I fired on them automatic, so you can't – You just spray the area on them and so you can't know how many you killed 'cause they were going fast. So I might have killed 10 or 15 of them.

Q: *Men, women, and children?*

A: Men, women, and children.

Q: *And babies?*

A: And babies ...

Q: *Why did you do it?*

A: Why did I do it? Because I felt like I was ordered to do it, and it seemed like that, at the time I felt like I was doing the right thing, because, like I said, I lost buddies...

Q: *What did these civilians – particularly the women and children, the old men – what did they do? What did they say to you?*

A: They weren't much saying to them. They [were] just being pushed and they were doing what they was told to do.

Q: *They weren't begging, or saying, "no ... no," or ...?*

A: Right. They were begging and saying "no, no". And the mothers was hugging their children, and ... but they kept right on firing. Well, we kept right on firing. They was waving their arms and begging ...

Some questions for you to think about or debate:

1 Why do you think that people obey orders from others?

2 Why do you think people obeyed orders in the situations depicted above?

3 Think of a situation when you obeyed an order and, as a consequence, you did something that you felt to be wrong. Why did you choose to obey? Why did you choose not to stick up for what you felt to be right?

Obedience to authority: an outcome of social influence where an individual acts according to the orders of some authority figure. It is assumed that without such an order the person would not have acted in this way.

Ecological validity: the degree to which the findings from a study can be generalized beyond the context of the investigation. Problems with ecological validity tend to emerge only when other researchers try to rerun the study in different situations.

Experimental (internal) validity: a measure of whether the experimental procedures actually worked and the effects observed were genuine (i.e. caused by the experimental manipulation). The conclusions of a study are justified when there is a high level of experimental validity.

WHAT IS OBEDIENCE?

Obedience is the result of social influence where somebody acts in response to a direct order from an authority figure (Cardwell 2000). It is assumed that without such an order the person would not have acted in this way. (The panel below explains how obedience differs from conformity.) Obedience may sometimes be destructive, as when people comply with the orders of a malevolent authority.

> **«**Obedience as a determinant of behaviour is of particular relevance to our time. It has been reliably established that from 1939 to 1945, millions of innocent persons were slaughtered on command; gas chambers were built, death camps were guarded, daily quotas of corpses were produced with the same efficiency as the manufacture of appliances. These inhumane policies may have originated in the mind of a single person, but they could only have been carried out on a massive scale if a very large number of persons obeyed orders.**»** (Milgram 1963, p. 371)

Similarly appalling events have occurred since then (e.g. the My Lai massacre during the Vietnam War, the slaughter of Kurds in Iraq and ethnic cleansing in

Kosovo). The list goes on. What induces people to obey their leaders' orders to torture and kill innocent human beings? Milgram was one of the first psychologists who tried to answer this question. He placed the issue of obedience in a social-psychological context, proposing that it is a normative process, a basic feature of human interaction.

The differences between conformity and obedience

Both obedience and conformity are outcomes of social influence. In the case of obedience, social influence takes the form of orders from an authority figure. In the case of conformity, the social norms of the majority exert influence on an individual to go along with the behaviour and attitudes of the group.

Public compliance and private change

Obedience often involves no more than public compliance, with private attitudes left unchanged. Conformity, however, may involve a long-lasting and fundamental shift of attitudes and beliefs, if the conformity takes the form of identifying with the group or internalizing the views of the majority.

Conscious vs unconscious effects

Figures who command obedience often display signs of their authority (e.g. uniforms) and individuals are usually well aware when they have obeyed such a figure. Indeed, many people have pleaded "I just did what I was told" as an excuse for carrying out reprehensible acts.

In the case of conformity, however, individuals are often unaware that they have been subjected to conformity pressures and may refute the idea that others have influenced them to modify their views or behaviour.

MILGRAM'S STUDIES OF OBEDIENCE

Stanley Milgram carried out a series of studies to try to shed some light on this aspect of human behaviour. In all, he studied over 1,000 participants who were representative of the general population. He discovered that, under certain situational influences, most of us would obey orders that went against our conscience.

His original study took place in a laboratory at Yale University in the USA (see key study, *Obedience*, on p. 172). The experimenter, who wore a grey laboratory coat to reinforce his status and authority, introduced two participants to each other and they each drew lots to determine who would be the 'teacher' and who would be the 'learner'. The learner-accomplice was a mild-mannered 47-year-old man who mentioned that he had had a heart complaint in the past, but that he was willing to participate in the study nonetheless.

As the learner-accomplice began making mistakes, the level of shock administered increased and he was heard to protest until, at 180 volts he shouted that he could bear the pain no longer. At 300 volts he screamed and complained that his heart was troubling him. At 315 volts he refused to continue and from then on he made no responses to the teacher's requests that he answer. In reality, of course, the accomplice never received any shocks. His responses and pleadings were prerecorded.

You will not be surprised to learn that this procedure was very stressful for the 'teacher' participants. Most protested and wanted to stop. Many showed signs of extreme anxiety, biting their lips and trembling. However, whenever the teacher hesitated, the experimenter gave standardized prompts to encourage him to continue:

Prod 1: "Please continue" or "Please go on"

Prod 2: "The experiment requires that you continue"

Prod 3: "It is absolutely essential that you continue"

Prod 4: "You have no other choice, you must go on".

ACTIVITY

Other people's estimates of Milgram's results

Milgram described this experiment to three different groups of people: psychiatrists, college students and middle-class adults. He asked them to guess how people would respond.

1 Before reading on to find out what they said, how do *you* think that people would be likely to respond? The maximum number of shocks that could be delivered to the 'learner' was 30, starting at 15 volts and going up to 450 volts. How many shocks do *you* think the participants would be prepared to deliver?

2 Describe the study to at least ten other people (class members, friends or family members). Ask them how many shocks they think someone would be prepared to deliver in this kind of situation. Note down each of their answers.

3 Now calculate the average score (the mean score) by adding up all the scores (including your own) and dividing by the total number of scores, or combine your answers with those collected by other members of your class so you have many more scores and then calculate the average. What is your answer?

The learner-accomplice is strapped to the 'shock generator'

On average, the people Milgram spoke to estimated an average of 9 out of the possible 30 shocks (i.e. 135 volts) and predicted that the participants would rebel against the instructions once that level was reached. Only a tiny handful predicted that participants would administer the maximum shock of 450 volts, which was labelled 'Danger, severe shock'.

Now read on to find out just how many shocks the participants actually delivered in Milgram's study.

original study by Milgram (1963)

Aim >>

To find out whether ordinary Americans would obey an unjust order from a person in authority to inflict pain on another person. Milgram wanted to discover what factors in a situation led people to obey.

Procedures >>

- 40 male volunteers, each paid $4.50, were deceived into thinking they were giving electric shocks.
- The participants were told that the study concerned the role of punishment in learning. The genuine participant always had the teacher's role and a confederate played the part of the learner. His task was to memorize pairs of words. When tested, the 'learner' would indicate his choice using a system of lights. The 'teacher's' role was to administer a shock every time the learner made a mistake. The teacher sat in front of the shock generator that had 30 levers, each of which indicated the level of shock to be given. The participant watched the confederate being strapped into a chair in an adjoining room with electrodes attached to his arms.
- To begin with the accomplice answered correctly and then began to make mistakes. Every time he made an error, he was to be given an electric shock administered by the participant. Shocks started at 15 volts and rose in 15-volt increments to 450 volts. If the teacher hesitated in administering the shocks, the researcher encouraged him to continue.
- **No shocks were actually administered.**
- The experiment continued either until the teacher refused to continue or until 450 volts were reached and given four times. The participant was then debriefed and taken to meet the learner–accomplice (as shown in the photo).

Findings >>

- All participants went to at least 300 volts on the shock generator.
- 65 per cent of participants went to the end of the shock generator. That is, they believed they had administered the full 450 volts!
- Most participants found the procedure very stressful and wanted to stop, with some showing signs of extreme anxiety. Although they dissented verbally, they continued, however, to obey the researcher who prodded them to continue giving the shocks.

Conclusions >>

- Under certain circumstances, most people will obey orders that go against their conscience.
- When people occupy a subordinate position in a dominance hierarchy, they become liable to lose feelings of empathy, compassion and morality, and are inclined towards blind obedience.
- Atrocities such as those carried out in World War II may be largely explained in terms of pressures to obey a powerful authority.

Criticisms >>

- The study has received many criticisms, most relating to the potential harm that might have been done to participants.
- Did participants really believe that they were giving electric shocks? Orne and Holland claimed that the study lacked experimental (internal) validity; participants were only 'going along with the act' when they 'shocked' the learner, that they were not really distressed, just pretending in order to please the experimenter. Orne and Holland also claimed that the situation within Milgram's laboratory bore little resemblance to real-life situations where obedience is required and so it lacked ecological validity (see p. 175 for a fuller discussion of the experimental and ecological validity of this study).

The potential harm to those participating in Milgram's study

In the key study opposite, the first criticism of Milgram's study is about the potential harm to participants.

Pause for a moment to imagine what it might have felt like to participate in this study and make a note of the ways in which you feel those involved might have been harmed by the experience. Think especially about the issues of respect, deception and any possible long-term harm.

Milgram's main results

Although most participants dissented verbally, they obeyed behaviourally, and 65 per cent of participants went to the end of the shock generator, believing they had administered 450 volts to the 'learner'. Milgram was as surprised by these results as anyone since the people he had spoken to about the procedure before carrying out his study thought only a tiny handful would proceed to 450 volts. They were wrong. What was it about the situation that caused the participants to obey?

You may be surprised that Milgram claimed that he had no way of knowing beforehand that his study would cause distress. His follow-up procedures with his participants also showed that many said they were glad that they had taken part because they felt they had learned something important about themselves. (See p. 184 for a more detailed discussion of the ethical issues raised by Milgram's study.)

Variations on Milgram's basic procedure

Milgram systematically varied a number of the features of his procedure in order to discover what elements of the situation made it more or less likely that participants would obey. These variations and their consequences for the participants' behaviour are listed in Table 5.2. It is clear from these results that obedience levels in a laboratory setting can be manipulated by controlling situational variables:

● When participants were relocated to less prestigious surroundings, obedience levels fell.

● When the participant knew that the learner had agreed to only a limited contract, obedience levels fell.

● When participants were forced to see, as well as hear, the pain and distress caused by their actions, obedience levels fell.

● When participants were required to use physical force personally to administer the shocks, obedience levels fell even further. As the participants became increasingly aware of the pain and distress inflicted on the learners, they were more likely to disobey the experimenter's orders to continue giving shocks (see photo on p. 181).

● When others modelled disobedience for them, participants conformed, followed suit and obedience levels fell.

● When the experimenter supervised participants less closely, obedience levels fell.

● When someone else 'did the dirty work' of throwing the switches, obedience levels soared.

Now read the 'Expert interview' with David Mandel on p. 174 for a discussion about the limited applicability of these findings to what actually happened during the Holocaust (the genocide of European Jews).

Table 5.2 >> Variations on Milgram's basic procedure

Variation	Obedience rate (those going to 450 volts)
>> Original experiment	65%
>> Venue moved to seedy offices in nearby town (Bridgeport)	47.5%
>> Learner agreed to participate on the condition that "you let me out when I say so"	40%
>> Teacher and learner in the same room	40%
>> Teacher had to force learner's hand on to plate to receive shock	30%
>> Teacher given support from two other 'teachers' (confederates) who refuse	10%
>> Experimenter left the room and instructed the teacher by telephone from another room	20.5%
>> Teacher paired with an assistant (confederate) who threw the switches	92.5%

Source: Milgram (1963)

Unit 5 // Social Influence

The obedience *alibi*

Dr David R. Mandel is an Associate Professor of Psychology at the University of Victoria (British Columbia, Canada). His academic background is in the fields of cognitive and social psychology. Dr Mandel's current research interests focus on the social psychology of collective violence and on topics in decision science that address how (and how well) people make judgements and decisions.

Q What aspects of Milgram's research have been used to explain events in the Holocaust?

A In Milgram's best-known 'voice feedback' experiment, 62.5 per cent of participants obeyed the experimenter's request to administer shocks to the 'learner' even at dangerously high voltage levels that apparently caused the learner harm. This key finding has been used as evidence in support of the idea that Holocaust perpetrators, like Milgram's participants, were ordinary citizens who succumbed to the influence of malign authority figures. According to this explanation, Holocaust perpetrators were motivated primarily by a need to fulfil their duties to their superiors. In short, they were 'just following orders'.

Q Are these conclusions justified?

A No, they are unjustified for several reasons. First, there is the obvious difference that whereas Milgram's participants were told that the shock procedure was not harmful, Holocaust perpetrators knew that they were killing unarmed civilians. Second, when Milgram's participants were subtly made aware of limits that the learner put on his consent to participate, obedience rates declined substantially. Holocaust victims obviously did not consent to be tortured and murdered, and any reasonable extrapolation suggests that very few of Milgram's participants would have tortured victims against their will. Third, when participants had discretion over the shock levels they administered, the vast majority were unwilling to give shocks that (apparently) caused the learner pain. In contrast, historical records reveal that Holocaust perpetrators were willing – sometimes eager – to torture and humiliate their victims before killing them. This finding alone suggests that perpetrators' motives to kill went far beyond 'just following orders'.

Q What potential harm is there in trying to use Milgram's research in this way?

A Although Milgram's findings are an important contribution to social psychology, their relevance to explaining the Holocaust has been greatly overstated. One danger is that an exclusive focus on obedience to authority detracts attention from other important factors including racism, prejudice and discrimination. Another danger is that the obedience explanation can be easily misused as an alibi to exonerate perpetrators of the Holocaust or other genocides.

David Mandel

ACTIVITY

David Mandel speaks out!

Exam questions in social psychology occasionally ask you to consider how far the conclusions drawn from a particular research area apply to the real world. The interview with David Mandel gives you some insights into the problems of extending Milgram's research to the behaviour of Holocaust perpetrators. Mandel's account of the Holocaust and the relevance of Milgram's work to it is available on the Internet at http://web.uvic.ca/psyc/dmandel/ak98paper.html Read this article and answer the following questions:

● Draw up a table that shows some of the variations of Milgram's basic study (e.g. the presence of an authority figure, the proximity of the victim) and equivalent Holocaust events. Do Milgram's findings reflect what actually happened in these Holocaust events?

● What does this tell us about the external (ecological) validity of obedience research?

● What, according to Mandel, are the theoretical limitations of an obedience perspective to explaining events in the Holocaust?

Evaluating Milgram's work

Ethical issues about deception, consent and protection of participants are dealt with on pp. 182–4.

Orne and Holland (1968) have criticized Milgram's studies on two other counts:

● lacking experimental (internal) validity
● lacking ecological validity.

Read the panel on the right for an overview of these aspects of Milgram's research.

Hofling *et al.* (1966) – obedient nurses

The situation used was a hospital. They arranged for a nurse (the participant) to receive a phone call from an unknown doctor who asked her to administer 20 milligrams of a drug called Astroten (a drug not known to these nurses) to a patient so that it would have taken effect before he arrived. If the nurse obeyed, she would be breaking several hospital rules:

● giving twice the maximum dose allowable for the drug
● administering a drug that was not on the ward stock list for that day
● taking a telephone instruction from an unfamiliar person
● acting without a signed order from a doctor.

Despite all this, 21 out of 22 of the participants started to give the medication (which was in fact a harmless placebo) until another nurse, who had been stationed nearby but out of sight, stopped them.

When interviewed afterwards, all the nurses said that they had been asked to do this type of thing before and that doctors became annoyed if they refused. These results are important as they highlight that pressures to obey are greater than most people imagine. When Hofling and colleagues asked nurses (not those in the study) what they thought the rate of obedience would be in this situation, they were all convinced that nurses would refuse to obey!

This study showed that high levels of obedience can be obtained in real-life settings and so appeared to provide support for the ecological validity of Milgram's findings. However, not all studies conducted in real-life settings do so.

Experimental (internal) validity

Experimental (internal) validity is a measure of whether experimental procedures actually work and whether the effects observed are genuine (i.e. caused by the experimental manipulation). Orne and Holland claimed that the participants in Milgram's studies were 'going along with the act' when they 'shocked' the learner. They argued that participants did not believe they were really giving electric shocks and that they were not really distressed, just pretending in order to please the experimenter and to continue to play their role in the study.

Milgram disputed both these claims. He cited evidence from films made of some of his investigations that clearly showed participants undergoing extreme stress. He also referred to evidence from post-experimental interviews and questionnaires to support his belief that the majority of participants believed they were administering real shocks. Furthermore, Orne and Holland do not explain why some participants refused to continue giving shocks if they were merely role-playing in the first place or why altering the location of the study (to run-down Bridgeport) reduced the levels of obedience.

Ecological validity (mundane realism)

Ecological validity is the degree to which the findings from a study can be generalized beyond the context of the investigation. Milgram's procedures have been replicated in other countries, with higher levels of obedience found in Germany and lower levels found in Australia (see p. 177). In a Jordanian study, children aged between 6 and 16 exhibited high levels of obedience, with 73 per cent believing that they were administering the full 450 volts (Shanab and Yahya 1977). Therefore, there is plenty of evidence to support Milgram's contention that high levels of obedience can readily be obtained in laboratories other than his own.

However, Orne and Holland have challenged the generalizability of Milgram's findings, claiming that the situation within Milgram's laboratory bore little resemblance to real-life situations where obedience is required. Given this criticism, the results of the study by Hofling *et al.* (1966) are interesting. This study appeared to provide support for the ecological validity of Milgram's findings by showing that blind obedience to an authority figure could occur just as readily in real life. However, Rank and Jacobson's later study (1977) called into question the ecological validity of the Hofling study!

Criticism of the study by Hofling and colleagues

1 Did you notice any weakness in the way that Hofling and colleagues designed and carried out their study? Clue: think about the way that nurses might normally operate when asked to administer a drug that they did not know about from a doctor who was not known to them.

2 If the design of the study was changed to enable nurses to respond as they would normally, do you think the results would be any different?

3 If your answer is 'yes', what does this tell us about the importance of the design of a study and the conclusions that are drawn?

Rank and Jacobson (1977): not so obedient nurses

Rank and Jacobson were uneasy about two aspects of Hofling's study – that the nurses had no knowledge of the drug involved and that they had no opportunity to seek advice from anyone of equal or higher status. In most hospital situations, they argued, nurses would either have knowledge about a drug or would have time to seek advice. Therefore, they replicated the

procedure, but this time the doctor required the nurse to use the common drug Valium at three times the recommended level. The doctor who telephoned gave the name of a real doctor on the staff and nurses were able to speak to other nurses before they proceeded. Results showed that only two out of 18 nurses proceeded to prepare the medication as requested. Rank and Jacobson concluded that "nurses aware of the toxic effects of a drug and allowed to interact naturally ... will not administer a medication overdose merely because a physician orders it" (p. 191).

Bickman (1974): the power of uniforms!

Before reading any further, do the activity below.

In this interesting field study, Bickman found that visible symbols of authority, such as uniforms, increased levels of obedience. Three male experimenters dresser either in uniform (as a milkman or a guard) or as a civilian (in a coat and tie) made requests of passers-by in a street in New York. For example, they asked them to pick up a bag for them or provide money for a parking meter. People were most likely to obey the experimenter who was dressed as a guard and least likely to obey the experimenter dressed as a civilian. A strength of this study is its real-life setting. However, the opportunity sample of participants (i.e. those people who just happened to be available) may have affected the findings. The results, nevertheless, supported those of Milgram who found higher levels of obedience at the visibly prestigious Yale University than at the run-down office in Bridgeport.

The power of uniforms

In these photographs the same man is dressed in three different ways. If he asked you to do something, such as wait inside a shop and stay there until told to, in which situation would you be most likely, and least likely, to obey? Explain your answer.

WHY PEOPLE OBEY

Why do people obey? A number of explanations have been offered that look at the psychological processes involved in obedience.

Legitimate authority

One suggestion is that we feel obligated to those in power because we respect their credentials and assume they know what they are doing. Legitimate social power is held by authority figures whose role is defined by society. This usually gives the person in authority the right to exert control over the behaviour of others, and others usually accept it (see the study by Hofling and colleagues described on p. 175). Although respect for authority permits orderly social interaction, there is the danger that it may be so deeply ingrained in us that we obey, even when we believe we are being asked to do something unethical or immoral. Clearly, the authority conveyed by a legitimate researcher at a prestigious university impressed the participants in Milgram's original experiment. When the location of the study was moved to a run-down office building, the level of obedience dropped (see Table 5.2, p. 173). Bickman's study also showed that people are more inclined to obey those who display visible symbols of authority such as uniforms.

Respect for authority varies from country to country. For example, in a study in Australia, where there is a greater tradition of questioning authority than was the case in the USA in the early 1960s, only 40 per cent of participants went to 450 volts on the shock generator. On the other hand, Mantell (1971) found 85 per cent obedience levels in Germany.

Gradual commitment

An important feature of Milgram's procedure was the gradual way in which participants became sucked into giving greater and greater levels of shock. They found it difficult to decide when to disengage from the procedure because each voltage increment was fairly small. Psychologists call this gradual commitment the 'foot-in-the-door' effect. Once people comply with a trivial, seemingly harmless, request they find it more difficult to refuse to carry out more serious, escalating requests. This is explained by the desire to appear consistent. Milgram also pointed out that participants felt that they had 'contracted' to help with the study. By coming along to the laboratory, they saw themselves as helpful people, willing to aid scientific research. If they then were to refuse to continue, they might have to re-evaluate this flattering self-perception.

Agency theory

Milgram's agency theory states that people operate on two levels:

- as autonomous individuals, behaving voluntarily and aware of the consequences of their actions

- on the agentic level, seeing themselves as the agents of others and not responsible for their actions.

The consequence of moving from the autonomous to the agentic level (known as the agentic shift) is that individuals attribute responsibility for their actions to the person in authority. At this agentic level, Milgram argued, people mindlessly accept the orders of the person seen as responsible in the situation. Milgram believed that this explained the behaviour of the participants in his study; they denied personal responsibility, claiming that they were merely "doing what they were told". You probably know that when those responsible for atrocities during World War II were asked why they did what they did, their answer was simply: "I was only obeying orders" (Arendt 1963). Similar defences have been offered more recently by ex-torturers at the South African Truth and Reconciliation Commission.

What causes people to undergo the agentic shift? Milgram suggested that it is part of the socialization process: we train children from a very early age to be obedient to authority at home, in school and in society. Many rules and regulations exist to reinforce obedience, so that eventually we tend to accept unquestioningly what we are told to do because most requests are perceived to be both reasonable and appropriate. Additionally, there are factors that operate to keep one in the agentic state. These are known as binding factors. They include:

- fear of appearing rude or arrogant by disrupting a well-defined social situation such as a laboratory experiment – this would involve a breach of etiquette and require courage

- fear of increasing one's anxiety levels (likely to be high already among Milgram's participants) by challenging the authority figure.

Buffers

The term 'buffer' is used here to describe any aspect of a situation that protects people from having to confront the consequences of their actions. Remember that the participants in Milgram's studies did not enjoy what they were doing. Why then did they continue? Milgram suggested that buffers acted as a mechanism to help people reduce the strain of obeying an immoral or unethical command. In turn, these buffers served to facilitate obedience. In the original Milgram study, the 'teacher' and 'learner' were in different rooms; the teacher was buffered (protected) from having to see his victim. In some real-life situations where obedience is required, the person merely has to press a button – the resulting destruction may not even be observed. In other cases, those carrying out orders are not told full details of their mission. This was the case with the aircrew who dropped the atomic bomb on Hiroshima.

Personality factors

Unlike the preceding situational factors, some dispositional (personality) factors have been proposed to explain Milgram's findings.

- **Authoritarian personality** – An authoritarian person has rigid beliefs, is intolerant and yet submissive to those in authority. Milgram (1974) found that participants who were highly authoritarian tended to give stronger shocks than those who were less authoritarian.

- **Psychopathic personality** – Miale and Selzer (1975) claimed that the obedience of Milgram's participants was a socially acceptable expression of their psychopathic (violent and psychologically disordered) impulses. Milgram refuted this account completely. He reminded us that when participants were able to select their own voltage levels, they gave lower levels of shock. Hannah Arendt agreed with Milgram. She covered the trial of the Nazi war criminal Adolf Eichmann for crimes against humanity. She wrote:

«It would have been comforting indeed to believe that Eichmann was a monster ... The trouble with Eichmann was precisely that so many were like him and the many were neither perverted nor sadistic ... [but] terribly and terrifyingly normal.**»**
(1963, p. 276)

Remember that the main conclusion of Milgram's findings is that situational factors are important in derailing normally decent people from the moral straight and narrow.

Adolf Eichmann as a young officer in the Austrian army and on trial in 1961. Is this the face of a monster? Would you have 'followed orders' in the same way as so many Nazi officers did?

RESISTING PRESSURES TO OBEY

So far in this topic, we have focused on the power of social influence to make people obey, but it is important to remember that some participants did actually disobey the instructions given them. The panel below lists describes how and when people resist obedience to a malevolent authority.

People resist obedience to a malevolent authority:

- when they feel responsible for their own actions
- when they observe others being disobedient (conformity effects)
- by questioning the motives of those giving the orders
- when they have time to think about what they are being asked to do
- when orders are so heavy handed and restrictive that people react against their freedom being threatened
- by using high levels of moral reasoning (though this does not guarantee moral actions).

The following paragraphs look in more detail at these types of situation.

Feeling responsible

In Milgram's study, some participants disobeyed the experimenter and refused to continue giving shocks when they thought the learner was in distress. One such participant in a follow-up study, when asked why, said that she had experienced too much pain in her own life, having grown up in Nazi Germany, and did not wish to inflict pain on someone else. According to Milgram, the triggering of painful memories had 'awakened' her from her agentic state. She felt responsible for any harm produced. The arrangement whereby the learner was in a separate room was an insufficient buffer for this particular participant who could imagine all too clearly the pain he must be suffering.

Disobedient models

Exposing people to the actions of disobedient models, i.e. seeing others refuse to obey instructions from an authority figure, encourages disobedience. For example, when confederate teachers refused to continue giving shocks, only 10 per cent of participants in Milgram's experiment continued (see Table 5.2 on p. 173).

Questioning motives

Questioning the motives, legitimacy and expertise of authority figures has been proposed as a way to prevent automatic obedience. Remember that when Milgram's study was transferred to a run-down office block, the levels of obedience dropped (see Table 5.2). The lack of prestigious surroundings made it easier for participants to question the legitimacy of the experimenter. See also the study by Gamson and colleagues that follows next.

Time for discussion

In a study conducted by Gamson et al. (1982) to investigate under what circumstances people will refuse to go along with an unjust authority, participants were involved in making a video and signing statements that could be used in court proceedings. Participants, who worked in groups, gradually became suspicious about the true purpose of the study and refused to obey the requests of the experimenter. They realized that they were being manipulated into producing tapes that an oil company could exploit in court. However, in this study, participants had plenty of time to share information and to discuss their suspicions. They eventually began to question the legitimacy and the motives of the authority figures. One explanation given for their disobedience was the psychological process called reactance (see below).

Participants reported feeling very anxious and stressed in this study. Therefore, the research raises ethical concerns about protecting participants from psychological harm. After running 33 groups the researchers felt obliged to abandon their plans to run the 80 groups they had originally intended.

Reactance

The process of reactance may occur when we want to protect our sense of freedom. Gamson and colleagues found in their study that once someone had voiced their concern about what they were being asked to do, others quickly joined in and this was the start of rebellion against the unjust authority.

Blatant attempts to restrict people's freedom can sometimes produce a boomerang effect, causing people to do the opposite of what is being asked. It has been suggested that reactance might contribute to underage drinking and the increase in cigarette-smoking among young people, although peer pressure and conformity effects probably play a part as well.

Individual differences

● *Moral reasoning* – Kohlberg (1969), a colleague of Milgram's, found that those who used more advanced stages of moral reasoning were more able to resist the exhortations of the experimenter and so showed higher levels of disobedience. However, other research has shown that there is not an exact correspondence between moral reasoning and moral actions: "One can reason in terms of principles and not live up to those principles" (Kohlberg 1973).

● *Gender differences* – Milgram reported no differences between men and women's levels of obedience to authority. Most of the research investigating gender differences has looked at differences in levels of conformity (rather than obedience). Overall there appears to be no difference in the susceptibility of males and females to social influence.

✓ CHECK YOUR UNDERSTANDING

Check your understanding of obedience to authority by answering these questions. Try to do this from memory at first. You can check your answers by looking back through Topic 2.

1 What do you understand by the terms 'obedience to authority', 'ecological validity' and 'experimental validity'?

2 Outline two differences between conformity and obedience.

3 Describe the procedures and conclusions from Milgram's original study of obedience.

4 What effects did changing situational factors make on the levels of obedience Milgram found?

5 Outline the criticisms levelled against the experimental validity of Milgram's studies.

6 How did Milgram respond to this criticism?

7 To what extent does later research support the ecological validity of Milgram's studies?

8 Describe two psychological processes that help explain why people obey authority.

9 Outline two reasons why people sometimes resist obedience.

10 To what extent do Milgram's findings on obedience provide a credible explanation for atrocities committed in the real world?

REVISION SUMMARY

Having covered this topic, you should be able to:

✓ define 'obedience to authority', 'ecological validity' and 'experimental validity'

✓ explain why people obey

✓ outline differences between conformity and obedience

✓ describe and evaluate research carried out into obedience to authority, including issues of experimental and ecological validity

✓ describe the aims, procedures, findings, conclusions and criticisms of a key study in obedience.

✓ explain how people might resist obedience.

GETTING YOU THINKING...

Milgram's well-known study of obedience continues to stimulate heated debate between psychologists. Consider the following statement:

《In Milgram's research on obedience, the ends justified the means.》

1 If you are working in a group, you could debate this statement with other members of your class. Divide yourselves into two groups, one supporting the statement and the other opposing it, with each group preparing arguments to present to the other group. Use this textbook as a resource. Include an opportunity for each group to ask the other group questions on their arguments.

At the end of the debate, take a vote to see how many people support the statement and how many are opposed to it. Find out whether or not anyone has changed their views as a result of the debate.

2 If you are working on your own, prepare your own summary of arguments for and against the statement. Which arguments do you find most compelling? Do the ends justify the means?

In one of the variations to Milgram's original procedure, participants were required to use physical force to administer the shocks

KEY TERMS

Deception: withholding information or misleading research participants. Deception may be trivial when only a few details of a hypothesis are withheld. On the other hand, deception is of more ethical concern when it involves deliberately providing false information that may influence a participant's willingness to take part.

Ethical issue: an ethical issue will arise in research where there is a conflict between the rights and dignity of participants and the goals and outcomes of research. For example, there may be conflict between the rights of participants to give fully informed consent and the importance of studying behaviour in as natural a setting as possible.

Ethical guidelines: the prescriptive guidance given by professional associations (such as the British Psychological Society) on how psychologists should practise (e.g. as clinical psychologists) or carry out their research. Guidelines attempt to deal with the key issues that face psychologists in their work with humans and animals. They are regularly updated by the organizations that issue them.

Informed consent: an ethical requirement that participants should have sufficient information about a research study to enable them to make an informed judgement as to whether or not to take part.

Protection of participants from psychological harm: an ethical requirement that research participants should be protected from undue risk during an investigation. Risks they should be protected from include humiliation, embarrassment and loss of dignity or self-esteem.

ETHICAL ISSUES IN SOCIAL INFLUENCE RESEARCH

Ethics can be defined as a consideration of what is acceptable or right behaviour in the pursuit of a particular personal or scientific goal (Cardwell 2000). Because human participants are used in much psychological research, ethical issues are a major concern within psychology and have primarily been about the dignity and rights of participants. The need for a clear and unambiguous set of guidelines for research psychologists led to the development of the ethical principles that underlie all psychological research today. To describe something as unethical, therefore, not only describes a practice that is morally wrong, but also one that is professionally unacceptable. The guidelines drawn up by the British Psychological Society (BPS) (2000) stress that psychologists must carry out their work in a way that respects the rights and dignity of all research participants.

The work of Milgram and Zimbardo, in particular, has raised many ethical issues, including concerns about:

- the inability of participants to give fully informed consent
- the use of deception
- the adequacy of the debriefing process
- the possible harm that might be done to participants.

Informed consent

Informed consent is an ethical requirement that participants should have sufficient information about a research study to enable them to make an informed judgement about whether or not to take part. Gaining a participant's informed consent is a very important aspect of any research investigation. Without full disclosure prior to obtaining their consent, it becomes impossible for participants to make a fully informed decision about their willingness to take part. Sometimes, participants who initially give their consent to take part in a study, later wish to withdraw that consent and have their own data destroyed. They must be free to do so, even if they have previously accepted payment for their participation. Of course, we might argue that full disclosure (of procedures to be used, reasons for the research, and so on) might invalidate some psychological research. One way that psychologists have tried to deal with the problems associated with getting fully informed consent is by finding alternatives to it (see the panel below, *Alternatives to fully informed consent*).

Deception

Deception involves withholding information or misleading research participants. By deceiving research participants, we may also remove their ability to give fully informed consent to take part in the investigation we have in mind. This is not an open and shut case, however, as total honesty throughout an investigation may lead participants to modify their behaviour in some way because of the knowledge they have about the real aims of the investigation. Social psychologists face particular ethical dilemmas over the use of deception in their research. Consider the implications of complete research honesty in the investigation carried out by Milgram on obedience to authority.

There are clearly some situations where deception is inappropriate and some where it may be acceptable. There is a difference, for example, between withholding some of the research details and deliberately misleading the participants into believing the purpose of the research is more innocent than it actually is.

Alternatives to fully informed consent

There are alternatives to informed consent that may be used in situations when revealing the purpose of the investigation to participants would invalidate the study:

>> Presumptive consent

For example, we may take a large random sample from the population to be studied and introduce them to the research design, including the use of deception. If they agree that they would still have given voluntary informed consent had they known the true aims of the investigation, then we may assume that they represent the views of that population group. Another sample from that population would then be selected for use in the study without being told its true purpose.

>> Prior general consent

In this case, people who might be used as participants in a study are told that *sometimes* participants are misinformed about the true purpose of a study. Only those who agree that such a practice is acceptable would be selected as participants for this type of study. Therefore, they have given general informed consent, but they do not know whether or not the actual study they participate in uses misleading information.

There are a number of issues here:

- Some deceptions have more damaging consequences than others. The amount of discomfort or anger expressed by participants when deception is revealed is normally a good guide to this. The majority of psychologists believe that some temporary deception is justifiable provided safeguards are adopted. When participants have been asked, most report that they think minor deception is acceptable.

- Deception in investigations of a trivial nature is less acceptable than in investigations that make significant contributions to psychological knowledge. Although this may seem a case of the ends justifying the means, it should be clear that the importance of some research means that the ethical concerns spread far beyond the immediate context of the investigation. Consider how Milgram might have justified deceiving his participants.

Some psychologists have tried to deal with the ethical problems that arise when participants are deceived by using alternative strategies (see the panel on the right).

Debriefing

An important aspect of any research design, *especially when deception has taken place*, is the process of debriefing. This is an ethical requirement where participants are aware that they have taken part in an investigation. Debriefing is carried out after data have been collected. It involves providing information to participants and discussing their experience of the research. Sometimes it is seen as sufficient merely to inform participants of the true nature of the investigation, but at other times such perfunctory debriefing would be inadequate. Consider again Stanley Milgram's research into obedience. His research participants either obeyed (i.e. gave the maximum electric shock) or disobeyed and declined to give further shocks. Either way, the participants had done something they may have perceived as being wrong. (See p. 185 for an account of the debriefing measures used by Milgram.)

Debriefing is an essential part of research. What would the effect be on a participant if they took part in upsetting or challenging research and were sent home without any chance to talk through their experience?

Alternatives to using deception

>> Complete information

Provide participants with *complete information* about the purpose of the investigation. In a study by Gallo *et al.* (1973), participants were told that the study concerned the extent to which people would conform. The results for these informed participants were no different from those for deceived participants who thought they were involved in an investigation of depth perception. However, a second study by the same researchers produced opposite findings.

>> Prior general consent

Tell participants about the general nature of the study (though not the detailed hypothesis being tested) and ask them to role-play the experimental procedure as though they were naive participants. Mixon (1972) used this method in a set-up similar to that used in Milgram's obedience studies. He found that provided the role-playing participants were led to believe that the experimenter carried the responsibility for any distress caused to the 'learner', they behaved much as Milgram's participants did. However, if the role-players were led to assume responsibility, their levels of obedience were significantly lower than those found by Milgram. More often than not, studies using role-play procedures result in different findings from those where investigators have concealed their true purpose from participants.

As a general rule, debriefing aims:

● to restore participants to the same state as when they entered the investigation. Take a situation, for example, where participants arrived in a happy mood to take part in an experiment. If the experiment resulted in participants becoming upset or agitated, it is important that they receive adequate explanation and reassurance before leaving the experimental setting so that their previous happy mood is restored

● to provide an opportunity for the researcher to give participants additional information about the research so that the whole thing becomes an educational experience for them.

Debriefing does not, of course, provide a justification for any unethical aspects of the investigation. A good researcher regards participants as colleagues, not as objects to be used solely for the purposes of research.

Protection of participants

Protecting participants from psychological harm is an ethical requirement that research participants should be protected from undue risk during an investigation. Thus, the risks that an individual may be exposed to during a psychological investigation should not be greater than the risks they might already be expected to face in their everyday life. Risks they should be protected from include humiliation, embarrassment and loss of dignity or self-esteem. You might like to consider whether the risks to self-esteem encountered by Asch's, Milgram's or Zimbardo's participants were greater than those you would expect them to meet in their normal life.

The question is often asked whether the scientific knowledge gained or the moral lessons learned by social influence research have outweighed the costs and potential harm done to participants. The studies carried out by Milgram and Zimbardo have received most attention.

ACTIVITY

The case for and against the research of Asch, Zimbardo and Milgram

Reread the descriptions of three well-known studies – Asch's study of conformity which involved accomplices, Zimbardo's prison simulation study and Milgram's research on obedience. Think carefully about issues such as informed consent, the use of deception, the use of debriefing, and possible harm to participants. Make a list of all the reasons you can think of why it was important for them to carry out their studies.

Now, make a second list of any reasons why you think that these three psychologists should not have been allowed to carry out their research.

When you have done this, compare your ideas with the points made below.

ETHICS IN MILGRAM'S OBEDIENCE STUDIES

Milgram's procedures have attracted much criticism. His work, however, has also received considerable support and has been stoutly defended by Milgram himself.

The case for the prosecution

● Baumrind (1964) believed that Milgram showed insufficient respect for his participants, that there were inadequate steps taken to protect them and that his procedures had the potential for causing long-term harm. The studies, it has been claimed, involved lack of informed consent, deception and possible psychological harm to his participants.

● Voluntary informed consent and lack of deception are important principles to be adhered to if psychological research is to be ethical. Without doubt, Milgram's participants did not know the true purpose of his experiment and therefore they could not give informed consent. For the experiment to work, deception was essential. The point at issue, however, is whether or not the deception can be justified in this case. Some researchers have

advocated the use of role-playing to avoid the need for deception (see p. 183).

● The criticism most often levelled against Milgram's experiments concerns the psychological harm that might have been done to participants. This harm, it is claimed, could result from several aspects of the procedure, including the stress of carrying out the instructor's orders to continue giving the shocks to the learner. For example, Milgram (1963) recorded that his participants often trembled, stuttered and sweated. Furthermore, there were the possible long-term psychological effects of learning that they had been willing to give potentially lethal shocks to fellow human beings, and feeling stupid and 'used' when they learned the true nature of the experiment and how they had been deceived. Allied to this is the likelihood that they would not trust psychologists or people in authority in the future.

- John Darley (1992), in his thought-provoking paper, *Social organization for the production of evil*, argues that the possibility of being evil is latent in all of us and it can be made active by a conversion process. He invites us to consider the possibility that Milgram may have begun the process of converting innocent participants into evil people. To support this theory, he points to Lifton's (1986) interviews with physicians who participated in the Nazi death camps. He reported that the Nazi doctors were initially banal, ordinary individuals. What they did, however, was not ordinary, and in performing their evil acts, they changed. Their encounter with a 'demonic killing machine' began a process that morally altered them. Could the same be true of those people who gave 450-volt shocks to the learners in Milgram's experiments?

- David Mandel (1998) has argued convincingly that the misapplication of Milgram's findings has led to an oversimplified explanation of the atrocities committed during the Holocaust. According to Mandel, to attribute the horrors of the Holocaust entirely to the sort of situational factors that caused obedience in Milgram's laboratory is oversimplified and misleading (see the Expert interview on p. 174). It ignores other important factors that motivated the perpetrators of atrocities, including the chances for professional advancement and the opportunities for lucrative personal gains by plundering Jews and their corpses. Analysis of the behaviour of those who killed and tortured Jews has revealed some facts that do not accord with Milgram's laboratory findings:

  - Perpetrators did not require close supervision by their superiors.
  - They were not inhibited by seeing the pain (and even the death) of those they victimized.
  - They were often willing to continue killing even when offered the opportunity to quit.

Case for the defence

Milgram has responded to his critics. The major plank of his defence is that participants themselves do not agree with the criticisms.

- Milgram responded to Baumrind's accusation that he had not respected his participants sufficiently by drawing attention to the questionnaire distributed to participants. Eighty-four per cent replied that they were glad they had been involved. Seventy-four per cent said they had learned something of personal importance. Only 1.3 per cent reported negative

Stanley Milgram with the 'shock' generator

feelings. Furthermore, one year after the study, a university psychiatrist interviewed 40 participants and reported no evidence of emotional harm that could be attributed to participation in the study.

- After each experimental session, a careful debriefing session was held when the reasons for the deception were explained and the true purpose of the study was revealed. Milgram claimed that the debriefing process was instrumental in helping to reassure and protect the participants. Obedient participants were reassured that their behaviour was the norm in that investigation (i.e. there was nothing wrong with them). Disobedient participants were reassured that their behaviour was actually socially desirable, because they had stood up against a malevolent authority figure trying to coerce them into doing something they felt was wrong.

- As regards the criticism that people might be distrustful of psychologists or others in authority in the future, Milgram (1964) replied that he thought it would be "of the highest value if participation in the experiment could inculcate a scepticism of *this* [inhumane] kind of authority" (p. 852).

- Supporters of Milgram have rallied to his defence, agreeing with him that if the results of his studies had been different, with participants declining to continue at the first sign of learner discomfort, no one would have protested. But, of course, we cannot be sure what the results of research will be. Milgram had not intended to cause discomfort to his participants. Indeed, the survey carried out beforehand predicted that few people would give shocks after the learner began to protest. Therefore, few participants should have experienced any discomfort. Even when participants did show distress, however, Milgram did not believe it sufficient to justify stopping the experiment. After Milgram's research was published, the American Psychological Association investigated it and found it ethically acceptable. He was, in fact, awarded a prize for his outstanding contribution to social psychological research.

- Elliot Aronson (1999) has suggested that psychologists face a particularly difficult dilemma when their wider responsibility to society conflicts with their more specific responsibilities to each individual research participant. This conflict is greatest when the issues under investigation are issues of social importance. Do the potential benefits of the research outweigh the costs to the individual participants? Unfortunately this 'costs–benefits' dilemma is not easy to resolve, as it is difficult to predict either costs or benefits before a study begins. Also, participants and investigators may have very different views as to what is an acceptable cost or a worthwhile benefit.

- Darley's proposition that those who took part in Milgram's experiments may have stepped onto the slippery slope towards evil was made after Milgram's death (1984) and so Milgram did not have an opportunity to respond. He did, however, as already mentioned, arrange for a psychiatrist to interview a sample of his participants to see if any psychological damage could be detected. None was reported.

- A positive outcome of Milgram's experiments has been the increased awareness among *psychologists* since then concerning how they should treat their participants. This, in turn, has led psychologists to draft guidelines to be used for research. Remember that the sort of ethical guidelines used by research psychologists today were not formulated when Milgram carried out his research.

ETHICS IN ZIMBARDO'S PRISON SIMULATION STUDY

Harm to participants

Savin (1973) criticized Zimbardo's prison simulation study for the way it humiliated its participants (see p. 163 for more detail). After six days the simulation, originally planned to last two weeks, was ended because of the unexpectedly extreme emotional and behavioural effects. Did the knowledge gained justify the means by which it was acquired? Savin thinks not; Zimbardo thinks it did. He reports that follow-ups over many years revealed no lasting negative effects; that student participants were healthy and able to bounce back from their 'prison' experience; that they had learned the important lesson that even the most intelligent and well-intentioned among us can be overwhelmed by social influences.

Need for independent surveillance

In recent years, Zimbardo has acknowledged that he should not have acted as 'prison superintendent' as well as principal researcher, because he became trapped by the day-to-day business of his superintendent role, rather as the 'guards' and 'prisoners' became trapped in their roles. However, he argues that instead of banning research of this type, what is needed is better research – that is, where experiments are ethically sensitive, there should be an independent monitor and more vigilant surveillance by the institution concerned. In this way, he claims, participants could be protected while valuable information was acquired.

Deceiving participants

Some critics of both Milgram and Zimbardo have suggested that deceiving participants is really not necessary in research and is particularly unethical when it might leave them feeling foolish or humiliated. They have proposed that other more ethically acceptable methods could be used, such as asking people to imagine how they or others would behave in certain situations. However, you may recall that Milgram did this by asking people how many participants they thought would go to 450 volts on his shock generator. Their predictions grossly underestimated the levels of obedience found by Milgram in his actual experiments. Zimbardo is scathing about the use of 'as if' procedures to replace simulations or experiments. Read what he has said in the panel on p. 187.

Did the knowledge gained from Zimbardo's prison simulation justify the emotional distress caused to participants during it?

Zimbardo: Ethics and research in social psychology

In an interview with Mark McDermott (1993), Zimbardo said:

« One of the subtle dangers arising out of the increase in concern for the ethics of experiments is it gives social psychologists an easy out. To do behavioural experiments is very difficult. Its time consuming, it's labour intensive and you can replace it with an 'as if' paper-and-pencil, 30-minute self-report. The question arises, 'is that the same thing?' If, in fact, you could discover the same things about human nature from asking people to imagine how they would behave in a situation instead of observing how they do, it clearly doesn't make sense to do the behavioural simulation. I think what you get from the Milgram study and my Prison study is very different from self-report-based ones. Indeed, Milgram asked 40 psychiatrists how people would behave in his conformity experiment. To a person they all got it wrong: they predicted that fewer than one per cent of the subjects would go all the way in shocking the innocent victim, when in actuality two-thirds blindly obeyed the unjust authority figure. There are situations you cannot imagine what it would be like until you are in them. So, if we are going to have a psychology of 'as if', of 'imagine this were the situation and how would you predict you would behave?', I think you are missing out on some of the powerful yet subtle dynamics of situational control ... »

« The contribution social psychologists make is [in] understanding what people will or won't do in certain situations. Typically, even if you describe the situation, people will underestimate its power. There is no way until you are in it, that you begin to feel and become entrapped in the power of the situation. »

ETHICAL GUIDELINES

As well using strategies such as role play and prior general consent (see p. 183), psychologists have also attempted to deal with ethical concerns by devising sets of ethical guidelines.

Ethical guidelines (the guidance given by professional associations, such as the British Psychological Society, on how psychologists should carry out their research) are necessary to clarify the conditions under which psychological research is acceptable. Nowadays, psychology departments in universities, colleges and hospitals have ethical committees that approve or reject proposed research. The decisions of these committees are strongly influenced by the criteria laid down in the ethical guidelines published by bodies such as the British Psychological Society (BPS). A summary of the BPS guidelines is shown in Table 5.3. This provides an outline of the guiding principles or 'rules' by which research psychologists operate.

Unfortunately, the mere existence of ethical guidelines does not guarantee ethical practice. Ethical codes have to be implemented conscientiously for this to happen. Furthermore, our views of what constitutes ethical conduct are not fixed for all time and so ethical guidelines require updating from time to time.

ACTIVITY

Your views on the BPS ethical guidelines

After you have read Table 5.3, *A summary of the ethical guidelines for research with human participants* (BPS 2000), discuss the following questions with others in your class.

1 To what extent do you think that the BPS Ethical Guidelines adequately protect the interests of those who choose to participate in psychological research?

2 These guidelines were published in 2000 and they were a revision of those published in 1993. Why do you think that ethical guidelines need to be revised at fairly regular intervals?

3 Should all psychologists who undertake research be compelled to follow a strict ethical code? If so, how could this be done? What do you think should happen to anyone who does not follow the code?

Table 5.3 >> A summary of the ethical guidelines for research with human participants (BPS 2000)

1 Introduction

Psychologists owe a debt to all those who take a part in their studies and so all participants should be treated with consideration and respect. This is reflected in the change from the term 'subjects' to 'participants'. Good psychological research is possible only if there is mutual respect and confidence between investigators and participants. Although investigators are potentially interested in all aspects of human behaviour, for ethical reasons some areas of human experience and behaviour may be beyond the reach of psychological investigation. Ethical guidelines are necessary to clarify the conditions under which psychological research is acceptable.

2 General

In all circumstances investigators must consider the ethical implications and psychological consequences for the participants in their research. The essential principle is that the investigation should be considered from the standpoint of all participants; foreseeable threats to their psychological wellbeing, health, values or dignity should be eliminated. Where investigations involve individuals of different ages, gender and social background, the investigators may not have sufficient knowledge of the implications of any investigation for the participants. The best judges of whether an investigation will cause offence may be members of the population from which the participants in the research are to be drawn.

3 Consent

Whenever possible, investigators should inform all participants of the objectives of the investigation and of all aspects of the research or intervention that might reasonably be expected to influence their willingness to participate. Research with children or with other vulnerable participants requires special safeguarding procedures. Where possible, the real consent of children and of adults with impairments in understanding should be obtained. In addition, where research involves people who are under 16 years of age, consent should be obtained from parents or from those *in loco parentis*. If this is not possible, approval must be obtained from an Ethics Committee. Investigators are often in a position of authority or influence over participants who may be their students, employees or clients. This relationship must not be allowed to pressurize the participants to take part in, or remain in, an investigation. The payment of participants must not be used to induce them to risk harm beyond that which they risk without payment in their normal lifestyle.

4 Deception

Withholding information or misleading participants is unacceptable if the participants are typically likely to show unease once debriefed. Where this is in any doubt, appropriate consultation must precede the investigation. Intentional deception of the participants over the purpose and general nature of the investigation should be avoided whenever possible, although it may be impossible to study some psychological processes without withholding information about the true object of the study or without deliberately misleading participants.

5 Debriefing

In studies where the participants are aware that they have taken part in an investigation, when the data have been collected, the investigator should provide the participants with any necessary information to complete their understanding of the nature of the research. The investigator should discuss with the participants their experience of the research in order to monitor any unforeseen negative effects or misconceptions. Debriefing does not provide justification for unethical aspects of an investigation.

6 Withdrawal from the investigation

At the outset, investigators should make plain to participants their right to withdraw from the research at any time, irrespective of whether or not payment or other inducement has been offered. In the light of experience of the investigation or as a result of debriefing, the participant has the right to withdraw retrospectively any consent given, and to require that their own data, including recordings, be destroyed.

7 Confidentiality

Except in circumstances specified by the law, information obtained about a participant during an investigation is confidential unless otherwise agreed in advance. Participants in psychological research have a right to expect that information they provide will be treated confidentially and, if published, will not be identifiable as theirs. Where confidentiality or anonymity cannot be guaranteed, the participant must be warned of this in advance of agreeing to participate.

8 Protection of participants

Investigators have a primary responsibility to protect participants from physical and mental harm during the investigation. Normally the risk of harm must be no greater than in ordinary life. Where research may involve behaviour or experiences that participants may regard as personal and private, the participants must be protected from stress by all appropriate measures, including the assurance that answers to personal questions need not be given. In research involving children, great caution should be used when discussing results with parents, teachers or those in *loco parentis*, since evaluative statements may carry unintended weight.

9 Observational research

Studies based upon observation must respect the privacy and psychological wellbeing of the individuals studied. Unless those being observed give their consent to being observed, observational research is only acceptable in situations where those observed would expect to be observed by strangers. Additionally, particular account should be taken of local cultural values and of the possibility of intruding upon the privacy of individuals who, even while in a normally public space, may believe they are unobserved.

continued on next page

Table 5.3 >> Summary of ethical guidelines continued

10 Giving advice

During research, an investigator may obtain evidence of psychological or physical problems of which a participant is apparently unaware. In such a case the investigator has a responsibility to inform the participant if the investigator believes that by not doing so the participant's future wellbeing may be endangered. If the issue is serious and the investigator is not qualified to offer assistance, the appropriate source of professional advice should be recommended.

11 Colleagues

Investigators share responsibility for the ethical treatment of research participants with their collaborators, assistants, students and employees. A psychologist who believes that another psychologist or investigator may be conducting research that is not in accordance with the principles above should encourage that investigator to re-evaluate the research.

Source: British Psychological Society (2000)

Evaluation of ethical guidelines

- *Only guidelines* – Guidelines are simply guidance (not hard-and-fast rules) and they are sometimes accused of being vague and difficult to apply.

- *Guidelines across cultures* – Different guidelines exist in different countries, e.g. the guidelines of the American Psychological Association (APA) are more detailed than those drawn up by the BPS. Most codes concentrate on the protection of participants from physical and psychological harm and on the confidentiality of the data they provide. On other matters, however, there is more variation between codes. In Holland, the guidelines deal with general advice to investigators, while the British guidelines are more concerned with the details of research procedures. In Canada, the guidelines advise going beyond the immediate concerns of the participants to analysing any long-term risks or benefits to both groups and individuals that might be affected. Therefore, we see that there is no universal set of guidelines applied to all psychologists worldwide.

- *Limited scope of BPS guidelines* – Condor (1991) has criticized the BPS guidelines for limiting its concerns to the relationship between the investigator and the participant and for ignoring the role of psychologists in society at large. Others accuse psychologists of perpetuating negative stereotypes (e.g. of elderly people) in books and research papers, and believe that ethical issues in psychology go beyond the traditional issues of confidentiality, deception or privacy (Gale 1995).

- *Role of ethical committees* – Most universities and other institutions that carry out research have ethical committees to scrutinize research proposals to ensure the rights of participants are being respected. The effectiveness of ethical guidelines and codes of conduct depends upon the rigour of these ethical committees. It is important that such committees include non-psychologists within their membership to represent the lay person's point of view.

- *Enforcing the guidelines* – Enforcement of ethical standards depends upon psychologists being willing to punish those who contravene the guidelines. The BPS and the APA impose penalties on their members if they infringe the ethical codes. However, every year A-level psychology students carry out investigations and these are not always supervised by BPS members or even psychologists. Therefore, there is potential for ethical guidelines to be breached. (Examination bodies, of course, provide guidance for conducting psychology practicals.)

- *Revising the guidelines* – Ethical codes are revised regularly to keep pace with social change. This is essential as society's views about morality change over time. The interests of psychologists also change, so that new ethical issues may arise (e.g. when to maintain confidentiality in research in the area of child abuse). The need for such revisions reminds us that ethical codes are not entirely dependent upon universal, unchanging truths.

ACTIVITY

Eliot Aronson on ethical issues

In the interview with Elliott Aronson on p. 190, you will learn the views of one of psychology's most distinguished scholars concerning the ethics of social influence research. Aronson focuses on the ethical dimension of these studies, but also makes the point that we have learned a great deal from such research.

Justifying individual studies in terms of a cost–benefit analysis is not always a straightforward task. Look again at the key studies you have covered in this unit.

- What were the 'costs' to the participants in each study, and what were the 'benefits' of the research?

- Did the benefits justify the costs?

- What other precautions might have been used to protect the participants in each study?

Ethical *dilemmas*

Elliot Aronson is Distinguished Visiting Professor at Stanford University. He graduated from Brandeis University in 1954, where he was influenced by Abraham Maslow. He has published 18 books (including the Handbook of Social Psychology *and* The Social Animal*) and more than 130 research articles. He is the only person in the 109-year history of the American Psychological Association to have been awarded all three of its highest academic prizes: For Distinguished Teaching (1980), for Distinguished Writing (1973) and for Distinguished Research Contributions (1999). In 2002 he was named as one of the 100 most eminent psychologists of the twentieth century.*

Q Does the importance of social influence research justify the methods used in its investigation?

A First, let me state that I believe that much (but certainly not all!) of the research on social influence is extremely important.

Second, I believe that we human beings are not fragile. Rather, we are extraordinarily resilient organisms. By that, I mean we can absorb an enormous amount of emotional discomfort without long-lasting negative effects.

Putting these two beliefs together, leads me to the following conclusions:

1 If the research is important, and well designed, and

2 If it is the best and perhaps the only way to get a peek at the phenomenon, and

3 If the degree of discomfort imposed by the experimenter on the participant is not extreme and is of short duration, then

4 I would conclude that the research is justified.

Elliot Aronson

For example, in Solomon Asch's experiment on conformity, we learned something both new and important: ordinary people will conform to implicit group pressure. I believe the research was justified because the question was an important one, the experiments were well designed, the results were clear – *and* the participants suffered a minimum of discomfort. Yes, it is discomforting to be in the minority, to have the data from your visual sense disconfirmed by the behaviour of others. But as discomforts go, this is minor. To spend an hour wondering about where you stand *vis-à-vis* the group is not an earth-shattering experience. Moreover, in the real world, we frequently find ourselves in disagreement with others, and it is no big deal.

At the other extreme, let us look at Philip Zimbardo's research on a simulated prison. I like to discuss this research in class because it is highly dramatic. But I don't think the experiment was justified. First, the discomfort was enormous. Second, the discomfort went on for six full days.

Third, because the investigators became captives to their role they were not sufficiently removed from the situation to protect the 'prisoners' from the excesses of the guards. Finally, although the situation was dramatic, I don't think we learned that much about prisons. We learned about the power of the social situation, of course – and that is important. But there are a great many experiments that have taught us that (albeit in less dramatic ways) that didn't produce such a high degree of anguish in the participants.

Q What about Stanley Milgram's experiment on obedience?

Here I am not quite sure. I think the research is extremely important. We learned for the first time that ordinary people (not just Nazis!) will go to great lengths in blind obedience to authority.

I also believe that there is no better way to get at the idea of obedience to authority than by doing it experimentally in a way similar to what Milgram did. Whenever I outline the situation to students in my class and ask them how they think they would have behaved, only 1 per cent think they might have gone all the way – while, as you know, in Milgram's experiments, about two out of three go all the way.

Thus, for me, the key issue is: "Did Milgram cross the line and make his participants too uncomfortable?" We know they sweated, strained and stuttered. We know many felt awful afterwards about what they had done. Yet, we also know that almost all of them were glad they participated. They felt they learned something extremely important. None suffered emotional disturbances.

Q Did Milgram have the right to provide them with this learning experience without their informed consent?

I think not. But I am glad he did! As a soft humanist, I think he went too far. But as a scientist interested in human behaviour, I am pleased that we have learned what we now know about obedience. In the balance, my belief in the resiliency of human beings tips the balance. No one was damaged by Milgram's experiment. I'm glad he did it – but I don't want anyone going quite that far again.

AS Social Psychology

Check your understanding of ethical issues in psychological research by answering these questions. Try to do this from memory at first. You can check your answers by looking back through Topic 3.

1 What do you understand by the terms: 'ethical issues', 'ethical guidelines', 'deception', 'informed consent' and 'protection of participants from psychological harm'.

2 Describe one alternative procedure that is used when it is not possible to gain fully informed consent.

3 Give two reasons why it is unwise to deceive participants.

4 Describe a procedure used to avoid deceiving participants.

5 What does the term 'debriefing' mean? Give its main aim.

6 The BPS guidelines state that participants should be protected from undue risk. What is meant by 'undue risk'?

7 Outline and evaluate two ethical criticisms made of Milgram's procedures.

8 Outline Milgram's response to one of these criticisms.

9 Are the studies of Milgram and Zimbardo justified in terms of the ethical issues that they raise?

10 To what extent have psychologists been successful in resolving the ethical issues raised by social influence research?

REVISION SUMMARY

Having covered this topic, you should be able to:

✓ define the following terms: 'ethical issue', 'ethical guidelines', 'deception', 'informed consent' and 'protection of participants from psychological harm'

✓ describe the key ethical issues associated with research on social influence

✓ discuss whether social influence research is justified in terms of the ethical issues that it raises

✓ outline and evaluate ways in which psychologists have dealt with ethical issues.

UNIT SUMMARY

Topic 1: Conformity and minority influence

- **Conformity** is the process of yielding to **majority influence**.

- **Compliance**, **identification** and **internalization** are types of conformity.

- People yield to majority influence because they wish to be liked (**normative social influence**) and because they wish to be right (**informational social influence**).

- Research into majority influence has found that there is strong group pressure to conform, especially if the majority is **unanimous** (**Asch**).

- **Zimbardo's prison simulation study** has shown that conformity to social roles plays an important part in shaping behaviour.

- More recent research has underlined the importance of **historical** and **cultural factors** in levels of conformity.

- **Minority influence** is a form of social influence where a persuasive minority successfully exerts pressure to change the attitudes, beliefs or behaviours of the majority. Those who yield to minority influence undergo a process of conversion.

- The **dissociation model** explains why minority influence may work slowly. Time is needed for minority ideas to become detached from their source before they are adopted openly by the majority.

- Research into minority influence has shown that minorities must behave **consistently** if they are to be influential (**Moscovici**).

- The **behavioural style** required for a minority to be influential is as follows:
  - consistent but not rigid
  - principled and willing to make sacrifices
  - similar in age and social standing to the majority
  - espousing views in line with current social trends.

- Some psychologists believe that majority and minority influences involve **different psychological processes**: majorities use normative processes to achieve compliance; minorities use informational processes to achieve conversion. Majority influence may produce quick effects, but minority influence may have more long-lasting effects.

Topic 2: Obedience

- **Obedience** is a type of social influence where somebody acts in response to a direct order from an authority figure.

- **Explanations** offered for obedience include:
  - gradual commitment to a legitimate authority
  - an agentic shift whereby individuals surrender autonomy and see themselves as agents of the person giving orders
  - the effect of buffers to protect individuals from the consequences of their actions
  - passivity that arises from a desire to avoid confrontation or upset
  - personality factors such as authoritarianism and psychopathy.

- **Differences** between obedience and conformity include:
  - different types of social pressure (orders in the case of obedience and social norms in the case of conformity)
  - different outcomes: public compliance (obedience) and private change (conformity where it takes the form of internalization)
  - conscious versus unconscious effect: we know when we have obeyed but we may not be aware of having conformed.

- **Milgram's** research on obedience found that when people occupy a subordinate position in a dominance hierarchy, they are inclined to blind obedience and that manipulating situational factors can influence obedience levels.

- Some psychologists have challenged the experimental (internal) validity of Milgram's studies but he has refuted any notion that his participants were merely role-playing.

- There is evidence from later studies (e.g. **Hofling and colleagues**) to support the ecological validity of Milgram's research.

- **Explanations** for resisting obedience include:
  - feeling responsible for one's own actions
  - observing others being disobedient
  - questioning the motives of those giving orders
  - having time to think about what is being requested
  - reacting against too blatant attempts to restrict one's freedom
  - high levels of moral reasoning.

Topic 3: Ethical issues in psychological research

- **Ethical issues** arise in research when there is a conflict between the rights and dignity of participants and the goals and outcome of research.

- Key ethical issues associated with social influence research include:
  - **informed consent**: an ethical requirement that participants should have sufficient information about a research study to enable them to make an informed judgement about whether or not to take part
  - **deception**: withholding information or misleading research participants
  - **protection of participants from psychological harm:** research participants should be protected from undue risk during an investigation.

- Is social influence research justified? Critics of Milgram and Zimbardo have accused them of deceiving and subjecting their participants to psychological harm. Others have defended their actions by referring to the importance of the findings and the extensive debriefing and follow-up procedures.

- Ways of dealing with ethical issues include:
  - gaining **prior general consent** or **presumptive consent** as ways of replacing the need for fully informed consent in situations where this is problematic
  - development of **ethical guidelines** by professional bodies to provide guidance on how psychologists should carry out research ethically.

- Guidelines, however, only offer guidance, and rigorous ethical committees are required to implement them. Society's views about what is moral continue to evolve and so ethical guidelines need to be updated periodically.

Answering exam questions on Social influence

For sample examination questions and answers on Social influence, together with examiners' comments on the answers, see pp. 259–61.

6 UNIT

QUANTITATIVE & QUALITATIVE Research Methods

PREVIEW

After you have read this unit, you should be able to:

>> describe three main types of experiment – laboratory experiments, field experiments and natural experiments – and discuss the main advantages and weaknesses of each

>> describe investigations using correlational analysis, and discuss the advantages and weaknesses of this research method

>> describe three non-experimental research methods – naturalistic observation, questionnaire surveys and interviews – and discuss the advantages and weaknesses of each

>> discuss the use of ethical guidelines in psychology.

INTRODUCTION

Psychologists use a wide range of research methods and techniques that allow them to gather and make sense of the data they produce. The data can be either quantitative or qualitative. Quantitative data have a numerical basis (e.g. time in seconds, stress ratings), whereas qualitative data are non-numerical (e.g. verbal reports of how research participants feel about something).

This unit is divided into two topics. Topic 1 focuses on the different types of experimental research, while the second topic examines the nature of non-experimental research. For many years the experiment, and in particular the laboratory experiment, has been the main research method used by psychologists. However, increasing dissatisfaction with the lack of realism of the findings from experimental research carried out in laboratories and their lack of relevance to everyday life has led psychologists to use alternative methods. This has resulted in an increase in the use of non-experimental methods producing qualitative data. It is now recognized that both experimental and non-experimental research methods have their place and can be considered to complement to each other.

As we examine the different research methods, we will consider the major ethical issues associated with each one. You will already appreciate the importance of ethical questions, for example, from reading about Milgram's studies of obedience and Zimbardo's prison simulation study in Unit 5, *Social influence*). These are two of the most hotly debated studies in psychology, because people disagree about whether they should have been carried out.

This unit discusses only some of the research methods that you are likely to meet as an AS-level student. Although research methods can be divided into specific categories, these methods can merge into each other. For example, the boundary between experimental and non-experimental research is far from clear cut. What really matters is that the most appropriate research method is used to investigate a particular problem or research question.

Graham Davies

The range of research methods psychologists use to study aspects of human and non-human behaviour include experiments, observations, questionnaire surveys and interviews. Which research method would you use to investigate each of the areas listed below? Note down the reasons for your choice:

1 the effects of day care on children's social and cognitive development

2 the effect of learning multiplication tables by heart on children's ability to solve mathematical problems

3 children's views on pocket money

4 the effect of playing violent computer games on levels of aggression in adolescents

5 children's behaviour in school playgrounds.

What problems might arise when using your chosen research method? How could you overcome these problems?

KEY TERMS

Quantitative data: information collected in the course of a research study that is in a quantified (numerical) form (e.g. speed of response in milliseconds).

Qualitative data: information collected in the course of a research study that is in non-numerical, narrative form, such as the transcript of what was said during a series of interviews.

Experiment: an investigative technique involving changes to one variable (the independent variable) in order to see its effect on another variable (the dependent variable), and to establish cause-and-effect relationships.

Laboratory experiment: an experiment carried out in a laboratory, allowing the researcher to exert a high level of control over the independent variable, and to eliminate or control for confounding variables.

Field experiment: an experiment carried out in a real-world setting (such as a classroom) rather than the more artificial setting of the laboratory.

Natural experiment: a type of quasi-experiment where the allocation of participants to the different experimental conditions is outside the control of the researcher, but rather reflects naturally occurring differences in the independent variable (e.g. two schools using different methods to teach reading).

Ethical guidelines: prescriptive guidance given by professional associations (e.g. the British Psychological Society) on how psychologists should practise or carry out their research.

EXPERIMENTAL RESEARCH IN PSYCHOLOGY

When carrying out an experiment, a researcher intervenes directly in the situation being investigated. The experimental method is regarded as being the most powerful research method used by psychologists because of its potential to investigate the causes of events, and thus to identify cause-and-effect relationships. A true experiment has three key features:

● The researcher manipulates an independent variable (IV) in order to investigate whether there is a change in a second variable, known as the dependent variable (DV).

● All other variables, which might influence the results, are either held constant or are eliminated.

● Participants are allocated to the experimental conditions randomly.

A variable is simply anything that can change (or vary). Examples include weight, response times, reading scores and IQ scores. In the simplest experiments, the researcher deliberately changes the IV, in order to see whether this manipulation affects the DV. For example, consider an experiment set up to investigate which of two methods is more successful at teaching young children to read. The IV would be the teaching method that the participants (i.e. the children taking part in the study) were exposed to. The DV would be some measure of their reading ability (for example, scores derived from a standard test of reading ability).

To be sure that it is the IV that has produced any change in the DV, the researcher must ensure that all other variables are held constant. If they cannot be held constant, then the effect of these variables needs to be eliminated. These unwanted variables are known as confounding variables, and might include the following:

● differences in the instructions given by an experimenter or in the stimulus materials being used – this can be overcome by standardizing the instructions and materials for all participants in the experiment

● differences between participants, e.g. in their age – this can be eliminated by using a single age group, or can be held constant by ensuring that the age structure of each of the groups taking part in the experiment is similar).

The logic of the true experiment is that, if all variables other than the IV have either been controlled or eliminated successfully, then any change that is produced in the DV must be the result of manipulating the IV.

As a principle of good experimental design, researchers must either allocate participants randomly to groups (i.e. give all those taking part an equal chance of being selected for each group) or permit all participants to experience each condition.

Sometimes, however, it is not possible to meet all three of the requirements for a true experiment. The term 'quasi-experiment' (the prefix 'quasi' means 'resembling but not really the same as') is used to describe an experiment where the investigator lacks complete control over the IV and/or the allocation of participants to groups. For example, if a psychologist was interested in studying the effectiveness of an anti-truancy strategy in schools, it probably would not be possible to introduce the strategy for some pupils but not for others. An alternative approach would be to undertake a quasi-experiment by comparing the truancy levels in schools where the strategy has been applied with the truancy levels in similar schools where it has not. This is a quasi-experiment because the researcher has no control over the allocation of participants to the two conditions – exposure to the anti-truancy strategy or no exposure to the anti-truancy strategy.

Evaluation of the experimental method

● By holding all variables constant between groups except for the IV, an experimenter may be able to establish a cause-and-effect relationship between the IV and the DV. No other research method can do this directly.

● The use of experiments means that researchers do not have to wait for natural events to reproduce the appropriate scenario needed to investigate a particular issue. It allows psychologists to study behaviour that rarely occurs or that cannot easily be studied in another way, such as bystander attitudes to an emergency. Also, it allows the researcher to select when, and possibly where, to undertake an experiment.

● An experiment generates quantitative data (numerical measures of the DV) which can be analysed using inferential statistical tests. These statistical tests (which are beyond the specification requirement for AS) allow the researcher to state how likely the results are to have occurred by chance, rather than by manipulating the IV.

● Once the data have been obtained and analysed, it is possible to generalize the findings from experimental research to the rest of the population from which the sample of participants has been drawn, provided that a representative sample of participants was selected to take part in the original study. However, the participants in many experimental investigations reflect an over-representation of males and of specific cultures, and have often been volunteers drawn from university campuses. You may, therefore, question how far it is reasonable to generalize the results of such experimental studies to groups of people beyond those represented by those taking part.

Identifying independent and dependent variables

After reading the brief descriptions below of three memory studies, identify the IV and DV in each one. The answers to this activity can be found on p. 211.

1 Baddeley (1986) investigated the effects of acoustic similarity on serial memory recall performance by presenting participants with a list of five short words that sound alike (e.g. *man, mat, map, can, cap*) and five short words that do not sound alike (e.g. *pen, day, few, cow, pit*).

2 Tyler *et al.* (1979) gave participants two sets of anagrams to solve: one set was easy (e.g. *doctro*), while the other was more difficult (*cdrtoo*). They were then unexpectedly asked to recall as many of the words as possible. The aim was to test the hypothesis that it is the amount of processing effort, rather than depth of processing, that affects memory retention.

3 Psychologists have been interested in the effects of the learning environment on memory recall. Smith (1979) gave participants a list of 80 words to learn while sitting in a distinctive basement room. The following day he tested some of the participants in the same basement room, others in a fifth-floor room with very different décor, and a third group in another upstairs room where participants were instructed to imagine themselves back in the basement room.

LABORATORY EXPERIMENTS

Laboratory experiments provide psychologists with the highest level of control over variables and are widely used in psychology. The psychology laboratory may be the only place where some sophisticated technical equipment can be used and accurate measurements made. Researchers interested in memory and cognitive processes often carry out laboratory experiments. For example, Stroop (1935) carried out a well-known series of laboratory experiments. He studied how colour-name words have an interfering effect on the time taken to name the ink colours of non-matching colours. For example, naming the ink colour of the word 'blue' written in green ink takes longer than it does for the same word written in blue ink. This effect has become known as the Stroop effect (see the activity below).

A participant is briefed in Milgram's research into obedience (see p. 171) – a classic laboratory experiment

The Stroop effect

In one experiment, Stroop (1935) selected five colour names – red, blue, green, brown and purple. For the experimental group, each word was printed several times in a grid, but never in the colour it named; instead, it appeared an equal number of times in each of the other four colours. A second sheet was produced of the same words in reverse order.

The control group experienced the same arrangement of ink colours, but this time each ink colour was represented by a coloured block. The researcher manipulated whether the stimulus sheets consisted of words in ink colours that conflicted with the colour names or were in the form of colour blocks.

The times taken to name the ink colours for each condition were compared. On average, it took participants 47 seconds longer to name the ink colours of a stimulus sheet in the experimental condition than in the control condition.

1 What is the IV in this experiment?

2 What is the DV?

3 How many conditions are there in this experiment?

4 Are the data collected quantitative or qualitative?

5 What cause-and-effect relationship does this study investigate?

Compare your answers with those on p. 211.

Advantages of laboratory experiments

- **Replicability of procedures** – A laboratory experiment that is well carried out and clearly reported can easily be repeated (replicated) by other researchers to see if they obtain similar results. If this happens and the findings are similar, then confidence is increased in the results. Without this ability to replicate studies fairly easily in a laboratory setting, researchers would have to wait indefinitely for the precise set of circumstances required for a particular experiment to recur.

- **Control over variables** – It is easier to control potential confounding variables in the laboratory than in any other setting or with any other research method, so high levels of precision can be achieved. If all variables other than the IV are controlled successfully or eliminated, then cause and effect can be established.

Weaknesses

- **Loss of validity** – By establishing high levels of control, and narrowly defining IVs and DVs, an experimental situation can become artificial and recognizably different from real-life situations. Laboratory studies were originally designed for use in the natural sciences such as chemistry and physics, where matter reacts in exactly the same way to external events under a given set of conditions. Human behaviour is far more complex and is affected by internal factors such as awareness, emotions and motives relating to human consciousness, as well as external variables that can be manipulated by the researcher.

  Ecological validity is concerned with the extent to which results may be generalized to settings other than the one in which the research took place, such as those outside the laboratory. For example, memory experiments have often been conducted using word lists, which are rarely learned in everyday life. However, in some research the artificiality of the laboratory situation may not really matter, such as when carrying out research on newborn infants or on auditory perception. Ecological validity is discussed more fully in Unit 7 (see p. 227).

- **Demand characteristics** – These occur when participants try to make sense of the research situation they find themselves in and act accordingly (Orne 1962). These can seriously threaten the validity of an experiment. The demands placed on participants in a laboratory situation are not helped by the experimenter sticking rigidly to a standardized procedure and acting in an unemotional way, which is necessary if confounding variables are to be avoided. Participants may respond to specific cues made by an investigator, such as differences in the tone of voice used or non-verbal signs of encouragement. Participants may also try to behave

in a way that they believe will be helpful to the researcher. Or, if feeling awkward or irritated by what is happening, they may set out deliberately to confound the results.

Other potential problems include evaluation apprehension, where participants demonstrate concern over what an experimenter might find out about them, or social desirability effects, where participants change their everyday behaviour so that they may be perceived more favourably by others.

Ethical issues

- **Consent** – In all psychological research, the fully informed consent of all the participants must be obtained. However, once in the laboratory setting, participants might become so overawed by the environment that they feel unable to withdraw from the procedure even if they wanted to. So, it is vital to abide by the guidelines about participants' right to withdraw from an investigation (see p. 188).

- **Deception** – Some experiments undertaken by social psychologists involve deception; in these situations, it is important to debrief participants about the true nature of the study and to obtain their consent to use the data collected (for example, turn to pp. 184–6 to remind yourself of the ethical issues raised by Milgram's research on obedience).

- **Use of animals** – Animals are often used in laboratory experiments as this offers greater opportunities for experimental control in research procedures, compared to research with humans. For example, Harlow and Harlow's deprivation studies with rhesus monkeys (see p. 53), could not have been carried out on humans. Since animals are not able to consent to their involvement in research, they must not be subjected to unnecessary suffering.

Now there's nothing to be worried about - it's a perfectly harmless experiment

FIELD EXPERIMENTS

Field experiments are experimental investigations carried out in the natural environment of those being studied, e.g. in homes, schools or on the street. These experiments attempt to improve the realism of the research. As with the laboratory experiment, an IV is still deliberately manipulated by the researcher to produce a change in a DV. Therefore, much of what has been written in the previous section about the laboratory experiment also applies to the field experiment, so here we focus on the key differences.

The field experiment is used in situations where it is considered particularly important for research to take account of the natural environment. For example, the method is used widely when studying non-human animals.

Field experiments are often more costly to undertake than those carried out in laboratory settings and may also take longer to complete. In addition, it may be more difficult to use sophisticated technical equipment outside a laboratory.

Advantages of field experiments

● *Improved ecological validity* – By avoiding the artificiality of the laboratory environment, the field experiment helps to eliminate the common criticism made of the laboratory experiment that it may be difficult to generalize the findings to real-life situations.

● *Reduction of demand characteristics* – Participants may be unaware that they are taking part in a research study, and so the influence of demand characteristics may be minimized.

Weaknesses

● *Establishing controls* – It is difficult to establish high levels of control in a field experiment, not only over IVs and in measuring DVs, but also over any potentially confounding variables. For example, non-participants may intrude through conversation

ACTIVITY

Field experiments

Read the accounts of the two field experiments below. In each case, why do you think that a field experiment was used in preference to a laboratory experiment?

Two examples of field experiments

Mating success of long-tailed widow birds (Andersson 1982)

In this experiment, Andersson demonstrated the importance of tail length to the mating success of the long-tailed widow bird, a species in which the males have very long tails (see photo right). The IV was tail length – some birds had their tails lengthened, others had them shortened and some had normal-length tails as controls. Mating success was measured by the average (mean) number of nests per male (this was the DV). Those with the longest tails were the most successful in terms of their mating success, whilst those with the shortest tails had the least mating success.

Bonding between mother and infant (Klaus and Kennell 1976)

In this field experiment, the IV was the random allocation of mothers to one of two groups, following the birth of their babies. In one group, mothers were allowed extra contact with their babies immediately following the birth. In the second group, the babies were separated from their mothers until the time for their first feed (the standard hospital procedure). The DV was how the mothers subsequently reacted towards their babies. Amongst the findings from this research study were that mothers in the group who had had extra contact reacted more positively to their babies in a number of ways (e.g. holding their babies closer and establishing eye contact more often) compared with mothers in the other group.

or simply by being present where the experiment is taking place. Because of the increased difficulty of establishing controls, it may be more difficult to replicate precisely a field experiment than a laboratory experiment.

● *Generalizing to other situations* – Although realism is high in a field experiment, the results cannot be generalized to other real-life situations that differ from the one in which the field experiment took place.

Ethical issues

● *Consent* – Ethical issues relating to informed consent and participants' right to withdraw are similar to those for laboratory experiments.

What steps can researchers in field experiments take to minimize disruption to the natural environment?

● *Confidentiality* – Since field experiments are undertaken in real-world settings, such as schools and hospitals, the identity of any organizations and participants involved must be protected. Simply removing the names of organizations or people, and substituting descriptive characteristics (such as 'a large teaching hospital in Nottingham', or by referring to the age, gender of participants) may not be good enough to guarantee anonymity. Where confidentiality or anonymity cannot be guaranteed, the participants must be warned of this in advance.

● *Use of animals* – When animals are used in field experiments, their natural environment is being altered in some way because of the very nature of a field experiment. Such tampering with nature in order to understand it places great responsibilities on researchers to ensure that they minimize the disruptive effects of any manipulation.

NATURAL EXPERIMENTS

In a natural experiment, the researcher exploits naturally occurring differences in the independent variable; the researcher does not directly control the IV. The approach is therefore best described as a quasi-experiment (see p. 196), although some purists might even regard it as non-experimental.

Examples of natural experiments can be found in the adoption studies discussed in Unit 2 (see p. 62, for example). Occasionally, an unforeseen event in the environment permits a natural experiment to be undertaken, such as the effect of widespread witnessing of violent crime on levels of violence subsequently recorded. Berkowitz (1970) hypothesized that witnessing violence makes people more violent. He recorded and examined data on violent crime before and after the assassination in 1963 of President Kennedy in the USA, which appeared on TV in America and throughout the world. Berkowitz was able to demonstrate a sudden rise in violent crime after the assassination, thereby supporting his hypothesis.

Advantages of natural experiments

● *Reduction of demand characteristics* – Participants may be unaware that they are taking part in an experiment, and so demand characteristics are avoided.

● *Lack of direct intervention* – The experimenter does not intervene directly in the research situation, although it is possible that the researcher's mere presence may still produce an effect on the participants' behaviour.

Weaknesses

● *Loss of control* – Since the IV is not directly controlled by the investigator, the degree of control exercised is less than in either the laboratory experiment or the field experiment. This reduces the likelihood of cause and effect being established.

- *Likelihood of the desired behaviour being displayed* – The naturally occurring situation that the researcher wishes to study may occur only rarely, thus reducing the available opportunities for research. This is illustrated in the study of violent crime by Berkowitz (1970) outlined above.

Ethical issues

- *Consent* – Ethical issues relating to obtaining fully informed consent and safeguarding participants' right to withdraw from a natural experiment are similar to those for field experiments.

- *Protection of participants* – This is also essential. For example, probing participants' views about the death penalty, following an increase in widely reported murders or terrorist atrocities might increase anxiety levels and lead to unwarranted distress associated with the study.

- *Confidentiality* – Participants in natural experiments have the right to expect that information they provide will be treated confidentially and, if published, will not be identifiable as theirs. Where confidentiality or anonymity cannot be guaranteed, participants must be warned of this in advance.

✓ CHECK YOUR UNDERSTANDING

Check your understanding of the nature of experimental research by answering these questions. Try to do this from memory at first. You can check your answers by looking back through Topic 1.

1 What are (a) qualitative data (b) quantitative data?
2 Why are ethical guidelines important?
3 List the three key features of a true experiment.
4 What is meant by the term 'demand characteristics'?
5 Give two advantages and two weaknesses of laboratory experiments.
6 What is a field experiment?
7 Give two advantages and two weaknesses of field experiments.
8 What is a natural experiment?
9 Give two advantages and two weaknesses of natural experiments.
10 Define what is meant by (a) an independent variable (b) a dependent variable.

REVISION SUMMARY

Having covered this topic you should be able to:

✓ define the following terms: 'quantitative data', 'qualitative data', 'experiment', 'laboratory experiment', 'field experiment', 'natural experiment', 'ethical guidelines'

✓ distinguish between quantitative and qualitative data

✓ identify three main types of experiment – laboratory, field and natural experiments

✓ describe the key features of a laboratory experiment

✓ describe the key features of a field experiment

✓ describe the key features of a natural experiment

✓ discuss the main advantages and weaknesses of these three types of experiment

✓ describe the ethical issues associated with laboratory experiments, field experiments and natural experiments.

GETTING YOU THINKING...

Dramatic Increase in Bullying in Local School

Imagine that you have just read a newspaper article with this headline. It reports that a short questionnaire was circulated to pupils of all the five secondary schools in your town. Sixty-five per cent of respondents stated that they had been bullied at school during the past two years. The article suggests that this dramatic increase is the result of poor discipline in the schools and holds the teachers responsible for this terrible state of affairs.

You have decided to contact the researcher and ask some questions, in order to prepare a report for your school magazine about this research.

1 Make a list of questions to ask the researcher who carried out the study. You want to find out whether you can be confident that the findings reflect the true incidence of bullying in the schools.

2 The newspaper article accuses teachers of using poor discipline. How might you go about researching whether or not this is true?

3 Imagine you discover that bullying is more common in schools with poor discipline. Can you be sure that the poor discipline causes the bullying? If not, why not and what other factors might be involved?

KEY TERMS

Investigation using correlational analysis: an investigation using a type of analysis that measures the extent of the relationship between variables that are thought likely to co-vary (e.g. height and weight).

Naturalistic observation: an observational technique where behaviour is observed in its natural context without intrusion by the person who is doing the observing.

Questionnaire survey: a technique, using a structured set of questions, for asking a large sample of people about their views and behaviours, etc. Questionnaire surveys may be conducted in person, by telephone, by post, via the Internet, etc.

Interview: any face-to-face situation where one person (the interviewer) asks a series of questions of another person (the respondent). These questions may be structured, semi-structured or unstructured.

In this topic we will examine research in which an IV is not deliberately manipulated by a researcher. Each of the research methods outlined here allows psychologists to study behaviour in more natural settings. However, this potential benefit has its costs – as a result of reduced levels of control, it is not possible for the researcher to reach any definite conclusion concerning cause-and-effect relationships, which is important if we are to understand behaviour as fully as possible.

The non-experimental methods discussed here are investigations using:

● correlational analysis
● naturalistic observations
● questionnaire surveys
● interviews.

CORRELATIONAL ANALYSIS

The term 'correlation' refers to a descriptive statistical technique that measures the relationships between variables. Literally, these techniques measure co-relationships between variables – that is, the extent to which high values on one variable are associated with high values on another (known as a positive correlation), or the extent to which high values on one variable are associated with low values on another (a negative correlation). Many correlational techniques calculate a correlation coefficient, a statistic that has a value on a scale between +1 (known as a perfect positive correlation) and –1 (known as a perfect negative correlation). The strength of a correlation (i.e. the degree of the relationship) increases as a calculated correlation coefficient moves away from zero and becomes closer to +1 or –1. Correlation coefficients are discussed more fully on pp. 241–2.

As it is a statistical technique, correlation is not strictly a research method, but the term is also used to refer to the overall design of non-experimental investigations that specifically try to identify relationships between variables.

Uses of correlational analysis

Correlational research is often used to investigate the extent of relationship between variables that are thought likely to co-vary. For example, Murstein (1972) was interested in whether we select partners who are of similar physical attractiveness to ourselves (see the panel below).

Another major use of correlation is in the early stages of research into a particular area, especially where it is desirable to isolate relationships from a web of complex variables. For example, studies using Holmes and Rahe's Social Readjustment Rating Scale (1967) have found a correlation between Life Change Units (scores derived from using the scale) and the incidence of illness (see p. 89).

Correlational techniques also play a major role in establishing the reliability and validity of psychological measuring instruments, such as psychometric tests of intelligence and personality. The concepts of reliability and validity are discussed further in Unit 7 (pp. 226–8).

Physical attractiveness and marital choice (Murstein 1972)

Murstein hypothesized that individuals tend to select marital partners of comparable physical attractiveness to themselves. He set out to investigate whether partners forming premarital couples were more similar in terms of their physical attractiveness than one would expect by chance.

Ninety-eight couples who were described as 'engaged' or 'going steady' participated as paid volunteers in his research. All participants were asked to rate the physical attractiveness of their partner and also to estimate their own physical attractiveness using a five-point scale.

Photographs were also taken of all the participants. Independent judges were asked to rate the physical attractiveness of each pair of couples.

The following correlation coefficients were obtained:

Relationship between:	Correlation coefficient
Male participants' perception of their own and their partners' attractiveness	+0.50
Female participants' perception of their own and their partners' attractiveness	+0.45
Independent judges' ratings of the physical attractiveness of partners	+0.38

All the correlation coefficients were highly significant (p < 0.01), meaning that the likelihood of these results occurring by chance was highly unlikely, at less than 1 in 100. The data therefore supported Murstein's hypothesis about the relationship between physical attractiveness and marital choice.

Does Murstein's research explain why highly attractive celebrity figures are often attracted to each other?

Analysis of Bowlby's '44 thieves' study

Reread the description of Bowlby's (1944) study of 44 juvenile thieves on p. 60. Then answer the questions below:

1 What type of study did Bowlby undertake?

2 What hypothesis was being tested?

3 Did the findings support the hypothesis?

4 What type of data did Bowlby collect in this study?

5 Do the results allow us to conclude that there was a link between frequent early separations and emotional maladjustment, or that frequent early separations cause emotional maladjustment?

6 Would it be possible to design an experiment to demonstrate a causal relationship between early separation and subsequent emotional maladjustment? Give reasons for your answer.

Advantages of correlational analysis

● *Measuring the strength of relationships* – Correlational techniques provide a precise quantitative measure of the strength of the relationship between specific variables.

● *Value to exploratory research* – Correlational techniques allow for the measurement of many variables and the relationships between them at the same time. They are useful, therefore, when trying to unravel complex relationships and are a powerful tool for exploratory research.

Weaknesses

● *The issue of causality* – It is impossible to establish cause and effect through research investigations using correlational analysis; it can only measure the degree of interrelationship between different variables. For example, Snedecor (1956) reported a near perfect negative correlation of -0.98 between the production of pig iron in the USA and the birth rate in Britain for the years 1875 to 1920! This ability to identify spurious relationships is a real drawback of the technique.

To illustrate the problem, there is a well-established correlation between the presence of symptoms of schizophrenia and the high availability of the neurotransmitter dopamine. However, there is insufficient evidence to state that excess dopamine causes schizophrenia. It remains possible that it is schizophrenia that causes the increase in available dopamine or, indeed, that there may be other links in the causal chain which have yet to be discovered. Nevertheless, the existence of this correlation has provided a useful avenue for further research.

● *Measurement of non-linear relationships* – Non-linear relationships cannot be measured by commonly used correlational techniques. For example, Fig. 6.1 shows the relationship between time of day and attention level in a group of students. Initially, there is a positive correlation between the two variables, but as lunchtime approaches this changes into a negative relationship. The result is that when such data are analysed statistically, the positive and negative relationships tend to cancel each other out, with the result that no meaningful relationship is indicated by the calculated correlation coefficient. It is important therefore to plot non-linear relationships visually in order to understand better what is happening.

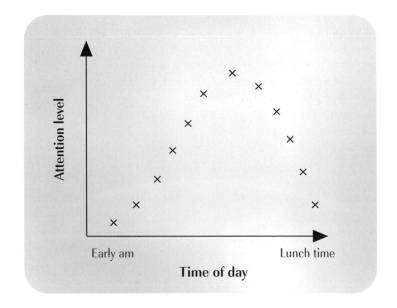

Figure 6.1 >>
Relationship between time of day and attention level in students

Ethical issues

- *Consent* – The same issues of fully informed consent and right to withdraw (as discussed under 'Natural experiments') apply here.
- *Use of findings* – In socially sensitive research, such as an investigation of sexual offences against children or drug abuse, the question of who 'owns'

the data is very complex. It raises possible concerns about research findings being used for reasons other than those for which they were originally intended. Researchers must, therefore, consider in advance how their research might be used. Participants can then give their informed consent not only to their participation in the study, but also to the ways in which the findings will be disseminated and used.

NATURALISTIC OBSERVATION

In naturalistic observation, behaviour is observed and recorded in its natural setting and there is no deliberate manipulation of variables. This research method provides a counter to tightly controlled research methods such as the laboratory experiment. The emphasis is placed on how people or non-human animals behave in natural situations; no attempt is made to influence the behaviour being investigated. The method can therefore be used in situations where intervention would be inappropriate (e.g. when studying weddings or funerals) or unethical (e.g. interventions with children).

Naturalistic observation may nevertheless be laboratory based. Some species (e.g. rats) appear to adapt well to laboratory conditions and the behaviour displayed in psychological laboratory settings may be considered sufficiently natural for naturalistic observational research to be undertaken.

Psychological laboratories can also be designed to resemble playrooms. Once children have become completely accustomed to such a room, their behaviour there may be sufficiently natural for naturalistic observational research to be undertaken.

A distinction is often made between participant observation, in which the observer actually joins the group of people being studied, and non-participant observation, in which the observer remains external to those being observed. Observers may choose whether to remain disclosed or undisclosed, so that participants are either made aware or remain unaware of the research taking place.

Uses of naturalistic observation

The wide range of uses of naturalistic observation includes topics such as driver behaviour, the behaviour of children in school settings and studies of the workplace. It is also useful where behaviour might be difficult to recreate in a laboratory setting or as a preliminary to laboratory investigation. An example of naturalistic observational research is that by Rosenhan (1973) described in the panel on the right.

Naturalistic observation has always been popular in research carried out on non-human animals. Examples include the classic research by Lorenz on imprinting (see p. 54). The method is particularly useful when studying

On being sane in insane places (Rosenhan 1973)

Eight people who were entirely free of any psychiatric symptoms presented themselves to different psychiatric hospitals in the United States of America. All reported the same symptom – they said that they heard a voice say "dull", "empty" and "thud". Apart from this single symptom they were all instructed to behave normally and to give honest answers to any other questions they were asked. All were believed to be genuine patients and were admitted to the psychiatric hospitals concerned, seven with a diagnosis of schizophrenia. Once admitted into hospital, they immediately stopped reporting that they had been hearing voices. They were later discharged 7 to 52 days later with diagnoses of "schizophrenia in remission". Rosenhan attributed these diagnoses to the context in which their behaviour was observed. None actually displayed symptoms of schizophrenia, but the context in which the symptoms were reported led to an expectation that these 'pseudopatients' were indeed mentally ill.

species that do not thrive in, or adapt to, laboratory conditions (e.g. red deer or marine mammals).

Advantages

- *Value as a preliminary research tool* – Careful use of naturalistic observation can lead to the identification of appropriate hypotheses for further investigation or may, on the other hand, help to prevent time being wasted in carrying out unrealistic experiments. It is a useful technique for studying unknown or little-known behaviours. For example, Clutton-Brock and colleagues have provided much of our knowledge about the behaviour of red deer through their pioneering studies carried out on the island of Rum in the Hebrides (e.g. Clutton-Brock and Albon 1979).

Why is naturalistic observation a popular method for research into the behaviour of non-human animals?

● **Validity** – Naturalistic observation can provide a useful check on whether experimental findings apply outside laboratory conditions. Realism and ecological validity can be good, provided that the observer remains undetected. The overall quality of the research may be improved through increased familiarity with the research setting, i.e. the researcher can become a "predictable and familiar part of the environment" with both human and non-human participants (Coolican 1999). Demand characteristics are minimized because behaviour is not affected either by anxiety or by inhibition that results from being in a laboratory situation. Also, with undisclosed naturalistic observation, there will be no feeling of a need to impress the researcher, as long as the observer remains undetected.

Weaknesses of naturalistic observation

● **Control** – The level of control over potentially confounding variables is poor, although some degree of control is often possible by, for example, limiting the focus of the study. This means that cause-and-effect relationships cannot be established with any certainty. Replication may be difficult, due to the problems that arise in controlling variables such as differences between naturalistic settings. Problems may sometimes be minimized with the appropriate use of sound or video recordings, so that a record exists that can be used by others to check the researcher's own interpretation of observed behaviours.

● **Observer effects** – It is possible that the presence of an observer may change participant behaviour, especially when a small group is being studied. This can also be an issue when observing non-human animals. For example, breeding patterns may be disturbed by the mere presence of an observer. Additionally, the potential exists for bias on the part of observers themselves, deriving from their expectations or interpretations of events.

● **Costs** – There may be problems with costs, such as those for travel or of transporting equipment.

● **Categorization of data** – There may be limitations concerning how the data gathered are categorized, affecting the interpretations of behaviour made – a behaviour may be observed that does not easily fit into the categories used. For example, identical behaviour in children might be classified as 'aggressive' by one researcher and as 'rough and tumble play' by another.

● **Replicability** – Because of the uniqueness of each observational situation, it may be difficult or even impossible to generalize results to other occasions or other settings.

Ethical issues

● **Privacy** – Studies based on observation must respect the privacy and psychological wellbeing of the individuals studied. Unless those being observed give their consent to being observed, observational research is only acceptable in situations where those observed would expect to be observed by strangers (e.g. in the high street of a major town). Particular account should be taken of local cultural values and of the possibility of intruding upon the privacy of individuals who, even while in a normally public space, may believe they are unobserved. Those observed have the right to expect that any information they provide will be treated confidentially and, if published, will not be identifiable as theirs.

● **Confidentiality and consent** – If researchers do not disclose that they are undertaking observational research and collect data in a non-public setting, such as a hospital ward or a school playground, they should subsequently inform those who were observed about the study and obtain their consent to use the data collected. If confidentiality or anonymity cannot be guaranteed, the participant must be warned of this in advance.

● **Use of findings** – The same issues arise as discussed under 'Correlational analysis' on p. 203.

QUESTIONNAIRE SURVEYS

A survey involves the systematic gathering of data from large numbers of people, usually by means of questionnaires. Vast amounts of data are regularly collected by large-scale surveys from households across the UK and are published in tables and charts in reports such as *Social Trends*. This provides a range of fascinating social and economic data about British society today, including population statistics, data about households and families, education, the labour market, health and lifestyles. You can access *Social Trends* electronically via the National Statistics website (see p. 213 for address).

Most surveys are carried out on carefully selected representative groups (referred to as 'samples') so that the researcher can generalize to the wider population from which any such group was drawn. The main exception is the national census that is carried out every ten years and involves every adult in the UK (i.e. the total adult population) and not a sample.

Questionnaire surveys can be used in a wide range of research situations. They allow researchers to ask participants questions about, for example, their attitudes, behaviours or intentions. They can be used where a pen-and-paper method is appropriate, allowing the researcher to gain information from a large sample of participants relatively quickly and efficiently. The researcher does not need to be present when the questionnaire is administered, although the researcher's presence may be helpful to answer any queries that the respondent has. Questionnaire surveys can be conducted face to face, by post, by telephone, via the Internet or left for participants to collect from some central point. As we shall see, both qualitative and quantitative data may be produced.

Questions can be of two broad types:

● *Closed questions* are those where the researcher determines the range of possible answers; respondents often reply by ticking boxes or circling appropriate answers. These questions are best used when factual information is required. They produce information that is easy to quantify and analyse, but which may lack realism due to the forced choices of answers available to the respondents. Examples of different forms of closed questions are shown in the panel below.

● *Open-ended questions* are those in which the researcher does not restrict the range of available answers. So, for example, a researcher might start an interview by asking: "What are your views on the use of corporal punishment by parents?" Open-ended questions produce a greater depth of qualitative information, but at a cost – answers are more difficult to analyse because the range of possible answers is so wide.

Some examples of closed questions

● *Checklists* – respondents tick any items that apply.

For example: Please tick the subjects in the following list that you studied at GCSE level.

☐ Art   ☐ English   ☐ History

☐ Geography   ☐ Mathematics   ☐ Psychology

☐ Science   ☐ Sociology

● *Placing items in rank order*

For example: Place a number against each of your GCSE subjects, placing them in rank order from most liked (given the number 1) to least liked.

● *Attitude scales*

For example: Underline the response that best reflects your attitude to the statement: 'A university education is essential if you are to succeed in the employment market.'

Do you: – strongly disagree?
– disagree?
– neither disagree or agree?
– agree?
– strongly agree?

● *Likert scales* – based on a numerical rating.

For example: How important are the following factors to the relationship between you and your partner? (Please circle the appropriate number.)

	Very Important	Neither important nor unimportant	Very unimportant
Sense of humour	1	2	3	4	5
Common interests	1	2	3	4	5
Mutual respect	1	2	3	4	5

● *Semantic differential scales* – where respondents are asked to rate items on scales based on a series of pairs of opposite adjectives.

For example: How would you rate your feelings about your AS-level Psychology course? (Place a tick at the appropriate point on each scale.)

Warm	I I I I I I I I	Cold
Satisfied	I I I I I I I I	Dissatisfied

When carrying out questionnaire surveys, it is good practice to keep the number of questions to a minimum, use short questions and phrase these questions very clearly in order to avoid any ambiguity or misunderstandings. Questions that are emotionally charged should be avoided.

Ideally, any questionnaire should be carefully piloted before it is administered (pilot studies are discussed in Unit 7, see p. 226).

Questionnaire surveys produce descriptive and/or explanatory information that can be tailored to fit a wide range of research situations. They can be carried out as a 'one-off' or, more powerfully, they can be conducted both before and after some event in order to examine the impact of that event. Their flexibility means that they are valuable both as a preliminary research tool and as a source of in-depth information on some topic of interest.

Examples of well-known questionnaires include the Social Readjustment Rating Scale (Holmes and Rahe 1967; see pp. 89–91) and the Hassles and Uplifts Scales developed by Kanner *et al.* (1981; see pp. 91–2).

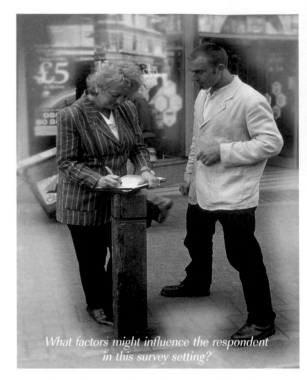
What factors might influence the respondent in this survey setting?

Advantages of questionnaire surveys

- **Simplicity** – Once constructed and piloted, questionnaires can be carried out with a minimum of training. Quantitative data obtained from closed questions are usually straightforward to analyse, so it is often easy to compare answers from different individuals or groups of respondents.

- **Speed** – Response rates (i.e. the proportion of people sent the questionnaire who choose to respond) tend to be quite low – around 30 per cent or fewer of those who were sent the questionnaire. However, large amounts of information can be gathered cheaply from a large number of respondents within a fairly short period of time.

Weaknesses

- **Problems with question wording** – If the wording of questions is ambiguous, then respondents may interpret the question in different ways and their answers may reflect this. Meaningful analysis of the responses therefore becomes difficult.

  Leading questions may also influence the responses given. For example, it is clear what answer is being encouraged by the question: "Don't you think that spending money on education is good?" Different interpretations of language can also be problematic. For example, there may be different interpretations of the term 'rarely' when used in a question about days off work due to illness. To one person, 'rarely' may mean once or twice a month; to another, once or twice a year. Finally, social desirability bias may be an issue – respondents may not provide truthful answers, especially to personal or potentially

embarrassing questions. They may wish their answers to be seen in the best possible light.

- **Researcher effects and biases** – If a researcher administers the questionnaire personally, then respondents may be influenced by factors such as the researcher's ethnic origin, age, appearance, gender or mode of dress. Even unintentional nods, smiles or frowns can have an effect on the results.

  Researcher bias may be a problem when analysing the data. For example, a researcher might interpret one possible answer option on a questionnaire as being more socially desirable than other possible answers. Responses in this category might be wrongly interpreted as providing genuine support for the researcher's particular (biased) viewpoint. (See Unit 7 for further detail about the wording of questionnaires.)

Ethical issues

- **Privacy** – Studies based on questionnaire surveys must respect the privacy and psychological wellbeing of all those who agree to complete the questionnaire. Those responding have the right to expect that any information they provide will be treated confidentially and, if published, will not be identifiable as theirs. If confidentiality or anonymity cannot be guaranteed, the participant must be warned of this in advance.

- **Consent** – Researchers need to safeguard respondents' right to withdraw some or all of their data from the study, and respondents should give their consent for their data to be included in the findings.

- **Risk of harm** – Investigators have a primary responsibility to protect respondents from psychological harm during an investigation. Normally, the risk of harm must be no greater than in ordinary life. Where a questionnaire probes behaviour or experiences that respondents may regard as personal and private, the respondents must be protected from stress by a range of appropriate measures, including the assurance that answers to personal questions need not be given. In research involving children, great care should be taken when discussing results with parents, teachers or those *in loco parentis*, since evaluative statements may carry unintended weight and, again, may cause distress.

- **Debriefing and support** – Questions on socially sensitive topics can cause distress to respondents, and appropriate debriefing and support mechanisms must be made available. However, survey researchers must also be vigilant regarding any questions that could appear straightforward, such as asking parents about their views on disciplining children. Such questions could trigger psychological distress in some respondents, who may subsequently require debriefing and support.

INTERVIEWS

<< Conducting interviews is a complex, labour intensive and uncertain business, fraught with tricky issues that social scientific researchers, and particularly psychologists, are often ill-equipped to address.>> (Banister *et al.* 1994)

Despite these difficulties, the interview is a common way of carrying out research; it may form the basis of a case study or may be used as one of the ways of conducting a survey.

Most research establishes some kind of distance between the researcher and the researched, but this kind of approach is challenged by the face-to-face nature of the interview, which is both personal and public. In order to encourage the flow of information from the interviewee to the interviewer, the interview needs an explicit purpose and aims.

Interviews also need very careful planning and piloting (see Unit 7). In some instances the focus of an interview is determined by the researcher; in others it may be negotiated between the interviewer and the interviewee.

- **Structured interviews** usually aim to produce quantitative data and include questions that are decided in advance with the aim of structuring the interviewee's responses. In this sense, they are similar to experimental research because the researcher largely determines the focus.

The structured approach has several advantages. The interviewer and interviewee are less likely to deviate from the topic that is the desired focus of the interview. Also, data analysis may be simpler, results are easier to generalize, less training is needed for interviewers, and there is less risk of the results being affected by interviewer bias, since the interviewer is more likely to be objective. However, there are costs as well as benefits. The researcher cannot follow up any new lines of enquiry that become apparent during the interview, and validity may be threatened by participants reacting to the formality of the research situation.

- **Unstructured interviews** are far less rigid and very little, if anything, concerning their nature will be decided in advance. They often start with one or two set questions, with further questions picking up on issues that the interviewee raises. These interviews can be more difficult to analyse, but have greater validity, as interviewees will be more likely to report whatever they wish to say and the interviewers can be flexible in their approach.

- The **semi-structured interview** is often the most successful approach, with the use of some prepared questions by the interviewer, supplemented by opportunities for the interviewee to expand on their answers.

The diversity of interviews also means that interviewing is a skill that requires careful development in those using this research method.

Interviews may be used to provide information in addition to that obtained by other research methods. For example, Milgram (1963) enriched his work on obedience (see Unit 5) by interviewing his participants after the experiment. Two areas where the approach has been of particular value are social psychology (see, for example, the use of interviews in the research on conformity by Asch, also discussed in Unit 5) and psychopathology (for example, in exploring the family histories of sufferers from anxiety disorders).

ACTIVITY

Interviews

Carry out two interviews on a topic of your choice. Use a structured interview with one person (i.e. a set series of five or six questions about the chosen topic) and an unstructured interview with another person.

What differences do you note in your findings?

The description of Lynch's (1960) work on 'Cognitive maps' (on the right) provides another example of the practical use of interviews.

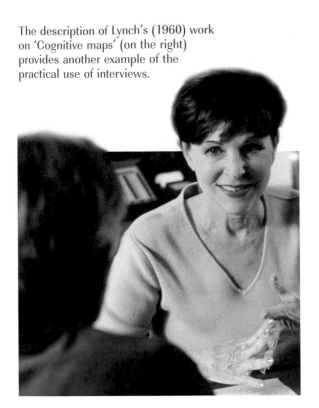

Cognitive maps (Lynch 1960)

Lynch was interested in environmental perception and, in particular, in the cognitive maps people create of their home areas. He carried out a series of interviews with the residents in three US cities – Boston, Jersey City and Los Angeles – about their feelings about local landmarks, and also about major routes and the areas that they passed through when driving around. He used the interview data to produce a general image of each city that identified the basic units of the urban landscape. Participants often mentioned distinctive features of their urban landscape that were not always the tallest or skyline features, but rather things on a more human scale, such as a well-known building or open space. Some interviewees had been to areas in their local city which they were unable to describe. Information gathered through such interviews has been used in urban planning.

Advantages of interviews

- *Flexibility* – Interviews can enable the researcher to explore complex issues that may be difficult to investigate through experimental techniques, questionnaire surveys or observation research. The interviewer can tailor questions to the responses of an interviewee so that issues can be explored in depth.

- *Tackling sensitive topics* – Interviews allow researchers to identify aspects of behaviour that are private or personal to the individuals concerned. This can be difficult with more impersonal research methods.

Weaknesses

- *Interpreting data* – Misinterpretation or partial interpretation of data may take place. Ideally, the interviewer needs to be detached from the interviewee, which can be difficult to achieve in face-to-face situations with their potential for bias. Qualitative data obtained from unstructured interviews can also be difficult to analyse.

- *Limitations in interviewees' responses* – Interviewees may be unable to articulate their thoughts clearly. Demand characteristics may also occur, such as social desirability bias.

Qualitative data comes in many forms and can be difficult to analyse

Ethical issues

The ethical issues associated with interviews are similar to those associated with questionnaire surveys (see p. 208), expecially with regard to the following:

- respecting the privacy and psychological wellbeing of interviewees

- obtaining informed consent from participants and respecting their right to withdraw some or all of their data
- maintaining confidentiality and anonymity
- protection from harm
- debriefing and support.

ANSWERS TO ACTIVITIES

Activity, p. 197 (top)

1 IV – the acoustic similarity of the words

DV – serial memory recall scores

2 IV – level of difficulty of the anagrams (i.e. easy or difficult)

DV – memory retention (i.e. memory scores)

3 IV – location of the memory test/instructions to imagine a particular environment

DV – the number of words correctly recalled.

Activity, p. 197 (bottom)

1 The IV is whether the stimulus sheets consisted of coloured words printed in conflicting coloured inks or coloured ink blocks.

2 The DV is the time taken to name the ink colours.

3 There were two conditions: experimental and control.

4 The data were quantitative.

5 The relationship investigated is that colour names written in a conflicting ink colour affect the length of time it takes to read the colour names.

✓ CHECK YOUR UNDERSTANDING

Check your understanding of non-experimental investigations in psychology by answering these questions. Try to do this from memory at first. You can check your answers by looking back through Topic 2.

1 What is correlational analysis and when is it used in psychology?

2 Give two advantages and two weaknesses of using correlational analysis.

3 What is naturalistic observation and when is it used in psychology?

4 What is meant by the term 'participant observation'?

5 Give two advantages and two weaknesses of using naturalistic observation.

6 What is a questionnaire survey and when is it used in psychology?

7 What is meant by an 'open-ended question' in a questionnaire?

8 Give two advantages and two weaknesses of using a questionnaire survey.

9 Define what is meant by an interview and describe when it is used in psychology.

10 What are the main differences between structured, unstructured and semi-structured interviews?

11 Give two advantages and two weaknesses of using interviews.

REVISION SUMMARY

Having covered this topic you should be able to:

✔ define the following terms: 'correlational analysis', 'naturalistic observation', 'questionnaire survey', 'interview'

✔ describe the key features of investigations using correlational analysis, and discuss their main advantages and weaknesses

✔ describe the key features of naturalistic observations, and discuss their main advantages and weaknesses

✔ describe the key features of questionnaire surveys, and discuss their main advantages and weaknesses

✔ describe the key features of interviews, and discuss their main advantages and weaknesses

✔ describe the ethical issues associated with investigations using correlational analysis, naturalistic observations, questionnaire surveys and interviews.

UNIT SUMMARY

Topic 1: Experimental investigations in psychology

● Psychologists use a range of research methods to investigate their subject matter. For many years the **experiment**, and in particular the **laboratory experiment**, has been their main research method. However, no single method is appropriate or successful in all circumstances and in all contexts.

● When carrying out an experiment, a **researcher intervenes** directly in the situation being investigated. The experimental method is regarded as being the most powerful research method because of its potential to identify **cause-and-effect relationships**.

● The true experiment has three key features:

 (a) The researcher manipulates an **independent variable** (IV) in order to investigate whether there is a change in the **dependent variable** (DV).

 (b) **All other variables** that might influence the results are either held constant or are eliminated.

 (c) Participants are **allocated randomly** to the experimental conditions.

● Experiments provide the highest levels of control, but at the possible cost of a reduction in the **ecological validity** of the research and the **generalizability** of the findings.

● The experimenter usually has greatest control when undertaking a laboratory experiment. **Field experiments** can give greater validity, but usually this is achieved at the cost of some degree of control over the key variables and possibly ease of replicability.

● The term **quasi-experiment** is used to describe an experiment where the investigator lacks complete control over the IV and/or the allocation of participants to groups. **Natural experiments** are sometimes regarded as quasi-experiments because they use naturally occurring events over which the researcher does not have full control.

● **Ethical guidelines** provide guidance on how psychologists should carry out experimental research in order to protect the people or animals that take part in their studies.

Topic 2: Non-experimental investigations in psychology

- **Non-experimental research methods** enable psychologists to study behaviour in more **natural settings**. However, this potential benefit has its costs – as a result of reduced levels of control, it is not possible for the researcher to reach any definitie conclusions concerning cause-and-effect relationships.

- Investigations using **correlational analysis** allow researchers to obtain measures of the relationship between variables, but do not allow the research to establish cause-and-effect relationships.

- In **naturalistic observation**, behaviour is observed and recorded in its natural setting and there is **no deliberate manipulation of variables**. Studies involving naturalistic observation provide the researcher with an **ecologically valid technique**. However, establishing controls may be difficult, making it difficult to generalize the results.

- **Questionnaire surveys** allow the researcher to ask people questions about, for example, their attitudes, behaviour or intentions, and to gather large amounts of information quickly and efficiently. Most surveys are carried out on carefully selected representative groups (referred to as **samples**) so that the researcher can generalize to the wider **population** from which the subgroup was drawn.

- **Interviews** need careful planning and piloting, but allow the flexible exploration of detailed issues, including complex ones. Interviews may be **structured**, **semi-structured** or **unstructured** and may generate **quantitative** and/or **qualitative data**.

- **Ethical guidelines** provide guidance as to how psychologists should carry out non-experimental research in order to protect the people or animals that take part in their studies.

Answering exam questions on Research methods

For sample examination questions and answers on Research methods, together with examiner comments on the answers, see pp. 262–5.

WEBSITES

www.statistics.gov.uk/socialtrends
Fascinating social and economic data about British society today.

http://universe.indiana.edu/clp/RF/experiment.htm
Useful guidance on a range of issues relating to experimental design.

http://kancrn.kckps.k12.ks.us/guide/nonexperimental.html
A site focusing on descriptive surveys.

www.mapnp.org/library/evaluatn/intrview.htm
Information on different types of interview, and how to prepare for and carry out inteviews.

www.slais.ubc.ca/resources/research_methods/question.htm
A range of resources relating to questionnaire survey research.

http://writing.colostate.edu/references/research.cfm
A range of guides on quantitative and qualitative research methods addressing research issues relevant to Units 6 and 7.

7
UNIT

RESEARCH DESIGN & IMPLEMENTATION
& Data Analysis

PREVIEW

After you have read this unit, you should be able to:

>> describe how aims are generated and how hypotheses are formulated

>> describe different research designs: experimental (independent groups, repeated measures and matched participants) and non-experimental (naturalistic observational studies, questionnaire surveys and interviews)

>> outline factors associated with research design: the control of variables, operationalization of independent and dependent variables, conducting pilot studies, techniques for assessing and improving reliability and validity, ethics

>> discuss different methods of selecting participants

>> explore the relationship between researchers and participants

>> describe the analysis of qualitative data derived from naturalistic observational studies, questionnaire surveys and interviews

>> use descriptive statistical techniques, including measures of central tendency and measures of dispersion

>> use and interpret graphs and charts

>> discuss the nature of positive and negative correlations, and the interpretation of correlation coefficients.

INTRODUCTION

Unit 6 discussed some of the research methods most widely used by psychologists. This unit covers a wide range of issues associated with the design and implementation of these research methods. You will start in Topic 1 by considering how to generate appropriate aims and formulate appropriate hypotheses. The unit then moves on to examine different experimental designs, as well as the design of non-experimental investigations. A range of factors associated with research designs are discussed, including the operationalization and control of variables, the nature of pilot studies and how two extremely important factors in research – reliability and validity – can be assessed and improved. The major sampling methods that psychologists use to obtain their participants are discussed. The unit continues by examining the relationship between researchers and participants in psychological research.

Topic 2 examines some of the ways in which psychologists analyse their data, and some of the issues that arise from this analysis. It examines how quantitative data can be interpreted using descriptive statistical techniques, as well as how qualitative methods of analysis are used in association with naturalistic observational studies, questionnaire surveys and interviews.

Graham
Davies

GETTING YOU THINKING...

Look at this image from the popular comic *2000 AD*. Do comics such as this increase levels of violence in children? How could you find out?

Imagine that you have been commissioned to find out whether there is any link between reading 'violent' comics and levels of aggression in children.

Think of as many different ways as possible of researching this topic and write brief notes about what each study would involve. This activity will revise the material you studied in Unit 6. If possible, discuss your ideas with your teacher or other students in your class.

Keep your notes safely because you will be returning to your ideas later in this unit.

KEY TERMS

Aim: the intended purpose of an investigation, i.e. what the research investigation is actually trying to discover.

Hypothesis: a testable statement. A research hypothesis is a general prediction made at the beginning of an investigation about what the researcher expects to happen.

Null hypothesis: predicts no differences between the results from the different conditions of an experiment (it predicts no correlation in an investigation using correlational analysis). Under the null hypothesis, any difference (or correlation) found is due to chance alone.

Alternative hypothesis (may be referred to as the experimental hypothesis in an experiment): predicts that something other than chance alone has produced the results obtained; in a well-designed experiment this should be the effects of the independent variable.

Directional hypothesis: an alternative hypothesis which predicts the direction in which any differences (or any correlation in an investigation using correlational analysis) in the results of an investigation are expected to occur.

Non-directional hypothesis: an alternative hypothesis which does not predict the direction in which any differences (or any correlation in an investigation using correlational analysis) in the results of an investigation are expected to occur.

Independent groups design: an experimental design which involves using different participants in each condition of the experiment.

Repeated measures design: an experimental design which involves exposing every participant to each of the experimental conditions, so, in effect, participants are used as their own controls.

Matched participants design: an experimental design which involves matching each participant in one of the experimental conditions as closely as possible with another participant in the second condition on variables considered to be relevant to the experiment in question.

Operationalization: the process of achieving precise descriptions of particular key terms in research – for example, what researchers understand by key variables such as the independent variable and the dependent variable. Operationalizing these variables usually results in a narrowing down of the research focus.

Pilot study: a small-scale prototype of a research investigation. It is carried out on a small number of participants in order to find out whether there are any problems with the design, the instructions for participants, the measuring instruments used or any other aspect of the proposed study.

Ethics: in psychology these are fundamental principles that respect the rights and feelings of those taking part in research.

Reliability: a term that means dependability or consistency. If the findings are replicated consistently, then the outcome can be said to be reliable.

Validity: a concept that is concerned with the extent to which a research instrument measures what it sets out to measure. A distinction may be drawn between different types of validity, including internal validity, external validity and ecological validity.

Internal validity: is concerned with the extent to which we can be sure that research findings are due to the mechanisms suggested, such as manipulation of the independent variable in an experiment, and not to the action of some other unwanted variable, such as individual differences or the effects of practice.

External validity: is concerned with the extent to which results can be generalized to other settings beyond that of the study concerned. A distinction can be drawn here between population validity (the extent to which results from research can be generalized to other groups of people) and ecological validity (the extent to which research findings can be generalized to situations outside the research setting).

Target population: a group of people that share a given set of characteristics, about which a researcher wishes to draw conclusions.

Sample: a subset of a target population which shares the characteristics of the population despite its smaller size.

Random sample: a subset of a target population in which every person or item stands an equal chance of being selected for inclusion. This requires the researcher to be able to identify every person or item in the target population before selection of a sample takes place. The selection process therefore takes place in a completely unbiased way.

Opportunity sample: a type of sample where the researcher selects anyone who is available to take part from a given population.

Demand characteristics: occur when participants try to make sense of a research situation that they find themselves in and act accordingly.

Investigator effects: result from the effects of a researcher's behaviour and characteristics on an investigation. They include expectation effects and the effects that the presence of a researcher can have on the behaviour of participants, resulting in their behaving in ways different from those that would normally be displayed.

AIMS AND HYPOTHESES

Generating appropriate aims

The starting point for any psychological research study is to generate appropriate aims for the idea that you wish to investigate. In order to generate these aims successfully, you need to know the intended purpose of the investigation, i.e. what the research investigation in question is actually trying to discover. In some non-experimental studies, the aims may be fairly broad, particularly in investigations in which qualitative data are being analysed. For example, the aim might be: "To describe the incidence of cigarette smoking in 10- to 16-year-olds living in Greater Manchester". In experimental investigations and, indeed, in others where quantitative data are produced, the aim may be to test one or more hypotheses.

Formulating hypotheses

A hypothesis can be defined simply as a testable statement. A research hypothesis is a general prediction made at the beginning of an investigation about what the researcher expects to happen. However, in order to

assist the analysis of data obtained from any research investigation, it is essential to phrase the hypothesis carefully, so that it is both clear and testable. This is the process of hypothesis formulation, i.e. refining the hypothesis so that it is stated in precise terms.

For example, consider the research hypothesis that "leading questions affect eyewitness testimony". In the form presented here, this begs too many questions to be tested precisely. For instance, what kind of leading question are we talking about, or in what ways is the testimony of witnesses affected? If this statement is to be converted into a format useful for the analysis of results data, then its wording must be completely unambiguous. A more tightly worded statement would be: "More witnesses report seeing a knife in a given scene when a leading question suggests the existence of a knife as a murder weapon." This formulation process highlights a fundamental issue concerning experimental research. On the one hand, the original research hypothesis is so general in its nature that it is difficult to test precisely. On the other hand, the version based on operationalized variables may be more clearly defined and testable, but may lack more general application (see p. 225 for a discussion of the operationalization of variables).

Researchers refer to two different hypotheses when analysing their data – the alternative hypothesis and the null hypothesis.

Alternative hypothesis

The alternative hypothesis (in an experiment this may be termed the experimental hypothesis) predicts that something other than chance alone has played a part in producing the results obtained. For example, imagine an experiment investigating the effect of an mnemonic on memory recall (a mnemonic is a device for aiding memory, such as using the phrase 'Richard Of York Gave Battle In Vain' to remember the order of colours in a rainbow). In such an experiment, the alternative hypothesis would predict a difference between the results from the two conditions, where those in the experimental condition would use a mnemonic and those in a second group would not. Only if the design of an investigation is completely watertight will the researcher be left with just one explanation for the results (i.e. that the independent variable is responsible for the outcome). In practice, reaching such a definite conclusion can be difficult.

An alternative hypothesis can be described as being directional or non-directional:

- A *directional hypothesis* predicts the direction in which results are expected to occur. For example, "More words are recalled from a list when using rehearsal as a mnemonic technique than when no mnemonic technique is used". In this case, we are predicting not only that there will be a difference in the number of words recalled, but that more will be recalled in one condition, i.e. when a mnemonic technique is used.

- A *non-directional hypothesis*, on the other hand, does not predict the expected direction of outcome. For example, "There is a difference in the number of words recalled from word lists presented with or without the presence of background music". Here a difference is predicted, but no prediction is made as to which of the two conditions results in a greater number of words recalled.

Directional and non-directional hypotheses are sometimes referred to as 'one-tailed' and 'two-tailed' hypotheses respectively. However, the terms 'directional' and 'non-directional' hypothesis are preferred.

Null hypothesis

The null hypothesis predicts that the results obtained from an investigation are due to chance alone. For example, in an experiment investigating the effect of an mnemonic on memory recall, the null hypothesis would predict no differences between the results from the two conditions. If any differences in observed outcome do occur, these are due to chance, rather than to the effect of the independent variable (in this case the use of a mnemonic). The researcher's task is to decide whether their null hypothesis should be retained or rejected. If the likelihood of the results occurring by chance is remote, then the null hypothesis can be rejected and we may prefer to accept the alternative hypothesis.

The null hypothesis can thus be regarded as the hypothesis which states that the alternative hypothesis is untrue. It is the more important of the hypotheses, because it is the null hypothesis that is actually tested when the quantitative data are analysed statistically.

ACTIVITY

Writing hypotheses

For each of the following studies, write a suitable alternative hypothesis and null hypothesis, and indicate whether your alternative hypothesis is directional or non-directional.

1 Tulving and Osler (1968) – experiment on retrieval cues (Unit 1, p. 24)

2 Brewer and Treyens (1981) – schemas and memory errors (Unit 1, p. 32)

3 Harlow and Harlow (1962) – formation of love in infant monkeys (Unit 2, p. 53)

4 Cohen *et al.* (1993) – study on stress (Unit 3, p. 86)

5 Johansson *et al.* (1978) – stress in a Swedish sawmill (Unit 3, p. 94)

An example is given below.

Study	Alternative hypothesis	Directional (D) or Non-directional (ND)	Null hypothesis
Baddeley (1966) – acoustic coding in short-term memory (Unit 1, pp. 8–9)	Words that sound different will be recalled better than words that sound similar.	D	Words that sound different will not be recalled better than words that sound similar.

RESEARCH DESIGNS: KEY DECISIONS

When undertaking research, a number of key decisions need to be taken. These may include the following:

- Deciding on an *appropriate research method* – Unit 6 focuses on the most appropriate research methods for different types of research and how they can best be used.

- Deciding *how many participants* to use – Researchers conducting an experiment or questionnaire survey usually have a choice when deciding how many participants to use. As a general rule, the larger the sample, the less biased it is likely to be; a sample of 25 or 30 participants is often regarded as a reasonable number in a small-scale study when quantitative data are to be collected and analysed. However, the non-experimental researcher sometimes has no control over sample size and may need to use whoever is available. Indeed, in some examples of qualitative research (e.g. research based on unstructured interviews), there may be only a few participants.

- Using an *appropriate sampling method* – This is essential where a sample of participants is selected to represent a larger population. The researcher also needs to decide how representative the participants are of a particular target population. (Sampling methods are discussed later in this unit.)

- Deciding *how to brief participants* – An important question is whether participants should be aware or unaware of taking part in research, or of the specific nature of the investigation. This raises the ethical issue of informed consent (see Units 5 and 6). Sometimes researchers disclose their intent to participants (this is usual in the case of questionnaire surveys, interviews and many experiments). They may even spend a period of time getting to know them before the research is carried out. It is hoped that this process encourages more natural behaviour. With naturalistic observation, the researcher may choose whether or not to let participants know that an investigation is being carried out on them. Where informed consent is not given, the researcher needs to consider very carefully the ethical issues that arise.

- Deciding the *medium for recording data* – A written record may be made (often by the participant in the case of questionnaire surveys and some experiments), or behaviour may be recorded for subsequent analysis, e.g. on video/audio tape or via computer. A combination of these methods is commonly used. The researcher also needs to decide which behaviour to record and which to ignore. If a written record is made, the researcher may need to devise an appropriate coding system for recording behaviour (an example is provided later in this unit in Fig. 7.2, p. 222).

- Deciding the *techniques for recording behaviour* – The method used may be highly structured (as in many experiments, questionnaire surveys and some naturalistic observational studies), or it may be unstructured (as in some interviews). The aim is to obtain data that are sufficiently explicit to enable appropriate analysis of the results.

A combination of different methods can be used for recording data ... the key is choosing the most suitable

DESIGNING EXPERIMENTS

Selecting an appropriate experimental design is essential for the success of any experimental investigation. It involves balancing the advantages and disadvantages of the different designs available. The aims of a successful experimental design are to:

- provide an overall plan for the experiment
- ensure precision of measurement
- enable results to be analysed to their full potential
- avoid potential sources of ambiguity or confusion
- ensure high levels of control over the different variables.

When deciding on an appropriate design, the researcher must consider carefully the precise nature of the experimental task, how to control relevant variables and the availability of participants. This section considers three experimental designs that you are likely to come into contact with:

- the independent groups design (different participants are used in each condition of the experiment)
- the repeated measures design (the same participants are used in each condition of the experiment)
- the matched participants design (participants are matched in each condition on variables relevant to the experiment).

Independent groups design

An independent groups design involves using different participants in each condition of the experiment (this may also be referred to as an 'independent measures/participants/subjects/samples design', or as a 'between groups/participants/subjects/samples design').

Experiments with this design may consist of:

- a control condition and one or more experimental conditions, or
- two (or more) experimental conditions.

See Table 7.1 for an example of how this design might appear in practice. In the former case, the group of participants that is given the experimental treatment is referred to as the 'experimental condition', and the group that exists for comparison and which receives no experimental treatment is the 'control condition'. Participants should be allocated randomly to each of the conditions (i.e. allocated in such a way that each participant stands an equal chance of being selected for each condition).

This procedure aims to ensure that characteristics of the participants (the participant variables) do not differ systematically between each condition. Otherwise, individual differences relevant to the experiment concerned might lead to results being confounded. (A discussion of confounding can be found on p. 225.) For example, in an experiment on learning ability it would be undesirable to have all the fastest learners

allocated to the same condition. This does not mean that random allocation will produce groups of participants that have identical characteristics. You may still, through chance, fail to eliminate individual differences as a factor and allocate all the fastest learners to one group. However, the chance of this happening is minimal. For example, imagine the likelihood of the numbers 1 to 6 inclusive coming up in that order on the National Lottery, or the probability of dealing out all four suits of a pack of cards in both suit and number order. The chances of events such as these happening are extremely remote, but of course any single combination, such as those just described, is as likely to happen as any other single combination.

By randomly allocating participants, researchers avoid any conscious or subconscious bias in participant allocation. Provided that an independent groups design is suitable for the proposed experiment and that enough participants have been used, then individual differences are unlikely to be significant as a confounding factor.

> ## Table 7.1 >> Allocation of participants in three different experimental designs
>
> 1 **The independent groups design:**
>
> Participants (Ps) may be allocated to the conditions randomly. For example:
>
> | Condition A | Condition B |
> |---|---|
> | P1 | P3 |
> | P2 | P5 |
> | P4 | P6 ... *and so on.* |
>
> 2 **Repeated measures design:**
>
> Each participant undertakes all conditions of the experiment. For example:
>
> | Condition A | Condition B |
> |---|---|
> | P1 | P1 |
> | P2 | P2 |
> | P3 | P3 ... *and so on.* |
>
> 3 **Matched participants design:**
>
> Pairs of participants are matched on appropriate variables relevant to the experiment; the members of each pair are then allocated to each condition (sometimes randomly). For example:
>
> | Condition A | Condition B |
> |---|---|
> | P1a | P1b |
> | P2a | P2b |
> | P3b | P3a ... *and so on.* |

The random allocation of participants to conditions can be achieved in several ways. The simplest method is to draw names from a hat. More sophisticated ways include use of a random number table or a computer programme capable of drawing and allocating random numbers.

In natural experiments (see p. 200), the allocation of participants to conditions is decided by the naturally occurring event that is treated as the independent variable. For example, if the independent variable is the management style of two different hospital wards, then the experimenter does not have complete control over the allocation of participants to conditions.

See Table 7.3 for the advantages and disadvantages of an independent groups design.

Repeated measures design

A repeated measures design involves exposing every participant to each of the experimental conditions, so, in effect, participants are used as their own controls. (You may also see this referred to as related measures/samples, or within participants/subjects design.) Table 7.1 gives an example of how participants might be arranged in an experiment using this design. One of the conditions in experiments using this design may be a control condition, which serves the same purpose as the control condition in an independent groups design, i.e. to provide a baseline against which responses from any experimental condition can be compared.

Table 7.3 summarizes the advantages and disadvantages of a repeated measures design. The disadvantage associated with order effects can be minimized in two ways: counterbalancing and randomization.

- *Counterbalancing* involves equal numbers of participants undertaking the tasks required of them in different orders. Table 7.2 shows two examples of how this might take place, with participants performing the conditions alternately until all participants have been tested. Note that there needs to be an even number of participants if counterbalancing is to be implemented fully. In the first example in Table 7.2, a multiple of two participants would be required and in the second a multiple of six, reflecting in each case the number of possible task orders.

Occasionally, however, it is not possible to apply counterbalancing as a strategy for minimizing order effects. Problems can occur, for example, when performing one condition helps the performance of another more than the other way round.

Consider the following memory experiment:
- Condition A: Learning a set of words presented randomly
- Condition B: Learning a matched set of words using a mnemonic technique to assist memory.

Table 7.2 >> Examples of counterbalancing in two- and three-condition experiments

Counterbalancing in a two-condition experiment:

Participant number	First condition undertaken	Second condition undertaken	
1	A	B	
2	B	A	
3	A	B	
4	B	A	... and so on

Counterbalancing in a three-condition experiment:

Participant number	First condition undertaken	Second condition undertaken	Third condition undertaken
1	A	B	C
2	B	C	A
3	C	A	B
4	A	C	B
5	B	A	C
6	C	B	A
			... and so on

There may be no problem when participants undertake Condition A first, followed by Condition B. However, when Condition A is presented after Condition B, it is likely that participants still have the mnemonic technique fresh in their minds. As a result, Condition B might help performance on Condition A more than A helps B, which is likely to lead to confounding of the results. In such circumstances, counterbalancing would be inappropriate and a researcher would be advised to use an independent groups design.

- *Randomization* involves adopting a random strategy for deciding the order of presentation of experimental conditions by, for example, drawing lots or tossing a coin. This procedure, however, fails to provide a guarantee that presentation order of conditions will not influence results, because it is still possible, through chance, that differences will remain in the numbers of participants experiencing the conditions in particular orders.

Randomization can also be used as a technique for deciding the order of presentation of, for example, individual stimuli within experimental conditions. It works best when there is a large number of items within each condition. For example, suppose an investigation involves each participant rating 20 photographs for their attractiveness. If the same presentation order is followed by all participants, then some biases in rating may occur (for example, the picture presented first is likely to be given an average rating by many participants, simply because they are rating this picture averagely as they feel they may wish to use more extreme ratings for subsequent photos).

Finally, it is possible to combine an independent groups and a repeated measures design. For example, children from two different age groups might be given two different cognitive tasks. The independent groups element of the design would involve a comparison of the two age groups, and the repeated measures element would be a comparison of performance on the two cognitive tasks.

Matched participants design

A matched participants design (or matched subjects or matched pairs design) aims to gain the key advantages of both an independent groups design (i.e. no problems with order effects as different people are used in each condition), and a repeated measures design (i.e. a greatly reduced risk of problems resulting from individual differences as participants are matched). It involves matching each participant in one of the experimental conditions as closely as possible with another participant in the second condition on all the variables considered to be relevant to the experiment in question. For example, pairs of participants might be matched for age, gender and their scores from intelligence and reading tests. Once pairs of participants have been identified, members of each pair can be randomly allocated to the conditions (see Table 7.1). The assumption made is that members of each pairing are so similar on the relevant variables that they can, for research purposes at least, be treated as if they are the same person. At the same time, however, participants perform in one condition of the experiment only, thereby eliminating the problem of order effects. See Table 7.3 for the advantages and disadvantages of a matched participants design.

Table 7.3 >> Advantages and disadvantages of different experimental designs

Independent groups design

>> *Advantages*   There is no problem with order effects, which occur when participants' performance is positively or negatively affected by their taking part in two or more experimental conditions. For example, performance in a second or subsequent condition may be improved through practice of a task done in a previous condition. Equally, negative effects may result from fatigue or boredom. Independent groups design has a wide range of potential uses and can be used where problems with order effects would make a repeated measures design impractical.

>> *Disadvantages*   There is the potential for error resulting from individual differences between the groups of participants taking part in the different conditions. Also, if participants are in short supply, then an independent groups design may represent an uneconomic use of those available to participate, since twice as many participants are needed to obtain the same amount of data as would be required in a two-condition, repeated measures design.

Repeated measures design

>> *Advantages*   Individual differences between participants are removed as a potential confounding variable. Also, fewer participants are required, since data for all conditions are collected from the same group of participants.

>> *Disadvantages*   The range of potential uses is smaller than for the independent groups design. For example, it is inappropriate to use two different reading schemes to teach young children to read within the same group of children – only an independent groups design could be employed in this case.

Order effects may result when participants take part in more than one experimental condition.

Matched participants design

>> *Advantages*   A matched participants design combines the advantages of both an independent groups and a repeated measures design.

>> *Disadvantage*   Achieving matched pairs of participants is difficult and time-consuming. It depends on the use of reliable and valid procedures for pretesting participants to obtain the matched pairs. Complete matching of participants on all variables that might affect experimental performance can rarely be achieved. Matched participants designs are, therefore, relatively uncommon, with their use being restricted to specific situations where a matching process is highly desirable in order that experimental success can be achieved.

DESIGNING NON-EXPERIMENTAL RESEARCH

The non-experimental methods of naturalistic observations, questionnaire surveys and interviews were introduced in Unit 6.

Naturalistic observational studies

A key design issue with naturalistic observational studies is deciding how to sample the behaviour to be studied. The possibilities include:

- *time interval sampling* – observing and recording what happens in a series of fixed time intervals
- *time point sampling* – observing and recording the behaviour that occurs at a series of given points in time
- *event sampling* – observing and recording a complete event each time it occurs.

A further issue is how data are to be recorded. Likely methods are written notes, producing a checklist or tally chart, or using a rating scale. Figure 7.1 shows a simple tally chart, developed for an observational study on the state of a baby. Figure 7.2 is a simplified example of the tally chart devised by Bales (1970) as part of his technique of Interaction Process Analysis (IPA) and is used for plotting changes in the interactions within small groups.

Figure 7.1 >> *Specimen checklist of behaviours and tally chart (behaviour categories taken from Bee 1999)*

State of baby during 30-second time period	No. of observations
Deep sleep:	JHTI JHTI I
Active sleep:	JHTI JHTI JHTI JHTI I
Quiet awake:	JHTI JHTI JHTI JHTI JHTI II
Active awake:	JHTI III
Crying, fussing:	JHTI JHTI III

Figure 7.2 >> *Simplified version of a tally sheet used by Bales (1970)*

Each observer records the interactions of one participant for the period of the discussion, which lasts for 10 minutes. This 10-minute period can be divided into two 5-minute halves to allow comparison between behaviours over time. From this sheet, the total number, type and direction of a participant's interactions can be calculated and compared with those of other participants.

Name of observed person _____

	Person being addressed											
	Person A		Person B		Person C		Person D		Person E		The group	
Categories	1st half	2nd half	1st half	2nd half	1st half	2nd half	1st half	2nd half	1st half	2nd half	1st half	2nd half
Seems friendly												
Jokes												
Agrees												
Gives suggestion												
Gives opinion												
Gives guidance												
Asks for guidance												
Asks for opinion												
Asks for suggestion												
Disagrees												
Shows tension												
Seems unfriendly												

Questionnaire surveys and interviews

Questionnaire surveys and interviews can produce qualitative and/or quantitative data, and the range of design options available to the researcher is wide. Some of the design decisions that need to be taken into account when designing questionnaires are outlined in Table 7.4 below.

Table 7.4 >> Design issues in questionnaire surveys

● **Open or closed questions?**
See Unit 6, p. 207, if you need to remind yourself of this issue or the different types of closed question available.

● **Question order**
It is usual to ask questions on demographic data (e.g. age, gender) at the end of a questionnaire. Questions asking about any highly sensitive issues are rarely placed right at the start.

● **Avoid unnecessary jargon**
For example: "Do you favour affirmative action in employment practices?" Your respondents need to be familiar with the language used for phrasing the questions. Plain English should be used wherever possible, or an explanation of terms given before the question is asked.

● **Avoid leading questions or value judgements**
For example: "Was the suspect's shirt blue or green?" A question should not lead the respondent towards a particular response.

● **Avoid double-barrelled questions**
For example: "Do you think that life is generally more stressful than it was 30 years ago, or do people find that modern technology reduces the stresses of life?" Don't include more than one item within the same question, as participants may wish to give different answers to each part.

● **Avoid emotive questions**
For example: "Do you think that the killing of defenceless animals in laboratories should stop?" Emotive language may bias the response made.

● **Avoid vagueness or ambiguity**
For example: "Do you take time off work? (please tick one)"

Never ☐ Rarely ☐ Sometimes ☐ Often ☐

These categories may mean different things to different people. All participants need to treat any particular question in the same way if the data collected are to be meaningful.

● **Avoid inappropriate assumptions**
For example: "What is your occupation?" may cause embarrassment if people are unemployed.

Asking suitable questions

1 Look at each of the questions included in Table 7.4 and see if you can suggest a more suitable question wording in each case.

2 Prepare a brief questionnaire (no more than ten questions) designed to investigate the respondent's health over the last six months. Check all the design issues raised in Table 7.4 and review your questions. Have you asked each question in the best possible way?

Table 7.5 below contains a checklist for interview planning, while Fig. 7.3 overleaf shows an example of an interview schedule prepared for a study of gender identity that would produce qualitative data. This schedule of questions is on the subject of the

---

Table 7.5 >> A checklist for planning interviews (based on Dyer 1995)

1 The preliminaries to the interview
Have you:
● clearly described the research problem?
● stated the aim of the interview?
● linked the problem to an appropriate theory?
● identified the general categories of data that you will need to collect?

2 The questions
Have you:
● generated an appropriate set of questions?
● planned the order in which the questions will be presented?
● planned the interview to obtain the required balance between structured and unstructured interviewing?

3 The interview procedure
Have you:
● considered the issues of self-presentation?
● identified and approached potential respondents?
● planned the pre-interview meeting?
● planned the post-interview debriefing?
● decided how the information is to be recorded in the interview?
● considered the ethical issues raised by the proposed research and sought advice if necessary?

contribution of early school experience to the development of gender identity. The extreme right-hand column is used to place a tick against each question as it is asked, to prevent the embarrassing possibility of asking the same question twice. The clear heading ensures that you have a record of the basic details of the research stored with the questions, and the range of question types covered.

Figure 7.3 >> *An example of an interview schedule (Dyer 1995, p. 72)*

Title of project: A study of the development of gender identity

Topic: Contribution of early school experiences

Date of interview:

1　Can you begin by giving me a general description of the school you attended at the age of 5, so I can begin to understand what kind of a place it was?

2　Looking back, how did your school deal with the issue of gender in general? For example, were boys and girls treated in different ways? Could you give me some examples of that?

3　How did this compare with what you experienced at home?

4　How was children's behaviour dealt with? For example, was a clear distinction made between what was considered appropriate behaviour for boys compared to girls?

5　Did the school generally reinforce or challenge stereotyped gender definitions? Can you give me some examples of that?

6　How do you now think this affected you during your early school life? Can you give me some examples?

7　Can you give me some examples of the kind of thing that would have happened if a boy behaved in a way the teachers thought was more appropriate to a girl?

8　Can you give me any examples of the ways in which the rules about appropriate behaviour were enforced? How do you feel about them now?

9　What would have happened if you had been found breaking a rule like that?

FACTORS ASSOCIATED WITH RESEARCH DESIGN

This section examines some of the key factors that are associated with research design. It looks at:

- how variables in research can be defined, controlled and operationalized
- how pilot studies help to improve research quality
- techniques for assessing and improving reliability and validity
- ethical issues associated with research.

Defining variables

As you will be aware from Unit 6, a variable is anything that may change or alter in any way. The control, manipulation and observation of variables are central to psychological research. Psychologists need to be able to define variables successfully if their research is to be treated as scientifically worthwhile. This is by no means an easy task.

Try the next activity for yourself.

ACTIVITY

Defining variables

What do you understand by the term 'aggressive behaviour'? Imagine that you are one of a team involved in designing an observational study of aggressive behaviour in young children in school playgrounds. You have been asked to prepare a definition of the term 'aggressive behavior' that could be used by the research team.

When you have decided on your definition, compare your ideas with those of another psychology student. How are they similar and how do they differ. Try to agree a single definition that you are both happy with.

When you thought about your definition, you probably included different forms of violent behaviour – but did you include things such as spitting, swearing, glaring or invading personal space? Even a smile can sometimes have aggressive intent! It is even harder to define variables when they are less tangible – for example, 'stress' or 'concentration levels'. We may be able to measure the visible signs of their effect on a person, and we may strive to measure their effects on an aspect of behaviour, but can we be confident that we are actually measuring the variable itself?

Operational definitions of variables or factors being investigated are precise descriptions of what researchers understand by particular terms.

Operationalizing variables

In experimental research, the key variables are the independent variable and the dependent variable (see Unit 6). Operationalizing these variables usually results in a narrowing down of the research focus. For example, the general statement that 'mnemonics improve memory' might be refined into an independent variable that specifies the presence or absence of imagery, and a dependent variable that specifies the number of words correctly recalled. This process has important implications for the extent to which research findings can be generalized because the narrower the research focus, the more limited the extent to which results can be generalized.

ACTIVITY

Operationalizing definitions

Refine the definition of 'aggressive behaviour' that you generated in the previous activity into a fully operationalized definition that could be used in an observational study of aggressive behaviour in young children.

The control of variables

Unwanted variables (i.e. those that cause the potential confounding of results) are also known as extraneous variables. They may obscure the effect of an independent variable on a dependent variable, or provide a false impression that an independent variable has produced changes when in fact it has not. If a variable other than the independent variable produces a change in a dependent variable, then results are said to be confounded. Unwanted variables can result from either random error or constant error, and need to be eliminated or controlled as far as possible.

● *Random errors* – The effects of random errors cannot be predicted. Possible sources of random errors might include:

– a participant's state of mind
– a participant's level of motivation
– incidental noise
– room temperature
– previous experiences on the day of the experiment.

It is hoped that random errors that might result from variables such as these will not systematically affect one condition of an experiment more than another. By allocating participants randomly to experimental conditions, psychologists will assume that random errors balance out across the experimental conditions. Such errors might, however, result in some loss of sensitivity.

The effects of random errors cannot be predicted ...

● *Constant errors* – Constant errors affect the dependent variable in a consistent way and are, therefore, a much more serious problem for the researcher than random errors, since they may not affect all conditions of an experiment equally.

Constant errors might include:

– a failure to counterbalance or randomize the presentation order of experimental conditions
– participant differences
– errors of measurement that affect one condition more than another.

Wherever possible, such sources of error should be eliminated by good experimental design.

Conducting pilot studies

A pilot study is a small-scale prototype of a particular research investigation, carried out on a small number of participants. The aim is to find out whether there are any problems with the design, the instructions for participants or the measuring instrument(s) used. Also, a pilot study may provide information on how long the study takes to complete, and enable the researcher to practise carrying out the research task.

The researcher can inform participants that it is a pilot study, and may ask them to draw attention to any problematic areas or ambiguities that they come across. In the light of experience gained with the pilot study, the researcher can make revisions before the final research is carried out.

A questionnaire survey or interview-based investigation will need to be piloted on people from the appropriate target population.

ACTIVITY

Piloting your questionnaire

Pilot the short questionnaire that you prepared as part of the activity on p. 223 with two or three members of your family or friends.

What did you learn from this pilot? How would you change the questions in the light of your pilot? Why is it important to carry out a pilot before embarking on a research project?

Assessing and improving reliability

The term 'reliability' means dependability or consistency – vital if the psychologist is to obtain meaningful data. The term can be applied in a general way to the findings from psychological research. If the findings are replicated consistently, then the outcome can be said to be reliable. The term is also used in specific contexts. There are several ways in which reliability can be assessed and improved, and this section will consider some of these. Assessing reliability often involves using a correlational analysis in order to assess the consistency of observer ratings, or psychological measuring instruments such as psychometric tests. Check that you know the meaning of the term 'correlation' (including 'positive correlation') before reading on (refer back to pp. 203–5, if necessary).

Assessing and improving observer reliability

Observer reliability is assessed by measuring the extent to which researchers, scoring the same participants, achieve consistency of measurement between each other. Scorers record their own data individually, and then the sets of data obtained from each scorer are correlated. Observer reliability is achieved if highly significant positive correlations are obtained between the scorers.

Ideally, in observational studies, more than one observer should be used. 'Inter-rater reliability' is a procedure that allows a researcher to measure the extent to which observers agree on the behaviours they have observed. Independent checks for reliability can often be made easier by the use of audiotaping or videotaping. Correlational analysis is often used to establish inter-rater reliability.

There are ways of improving observer reliability. For example, observers should be trained thoroughly in the techniques being used. Also, operational definitions of the key terms involved in the research should be both clear and understood fully by all the observers involved in gathering data. Consider, for example, an observational study of aggressive behaviour in children's playgrounds. If more than one observer is being used, it is important that they all understand exactly which behaviours can be categorized as examples of 'aggressive behaviour'. In other words, they need to operationalize the term 'aggressive behaviour', as you were asked to do in the activity on p. 225.

Assessing and improving test reliability

Another important aspect of reliability concerns the reliability of tests, such as those which attempt to measure intelligence or personality. Several methods are used by psychologists, including the split-half method and the test–retest method.

- *The split-half method* – This can be used as a way of assessing the extent to which individual items in a particular test or questionnaire are consistent with other items in the same test. The method involves splitting the test or questionnaire concerned into two parts after data have been obtained from the participants. This splitting might be done by, for example:

  - comparing the results obtained from odd- and even-numbered questions

  - comparing the results from the first half of the test with those from the second half

  - splitting the test into two at random.

  The two sets of responses (however they are obtained) are then correlated. A highly significant positive correlation between the two sets of responses would indicate reliability. If the correlation is not high enough, the researchers would need to check the procedure used for constructing the test carefully and very possibly revise the test items. The aim of the revision would be to produce an improvement in the reliability of the particular test or questionnaire.

- *The test–retest method* – This is used to assess another important aspect of consistency – the stability of a test or questionnaire over time. This method involves presenting the same participants with the same test or questionnaire on different occasions, with no feedback given after the first presentation. The time interval between presentations needs to be selected carefully. If it is too short, participants may remember their previous answers, but if it is too long, then the participants may possibly have changed in some way relevant to the test or questionnaire. Once again, correlational techniques are used to indicate the test stability. If there is a highly significant positive correlation between the scores obtained from the test and retest phases, then the test is deemed to be stable. Test items and/or testing procedures can be revised (e.g. by rephrasing instructions) if a sufficiently high correlation is not obtained.

Assessing and improving validity

Validity is concerned with the extent to which something measures what it sets out to measure. This is not as simple as it might first appear. For example, there is considerable debate over issues such as whether personality tests are valid measures of personality, or whether diagnostic classification schemes used in the mental-health field really are valid. A distinction may be drawn between internal validity, external validity and test validity.

Internal validity

Internal validity is concerned with the extent to which we can be sure that research findings are due to the mechanisms suggested. For example, in an experiment the key issue might be whether we can be certain that differences in the results obtained are due to manipulation of the independent variable and not to the action of some other unwanted variable, such as individual differences or the effects of practice. Internal validity is also compromised if no effect is found within research when in fact an effect actually exists.

External validity

External validity is concerned with the extent to which results can be generalized to other settings beyond that of the study concerned. A distinction can be drawn here between the following:

- *population validity* – the extent to which results from research can be generalized to other groups of people

- *ecological validity* – the extent to which research findings can be generalized to situations outside the research setting.

Note that laboratory experiments do not automatically lack ecological validity by the mere fact that they are carried out in laboratories. They sometimes do, but many laboratory studies are ecologically valid and have results that can be generalized beyond the lab. Similarly, the fact that research is carried out in a natural setting does not guarantee ecological validity. This may or may not be achieved – it all depends on whether or not the results can be generalized.

Test validity

There are several different techniques available to help the psychologist assess test validity, including:

- *Face validity* – the simplest technique is concerned with assessing whether a measuring instrument looks correct in the eyes of independent experts, who may suggest improvements to the researcher. Because of its subjectivity, assessment of face validity usually only takes place in the earliest phases of constructing a measuring instrument, e.g. when a draft examination paper is submitted for approval.

- *Content validity* is superficially similar to face validity. Again, independent experts are asked to assess the validity of the measuring instrument concerned. This time, however, the procedures are more rigorous, and there is a detailed and systematic examination of all the component parts of the measuring instrument concerned.

- *Concurrent validity* involves obtaining two sets of scores at the same time: one from the new procedure with unknown validity, and the other from an alternative procedure or test for which validity has already been established. The scores obtained from both of these measures will be correlated with each other to assess the validity of the new procedure. A highly significant positive correlation would suggest that the new procedure or test is valid. For example, a new procedure for the diagnosis of a psychopathological condition might be compared with an existing method of diagnosis for which the success rate is already known. Further refinement of the criteria in order to improve concurrent validity might be necessary if the correlation obtained is not sufficiently high.

- *Predictive validity* involves a similar strategy, but this time the two sets of scores are obtained at different points in time. An example from abnormal psychology might be correlation of initial diagnoses with information gained in the light of experience with the patients concerned over a period of time. In other words, a diagnostic procedure or test with high predictive validity would allow fairly accurate forecasts to be made about future behaviour. If the test indicates that certain behaviours should occur, and they do not occur, then the test has low predictive validity.

Ethics

The ethical issues associated with research are dealt with in other units. Topic 3 in Unit 5 includes a section on ethical guidelines and Unit 6 discusses particular issues in association with the different research methods. The next activity will enable you to check your memory of key ethical issues. If you find this activity difficult, then be sure to go back and reread the relevant sections of Units 5 and 6.

ACTIVITY

Ethical issues

Describe in as much detail as you can at least one ethical issue that is important in relation to each of the following research methods:

1. laboratory experiment
2. naturalistic observation
3. questionnaire survey
4. interview.

Select a different ethical issue for each method.

SELECTING PARTICIPANTS

A 'target population' is a group of people that share a given set of characteristics about which a researcher wishes to draw conclusions (e.g. all students registered for AS-level Psychology examinations in a given year). However, a target population is usually too large for each individual to be investigated, so a subset of the population – a sample – is investigated instead. A 'representative sample' forms part of a target population, sharing the characteristics of the population despite its smaller size. If, and *only* if, a sample is truly representative, can it be used by psychologists as a basis for generalizing their conclusions to the remainder of the target population. It follows from this that a sample that is not truly representative may result in wasted time and effort.

A general principle is that the larger the sample, the more likely it is to give an accurate estimate about the nature of the population from which it has been drawn. Deciding sample size, therefore, reflects a delicate balancing act between the need to represent accurately the target population on the one hand, and practical considerations, such as saving time and money, on the other. In practice, some degree of sampling error is likely to result – the researcher's task is to minimize this error. Statistical tables can be used to advise on the sample size needed to achieve acceptable levels of

sampling error in target populations of different sizes. Samples can be taken in several different ways. We shall discuss two main methods of sampling below: random and non-random.

Random sampling

In a random sample, every person or item in a given target population stands an equal chance of being selected for inclusion. This means that it is necessary to have a list that identifies every person or item in the target population in order to generate the random sample. Selection then takes place in a completely unbiased way. However, selecting a random sample does not guarantee the researcher a sample that is totally representative of the population concerned. Nor does it mean that any two random samples drawn from the same target population will share identical characteristics. By its very nature, a random sample can only come with a guarantee that it has been selected in an unbiased manner (e.g. by using one of the techniques for randomly allocating participants to conditions described earlier on p. 219). However, as long as the target population and sample size have been chosen carefully, the laws of probability predict that the chance of selecting a biased sample through random sampling techniques is minimal.

Non-random sampling methods

There are other possible sampling methods, most of which are beyond the requirements of the AS Psychology specification. Two that you may come across, however, are the 'self-selected (or volunteer) sample' and the 'opportunity sample'.

- *Self-selected samples* – This involves participants selecting themselves for the research concerned, often by replying to an advertisement. This type of sampling is widely used in university research. A well-known example was in Milgram's research on obedience in the 1960s (see Unit 5). Potential disadvantages of using a self-selected sample are that the majority of a given target population are unlikely to respond, and that those who do respond may be atypical of the target population in some way. Thus, the data gathered from this potentially biased sample are unlikely to be representative of the target population.

- *Opportunity (or opportunist) sample* – This is a widely used but easily biased method, involving the researcher selecting anyone who is available to take part from any given population, such as available staff or students within a college. Again, data gathered from an opportunity sample are unlikely to be representative of the target population because certain subgroups may not be available for inclusion – for example, if a researcher was selecting an opportunity sample from a school on a day when all Year 6 pupils were away on a field trip.

THE RELATIONSHIP BETWEEN RESEARCHERS AND PARTICIPANTS

The research situation is not without a social dimension, and it is to be expected that a relationship will develop between researchers and participants. As a social situation, a research investigation is liable to be influenced by those taking part in it. Research participants may be affected by demand characteristics, while investigators themselves may have unintended effects on the outcome of research – known as 'investigator effects'.

Demand characteristics

Demand characteristics occur when participants try to make sense of the research situation that they find themselves in and act accordingly. These characteristics have already been described in the section on laboratory experiments (Unit 6, p. 197), but they may occur in any research scenario in which the participants are aware of taking part. They become a problem as soon as participants act differently from the way that they would outside the research situation. Well-designed research will aim to minimize their effects as much as possible.

Demand characteristics might include the following participant behaviour:

- *trying to guess the purpose of the research* and acting in a way that they feel is helpful to the researcher – or indeed, unhelpful

- *acting nervously and out of character* because of being in a research situation – for instance, participants may feel that they are being evaluated in some way (e.g. that their personality is being assessed) and feel worried about this

- *displaying a social desirability bias*, wishing themselves to be seen in the most favourable light possible, e.g. in the responses given to a questionnaire on moral standards.

Investigator effects

Investigator effects result from the effects of a researcher's behaviour and characteristics on an investigation. There is a wide range of possibilities here. Expectation effects can occur where a researcher is deeply committed to achieving a particular outcome. This may be a particular problem when observing events that can be interpreted in more than one way (an example might be the difficulty in distinguishing between children fighting or indulging in rough-and-tumble play). Alternatively, even overt fraud ('massaging the data') is a possibility, however remote.

In naturalistic observational studies, the presence of the observer can cause participants to behave in ways different from those that would normally be displayed. For example, behaviour may be more restrained than usual. When research is carried out using questionnaire surveys or interviews, then many different aspects of the investigator may have an influence, including the investigator's age, gender, ethnic group, appearance, expression and communication style.

Check your understanding of research design and implementation in psychology by answering these questions. Try to do this from memory at first. You can check your answers by looking back through Topic 1.

1 What is a research hypothesis?

2 What is a null hypothesis?

3 Name the experimental design where all participants take part in all the conditions of the experiment.

4 Give one advantage and one disadvantage of an independent groups design.

5 What does the term 'event sampling' mean in observational research?

6 What is a pilot study and why is it important to carry one out?

7 Describe one way in which observer reliability can be assessed.

8 Suggest one way in which observer reliability might be improved.

9 Name two techniques for assessing test reliability.

10 Explain what the term 'external validity' means.

11 Name three of the techniques that can be used by a psychologist to help assess test validity.

12 What does a 'target population' mean in the context of psychological research?

13 Define the term 'random sample'.

14 Why is an opportunity sample likely to be unrepresentative?

15 What is meant by the term 'demand characteristics'?

REVISION SUMMARY

Having covered this topic you should be able to:

✓ define all the key terms listed on pp. 215–16

✓ describe the following experimental designs – independent groups, repeated measures and matched participants designs

✓ discuss key design issues in non-experimental research – naturalistic observations, questionnaire surveys and interviews – including deciding how behaviour is sampled, the method(s) used for recording data, and the phrasing and organisation of questions

✓ explain why independent and dependent variables need to be operationalized

✓ describe the importance of conducting pilot studies and controlling variables

✓ outline techniques for assessing and improving reliability

✓ discuss the ethical issues relating to psychological research and the importance of respecting the rights and feelings of those taking part

✓ describe different sampling techniques to select participants for research investigations from the target population of interest

✓ discuss the relationship between researchers and participants, including demand characteristics and investigator effects.

GETTING YOU THINKING...

Look at the two graphs carefully and answer the questions that follow:

1 Describe in words what Graph A tells you.

2 Describe in words what Graph B tells you.

3 Which graph do you find the more accurate and informative? Why?

4 What changes would need to be made to the graph you considered less informative in order to make it more informative?

Look at some newspapers or magazines and try to find at least one good example of graphical presentation of numerical data and one poor example. Write a few notes about each one, highlighting what you feel to be the good and less good features of each example. Discuss these with another student on your course and/or your teacher.

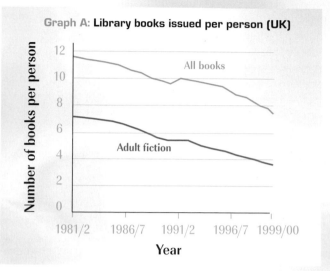

Graph A: **Library books issued per person (UK)**

Graph B: **Long-lasting efficacy** – The best way to eliminate dandruff and prevent it recurring

KEY TERMS

Measure of central tendency: a descriptive statistic that provides a single value which is representative of a set of numbers by indicating the most typical (average) value. The mode, median and mean are measures of central tendency.

Mode: the most frequently occurring value in a data sequence.

Median: the middle value of a set of scores arranged in ascending or descending order.

Mean: the arithmetic average of a set of scores, calculated by adding all the scores together and dividing by the number of scores.

Measures of dispersion: descriptive statistics that enable us to examine the variability within sets of data; they help us to understand whether scores in a given set of data are similar to, or very different from, each other. The range and standard deviation are measures of dispersion.

Range: the difference between the highest and lowest scores in a given set of data.

Standard deviation: used to measure the variability (i.e. the typical deviation) of a given sample of scores from its mean; the most powerful of the measures of dispersion available to the researcher.

Correlation: a term that refers to the extent to which values on (usually two) different variables co-vary.

Correlation coefficient: a descriptive statistic with a numerical value on a scale between −1 and +1. It demonstrates the strength of any relationship that exists between two sets of data.

Positive correlation: a measurement of the extent to which high values on one variable are associated with high values on another. A positive correlation is indicated by a correlation coefficient between zero and +1.

Negative correlation: a measurement of the extent to which high values on one variable are associated with low values on another. A negative

correlation is indicated by a correlation coefficient between zero and −1.

Histogram: a form of graphical representation used to present data on interval or ratio levels of measurement. It consist of a series of vertical bars of equal width, which represent the frequencies of the variable placed on the x-axis.

Bar chart: a series of vertical bars of equal width used to illustrate the frequencies of a non-continuous variable displayed on the x-axis. It is superficially similar to a histogram.

Frequency polygon: a form of graphical representation used to present data on interval or ratio levels of measurement. It consists of a line linking points that represent the frequencies of the variable placed on the x-axis.

Scattergraph (or scattergram): a graphical technique used to illustrate sets of data that are being correlated with each other. Data from one of the variables being correlated are presented on the x-axis, and data from the same individual for the second variable on the y-axis.

This topic looks at ways of analysing and interpreting both qualitative and quantitative data. It starts by focusing on the analysis and interpretation of qualitative data derived from naturalistic observational studies, questionnaire surveys and interviews. These research methods often also produce quantitative data; indeed, with questionnaire surveys, these may often be the only kind of data produced.

The final section of this topic introduces the use of descriptive statistical techniques to analyse quantitative data. Further analysis of quantitative data using inferential statistical tests is outside the scope of the AS-level Psychology specification. If you continue your study of psychology to A level, you will be using inferential statistical tests to help you analyse your coursework data.

ANALYSING QUALITATIVE DATA

Qualitative data include data generated from observational research, interviews and questionnaires that are not in the form of numbers. The task of the researcher, therefore, is to analyse large volumes of narrative accounts, including transcripts from interviews, detailed descriptions of what was observed or the written answers to questionnaires.

When analysing qualitative data, the researcher is usually concerned with searching for the underlying meaning in what people do or say, and this relies heavily on the researcher's interpretive skills. Researchers use a number of different techniques to analyse qualitative data, involving categorizing the data and trying to identify themes within the data. This is very different from the use of statistical tests to analyse quantitative (numerical) data.

Data from naturalistic observational studies

The use of naturalistic observational techniques is discussed in Unit 6. These techniques differ widely both in terms of the approaches used and in the ways in which behaviour is recorded and classified, so it is hardly surprising that they also differ widely in terms of how behaviour is analysed and presented. Data interpretation may also produce ideas for hypotheses that can be tested using other research methods.

When qualitative data are obtained, these may be presented in different ways, including diary descriptions and specimen descriptions of behaviour. An example of a diary description from an observational study is shown in the panel opposite; it illustrates the social rituals through which a child's ability to name can arise.

Diary description

Mary, aged 11 months: Mother takes Mary out of her high-chair and puts her on the potty. Her toys are all in a box on the table in front of her chair.

Mother (spontaneously): "Do you want Teddy?"

Mary: "aah"

Mother: "Where is he?"

Mary looks around and makes to get off her potty and go to the table, but Mother restrains her. Mary looks at the table and points.

Mother (going to table opposite and bringing down the box of toys): "That's right, he's there, isn't he? Here he is. What does he say? What does Teddy say?"

Mary: "aah"

Mother: "Yes, he does, doesn't he?"

Mary: "aah"

Mother pats Teddy.

Mary: "aah"

Mary's attention moves to the box containing her other toys, which Mother has placed on the floor near her.

Mother: "Oh, what can you see in there? Doggie? (takes doggie out) Let's see who else is in here. Who's that? Is it duckie? and what does the duck say?"

Mother squeaks the duck.

Mary: "aah"

Mother: "He doesn't! What does the duck say? What does he say?"

Mary: "argh" *(reaching towards it)*

Mother: "Yes, I know you want it. What does he say?"

Mary: "woraghagh"

Mother: "He doesn't, he says *(she squeaks it concurrently)* 'quack, quack, quack', doesn't he? 'quack, quack, quack'."

Mary: "gh, gh"

Mother: "Yes, he does."

Mary (looking at Teddy): "aah"

Mother: "And that's aah is it, that's aah Teddy?"

Mary: "aah"

Mother: "And who's this, what does he say? What does duck say? What does duck say?"

No response from Mary. Mother squeaks duck.

Mary: "gah"

Mother: "Quack!"

Mary: "gah"

Mother: "Ooh, aren't you clever."

Source: Lock (1980, p. 110)

Although ecological validity may be a strength of observational studies, the categorization of behaviours that takes place in them (and also in interview-based research, discussed later) may challenge their validity. Are the operational definitions used the best ways of defining behaviours? For instance, are the definitions comprehensive enough, or too comprehensive? It is important, therefore, that the structure of a study is fully justifiable in terms of its theoretical basis, and also sufficiently complete, i.e. it should include all the behaviours of interest.

Other potential threats to validity are:

- *inadequate sampling* (e.g. too few samples, or sampling undertaken at inappropriate times)
- *mishandling* or *inadequate handling* of the system used (e.g. through pressure or lack of familiarity in a research situation).

These challenges to validity highlight the need for careful analysis and presentation of observational data if the potential benefits from the richness of the data gathered are not to be compromised.

Data from questionnaire surveys

Much of the information that is gained from conducting research using questionnaire surveys is analysed using quantitative methods. However, data from appropriate open questions that invite participants to give different responses may be analysed qualitatively. In contrast to closed questions, the use of open questions may serve to reduce researcher bias and the impact of the researcher's own views on the design of the survey. The result is a means of analysis that is both flexible and interpretative.

A further possibility for the analysis of data derived from questionnaire surveys is to convert qualitative data to quantitative by, for example, counting the number of times that a particular item is mentioned. This is a fairly common way of analysing data and shows the extent to which qualitative and quantitative data may be interdependent.

Data from interviews

Interviews are often just one of the techniques used by the researcher in association with other methods in a particular piece of research. As such, they may help to provide a validity check on the results obtained. Interpreting the information gained from interviews is a complex procedure.

Qualitative data might include many elements which need to be taken into account when interpretation takes place. These include description of features of interest, such as:

- the actual behaviour observed by the interviewer
- the context(s) in which the behaviour occurs
- self-reports of behaviour by the participant(s)
- self-reports of cognitions that cannot be observed directly – for example, the feelings, thoughts and attitudes of the participants in the study
- interpretations made by the researchers
- implications of the study for any theory.

From this list it can be seen that distinctions need to be made between the aspects of a report that:

- describe what actually happened
- are based on the interpretations and inferences made by the researcher
- are based on the interpretations and inferences of the participant(s).

If reporting is to be objective, the distinctions between these need to be made clear to the reader when a report of an investigation is published. Inevitably, the potential for bias in reporting is considerable. For example, researchers might report only those aspects of behaviour that support their own theoretical standpoint, or are particularly relevant to their research. Also, decisions about what information to include and what to leave out may be subjective. Carefully reported investigations should always make clear to the reader the criteria used to select participants and how decisions were made about what information to present.

The close, and often prolonged, relationship between the researcher and the participant(s) in interview-based research may heighten the importance of interpersonal interaction. This interaction may be very productive or it may reduce objectivity by introducing subjectivity.

Whilst the qualitative data generated by interview-based research may add to our existing understanding, they can also produce evidence that challenges theory or our existing understanding, thereby stimulating further research and, perhaps, a new theoretical perspective.

The nature of the data obtained often reflects the extent to which the interview was structured or unstructured (see Unit 6, p. 209). Where data are qualitative, the researcher is able to present results more flexibly, but the problem exists of how to organize and present a mass of descriptive data in a meaningful way. Some of the issues the researcher might consider are listed below.

- Examine carefully the background theory for a study involving interviews before the research is undertaken, and then decide how the data can be categorized appropriately.
- Solicit opinions from the interviewees on how they would wish the material to be presented. Has material been presented in the spirit in which it has been told?
- Decide how any selection or paraphrasing of material is going to be undertaken. (Particular care needs to be taken with this if bias in reporting is to be avoided.)
- Decide whether quotations will be used to enrich the presentation of data. If so, how will they be selected?

Categorization of qualitative data is an important task for the person reporting an interview. It involves the grouping of like items together, e.g. statements by the interviewee concerning particular subjects. A good computer database can be helpful when doing this.

Perhaps inevitably, because of their nature, the interpretation of interview data is partial or incomplete. Something may be lost in terms of reliability, and something gained through the sensitivity and depth of the approach. They may have the important benefit of providing a new basis for interpretation. See the panel opposite for an example that provides interesting insights on the Bristol riots of the early 1980s derived from interviews.

DESCRIPTIVE STATISTICAL TECHNIQUES

Descriptive statistical techniques provide ways in which the researcher can obtain summary descriptions of sets of quantitative data. Two types of descriptive statistical techniques are measures of central tendency, which give average values, and measures of dispersion, which look at the variability of scores. Each of these techniques provides a single value that can help us to summarize a set of data which might otherwise be

difficult to interpret. This potential benefit, however, is not without its cost. When any single value is obtained, the process of summation inevitably produces a loss of individual information.

Measures of central tendency and measures of dispersion are also valuable to the psychologist in that they form the basis for analyses using inferential statistics.

Riots and representations: the Bristol riots of the 1980s

In-depth interviews that generate qualitative data can add a great deal to our understanding of social processes, and can illuminate events that appear, at first sight, to be incomprehensible. A series of street disturbances in Britain in the early 1980s, for example, raised the spectre of 'mob rule', and the idea that people who get together in crowds are overtaken by a 'group mind'.

Journalists tend to see people in crowds (particularly when they attack the police) as if they were animals who have been stripped of the veneer of civilization that usually holds them in check. Social psychologists who have been influenced by the theories of the French

writer, Gustave LeBon, have been just as negative. LeBon (1947, but first published in 1895) argued that the behaviour of people in crowds fell several rungs down the evolutionary ladder, to the level of "beings belonging to inferior forms of evolution, women, savages, and children, for instance" (LeBon, 1947, p. 36). These ideas take on a quite nasty political flavour when they are used to describe 'riots' by black people in inner-city areas, and the task of the psychologist should be to look at how popular images work, and how people in the crowd understand their actions. In-depth interviewing can move to an 'insider' perspective on these events, and so assist in this task.

One of the first 'riots' in the 1980s, in the St Paul's area of Bristol, was studied by Reicher (1984), a social psychologist whose training had been in the experimental tradition. Reicher was carrying out research on social identity at Bristol University when the April 1980 'riot' broke out, and he was able to interview participants. Their accounts did not correspond with either standard social psychological or journalistic images of people who had lost their minds, and the 'inside' story was of a community trying to defend itself against the police. One of the striking aspects of the insider accounts was that both black and white people who were in the crowd refused to accept the outsider claims that this was a racial disturbance.

Private homes and shops within the community were left untouched, whereas the banks and the unemployment office were seen as legitimate targets. The stories collected in these interviews also corresponded with the descriptions of the damage given by the authorities. An examination of the accounts of outsiders and insiders by Reicher and Potter (1985) illustrated the ways in which traditional 'scientific' explanations of crowd behaviour fail to account for the insider perspective which, in the case of St Paul's, stressed the meaningfulness of crowd action, and the feelings of solidarity and emotional warmth that came with defence of the community.

Source: Foster and Parker (1995)

Measures of central tendency

You are probably already familiar with measures of central tendency and refer to them as averages. A measure of central tendency provides a single value that is representative of a set of numbers by indicating the most typical value. Three measures of central tendency are discussed here:

- The *mode* is the most frequently occurring value.
- The *median* is the middle value of scores arranged in ascending or descending order.
- The *mean* is the arithmetic average.

Each has its own particular uses – and hence advantages and disadvantages – for particular sets of data.

The mode

The mode is the value in any set of scores that occurs most frequently. For example, with the following series of numbers:

2   4   6   7   7   7   10   12

the most frequently occurring number is 7, and so the mode = 7.

Although the mode provides information on the most frequently occurring value, it has its limitations and is not widely used in psychological research. One reason for this is that when there are only a few scores representing each value, then even very small changes in the data can radically alter the mode. For example:

3	6	8	9	10	10	Mode = 10
3	3	6	8	9	10	Mode = 3

A further possible problem is that there may not be a single modal value. For example, take the series of numbers:

3   5   8   8   8   10   12   16   16   16   20

In this situation, there are two modal values (8 and 16), known as the 'bimodal values'. With cases such as this, the bimodal values may still provide a useful summary statistic. It is, of course, possible to have several modal values, in which case the distribution is referred to as 'multimodal' and the value of the statistic becomes even more limited. For example:

2   2   4   7   7   8   8   10   11   11   13   13

Here, five values occur twice.

The mode has an advantage in that it is a figure that actually does always occur in a given sequence, which may not be true of other measures of central tendency. However, its disadvantage is that it tells us nothing about the other values in the distribution concerned.

The median

The median is the middle value of a set of numbers that has been placed in numerical order (i.e. in order from lowest to highest score, or highest to lowest). Therefore, half of the scores in a given set of data will lie above the median, and half below it. When there is an even number of scores, however, there will be two middle values. In these circumstances, the median is calculated by adding the two central values together and dividing by two. The panel below provides an example of both situations.

When calculating the median, you may find it helpful to cross out the lowest and highest values alternately until you are left with the middle value(s).

The main advantage of the median is that it remains relatively unaffected by any outlying values. It is therefore a safe measure of central tendency to use when we are unsure about the reliability of extreme values. Also, it can be used with data from skewed distributions – that is, where there is a cluster of values at one end of the range (see the panel opposite). Unlike the mean, it can be used when data are on an ordinal level of measurement: first, second, third, etc. (for example, rating scales where data are not measured in fixed units with an equal distance between each point on the scale concerned).

A disadvantage of the median, however, is that it does not work well with small data sets and is affected by any alteration of the central values in a set of values. For example: if we have two sets of data:

10	12	13	14	18	19	22	22	**and**
10	12	13	14	15	19	22	22	

the median would be 16 in the first case and 14.5 in the second, despite only one value being different in the two sets of data.

The mean

The mean is the arithmetic average of a set of data, and is probably the measure of central tendency with which you are most familiar. It is calculated by adding all the values together and dividing the total by the number of scores. An example is shown in the panel below.

The main advantage of the mean is that it makes use of all the available data. As such, it is the most powerful of the measures of central tendency available. However, it needs to be used with a certain amount of caution. One limitation of the mean is that when it has been calculated, decimal points may be less meaningful if all the data consist of whole numbers (as in the example shown below).

Also, the distribution of values needs to be taken into account. The mean can be used appropriately as the measure of central tendency with sets of data (such as

Calculating the median

To calculate the median when there is an **odd** number of scores:

Place scores in numerical order

2   4   5   ⑥   8   10   11

Median = 6

To calculate the median when there is an **even** number of scores:

Place scores in numerical order

2   4   5   ⑥ 8   10   11   13

Median = $\dfrac{6 + 8}{2}$

Median = 7

Calculating the mean

To find the mean of:

2 4 5 5 6 6 6 7 8 10

Add all the values together:

$2 + 4 + 5 + 5 + 6 + 6 + 6 + 7 + 8 + 10 = 59$

Divide this sum by the number of scores (there are 10 scores):

Mean $= \dfrac{59}{10}$

Mean $= 5.9$

Normal and skewed distributions

A normal distribution curve is a bell-shaped curve which is symmetrical about its mean, median and mode (see diagram below). It is called 'normal' because it describes the theoretical distribution of a great many naturally occurring variables. Various characteristics of individuals are considered to be normally distributed (e.g. height and body weight) and sometimes a particular measure is deliberately constructed in a way that a normal distribution of scores results (e.g. some intelligence tests). In theory, a normal distribution curve should result when a large random sample of measurements is taken from an appropriate population. In practice, however, it would be very rare for a distribution to fit a normal distribution curve precisely – there are always likely to be at least some minor irregularities.

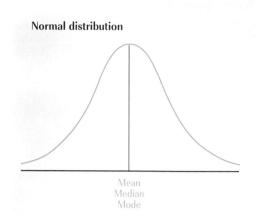

Normal distribution

Mean
Median
Mode

Notice the key features of this curve:

- The curve is symmetrical about its mean value, which occurs at the central point of the distribution. (This value is also the median and mode.)

- The curve has a characteristic bell shape, curving downwards close to the mean and outwards further away.

- The outer extremities of the distribution (known as the tails) will never touch the horizontal axis.

- The properties of this distribution mean that certain statements about probability can be made – a very important feature when a researcher wishes to express clearly the relationship between sample data and data from the population that the sample represents.

However, all variables are not normally distributed; some distributions can be best described as skewed (see below).

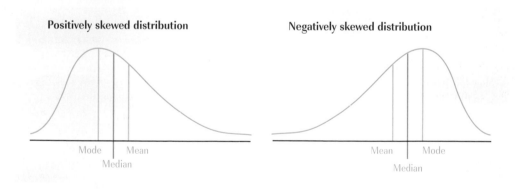

Positively skewed distribution

Mode | Mean
Median

Negatively skewed distribution

Mean | Mode
Median

normally distributed data – see the panel above) which do not have extreme outlying values. When such extreme values are present, the median should be used instead.

For example, calculate the mean of 8, 10, 10, 12, 60. What does the mean tell us about any of these scores?

In this example, the mean is 20, which tells us very little about the four low scores and the single high score. In circumstances where such 'outliers' occur, it would be more appropriate to use the median (10), which at least would summarize the first four values

reasonably successfully (coincidentally, 10 is also the mode in this example).

The mean can be used most successfully with data on interval or ratio levels of measurement (i.e. data measured in fixed units, where each point on the scale of measurement concerned is an equal distance apart). Caution needs to be used if the mean is used with data on ordinal levels of measurement, where data are capable of being placed in rank order, but no assumptions can be made about points on the scale concerned being an equal distance apart.

For example, consider the situation where a teacher rates pupils on a seven-point scale that measures how hard they have worked on their psychology coursework. Students are rated from 1 ('very hard-working') to 7 ('no effort'). Given the arbitrary nature of the scale, we have no way of knowing for certain whether all those rated at 4 on this scale ('average level of work') actually put in precisely the same amount of work, or whether all the points on the scale are at an equal distance apart. Therefore calculating the mean would be inappropriate. In a similar way, it would be wholly inappropriate to work out a mean GCSE grade – these grades are measured on an ordinal level, as some mark bands cover a wider range of marks than others.

Using a measure of central tendency is insufficient on its own to describe a set of data. Take, for example, the following scenario:

Data set A	Data set B
100	100
101	40
99	120
102	60
98	180
100	100

The mean for each set of data is 100, yet the distribution of scores is very different in each case. In data set A, the scores are all very close to 100, while in data set B, they are dispersed much more widely. This is where measures of dispersion have an important role to play.

Measures of dispersion

Measures of dispersion enable us to examine the variability within our data sets, and help us to understand whether scores in a given set of data are similar to, or very different from, each other.

The range

The range is easy to calculate because it is simply the difference between the highest and lowest scores in a given set of data, with 1 added if the scores are all whole numbers. A sample calculation is shown in the panel below.

Calculating the range

To calculate the range of:

3 7 8 10 11 16 18 21 22 26

Find the difference between the highest score (26) and the lowest (3), and add 1.

Range = 26 – 3 + 1 = 24

Similarly, if values are recorded to one decimal place, then the range is the difference between the lowest and highest values with 0.1 added (to two decimal places, it is the difference plus 0.01, and so on). If values are recorded to the nearest half unit, then the range has 0.5 added to the difference between the lowest and highest value.

The range has the advantage of being quick to calculate, but has some important limitations. It does not provide any idea of the distribution of values around the centre, nor does it take individual values into account (remember that the only values used when the range is calculated are the two most extreme values). Following on from this point, the range is therefore seriously affected by any outlying values in a given set of data.

The interquartile range

In an attempt to overcome the potential effect of outlying values, calculating the interquartile range is often preferred. The interquartile range measures the spread of the middle 50 per cent of values when they are placed in numerical order. The top 25 per cent and the bottom 25 per cent of values are ignored, which has the effect of removing the influence of outlying values, and providing an indication of grouping around the central value. The panel below explains how this is calculated.

Calculating the interquartile range

Calculate the interquartile range for the following data:

2 3 7 8 10 11 16 18 21 22 26 26

We first need to calculate the median:

$$\text{The median} = \frac{11 + 16}{2}$$

Median = 13.5

There are six scores above the median, and six below it. The interquartile range will therefore include the six scores that lie closest to the median, and exclude the remaining six. So, for the scores lying above the median, this means that 16, 18 and 21 will be included within the interquartile range, and 22, 26 and 26 excluded.

The upper boundary of the interquartile range will therefore be the mean of the values immediately below it (21) and immediately above it (22), i.e. 21.5. Similarly, the lower boundary will be the mean of 7 and 8 (i.e. 7.5). The interquartile range is, therefore, the difference between 21.5 and 7.5 (i.e. 14).

The standard deviation

The standard deviation is a measure of the variability (i.e. of the typical deviation) of a given sample of scores from its mean. Calculation, as with the mean, involves using all the scores in a given set of data; this makes the standard deviation the most powerful of the measures of dispersion available to the researcher. Calculation is beyond the scope of the AS-level Psychology specification, although if you continue to A level, you may need to calculate it for data sets in your coursework.

The standard deviation allows us to make statements of probability about how likely (or how unlikely) a given value is to occur. This ability to make inferences is based on the relationship between standard deviation and a normal distribution curve (refer back to p. 237). The meaningful use of the statistic not only requires data that are approximately normally distributed, but also data measured on interval or ratio levels of measurement (i.e. data measured in fixed units, where each point on the scale of measurement concerned is an equal distance apart). Standard deviation becomes a less effective measure when there are any outlying scores that skew the data distribution.

The percentages of values that lie between the mean and a given number of standard deviations above and below the mean are fixed properties which help to make the standard deviation a particularly useful measure. These fixed properties are:

- 68.26 per cent of all values lie within one standard deviation either side of the mean
- 95.44 per cent of all values lie within two standard deviations either side of the mean
- 99.74 per cent of all values lie within three standard deviations either side of the mean.

Figure 7.4 illustrates how this works with some data where the calculated standard deviation is 10. As the mean value is 100, this means that 68.26 per cent of the psychology test scores in the population can be inferred as lying between 90 (minus one standard deviation from the mean) and 110 (plus one standard deviation from the mean), while the percentage of test scores lying between 70 and 130 is 99.74 per cent (three standard deviations either side of the mean).

Figure 7.4 »
The percentage of scores that lie between a given number
of standard deviations either side of the mean

Psychology test scores

USING AND INTERPRETING GRAPHS AND CHARTS

Graphs and charts act as visual aids which help to make sense of the data obtained from psychological investigations. They aim to provide an overall picture that helps to summarize the results; when well constructed, they can show us at a glance any patterns which occur in the data.

Be warned, though, that the careful manipulation of the way that the axes in graphs or charts are drawn can easily bias the interpretation. Before reading on, try the activity below, which illustrates the kind of visual deception that can occur.

ACTIVITY

Presenting data

A psychology software publisher asks one of its sales representatives to present her sales figures for the last three years to the company's senior management. Her sales are:

2000   1,000 items

2001   1,001 items

2002   1,002 items (evidently a sales boom!).

The company is dissatisfied with the sales performance, but the sales person is desperate to keep her job. Both parties decide to present the sales figures by means of a line graph, with the years 2000 to 2003 on the x-axis (horizontal) and number of items sold on the y-axis (vertical). The sales person draws a graph with 3 cm representing one year, the management opt for 4 cm = one year. The y-axis of the sales person's graph is 16 cm long and extends from 1,000 items sold to 1,002. However, the management draw their y-axis 10 cm long, and label it from 0 items sold to 10,000. Draw or sketch the two graphs and see the bias created.

The graphs will produce very different impressions, even though they are based on identical data – see Figs 7.9 and 7.10 on p. 243, which show the graphs at half actual size. Shortening or extending the axes, or manipulating their labelling, can convey a desired impression and may be highly misleading to the observer. The important lesson from this exercise is that there is no single correct way to select the scales that are used on the axes of graphs. However, there are certain conventions that serve both to assist the author to present their information in an unbiased way, and to reduce the risk of misunderstandings.

- Plot frequency of scores on the y-axis (as in the examples that you have just drawn). This is the conventional mode of presentation, but is not a hard and fast rule – sometimes horizontal bars can provide a pleasing alternative.

- Adopt the three-quarter high rule. This states that when frequencies are plotted, the length of the y-axis should be determined in the following way. It should be organized so that the distance of the highest point on the graph (i.e. the point that represents the score with the highest frequency) from the x-axis is approximately equal to three-quarters of the total length of the x-axis.

- It is possible to break the x-axis or y-axis of a graph if labelling of the axis from zero would give a poor visual impression due to the large amount of empty space that would result.

- Remember that all graphs and charts need to have each axis clearly labelled and have an informative title.

Ideally, someone looking at a graph or chart should be able to understand what it is about without any additional explanation. It is also important when reading other people's work to look out for examples of graphs and charts that are misleading.

Histograms

Histograms and bar charts are two of the most widely used graphical techniques. Simple forms of these are discussed here, but alternative forms exist, such as compound or three-dimensional ones which show data from more than one condition simultaneously.

Histograms are a useful form of graphical representation which can be used when presenting data on interval or ratio levels of measurement.

Figure 7.5 >>
Histogram showing the number of words recalled in a memory experiment

A histogram consists of a series of vertical bars of equal width, which represent frequencies of the variable placed on the x-axis. The height of each bar represents the frequency of occurrence for each point on the scale or each category. A histogram is drawn with the bars representing the frequencies actually touching each other. An ideal number of bars to use is between six and eight. Sometimes, single values can be used for each bar, but if the scale used on the x-axis has a large number of points, then the data can be placed into class intervals.

Bar charts

A bar chart is superficially similar to a histogram, and consists of a series of vertical bars of equal width, which can be used to illustrate the frequencies of a non-continuous variable on the x-axis. They are often used to depict data measured on nominal (placed in categories) or ordinal levels of measurement or, for example, to illustrate the means from different samples. Unlike the histogram, it is usual to draw each bar separated from each of the others so that a continuous variable is not implied on the x-axis (as in Fig. 7.6).

Figure 7.6 ≫
Bar chart showing the number of observations of different behaviours in a group of children

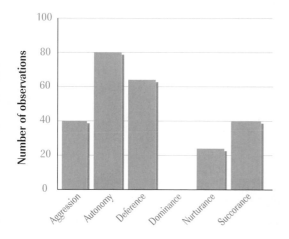

When data are at a nominal level, bias should be avoided in the order in which the bars are presented, as these can logically be presented in any order. They are often presented in alphabetical order to avoid such bias. However, when data are treated at an ordinal level, the x-axis can be drawn using the order of the points on the scale concerned.

Frequency polygons

The frequency polygon is a particularly useful technique when you want to compare two or more frequency distributions. It is used as an alternative to the

Figure 7.7 ≫
Frequency polygon showing the number of words recalled in a memory experiment

histogram. Indeed, a frequency polygon can be drawn by linking the midpoints from the top of each bar contained in a histogram, as in the example in Fig. 7.7. A frequency polygon may be the preferred technique when you need to depict results from two or more conditions of an investigation at the same time; this is because two or more lines can be drawn on the same graph to show direct comparison of results.

Scattergraphs and the interpretation of correlation coefficients

Before reading on, try the activity on the next page.

The term 'correlation' was introduced in Unit 6 (pp. 203–5), where the concepts of correlation coefficients, and positive and negative correlations were introduced. Reread that section now to refresh your knowledge of these terms. As far as interpreting correlation coefficients is concerned, the strength of a correlation increases as the obtained coefficient becomes closer to +1 or −1. An important way of depicting correlational relationships is the scattergraph (or scattergram). Data from one of the variables being correlated are presented on the x-axis and data from the second variable on the y-axis (see Fig. 7.8).

Study the examples of scattergraphs in Fig. 7.8 and then try the activity on interpreting scattergraphs on p. 243.

In order to interpret a correlation coefficient fully, it is necessary to test the correlation coefficient obtained for statistical significance. This is because the significance of a correlation coefficient is linked directly to the key variable of the number of pairs of scores being correlated. If you go on to study psychology at A level, you may have the opportunity to carry out a correlational study and to analyse the results taking this factor into account.

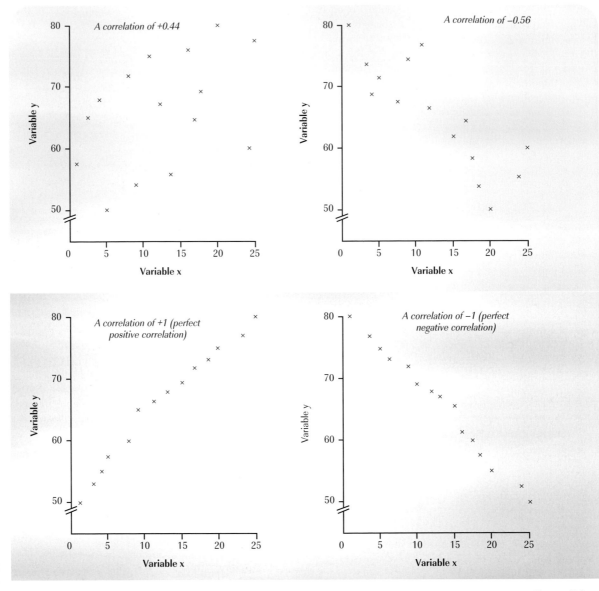

Figure 7.8 >>
Scattergraphs illustrating different correlation coefficients

ACTIVITY

Correlations

For each of the following correlations (relationships), decide whether they are positive or negative.

1 The more aggressive parents are, the more aggressive their children tend to be.

2 The hotter the weather, the fewer the clothes people wear.

3 The more expensive the petrol, the less petrol people buy.

4 The hotter the weather, the more clothes people remove.

5 The fewer sweets eaten, the fewer fillings needed.

6 The colder the weather, the higher people's fuel bills.

7 The more people exercise, the less risk they have of a heart attack.

8 More extrovert people get more party invitations.

9 The shorter the hours of daylight, the greater the incidence of depression.

10 As children grow older they become more independent.

Interpreting scattergraphs

Below is a scattergraph showing the relationship between scores derived from questionnaires measuring ill health and stress levels. How would you interpret this correlation?

(See below for answer.)

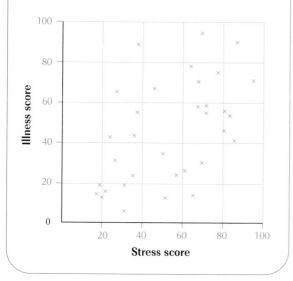

Planning a study

Now that you have reached the end of this unit and have learned more about the factors involved in designing research and analysing data, look back to the 'Getting you thinking...' on p. 215. Choose just one research method to investigate whether there is any link between watching violent cartoons and levels of aggression in children.

Use what you have learned in this unit to prepare a plan. Issues to consider when planning a research study are:

1 the aim of the study and any research hypothesis (for experimental research)

2 who the participants will be – how many and how you would select them

3 what design you will use, if you plan to undertake experimental research

4 whether you will need to carry out a pilot study

5 what the main ethical issues associated with the proposed study and are how you would address them (Units 5 and 6 should help you)

6 what type(s) of data you will collect and how you will analyse the data.

ANSWERS TO ACTIVITIES

Activity, p. 240

Figure 7.9 »
Graph produced by salesperson

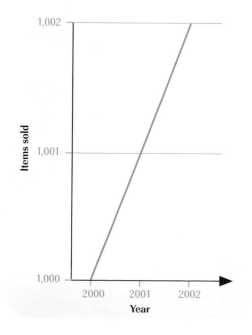

Figure 7.10 »
Graph produced by management

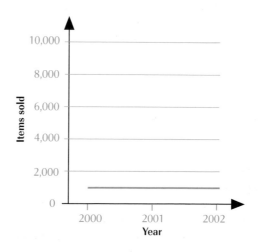

Activity, this page (top left)

The scattergraph illustrates that stress and illness scores tend to be positively correlated. In other words, when stress scores increase, then so, generally speaking, do illness scores. The correlation coefficient is in fact around +0.6.

Check your understanding of data analysis by answering these questions. Try to do this from memory at first. You can check your answers by looking back through Topic 2.

1 Name three measures of central tendency.

2 Which measure of central tendency is the middle value of a set of numbers placed in numerical order?

3 What are the main properties (characteristics) of the normal distribution curve?

4 Explain what is meant by the term 'measure of dispersion'.

5 Name two measures of dispersion.

6 When might the interquartile range be used rather than the range?

7 What is the main difference between a histogram and a bar chart?

8 When might a frequency polygon be used instead of a histogram to present frequency data?

9 Does the following statement indicate a positive or a negative correlation?

<< The more people exercise, the less risk they have of a heart attack. >>

10 What is a scattergraph (or scattergram)?

REVISION SUMMARY

Having covered this topic you should be able to:

✓ define the key terms listed on pp. 231–2

✓ describe ways in which qualitative data from naturalistic observations, questionnaire surveys and interviews may be analysed

✓ discuss the appropriate use and interpretation of three measures of central tendency – median, mean and mode – and two measures of dispersion – range and standard deviation

✓ explain the nature of positive and negative correlations and the interpretation of correlation coefficients

✓ describe the appropriate use and interpretation of histograms, bar charts, frequency polygons and scattergraphs.

UNIT SUMMARY

Topic 1: Research design and implementation

● At the start of any psychological investigation, appropriate **aims** and **hypotheses** of the study should be **generated** and clearly stated. Hypotheses are **testable statements**. A **null hypothesis** predicts no difference or no correlation, and if any difference or correlation is found, it is due to chance variation alone. An **alternative hypothesis** attributes results to some factor other than chance, such as the independent variable in an experiment. Alternative hypotheses may be **directional** (predicting the likely direction of outcome) or **non-directional** (not predicting the likely direction of outcome).

- The **experimental designs** available to the researcher include independent groups, repeated measures and matched participants designs. Key design issues with **non-experimental** research (e.g. naturalistic observations, questionnaire surveys and interviews) include deciding how behaviour is sampled, the method(s) used for recording data, and the phrasing and organization of questions.

- The **control of variables** is fundamental to scientific research in psychology. Psychologists need to **define precisely** all the variables that they are investigating to ensure that these are properly **operationalized**, including both **independent** and **dependent variables**.

- Small-scale **pilot studies** can be carried out before research takes place in order to identify any potential problems.

- Researchers need to **assess** and, where necessary, **improve** the reliability and validity of their research measures and techniques. **Reliability** refers to the consistency of a test or procedure. Key aspects of it are observer reliability and test reliability. The **validity** of measuring instruments can be established by the extent to which they measure what they set out to measure. Key aspects are internal, external (ecological) and test validity.

- It is essential that all psychological research is carried out **ethically**, i.e. it respects the rights and feelings of all those taking part.

- Different sampling techniques can be used to **select participants** for research investigations from the **target population** of interest. In a **random sample**, every person in the target population has an equal chance of being selected. In an **opportunity sample**, the investigator chooses whoever is available from the target population.

- The **relationship** between researcher and participant can affect an investigation. **Demand characteristics** occur when research participants attempt to make sense of the research situation that they find themselves in. **Investigator effects** result from the effects of a researcher's behaviour and characteristics on an investigation.

Topic 2: Data analysis

- **Naturalistic observational studies, questionnaire surveys** and **interviews** may produce **qualitative** (non-numerical) or **quantitative** (numerical) data. Qualitative data can provide a richness of detail which may not be achievable with quantitative data. However, quantitative data are often easier to analyse.

- Descriptive statistical techniques used to analyse quantitative data include **measures of central tendency** (averages). These are the **mode** (the most frequently occurring value), the **median** (the middle value when data are placed into rank order) and the **mean** (where all values are added together and divided by the number of scores).

- **Descriptive statistical techniques** also include **measures of dispersion**, such as the **range** (a measure of the difference between highest and lowest values in a data set) and **standard deviation** (the average deviation of scores from the mean).

- **Graphs and charts** that can be used by a researcher include **histograms, bar charts, frequency polygons** and **scattergraphs**.

- **Correlation** is a statistical technique for measuring relationships between sets of data. Correlations can be described as **positive** (high scores on both variables) or **negative** (high scores on one variable, low scores on another). The strength of a positive or negative correlation increases as the obtained **correlation coefficient** becomes closer to +1 or −1 respectively. The nature of the relationship (correlation) can be shown on a **scattergraph**.

Answering exam questions on Research methods

For sample examination questions and answers on Research methods, together with examiner comments on the answers, see pp. 262–5.

8 UNIT

PREPARING FOR THE
AS Examination

PREVIEW

In this unit you will be looking at:

>> the nature of the AS examination

>> how your examination work will be marked

>> sample examination answers and examiner comments

>> how to perform to your full potential in the examination.

INTRODUCTION

The Advanced Subsidiary (AS) is set at a level midway between GCSE and GCE Advanced Level, and the skills that you will need to demonstrate will be different from those at these other levels. It is our aim here to give you the fullest possible understanding of how the examination 'works' – for example, by looking at how questions are set and marked, so that you can prepare for the exam with these factors in mind. If you use this unit in conjunction with the other units that contain the psychological knowledge, topic by topic, you should be ideally prepared to achieve your best possible grade.

You will start, in Topic 1, by looking at the nature of the AS examination. Here, we focus on the different types of questions that are set in the exam and the different skills they are designed to test: labelled AO1, AO2 and AO3. Topic 2 goes on to describe what examiners will be looking for when they mark your answers.

In Topic 3, we see how this works in practice by looking at some sample exam questions, together with two candidates' responses to these questions. By examining what these candidates have done right and wrong, you will see how to score well in the answers you write.

Finally, Topic 4 contains ten top tips for doing well in psychology.

Paul Humphreys

Mike Cardwell

AO1, AO2 AND AO3

AS-level questions set for AQA Psychology Specification A assess three types of skill. These skills, known as 'Assessment Objectives' are as follows:

● *Knowledge and Understanding* (AO1)

● *Analysis and Evaluation* (AO2)

● *Designing, Conducting and Reporting* (AO3).

AO3 questions are restricted to Research Methods questions, but AO1 and AO2 questions are present in all other sections. Each question is worth 30 marks, with the AO1 parts of the question being worth 18 marks and the AO2 component of each question being worth 12 marks.

The first two parts of each question (except for Research Methods) are always AO1 and the last part always AO1 *plus* AO2. This is important because different types of question require different types of answer. AO1 questions require more *descriptive* responses, whereas AO1 + AO2 questions require more *evaluative* responses.

Assessment Objective 1 (AO1)

AO1 is the demonstration of knowledge and understanding through clear and effective communication. Are knowledge and understanding the same thing? No, they are not! I know that in order to make my car go faster, I have to press my foot down on the accelerator pedal, but I must confess I don't understand how this 'works'. By same token, I may 'know' what the main features of Bowlby's theory of attachment are (pp. 53–6), but this knowledge may be quite superficial with no real understanding underpinning it. Take the non-understanding student away from their rote-learning list, and they're lost.

Conversely, if you really understand something, you can look at it from any angle – not just a prelearned sequence – and still feel totally at ease with it. Understanding leads to insight: having a real grasp and comprehension of the thing in question. If you depend on memory, it may well let you down, especially if you are anxious about it; understanding will never let you down.

Assessment Objective 2 (AO2)

AO2 is analysis and evaluation. We are using the term 'analysis' in the same sense as it is used in psychoanalysis. Freud was interested in analysing the psyche, or the mind, using such questions as:

"What are the elements that make it up?" – "How do they work together?" – "How do they interrelate?"

In the same way, we can take any theory apart, examine the individual parts of it, and then put it back together. Think of analysis as taking something apart, stripping it down to its basic elements and then carrying out a detailed examination of these.

There is another aspect of analysis that is not immediately apparent from a literal definition of the word. Imagine you go to see your football team play a match. The odds are you will get sucked into the 'theatre' of the match, and will watch it with the heart more than the mind. A football writer, on the other hand, will be watching your team and the game *analytically*. There is, then, a component of critical consideration to analysis too.

What about evaluation? By this term we mean making an informed judgement about the value or worth of something. It is one thing to know the 'factual features' of Bowlby's theory of attachment, quite another to make an informed judgement about its quality or worth.

Two important points need to be made. You may have noticed that the phrase used was *informed* judgement. This means the judgement is not a whim or 'pulled out of thin air', but is based on solid information and can be substantiated. "Milgram's work was ethically unforgivable" is an evaluation of sorts, but has no substance.

The second point is that evaluation should be *two-sided*. Few things in psychology and life are so one-sided that they have nothing that can be said in their favour or nothing that can be said against them. In most circumstances, there are two sides to a question and both need evaluating. Evaluation does not mean 'slagging off'; it means giving a balanced appraisal. Try always to give both the pros and the cons.

Assessment Objective 3

Assessment Objective 3 (AO3) relates only to the Research Methods questions. In each Research Methods question, all but 9 of the marks are awarded for AO3 skills. This assesses your ability to think on your feet concerning the stimulus material rather than trotting out some rote-learned material without considering the context of the question. For example, *why* did the researchers use a matched participants design, or *how* could the design of this study be improved?

TYPES OF QUESTIONS

The following are *examples* of the types of questions that are used to assess AO1 and AO2 (this book contains many more such examples). At the end of each topic we have given you a revision summary so you know the specific question types that will apply to that topic. Remember that each mark is equivalent to approximately one minute of thinking and writing, so it is vital to use this time wisely, neither extending it nor skimping on it.

AO1

These questions assess your *knowledge and understanding* of the specification material. They are the first two parts of each question (except Research Methods). There is also an AO1 component in the final part of each question. We will deal with that later. Examples of these questions are shown in the panel on p. 248.

Examples of AO1 questions

- **What is meant by** the terms conformity, minority influence, and obedience? (2 + 2 + 2 marks)
- **Outline two reasons why** people yield to majority influence. (3 + 3 marks)
- **Describe two differences** between short-term (STM) and long-term (LTM) memory. (3 + 3 marks)
- **Describe the aims/procedures/findings/ conclusions/criticisms*** of one study of majority influence. [*any combination of two of these aspects of the study] (6 marks)
- **Outline findings of research** into the effects of day care on children's social development. (6 marks)
- **Describe one explanation** of attachment (e.g. Bowlby's). (6 marks)
- **Outline two explanations** of forgetting in short-term memory. (3 + 3 marks)
- **Outline two limitations** of the definition of abnormality as 'deviation from ideal mental health'. (3 + 3 marks)
- **Give two criticisms** of the levels of processing theory of memory. (3 + 3 marks)

AO1 + AO2

The AO1/AO2 question is your chance to show that you can *think* about the specification content in such a way as to answer a slightly more challenging question about the topic in question. This final part is assigned 18 of the 30 marks available for the total question. Six marks are given for the AO1 content and 12 are for the AO2 content. It is vitally important to remember this mark division when planning your response, so that one-third of your answer is AO1 and two-thirds AO2.

What do they look like?

The AO1 + AO2 questions tend to follow a fairly similar format in that you are asked to do something descriptive for 6 marks and then something more evaluative for the remaining 12 marks. Sometimes this AO1 division is fairly obvious, as in the following examples:

- 'Outline and evaluate ...'
- 'Give a brief account of and evaluate ...'

Sometimes it is up to you how you will divide your answer into AO1 and AO2. For example:

- 'To what extent does research support ...'
- 'Consider the view that ...'

It is always worth spending a couple of minutes 'deconstructing' the question so that *you* are clear what is the AO1 requirement and what is the AO2 requirement, and planning your response strategically along these lines. Take a look at the three questions in the panel below, and decide what the AO1 and AO2 requirements of each question might be.

Examples of AO1 + AO2 questions

- To what extent has psychological research shown eyewitness testimony to be unreliable? (18 marks)
- Give a brief account of, and evaluate the use of ethical guidelines as a way of resolving ethical issues in psychological research. (18 marks)
- *"What is considered 'normal' or 'abnormal' cannot be understood without also considering the cultural context of the behaviour being evaluated."*

  Consider how attempts to define abnormality might be influenced by cultural differences. (18 marks)

WHAT IS THE EXAMINER LOOKING FOR?

There is no one right route through these questions, but, as we shall see in the next topic, examiners have different criteria that they use when deciding how many marks to award for a particular answer. For these questions, they have separate criteria for the AO1 component and the AO2 component.

AO1 (0–6)

- *Accuracy* – is the material accurate, partially accurate or inaccurate?
- *Detail* – is the material sufficiently elaborated or does it lack detail?

AO2 (0–12)

- *Informed commentary* – are you saying something about the material that is both psychologically informed and shows engagement with the material?
- *Analysis* – what are the raw ingredients of your argument and how do these blend together?
- *Effective use of material* – have you made the most of your material?

AO3 questions

The Research Methods question carries 30 marks, as do all the questions, but there are some key differences. For example, there is no choice – just the one question, which you will be required to answer. Perhaps more importantly, there is no guaranteed structure to the Research Methods, as there is with the others. What we can say with confidence is that some of the questions will require very short answers (1 or 2 marks) whereas others will require more from you and may carry, say, 6 or 7 marks. Bear in mind that the higher the number of marks allocated to each question, the more time you spend answering it. The notional idea of 'a mark a minute' discussed earlier is still a good rule of thumb. The Research Methods question will always begin with a short piece of stimulus material – usually describing a hypothetical study – and the questions will then be based around this.

A key determinant of success is having a sound understanding of what the examiner is looking for – or to put it another way, how they mark your work. The uninformed student will write *hoping* that this is what the examiner is looking for; the informed student will write *knowing* that it is what the examiner is looking for.

Before they mark any exam papers (or *scripts,* as they are technically known), all examiners attend a full day's standardization meeting in which they work through a large number of candidates' answers. They work alongside all the other examiners and are led by the Principal Examiners who set the question papers. Two factors that will be significant to you emerge from this:

● This process ensures that all examiners mark to the same standard, so it makes no difference which examiner marks your work. There are no hard or soft markers!

● All the examiners mark to the same set of criteria or guidelines. This is the critical factor, because these criteria are made public by the examining board so you can know in advance what the examiners are looking for.

We will look at the marking criteria shortly, but three other important general points need to be made first.

● Examiners mark according to a standard that it is reasonable to expect a notional 17 year old to display working under exam conditions. They appreciate that you will be anxious and tense, have limited time, are answering questions that you have only just seen and are not allowed to consult your books, notes, etc. Clearly, an exam is a very different exercise from writing an essay for classwork, and you can rest assured that the examiner will always be mindful of this.

● In psychology there are rarely single, right answers (other than occasionally for Research Methods questions). The consequence of this is that there is no single answer to learn when preparing for questions and, perhaps most importantly, no single answer that the examiner is looking for.

● Examiners do not mark with pass or fail in mind. They do not even mark with grades in mind. Grades are decided by an Awarding Committee of examiners and teachers after the marking has been completed. Examiners award marks solely according to the marking criteria, which we will now explore.

HOW ARE THE MARKS AWARDED?

Here, we give an insight into how the marks are awarded for the most common of the AQA Specification A question types used in the AS-level psychology exam. These are summaries of the marking allocation tables used by examiners, but they contain the same mark divisions and criteria.

In the AO1 questions, the emphasis is on the amount of relevant material presented (e.g. 'limited' or 'basic'), the amount of detail given (e.g. 'lacking detail') and the accuracy of the material (e.g. 'muddled').

In the AO1 + AO2 part of the question, the emphasis is not only on the descriptive content (AO1), but also on the amount and level of the critical commentary (e.g. 'superficial'), its thoroughness (e.g. 'reasonably thorough') and how effectively it has been used (e.g. 'highly effective'). This is the AO2 component of the question, and in the final part of each question this is worth 12 of the 18 marks available.

AO1 questions

The table on the right and the one on p. 250 show how marks are awarded for different AO1 questions.

> ### AO1: 2-mark questions
>
> #### Example
> "What is meant by the terms conformity, minority influence, and obedience? (2 + 2 + 2 marks)"
>
> | >> 2 marks | Accurate and detailed |
> | >> 1 mark | Basic, lacking detail, muddled or flawed |
> | >> 0 marks | Inappropriate or incorrect |

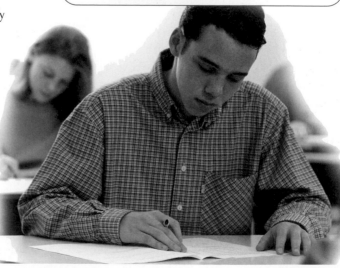

AO1: 3- and 6-mark questions

Examples

Outline two explanations of forgetting in short-term memory. (3 + 3 marks)

Outline findings of research into the effects of day care on children's social development. (6 marks)

3-mark questions	6-mark questions	Criteria
3	6–5	>> Accurate and detailed
2	4–3	>> Limited, generally accurate but less detailed.
1	2–1	>> Basic, lacking in detail, muddled or flawed.
0	0	>> Inaccurate or inappropriate

AO1 + AO2 questions

As all AO1 + AO2 questions are worth 18 marks (6 marks for AO1 and 12 for AO2), the following table applies to the AO2 component in all the questions that you will meet in the exam. The heading 'commentary' applies to the specific AO2 requirement of the question (e.g. 'evaluate' or 'to what extent?').

AO1 + AO2 questions

Marks	Commentary	Analysis	Use of material
12–11	>> Informed	>> Reasonably thorough	>> Effective
10–9	>> Reasonable	>> Slightly limited	>> Effective
8–7	>> Reasonable	>> Limited	>> Reasonably effective
6–5	>> Basic	>> Limited	>> Reasonably effective
4–3	>> Superficial	>> Rudimentary	>> Minimal interpretation
2–1	>> Just discernible	>> Weak and muddled	>> Mainly irrelevant
0	>> Wholly irrelevant	>> Wholly irrelevant	>> Wholly irrelevant

Quality of Written Communication (QoWC)

As indicated earlier, all examinations now include an assessment of your written communication skills. There are up to two marks awarded in each unit paper. That isn't a great deal, but it helps to know that they are there and how you can make sure you get them! The table on the right may help in this respect.

Quality of Written Communication

>>	2 marks	Accurate and clear expression of ideas, a broad range of specialist terms and only minor errors in grammar, punctuation and spelling.
>>	1 mark	Reasonable expression of ideas, a reasonable range of specialist terms and few errors of grammar, punctuation and spelling.
>>	0 marks	Poor expression of ideas, limited use of specialist terms and poor grammar, punctuation and spelling.

MODULE 1: COGNITIVE & DEVELOPMENTAL PSYCHOLOGY

Cognitive psychology: Human memory

(a) Give three differences between STM and LTM.   (2 + 2 + 2 marks)

Answer 1

STM has limited capacity but LTM is unlimited.

STM stores information for a brief period, but LTM stores it forever.

STM is encoded in sounds and LTM is what they mean.

Answer 2

The capacity of STM is limited (7 ±2 items) whereas the capacity of LTM is thought to be unlimited.

STM stores information for a very short period of time unless it is rehearsed, whereas LTM stores information more or less permanently.

STM involves acoustic coding (i.e. by sound) whereas material in LTM is encoded semantically (i.e. by meaning).

● *Answer 1:* Each of these differences is generally accurate, but lacking in detail. Each of these would get 1 mark, for a total of 3 marks.

● *Answer 2:* Not a lot more words, but greater clarity and the right amount of elaboration mean that this answer gets all 6 marks available.

(b) Outline two explanations of forgetting in LTM.   (3 + 3 marks)

Answer 1

One reason for forgetting in LTM is through decay. Over time we lose the ability to remember things that we have learned when we were younger. They just decay from memory.

Another reason is displacement. New memories displace older ones, so we forget them.

Answer 2

One explanation of forgetting in Long Term Memory is interference. One set of information interferes with another. Sometimes interference is proactive, where previously remembered information interferes with new information, making it more difficult to remember. Sometimes it is retroactive, where new information makes it more difficult to recall older, similar information already in memory.

A second explanation is retrieval failure, where forgetting is a result of the absence of appropriate retrieval cues. If we are in a different psychological state (e.g. sober) or the context in which we try and remember is different (e.g. in an examination), we find it more difficult to recall information than if we were in the same state and context as when we first learned it.

● *Answer 1:* The first explanation is generally accurate but lacks the precision necessary for full marks. The term 'decay' is never really explained. The second explanation is wrong – they might have been describing interference, but they have used the term 'displacement' which is an explanation of STM forgetting. These answers would be worth 2 + 0 marks, for a total of 2 marks.

● *Answer 2:* These are two accurate and detailed accounts of forgetting in LTM. This answer makes full use of the time available and contains an appropriate amount of elaboration for the full 6 marks. The use of appropriate examples in the second explanation helps to demonstrate the difference between internal and external cues.

Answer 1

The multi-store model was proposed by Atkinson and Shiffrin (1968). It suggests that memory flows through the system going through sensory memory (SM), short-term memory (STM) and finally long-term memory (LTM). Atkinson and Shiffrin found that at each of these three stages, information can be lost through forgetting. They found that in SM information is lost because of decay. In STM, information is lost through displacement, and in LTM it is lost through interference.

Atkinson and Shiffrin also found that there were differences in the way the information was coded in each of the stores. In the STM, for example, they found that coding was acoustic (the way things sounded) and in LTM it was semantic (the meaning of things). Many other studies have demonstrated this distinction between STM and LTM, and so support the multistore model.

Other research findings have also supported Atkinson and Shiffrin. For example, the case of KF, who had become brain injured after an accident showed that he could remember some things in his long-term memory and also remember new things, but he could not remember things in the short term. This supported the idea that LTM and STM are different parts of the memory, because KF had damaged the part of his memory connected with STM, but the part of his brain connected with LTM was undamaged, so accounting for his memory impairment.

Answer 2

Atkinson and Shiffrin (1968) explained memory in terms of three distinct stores. These were the sensory memory, which holds information for a very brief period, short-term memory (STM), which has limited capacity and relatively short duration, and a long-term memory (LTM) which has potentially unlimited capacity and duration. If a person's attention is focused on material in the sensory memory, then this material would get transferred to STM. Atkinson and Shiffrin claimed that information was transferred from STM to LTM through the process of rehearsal. They proposed a direct relationship between rehearsal in STM and the strength of the long-term memory – the more the information is rehearsed the better it is remembered.

Research studies have supported Atkinson and Shiffrin's view that the stores are different in terms of capacity, encoding and duration. The existence of separate stores in memory is also supported by the use of modern brain scanning techniques (such as PET scans). These have shown, for example, that the prefrontal cortex is active when individuals are working on a task in immediate (i.e. short-term) memory whereas the hippocampus is active when LTM is engaged. The idea that there is a different physiological basis for short-term and long-term memory is further supported by the study of a man called HM (Milner 1966) who had to have both hippocampi removed due to a tumour. After this surgery he was unable to form any new long-term memories though he could perform STM tasks.

Despite this research support, the multi-store model is probably an oversimplification of memory processes. The multi-store model just proposes one long-term store whereas research suggests several different forms of LTM (e.g. episodic, semantic and procedural memory). This model also proposes just one short-term store whereas Baddeley and Hitch's working memory model shows that this too is an over-simplification. Finally, the multi-store model proposes one mechanism for how data is stored in LTM – rehearsal. Despite Atkinson and Shiffrin's claim, it is unlikely that rehearsal is the only way that information finds its way into LTM. Flash-bulb memories, for example, are extremely long-lasting, without any form of rehearsal taking place.

● *Answer 1:* Most of this material is descriptive, so it picks up fairly decent marks for the AO1 component of this question (accurate and detailed, so 5 of the 6 marks available), but there is little evidence of AO2 material. Some of this is speculative (e.g. "many other studies have demonstrated this distinction"), and is not particularly effective as 'commentary' on the multi-store model. The material on KF does address the validity of this model, but overall the AO2 material is superficial and would only receive 3 of the 12 marks available.

● *Answer 2:* This answer is clearly divided into three distinct paragraphs. The first of these is an accurate and well-detailed précis of the multi-store model. The next two paragraphs are purely evaluative, the first being evidence for the multi-store model and the second evidence against. This is very effective evaluation. The entire answer is extremely well organized and is structured so as to capture the full 6 marks available for AO1 and the full 12 marks available for AO2.

Developmental psychology: Attachments in development

(a) Explain what is meant by the terms 'secure' and 'insecure' attachment. (3 + 3 marks)

Answer 1

Secure attachment means that the child is better balanced and happier than an insecurely attached child. They are more likely to cope better with relationships later on in their life compared to insecurely attached children who lack the security of having someone they can trust to look after them.

● *Answer 1:* These explanations have a 'whiff of truth' about them so are obviously worth more than zero marks, but the lack of detail and the general imprecision means that they are restricted to 1 mark each. The student has presented a comparison by way of explaining each of these terms, but may have been better off explaining each term independently.

Answer 2

Securely attached infants feel content to explore a strange environment using their caregiver as a safe base. They show some distress when left by their caregiver but are relatively easily comforted and greet the caregiver enthusiastically at reunion.

Insecurely attached children show disturbed behaviour during separation from the caregiver and also when reunited. 'Resistant-insecure' children are distressed on separation and resist attempts at reunion with their caregiver. 'Avoidant-insecure' children are indifferent at separation and avoid contact on reunion.

● *Answer 2:* Although relatively brief, these two explanations are accurate and detailed. This demonstrates a good understanding of the terms and would be worth the full 3 marks for each term.

(b) Outline research into the effects of privation. (6 marks)

Answer 1

Rutter studied privation to see if its effects were far reaching. He found that privation could produce a number of different types of retardation including intellectual retardation and possible anti-social behaviour later in life. The case of Genie found that she too suffered later in life as a result of her earlier privation, and failed to recover once the privation was removed. The Czech twins (Koluchova, 1976), despite extreme privation when young, nevertheless recovered well when placed in a foster home at the age of 7 years. Tizard and Hughes studied children who were put in a children's home before they were 4 months old. Those who were later adopted fared much better than those who were not.

● *Answer 1:* The studies quoted are accurate but each lacks sufficient detail. Possibly it would have been more effective to have covered less and added a little more detail on each. There is an occasional lack of clarity which probably also stops this answer from getting into the top mark band, but this would receive 4 of the 6 marks available.

Answer 2

Spitz (1945) discovered, that despite hygienic surroundings and a good diet at a foundling home, babies received minimal social or physical stimulation and frequently died. Goldfarb's studies of children cared for in institutions and those removed to foster homes also showed abnormal development in the institutionalized children in areas of intelligence, motor co-ordination, behaviour, and language. Provence and Lipton (1966) found that institutionalized children showed impairment in a number of areas including reaction to peers and impulse control. More recently, studies of Romanian orphanages have shown that the majority of these children had suffered from extremes of privation and as a result were severely delayed in their development. They found that many of the older children preferred to take care of themselves and this created barriers to closeness with parents or other adults.

● *Answer 2:* This is clearly focused on the effects of privation. The earlier studies of Spitz and Goldfarb are reinforced with the more contemporary study of Romanian orphanages. There are enough studies to have a breadth of research findings, yet not too many that there is no detail in the answer. The occasional lack of a date or name is not important and does not stop the answer getting the full 6 marks.

(c) To what extent has day care been shown to have beneficial effects on children's cognitive and/or social development? (18 marks)

Answer 1

Day care is where a child is cared for outside the home by someone who isn't a family member. Day care isn't the same as institutional care, such as in a residential nursery because this is 24-hour care. Examples of day care would include child-minding, and is available for children below school age. Cognitive development is defined as changes in mental abilities as a result of age (or experience). Social development is defined as changes in social behaviour (e.g. with peers) as a result of age or experience. Day care is thought to affect both cognitive and social development because it provides the right sort of experience for children to develop these skills.

There hasn't been a lot of research into the effects of day care on children's cognitive development, therefore it is difficult to draw any firm conclusions about whether it might be good or bad for the development of mental abilities. If day care is stimulating for the child however, then it stands to

reason that it would be good for them and that it would cause beneficial effects for their cognitive development. Good child-minders spend lots of time stimulating the children they are looking after, and this has beneficial effects. However, different children react differently to this stimulation therefore what is beneficial for one child might not be beneficial for another.

There has been a lot more research on the effects of day care on children's social development, but the results are just as inconclusive. It makes sense that if children are allowed to play with others they learn how to get on with each other therefore their social skills improve. However, there is some evidence that day care can actually have harmful effects on children's social development. For example, in one study in America, the researchers found that children who had had a lot of day care when they were younger were more aggressive when they were older.

Answer 2

Although there is a lot of evidence to suggest that day care can have negative effects on children's social development, there is also evidence to suggest that it does have some positive effects. Clarke-Stewart et al. (1994) found that children who had attended day care coped better with social situations in their first year at school and got on better with their peers. Enrichment programmes such as the High/Scope Perry Preschool Project have also produced positive effects on social development over a much longer period. Schweinhart et al. (1993) found that children who had taken part in this day care programme had lower delinquency rates in adolescence and were less likely to have a criminal record when older compared to a control group who did not take part in this project.

The positive effects of day care on social development must be balanced against the possible negative effects of day care. Belsky (2003) claims that the more time that children spend in day care during their pre-school years, the more likely they are to display aggressive and disobedient behaviour as 4–8 year olds. He argues that children who experience poor-quality day care are more likely to experience these negative effects, as they fail to develop the secure sense of self that comes from the loving and attentive care needed for positive development. However, a study that evaluated the consequences of working mothers

on the development of their children found that they suffered no permanent harm because of the mother's absence (Harvey 1999). Harvey concluded that whether or not day care had a positive (or negative) effect on children's social development depended on the quality of the parent–child relationship and the quality of the day care arrangement.

It is difficult to state conclusively that day care has either positive or negative effects on children's social development. This is because a lot depends on individual differences in the children themselves, and on the quality of the day care experience. Belsky suggests that some children are particularly vulnerable to the adverse effects of poor-quality day care. Research suggests that boys are more vulnerable than girls and so are more likely to show negative effects in their later social development. Pennebaker et al. (1981) found that shy children are more likely to find day care threatening and are less likely to benefit from the experience. It is also important to point out that some research fails to support the claim that 'high intensity' day care has inevitable negative effects on children's subsequent development (e.g. Clarke-Stewart et al. 1994). Therefore, any conclusions that we draw about the effects of day care on social development can only be tentative.

Answer 1: This answer does not actually say anything that is wrong, but a lot of it is either irrelevant or unsubstantiated. The definitions in the first paragraph are not required (they do not really address the specific question). The last sentence does make a statement about the effects of day care on development, and therefore would count as basic and lacking detail. The AO1 content would be worth just 1 mark. The AO2 content is a little better, but still contains a lot of speculation. However, there is an awareness of why day care might have positive effects, the importance of individual differences in children exposed to day care, and the existence of contradictory research evidence. The AO2 material would be worth 5 marks (basic with limited analysis). This would have been vastly improved if actual research evidence had been used to support the claims being made. That gives a total of just 6 marks.

Answer 2: This answer is far more focused and has sufficient material to address only the effects of day care on social development. The opening paragraph again contains all the AO1 material, but this time it is a clear, accurate and detailed description of appropriate research studies. This would receive the full 6 marks for AO1. The next two paragraphs are full of evidence and arguments that show good critical engagement with the topic. Much of this revolves around a counter argument that day care may, in some circumstances, have negative effects for a child's social development. This is fine, provided that it is used (as it is here) as part of a wider engagement with the requirements of the question set. This is informed and reasonably thorough, so would receive the full 12 marks for AO2. This gives a total of 18 marks for the question.

MODULE 2: PHYSIOLOGICAL PSYCHOLOGY & INDIVIDUAL DIFFERENCES

Physiological psychology: Stress

(a) Outline two ways in which the body responds to stress.   (3 marks + 3 marks)

Answer 1

The body reacts to stress by the General Adaptation Syndrome. This involves three stages, which are alarm, resistance and exhaustion. The body adjusts to stress, but if it is prolonged the body can no longer cope. This is the stage of exhaustion.

The second way is through the action of the autonomic nervous system. One part of this is the sympathetic nervous system, which is activated when the body encounters a stressor. This causes many different physiological changes that are associated with fight or flight.

Answer 2

When you are aroused, your pituitary gland releases adrenocorticotrophic hormone (ACTH) into the bloodstream. This travels to the adrenal cortex, which releases corticosteroids. These mobilize energy resources and maintain blood flow and heart rate to get oxygen to the muscles that may be needed in a 'fight or flight' response.

During arousal, the sympathetic division of the autonomic nervous system stimulates the adrenal medulla to release the hormones adrenaline and noradrenaline into the bloodstream. These hormones, in conjunction with corticosteroids, reinforce sympathetic arousal by stimulating heart rate and mobilizing further energy resources in the body. This enables the body to deal with the stressor by activating a 'fight or flight' response.

Comment

Answer 1: Both of these are accurate, but both lack sufficient detail to earn the full 3 marks. We might ask of the first "what goes on in these three stages?", and of the second, "what specific physiological changes are initiated by the sympathetic nervous system?" They would receive 2 marks each.

Answer 2: These outlines of two ways in which the body responds to stress are both accurate and detailed. Each is a very good précis of what is quite complicated biology – remember though, that this question might have asked for a description of one way rather than an outline of two. This would receive the full 6 marks.

(b) Outline the *procedures* and *findings* of one study of the relationship between stress and cardiovascular disorders.   (6 marks)

Answer 1

A study was done which divided over a thousand men into Type A or Type B. They were then watched for 8 years to see how many would have heart attacks. When they looked to see who had heart attacks, 70% were Type A. These are people who are rushed and pressured and this study shows that they are more likely to die of heart attacks.

Answer 2

Rosenman studied 3500 middle-aged men for eight years. First of all he interviewed them in order to classify them as either Type A (always rushing, competitive and time pressured) or Type B (the opposite of this), or Mixed Type A/Type B. Before the study began, he checked to see if any of the men had a history of heart disease. None had.

During the course of the study about 7% of the men had heart attacks. Of these, about 70% had previously been classified as Type A. The remaining 30% were those who had been classified as being mixed Type A/Type B, and none of the Type B men had a heart attack in the same period.

- *Answer 1:* Although brief, this answer has a reasonable amount of information about the procedures and findings of this study. Detail and accuracy are not really as they should be, but there is just enough of each of these to move this beyond the bottom mark band and to achieve 3 marks out of 6.
- *Answer 2:* Although there is a fair bit of 'rounding up' and 'rounding down' when describing the figures in this study, we get the point nonetheless. Procedures are carefully described (3,500 middle-aged men, classified as Type A, followed for 8 years and so on) and in detail. The findings are also accurate and the extra detail (e.g. we are also told the outcomes for the Type B group) is appropriate elaboration. This is worth the full 6 marks.

> **(c)** Outline and evaluate attempts to explain the relationship between life changes and stress. (18 marks)

Answer 1

The Social Readjustment Rating Scale of Holmes and Rahe is an attempt to measure the number of life events that a person has experienced and the seriousness of those life events. This information can then be used to see if there is a relationship between stressful events and illness. The trouble with this is that it doesn't tell us much about the possible causal association between two things. For example, if a person has been divorced and they also have had depression, it is tempting to say that they are depressed because they are divorced. However, it is possible that it might work the other way, and that they became divorced because their partner got fed up with their depression!

Unfortunately the SRRS does not distinguish between a positive life event and a negative event. For example,

getting married and being fired at work have virtually the same score, yet one is surely positive and the other negative. The scale relies on people's retrospective reports of their life events in the previous two years. However, human memory is fallible! A study by Raphael et al. found that people tended to recall different life events when asked at different times. Some people may believe that there is a relationship between life events and illness, and therefore in their own mind they will have already made the connection, making a particular life event or events easier to recall. For others though, who believe that things like depression are just physical illnesses, the connection will not be made so easily. All of these criticisms mean that the SRRS is not a particularly valid way of relating life changes with stress.

Answer 2

The Social Readjustment Rating Scale (SRRS) was developed by Holmes and Rahe (1967). This scale uses a variety of life events rated on a 0–100 scale, with death of a spouse at 100 the most stressful of the events on the scale. The values of all the experienced events are then added tgether to give a total stress score. A number of studies have shown that people's illness rates increase following increases in stress scores. However, a number of the items on the scale are vague e.g. 'personal injury or illness' appears to suggest that someone could have the same score for flu and cancer. Second, there is a general failure to consider the impact of an event on the individual. Christmas is considered to be only mildly stressful, yet to many, Christmas is extremely stressful, perhaps because it emphasizes their loneliness. There is also a failure to distinguish between desirable and undesirable events. For example, pregnancy could be much desired if a couple are planning a family or viewed as a disaster to a single mother who is struggling to make ends meet. This is

critical, as research has shown that undesirable life events are correlated with illness, but desirable events are not.

There are other problems in the use of this scale. For example, there is a problem of inferring cause and effect, as the scale only suggests that the life events and illness are correlated. These major life events are also relatively rare and therefore cannot be a major cause of our day-to-day stress. According to Hopson (1981), there are different transitional routes for individuals coping with positive and negative life events. Each has the same potential for a later crisis because they are 'life stressors', but the likely adjustment outcomes are different. Hopson's model is important because, unlike the Holmes and Rahe model, it distinguishes between responses to positive and negative events, and focuses on transition and recovery rather than a static relationship between life event and stress reaction. It also acknowledges that positive life events such as marriage or the birth of a child have as much potential for psychological disruption as negative events.

● *Answer 1:* This is a good response to the question, but more than one 'attempt' is asked for. This is what examiners refer to as a 'plurality requirement'. This answer only includes one 'attempt' (the SRRS), so unfortunately there is a maximum of 4 out of 6 for the AO1 component, and 8 out of 12 for AO2. In this answer, there is little in response to the 'outline' instruction, so just 2 out of 6 marks for AO1, but the AO2 is a lot better, so 7 out of 12 (8 maximum remember) giving a total of 9 marks out of 18.

● *Answer 2:* This answer satisfies the plurality requirement of this question. The description of the SRRS has been kept suitably brief, and is followed by some excellent evaluative points. Hopson's transitional model is outlined accurately, and the positive evaluation of this model is effective AO2. This answer has fully addressed the requirement to outline and evaluate more than one 'attempt', which is where Answer 1 came unstuck.

Individual differences: Abnormality

(a) Outline the clinical characteristics of bulimia nervosa. (6 marks)

Answer 1

There are two main eating disorders, anorexia and bulimia. They are becoming more common and sometimes affect famous people like Princess Diana. Anorexia means loss of appetite but this is not quite right because people with anorexia are often hungry although they do not eat enough. Bulimia is different because they eat a lot and then vomit. They don't die of starvation but they damage their bodies, e.g. their teeth go bad and they get puffy faces.

Answer 2

The main characteristics of bulimia nervosa are:

- Recurrent episodes of binge eating.
- Inappropriate compensatory behaviours to prevent weight gain, e.g. vomiting or the use of laxatives.
- Behaviours occurring on average at least twice a week for a period of three months or more.
- Self-evaluation being unduly influenced by body shape and weight.
- An awareness of hunger and of the disorder.
- More antisocial behaviour.
- Irregular menstruation.
- Often a perceived intense family conflict.

● *Answer 1:* There is a fair amount of irrelevant information in this answer. The question is specifically related to bulimia nervosa and not eating disorders in general. There is no credit, therefore, for the material on anorexia nervosa. The outline of the characteristics of bulimia nervosa are basic and lacking detail, and would receive just 2 marks.

● *Answer 2:* Eight points are made here. All are accurate and pertinent specifically to bulimia nervosa rather than eating disorders in general. For this type of question (i.e. a list of characteristics) it is acceptable to write in bullet points. At other times, answers should be in continuous prose. This answer receives 6 marks.

(b) Outline assumptions made by the biological (medical) model in terms of the treatment of abnormality. (6 marks)

Answer 1

The biological model has a number of treatments of abnormality. The first of these is treatment through drugs. Drugs are used for the treatment of stress (e.g. beta blockers), and other disorders (such as schizophrenia). Beta-blockers reduce activity in the autonomic nervous system. Anti-schizophrenic drugs reduce the activity of the neurotransmitter dopamine. The second type of treatment is electro-convulsive therapy (ECT), which is used with severely depressed patients. The third type of treatment is psychosurgery. This is a last resort, but can be used to treat very violent patients or those with particular kinds of disorder that don't respond to other forms of treatment.

● *Answer 1:* This is a common misunderstanding of this question. It does not ask for an outline of treatments, but an outline of the assumptions of the model regarding treatment. Under current AQA marking criteria, this answer would receive 4 marks and would need more explicit focus on the assumptions for the full 6 marks.

The main treatment associated with the biological model is drug therapy. This is based on the assumption that a chemical balance in the brain is the main cause of the problem. By administering drugs, it is possible to alter this chemical imbalance and so restore normal levels of brain functioning. A second form of treatment is ECT (electro-convulsive therapy), where an electrical current is passed through the brain for approximately half a second. This form of therapy works on the assumption that severe depression is caused by a depletion of certain neurotransmitters that are involved in the regulation of mood. Psychosurgery, although rarely used nowadays, might be appropriate if a particular mental disorder is thought to stem from dysfunction of particular areas of the brain. Removal or isolation of these areas may then be possible to restore normal behaviour.

● *Answer 2:* This answer addresses the question in a much more direct way. It is the assumptions themselves that are the main focus of the answer (e.g. "...a particular mental disorder is thought to stem from dysfunction of particular areas of the brain"). This is accurate and detailed, and would receive the full 6 marks.

[c] "The main problem with abnormality as a concept is that we cannot agree exactly what constitutes abnormal behaviour."

Outline and evaluate two or more attempts to define abnormality. (18 marks)

Answer 1

There are approximately four definitions of abnormality, including deviation from ideal mental health, deviation from social norms and statistical infrequency. Deviation from social norms suggests that abnormality resides in the way that a person's behaviour and actions are different from the accepted norm of society. Different societies possess different values and opinions, so for example, in British society, we may see running around naked in public as abnormal behaviour, but some other societies may not. Also, different cultures have different views on abnormality, and these always differ from accepted behaviour in other cultures. This weakens the value of this definition of abnormality because it can't accommodate differences between cultures in what is considered acceptable behaviour.

Statistical infrequency offers the view that there is a distinct 'line' of normal behaviour and abnormal behaviour, and every person can be categorized somewhere on this line. What is considered 'normal' would be in the middle and

behaviours further away from the middle are less frequent, and therefore abnormal in this sense. However, one main criticism of this definition is that both genius and mental retardation are rare in society, but only mental retardation is considered to be abnormal. Another problem with this definition is that some disorders, such as depression, are not particularly infrequent in western societies, so would not be counted as abnormal under this definition.

Deviation from ideal mental health suggests that there is a lack of coping with the environment for the person. This could mean that they can't form emotional relationships with other people, or don't have a good perception of reality. A major problem with this definition is that many people would be excluded from what might be thought of as 'ideal' mental health because they have difficulties forming relationships or are neurotic in some way. It is difficult to know where to draw the line, and ideas about what is ideal mental health will always change over time.

● *Answer 1:* The AO1 content of this answer is limited and generally accurate (e.g. the description of statistical infrequency is not particularly precise). It would be worth 4 marks. The AO2 material is also limited (being restricted to just a couple of critical points on each of the three definitions covered), but has been used in a reasonably effective manner. If these critical points had been developed a little more, to constitute a more thorough analysis of the definitions being offered, then the AO2 mark would have been a lot higher. However, this is still worth 8 marks, to give a total for this part of the question of 12 marks.

● *Answer 2 (next page):* This is a very well structured answer. It does not try to do too much and restricts its focus to just two definitions. This is advantageous here because it gives the opportunity to add more detail in the outline and evaluation of the two 'definitions' that are chosen. The AO1 is no more than is required (and is accurate and detailed) and by keeping it all in the first paragraph you can 'manage' the whole answer much more effectively. The next two paragraphs are all AO2, neatly divided into evaluation of each definition in turn. The evaluation is clearly informed and effective and so deserves full marks. This would receive the full 18 marks for this part of the question.

Answer 2

The deviation from social norms definition of abnormality sees abnormality as departure from rules and standards considered normal within society. Some rules are explicit, but others are implicit in that they refer to expected standards of behaviour (such as not standing too close to someone in a social gathering). These rules become established within society and anyone who breaks them is considered deviant or 'abnormal'. The deviation from ideal mental health definition sees abnormality as deviation from six criteria that characterize a psychologically healthy person. These include having a positive self-concept, striving to fulfil our full potential (self-actualization) and showing resistance to stress. According to Jahoda (1958), anyone who does not show evidence of these criteria would be considered 'abnormal' and would be vulnerable to developing a mental disorder.

There are advantages to the deviation from social norms approach. It helps us to identify mental disorders because we know what to expect from people. Anyone whose behaviour departs drastically from social norms might have a mental disorder. Because many people with mental disorders are not motivated to help themselves by seeking help, others can more easily detect abnormal behaviour and act on their behalf. However, some behaviour clearly departs from social norms but is considered 'eccentric' rather than 'abnormal', and so would not be thought to indicate an underlying mental disorder. This definition also fails to acknowledge that rules and standards of acceptable behaviour change over time. What is considered acceptable behaviour in one generation (e.g. homosexuality) may well have been considered abnormal in previous generations.

The main limitation of the 'deviation from ideal mental health' approach is that few people would be able to meet all six criteria suggested by Jahoda. For example, few people manage to reach their full potential in life. So, if self-actualization is a criterion for ideal mental health, few people would be regarded as mentally healthy. Showing resistance to stress also assumes that all stress is harmful. Briner (2003) argues against this assumption. He believes that many people actually work more efficiently when under conditions that are moderately stressful. This definition is also culturally biased in that it reflects a Western preoccupation with personal fulfilment. This is not necessarily the case in non-Western cultures where people are more concerned with collective interests than individual interests.

MODULE 3: SOCIAL PSYCHOLOGY & RESEARCH METHODS

Social psychology: Social influence

(a) Outline two differences between majority and minority influence.　　(3 + 3 marks)

Answer 1

Majority influence is conforming in public and minority influence is conforming in private. For example we might go along with others in public to save face but in private we don't have to worry about what others think and so we can change our mind without worrying about what others think.

Majority influence tends to happen straight away, but minority influence is only felt after a period of time, after the person has had time to think about the minority point of view.

Answer 2

Majority influence involves public compliance, where the person is more concerned with being accepted by others (normative social influence) than what is necessarily the right course of action. Minority influence, on the other hand, involves private acceptance of the minority position. The majority are more likely to examine the minority's arguments closely in private. Thus, they are more likely to be affected by informational social influence and so be converted to the minority position.

- *Answer 1:* The first difference is accurate and the example is quite appropriate as a way of fleshing out the answer sufficiently for a second mark. It would have been relatively simple to add a little more detail to earn the full 3 marks. The second answer is slightly better, but this is still lacking detail. This would get 2 marks for each answer, a total of 4 marks.

- *Answer 2:* This answer takes the same two differences but adds detail. It used the time allocated wisely and therefore ensures that all 3 marks for each difference are gained, for a total of 6 marks overall.

(b) Describe the findings and conclusions from one study of obedience. (6 marks)

Answer 1

Milgram in his classic study of obedience found some staggering results. All of the participants went to 300 volts and an amazing 65% went to the highest of 450 volts. In variations on this study, the findings were just as conclusive. He changed from a prestigious Yale University to a seedy office in town, and the obedience rate fell to 47.5%. When the teacher had to force the hand of the learner onto a metal plate to receive the shocks, the rate fell to 30%. When somebody else threw the switches at the instruction of the teacher, the rate rose to 92.5%. Milgram concluded that people will obey even sometimes against their better judgement or when they have said previously that they would not.

Answer 2

Milgram's study of obedience (Milgram 1963) found that all participants were willing to deliver at least 300 volts to the learner, and that 65% of these participants were willing to deliver the full 450 volts when told to do so by the experimenter. Milgram also found that the participants found the procedure very stressful, displaying signs of extreme anxiety. Although they dissented verbally, they tended to show obedient behaviour when 'prodded' by the experimenter to continue.

Milgram concluded that in some circumstances, particularly when in a subordinate role in a power hierarchy, people will obey orders even if they go against their conscience. Milgram believed that such 'blind obedience' could explain many of the atrocities carried out in wartime, with the pressure to obey superiors being greater than any feelings of empathy or compassion for the victim.

- *Answer 1:* This is a good description of the percentage rates obtained by Milgram in (some of) the variations on his base rate study of obedience. Although these might technically be seen as coming from separate studies, they would be counted as part of one extended study of the same phenomenon. The conclusions (last sentence only) do not really add much, but do consolidate a mark of 4 for this question. Another sentence or two relating the findings to the overall aims of Milgram's study might well have secured the full 6 marks.

- *Answer 2:* This answer is fairly evenly balanced across both findings and conclusions. It is an accurate representation of Milgram's base-line study of obedience. The description of how participants behaved (including their own anxiety during the procedure) is relevant as a research 'finding'. The conclusions take us beyond the studies findings and display a real understanding of what this study actually told us about obedience to authority.

(c) "The unacceptability of research into obedience is that it tells us very little about obedience in the real world."
To what extent have studies of obedience been shown to lack validity? (18 marks)

Answer 1

The key study to be examined for validity concerning obedience is Milgram. This study has been questioned both ethically and regarding validity. It initially consisted of the participant meeting a supposed other participant and then both being separated. The participant was informed and instructed to give the 'other participant' (really an accomplice) electric shocks beginning at 15 volts and going up to 450 volts, when they made incorrect answers. The participant was subjected to screams of the imposter participant (actually a recording) during the experiment. An alarmingly high result showed that all participants went up to 300 volts simply because they were instructed to do so.

However, many have criticized Milgram's work for lacking ecological validity, i.e. how true it is to real life situations. The question is, would this situation really occur in daily life? Critics have suggested that because the participants were paid, then they felt obliged to continue and so the research loses some validity here. Milgram replied by arguing that in everyday situations, people are continuously put upon by employers, colleagues etc., and so this factor increased the validity of the study. Further studies by Milgram, varying the conditions, e.g. in a seedy room instead of Yale University, allowing the participants support from others, support the claim for validity. The fact that participants were asked to continue when they showed signs of resistance has also been criticized, as interference from the researcher lacks experimental validity. His study was repeated many times, and so validity seems to be evident here.

Hoflings study of nurses obeying doctor's orders over the phone displays an extremely high rate of obedience. This was carried out in a real life setting, with unsuspecting nurses. However, although ecological validity is very high in this case, experimental validity has to be brought into question. Many ethical issues are also raised, e.g. informed consent, distress and humiliation when they realized what they had done. Both of these studies provide a good insight into the conditions needed for obedience and also act as a warning to people to question authority. However, as displayed above, if under good experimental conditions this can often produce good ecological validity.

Answer 2

There are two main issues of validity in obedience research. The first of these is experimental (or internal) validity. This is a measure of whether the procedures used in the study actually work. In the case of Milgram's study of obedience, Orne and Holland claimed that participants 'saw through' the deception and were merely playing out their role as naïve participants. The second issue is that Milgram's study lacked ecological validity, in that the findings of the study could not be generalized beyond the context of the investigation. Other critics of Milgram's study have argued that Milgram's claim that he had discovered the processes by which people could have committed the atrocities of the Nazi death camps (i.e. they were simply obeying orders) was unfounded (Mandel 2003).

Milgram defended his original claim through evidence from debriefing sessions where participants admitted they had believed they were giving shocks, and through film evidence where participants appeared in considerable distress when delivering the shocks. If participants truly did not believe that they were giving shocks, then this does not explain why some participants (35%) refused to deliver the full range of shocks. However, the way in which Milgram's study was carried out may have been sufficient to allow some participants to recognize that they, rather than the victim, were the real subjects of the experiment. The fact that the experimenter appeared unconcerned about the learner's distress was one clue for the participants that this was not a 'real' situation.

Milgram's critics argued that being ordered to give electric shocks to poor learners did not involve the same psychological processes as those which affected German prison guards in concentration camps. Milgram did not accept this criticism. He, argued that even though the circumstances were less severe superficially, the psychological processes were similar enough to allow us to draw inferences from the laboratory and apply them to real life. However, Mandel (2003) argues that Milgram's conclusions about obedience and the behaviour of Holocaust perpetrators were unjustified because the two situations were so dissimilar. In Milgram's study, when participants could choose what level of shock to give, they tended to choose less painful shock levels. In contrast, Holocaust perpetrators were often willing to torture their victims before killing them. This suggests that their motives went far beyond merely 'obeying orders'.

● *Answer 1:* Too often students throw in everything they know about a topic without thinking whether it really is relevant to the question asked. This question requires a short description of aspects of obedience research that might (or might not) show questionable validity, followed by two-thirds of the answer engaging critically with these claims. This student has presented a limited outline of Milgram's study that doesn't really give us much to go on when assessing validity later on. There is some confusion about what constitutes 'ecological validity' and the claims made (e.g. "and so validity seems to be evident here") are not really substantiated. The treatment of Hofling's study is also rather vague, with the erroneous claim that this study has greater validity simply because it takes place in a real hospital with real nurses. The evaluation is not particularly effective. This would receive 3 marks for AO1 and 5 for AO2, a total of 8 marks.

● *Answer 2:* This is a clearly structured answer. The AO1 material (in this case a statement of the arguments relating to the validity of obedience research) are clearly laid out in the first paragraph. These are arguments relating to internal validity and ecological validity. These are accurate and detailed, and would earn the full 6 marks for AO1. The next paragraph gives a balanced critical evaluation of the claims for lack of internal validity. Although it is not necessary to present both sides of the argument, that has been done effectively here. The third paragraph has been conducted in the same way, with good use of Mandel's supporting arguments concerning obedience and the Holocaust. This would receive the full 12 marks for AO2, for a total of 18 marks.

Research methods

Total for this question 30 marks

Psychologists have recently become interested in the therapeutic effects of gardening among adults suffering from stress-related health problems. Earlier research had suggested that gardening, in conjunction with stress counselling, produced greater therapeutic gains in adults suffering from stress-related symptoms than counselling alone.

Two psychologists independently interviewed 20 young adults who attended weekly stress clinics. They then divided these adults into two matched groups based on age and severity of stress-related symptoms. Each participant was given a score based on the severity of their stress-related symptoms, with 1 being very low and 100 being very high. For the next ten weeks, the 10 adults in Group A received their weekly stress-counselling session with one of the psychologists, followed by an afternoon of light gardening work in the clinic garden. The 10 adults in Group B also received their weekly stress-counselling session with one of the psychologists but then simply returned home.

Table to show change in stress-related symptoms after 10 weeks

Group A (counselling plus gardening)		Group B (counselling alone)	
Score at Week 1	Score at Week 10	Score at Week 1	Score at Week 10
32	19	30	21
46	28	47	33
53	29	54	38
58	31	58	36
60	40	61	43
68	40	67	51
71	44	70	53
71	41	73	57
77	37	75	49
84	46	84	59

At the end of the 10-week experiment, each participant was again interviewed in order to establish the current severity of their stress-related symptoms. The results are shown in the table above.

(a) Give an appropriate experimental/alternative hypothesis for this study. **(2 marks)**

Answer 1

Adults who garden will feel better than those who don't.

Answer 2

Adults suffering from stress-related symptoms who receive counselling and gardening therapy for a ten-week period show greater improvement of these symptoms than adults who receive counselling alone.

● *Answer 1:* With 2 marks available, it is wise to think how the examiner would discriminate between a 1-mark and a 2-mark answer. This is accurate but just lacks detail, so would receive 1 mark only.

● *Answer 2:* In this answer, a full and technically accurate hypothesis is given that makes reference to both independent and dependent variables and a comparison between the two conditions. It would receive 2 marks.

(b) State whether the hypothesis given in response to part (a) is directional or non-directional and justify your choice. **(3 marks)**

Answer 1

It is directional because it states which way the results will go (that the gardening group will do better).

Answer 2

It is directional. A directional hypothesis is justified because previous research had found that gardening, in conjunction with stress counselling, produced greater therapeutic gains in adults suffering from stress-related symptoms than counselling alone.

● *Answer 1:* The identification of direction is correct, but this is a definition of a directional hypothesis not a justification. Only 1 mark is given.

● *Answer 2:* Both identification and justification are accurate and appropriately detailed, so all 3 marks are awarded.

(c) (i) What is meant by an 'independent variable'? (2 marks)
(ii) Identify the independent variable in this study. (1 mark)

Answer 1

(i) It is the change in a participant's behaviour as a result of the experimental manipulation.

(ii) The change in stress-related symptoms over the 10-week period.

Answer 2

(i) It is the something that an experimenter can vary in some way in order to see its effect on some aspect of behaviour – the dependent variable.

(ii) It is the gardening therapy.

● *Answer 1:* (i) No, this is a *dependent variable*, so 0 marks. (ii) This is also a measurement of the dependent variable, so again 0 marks.

● *Answer 2:* (i) An accurate and detailed definition that makes sure of both marks. (ii) Accurate – all that is needed for the 1 mark available.

(d) Suggest one advantage and one disadvantage of using a matched participants design in this study. (2 + 2 marks)

Answer 1

An advantage is that it overcomes participant variables (such as age) that might affect the outcome of the study.

A disadvantage is that it is difficult to do.

Answer 2

An advantage is that because participants are matched in important variables, any effect they might have on the dependent variable is the same for both conditions.

A disadvantage is that the researcher can never match in terms of all possible participant variables that might affect the dependent variable. Therefore it is only partially successful at controlling the influence of these variables.

● *Answer 1:* The advantage is fine – it identifies an advantage and elaborates it for the full 2 marks. The disadvantage has a 'whiff of psychology' about it, so would just about be worth 1 mark.

● *Answer 2:* This answer has enough detail to ensure both marks for the advantage and disadvantage, so 2 marks for each.

(e) Why was it necessary for both psychologists to interview participants before allocating them to Group A or Group B? (3 marks)

Answer 1

It was important so they knew how to match them into the two groups. For example, they would not want to put all the really stressed people in one group.

Answer 2

This was necessary so they could have some degree of inter-rater reliability when deciding the degree to which each of the adults showed stress-related symptoms (an important consideration when matching across conditions). This would help them to include only those participants for whom there was agreement concerning the severity of their stress-related symptoms.

● *Answer 1:* This is one reason, but not the main reason. One psychologist working alone could have made decisions about matching, so only partially accurate for 1 mark.

● *Answer 2:* An accurate and detailed answer that shows awareness of the need for inter-rater reliability in the assessment of the participants' stress-related symptoms. As the study is concerned with therapeutic outcomes, it is important to get agreement on the initial assessment.

(f) Identify one ethical issue that the researchers do not appear to have considered and explain how this ethical issue could have been dealt with. (3 marks)

Answer 1

The experimenters have deceived the participants by not telling them they were part of a study. They could have told them all about the study at the beginning and asked their permission.

Answer 2

An uncontrolled ethical issue is informed consent. It would be necessary for the researchers to give enough information (e.g. about the gardening therapy) at the beginning of the study for the participants to make an informed decision about whether they wanted to take part.

- *Answer 1:* We can only assume that this was the case, but it seems reasonable here. The resolution of this issue is a little vague and needs clarification and development. This would receive 2 marks.

- *Answer 2:* Again we can only guess at whether participants gave their informed consent but, as it wasn't stated in the stimulus material, it's okay to assume that they didn't. An appropriate and detailed account of how to deal with it brings a total of 3 marks.

(g) Explain two conclusions that might be drawn from the data in the table. (3 + 3 marks)

Answer 1

Both groups got better but Group A improved more than Group B.

At the end of the experiment, Group A (the gardening therapy group) showed less stress symptoms than Group B.

Answer 2

At the end of the 10-week period, Group A (gardening therapy plus counselling) show, on average, a greater improvement in terms of the severity of their stress-related symptoms than Group B (counselling alone).

The greatest improvement in participants who undertook the gardening therapy was in those who initially had the most severe stress-related symptoms. Those with less severe stress-related symptoms appeared to profit less from the gardening therapy.

- *Answer 1:* The first conclusion is actually two conclusions, but could be counted as elaborated into one conclusion that is just about worth 2 marks. This second conclusion is actually an extended version of the second part of the previous one. Therefore if we ignore the second half of the first conclusion we can give 1 mark for that and 2 marks for the second conclusion (this is a case of the examiner working hard for the student!).

- *Answer 2:* Both these conclusions are accurate and detailed, and the student has looked within the sets of data to work out that the gardening therapy has a differential effect dependent on the initial severity of the stress symptoms. Full marks again.

(h) Other than ethical issues, explain two ways in which the design of this study might have been improved. (3 + 3 marks)

Answer 1

It would be better if there were more participants. Twenty is not really enough for a study like this. It would be better if the psychologists had used 100 in each group. That way they would have got results that were more reliable and valid.

A second improvement would be if they had looked at the occupations the people did and matched them in terms of that as well as just age and stress symptoms.

- *Answer 1:* There is a common belief that more is better in experimental research. This is not always true, and we are not told why having 100 participants would be a design improvement over having just 20. Words such as 'better' and 'more reliable and valid' are thrown around without really being appropriate in this context. This first 'improvement' would not get any marks. The second suggestion is better, as the student correctly identifies that some of the participants may have more stressful occupations (which would aggravate their stress symptoms) therefore they need to be matched in this variable as well. There is just enough here for 2 marks.

Answer 2

A design flaw in this study is that participants are rated at the end of the study by the same psychologists who gave them counselling during it. In order to avoid bias, it would be necessary for participants to be interviewed by an impartial psychologist who would not know whether they had been in Group A or Group B during the study.

Because the gardening therapy is the independent variable in this experiment, it would be important to test whether it really was the gardening that caused the improvement or simply the extra time spent 'in therapy'. Therefore Group B should be given extended counselling time so that each group spent the same time with a psychologist every time they attended the clinic.

● *Answer 2:* There are two clear design flaws isolated in this answer. Both are explained first so that the resolution makes more sense. These are accurate and detailed, and it shows very efficient use of the time available to provide answers to this final part of the question. This would get the full 3 + 3 marks.

FINAL COMMENT

We have looked at how two hypothetical students have tackled a complete AS psychology paper. Answer 2 in each case is a full marker so that student would clearly get a Grade A. But what about the other 'student' (Answer 1 to each question)? It is difficult to be certain about what grade this level of performance would get as the grade boundaries change slightly year by year, but the table (right) gives you some idea of what you might expect with these marks for each of the unit papers. We will assume a mark of 2 for QoWC (Quality of Written Communication) for each paper, so the total mark per paper is 62.

Unit paper	Mark (out of 62)	Approx. grade
>> Cognitive and Developmental Psychology	27	D
>> Physiological Psychology and Individual Differences	36	B
>> Social Psychology and Research Methods	31	C

Topic 4 >> Doing well in psychology: 10 exam success tips

Top sportspeople such as Ellen MacArthur are renowned for their determination to succeed, but would be the first to admit that determination on its own is not enough. Sailing round the world single-handed takes a great deal of planning. Like many others before her, Ellen *wanted* to achieve, but knew that to do so, she would have to *prepare* for the task ahead in the most efficient way. The same is true for the AS examination:

Determination + Planning = Success

So, our focus throughout this unit is on *efficient* preparation and performance, not tears and toil. This final topic presents our 'Top 10' exam success tips.

Exam tip 1: Organization and planning

One of the best examples of *efficient* preparation concerns organization and planning. Good students break their work up into manageable chunks and set themselves goals to achieve. These goals may correspond to what your tutor will know as *learning outcomes*. Examples would be:

● "By the end of my revision today I will be able to write an accurate and detailed description and evaluation of Bowlby's maternal deprivation hypothesis."

● "By the end of my revision today I will be able to explain physiological approaches to stress management."

It helps to make a chart so that you know *exactly* what you need to demonstrate in the exam. We have included revision summaries at the end of each topic so you can do this. For Developmental psychology, Topic 1, your revision summary (see p. 57) can be broken down and set out in a chart in the format shown on p. 266.

By breaking your topics into small and more tangible skills, you can keep a careful eye on your own progress. The three columns roughly equate to the division of marks, so a *basic* performance might get you 1 out of 3 marks or 2 out of 6 marks. A *reasonable* performance might get 2 out of 3 or 3/4 out of 6 marks, and a *good* performance would get 3 out of 3 or 5/6 out of 6. It may help motivate you to know that it *is* possible to get a Grade A on just two-thirds of the marks available, so don't get too dispirited if you don't get too many ticks in the third column. You must, however, aim for at least a tick in the second column for every item.

Setting yourself tangible targets will motivate you and will help you keep a check on how you are progressing, what you have achieved and what still remains for you to do. Two final points:

● Don't set yourself huge, impossible goals, e.g. "Tonight I will learn everything about abnormality".

● Remember to revisit what you have already learned. If skills and knowledge are not regularly re-addressed and reviewed, they can decay. This review often only takes a matter of a few minutes. Do this regularly for maximum impact.

	Tick if you could make only a basic attempt	Tick if you could make a reasonable attempt	Tick if you have complete mastery of this
Definition of attachment			
Definition of secure attachment			
Definition of insecure attachment			
Definition of cross-cultural variations			

Exam tip 2: Gain access to materials

The AQA examining board (at Stag Hill House, Guildford, Surrey GU2 5XJ) makes available a wide range of support material for the AS examination: specimen examination papers, marking schemes, suggestions for reading, and much, much more. Most of this is written for tutors but if you believe (as I think you should) that you should make sure that as much of your future is in your own hands as possible, then reading these will put you in the driving seat. The Chief Examiner writes a highly detailed report at the end of each exam series and by reading this you will be aware of the shortcomings of fellow students in the previous exam and so be able to avoid these yourself. Most important of all, get yourself a copy of the relevant specification for this exam. Know the specification and there will be no unpleasant surprises in the exam. You can download this free from **www.aqa.org.uk** (follow the links to AS Psychology, Specification A).

Exam tip 3: Use a wide variety of sources

Of course the writers of this book want to include everything possible that you will need in order to do well, but it is always good practice to cast your net wide. There are a number of magazines and periodicals written for psychologists and psychology students, and you should aim to make good, intelligent use of the Internet. As well as a lot of unmitigated junk, the Internet also contains a wealth of superb and bang-up-to-date material which cannot fail to impress your examiner, as well as increasing your interest and involvement with the topic. You may, of course, find some of the material held on these sites to be quite advanced (a good deal will be written for undergraduates and professionals) but there *will* be plenty to interest and help you.

Exam tip 4: Get plenty of exam practice

There is no substitute for practising the skills on which you will finally be assessed, in the actual situation in which they will be assessed. If you practise answering questions from mock papers under exam conditions – no books, with time limits, answering questions you have not seen before – every week during your revision, building up to the exam, the exam will hold no terrors for you.

As the exam approaches you should spend at least two hours a week doing 'mock exams' on your own. Your teacher will be able to supply you with typical exam questions and you should aim to work on these under exam conditions, two questions in one hour, with no books and so on. When you have finished, you should

check your answers through – with your books this time – and seen how accurate and detailed your answers are. If you read the sample answers and examiner comments, you and your friends can assess each others' answers and talk about the merits and shortcomings of each one. It may be a bit embarrassing to start with, but it soon gives you mastery over the assessment side of the specification.

Exam tip 5: Know what will come up in the exam

We have already discussed the skills and content areas you will need to know about. But we can be even more specific. The detail of the specification shows *exactly* what you need to know. Put simply, if it's not in the specification, it can't be in a question.

If you have a copy of the specification, you can get inside the head of the Principal Examiner who sets the questions for each examination. He or she does not try to trip you up, but merely samples different areas of the specification for each examination. Remember that you cannot ignore *any* part of the specification because each subsection (e.g. stress as a bodily response, stress and illness, stress management) is sampled in every examination. However, because questions are set to the wording of the specification, you have a pretty good idea what a question in a particular area will look like.

ACTIVITY

Predicting examination questions

Use the information in Topic 1 in this unit to work out what questions could be asked for the following subsection of the specification, and compare your list with that of a friend.

Defining psychological abnormality

Attempts to define abnormality in terms of statistical infrequency, deviation from social norms, a failure to function adequately, and deviation from ideal mental health. Limitations associated with these attempts to define psychological abnormality (including cultural relativism).

Exam tip 6: Answer the question

This may sound obvious – even patronizing – but many candidates simply don't answer the questions set. Some candidates seem to think that the actual wording of a question doesn't really matter too much, as long as they write an answer 'in the general area'. Others seem to prepare too rigidly and go into the exam hall simply intent on reproducing 'prewritten' answers. For whatever reasons, the answers do not 'fit' the questions. You must go into the exam hall prepared to be flexible and deal with the specific demands of the paper in front of you.

To use two analogies, *don't* think of yourself as an actor in a play whose task it is to repeat the lines they have learned, word perfect. *Instead,* think of yourself as a doctor who has to deal with whatever comes your way in a particular surgery session.

Make sure you read the questions carefully, and don't start writing your answers until you have really thought about what you are being asked to do and planned your responses. Remember, it isn't just what you put into your answers; it's also to do with what you leave out. Almost certainly you will know a lot more psychology than you can write down in the exam. The trick is to make sure that you offer the examiner those parts of your psychological knowledge that are most relevant to the questions in front of you. Don't fall into the trap of writing what you want to; write what the examiner wants.

Exam tip 7: Plan your AO1 + AO2 response *carefully*

Choose carefully

The final part of each question carries the most marks, so it is wise to spend a bit of time at the beginning of the examination choosing which one you will answer. You will have a choice of one from two in Cognitive, one from two in Developmental, and so on. Don't be seduced by the relatively easy first part of each question; try to work out how well you could perform over all three parts, *particularly* how well you are likely to perform on the final part. The key then is to make the right choice *before* you begin writing.

The three paragraphs technique

This is probably the most straightforward way of responding to the AO1 + AO2 questions. You may remember that these questions are one-third AO1 and two-thirds AO2. By packing all your AO1 into the first paragraph and your AO2 into the two subsequent paragraphs, you can be confident that you have presented your material with the right balance (so making it more likely that you pick up more of the marks available for these two skills). Take the following question, for example:

> Outline and evaluate the physiological approach to stress management. (18 marks)

The three paragraphs could contain the following:

- *Paragraph 1:* An outline of the use of drugs and biofeedback in stress management.

- *Paragraph 2:* An evaluation (preferably the strengths and limitations) of drugs as a way of managing stress.

- *Paragraph 3:* An evaluation (preferably the strengths and limitations) of biofeedback as a way of managing stress.

The other advantage of using this approach is that you can impose neat time and space divisions on your work. If you allow 15 minutes of writing time for this part of the question, that's 5 minutes (100 to 120 words) for each paragraph. Having to write 100 words on one small area (e.g. evaluation of drugs as stress management) *appears* far less intimidating that having to write a mini-essay (of 300 to 360 words) on the physiological approach to stress management.

Working backwards from your conclusion

If you want to get somewhere, it is often a good idea to look on a map to find the place you're going, and then work backwards in an attempt to plan your route. Take a look at the question above – what do *you* think of the physiological approach to stress management? Is it good, bad, or are there good points and bad points? Think about this for a while, and then decide what arguments you will put together to justify that conclusion. There are three stages to this approach:

- What is my conclusion?
- What evidence would lead to that conclusion? This might be research evidence that supports your point of view or challenges others'. It might be the views of critics or supporters of this point of view.
- What arguments (or evidence) might I meet along the way, and how would I discount them?

The debate

As you develop your interest and involvement with psychology, you will become aware that not everybody agrees with a particular point of view. There are very few 'facts' in psychology, and psychologists spend a great deal of time arguing for their own views on a topic. You can represent that tension within a topic area by presenting your AO1 + AO2 response in the form of a debate. This works as follows:

- Begin by marshalling together everything you feel is relevant to a two-sided discussion. This includes 'facts', research evidence, points of view, alternative explanations, strengths, limitations, etc.
- Remember that when you describe something, this counts as AO1.
- If you comment on it, this counts as AO2.

Take the following question, for example:

> Consider the levels of processing model as an explanation of human memory. (18 marks)

Now look at the sample answer on the next page.

This was supported in research by Craik and Tulving (1975) who found that participants remembered most words from a list that had been processed for meaning and least from those that had simply been processed for their structure. This showed that deeper processing led to enhanced memory, a key assumption of the model.

However, many psychologists question the idea of 'depth'. To say that something is remembered if it is deeply processed and that deep processing leads to better memory is a circular definition.

This criticism may not be entirely fair as subsequent research extended what is meant by 'depth' to include organization, distinctiveness, elaboration and effort. Research by Eysenck and Eysenck (1980), for example, provided evidence for the importance of elaboration as an aspect of deeper processing.

This extract from an answer to this question shows how the argument moves from one side to the other, providing a critical overview of the agreements and disagreements within psychology concerning the value of levels of processing theory. Notice how the answer uses 'AO2 phrases' (such as 'this was supported in research', 'question the idea of ', 'this criticism was not entirely fair') to contextualize the material. In this way the answer *evaluates* levels of processing theory rather than simply providing more AO1 descriptive material.

Finally, and perhaps most importantly, is the effective use of material. This is what causes students most problems. Students frequently *describe* studies that are relevant and the examiner is aware that there is a link between the study and the point the candidate was trying to make, but the student *does not make that link*! In other words, they have the material but don't *use* it.

Exam tip 8: Good time-management

As we have seen, all the AS questions (excluding those on Research Methods) are set to a specific formula: the allocation of marks is always 18 for AO1 and 12 for AO2.

You must divide your answer to map that of the question. For your answers, you will have a little less than a minute per mark (30 marks available per question; 30 minutes allowed – but reading the questions, planning your answers and then checking them through at the end will, of course, use some of that time allowance, so let's say you have 25 minutes *writing* time). Alternatively, think of it another way: the average candidate is probably capable of writing around 500 words in 25 minutes.

What this means is that each 6-mark unit should be allocated approximately five minutes of writing time and should generate around 100 words.

Exam tip 9: Make your answers 'psychological'

The exam is in psychology, so, naturally enough, you will be judged on the quality of your psychology! Again, this may seem an obvious point, but senior examiners know from experience that a large number of candidates ignore this point.

You should try to avoid writing your answers in a chatty, anecdotal way, but should write in the third person ('it can be argued' rather than 'I reckon', for example). Try to write in an objective, logical manner and remember that you should always aim to give evidence to support what you

are saying. The bloke down the pub may be able to say "girls have eating problems these days because all the magazines are stuffed with photos of stick-like dolly birds," but you can't. You need to say, "Psychological research such as that carried out by XXX has shown that ..."

You may find this difficult to begin with, but it is a classic instance where practice can make perfect, as you will discover.

Exam tip 10: Performing well in Research Methods

This part of the exam is very different to the others. It focuses on how psychological research is carried out and is what we might call problem-driven.

There are two significant differences between how you need to write your Research Methods answers and how you answer other questions:

● In Research Methods, you need not write in complete sentences/paragraphs. However, do note what we have just said about brief answers (getting 1 instead of 2, when 2 is available), so you should not aim to be too frugal with your words. The key point is that there is no point in merely putting in words for the sake of it.

● In all other aspects of the exam, examiners use something known as 'positive marking'. What this means is that if you make a mistake, the examiner ignores it and doesn't take any marks away. The logic is that in writing something inaccurate, candidates penalize themselves because they have wasted precious time when they could have been writing something which would earn credit. 'Knocking marks off' would therefore be a double penalty. However, this logic isn't used in Research Methods.

For example, a question could ask you to identify a method used in a study; you could write 'survey, interview, experiment, correlation, observation'. Under the principles of positive marking, you would get the mark because you have given the right answer, albeit embedded in a list. However, the whole list would have taken you only seconds to write. This isn't allowed. The examiner is told to mark only the first answer you give in situations like this.

So there you have it. Now you know everything you need to know. All that is left is for you to put what you have learned in this unit into practice. *Good luck!*

Psychology

FOR A2-LEVEL

9 UNIT

SOCIAL Cognition

PREVIEW

After you have read this unit, you should be able to describe and evaluate:

>> explanations of the attribution of causality, including errors and biases in the attribution process

>> social and cultural influences on our perception of the social world, including social representations and stereotyping

>> the origins and maintenance of prejudice and discrimination, and explanations and research relating to the reduction of prejudice and discrimination.

INTRODUCTION

Social cognition refers to the area of social psychology that is concerned with how people think about other people or groups of people. Although this field shares many similarities with the field of cognitive psychology, there is an assumption that the way in which we think about other people (i.e. our *social* world) differs in important ways to the way in which we think about the physical world.

Topic 1 is concerned with the attribution of causality – seeking explanations for our own behaviour and the behaviour of others. This is probably the area closest to a popular understanding of psychology. Different theorists have attempted to unravel the rules that we use to make causal attributions about each other's behaviour. This is not as clear cut as it might at first appear, as much of our attributional thinking is biased in ways that both reflect a particular perspective and also serve our own best interests.

The tendency to take mental short cuts in processing information from our social world is illustrated by the process of stereotyping – mentally placing people into pre-existing categories – which enables us to apply general evaluations based on our existing 'knowledge' about that category and its members. In recent years, social psychology has moved increasingly away from the laboratory to an exploration of the truly *social* aspects of human behaviour, as you will discover in Topic 2. Social representations theory represents our attempt to discover how common-sense representations of the world become so widely spread and shared by most members of a culture.

One of the inevitable consequences of the process of categorization is the fact that we will judge some people more negatively than others. Theorists have puzzled over the problems of prejudice and discrimination for many years and, at various times, have explained this tendency in terms of personality differences, the pressures of intergroup competition and the need to preserve a positive social identity. Attempts to reduce prejudice have not always met with success, but this does not stop us looking for solutions to this most insidious aspect of social cognition. Prejudice and discrimination are the focus of Topic 3.

Mike Cardwell

Social cognition is the study of how people make sense of their social world. Much of this unit concerns the short cuts that people take as part of this process. Although useful and efficient as ways of understanding the world around us, such cognitive short cuts can sometimes hurt when they are applied to us. This simple exercise is designed to allow you to experience at first hand the impact of stereotyping.

1 As a class, discuss some of the common stereotypes that people hold about different gender, ethnic and occupational groups. For example, what common stereotypes are held about the people in the photographs?

2 Each member of your class can then be given a label (by the teacher) with a gender, ethnic or occupational group on. These might include 'woman', 'old man', 'White', 'Black youth', 'student', 'doctor' or 'estate agent'.

3 Find another person and (with their permission), stick your label on their back (so they can't see it).

4 Interact with each other according to the labels that people are wearing for a few minutes, making use of some of the common stereotypes for that group of people.

5 Remove the labels and share your experiences – how readily did people recognize the stereotypes associated with their label? How did it make them feel?

Attribution of causality: the way in which we infer the causes of our own or another person's behaviour according to a set of cognitive rules and biases. As a result of these strategies we decide whether a person's behaviour is caused by their own stable characteristics, or whether it is a result of situational influences.

Dispositional attribution: inferring that the reason for a person's behaviour is something about themselves such as their personality.

Situational attribution: inferring that a person's behaviour is caused by something about the situation they are in.

Social perception: how we come to form impressions and make inferences about others.

Social representations: the common-sense explanations that are shared by and shape the understanding of members of a particular group or culture.

Stereotyping: generalizing about a group of people so that the same characteristics (often unflattering) are assigned to all members of the group regardless of individual variations between members. Stereotyping may underlie prejudice and discrimination.

Prejudice: prejudging individuals on the basis of their membership of a particular category or group.

Discrimination: a way of behaving towards members of a categorized group such that all members of that group are treated in the same (usually unfair) way, i.e. the behavioural expression of prejudice.

People have an overwhelming desire to form a coherent understanding of their world and to control their social environment. One aspect which is fundamental to this is that of 'causality' – that is, what causes particular events or behaviours to occur. An 'attribution' is the end result of a process in which people use available information to make inferences about the causes of a particular behaviour. Attribution theory is concerned with explanations of how each of us attributes causes for our own and others' behaviour. When we process social information, we are apt to take short cuts and as a result we do not process information as accurately or completely as we could. In other words, we might be seen as 'cognitive misers'. As a result of this tendency, biases may occur in the attribution process.

According to attribution theorists, our explanations for a person's behaviour will generally refer either to factors stemming from within that person or to factors that are external to that person, such as their environment. Causes can therefore be of two types:

- *dispositional* (internal) attribution – we explain people's behaviour in terms of it being a result of 'something about them' (such as their 'nature' or mood)
- *situational* (external) attribution – behaviour is explained in terms of something about the environment or social world (such as the weather or the influence of a third person).

ATTRIBUTION THEORIES

A number of attribution theories have been developed. These include:

- the *correspondent inference theory* (Jones and Davies 1965)
- Kelley's (1967) *co-variation model*
- Kelley's subsequent (1972) refinement, the *causal schemata model*
- Weiner's model of *achievement attribution* (1979).

Rather than being seen as competitors, each seeking to explain the same thing in the best way, it is more fruitful to see attribution theories as being complementary. They differ according to the kind of explanation that is required and the information that is available to the person doing the explaining. In this unit the models of Kelley (1967 and 1972) and Weiner (1979) will be discussed.

The co-variation model: Kelley's first attribution theory

The co-variation model (Kelley 1967) applies to the explanations we give for the behaviour of people we know. Kelley argues that when we make such attributions, we take our information from two sources. The first of these is what we know about the person and their previous behaviour. The second is the way in which the person's behaviour compares with that of other people. According to the principle of co-variation, we take three types of causal information into account when arriving at an explanation, the first two derived from the previous behaviour of the person and the third from the behaviour of other people. The extent to which these three types of information co-vary results in us making a dispositional (internal) attribution, a

situational (external) attribution, or a combination of the two. The three types of information are about:

- *Consensus* – This refers to the extent to which other people behave in the same way towards the same stimulus (or 'entity') as the person whose behaviour we are trying to explain. For example, suppose that we are asked to explain why a person is afraid of a dog. If most people are afraid of this particular dog, then consensus is high. However, if few people are afraid of the dog, consensus is low.
- *Consistency* – This refers to the extent to which the person in question has behaved in the same way in the past towards the stimulus in question. If the person has been afraid of the dog on other occasions, consistency is high. However, if the person has not shown fear before, then consistency is low.
- *Distinctiveness* – This refers to the extent to which the person behaves in the same or a similar way to other stimuli. If, for example, the person is not afraid of other dogs, then the behaviour of being afraid of this dog is a highly distinctive one. Thus, distinctiveness is high. If the person is afraid of all other dogs and, perhaps, all other animals, then the behaviour of being afraid of this dog is not particularly distinctive. Hence we can say that distinctiveness is low.

Kelley argued that if consensus was low, consistency was high and distinctiveness was low, then we would tend to make a dispositional (or internal) attribution for behaviour. So, if Rob was afraid of the dog and we knew that very few other people were afraid of the dog (low consensus), that Rob had been afraid of the dog before (high consistency) and that Rob was afraid of other dogs as well as this one (low distinctiveness), we would tend to explain his behaviour in terms of 'something about him'. Perhaps, for example, we might describe him as being 'timid'.

If consensus, consistency and distinctiveness were all high, Kelley argued that an attribution to the 'entity' would be made. For example, suppose that Chris had failed to win a prize on a particular radio quiz show; everyone else he knew had failed to win a prize on the same quiz; he had also failed to win a prize on the quiz when he had taken part in it before, but he had won prizes on other quiz shows. We would explain his behaviour in terms of the quiz show. Perhaps, for example, his failure could be explained in terms of the quiz being very difficult.

In circumstances, however, when consensus is low, consistency is low, but distinctiveness is high, Kelley argued that the cause of behaviour would be most likely to be attributed to a particular set of special circumstances. See Table 9.1 for a summary of the co-variation model.

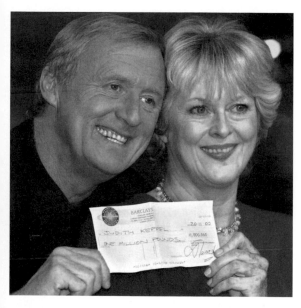

Judith Keppel was the first person to win a million pounds on a TV quiz show. How would you explain her quiz-winning behaviour using the co-variation model?

Research studies of the co-variation model

Two research studies – into attributions of alcohol relapse and youth crime – are described below.

Attributions of alcohol relapse (Seneviratne and Saunders 2000)

Seneviratne and Saunders studied the attributions made by alcohol-dependent individuals for their own and others' relapses. They found significant differences for the attributions made by individuals for their own relapses compared to how they attributed the relapses of others. The relapses of others were seen as being predominantly due to internal factors (such as lack of personal control) whereas their own relapses were attributed to external factors (e.g. high stress levels). In this case, consensus was low (not all alcoholics relapsed) and consistency was high (others were seen as having a history of alcohol abuse), therefore a dispositional (or internal) attribution for the relapse behaviour of others was appropriate.

Attributions of youth crime (Pfeffer *et al.* 1998)

Pfeffer and colleagues examined perceptions of youth crime among British and Nigerian children. Children between the ages of 7 and 10 were asked to respond to the question: 'Why do you think young people commit crime?' The Nigerian children used significantly more situational explanations (e.g. poverty) and fewer dispositional explanations than the British children. The most frequently occurring explanation for the British children was dispositional (e.g. 'for fun' or 'for drugs'). These results indicate cultural differences in children's attributions for youth crime which may be explained by the difference in emphasis placed on personal responsibility in Western societies and collective responsibility in non-Western societies. For the Nigerian children, crime was seen as a distinctive response of only a few people (i.e. low consensus) to a specific set of circumstances (high distinctiveness) that would not continue if those circumstances did not exist (i.e. low consistency).

Table 9.1 >> Summary of the co-variation model (Kelley 1967)

	Attribution to the person (internal)	Attribution to the 'entity' (external)	Attribution to special circumstances (external)
>> *Consensus*	Low	High	Low
>> *Consistency*	High	High	Low
>> *Distinctiveness*	Low	High	High

Evaluation
the co-variation model

● *Is co-variation information always useful?* –
Garland *et al.* (1975) have shown that when given
a choice about the information necessary to arrive
at an attribution, some people choose information
about things like 'personality' and/or the context
in which the behaviour is occurring rather than
consensus, consistency or distinctiveness
information. Indeed, in one study, it was
discovered that people only use information about
distinctiveness and consistency when no
information about context or situation is available.
Other research (e.g. Alloy and Tabachnik 1984)
has shown that even when information about
consensus, consistency and distinctiveness is
available, people are not particularly adept at
using it in a systematic way, and therefore
its usefulness in making accurate attributions
is diminished.

● *Co-variation analysis is cognitively expensive* –
it takes a great deal of mental effort to assess
information on consensus, consistency and
distinctiveness (even when these sources of
information are readily available). Just because
people's attributions seem to fit the predictions
made by the co-variation model, does not
mean that people are actually calculating the
co-variation between consensus, consistency, and
distinctiveness in their heads. As noted before in
this unit, we tend to act as 'cognitive misers' and
rather than spend time searching for information,
we often jump to 'quick-and-easy' conclusions
regarding the causes of behaviour.

● *A simpler alternative, the abnormal conditions
focus model* – Hilton and Slugoski (1986) offer a
simpler interpretation of the way in which people
might use information about consensus,
consistency and distinctiveness. In their abnormal
conditions focus model, they suggest that each
type of information 'goes with' a particular type
of attribution. Consensus information affects
primarily internal attributions, distinctiveness has
an important role in situational (external)
attributions, and consistency affects attributions
according to circumstance. Hilton and Slugoski
describe how people would make attributions
according to information that 'stands out' (i.e. is
'abnormal'). For example, if Mark is the only
person to order fish (i.e. low consensus), this
stands out and we are likely to make an internal
attribution (he likes fish). If he only eats fish at
this particular restaurant and never orders it
elsewhere (i.e. high distinctiveness), then this too
stands out and we are more likely to make an
external attribution (the fish must be particularly
good in this restaurant).

Causal schemata: Kelley's second attribution theory

Largely because of the criticisms that were made of the
co-variation model, Kelley (1972) advanced a second
attribution theory. The 'causal schemata model' applies
to behaviour observed *on a single occasion* and about
which there is no consensus, consistency or
distinctiveness information. Kelley argued that if we do
not know a person and have no information about their
previous behaviour, then we can only rely on our causal
schemata. Causal schemata are, according to Kelley,
'general conceptions a person has about how certain
kinds of causes interact to produce a specific kind of
effect'. He proposed that causal schemata, along with
the processes of 'discounting' and 'augmenting' are
used as follows:

● *Multiple sufficient causes* – This type of causal
schema applies when a behaviour may have a
number of causes for it and when we are satisfied
that any one of them is a sufficient explanation of it.
For example, suppose that your neighbours have just
moved house. They might have moved because they
want to live in a larger or smaller house, because
they want a bigger garden, because the house is
about to be repossessed or because they do not like
you playing music loudly and having rowdy parties.
Each cause is sufficient in itself to explain the
behaviour of moving house.

● *Discounting principle* – On some occasions, we
may have reason to favour one in particular of these
sufficient explanations, which leads us to add weight
to it and dismiss or discount the others. Kelley calls
this the discounting principle. For example, suppose
that a well-known celebrity appears on television
advertising a particular brand of crisps. The celebrity
may really like the crisps and be advertising them for
that reason. He may, however, be doing the
manufacturer a favour because of a personal
friendship with the head of the company. It might
even be the case that the celebrity had been paid
£100,000 to endorse the crisps. It is likely that most
of us would discount two of the three sufficient
causes presented above, and opt for the last one.
The discounting principle demonstrates that people
tend towards simplicity in their social perceptions.

● *Multiple necessary causes* – This type of causal
schemata applies when two or more factors are
necessary for an attribution to be made to explain a

particular behaviour. For example, in order to be successful in the London Marathon, it is not sufficient to wear running shoes; the runner must also be fit. If the marathon was completed, we would conclude that the runner not only wore running shoes, but was also a physically fit athlete.

- *Augmentation principle* – This applies to both multiple sufficient and multiple necessary causal schemata. It proposes that the role of a given cause is augmented (increased) if the effect occurs in the presence of an inhibitory cause. For example, someone who does well in an examination despite poor teaching and prolonged illness is more likely to have their success confidently attributed to their ability and hard work (i.e. dispositional factors). The strength of this conviction will be increased by the fact that such difficult circumstances must be overcome in order to succeed.

Research studies of the causal schemata model

Attribution of responsibility to a rape victim

Bolt and Caswell (1981) presented female psychology students with descriptions of a fictional female worker who had been raped whilst walking through a wooded park on her way home from work. The four conditions presented to participants varied by *time* (either 5.30pm or 11.30pm) and whether the victim was *acquainted* with her assailant. Participants were asked to indicate the degree to which the victim might be considered as causally responsible for the attack. Highest ratings of victim responsibility were given when in the 'unacquainted/late' condition, and lowest in the 'acquainted/early' condition. In the former case, the perceived carelessness of the victim (walking through a wooded park late at night) was seen as a contributory factor. In the latter case, and consistent with Kelley's discounting principle, the setting was seen as less relevant and therefore discounted as a contributory factor.

Attribution and magnitude of events

Kun and Weiner (1973) tested the hypothesis that the more extreme an effect to be attributed, the more likely the attributor was to assume multiple *necessary* causes. Confirming this, they found that success at a difficult task (a relatively uncommon event) was believed by participants to require *both* high ability *and* high effort. On the other hand, success at an easy task (a relatively common event) was seen as caused by *either* high ability *or* high effort (i.e. multiple *sufficient* causes rather than multiple *necessary* causes).

Evaluation
the causal schemata model

- *Causal schemata are important* – Manstead *et al.* (1995) believe that causal schemata are important for three main reasons:

  1 They help the perceiver to make attributions even when information is incomplete.

  2 They are general ideas of causes and effects that may apply across different content areas.

  3 They provide the perceiver with a form of 'causal shorthand' which enables them to carry out complex attribution inferences quickly and easily.

- *Strengths of the model* – Kelley (1972) believed that the main strength of this model is that causal schemata were more likely to be used to make causal attributions when there was little information available about the target person. There is certainly some research that supports the main assumptions of the model (e.g. Kun and Weiner 1973, Bolt and Caswell 1981).

- *Limitations of the model* – According to Fiedler (1982), the research in support of causal schemata is highly artificial. Although the theory is plausible, it lacks consistent empirical support in more natural settings.

Weiner's model of achievement attribution

Weiner (1979) was interested in the sorts of attribution that people make when determining the reasons for success and failure on a task (such as in a driving test or psychology examination). Weiner believed that when explaining success or failure, we attribute it to one or more of four basic causes – ability, effort, task difficulty and luck. We arrive at a causal attribution for success or failure by considering where a particular event lies along three different dimensions:

- *Internal/external* – the locus of the cause may be something about the person (i.e. internal) or about the situation (external). For example, ability and effort are internal causes of an event, but help from friends or bad luck are external causes.

- *Stable/unstable* – the degree to which the cause is likely to change or stay as an enduring feature.

Table 9.2 >> Weiner's achievement model of attribution (Weiner 1979)

| | Internal | | External | |
	Stable	Unstable	Stable	Unstable
>> **Controllable**	Typical effort	Unusual effort	Consistent help or hindrance from others (e.g. friends)	Unusual help or hindrance from others (e.g. strangers)
>> **Uncontrollable**	Ability	Mood	Task difficulty	Luck

For example, intelligence may be seen as a stable (enduring) feature, whereas mood is more unstable (changeable).

- *Controllable/uncontrollable* – the extent to which a person has control over the cause. For example, students have a good deal of control over the amount of effort they put into their revision, but very little over how difficult the exam is going to be.

These three dimensions then produce eight different types of explanation for the event being explained (see Table 9.2). For example, failure to pass a driving test might be attributed to the weather (bottom right in Table 9.2), if a person considered themselves a good driver and the weather conditions were unusually bad. In this example, failure is *external* (because it is not about their driving ability, and weather conditions were bad, i.e. unstable and uncontrollable).

According to this theory, people first assess whether someone – or they themselves – has succeeded or failed at some task. This leads to either a positive or negative emotion (if we succeed at something, we generally feel pleased; if we fail, we are disappointed or upset). Following our causal attribution, we then experience more specific emotions. For example, we may feel pity for a person's homelessness if we feel that their plight was beyond their control. Each of the three dimensions has different consequences for future behaviour:

- The *stability dimension* is important in shaping our expectations of how well someone might perform in the future. If we believe that someone's poor performance in a sports event is due to their lack of ability, we would expect them to continue to perform poorly in similar events in the future. We may consequently wonder why a football manager continues to select a player whom we have branded as 'useless'.

- The *internal/external dimension* determines the rewards or punishments that might follow an event. If we believe that someone's success has been a product of their hard work, we might reward them for their efforts. If they failed through lack of effort, we might exercise our right to punish for the same reasons. However, if success or failure was perceived to be the product of external forces, then we are

more likely to withhold any rewards and refrain from punishing the person who has failed.

- The *controllability dimension* concerns the potential for change in the future. If we believe our success to be a matter of good fortune (i.e. uncontrollable), we may not feel confident about predicting similar success in the future. Alternatively, when we believe that we have controlled the successful outcome ourselves, we are often highly enthusiastic and optimistic about repeating the experience.

Research studies of Weiner's model

Romantic jealousy

Bauerle *et al.* (2002) examined Weiner's theory as an explanation of romantic jealousy. Participants from the general population recalled jealousy episodes in their lives, then made attributions for the events and categorized them using Weiner's dimensions. Jealousy was more likely when the cause of a partner's indiscretion was perceived to be internal, controllable and intentional. The findings were consistent with Weiner's model in identifying the blame conditions that trigger jealousy responses.

Attitudes to people with HIV/AIDS – who's to blame?

Cobb and de Chabert (2002) examined the beliefs of social-service providers who work directly with individuals affected by HIV/AIDS. Forty-six HIV/AIDS social-service providers were asked to read a hypothetical scenario depicting an individual at risk of HIV/AIDS because of multiple high-risk behaviours. Results of the study show that participants who perceived individuals as more responsible for their illness report increased anger, attributed more blame and expressed less willingness to help those at risk of HIV/AIDS.

Cross-cultural studies

Several studies have shown that at least some aspects of Weiner's model apply to non-Western as well as Western cultures. In one study (Schuster *et al.* 1989), participants in Belgium, Germany, India, South Korea and England were given details of a person who had failed to get a particular job. Participants rated each of 22 causes for the person's failure to get the job (i.e. their ability, effort, interest, luck and so on) on the dimensions of control (to what extent was it controllable by the person?), stability (to what extent was it changeable?) and locus (did it exist internally or externally to the person?). Schuster and colleagues found considerable consistency across the different cultures in how controllable, stable and internal/external each of these 22 causes was perceived to be. The one exception to this was the Indian sample who consistently rated all causes as being more uncontrollable, unstable and external than samples from the other four cultures.

AO2

Evaluation
Weiner's model

- **Research support** – Weiner's model has received considerable empirical support. Research has shown that category-based expectancies (e.g. male/female, Black/White) may affect the attributions that are made. For example, members of both sexes are more likely to attribute a woman's success to temporary factors but to attribute a man's success to his ability (Deaux 1976). Similarly, White Americans were more likely to see ability as responsible for success in a White than in a Black person (Yarkin *et al.* 1982).

Do you think that 'category-based expectancies' have changed since Deaux's 1976 research?

- **Practical applications** – The model can also be applied to our behaviour when working at a task. Adults and children who attribute their failure in a task to an internal, stable cause (such as a lack of ability or a character defect) are less likely to persist with it. For example, if we can attribute our failure to land a favoured job to unfair selection practices or the ignorance of the interviewer (i.e. uncontrollable external causes), we are likely to continue to apply for similar jobs in the future (Crocker and Major 1989).

- **Beyond simple internal/external attributions** – Weiner's model recognized the importance of dimensions beyond the simple internal/external dimension. For example, a person's failure in an examination or in a sporting event may be attributed to lack of ability or lack of effort, both internal attributions. However, the consequences that follow these attributions may be very different, since lack of ability is a stable characteristic whereas lack of effort may be unstable (and therefore changeable).

- **Individual differences** – Although there is a great deal of empirical support for Weiner's views on attribution, there is some doubt over whether everybody uses his three dimensions in quite the same way. For example, Krantz and Rude (1984) found considerable variation in the ways in which participants classified a particular cause along these dimensions. Intelligence, for example, may be seen as a stable characteristic by some people but a highly changeable characteristic by others. What this research suggests, then, is that we all perceive human attributes in very different ways and this, in turn, affects the attributions that we make.

Kelley's and Weiner's theories, along with others we have not discussed, assume that we are motivated to explain the behaviour of others in a logical and rational manner. Because these theories describe the ways in which we should normally make attributions, they are referred to as 'normative' models of the attribution process. However, as stressed earlier, people do not process every piece of social information in a logical and rational manner. The short cuts we take when arriving at explanations for behaviour lead to biases in our processing of information.

BIASES IN THE ATTRIBUTION PROCESS

Psychologists have discovered that people can be biased in a number of ways when they make attributions. An attributional bias can be defined as a distortion in perception or judgement about the causes of our own or other people's behaviour. This section looks at several of these biases.

The fundamental attribution error

The nature of the fundamental attribution error

Ross (1977) defines the fundamental attribution error (FAE) as 'the tendency to underestimate the importance of situational determinants and overestimate the degree to which actions and outcomes reflect the actor's dispositions'. What this means is that we have a tendency to make internal (or dispositional) attributions for people's behaviour even when external (or situational) attributions are equally likely to explain the behaviour. For example, if someone was to spill coffee over us, our explanation of their behaviour would probably be in terms of their 'being clumsy', even when a situational explanation (the person had been pushed by somebody else) was equally likely. It has been suggested that our 'miserly' approach to cognitive processing leads us to ignore situational influences unless we are directly alerted to them. This results in our emphasizing factors concerned with the person. If we are satisfied that our dispositional attribution is adequate, we feel we have no need to make matters more complex by considering additional information.

Explanations of the FAE

An interesting explanation of the FAE concerns the role of linguistic factors. Nisbett and Ross (1980) suggest that the English language is constructed in such a way that it is relatively easy to describe an action and the actor in the same way. For example, we may speak of a person as being kind or honest, but it is more difficult to describe a situation in those terms.

When we perceive a particular behaviour, we focus on the person who is behaving, not the situation. It is not surprising, therefore, that the actor is overrated as causally important. When people are primed, however, to pay attention to situational factors, the FAE is less likely (Rholes and Pryor 1982).

Bierbrauer (1979)

Bierbrauer had participants watch a film of Milgram's obedience experiments in which one participant (the 'teacher') apparently gives a series of increasingly severe electric shocks to another (the 'learner'). When asked to explain the behaviour of the teacher, participants underestimated situational factors (such as the presence of the experimenter) in favour of dispositional ones (such as 'the teacher was cruel') in their explanations.

Evaluation the FAE

- **Research support** – Support for the FAE has come from studies by Bierbrauer (1979) and Ross *et al.* (1977) (see panels above and on p. 279).

- **The FAE as cultural bias** – From a cultural perspective, the FAE might be seen as an indication of the pervasive individualism of modern Western societies (Moghaddam 1998). Moghaddam also believes that rather than the FAE being an 'error', it is in fact a cultural 'bias' to perceive causes as internal rather than external to individuals. Support for this assertion comes from Miller (1984) who found that whereas children growing up in Western cultures tend to attribute causes of others' behaviour to dispositional factors, children growing up in India show the opposite trend, attributing them more to situational factors, i.e. things outside their control. This was particularly evident when children were asked to explain the actions of someone who had done something wrong.

- **The ultimate attribution error** – The FAE may arise in a slightly different form when we are making causal attributions about in-group and out-group behaviours. When it operates at the group level, this form of attributional bias is known as the 'ultimate attribution error' (Pettigrew 1979). It involves perceiving desirable actions by one's own group arising as a result of group (internal) characteristics and undesirable actions being a product of external forces. Conversely, desirable actions performed by other groups are 'explained away' in terms of situational factors (e.g. 'they were lucky') rather than being seen as a product of dispositional characteristics of the group. Undesirable actions, however, are seen as reinforcing our stereotype of the out-group and are therefore attributed to the inherent group characteristics. A supporter of Liverpool FC, for example, might explain unruly behaviour among Liverpool fans as the result of provocation or media hysteria, while being quick to condemn the disgraceful behaviour of 'hooligans' who support other teams.

Ross *et al.* (1977)

In their experiment, participants were randomly assigned to be either questioners or contestants in a general knowledge quiz. The questioners were allowed to make up questions based on their own specialized knowledge which, of course, would mean that contestants would often struggle to provide correct answers. The 'quiz' was observed by other participants and at the end of it the observers, questioners and contestants were asked to rate the general knowledge of the questioners and contestants. Both the observers and contestants considered the questioners to have superior knowledge. The questioners, however, did not consider themselves to have superior knowledge. Ross and his colleagues argued that the observers and contestants had ignored the fact that the questioners had an unfair situational advantage (they had compiled the questions) and had overestimated dispositional factors in making their judgements.

Actor/observer biases

The nature of actor/observer biases

The FAE occurs when we are explaining the behaviour of other people. Thus, when we are observers of behaviour, we tend to make dispositional attributions about causes rather than situational ones. For example, when we see someone trip up whilst walking down the street, we tend to explain that behaviour in dispositional terms ('what a clumsy person!'). Suppose, however, that we were to trip up whilst walking down a street. Would we explain our own behaviour in dispositional terms? According to the evidence, the answer is 'no'; when we are the actors, we tend to explain our behaviour in situational terms. In the case of tripping up, we might explain our behaviour in terms of 'uneven paving stones'.

Explanations of actor/observer biases

● Jones and Nisbett (1971) have argued that one reason for the differences between actors' and observers' attributions is that different aspects of information are available to those concerned. The actor, who has performed the behaviour, has more direct information available about the event than does the observer. The observer may be at some distance from the actor and may not be able to see the actual situational cause (in the example we used above, the uneven paving stone). The actor also knows more about their own previous behaviour than does the observer (i.e. we have more *privileged* information about ourselves than does an observer). We may know, for example, that we have very rarely tripped up while walking down the street. The observer, by contrast, does not have this knowledge and may assume that the behaviour is typical of the person observed.

● The *focus of attention* is different for the actor and observer. Actors focus outwards away from themselves towards the situation (and therefore cannot 'see' themselves behaving) and so are likely to locate the cause of their behaviour there (actor bias). Observers, on the other hand, focus their attention on the actor, bypassing situational factors, and are, therefore, more likely to attribute the cause of behaviour to the actor (observer bias).

● Research has highlighted the importance of *prominence* in causal attributions. McArthur and Post (1977) found that observers tended to make more dispositional attributions when the actor was strongly illuminated than when they were dimly lit.

Evaluation
actor/observer biases

● *Research support* – There is a great deal of support for the actor/observer effect, but the effect is not always consistent and can be reversed. An analysis of such cases suggests that the effect is actually influenced by the cultural norms of presenting oneself as 'positive' and 'autonomous' (Moghaddam 1998). For example, actors have been found to attribute their own positive behaviours to dispositional factors and their negative behaviours more to situational factors (Chen *et al.* 1988).

● *Strong and weak forms* – It appears that evidence cannot support a 'strong' view of either the FAE or the actor/observer effect. However, a 'weak' form of both is consistent with the research findings. In this, observers do not make either a dispositional or a situational attribution, but use both types of factor when determining the cause of events around them. They may rely on one relatively more than the other, depending on their particular perspective of events.

● *Cross-cultural evidence* – This suggests that people must learn the attributional accounts that are favoured by that particular culture. This learning then becomes so efficient that particular attributional accounts become automatic and unthinking (Augoustinos and Walker 1995).

Attributions of success and failure: self-serving biases

The nature of self-serving biases

Although the actor/observer bias suggests that we emphasize situational factors in explaining our own behaviour, there are occasions on which this bias can be overturned. One of these is when we are asked to explain why we were successful at something, such as passing an exam. The actor/observer bias suggests that such behaviour would be explained in situational terms, such as 'an easy exam paper'. However, most people do not explain their successes in this way. People who pass exams usually explain their success by reference to all the hard work they did, how intelligent they are, and so on – in other words, to dispositional attributions.

It seems, then, that we are quite happy to make dispositional attributions for behaviour when we are successful, and this has been termed the 'self-enhancing bias'. However, we tend to avoid taking responsibility when we are unsuccessful (the 'self-protecting bias'). Miller and Ross (1975) use the general term 'self-serving bias' to describe both these biases.

Explanations of self-serving biases

- Taking responsibility for success allows us to present ourselves in the best possible light to others (the 'impression management' explanation). Denying responsibility for unsuccessful outcomes allows us to protect our self-esteem, whereas taking responsibility for success enhances it.

- An implicit assumption of the self-enhancement explanation is that it is normal and biologically adaptive to maintain a positive self-esteem (Augoustinos and Walker 1995). One of the adverse consequences of a chronically low self-esteem is depression, which may be marked by feelings of helplessness and hopelessness.

Attributional retraining

The finding that depressives possess a particular attributional style has led to the development of attributional retraining programmes in which depressives are taught how to make more self-serving attributions for their own behaviour. Interestingly enough, some evidence (e.g. Lewinsohn *et al.* 1980) suggests that relative to non-depressed people, depressives tend to make more realistic attributions about their own performances. As a result of attributional retraining, the realism of this self-view tends to diminish, to be replaced by the 'illusory warm glow in which one sees oneself more positively than others see one' (Lewinsohn *et al.* 1980). Perhaps this is a small price to pay for a positive sense of self-worth!

Evaluation
self-serving biases

- ***Attributional style and depression*** – A large number of research studies have now firmly established a link between attributional style and depression. It is argued that depressives possess a particular attribution style in which failures and other negative events are attributed to internal, stable and global (i.e. all-embracing) causes (Augoustinos and Walker 1995).

- ***Teachers' attributions*** – Johnson *et al.* (1964) asked teachers to attribute responsibility for the performance of their pupils. The researchers found that teachers saw poor performance by their pupils as the responsibility of the pupils. However, this view changed when the children improved over time, such that the teachers saw themselves as being responsible for their pupils' improved performance!

- ***Cultural differences*** – Evidence suggests that the pattern of self-serving biases found in individualist societies (such as the USA and UK) is not always found in other societies (such as Japan and China) where interdependence is more highly valued than independence. In such societies, individuals learn that they are more likely to be positively evaluated by others if they present themselves in ways that are more self-effacing than self-enhancing. For example, a study of Japanese and American students found that Japanese students estimated that 50 per cent of their peers were intellectually more capable than themselves; the figure for American students was only 30 per cent (Markus and Kitayama 1991).

Self-handicapping

In some cases we might accept responsibility for failure if it can be attributed to a factor that is evident to others, and we know that we can control that factor and thus improve our performance at a later date. However, when this is not possible, we may invent reasons for the failure before the event has taken place. This is called 'self-handicapping' (Berglas and Jones 1978), a strategy we use to maintain an image of competence when things go wrong. In exams, for example, we may know that we don't have the ability to pass. By self-handicapping, we are able to provide a creditable explanation for likely failure in situational rather than dispositional terms.

ACTIVITY

Self-handicapping

Think about the time immediately before an examination when you are waiting to go into the examination room. Your fellow students are all there and you begin talking about your prospects in the exam.

1 What sorts of things do you and your fellow students talk about?

2 Do you talk about how little revision you've done and how, as a result of this, your chances in the exam are very slim?

3 What other reasons do people come up with for possible failure in the exam?

 CHECK YOUR UNDERSTANDING

Check your understanding of attribution of causality by answering these questions from memory. You can check your answers by looking back through Topic 1.

1 What is the difference between a 'dispositional attribution' and a 'situational attribution'?

2 Suggest two causal factors that might constitute dispositional explanations of behaviour, and two that might constitute situational explanations.

3 Construct a descriptive 150-word précis of Kelley's co-variation theory as an explanation of attribution.

4 Construct a 150-word critique of Kelley's causal schemata model.

5 Summarize in 100 words the findings from cross-cultural research into Weiner's attributional theory.

6 Select two other research studies relating to Weiner's attributional theory. In what way(s) do these support or challenge the assumptions of this theory?

7 Identify three types of attributional error/bias.

8 Look at question 5 in the Example Exam Questions on p. 282. If you had six 100-word paragraphs to answer this question, what would go in each paragraph?

9 What is the difference between a 'self-serving bias' and a 'self-handicapping' bias?

10 What is the link between attributional style and depression, and what is the aim of attributional retraining for depressives?

REVISION SUMMARY

Having covered this topic, you should be able to:

✔ describe and evaluate at least two theories of attribution of causality

✔ describe and evaluate research studies related to these theories, and use these studies effectively as AO2 commentary on each of the theories studied

✔ describe and evaluate research (theories and/or studies) into errors and biases in the attribution process.

Unit 9 // Social cognition

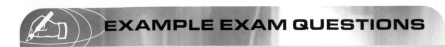
Below are some **possible examination questions** set on this topic, along with hints to help you understand and approach each question effectively:

1 Describe and evaluate **one** theory of the attribution of causality. (24 marks)

Occasionally questions ask you to concentrate on just *one* theory. The question might even include suggestions concerning appropriate theories. You need to be prepared for this eventuality and have at least one theory that you could expand in response to such a question, i.e. be able to present 12-marks-worth of description and 12-marks-worth of commentary. The evaluation here could use research studies (provided these are *used* as part of an evaluation rather than simply described) or general critical points (as we have included in the 'AO2 Evaluation' panels in the text).

2 Outline and evaluate **two** theories of the attribution of causality. (24 marks)

A more common question is to ask for an *outline* of two theories. This requires a précis (just the most pertinent points) rather than the lengthier response to the question above. Although the word 'evaluate' is the same as for question 1, it is implicit in this question that this is an 'outline' evaluation. Remember though, that there must be some degree of elaboration to make your evaluation *effective*. You will receive little credit for simply stating that the theory has empirical support; you need to explain why this is a strength and give an example of such evidence. The evidence itself need not be *described* in detail. See p. 937 for information on 'Innovative and effective AO2'.

3 Describe and evaluate research studies relating to the attribution of causality. (24 marks)

Given the wording of the specification, this is a legitimate question. Questions may specifically be asked about 'research studies' wherever this phrase appears in the specification. There is no minimum requirement for a specific number of studies, so it is up to you. In this unit there are studies attributed to each theory, which can be combined to form a response to this question. There is also no maximum number of studies, but the more studies you attempt to describe and evaluate, the less detail you can provide for each. Both breadth and detail are important for high marks, so you must balance them – not too much breadth and just enough detail to demonstrate your knowledge and understanding.

4 (a) Outline **two or more** theories of the attribution of causality. (12 marks)
   (b) Evaluate the theories of attribution of causality that you outlined in part (a) in terms of relevant research studies. (12 marks)

The (a) part of this question mirrors question 2 above, but the (b) part requires more than just a description of relevant research studies; it requires an evaluation of your chosen theories *using* those research studies – they must be used to indicate the strengths and/or limitations of your theories. Remember that both theories must receive this treatment, otherwise you would be demonstrating 'partial performance' in part (b), and would limit the number of marks you could gain (a maximum of 8 out of 12 marks for AO2). Partial performance criteria also apply to part (a) if a candidate only outlines one theory (a maximum of 8 marks for AO1).

In parted questions, material that is *peripherally relevant* or *irrelevant* to one part of the question and would earn marks in the other part, is then '*exported*' (when determining marks) to that part. Even so, it is important to retain a clear focus on the different parts of the question.

5 Discuss research (theories **and/or** research studies) relating to errors and biases in the attribution process. (24 marks)

This is a wide-open question that allows for any combination of the nature and explanations of attributional biases for your AO1 and research support/commentary for AO2. There is no minimum (or maximum) requirement for the number of errors/biases you discuss, but remember the depth/breadth trade-off. The phrase 'errors and biases' does not mean that you have to write about both, but merely indicate that sometimes these are referred to as errors, and at other times biases. Note that it is made clear that research refers to theories or even explanations (such as the fundamental attribution bias) or to studies. If you *describe* a theory, then you may use studies as a means of evaluation, or vice versa.

<< An attempt, using the models and methods of cognitive psychology, to discover how cognition influences social behaviour. >> (Manstead *et al.* 1995)

Social perception is that area of social psychology that deals with our attempts to make sense of the world around us, and as such is strongly influenced by social and cultural forces, such as family, friends and the media. Perceivers typically go beyond the information given in any social encounter and so rely on existing models of the social world to guide their perception of events in it.

FEATURES OF SOCIAL PERCEPTION

Cognitive misers and motivated tacticians

The cognitive miser

People often choose the path of least resistance, i.e. they choose the approach that will allow them to reach their goal with the minimum of effort. In terms of cognition, individuals are usually unwilling to expend more than the minimum amount of cognitive effort (i.e. they are 'cognitive misers'). Cognitive misers make extensive use of 'heuristics' (or 'rules of thumb') to guide their social perception. One example of a heuristic is the 'false consensus effect', the tendency to see one's own behaviour as being more typical than it actually is (Hogg and Vaughan 2002). Heuristics provide a quick and simple way of dealing with large amounts of information and are reasonably accurate most of the time.

The motivated tactician

This approach represents the individual as a 'fully engaged thinker' who chooses between alternative information-processing strategies on the basis of current motives and needs. Fiske and Neuberg (1990) proposed that:

- people first of all categorize others by relying on their own stereotypes
- if any information contradicts the initial categorization, people are motivated to recategorize or sub-categorize the person

- the model assumes that there is a correct judgement to be made.

Social categorization

Social categorization involves matching a person to an existing social category. This categorization may take several forms such as race, gender or age. Rather than try to process all the stimulus information available, perceivers simply assign individuals to social categories on the basis of shared or common characteristics. Following categorization into different category groups, we tend to ignore similarities and exaggerate differences between those individuals. Once a person has been categorized, it is assumed that they possess characteristics of the group even though such characteristics were not evident during initial categorization.

Consequences of social categorization

- If a person belongs to (i.e. identifies with) one of the groups involved, the effects of social categorization, as described above, are accentuated. This is the basis for prejudice against members of the 'out-group', that is, as a means of bolstering the self-esteem of oneself and one's group.
- People tend to be more aware of differences between 'in-group' members and represent them as more complex than members of an out-group.

SOCIAL REPRESENTATIONS

One of the consequences of taking a truly *social* view of human behaviour is to discover that whole cultures often share the same view of the world around them. These shared or 'social representations', passed from person to person in everyday language and embellished by the popular media, allow ordinary people to turn the unfamiliar into the familiar and the complex into the more easily understood. They rapidly become established as unquestioned, common-sense explanations which are shared by, and shape the understanding of, members of a particular group or culture. Social representations, therefore, have *two main functions*:

- to enable us to make sense of our world
- to aid communication within it.

Social representations theory

The theory of social representations (Moscovici 1981) emerged out of the need to reintroduce a *social* focus to social psychology, and in particular to understand an individual's psychological functioning by placing them in their social and cultural context. Moscovici's theory was largely based on Durkheim's (1898) idea of 'collective representations'. Collective representations were seen as those views and beliefs that were widely shared by members of a society, that were social in origin and were generally about society. These representations, such as myths, legends and traditions, were phenomena with their own distinctive characteristics, independent from the individuals who expounded them and requiring explanation at the sociological, or societal, level (Lukes 1975).

Moscovici's ideas about social representation, whilst sharing many of the features of Durkheim's collective representations, differ in two important ways:

1 Social representations are seen as dynamic and constantly changing.

2 Many different types of representation exist within the sub-groups and other collectives that make up Western society.

The role of these representations is to 'conventionalize' objects, persons and events by locating them within a familiar categorical context. Once formed, these representations become prescriptive in nature, determined by tradition and convention, and imposing themselves on the way we think about the world around us. Because we are often unaware of how shared prejudices and social factors determine our thinking, we may choose instead to explain our way of perceiving the world as 'common sense'. Indeed, Moscovici suggested that social representations may be the contemporary equivalent of common sense (Moscovici 1981). What makes social representations truly *social* is that they are created and generated through continued social interaction and communication by individuals and groups. Social representations, therefore, are the ...

> << ... ideas, thoughts, images and knowledge which members of a collectivity share: consensual universes of thought which are socially created and socially communicated to form part of a 'common consciousness'. Social representations refer to the stock of common-sense theories about the social world. They are comprised of both conceptual and pictorial elements. Through these, members of a society are able to construct social reality. >>
> (Augoustinos and Walker 1995, p. 135)

Anchoring and objectification

Two central ideas in Moscovici's view of social representations are 'anchoring' and 'objectification'. These two processes help us to transform unfamiliar objects or events into something more familiar. Moscovici believed we are motivated to perform this transformation because, if we can make sense of and understand an unfamiliar object, then it becomes less threatening and frightening.

● *Anchoring* – the tendency to classify and name unfamiliar objects and events by comparing them with our existing stock of familiar categories. To accomplish this, we compare an unfamiliar object with a prototype (i.e. something that typifies a more familiar object or event). If it fits, or can be adjusted to fit this prototype, then its similarity to it renders us able to predict other characteristics based on our knowledge of the prototype. For example, faced with somebody behaving in a bizarre manner in a public place, we may be relieved when someone explains that they are 'mentally ill'. By classifying and naming this event, we are then able to recognize and understand it within our own representation of the term 'mental illness'.

● *Objectification* – the process by which unfamiliar and abstract notions, ideas and images are transformed into more concrete and objective common-sense realities (Augoustinos and Walker 1995). Moscovici's (1961) own research looked at the way in which psychoanalytic concepts such as 'neurosis' and 'complex' were represented throughout French society. He showed how lay people adopted these terms and used them to explain their own behaviour and the behaviour of others. In the course of establishing these social representations of Freudian psychology, abstract constructs such as 'unconscious' and 'ego' were perceived as physical entities, and 'complexes' and 'neuroses' as objective conditions that afflict people.

According to social representations theory, as humans, we have the tendency to simplify complex information into a core of pictorial and cognitive elements that are stored in memory and accessed when required (Augoustinos and Walker 1995). This popularization of scientific concepts has been accelerated through the mass media. Media representations enable people with little scientific training to discuss issues such as the greenhouse effect, schizophrenia or the ozone layer.

Knowledge may be 'objectified' into a social representation through three different processes:

● *Personification* of knowledge links an idea or concept to a particular person. For example, describing someone as a 'Blairite', or linking together a theory (e.g. psychoanalysis) to one person (e.g. Freud) gives the concept a concrete existence.

● *Figuration* is the process by which we use a metaphorical image to help us understand an abstract notion. For example, during the 1980s, food surpluses within the European Community were described as 'milk lakes' or 'butter mountains', and during the Gulf War in the early 1990s, Saddam Hussein's hostages were described as 'human shields' (Augoustinos and Walker 1995).

● *Ontologizing* is the process by which an abstract notion is interpreted as a material phenomenon. For example, the abstract notions of a 'mind' or a 'neurosis' may be better understood if they are interpreted in some concrete and physically meaningful way (such as describing someone as 'mechanically minded' or having a 'nervous breakdown').

Social representations research

Critics of social representations have argued that the concept is too vague and loosely defined, and therefore difficult to translate into scientific research. Moscovici himself (1985) suggests that he has somehow violated a taboo of scientific psychology by not attempting to imitate the rigour of standard scientific theories, and by instead presenting his ideas as a series of essays and speculations.

Representations of health and illness

One of the most widely reported studies of social representations is Herzlich's (1973) study of the representations of health and illness in France in the 1960s. She interviewed 80 people, half of whom were described as professional people, and the other half as middle class. Most of the respondents lived in Paris, although 12 lived in a small village in Normandy. Using an interview method structured around themes

identified in an earlier pilot study, Herzlich discovered the dominant view that the urban way of life was a primary cause of illness. Living in a city was seen as resulting in fatigue and nervous tension, and as a direct cause of mental disorders, heart disease and cancer. Respondents made frequent references to the 'constraining' noise and rhythm of urban life which were forced upon the individual who was powerless to change them. In contrast, life in the country was seen as healthier, with water and air being cleaner, and the pace of life slower and calmer. Whether or not an individual could resist the onset of illness and remain healthy was, by contrast, seen as a product of internal factors such as the individual's predisposition to illness or their temperament. Illness was, therefore, seen as generated by an external environment, with the individual being the source of health. However, in a cautious postscript to this study, Farr (1977) warns against reading too much into its findings. He claimed that the finding that illness is associated with society and health is associated with the individual is evidence of the self-serving bias discussed earlier in this unit. Farr suggests that whenever respondents are asked to explain favourable (i.e. health) as opposed to unfavourable (i.e. illness) accounts, there is a strong tendency to adopt such an attributional bias.

KEY RESEARCH >> SOCIAL REPRESENTATIONS

Social representations of smoking in adolescent girls (Lucas and Lloyd 1999)

Relatively few studies have attempted to describe adolescents' social representations of young cigarette smokers and non-smokers. Kevin Lucas and Barbara Lloyd studied a large group of 11- to 14-year-old adolescents from secondary schools in East Sussex to find out whether the social representations of smoking were different for smokers and non-smokers, and whether this might explain why they identified with one group rather than another. Qualitative data was gathered from girls recruited from friendship groups in years 7 and 9, and their perceptions of smokers and non-smokers noted. Each group was homogeneous in their smoking behaviour: either all members of the group smoked or all members did not smoke.

Among groups of non-smokers, girls who belonged to smoking groups were consistently described as being more active (e.g. smoking was seen as a way of attracting boys), predatory (they are seen as applying pressure to make others smoke) and demanding conformity in their smoking behaviour (non-smoking members were not tolerated). Smoking itself was represented by non-smokers as being analogous to a highly contagious disease. A smoking 'outbreak' is described thus:

continued on next page

<< It was in year 8, I think, that they started going to clubs and then more girls started. Just recently, more girls started smoking 'cos a big group of them go down to the leisure centre, and then one started smoking who came to this school just recently, and then they all started smoking. >>

Non-smoking groups identified two ways in which this 'infection' was transmitted to others. The first involved an experimental episode, resulting largely from curiosity, the second, and more likely, was predation by a smoking group. Many reasons were given for avoiding smokers, but all represented smokers as having 'gone bad' in some way.

In contrast, smokers noted the desire to be active and out in the world with their friends rather than being bored. Smoking gave them the opportunity to 'go off to the woods and have a laugh'. Despite the fact that adolescents are often told that smoking for the first time is unpleasant, girls in groups of regular smokers did not always describe the experience as such. Smokers tend to be seen by their peers as fun-loving and non-conformist, and cigarettes are seen as a passport to an exciting and popular lifestyle.

Although it is evident that adolescent girls who never smoke have incorporated and accepted the representations of smoking and non-smoking by the age of 17, there are still substantial numbers who share quite different representations which resist conventional attempts to change their behaviour.

Evaluation
social representations theory

● **Attributions as social representations** – Social representations theory provides a plausible explanation for many of the attributional biases discussed earlier in this unit. We noted that there are clear cultural differences in the way in which people from different cultures explain their own behaviour and the behaviour of others. In Western cultures, we show a preference for dispositional over situational causes, whereas the reverse is true for many other societies (Slugoski 1998). Slugoski argues that this might be explained in terms of the shared social representations of persons within these different societies. In the West, we tend to see the individual as the primary causative agent in behaviour, whereas in non-Western cultures, shared representations tend to emphasize the social and contextual embeddedness of all human activity. Indeed, as we have seen, the FAE appears to be primarily a Western phenomenon, shared, we are led to believe, by all members of Western cultures.

● **Are social representations truly 'social'?** – Parker (1987) criticizes Moscovici's concept of social representations because, unlike Durkheim's notion of collective representations, social representations are cognitive structures that reside in the mind of each individual, making subjective meaning more important than the socially shared nature of the content. Parker is also critical of the way social psychologists tend to use sociological theory to override the problems that have traditionally plagued social psychology since its days as an experimental science. He argues that

the theory of social representations can easily be absorbed by mainstream psychology rather than being seen as more 'social' and therefore distinct from it. To critics such as Parker, the cognitive focus of social representations strips them of any true social or collective character.

● **The consensual nature of social representations** – A final problem with social representations theory is in determining the degree to which social representations are truly *consensual* (i.e. shared by all members of a group). Critics such as Potter and Litton (1985) argue that empirical studies (such as the Herzlich study discussed earlier) assume consensus and ignore diversity. They argue that it is essential to differentiate between different levels of consensus. In their analysis of social representations that emerged during the St Paul's riots in Bristol in 1980, they found considerable consensus regarding the range of explanations that could account for the riots (Litton and Potter 1985). However, there also appeared to be considerable variation as to whether people fully accepted, partially accepted or rejected these accounts as legitimate explanations. Litton and Potter draw an important distinction between the 'use' of an explanation and the 'mention' of an explanation. The former is used to make sense of an event and implies acceptance by the person using it. The latter refers to an explanation that is not actually used, but is referred to as an available explanation. Many of the people interviewed following the St Paul's riots revealed their preferred explanations whilst also mentioning other explanations that they might have rejected. Litton and Potter suggest that rather than demonstrating consensus, studies such as this actually demonstrate both conflicting and contradictory social representations.

SOCIAL AND CULTURAL STEREOTYPING

Stereotypes

In an early study, Katz and Braly (1933) demonstrated the existence of stereotypes about members of different ethnic groups. Subsequent research showed that whilst certain stereotypes had changed over time, they were still prevalent (Karlins *et al.* 1969).

From the list of words below, select five that you think are typical of:

(a) Americans   (b) Germans
(c) West Indians   (d) Chinese.

Place them in order, putting the word you think is most typical first. You may use the same words to describe the members of different nationalities.

Superstitious	Industrious	Sly
Intelligent	Musical	Sensual
Materialistic	Ignorant	Stolid
Methodical	Ambitious	Loyal to family
Impulsive	Passionate	Lazy
Religious	Sportsmanlike	Scientifically minded
Happy-go-lucky	Tradition-loving	

Now compare your responses with those of other people. Do you see any similarities? Karlins and colleagues found that in 1969, Americans were mostly seen as 'materialistic', whereas 'industrious' was the stereotype most typical of Germans. West Indians were seen as 'musical' and the Chinese as 'loyal to family'.

The nature of stereotyping

The notion of *stereotypes* can be traced back to Lippmann (1922), who believed that these 'pictures in the head' represented an 'ordered, more or less consistent picture of the world, to which our habits, our tastes, our capacities, our comforts, and our hopes have adjusted themselves'.

A stereotype is a mental representation of a social group and its members (Hamilton and Sherman 1994). Research on stereotypes has helped us to understand how different groups see each other, e.g. the 'humourless German' or the 'mean Scot'. Stereotypes and stereotyping are of interest to social psychologists because stereotypes are frequently and easily activated, and this activation influences how we react to group members – in particular members of disliked groups.

The functions of stereotypes

Stereotypes also serve the important cognitive function of organizing incoming information, directing our attention towards some events and away from others, and, in so doing, they often alter the retrieval of that information.

Augoustinos and Walker (1995) argue that stereotypes are a form of 'schema' – that is, they direct our mental resources, guide the encoding and retrieval of information, and save cognitive energy. We will now consider each of these in turn.

- *Stereotypes direct attention* – We are unable, or unwilling to attend to more than a small proportion of the vast amount of information that we receive from our social environment. Furthermore, the stimuli that we do attend to we categorize and then process accordingly. For example, in a study carried out by Taylor *et al.* (1978), participants were asked to identify which member of a mixed group made a particular comment. They tended to recall the *category* the person was from (e.g. it was a *woman* or a *Black* person), rather than which individual had made the comment. This supports the idea that our attention is directed at category-based stereotypes rather than individuals within those categories.

- *Stereotypes guide the encoding of information* – Stereotypes and stereotyping are by their very nature social, since they are about a social category (such as women, students, Australians, etc.) and are shared by a large proportion of our own culture. In this sense, they might be considered to be a social representation – but more about that later.

- *Stereotypes guide the retrieval of information* – A number of studies have reported that participants tend to recall more information about target groups when that information is congruent (in agreement) with their prior impressions of the group. Although many of these studies have used artificial (i.e. fictitious) groups, some using real groups (such as football fans or salespeople) have also confirmed this. The degree to which information about a target group fits with a previously held stereotype will influence the likelihood of that information being remembered (Cano *et al.* 1991).

- *Stereotypes save cognitive energy* – We saw earlier that schemas 'simplify detail and speed up processing', or put another way, they conserve mental energy. By using stereotypes, we effectively free up cognitive resources that we would otherwise use processing information about the object of the stereotype (Augoustinos and Walker 1995).

Explaining stereotyping

Grain of truth hypothesis

We may ask where a stereotype originated from in the first place. One explanation is the 'grain of truth' hypothesis – that for at least some members of the target group, the stereotypes are actually true. Social psychologists have not always been keen to tackle this idea, partly because many negative stereotypes are associated with groups who are already victimized within society. To carry out such research, argue Sieber and Stanley (1988), would be to 'lend scientific integrity to the prevailing prejudice'. The fact that stereotypes might indeed contain a grain of truth is explained by Augoustinos and Walker (1995). They suggest that instead of stereotypes being seen as an intrinsic part of the group themselves, they reflect the social and economic position of the group at the time the stereotype was formed. They give an example purportedly written by Cicero to Atticus during the time of the Roman invasion of Britain:

<< Do not obtain your slaves from Britain, because they are so stupid and so utterly incapable of being taught that they are not fit to form part of a civilized household. >>

Illusory correlations

Another explanation of stereotypes relates to 'illusory correlations', i.e. perceiving relationships between two events when, in fact, none exists. For example, people may perceive a relationship between a particular ethnic group and violent crime or between travellers and petty crime even though none exists. Hamilton and Gifford (1976) have argued that we perceive a correlation between two such events because they are both unusual and therefore distinctive. When both events occur together, we tend to assume that they are linked (see Fig. 9.1). In their research they presented participants with scenarios depicting desirable and undesirable actions of hypothetical groups. They found that participants typically overestimated the number of undesirable actions from members of the smaller (minority) group.

Illusory correlations may play a key part in the development of prejudice because they lead people to assume that the relationship between two events (particularly if one is negative) is higher than it actually is. They may also lead people to ignore the many other factors that may be responsible for the relationship that have nothing to do with any inherent qualities of the target group. For example, it may well be true that members of a particular minority group commit a disproportionate percentage of violent crimes, but this may be due more to other social factors, such as unemployment or antagonism by majority group members, rather than the inherent qualities of the group.

Figure 9.1 >> *Illusory correlations*

Evaluation
social & cultural stereotypes
(A02)

● *The inevitability of illusory correlations* – Despite the widespread persistence of illusory correlations, they are not inevitable. If perceivers are able to direct careful attention to information about two events, or if they are distracted from giving it much attention, then the likelihood of illusory correlations is reduced. Illusory correlations are most likely to occur when perceivers have a moderate amount of cognitive resources for processing information about the two events. Unfortunately, argue Baron and Byrne

(1994), individuals appear to operate at exactly that critical level. They pay just enough attention to information they receive to form erroneous perceptions of the social world. For example, an employer who believes that 'being blonde' and 'having fun' are related, may believe also that blondes are poor employment prospects for responsible jobs because they are too busy having fun (Baron and Byrne 1994).

● *Stereotyping and prejudice* – Stereotypes have received much attention from social psychologists because of their social consequences, which are often negative, and which may lead to prejudice and discrimination. People's tendency to take

continued on next page

Evaluation continued
social & cultural stereotypes

cognitive short cuts means that, when asked to recall a person's characteristics, we may do so according to the general category in which we placed them, i.e. we tend to recall through stereotypes. We also tend to accept information which confirms the stereotype and refute information which challenges it. For example, when a prejudiced person meets a pleasant or likeable member of a rejected group, that member is perceived to be 'an exception to the rule' rather than as evidence of a misconception. As a result, our stereotypes remain unchanged, the bias in our processing becomes self-confirming, and prejudice is maintained. According to Billig (1985), social cognition theories see stereotyping as an almost inevitable consequence of social information processing. Although Billig accepts that it is functional for us to categorize, he points out that we have the ability to particularize. In Billig's view, the focus of research on prejudice and prejudice reduction should be 'category selection', that is, identifying the categories used by prejudiced and non-prejudiced thinkers.

● **Stereotyping and the cognitive miser** – Stereotypes are not always used as a basis for social judgement. Manstead *et al.* (1995) argue that in their role as 'cognitive energy conserving' devices, they are more likely to be employed in situations that are cognitively demanding. Likewise, when perceivers are in extreme emotional states, their information-processing capacity is reduced and they are more likely to rely on stereotypes. However, when perceivers are motivated to make individual judgements about others or are held accountable for their perceptions, stereotypes are less likely to be used.

● *How useful are stereotypes?* – The traditional view of stereotypes sees them as generally incorrect. This view has been strengthened by research evidence which has exposed significant biases in the way we see and make judgements about our social world. Moghaddam (1998) suggests that a suitable way of summing up our current view of the accuracy of stereotypes is to see them as '... generally inaccurate and systematically biased'. A more social view of stereotypes sees them from a different perspective. A social perspective acknowledges that stereotypes serve important functions for society as well as for cognitively slothful individuals. Jost and Banaji (1994) suggest at least three important functions of stereotypes:

– *ego justification*, i.e. protecting our own status

– *group justification*, i.e. protecting the status of our own group

– *system justification*, i.e. legitimizing existing status hierarchies so that those with high status are seen as superior to those with low status, who are seen in a more negative light.

CHECK YOUR UNDERSTANDING

Check your understanding of social perception by answering these questions. Do this from memory at first. You can check your answers by looking back through Topic 2.

1 What is the difference between a 'cognitive miser' and a 'motivated tactician'?

2 Suggest two consequences of social categorization.

3 What is meant by a 'social representation'?

4 Briefly explain the nature of anchoring and objectification, and give an example of each.

5 Why do adolescent girls smoke? Construct a 100-word response to this question using insights from social representations theory.

6 What is a stereotype?

7 Identify the four functions of stereotypes.

8 What is an illusory correlation? Give an example of an illusory correlation.

9 Briefly outline (100 words) the link between stereotyping and prejudice.

10 If you decided to answer question 3 in the Example Exam Questions on p. 290 in terms of social *and* cultural stereotyping, what would go in each of six 100-word paragraphs?

REVISION SUMMARY

Having covered this topic, you should be able to:

✓ describe and evaluate research (theories/studies, etc.) into social representations

✓ describe and evaluate research (theories/studies, etc.) into social and cultural stereotyping.

 EXAMPLE EXAM QUESTIONS

Below are some **possible examination questions** set on this topic, along with hints to help you understand and approach each question effectively:

1 Discuss research (theories **and/or** research studies) into social **and/or** cultural influences on the perception of the social world. (24 marks)

> This 'general' question gives you considerable freedom over what you might include in an answer. You might choose to answer the question in terms of either of the topics that follow it (i.e. social representations and stereotyping), or in some other way that illustrates how social and/or cultural factors influence the way in which we perceive our social world. In the AQA specification, the topics of social representations and stereotyping are preceded by the word 'including'; this means that they may be prescribed in an exam question, but this question offers the opportunity to use them in a rather different way.

2 Critically consider research (theories **and/or** research studies) into the nature of social representations. (24 marks)

> The term 'critically consider' can be treated in the same way as 'discuss', i.e. it means 'describe and evaluate'. In this case the question focuses on the specific area of social representations rather than the wider topic of social perception. You may include discussion of *any* aspects of social representations (e.g. social representations theory, studies, etc.). Where you have described a theory, you may use studies as one form of evaluation, or vice versa. Evaluation may also be achieved by criticizing the methodology used in any study or other forms of theoretical criticism. Remember that evaluation can be positive or negative.

3 Discuss research (theories **and/or** research studies) into the nature of social and/or cultural stereotyping. (24 marks)

> As in the two previous questions, the term 'research' allows you to use theories and/or studies in your answer. The term 'and/or' allows you to cover social or cultural stereotyping (or both). Even when questions say social *and* cultural stereotyping, this is simply to reflect the wording of the specification and is not meant to suggest that both must be covered (it is difficult to determine what is a *cultural* stereotype and what a *social* stereotype). Like question 2, this question focuses on a specific topic within social perception, this time stereotyping. Material on social perception in general may only be creditworthy where it has been made relevant to this question.

4 (a) Outline research (theories **and/or** studies) into social perception. (12 marks)

(b) To what extent does the research outlined in part (a) support the view that perception is a social process? (12 marks)

> The first part of this question serves to remind you that questions can be set on the topic title ('social perception') as well as the specification contents of the topic. The danger with such a question is the potential breadth of material that could be included. In part (b) you must limit yourself to the research described in part (a) and then *use* this to judge whether the way we view the world is a social process (bearing in mind the point made above that 'social' overlaps with 'cultural'). There is no requirement to reach a conclusion about whether or not perception is a social process. It would be sufficient to examine the evidence that it is a social/cultural process without venturing into the possible evidence against this (i.e. when perception is physically determined or when it is not learned).

Topic 3 >> Prejudice and discrimination

Zimbardo *et al.* (1995) have defined *prejudice* as 'a learned attitude toward a target object, involving negative affect (dislike or fear) and negative beliefs (stereotypes) that justify the attitude'. They define *discrimination* as 'the behavioural intention to avoid, control, dominate or eliminate those in the target group'. Note that prejudice is an attitude, whereas discrimination is a behaviour.

There is no doubting the existence of prejudice in modern society, and many people have been victims of prejudiced attitudes because of their sex, age, disability, sexuality, physical appearance and/or membership of an ethnic group. Some people have also been victims of discrimination. Much of the early research in this area of social psychology was conducted by Allport (1954), who outlined five *behavioural stages* of ethnic prejudice. These are:

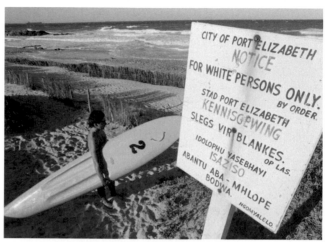

How does this sign, from South Africa during the Apartheid era, demonstrate discrimination?

- **antilocution** or *verbal denigration*, such as the telling of racist jokes
- **avoidance** of the ethnic group by, for example, segregation
- **discrimination**, or the inequitable treatment or exclusion of those belonging to an ethnic group
- **physical attack**, that is, actual violence against people and their property
- **extermination** of the ethnic group, as, for example, in the case of the attempts by Nazis to exterminate the Jewish race.

Prejudice is an example of an attitude and, as such, has three components:

- **affective** – our feelings or emotions towards the target group
- **cognitive** – the beliefs, thoughts and ideas we have about the members of the target group
- **behavioural** – our predisposition to behave in certain ways towards the target group.

Usually, these three components are in balance: for example, if our beliefs about the target group are negative, our feelings and behaviours are also negative. This is because we prefer consistency in our social world and this allows us to interact successfully in it.

In some cases, however, the components may not be in balance. In their theory of 'reasoned action', Fishbein and Ajzen (1975) argued that, although attitudes are often correlated with both behavioural intentions and actual behaviour, this is not always the case. Thus, a person may hold prejudiced beliefs but may not necessarily apply those beliefs by engaging in discrimination. Equally, discrimination may occur without this reflecting prejudice. In many schools, for example,

physical education is taught separately to boys and girls, an example of discrimination without prejudice.

In this section we will focus on racism, which is one of the most pervasive forms of prejudice and discrimination. *Racism* can be defined as any attitude, action or institutional structure that exerts power unjustly over others because of their race. It is important to note that our definition includes reference to both *individual* and *institutional* racism, where, as Cray (1995) has observed, the political and economic structure of an organization is such that it discriminates. Jobanputra (1995) has argued that psychology itself has always been affected by the racism of society in general. For Bhavnani and Phoenix (1994) three forms of racism in psychology are most evident:

- **Biological racism** – This assumes that some groups are naturally inferior to others, and has been most clearly demonstrated through the use of IQ testing in which attempts have been made to demonstrate White superiority.

- **Common-sense racism** – This refers to work on social identity theory in which it is often assumed that members of the in-group will automatically discriminate against the out-group (a point we will return to later on in this unit).

- **New or modern racism** – This does not view other groups as being explicitly deficient in physical or intellectual terms (as is the case in biological racism), but attempts to justify inequalities in more subtle ways, such as viewing people as being 'different' in terms of their culture and their non-traditional values. For Jobanputra (1995), this type of racism is the most harmful because it can be cleverly disguised and therefore more difficult to detect and 'prove'.

ORIGINS AND MAINTENANCE OF PREJUDICE AND DISCRIMINATION

Personality theories of prejudice

The authoritarian personality

A popular explanation of prejudice is to attribute it to a particular type of personality. The best-known attempt to link prejudice with personality was Adorno et al.'s (1950) 'authoritarian personality theory'. This theory explained why some people were more receptive than others to racist or fascist ideas that may be common in society at that time.

Adorno and colleagues believed that these personality differences could be traced back to the family in which the child was socialized. Parents who imposed a strict regime and were overly concerned with 'good behaviour', and who used harsh disciplinary measures to punish transgressions, produced children who harboured retaliatory urges towards them. As the child's aggression could not be directed towards the parents (because of the obvious consequences), it had to be displaced onto substitute targets. These 'scapegoats' were inevitably those who were seen as weaker than the individual themselves, and were thought to include members of minority ethnic groups or any other socially devalued group.

Adorno and colleagues also believed that this personality syndrome shaped the way in which prejudiced attitudes were constructed and expressed. As a direct result of the parents' strict conventional morality, the child developed a simplistic way of thinking about the world. People and their actions were rigidly categorized into 'right or wrong'. This tendency was thought to develop into a cognitive style where there was little 'fuzziness' between categories (such as social groups), and where the development of distinctive and immutable stereotypes about them was

almost inevitable. As a result, the authoritarian personality, overly deferential towards authority figures (who symbolically represented the parents), at the same time saw the rest of the world in black and white, and was overtly hostile to anyone who was not an in-group member.

The development of a personality inventory (the F scale which measured authoritarianism) subsequently established reliable correlations between:

- authoritarianism and anti-Black prejudice (Pettigrew 1959)
- ethnocentrism (considering one's group to be at the centre of everything (Meloen et al. 1988)) and sexual aggression towards women (Walker et al. 1993). Some of the items appearing on the questionnaire are shown in the panel below.

> ## Examples of items from the F scale
> (used to measure authoritarianism)
>
> Respondents are asked to indicate if they agree or disagree with each item
>
> - 'Most of our social problems would be solved if we could somehow get rid of the immoral, crooked and feeble-minded people.'
> - 'Obedience and respect for authority are the most important virtues a child should learn.'
> - 'An insult to our honour should always be punished.'
> - 'It is only natural and right that women be restricted in ways in which men have more freedom.'

Evaluation
authoritarian personality theory

- **Problems with the F scale** – Some of the fundamental problems associated with this approach arise from the instruments used to measure the degree of authoritarianism in the first place. Adorno and colleagues' F scale contained 30 items, all worded in such a way that agreement with them indicated an authoritarian response. Brown (1965) suggested that any authoritarianism so measured by the F scale could not be distinguished from the more general tendency to agree with authoritative-sounding statements.

- **Limited application** – Adorno and colleagues' concept of the authoritarian personality is also criticized because it only deals with right-wing authoritarianism. The theory (and the F scale) dealt only with prejudice towards 'conventional' targets such as Communists, Jews and other 'deviant' or minority groups (Brown 1995). Rokeach (1956) developed the alternative hypothesis that some people were more *dogmatic* or close-minded and were therefore more predisposed toward prejudice than more open-minded people. Dogmatic individuals are those who have a highly organized set of attitudes which are resistant to change in the light of new information. They are, therefore, rigid

continued on next page

and intolerant thinkers. The rejection of Trotskyites by supporters of Stalin in the 1930s is a prime example of how intolerance and mental rigidity can also be observed in extreme left-wing political groups.

● *Prejudice as personal or social pathology?* – Locating prejudice within the individual means that it is seen as a 'personal pathology ... rather than a social pathology' (Wetherell and Potter 1992). Prejudiced individuals are seen as irrational and illogical, and requiring 'rehabilitation'. Wetherell and Potter argue that this has the effect of 'deflecting attention from the political necessity of societal and structural change'.

Realistic conflict theory

It has long been recognized that, as well as the needs and personalities of individual group members, the common goals and interests of the group as a whole are potent influences on behaviour (Vivian and Brown 1995). If members of one group believe that their interests can only be satisfied at the expense of some other group, then hostility develops between the groups concerned. When groups are engaged in reciprocally competitive and frustrating activities, each group will develop negative stereotypes about and enmity towards the other group (the out-group). The theory was first formulated by Muzafer Sherif (1966) and colleagues who carried out some of the earliest studies in this area. The initial hypotheses of the theory were validated by the first stage of the 'Robbers' cave' experiment (Sherif and Sherif 1953) involving 11- to 12-year-old boys at a summer camp (see Key research below). As a result of this experiment, Sherif concluded that intergroup bias and hostility develops through competition and can be reduced through cooperation in pursuit of higher goals.

Why do members of gangs build up strong 'in-group' identities and emphasize hostility to 'out-groups'?

KEY RESEARCH >> REALISTIC CONFLICT THEORY

Intergroup conflict (Sherif and Sherif 1953)

In a classic study, Sherif and Sherif (1953) demonstrated just how easy it is for intergroup conflict to develop. In the first stage of their study, boys who had arrived at a summer camp were randomly divided into two groups. For the first week, each group worked separately and on their own. One of the groups called themselves 'the Rattlers' and the other called themselves 'the Eagles'. In the second stage of the study, the groups were set against each other. Although the researchers had planned to introduce intergroup rivalry through various tasks, the tasks were not needed. For example, when the Rattlers won a tug of war competition, the Eagles responded by burning the Rattlers' flag! The Rattlers retaliated by raiding the Eagles' camp, damaging their property.

By the end of the second week, the two teams were arch enemies. Support for their own group (the in-group) was high. In written tests, those in the in-group were considered to be 'friendly', 'tough' and 'brave'. Those in the out-group, however, were perceived in strongly negative ways and were described as 'sneaky', 'bums' and 'cowards' (strong terms for the 1950s). In a very short time, then, the competitive structure created by the Sherifs had led to hostility between the groups. In a subsequent condition of the experiment, researchers were able to reduce the hostility between the groups by replacing the competitive goals with goals that could only be achieved by members of the two groups cooperating together.

Although Sherif and Sherif's study has been replicated in a number of different cultural settings, a study by Tyerman and Spencer (1983) failed to produce the same degree of intergroup conflict in a scout group in the UK. They also found that it was relatively easy to increase cooperation between different scout patrols, even in the absence of a higher goal. Tyerman and Spencer suggest that this may be due to the fact that, unlike the groups in Sherif and Sherif's experiment, the scout group already possessed an existing higher goal (i.e. being members of the larger scout movement and subscribing to its values and goals).

(A02) Evaluation
realistic conflict theory

● *Advantages* – Realistic conflict theory has a number of advantages over other explanations of prejudice. Particularly important in this respect is its ability to explain the 'ebb and flow' of prejudice over time or different social contexts – these can be attributed to changes in the political or economic relations between the groups concerned (Brown 1995). One could usefully apply realistic conflict theory to the conflict between Serbs and Croats or, more recently, between Russia and Chechnya.

There are, however, a number of problems with the theory which, Brown suggests, means it is unlikely by itself to provide a complete explanation for all forms of prejudice (Brown 1995):

● *Problems of eradicating in-group bias* – A number of experiments have demonstrated that in-group bias is extremely difficult to eradicate even when both groups have a vested interest in its elimination. Whilst it is not difficult to understand the resilience of such favouritism when groups are engaged in competition for some scarce resource, it is harder to explain when no such competition exists.

● *Prejudice in the absence of competition* – Competition does not even appear to be necessary for in-group favouritism to develop. In Sherif and Sherif's studies, the different groups were already trying to assert their dominance long before the competitive activities were introduced. It appears that people will favour their group over another merely as a result of being categorized in that group rather than another (Tajfel *et al.* 1971). This finding gave rise to a number of experiments which demonstrated that simply belonging to a group was sufficient to produce strong and resilient prejudices for one's own group and against members of other groups (see next section and Fig. 9.2 below).

● *Real or imagined conflict?* – Another problem concerns whether conflict between groups must, by necessity, be concrete and real, or whether it can be more abstract or imagined. Brown (1995) points out that racial prejudice often takes the form of 'they (immigrants) are taking all our jobs/houses', even though rates of unemployment and homelessness might be considerably higher among immigrant groups than among the host community.

● *The power of conflict* – The power of conflict in shaping and developing prejudicial attitudes can be demonstrated in many different studies. For example, Brewer and Campbell (1976) carried out a study of 30 tribal groups in East Africa. Of these, the vast majority rated their own group more favourably than other groups. The degree of bias and hostility towards other groups was determined by the proximity of the groups being rated. Groups that were geographically closer were rated less favourably than those further away. This finding is consistent with realistic conflict theory, as groups in close proximity with each other would be more likely to be involved in disputes over territory and access to scarce resources such as water and grazing rights.

Figure 9.2 >> *A social identity theory explanation of prejudice and discrimination*

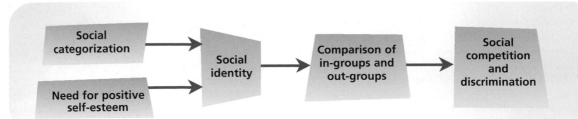

Social identity theory and prejudice

According to social identity theory (Tajfel 1981):

- People divide their social world into distinct *social categories*. They then locate themselves and others within this system of social categorization. A person's *social identity* consists of how they define themselves in each social category (gender, age, ethnic group, social class, occupation, etc.).

- We use this *categorization* in order to enhance our self-esteem. People strive for a *positive* social identity, and as this is derived from our group membership, a positive social identity is the outcome of favourable social comparisons made between the in-group and other social groups. When we compare ourselves with others, we highlight any qualities that support our own in-group values (termed 'in-group favouritism') and we point out any weaknesses that may appear to exist in the out-group (termed 'negative out-group bias').

- *Ethnocentrism* occurs when the in-group considers itself to be at the centre of everything, and any out-group is judged according to the in-group's standards. According to Pettigrew (1979), ethnocentrism is the ultimate attributional bias: group members see their own desirable behaviour as being dispositional and stable, whilst desirable behaviour in an out-group is attributed to situational factors. The reverse of this is true in the case of undesirable behaviour.

Social identity theory and the minimal group paradigm

Contrary to the claims of realistic conflict theory, the mere fact that two distinct groups exist seems sufficient for the creation of group identities which take precedence over group members' individual identities. Simply *being* in a group is sufficient to develop bias towards one's own group (the in-group) and against other groups (the out-groups). In the absence of anything but a category label (hence the expression 'minimal groups'), it is difficult to imagine that the identity comparison and evaluation process would take place. Tajfel's research on minimal groups (see panel below) clearly shows that they do. Mere categorization was sufficient to elicit intergroup discrimination.

Social identity and self-esteem

Social identity theory assumes that we are motivated to understand and evaluate ourselves and to enhance our self-esteem. As long as our membership of a particular group enables us to do this, we will remain a member of that group. However, Tajfel (1978) argues, if the group fails to satisfy this requirement, we may:

- try to change the structure of the group (*social change*)

- seek new ways of making comparisons, which favour our group and thus reinforce our own social identity – an example of this *social creativity* would be the 'Black is beautiful' movement in the USA in the late 1960s

- leave the group with the desire to join the 'better' one.

Tajfel also suggests that it is difficult for a member of a minority group to achieve a positive social identity, given that minority groups always have an inferior status compared to the majority. Minority groups do not, therefore, tend to contribute to their members' self-esteem (Turner 1982). Tajfel has even observed that a significant proportion of minority group members may exhibit high levels of self-hatred (Tajfel 1981).

The minimal group paradigm (Tajfel 1970)

Tajfel has demonstrated how easily people will discriminate against others whom they perceive to be in a different group. Some schoolboys from Bristol were placed into groups in a purely random fashion. There was no face-to-face contact between any of the boys. Under the pretext that they were participating in an experiment on decision-making, the boys were required to allocate points, which could later be converted to money, to both their own group (the in-group) and another group (the out-group). In-group favouritism was shown with the boys allocating more points to their own group. Most interestingly, the boys maximized the differentials between the groups, even when this meant disadvantaging their own group in terms of the absolute number of points allocated.

Although it is tempting to conclude that the very act of categorizing people as members of even the most nominal (minimal) group is sufficient to cause in-group favouritism and out-group discrimination, the minimal group paradigm has been criticized. For example, the members of the groups in Tajfel's studies may have been subjected to 'demand characteristics' and felt that they had little choice but to discriminate against the out-group members. Nevertheless, the findings from minimal group studies are remarkably robust, having been replicated many times in several countries and using adult as well as child participants.

Evaluation
social identity theory

● **Does group membership have implications for one's social identity?** – This assumption has been demonstrated in a number of studies, both in the laboratory and in more natural settings. An example of the latter type of study comes from Cialdini *et al.* (1976). He observed supporters of an American college football team on the days immediately following intercollegiate games. If their team had won, college scarves and insignia were much more in evidence than if they had lost. This suggests that one's willingness to be associated with a group is associated with the group's fortunes in intergroup encounters (Brown 1995).

● **Do people evaluate their group in terms of intergroup comparison?** – There is a great deal of evidence that people will engage in comparisons of this sort when asked to do so, but little evidence of spontaneous comparisons as predicted by the theory. An exception to this is the study carried out by Haeger (1993) who asked participants (as part of a survey) from six European countries to write whatever came into their mind when they thought of their own country. Analysis of their responses showed that 20 per cent had spontaneously included references to other countries when judging their own, e.g. 'people are free and have a comfortable standard of living compared to other countries'.

REDUCING PREJUDICE

The reduction of prejudice is clearly an important goal for society. Traditionally, the way to reduce prejudice was to take one of two approaches:

● intergroup contact

● social education (or socialization).

The contact hypothesis

The aim of this approach is to increase contact between different groups and thereby reduce prejudice. Research indicates that mere contact between groups is not sufficient, and that it must be interdependent and cooperative rather than competitive.

Research studies of the contact hypothesis

Early studies showed that when contact is increased, prejudice is reduced. For example:

● **Stouffer et al.** (1949) showed that mixed race units in the American army produced less prejudice than segregated race units. This occurred because actual contact allowed negative stereotypes to be removed, increased cooperation rather than competition, and led to the formation of a single in-group fighting a common enemy. Effects were not generalized, however, to situations beyond the army.

● In another study, **Deutsch and Collins** (1951) showed that a group of White residents, moved to an integrated housing programme, showed less prejudice towards Blacks than White residents who moved to a segregated housing programme. Note that the residents in the integrated housing were of equal status and no conflicts existed between them prior to the start of the programme.

The results of studies such as these led other researchers to set up situations in which people could be manipulated into being prejudiced and were then exposed to strategies designed to reduce prejudice.

● **Sherif and Sherif** (see Key research, pp. 293–4) found that bringing the leaders of the two groups of boys together did not produce any effect, nor did bringing the groups together. For example, when the groups were invited to eat together they simply threw food at one another. Mere contact, then, was not enough to reduce prejudice. What did seem to be effective was the creation of higher goals, i.e. goals that can only be achieved through cooperation. Thus, when the water supply was damaged and the two groups had to work together to repair it, and when a truck 'broke down' and both groups had to pull it with ropes to get it restarted, the prejudiced feelings that had developed were significantly reduced. Indeed, at the end of the summer camp a party took place which was enjoyed by both groups together.

Changing cognitions

So how do these approaches relate to social cognition and categorization? We have already pointed out that through equal-status contact, people have the opportunity to gain direct experience of other groups. However, unless this is prolonged (as in the case of an integrated housing project), it has been found that negative stereotypes will actually be reinforced rather than reduced.

Increased contact can help to reduce prejudice, however, in three ways:

● It can lead to the recognition of similarities between groups.

● Negative stereotypes can be changed if sufficient information about a group is provided.

- The out-group homogeneity effect may be challenged (i.e. all out-group members are *not* all the same).

According to Fiske (1989), when people are instructed to pay close attention to others, they do perceive those others in terms of personal rather than stereotypical attributes. In fact, Fiske and Neuberg (1990) suggest that we can engage in a number of strategies, ranging from total dependence on stereotypes (least cognitive effort involved) to dependence on the unique features of a person (most cognitive effort involved). Dependence on the unique features of a person matches Billig's idea of particularization (see p. 289). What is important is to address how we prevent people from taking short cuts in their cognitions and focus instead on individual differences.

If intergroup contact is possible, then new in-groups may form, but contact alone is not enough. According to Allport (1954), six conditions are necessary for prejudice reduction:

- *Equal-status participants* – Prejudice will continue if one group regards itself as being superior. If members of different groups can be brought together on equal terms, a basis for cooperative action is provided and prejudiced attitudes may be revised.
- *Mutual interdependence* – Members of two or more different groups must depend on each other in order to accomplish a task.
- *A common goal* – Groups must work towards a common goal that is important to both groups.
- *Multiple contacts with non-stereotypical individuals* – The more people we meet who do not fit into our stereotypes about their group, the more likely that our prejudices about the group will change, provided that we perceive the individuals as *typical* of the group, and not just *exceptions* to it.

Intergroup contact is most effective at reducing prejudice when members are working towards a common goal

- *Informal interpersonal contact* – Getting to know someone on a personal basis may reduce the out-group homogeneity effect; this, in turn, may help us to appreciate members of the so-called out-group as individuals.
- *Social norms for equality* – Contact can only be effective if there is support from the authorities and the community. For example, racial prejudice is less likely to find expression in a workforce where a company has a well-publicized policy of equal opportunities and anti-racism which is implemented openly from the top down.

(A02) Evaluation
the contact hypothesis

- *Research support* – Studies relating to Allport's six conditions have shown support for the effectiveness of increased contact in reducing prejudice. For example, a study of the attitudes of Hindu and Muslim students towards each other was carried out in Bangladesh (Islam and Hewstone 1993). Included in the questionnaire were questions about the frequency of contact with members of the other group and the quality of this contact (e.g. equal status or not, cooperative or competitive). Islam and Hewstone found that both the quantity and quality of interaction were directly related to a more positive attitude toward the out-group.

- *Competitive versus cooperative reward structures* – A major problem in this area of research is that reducing intergroup conflict can only be achieved if it is possible for both groups to have their needs satisfied. According to Deaux *et al.* (1993), we need to look at the reward structure when considering the interaction between two individuals or two groups. A competitive reward structure, for example, is totally inappropriate for prejudice reduction since success for one person must mean failure for the other. Much more appropriate for the reduction of prejudice is a cooperative reward structure. In this, an individual or a group can only achieve success if the other individual or group also achieves success. A cooperative reward structure was employed by Aronson and his colleagues in their jigsaw technique study (see p. 299) and by Sherif and Sherif when they devised higher goals for their groups (see p. 293).

Unit 9 // Social cognition

Social identity theory and the reduction of prejudice

Decategorization

Variations of the contact hypothesis have been developed. These new models have their origins in social identity theory and recognize that group memberships become incorporated into a person's self-concept. This has important consequences for the person's behaviour towards members of other groups. For example, Brewer and Miller (1984) suggest that if boundaries between groups can be made less rigid, then all contact would be at an interpersonal rather than an intergroup level. In this 'personalized' form of contact, they argue, people would be more likely to attend to information about the individual rather than group-based (i.e. stereotypical) information. With repeated contacts of this kind, the usefulness of category identity as a basis for future interactions is undermined, and permanent changes would occur in social interaction with out-group members (Brewer and Miller 1984).

Recategorization

Whereas Brewer and Miller see *decategorization* as the best way of reducing intergroup prejudice, Gaertner *et al.* (1993) suggest that drawing the in-group and out-group together into a new superordinate category (i.e. a process of *recategorization*) would be more effective. After the terrible earthquake in India in 1993, both Hindus and Muslims helped each other. A typical response from a Hindu helping dig out a Muslim family from beneath their collapsed house was: 'That is not a Hindu or a Muslim down there; it is a human being.'

Research support for social identity theory explanations

Research support for this model has been encouraging.

Bettencourt *et al.* (1992)

In this study, two artificial participant categories were created and then members of the two categories were brought together into cooperative work groups. Groups were given different instructions, with one group being encouraged to focus on each other 'to find out what other team members really are like' and the other being told to concentrate solely on the task in hand. The dependent measure in this study was the degree to which participants would, once the task was completed, assign rewards to other members of their group and also to members of another group, unknown to them and shown only on a short video clip. In line with the predictions of the model, participants who had been encouraged to 'focus on each other' were far more likely to share the rewards fairly within their own group and also between the two groups. Conversely, participants who had simply been told to 'concentrate on the task' showed a significant bias towards their own category and their own group.

Gaertner *et al.* (1990)

To test the assumption that recategorization is important in reducing prejudice, Gaertner and colleagues carried out a number of experiments which created artificial categories, then varied the amount of interdependence between the groups. Typically, they have found that where the participants perceived the situation as having one superordinate group (such as 'students'), they showed far less intercategory bias than when they judged the situation one in which there were two groups (such as 'arts and engineering' students) (Gaertner *et al.* 1990).

Reducing prejudice through education

Changing attitudes through targeting children at home has, unfortunately, not met with much success. Targeting the home can only work when parents realize that their views are prejudiced – and often they think such views are justified. So what can be done? One possibility is to enrich the school curriculum to enable children to be exposed to other viewpoints (see the panel below and the Key research opposite).

Verona High School, New Jersey, USA

Over the past few years, Verona High School has achieved national, state and local recognition as a leader in the fields of prejudice reduction. The objectives of the programme are:

- to provide students, teachers and staff with sufficient opportunity to discuss equity issues
- to understand that equity and diversity represent challenges and opportunities for individuals and society as a whole
- to align the specific content area of instruction with equity issues: disability, race, gender, religion, ethnicity or age.

The programme helps prepare students to live effectively in a society that is culturally and ethnically diverse.

Martin Luther King Jr day is set aside for the purpose of this programme. Called Diversity day, classes are dedicated to the programme. Challenging questions are asked of the students concerning how they would react to specific situations involving bias and other ethical issues involving diversity. Each year places a different theme on the day to focus the studies.

The entire high school staff has been trained by the Anti-Defamation League's 'World of Difference' Programme to become aware of stereotyping and biases, and to enhance their ability to work with students cross-culturally.

Brown eyes, blue eyes (Elliot 1977)

A classroom-based study conducted by Elliott attempted to show children what it was like to be discriminated against. One day Elliott, a school teacher, told her pupils that blue-eyed children were 'inferior'. Within a day, the blue-eyed children in the class were doing poorly at their work and described themselves as 'sad', 'bad', 'stupid' and 'mean'. In the meantime, the brown-eyed pupils in the class had become what Elliott described as 'nasty, vicious, discriminating little third graders'. Fights broke out because one child called another 'blue eyes'. The following day, Elliott told the children that she had made a mistake and it was actually brown-eyed children who were inferior and not those with blue eyes. Within a very short time, attitudes and behaviours reversed completely! On the third day, the children were told the truth of the matter.

Studies such as Elliott's give children direct experience of what it is like to be discriminated against. It was believed that the effects of the experience would be temporary because school-based studies are done in isolation from the home environment. However, in a ten-year follow-up of the original pupils in her class, Elliott (1990) found that they were more tolerant of group differences and were actively opposed to prejudice.

Why do you think experiences of being bullied made the subjects of this study actively opposed to prejudice as adults?

The jigsaw technique

In order to change the atmosphere of the classroom so that it met Allport's six conditions (see p. 297), Aronson *et al.* (1977) developed the 'jigsaw technique'. These researchers believed that the competitive nature of school ensures children will not learn to like and understand each other. Rather than compete, they argued, children should be encouraged to cooperate in the pursuit of common goals. The jigsaw classroom is a setting specifically designed to reduce prejudice and raise the self-esteem of children by placing them in small desegregated groups and making each child dependent on the other children in the group to complete a task. Each member of a group is given a different section of material to learn. Group members have to interact with each other, learning their part and communicating it to the others. The parts then combine to produce a whole. The research by Aronson and colleagues has generally demonstrated that children in jigsaw classrooms perform better and show greater increases in self-esteem than those in traditional classrooms.

Reducing stereotypes in the classroom

In a study by Harris *et al.* (1992), 7- to 10-year-old children were required to complete a variety of tasks (such as building a Lego tower and colouring pictures). Half of the boys had been diagnosed as hyperactive, and were paired with non-hyperactive children with whom they were previously unacquainted. Of the non-hyperactive children, half were told of their partner's 'condition' (that he disrupted the class, talked a lot and got into trouble) and half were not. Results were as expected. Boys who had been told of their partner's hyperactivity were less friendly towards them. As a result, their partners enjoyed the task less, and took less credit for any task success. Harris and colleagues also found that being with a known hyperactive partner also meant that the non-hyperactive children also enjoyed the task less than the children who had not been told of their partner's hyperactivity. Prejudice, it seems, is a two-edged sword, with not only the victims being harmed but also those who are the instigators of prejudice. Baron and Byrne (1997) suggest that educating parents about these harmful effects may well make them think twice before exposing their children to their own prejudiced views. Parents might also encourage self-examination in their children, and stress the importance of seeing people as *individuals* rather than *group representatives* (Hogg and Vaughan 1998).

Evaluation
reducing prejudice through education

● **Does the jigsaw technique work?** – Aronson and his colleagues found that whilst it took some children longer than others to realize the value of cooperation, children from different ethnic groups cooperated and learned from each other when exposed to the jigsaw technique. The strategy appeared to be effective because it made the children mutually interdependent as well as teaching them about cooperation.

● **Why does it work?** – Gaertner *et al.* (1990) suggest that the reason why the jigsaw technique is so effective is because it breaks down in-group and out-group categorization and fosters the notion of a single group. The jigsaw method also ensures that children from different ethnic groups are of equal status during the task (see previous section on the contact hypothesis). Without this equality of status, the jigsaw method would not be as effective.

● **Overcoming stereotypes** – The Harris *et al.* study confirmed that negative and stereotypical reactions to stereotyped individuals may be part of a mental 'knee-jerk'. If children could be taught to see others as complex individuals rather than as stereotypes, then these stereotypical reactions might be reduced. Langer *et al.* (1985) supported this idea in the context of young children's attitudes towards disabled people. Children who had been specially trained to be more aware of others as *people* were more positive about disabled people as a result.

CHECK YOUR UNDERSTANDING

Check your understanding of prejudice and discrimination by answering these questions from memory. You can check your answers by looking back through Topic 3.

1 What is the difference between 'prejudice' and 'discrimination'?

2 What are the three components of a prejudicial attitude?

3 Construct a descriptive 150-word précis of the authoritarian personality theory.

4 What, according to realistic conflict theory, is the main cause of prejudice?

5 What is the minimal group paradigm, and why is it important to a social identity theory explanation of prejudice?

6 Allport (1954) lists six conditions that are necessary for prejudice reduction. What are they?

7 What is the difference between 'decategorization' and 'recategorization'?

8 Briefly outline (in 100 words) how the jigsaw technique works.

9 *Why* is the jigsaw technique thought to work?

10 Construct a 200-word argument to convince a sceptic that psychology has produced worthwhile insights into the reduction of prejudice.

REVISION SUMMARY

Having covered this topic, you should be able to:

✔ describe and evaluate at least two theories of the origins/maintenance of prejudice and/or discrimination

✔ describe and evaluate at least two explanations relating to the reduction of prejudice and/or discrimination

✔ describe and evaluate research studies relating to the reduction of prejudice and/or discrimination, and use these studies effectively as AO2 commentary on each of the theories studied.

Below are some **possible examination questions** set on this topic, along with hints to help you understand and approach each question effectively:

1 Outline and evaluate **two or more** theories of the origins **and/or** maintenance of prejudice **and/or** discrimination. (24 marks)

> It is wise to be strategic when planning your response to this question. The question allows for 'two or more' theories, but as you only have 30 minutes, two is usually enough. In 30 minutes you would probably be able to write 600 words, so that's 300 on each theory, and that would be further divided into 150 words of AO1 and 150 words of AO2. If you cannot write that much for each theory, this question gives you the option of including a third theory. The question is also generous insofar as there is no distinction made between origins and maintenance (you can write about one or both of them – and the same for prejudice and discrimination). If you only present one theory then partial performance penalties would apply for AO1 and AO2 (allowing a maximum of 8 marks out of 12 for each assessment skill).

2 Describe and evaluate **one** theory of the origins of prejudice. (24 marks)

> Given the wording of the specification, a question could be asked about only one theory and be specified as a theory of prejudice. Note that, in this question, the AO1 term used is 'describe', to reflect the fact that more detail is expected where only one theory is required as distinct from less detail when 'outline' is used. If you introduced a second theory, that would gain credit only if you used it as a form of *sustained critical commentary*. In other words, it is not enough to say 'In contrast, there is theory 2 …' and then merely offer a description of the second theory.

3 Outline and assess **two or more** explanations relating to the reduction of prejudice **and/or** discrimination. (24 marks)

> When answering a question such as this, don't be seduced into providing long drawn-out explanations that have more to do with the *origins* of prejudice than its reduction. Material about origins of prejudice has some relevance, as many of the problems faced when trying to reduce prejudice are a consequence of the reasons why people are prejudiced in the first place. However, this material should be used carefully, and is more helpful as a point of critical commentary on the effectiveness of a particular strategy. Do not take the approach of saying 'We can explain the reduction of prejudice in terms of how it is caused …' and then proceed to write an essay entirely on origins. This would gain little or no credit. Note that the term 'assess' has been used instead of 'evaluate' as an AO2 term. The two terms have equivalent meanings (see Table 32.1 on p. 937).

4 Discuss research (explanations **and/or** research studies) relating to the reduction of prejudice **and/or** discrimination. (24 marks)

> This is effectively the same question as question 3, but with the added bonus that you can include (if you want to) research *studies* alongside your explanations. Remember that if you do this, then explanations can form some of your AO2 content as long as they are *effectively* used as commentary.

5 (a) Outline **two explanations** relating to the reduction of prejudice **and/or** discrimination. (12 marks)

  (b) Evaluate the **two** explanations relating to the reduction of prejudice **and/or** discrimination that you outlined in part (a) in terms of relevant research studies. (12 marks)

> The (a) part of this question is similar to question 3 above, but the (b) part requires more than just a description of relevant research studies; it requires an evaluation of your chosen explanations *using* those research studies. There would be little credit for any description of these studies, which would be AO1 material and not creditworthy in part (a) or part (b). You must consider what such studies tell us (good or bad) about the explanations. Both explanations must receive this treatment, otherwise you would be demonstrating 'partial performance', and would lose marks.

Topic 1: Attribution of causality

- Attributions **of causality** of our own behaviour and the behaviour of others may be dispositional (something about the person) or situational (something about the environment).

- **Kelley's co-variation theory** stresses the way that we reach causal decisions when we have information about the person and their previous behaviour, and about the behaviour of others in the same situation. For instance, when someone acts consistently across time and across similar situations, and when others do not respond in the same way, a dispositional attribution is made. When someone acts differently in one situation compared to how they act in other similar situations, and when everybody else acts in the same way, a situational attribution is made.

- **Kelley's causal schemata model** explains how people reach causal attributions based on more limited information. When there are a number of possible causes and one is present, other possible causes may be discounted. If more than one cause is necessary to complete a task, the presence of one is taken to indicate the concurrent action of the other.

- **Weiner's model of achievement attribution** sees causal attributions for success or failure being a product of where an event lies along the dimensions of internal/external, stable/unstable and controllable/uncontrollable. These three dimensions produce different types of explanation for the event being explained.

- **Attributional biases** are distortions in perception or judgement concerning the causes of our own or other people's behaviour. These include the **fundamental attribution error** (FAE) (over-estimating the importance of dispositional factors), actor/observer differences (seeing the causes of others' behaviour in dispositional terms, but our own in situational terms) and **self-serving biases** (which internalize the causes of success but externalize the causes of failure).

Topic 2: Social perception

- **Social perception** involves the use of social schemata such as heuristics (problem-solving strategies which involve taking the most likely option) and categorization (categorizing incoming information into meaningful units).

- **Social representations** allow us to make sense of our social world and to communicate with others about social issues. They make up a 'common-sense' view of the world that is shared by most members of a group.

- Stereotypes are mental representations of a group and its members. Because they are often negative, **social and cultural stereotyping** may lead to prejudice and discrimination. Stereotypes may also serve an important cognitive function, in that by directing and guiding the encoding and retrieval of information, they save considerable cognitive effort.

Topic 3: Prejudice and discrimination

- Personality explanations of **prejudice** have explained prejudice as rooted in the individual. Adorno's 'authoritarian personality' model sees prejudice as one possible consequence of a particular type of socialization experience and the individual's subsequent reaction to it.

- **Realistic conflict theory** explains prejudice in terms of competition between groups, usually over some scarce resource. When groups are engaged in competitive and frustrating activities, each group develops negative stereotypes about the other group.

- **Social identity theory** explains prejudice as being a consequence of our search for positive self-esteem. This may be achieved by comparing our own group (the in-group) with other groups and their members (the out-group). In order to achieve a positive self-esteem, these comparisons tend to see the in-group as superior and the out-group as inferior, which can lead to **discriminatory** consequences for the out-group.

- Attempts to **reduce prejudice** have met with mixed success. Increased intergroup contact (**contact hypothesis**) may be successful if the contact is interdependent and cooperative, rather than competitive. Increased contact can help to reduce prejudice if it leads to the recognition of similarities between groups and if sufficient positive information is provided about the target group.

- Educational interventions to reduce prejudice have stressed the importance of cooperation (the jigsaw method) in pursuit of **common goals**, of reducing stereotypes and of providing direct experience of prejudice.

- Social identity theory suggests prejudice can be reduced by 'decategorizing' (concentrating on the individual rather than the category) and drawing the in-group and out-group together into a new superordinate category.

FURTHER RESOURCES

Hogg, M.A. and Vaughan, G.M. (2002) *Social Psychology* **(3rd edn), London: Prentice Hall.**

A comprehensive and readable text that covers all the issues in this unit in detail.

Moghaddam, F.M. (1998) *Social Psychology: Exploring Universals across Cultures,* **New York: W.H. Freeman.**

This text integrates a comprehensive coverage with fascinating insights about cultural diversity in social behaviour.

Pennington, D.C., Gillen, K. and Hill, P. (1999) *Social Psychology***, London: Arnold.**

An ideal extension text for the material in this unit.

Websites

http://www.socialpsychology.org

Social psychology network – a searchable database with links to lots of other social psychology sites on the web.

http://mentalhelp.net/psyhelp/

An interesting self-help guide, with Chapter 7 having a good section on explaining and reducing prejudice.

10

UNIT

Relationships

PREVIEW

After you have read this unit, you should be able to describe and evaluate:

>> explanations and research studies relating to interpersonal attraction

>> theories and research studies relating to the formation of relationships

>> theories and research studies relating to the maintenance and dissolution of relationships

>> psychological explanations of love

>> explanations and research studies relating to differences in relationships between Western and non-Western cultures

>> understudied relationships (such as gay and lesbian relationships, and 'electronic' friendships).

INTRODUCTION

If we think about the times in our lives which we associate with great happiness and great sadness, it is highly likely that the majority of them have involved other people. They might include falling in love, the loss of a loved one, the birth of children, the pain of a divorce or being told that our parents were splitting up. Even the significant moments in our personal histories which we might think of as personal triumphs or disasters (e.g. getting good A-level results, missing a critical volley in the final of a tennis competition) involve at least some social dimension (e.g. the class you studied with or your opponent in the tennis final). It follows from this that one of the most important aspects of psychology – and social psychology, in particular – is the study of the relationships that we have with others.

In the past, much research into relationships has focused on what we might call their 'bright' side – what Duck (1999a) disparagingly calls 'the deliriously cheerful emphasis on the delights of relationships'. He continues, however, to point out: 'Research of recent years has discovered the dark side of life generally and of relationships in particular, including consideration of ... relational anger and shame and the management of the daily routine relational hassles that we all experience or the drag of long-term relational obligations.' (Duck 1999a, p. 4)

We may define a *social relationship* as an 'encounter with another person or with other people which endures through time'. It is likely to be characterized by many features, such as expectations, responsibilities, rules, roles, and giving and taking. It may be institutionalized (as in the case of marriage). It may be permanent or impermanent, formal or informal. At least some of our relationships with others will constitute the most important aspects of our social lives.

So why do we engage in relationships? What do we get out of it for ourselves and what do we give to others? Why do we seek to begin some relationships and end others? What determines which are the relationships from which we derive the most, or least, satisfaction?

These are just some of the questions which psychologists have considered in their attempts to build general explanatory models of relationships and which you will consider in this unit.

Mike Cardwell
Paul
Humphreys

1 Friends occupy a particularly important role in our lives, but how selective are we when choosing our friends? What do we look for in a friend, and what do they give us in return? What would you say is the function of a friend?

2 Do you keep a profit and loss account in your romantic relationships? What were the profits and costs of your last relationship? How important is it that you get at least as much out of a relationship as you put in?

Matching hypothesis: proposal that people tend to select partners who are alike in terms of physical attractiveness, background, etc.

Sociobiological theory: the explanation of social behaviour in evolutionary terms, e.g. according to this theory, males place a high value on female physical attractiveness because youth and health indicate someone likely to produce healthy babies and so pass on the father's genes.

Reinforcement-affect model: the theory that we find people attractive (a) because they were around when positive things happened and so we associate them with feeling good, or (b) because they are themselves reinforcing, e.g. by being helpful and friendly.

Social exchange theory: an explanation of why some relationships continue while others end, based on the notion that people remain in relationships as long as the rewards of staying outweigh the costs.

Equity theory: proposition that people stay in relationships as long as they perceive them to be fair. Equity is not the same as equality. If one partner gives more in a relationship but also benefits more than the other person does, then the relationship may still be equitable.

Romantic (passionate) love: an intensely emotional state characterized by physical longing when object of passion is absent, joy when relationship is going well and anguish when it goes wrong.

Companionate love: the emotional state that combines feelings of affection and attachment characterized by mutual concern for each other – less intense than romantic love.

Collectivistic cultures: cultures that value group loyalty, prefer group to individual decisions and where the needs of the group outweigh the concerns of the individual.

Understudied relationships: relationships that have, until recently, received little attention by researchers, e.g. gay relationships, relationships formed via the internet.

Computer-mediated communication (CMC): interpersonal interactions over the internet, e.g. via e-mails and chat rooms.

EXPLANATIONS OF INTERPERSONAL ATTRACTION

ACTIVITY

Your experience of attraction

In your life you will have felt attracted to many people; some may have returned your feelings, others will not have. Think of three people whom you have felt particularly attracted to. What, if anything, did they have in common?

When you reach the end of this topic, ask yourself how well you feel the psychological explanations and research described match your subjective experience of being attracted to other people.

A filter model of attraction

Kerckhoff and Davis (1962) believed that people rely on a number of social and personal factors to filter potential relationships from the 'field of eligibles' (i.e. all those with whom we might potentially form a relationship). We narrow down this field through a series of selection filters. Different criteria tend to be used at different stages, beginning with social variables, such as ethnicity/race, class and religion. We then move to use internal values and then to personality traits to make our selection. Although we may seek similarity in social variables and values (e.g. we may be drawn to other Christian, vegetarian types), we may be attracted to personality traits that are complementary (rather than similar) to our own. Criteria shown to be important during this process include the following:

- *Proximity* – Physical proximity is perhaps the most obvious filter in initial attraction. Most people form relationships with other people who live close by. This is not surprising as physical proximity will influence who becomes aware of each other.

- *Similarity* – Social and/or cultural similarity is also thought to narrow down our 'field of eligibles'. It is more likely that people will talk to and come into contact with others of the same ethnicity, background, occupation, etc. Once this initial stage of filtering has taken place, people may shift to considering whether other people share similar attitudes. If they do, then the relationship is more likely to be pursued (Duck and Gilmour 1981).

- *Physical attractiveness* – Physical attractiveness plays a particularly important role in attraction. In their 'computer dance study', where couples had been supposedly randomly assigned to each other, Walster *et al.* (1966) found physical attractiveness to be the single best predictor of how much each person liked his or her assigned partner (see p. 309).

- *Complementarity of needs* – Although people may be initially drawn together because of their *similarity*, it may then become apparent that one has characteristics the other lacks and vice versa. Someone who is domineering may be attracted to someone who is submissive, while someone with a strong need to care may be attracted to someone with a strong need to be cared for.

- *Competence* – People tend to be more attracted to others who appear intelligent and competent than those who are less so. There is, however, the possibility that another person may appear to be *too* perfect. Aronson (1976) suggests that it is better to have one glaring fault which will make a person appear at least 'human'.

The matching hypothesis

Physical attractiveness and matching

We have already seen how important physical attractiveness is in initial attraction, yet people do not always gravitate towards the most attractive person available. According to the matching hypothesis (Walster *et al.* 1966), people are attracted to others who have a similar level of physical attractiveness to their own. Furthermore, we are likely to seek out people similar to ourselves in other attributes, such as intelligence, athleticism, etc. There are many possible reasons why we should be attracted to physically attractive people (e.g. there is a great deal of prestige to be gained in dating a physically attractive person), but there are also the potential costs of rejection from someone who does not see *us* as physically attractive. Self-esteem also affects this process. When a person is feeling low in self-esteem, it is more likely that they will target someone who is less likely to reject them. If, however, their self-esteem is high, then they may believe that no one will reject them and may target people that they might otherwise consider as being 'out of their league'.

The consequences of mismatching

Of course, there are plenty of couples who appear physically *mis*matched, but proponents of the matching hypothesis argue that such 'mismatched' couples balance out in other areas. However, in relationships where partners *are* mismatched, there are several possible consequences. The less attractive partner may feel insecure and jealous of the attention given to their partner, or the less attractive partner may feel unattractive compared to their partner. It follows, then, that mismatching may place strains on a couple and threaten the long-term success of that relationship.

THEORIES OF RELATIONSHIP FORMATION

Sociobiological theory

Sociobiology refers to the use of evolutionary ideas to explain the social behaviour of animals (Cardwell 1996). In non-human relationships, such as those found among insects or birds, much is genetically programmed. However, the further we move up the phylogenetic (evolutionary) scale, the less this appears to be the case. Some efforts have been made to explain in purely genetic terms aspects of relationships between people, such as lovemaking – usually called mating in this context! – and dominance.

Wilson (1975) argues that human sexual attraction and behaviour may be explained through an understanding of 'survival efficiency'. He argues that there is a 'bargaining' between men and women, which characterizes and defines their sexual relationships. It is, he says, in the 'interests' of the male to impregnate as many women as possible, as this increases the chances of his genes being handed down as copiously as possible into the next generation. The reasons for this lie in the vast number of sperm that a man is capable of producing in his lifetime.

Conversely, a woman may produce only one egg per month. Whereas the male is capable of fathering an almost infinite number of children in a relatively short period of time, the woman usually carries just one pregnancy at a time. The best chance of her genes surviving into the next generation is for her to ensure the healthy survival of the (relatively) few offspring that she is capable of producing during her reproductive lifetime.

Mormon multiple marriage: what does the man get out of this arrangement? And what about his five wives and 24 children?

Evaluation
sociobiological theory

- *Overemphasis on reproduction* – The above theory presumes that sexual attraction and behaviour is about reproduction. For many people, most sexual unions are not directed towards bearing children. Many people now elect to be childless. The theory also presumes heterosexuality. Explaining *homosexual* relationships in the same way is clearly problematic, as such relationships are not linked to reproductive advantages for either partner.

- *Evolutionary advantages* – This theory does, however, offer a plausible explanation for the evolution of specific mate preferences that exist today. In our evolutionary past, men who selected partners who were low in reproductive capacity would have experienced lower reproductive success than men who selected mates with 'peak' reproductive value. Likewise, women who selected men who were unable or unwilling to invest resources in their offspring, would experience lower reproductive success than those who placed a premium on these qualities (Buss 1995).

- *Supporting gender stereotypes* – There is an ethical concern that the sociobiological theory may be seen as supporting divisive gender stereotypes and endorsing behaviours which perpetuate the so-called 'double standard', allowing men sexual 'privileges' and freedoms which women are denied.

- *Lack of relevance in a modern world* – Some psychologists take the view that the old sociobiological explanation may once have suited male/female relationships, but that it would not necessarily suit those of today, or even that sociobiological needs have changed. For example, Lord (1997, p. 347) says:

  <<The world today ... is a far different environment than existed millions of years ago. In the past, it might have been adaptive for men to mate with every attractive woman and for women to prefer dominant men who controlled resources. It may not be as adaptive to do so today (Ickes 1993) ... It might have been effective in the past for men to acquire resources and women to stay home and feed babies. This division of labor may not be the most effective today (Eagly 1987). Both men and women in technologically advanced cultures can learn how to do both – amass resources and feed babies. >>

The reinforcement-affect model (Byrne and Clore 1970)

It is possible that the reason why we spend so much of our time in social relationships is that we find them rewarding (i.e. positively reinforcing) or that we find life alone unpleasant and unrewarding. This model tries to explain social relationships in terms of the influence (affect) that reinforcing behaviour has over us, using conditioning as its basis (see Unit 21). Other people may reward us directly (operant conditioning), perhaps by meeting our psychological needs, such as the need for friendship, love and sex, etc. Or perhaps they reward us indirectly (classical conditioning), in that they are associated with pleasant circumstances. Because some individuals are directly associated with reinforcement (i.e. they provide it), we like them more, and are more likely to enter into a relationship with them. If we meet someone when we are in a good mood (i.e. we are happy), we may associate that person with our good mood and therefore find them more attractive. If we meet someone when we are in a negative emotional state, however, and they help us to escape that state, we may associate them with negative reinforcement, which also increases both our liking for them and the likelihood that we would form a relationship with that person.

Argyle (1992) points out that individuals who are rewarding (because they are friendly, helpful and cheerful) tend to be liked most. Positive non-verbal signals, such as smiling, are signs of liking and are particularly important. A different way of looking at how relationships may be reinforcing is to consider how they may satisfy our social needs. Argyle (1994) has identified motivational systems which he claims are at the roots of social behaviour (see Table 10.1). Read through the table and think about how far you agree with Argyle.

Table 10.1 >> Human needs affecting social behaviour

Needs/motives	How relationships help meet needs
>> Biological needs	e.g. collective eating and drinking behaviours
>> Dependency	e.g. being comforted or nurtured
>> Affiliation	e.g. seeking the company and approval of others
>> Dominance	e.g. making decisions for other people, being 'bossy'
>> Sex	e.g. flirting, making love
>> Aggression	e.g. engaging in football violence
>> Self-esteem and ego identity	e.g. being valued by others

Source: adapted from Argyle (1994)

ACTIVITY

Your social relationships

Note down three important social relationships in which you are involved. Under each of the three, list the social needs you feel are met by these different relationships. In being explicit in this way and producing lists, you may be surprised at the similarities and differences in these relationships.

Evaluation
reinforcement-affect model

- *Giving and receiving reward* – Hays (1985) found that in examining student friendships, as much value was given to rewarding the other person as being rewarded oneself. The key factor was the totality of both giving and receiving, not merely the latter in isolation. Participants in relationships are often more concerned with equity and fairness in rewards and demands than with the desire to maximize their own benefits (see later section on equity theory, p. 314).

- *Limitations* – Many social relationships which are more commonly found in non-Western,

collectivist cultures show little concern for the receipt of reinforcements. For example, Hill (1970) showed that kinship bonds are very influential, resilient and are not dependent upon reinforcement. (See p. 325 for more on individualist and collectivist cultures.)

- *Gender differences* – There is evidence of gender as well as cultural differences. It has been shown that in many cultures women are socialized into being more attentive to the needs of others (such as husbands and children), rather than being oriented towards the gratification of their own needs (Lott 1994). It could be argued, of course, that this 'meeting the needs of others' might in itself be reinforcing.

RESEARCH STUDIES OF INTERPERSONAL ATTRACTION AND RELATIONSHIP FORMATION

Much of the psychological research into social and interpersonal relationships has focused on romantic relationships. This is not surprising, given that much of the research has been carried out in North America, where a high value is placed on romantic attachment as a basis for marriage and cohabitation. A number of specific factors have been investigated by researchers as possibly important in initial attraction and the subsequent formation of relationships.

Physical attractiveness

Many studies have shown that, in Western cultures at least, physical attractiveness is one of the major determinants of whether we express a wish to develop a relationship (romantic or platonic) with another person. See the Key research and panel above.

Frequency of interaction

Much of the early work into friendship and attraction (e.g. Festinger *et al.* 1950) emphasized the importance of proximity (physical/geographical closeness) and the frequency of interaction which is very often associated with this. A later study illustrated the power of familiarity which arises out of continued contact. Saegert *et al.* (1973) found that women who were simply in the company of certain other women as part of a series of drink-tasting studies, came to prefer them to those whom they met only once.

Why, according to psychological research, is it not unusual for relationships to form at work?

Matching and attraction

A study carried out by Murstein (1972) supports the matching hypothesis. In this study, photographs of the faces of 'steady or engaged' couples were compared with random couples (i.e. pairs of individuals who were only together for the purpose of the photograph). The real couples were consistently judged to be more similar to each other in physical attractiveness than the random pairs. Murstein summarized the findings of the study thus: 'Individuals with equal market value for physical attractiveness are more likely to associate in an intimate relationship such as engagement, than individuals with disparate values.'

KEY RESEARCH >> PHYSICAL ATTRACTIVENESS & RELATIONSHIPS

the computer dance studies (Walster *et al.* 1966)

In this study by Walster *et al.* (1966), known as the computer dance study, 752 'fresher' students at the University of Minnesota took part. They initially had to fill out a questionnaire. They were then told that on the basis of the data gathered from these, each student had been allocated an ideal partner for the evening of the dance. In fact, the pairings had been made at random (by a computer).

Unbeknown to the students, they had all been rated for their physical attractiveness. Students were asked how much they had liked their 'date' and how much they wanted to go out with them again. Physical attractiveness was the single biggest predictor of how much each date had been liked (by both males and females) despite having spent several hours in each other's company. The desire for another date was determined by the

attractiveness of the woman, irrespective of the attractiveness of the male. Clearly the males wanted the best lookers, whatever their own rating in the beauty stakes!

The original study was criticized for its lack of relevance for real-life relationships because people in North America are rarely assigned dating partners (unlike arranged marriages in some Asian cultures, as we shall see later). Consequently, Walster and Walster (1969) carried out another 'computer dance' study, but this time the students were able to meet each other first and state what kind of dating partner they wanted (in terms of physical attractiveness). This made a critical difference. This time the students chose someone of *comparable* physical attractiveness to themselves, supporting the matching hypothesis.

Similarity

There is considerable evidence to support the view that 'alikes' rather than 'opposites' attract. It would appear that similarity of values, attitudes, beliefs and ways of thinking are common indicators of strong friendships and attraction (e.g. Lea and Duck 1982).

In one survey study, it was found that the more similar a husband and wife, the more satisfied they tended to be with their marriage (Caspi and Herbener 1990).

Similarity in friendship and attraction

Researchers offered free accommodation to male students who were strangers to each other and who volunteered to let the researchers allocate them to their living quarters for the year. Students were randomly allocated a room mate. The most stable friendships developed between room mates who came from similar backgrounds and who shared similar attitudes (Newcomb 1961).

Boyden et al. (1984) found that gay men who scored highly on stereotypical male traits desired a partner who was most of all logical (a stereotypical masculine trait). On the other hand, gay men who scored highly on stereotypical female traits desired a partner who was expressive (a stereotypical feminine trait).

Rubin (1973) gives the following reasons for why we are attracted to those who are similar to us:

- We are 'drawn' to the possibility of engaging in the same activities.
- We seek social validation of our beliefs.
- If we like ourselves, it should logically follow that we will like others who are similar to us.
- It may facilitate communication if certain fundamentals are shared.
- We may presume that people who are similar to us will like us.

In arguing for the view that opposites attract, Kerckhoff and Davis's 'filter theory of mate selection' (1962) (see p. 306) takes a longitudinal view of relationships and contends that in the early stages of a relationship, similarity in values may be important, but in the later stages of an established relationship, complementary needs are more important.

The reinforcement-affect model

Some research has suggested that people may be liked (found rewarding) because they happen to be associated with something pleasant. For example, May and Hamilton (1980) asked female students to say how much they liked the look of male strangers whose photographs they had. While some students looked at the photographs, pleasant music was played. Others looked at the same photographs while unpleasant music was played. A comparison (control) group viewed the same pictures but no music was played. As predicted, the students who had heard the pleasant music while looking at the photographs liked the men best and rated them as better looking. This and many other experiments (e.g. Cunningham 1988) have shown that positive affect (feeling) can lead to attraction.

Suitability: advertising for a mate

How do people placing advertisements in the personal columns try to sell themselves and what do they look for in the responses they receive? Cameron et al. (1977) found that men tended to sell themselves on characteristics relating to status (e.g. income, job), whereas women mentioned physical appearance more often. Harrison and Saeed (1977) found that women stressed the need for sincerity and genuineness in replies and tended to seek dates with men older than themselves, whereas men sought attractive women who were younger than themselves. Much of this fits neatly with predictions from sociobiological theory (see p. 307). However, Koestner and Wheeler (1988) suggest that, at least in personal ads, people tend to offer the attributes that their culture suggests will be attractive to the opposite sex. Duck (1999) puts it thus:

'Advertisers have to present their positive side in a way that is easy to assimilate and economical in terms of space ... such needs encourage people to play concisely towards cultural norms and stereotypes ... they develop reasonably clear ideas about the sorts of cues that should be mentioned in ads.' (Duck 1999, p. 32)

A study by Dunbar and Waynforth (1995) found evidence of many of the predictions of sociobiological theory (see panel below).

Personal ads: what men and women say

Dunbar and Waynforth (cited in Dunbar 1995) analysed nearly 900 ads in four USA newspapers. Forty-two per cent of male advertisers sought a youthful mate, as opposed to only 25 per cent of female advertisers. Forty-four per cent of males sought a physically attractive partner, whereas only 22 per cent of women stated this. There were also consistent differences, again in line with sociobiological explanations, in how men and women tried to 'sell' themselves. In the wording of their ads, 50 per cent of women used terms such as 'pretty', 'curvaceous' and 'gorgeous', but only 34 per cent of males used comparable terms (such as 'handsome'). Men were more likely to advertise their economic status and earning power.

Dunbar and McGuiness (cited in Dunbar 1995) found similar outcomes when they analysed 600 ads in two London magazines. For example, 68 per cent of women advertisers described their physical attractiveness, compared to 51 per cent of the men. These results support those found by Cameron et al. (1977) and Harrison and Saeed (1977) described above.

Evaluation
attraction and relationship formation research

- *Artificiality* – Much of the research is highly artificial and 'leaves out most of the things people do in everyday life' (Duck 1999). In the case of some studies, the artificiality of the situation is so 'rigged' that physical attraction is all the participants had to go on.

- *Lack of emphasis on change and variability* – Much of the research, especially that carried out in the 1960s and 1970s, focused too heavily on snapshots of relationships (as if frozen at a moment in time). This takes insufficient account of change and variability. We all have bad days, even in good relationships.

- *The relative nature of personal characteristics* – No characteristics or attributes are absolute; all are relative. For example, a characteristic we find attractive in someone at one point in a relationship may be viewed negatively at another time. We may adore someone's unpredictability when we fall in love with them, but see it as irresponsibility as we fall out of love with them.

- *The influence of others* – By focusing upon the individual or the couple, a lot of the earlier research failed to take account of third parties, such as parents or friends, who may have enormous influence on whom we form relationships with. There needs to be clearer

recognition of the fact that relationships do not 'stand alone'. In the real world, as opposed to the psychology laboratory, all of us engage in several relationships simultaneously. In polygynous cultures, for example, a man will have sexual relationships with several wives concurrently. Even in monogamous Western cultures, this occurs when people have extramarital affairs.

- *Overemphasis on romantic relationships* – There has been too much emphasis on romantic relationships at the expense of cross-sex and same-sex platonic friendships, for example, which figure largely in the lives of most people.

- *Overemphasis on physical attractiveness* – Few of us would deny the importance of physical attractiveness but, equally likely, most of us will have encountered physically attractive people who repel rather than attract because of their vanity and self-obsession.

- *Does familiarity always lead to liking?* – Despite the wealth of supportive evidence showing the importance of familiarity, there does appear to be ambivalence about the direction of the effect. Do we like people more because we spend time with them, or do we spend more time with them because we like them? Frequency of interaction does not always lead to greater liking. Warr (1965) demonstrated that it can also produce more disliking. Thus it may be that frequency of interaction results in greater intensity of feelings between people, but that these feelings may be either positive or negative.

CHECK YOUR UNDERSTANDING

Check your understanding of attraction and the formation of relationships by answering these questions. Do it from memory at first. You can check your answers by looking back through Topic 1.

1 What is the central proposition of the filter theory of attraction?

2 Identify five criteria used by people to 'narrow down the field of eligibles' in initial attraction.

3 What is the central proposition of the matching hypothesis?

4 What, according to the matching hypothesis, are the possible consequences of 'mismatching'?

5 Much of the research on attraction was carried out in the 1960s and 1970s. Why does this present a problem for our understanding of attraction in 2004 (and beyond)?

6 Construct a descriptive 150-word précis of sociobiological theory as an explanation of the formation of relationships.

7 Identify three critical (i.e. AO2) points relating to sociobiological theory as an explanation of the formation of relationships, and explain *why* these pose problems for the theory.

8 What is the link between need satisfaction and the formation of relationships?

9 Briefly describe one study relating to the reinforcement-affect theory of relationships, and explain how this supports the specific assumptions of that theory.

10 Identify three critical (i.e. AO2) points relating to reinforcement-affect theory as an explanation of the formation of relationships, and explain *why* these pose problems for the theory.

REVISION SUMMARY

Having covered this topic you should be able to:

✓ describe and evaluate at least two explanations relating to interpersonal attraction

✓ describe and evaluate research studies of interpersonal attraction, and use these studies effectively as AO2 commentary on each of the explanations studied

✓ describe and evaluate at least two theories relating to the formation of relationships

✓ describe and evaluate research studies of the formation of relationships, and use these studies effectively as AO2 commentary on each of the theories studied.

EXAMPLE EXAM QUESTIONS

Below are some **possible examination questions** set on this topic, along with hints to help you understand and approach each question effectively:

1 Describe and evaluate **one or more** explanations of interpersonal attraction. (24 marks)

> There is a general rule when setting exam questions that the injunction 'describe' is used when asking for one explanation and 'outline' when asking for more than one. In this case you are invited to write about 'one or more' This is very much your choice, as full marks are available for a good answer that is restricted to just one explanation. A 'good answer' would probably be about 600 to 700 words in length, half of which is description and half evaluation. If you feel that you cannot write 300 words describing your chosen theory, then you have the option of writing about a second or even third theory. If you do describe several theories, there is no requirement to evaluate them all.

2 Discuss psychological research (explanations **and/or** studies) into interpersonal attraction. (24 marks)

> The term 'research' here allows you to use either explanations *or* studies *or* both in your answer. In this question, the actual explanations are not specified. The matching hypothesis appears as an *example* in the specification, but cannot be asked for in a question. A question could say '(for example, matching hypothesis)', but even then you don't have to include the matching hypothesis. 'For example' means what it says – this is a possible example. You may use studies as a means of evaluating your explanations or vice versa. In this essay, AO2 marks are determined by the way that material is *used* – either descriptively or as commentary.

3 (a) Outline **two** explanations of interpersonal attraction. (12 marks)

   (b) Assess the **two** explanations of interpersonal attraction you described in (a) in terms of relevant research studies. (12 marks)

> What is required in part (a) is a précis of two explanations of interpersonal attraction. Part (b) requires more than just a *description* of relevant research studies; it requires an evaluation of your chosen theories *using* those research studies. Both explanations must receive this treatment, otherwise you would be demonstrating 'partial performance', and would lose marks.

4 Critically consider **two** theories of the formation of relationships. (24 marks)

> The term 'critically consider' is an AO1 + AO2 term. The AO1 component is clearly a description (or probably just an outline) of two theories, but the AO2 can include criticisms, research support, cultural variations, implications, etc., provided these are *used* as part of your AO2 commentary on the two theories rather than just being described in their own right. It is important to restrict your answer to theories of formation and not consider those related to maintenance or dissolution, though knowledge of the latter kinds of theory might be used as part of your commentary.

5 Describe and evaluate research studies relating to the formation of relationships. (24 marks)

> Questions may specifically be asked about 'research studies' if this phrase appears in the specification. The number of research studies is up to you. In this unit there are research studies provided for each theory, but the more studies you attempt to describe and evaluate, the less detail you can provide for each.

MAINTAINING RELATIONSHIPS

Many studies of relationship maintenance assume that the people involved are committed to the survival of the relationship. The problem of this assumption is highlighted by a study carried out by Ayres (1983), who was also concerned with the strategies people use to maintain their relationships. The study showed that strategies vary according to the direction the people want the relationship to move in:

● *Avoidance strategies* tended to be used by a person who is resisting an attempt by the other to change the relationship. They might pretend that the other

person's concerns are mistaken or trivial, or they might just refuse to talk about them at all (e.g. 'It's just all in your imagination, there's nothing wrong').

● *Balance strategies*, such as putting in more or less effort, were used by those who wanted a relationship to change. The level of effort depended on the desired direction of change.

● *Directness* usually involved talking about issues and was generally associated with a desire for the status quo.

THEORIES OF RELATIONSHIP MAINTENANCE AND BREAKDOWN

How you maintain relationships

As we noted at the beginning of the unit, even the best relationships have their 'dark' moments. Think of the ways in which you have worked on relationships to ensure that they are maintained and survive. What strategies did you use? Which ones have been the most successful? Did you find that you had to use different strategies for different people/relationships?

Two of the most influential theories which have been used to help us understand why we maintain certain relationships and close others down are 'social exchange theory' and 'equity theory'. They are known as 'economic theories' of social relationships.

Since their introduction in the late 1950s, economic theories have been highly influential and have generated a great deal of empirical research. They are so called because they assume a view of social relationships analogous to economic activity, such as cost/benefit analysis: What do I gain? What do I lose? What do I give? What do I receive?

Economic theorists argue that we run our relationships according to a balance sheet principle – we aim to maximize our gains or profits, and minimize our losses. The majority of economic theories are exchange theories because they employ a metaphor of typical marketplace activity where we haggle/negotiate and try to drive the best bargain we can. We exchange the rewards we give to others for the ones that we wish them to give to us, whilst at the same time trying to 'stay ahead' (receiving more than we give). Blau (1964) argued that our social interactions are 'expensive' (they

take energy, time, commitment and other 'valuable', finite personal resources) and so what we get out of the relationships must at least pay us back in equal amount (but preferably give us a profit).

Social exchange theory

This was the first of the economic theories and was developed by Thibaut and Kelley (1959).

Profit and loss – the payoff matrices

The theory was concerned with the construction of so-called 'payoff matrices'. These are the calculations of the possible activities a couple could engage in and the profits and losses for each person for all the possible permutations of activities. Thibaut and Kelley believed that individual members of a relationship (a particular type of social exchange) were motivated to maximize their rewards and minimize their costs. Possible rewards include companionship, being cared for, sex, etc. Possible costs include effort, financial cost and missed opportunities. For a successful relationship, according to this model, rewards minus costs should result in a positive outcome for each individual.

Comparison levels

On the basis of this, Thibaut and Kelley proposed a four-stage model of long-term relationships (see Table 10.2). They also recognized the importance of influences beyond an analysis of the relationship itself (called the 'reference relationship'). They introduced two 'reference' levels: comparison level (CL) and comparison level for alternatives (CL alt):

● *CL* is concerned with the past and the present; that is, the comparison between the rewards and costs of the reference (current) relationship and what we have been used to in the past. If the reference relationship compares favourably, we are motivated to stay in the relationship.

Table 10.2 >> Thibaut and Kelley's four-stage model of long-term relationships

1 **Sampling**   The couple explore the rewards and costs in a variety of relationships.

2 **Bargaining**   The couple 'cost out' the relationship and identify sources of profit and loss.

3 **Commitment**   The couple settle into a relationship. The exchange of rewards becomes relatively predictable.

4 **Institutionalization**   The interactions are established. The couple have 'settled down'.

Source : adapted from Thibaut and Kelley (1959), Kelley *et al.* (1983)

● *CL alt*, on the other hand, is concerned with possible alternative relationships. Here we compare the reference relationship with others which we could be in. If we feel that we could do better in another relationship, we may be motivated to finish the current one.

The social exchange model was modified in several respects by Homans (e.g. 1974) and a major redrawing of social exchange theory began to take shape, which eventually resulted in equity theory.

Equity theory

Equity theory assumes that people strive to achieve fairness in their relationships and feel distressed if they perceive unfairness (Messick and Cook 1983). Unlike social exchange theory, where individuals are seen as trying to maximize their rewards and minimize their costs, in equity theory it is *inequity* in relationships that is seen as having the potential to create dissatisfaction. People who contribute a great deal in a relationship and receive little in return would perceive inequity, as would those who *receive* a great deal and give little in return. Both of these relationships would be perceived as inequitable, and would have the same consequence

for both partners – dissatisfaction. Note that equity does not necessarily mean equality; rather it refers to balance and stability. Furthermore, equity may be defined by each member of the social relationship or by outsiders, and these definitions may, of course, differ. Walster *et al.* (1978) offered four principles of equity theory:

● People try to maximize their rewards and minimize negative experiences within any relationship.

● The distribution of rewards is negotiated to ensure fairness. This may be achieved through trade-offs or compensations (i.e. a 'favour' or 'privilege' for one person is paid back by an equivalent favour/privilege).

● Unfair (or inequitable) relationships produce dissatisfaction. Not surprisingly, the dissatisfaction is felt more acutely by the 'loser', and the greater the degree of perceived unfairness, the greater is the sense of dissatisfaction.

● As long as the 'loser' feels there is a chance of restoring fairness and is motivated to save the relationship, he or she will endeavour to re-establish equity. Furthermore, the greater the degree of inequity the loser perceives, the greater will be the effort at realignment.

KEY RESEARCH >> MAINTENANCE & DISSOLUTION OF RELATIONSHIPS

the investment model of relationships (Rusbult 1983)

Caryl Rusbult (1983) found that when people were deciding whether to end a relationship, not only did they weigh up the rewards and costs of the relationship and the possible alternative relationships available to them, but they also considered how much they had invested in the relationship. She defines investment as 'anything a person puts into a relationship that will be lost if they leave it'. This may include such things as possessions, children's welfare and emotional energy. To test this hypothesis, Rusbult asked college students in heterosexual relationships to complete questionnaires over a seven-month period. They kept notes about how satisfactory their relationship was, how it compared with possible alternatives and how much they had invested in it. Students also noted how committed they felt to the

relationship and whether it had ended. The graph in Fig. 10.1 shows the results.

We can see, therefore, that satisfaction, comparison and investment all contributed to commitment and to break-up. High satisfaction and investment are important in committed relationships. The existence of an attractive alternative features large in deciding to end a relationship.

More recently, Rusbult and Martz (1995) applied this model to abusive relationships. They asked women who were living in refuges why they had stayed with abusive partners instead of leaving as soon as the abuse began. As predicted by the model, women had felt the greatest commitment to their relationship when their economic alternatives were poor and when their investment was great.

Satisfaction with relationship

Comparison level for alternatives available

Level of investment in relationships

Figure 10.1 >> *Factors that contribute to a committed relationship versus a relationship breakdown*

Evaluation
economic exchange theories

AO2

- *Contrived methodologies* – Many of the studies associated with exchange theories have been characterized by rather contrived methodologies, which have little ecological (real-world) validity. Argyle (1988) points out that social exchange theory 'has led mainly to very artificial experiments ... Research on real-life relationships has been hampered by the difficulty of scaling rewards' (p. 224).

- *Emphasis on short-term relationships* – The majority of techniques that have been used to test exchange theories have been short term and did not examine the dynamics of relationships through time (i.e. only fairly immediate effects and consequences were identified). See, however, the relatively longitudinal study of Rusbult in the Key research panel to the left.

- *Lack of consistent empirical support* – For example, Clark and Mills (1979) have identified two different styles of couples: the 'communal couple' and the 'exchange couple'. In the former, giving is motivated by concern and positive regard for the other; only in the latter is there the kind of 'score-keeping' predicted by exchange theory. People in communal relationships do

have some concerns over equity, but they are more relaxed over what it comprises. They tend to think that in a relationship, rewards and costs eventually balance out and equity is achieved.

- *Limited application of equity theory* – For example, Hatfield *et al.* (1979) showed that equity might be more important for females than for males, and Murstein *et al.* (1977) also showed that equity is an issue of concern only in 'problematic' marriages. Both of these factors (i.e. gender and 'health' of relationship) were confirmed as important more recently in a longitudinal study of 736 married couples, carried out by Van Yperen and Buunck (1990).

- *Cultural bias* – Work carried out in societies other than North America tends to give little support for equity theory. For example, Lujansky and Mikula (1983) found no equity effects upon romantic relationships in Austria, while Gergen *et al.* (1980) found that whereas American students preferred equity (a constant ratio of rewards to inputs), European students preferred equality. Moghaddam *et al.* (1993) argue that the emphasis on exchange and equity is a reflection of the dominant values of North America, where these theories of social relationships were developed. They claim that these theories reflect the highly individualistic, capitalist and Protestant work ethic of North America.

RESEARCH INTO MAINTENANCE STRATEGIES

Important research into maintenance strategies has been done by Dindia and Baxter (1987) – see panel below.

Maintenance strategies (Dindia and Baxter 1987)

Dindia and Baxter interviewed 50 married couples and asked about their maintenance strategies. Partly because of the nature of the questions asked and partly because of the behaviours of the couples, two types of strategies emerged: maintenance and repair. Repair strategies are those used to make good damage. Maintenance strategies may be likened to preventive medicine.

Dindia and Baxter identified a total of 49 different strategies. The maintenance ones (e.g. 'spending time together in the evenings', 'talking about the day', 'telephoning when I'm away') tended to focus on doing things together, whereas the repair strategies (e.g. 'talking over the problem' or 'issuing an ultimatum') tended to focus on the nature or mechanics of the relationships itself, and thus were more inward-looking and analytical. There were interesting differences in the responses given by the couples that had been married for long periods compared to those who had only recently married. The former reported using fewer maintenance strategies than the relatively newly-wed couples. There are a number of possible explanations for this:

- It may be related to the beneficial effects of familiarity (knowing the other so well) – a lot of the groundwork will already have been done and the relationship will 'run itself'.

- There may be a negative 'taking-for-grantedness' in the relationship.

- It may be an issue of awareness: perhaps the long-term partners are so used to the relationship and the things that they do within it, that maintenance becomes 'second nature' and somewhat invisible to them. For this reason, it was not reported to the researchers.

THE ENDING (DISSOLUTION) OF A RELATIONSHIP

The ending of a relationship can be one of the most emotionally demanding times of our lives. We must, however, be mindful of the different needs of the people in the relationship. The end of a relationship may be a catastrophe for some, but for others it can be a liberating restart. It can also be the case, that a relationship ends even though both partners wish it to continue or even develop (e.g. lovers thwarted by parental prohibition, geographical separation or the death of one of the partners).

Why do relationships break down?

ACTIVITY

Your experience of relationship endings

Think of the relationships in which you have been involved and which you ended. Were there common reasons or was each one different?

Now think of relationships which the other person ended. Were there common reasons or was each one different? If there was a common reason, what does this tell you about yourself?

Causes of relationship dissolution

There are many reasons for relationships ending. Some of those studied by psychologists are listed in Table 10.3.

Table 10.3 >> Reasons for relationships ending

- >> conflict (overt disagreement or dispute over an issue such as financial priorities)
- >> breaking agreed rules (e.g. about confidentiality, support, fidelity)
- >> dissatisfaction or boredom with the relationship
- >> lack of stimulation or novelty
- >> an attractive alternative relationship (see exchange models)
- >> costs outweighing rewards (see exchange models)
- >> perceived changes in the relationship (for example, one partner believing that they no longer share key common interests)
- >> interference from other relationships
- >> problems of abuse (e.g. alcohol, sexual, monetary)
- >> changes in self or other person
- >> falling out of love
- >> saving face (e.g. finishing a relationship before the other person does).

Duck (1981) suggested that causes for relationships breaking down can be divided into two categories:

- *predisposing personal factors*, such as distasteful personal habits or emotional instability
- *precipitating factors*, such as:
  - exterior influences on breakdown (e.g. a rival)
  - process/behavioural/management features (e.g. incompatible working hours)
  - emergent properties of relationships that cause decline (e.g. 'the relationship was going nowhere' or 'it just got too intense')
  - attributions of blame (e.g. 'what went wrong?', 'who was to blame'?).

Why might incompatible working hours be a precipitating factor in relationship breakdown?

Maintenance difficulties

Like many other things in life, a healthy relationship requires constant maintenance. For some people, it is the difficulty of maintaining a satisfactory relationship that eventually leads to its breakdown. In some circumstances, relationships become strained simply because partners cannot maintain close contact. Living and working apart, going away to university and other situations where the day-to-day maintenance strategies become more difficult, place a great strain on existing relationships (Shaver *et al.* 1985). Whilst we all hope that our romantic, and indeed other relationships, should be strong enough to survive the pressures of decreased daily contact, it is evident that for many this is not the case.

Rule violation

Argyle and Henderson's (1984) research on the 'rules' of friendship provided insight into those aspects of rule violation that are particularly relevant to the breakdown of friendships. In their research, they asked people to think of a friendship that had lapsed for reasons that might be attributed to the relationship itself (rather than maintenance difficulties). They then asked participants to rate the extent to which any failure to keep friendship rules had contributed to the breakdown of that relationship. The specific rule violations discovered to be most critical in relationship breakdown included:

- jealousy
- lack of tolerance for a third-party relationship
- disclosing confidences
- not volunteering help when needed
- criticizing the person publicly.

A model of relationship dissolution (Duck 1988)

Duck (1988) has developed a four-phase model of the termination of close or intimate relationships:

1 *Intra-psychic phase* – This is where one of the partners or friends becomes increasingly dissatisfied with the relationship. If the dissatisfaction is sufficiently great there is 'progression' to the next phase.

2 *Dyadic phase* – Here the other person becomes involved. If the dissatisfaction is not acceptably resolved, there is progression to the next phase.

3 *Social phase* – This is where the break-up is 'aired' and made public, for example to friends and family. It is also where the social implications (such as care of children) are negotiated. If the relationship is not saved here (perhaps by the intervention of family), it goes to the final stage.

4 *Grave-dressing phase* – Here the ex-partners begin the organization of their post-relationship lives and begin publicizing their own accounts of the breakdown and what (if any) is the nature of the new relationship with the ex-partner. Partners who develop their own versions of where the blame for breakdown actually lies, frequently employ the self-serving attributional bias (see Unit 9, p. 280).

Stages in the breakdown of relationships (Lee 1984)

From a survey of 112 break-ups of premarital romantic relationships, Lee (1984) discovered evidence for five distinct stages, illustrated in Fig. 10.2.

Lee found that exposure and negotiation tended to be experienced as the most intense, dramatic, exhausting and negative aspects of the whole experience, although in some cases individuals missed out these stages and simply went direct from D to T (i.e. they just walked out). Those who took this direct route to termination reported having felt less intimate with their partner even when the relationship *was* satisfactory.

On the other hand, those who reported a particularly long and drawn-out journey from D to T reported more attraction for their former partner and experienced the greatest loneliness following the break-up.

1 Partners discover that they are *dissatisfied* with the relationship.

2 Dissatisfaction is then *exposed*.

3 Exposure of dissatisfaction may lead to *negotiation* with the other partner concerning the nature of the dissatisfaction.

4 Attempts are made to *resolve* the problem.

5 If attempts to resolve the problem fail, the relationship is *terminated*.

Figure 10.2 >> *Five stages in the breakdown of relationships*

ACTIVITY

Expert interview

Read the Expert interview given by Steve Duck on p. 319 and then consider:

1 Duck's views on the differences between Western and non-Western relationships

2 how the close social networks found in non-Western cultures might affect what happens when relationships are threatening to break down

3 whether your observations or own experiences lead you to agree with the research findings about sex differences in the reasons for relationships breaking down.

Evaluation
research into relationship dissolution
AO2

● *Similarities between the models* – Duck's and Lee's views of relationship breakdown share some similarities, with both seeing breakdown as a *process* that proceeds through a number of stages before termination, rather than seeing it as a single step. The main difference between the two models is one of emphasis. In Lee's model there is more emphasis on the early stages of the process, particularly on the painful stages of exposure and negotiation. In Duck's model there is more focus on the beginning and end of this process, with particular emphasis being placed on how people might react after the relationship is over.

● *Rule violation* – Argyle and Henderson's research discovered some important individual differences with regards tolerance of rule violation in friendships. Women identified lack of emotional support as a critical factor in dissolution, whereas men thought absence of fun was of greater importance. Younger participants (late teens and early 20s) attributed more importance to being criticized in public, whereas older participants (early 30s) felt lack of respect was more important.

● *Research in non-Western cultures* – Moghaddam *et al.* (1993) believe that Western and non-Western relationships are dominated by different concerns and features which would affect the dissolution process. They argue that North American relationships are predominantly individualistic (concerned with the needs of the self rather than those of a broad group of people), voluntary (rather than determined by kin or family) and temporary (with the majority of relationships able to be terminated). Conversely, most non-Western relationships are collective, obligatory and permanent.

● *The impact of relationship dissolution* – Akert (1992) found that the role people played in the decision to end the relationship was the single most powerful predictor of the impact of the dissolution experience. Akert discovered that the partners who did not initiate the break-up tended to be the most miserable, reporting high levels of loneliness, depression, unhappiness and anger in the weeks after the termination of the relationship. Those who initiated the break-up of the relationship found the end of the relationship the least upsetting, the least painful and the least stressful. Although they did report feeling guilty and unhappy, they had fewer negative symptoms compared to partners who were less responsible for the break-up of the relationship.

The dissolution of **relationships**

Steve Duck was born in Keynsham and studied psychology at Oxford University (MA) and Sheffield University (PhD) before teaching at Glasgow and Lancaster Universities. In 1986, he was invited to take the Daniel and Amy Starch Distinguished Research Chair at the University of Iowa in the USA and has been there ever since. He has published approximately 40 books on friendship and relationships, was the founding editor of the Journal of Social and Personal Relationships *and was the first President of the International Network on Personal Relationships.*

Q Western relationships are generally represented as being temporary and non-Western relationships as more permanent. Is this an unjustified generalization or a fair reflection of real and enduring cultural differences?

A Western and non-Western relationships are generally regarded as being based on different philosophies: individualism in the first case (freedom to seek individual gratifications) and collectivism in the second (attention to group membership and responsibilities). In the West, the main feature of romances nowadays is freedom of choice. In non-Western cultures, there is more emphasis on duty to parents, obligations to family and obedience to authority, so they are given less freedom of choice in their romantic relationships. However, there is also a considerably lower divorce rate in those cultures (about 1 per cent) whereas in the West it is closer to 50 per cent. In views about friendship, the West emphasizes choice, 'value-for-money', convenience and abandoning friendship bonds when these criteria are no longer met. Non-Western cultures place more emphasis on loyalty, duty and sticking things out through thick and thin.

Steve Duck

Q You are well known for your model of relationship breakdown (see p. 317). Has research justified your faith in this model?

A Not exactly, though I still believe in the basic framework. I still like the focus on extended processes of breakdown, but the original model left out the importance of communication. For example, in the Dyadic process, communication is localized to 'partner talks' or talks about 'our relationship', and so the partners withdraw from discussion with friends and acquaintances to spend time talking things out together. So, researchers should find not only that the amount of time spent with people outside the dyad declines sharply, but also that the discussed topics focus on the relationship rather than outside.

Q Would you regard this as a 'universal' model of relationship breakdown or does it only apply to Western relationships?

A I do not really know if it works anywhere but in the West. One of my PhD students, Masahiro Masuda, did a good thesis on relationships after a break-up and he thought it was relevant to his culture (Japan) but there are ways in which it works differently. In cultures that emphasize collective group responsibility more than in the West, there are many subtle differences in the way that the social network plays a role in breakdown of relationships: for example, the social network offers more relational support to help the couple work through problems, and also it may exert closer scrutiny that prevents problems getting out of hand.

Q Has research demonstrated significant sex differences in the main reasons for relationship breakdown?

A This depends on the kind of relationship that we are thinking about. Broadly speaking, research shows that men and women have different approaches to love relationships, with men placing more emphasis on the beginning of a relationship and women thinking further ahead to the way in which they develop. In respect of the breakdown of relationships, women have been shown to pay more attention to relationship details than men do and to be more sensitive to the ways in which it may be failing to live up to expectations. But the reasons given for breaking up relationships are pretty much the same in both sexes: boredom, betrayal, incompatibility and better alternatives.

PSYCHOLOGICAL EXPLANATIONS OF LOVE

Romeo and Juliet, Antony and Cleopatra, David and Victoria Beckham – all legends of love. But what, exactly, do we mean by the term 'love'? Beall and Sternberg (1995) say: 'It is difficult, if not impossible, to answer the question 'What is love?' because any answer must reflect its time, period and place.' Lord (1997) traces the history of love, in its various and changing socially acceptable forms all the way back to Athenian Greece and Ancient Rome, but we can be fairly confident that it will have been a characteristic of human life since the dawn of our species' existence. And yet, as we shall see, even at the dawn of the twenty-first century, what people understand by the term 'love' and how they interpret its experience vary considerably.

> « Most North Americans believe that romantic love is natural, desirable and necessary for marriage. However, most Chinese words for love have negative connotations: infatuation, unrequited love, sorrow. In China ... romantic love is viewed with some suspicion, as illicit and socially disruptive. »
> (Smith and Mackie 2000, p. 447)

Even within a particular relationship, the expression and form of love may – and almost certainly does – change. Relatively early stages may be characterized by feelings of sheer exhilaration in the presence of the other, perhaps even panic at barely being able to control one's feelings and perspiration levels! But the fireworks of passionate sex may be replaced by the contentment of lifelong partnerships, and intimacy and exchange which may be more psychological than physical.

Romantic and companionate love

Hatfield and Walster (1981) differentiate, as many other psychologists have done since then, between *passionate* (or *romantic*) love and *companionate* love. Hatfield (1987, p. 676) puts it thus:

> « Passionate love is an intensely emotional state and confusion of feelings: tenderness, sexuality, elation and pain, anxiety and relief, altruism and jealousy. Companionate love, on the other hand, is a less intense emotion, combining feelings of friendly affection and deep attachment. It is characterized by friendship, understanding, and a concern for the welfare of the other.»

Hogg and Vaughan (2002, p. 513) give the following account of romantic love which really seems to capture its essence:

> « ... thinking of the lover constantly, wanting to spend as much time as possible with him or her and often being unrealistic in judgements about the lover. This usually results in the lover becoming the focus of the person's life, to the exclusion of other friends. It is perceived as a very intense emotion,

and, moreover, one over which the individual has very little control. »

Liebowitz (1983) showed that the physiological arousal associated with passionate (romantic) love is comparable to the 'rush' of excitement produced by such drugs as amphetamine and cocaine. Furthermore, 'withdrawal' symptoms may also be comparable. Perhaps it is possible to understand Romeo and Juliet at a physiological level too!

Contrast all of this with what Lord (1997 p. 354) says about companionate love:

> « [It] is fueled by rewards and positive associations. People who are in companionate love enjoy intimacy and care about each other's wellbeing. They want to get close to each other, to explore similarities and differences in their personal histories, values, hopes and fears. They reveal themselves to one another, feel responsible for each other, and quietly display their gentle, tender feelings for each other. »

Companionate love is committed and intimate

Hatfield and Walster's (1981) three-factor theory of love

According to Hatfield and Walster (1981), three factors need to be present for us to 'fall' in (romantic) love:

● *Physiological arousal* – Schachter and Singer's (1962) classic studies have shown that, in certain circumstances at least, emotions are determined by a general arousal state which the individual then interprets by 'referring' to external factors or cues.

We may feel angry or sexually aroused, according to this explanation, depending on whether we are in the presence of an enemy or a desired lover – even though the physiological arousal itself may be very similar in both situations. The term 'being turned on' seems to fit this component very nicely!

- *Appropriate love object* – Feeling aroused is all very well, but in order to fall in love (as opposed to being merely 'turned on'), we need a recipient for our desires. Feelings of passion and arousal may disappear quite rapidly unless we have someone appropriate to direct them towards. People may be inappropriate for many reasons: we may find them not attractive enough (or too attractive! – refer back to the matching hypothesis); they may already be committed to someone else; they may be of an inappropriate class or caste.

- *Cultural exposure* – Our culture needs to have a model of love for us to use in order to make sense of our experience (many non-Western cultures do not). These cultural beliefs point our attention and perceptions in certain directions. One tends to see what one is looking for. Research has shown that the more you think about love, the more likely you are to fall in love (Tesser and Paulhus 1976), and the more you believe in there being such a thing as 'love at first sight', the more likely it is that it will happen to you (Averill and Boothroyd 1977).

Figure 10.3 >> *Sternberg's triangle of love*

Passion
the hot point of love, e.g. arousal, intense feelings, physical attraction, sexual consummation

Intimacy
the warm point of love, e.g. close and bonded feelings, helping, depending on, supporting, caring and sharing

Decision/ commitment
the cool point of love – a deliberate choice about loving, and staying with, someone

Sternberg's 'Triangular theory of love'

According to Sternberg (1986, 1988), types of love are determined by three points of a triangle (see Fig. 10.3). When love has only passion, we often refer to it as 'infatuation'; when love has only intimacy, we may think of it as 'liking'; and when love has only commitment, it may be seen as 'contractual' or 'economic/market love'.

Sternberg identifies another kind of love, 'consummate love', which occurs when all three of the above operate. Hogg and Vaughan (2002) show how, by combining the points of the triangle in different ways, different types of love can be identified (see Table 10.4). Problems clearly will arise when, for example, one person experiences romantic love for another, who feels only companionate love for them.

Table 10.4 >> Hogg & Vaughan's variations of love

	Passion	Commitment	Intimacy
>> *Infatuation*	Present	Absent	Absent
>> *Empty love*	Absent	Present	Absent
>> *Liking*	Absent	Absent	Present
>> *Fatuous love*	Present	Present	Absent
>> *Romantic love*	Present	Absent	Present
>> *Companionate love*	Absent	Present	Present
>> *Consummate love*	Present	Present	Present
>> *No love*	Absent	Absent	Absent

Hendrick and Hendrick's six styles of love

Hendrick and Hendrick's (1986) model focuses on the types of love styles that people enter relationships with:

- *Game-playing* – treating love like a game, a sport or a competition
- *Possessive* – trying to tie the partner into a long-term relationship
- *Logical* – treating love as a practical, logical decision-making process
- *Altruistic* – making sacrifices; putting the other person's happiness above your own
- *Companionate* – sharing loving affection and friendship which develops over time
- *Erotic* – desiring hedonism and sexual pleasure.

Research has shown that real-life couples show much similarity in their love styles and that lasting romantic relationships scored high on erotic love, but low on game-playing (Hendrick and Hendrick 1992).

Now try the following activity.

Sub-cultural differences in love styles in the USA

Hendrick and Hendrick (1986) studied differences in the frequency with which men and women were positively disposed to, and displayed such love 'styles' in the USA in the mid-1980s. Using their six styles of love, try and predict the sex biases they found. We can think of gender differences as an example of sub-cultural differences (i.e. differences within a culture, such as the USA, as opposed to differences between two or more cultures). Other examples of sub-culture differences include class and ethnicity.

Answers to the activity are given on p. 337.

Evaluation
psychological explanations of love

- *Sternberg's typology of love* – One of the limitations of Sternberg's theory was that it identifies a particular type of love, but does not explain how this developed in the first place. In order to do this, he extended his theory to take account of the 'stories' that people develop concerning what they believe love should be (Sternberg 1998). Sternberg interviewed college students about their romantic expectations and identified 25 common stories that people use to describe love. These included the fairy-tale story ('love is a story about a prince and a princess'), and the gardening story ('any relationship that is left unattended will not survive'). When he applied this analysis to couples, those with similar profiles tended to be more satisfied than those with less similar profiles.

- *The prototype approach* – Fehr (1988) argued that much of the confusion in trying to define love has arisen from the search for a classical definition which may not actually exist. Some researchers, rather than following the theoretical 'top-down' approach adopted by Sternberg, Hendrick and Hendrick (and others), have taken a 'bottom-up' approach to determine the nature of love. One such technique, the prototype approach, involves collecting data directly from people about their knowledge and beliefs concerning the nature of love. Fehr (1988) asked one group of participants to list the characteristics of 'love' and a second group to rate how central each feature was to the concept of love. Features that her participants believed were central or 'prototypical' to love included: trust, respect, concern for the other's well-being, loyalty and commitment. Features that were considered peripheral or unimportant to the concept of love included: seeing only the other's good qualities, uncertainty and dependency.

- *Reconciling the two approaches* – Aron and Westbay (1996) extended Fehr's work by exploring the underlying structure of this prototype of love. They found evidence that the prototypic love features identified by participants in Fehr's study could be reliably reduced to three dimensions that resembled those in Sternberg's triangular love typology: passion, intimacy and commitment. This suggests that the experiences of many men and women do indeed reflect the three basic dimensions proposed by Sternberg.

Commentary
differences in love between cultures

- *How universal is romantic love?* – In the West, we have become accustomed to the idea that one should marry for love, and that falling out of love is a prerequisite for the dissolution of a relationship. As non-Western societies become more industrialized and individualistic, the percentage of people who believe that love should precede marriage has also increased (Moghaddam 1998). There are still differences, however, with one study of young people in 11 countries revealing that a higher percentage of people in collectivist cultures (such as Pakistan and India) were willing to marry someone who had all the qualities they desired but whom they did not love (LeVine *et al.* 1995).

- *Love and sexual motivation* – Psychological writings abound with the notion that sexual motivation is a key human drive that influences much of our thinking and behaviour (think of the Eros instinct in Freudian psychology, for example). In the Dani society of western New Guinea, however, there is indifference to sexual activity (Heider 1976). Premarital and extramarital affairs are rare, and married couples usually wait about two years after marriage before having intercourse.

REVISION SUMMARY

Having covered this topic you should be able to:

✓ describe and evaluate at least two theories relating to the maintenance of relationships

✓ describe and evaluate research studies of the maintenance of relationships, and use these studies effectively as AO2 commentary on each of the theories studied

✓ describe and evaluate at least two theories relating to the dissolution of relationships

✓ describe and evaluate research studies of the dissolution of relationships, and use these studies effectively as AO2 commentary on each of the theories studied

✓ describe and evaluate at least two psychological explanations of love.

EXAMPLE EXAM QUESTIONS

Below are some **possible examination questions** set on this topic, along with hints to help you understand and approach each question effectively:

1 Outline and evaluate **two or more** theories relating to the maintenance of relationships. (24 marks)

> Whatever theories you choose in response to this question, you must stress the maintenance of relationships rather than their formation or dissolution. There is no minimum or maximum requirement for a specific number of theories, but the more theories you attempt to describe and evaluate, the less detail you can provide for each. Both breadth and detail are important for high marks so you must balance them – not too much breadth and just enough detail to demonstrate your knowledge and understanding. If you only present one theory, your marks are restricted by the partial performance criteria maximum of 8 out of 12 marks for AO1.

2 Discuss psychological research (theories **and/or** studies) into the maintenance of relationships. (24 marks)

> The term 'research' here allows you to use either explanations or studies, or both, in your answer. If you choose to discuss explanations only, then your answer could be the same as the one to question 1 above. If you choose to include research studies as part of your AO1 content, then you must also offer some AO2 evaluation for these studies. Alternatively, you might use your research studies as part of an evaluation of your explanations. Any description of studies will be credited as AO1. Any explanation as to what these studies show us, or criticisms of the studies will be credited as AO2.

3 (a) Outline **two** theories relating to the dissolution of relationships. (12 marks)

  (b) Evaluate the **two** theories relating to the dissolution of relationships you described in (a) in terms of relevant research studies. (12 marks)

> What is required in part (a) is a précis of two theories of the dissolution of relationships; a précis is not simply a shortened version, but a short account that focuses on carefully selected, essential points. It is useful to practise writing such précis: prepare a 15-minute description of each theory and a $7\frac{1}{2}$-minute version. Part (b) requires more than just a description of relevant research studies, it requires an evaluation of your chosen theories using those research studies. Both theories must receive this treatment, otherwise you would be demonstrating 'partial performance', and would lose marks.

4 Discuss research (theories **and/or** studies) relating to the dissolution of relationships. (24 marks)

> The term 'discuss' allows for a much more discursive and wide-ranging response to this question. The AO1 component is clearly a description (or probably just an outline) of theories and/or studies of the dissolution of relationships, but the AO2 can include criticisms, research support, cultural variations, implications, etc., provided these are used as part of your AO2 commentary on the two theories rather than just being described in their own right. It is not enough to offer a linking sentence such as 'the theory can be criticized by contrasting it with another theory, such as ...' and then to go on and describe the second theory. Any features of the second theory that you introduce must be used as commentary on the first theory (e.g. you might look at similarities and differences).

Check your understanding of the maintenance and dissolution of relationships by answering these questions. Check your answers by looking back through Topic 2.

1 What is the main difference between 'avoidance' and 'balance' strategies of relationship maintenance?

2 Why are social exchange and equity theory known as 'economic' theories of relationships?

3 What is the main difference in emphasis between these two theories?

4 Identify four evaluative points relevant to economic theories of relationship maintenance.

5 Identify five reasons why relationships have been shown to break down.

6 Put these phases of relationship dissolution into the correct order: Social, Grave-dressing, Intra-psychic, Dyadic.

7 In Lee's model of relationship breakdown, what do the letters D E N R T stand for?

8 Distinguish between 'romantic' and 'companionate' love.

9 What kind of love is characterized by commitment and intimacy but no passion?

10 Is romantic love a universal phenomenon?

Topic 3 >> Cultural and sub-cultural differences in relationships

Sub-cultural differences are those which are found within a particular culture, society or country. In contemporary Britain they include, for example, differences between:

● men and women

● homosexuals and heterosexuals

● Asians, African-Caribbeans and Whites

● old and young.

Culture has been defined by Hofstede (1994) by way of a computing analogy when he says it is 'the collective programming of the mind which distinguishes one group or category of people from another'. It also 'travels' through time and physical distance (although cultural values do, of course, change too) to provide relatively stable sets of values and rules by which people live their lives. Culture may be largely 'land-locked' within a particular country, especially before the advent of modern travel and communication, or it may not be (such as with Jewish culture).

DIFFERENCES IN RELATIONSHIPS: EXPLANATIONS & RESEARCH

Moghaddam *et al.* (1993) contend that whereas social relationships in Western cultures tend to be individualistic, voluntary and temporary, those in non-Western cultures tend to be collective, obligatory and permanent. It follows from this distinction that a great deal of what we have just been considering is simply not applicable or relevant to non-Western cultures. Moghaddam and colleagues go on to say:

《The cultural differences in interpersonal relationships remind us that scientists, like everyone else, are socialized within a given culture. As a result, their theories and research are inevitably affected by this cultural experience. The cultural values and environmental conditions in North America have led North American social psychologists to be primarily concerned with first-time acquaintances, friendships, and intimate relationships, primarily because these appear to be the relationships most relevant to the North American urban cultural experience.》 (p. 103)

They suggest that in non-Western cultures where people cannot enter and leave relationships at will, key questions might be very different indeed.

Categorizing cultures

Let us begin our journey into cultural and sub-cultural differences in relationships by examining how different cultures may be classified.

In some of the largest studies ever carried out in the social sciences, Hofstede (between 1980 and 1994) analysed data on work experience from over 100 000 employees, working in 50 different countries. On the basis of the analysis, he contended that over half of the variance between countries was accounted for by four dimensions:

1 Individualism/collectivism

In individualistic cultures, the emphasis is upon the individual person and his or her rights, goals, behaviours, etc. Individual performance and achievement are praised, while dependence on others is not seen as particularly desirable. People in individualist cultures strive for autonomy and there is emphasis on the 'I' rather than the 'we'. When there is conflict between the individual and the collective (e.g. the group or the family), individual desires are deemed more important by the individual. In contrast, collectivist cultures value the 'we' over the 'I'. Ties between, and responsibilities to, collective units (e.g. the family or the community) are seen as more important than the desires of particular individuals. Thus, for example, a marriage is seen as a union between families as much – if not more – than between individuals.

What is it that makes some cultures individualistic and others collectivist? Goodwin (1999) offers the following possibilities:

- *Economic wealth* – In affluent countries there are likely to be many avenues for individuals to pursue personal economic security and autonomy, whereas in poorer countries people may have to pool resources far more and be more dependent upon others. More developed (and probably richer) countries may have broader social networks and geographical freedom to roam; this may lead to individuals moving away from pre-existing community groups.

- *Religion* – The ancient Eastern philosophy of Confucianism puts a very high value upon collective harmony and wellbeing, whereas Christian churches may put more emphasis on individuals making their own unique relationship with God.

- *Geographical proximity* – Individualism and collectivism each tend to cluster globally. Amongst other factors this may be related to climate. For example, Hofstede (1994) argues that in colder climates, survival may be largely down to individual initiative.

2 Power-distance

This concerns the extent to which members of a culture accept that power in an organization or institution should be distributed unequally between its members. High power-distance cultures are characterized by a belief that power is properly vested in formal positions which reflect status differentials. People in low power-distance cultures believe that power should only be deployed when it is necessary and can be justified. Individualistic cultures tend to be low on power-distance, and collectivist cultures high.

3 Masculinity and femininity

Even cultures can be sexed/gendered. Hofstede (1983) describes masculine cultures as reflecting 'a preference for achievement, heroism, assertiveness and material success', as opposed to feminine cultures which show 'a preference for relationships, modesty, caring for the weak and the quality of life'.

4 Uncertainty avoidance

This reflects 'the extent to which members of a culture feel threatened by uncertain or unknown situations' (Hofstede 1994). In high uncertainty-avoidance cultures, there is emphasis on consensus, predictability and planning. There tend to be clear and explicit rules for dealing with deviance from acceptable behaviour. In low uncertainty-avoidance cultures, unpredictability and 'voyages into the unknown' are viewed with curiosity and interest, rather than with fear and apprehension.

Bond (1988), working with Chinese social scientists, found a fifth dimension that emerged from his analysis: *Confucian dynamism*. This tends to be characteristic of collectivist cultures and concerns long-term perspectives, perseverance, strict social ordering, thrift and a sense of shame in the context of social responsibility to one's self and others.

Based on Hofstede (1994), Goodwin (1999) gives us the following table on the highest- and lowest-scoring countries on the five cultural categories (see Table 10.5).

Table 10.5 >> Highest- and lowest-scoring countries according to five cultural categories

	Individualism/ collectivism*	Power-distance	Masculinity/ femininity**	Uncertainty avoidance	Confucian dynamism
>> *Highest three countries (in order)*	USA Australia Britain	Malaysia Guatemala Panama	Japan Austria Venezuela	Greece Portugal Guatemala	China Hong Kong Taiwan
>> *Lowest three countries (in order)*	Guatemala Ecuador Panama	Austria Israel Denmark	Sweden Norway Holland	Singapore Jamaica Denmark	Pakistan Nigeria Philippines

* Individualism scores high; collectivism scores low. Therefore, USA was most individualistic; Guatemala was most collectivist.

** Masculinity scores high; femininity scores low. Therefore, Japan was most masculine; Sweden was most feminine.

- *Origin of research* – Apart from Confucian dynamism, the categories have been based on concepts which have emerged largely from Western research.
- *Nature of the categories* – Schwartz (1997) has been critical about the 'purity' of the categories. He argued that there are many variations within, as well as between, cultures.
- *Situational variables* – The model can be said to fail to account sufficiently for situational or contextual variables. We can be individualistic in certain situations and collectivist in others (Schneider *et al.* 1997).
- *Individual differences* – Tables such as Table 10.5 focus on the statistical average of people's responses within a particular culture, but there is considerable room for individual variation and diversity (Cha 1994).

Voluntary and involuntary relationships

Marriage 'arrangements' around the globe range from those where partners have no choice whatsoever in whom they marry, to those where the choice is totally determined by the partners themselves. Rosenblatt and Anderson (1981) contend there are few societies characterized by such extremes; the majority have variable characteristics of both. While many Western countries subscribe to the 'Cupid's arrow' model of love (we 'fall' in love; it is something that 'happens' to us), in many non-Western, collectivist cultures the marriage is seen as a match between families.

It is worth noting, however, that in Western cultures people increasingly say that it is important to love someone before marrying them. Simpson *et al.* (1986)

compared responses to the question: 'If a man (woman) had all the qualities you desired, would you marry this person if you were not in love with him (her)?' The biggest changes were between the first two samples for both men and women. In 1967, just over 60 per cent of men responded 'no'; the figure rose to over 80 per cent in 1976 and then fell back slightly in 1984. Slightly over 20 per cent of women responded 'no' to the question in 1967. By 1976, this figure had approximately quadrupled, and further increased (slightly) in 1984 by which time men and women responded almost identically (Hogg and Vaughan 1998).

However, the most common form of marriage partner selection worldwide is by arrangement, with parents having the most significant say, although family and friends are also often influential (Ingoldsby 1995). There is considerable variation in how much weight is given to the views of the potential partners themselves.

The bride-price and dowry systems

In two-thirds of the world's societies, a man (or his family) must pay (a bride-price) to marry a woman (Stephens 1963). It is particularly common in Africa where the bride's family are paid by the groom's family 'in return for her labour and reproductive powers' (Goodwin 1999). Mwamwenda and Monyooe (1997) found huge support (88 per cent) for the bride-price system amongst Xhosa-speaking graduate students in South African universities. It was seen as a statement of appreciation by the groom about the value of the bride and her dignity.

The dowry has been a feature of arranged marriages in Europe and some Asian cultures. Here the bride brings gifts with her from her family, often to help 'set up' the new home. This is seen as an exchange for the groom's earning power. Dowries often operate in societies which have traditionally accorded relatively low status to women.

Women from an African bride's family count the items that will contribute to her dowry

Marital choice among British Asians

How, if at all, do British immigrant families adapt their cultural values and lifestyles to those of their new society? The results of some interesting research are summarized below:

- In a study looking at Sikhs, Hindus and Muslims living in Britain and Canada, it was found that the practice of arranged marriages was common. Marriages were determined by families and intermediaries, with the chief criteria being caste, social class and religion. Asian parents were particularly protective of daughters and this was leading to cross-generational conflict as the young people in the Westernized cultures valued individual partner choice far higher than their family (Ghuman 1994).

- Hindus and Sikhs were more likely to accept arranged marriages than Muslims.

Permanent or impermanent? The issue of divorce

Almost all cultures have provision for divorce, although there is greater stigma attached to divorce in cultures with traditional arranged marriages. Betzig (1996) studied divorce in 160 countries and found that the most common grounds for divorce (in descending order) were:

- infidelity (particularly women's rather than men's)
- sterility
- cruelty and/or maltreatment (usually of the husband towards the wife).

Other writers have argued that economic and social developments are the factors which put most strain on marriages. Changes in the roles of women have led to increases in divorce rates in many cultures (McKenry and Price 1995).

There is considerable cross-cultural variation in reasons for marital breakdown and divorce. The following are some of those discussed by Goodwin (1999):

- In Poland, where divorce rates are low compared to most of Europe, it is usually women who file for divorce, mainly due to maltreatment caused by husbands' alcohol abuse.

- In African societies, such as Ghana and Nigeria, social and economic changes such as industrialization, increased urbanization and greater education for women have led to increases in divorce rates (McKenry and Price 1995).

- In Saudi Arabia, a man does not have to give a reason for divorcing his wife, but the wife can only initiate a divorce if this is specifically stated in their marriage contract. After divorce, the children remain with the father who stays in the family house. The wife returns to her parents' house (Minai 1981).

- In China, the divorce rate is very low (less than 4 per cent) and carries shame for both parties and the family. This is a clear example of collectivist cultural values in operation.

In a historical analysis, Simmel (1971) argues that individualism is associated with higher divorce levels as it encourages the individual constantly to seek their ideal partner.

How does the Chinese emphasis on collectivist cultural values explain this family set-up?

Sub-cultural differences in relationships

Work by many psychologists has demonstrated clear and consistent class differences in relationships in Britain. Argyle (1994) includes the following:

- Friendship is more important to the middle classes than the working classes, for whom there is more emphasis on kin.

- Differences in the nature of friendship: 'Middle-class friends have similar interests and attitudes, and come from work, leisure groups, voluntary work or other activities. Working-class friends are chosen more because they live nearby and can provide help when needed, they form tight-knit groups with neighbours, and see each other in social clubs and pubs.' (p. 157)

- Middle-class marriages are more symmetrical with more shared friends and leisure and decision-sharing.

- Middle-class families are more child-centred, with the father playing a more significant part than in working-class families.

- Working-class families are more authoritarian in child-rearing practices, whereas middle-class families are more egalitarian.

Evaluation
research into Western and
non-Western relationships
AO2

● *Voluntary or involuntary relationships?* – In those societies where geographical and occupational mobility is limited, 'non-voluntary' (arranged) marriages seem to be the accepted alternative to Western voluntary relationships. But how common are arranged marriages? In a study of 70 Hindu Gujarati couples living in Leicester, it was found that only 8 per cent had completely 'arranged' marriages. Three-quarters had been introduced by a third-party and had been given the option of refusing their partner. Often they had met each other at large social events (although they had been given little opportunity for close interaction). Hindu Gujaratis, in fact, had a considerable choice about the timing of their marriage (Goodwin *et al.* 1997).

● *Permanent or impermanent relationships?* – The shift to more non-permanent relationships in the West is relatively recent. Fifty years ago divorce was relatively rare in the West, but with greater urbanization and mobility, the impermanence of relationships has become a feature of urban societies. The collectivist/individualist dimension in this area is well illustrated in a study by Brodbar-Nemzer (1986) of more than 4,000 Jewish households in

New York. He asked participants about their denomination (orthodox or liberal); their behaviour (e.g. attending synagogue) and their friendship networks (the proportion of their closest friends who were Jewish). He found a strong link between Jewish commitment and disinclination to divorce, attributing this to a stronger sense of social integration and more favourable attitudes towards the family found in the more 'committed' members of the Jewish community.

● *Communication difficulties in cross-cultural research* – For example, literal translations of studies may fail to take into account differences in emphasis or nuance, which can often be important.

● *Cultural bias in research* – There is a danger of making cross-cultural psychology just 'doing psychology in exotic places', i.e. taking issues and phenomena which are of interest to (dominant) Western psychology and seeing if they replicate in other cultures. Clearly this agenda-setting takes no account of what is important in that 'other' culture. Kim and Berry (1993) address this problem with a call for indigenous psychologies, which study factors that have developed/emerged within particular cultures and are seen as important and functional to those cultures (rather than risking a psychology of North American self-interest).

UNDERSTUDIED RELATIONSHIPS

Gay and lesbian relationships

This section does not aim to address the question: what makes a person homosexual? This is because no one really knows – it is highly likely that there are multiple factors (Garnets and Kimmel 1991). It is also important to avoid anything that encourages thinking of any kind of sexuality other than heterosexuality as a 'deviation from the norm'. How many people who are straight have been asked what makes them heterosexual or why they are not homosexual? The converse, however, is a common and recurrent event for many gays and lesbians. Furthermore, unlike most ethnic minority groups, gays and lesbians often grow up surrounded by negative stereotypes held about them by their own families and friends.

Homosexuality is still illegal in many countries in the world today and only as recently as 1973 was it removed from the DSM. It is still a part of the ICD (see Unit 24) . However, there are certain cultures where homosexual practice is positively encouraged (although often only in certain, prescribed situations),

and there have been historical periods, such as that of the classic Greco-Roman civilization, where homosexuality was considered quite normal practice. Things are not that easy for gay men and lesbians, even in the liberal West at the turn of a new century. Many politicians and people in the public eye (such as entertainers) have had their careers effectively ruined on being 'outed' (Humphreys 1997).

Forming gay and lesbian relationships

One great difficulty for gay men and lesbians, then, is recognizing each other. A practical solution lies in venues aimed specifically at gay clients, such as cafés, pubs and bars. These exist in every major town and city, and can serve many functions:

<< Some [gay men] are there to meet with friends. Some are there to drink, make new friends and conversation. Others are there for sex. Some passively observe the environment while others actively participate in it. Whatever the reason one goes to a gay bar, there is common ... excitement in

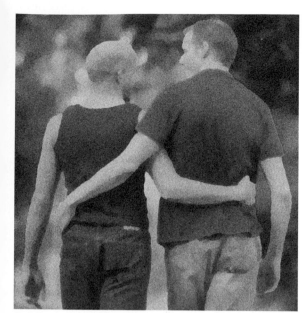

Public signs of affection between gay couples may be met with disapproval or even abuse from onlookers

the fact that it is one of the few places in society where by their mere presence all patrons can be assumed gay. » (Shaw 1997, pp. 136–7)

Women face an additional problem when trying to form a same-sex relationship. Women have been socialized into being more *reactive* than *proactive* in relationships, meaning that neither woman may feel comfortable making the first move.

Personal advertisements in newspapers and contact magazines are a source of information concerning what men and women offer to a potential same-sex partner, and what they seek in return. Gay men appear to seek specific physical attributes in a partner (attractive face, athletic body) and may also value many of the 'status symbols' (e.g. a well-paid or 'masculine' career) that go with the male role in Western cultures (Davidson 1991). Lesbians are more likely to emphasize personality characteristics than physical appearance, although more recently many lesbians have begun to value self-sufficiency and strength in a long-term partner (Huston and Schwartz 1995).

Maintaining gay and lesbian relationships

We have already seen that there are a number of strategies used by partners to maintain a healthy interpersonal relationship. For lesbian couples these include a high degree of emotional intimacy and an equitable balance of power (Eldridge and Gilbert 1990). For male couples, these include minimal conflict and high appreciation of the partner (Jones and Bates 1978).

Conversation as a maintenance strategy tends to be used differently by gay and lesbian partners. For women in same-sex relationships, conversation is used to establish and maintain intimacy between the two

partners. Aspects of communication that act as barriers to the building of intimacy (such as challenges) are avoided. For men in same-sex relationships, conversational challenges are frequently used as a way in which one partner might get his own way over his less powerful partner (Huston and Schwartz 1995).

Difficulties faced by same-sex partners

Homosexual people occasionally do not 'correct' people's assumptions about their not being heterosexual and instead conceal their sexuality. Concealing a homosexual identity is also known as being 'closeted'. As gay men and lesbians do not differ in appearance from straight people, they are usually presumed to be heterosexual and are treated as such. This invisibility also allows them to pretend to be heterosexuals – an invaluable survival strategy at times and sites of political intolerance (such as Hitler's Nazi Germany). However, concealment may come at a great cost. Gay men and lesbians who do this have to 'seal off' and hide away whole sections of their lives and, if partnered, live in constant dread of being discovered.

For many gay men and lesbians, it is a lose/lose situation. If they are 'out', they may be marginalized and rejected. If they are not, their invisibility will also be problematic. They will not be able to share the joys of openly loving and being companionate, which heterosexuals can enjoy. This will carry many additional burdens such as:

- being thrown back on the constant support and sympathy of the (hidden) partner
- the fear of being 'outed' – whether deliberately or by accident (e.g. a confidant lets something slip)
- family members and friends' unrealistic expectations about the possibility of their developing heterosexual relationships.

For obvious reasons, many gay men and lesbians choose to spend most of their social lives in the company of other gay people, but for those who have children, this option in not so easily available. They have to negotiate a world of schools and child-orientated networks. In all of this they are faced with the task of safeguarding the integrity of their living arrangements, protecting their privacy and also being supportive to the needs of their child(ren).

« Those who are involved in shared custody arrangements with a former heterosexual spouse often face the realistic danger of having the courts remove their children from their custody if the true nature of their relationship is exposed. The problem of maintaining secrecy in families in which a gay or lesbian parent is not out is complex. » (Greene 1994, p. 15)

Difficulties of forming and maintaining gay and lesbian relationships

Among the pressures experienced by gay people that may affect their relationships are:

- the psychological effects of growing up in a (heterosexual) society that characterizes homosexuality and lesbianism as unacceptable
- the way few happy and successful gay relationships are presented by the media – gay characters tend to be secondary to the plot (unless it is a 'gay drama') and gay relationships are often presented as superficial, unstable or problematic
- difficulties in personal counselling if one turns to a professional for help – Markowitz (1991) says that many therapists will impose female/male models on gay/lesbians as there are no equivalents for same-sex pairs. Peplau (1991) lists a number of commonly heard stereotypes about gay/lesbian couples, e.g. that they are incapable of sustaining a long-term relationship and experience inferior versions of heterosexual relationships. Greene (1994) says 'such stereotypes are tenaciously held by many therapists despite the absence of any credible evidence to support them'.

Greene (1994, p. 10) sums up the position:

>> Many [gays and lesbians] endure painful isolation from their families of origin who do not accept their identity, as well as the painful process of rejection that often precedes it. They face internalized homophobia in themselves, which can negatively affect their psychological adjustment ... 92 per cent of lesbians and gay men report being targets of anti-gay verbal abuse or threats, and ... 24 per cent report physical attacks, of which some result in death (Herek 1989). Both lesbians and gay men face the realistic potential for physical abuse and violent attack (gay bashing) that can be life threatening. >>

Commentary

AO2 — differences between gay and straight romantic relationships

- *Emotional intimacy* – Nardi and Sherrod (1994) argue that the avoidance of emotional expressiveness is actually a characteristic of heterosexual males, socialized into heterosexual masculinity. Nardi and Sherrod's research found no differences between levels of openness and self-disclosure in the same-sex relationships of lesbians and gay men.

- *Heterosexual bias* – Much of what we know about personal relationships is based on assumptions that are more appropriate to heterosexual relationships than those between same-sex partners. This has resulted in a relative ignorance about relationships that fall outside this heterosexual research bias (Griffin 2002).

- *Public vs private* – Straight couples can openly show their affection (and celebrate their 'coupledom') in public, e.g. by kissing or holding hands. Such public signs of affection between same-sex couples may be met with disapproval or even abuse, so few gay couples dare to try it except in 'safe' contexts, such as gay-only or gay-friendly venues, or among friends.

- *Shared social worlds* – Despite the differences between the social worlds of heterosexual and homosexual couples, there are many areas where there is a considerable overlap. Indeed, many lesbians and gay men live happily in relationships in what is a predominantly heterosexual world, although this is sometimes achieved by their 'pretending' to be, or being taken for, heterosexual. However, in an age of greater tolerance, it is increasingly the case that gay and straight couples are able to live side by side with mutual respect for each other's relationships and enjoyment of each other's company – without anyone feeling the need to keep up false pretences about their sexuality.

- *After the relationship is over* – Research suggests that, unlike heterosexual couples, lesbians and gay men are more likely to remain friends after a relationship has finished (Nardi 1992). Although there is relatively little research in this area, it does suggest that the distinction between platonic and sexual relationships is not the same for lesbians and gay men as it is for heterosexual couples. For the latter, sexual intimacy is likely to end a friendship, whereas for lesbians and gay men, sex is more likely to lead to continuing friendship (Nardi 1992).

Electronic friendships and computer-mediated communication (CMC)

To start this section, read the case study of 'Joan' in the panel on the next page.

Computer-mediated communication (CMC) includes all types of interpersonal interaction over the internet. It can take many forms, such as e-mail, virtual notice boards, chat rooms, e.g. IRC (Internet Relay Chat), and the relatively sophisticated MUDs, MOOs and MUSHs. These are computer programs where users assign themselves a character and then are able to navigate around a metaphorical building or neighbourhood, instigating conversations and joining in – or just listening to – on-going discussions in the 'rooms'.

'Joan'

'Joan ... was a New York neuropsychologist in her late twenties, who had been severely disfigured in a car accident that was the fault of a drunken driver. The accident had killed her boyfriend. Joan herself spent a year in the hospital being treated for brain damage which affected both her speech and her ability to walk. Mute, confined to a wheelchair, and frequently suffering intense back and leg pain, [she] had at first been so embittered about her disabilities that she didn't want to live. [Then she was given] a computer ... to be used specifically to make friends online.

'... Joan could type ... and she had a sassy, bright, generous personality that blossomed in a medium where physicality doesn't count. Joan became enormously popular ... Over the next two years, she became a monumental online presence who served both as a support for other disabled women and as an inspiring stereotype-smasher to the able-bodied. Through her many intense friendships and (in some cases) her online romances, she changed the lives of dozens of women.

'Thus it was a huge shock when, through a complicated series of events, Joan was revealed as not being disabled at all. More to the point, Joan, in fact, was not a woman. She was really a man ... a prominent New York psychiatrist in his early fifties engaged in a bizarre, all-consuming experiment to see what it felt like to be female, and to experience the intimacy of female friendship.' (Van Gelder 1985, cited in Lea and Spears 1995, pp. 197–8)

Shocked? Most people are. Leaving aside the appalling ethics of what the American psychiatrist did, this case study tells us a good deal about CMCs. Perhaps Cherny (1998) put it best when she said 'what you see is what I say'.

Behind the guise of a computer, you can be whoever you want to be

ACTIVITY

Your experience of CMC relationships

Are you a regular computer-user and e-mailer? Think of someone you have both a face-to-face and CMC relationship with:

- How differently do you interact with the person in these two modes?
- Are there things you say in e-mail or via online that you would not say face-to-face (or vice versa)?
- Is e-mail easier or harder than face-to-face talk?

CMC relationships can be contrasted with face-to-face (FtF) or corporeal relationships. The term 'corporeal' emphasizes physicality, one of the things that CMC most clearly does not have, as the case study of Joan illustrates so dramatically. Online interaction is performed in an environment that is mostly text based. This means that many of the dimensions that characterize FtF relationships (such as body language and eye contact) are absent in CMC relationships. CMC allows for both 'synchronous' (users are online at the same time and can read and respond to messages immediately) and 'asynchronous' communication. With asynchronous CMC (such as e-mails) users read and respond to messages at different times. Lenhart *et al.* (2001) found that a significant proportion of American teenagers claim that the internet helps their relationships with their friends, or helps them make new friends. Lenhart and her colleagues also found that a substantial proportion of teenagers use instant messaging to maintain relationships with their friends, with a significant number having used instant messaging as a way of starting or finishing a relationship.

The nature of internet relationships

CMC is generally seen as being inferior to FtF communication because it offers communicating partners fewer cues to work with when developing a relationship. 'Reduced cues theory' (Culnan and Markus 1987) claims that CMC filters out important aspects of communication that participants in FtF communication have access to (e.g. intensity, volume and body language), leaving a conversation in a 'social vacuum'. The reduced cues available to each partner in the communication may lead to deindividuation (a lack of individual identity), which in turn undermines social and normative influences, leading to uninhibited behaviour. Because CMC lacks the norms and standards that regulate FtF behaviour, users can become more aggressive and impulsive when communicating with others. Examples of such 'deregulated' behaviour include 'flaming', in which the writer attacks another participant (perhaps by the use of profanity or excessive use of capitals and exclamations) that would not typically happen in FtF interaction. In CMC interactions, participants may feel less connected to the interaction and so are less concerned about their detachment from it. They may, for example, abruptly exit a conversation or deliberately ignore others who are trying to communicate with them.

Commentary
AO2 differences between CMC and FtF relationships

- *Creating a good impression* – Physical appearance has been shown to be very important in interpersonal attraction, particularly for romantic relationships. However, in CMC interaction, a person's impressions of an online partner are based instead upon whatever information the partner has chosen to reveal about themselves. The impression created is therefore likely to be more positive than if the interaction had occurred offline.

- *Asynchronous communication* – In contrast to the synchronicity of FtF communication, asynchronous modes of CMC, where there are delays between communications, allow partners more time to reflect upon and prepare their messages at their own pace. As a result, CMC partners may be able to communicate in a more socially desirable and effective manner than is possible in FtF interactions, thus further improving their self-presentation to their partners.

- *Entrainment* – For FtF relationships to be effective, the partners have to engage in 'entrainment', the synchronization between partners of their activities in order to be co-present. The entrainment necessary to maintain a FtF relationship can be both inconvenient and challenging to the partners. In CMC, losing the need for entrainment may provide partners with a sense of personal space and control over their relationship. This may be particularly attractive for those who avoid intimate relationships through fears of losing their freedom. CMC relationships may be attractive to them because they are free to engage and disengage when they want to (Cooper and Sportolari 1997).

Initiating relationships

CMC offers an unusual opportunity in the initial stages of relationship formation, in that individuals can maintain much more control over their self-description and representation. Sprecher and McKinney (1987) claimed that the most common obstacles to beginning a relationship are traditional sex roles (women are socialized into being more *reactive* than *proactive* in initiating relationships), shyness, and lack of confidence in one's physical appearance. In CMC, because self-representation is entirely within one's own control, some of these barriers appear to be diminished. A study of an online matchmaking service found that patterns of relationship initiation among online users were indeed different in this medium (Scharlott and Christ 1995). CMC was found to have a beneficial effect on all three barriers to relationship initiation.

Sexual relationships on the internet

CMC also provides a context for *sexual relationships*. A Wired Top 10 survey carried out in 1994 of the ten most populated chatrooms created by America On-Line (the biggest provider in the USA) showed that three were gay, one was lesbian, one was 'swingers or groups' and the remaining five were heterosexual. CMCers also have one-to-one sexual relationships online, exchanging sexual banter and simulating sex. 'Julie' (*Marie-Claire* 1993, p. 26) said:

>> Typing back and forth is as far as I want to go for now. I'm a lot bolder than I would be in person; I'd never do that kind of talking face-to-face, or get into any of my fantasy roles. What I enjoy is that they'll never know who I am, yet we can talk about the most personal and specific things. >>

Gay men and CMC

Shaw (1997) interviewed twelve gay men about their CMC. Some were interviewed by Internet Relay Chat, others by e-mail, others by telephone. He says: 'While my sample does not purport to be statistically significant, my research role ... afforded me the opportunity to establish a bond of trust with the users (and produced) some keen insights.' Most of the men said they averaged 10 to 15 hours per week on IRC.

He draws the following intriguing parallels between CMC and the (corporeal) gay bar (see pp. 328–9).

>> Entering the (online) community via the gaysex channel, users find themselves in a large 'room' with as many as 70 other gay men. Not all of the men ... are contributing to the dialogue: some 'lurk' (observing and waiting for the right moment to join it), and some 'whisper' (sending private messages to one another). For those participating in the dialogue there is political talk ... GIFs (electronically scanned photographs sent over the internet) being exchanged, advice seeking, and just about everything else imaginable. As texts scroll up their screens, users can eavesdrop on many conversations at once. While heterosexuals wander into the channel from time to time, ... there is comfort in the fact that the regulars are gay men ... The results are a mixed bag of excitement and disgust, promise and letdown, nonchalance and embarrassment. >> (pp. 136 and 140)

(AO2) **Evaluation**
'electronic friendships'

- *The SIDE model* – The SIDE (Social Identity Model of Deindividuation Effect) offers an alternative to the reduced cues theory claim that CMC will free individuals from social constraints and norms and lead to anti-normative behaviour. Instead, proponents of SIDE claim that CMC actually reinforces existing social boundaries (Postmes *et al.* 1998). Anonymous individuals in CMC are inclined to accept 'in-group' norms and reject 'out-group' norms. This results in increases in in-group favouritism and bias against members of out-groups. This model has been applied to social categories such as gender, nationality and sexuality. If anonymity is maintained but some other identity is revealed (such as gender) in CMC, individuals tend to behave in terms of the prevailing norms of that social identity.

- *Advantages of CMC relationships* – CMC can provide opportunities for friendship and support. Simply because people have not met face to face does not make CMC relationships any less 'real' or significant. Two people who met on Presbynet (a conferencing resource provided by the Presbyterian church) said that after two months online 'I know some of these people better than some of my oldest and best friends' and 'I'm constantly amazed at the companionship and warmth one can find at the computer terminal' (Wilkins 1991). A person on another service said 'I have talked to some people for years without knowing where they live or their real names. Yet they are as much a presence in my life as if they were right in the room' (Kerr 1982).

- *Problems with internet relationships* – Although there are some positive effects that arise from CMC relationships, there are also some potentially negative consequences:

  – Individuals may become overly reliant upon CMC for initiating relationships, leading to less well-developed FtF relational skills. Individuals may have less incentive to develop social skills or overcome shyness if they can develop relationships online.

  – Because individuals can control how they present themselves (their self-representation), this can lead to abuse. This is dramatically illustrated in an example described by Reid (1998) (see panel overleaf).

  – Technology can be used to assist people in experiencing initiation without the traditional barriers associated with it. Concurrently, technology ought not be viewed as a 'cure all' for issues such as shyness and low self-esteem, which require separate attention.

- *Ethical issues in internet research* – As a result of the growing tendency for researchers to use the internet in their research, there is growing concern about the potential harm to online users unaware they have become research participants when they discuss their relationships. Failing to get consent before monitoring internet chat rooms, for example, amounts to an invasion of privacy. Ethical guidelines generally prohibit experiments on humans without consent, though some observations in public settings are acceptable. But when is a public group considered private and a private group considered public? Many discussion groups are open to allcomers, but participants generally assume that fellow members join because they have similar interests or concerns. That makes such groups less like a public square and more like someone's living room. Ess (2000) suggests that the online world is still new and opens up all sorts of ways of doing research: 'It's much easier to lurk in a chat room undetected than it is to stand in a room and take notes.'

Abuse on the internet (Reid 1998)

JennyMUSH was a virtual help centre for people who had been sexually assaulted or abused. Users developed a strong common bond. However, one person was able to destroy all the trust which had been built up and inflict further trauma on the members of the community. After being in the system for only two weeks, this user was able to transform himself into a virtual manifestation of every other user's fears. He changed his initial virtual gender to male (he had joined as a woman) and his name to 'Daddy' and then by using the 'Shout' command, was able to send obscene messages to all other users, describing assaults in graphic and violent terms. Many took the most direct form of defence and logged off the system, but others stayed and tried to stop the attacks. Many pleaded, others used threats, but all of them were powerless.

The administrators of JennyMUSH eventually took charge of the system once they saw what was happening. Daddy was isolated but where there had previously been trust and privacy, there was suspicion, distrust and wariness. JennyMUSH did not survive and was closed down in 1995.

REVISION SUMMARY

Having covered this topic you should be able to:

✓ describe and evaluate at least two explanations relating to differences in relationships between Western and non-Western cultures

✓ describe and evaluate research studies relating to differences in relationships between Western and non-Western cultures, and use these studies effectively as AO2 commentary on each of the explanations studied

✓ describe and evaluate research (theories and/or studies) into at least two types of 'understudied' relationship.

CHECK YOUR UNDERSTANDING

Check your understanding of cultural and sub-cultural differences in relationships by answering these questions. Try to do this from memory at first. You can check your answers by looking back through Topic 3.

1 What is the difference between individualist and collectivist cultures?

2 Summarize two differences between relationships in Western and non-Western relationships.

3 Identify three critical points that might be applied to research into Western and non-Western relationships.

4 Identify two factors that have been found to influence the formation of lesbian relationships, and two that have been found to influence the formation of relationships between gay men.

5 In what ways do gay men and lesbians use conversation to maintain their same-sex relationships?

6 Identify three differences between same-sex and opposite-sex romantic relationships.

7 Briefly summarize the proposed relationship between reduced cues and deindividuation in CMC.

8 Identify three differences between CMC and FtF relationships.

9 Give a brief précis of the SIDE model of CMC.

10 Identify and briefly summarize two problems with internet relationships.

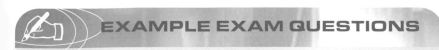

Below are some **possible examination questions** set on this topic, along with hints to help you understand and approach each question effectively:

1 Outline and evaluate **two or more** explanations of differences in relationships between Western and non-Western cultures. (24 marks)

> This is a tricky question to plan as it requires a very specific response. The wording of the specification particularly refers to explanations of differences between Western and non-Western relationships. You must outline these differences; the term 'outline' is used to indicate that you may have a lot to do and will need to use less detail than if the term 'describe' was used. Then you must also offer some critical commentary on these explanations for the AO2 component of the answer. This is where you can be creative with the material you weave into a commentary on your chosen explanations. One way to produce commentary is to use the useful list of phrases (see 'Innovative and effective AO2' on p. 937), or simply to ask yourself 'so what?'.

2 Discuss research (explanations **and/or** studies) into differences in relationships between Western and non-Western cultures. (24 marks)

> This is effectively the same question as question 1 above, except you can also include research studies in your response. If you choose to include research studies as part of your AO1 content, then you must also offer some appropriate AO2 evaluation for these studies – for example, you might consider methodological flaws that challenge the validity of the conclusions or you might consider how the findings could be applied in the real world. Alternatively, you might use your research studies as part of an evaluation of your explanations.

3 (a) Outline **two** theories relating to the formation of relationships. (12 marks)

(b) To what extent have research studies demonstrated differences in relationships between Western and non-Western cultures? (12 marks)

> This question combines two topics in this unit. Part (a) draws on your knowledge of formation of relationships (Topic 1) and part (b) relates to Topic 3. Part (a) is entirely AO1 and is straightforward if you bear timing in mind – you have about 7 minutes to write each of your theories. If you know more about one theory than another, this may still attract full marks as there is no expectation of balance (i.e. each theory is not worth 6 marks). Part (b) is more challenging because if you include descriptive material, you will get only minimal credit for that. You must use your knowledge of different cultures to consider whether there are differences in the way relationships form. You don't have to present a conclusion but this would gain credit as long as you don't just repeat points you have already made.

4 Discuss research (theories **and/or** studies) into **two** types of understudied relationship. (24 marks)

> The term 'research' here allows you to use either theories or studies or both in your answer. There are many permissible combinations of 'understudied relationship', e.g. gay and lesbian relationships can count as two separate types of relationship or as one type (i.e. homosexual relationships). Likewise, CMC relationships and 'text' relationships can count as two separate types or as one type (i.e. mediated relationships).

5 (a) Describe research studies into **any two** types of 'understudied' relationship (e.g. gay and lesbian; 'electronic' friendships). (12 marks)

(b) Assess the research studies that you have described in part (a). (12 marks)

> In part (a) some examples have been provided (these are examples that appear in the specification). Examples are intended to remind you about what you *might* include, but remember that you don't *have to* include them. If you were to write nothing about gay, lesbian or electronic friendships, but instead wrote about other understudied relationships such as same-sex friendships, this would be equally creditworthy. However, you must insure that you consider two types, or you will incur a partial performance penalty (maximum of 8 marks for AO1 and for AO2).

Topic 1: Attraction and the formation of relationships

● Kerckhoff and Davis believed that in **interpersonal attraction**, people rely on a number of social and personal factors to filter potential relationships from the 'field of eligibles'.

● Psychological research into interpersonal attraction in the US in the 1960s and 70s concentrated on **physical attraction** and resulted in the **matching hypothesis**. However, much research was seen as unlike real life. Research using dating advertisements found culture-specific ideas of attractiveness in use. Frequency of interaction and similarity of values were also found to be important, at least in short-term relationships. Variety between and within relationships is often not taken into enough consideration.

● **Sociobiological theory** uses evolutionary ideas to explain human behaviour during **relationship formation**, favouring stereotypical gender roles and determinism. **The reinforcement-affect** model of relationship formation explains that we spend so much of our time in social relationships because we find them rewarding (i.e. positively reinforcing) or that we find life alone unpleasant and unrewarding.

● Much of the psychological research into social and interpersonal relationships has focused on romantic relationships, reflecting the North American interest in the factors that influence attraction and the formation of relationships. Research includes Walster *et al.*'s computer dance study, Murstein's matching study, and Dunbar and Waynforth's analysis of newspaper advertisements.

Topic 2: Maintenance and the dissolution of relationships

● People use different strategies within relationships to **maintain them**. These vary according to whether the participants want the relationship to strengthen, weaken or stay unchanged.

● The **maintenance** and breakdown of relationships have been described by **social exchange** and **equity theories** as analogous to economic cost/benefit situations, with investment, satisfaction, comparisons with others and principles of equity as important factors. However, these theories are difficult to test in real-life and long-term situations. They also appear to reflect predominantly North American values.

● Many factors contribute to the breakdown and **dissolution of relationships**. Duck divides these into predisposing personal factors and precipitating factors. Duck has also developed a four-phase model of dissolution, while Lee identified five stages in the breakdown of relationships. Both models see breakdown as a *process* that proceeds through a number of stages before termination, rather than seeing it as a single step.

● Hatfield and Walster's **psychological explanations** divide love into passionate (**romantic**) and **companionate**, with various factors needed for love to occur. Sternberg also includes consummate love and sees love as determined by the various combinations of passion, intimacy and commitment. Hendrick and Hendrick's model focused on the love styles that people enter relationships with.

● Comparisons of cultural groups and love styles show support for Lee's six basic love styles, though with variations within and between **cultures** and **sub-cultures**. While there are some cross-cultural similarities, cultures have also been shown to vary enormously in their accepted love and sexual practices.

Topic 3: Cultural and sub-cultural differences in relationships

● Hofstede categorized relationships in different countries along four dimensions, with a fifth added later, the most important being **individualistic/collectivist**.

● Research has shown a vast array of marriage arrangements in **Western** and **non-Western cultures** from extremes of partners having no choice, to partners having total choice of whom they marry.

● Even in the most common form of marriage, i.e. by parental arrangement, there is a considerable range from **voluntary** to **involuntary**, as research among British Asians has shown.

● The issue of **permanence/impermanence** in relationships has been studied through the cross-cultural variations in reasons for, and prevalence of, divorce.

- Much of the research into relationships has itself been conducted from a Western cultural standpoint, and it has often not taken into consideration internal, individual and cultural variation and diversity, nor necessarily understood the nuances of the other cultures and sub-cultures it has investigated.

- It is difficult to make comparisons in **'understudied' relationships** such as **gay and lesbian relationships**, which are, because of the pressures of societies' laws and prejudices, relatively hidden. However, misconceptions about stereotypes and a unitary culture have been investigated by, for example, Markowitz and Greene. There are notable differences between same-sex and opposite-sex relationships, although the overall desire for intimacy and love are universal.

- **Electronic friendships** are a newer area of study, with interesting comparisons to be made with face-to-face relationships, especially in the areas of support, potential for harm, disguise and freedom of expression.

FURTHER RESOURCES

Duck, S. (1999) *Relating to Others* **(2nd edn), Buckingham, Open University Press.**

A highly readable yet scholarly account of recent research by the professor who has done most to establish the credentials of relationships as a topic for serious psychological study.

Goodwin, R. (1999) *Personal Relationships Across Cultures*, **London: Routledge.**

An up-to-date and thorough account of cultural and sub-cultural differences (and similarities!) in this complex field of human relationships. An excellent eye-opener.

Greene, B. and Herek, G.M. (1994) *Lesbian and Gay Psychology: Theory, Research and Clinical Applications*, **Thousand Oaks, CA: Sage.**

A book which offers a multi-faceted approach to the psychological study of people who are non-heterosexual. Long overdue.

Gackenbach, J. (ed.) (1998) *Psychology and the Internet*, **San Diego, CA: Academic Press.**

A fascinating set of articles on the new area of psychology which is currently sparsely resourced.

Websites

www.ascusc.org/jcmc/

The website of the *Journal of Computer Mediated Communication*, and *On-the-Web Quarterly*. Edited by McLaughlin and Rafaeli at Annenberg, School for Communication, University of Southern California. Topics covered since it began in June 1995 include play and performance in CMC, virtual environments and persistent conversation.

ANSWERS TO ACTIVITIES

Sub-cultural differences in love styles in the USA, p. 322

- *Game-playing* – Men used this type more often than women.
- *Possessive* – Women's lives were more characterized by this type of love than were men's.
- *Logical* – More characteristic of women than men.
- *Altruistic* – No difference found between men and women.
- *Companionate* – Valued slightly higher by women than men.
- *Erotic* – No difference found between men and women.

PRO- & ANTI-SOCIAL
Behaviour

INTRODUCTION

Although we are used to reports on the television and in the newspapers about increasing levels of *anti-soc*ial behaviour, the term *pro*-social is less widely used. Psychologists use the term 'anti-social' to refer to any behaviour that is considered harmful or disruptive within a group or society. Although what might be considered anti-social is rather subjective, there is little doubt that aggressive behaviour, particularly when it is directed towards other human beings, would be considered anti-social. Psychologists are divided as to the causes of aggressive behaviour. In Topic 1 we examine the nature and causes of aggression, restricting our focus to *social* explanations of aggression rather than biological explanations.

If anti-social behaviour is considered harmful and disruptive, then *pro*-social behaviour can be thought of as any act that helps or benefits others. When people help others with no apparent benefit to themselves, we may describe their behaviour as being pro-social (Cardwell 2003). In Topic 2 we examine two different, yet closely related, forms of pro-social behaviour – *altruism* and *bystander behaviour*. Altruism refers to the apparent human tendency to help others without consideration of our own needs. A particular form of altruistic behaviour concerns the behaviour of bystanders in emergency situations. Why is it that some people are more likely than others to intervene in emergencies, and why is it that some situations are more likely to elicit helping behaviour than others? Psychologists offer a number of explanations that might shed light on these questions.

It is important to consider the extent to which the media influence our behaviour. Although the 'media' encompass a number of different forms, most research has concentrated on television (and video/DVD) and, more recently, on computer games. Some studies have suggested that exposure to television violence is positively correlated with violent behaviour, yet other studies suggest that any relationship is weak. It is also argued by some that television and other media can be used to reduce aggression and encourage pro-social behaviour, and that the educational value of these media is more important than their possible anti-social effects.

**Mike
Cardwell**

1 What makes some forms of behaviour pro-social and others anti-social? Football violence (see photo right) is clearly an example of the latter, but how should we classify peaceful protest (as in the photo below)?

2 What criteria should we use to decide if behaviour is pro- or anti-social?

3 On 13 January 1982, moments after take-off in Washington DC, a commercial jet hit a crowded bridge and plunged into the icy waters of the Potomac river. A 28-year-old man named Lenny Skutnik stopped and watched from the shore as rescuers tried to pull survivors out of the river. When Priscilla Tirado lost her grip on a helicopter lifeline and started to sink, Skutnik risked his own life by jumping into the water and pulling her to safety. Why did he behave in this pro-social way?

KEY CONCEPTS

Aggression: an action or a series of actions where the aim is to cause harm to another person or object.

Deindividuation: the process that occurs when one loses one's sense of individual identity so that social, moral and societal constraints on behaviour are loosened.

Relative deprivation: the state that people experience when they perceive a gap between what others have and what they have themselves, i.e. others are seen as relatively better off.

Environmental stressors: aspects of the physical environment (such as noise or crowding) that may contribute to aggression.

Altruism: helping behaviour that is voluntary, costly to the altruist and motivated by something other than the expectation of material or social reward.

Empathy: feeling an emotional response that is consistent with another's emotional state or condition (i.e. feeling sad when we meet someone who is sad).

Egoism: the tendency to act out of self-interest.

Diffusion of responsibility: a decrease in an individual's sense of responsibility for helping in an emergency because other bystanders are present.

Pluralistic ignorance: the phenomenon where bystanders to an emergency define the situation wrongly as one that does not require intervention because other bystanders do not seem concerned.

Unit 11 // Pro- and anti-social behaviour

Different types of aggressive behaviour include:

- *anti-social aggression* – defined by Penrod (1983) as 'all behaviour that is intended to inflict physical or psychological harm on another individual who does not want to be so treated'
- *pro-social aggression* – e.g. when the police shoot a terrorist who has murdered hostages and is threatening others

- *sanctioned aggression* – such as self-defence, e.g. when a woman injures a rapist while defending herself.

A further distinction is made between aggressive *behaviours*, which are overt, and aggressive *feelings*, such as anger, which are covert. Frustration frequently makes people angry, but angry people do not always behave aggressively.

SOCIAL PSYCHOLOGICAL THEORIES OF AGGRESSION

There are many ways of explaining aggressive behaviour in humans. Some theories view aggression as an important part of our evolutionary heritage, others as an imbalance in hormones or neurotransmitters in the brain. Early psychological theories of aggression explained aggressive behaviour as an automatic consequence of personal frustration. Social psychological theories see the cause of our aggressive behaviour as arising out of our interactions with others in our social world. We will now look at three very different ways in which social psychologists explain aggressive behaviour.

Social learning theory

According to Berkowitz (1989) and Bandura (1965), although the aggressive behaviour of nonhuman animals can be explained in terms of instinctual drives, aggression in humans is the product of learning. They claim that aggressive behaviour is learned either through direct experience or by observing others.

- *Learning by direct experience* is derived from Skinner's principles of operant reinforcement (see Unit 21). In other words, if a child pushes another child and as a result gets something they want, the action is *reinforced* and is more likely to occur in similar situations in the future.
- *Learning by vicarious experience* derives from social learning theory. This form of observational learning occurs when a

child sees a role model behaving in a particular way and reproduces that behaviour. The child is then said to be imitating the behaviour of the model.

Reinforcement

Social learning theorists emphasize that for behaviour to be imitated, it must be seen to be rewarding in some way, i.e. it is *reinforced*. The likelihood of a person behaving aggressively in a particular situation is determined by:

- their previous experiences of aggressive behaviour – both their own and that of others
- the degree to which their aggressive behaviour was successful in the past
- the current likelihood of their aggressive behaviour being rewarded or punished
- other cognitive, social and environmental factors that are operating at the same time – aggressive behaviour may increase under hostile environmental conditions (e.g. very noisy situations), but fear of retaliation from the 'victim' may inhibit the expression of aggression.

Media violence and aggressive behaviour

Social learning theory leads us to consider the various ways in which children might be exposed to aggressive models. In particular, television has been examined as a powerful source of imitative learning. Huesmann (1988) suggests that children may use television models as a source of 'scripts' that act as a guide for their own behaviour. For example, if they see a movie hero beat up the bad guys that get in his way, this may become a script for any situation in which it might be deemed appropriate. These scripts are stored in memory, and are strengthened and elaborated through repetition and rehearsal.

The relationship between observation of aggression in the media and subsequent aggressive behaviour is a complex one (see pp. 366–70 for a discussion of this).

Do you think most bullies learn their behaviour through reinforcement or imitation?

It appears to be influenced by several variables including the following (Manstead *et al.* 1995):

- If the observed violence is thought to be real behaviour (e.g. in more 'believable' story lines and 'domestic' drama), it is more likely to elicit aggression than if it is considered to be fictional or fantasy violence.

- If viewers identify with the aggressor in some way, they are subsequently more aggressive than if they do not identify with the aggressive model. Heroes are therefore more powerful models than villains.

- Observing unsuccessful aggression, in which the aggressor is punished tends to inhibit aggressive behaviour in the observer.

Research related to social learning theory

Bandura and his colleagues carried out a series of experiments involving children exposed to the aggressive behaviour of an adult model (see Key research below). By varying the conditions under which the model was viewed, as well as the consequences for the model's aggressive behaviour, Bandura was able to develop a social learning model of aggression. He found that children were more likely to imitate the aggressive behaviour of a model under the conditions expressed in Fig. 11.1.

Figure 11.1 >> *The social learning view of aggression (Bandura 1965)*

Children observe aggressive behaviour

The model is rewarded for their aggressive behaviour

Other adults show approval of the model's aggressive behaviour

Other children imitate the behaviour of the model

Each of these instances increases the likelihood that the observing child will imitate the aggressive behaviour of the model.

KEY RESEARCH >> DO CHILDREN LEARN AGGRESSION?

the Bobo doll studies (Bandura *et al.* 1963)

Bandura *et al.* (1963) divided 66 nursery school children into three groups. All three groups watched a film where an adult model kicked and punched a Bobo doll (see illustration).

- *Condition 1*: Children saw the adult model being rewarded by a second adult.

- *Condition 2*: Children saw a second adult telling off the adult model for the aggressive behaviour.

- *Condition 3*: The adult model was neither rewarded nor punished.

The children were then allowed to play in the room with the Bobo doll whilst experimenters watched through a one-way mirror.

Results showed that children in Condition 1 behaved most aggressively, and those in Condition 2 behaved

least aggressively. However, an important distinction must be made between learning and performance. All the children learnt how to behave aggressively, but those in Condition 2 did not perform as many aggressive acts until later, when they were offered rewards to do so. When this happened, they quickly showed that they had learned (acquired) as many aggressive techniques as the children in Condition 1.

Unit 11 // Pro- and anti-social behaviour

341

Evaluation
social learning theory

- **Methodological problems with the Bobo doll studies** – Social learning theories of aggression rely heavily on experimental evidence and field studies of observational learning. There are, however, some methodological problems in the experiments described by Bandura and colleagues. A Bobo doll is not, after all, a living person and does not retaliate when hit. Other investigators have also cast doubt on the conclusion that Bandura's child subjects had learned their aggressive behaviour from watching an aggressive model on film. In one study, nursery school children who behaved most violently towards the doll were also rated by their teachers and peers as being more violent generally (Johnston *et al.* 1977).

- **Explaining inconsistencies in aggressive behaviour** – Social learning explanations can, however, account for the lack of consistency in people's aggressive behaviour. If someone is assertive and domineering at home but meek and submissive at work, it means they are *reinforced* differently in the two situations. They have *learned* to behave differently in the two situations because assertiveness brings rewards in one context but not in the other.

- **Social learning or biology as primary causal agent?** – Biological explanations of aggression have stressed factors quite unrelated to social learning. The presence of higher levels of the male hormone testosterone has been cited as a primary causal agent in aggressive behaviour. Premenstrual syndrome has even been cited in criminal trials as a reason for aggressive behaviour (Flanagan 2000). These, together with other biological explanations, cast doubt on aggression being purely a *learned* behaviour. In defence of this position, however, social learning theorists point to societies that have no aggressive behaviour (such as the Amish in the USA) as powerful evidence of the dominant role played by learning over biology. Interestingly, in most societies where nonaggressive behaviour is more prevalent than aggressive behaviour (such as the Arapesh of New Guinea and the Pygmies of central Africa), there are few distinctions made between males and females. Although differences between the roles of males and females do exist in these societies, no attempt is made to project an image of brave, aggressive masculinity (Deaux *et al.* 1993).

Deindividuation

Hogg and Vaughan (1998) define deindividuation as: 'a process whereby people lose their sense of socialized individual identity and engage in unsocialized, often anti-social behaviours'.

People normally refrain from acting in an aggressive and selfish manner in part because they are easily identifiable in societies that have strong norms against such 'uncivilized' behaviour. In certain situations, such as in crowds, these restraints may become relaxed and we may engage in 'an orgy of aggressive, selfish and anti-social behaviour' (Hogg and Vaughan 1998). In his study of the situational determinants of destructive obedience, Milgram (1965) found that participants were more likely to give higher levels of shock when they could not see their victim. When the 'victim' was in the same room, the participants were more reluctant to deliver high levels of shock to someone they could see (and who could see them).

Individual and deindividuated behaviour

Zimbardo (1969) distinguished between *individual* behaviour, which is rational and conforms to acceptable social standards, and *deindividuated* behaviour, which is based on primitive urges and does not conform to society's norms. According to Zimbardo, being part of a crowd can diminish awareness of individuality.

In a large crowd, each person is faceless and anonymous. There is diminished fear of retribution and a diluted sense of guilt. Conditions that increase anonymity serve to minimize concerns about evaluation by others and thus weaken normal controls based on guilt, shame or fear. The larger the group, the greater the anonymity and the greater the difficulty in identifying a single individual.

Malamuth and Check (1981) questioned male students at an American university and found that almost one-third admitted that there was a chance they would rape if there was no chance of being caught.

Public and private self-awareness

More recent developments of the concept of deindividuation have distinguished between the effects of reduced public self-awareness (being anonymous to others) and reduced private self-awareness. A person who is self-focused tends to act according to internalized attitudes and moral standards. If the person submerges themselves within a group, they may lose this focus and become less privately self-aware. It is this reduction in private self-awareness that is associated with increased anti-social behaviour rather than the anonymity of public self-awareness (Prentice-Dunn and Rogers 1989).

Research related to deindividuation

The Stanford Prison experiment

Zimbardo was interested in finding out whether the brutality reported among guards in American prisons was due to the sadistic personalities of the guards or had more to do with the prison environment (Zimbardo *et al.* 1973). The 'prison' environment, in which 'prisoners' were dressed only in smocks and nylon caps, and addressed only by their number, appeared to be an important factor in creating the brutal behaviour of the 'guards'. The dehumanization of the prisoners by the guards, together with the relative anonymity of each group, made it easier for the guards to treat the prisoners in such a brutal manner that the study had to be stopped after just six days.

Commentary
deindividuation

Much of the early evidence for deindividuation was supportive, but the concept is not without its problems, not least of which is the finding in some studies that deindividuation may produce increases in *pro-social* behaviour (e.g. expressions of collective good will at religious rallies) rather than anti-social behaviour (Diener 1980).

- *The role of anonymity* – Researchers have often failed to distinguish between the effects of anonymity of those being aggressed against, e.g. when we aggress against a 'faceless' enemy or victim, as opposed to those doing the aggressing, e.g. hooded terrorists who cannot be identified by their victims. This also raises the question of whether 'identifiability' is in respect of the in-group or out-group. In other words, does the likelihood of aggression increase if our *in-group* cannot recognize us, or if the *out-group* cannot. Manstead *et al.* argue that anonymity among the in-group does not really reflect the reality of most crowd situations (Manstead *et al.* 1995).

- *Social norms and behaviour* – According to the deindividuation perspective, when we are submerged in a group, this undermines the influence of social norms. This is in sharp contrast to social psychological research that has demonstrated the strong normative hold that groups have on individual members. Rather than individuals pursuing behaviour 'based on primitive

The 'baiting crowd'

Mann (1981) has used the concept of deindividuation to explain a particular form of collective behaviour, the 'baiting crowd'. The 'baiting' or taunting crowd has been reported in some American studies and lends support to the notion of the crowd as a mob. Mann analysed 21 incidents of suicides reported in American newspapers in the 1960s and 1970s. He found that in 10 of the 21 cases where a crowd had gathered to watch, baiting had occurred (i.e. the crowd urged the potential suicide to jump). These incidents tended to occur at night, when the crowd was large and when the crowd was some distance from the person being taunted (particularly when the 'jumper' was high above them). All of these features, claimed Mann, were likely to produce a state of deindividuation in the individual members of the crowd.

urges and not conforming to society's norms', they might be seen as conforming to a 'local' group norm (Manstead *et al.* 1995). This norm need not necessarily be anti-social, and could thus account for some apparently contradictory findings that show an increase in *pro*-social behaviour when deindividuated (e.g. Diener 1980).

- *Deindividuation and football crowd violence* – It is tempting to apply the concept of deindividuation to crowd violence in British football. Stereotypical images of football fans on the rampage make all too familiar reading in the press and do suggest a faceless crowd engaged in an 'orgy of aggressive, selfish and anti-social behaviour'. A study of football hooliganism by Marsh *et al.* (1978) tells quite a different story. Marsh and colleagues found that what might appear to be an undisciplined mob on match days, can actually consist of several different groups, each with their status. They also found that much of the violence displayed was highly ritualized rather than physically violent.

- *The Zimbardo et al. prison study* – It is sometimes concluded that the brutality of the guards in this study indicates the power of deindividuation to produce aggressive behaviour. However, the guards' brutality, together with the relative submission of the prisoners, suggests that they were acting in terms of *perceived* social roles rather than losing 'their sense of socialized individual identity'. The study failed to tell us much about how *real* guards behave, but rather how people behave when they are asked to *act* like guards.

Relative deprivation theory

The root cause of conflict, according to relative deprivation theory (Stouffer *et al.* 1949), is the unacceptable discrepancy between what people think they have a right to expect (e.g. a good education and

comfortable standard of living) and what, given current social conditions, they estimate they are realistically capable of attaining. This is accentuated by comparing their own position to that of others whom they feel are not so deprived. The gap between what they feel they have a right to and what they actually get is frequently described as 'perceived relative deprivation', because what a person believes subjectively may be more important than measurable objective criteria.

Social conditions and relative deprivation

If people feel deprived of something to which they feel entitled, they feel frustration. Berkowitz (1972) claimed that subjective frustration due to perceived relative deprivation can incite aggression. This relative deprivation will be felt most keenly in modern industrialized societies where the life opportunities and comparative wealth of one sector of society may be markedly and visibly different to the conditions enjoyed by less privileged groups within these societies. The 1992 riots in Los Angeles, which resulted in more than 50 deaths, was an example of this scenario. The spark for these riots was the acquittal by an all-White jury of

four Los Angeles police officers who had been accused of beating a Black motorist. With a background of rising unemployment and increasing disadvantage, this was seen as an expression of the low value placed by White America on American Blacks.

A sense of perceived relative deprivation can also come about as a *result* of improvement in the resources and opportunities made available to a group. One aspect of human nature seems to be that when things do get better, we expect even greater improvements. Although conditions might be improving, expectations increase even faster. Consider what happened at the end of the Cold War, when Eastern European countries, once Soviet-controlled, became independent. Expectations rose faster than improvements and in many cases violence and crime became widespread.

Egoistic and fraternalistic relative deprivation

Runciman (1966) has drawn a distinction between two different types of relative deprivation:

- *Egoistic relative deprivation* – experienced if an individual feels deprived relative to other similar individuals. If our colleagues all seem to be better off than we are, we may feel deprived in comparison to them. An important part of this process is that comparisons are realistic. Comparing our standard of living with the rich and famous is a pretty futile exercise, and these unrealistic exercises do not leave us with enduring feelings of relative deprivation.

- *Fraternalistic relative deprivation* – experienced when members of one group compare themselves to members of another group. If the general conditions in the two groups are such that one group feels that they are worse off than the other, feelings of relative deprivation may arise.

The Los Angeles riots were triggered by a perceived injustice in a court of law, but would not have happened without the relative deprivation background

Commentary
relative deprivation theory

- *Fraternalistic deprivation and social unrest* – Runciman's distinction between egoistic and fraternalistic relative deprivation is important. Many studies have supported the belief that social unrest and aggression are more a product of the latter than the former. For example, Abèles (1976) found that Black militancy in the USA was closely associated with intergroup comparisons between Blacks and Whites. Abèles also found that levels of militancy tend to be greatest in Blacks with the highest socioeconomic and educational status. Remember that relative deprivation is a *subjective* rather than an *objective* experience. These individuals were more acutely aware of the discrepancies between the group (i.e. Blacks) as a whole and the dominant White group with whom they compare (i.e. fraternalistic relative deprivation).

- *Relative deprivation and unemployment* – Walker and Mann (1987) in a study of unemployed workers in Australia, found that they were more likely to engage in militant protest (such as destruction of private property) when they felt that their group had not attained what they deserved relative to other groups. Those workers who felt more egoistically deprived reported symptoms of stress (e.g. headaches, sleeplessness) rather than militancy and aggression.

- *Cultural differences* – The discrepancy between what people feel they deserve and will realistically achieve tends not to be as great in traditionally agricultural societies. For most people in these societies, expectations tend not to exceed achievements and so do not result in feelings of relative deprivation. Indeed, many anthropologists have reported a relative lack of violence in such societies compared to modern complex societies.

Theories in précis

Most textbooks arm you with much more information than you can reproduce in an exam. We will look at how to structure exam questions at the end of this topic (see pp. 348–9), but it is worth thinking about this problem now. In an exam, you might be asked to 'describe and evaluate' one theory, but you might also be asked to 'outline and evaluate **two** theories'. You don't get any extra time for the extra theory, so it is clear that your answer must take a different approach.

For *each of the three theories* of aggression that we have just covered:

● Construct a 150-word précis that covers the central claims and assumptions. Try to make the word length as exact as possible. Edit and re-edit this précis to make sure you are using your word allowance in the most efficient way.

● Do the same for the *evaluation* of each theory, sticking to just 150 words that you feel offer a good critical commentary on that theory.

● You may find it easier to use bullet points for this activity (to help you appreciate discrete points of description and evaluation), but in an exam, remember to write in continuous prose.

THE EFFECTS OF ENVIRONMENTAL STRESSORS ON AGGRESSIVE BEHAVIOUR

Environmental stressors and you

In this section we will be looking at research into the effects of environmental stressors such as temperature, noise and crowding on aggression. You will see what psychologists have discovered about this relationship, but how do they make *you* feel?

1 Cast your mind back to the heatwave in August 2003. How did you and those around you cope with the soaring temperatures? Did you witness more irritability and bad temper when temperatures were at their highest?

2 What effect does loud noise have on you? Does it depend on whether you can control or escape from the noise? Does it depend on who is responsible for the noise?

3 We all have to face crowds at some point. This might be at a football game, braving the New Year sales, clubbing at a crowded nightspot, or just sitting in an overcrowded lecture hall. Do different conditions make you feel exhilarated or aggressive?

The idea that aggression may be a product of aspects of the physical environment is not a new one. Environmental stressors (also known as 'ambient' stressors) may cause an increase in arousal (a generalized state of physiological and psychological excitation). This in turn may evoke negative emotions and thus hostile thoughts and even aggressive behaviour. These environmental stressors may cause stimulus overload, interfering with whatever a person is trying to

accomplish, and therefore leading to frustration. Several stressors in the environment have been shown to relate to aggressive behaviour. We will examine two of these: temperature and crowding.

Temperature

The effects of high temperatures on aggression have been demonstrated in a number of studies, both in the laboratory and also in the natural environment. Hotter regions of the world tend to have more aggression than cooler regions, and hotter years, seasons and days tend to have more incidents of violent crimes than cooler ones (Anderson 1989). Other studies have demonstrated the effects of high temperatures on drivers' aggression. In one study (Kenrick and MacFarlane 1986), drivers honked their horns more in response to a car blocking the road at a traffic light as the temperatures rose.

Laboratory studies of the temperature/ aggression relationship

Laboratory studies of the relationship between heat and aggression have tended to yield a slightly different finding. Halpern (1995), in a review of studies of this area, found evidence for an 'inverted-U' relationship between heat and aggression. In other words, maximum aggression is elicited by moderate temperatures (see Fig. 11.2 overleaf). As temperature rises, so does aggression, but only to a certain level, after which it begins to decline. It is possible to explain this in terms of the action of two different motives, each linked to changes in temperature. Over the low to moderate temperature range, the motivation to engage in aggressive behaviour (even if this is only thinking hostile thoughts) increases as we experience an increase in our negative emotions. At higher temperatures, however, the motivation to escape the heat replaces the motivation to aggress.

Figure 11.2 >>
The relationship between heat and aggression

'Whoa there, hang on, I'll just turn the central heating off'.

Heat and violent crime

Anderson (1987) examined crime statistics to see whether there was a relationship between heat and aggressive behaviour. Anderson found that violent crimes (such as murder, rape and assault) were more common in hotter months and in hotter years. Non-violent crimes (such as burglary and car theft) did not follow the same trend.

Explaining the temperature/aggression relationship

The 'negative affect escape theory' (Bell and Baron 1976) claims that aggression is a *direct* consequence of uncomfortably high temperatures. Negative affect (anger, irritability) increases as the temperature rises,

which in turn leads to an increase in aggressive and escape motives. If escape is not possible, then aggressive behaviours are displayed.

Other explanations focus more on the *indirect* relationship between heat and aggression. 'Routine activity theory' (Cohen and Felson 1979) states that the opportunities for interpersonal aggression increase in hot weather because people are more likely to be out of doors and so come into contact with other people. Hot weather is also associated with increases in alcohol consumption, which in turn compounds this relationship.

Commentary
temperature and aggression

● *Hotter climates and aggressive behaviour* – Field research has established a relationship between hotter regions and aggression, but Moghaddam (1998) warns against taking these results too literally. He quotes studies by Lombroso (1911) who found higher murder rates in southern Italy, and Brearley (1932) who found similar trends in the southern United States, each compared to the northern areas of these countries. Moghaddam argues that the northern and southern regions of Italy and the USA differ in many other ways, each of which might feasibly explain the different rates in murder and other violent crimes.

● *Heat and violent crime* – Cohen and Felson (1979) explain seasonal variations in violent crime by the increased likelihood of people coming into contact with each other during the hotter summer months. In other words, increases in temperature alone may not be responsible for the concurrent rise in aggressive behaviour. This conclusion is also

supported by the American homicide statistics, which show that there are two peak periods in homicide rates – late summer and December (around Christmas time, when people are more likely to be socially active) (Moghaddam 1998).

● *Laboratory studies of the temperature/ aggression relationship* – These have failed to establish a clear-cut relationship between temperature and aggression. Some studies have found an increase in aggression with increasing temperatures, and others have found a decrease in aggressive behaviour. Some studies that have attempted to incorporate anger as a variable into this relationship have found that participants who are cold and angry display more aggressive behaviour than those who are hot and angry (Baron and Bell 1976).

● *Review of research findings* – Moghaddam (1998) reviewed research findings in this area and suggests that the most important general conclusion that can be drawn is that high temperatures can change the way in which people interpret ambiguous situations and may, therefore, predispose a person towards an aggressive response.

A2 Social Psychology

Crowding

Crowding refers to the psychological state of discomfort that is induced if our expectations about the use of space are violated by the presence of others. As a result of this discomfort, emotional distress may arise and a number of behavioural adjustments aimed at preserving one's personal space may occur (Kaya and Erkíp 1999). High density usually affects social interaction between individuals. When an increase in social density is seen as undesirable, social outcomes are generally negative, and more aggression and less cooperation occur (Horn 1994). Individuals subjected to high density often respond by withdrawing from social interaction and avoiding social contact (you may see this taking place next time you travel in a crowded lift).

Although the role of crowding or population density has also been proposed as an environmental stressor, the evidence is not particularly strong. There is, however, some evidence that increased density of people (e.g. in heavily congested traffic routes) and violations of personal space may produce an aggressive response (Geen 1990).

Crowding in nightclubs

Macintyre and Homel (1997) studied the effects of crowding in six Australian nightclubs. The more crowded venues also tended to be the more violent, with higher levels of observed aggressive incidents. This was the case even when levels of male drunkenness and staff interactions with club-goers were taken into account.

Gender differences

Research into the relationship between increased density and adult aggression has shown that increased density is related to increased aggression in males but not in females. For example, Stokols et al. (1973) studied same-sex groups of eight in either a small room or a large room, and found that males rated themselves as more aggressive in the small room whereas the opposite was true for females. In another study, Schettino and Borden (1975) used a ratio of people in a classroom to total number of seats as a measure of density. Males reported an increase in feelings of aggression as density increased, but the opposite was true for females.

Explaining the crowding/aggression relationship

Stokols (1976) identified ways of explaining why crowding might lead to increased levels of aggression. These are as follows:

- **Stimulus overload** – High density can be aversive because it may cause us to be overwhelmed by sensory inputs. When the amount of stimulation produced by high density exceeds our ability to deal with it, negative consequences occur.

- **Behavioural constraint** – High density is aversive because it may lead to reduced behavioural freedom (e.g. waiting in a queue for the ladies, or being stuck in a traffic jam). Whether or not we experience negative effects depends on what we want to do and whether high density constrains us from doing it.

- **Ecological model** – This assumes that high density will produce negative consequences since it may result in insufficient resources for people in that setting (e.g. fighting for food at a famine relief centre). Resources are broadly defined and may include both materials (such as food) and privacy.

One element common to all three of these perspectives is that conditions that produce a loss of control are more likely to produce negative consequences.

(A02) Commentary
crowding and aggression

- **Effects of crowding on aggression** – Research into the effects of crowding on aggression allows us to draw several tentative conclusions. Higher densities of people may lead to less liking for both people and places, and greater withdrawal. This effect appears stronger for males than for females.

- **Social versus spatial density** – Social density refers to the number of people in a space. Spatial density refers to the amount of space available. Research has produced inconsistent results suggesting only a weak relationship between high densities and aggressive behaviour. Specifically, high social density will produce negative effects more consistently than high spatial density. Social density manipulations are generally aversive, but spatial density manipulations are only problematic among males in same-sex groups (Paulus 1977).

Do crowded places have a greater impact on males than females?

- **Crowding in cities** – Some studies have shown that cities contain more stressful environmental features, such as increased temperature, noise, crowding and inconvenience. Urban dwellers typically report being affected far more adversely by these physical stressors than do rural dwellers.

Check your understanding of the nature and causes of aggression by answering these questions from memory. Check your answers by looking back through this first topic.

1 What do you understand by the terms 'pro-social behaviour' and 'anti-social behaviour'?

2 What is the difference between 'direct' and 'vicarious' experience?

3 List four assumptions of the social learning theory of aggression.

4 Construct a descriptive 150-word précis of deindividuation theory as an explanation of aggression.

5 Identify three critical (i.e. AO2) points relating to deindividuation theory as an explanation of aggression, and explain *why* these pose problems for the theory.

6 What is the difference between 'egoistic' and 'fraternalistic' relative deprivation?

7 In what ways do these have different effects on individuals?

8 Summarize two explanations of the temperature/aggression relationship.

9 Does crowding lead to aggression? Construct a 300-word précis that responds to this question (150 words of AO1 and 150 words of *effective* AO2).

REVISION SUMMARY

Having covered this topic you should be able to:

✓ describe and evaluate social learning theory, deindividuation theory and relative deprivation theory as explanations of aggression

✓ describe and evaluate research studies related to these theories, and use these studies effectively as AO2 commentary on each of the theories studied

✓ describe and evaluate research (theories and/or studies) into the effects of temperature and crowding as environmental stressors.

EXAMPLE EXAM QUESTIONS

Below are some **possible examination questions** set on this topic, along with hints to help you understand and approach each question effectively:

1 Describe and evaluate **one** social psychological theory of aggression. (24 marks)

In exam questions, the term 'describe' is used when asking for one theory and 'outline' when asking for more than one. Any one of the three theories covered in this topic would be suitable here. A good idea is to break your answer into four 150-word paragraphs, with the first two being AO1 and the second two being AO2. You will select the theory you know best to present as AO1 but may decide to use your knowledge of another theory as AO2. You may use a second theory in this way as long as it is used as a form of *sustained critical commentary*. In other words, it is not enough to say 'In contrast there is theory 2 …' and then just give a description of the second theory. You might, for example, consider similarities and differences between the two theories.

2 Outline and evaluate **two** social psychological theories of aggression. (24 marks)

> What is required here is a précis of two theories and a summarized evaluation of each. A good précis selects key points and expresses these clearly. It may help you to practise writing 12-mark and 6-mark versions of your theories (and the same for evaluation) before the exam. Using the four 150-word paragraph technique gives you a neat division in your response. Remember, though, that your AO2 evaluation still needs to be effective, so it is better to cover just two or three critical points for each theory and leave yourself time to elaborate these points.

3 (a) Describe **one** social psychological theory of aggression. (12 marks)

   (b) Assess the social psychological theory of aggression you described in part (a) in terms of relevant research studies. (12 marks)

> For part (b), you are required to use research studies as AO2 evaluation of theories. Simply *describing* a research study is insufficient – you will get very little credit for material that poses as AO2 but is really just more AO1 description. Also, in order to make a research study work as AO2, it needs to be used as part of a *sustained* critical argument. The secret to effective use of research studies in your AO2 commentary is to focus on the *relationship* between theory and study, and state the link. Why do psychologists carry out research in the first place? One important reason is to put theoretical assumptions to the test. It is up to you to make the results of that 'test' explicit to the reader.

4 Discuss social psychological research (theories **and/or** studies) into aggression. (24 marks)

> The term 'research' here allows you to use either theory *or* studies *or* both in your answer. Note that in this question, the actual theories are not specified in the question. You are free to include any theories you wish, though you must present at least two as 'theories' is plural. If you only cover one theory then you will incur a partial performance penalty of a maximum of 8 marks for AO1 and the same for AO2. If you describe two theories but only evaluate one of them, then you would be restricted to 8 marks for AO2.

5 Describe and evaluate research (theories **and/or** studies) into the effects of **two or more** environmental stressors. (24 marks)

> The instruction 'two or more' invites you to include both environmental stressors covered in this unit. Two is plenty, as you don't get more marks if you include three. Also, focusing on two means that you have more time to make your AO1 description *detailed* and your AO2 evaluation *effective*. This is called the 'depth-breadth trade-off'. The more environmental stressors you cover, the less detail you can present in AO1 and the less elaboration you can provide for AO2.

Topic 2 >> Altruism and bystander behaviour

In 1964, New Yorker Kitty Genovese was returning home from work. As she neared home, a man jumped out of the shadows, attacked and killed her. She screamed and tried to defend herself. Although 38 people heard her screams and many looked out of their windows and saw the attack, which lasted for over 40 minutes, no one went to her rescue and no one called the police. Why not? This topic explores the question of what causes people to act in a 'pro-social' way.

What is pro-social behaviour?

● *Helping* is a general term, which describes giving assistance to another person.

● *Altruism* is more specific and considers the motives for helping. Walster and Piliavin (1972) define altruism as 'helping behaviour that is voluntary, costly to the altruist and motivated by something other than the expectation of material or social reward'. Altruism is therefore different from helping, in that there is a regard for the interest of others, without apparent concern for one's self-interest.

● Both altruism and helping are forms of *pro-social behaviour* which can be defined as 'any actions that benefit another regardless of the benefits or self-sacrifices of the actor' (Wispe 1972).

Your response to distressing situations

1 Imagine you are sitting watching your 5-year-old son playing the part of a shepherd in the school nativity play. He has just one line to say, but when his time comes, he freezes. Everybody waits, but nothing comes out. And then, unseen by everybody but you, he begins to cry. What do you feel like doing?

2 You are flicking through a magazine when you come across a story about a terrible famine in East Africa. The article is accompanied by disturbing photos of emaciated children and adults.

Are you haunted by those images for the rest of the day, or do you quickly turn the page to escape the distressing situation?

ALTRUISM

The primary motivation for altruistic behaviour is seen as a desire to improve the welfare of another person rather than the anticipation of some reward or for any other reason that might indicate self-interest (Cardwell 2003). One of the major problems for psychologists has been determining what is truly *altruistic* and what might better be explained in terms of *egoism* (i.e. self-interest). Consider a child who helps to clear snow off an elderly neighbour's drive, and is then given money as a reward. How can an observer know if the child's helpful behaviour was altruistic (i.e. motivated by a desire to help the neighbour) or egoistic (i.e. motivated by a desire to make money or to avoid parental condemnation for not helping)?

Batson's empathy–altruism hypothesis

Empathy

Batson's 'empathy–altruism hypothesis' (Batson 1991) explains altruistic behaviour as a consequence of 'empathy'. Empathy involves feeling an emotional response that is consistent with another's emotional state or condition (i.e. feeling sad when we meet someone who is sad). Batson added that this empathy will also result in feelings of sorrow, concern or compassion *for the other person*. Witnessing another person in distress, therefore, will create empathic concern (e.g. sympathy) and helpers will then be motivated to help alleviate the other person's distress.

Empathy involves a number of different components, including:

● **perspective taking** – the ability to take another person's point of view that leads to empathic concern. If the perspective of the other person is not taken we experience only personal distress, rather than empathic concern

● **empathic concern** – feeling compassion for the welfare of another person who is suffering

● **personal distress** – an emotional reaction experienced when we see someone else suffering, coupled with self-orientated concerns to diminish the emotional reaction rather than altruistic

concerns for the other person. Any actions we take will be based on a desire to reduce our distress (i.e. egoistic motives) (see Fig. 11.3).

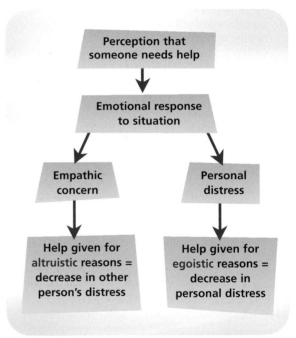

Figure 11.3 >> *The empathy–altruism model*

Research studies relating to the empathy–altruism model

Research in this area has found that people high in empathic concern are more likely to help others even when they are in a position to escape from this responsibility (see panel on Batson *et al.* 1981).

There is always the possibility that people help others in distress to avoid the disapproval of others who witness them not helping. Fultz *et al.* (1986) investigated the possibility that an expectation of negative social evaluation is a prerequisite for the empathy–altruism model of helping. Empathy was again manipulated, with participants being asked either to

study of the 'empathy condition' by Batson *et al.* (1981)

In one intriguing study, Batson *et al.* (1981) had female college students watch while another student (actually a confederate of the experimenter) received random electric shocks. To manipulate emotional reactions, the participants were told that they were either very similar to the student receiving the shocks (high-empathy condition) or very dissimilar to them (low-empathy/personal distress condition). In addition, half of the participants were told they were free to go after watching the participant for two trials, while the other half were told they could go after ten trials. After two trials the confederate appeared to become distressed and revealed a childhood fear of electric shocks. Participants were then faced with a difficult decision – take her place (showing empathetic concern) or leave (showing personal distress). Batson and colleagues found that those in the high-empathy condition were more likely to take her place. Additionally, participants in this condition who were free to leave after the second trial were more likely to stay and take her place. Among the 'personal distress' participants, only those who had been told to watch all ten trials tended to offer to replace the confederate. Those in the 'personal distress' condition who were free to leave tended to take the easy way out, and left.

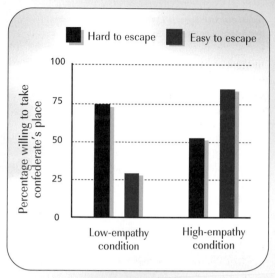

Figure 11.4 >> *Results of Batson et al.'s 1981 study*

imagine how the other person felt (high-empathy condition) or simply to observe the other person's behaviour (low-empathy condition). The possibility of social evaluation was also manipulated into high (public) and low (i.e. anonymous) conditions. As with the study by Batson and colleagues, there was more helping in the high-empathy than in the low-empathy condition. The possibility of social evaluation did not increase helping in the high-empathy participants (in fact the level of helping among high-empathy

participants was higher in the *low* social evaluation condition). Among low-empathy participants, however, the level of helping was lower in the anonymous condition than it was in the public condition. Consistent with the assumptions of the empathy–altruism model, this study suggests that when empathy is aroused, people do not help for purely egoistic reasons. However, in the absence of empathy, egoistic factors are more influential in determining whether or not help is given.

 ## Commentary
empathy–altruism model

● **Research support** – In their initial studies, Batson and colleagues showed that people help for reasons other than the reduction of their own personal distress. Indeed, recent research on adolescent altruism (Roker *et al.* 1998, cited in Pennington *et al.* 1999) has found that British adolescents show a high level of altruistic and helping behaviour, often unbeknown to their parents. Studies such as Fultz *et al.* (1986) cast doubt on the claim that people who show empathic concern help others in order to escape social disapproval. Such studies also

contradict the underlying assumption that human nature is fundamentally self-serving (Batson and Oleson 1991).

● **Alternative explanations** – Most of the studies used to support the empathy–altruism model are concerned only with helping over the short term rather than investigating the more long-term commitment to altruistic behaviour found in many people. As a result, there may well be alternative explanations (e.g. demand characteristics) that would account for participant behaviour in these studies *without* involving the complexities of perspective-taking and empathic concern.

continued on next page

Unit 11 // Pro- and anti-social behaviour

Commentary continued
empathy–altruism model

- *Evolution and altruism* – Kruger (2003) compared the influence of altruistic factors, such as empathic concern, with more egoistic factors, such as degree of genetic relatedness (kin selection) and reciprocity, in order to predict participants' intentions to perform a risky rescue behaviour. Reciprocal altruism (doing a favour in the belief that it will be returned at a later date) and kinship were the strongest predictors of rescue intentions. Empathic concern made a small but significant contribution in predicting helping intentions. This provides evidence that some altruistic mechanisms, such as empathic concern, may operate within a genetically 'selfish' system. Kruger reasons that because our ancestors lived in

small kin-based groups, mechanisms that may formerly have been restricted to kin may now be generalized to non-kin.

- *Oneness* – Cialdini *et al.* (1997) believe that individuals help not because they feel more empathic concern for another person, but because they feel more at one with them, i.e. they perceive something of themselves in the other person (e.g. they may be related or part of the same group). Cialdini and colleagues claim that the same conditions that typically lead to empathic concern also lead to this state of oneness. This suggests, therefore, that empathy–associated helping is not selfless, but is rooted in the desire to help that part of the self that is located in another. Increases in empathy, according to this view, are related to increases in the presence of the self in the other. As a result, empathy-associated helping would no longer be seen as altruistic.

The negative-state relief model (Cialdini *et al.* 1987)

The negative state

The negative-state relief model proposes that when we experience negative states (such as sadness or guilt), we are motivated to alleviate this condition by helping others. This is personally rewarding and thus eliminates the negative state. People learn during childhood that helping others in need is a positive behaviour that will make them feel good about themselves. According to this view, therefore, the motivation for helping is egoistic, depending on the anticipated emotional consequences. For example, we may see someone begging for money while we are out Christmas shopping. This might make us feel guilty, so we hand over a pound and feel better.

Negative-state relief

According to the negative-state relief hypothesis, the primary objective in any behaviour that appears altruistic is actually the enhancement of our own mood. If we are experiencing negative emotions, we may be motivated to help someone else as a way of relieving these emotions. It doesn't really matter whether the emotions are already present *before* the opportunity to help arises, or are aroused by the situation itself. Either way, helping someone in need offers a powerful antidote to whatever negative feelings we may be experiencing. If we are offered a less costly route to the same end result, however, we should, according to this hypothesis, take it (see Fig. 11.5).

Figure 11.5 >> *The negative-state relief model*

Research studies relating to the negative-state relief model

Two important pieces of research were carried out by Cialdini et al. (1987) and Manucia et al. (1984).

Cialdini *et al.* (1987)

Cialdini *et al.* (1987) carried out a study in much the same way as Batson had done to test his empathy–altruism hypothesis. Participants were again given instructions designed to create high- or low-empathy conditions and then put into a situation where they might help another person who was receiving electric shocks. This time, however, just before the request for help was made, the researchers offered a surprise monetary 'bonus'. According to the empathy–altruism hypothesis, highly empathic participants should help regardless of any attempts to elevate their mood by other means. Cialdini and colleagues, however, found that when participants were given the surprise 'bonus', there was no difference between the likelihood of high-empathy and low-empathy participants helping when the request for help was made. That is, elevating the mood of the high-empathy participants reduced their tendency to help. This supports the negative-state relief model. This study demonstrates that under some conditions, experiencing a mood-lifting event (in this case receiving money) may lessen our motivation to relieve our negative state by helping others.

Manucia *et al.* (1984)

The research by Cialdini and colleagues established that emotional distress led to increases in helping behaviour. However, this research failed to demonstrate that people helped solely in order to feel better. Manucia *et al.* (1984) used a bogus mood-freezing manipulation in order to demonstrate precisely that. In this study, participants were asked to recall distressing memories (negative mood condition) or neutral memories (control condition). Participants were also given a placebo drug and some were told that it would have the side effect of making it impossible for them to change their mood for an hour or so. As this would make any attempt to change mood (e.g. by helping someone in need) useless, it should have eliminated any behaviours that were performed solely for this reason. In line with the negative-state relief hypothesis, Manucia and colleagues found that the mood-freezing manipulation eliminated any increase in helping by participants in the negative-mood condition, i.e. people helped only when they believed that giving help could improve their emotional state, and not otherwise. The implication of this study, as predicted by the negative-state hypothesis, is that people help others to improve their own mood.

Commentary
negative-state relief model

● **Good and bad moods** – People use helping behaviour not just to repair a bad mood, but also to keep their good mood going, and so people in a good mood are more likely to help. Isen and Levin (1972) carried out a study in a shopping mall where participants either found or did not find a dime (10 cents) in a phone booth. As the person emerged from the booth, a confederate walked by, dropping a sheaf of papers: 84 per cent of those who found the money helped pick up the papers, compared with only 4 per cent of those who did not find the money. The relationship between pro-social behaviour and positive mood challenges the view that altruistic behaviour has the purely egoistic function of relieving a person's *negative* mood.

● **Altruism or egoism?** – Both Batson and Cialdini agree that when we come across someone in need, we are likely to feel sad and after helping them we are likely to feel happier. The subtle difference between the two hypotheses lies in *why* we help. Cialdini's view is that we help people in need primarily in order to feel better about ourselves, whereas Batson's view is that we help others because the victim needs help and, by helping, we then feel better about ourselves. The problem of whether people help others in distress for altruistic

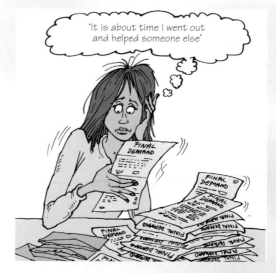

or egoistic reasons is not yet resolved. Batson (1991) does suggest one way in which these conflicting findings might be explained. He argues that we are more likely to feel empathic concern when we feel a close attachment to the person in need. On the other hand, we may feel only distress when we have no particular attachment or relationship with the person in need. In these conditions we may reduce our distress either by helping, or simply leaving the scene of the distress.

continued on next page

Unit 11 // Pro- and anti-social behaviour

- *Methodological limitations* – The *nature* of the research context in these studies is important. Most research on altruism has been carried out

with student volunteers and in laboratory simulations that bear very little similarity to helping in real-life situations. Cultural characteristics of individualist cultures, such as the USA, may well predispose individuals in such situations to be *less* helpful than individuals in cultures where *interdependence* is more the norm.

THE INFLUENCE OF OTHERS (BYSTANDER EFFECTS)

In the Kitty Genovese incident described on p. 349, there were 38 witnesses to her murder, yet no one helped or called the police. Some residents did turn on their lights and it is possible that one shouted from a window. This did not deter the attacker, who, despite the cries for help from his victim, continued his attack and killed her. Why had nobody helped in this situation? A large number of people witnessed the attack, which lasted over 40 minutes. Darley and Latané (1968) suspected that the fact that the number of possible helpers was so large might actually have contributed to their lack of intervention. They proposed a cognitive model of helping that might explain the reluctance of others to 'get involved' in situations such as the Kitty Genovese incident.

Latané and Darley's cognitive model

Diffusion of responsibility

When only one person is present, that person is 100 per cent responsible for giving help. When there are two people present, responsibility is divided. If there are ten bystanders, the onus of responsibility is diffused amongst all ten. In the Kitty Genovese case, witnesses assumed someone else had phoned for the police. Support for the notion of diffusion of responsibility comes not only from Latané and Darley's own research, but also from 'social loafing' research (Latané *et al.* 1979) where it has been shown that the more people who are present, the less effort each individual makes.

Pluralistic ignorance

When making a decision whether or not to help, we look to see what other bystanders are doing. If one person defines the situation as an emergency and helps, we are likely to follow and give assistance. If no one offers to give help, then we may conclude that the situation is not an emergency and do nothing. In effect, each bystander looks to the behaviour of others as a guide to their own behaviour. In the Kitty Genovese case, since no one was seen to be intervening, this tended to define the situation as one not requiring intervention from anyone.

The decision model

Latané and Darley (1970) formulated a five-stage model to explain why bystanders at emergencies sometimes do and sometimes do not decide to offer help. At each stage in the model, the decision 'No' results in no help being given, while the decision 'Yes' leads the individual closer to offering help (see Fig. 11.6). Latané and Darley argued that helping

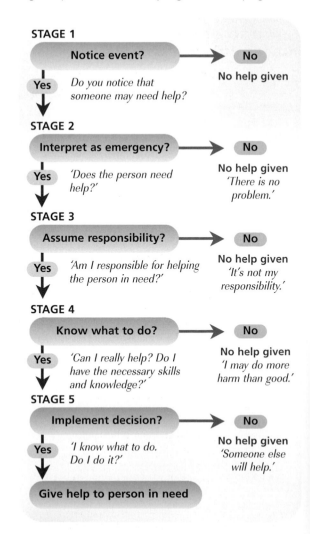

Figure 11.6 >> *Latané and Darley's cognitive model*

responses may be inhibited at any stage of the process. These 'inhibitions' and the stages they affect are:

- **Stage 1** – The bystander may not notice the situation.
- **Stage 2** – The situation may be ambiguous and not readily interpretable as an emergency. In this case the bystander may try to interpret the situation by observing the behaviour of other bystanders ('informational influence').
- **Stage 3** – The person may avoid taking responsibility by assuming that someone else will. This process is known as 'diffusion' and is likely to happen if the bystander sees danger in helping or if others are perceived as better able to offer help.
- **Stage 4** – Should the person wish to take responsibility for helping, they may not do so because they are neither trained nor competent to do so.
- **Stage 5** – Competent people may not help in an emergency because they perceive that it is against their interests to do so. For example, the recipient of help may be hostile or the situation itself may be dangerous (such as in assault cases).

Latané and Darley: research studies

Bystander effects in the laboratory

In their 'epileptic seizure' study, Darley and Latané (1968) used male students seated in cubicles connected by an intercom system. They had volunteered to take part in a discussion on college life. There were three conditions in the experiment. The students were led to believe that they were either alone with one other participant, who later would be heard to

Table 11.1 >> Bystander effects

Group size (no. of people)	% responding during fit	% responding at any point	Average response time (in seconds)
>> 1	85	100	52
>> 2	62	85	93
>> 5	31	62	166

Source: Darley and Latané (1968)

have an epileptic seizure, or that they were joined by either one *or* four other participants besides the apparent seizure victim. Once the discussion was underway, the victim clearly announced that he was experiencing a seizure. Help was less likely and slower to happen when participants believed that other potential helpers were present (see Table 11.1 above for results). That supports the concept of diffusion of responsibility.

Bystander effects in the natural environment

Latané and Darley (1970) found that when a person dropped some books in a lift, the probability of receiving help decreased with the number of people present: 40 per cent were offered help when there was one other passenger, but only 15 per cent when there were six others. Not all studies carried out in a natural environment, however, have found that large numbers mean little helping (see research studies relating to Piliavin's arousal: cost–reward model on p. 356).

Commentary
cognitive model

- **Research support** – Bickman (1972) has shown that the more ambiguous the situation, the less likely it is that help will be offered. Latané and Nida (1981) found that the helping response is inhibited when situations are manipulated to increase their ambiguity. As would be expected, people who have the responsibility of group leadership, or are trained and competent to deal with emergency situations, are more likely to help. Maruyama *et al.* (1982) found that increasing personal responsibility leads to an increase in helping. Clark and Word (1974) have shown the importance of necessary skills, and found that those with 'electrical' experience helped those who had apparently suffered an electric shock. It has been shown, however, that where there are no other people present, individuals will still help despite their lack of competence.

- **Bystander effects** – One well-established finding is that the presence of other observers reduces the likelihood that any one person will proffer a helping response (Latané and Nida 1981). This is consistent with the diffusion concept, suggested by Latané and Darley (1970). However, this effect does not appear to hold if a helping response is first modelled by an observer. Bryan and Test (1967) showed that people were more likely to help a person in distress if the specific behaviour has previously been modelled to them. This finding is interesting because it seems to be inconsistent with the notion that the presence of others inhibits helping. The process of conformity to social norms may explain this. That is, people use the actions of others as cues to decide what are appropriate responses to specific situations. When others help, this stimulates helping behaviour, but when others do not help, this inhibits helping behaviour.

The arousal:cost−reward model

Latané and Darley's model was an example of a *cognitive* approach to explaining bystander behaviour. An alternative theory is the arousal:cost−reward model, developed by Piliavin *et al.* (1981) to explain the results of their 'subway Samaritan study' (discussed below and on p. 357). This theory suggests that when people come across someone in need, they experience three stages before they either respond or walk away.

Physiological arousal

When we see someone in distress, we become physiologically aroused. The greater the arousal, the more likely it is that we will help. Gaertner and Dovidio (1977) found a strong positive correlation between the speed at which participants responded to an 'emergency' in a laboratory, and their heart rate – the faster the heart rate, the faster the speed of response.

Labelling the arousal

Physiological arousal, however, does not automatically produce specific emotions. How we interpret the arousal plays a critical role in determining the actual emotion that we feel. As we saw in the previous section on altruism, seeing someone else in distress elicits two kinds of responses: personal distress and empathic concern. Piliavin believed that physiological arousal was more likely to be labelled by bystanders as personal distress, especially if they did not have a close personal relationship with the person in need of help.

Cost−benefit analysis: evaluating the consequences of helping

After interpreting arousal, whether help is given or not depends on how one weighs up both the costs and benefits of helping, according to Piliavin.

The *costs of helping* may include:

- effort – e.g. helping may be physically demanding
- time – e.g. being late for work or an appointment
- loss of resources – e.g. damaging clothes or losing earnings
- risk of harm – e.g. risking life and limb
- negative emotional response – e.g. feeling physically sick.

All these factors are weighed against the *benefits of helping* such as:

- social approval – e.g. thanks from victim (and crowd, if there is one)
- self-esteem – e.g. feeling that one is a kind person
- positive emotional response – e.g. feelings (such as elation) elicited by successful rescue.

Figure 11.7 >> *How Piliavin et al.'s model might explain some real-life situations*

It is argued by Piliavin and colleagues that such a cost−benefit analysis is performed to reduce negative emotional arousal, and in addition to the above factors, the costs of *not helping* must also be assessed. These may include:

- disapproval – e.g. no rewards from victim or crowd
- damaged self-esteem – e.g. feelings that one is not a kind person
- negative emotional response – e.g. not helping may cause feelings of guilt.

The Piliavin model has been demonstrated in a number of studies which have found that increasing various costs will lead to a decrease in helping, whilst increasing the benefits will lead to an increase in helping. Some examples of situations that might be explained by this model are described in Fig. 11.7.

Research studies relating to the arousal:cost−reward model

The 'Subway Samaritan'

Piliavin *et al.* (1969) conducted a study to investigate the effects on helping of the type of person who is in need. They looked at the effect on help offered of (a) the victim appearing ill or drunk, and (b) the race of the victim (Black or White). During a seven-and-a-half minute journey on a busy New York subway train, the 'victim' accomplice collapsed on the floor of the train and remained there until someone helped. The major findings of the study are as follows:

- Those appearing to be ill were more likely to be helped than those appearing to be drunk.

- The race of the 'victim' had little effect on the helping.
- The expected diffusion of responsibility effect did not occur.

Why was this? Piliavin and colleagues suggest that in the laboratory studies, participants could *hear* but not *see* the 'victim', whereas in this study, participants could both see and hear the 'victim'. Participants could also see what bystanders were *actually* doing.

Characteristics of the person in need

Undoubtedly we perceive certain types of people to be more deserving of help than others. We help those to whom we are related and those for whom we feel responsible. Research (e.g. Piliavin *et al.* 1981) has generally shown the following:

- We are more likely to help those who are perceived to be similar to ourselves.
- We are more likely to help those we perceive as less able to help themselves, e.g. children and elderly people.
- We are more likely to help those to whom we are physically attracted.
- We are less likely to help those who are not attractive, particularly those who are disfigured (unless we are also disfigured).
- We are less likely to help those whom we perceive as responsible for their own plight.

Characteristics of the potential helper

- *Helping personality* – In an attempt to answer this question, Bierhoff *et al.* (1991) compared the personal characteristics of those who witnessed a road traffic accident and provided first aid, with those who witnessed such an accident and did not provide help. The results of this study are shown in Table 11.2.
- *Mood* – Other research has concentrated on more transitory psychological states, such as the *mood* someone is in when they encounter another person in need. Being in a good mood may lead to helping if the consequences of helping are likely to be pleasant and where there is little ambiguity about help being needed. If, however, the need is ambiguous and the consequences of helping are likely to be unpleasant, then people in a good mood tend not to help. According to Isen (1984), this is because they do not want to spoil the good mood they are currently enjoying. Likewise, being in a bad mood may help pro-social behaviour. A bad mood, especially if it is due to guilt, might be alleviated by helping someone (the negative-state relief hypothesis, see p. 352).

- *Alcohol consumption* – Steele and Southwick (1985) have even shown that the consumption of alcohol sometimes leads to helping behaviour. This may happen because alcohol reduces inhibitions and awareness of potential dangers.

The relationship between helper characteristics and the likelihood of helping is a complex one. The characteristics of the situation, the need for help and the personal characteristics of the helper interact in complex ways that determine whether or not help will be given.

> ### Table 11.2 >> Components of the helping personality
>
> **Characteristics of those who did help**
> >> had high internal locus of control
> >> held belief in a 'just world'
> >> felt socially responsible
> >> possessed ability to empathize
> >> were less egocentric
>
> **Characteristics of those who did not help**
> >> had low internal locus of control
> >> held less belief in a 'just world'
> >> felt less socially responsible
> >> possessed less ability to empathize
> >> were more egocentric
>
> *Source: adapted from Bierhoff et al. (1991)*

Commentary
arousal : cost–reward model

- *Research support* – There is considerable support for the claim that people are aroused by the distress of others. Such a reaction is seen quite early developmentally and also appears across many different cultures, suggesting that this is a biologically inherited capacity (Manstead *et al.* 1995). There is also support for the claim that arousal increases the likelihood of helping in an emergency, although there is less agreement about whether people help to reduce their personal distress or because of empathic concern.

continued on next page

● *Modification to arousal:cost–benefit model* –
Piliavin later acknowledged that in very serious
emergencies, where lives may be lost and when
arousal is very high, people may offer help
without carrying out a cost–benefit analysis.
In such situations, people may rush to help
impulsively without taking account of the costs
they might incur.

● *An alternative explanation* – Weiner (1986) has
proposed an attributional explanation of when we

are likely to help another person in distress
(see pp. 276–7). When we come across someone
in distress, we search for possible causes of their
plight. If we decide their plight is a product of
uncontrollable causes (e.g. an accident), we feel
sympathy and are more likely to help. On the
other hand, if we feel their plight is more a
product of controllable causes (e.g. their
drunkenness), we feel anger or irritation, and are
less likely to help. According to this perspective,
determining the possible costs and rewards of
helping is insufficient when deciding whether or
not to help.

CULTURAL DIFFERENCES IN PRO-SOCIAL BEHAVIOUR

Differences *between* cultures

Individualism and collectivism

Individualist societies tend to stress the need for
individual achievement and independence, whilst
collectivist (communal) societies stress
interdependence, where individuals depend on each
other. Miller (1994) compared the Hindu culture of
India (a collectivist culture) with the United States (an
individualist culture) in their attitudes towards helping
others. She found that Hindu Indians feel a general
obligation to respond to others' needs, whereas
Americans feel that any such obligation is more
dependent upon the nature of the relationship (e.g.
helping a family member or someone that they *liked*).

In a test of the assumed differences between
individualist and collectivist cultures, Nadler (1986)
compared Israeli urban dwellers with those living on a
kibbutz in terms of their attitudes to helping. Nadler
found that those who had been raised communally
were more likely to help and seek help than those
raised in a city, especially when the help was seen to
benefit the group rather than just the individual. In
order to test whether these results really were the
product of individualist or collectivist experiences,
Nadler (1993) compared these two groups with recent
immigrants to Israel, one group from the US (an
individualist culture) and one from the Soviet Union
(then generally considered a collectivist culture). As
before, the kibbutz dwellers were *most* likely to seek
help, and the US immigrants and Israeli city dwellers
less likely to do so. The Soviet immigrants were *least*
likely to seek help – within the former Soviet Union,
people tended only to seek help from those to whom
they felt close and intimate, avoiding interactions
outside this small circle of family and friends. This tells
us that interdependence may be more narrowly defined

to include only those individuals who can offer
reciprocal help when needed.

Pro-social behaviour and the regulation of social relationships

An example of the role that pro-social behaviour, or
specifically helping behaviour, plays in the
establishment of social relationships can be found in
the Chinese custom of *guanxixue* (guan-shee-shwe),
meaning 'doing favours for people' (Moghaddam 1998).
This involves 'the exchange of gifts, favours, and
banquets; the cultivation of personal relationships and
networks of mutual dependence; and the manufacturing
of obligations and indebtedness' (Yang 1994).

Through *guanxixue*, individuals can create extensive
social networks involving many others who are morally
obligated to them. A cultural perspective of pro-social
behaviour, therefore, allows us to see that helping and
being helped involves much more than just
instrumental benefits. Culture also provides the rules
and norms concerning when it is appropriate to seek
and to offer help. If the objective of pro-social
behaviour was simply to maximize benefits, then we
would expect people to seek help and take it whenever
it is offered.

ACTIVITY

Individualism, collectivism and rewards

Read through the Key research below.

● What are the main conclusions of this study?

● Do these results show evidence of an equity rule,
an equality rule or both in operation in these two
cultures?

● How would you respond if you were the person
responsible for the reward allocation?

individualism, collectivism and reward allocation: a cross-cultural study

Underlying much of the theorizing about individualism and collectivism is the idea that collectivism involves the equal sharing of rewards from collaborative efforts, whilst individualism entails the maximization of personal gain.

Recent studies carried out in Hong Kong and other collectivist Asian cultures have found evidence for a distribution of rewards based on equality (i.e. rewards are shared equally regardless of the amount of any one individual's contribution), whereas for members of individualist cultures, the equity rule is favoured (those who contribute the most deserve the most rewards).

Members of collectivist cultures do not, however, appear to apply the equality rule beyond the confines of their own group but, on the contrary, make greater use of an equity rule. Members of individualist cultures tend to apply the equity rule both to in-group members and out-group members, demonstrating the priority of personal goals over in-group goals. Russia is a country which historically has embodied the values of collectivism, therefore it might be hypothesized that Russians would behave in similar ways to members of other collectivist cultures in their preferred patterns of reward allocation.

This study compared British and Russian participants with respect to their use of equity and equality rules when sharing rewards after a hypothetical collaborative task. The researchers predicted that the British participants would be influenced only by the levels of task performance, allocating more rewards for more work (the equity rule). In contrast, they expected the Russian participants to be influenced by the levels of task performance (i.e. an equity rule) only when the co-worker was a stranger. When the hypothetical co-worker was a friend, they would be more likely to share any rewards equally with them regardless of the amount they had contributed to the task (the equality rule).

The main results are described in the table below. Note that each of these percentages refers to the allocation that the participants allocated to themselves. The levels of task performance were always manipulated so that the person doing the allocating either contributed 80 per cent of the task involvement (high performance) or 20 per cent (low performance). Therefore, if participants made equitable distributions they would allocate 80 per cent of the reward to themselves under the high performance condition, and 20 per cent under the low performance condition.

	Britain	Russia
	% given to self	% given to self
High performance		
>> Friend as co-worker	68.25	58.00
>> Stranger as co-worker	64.00	73.00
Low performance		
>> Friend as co-worker	33.15	20.10
>> Stranger as co-worker	33.30	19.60

As a conclusion to this study, Tower and colleagues gathered qualitative data from focus group discussions with the two sets of participants. The following explanations were typical of responses from the two groups.

'She is my very close friend. Situations and circumstances might differ. One day I might need some help and understanding too. I trust my close friends.' (Russian participant)

'What you put in is what you get out – this is fair. If the mate was a close friend, I'm sure that he/she would understand.' (British participant)

Source: Tower *et al.* (1997)

Differences *within* cultures

Gender differences

● **Giving help** – Girls have sometimes been shown to be more helpful in a variety of different tests of pro-social behaviour (e.g. Eisenberg *et al.* 1991), although research findings in this area are not always consistent. Why might this be? One possibility is that differences in pro-social behaviour between the sexes can be attributed to differences in the social roles typically adopted by men and women. Eagly (1987) suggests that the uneven distribution of men and women into particular social roles is determined by gender-role differences. Because of these differences in gender-role behaviour, men are more predisposed to occupations where a certain amount of risk-taking is the norm. One might assume, therefore, that men are more likely to intervene in dangerous situations, an assumption that is supported by research (Piliavin *et al.* 1969). Indeed, contrary to the popular stereotype, men appear to be more helpful than women. In a meta-analysis of 99 different studies, 62 per cent of the studies found males were more helpful than females (Eagly and Crowley 1986).

● **Seeking help** – Cultural rules governing gender relations may account for the fact that, in most cultures, women *seek* help more than men (Moghaddam 1998). Cultural rules allow women to present themselves as 'in need', whereas male concerns for 'toughness' and 'independence' may prevent them from seeking the help of others. Glick and Fiske (1996) coined the phrase 'benevolent sexism' to describe the stereotypical protective attitude that many men have towards women, which contributes both to the higher percentage of males *offering* help, and the higher percentage of females *seeking* help.

Urban–rural differences

One of the enduring assumptions about increasing urbanization is that it interferes with the natural patterns of living together that characterize people in smaller communities (Bierhoff 2002). Early research certainly appeared to confirm this assumption. For example, people living in rural areas of Massachusetts were more likely to help callers who had dialled a wrong number or to mail apparently lost postcards, than were people living in the city of Boston (Korte and Kerr 1975). More recent studies (e.g. Levine *et al.* 1994), however, suggest that population *density* (i.e. population per square mile) is a better predictor of helping than population *size*. These results may be explained in two ways:

● **Diffusion of responsibility** (Latané and Darley 1970) – Higher densities would indicate a higher diffusion of responsibility and therefore lead to less individual responsibility for helping.

● **The information-overload hypothesis** (Milgram 1970) – People from cities are so familiar with emergency situations that they treat them as everyday occurrences – these situations are less likely to attract interest and so people do not help. According to this view, urban residents restrict their attention to personally relevant events and so the needs of strangers may go unnoticed. People from small towns, however, do not witness emergencies very often, so that when these situations occur, their novelty is more likely to attract attention and help. This claim is supported in numerous studies (e.g. Gelfand *et al.* 1973), which show that people with small-town backgrounds are more likely to help in an emergency than those from larger cities.

ACTIVITY

Using the Internet to find research

Using the Internet, identify and summarize the results of one study that has explored urban–rural differences in pro-social behaviour, and one study that has explored gender differences in pro-social behaviour.

Using a search engine such as *Google*, try typing in words such as 'research urban-rural differences pro-social behaviour'. It might be worth trying alternative spellings, such as 'prosocial' or the American 'behavior'.

Commentary
cultural differences in pro-social behaviour

● **Laboratory and field studies** – These studies often produce contradictory results concerning the likelihood of helping and seeking help. Laboratory studies typically find that people will go out of their way to avoid seeking help from others, yet field studies find that people are more disposed to help others and will go out of their way to seek help (Wills 1992). Laboratory-based studies tend to lack the *social* context of help-seeking. Faced with a limited time period with anonymous fellow participants, there would seem little point in trying to develop a social relationship in such a context. In the real world, however, people actively help and seek out the help of others to *extend* their social relationships (Moghaddam 1998).

continued on next page

Commentary continued
cultural differences in pro-social behaviour

AO2

- Much of the research on human altruism that is carried out in the West is done in laboratories, whereas much of the research carried out in non-Western cultures is field research. Therefore, this difference in type of research may give us a false impression of cultural differences in pro-social behaviour.

- *Short and long-term help* – Although many of the studies of gender differences appear to contradict the popular gender stereotype that women are more helpful than men, we should guard against accepting this conclusion without reservation. Most studies concentrate on the help given to

strangers in short-term encounters, and largely neglect the longer-term help offered to friends and family members (Bierhoff 2002). Research on gender differences in helping behaviour, therefore, does not represent all forms of helping equally.

- *Urban–rural differences* – Research has generally supported the assumption that people in rural communities are more inclined to act pro-socially than people in urban areas, but rural areas may also be characterized by a reluctance to act pro-socially in some circumstances (Steblay 1987). Milgram's information-overload hypothesis may only be valid, therefore, if additional factors are also taken into account. One of these concerns the strength of in-group favouritism shown by members of smaller communities (which would, therefore make them less likely to help an outsider).

✓ CHECK YOUR UNDERSTANDING

Check your understanding of altruism and bystander behaviour by answering these questions from memory. Then check your answers by looking back through Topic 2.

1 What do you understand by the terms 'altruism' and 'bystander behaviour'?

2 What is the difference between 'altruistic' and 'egoistic' behaviour?

3 Construct a descriptive 150-word précis of the empathy–altruism model and a 150-word précis of the negative-state relief model.

4 What are the main differences between these two explanations of altruism?

5 Identify three critical (i.e. AO2) points relating to the empathy–altruism model, and explain *why* these pose problems for this explanation.

6 How would the cognitive model of Latané and Darley explain the Kitty Genovese incident?

7 Identify two research studies relating to bystander behaviour and offer a brief critical commentary (i.e. AO2) on each study.

8 Briefly outline two explanations for urban–rural differences in pro-social behaviour.

9 How confident can we be in stating that there are gender differences in pro-social behaviour? Justify your answer.

10 Are there cultural differences in pro-social behaviour? Construct a 300-word précis that answers this question (150 words of AO1 and 150 words of *effective* AO2).

REVISION SUMMARY

Having covered this topic you should be able to describe and evaluate:

✓ explanations of human altruism

✓ research studies relating to human altruism

✓ explanations of bystander behaviour

✓ research studies relating to bystander behaviour

✓ cultural differences in pro-social behaviour.

Below are some **possible examination questions** set on this topic, along with hints to help you understand and approach each question effectively:

1 Critically consider **two** explanations of human altruism. (24 marks)

'Critically consider' is an AO1+AO2 term indicating that you must both describe and evaluate your explanations. As two explanations are required, there would be a partial performance penalty if you provided only one. However, there is no need for your answer to be exactly balanced – you may describe (and evaluate) one theory in more detail than the other. For full marks, however, you should not focus almost exclusively on one theory but should try to offer more or less the same coverage of each explanation. Question 3 in 'Check your Understanding' will help you prepare for this.

2 (a) Describe **one** explanation of human altruism. (12 marks)
   (b) Evaluate the social psychological theory of human altruism you described in (a) in terms of relevant research studies. (12 marks)

Part (a) requires an extended descriptive coverage of just one explanation. If you have difficulty presenting enough material on your explanation for 12 marks worth (about 300 words), you could introduce some research studies to display your understanding of the theory more clearly. Don't make the mistake of padding out your essay with an introduction or a definition of altruism; neither would gain credit. In part (b), *description* of research studies would not be creditworthy. You must *use* the studies to evaluate the explanation. Any evaluation of the research studies could also be credited as AO2. For example, you might consider the participants used in the study and whether this reduces the validity of the findings and conclusions of the study.

3 Outline and evaluate **two or more** research studies relating to human altruism **and/or** bystander behaviour. (24 marks)

Questions in this area often give you the choice of writing about altruism and/or bystander behaviour. There are no tricks in this question – the choice really is yours. If you feel you know enough about *either* altruism *or* bystander behaviour, then choose that option as you are more likely to have detail and elaboration in your answer. If you don't have enough to write, then choose the 'and' option. As the question refers explicity to 'research studies', then explanations would not receive credit except inasmuch as they might offer commentary on a study. Note that you are restricted in this question to human behaviour, so research studies that involve non-human animals would not be creditworthy. However, again, such research might be introduced as commentary but must be done so *explicitly*.

4 Discuss cultural differences in pro-social behaviour. (24 marks)

Each question has 24 marks, 12 for AO1 and 12 for AO2. That means that half your answer to this question should be AO2 commentary. To make this *effective*, the points made should always be elaborated so the examiner is clear about what you mean. Guidance about innovative and effective AO2 is provided on p. 937. Don't forget that you can include sub-cultural (i.e. *within* cultures) differences in your answer, as sub-cultures are a form of culture.

5 (a) Outline **one or more** explanations of human altruism **and/or** bystander behaviour. (12 marks)
   (b) To what extent are there cultural differences in pro-social behaviour? (12 marks)

In part (a), you are offered a choice of presenting one or more explanations. This tells you that you can gain full marks if you only cover one explanation. However, if you feel that you cannot write enough on one explanation, you can opt for greater breadth and describe more than one explanation. There is no credit in this question for an evaluation of your explanation(s) unless the focus is on cultural differences. In some parted questions material can be 'exported' from one part to another, if it is relevant. Any evaluation in part (a) could be exported, as long as it related to cultural differences. As with question 2(b) above, part (b) of this question requires more than just a *description* of cultural differences in pro-social behaviour, but a *commentary* on them (e.g. research support for cultural differences, explanations for them, methodological difficulties, etc.). Any descriptive material may be 'scene-setting' and gain a small amount of credit.

MEDIA INFLUENCES ON PRO-SOCIAL BEHAVIOUR

The late 1950s and early 1960s produced a growing concern over the portrayal of violence on television and its potential effects, particularly on the behaviour of children. While the majority of the literature has focused on the effects of viewing violent behaviour, a substantial number of studies have provided evidence for the potential value of the media for developing pro-social behaviour. These studies have demonstrated that children imitate forms of pro-social behaviour, such as altruism, helping, delay of gratification and positive interaction with others, when exposed to models displaying such behaviours.

Explanations of media influences on pro-social behaviour

Exposure to pro-social messages

Although there are periodic moral panics concerning the exposure of children to violence on television, children are also exposed to a fair proportion of pro-social acts as well. An early content analysis of US broadcasting found that, on average, there were eleven altruistic acts and six sympathetic behaviours per hour of programming (Liebert and Poulos 1975). However, as in real life, these pro-social acts frequently appeared in the context of *anti-social* behaviour, with one study finding that among the favourite television programmes of 8- to 12-year-olds, there were an average of 42.2 acts of anti-social behaviour and 44.2 acts of pro-social behaviour in an average hour (Greenberg *et al.* 1980). Although there have been relatively few recent content analyses of pro-social content on television, studies have continued to demonstrate that pro-social content on television is clearly as evident as anti-social content.

Social learning theory

How might children learn pro-social messages having been exposed to them? Bandura's social learning theory (Bandura 1965, see p. 341) suggests that children learn by first observing a behaviour, then later imitating it if the expectation of reward is greater than the expectation of punishment for that behaviour. The process of social learning works in the same way for learning pro-social

acts seen on television as it does for learning anti-social acts. Unlike the depiction of *anti-social* acts, however, the depiction of pro-social acts (such as generosity or helping) is likely to be in accord with established social norms (e.g. the need to be generous and helpful to others). Assuming that these social norms have been internalized by the viewer, the imitation of these acts, therefore, is likely to be associated with the expectation of social reinforcement, and so the child is motivated to repeat these actions in their own life.

Developmental trends in pro-social influence

We might expect there to be developmental trends in the influence of pro-social messages because many of the skills associated with pro-social reasoning develop with age (see discussion of Eisenberg's theory on p. 364). Pro-social behaviours have been shown to be contingent on the development of pro-social skills, such as perspective-taking, empathy and level of moral reasoning, which continue to develop throughout childhood and into adolescence (Eisenberg 1990). For example, research has shown that young children are less able to recognize the emotional state of others (Hoffman 1976) and are less sure of how to help (Barnett *et al.* 1987, cited in Mares 1996). It is also evident from research that young children have more difficulty understanding abstract pro-social messages, and may be less affected by pro-social messages if these portrayals are more complex than the simple modelling of a specific behaviour (Mares 1996).

Commentary
explanations of media influences

- **Exposure to pro-social messages** – A number of studies have found that the pro-social messages in programmes such as *Sesame Street* and *Mr Rogers' Neighbourhood* are getting through to children and are influencing their values and behaviour. Evidence from the meta-analyses carried out by Hearold (1986) and Mares (1996) add testimony to this claim. Many of these studies, however, have demonstrated that children fail to

generalize from the specific act seen on screen to new and different situations. Some specially constructed pro-social programmes, used primarily in educational settings, have been criticized for not being of the same production quality as broadcast material, and for failing to provide sufficient opportunity for children to rehearse the key behaviours being portrayed (Zielinska 1985). Pro-social behaviours depicted in educational programming seem only to enhance the extent to which young children exhibit similar behaviours if sufficient opportunities are provided for rehearsing these behaviours (Gunter and McAleer 1997).

continued on next page

Commentary continued
explanations of media influences

- **Social learning theory** – Exposure to filmed models has less effect than exposure to real-life models. Pro-social programming *does* appear to have an effect, but the effect tends to be relatively short-lived and may not generalize to new settings. Nonetheless, although filmed models may have less influence on pro-social behaviour than live models, it is likely that prolonged viewing of pro-social programming could result in substantial and enduring increases in children's pro-social behavior (Eisenberg 1983). Social learning theory also requires that children *notice* a particular act or message, and must then remember it so that they can recreate it some time in the future. A characteristic of many anti-social acts is that they have high impact value, whereas pro-social acts tend to be more subtle and abstract, and therefore less memorable. An additional problem for young children arises when two segments of a story line are separated by adverts, and therefore lose some of their impact.

- **Developmental trends in pro-social influence** – Research has tended to show that pro-social messages have a greater effect on young children than on adolescents. This is contrary to what we might expect given the development of pro-sociality proposed by Eisenberg (1987). However, when younger and older children do imitate pro-social behaviours they have seen modelled on television, their motives might be quite different. Midlarsky and Hannah (1985) suggest that younger children have more egocentric motives in that they may imitate pro-social behaviours if they believe these will bring them reward or help them avoid punishment. In contrast, adolescents are better able to understand the underlying principle of abstract pro-social messages and are more likely to act for altruistic reasons (Roker *et al.* 1998).

Research into media influences on pro-social behaviour

Lovelace and Huston (1983) have identified three modelling strategies used by researchers for the transmission of pro-social messages:

- **pro-social only** – only pro-social behaviours are modelled

- **pro-social conflict resolution** – pro-social behaviours are presented alongside anti-social behaviours

- **conflict without resolution** – problems are presented that *suggest* pro-social solutions.

Although these strategies have the potential for pro-social effects on adults, most of the attention has been directed towards their effect on children. Each of these strategies is based on *social learning theory*, which holds that viewing modelled behaviours, particularly if the consequences of such behaviours are personally desirable, results in an imitation of those behaviours.

Pro-social behaviour only

Research using this strategy has focused on media models who show pro-social or courageous behaviour. Several studies (e.g. Sprafkin *et al.* 1975) have demonstrated the positive effects of pro-social models on television on children's helping behaviour. In particular, these studies have found that children's willingness to help can be increased through viewing a televised example of a *specific* pro-social behaviour. This supports the predictions of social learning theory, that the effects of a televised example will be mediated by specific modelling cues rather than the general pro-social format of the show.

Pro-social conflict resolution

Television programmes that present only pro-social behaviour are rare. Typically, pro-social behaviour is presented alongside or in contrast to anti-social behaviour. Several studies have investigated the effectiveness of pro-social messages when they are presented in this context. Paulson (1974) investigated the effects of modelling pro-social alongside anti-social behaviour. This was part of a *Sesame Street* programme (see photo below) designed to teach cooperation (a pro-social behaviour). Findings of this study, which took place over a six-month period, indicated that children who saw the programmes recognized cooperation when they saw it, and subsequently scored higher on measures of cooperation compared to children who had not seen the programmes. Unfortunately, the researchers found no evidence of an increase in the general level of these children's pro-social behaviour during free play.

Conflict without resolution

In the third type of modelling strategy, unresolved conflicts are presented to children via the media. Programme content frequently deals with problems that are likely to be encountered when growing up, such as parental pressure, male–female relationships, privacy and friendship. A character is seen as struggling with a particular problem (for example, should she continue seeing someone of whom her parents clearly disapprove), but no decision is made. Children are encouraged to discuss how they would resolve the problem faced by the central character.

Meta-analyses of media influences on pro-social behaviour

A meta-analysis allows researchers to compare results across many different studies, and to establish an average 'effect size' (i.e. the size of the difference between an experimental and control condition in a research study) for a particular aspect of pro-social behaviour. Hearold (1986), carried out a meta-analysis of 230 studies of the effects of television and found the following:

> <<Although fewer studies exist on pro-social effects, the effect size is so much larger, holds up better under more stringent experimental conditions and is consistently higher for both boys and girls, that the potential for pro-social overrides the small but persistent effects of anti-social programmes.>>

A more recent meta-analysis in this area was carried out by Mares (1996). Mares included four different categories of pro-social behaviour in her analysis, spread over 39 different studies. These are the main findings and the effect size for each category of pro-social behaviour:

- **Positive interaction** – This included friendly/nonaggressive interactions, expressions of affection and peaceable conflict resolution. Children who viewed positive interactions tended to act more positively in their own interactions with others, compared to those who viewed neutral or anti-social content. The effect size was found to be moderate.

- **Altruism** – This included sharing, donating, offering help and comforting. Children who viewed explicitly modelled altruistic behaviours tended to behave more altruistically than those who viewed neutral or anti-social content. The effect size was found to be moderate to large. Where altruism was not explicitly modelled, but required generalization from one context to another, the effect size was much smaller.

- **Self-control** – This included resistance to temptation, obedience to rules, ability to work independently and persistence at a task. Children who viewed models exercising self-control tended to show more self-control in their own behaviour, particularly when compared to those who saw a model behaving *anti-socially* (e.g. disobeying rules). The effect size was moderate when comparisons were made with neutral content, but large when comparisons were made with anti-social content.

- **Anti-stereotyping** – This included the effects of counter-stereotypical portrayals of gender and ethnicity on attitudes and beliefs. Children who viewed counter-stereotypical themes showed less evidence of stereotyping and prejudice in their own attitudes and beliefs. The effect size was moderate, but was much larger when exposure to counter-stereotypical themes in the context of a school classroom was accompanied by extra classroom activities designed to expand on the issues viewed.

Evaluation
research into media influences

The 'pro-social only' model

- **Limited generalization** – The measures of pro-sociality are typically taken in an artificial and contrived environment, limiting their application to children's behaviour in real-life settings. Thus, generalizations to other situations may be limited.

- **Short-lived effects** – It is also evident that many of the effects that have been produced by these interventions have been very short-lived (Rushton and Owen 1975).

The pro-social conflict resolution model

- **Conflicting messages** – It is also possible that children might adopt the anti-social behaviours that are modelled alongside the pro-social behaviours in such programmes. In fact, some research studies have found increases in assertiveness and aggression when children have been exposed to *Mr Rogers' Neighbourhood* as part of a 'Head Start' intervention programme (Friedrich-Cofer *et al.* 1979).

- **Justifying aggression** – Lovelace and Huston (1983) also observed that negative effects might occur if the pro-social behaviours were not shown in clear contrast to the anti-social behaviours. A study by Liss and Reinhardt (1979) supported this conclusion. They found an increase in aggressive behaviour in children who had watched a cartoon series *Superfriends*. Although both pro-social and anti-social behaviours were modelled in this series, characters usually demonstrated some justification for their aggressive behaviour, and so legitimized it for those watching.

continued on next page

The 'conflict without resolution' model

● *Research support* – Some research has indicated that children do understand and learn the programme content and are able to generate pro-social rather than anti-social solutions to the problems faced in the plot (Rockman 1980).

● *Conflicting evidence* – Other studies have indicated limited potential for pro-social change with this kind of programme, and that children younger than 8 might not benefit from this type of modelling as effectively as older children (Lovelace and Huston 1983).

Meta-analyses of pro-social effects

● *Hearold (1986)* – Comstock (1989) has explained Hearold's findings thus: pro-social messages are generally *designed* to have an influence on viewers, whereas anti-social messages are not specifically designed for that purpose. Hearold's study did not, however, contain age comparisons, although she did report that after the age of 6, pro-social messages in television appeared to have a stronger effect on girls than on boys.

● *Mares (1996)* – As with Hearold's study, in most of the studies analysed by Mares, results were not broken down by sex. However, in those that were, and consistent with Hearold's findings, more positive effects were discovered for girls. Also, pro-social messages have a greater effect with primary age children than with adolescents. Many studies have found that pro-social effects were limited to those situations which were similar to the pro-social act seen in the television programme. This perhaps highlights the need to be specific when attempting behaviour change through this medium, and contrasts with the typical finding that viewers are able to generalize *anti-social* behaviours from one context to another more readily than they can *pro-social* behaviours.

MEDIA INFLUENCES ON ANTI-SOCIAL BEHAVIOUR

<<There can be no longer any doubt that heavy television violence is one of the causes of aggressive behaviour, crime and violence ... Television violence affects youngsters of all ages, of both genders, at all socio-economic levels and all levels of intelligence ... The causal effect of television violence on aggression, even though it is not large, exists.>> (Eron 1992)

<<What, then, can be seen as the 'different' factor that has entered the lives of countless children and adolescents in recent years? This has to be recognized as the easy availability to children of gross images of violence on video.>> (Newson 1994)

These statements, from influential psychologists either side of the Atlantic, give you an idea of the way in which many people, psychologists included, view the media/violence debate. For many, there is simply no question that television and other forms of media are responsible for today's violent behaviour in society, particularly in children. For others, the debate is far from clear. In this next section we will look at the evidence and examine critically the claims of such a 'media effects' model.

Studies into the effects of exposure to television violence

Correlational studies

The weight of evidence from correlational studies is fairly consistent: viewing and/or preference for violent television is *related* to aggressive attitudes, values and behaviours. Atkin *et al.* (1979) gave 9- to 13-year-old boys and girls situations such as the following: 'Suppose that you are riding your bicycle down the street and some other child comes up and pushes you off your bicycle. What would you do?' The response options included physical or verbal aggression, along with options to reduce or avoid conflict. These investigators found that physically or verbally aggressive responses were selected by 45 per cent of heavy viewers of television violence, compared to only 21 per cent of those who watched little television violence.

Although correlational studies suggest a link between watching television violence and engaging in violent behaviour, they do not demonstrate a *causal* relationship between the two. To investigate this, psychologists must choose methods which give them more control over the conditions in which violence is viewed and the behavioural measurement of violence.

Experimental studies

Bandura *et al.* (1963) (see Key research, p. 341) showed that children who had viewed an aggressive model on film were more aggressive in their play than those who had not observed the aggressive model. Early studies such as this were criticized on the grounds that the aggressive behaviour was not meaningful within the social context and that the stimulus materials were not representative of available television programming. Addressing this criticism, Liebert and Baron (1972) investigated young children's willingness to hurt another child after viewing videotaped sections of aggressive or neutral real television programmes. The boys and girls were in two age groups: 5 to 6, and 8 to 9. The aggressive programme consisted of segments of *The Untouchables*, while the neutral programme featured an athletics race. The main findings were that the children who viewed the aggressive programme demonstrated a greater willingness to hurt another child.

It is clear from experimental studies such as these that we can produce an increase in aggressive behaviour following a fairly brief exposure to televised violence, but the question remains as to whether the heightened aggression observed in the laboratory would spill over into everyday life. To investigate this, the impact of violence in the media has to be studied in more natural settings.

Field experiments

Field experiments retain the advantages of experimental design, but avoid the problem of demand cues since participants do not usually know they are being studied. In the typical field experiment, the investigator presents television programmes in the normal viewing setting and observes behaviour where it naturally occurs. The investigator typically controls the television diet of the participants by arranging a special series of programmes. An example is described in the panel below.

Study of aggression by Parke *et al.* (1977)

Parke *et al.* (1977) found heightened aggression among both American and Belgian teenage boys following exposure to aggressive films. In the Belgian study, teenage boys living in a minimum-security institution were presented with a diet of either aggressive or neutral films. This study included a one-week baseline observation period, followed by one week of film viewing, and a one-week post-viewing observation period. There were four cottages involved. Two cottages contained boys with high levels of aggressive behaviour; two contained boys with low levels of aggression. One of each pair of cottages was assigned to the aggressive film condition, while the other two viewed the neutral films. Only the boys in the initially high-aggressive cottage who saw the aggressive movies increased their level of aggression. Those who were exposed to the neutral films reduced their level of aggression.

Natural experiments

These studies take advantage of the fact that television was introduced at different times in different locations. They assume that people who are exposed to television will also be exposed to a high dose of television violence. This is probably a reasonable assumption

given the extremely high correlation between television viewing and exposure to television violence (Milavsky *et al.* 1982).

Williams (1986) had the opportunity to evaluate the impact of televised violence on the behaviour of children before and after the introduction of television in a Canadian community. They compared children living in the before/after television town with their peers in two other towns where television was well established. The three towns were called Notel (no television reception), Unitel (receiving only CBC) and Multitel (receiving CBC and three American commercial networks). Children in all three towns were evaluated at Time 1 when Notel did not receive a television signal and again at Time 2 when Notel had had television for two years (it had received CBC). Results indicated that only children in the Notel town showed any significant increase in physical and verbal aggression from Time 1 to Time 2.

A more recent natural experiment, however, produced very different findings. It was carried out in St Helena, a small British colony in the South Atlantic, made famous as the place where Napoleon Bonaparte was exiled. St Helena received television for the first time in 1995. Despite fears that the introduction of television would be accompanied by a corresponding increase in aggressive behaviour, this proved not to be the case. Researchers found that very little changed in the post-television period, and even discovered some increases in *pro-social* behaviour on some behavioural measures (Charlton *et al.* 2000).

ACTIVITY

Using the Internet to find research

Using the Internet, try to find out some more information about the St Helena study. As this is such a recent and ongoing study, it is well-documented on the Web. Try searching for the St Helena Link Project, and following the links to 'Behavioural research' and 'Frequently asked questions'.

Longitudinal studies

We get a clearer picture about the extent of the effects of television violence when we examine exposure over a much longer period. A study by Belson (1978) helped to pin down which types of programme have the most influence. Belson interviewed 1,565 youths who were a representative sample of 13- to 17-year-old boys living in London. These boys were interviewed on several occasions concerning the extent of their exposure to a selection of violent television programmes broadcast during the period 1959 to 1971. It was thus possible to obtain, for each boy, a measure of both the magnitude and type of exposure to televised violence (realistic, fictional, etc.). When Belson compared the behaviour of boys with higher exposure to televised violence to those who had lower exposure, he found that the high-violence viewers were more involved in serious violent behaviour. Moreover, he found that serious interpersonal violence was increased by long-term exposure to (in order of importance):

1 plays or films in which personal relationships are a major theme and which feature verbal or physical violence

2 programmes in which violence seems to be thrown in for its own sake or is not necessary to the plot

3 programmes featuring fictional violence of a realistic nature

4 programmes in which the violence is presented as being in a good cause

5 violent westerns.

It is notable that no significant relationships between early viewing exposure and later aggression were obtained for girls.

A meta-analysis of media influence research

The most recent meta-analysis of media violence research involved 217 studies (mostly experimental research) of media violence and aggressive behaviour published between 1957 and 1990 (Paik and Comstock 1994). This analysis provided clear evidence that brief exposure to violent dramatic presentations on television or in films caused short-term increases in aggressive behaviour, particularly among young people. The largest effect was among pre-school children, and the effect on males was slightly larger than the effect on females.

Explanations of media influences on anti-social behaviour

Cognitive priming

Aggressive ideas in violent films can activate other aggressive thoughts in viewers through their association in memory pathways (Berkowitz 1984). Immediately after a violent film, the viewer is primed to respond aggressively because a network of memories involving aggression is retrieved. Huesmann (1982) suggests that children learn problem-solving scripts in part from their observations of others' behaviour. These scripts are cognitive expectations about a sequence of behaviours that may be performed in particular situations. Frequent exposure to scenes of violence may lead children to store scripts for aggressive behaviour in their memories, and these may be recalled in a later situation if any aspect of the original situation – even a superficial one – is present.

Observational learning

Bandura (1986) has argued that television can shape the forms that aggressive behaviour takes. Television can teach skills that may be useful for committing acts of violence, and it can direct the viewer's attention to

behaviours that they may not have considered. For example, young people may mimic martial arts moves or may learn effective tactics for committing violent crime. There is frequent anecdotal evidence that bizarre violent events have followed soon after their depiction on television, suggesting a form of copycat behaviour.

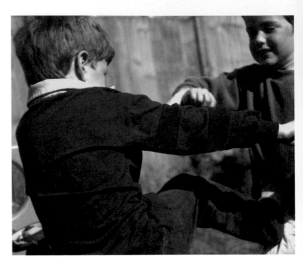

Does television teach children the skills of violence?

Desensitization

This argument assumes that under normal conditions, anxiety about violence inhibits its use. Those who are not used to media violence would, presumably, be shocked at witnessing an act of violence in the real world, yet frequent viewing of television violence causes such events to appear more commonplace and so may cause viewers to be less anxious and sensitive about *actual* violence. Therefore, someone who becomes desensitized to violence may perceive it as more 'normal', become less likely to intervene when they witness violence and be more likely to engage in violence themselves. Related to this view is the finding that boys who are heavy watchers of television violence show lower than average physiological arousal to new scenes of violence, i.e. they are less shocked by violence and less inhibited about using it themselves.

Justification

It has been suggested that violent individuals may enjoy violent media because it justifies their own actions and behaviour as normal and acceptable. A child who has behaved aggressively may choose to watch violent television because it relieves their guilt and justifies their aggression. As a result of this justification, the child then feels less inhibited about aggressing again. This process may well work in conjunction with the process of desensitization. If a child becomes desensitized to aggression, then their guilt for acting aggressively also diminishes. As a result, the child will view their aggressive behaviour as the norm and feel justified in acting in this way.

Evaluation
media influences on anti-social behaviour

● *The inconclusive case for media violence effects* – More than almost any other area of social psychology, the issue of media violence provokes fierce debate between those who believe that violence on the screen *does* promote violence in those who are exposed to it (e.g. Huesmann and Moise 1996), and those who believe evidence does not support this conclusion (e.g. Freedman 1996). Table 11.3 on p. 371 presents some of the points and counterpoints of this debate, based on the views of these protagonists.

● *The nature of the audience* – Psychological research into media effects has tended to represent young media users as 'the inept victims of products, which can trick children into all kinds of ill-advised behaviour' (Gauntlett 1998). Research which seeks to establish exactly what children can and do understand about the media has shown that children are able to talk intelligently (and cynically) about the media (Buckingham 1996) and that children as young as 7 are able to make thoughtful, critical and 'media literate' utterances themselves. A further complication for those who subscribe to the media effects model is the finding by Hagell and Newburn (1994) that young offenders watched *less* television and video than their non-offending counterparts, had less access to the technology in the first place and had no particular interest in specifically violent programmes.

● *Methodological problems with media violence research* – Because experiments are narrowly focused on specific causal hypotheses, they tend not to examine the real-world influences that might actually lessen or even eliminate the aggressive reactions observed in experiments. Participants may also react differently in the laboratory when they realize that their expressions of aggression will not be punished (Gunter 1983). In addition, claims Freedman (1992), many participants may choose to provide the responses they believe the researcher wants (demand characteristics). It is particularly problematic that the more naturalistic or 'ecologically valid' a research design, the less likely it is that any effects will be observed, suggesting that beliefs or behaviours learned under experimental conditions cannot be generalized to viewers' everyday lives (Livingstone 2001).

● *Desensitization* – The desensitization hypothesis claims that excessive media violence diminishes the distaste with which we normally view violence and makes us more blasé about its consequences. Research fails to support this fundamental claim. Indeed, some research shows the exact opposite. Goldstein *et al.* (1976), for example, found that immediately after seeing a violent movie, men were *more* concerned about murder, and more punitive towards those who commit murder. This finding was confirmed across four different countries, and showed no support for the desensitization hypothesis. Furthermore, in a comparison of towns with and without television, those *with* television scored higher in terms of their anxiety about aggression compared to those *without* television (Schramm 1961).

● *Observational learning* – The kinds of media violence that are typically condemned by the 'effects model' are limited to fictional programmes. The acts of violence that appear daily on our television screens on news programmes are somehow exempt from this condemnation. There is an inconsistency to this argument. If anti-social acts shown in television drama have such a profound effect on viewers, it is puzzling that the anti-social activities that are so frequently in the news and other documentaries do not have similar effects. This is even more puzzling when we consider the fact that in fictional drama, most anti-social acts have negative consequences for the perpetrator, but in documentary depictions of violent acts there are few apparent negative consequences for those who perform them. The basic question of why the media should induce people to imitate its content has never been answered (Gauntlett 1998).

ACTIVITY

Expert interview: Guy Cumberbatch

Read the Expert interview given by Guy Cumberbatch on p. 370 and then answer the following questions:

1 According to Cumberbatch, why is it difficult to arrive at confident conclusions about the anti-social effects of the media?

2 In your own words, try to explain why Cumberbatch thinks that TV has more potential for good than for harm.

3 Do you agree that media violence is irrelevant when it comes to explaining people's 'nasty' behaviour? Justify your point of view by referring to the research you have read about in this unit.

Media violence and *aggression*

Guy Cumberbatch is a Chartered Psychologist who is Director of The Communications Research Group in Birmingham (UK), which is funded equally by broadcasters and the regulatory bodies. Since 1990, he has carried out all the annual monitoring of television for the Broadcasting Standards Commission. Guy has specialized in media violence for the past 30 years.

Q Reading the research on the anti-social effects of the media creates a confusing picture. Some research seems to suggest clear effects, while other researchers report no such effects. What are we to make of this?

A The more popular conclusion has been that media violence causes aggression in real life. But the controversy is about the research evidence and what conclusions can be drawn. Here, the consensus claimed by some appears based on findings which appear weak, inconsistent and even contradictory to other reviewers. A particular worry is that so many reports gloss over non-significant findings. Measures are often mentioned in the design sections of studies, but then no results are reported. You have to look carefully to see that.

Part of the problem must also be that researchers who investigate the anti-social effects of the media are likely to believe they might find something.

Q Is there evidence to suggest that some individuals are more prone to media effects than others?

A Even the strongest claims made about media effects usually add the disclaimer that 'not everyone who watches a violent movie or plays a violent video game will become a killer'. Some killers do watch and enjoy violent movies, but there is no convincing evidence that anyone has been influenced by the media to commit a serious violent crime. It has been claimed that some people are more likely to become violent because of media violence. Risk factors include children who have suffered parental neglect and abuse and have older siblings involved in crime. However, while such factors are certainly predictors of anti-social behaviour, they do not in any way indicate that such factors make people any more or less vulnerable to media effects. Thus, the suggestion that such factors mediate media effects is entirely speculative.

Q The moral panic over television's potential anti-social effects distracts attention away from its potential as an educator. Is there more of a case for television's pro-social effects?

A The moral panic about TV violence began with the rapid growth of violent crime in the 1960s and 70s when television also grew rapidly in homes. Despite clear evidence that crime rates have shown massive drops in the last decade, the moral panic continues. At a more general level, we should note that there is an asymmetry between anti-social and pro-social behaviour. We don't need to watch TV violence to want to punch someone on the nose or learn how to do it. However, the ability to resolve conflict situations without using violence is not instinctive: it is a higher-level, learned behaviour. Thus, I think TV has great potential for good, but little potential for harm.

Q In 1994, you wrote that 'it would be more economical to conclude that media violence is essentially an irrelevant issue in understanding why some people are so nasty and most of the rest of us are not nicer.' Ten years on, is this still a view you hold?

A Yes. I think we know enough about the development of nice and nasty behaviours to have some confidence in what's important. Research indicates that problem behaviours are well established by pre-school age. Thus, concerns about what children watch when they are older than this is somewhat misplaced. By the age of 10 or 11, problem children are out on the streets hanging around with their delinquent peers, becoming socialized into crime and violence. The problem is not that such children are spending too much time playing video games or watching television – violent or otherwise – but that they are not at home engaged in such pursuits!

Guy Cumberbatch

Table 11.3 >> Does media violence promote aggression? Key points of the debate

Huesmann and Moise (1996)

>> The relationship between aggression and exposure to media violence has been supported by a wide variety of experiments conducted in different countries by researchers with different points of view.

>> Despite Freedman's insistence that the correlation between aggression and exposure to violence is statistically small, its impact has real social significance.

>> Because media heroes are admired and have special authority, children are likely to imitate their behaviour and learn that aggression is an acceptable solution to conflict.

>> Children younger than 11 do not make the distinction between fiction and reality very well.

Freedman (1996)

>> Most of the studies of the relationship between aggression and exposure to media violence have serious methodological flaws and have yielded inconsistent results.

>> The correlations between aggression and violence exposure are quite small, accounting for only 1 to 10 per cent of individual differences in the aggressiveness of children.

>> If children are learning anything from the media, it is that the forces of good will overcome evil assailants, who are the first to use violence.

>> Children are able to recognize fiction as early as the age of 5; those watching retaliatory violence do not believe they could act successfully by engaging in such behaviours.

✓ CHECK YOUR UNDERSTANDING

Check your understanding of media influences on pro- and anti-social behaviour by answering these questions. Check your answers by looking back through Topic 3.

1 How do media researchers operationalize the term 'pro-social behaviour' in this context?

2 How might the influence of pro-social content on television be limited by the developmental stage of the child?

3 Define each of Lovelace and Huston's three modelling strategies used for the transmission of pro-social messages.

4 Briefly outline the main findings, and the effect size for each category of pro-social behaviour used in the Mares (1996) meta-analysis.

5 What is a meta-analysis and why is it useful in this context?

6 In the Belson (1978) study, what were the top five most influential types of programme in terms of their effect on aggressive behaviour in boys?

7 Briefly summarize the desensitization and justification explanations for media influence.

8 Huesmann and Moise (1996) believe that 'because media heroes are admired and have special authority, children are likely to imitate their behaviour and learn that aggression is an acceptable solution to conflict'. What is Freedman's counterpoint to this?

9 Freedman (1996) believes that 'children are able to recognize fiction as early as the age of 5; those watching retaliatory violence do not believe they could act successfully by engaging in such behaviours'. What is Huesmann and Moise's counterpoint to this?

10 In what way did Hagell and Newburn's research with young offenders challenge the view that media violence *causes* violent behaviour?

REVISION SUMMARY

Having covered this topic you should be able to describe and evaluate:

✓ explanations and research studies relating to media influences on pro-social behaviour

✓ explanations and research studies relating to media influences on anti-social behaviour.

Below are some **possible examination questions** set on this topic, along with hints to help you understand and approach each question effectively:

1 Outline and evaluate **two or more** explanations of media effects on pro-social behaviour. (24 marks)

> It is vital to focus on the particular demands of a question. This question involves media effects but is only concerned with media effects on *pro*-social behaviour. It is easy to miss the fact that this is a question on *pro-social* behaviour, not *anti-social* behaviour. You are required to describe and evaluate at least two explanations, or otherwise incur a partial performance penalty. Furthermore, you must note that the question is concerned with *explanations* of how these effects occur. This means that you should restrict your answer to explanations rather than research studies. This also applies to AO2, so your commentary should also focus on explanations but of course you can use the research studies to support or challenge the explanations. What you must not do is to describe the studies in anything more than the barest detail. Focus on the *conclusions* of the studies and how these relate to the explanations.

2 (a) Outline and evaluate **one or more** studies relating to media influences on pro-social behaviour. (12 marks)
　(b) Outline and evaluate **one or more** studies relating to media influences on anti-social behaviour. (12 marks)

> This is an unusual question because there is AO1 and AO2 in each part of the question (as indicated by 'outline and evaluate' in both parts). This means that in part (a) there are 6 marks AO1 and 6 marks AO2. The whole question can be conveniently split into four parts: (a) AO1 and AO2, (b) AO1 and AO2. This makes planning a response reasonably straightforward – four 'chunks' each of about 150 words. The 'one or more' instruction allows for a more general response covering as many (or as few) studies as you like. Evaluation can then be *specific* (i.e. related to specific studies) or *general* (i.e. related to appropriate research studies in general).

3 Discuss research (explanations **and/or** studies) relating to media influences on anti-social behaviour. (24 marks)

> This is the question that everybody dreams about. Just about anything goes in this question (so long as you make the focus anti-social behaviour), but that can also be your downfall. Planning a response (just about 600 words) to an open question like this should be done well in advance, otherwise you will struggle in the exam to decide what to put in your answer and what to leave out. Remember that *selectivity* is an important skill to develop. The examiner recognizes that you will not have time to include everything you know but gives credit to your ability to *select* the most important things.

4 (a) Outline **two or more** explanations of media influences on anti-social behaviour. (12 marks)
　(b) To what extent do research studies support the view that the media is responsible for anti-social behaviour? (12 marks)

> Part (a) of this question is straightforward (see comments for question 1 above). Part (b) takes some thinking about. It does *not* ask you for a description of research studies, but asks you to make a considered appraisal of whether research really has shown that media violence causes violent behaviour. Your answer should consist mainly of commentary, with some necessary but brief descriptions of the studies as 'scene-setting'.

5 Critically consider explanations **and** research studies relating to media influences on anti-social behaviour. (24 marks)

> This would be a legitimate question given the fact that the terms 'explanations' and 'research studies' are in the specification. It means that you must outline *both* explanations and research studies, and must outline at least two of each, as the terms are in the plural. You are unlikely to have time for more than two of each or would lose the detail required to gain high marks. Failure to present both explanations and research studies and to provide two of each would result in partial performance penalties! One problem (for you and the examiner) in a question such as this, is to make sure it is clear whether you are *describing* the explanations/research studies (and thus should gain AO1 credit) or are using the material as commentary (and thus should gain AO2 credit), so try and make the distinction as clear as possible.

Topic 1: Nature and causes of aggression

- **Social psychological theories of aggression** stress the role of factors outside the individual in determining aggressive behaviour.

- The **social learning theory** of aggression sees aggressive behaviour as being learned either through direct experience or by observing others who model it.

- **Deindividuation theory** explains aggression as a result of a temporary loss of personal identifiability, which may result in an increased tendency to act in anti-social ways.

- **Relative deprivation theory** explains aggression as being the result of an unacceptable discrepancy between what people think they have the right to expect and what they realistically are likely to achieve.

- Aggression may be a response to **stressors in the environment**. These include temperature and crowding. Although research is inconclusive regarding the negative effects of these stressors, it does suggest that negative effects are more likely if people feel they do not have control over the source of the stress.

Topic 2: Altruism and bystander behaviour

- Explanations of **human altruism** differ according to whether pro-social behaviour is seen as a product of personal distress (egoistic behaviour) or empathic concern (altruistic behaviour). Cialdini and colleagues' **negative-state relief** model is an example of the former, and Batson's **empathy–altruism** model an example of the latter.

- The tendency to help in an emergency may be lessened by the presence of others if diffusion of responsibility occurs.

- Theoretical explanations of **bystander behaviour** focus on the decision-making stages that bystanders must go through before deciding whether to help. Latané and Darley's model focuses on the cognitive interpretation of the incident and our possible role in helping, whereas Piliavin and colleagues' arousal:cost–reward model emphasizes a more egoistic concern with the costs and benefits of helping.

- Comparisons of **different cultures** concerning their **pro-social behaviours** have typically focused on the differences between individualist and collectivist cultures. The behavioural differences of individuals may be interpreted in terms of the dominant cultural characteristics of their society.

Topic 3: Media influences on pro- and anti-social behaviour

- Although the vast majority of research studies have focused on the **anti-social influences of the media**, a number of studies have suggested the **media's potential as a source of pro-social socialization**. The effectiveness of the media in this role is determined by the way in which pro-social behaviours are modelled.

- Research into the potential anti-social effects of the media has not always produced consistent results, although many do suggest a relationship between exposure to media violence and violent behaviour.

- Possible explanations of the media–violence relationship include the idea that children learn aggressive scripts from television or they become desensitized as a result of their exposure to violence in the media.

- The media effects model is criticized for being based on problematic assumptions about the media and its viewers.

12
UNIT

BRAIN AND
Behaviour

PREVIEW

After you have read this unit, you should be able to:

>> describe and evaluate methods used to investigate the brain, including invasive and non-invasive methods, and the strengths and limitations of these methods

>> outline the functional localization of the cerebral cortex, including the primary motor, sensory and association areas

>> describe and evaluate the alternative idea of functions being distributed across the cerebral cortex – so-called 'distributed functions'

>> explain the lateralization of function in the cerebral cortex, including the organization of language in the brain and other hemisphere asymmetries of function.

INTRODUCTION

The functions of the cerebral cortex represent the final frontier for neuroscientists. It is the most complex structure of the brain, containing over 90 per cent of all the neurons of the forebrain. It is involved in all our higher cognitive abilities, as well as functions such as consciousness and personality. Although we know a reasonable amount about some functions, such as perception and language, others still remain a mystery. It is also unusual in that some aspects of cortical organization are specifically human, related to the evolution of language, while others such as perception can be modelled using findings from work with animals.

You may have noticed the current media interest in the brain, particularly the effects of brain damage. These can often be dramatic, such as the loss of speech or a failure to recognize family and friends after a stroke. But the organization of the undamaged brain is also relevant to behaviour. Are gender differences (e.g. in aggression or verbal abilities) innately built into the brain? Are the brains of left-handed individuals organized in the same way as those of right-handers? Are anti-social and psychopathic behaviours caused by problems in parts of the brain, rather than by upbringing and environment? As we shall see, brain research investigates all of these problems and many others, using a variety of sophisticated methods.

In Topic 1, we consider the most popular methods used to investigate the brain. These have changed dramatically over the last 20 years or so and much of what we know about brain and behaviour today has emerged during that time. In Topic 2, we go on to review the localization of functions in the cerebral cortex, which helps to explain the consequences of brain damage, and discuss the alternative idea of functions being distributed across the cortex rather than being localized to specific areas. This is followed, in Topic 3, by a detailed description of the lateralization of some brain functions, especially language. This idea of functional asymmetry can then help to explain differences in behaviour between left- and right-handed people or between males and females.

Simon
Green

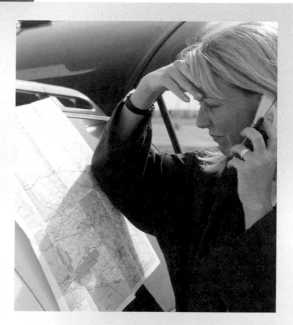

1 Ask a few of your friends whether they think there are any differences between the way that males and females perform certain tasks such as reading a map and solving problems. Make a list of the activities that most people think males typically perform better and those that females tend to perform better.

2 When large groups of males and females are tested, males tend to perform better on non-verbal tests such as solving mazes (these are also called 'visuo-spatial' tasks) and females do better on verbal tasks such as solving anagrams. As we shall see, research shows that language (verbal) abilities are usually located in the left cerebral hemisphere, and visuo-spatial abilities in the right hemisphere. What do these observations suggest about the functional organization of the cerebral cortex in males and females?

KEY CONCEPTS

Invasive methods: techniques for investigating the brain that involve penetrating through the skull into brain tissue. Examples include electrical stimulation and lesions.

Non-invasive methods: techniques for investigating the brain that do not penetrate the skull. Examples include the electro-encephalograph (EEG) and modern brain scanners.

Sensory cortex: areas of the cerebral cortex specialized for processing sensory input such as vision and hearing.

Motor cortex: areas of the cerebral cortex specialized for controlling movement of the body muscles. Motor cortex occupies the precentral gyrus.

Association cortex: areas of cerebral cortex not directly involved with sensory input or motor control, but with higher cognitive functions, such as language or problem-solving.

Localization of function: the principle that specific functions are localized to specific areas of cortex, such as the role of Wernicke's area in understanding speech.

Distributed functions: the principle that specific functions involve combined activity across many regions of the cortex. An example would be the way in which visual perception depends upon processing distributed across several brain regions.

Lateralization of function: an aspect of the organization of the human brain in that functions are primarily controlled by one hemisphere or the other. An example is the left hemisphere control of language and the right hemisphere specialization for visuo-spatial functions. Also referred to as **functional asymmetries**.

Unit 12 // Brain and behaviour

Many of the procedures used today by researchers to investigate brain function involve implanting electrodes (usually made of very thin wire) accurately into the brain. In other areas, such as neurosurgery (i.e. performing surgical operations on the brain), it is also important to know exactly where structures are located within the brain. For humans and all experimental animals, we now have stereotaxic atlases – when the skull is fixed (painlessly) in a rigid steel frame, known as a 'stereotax', the atlas can be used to provide three-dimensional coordinates for any brain structure. Surgeons or researchers can then carry out their procedures, confident that they are in the correct area of the brain.

TRANSMISSION OF INFORMATION IN THE NERVOUS SYSTEM

The two basic processes underlying information transmission in the nervous system are:

- electrical transmission along the neuron
- chemical transmission across the synapse.

Some of the most popular methods used to investigate brain function are based on our knowledge of these two basic processes, so it is important to have an outline understanding of them.

Neurons and electrical transmission

Neurons, or nerve cells, have three main components: the cell body, dendrites and axon. As you can see from Fig. 12.1, the cell body extends into a set of short processes on one side (the 'dendrites') and into a single, longer branching process on the other (the 'axon'). The cell body contains the nucleus, in which we find the chromosomes, the genetic material. Every cell in the body contains an identical set of chromosomes, and, besides allowing us to pass characteristics on to our offspring, the genetic material also controls the activity of the cell containing it.

The outer covering of the neuron is the cell membrane. This is a complicated layered structure made up of protein and fat molecules, and is crucial to information transmission. The fluid inside the neuron ('cytoplasm') and the fluid surrounding it ('extra-cellular fluid') contain concentrations of electrically charged particles known as ions, which include positively charged ions such as potassium and sodium, and negatively charged ions such as chloride. When the membrane is in its resting state, the distribution of ions means that there is an electrical charge or potential across the membrane of –70 millivolts (thousandths of a volt); this is called the 'resting potential'.

When the membrane is disturbed, the electrical potential across it changes rapidly from –70 to +40 millivolts. This very rapid and violent swing in the membrane potential is called the 'nerve impulse' or 'action potential' (see Fig. 12.2).

Figure 12.2 >> *Action potential*

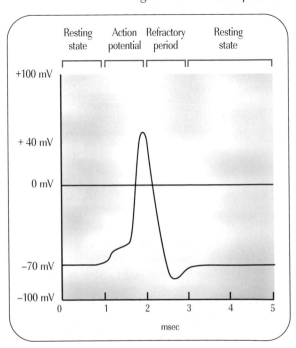

Figure 12.1 >> *Standard neuron*

Another feature of the structure of the cell membrane is that when a nerve impulse is produced by some sort of stimulation at one point on the membrane, it automatically travels along the membrane by a process called 'propagation'. A thin wire or glass electrode can be used to record the nerve impulse at one point on the cell membrane as a momentary blip of electrical potential. Before and after the nerve impulse, that point on the membrane is at its resting potential. If nerve impulses are repeatedly stimulated, they travel in sequence along the membrane and will be recorded by an electrode as a sequence of blips. Each nerve impulse disturbs the membrane for about 4 milliseconds, so the maximum rate of impulse transmission is about 250 per second.

Many neurons in the nervous system operate in this way. However, others have become modified to allow even faster rates of transmission. These neurons, including most of those in the brain, have axons which are covered in a fatty layer called a 'myelin sheath' (see Fig. 12.3). At intervals along the sheath, the axon membrane is exposed; these points are called 'Nodes of Ranvier', and, by complicated electrical processes, the nerve impulse can 'jump' from node to node. This is known as 'saltatory conduction' and is much faster than conventional propagation of impulses along the neuronal membrane. Faster transmission clearly increases the rate of information processing, and myelination was an important step in the evolution of advanced brains.

Figure 12.3 >> *Myelinated neuron (saltatory*

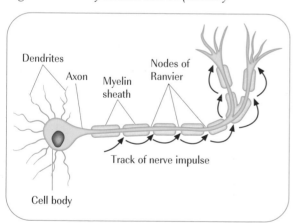

Dendrites
Axon
Myelin sheath
Nodes of Ranvier
Track of nerve impulse
Cell body

Each impulse, wherever it is recorded, has exactly the same electrical properties as any other. This is important because we know that information handled by the nervous system, which is in effect everything it does, is coded by these signals. As they are electrically identical, then different types of information must be coded by the frequency and patterning of impulses (i.e. whether they come in steady streams or in bursts of activity), and where in the nervous system they occur.

Information in the nervous system is carried along neurons in sequences of nerve impulses. In the nervous

system there are something like 100 billion neurons, most of which are in the brain. If these neurons were physically connected, nerve impulses would automatically travel to all parts of the system because neurons are specialized to transmit impulses, and the whole system would be one enormous electrical circuit. This would not allow specialized processing in different parts of the brain. The reason it doesn't happen is because in between neurons there is a tiny gap, called the 'synapse'.

The synapse and chemical transmission

These gaps between neurons, usually separating the end of an axonal branch from a dendritic surface, are minute. They are only visible using an electron microscope and are measured in microns (billionths of a metre), but even so they represent a physical gap which the electrical nerve impulse cannot cross. Transmission across the synapse has to involve other processes that are chemical in nature.

The end of each axon branch (the 'presynaptic terminal') contains molecules of chemicals called neurotransmitters. When nerve impulses travelling along the axon reach the presynaptic terminal, a complicated set of events results in the neurotransmitters being released into the synaptic gap. Because the gap is so small, the molecules of neurotransmitter can drift or diffuse over to the membrane of the dendrite. On this postsynaptic membrane we find receptors. These are molecules attached to the membrane, with a structure that matches that of the neurotransmitter molecule, in the same way that a door key is shaped to fit a particular lock. Neurotransmitter molecules attach themselves to receptors and, although the combination is very brief, it is sufficient to disturb the postsynaptic membrane, allowing ions to pass through it. This passage of ions is the basis of the nerve impulse, as described earlier, and if sufficient neurotransmitter is released into the synapse then a nerve impulse will be triggered in the postsynaptic neuron. Figure 12.4 outlines the basic structures involved in the chemical neurotransmission across the synaptic gap.

The amount of neurotransmitter released depends on the frequency of nerve impulses arriving at the presynaptic terminal. If the frequency is not sufficient, a nerve impulse is not triggered in the postsynaptic neuron, and the information coded by activity in the presynaptic neuron is lost.

The synapse represents an opportunity for information to be processed and integrated, as neurons have around a thousand synaptic connections with other neurons; so the activity in one neuron represents inputs from thousands of other neurons. It is an opportunity for information, in the form of nerve impulses, to be integrated with other pathways, or lost (when they do not cross the synapse), or processed in other complex ways. The 100 billion or so neurons in the nervous system each make on average about 1000 synaptic connections, so the complexity of the entire network of neurons is such that it is almost impossible to imagine.

Over the last 30 years we have learnt a great deal about the neurotransmitters released from neurons. Each neuron releases the same one from all of its axon branches, but different neurons can release different neurotransmitters. We believe there may be 20 to 30 neurotransmitters involved in synaptic transmission, and you will meet some of these in other parts of the course – for instance, the relationship between schizophrenia and the neurotransmitter dopamine in Unit 25.

This outline of electrical and chemical neurotransmission in the nervous system serves as a background to the different methods used to investigate

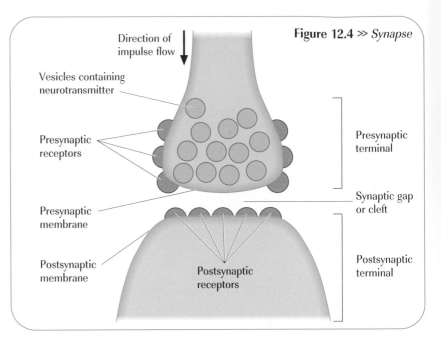

Figure 12.4 >> *Synapse*

Direction of impulse flow

Vesicles containing neurotransmitter

Presynaptic receptors

Presynaptic membrane

Postsynaptic membrane

Postsynaptic receptors

Presynaptic terminal

Synaptic gap or cleft

Postsynaptic terminal

brain function. Others use a range of sophisticated technologies to scan or take pictures of the brain.

Before reading on, try the next activity that is designed to help you remember some of the key terms that you have encountered relating to the electrical and chemical transmission of information in the nervous system.

ACTIVITY

Key terms

What term is used to describe the following:

1 the outer layer of a neuron?

2 the spherical structure of the cell that contains the genetic material (the chromosomes)?

3 gaps in the myelin sheath?

4 the chemical released into the synaptic gap?

5 molecules on the postsynaptic membrane that bind to **4**?

6 electrically charged particles?

7 the normal electrical state of the neuronal membrane?

8 a rapid and violent swing in the membrane potential?

INVASIVE METHODS OF INVESTIGATING THE BRAIN

Methods used to investigate brain function can be broadly divided into invasive and non-invasive. Invasive methods involve direct interference with the brain – for example, by physical damage using lesions, placing electrodes through the skull into the brain, or giving drugs which act directly on brain synapses.

Electrical stimulation

Thin wire electrodes can be implanted in the brain and used to stimulate brain neurons artificially in order to investigate their effects on behaviour. The currents used

have to be in the range found within the brain (thousandths of an amp), but as the brain does not possess pain receptors, this technique can be used in conscious human participants, as well as in non-human animals. For example, Penfield (1958) stimulated the temporal lobe in humans and some individuals reported experiencing vivid memories from their childhood. Stimulation in the visual cortex can produce a sensation of flashes of light, whilst auditory cortex stimulation may lead to a 'buzzing' sound sensation. Movement of skeletal muscles can be produced by electrical stimulation of the motor cortex.

Strengths

● *Advances in knowledge* – Since the early 1900s, the greatest strength of electrical stimulation has been in providing a huge amount of information on brain function.

Limitations

● *Difficulty of generalizing results from non-human animals to humans* – This invasive

procedure has mainly involved non-human animals, and there is the problem of generalizing results to the human brain. For instance, where the visual system is concerned, work on non-human primates has been largely confirmed by studies of humans with damage to the visual cortex, and much of our knowledge of our sensory and motor systems has come from animal work. But in the area of cognitive functions, such as memory, planning and problem-solving, our abilities are so different from other animals that generalizing the findings is far less justified.

Chemical stimulation

Earlier, we briefly reviewed chemical transmission across the synapse. Many of the most dramatic effects of drugs on behaviour can be explained by our knowledge of how they act at the synapse. As a given synapse involves a specific neurotransmitter and its specialized receptors, we can design drugs that are highly specific for particular types of these synaptic receptors. Such drugs can either stimulate the receptor ('stimulants' or 'agonists' – these drugs usually have a structure very similar to the natural neurotransmitter) or, by combining with the receptor, they inactivate it ('blockers' or 'antagonists'). We can then relate the effects of the drug on behaviour to their effects on

synaptic neurotransmitters and so increase our understanding of the functions of brain neurons and their neurotransmitters on behaviour.

So, if we wish to investigate the role of dopamine synapses in behaviour, we can give animals drugs that specifically stimulate or block dopamine receptors. By observing the behavioural effects, we can then draw some conclusions about what the dopamine system may be doing. Similarly, if we think that the acetylcholine system is involved in memory, drugs that stimulate cholinergic receptors should improve memory and learning in animals, while cholinergic antagonists, which block the receptors, should impair memory and learning.

Strengths

● *Dramatic increase in knowledge* – Investigating the chemistry of neurotransmitters is helping us to gain a more complete picture of brain function. Although the majority of the work has again been carried out on non-human animals, advances in our knowledge over the last 30 years have been dramatic. The finding that anti-psychotic drugs such as chlorpromazine, used to treat schizophrenia, acted by blocking dopamine receptors was largely based on work with rats. Recently introduced anti-depressant drugs such as Prozac (from the drug group known as selective serotonin reuptake inhibitors or SSRIs) were developed on the basis of our increased understanding of serotonin synapses and their role in brain function; this research was also largely undertaken on non-human animals.

● *Insights into chemical dependence* – Through chemical stimulation we now have a greater understanding of brain function and of how drugs work in the brain, including drugs of abuse such as alcohol, heroin and ecstasy. This may allow us to understand their appeal and also the problems of dependence and its treatment.

Limitations

● *Scarcity of studies* – Direct studies of neurotransmitters in humans are rare. Apart from the PET scanners (discussed later), studies would have to be invasive and there is no technique for doing this on living people. Thus, direct investigations of links between behaviour and neurotransmitters in humans have been scarce, and generalizing results from non-human animals is one of the most important problems in this area. Fortunately, the work that has been undertaken suggests that neurons and synapses in the non-human animal brain operate in the same basic way as in the human brain.

Physical destruction of brain tissue by ablation and lesioning

This was the original approach to the experimental study of brain function in non-human animals. Hundreds of thousands of experiments have been carried out and the technique is still popular. At first, the techniques were performed using needlepoints or knife cuts. Nowadays, localized areas of damage, or 'lesions', are usually produced using thin wire electrodes. A current is passed through which heats the tip of the electrode and the heat creates a small sphere of destruction around the tip.

Several decades ago, large lesions, or 'ablations', were popular and frontal lobotomy (that is, destruction of the frontal lobe) was even used in humans as a 'treatment' for schizophrenia. As more was discovered about the links between brain structure and behaviour, interest shifted to smaller units of the brain. Whereas in the past we might have ablated the whole visual cortex, now we would confine damage to smaller zones within the area. One of the latest lesion techniques used in research with non-human animals involves chemicals called 'neurotoxins'. These are specific to particular neurotransmitters, so they destroy only those neurons releasing that neurotransmitter at their synapses when they are injected into a part of the brain.

The logic behind the use of ablations and lesions to study brain function is that if damage to a particular area of the brain affected one particular aspect of behaviour, then we could conclude that the brain area was involved in that aspect of behaviour. An excellent example was the demonstration that lesions to the ventro-medial hypothalamus led to overeating in rats, eventually causing them to become obese (see Unit 14). Lesions to the lateral hypothalamus produced rats that did not eat at all. These results supported the popular model of eating as regulated by hunger and feeding centres in the hypothalamus.

As well as systematic damage in non-human animals, we can also study accidental damage in humans. Brain tumours, strokes, car crashes and other accidents, can all damage brain tissue and produce effects on behaviour that can be studied systematically. This is an area called 'cognitive neuropsychology'.

Evaluation
ablation and lesion studies

Strengths

● *Depth of knowledge provided* – Lesion studies in non-human animals and the study of the brain-damaged humans have contributed enormously to our understanding of brain function. Some examples were given earlier, and the work on language disorders, following brain damage in humans by Broca and Wernicke (discussed later), led to the first model of language mechanisms in the brain.

● *Increasing accuracy in techniques* – Increasingly, we can accurately lesion smaller and smaller components of the nervous system, down to single pathways and specific clumps of neurons, which allows us to link the lesion sites to behaviour more reliably.

Limitations

● *Difficulty of linking effects of brain damage to area of brain damaged* – The main limitation of ablation and lesion studies is that the simple notion that the effects of brain damage can be identified with the area of brain damaged is unjustified. A useful analogy is that of sticking a potato in a car exhaust. This stops the engine, but to conclude that the exhaust makes the engine go is obviously incorrect. However, if you perform lots of studies on car engines by removing the distributor, carburettor, pistons, etc., to see what happens, you might eventually produce a model of how all the components interact. This is the main justification for ablation and lesion studies.

● *Difficulty of interpreting findings* – The brain is infinitely more complicated than a car engine. Even a small lesion destroys not just neurons at that site, but possibly pathways travelling through. Even the destroyed neurons have connections to many other neurons, and these in turn will be affected by the damage. All neurons are part of intricate circuits, and so lesion effects are never restricted to the site of damage. Interpreting the findings of such studies can therefore be very difficult.

NON-INVASIVE METHODS OF INVESTIGATING THE BRAIN

Unlike the invasive methods described so far, non-invasive methods do not involve direct interference with the brain. Instead they record electrical activity from the skull surface or create images of the brain using a variety of scanners.

Electrical recording

The 'electroencephalograph' (EEG), introduced in 1929 by Berger, records the electrical activity of billions of cortical neurons using a number of small metal electrodes on the surface of the skull. This is non-invasive, with no need to penetrate brain tissue.

The EEG can be 'synchronized', with a recognizable and repeated waveform, or 'desynchronized', with an apparently random pattern of waves and spikes. It also has a frequency or number of waves or spikes per second (measured as 'hertz'). Certain patterns correlate highly with behavioural states. For example, alertness and activity produce a fast, desynchronized EEG, while drowsiness leads to a synchronized pattern called the 'alpha rhythm', with a frequency of 8 to 12 hertz. Wave frequency gradually slows as you fall asleep, but is then interrupted by the faster, desynchronized EEG associated with REM sleep (this is discussed in more detail in Unit 13).

Besides behavioural states, 'event-related potentials' (ERPs) can also be recorded using the EEG. Repeated presentations of a specific stimulus, such as different facial expressions, produce ERPs that can be identified in the EEG recording. Moreover, because EEG recording involves the whole cortical surface, the relative size of ERPs can be used to localize processes, such as recognition of facial expressions, to different parts of the cortex.

Evaluation
electrical recording

Strengths

- **Useful non-invasive procedure** – As procedures in humans must, for ethical reasons, be non-invasive, the EEG and ERPs are popular techniques and have provided insights into areas such as sleep and attentional processes.

- **Real-time recording** – Electrical recording also has the advantage that it is in 'real time' – the electrical impulses produced by neurons are directly recorded, providing a moment-by-moment picture of brain activity.

- **Use of ERPs** – ERPs are more specific than EEGs and so can be used to investigate the rapid processing underlying, for instance, selective attention. By presenting sequences of stimuli and recording the responses in different areas of the brain, we can generate models of where in the brain different aspects of attention and perception occur.

Limitations

- **Difficulty of localizing EEG recordings** – There is a problem with interpreting EEG records because we do not know how the electrical activity of populations of neurons combines to form the overall EEG recording. Therefore, localizing EEG recordings to particular regions of the brain is extremely difficult.

- **Limited suitability of ERP technique** – Precise localization is still difficult, even with ERPs, and the need to present stimuli repeatedly in order to identify ERPs means that this technique is only suitable for certain types of study such as investigations of attention and perception.

Scanning and imaging

Brain scanning and imaging has become the main source of information on human brain function since the relevant technology was developed in the early 1970s. This era began with the introduction of the well-known CT (formerly CAT) scanner.

- **Computed [axial] tomography (CT scanning)** – CT scanners use multiple X-rays and a computer to produce images of horizontal sections of the brain.

- **Magnetic resonance imaging (MRI scanning)** – A later technique was MRI scanning (see the photo on p. 382). The procedure involves placing the head in a powerful magnetic field and bombarding the brain with radio waves. Molecules in the brain vibrate in response to the radio waves and emit radio waves of their own. These are recorded, computerized and assembled into a three-dimensional picture of brain structures. Overall, the level of detail is better than with the CT scanner and it also avoids subjecting the patient to X-rays.

- **Positron emission tomography (PET scanning)** – This is a more complicated but more valuable procedure. The usual procedure involves injecting radioactive glucose into the bloodstream. This reaches the brain and as the glucose is used as an energy source by cells, it is taken up by neurons. The brain is then scanned by a battery of detectors which pick up the radioactivity emitted by the glucose (the doses of radioactivity used are tiny and harmless). Parts of the brain that are more active take up more glucose and emit more radioactivity and a computer is used to provide an activity map of the brain. This procedure can be used to identify those parts of the brain which are most active, for instance, during speech, problem-solving or recognizing faces. This ability to correlate activity in different brain areas with psychological functions makes PET scanning the most useful of current computer-based techniques. It can also be used with radioactive chemicals that combine with synaptic receptors; measuring receptor activity can tell something about neurotransmitter function in the brain. An example would be studies of changes in dopamine and serotonin receptor numbers in schizophrenia.

A three-dimensional MRI scan. Red indicates an area of high activity, while blue (and green) indicates less activity

- *Functional MRI (fMRI)* – One of the early problems with scanning techniques was that they took so long (up to half an hour) to produce a picture of the brain that fast psychological processes, such as those involved in selective attention or emotional reactions, could not be studied. However, technical advances now allow changes in the brain correlated with psychological reactions of a few seconds to be studied, using modern PET scanners or functional MRI (fMRI).

- *Magnetoenecephalography (MEG)* – A recent addition to the battery of scanning techniques is MEG, which involves recording the tiny magnetic fields produced by active neurons. One clear advantage that MEG has over other scanning techniques is that the magnetic fields are produced by nerve impulse activity so that the MEG scan reflects moment-by-moment neural activity in the brain, down to thousandths of a second.

Evaluation
brain scanning and imaging

Strengths

- *Non-invasive investigation of living humans* – It is impossible to overestimate the significance of scanning. Up to the early 1970s, neuropsychology and psychobiology were dominated by work with non-human animals. With scanners it became possible to investigate the human brain in living participants. Initially, studies were limited to structural pictures, such as X-rays, which could show up tumours, areas of large damage after cerebral haemorrhage or degeneration. Now we can look at function as well as structure, using PET, fMRI and MEG, and our knowledge of human brain function has increased dramatically.

- *Ethical issues* – Using scanners eliminates the ethical problems of using non-human animals and practical issues such as generalizing from animals to humans.

Limitations

- *Limited spatial resolution* – The spatial resolution (i.e. how small an area of brain tissue

can be identified) of scanning techniques is still not ideal, with localization only possible to the level of relatively large areas of cortical or sub-cortical tissue, but this is improving every year.

- *Limited temporal resolution* – Temporal resolution (what *frequency* of brain activity can be identified) has been a problem when studying the brain, which operates in milliseconds. However, with the introduction of fMRI and MEG, as mentioned above, we can now study brain events taking place over milliseconds rather than minutes, which significantly increases the range of processes that psychologists can investigate.

- *Practical issues* – PET, MRI and fMRI scanners involve recording over long periods (usually hours) with the participant's head enclosed in the tube-like scanning machine. Procedures are highly technical, expensive and time-consuming, involving as many as 30 people in a given study. MEG recording uses a net of recording electrodes over the skull, and so eliminates the scanning tube. However, it is highly sensitive to environmental magnetic fields and so recording has to take place in magnetically shielded laboratories, preferably at night.

ACTIVITY

Key terms

You have just read about a number of invasive and non-invasive techniques used to investigate brain function. Create a table of all the techniques, with a brief description of each technique and its main advantages and disadvantages. This table should help you when you revise this topic and also when you come to decide what techniques to include when answering exam questions.

A2 Physiological Psychology

Check your understanding of methods of investigating the brain by answering these questions from memory. You can check your answers by looking back through Topic 1.

1 What causes a nerve impulse?

2 What is the myelin sheath on a neuron and what is its purpose?

3 Name the chemicals released by a neuron that cross the synaptic gap and are received by special receptors on the next neuron.

4 What are the two basic processes underlying information transmission in the nervous system?

5 Give one advantage of the EEG and name one area of research where it has been widely used.

6 In 100 words outline one example of how our knowledge of the synapse and neurotransmitters

has helped to explain drug effects on human behaviour.

7 Write a 100-word précis of one invasive method of investigating the brain, and give a brief account of two critical (AO2) points relating to this method.

8 Write a 100-word précis of one non-invasive method of investigating the brain. Outline two advantages and two disadvantages of using this method.

9 Describe two examples of findings from scanning studies of the human brain.

10 Construct a 150-word précis comparing invasive and non-invasive methods of investigating the brain.

REVISION SUMMARY

Having covered this topic, you should be able to:

✓ outline the electrical and chemical transmission of information in the nervous system

✓ describe and evaluate invasive techniques for investigating the brain, such as the physical destruction of brain tissue and electrical/chemical stimulation

✓ describe and evaluate non-invasive techniques for investigating the brain, including electrical recording, scanning and imaging

✓ evaluate the contribution of modern brain scanning and imaging techniques to our understanding of brain function.

EXAMPLE EXAM QUESTIONS

Below are some **possible examination questions** set on this topic, along with hints to help you understand and approach each question effectively:

1 (a) Outline **two** non-invasive (e.g. electrical recording, scanning, imaging) methods used to investigate the brain. (12 marks)

    (b) Assess the **two** methods you have outlined in (a) in terms of their strengths and limitations. (12 marks)

> Normally, you are not specifically asked for strengths and limitations, but just for general evaluation. In this case 'strengths and limitations' forms part of the specification. If the question is divided into two parts – (a) and (b) – follow the instructions, especially if (a) is AO1 and (b) is AO2. Mixing the two parts makes the examiner's job much harder! Examiners do export material from one part of the question to another for the purpose of determining marks but only if it is not relevant where it is.
>
> Note that *two* methods are required in part (a). Two different scanning techniques would be allowable, as long as you present them as two separate methods. If you only outline one method, then partial performance penalties would apply (a maximum of 8 marks for AO1). In part (b), there is a double partial performance penalty because you must evaluate both methods in part (a) and must include strengths *and* limitations. If only one strength is given for one method, the maximum mark for AO2 would be 4.

2 Outline and evaluate **two** invasive (e.g. electrical/chemical stimulation, ablation, lesioning) methods used to investigate the brain. (24 marks)

> This is similar to the first question, but slightly more demanding because you need to balance carefully your AO1 and AO2 material within your answer. You also must cover *invasive* methods only this time. Choose your methods so that evaluation is easier; strengths and limitations of ablations and lesions would be quite similar and repetitive, so lesions and electrical or chemical stimulation would probably be easier to tackle. The examples given in the question are taken from the specification. They are placed there to help you to focus on the right techniques, but you should not do all three because only two are required. If you do cover all three, they will all be read and the best two methods given credit.

3 (a) Outline and evaluate **one** non-invasive method used to investigate the brain. (12 marks)
  (b) Outline and evaluate **one** invasive method used to investigate the brain. (12 marks)

> This is an unusual question because there is AO1 and AO2 in each part of the question (as indicated by 'outline and evaluate' in both parts). This means that in part (a) there are 6 marks AO1 and 6 marks AO2. This question can be conveniently split into four parts – (a) AO1 and AO2, (b) AO1 and AO2 – which makes planning a response straightforward, i.e. four 'chunks' each of about 150 words. You may well know more than 150 words of description (or evaluation) for each component, so you must be *selective* about the points you include. Focus on a few good points rather than trying to impress the examiner with the breadth of your knowledge and show very little understanding.

4 Discuss **two or more** methods used to investigate the brain in terms of their strengths and weaknesses. (24 marks)

> This looks like a very straightforward question that allows you to select any method, but you need to be careful in your choice. You need to balance your AO1 and AO2 material, so make sure the methods you choose give you the best chance of scoring high marks under both headings. Try to develop a four-paragraph approach to your answer, i.e. two paragraphs of AO1 and two of AO2. This allows you to check easily on the balance between the AO1 and AO2 material.

5 Critically consider methods used to investigate the brain. (24 marks)

> The term 'critically consider' is an AO1+AO2 term (see Table 32.1 on p. 937). It can be treated in the same way as 'discuss', i.e. it means 'describe and evaluate'. Therefore this question is similar to the one above except that there is no requirement to produce both strengths and limitations. However, there still is a partial performance because 'methods' is in the plural so at least two are required.

Topic 2 >> Localization of function in the cerebral cortex

It might seem obvious that behavioural functions should be localized to particular structures and regions of the brain, but there is actually no particular reason why they should be. If we approached the brain knowing only the arrangement of neurons and how they worked, we would have no immediate way of knowing, for example, how language might be organized. Would it be spread over large regions of the cerebral cortex, or would it be restricted to small, highly specialized areas?

The principle of localization of function states that psychological functions are located in specialized areas, so that damage to the relevant area causes a drastic loss of that function. It can be contrasted with the view that functions are widespread, or distributed across large regions of the brain, so that damage to any one small area causes only a small loss of function.

We now have a huge amount of experimental data that goes a long way towards answering this question. The hypothalamus – a small structure buried deep within the brain – contains important centres for the control of physiological function such as feeding and temperature control, and this type of strict localization seems to apply to other physiological functions. An interesting question is whether the higher cognitive functions of the cerebral cortex are similarly localized.

A2 Physiological Psychology

FUNCTIONAL ORGANIZATION OF THE CEREBRAL CORTEX

The cerebral cortex contains most of the neurons in the forebrain and controls many complex functions. The simplest way to approach the organization of these functions is to divide them into categories, linked to the areas of the cortex that contain them:

- *Sensory functions*, such as vision and hearing, are related to the processing of sensory input and are located in the *sensory cortex*.
- *Motor functions* are concerned with the planning and execution of movement and are located in the *motor cortex*.
- There is a large category of *cognitive functions*, such as language, thought, planning and problem-solving, perception and so on, which together make up our higher cognitive abilities; these are located in areas of the *association cortex*. Association cortex is so called because its function is to 'associate' or relate sensory input to motor output in some way.

Sensory and motor functions in the cerebral cortex

It has been known since the early years of the 20th century that electrical stimulation or lesions of various parts of the cerebral cortex in animals can affect sensory and motor abilities. This has been confirmed by the effects of accidental damage to the cerebral cortex in humans, or by some rare cases where electrical stimulation has been carried out on human patients (usually to check that a subsequent surgical procedure will not damage, or impair, important functions). Many findings have also been confirmed by modern brain scanning studies.

The result of all this work is that we can now plot the cortical organization of these sensory and motor functions on to the cerebral cortical surface of the hemispheres. Figure 12.5 shows such a map. In each of the areas, electrical stimulation will mimic the function to a greater or lesser extent, while damage will impair the function.

Visual and auditory cortices

You will immediately notice that our most complex and important sensory abilities – vision and hearing – have specialized cortical areas dedicated to them. This is because visual and auditory (hearing) processing is far more complex than, say, the perception of touch or taste, and therefore requires more neurons. Stimulation in these areas produces either visual sensation (e.g. a flash of brightness) or auditory sensation (e.g. a buzzing noise), while damage may impair vision or hearing.

Somatosensory cortex

The somatosensory cortex in the postcentral gyrus (so-called because it lies behind the central fissure, which is one of the brain's main anatomical landmarks)

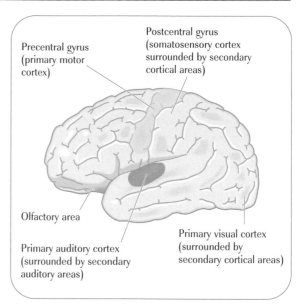

Figure 12.5 >> *Side view of left hemisphere showing sensory and motor areas*

contains our general body senses, mainly dealing with stimuli on the skin such as touch, pressure, heat, cold and some aspects of pain. Stimulation here gives rise to the experience of touch or pressure on part of the skin. It seems that there is a point-for-point representation of the body surface on the cortical surface; this arrangement is called a 'topographical map'. As you stimulate parts of the somatosensory cortex, so the reported sensation of touch moves up and down the body. The map is upside down, with the skin of feet and legs dealt with by the cortex at the top of the brain. Damage to somatosensory cortex leads to a loss of sensation (anaesthesia) from the body.

Primary, secondary and tertiary cortical areas

The visual, auditory and somatosensory cortex are the target zones for neuronal pathways carrying information from sensory receptors into the central nervous system. As the receiving areas for these pathways, they are called the 'primary sensory cortex'. Of course, there are a number of stages between basic sensation and complex perception. After arrival at the primary cortex, sensory information is passed on to secondary and even tertiary cortical areas where increasingly complex processing occurs. These secondary and tertiary cortical areas, where sensation becomes perception, surround the primary receiving areas. You can see this change in the effects of brain damage. If the primary visual cortex is involved, loss can be drastic, such as complete blindness, because without the primary cortical areas the visual input cannot be transmitted on for further processing. If secondary or tertiary areas are involved, basic visual abilities may be intact, but some

Unit 12 // Brain and behaviour

high-level ability, such as face recognition, may be lost. The study of such syndromes (i.e. patterns of symptoms) that occur after damage to cortical areas outside the primary cortex is called 'cognitive neuropsychology'. It aims to use the pattern of cognitive loss after brain damage to build models of how normal cognitive functions are organized.

Motor cortex

The precentral gyrus in the frontal lobe (see Fig. 12.5) contains the motor cortex. This is the origin of pathways running eventually to the muscles of the skeleton to produce movement. Damage here can lead to paralysis, while stimulation can produce movement of individual muscle fibres. As with the somatosensory cortex, the motor cortex contains a topographical map of the body, which is also upside down, with muscles of the feet and legs controlled from areas at the top of the motor cortex. As our most complicated muscular control involves the muscles of the throat, larynx, pharynx and tongue used in speech, this area takes up more cortical surface. It is also important to remember that there are other parts of the motor system. The cerebellum and the basal ganglia have important roles in integrating and fine-tuning movement; damage to those areas affects smooth control, but does not eliminate movement completely.

Sensory and motor pathways to and from the cerebral cortex

Figure 12.5 shows the left hemisphere only. However, a map of the sensory and motor functions of the right hemisphere would look exactly the same, but the other way round. Humans, like all mammals, are what is called bilaterally symmetrical (bilateral means 'two-sided'); if divided vertically, you end up with two mirror-image halves. The presence of two legs, two arms and two cerebral hemispheres reflects this bilateral symmetry, which also explains why we usually find brain structures in pairs, one on each side of the brain.

The arrangement of sensory and motor pathways connecting the cerebral cortex of each hemisphere with the body reflects this fundamental organizational principle:

● *Motor and somatosensory pathways* connect each hemisphere with one side of the body only. For reasons that are currently unknown, these pathways are crossed ('contralateral'), with the left hemisphere connecting to the right side of the body, and the right hemisphere to the left. Cortical damage to the left hemisphere therefore produces a right-sided paralysis and loss of sensation. This arrangement is called a 'crossed' or 'contralateral' pathway.

● The *visual and auditory systems* have a more complicated arrangement. Each eye and ear has pathways connecting it with *both* hemispheres, i.e. a combination of crossed and uncrossed (or 'ipsilateral' – meaning 'same-side') pathways. This means that damage to only one hemisphere will not

destroy vision or hearing completely because the other hemisphere is still functionally connected to both eyes or to both ears. We discuss the visual pathways in more detail later.

Despite vision and hearing having crossed and uncrossed pathways, the arrangements are perfectly symmetrical in relation to the hemispheres themselves. For sensory and motor functions the two hemispheres have similar organizations, i.e. they show functional symmetry and so a description of one hemisphere also applies to the other.

The cerebral cortex of the two hemispheres also shows significant *localization* of sensory functions, with small areas of cortex carrying out specialized and specific functions. This is especially the case for the primary sensory receiving areas, as illustrated by the drastic effects of damage which is restricted to either the primary visual cortex or to the primary auditory cortex, which can lead to blindness or to deafness respectively.

Taking out the sensory and motor cortical areas leaves large parts of the cerebral cortex, known as association cortex, unaccounted for (see Fig. 12.5). As mentioned previously, we assume that higher cognitive functions are located in the association cortex.

Cognitive functions in the cerebral cortex

Since much of the early work investigating the organization of cognitive functions in the brain focused on language, we will start by looking at this aspect.

Broca, Wernicke and the study of the brain mechanisms of language

The search for the brain mechanisms associated with language began in the earliest days of brain research in the mid-19th century, when the systematic study of brain-damaged patients started. Paul Broca (see Key research opposite) and Karl Wernicke, who were particularly interested in how language was organized in the brain, made two of the most remarkable observations about language.

At about the same time as Broca was working, Wernicke (1874) was also studying brain-damaged patients and identified a syndrome with the opposite pattern of symptoms: these patients did not seem to comprehend speech, but could produce reasonably well-organized sequences of speech. As they could not understand speech, what they said was unrelated to any question or comment spoken to them. This syndrome is called 'Wernicke's aphasia', or 'sensory' or 'receptive aphasia'.

Both Broca and Wernicke were interested in the brain mechanisms of language and so they examined the brains of their patients after they had died. Broca consistently found that his patients had suffered damage to an area low down in the cortex of the frontal lobe, now known as 'Broca's area' (see Fig. 12.6 on

The work of Paul Broca: Broca's area and Broca's aphasia

Broca was a surgeon and anthropologist, as well as being a founding father of neuropsychology. In 1861, Broca reported on a patient, whose surname was Leborgne, who had been admitted to hospital after suffering a stroke. Tests showed that although Leborgne's general intelligence and ability to understand speech were unaffected – he could understand speech because he could follow instructions and answer simple questions with head movements – he had no fluent speech at all and the only recognizable word he could say was 'tan'.

Leborgne had lost his speech about 11 years earlier, and had gradually developed a right-sided paralysis, suggesting progressive brain damage. Leborgne, or 'Tan' as he is often called, died shortly after Broca's examination of him, so Broca was able to perform an autopsy on his brain. Although the damage to his brain was found to be extensive, Broca noted that it concentrated in the lower part of the left frontal lobe, so he proposed that the loss of speech was due to damage in that area.

Broca was able to report on a second case in the same year, where brain damage was much more localized but the symptoms were similar, with good speech comprehension but loss of speech production. The brain damage involved the same area of the lower frontal lobe. By 1865, Broca had found 10 similar cases with comparable symptoms of a lack of speech production, but with normal speech understanding or comprehension. He was able to confirm that loss of speech was associated with damage to the lower part of the left frontal lobe, in an area now known as 'Broca's area'. This syndrome is known as 'Broca's aphasia' (aphasia is the technical term for any speech problem encountered after brain damage). Alternative terms for Broca's aphasia are 'expressive' or 'motor aphasia'.

Interestingly, Leborgne's brain was rediscovered in the 1980s and subjected to a CT scan. This confirmed Broca's original observations, but also found that damage penetrated beneath the cortex to involve the basal ganglia – a part of the brain that deals with control of movement. Although Broca missed this area of damage, it is remarkable that his original description of Broca's aphasia, and the identification of the brain area that bears his name, has largely stood the test of time.

Leborgne's Brain, displayed in the Dupuytren Museum in Paris

p. 388). Wernicke's patients had damage to an area in the temporal lobe close to the primary auditory cortex (Fig. 12.6), now called 'Wernicke's area'.

Work since then, right up to recent studies using PET scans, generally confirms the original findings of Broca and Wernicke: damage to Broca's area severely impairs speech but leaves the comprehension of speech intact, while damage to Wernicke's area affects comprehension but leaves speech production quite fluent.

It seems that Wernicke's area in the temporal lobe contains a store of the sound representations of words that we use to recognize incoming speech. Broca's area is thought to contain the motor plans for words, e.g. the pattern of muscle movements of the throat and tongue, which are specific to each word. When we wish to speak, instructions are passed from Wernicke's area to Broca's area to activate the relevant motor plans, which are then transmitted the short distance to the motor cortex in the precentral gyrus. This sends instructions down the motor pathways to the muscles themselves. When Wernicke's area is damaged, we lose the store of word representations and so cannot recognize incoming speech, but if Broca's area is intact, motor plans can still be activated and speech produced. Conversely, if Broca's area is damaged, we can no longer produce speech but, as long as Wernicke's area is intact, we can still understand what is spoken to us.

Language and the left hemisphere

Besides the significant finding that speech production and comprehension seemed to be localized to particular areas of the cortex, Broca and Wernicke also confirmed a suggestion made earlier in the 19th century, that brain damage affecting language usually involved the left hemisphere. Damage to the right hemisphere rarely had any effect on language.

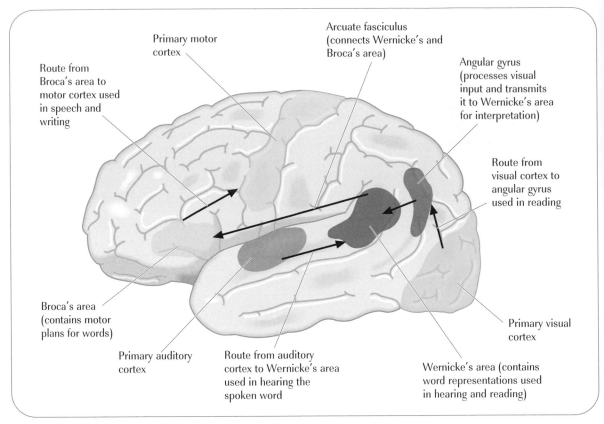

Figure 12.6 >> *Language mechanisms in the left hemisphere*

Labels in figure:

Route from Broca's area to motor cortex used in speech and writing

Primary motor cortex

Arcuate fasciculus (connects Wernicke's and Broca's area)

Angular gyrus (processes visual input and transmits it to Wernicke's area for interpretation)

Route from visual cortex to angular gyrus used in reading

Broca's area (contains motor plans for words)

Primary auditory cortex

Route from auditory cortex to Wernicke's area used in hearing the spoken word

Wernicke's area (contains word representations used in hearing and reading)

Primary visual cortex

The conclusion was that our language mechanisms are located in the left hemisphere.

Thousands of research studies since those pioneering observations have confirmed this general pattern, with some exceptions that we will consider later in this unit. The significance of the finding was that, in contrast to sensory and motor functions, language was not organized symmetrically across the two hemispheres of the brain, but represented a hemisphere asymmetry of function. From these beginnings, the study of hemisphere asymmetries of function has become one of the main research themes in psychology, and we review some of the findings in Topic 3.

Other cognitive functions in the association cortex

Various other cognitive functions are organized in the association cortex:

● *Frontal lobe syndrome* – Studies of damage to the frontal lobe of the cerebral cortex has led to the idea of a frontal lobe syndrome, with symptoms of impulsivity, a failure to plan ahead or to follow plans through to a conclusion, perseveration (repeating the same actions over and over again), and sometimes apathy and indecision. There can be a loss of creative or abstract thought. Generally, this area of the association cortex seems to control our capacity for forward-planning and goal-directed behaviour.

● *Object recognition and apraxias* – The association cortex of the parietal lobe contains many functions related to perception. Damage can lead to problems with object recognition and apraxias (particular problems with skilled sequences of actions, such as assembling a set of parts into a complete object).

● *Face recognition and the perception of surrounding space* – In the association cortex of the right-hemisphere parietal lobe, there appears to be an area specialized for face recognition, while damage to other areas in the right parietal cortex can lead to unilateral neglect. This is a bizarre syndrome in which patients ignore the space on their left, i.e. on the opposite side to the lesion. They will draw only one half of a clock, with all the numbers crowded together, or only dress one side of their body. It seems that the parietal lobe is involved in our perception of surrounding space.

● *Auditory perception and the identification and categorizing of objects* – The temporal lobe association cortex contains Wernicke's area, described earlier. It also contains regions of secondary and tertiary visual cortex, radiating out from the visual cortex of the occipital lobe. Damage to the temporal lobe can therefore also affect auditory perception (e.g. identifying sounds or voices), language and high-level visual perception such as identifying and categorizing objects – for example, being able to recognize that the object seen is an apple and that an apple is a fruit.

These syndromes, observed after brain damage, happen even though basic sensory and motor pathways are working properly. For instance, testing shows that patients with aphasia have normal vision, hearing and motor control, so the symptoms must be due to difficulties with higher-level cognitive processes.

Evaluation
functional organization of the cerebral cortex

Much of the material presented above goes beyond a straightforward description of cortical functions and could therefore be used as evaluation and commentary. Key points include the following:

- *Research evidence supporting assumptions about functional organization* – Excellent examples would be the work of Broca and Wernicke on language centres in the left hemisphere. The strengths of their studies include the use of human participants, the identification of Broca's and Wernicke's areas, and the support from many later studies. Limitations include the small number of patients studied by Broca and Wernicke, and the fact that the extent of brain damage would vary between different patients. This would make the precise localization of Broca's and Wernicke's areas difficult.

- *Effects of damage or stimulation* – Similarly, describing the effects of damage or stimulation to other areas, such as visual cortex lesions leading to blindness, would count as elaboration and commentary on functional organization. The strength of this approach is that combining these studies provides an overall picture of the functional organization of the cerebral cortex. Limitations include the reliance on many studies with non-human animals, making generalization difficult. Another important limitation is that our current knowledge of the sensory and motor areas of the cerebral cortex is far greater than our knowledge of the association cortex.

- *Range of evidence and methods* – Emphasizing the range of evidence and the methods used is a key point to make. Our current understanding of the functional organization of the cerebral cortex is based on work with non-human animals, brain-damaged humans and intact human participants. Methods include lesion, electrical stimulation and chemical stimulation and recording studies, and modern work using a range of brain scanning and imaging techniques. Although each method has its own strengths and limitations, as reviewed in Topic 1, the *overall* strength of brain research is that results from all these different methods can together provide a broad picture of the functional organization of the cerebral cortex.

- *Technical limitations* – An important limitation of studies of cortical organization would be the technical difficulties involved in studying the cerebral cortex. It is a vast network of many millions of interconnected neurons and is infinitely more complex than the most sophisticated modern computer. Although our methods are becoming more refined, they are still primitive compared to the brain's organization. For example, we may localize the understanding of speech to Wernicke's area in the temporal lobe, but we have no idea how the millions of neurons in that area are combined into circuits or how the meanings of words are stored in those circuits.

DISTRIBUTED FUNCTIONS

Different ideas on functional organization are a key issue for discussion and commentary. So far, we have focused on the localization of function, but an alternative approach considers functions as distributed *across* cortical areas.

Even when neuropsychologists talk about higher cognitive functions, they usually speak in terms of the localization of function. The frontal lobe syndrome occurs after damage to the frontal lobe, not to the parietal lobe. Problems with face recognition are seen after damage to the parietal lobe, rather than elsewhere in the cortex. However, this large-scale localization does not disguise the fact that we now know a great deal more about the detailed organization of psychological functions in the cortex, and this provides an alternative view of cerebral organization.

Memory as a distributed network

'Memory' provides a good example. For the psychologist there is no single thing called memory that can be localized; rather it can be broken down into short-term and long-term memory, retrieval processes, working memory, semantic and procedural memory, etc. These different aspects of memory will be processed in different parts of the brain, so while particular sub-processes such as short-term memory may be localized, our memory system as a whole depends on a *distributed network*. The efficient functioning of our memory system must therefore involve the integration of neural activity across many distinct areas, regions or pathways in the brain.

Parallel distributed processing

An even better example is the visual system and visual perception. It turns out that our visual system processes different characteristics of the visual stimulus independently. Starting with the visual stimulus being received on the retina of the eye, shape, colour and movement are processed through parallel but independent pathways of the visual system. Damage to different areas of the cerebral cortex can affect colour vision (the person sees the world only in black and white), or movement (in this strange situation, the person can see objects only when they are still; when they move, they disappear). Our experience is of seeing whole objects with shape, colour and movement integrated. But to achieve this the brain has to combine the results of this parallel distributed processing of the separate characteristics. So while we can talk about the localization of colour vision in pathways or cortical areas, it makes no sense to say that visual perception itself is localized in a particular part of the brain. It is probable that all our higher cognitive functions depend on parallel and distributed processing across many cortical areas.

Evaluation
localization vs distributed functions

- **Complementary, not alternative** – 'Distributed functions' are sometimes presented as an alternative to localization of function, but the examples above illustrate how they complement each other, rather than being alternatives. Even with language, the most heavily studied of our cognitive functions in the association cortex of the cerebral hemispheres, we can see how the two operate together.

- **Integration of processes** – Broca and Wernicke showed how speech production and speech comprehension were localized to particular areas of the association cortex. However, language could be considered as involving a range of activities, including speech production and comprehension, reading and writing, retrieving the appropriate words from our semantic memory, assembling them into meaningful sentences and then speaking or writing them in the right order. In this case we can see how 'language' is too complex to be localized to any one or two areas of the cerebral cortex. It depends on the parallel and distributed processing of many different aspects of language across many different cortical regions. Each sub-process may be localized, but our overall sophisticated language abilities depend on the integration of many sub-processes distributed across the cerebral cortex.

✓ CHECK YOUR UNDERSTANDING

Check your understanding of localization of function in the cerebral cortex by answering these questions from memory. Check your answers by looking back through Topic 2.

1 State the principle of localization of function

2 Give one example of a brain structure in which functions are highly localized.

3 In 150 words, outline a general division of the functions of the cerebral cortex.

4 What is the difference between functional symmetry and functional asymmetry? Give one example each of a cortical function organized in these ways.

5 Write a 150-word précis describing the original studies of Broca and Wernicke.

6 What aspects of language are controlled by Broca's area and Wernicke's area?

7 Construct a 100-word précis of the difference between Broca's aphasia and Wernicke's aphasia.

8 In 150 words, describe one effect of damage to the frontal lobes and one effect of damage to the parietal lobes of the cerebral cortex.

9 Identify and give a brief account of three critical (AO2) points that could be used to provide evaluation and commentary on localization of function in the cerebral cortex.

10 In 100 words, outline two pieces of evidence that suggest that visual perception represents distributed processing in the cerebral cortex rather than strict localization of function.

REVISION SUMMARY

Having covered this topic, you should be able to:

✓ describe, with examples, the division of the functions of the cerebral cortex into sensory, motor and cognitive

✓ outline the organization of sensory and motor functions, including primary and secondary cortical areas, and the principle of functional symmetry

✓ describe the methods and findings of the pioneering work of Broca and Wernicke into language organization in the cerebral cortex, including functional asymmetry

✓ use research evidence, the range of methods used and the different approaches to cortical organization in order to evaluate functional localization in the cerebral cortex

✓ outline how studies of the visual system suggest that the brain can process information in parallel distributed pathways, as an alternative to localization of function.

 EXAMPLE EXAM QUESTIONS

Below are some **possible examination questions** set on this topic, along with hints to help you understand and approach each question effectively:

1 Discuss the functional organization of the cerebral cortex. (24 marks)

> Like the previous topic, the specification for this topic is straightforward, and the range of questions that can be asked is quite narrow. AO1 material is easily available, covering sensory, motor and some cognitive processes. For AO2 commentary, you can use research findings from electrical stimulation, chemical stimulation, lesion and brain scanning studies (not forgetting that individual studies such as those of Broca have limitations as well as strengths), the range of methods used to gather evidence, the historical context, difficulties of studying the cerebral cortex, and hypotheses about the organization of the cortex such as localization versus distributed functions.

2 Describe and evaluate the organization of sensory and motor areas in the cerebral cortex. (24 marks)

> This question is similar to the last one but is more restricted, requiring more detail of sensory and motor areas (e.g. secondary sensory cortical areas). It is important to point out that after reaching the primary cortical reception area, sensory input is transmitted on to secondary areas for further processing; vision could be used as a good example. You could bring in cognitive functions as a contrast with sensory and motor functions, e.g. the fact that they do not seem so localized to particular cortical areas, or even that we do not know so much about them. If you use them in this way, support your commentary by including phrases such as 'In contrast to sensory and motor functions, cognitive functions …' or 'Cognitive functions such as language are far more complicated than sensory and motor processes …'.

3 Discuss research (explanations **and/or** studies) into the functional organization of the cerebral cortex (e.g. Broca's and Wernicke's areas). (24 marks)

> This question has the same requirements as question 1, but has been included to illustrate two further points. The term 'research' is not included in this part of the specification, but, as it is a rather general term, has been put in the question to help you focus your answer. As indicated in the first brackets 'research' includes explanations or studies. Second, examples have been provided in this question to prompt candidates who can't think what to write. Such examples are taken from the specification, but you are not obliged to cover these topics or to be limited to these topics.

4 Critically consider 'distributed functions' as an alternative to localization of function.　　(24 marks)

> This is quite a difficult question, but it could legitimately be asked because it is taken directly from the specification. You need to describe the 'distributed functions' approach. This is most easily done by using an example such as the way the visual system processes movement and colour separately, although we see a 'whole' object. You could mention the complexity of cognitive processes and how unlikely it is that all of the sub-processes essential for language functions will, for instance, be localized to just one area of the cerebral cortex. You could contrast this with the localization of sensory and motor processes. You can also use research evidence as part of your AO2 material; this could include general findings, such as the specific loss of colour or movement perception after brain damage, or specific studies such as those of Wernicke and Broca. Remember to *use* studies as effective commentary in order to gain AO2 credit.

5 (a) Describe the functional organization of the brain.　　(12 marks)
　　(b) To what extent is such organization localized?　　(12 marks)

> Parted questions aim to help you produce a more focused answer. In this case, your answer would contain elements from the answers above. For part (a), you could include similar descriptive material to that from question 1. For part (b), the AO2 content is restricted to the issue of localization, which is part of your answer to question 4 above. You might use the same evidence but the emphasis must be on how you *use* it, because it should be commentary and not description, in order to attract AO2 marks. As the question includes the phrase 'to what extent?' it might be appropriate to state some conclusion but this is not mandatory. Often candidates present conclusions which are little more than a summary of what has already been stated and therefore do not receive any further credit.

Topic 3 >> Lateralization of function in the cerebral cortex

The work of Wernicke and Broca demonstrated that some of the functions of the association cortex, such as language, seemed to be located in one hemisphere only; this is called an 'asymmetry of function', in comparison to sensory and motor functions which are organized symmetrically across the hemispheres. Since then, many experimental studies carried out on both normal individuals and brain-damaged patients have supported and extended these original findings. Roger Sperry (1982) carried out a very important series of studies, beginning in the 1950s and continuing until his death in 1980.

SPLIT-BRAIN STUDIES

Those participating in Sperry's studies were patients suffering from epilepsy. Epilepsy comes in many forms, but always involves an uncontrolled discharge of electrical activity in the brain. The discharge may originate in an area of scar tissue following accidental brain damage, often at birth, or during brain surgery, or perhaps from a developing cyst or tumour. When such a point of origin can be identified, it is called a 'focus' and it can sometimes be removed surgically. In other cases of epilepsy, there is no clear focus, but probably some imbalance in excitatory and inhibitory activity in the brain. Whatever the cause, once the discharge begins it is automatically transmitted along neuronal pathways. Severe epilepsy can involve many brain circuits and lead to convulsions and loss of consciousness. A patient may have several attacks a week or even a day and so it can be a disabling condition. Nowadays we have many drugs for the control of epilepsy, although there are still patients who do not respond and find it difficult to live a normal life. In the 1940s, when Sperry's interest began, there were far fewer drugs available and so many more patients suffered severely from the effects of epilepsy.

In most types of epilepsy, the attack usually begins in one hemisphere. Connecting the hemispheres is the largest pathway in the brain – the 'corpus callosum' – that consists of some 300 million neuronal fibres. This pathway interconnects areas of the cerebral cortex in each hemisphere, ensuring that the hemispheres communicate with each other and synchronize their activities. The corpus callosum also allows epileptic discharges to spread to the other hemisphere and so in the 1940s an operation was devised to prevent this spread; this involved cutting the corpus callosum. In this way the epilepsy was confined to one hemisphere only and its effects were therefore reduced.

Strangely, this operation (technically called a 'commissurotomy' because the corpus callosum is the largest of the 'commissures', which is the name given to the pathways travelling between the hemispheres rather than contained within one of them) seemed to have little effect on the person. Their sensory, motor and cognitive functions continued as before, but there was also an improvement in their epilepsy.

This finding intrigued Sperry. Surely the largest pathway in the brain must have important functions and its removal ought therefore to affect behaviour in some way? He decided to study these patients using careful experimental procedures based on the anatomy of the visual pathways. These are outlined in Fig. 12.7. Light strikes the retina at the back of the eye, which contains millions of visual receptor cells. The receptors trigger activity in axons making up the optic nerve (see Fig. 12.7), which runs via the thalamus to the primary visual cortex in the occipital lobe.

As Fig. 12.7 shows, in the retina of each eye the receptors in the outer half connect with fibres running to the visual cortex in the hemisphere on the same side of the brain – an ipsilateral pathway. Receptors contained within the inner half of each retina project to the visual cortex in the opposite hemisphere – a contralateral pathway. So each retina projects in a systematic way to both hemispheres, with the crossed pathways passing from one side to the other at the optic chiasma.

Figure 12.7 also shows how a stimulus presented out to the right of the patient (known as the 'right visual field' or RVF) is picked up. With the eyes pointing (or fixated) straight ahead, it hits the *left* side of the *left* eye and the *left* side of the *right* eye. If you look carefully at Fig. 12.7, you will see that these parts of each retina both project to the visual cortex of the *left hemisphere*. So a stimulus in the RVF, with both eyes fixated straight ahead, is seen first by the left hemisphere and by the same geometrical argument, a stimulus presented out to the left of the person (in the 'left visual field' or LVF) is seen first by the *right hemisphere*.

In normal participants, any information reaching one hemisphere first is rapidly and automatically transferred to the other hemisphere via the corpus callosum. However, for patients who have had a commissurotomy (often called informally 'split-brain patients'), the information cannot pass to the other hemisphere because the corpus callosum has been cut. So this experimental procedure, known as the 'divided field', enabled Sperry to present visual stimuli, knowing that they would be confined to the hemisphere to which they were transmitted. What sorts of thing could he demonstrate?

Testing the different hemispheres with verbal stimuli

The split-brain patient sits in front of a screen. A word is flashed up very briefly in the individual's RVF (if the exposure of the stimulus is too long, the eyes automatically move towards the stimulus, which may then be seen by both hemispheres). The word is transmitted to the left hemisphere and if you ask the patient to report what they saw, they will say the word. When the study is repeated with the LVF, the word travels to the right hemisphere. When asked to report what they have seen, the patient reports seeing nothing.

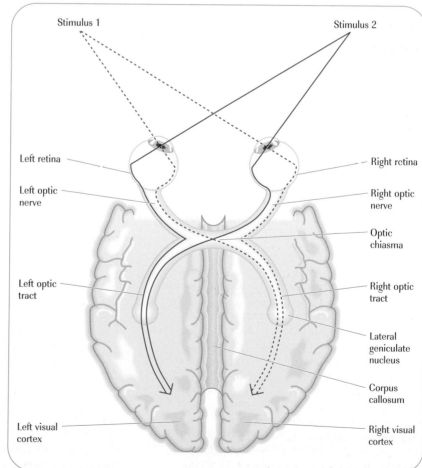

Figure 12.7 >> *Visual pathways in relation to split brain*

Stimulus 1

Stimulus 2

Left retina

Left optic nerve

Left optic tract

Left visual cortex

Right retina

Right optic nerve

Optic chiasma

Right optic tract

Lateral geniculate nucleus

Corpus callosum

Right visual cortex

The reason for this lies in way that language mechanisms in the brain are organized. In most people, the left hemisphere contains the language system, i.e. it can read words and speak. The word presented in the RVF goes to the left hemisphere where it can be read and reported by the patient. The word presented in the LVF goes to the right hemisphere, which does not have a highly developed language system and certainly cannot speak. Therefore the person has nothing to report. In fact, the experiment involves a *spoken* response which itself has to emerge from the left hemisphere. So, with the corpus callosum cut, the left hemisphere does not know what is going on in the right hemisphere, so the patient's left-hemisphere language system cannot comment on stimuli presented to the right hemisphere.

This type of study allowed Sperry to confirm that the left hemisphere controls reading and speech and that the right hemisphere apparently could not process verbal stimuli at all. But he was worried that because he used *verbal* questions and responses he was only testing the left hemisphere, as this was where the language system was located. As the right hemisphere had no language system he had to find an alternative way of testing it.

Testing the hemispheres with other stimuli

You may remember that the motor pathways are completely crossed, with each hemisphere controlling the muscles of the opposite side of the body. The right hemisphere controls the left arm and hand, and so Sperry used this system to test the right hemisphere. The experiment described above is repeated, except that in this case the left hand is placed behind a screen (so the participant cannot see what it is doing) among a collection of different objects. A word such as 'orange' is presented in the RVF. It goes to the left hemisphere and when the participant is asked whether they saw anything, they say 'orange'. Then 'banana' is presented in the LVF. This goes to the right hemisphere and when asked for a spoken response, the participant denies seeing anything. However, the left hand behind the screen emerges triumphantly holding a banana it has selected from the range of objects!

It appears that the right hemisphere can understand simple, concrete nouns and understand their meaning. This activated the left hand, controlled by the right hemisphere, to select the appropriate object. Meanwhile the left hemisphere, which can talk but has no access to the right hemisphere, has not seen the word and does not know why the left hand is holding a banana. When asked what is going on, the participant, using their left hemisphere to produce a spoken reply, will seem confused, or sometimes even deny that the left hand is theirs! The split brain represents a 'disconnection syndrome', in which brain damage disconnects functions that are normally integrated. Ask a normal participant, with their eyes shut, to say

whether two objects, one in each hand, are the same and they can do it easily. Ask a split-brain patient to do the same thing and they cannot even say whether they have an object in their left hand.

Using the left-hand response system, Sperry and other researchers could test the right hemisphere with various types of stimulus, while the left hemisphere could continue using its language mechanisms. Sperry concluded that the right hemisphere had some simple reading ability because it could read concrete nouns (i.e. object names), but not abstract words and could not produce language (writing or speaking). However, it was better at recognizing pictures and shapes, especially faces.

Conclusions

Work on the split brain demonstrated that although the right hemisphere may not be very linguistic, it does have important functions related to processing pictures and shapes (visuo-spatial stimuli). If two faces are presented simultaneously and split-brain patients are asked afterwards to choose from a selection of faces, they choose the one presented to the right hemisphere. The left hand/right hemisphere system is also better at copying abstract designs. It seems that we can divide the hemispheres into a verbal and linguistic left hemisphere and a visuo-spatial right hemisphere, and this has become a basic model of brain function, supported by thousands of subsequent studies with normal participants. Before looking at some of this later work, there are some problems with split-brain research that should be mentioned.

The right hemisphere cannot produce language, but is better at recognizing pictures and shapes, especially faces

Evaluation
split-brain studies

Limitations

- *Small sample* – Because it is such a drastic treatment, very few commissurotomies have ever been carried out – only about 80 in total – and they are extremely rare nowadays. Only about 20 of these individuals have been given psychological testing and most of the data have come from fewer than ten of them. This sample is too small to generalize to the whole population.

- *'Normality' of participants* – Some form of brain abnormality causes epilepsy and patients have to live with it for many years before surgery takes place. They are also likely to be on drug therapy and it is hard to argue that these were 'normal' participants before surgery. In fact, some of the patients showed good evidence of right-hemisphere expressive language, by writing with the left hand. So do we conclude that bilateral (two-sided) language organization is 'normal', or that their particular brains have been re-organized because of the presence of some sort of abnormality and should not be used to model the normal brain?

- *Uncontrolled variables* – There are too many uncontrolled variables for the split-brain patients to be considered a uniform group. They vary in relation to gender, age of onset of epilepsy, cause of the epilepsy, age at which surgery was performed and age at testing.

Strengths

For the key reasons listed above, it is unjustified to use experimental findings from split-brain patients only in order to build models of normal brain function. However, they have been very important, for various reasons:

- *Discoveries about cognitive functions of the right hemisphere* – From Sperry's earliest work onwards it seemed likely that the right hemisphere, previously thought to be unimportant compared to the 'verbal' left hemisphere, did contain important cognitive functions related to visuo-spatial stimuli such as shapes and faces.

- *Role of language* – Studies on split-brain patients show the central role of language in our conscious self-awareness. When asked to comment on their situation, they always refer to the experiences of the left hemisphere. Only under special experimental conditions can the right hemisphere express itself clearly.

- *Role of the corpus callosum* – Sperry was intrigued by the role of the corpus callosum in brain function. The disconnection syndromes seen in split-brain patients suggest that the corpus callosum enables each hemisphere to be aware of activities in the other. Each hemisphere seems to have its own specialized functions and, in the intact brain, the corpus callosum allows these to be coordinated and integrated, producing an integrated personality. Thus we can reflect (using left-hemisphere language) on our visuo-spatial abilities in the right hemisphere.

- *Sperry's divided visual field technique* – One underestimated contribution of Sperry's work was his development of the divided visual field technique used to test the hemispheres separately. As we shall see, this has become one of the most popular experimental procedures and has contributed significantly to our understanding of hemisphere function by allowing test stimuli to be presented to each hemisphere independently.

HEMISPHERE ASYMMETRIES: STUDIES WITH NORMAL PARTICIPANTS

In parallel with the split-brain work, thousands of studies were carried out on normal participants. Many of these relied on two basic techniques:

- Sperry's divided field
- dichotic listening.

Divided-field studies

As normal participants have an intact corpus callosum, the divided field cannot be used unmodified because a single stimulus presented to one hemisphere is rapidly communicated to the other. The simple modification is to present two different stimuli simultaneously, one in each visual field. With brief exposure (less than 100 milliseconds), the participant usually reports one stimulus only. If words are used, the word presented in the RVF and going directly to the left hemisphere and its language mechanisms would be the one registered by the participant; this is called 'RVF superiority'. If pictures or faces are used, then the one in the LVF going first to the right hemisphere is reported. The right hemisphere is better at analysing such visual stimuli. Although the results have to be passed to the left hemisphere to be reported verbally, this is faster than the processing of the stimulus in the RVF going to the left hemisphere, which cannot deal with it and has to pass it across to the right hemisphere to be analysed. Visuo-spatial stimuli therefore give an 'LVF advantage'.

The results of the many studies carried out with the divided visual field are reasonably consistent:

- Words, letters and digits give an RVF advantage, indicating superior processing by the left hemisphere.
- Recognizing faces and patterns, discriminating brightness and colours and depth perception all give an LVF advantage, indicating right-hemisphere processing.

Dichotic-listening studies

Dichotic listening is a similar procedure but designed for the auditory system. Two different sounds are presented simultaneously through headphones. Although each ear projects to both hemispheres, the crossed, contralateral pathway is dominant, so stimuli presented in the left ear are processed by the right hemisphere and vice versa. If words are used, the one in the right ear going to the left hemisphere is usually reported, giving a right-ear advantage (REA). If non-verbal sounds, such as animal noises, are used (a sort of auditory equivalent of visuo-spatial stimuli), then the sound in the left ear tends to be the one identified and reported; this is a left-ear advantage (LEA).

To summarize the main findings from dichotic-listening studies:

- Spoken words, digits, normal and backwards speech and nonsense syllables all give an REA (left-hemisphere processing).
- Recognizing environmental sounds and most aspects of music perception give an LEA (right-hemisphere processing).

Characteristics of the two hemispheres

So the pattern of visual field superiorities and ear advantages provide us with a picture of how the hemispheres process a range of stimuli. Table 12.1 summarizes some of the findings.

Table 12.1 >> Suggested characteristics of the two hemispheres

Left hemisphere	Right hemisphere
>> Verbal	>> Visuo-spatial
>> Sequential processing	>> Simultaneous, parallel positioning
>> Analytic	>> Gestalt, holistic
>> Rational	>> Emotional
>> Deductive	>> Intuitive, creative
>> Convergent thought	>> Divergent thought
>> Scientific	>> Artistic

Attempts have been made to characterize the hemispheres on the basis of such findings. As words and digits come in as a sequence of stimuli spread over time, the left hemisphere is better at *sequential* or time-based processing, and at segmenting and analysing input into its component parts. (Think of understanding speech, where we take in the sequence of sounds, but to understand them we need to identify each unit, be it a syllable or whole word, and then put the sentence together after analysing the parts.) Pictures and faces are usually identified as one whole stimulus, with all the features processed immediately in parallel; so the right hemisphere is better at 'Gestalt' or 'parallel processing'. ('Gestalt' means an integrated whole stimulus, not just a collection of parts.)

Some theorists have gone further, seeing the left hemisphere as analytic, scientific and rational, and the right hemisphere as creative, artistic and emotional. However, there is little solid experimental evidence to support these suggestions. As the role of the corpus callosum is to coordinate the activities of the two hemispheres, it is unlikely that any complicated human activity involves only one of them independently. Scientific activity, for instance, involves producing hypotheses and theories – clearly a creative enterprise.

Later research into hemispheres

While the original work of Wernicke and Broca, and Sperry's experiments on the split brain, can be criticized for studying too few participants and involving uncontrolled variables, the basic picture of hemisphere specialization that emerged has been confirmed by later and better-controlled studies. Bradshaw and Sherlock (1982), for example, used drawings of faces made up of geometric features such as triangular noses and rectangular eyes. Using a divided-field technique they found that the right hemisphere was better at processing the general arrangement of facial features (whether they were close together or spread far apart), but that the left hemisphere was better at analysing specific features, such as whether the triangular nose pointed up or down. These findings support the idea that the left hemisphere is better at analytic processing and the right hemisphere is better at Gestalt or parallel processing.

Language is localized to the left hemisphere, while the right hemisphere is specialized for the processing of visuo-spatial stimuli, of which the best example is faces. Other approaches, such as assessing the effects of 'lateralized' (one-sided) brain damage, give further support. Left-hemisphere damage following a stroke or accidental brain injury can affect language, leaving face recognition intact, while right-hemisphere damage can produce the opposite pattern.

Evaluation
divided-field and dichotic-listening studies

- **Good experimental design** – Divided-field and dichotic-listening techniques are highly controlled experimental procedures, so the results are reliable and have been replicated in many different psychological laboratories across the world.

- **Individual differences** – However, not all participants show the expected biases to one side or the other. Usually a group of participants overall will show an LVF advantage for faces and an RVF advantage for words, but some individuals may show no advantage or even a reversal of the normal pattern, with an LVF advantage for words and an RVF advantage for faces. So, although we have a general model of how the hemispheres are organized, we have to remember that there can be individual differences.

- **Real-life application?** – These methods are excellent for isolating the different functions of the hemispheres *experimentally*, but in everyday life we use both hemispheres all the time. The main purpose of the corpus callosum is to integrate the activities of the two hemispheres, and most of our behaviour will involve both hemispheres working together.

HANDEDNESS, GENDER AND HEMISPHERE ASYMMETRIES

What emerges from these studies is the picture of a 'standard' brain, with left-hemisphere language and right-hemisphere visuo-spatial ability. But how standard is this brain? The section above referred to possible individual differences, and some of these have been systematically studied. The left hemisphere controls language and the right hand, which is the dominant hand for most people: Do people who are left-handed show the same pattern of asymmetries? Does gender make any difference?

ACTIVITY

Handedness

1 If you are right-handed, close your eyes and stand on your right leg. Then repeat the exercise, but this time talk aloud while you do it (e.g. describe what has happened to you during the day, recite a poem or even talk about an area of psychology that you find particularly interesting!).

Some people find that standing on their right leg more difficult if they are talking at the same time. In theory, both right-leg balancing and talking are left-hemisphere functions and interfere with each other, hence the difficulty.

2 What type of task might interfere with left-leg balancing? Test it out by asking another right-handed person to carry out the same two-stage activity, but this time substituting a right-hemisphere activity. Did they find the simultaneous activity more difficult?

3 If you are left-handed, what result would you predict? Now test it out.

Handedness and hemisphere assymmetry

Depending on precisely how it is assessed, around 10 to 15 per cent of the population are left-handed. As right-handers seem to have a left hemisphere that controls language and the right hand, it would seem logical that left-handers should have right-hemisphere language, i.e. the reverse pattern. In fact, the picture is more complicated. Around 70 per cent of left-handers have left-hemisphere language, around 15 per cent have language in the right hemisphere and in 15 per cent language seems to involve both hemispheres, i.e. bilateral representation. In general, people who are left-handed are less lateralized in regard to language than those who are right-handed.

Does this have any implications for cognitive abilities? There were early suggestions that left-handers might be worse at visuo-spatial tasks than right-handers because the spread of language into the right hemisphere might somehow interfere with visuo-spatial abilities. However, there is no convincing evidence for overall differences in cognitive abilities between left- and right-handers.

Interestingly, left-handers are overrepresented amongst mathematicians and architects, but also amongst people with dyslexia and those suffering from learning difficulties. There are speculations that these observations are related to the unusual pattern of hemisphere development in left-handers.

Gender and hemisphere assymmetry

There is some evidence that females show a different pattern of hemisphere asymmetries to males – in particular, a higher frequency of bilateral representation of language across both hemispheres. This has been used to explain the superiority of females in language-based intelligence tests and their poorer performance on visuo-spatial tasks. It is argued that the increased development of verbal skills involving both hemispheres interferes with the development of visuo-spatial skills in the right hemisphere.

Although this biological argument has become popular, there is little experimental evidence to support it, and it ignores the wide range of social and cultural pressures during development which can influence cognitive abilities. For instance, there is a powerful correlation, regardless of gender, between academic performance in a particular individual and previous experience of that subject. This does not seem surprising, but biological theorists often ignore learning experience.

Interaction between gender and handedness

As people who are left-handed and females can show patterns of reduced asymmetry for language, you might argue that female left-handers should be the least asymmetrical of all. However, this is not consistently the case. Performance on tests of hemisphere asymmetries, such as the divided field and dichotic listening, seems to involve a complex interaction between gender and handedness. It also reflects the fact that differences in hemisphere organization between any two individuals, regardless of handedness

Do women have a higher frequency of bilateral representation across both hemispheres?

or gender, are probably greater than any systematic differences between groups of left- and right-handed people, or between males and females (Springer and Deutsch 1997).

Evaluation
research into asymmetries

- *Identifying effects of variables* – The main strength of research in this area is that it has shown how variables such as handedness and gender can affect the 'standard' pattern of brain organization.

- *Difficulty in interpreting results* – Interpreting the results of divided-field and dichotic-listening studies is complicated, unless handedness and gender are carefully controlled, i.e. unless studies are carried out on people of the same gender with the same handedness. However, research should ideally include gender and handedness. This means that it is difficult to speak of a 'standard' brain, because hemisphere organization is influenced by these variables.

REVISION SUMMARY

Having covered this topic, you should be able to:

✓ describe the methods and findings of Sperry's split-brain work

✓ evaluate the contribution of split-brain studies to our understanding of lateralization of function in the cerebral cortex

✓ outline methods and findings of studies of hemisphere asymmetries in normal participants

✓ outline the specialized functions of left and right hemispheres, including the *types* of processing each hemisphere is specialized for

✓ describe possible differences in hemisphere organization between left- and right-handed people and between males and females.

CHECK YOUR UNDERSTANDING

Check your understanding of lateralization of function in the cerebral cortex by answering these questions from memory at first. Check your answers by looking back through Topic 3.

1 What type of participants did Sperry use in his studies and what does the term used to describe these patients mean?

2 Where is the corpus callosum and what is its function?

3 In 100 words, outline the divided-field technique for testing hemisphere functions.

4 Construct a descriptive 150-word précis of three conclusions that Sperry drew from his studies of split-brain patients.

5 Identify and give a brief account of two reasons why Sperry's studies are considered important.

6 Identify and give a brief account of two limitations of split-brain studies.

7 Write a 100-word précis of the organization of functions across the two hemispheres.

8 How is language organized in the brains of left-handed people?

9 Outline the effects of gender on tests of language and visuo-spatial abilities.

10 Write a descriptive 150-word précis of the influence of gender on localization of function in the cerebral hemispheres.

EXAMPLE EXAM QUESTIONS

Below are some **possible examination questions** set on this topic, along with hints to help you understand and approach each question effectively:

1 Critically consider the lateralization of function in the cerebral cortex. (24 marks)

> A typical examination essay is likely to be 600 to 700 words long. Many candidates have difficulty in getting the balance of AO1 and AO2 right within this word limit. There are several strategies you might use to ensure a good balance. One way is to start every paragraph with a few sentences of AO1 and then present an equivalent amount of AO2. In this question you might use research studies as part of either the AO1 or AO2 material. Any *description* of a study would be given AO1 credit whereas if the study is used to offer commentary on a statement about lateralization of function then it would count as AO2. For example, you might state that language is lateralized in the left hemisphere and then support this with the conclusions of a research study.

2 Discuss the organization of language in the brain. (24 marks)

> This question is similar to the last one but is more restricted because it focuses on one example of lateralization – that of language in the brain. Nevertheless, this is a straightforward question that can be answered using the work of Broca, Wernicke and Sperry. Since it is broad, you can cover specific areas (the studies of Broca and Wernicke) and/or the concept of lateralization to the left hemisphere. AO2 commentary could cover the 'why?' of lateralization, including the evolution of language as a highly specialized function, or perhaps a comparison of language with symmetrical sensory systems. Other AO2 material could include supporting research evidence, an emphasis on the complexity of language systems and the range of methods used. If time permits, language organization in people who are left handed and in females could also be discussed.

3 Discuss hemisphere asymmetries of function. (24 marks)

> This is a very broad question so it is important to think carefully about what you are going to include in your answer. You need to discuss more than one asymmetry, so you cannot concentrate only on language, although it can be the main focus. You could also include visuo-spatial skills, for example. Research evidence could include Wernicke, Broca and Sperry, as well as reference to the many studies with normal participants. Commentary could include research evidence, the range of methods used, variations in hemisphere organization with handedness and gender, and perhaps a comparison with symmetrical sensory and motor functions.

4 (a) Describe hemisphere asymmetries of function (e.g. Sperry's research on the split brain). (12 marks)
 (b) Evaluate the hemisphere asymmetries of function that you have described in part (a). (12 marks)

> This question focuses clearly on the amount of AO2 material that you should provide. An example is provided from the specification. Sometimes examples can be misleading, as in this case because it suggests you only have to describe one asymmetry whereas the wording of the question indicates that at least two asymmetries must be covered.

5 (a) Outline and evaluate **one** method of investigating the brain. (12 marks)
 (b) Critically consider the use of the method you outlined in part (a) to investigate lateralization of function in the cerebral cortex. (12 marks)

> This question is included as a reminder that you can be asked one question on several of the topics in this unit. It also shows how problems may arise if a candidate does not read both parts of a question before beginning their answer. The method you choose to describe and evaluate in (a) must be applicable to the investigation(s) you wish to discuss in part (b).

UNIT SUMMARY

Topic 1: Methods of investigating the brain

● Many different methods are used to investigate the functioning of the brain.

● **Invasive methods** include **electrical stimulation** (implanting electrodes into the brain to record nerve impulses and to stimulate brain neurons artificially); **chemical stimulation** (using drugs which mimic the activity of neurotransmitters, or which stimulate or block synaptic receptors); and physical destruction of brain tissue (**lesioning** affects more localized regions and **ablation** removes larger areas of the brain).

● The main **strength of invasive methods** is that they have provided a huge amount of information about the brain and have contributed to current models of brain function. The use of chemical stimulation has allowed us to link behaviour to the brain's synaptic neurotransmitters, providing important insights into neurotransmitter abnormalities in schizophrenia and depression, for example.

● The main **limitation of invasive methods** is that for ethical reasons most of the work has been done on non-human animals, leading to the problem of generalizing the results to the human brain. Also, specifically human functions such as language cannot be studied with these methods.

● **Non-invasive methods** for studying the brain include **electrical recording** – recording the electrical activity of billions of cortical neurons using electrodes on the skull surface using EEG. **Scanning and imaging** techniques have also been widely used since the early 1970s. CT or CAT scans use multiple X-rays and computerized analysis to produce pictures of sections through the brain. MRI and fMRI scans involve bombarding the brain with radio waves to produce high-definition pictures of brain structures. PET scans record the radioactivity emitted by labelled glucose injected into the bloodstream and taken up by brain structures, creating an activity map of the brain. Finally, MEG scans reflect moment-by-moment neural activity by recording the tiny magnetic fields produced by neuronal activity.

Topic 2: Localization of function in the cerebral cortex

● Sensory and motor functions are localized to particular areas of the cerebral cortex – **the primary motor and sensory areas**. Each hemisphere is associated with the opposite side of the body, and the arrangement of sensory and motor functions within and across the hemispheres is identical and symmetrical. Motor and sensory pathways are therefore crossed (contralateral). Visual and auditory systems have pathways connecting to both hemispheres (a combination of contralateral and uncrossed or ipsilateral pathways), although the arrangement is perfectly symmetrical.

● Higher cognitive functions such as language are located in the association cortex and can be asymmetrically organized across the hemispheres. Broca identified an area of the brain, now called **Broca's area** which, if damaged, severely impairs speech production whilst leaving comprehension of speech intact. Wernicke identified an area in the temporal lobe, now known as **Wernicke's area**, which affects speech comprehension if damaged. Their work has helped to map the localized areas and routes underlying speech production and comprehension. Modern scanning techniques have generally confirmed their findings, locating language mechanisms in the left hemisphere of the brain.

● The **association area** of the cortex also controls other cognitive abilities such as the capacity for forward planning, goal-directed behaviour, perception (such as object recognition), sequences of action, face recognition, visual aspects of language and auditory perception. Damage to the association cortex can produce aphasias, apraxias and problems with perception, even though basic sensory and motor processes remain intact.

● Although sensory and motor functions are localized to specific areas of the cortex, especially primary sensory and motor cortex, higher cognitive functions require parallel and distributed processing. This means that although sub-processes such as language comprehension and colour perception may be localized to particular cortical areas, our language and visual abilities overall depend on the integration of these distributed functions. **Localization of function** and **distributed functions** are not therefore alternatives – together they describe the way that the sensory, motor and association cortex are organized in the hemispheres.

Topic 3: Lateralization of function in the cerebral cortex

● **Sperry** devised experimental techniques, such as the divided field, to show that in **split-brain** patients, the right hemisphere had superior visuo-spatial abilities, while the left hemisphere contained language mechanisms. In normal, intact people, the corpus callosum allows the two hemispheres to coordinate and integrate their functions.

● Subsequent studies using divided-field and dichotic-listening experiments in intact people have confirmed the **lateralization of function in the cerebral cortex**: the left hemisphere is specialized for the processing of language because it deals best with time-based, sequential stimuli, whereas the right hemisphere processes whole stimuli such as pictures and faces in parallel. However, studies of left-handedness and gender differences show some variation in patterns of **hemisphere asymmetries**, although the practical significance of this remains unclear.

FURTHER RESOURCES

Green, S. (1994) *Principles of Biopsychology*, Hove: Erlbaum.
Gives clear and comprehensive coverage of all the areas covered in this unit.

Springer, S.P. and Deutsch, G. (1997) *Left Brain, Right Brain* (5th edn), New York: Freeman.
Besides covering hemisphere functional asymmetries, this text also contains topics such as methodology in brain research, language disorders and some speculations on the nature of consciousness.

Websites
http://www.healthlinkusa.com/A.html
This is an extensive site covering a number of brain disorders, including aphasia.

http://thalamus.wustl.edu/course/sleep.html
Despite its address, this website provides a concise summary of the language mechanisms of the brain.

http://www.nimh.nih.gov/hotsci/mri.htm
A chance to see what an MRI scan looks like in a comparison of the brain of a person with schizophrenia and a non-schizophrenic individual. Also some interesting information about the usefulness of MRI scans.

http://www.nimh.nih.gov/events/petscan.htm
PET scans of people diagnosed with schizophrenia and non-schizophrenic individuals when performing a memory task.

Unit 12 // Brain and behaviour

BIOLOGICAL RHYTHMS, Sleep & Dreaming

PREVIEW

After you have read this unit, you should be able to:

>> describe and evaluate research studies into ultradian, circadian and infradian biological rhythms, including the role of endogenous pacemakers (biological clocks in the brain) and exogenous zeitgebers (environmental stimuli such as light and darkness)

>> explain the consequences of disrupting biological rhythms

>> describe and evaluate theories and research studies relating to the evolution and functions of sleep, including ecological and restoration accounts

>> discuss the implications of findings from studies of total and partial sleep deprivation for ecological and restoration theories of the evolution and functions of sleep

>> describe and evaluate research findings relating to the nature of dreams, including content, duration and relationship with the stages of sleep

>> describe and evaluate theories of the functions of dreaming, including neurobiological and psychological accounts.

INTRODUCTION

About one third of our lives is spent asleep, and yet there is still no clear agreement on what the functions of sleep may be. It represents one of our basic biological rhythms, and we know that disrupting sleep can have drastic effects on people. Sleep consists of a number of different stages and during one of these we dream – one of the strangest experiences we can have. Dreams contain imagery that is sometimes ordinary and occasionally bizarre. This has led to various theories of dreaming, ranging from wish fulfilment to information processing.

Topic 1 introduces biological rhythms and the interaction between endogenous (internal) pacemakers (i.e. biological clocks found in the brain) and exogenous zeitgebers (i.e. external or environmental stimuli vital to synchronizing biological rhythms with the outside world). This first topic also considers some effects of disrupting these rhythms.

The second topic describes the characteristics, evolution and possible functions of sleep, looking at research evidence and, in particular, at studies of total and partial sleep deprivation.

Various approaches to the study of dreaming are considered in Topic 3, including the relationship between dreaming and the stages of sleep. This topic also examines neurobiological and psychological theories of the functions of dreaming.

Simon Green

Many systems in the body show a rhythmic variation over 24 hours. These include physiological processes such as body temperature and urine production, and also more psychological characteristics such as arousal or alertness. This means that you tend to be most alert and lively at particular times of the day.

1 Think about your own patterns of alertness over several days. Do you feel livelier in the morning, afternoon, evening, or never! Do you think that it is reasonable to suggest that some people are 'morning' types and others 'evening' types?

2 Do your own patterns of alertness fit in with your sleep patterns? Do you sleep better by going to bed at around 10.00 p.m., or do you find there is no point in even trying to sleep until midnight or even later? Do your friends have similar patterns of sleeping and waking?

3 Finally, is your sleep pattern actually dictated by your social life and the need to stay up late with friends?

As we shall see, working against your natural biological rhythms can have negative effects on how you feel and even on how well you work.

KEY CONCEPTS

Biological rhythms: regular variations in the biological activity of living organisms. They include rhythms with a frequency or periodicity of less than one day (ultradian), those with a periodicity of 24 hours (circadian), and those with a periodicity of greater than 24 hours (infradian).

Endogenous pacemaker: biological 'clocks' in the brain controlling biological rhythms. The best example is the suprachiasmatic nucleus in the hypothalamus.

Zeitgeber: means 'timegiver', and refers to external stimuli that help in synchronizing biological rhythms to the outside world. The most important one is light.

Stages of sleep: sleep can be divided into slow wave sleep (SWS) and REM (or dreaming) sleep. SWS can be divided into four stages, each with characteristic EEG activity. REM sleep combines

an EEG characteristic of waking behaviour with deep sleep, and can therefore be referred to as paradoxical sleep.

Ecological theories: theories of the function of sleep that emphasize evolutionary and ecological aspects of animal behaviour. The simplest version proposes that sleep keeps an animal safe from predators.

Restoration theories: theories of the function of sleep that emphasize the recovery of physiological resources expended in waking behaviour. One version proposes that slow wave sleep is for recovery of the body, and REM sleep for recovery of the brain.

Theories of dreaming: theories of the function of dreaming. They divide roughly into those that see dream imagery as significant, and those that see dream content as an irrelevant by-product of brain activity.

The natural world is full of rhythms, such as the regular cycle of the seasons, the rise and fall of the tides, and the rising and the setting of the sun. The body also has its rhythms: some are obvious, such as the alternation of sleeping and waking and the menstrual cycle, while others are less obvious, such as the regular variations in body temperature over a single day.

Many of these rhythms are clearly related to the physical properties of the world we live in. The cycle of the seasons depends on the earth's orbit around the sun. The alternation of day and night is due to the earth's rotation about its axis, and tidal flow reflects the gravitational influence of the moon on the earth. It would therefore be logical to assume that the rhythms we observe in living organisms are directly controlled by these external stimuli. In fact, the situation is more complicated than that. For instance, beach-living algae (single-cell plants) stay under the sand at high tide, burrow to the surface as the water recedes to allow for photosynthesis in the sunshine, and then tunnel back under, just before the tide returns. Is this regular rhythm controlled by tidal flows? A simple way to test this is to keep the algae in a laboratory with constant light and no tides. Despite the absence of environmental stimuli, the algae still burrow to the surface just after the time of high tide at their home beach and tunnel back under, just before the tide returns.

In countries with severe winters, the squirrel population hibernates. If these squirrels are kept in a laboratory in a constant, warm environment, with alternating 12-hour periods of light and dark, they still go through the hibernation routine at the appropriate time of year, increasing food intake and body weight and decreasing body temperature. They also awake as spring approaches in the world outside.

These examples suggest that rhythmic activities can be 'endogenous' (i.e. in-built) and so persist even when the environmental stimuli are absent. Algae are single cells and the controlling endogenous pacemaker is probably in the genetic material of the cell nucleus. Squirrels are mammals with complex brains, and hibernation is a complex activity, probably controlled by pacemakers in the brain. However, even with these 'endogenous pacemakers' (or 'biological clocks'), behaviour in the real world has to be adapted to external events such as winter or night time, so that hibernation occurs at the right time. Where exogenous (external) events have a role in rhythmic activities, they are called 'exogenous zeitgebers' (meaning literally, 'external time-givers'). Much of the research into biological rhythms has focused on understanding the relationship between endogenous (internal) pacemakers and exogenous (external) zeitgebers.

DIFFERENT TYPES OF BIOLOGICAL RHYTHM

A general classification divides biological rhythms of the natural world into three main types:

● *circadian* rhythms
● *infradian* rhythms, including *circannual* rhythms
● *ultradian* rhythms.

Circadian rhythms

'Circadian' (from two Latin words for 'about' and 'day') biological rhythms occur once every 24 hours. The human sleep/waking cycle is a good example, and many other physiological systems, such as body temperature, operate to the same 24-hour rhythm. Our body temperature peaks in the late afternoon and is lowest during the early hours of the morning.

Mammals exhibit about 100 different circadian biological rhythms (Green 1994). These rhythms are particularly important to animals because they synchronize behaviour and body states to changes in the environment. The cycle of light and dark, for example, has great significance for survival. Nocturnal animals can avoid predators during the day by remaining hidden. Diurnal animals, on the other hand, are adapted to forage for food during the day. An endogenous pacemaker (or

biological clock) enables these animals to anticipate periodic events, such as the onset of darkness or sunrise, and engage in appropriate behaviour that adapts them to these environmental changes.

Research studies on the control of the sleep/waking cycle (covered in Topic 2) are directly relevant to the investigation of circadian rhythms.

Infradian rhythms

'Infradian' biological rhythms occur less than once every day – for instance, hibernation in squirrels and the human menstrual cycle. Some infradian rhythms occur on a yearly basis and are therefore also known as 'circannual rhythms'.

Circannual rhythms

Circannual biological rhythms occur on a yearly cycle. Examples include migration in birds and hibernation in squirrels and bears. Some of these changes in behaviour are driven by exogenous (external) factors, such as temperature or food availability. Research shows that many of these rhythms (such as seasonal fluctuations in body weight) will, however, still be maintained in the constant conditions of the laboratory. As with circadian rhythms, animals show annual rhythms of approximately 365 days even in the absence of external zeitgebers, suggesting the existence of endogenous, circannual biological clocks. These are sometimes referred to as 'free-running' biological rhythms.

Research by Zucker et al. (1983) explored the operation of both circadian and circannual rhythms in ground squirrels. These researchers measured activity levels, reproductive cycles and body weight in animals that had free-running circadian and circannual rhythms. Lesions in the suprachiasmatic nucleus (we will explore its role in more detail later in this topic) were found to disrupt circadian activity cycles, but tended not to have any effect on changes that operated on a circannual rhythm, such as body weight and reproductive status. This finding suggests that circannual rhythms must, therefore, involve a different underlying mechanism, i.e. a different endogenous pacemaker or biological clock.

Seasonal changes in behaviour are also evident in human beings. For some people, winter brings a particularly low period that may become a profound depression. This winter depression may alternate with a summer mania (Blehar and Rosenthal 1989). In winter, people affected by this fluctuation in mood become depressed, slow down, sleep a lot and overeat. When summer comes, they become elated, energetic and thinner (Rosenzweig et al. 1999). This syndrome has become known as 'seasonal affective disorder' (SAD).

Light treatment has been shown to be effective for some people suffering from SAD

Some studies have suggested a correlation between latitude (northern latitudes have more prolonged periods of winter darkness) and frequency of the incidence of SAD, although a study in Iceland, which is in the far northern latitude, did not confirm this suggestion (Magnusson and Stefansson 1993). One important function of light is that it suppresses melatonin, a hormone that may have an important role in the regulation of sleep. Exposure to darkness stimulates the synthesis of melatonin whereas light suppresses it. People with SAD are thought to have a high threshold for melatonin suppression, and a therapy that is effective in some cases of SAD is light treatment. This involves exposure to bright white light for at least an hour every morning. This must influence the activity of the suprachiasmatic nucleus, the pineal gland and the release of melatonin, but the precise mechanisms of this anti-depressant action are not yet fully understood.

Serotonin may also have an important role in SAD because a seasonal rhythm has been demonstrated for this brain neurotransmitter. We have lower levels of serotonin in the winter and spring than in summer and autumn (Egrise et al. 1986).

Ultradian rhythms

'Ultradian' biological rhythms have more than one complete cycle every 24 hours. An example of an ultradian rhythm that has been widely studied is sleep, which oscillates between stages of lighter and deeper sleep during a single night, each cycle lasting about 90 minutes. Research studies into the different types of sleep (slow-wave sleep and rapid eye movement sleep) are also directly relevant to ultradian rhythms in general. Ultradian rhythms are, of course, also seen in other behaviours such as food-seeking in non-human animals and hormone release.

Ultradian rhythms are also found in many complex human behaviours. For example, research studies show that when human participants perform tasks that require alertness, EEG recordings of alertness appear to vary with an ultradian rhythm. Destruction of the brain mechanisms that control circadian rhythms in animals does not appear to affect behaviours that have an ultradian rhythm. However, they are affected by lesions to specific areas of the hypothalamus in the brain (Rosenzweig et al. 1999). The periods of ultradian rhythms appear to be correlated with brain and body size – smaller animals tend to have more rapid cycles (Gerkema and Dann 1985).

ENDOGENOUS PACEMAKERS AND EXOGENOUS ZEITGEBERS

Endogenous pacemakers (or biological clocks) probably represent an inherited genetic mechanism. For example, regular rhythms of activity and rest can be measured in the unborn human embryo that has never been exposed to the outside world. But, as pointed out earlier, these

rhythms have to respond to exogenous zeitgebers if the behaviour they control is to be fully coordinated with the external world. One of the most influential zeitgebers is light, and its role in fine-tuning bodily rhythms has been reasonably well mapped out.

Role of the pineal gland

The most important endogenous pacemaker in the brain of birds and reptiles is probably the pineal gland. This structure contains light receptors that respond to external light, penetrating the thin layer of skull that lies above the pineal gland. In turn, these light receptors influence the activity of neurons in the pineal gland. These neurons have a natural rhythmic activity and also convert the neurotransmitter serotonin into the hormone melatonin. Melatonin is then released into the general circulation, which acts on many of the body's organs and glands, and seems to be responsible for the rhythmic nature of many activities. For instance, it acts on brainstem sleep mechanisms to help synchronize the phases of sleep and waking, and it has been shown that injections of melatonin can produce sleep in sparrows (Abraham *et al.* 2000). The manufacture and release of melatonin is regulated by the amount of light falling on the pineal gland, decreasing as light increases. Research has shown, for instance, that chickens wake and become active as dawn breaks and melatonin secretion falls (Binkley 1979). This means that although their waking is controlled by the biological clock in the pineal gland, it is adjusted to the actual time that morning begins, which varies throughout the year.

Role of the suprachiasmatic nucleus (SCN)

In mammals, including humans, the pathways are more complicated. The main biological clock seems to be a small area in the hypothalamus – the suprachiasmatic nucleus (SCN) – whose neurons have an in-built circadian rhythmic firing pattern. This nucleus regulates the manufacture and secretion of melatonin in the pineal gland via an interconnecting pathway. Another pathway connects the retina of the eye to the SCN. This allows the amount of light falling on the retina to influence the activity of SCN neurons and, indirectly, the release of melatonin from the pineal gland. So the link between light and melatonin production is maintained. A recent discovery is that light can reach the brain without passing through the eyes. Campbell and Murphy (1998) applied light to the back of the knees of human participants and were able to shift the circadian rhythm in body temperature and melatonin secretion.

The pineal gland and the SCN function jointly as endogenous pacemakers (or biological clocks) in the brain. There are many bodily rhythms, and it is likely that there are other structures involved in maintaining their regularity, as we shall see in Topic 2 in relation to sleep. Research has shown, for example, that animals fed on a regular basis soon become active just before their feeding time. This happens even in the absence of environmental cues and must therefore rely on some sort of internal clock. Rosenwasser *et al.* (1981) found that rats still showed this anticipation after their SCN was destroyed, so another biological clock must also be able to perform this function.

Although the SCN has a vital role in 24-hour biological rhythms, it has also has important functions in biological rhythms much longer than 24 hours, i.e. infradian rhythms. Male hamsters show annual rhythms of testosterone secretion, and these appear to be based on the amount of light that occurs each day. The breeding season of hamsters begins as the days lengthen and ends when the days get shorter again. Lesions of the SCN destroy these annual-breeding cycles, and male hamsters secrete testosterone all year round (Rusak and Zucker 1975). These lesions probably disrupt the annual cycles because they destroy the 24-hour clock against which daily light levels are measured to determine the season. If the period of light is less than 12 hours, it must be winter; if it is more than 12 hours, it must be summer (Carlson 1994).

Removing exogenous zeitgebers

The sensitivity to light of the pineal gland and the SCN, and the role of melatonin in controlling sleep and other activity, mean that despite the endogenous nature of biological clocks, their activity is synchronized with the light/dark rhythm of the world outside. Occasionally, slightly bizarre studies have allowed us to look at the effects of removing light as an exogenous zeitgeber, allowing these biological clocks to run free, i.e. without the influence of zeitgebers (see panel below). Studies

---

Research into free-running biological rhythms

The most famous study of free-running biological rhythms involved a French cave explorer called Michel Siffre who, in 1972, spent six months in an underground cave in Texas, separated from natural light/dark cycles. He was wired up so that various bodily functions could be recorded. When he was awake, the researchers put the lights on; when he went to bed, they turned the lights off. He ate and slept whenever he wanted. At first his sleep/waking cycle was very erratic, but it settled down to a fairly regular pattern of between 25 and 30 hours, i.e.

slightly longer than a 24-hour cycle. When he finally emerged, it was the 179th day, but by his 'days' it was only the 151st day since he went underground!

In a similar study, Aschoff and Weber (reported in Kleitman 1965) used an underground bunker. Student participants therefore had no cues to light and dark, and could select their own light-on active or light-off sleep periods. As with Siffre, the participants settled into regular sleep/waking cycles and again, like Siffre, the normal circadian rhythm extended slightly to between 25 and 27 hours.

such as these show that humans with free-running biological clocks settle into a rhythmic sleeping/waking pattern of between 25 and 27 hours, i.e. slightly longer than under normal conditions. So we can draw two conclusions:

- Endogenous mechanisms can control sleep/waking cycles in the absence of light.
- Light as an exogenous zeitgeber is necessary to reset the clock every day so that the biological rhythm is coordinated with the external world.

(A02) Evaluation
research studies into biological rhythms

- *Research findings* – A number of studies undertaken with both humans and non-human animals have established the existence of endogenous pacemakers regulated by exogenous zeitgebers. They have also shown how these processes play a vital part in regulating behaviour.
- *Generalizability of research* – Much of the work, especially on the brain mechanisms of

pacemakers, has been carried out on non-human animals, so it is important to be careful about generalizing the findings to humans.

- *Individual differences* – Studies of free-running biological rhythms in humans also show that there are significant individual differences in these mechanisms, i.e. that they may not operate in exactly the same way in all people.
- *Numbers of participants* – Some research, such as Siffre's cave study, has used very few or even single participants. This means that we can only generalize the findings with great care.

CONSEQUENCES OF DISRUPTING BIOLOGICAL RHYTHMS

The studies on free-running rhythms in humans indicate how we use stimuli around us to coordinate our biological clocks. The gradual lengthening and shortening of the days is reflected in gradual shifts in rhythms of activity and sleep/waking cycles. These biological processes are also influenced by other stimuli, such as outside temperature and social patterns. Inuit Eskimos have regular sleep/waking cycles, even though they have continuous daylight in summer and continuous darkness in winter, showing that for them the social rhythms of life are the dominant zeitgebers.

Usually, exogenous zeitgebers, such as light or social behaviour patterns, change very slowly, if at all. However, there are times when they change radically and quickly, and the usual coordination between our internally controlled biological rhythms and the outside world (the exogenous zeitgebers) breaks down. Modern living has led to two common examples – jet travel and shift work – which we will consider next.

Jet lag

If you travel by plane from East to West – for example, from the UK to the east coast of the USA, leaving the UK at noon – you arrive at about 7 p.m. UK-time, but it would be 2 p.m. USA-time. All your biological rhythms are working to UK-time, so that by 7 p.m. USA-time your internal clock is telling you that it is midnight and you are feeling ready to sleep – with a falling body temperature and decreasing bodily arousal. This dislocation of our physiological rhythms from the outside world produces the sensation of jet lag that many people experience and which lasts as long as it takes for the body to resynchronize. Studies have

shown that the quickest way to achieve this adjustment is to follow the local exogenous zeitgebers rather than your body, so in the example above you should force yourself to stay awake until 11 p.m. USA-time and also adjust your meal times and socializing patterns. If you follow your biological clocks, adjustment takes much longer.

Strangely, jet lag is more severe travelling from West to East (from the USA to the UK, for example) than from East to West. This may be because it is easier to adjust our body clocks when they are ahead of local time (called 'phase delay') than when they are behind (a situation when they have to 'phase advance'). Because of its role in controlling body rhythms, melatonin has been studied as a possible treatment for jet lag and other desynchronization problems and, although nothing very systematic has yet emerged, the research may eventually lead to an effective therapy. Recently, for instance, Takahashi *et al.* (2002) reported that melatonin speeded up the resynchronization of biological rhythms after an 11-hour flight and reduced the symptoms of jet lag.

Shift work

Organizations and industries that work around the clock require their employees to do shift work. This means that employees are required to work when they would normally sleep and to sleep when they would normally be awake. A classic pattern is to divide the day into three eight-hour shifts – midnight to 8 a.m., 8 a.m. to 4 p.m. and 4 p.m. to midnight. Switching shifts obviously disrupts links between external zeitgebers (light/dark, meals, social life, etc.) and biological rhythms, and, as with jet lag, some time is necessary for readjustment. Many shift patterns require a change every week, with workers moving back one shift every time. Studies of jet lag suggest that one week is barely enough time to allow for such a major resynchronization, so that the workers are in a permanent state of 'jet lag', impairing performance and increasing stress. The backward movement is the same as West to East jet travel, leading to the more difficult phase-advance situation. There is anecdotal evidence that performance, especially vigilance, is lowered at times when biological rhythms are pushing for sleep. For example, it is interesting to note that both the near-nuclear accident at Three Mile Island nuclear power station in Pennsylvania in 1979, and the actual nuclear disaster at Chernobyl (in the north east of Ukraine in the former Soviet Union) in 1986, occurred because of decision failures during the early hours of the morning.

Experimental support comes from a study of a chemical plant in Utah by Czeisler and colleagues in 1982. High incidence of health problems, sleep difficulties and work-related stress was noted in staff employed on short rotation shifts. Czeisler persuaded the company to change to a phase-delay system (moving a shift forwards every time) and to increase the shift rotation from seven to 21 days, allowing more time for adjustment. After nine months of the new system, worker satisfaction was significantly increased and factory output was higher. Alternative approaches to reducing the negative effects of shift work include the use of melatonin. Sharkey (2001) found that the hormone could speed up biological adjustment to shift patterns and increased sleep time during non-work periods.

The problems of jet lag and shift work are due to the way we have artificially dislocated the normal coordination between our biological clocks and the external world. We are the result of a long evolutionary history, in which the alternation of day and night has shaped the lives of all organisms. It is no surprise that we should still be under the same influence and suffer consequences when we interfere with things. Coren (1996) has pointed out that a culture shift occurred at the beginning of the 20th century when electric lighting became widely available. Factories and offices could operate around the clock, introducing widespread shift work and longer working hours. Social life also could extend late into the night. Coren estimates that on average we sleep for around one-and-a-half hours less than we did a century ago, so that many of us are in a constant state of mild sleep deprivation.

Evaluation
research on disrupting biological rhythms

- *Research findings* – A strength of this research is the consistent evidence for the idea that disrupting biological rhythms can have cognitive and emotional effects on people, sometimes leading to drastic consequences.

- *Methodological issues* – Much of the research evidence is generated by field studies that have high ecological validity. However, many confounding variables, such as personality and individual differences in biological rhythms, are not controlled.

- *Real-life significance?* – Although there are examples where disrupting rhythms has had drastic effects, many thousands of people carry out shift work without any obvious effects on their cognitive abilities, such as attention and concentration, or their emotional well-being.

REVISION SUMMARY

Having covered this topic you should be able to:

✓ give examples of circadian, infradian and ultradian biological rhythms, and explain the main differences between these various types of biological rhythm

✓ describe and evaluate research studies into biological rhythms

✓ use research studies to describe the role of endogenous pacemakers and exogenous zeitgebers

✓ give examples of how biological rhythms can be disrupted, and explain the consequences of disrupting biological rhythms, using examples from shift work and jet lag.

Check your understanding of biological rhythms by answering these questions. Do it from memory at first. You can check your answers by looking back through Topic 1.

1 In 100 words, outline what we mean by an endogenous pacemaker.

2 What is the name given to external events that play a role in rhythmic activities? Give an example.

3 Name four types of biological rhythm, describe each one briefly, and give an example of each.

4 Prepare an outline in 150 words of seasonal affective disorder (SAD).

5 Name two brain structures with important roles as biological clocks.

6 What hormone is involved in regulating our biological rhythms? Where is it released from?

7 Write a 150-word précis of the findings of studies of free-running biological rhythms and what they can tell us about the control of biological rhythms.

8 Identify and give a brief account of two critical (AO2) points relating to studies of free-running biological rhythms.

9 Outline in 100 words two examples of the disruption of biological rhythms in everyday life and their effects on behaviour.

10 Why is sleep deprivation more common in today's world than in previous generations?

EXAMPLE EXAM QUESTIONS

Below are some **possible examination questions** set on this topic, along with hints to help you understand and approach each question effectively:

1 Outline and evaluate research studies into **two** forms of biological rhythm (e.g. circadian, infradian, ultradian rhythms). (24 marks)

There are three important instructions in the question. First, you are asked to write about *research studies* of biological rhythms, rather than just describing what these rhythms are. Second, you are only required to *outline* these studies, so a detailed description would not be appropriate. Third, you are asked to write about *two* types of rhythm, so you must not write about more than two or about just one of them (which would result in a partial performance penalty of a maximum of 8 marks for AO1 and 8 marks for AO2). The examples are given to remind you what might be included.

2 (a) Outline research studies into **two** forms of biological rhythm. (12 marks)
(b) Assess the impact of disrupting biological rhythms in humans. (12 marks)

In this question, part (a) is AO1 and part (b) AO2, and you should divide your time equally between them. The form that the evaluation (AO2) is to take has been specified, i.e. you need to give a 'considered appraisal' of evidence that disruption has detrimental effects. This might include explaining *why* disruption of rhythms has such a detrimental effect, looking at the research evidence for these effects, or perhaps assessing the consequences of disruption over the longer term. Part (b) does not tie you to the same two biological rhythms that you outlined in the first part of the question. Your response to part (b) might be specific to one particular type of rhythm or it could be more general, taking in more than one type of rhythm.

3 Discuss the role of endogenous pacemakers and exogenous zeitgebers in biological rhythms. (24 marks)

The AO1 content of this question would consist of a description of endogenous pacemakers and exogenous zeitgebers and the relationship between them. The question is very general, so work with both humans and non-human animals can be used. You are required to discuss both pacemakers *and* zeitgebers; although coverage need not be perfectly balanced you will need to provide AO1 and AO2 for both. The most straightforward source of AO2 material would be research studies supporting and illustrating the role of pacemakers and zeitgebers in biological rhythms. However, you should remember that *description* of studies would count as AO1, so you must concentrate on *findings* and their *implications* for AO2 credit related to research studies.

EXAMPLE EXAM QUESTIONS

4 (a) Outline **two** types of biological rhythm. (6 marks)
  (b) Outline and evaluate research studies relating to biological rhythms (18 marks)

> Part (a) is AO1, making up a quarter of the essay, so it only needs to be an *outline* of two biological rhythms. This could consist of a definition and an example or two of each type of rhythm. In part (b), 6 of the 18 marks are for a description of research studies (in the plural). You must restrict yourself severely or you are in danger of reducing AO2 marks because of having no time for this component. Part (b) is three-quarters of the essay, i.e. about 450 words. If you covered three studies, you could write 50 words describing each study and 100 words of commentary on it. This means that you write an outline that covers the most important points and does not waste time on relatively trivial details.

5 Discuss the consequences of disrupting biological rhythms (e.g. shift work). (24 marks)

> In contrast with question 2 above, here you would gain credit for *describing* the consequences of disrupting biological rhythms. The example of shift work is given in the question. Jet lag is the other obvious possibility. You would not gain any credit for including studies relating to biological rhythms unless these are made explicitly relevant to disruption. You can gain AO2 credit by considering how to deal with consequences or you might consider the validity of any studies mentioned.

Topic 2 >> Sleep

The 24-hour cycle of sleeping and waking is our most obvious biological rhythm. We spend around 30 per cent of our lives sleeping, so it is an important part of our lives and for centuries we have speculated about its function. Other bodily processes, such as body temperature, urine flow and release of hormones from the pituitary and adrenal glands, also show a circadian rhythm, with one peak and one trough every 24 hours. However, it is the sleep/waking cycle that has been most widely studied. One of the features of sleep is that there are several different identifiable types of sleep, which we move between throughout the night in a regular pattern (see Fig. 13.1). This is an example of an ultradian biological rhythm.

One of the earliest debates in this area was whether sleep was simply the state the body fell into when it was not active, i.e. sleep as a passive process. You have probably read enough by now to realize that this is unlikely. The brain contains biological clocks that actively regulate physiological and behavioural processes. In the cave and bunker studies outlined in Topic 1, sleep/waking patterns settled down to a consistent pattern despite the absence of exogenous zeitgebers, while states such as hibernation are induced

Figure 13.1 >> *Pattern of sleep over one night*

by the brain at the appropriate time of year. Generally, biological rhythms reflect active control by brain mechanisms, and sleep is unlikely to be different. The main challenge is to identify the specific brain mechanisms involved in sleep and explain how they interact with the world outside. This may give us some indication of the functions of sleep.

TYPES AND STAGES OF SLEEP

The introduction of the electroencephalograph (EEG) in the 1930s was a crucial development, allowing us to investigate what is going on when someone is asleep. (This technique of studying brain function is described in more detail on p. 381.) Using it, Dement and

Kleitman in the 1950s were able to demonstrate that sleep, far from being a quiet and peaceful phenomenon, consisted of clearly identifiable stages of brain activity (Dement and Kleitman 1957).

Page 381 describes how EEG activity can be synchronized or desynchronized. When synchronized, there is a repeated waveform with a particular frequency, measured as cycles per second or herz (Hz); when it is desynchronized, there is no consistent waveform. The waking, alert EEG pattern consists of fast, desynchronized activity. As we relax prior to sleep, the EEG pattern becomes synchronized and 'alpha waves' appear with a characteristic frequency of 8 to 12 Hz. Heart rate slows, muscle tension reduces and body temperature begins to fall.

It is generally agreed that there are two main types of sleep: slow-wave sleep and rapid eye movement sleep.

Slow-wave sleep

The four stages of slow-wave sleep (or SWS) are described in the box on the right. It is called SWS because the EEG pattern is characterized by synchronized, slow-wave activity, although it is sometimes called 'non-rapid eye movement' sleep (or NREM). The stages of sleep we pass through during the night are an example of an ultradian rhythm.

Rapid eye movement (REM) sleep

Sleep is a dynamic process and after about 30 minutes in Stage 4 SWS, we ascend through the sleep stages to the light Stage 2 SWS. At this point, about an hour-and-a-half after going to sleep, the EEG activity suddenly shifts into the fast, desynchronized pattern of the aroused person. At this point, arousal thresholds are also very high (i.e. the individual is hard to wake up) and the skeletal muscles relax completely, leaving the person effectively paralysed. Heart rate and respiration increase and rapid movements of the eyes occur. For this reason, this type of sleep is called 'rapid eye movement' (REM) sleep. It is sometimes also referred to as 'paradoxical sleep', because it combines features of bodily relaxation with an aroused EEG pattern and rapid eye movements.

After 15 minutes or so in REM sleep, we move back into light SWS and then descend into the deeper

The four stages of slow-wave sleep

- In *Stage 1* of sleep proper, the alpha waves disappear to be replaced by slower and smaller desynchronized activity.

- In *Stage 2,* the EEG pattern becomes synchronized with larger and slower waves interrupted by bursts of fast spiking activity – the 'sleep spindles'. These last for a second or two and consist of high frequency (12 to 16 Hz) waves.

- *Stage 3* is dominated by large slow 'delta waves' (1 to 3 Hz), with sleep spindles becoming less common. Heart rate, body temperature, respiration and metabolic rate continue to fall.

- In *Stage 4,* the EEG recording consists only of delta waves, metabolic rate is at its lowest and the arousal threshold (a measure of how hard it is to wake the individual up) is very high.

Stages 3 and 4. This cyclical pattern, shown in Fig. 13.1, repeats itself about every 90 minutes, giving five or six cycles per night. Towards morning, we spend more time in light SWS, which seems to trigger more phases of REM sleep. As we shall see, REM sleep is associated with dreaming, so we tend to dream more as morning approaches.

As mentioned earlier, cycles of rest and activity recorded in the developing embryo reflect control by endogenous pacemakers. After a baby's birth, the activity of these biological clocks will become synchronized with the outside world, especially the light/dark cycle. The sleep/waking cycle and the patterning of the stages of sleep are fundamental biological rhythms. So, what are their functions?

THE EVOLUTION AND FUNCTIONS OF SLEEP

There is no simple explanation for the functions of sleep and there are many hypotheses based on a wide range of observations and experiments. Sleep is found throughout the animal kingdom, although it can be hard to recognize in reptiles and other cold-blooded animals. This is because arousal states in these groups depend so much on external temperature that it can be difficult to distinguish sleep from inactivity brought on by the cold. In addition, the EEG recordings used to identify sleep stages in mammals come from the cerebral cortex, which is poorly developed in reptiles, so we are not even sure what reptilian sleep would look like in terms of EEG activity. Sleep is clearly identifiable in birds and mammals and the fact that it is found in all

species studied suggests that it must have some important function. There are humans who can exist on very little sleep – in rare cases less than an hour – but, in general, we all need between six and eight hours. This has given rise to several accounts of the functions of sleep. We will consider two types here – ecological theories and restoration theories.

Ecological theories

The basis of any ecological explanation of sleep is that it serves an important adaptive function because it keeps animals inactive when they do not need to engage in activities essential for their survival.

In particular, it keeps animals safe from predators and conserves their energy. This approach emphasizes the need to look closely at the way animals live, in particular their 'ecological niche'. An animal's ecological niche refers to the environment they inhabit (e.g. terrestrial or aquatic, on the ground or in trees) and also their lifestyle (e.g. carnivores or herbivores, predators or prey, or whether they are active during the daytime or at night-time).

Although sleep can be identified with difficulty in reptiles, it is found in its characteristic complexity only in birds and mammals. Even in mammals, there are profound differences in total sleep time, amounts of SWS and REM sleep and cyclical organization. Many variables contribute to these differences, such as primitiveness (which is assessed in terms of brain development), body size and ecological niche (i.e. environment and lifestyle). This has led to a number of hypotheses about the general functions of sleep across the animal kingdom.

Predator or prey?

Meddis (1979) proposes that sleep evolved to keep animals inconspicuous and safe from predators when normal activities were impossible. The importance of the predator or prey status is emphasized by the observation that predators (lions, tigers, etc.) sleep for much longer than prey animals (cattle, gazelle, etc.). It is as though the more dangerous your world, the less time you can afford to spend asleep and in a vulnerable position. One slight complication is that prey animals tend to be herbivores, needing to spend huge amounts of time grazing in order to take in sufficient food and therefore have less time to sleep. But, of course, it still makes sense to be as inconspicuous as possible when not feeding.

Sleep in aquatic mammals

The precise ecological niche that an animal occupies can affect the organization of its sleep. Aquatic mammals, such as dolphins and porpoises, have particular problems because sleep under water is dangerous, given that they need to breathe air. The Indus dolphin gets around this by sleeping for a few seconds at a time repeatedly throughout the day and night (Pilleri 1979). Other marine mammals have adapted to the need for sleep in different ways. Both the bottlenose dolphin and the porpoise can 'switch off' one of their cerebral hemispheres at a time (Mukhametov 1984). This strategy allows one hemisphere to be alert while the other catches up on its sleep. During these periods of 'unilateral sleep', the animals continue to come up to the surface to breathe, so their sleep is not characterized by complete motor paralysis. Figure 13.2 shows the EEG records from the two hemispheres, and clearly demonstrates that SWS occurs independently in the two hemispheres. The lengths that animals go to in order to sleep, is a powerful argument in favour of sleep being an essential function.

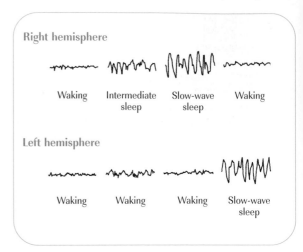

Figure 13.2 >> *Sleep in a dolphin*
The two hemispheres sleep independently, presumably so that the animal remains alert
Source: Carlson (1994, p. 261)

Sleep, body weight and metabolism

In land mammals, total sleep time is also related to body weight. Squirrels and shrews, for instance, sleep for about 14 hours a day, cows and sheep for about four. The smaller the animal, the greater its metabolic rate. Metabolic rate is an index of the activity in the body's physiological systems and the higher it is, the faster the body uses up its energy resources. So, sleep in smaller mammals may be important for conserving these resources, as well as keeping them safe from predators.

Because of the way that the pattern and duration of sleep seem to depend on brain development, body size, life style, etc., it is unlikely that any single explanation could account for the function of sleep in all animals. The giant sloth is relatively large and is not the most active of animals and should not, therefore, 'need' much sleep, yet it sleeps for around 20 hours a day. This goes against the supposed relationship between small bodies and the amount of sleep. Incidentally, it also goes against restoration ideas (discussed in the next section), because according to the restoration account, length of sleep should be related to energy expenditure.

Functions of different types of sleep

As sleep has several stages, it is even likely that different stages have different functions. For instance, REM sleep is most clearly identifiable in birds and mammals that are warm-blooded, and not in reptiles that are cold-blooded. It has been suggested therefore that REM sleep, during which brain metabolism is increased, may have evolved as a means of maintaining the brain's temperature during a period when it might otherwise fall to dangerously low levels.

Like all biological and behavioural phenomena, sleep is subject to evolutionary pressures, especially perhaps the ecological niche the animal occupies. Although there seems to be a fundamental drive to sleep, the precise patterning and organization of sleep may then become tailored to the particular lifestyle of the species.

A02 Evaluation
ecological theories of sleep

- **Is sleep the most adaptive approach?** – Although the ecological theory that sleep serves an important adaptive function seems to be a very plausible explanation, it is difficult to evaluate what kinds of evidence would support this proposition. It is also not clear why such a complex physiological mechanism as sleep would evolve, simply to keep vulnerable animals out of harm's way, when a state of behavioural inactivity would serve much the same purpose. Many animals do, indeed, 'play possum' by freezing when threatened by predators and you could argue that the safest state would be to remain inconspicuous but alert.

- **Why do vulnerable animals sleep less?** – An opposite view is that more vulnerable animals sleep less because of their decreased awareness of predators when asleep and this is supported by the fact that prey animals seem to sleep less than predators. In fact, there is a negative correlation between predatory danger and the amounts of both slow-wave and REM sleep.

- **Why hasn't sleep been selected out?** – A persuasive argument against the view that sleep serves an important adaptive function is the fact that sleep is found in species that would seem to be better off without it (Carlson 1994). For example, the Indus dolphin lives in the muddy waters of the Indus River in Pakistan. Over the years, this animal has become blind because good eyesight is unnecessary, given the extremely poor visibility of its environment. It does, however, have an excellent sonar system that it uses to navigate and to find prey. Despite the dangers of falling asleep (i.e. potential injury from floating debris and passing river traffic), sleep has not disappeared. Although the Indus dolphin never stops swimming, it sleeps in short naps of between 4 and 60 seconds for a total of around seven hours each day. If sleep merely served an adaptive function, then surely it would have been eliminated through the process of natural selection in the same way that vision was (Carlson 1994).

Restoration theories

If asked why they sleep, most people would answer that they sleep because they are tired. This simple explanation suggests that sleep is necessary to repair the body and restore the body to its full 'waking' capacity, making up for all the wear and tear of the day's activities. A specific way in which the body 'restores' the materials of the day comes from the finding that growth hormone is released during SWS. As well as being involved in growth processes, growth hormone has an important role in the metabolism of proteins. Protein synthesis is an important aspect of the restoration of body tissue and since these are relatively fragile, they must be constantly renewed and replaced during sleep. The highest concentrations of growth hormone in the blood are found during SWS, particularly in Stages 3 and 4.

Horne's (1988) core sleep/optional sleep model

In a review of the effects of sleep deprivation, Horne (1988) concluded from a number of controlled laboratory studies that sleep deprivation in normal participants produces only the mild range of effects seen in Randy Gardner (see the panel on the right), together with some sleep recovery concentrated mainly

Sleep deprivation record

Sleep deprivation studies have provided much of the research evidence for restoration theories. Some studies have used uncontrolled single cases. Dement (1978) reports the case of a 17-year-old schoolboy, called Randy Gardner, who stayed awake for 264 hours (11 days) in 1964 and holds the record for total sleep deprivation. He developed blurred vision and incoherent speech, some perceptual disturbances, such as imagining objects were people, and a mild degree of paranoia, imagining that others thought him to be stupid because of his cognitive problems. The effects seemed mild compared to the degree of sleep deprivation. However he recovered quickly when he eventually slept. The first night he slept for 15 hours and only recovered about a quarter of his overall lost sleeping time during the nights that followed. Recovery was specific to particular stages – two-thirds of Stage 4 SWS and a half of REM sleep were recovered, but little of the other stages of SWS (Dement 1978).

in Stage 4 SWS and in REM sleep. Although the effects of sleep deprivation were not dramatic, they did involve some problems with cognitive abilities, such as perception, attention and memory, while the recovery of Stage 4 SWS and REM sleep suggests that these are the critical phases. Horne therefore proposes that 'core sleep', consisting of Stage 4 SWS and REM sleep, is essential in humans for the normal brain functioning essential for our cognitive abilities, while the lighter stages of SWS are not essential, and he refers to these as 'optional sleep'. During core sleep the brain recovers and restores itself after the activities of the day.

Oswald's (1980) restoration model

This account is similar to the restoration model put forward by Oswald (1980). He suggests that the high level of brain activity seen during REM sleep reflects brain recovery, while an increase in the body's hormone activities (especially growth hormone) during SWS reflects restoration and recovery in the body. They both agree that REM sleep is essential for brain repair and restoration. This is supported by the high proportion of REM sleep seen in the newborn baby, where it makes up 50 to 60 per cent of sleep time, gradually falling to the normal proportion of about 25 per cent as the child grows.

The months before and after birth are a time of rapid brain growth and development, so if REM sleep is a time when such processes occur, it is logical that a baby should show increased amounts of REM sleep (see Fig. 13.3).

The main difference between the accounts of Horne and of Oswald concerns the proposed functions of slow-wave sleep. As total sleep deprivation produces few obvious effects on the body, Horne (1988) thinks that body restoration is not the purpose of sleep. He suggests that this occurs during periods of relaxed wakefulness, leaving core sleep to provide for the

About 50 to 60 per cent of newborn babies' sleep time is REM. How do researchers account for that?

restoration of brain systems. However, Horne is specifically discussing studies carried with human participants and it is quite possible that the sort of division between brain restoration and body restoration put forward by Oswald could apply to non-human animals. As there are significant differences between species in the precise details of their sleep/waking cycle, it is possible that no single hypothesis could cover them all.

Figure 13.3 >> *Changes in proportions of SWS and REM sleep with age*

ACTIVITY

Your experience of sleep deprivation

Think back to a time when you experienced significant sleep deprivation – perhaps during a hectic period of clubbing and partying, or a series of late-night revision sessions before important exams.

1　What was your experience? Did you feel tired? Did you notice any loss of concentration or any problems with your memory?

2　What does this suggest about the function of sleep? Does it support a restoration or ecological account of the function of sleep?

3　When you returned to your usual sleep routine, did you sleep for longer and recover all the sleep you had lost?

Often excitement or stress can override our biological clocks and keep us awake when the body wants to sleep, and the arousal of examinations, for instance, can minimize the effects of sleep deprivation on concentration and memory, at least for a while.

Challenges for restoration theories

- *Effect of energy expenditure* – It is perhaps surprising that the view that sleep has a vital restorative function is only weakly supported by research. One way of testing this hypothesis is by looking at the effects of pre-sleep activities on the duration of sleep. According to the restorative perspective, intense energy expenditure during the day should increase the duration of sleep in order to restore the resources used. For most people, intense exercise may cause them to fall asleep more quickly, but it does not cause them to sleep for longer (Rosenzweig *et al.* 1999). We have also seen earlier that the giant sloth sleeps for about 20 hours a day even though its energy expenditure is small.

- *Body function and sleep deprivation* – Sleep deprivation studies have also failed to provide conclusive evidence that sleep is necessary to keep the body functioning normally. Horne (1988) reviewed 50 studies in which humans had been deprived of sleep. He found that very few of these studies reported that sleep deprivation had interfered with the participants' ability to perform physical exercise. Neither was there any evidence of a physiological stress response to the sleep deprivation.

- *Growth hormone and sleep* – One of the most important claims for the restorative function of sleep was that growth hormone is released during SWS and that this has an important role in protein synthesis. However, Horne (1988) points out that as amino acids (the constituents of proteins) are only freely available for five hours after a meal, and most people eat several hours before going to bed, then the supply of available amino acids is low for most of the night. This implies that not much protein synthesis would go on during sleep.

Support for restoration theories

- *Animal studies* – Some support for restoration accounts comes from animal studies. Prolonged sleep deprivation in rats appears to cause them to increase their metabolic rate, lose weight and die within an average of 19 days (Everson *et al.* 1989). Allowing these animals to sleep within that time prevents their death. However, animal studies such as this do not allow us to separate the effects of sleep deprivation from the methods used to keep the animals awake. In order to keep animals awake they must be constantly stimulated, and hence stressed. Studies to isolate which organs are most affected by chronic sleep deprivation have failed to isolate one specific system that is affected to the exclusion of others. It is most likely that sleep deprivation in animal studies interferes with the immune system, which then leads to death. It is possible that sleep provides the only opportunity for tissue restoration in some species. For example, when rats are awake, they generally spend all their time foraging for food, seeking mates or avoiding predators. Humans, on the other hand, are capable of resting during the day. In fact, our metabolic activity when we are in a state of quiet restfulness is only 9 per cent higher than it is when we are asleep.

- *Fatal familial insomnia* – Some humans have a rare inherited defect that prevents them sleeping normally. People with this disorder, called 'fatal familial insomnia', sleep normally until middle age when they simply stop sleeping, leading to death within two years. Autopsies have revealed a degeneration of the thalamus, which may well be responsible for the onset of the insomnia. Although these cases support restoration accounts, they are very rare and such patients clearly have brain damage, making it difficult to generalize the findings.

- *REM sleep and restoration of brain neurotransmitters* – Stern and Morgane (1974) propose that REM sleep is specifically for the restoration of brain neurotransmitters. They observed that after REM sleep deprivation, participants show 'REM rebound', i.e. an increase in REM sleep when they are allowed to sleep normally. It is as if REM rebound is necessary for restoring something lost during REM sleep deprivation. They noted that anti-depressant drugs also reduce REM sleep, but that there is no REM rebound when people stop their drug treatment. They argue that the drugs increase the levels of brain neurotransmitters such as serotonin and dopamine that are normally a function of REM sleep. However, since people taking anti-depressant drugs have increased levels anyway, they do not need REM sleep and do not therefore show REM rebound when they stop taking the drugs.

Theories of *sleep*

Professor **Jim Horne** *runs the Sleep Research Centre at Loughborough University. He is also the editor of the* Journal of Sleep Research, *the world's main non-clinical scientific journal for sleep research. With a background in physiology and psychology, he is a Fellow of both the Institute of Biology and the British Psychological Society. His particular interests are the 'why' and 'how much' of sleep, as well as in sleepiness, especially driver sleepiness and the need public awareness about driving while sleepy.*

Q **In the 1990s your position was that sleep deprivation affected cognitive processes only – i.e. the brain. Is this still your position?**

A For cerebrally advanced mammals such as humans, sleep is mainly a function by and for the brain. Specifically, it's really the cortex, as most brain areas below the cortex don't sleep. Thus, the real effect of sleep deprivation is on our cortex, particularly the human frontal lobes, which comprise approximately 30 per cent of the cortex. This latter region works the hardest during wakefulness and can't go 'off-line'. It's the region that makes our behaviour 'human' – so, with progressive sleep loss, not only do we become more sleepy, but our behaviour becomes more like that of a zombie. We become creatures of routine, can't deal with anything new, have dull and stilted speech, and become forgetful. Personality changes include irritability, being less able to suppress our more basic emotions and to 'sense' the feelings of others – hence we become difficult for others to cope with. All these behaviours reflect frontal lobe failings.

Jim Horne

Q **Your work led to the idea of 'core sleep', made up of REM and Stage 4 SWS. Again, is this a position you still hold?**

A How much of our usual sleep is really necessary? After a night of no sleep, the next night we will regain less than half of that lost sleep, and feel fine. We regain all of the lost 'deep' sleep (Stages 3 and 4), found in the first five hours of normal sleep. I still refer to this as 'core sleep' – it seems to be of the most benefit to the slumbering cortex. After about six hours of good sleep, all core sleep has usually disappeared to be replaced with 'optional' sleep, which will maintain sleep until morning awakening. 'Optional' doesn't mean that we can dispense with it, but rather, it is much more adaptable than core sleep – perhaps a better term is 'elastic' sleep.

REM sleep can be removed entirely from sleep, for many months at a time, by medicines used for treating depression, without ill effects or any sign of big rebounds of REM sleep when treatment ceases. This refutes any idea that it is essential to memory processing. As so much of REM sleep seems to be dispensable, I don't see it as real sleep.

Q **We still do not have agreement on what the function of sleep is. Why is this?**

A Most sleep researchers are agreed that sleep provides recovery, but what exactly is recovered is another matter. Unfortunately, we haven't the technology to harmlessly get within living cells of the sleeping animal – particularly neurones or glial cells within the human cortex, where we know sleep is of particular importance. Besides, sleep must have several functions, evolved to suit the circumstances of various animals, and probably not the same for humans and mice, for example. For the mouse, sleep stops it running about aimlessly and conserves much energy by confining it to the insulation of its nest where it can huddle against other mice. It can't sit still and relax in wakefulness as this entails thinking, watching, reading, etc. – behaviours obviously beyond the repertoire of its simple cortex. We humans can easily do this, and so sleep is not necessary for our energy conservation. If, instead of sleeping over-night, we lie awake but relaxed, the extra energy needed is only the equivalent of eating an extra slice of bread – sleep would hardly be worthwhile. However, our large and complex cortex requires sleep rather than relaxed wakefulness for its recovery, whilst the mouse's simpler cortex probably needs little sleep in this respect.

Q **In all your work on sleep, you make little reference to dreams and dream imagery. Do you have views on what dreams are and whether they have any particular function?**

A Dreams are simply to keep the brain periodically occupied during sleep – they entertain, but are only the 'cinema of the mind'. We dream as we think, and they are a fascinating jumbled distortion of recent events and thoughts. Thus the only person that can really figure out what the dream might mean, is ourselves. Although for Freud dreams were the 'royal road to the unconscious' this was when society discouraged people from expressing their true selves and emotions, and perhaps dream analysis was the only way of approaching a troubled mind. Nowadays, in our more enlightened society, we can get to the deepest recesses of the mind by establishing rapport and talking to people at depth when they are awake.

Expert interview: Jim Horne on theories of sleep

In the course of his interview, Jim Horne mentions several possible functions of sleep. Make up a table. On the left, put a possible function of sleep. On the right, outline the evidence that Jim Horne refers to (e.g. 'maintaining the frontal lobes of the brain' on the left, 'effects of sleep deprivation in humans' on the right). Jim Horne also refers to differences between species in the nature and functions of sleep. Make up another table that summarizes these differences and why they occur. Then add to this table two examples from Topic 3 of this unit of how sleep patterns vary across different species.

✓ CHECK YOUR UNDERSTANDING

Check your understanding of sleep by answering these questions. Try to do this from memory at first. You can check your answers by looking back through Topic 2.

1 Name two different types of sleep.

2 How many stages of sleep are there? In which stages are delta waves found?

3 Write a 100-word précis of the ecological account of the functions of sleep.

4 Outline one observation that supports the ecological account, and identify and prepare a brief description of two limitations of the ecological theory.

5 In 100 words, outline the effects of total sleep deprivation.

6 Identify and give a brief account of three critical (AO2) points relating to the restoration account of sleep.

7 Outline one difference between the restoration accounts of Horne and Oswald.

8 In no more than 100 words, describe the differences between 'core' and 'optional' sleep.

9 What, according to Stern and Morgane, is the function of REM sleep?

10 What is meant by the term 'REM rebound' and when does it occur?

REVISION SUMMARY

Having covered this topic you should be able to:

✓ outline the ecological and restoration theories of the functions of sleep

✓ describe and evaluate research studies relating to the ecological account of the functions of sleep

✓ describe and evaluate research studies relating to the restoration account of the functions of sleep

✓ describe and evaluate studies of total and partial sleep deprivation

✓ outline the implications of studies of total and partial sleep deprivation for theories of the functions of sleep.

EXAMPLE EXAM QUESTIONS

Below are some **possible examination questions** set on this topic, along with hints to help you understand and approach each question effectively:

1 Describe and evaluate **one** theory of the functions of sleep. (24 marks)

It is important to remember that there are two components to this question. The term 'describe' invites you to demonstrate your knowledge and understanding of your chosen theory, and the term 'evaluate' invites you to make a judgment about the 'value' of that particular theory. For each component you should write about 300 words.

2 (a) Outline the restoration account of the functions of sleep. (6 marks)

(b) Outline and evaluate research studies relating to the restoration account of the functions of sleep. (18 marks)

> Questions can specifically be asked about the two accounts of sleep named in the specification, i.e. ecological and restoration. Here, you are asked to present a 6-mark version – about 150 words. The AO1 component of part (b), worth 6 marks, would consist of descriptions of research studies and then, for AO2, an evaluation of these studies. It is important to restrict the descriptive content because there are twice as many marks for evaluation of the studies. A minimum of two research studies are required because 'studies' is plural.

3 (a) Outline and evaluate the ecological account of the functions of sleep. (12 marks)

(b) Outline and evaluate the restoration account of the functions of sleep. (12 marks)

> This question illustrates a different mark split again. There are AO1 and AO2 marks in both parts of the question. Remember that evaluation involves you actively engaging with your written material – constantly challenging assumptions, critically examining evidence (does it support or challenge a particular point of view?) and suggesting alternative interpretations.

4 (a) Outline **two or more** research studies related to the ecological account of sleep. (12 marks)

(b) To what extent do such studies support the ecological account of sleep? (12 marks)

> In part (a), the instruction 'two or more' is an invitation for you to include as many research studies as you wish, but that two studies would be sufficient for full marks. The danger of writing about lots of studies is that you would sacrifice breadth for depth/detail, an important AO1 criterion. In part (b), you can consider the studies introduced in part (a) or any other studies. However, there are two provisos. First, the studies must be related to the ecological account and, second, you would not gain credit for any description of such studies. In part (b) you must *focus* on what the studies tell us, i.e. the conclusions and whether such conclusions support the ecological account.

5 Discuss the implications of findings from studies of total and partial sleep deprivation for theories of the functions of sleep. (24 marks)

> The AO1 content of this question would be a description of studies of total and partial sleep deprivation, focusing on their findings. AO2 material could include the immediate implications of such studies, e.g. Horne's view that effects are concentrated on cognitive processes, and how this leads to his theory of core and optional sleep. More general AO2 could discuss the fact that sleep deprivation is associated with a range of effects, so leading to the conclusion that sleep is necessary. However, a key part of the question is the implications for theories of the functions of sleep, so you will eventually have to focus on specific theories. The most straightforward approach would be restoration theories, and you can perhaps compare Horne's theory with Oswald's.

Topic 3 >> Dreaming

THE NATURE OF DREAMS

Dreams are often thought of as a series of visual images, although these are merely one part of the dream experience. We may also experience actions and emotions. Congenitally blind people also have dreams that are no less vivid than those of sighted people, even though they see nothing (Oswald 1980). The term 'nightmare' tends to be used for those dreams that occur during REM sleep in which a series of events are associated with anxiety. When a person awakes from a

nightmare, they are frequently aware of the muscle paralysis that accompanies REM sleep. Nightmares occur unpredictably during sleep but become more frequent when the person has experienced considerable anxiety during their waking hours. According to Oswald (1980), people who are depressed by day tend to have dreams that contain themes of failure and loss.

Hunt (1989) classified dreams into the following categories:

- personal dreams (with themes of direct personal relevance)
- medical dreams (health-related)
- prophetic dreams (related to future possibilities)
- spiritual dreams
- nightmares
- lucid dreams.

This last category of lucid dreams is the rare experience some people have of actually being conscious during a dream, i.e. they are aware that they are dreaming and can control the course of the dream.

Dreaming and REM sleep

Dreams are the most distinctive feature of REM sleep. Although people woken up during non-REM sleep may report dreaming, they are much more likely to report it if they are woken during a phase of REM sleep. Dreams can be bizarre and dramatic, and it is easy to assume that they must have some deep meaning. Before looking at some of the possibilities, we must first draw a distinction between REM sleep and dreaming. REM sleep is a physiological state of the brain and body that is defined using EEG recordings, eye movements, muscle tone, etc. The pioneering work of Aserinsky and Kleitman (1953) supported a close association between REM sleep and dreaming, so much so that for years afterwards it was perfectly acceptable to refer to REM sleep as 'dreaming sleep'. If REM sleep and dreaming were the same thing, we could call them 'isomorphic', meaning that talking about one would be the same as talking about the other. However, we now know that they are *not* isomorphic. Although REM sleep is a physiological state, it could only be isomorphic if dreams occurred *whenever* we went into REM sleep and *only* if we went into REM sleep.

However, dreaming also occurs in non-REM (NREM) sleep, and, although dreams during NREM sleep are generally less intense, less emotional and less vivid than dreams during REM sleep, they are sometimes indistinguishable (Moffitt *et al.* 1993). This supports the conclusion that REM sleep and dreaming are not identical. In fact, some of the theories of REM sleep discussed earlier concerning restoration of

neurotransmitter levels are purely physiological, with no role for dreams at all. But most researchers agree that there is a special relationship between REM sleep and dreaming, and, increasingly, theories of the function of REM sleep include a role for the dream imagery that accompanies it, or at least an explanation of it.

Aserinsky and Kleitman demonstrated that dreams take place in real time, i.e. they are not speeded up or slowed down, so if we dream for most of the time we are in REM sleep, then we would dream for around two hours per night. We do not recall all our dreams when we wake up. Since we spend more time in REM sleep as the night passes, we dream more towards morning and it is those images we usually remember best.

LaBerge and lucid dreaming

Lucid dreaming is the experience of being aware that you are dreaming while you are actually dreaming. Stephen LaBerge (1985) had been a lucid dreamer since the age of five but found, as he developed his career as a sleep researcher, that other psychologists did not believe in lucid dreams. He therefore devised a study to demonstrate the phenomenon. He knew from experience that lucid dreamers can move their eyes voluntarily during dreams. One night in the sleep laboratory while he was wired up to an EEG machine to record brain waves and eye movements, LaBerge entered a phase of lucid dreaming. Within the actual dream, he opened his eyes and moved them deliberately up and down, following movements of his finger. When he awoke colleagues checked the EEG and found large systematic eye movements recorded exactly when they had observed LaBerge's finger moving up and down. This was evidence that sleepers have some conscious control over finger and eye movements during lucid dreams. Since then lucid dreaming has been confirmed as a real phenomenon, although the mechanisms behind it are still unknown.

Interestingly, lucid dreams are evidence against the neurobiological theory of dreaming put forward by Hobson and McCarley (Hobson 1988). This theory explains dreams, using the essentially random activity of brainstem neurons, but lucid dreams must involve control by high-level cortical areas of the brain involved in conscious awareness.

THEORIES OF THE FUNCTIONS OF DREAMING

Early work on the significance and functions of dreaming was dominated by the ideas of psychoanalysts such as Freud. This was mainly because the highly subjective nature of dream content meant that it was impossible to use objective scientific methods. Psychology sees itself as a science and therefore had no way of investigating dreams. The discovery in the 1950s of the relationship between REM sleep and dreaming made it possible to link the scientific study of REM sleep, using EEG recordings, to hypotheses about the nature of dream content. Gradually, theories of the function of REM sleep

began to include speculations on the role of dream imagery. This process was helped by rapid developments in computer science, which led to the increased use of computer analogies to explain psychological phenomena, including REM sleep and dreams. We have therefore a wide range of hypotheses, ideas and speculations about the nature and functions of dreaming.

There is no particularly neat division of theories of dreaming into categories. Even the earliest ideas from Aristotle in 350 BC and Artemidorus in AD 200 are echoed in contemporary approaches, such as the dependence of dream imagery on the experiences of the previous day. Freud concentrated on the use of dreams to analyse relationships between our conscious and unconscious minds, but the idea of dream imagery reflecting an interaction between our daily experiences and our stored memories is also found in theories from modern experimental psychology.

Neurobiological theories of dreaming

In neurobiological models of dreaming, based on the brain's physiological activity during REM sleep, the interpretation of dream imagery is secondary to explaining the underlying cognitive function of REM sleep.

Crick and Mitchison and reverse learning

Computer metaphors, which are popular for describing the brain, have also been applied to dreams. Read the Key research of Crick and Mitchison (1983) below.

Hobson and McCarley and the activation-synthesis model

One of the striking characteristics of REM sleep is that during this phase, the brain is as physiologically active as when we are awake. This activity has stimulated the idea that something important must be happening during REM sleep and dreaming, as suggested by

Crick and Mitchison. A similar approach is taken by Hobson and McCarley (see Key research panel opposite). Their activation-synthesis hypothesis of dreaming is based on many years of intricate electrophysiological research into the brain mechanisms of REM sleep.

ACTIVITY

A dream diary

1 Keep a dream diary for two weeks, noting the content of even fragments of dreams that you remember. Try to categorize the dreams using Hunt's types on p. 419; do they all fit?

2 Several theories of dreams refer to the need to combine the day's experiences with stored memories. Does this match your dreams, in the sense that the day's events, feelings and anxieties feature prominently?

3 Reverse learning and activation-synthesis both predict that some dreams will be bizarre and disconnected sequences of random images. Do you have such dreams, or do they all have some kind of 'story line'? If so, is this a limitation of both these neurobiological theories?

KEY RESEARCH >> NEUROBIOLOGICAL MODELS OF DREAMING

Crick and Mitchison's (1983) reverse-learning model

Crick and Mitchison proposed that the brain is 'off line' during dreaming, and that during this phase it sifts through the information gathered during the day's waking activities and throws out all unwanted material. According to this model, we dream in order to forget and this involves a process of 'reverse learning'. The cortex cannot cope with the vast amount of information received during the day without developing 'parasitic' thoughts, which would disrupt the efficient organization of memory. During REM sleep, these unwanted connections in cortical networks are wiped out by impulses bombarding the cortex from sub-cortical areas. The actual content of dreams represents these parasitic thoughts as they are erased from memory.

One piece of indirect evidence to support this theory is from studies of the spiny anteater – echidna. This primitive, egg-laying

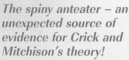

mammal, which belongs to a group known as the monotremes, has no REM sleep, but does have a very enlarged frontal cortex. Crick and Mitchison argue that it needed this excessive cortical development in order to store both adaptive memories and parasitic memories, which in more highly evolved animals are disposed of during REM sleep.

One problem for the reverse-learning theory is that dreams are often organized into clear narratives (stories). If they consisted only of disposable, parasitic thoughts, why should they be organized in this systematic way? Later, Crick and Mitchison restricted their theory to apply only to dreams with bizarre imagery and no clear narrative.

The spiny anteater – an unexpected source of evidence for Crick and Mitchison's theory!

A2 Physiological Psychology

Hobson and McCarley and the activation-synthesis model (Hobson 1988)

The activation component of the theory concerns the regular switching on of REM sleep as part of the cycle of sleep stages. The REM mechanism is based in the brainstem and when activated, it inhibits skeletal muscles, producing the characteristic 'paralysis' of REM sleep, and excites activity in the forebrain via pathways ascending from the brainstem. As part of this forebrain activation, sensory and motor information is internally and automatically aroused, and forms the basis of our dream experience. The dream itself represents the organization of all this sensory and motor activation into a coherent structure, with considerable input from an individual's past experiences and expectations.

The activation-synthesis hypothesis states that dreaming is an automatic part of the brain's sleep mechanisms and can be seen as an endogenous (in-built) process with a large genetic component. It may have no significance beyond the brain's natural drive to organize material into a coherent sequence.

However, this theory also allows for the brain to integrate sensory and motor information with individual memories and expectations, and this can happen in novel and creative ways. For example, when neurons fire in the part of the brain that handles balance, the cortex may generate a dream about falling. Likewise, when signals occur that would ordinarily produce running, the cortex may create a dream about being chased (Tavris and Wade 1995). In this way, the model can also account for any narrative aspect of dreams.

As stated previously, cells in the brainstem produce REM sleep, and these appear to be sensitive to the neurotransmitter acetylcholine. In support of this idea, Hobson (1988) points out that when sleeping volunteers are injected with drugs that increase the action of acetylcholine, REM sleep and dreaming both increased. On the other hand, when volunteers are injected with a drug which blocks the action of acetylcholine, REM sleep and dreaming were found to decrease (Gillin *et al.* 1985).

Evaluation
activation-synthesis model

- *Support* – Hobson and McCarley's model is broader than the reverse-learning theory and is also based on extensive experimental work. It provides a sound account of the brain mechanisms underlying REM sleep and dreaming. Basing psychological interpretation on the neurobiology of REM sleep and dream states does make it quite convincing.

- *Challenge* – The breadth of the model is a major problem when trying to validate it. Since dreams can be either meaningless or creative, it is difficult to explain any type of dream experience, i.e. it has little predictive power. This is not a problem confined to this model – dream research always runs up against the need for subjective interpretation of dream symbolism and it is virtually impossible to do this in a scientifically rigorous way.

Psychological theories of dreaming

In contrast to neurobiological theories, psychological approaches take the dream imagery itself as the issue to be explained.

Dreaming, REM sleep and learning

Anecdotal stories of problem-solving during dreaming have led to the suggestion that there is an association between REM sleep and learning and/or memory. A chemist called Kekule claims to have confirmed the structure of the benzene molecule (a ring) by dreaming of a snake biting its own tail. His daytime attempts at solving the problem appear to have been completed during REM sleep. Although such accounts are interesting, they do not provide reliable evidence.

Other psychologists have tried to study the relationship between sleep and learning more systematically (see panel on p. 422).

These studies provide direct evidence that some forms of very simple learning involve specific phases of sleep, especially REM sleep. Stickgold (1998) points out that participants often report dream imagery that includes elements of the task being learned, and so both dreams and the brain's electrical activity during REM sleep reflect the learning process.

Many investigators have noticed that during the phases of sleep, there is a huge amount of two-way communication (exchange of nerve impulses) between the cortex and the hippocampus in the limbic system. During SWS, it runs from the hippocampus to the cortex, and during REM sleep from the cortex to the

Studies of sleep and learning

- *Karni et al. (1994)* trained participants on a perceptual speed task. They had to report whether the background pattern to a letter in the centre of a computer screen was made up of vertical or horizontal lines. Response times were around 100 milliseconds and did not improve with practice. However, after a night's sleep, performance was found to improve by about 15 milliseconds and this improvement was sustained over several months. However, if participants were woken each time they entered REM sleep, so that they were effectively deprived of REM sleep, no such improvement occurred. This would suggest that REM sleep is essential for the improvement in performance and responsible for the delayed learning.

- *Stickgold (1998)* was interested in whether other stages of sleep were also important in this task. The technique he used was to allow participants to sleep normally and measure the amount of time they spent in each stage. It turned out that those who improved the most

had the greatest amount of REM sleep in the last two hours of sleep, but also the most SWS in the first two hours. He suggests that this sort of learning is a two-stage process, involving both SWS and REM sleep. He also demonstrated that participants have to sleep within 24 hours of training for this delayed learning to occur.

- *Smith (1999)* used two tasks in similar studies. In one, participants had to trace between the double outline of a triangle, and in the other they had to do the task while looking in a mirror (this is called 'reversed mirror-image drawing'). They were deprived either of SWS or REM sleep on the night following the training. Smith found that Stage 2 SWS deprivation affected only the simple version, while REM sleep deprivation affected the more complex task. He concludes that simple learning involving only slight modifications of previously acquired skills involves Stage 2 SWS, but that REM sleep is needed in order to learn new tasks.

hippocampus. An emerging view is that memories of the day's events are stored initially in the hippocampus and are integrated with experiences permanently stored in the cortex during sleep. The imagery of dreams, which is sometimes bizarre, reflects these attempts to link recent memories with past ones. One result of this may be improved learning of simple tasks, but the outcome may be more complicated.

Winson, dreams and survival behaviour

The work of Winson (1997) suggests a more complicated picture. He works with non-human animals, such as rabbits, cats and rats, which show a characteristic 'theta rhythm' of six cycles per second in EEG recordings from the hippocampus during REM sleep. This rhythm is also recorded when the animal is awake and engaging in what Winson calls 'species-specific survival behaviour', such as exploring new territory in rats, predating in cats, or when alert and apprehensive in rabbits. Winson's proposal is that theta rhythm during REM sleep is responsible for the reactivation of these memories, which are stored in the hippocampus, so that they can be integrated with previous experiences that are stored in the cortex, and so that new survival strategies can be developed. He speculates that humans have moved beyond behaviours such as simple exploration as a vital survival function, to a world where threats and anxieties are more complex – relationships, examinations, careers, etc. But the role of REM sleep has remained the same – as a time when the day's experiences are reactivated and incorporated with earlier memories, and when new

coping strategies are evolved. Dream imagery would then depend on the nature of the problems, individual coping strategies and previous experiences, but would often clearly reflect the day's experiences.

Winson also addresses the problems of the spiny anteater's forebrain (see p. 420) and the proportionately large amount of REM sleep found in a newborn child (see p. 414). The spiny anteater does not have REM sleep, and so needs to integrate new information with stored memories while it is awake.

To develop more effective survival strategies by processing more information, the frontal cortex would have to increase in size. The evolution of REM sleep meant that this function could be performed 'off line' and so reduces the demands on the cortex.

The infant is bombarded with information that is processed into basic memory structures that form the cognitive framework with which later experiences have to be integrated. Forming this bedrock of memories requires large amounts of REM sleep, which then declines as our basic cognitive structures emerge. From then, REM sleep takes on its lifelong function of integrating the day's experiences with our established memories.

Dreams and problem-solving

Winson's model suggests a major role for REM sleep in developing new coping strategies. The research is based on non-human animals, and so there is no defined role for dream imagery (the rabbit cannot report on its dreams). However, similar ideas have been proposed by other researchers working with humans, focusing more on problem-solving than on learning, and with a greater emphasis on dream imagery. Cartwright believes that dreams help us to adjust to major life changes, threats and problems. In one study involving divorced women, Cartwright (1984) found that women who were not depressed by their divorce had longer dreams that reflected the negative emotions aroused by the situation, and the story-lines often involved the dreamer in marital roles. In the depressed group of divorced women, on the other hand, dreams were shorter, usually with no reference to the divorce, and with far less emphasis on marriage. However, as the mood of the depressed women improved, their dreams began to resemble those of the non-depressed group. Cartwright suggests that moderate emotional reactions to life changes lead to more adaptive dreams, while strong emotional reactions seem to inhibit the adaptive role of dreaming.

As we move further away from the electrophysiological study of REM sleep, through psychological approaches such as Cartwright's, we end up with the psycho-dynamic approaches of Freud. This may seem rather unusual in a unit focusing on physiological psychology. However, the recent emphasis in experimental psychology on the interplay between REM sleep and dream imagery, and especially how dream imagery may reflect the possible role of REM sleep in integrating the day's experiences with previous memories, create a logical link between the two traditions.

Freud and dreams

Freud always felt that his work on the interpretation of dreams was fundamental to his whole psychodynamic approach: 'the interpretation of dreams is the royal road to a knowledge of the unconscious activities of the mind' (Freud 1955). He believed that a dream was the disguised fulfilment of desires repressed into the unconscious mind. It had to be disguised because the repressed desires could be sexual or aggressive urges unacceptable to the dreamer when awake. In that sense, the two functions of dreams are to protect the sleeper, but simultaneously to allow some expression of these repressed urges.

Because of this, the dream has a 'manifest content', which the dreamer reports and which the analyst has to interpret in order to reveal the 'latent content', which directly reflects the repressed urges. The transformation of deep-seated desires and anxieties into the manifest symbolism of the dream is called the 'dream work'. Several mechanisms can be involved, including condensation, displacement and considerations of representability.

- *Condensation* refers to the way a particular dream symbol acts as a focus for several different hidden thoughts or anxieties. A particular character from the past may have several different meanings – your relationship with your father, problems at school, or perhaps a recent argument with someone at work or college.

- *Displacement* occurs particularly with emotions. Sometimes the emotional reaction to a particular event in a dream is out of all proportion to the event itself. Freud would say that the emotion is, in fact, attached to some hidden wish or thought and has been displaced onto the dream image.

- Considerations of *representability* involve the visual nature of dreams. Hidden thoughts are translated into a visual form, so that a dream of panic or of running from an unknown terror may represent the hidden fear of instinctual sexual urges.

As Freud points out, the whole point of the dream work is to prevent the dreamer becoming aware of the hidden thoughts and anxieties, and the role of the analyst is to interpret the imagery and reverse the condensation, displacement, etc., and to reveal the latent meaning of the dream. To help interpretation, Freud developed a vocabulary of dream symbols. Drawing on cultural symbols found in stories, mythology, jokes, etc., he suggested, for instance, that dreams of flying represented sexual intercourse. He also emphasized that dream imagery usually contained representations of the previous day's events, which, although neutral in themselves, could be used to disguise the latent content. Freud was also happy to accept that sometimes dream imagery could be accepted at face value – sometimes a cigar is just a cigar!

Although Freud's theory of the nature and function of dreams has become more a part of popular culture than scientific psychology, recent research undertaken with patients with brain damage in the cortical-limbic circuit in the forebrain has shown that dream content may indeed reflect our unconscious wishes and desires, as predicted by Freud (see the panel on p. 424). Freud sees dreams and dream content as important in their own right. Dreams are a mixture of current events and emotions carried over from the day's experiences, mixed in with material from the unconscious mind. In a way, this is not so far from some contemporary models of REM sleep from experimental psychology, which emphasize the integration of current experiences with earlier memories. Of course, the psychodynamic framework is very different, but the problem of deciding which interpretation of dream imagery is correct is virtually impossible, whichever theory you follow. When studying dreams, the methodology has hardly varied – the researcher has to rely on the subjective report of the dreamer – and those modern psychologists, who are more interested in dream content than in REM sleep as such, are still using the methods that were pioneered by Freud.

Dream on, Freud

Sigmund Freud's idea that in our dreams we see our true desires, stripped of the polite concealments that social life imposes, has had a fairly rough ride from scientists ... But results reported at the American Association for the Advancement of Science (AAAS) in Anaheim, California suggest that Freud may not have been so wide of the mark after all.

Until now, scientists have seen dreams as the manifestation of a period of paradoxical sleep in which the sleeper's brain is aroused even though he or she is sound asleep. Because the eyes are moving, this type of sleep is known as REM, or rapid-eye movement sleep. On an average night we spend about a quarter of our sleeping hours in this condition. When woken from REM sleep, 70 to 95 per cent of people report dreams, whereas only 5 to 10 per cent do so when woken from non-REM sleep.

Dr Mark Solms, of St Bartholomew's and Royal London Hospital School of Medicine, told the conference that this is why REM sleep is seen as the physiological concomitant of dreaming. If so, then dreaming is merely an accidental by-product of REM sleep with no greater significance.

His own work with nine patients suffering a particular type of brain damage led him to doubt this ... In each case, a circuit in the forebrain called the cortical-limbic circuit had been damaged or destroyed. The patients reported to him that the result of the brain damage was to deprive them of dreams, but sleep studies showed that they still had normal REM sleep.

This sent Dr Solms back to the huge literature on the effect of prefrontal lobotomies, a once fashionable operation in which this very circuit was deliberately severed in order to treat mental disorders. He found what everybody else had forgotten, which was that 70 to 90 per cent of lobotomy patients reported loss of dreams. Since it is known that REM sleep is controlled from an entirely different part of the brain, in the brainstem rather than the forebrain, it became clear to him that REM sleep and dreams, though they may often coincide, are not one and the same.

The effect of a lobotomy was to make the patients listless and apathetic, because the circuit that was cut is connected with motivation and goal-seeking behaviour. It is particularly active in people with addictions to drugs, alcohol or even tobacco. This implies that dreaming is linked to the circuits in the brain which control our wishes and desires, strikingly close to what Freud himself claimed.

At the conference, he also found support from brain-imaging studies by Dr Allen Braun, of the US National Institute on Deafness and Other Communication Disorders, who concluded: 'Rather than implying that dream content is random, meaningless, this pattern suggests that it may constitute direct, albeit distorted, access to unconscious processes.'

Freud lives!

Source: Nigel Hawkes, *The Times*, 27 January 1999

Evaluation
dream research (A02)

● *Laboratory-based research* – Much of the research on REM sleep and dreaming takes place in a sleep laboratory. The participant comes into the laboratory, is wired up with electrodes to record EEG activity and then allowed to sleep. Not surprisingly, the dreams reported under such conditions can differ significantly from those reported under normal conditions. They tend to be shorter, less dramatic and with less emotional intensity; nightmares are virtually never experienced in a sleep laboratory. In fact, dreams often incorporate elements of the laboratory setting, such as wires, people in white coats and large complex machines (Van de Castle 1994). This 'laboratory effect' makes it impossible to argue that dreaming under these conditions represents dreams in the real world, although allowing the participants to sleep one night in the laboratory before recording takes place can lessen the effect.

continued on next page

Evaluation continued
dream research

● *Subjectivity of dreams* – To interpret dream imagery, whether you are a cognitive psychologist or a Freudian analyst, means that you have to rely on the subjective report of the dreamer. This goes against the 'scientific method' adopted by modern-day psychology, which normally requires that behaviour should be observable and objective. But since dreams are personal and inaccessible to others, dream researchers have to trust the accounts of their participants in order to carry out their research.

● *Enforced sleep deprivation* – Many studies of dreaming are carried out during which humans and non-human animals are deprived of stages of sleep, usually REM sleep. Studies of human problem-solving during REM sleep, discussed earlier, use exactly this approach. But we have to accept that waking humans and non-human animals up at intervals during sleep may well have other effects, causing, for instance, non-specific stress and anxiety, and disrupting other biological rhythms such as the secretion of hormones and brain neurotransmitters. The results may therefore be due to these non-specific effects rather than to selective deprivation of REM sleep.

CHECK YOUR UNDERSTANDING

Check your understanding of dreaming by answering these questions. Try to do this from memory at first. You can check your answers by looking back through Topic 3.

1 Give one difference between the dreams occurring in REM and those occurring in SWS.

2 Write a 100-word précis of the reverse-learning theory of dreaming and then prepare a brief account of two critical (AO2) points relating to it.

3 Write a 100-word précis of the activation-synthesis theory of dreaming and then prepare a brief account of two critical (AO2) points relating to it.

4 Outline one study of the role of REM sleep in memory and learning.

5 Where in the brain are the day's experiences first stored?

6 What sorts of behaviours did Winson suggest were reactivated during REM sleep?

7 Outline in no more than 100 words one problem-solving model of dreams.

8 Prepare a brief account of the Freudian concepts of latent and manifest content.

9 Identify and briefly describe one mechanism involved in the 'dream work'.

10 Give a brief account of two critical (AO2) points relating to the problems of carrying out research into dreams.

REVISION SUMMARY

Having covered this topic you should be able to:

✓ describe and evaluate research findings into the nature of dreams, including content, duration and relationship with the stages of sleep

✓ outline and evaluate two neurobiological theories of the functions of dreaming – reverse-learning and activation-synthesis

✓ describe and evaluate research studies into REM sleep and learning

✓ outline and evaluate psychological theories of the functions of dreaming, using research studies and alternative accounts

✓ discuss the problems of undertaking scientific research into dreaming.

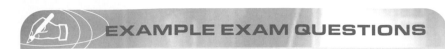

Below are some **possible examination questions** set on this topic, along with hints to help you understand and approach each question effectively:

1 Discuss research findings relating to the nature of dreams. (24 marks)

> This question looks quite limited, but you need to understand the use of terminology. The term 'research' can include *theories* and *data* collection, so it would actually be acceptable to discuss the 'findings' from theories of dreams and/or studies. However such theories and studies must be described so that they provide information about the *nature* of dreams rather than its functions in order to attract marks. AO2 material could include research support for a particular theory of dreams or, for instance, research into the relationship between dreams and the stages of sleep. You must not simply *describe* supporting studies, but embed them in a *sustained* commentary. It would also be legitimate to include general evaluation and commentary on the problems of doing research into dreams and dreaming; this could cover the laboratory effect and the problem of relying on the dreamer's self-report of their dream content.

2 Outline and assess neurobiological accounts of dreaming (e.g. Hobson and McCarley, Crick and Mitchison). (24 marks)

> In this question you must present at least two of the theories that are classed as neurobiological and can draw from the list of examples given, and/or use others. When evaluating (or assessing) these theories, you could use psychological theories as a contrast, so long as you do more than just offer a description of a psychological theory. Any features of the psychological theory that are introduced must be used as commentary and thus would be 'sustained'. Note that REM sleep is not the same as dreaming and any account of REM sleep must be explicitly linked to dreaming to gain credit.

3 Critically consider **two or more** psychological accounts of the functions of dreaming (e.g. Freud, Webb, Cartwright). (24 marks)

> Here, the term 'critically consider' demands an AO1+AO2 response. You are required to describe psychological accounts: a minimum of two accounts are required (or there would be a partial performance penalty). The use of the phrase 'two or more' is a reminder that two would be sufficient for full marks. Finally, this question says 'accounts of the functions of dreaming'. This means that your accounts must focus on function rather than, for example, the nature of dreams.

4 (a) Outline **one** theory of the functions of dreaming. (6 marks)
  (b) Outline and evaluate research (theories **and/or** studies) relating to the theory of the functions of dreaming you have outlined in (a). (18 marks)

> First, look closely at the mark split. Part (a) is worth 6 AO1 marks; this is only one quarter of the available marks, so this section must not be too long. Choose the one theory that allows you to do well on section (b). Reverse-learning, for instance, probably has less AO2 material that is easily accessible than activation-synthesis or Freudian approaches. In part (b), you can describe alternative theories or studies (to gain AO1 marks) as long as you can then use them (for your AO2 marks) to evaluate the theory in part (a). This could come in several ways. For instance describing the limitations and/or strengths of individual research studies.

UNIT SUMMARY

Topic 1: Biological rhythms

● **Biological rhythms** are found throughout the natural world, in both plants and animals, and may be classified into **circadian, infradian** and **ultradian biological rhythms** (circannual rhythms are examples of infradian rhythms).

● Evidence suggests that these rhythms are natural, controlled by **endogenous pacemakers** or biological clocks.

- These clocks can be set by external stimuli, referred to as **exogenous zeitgebers**, such as light and dark. In mammals, the main biological clock is the suprachiasmatic nucleus (SCN), which responds to light falling on the eye by altering the release of melatonin from the pineal gland.

- **Bodily rhythms can be disrupted** by jet travel and **shift work**, leading to behavioural disorganization and stress. Day-length changes are involved in seasonal affective disorder (SAD), which can be treated by exposure to bright artificial light during the day.

Topic 2: Sleep

- Using EEG recordings, we can identify two types of sleep – **slow-wave sleep** (**SWS**) and **rapid eye movement** (**REM**) sleep (also referred to as 'paradoxical sleep') – and also four stages of SWS.

- **Restoration accounts** of the functions of sleep concentrate on body, brain and hormonal recovery. **Studies of total and partial sleep deprivation** show that both Stage 4 SWS and REM sleep are important for normal growth and function of the brain. Neurochemical approaches show that REM sleep is important for the functioning of brain neurotransmitter pathways.

- Sleep patterns also depend on lifestyle and ecological niche, and **evolutionary** approaches focus on the variations between different species.

- Overall, there is unlikely to be a single explanation for the functions of sleep.

Topic 3: Dreaming

- Dreams occur mainly during REM sleep, but are not the same thing as REM sleep, which is defined physiologically. Research into the **nature of dreams** has looked at their **relationship with stages of sleep**, **duration** and **content**.

- **Theories of the functions of dreaming** range from those that see them as meaningless, to those that associate them with learning, problem-solving and integrating the day's experiences with stored memories.

- **Neurobiological approaches** often use computer metaphors to describe the brain's activity during dreaming, for example, for wiping out unwanted information by 'reverse learning' (**Crick and Mitchison**). **Hobson and McCarley** used electrophysiological research into brain mechanisms to formulate their activation-synthesis hypothesis. Modern **psychological accounts** include studies of dreams in relation to improvements in learning, survival strategies and problem-solving (**Cartwright**).

- Researchers have to rely on the subjective reports of dreamers in order to develop any theory of the functions of dreaming. Despite its emphasis on the unconscious, **Freud's** approach has some similarities with modern ideas from cognitive psychology.

FURTHER RESOURCES

Moorcroft, W.H. (2003) *Understanding Sleep and Dreaming*, New York: Plenum Press.

  An excellent survey of current research.

Coren, S. (1996) *Sleep Thieves*, New York: The Free Press.

  Very readable account of the mechanisms of sleep and how biological rhythms can conflict with modern life.

Winson, J. (1997) 'The meaning of dreams', *Scientific American*, Special Issue: *Mysteries of the Mind*, 7 (1), pp. 58–67.

  Reviews some modern information-processing theories of dreams.

Websites

www.sleepnet.com/

  A comprehensive guide to sleep, sleep-related issues (including dreams) and sleep disorders.

www.asdreams.org

  The home page for the Association for the Study of Dreams.

www.dreamgate.com

  A searchable site that includes a full-text online version of Freud's classic *Interpretation of Dreams*.

www.circadian.com/

  A useful site devoted to circadian rhythms.

Unit 13 // Biological rhythms, sleep & dreaming

14
UNIT

MOTIVATION AND
Emotion

PREVIEW

After you have read this unit, you should be able to describe and evaluate:

>> theories and research studies relating to the role of brain structures in motivational states

>> physiological approaches to explaining motivation

>> psychological approaches to explaining motivation

>> combined physiological/psychological approaches to explaining motivation

>> the role of brain structures in emotional behaviour and experience

>> physiological approaches to explaining emotional behaviour and experience

>> combined physiological/psychological approaches to explaining emotional behaviour and experience.

INTRODUCTION

Motivation and emotion are often discussed together in psychology textbooks. Both terms are used to explain large areas of human experience, particularly the way behaviour is activated and organized for some clear purpose. Everybody has a general idea about what these two terms mean. However, psychology has to define terms in such a way that they are clear and unambiguous, and this can sometimes produce research and theories that can seem a long way from everyday life. Much of the work on the physiology of motivation and emotion has been done with non-human animals, and so we also have to consider whether applying the results to humans is justified.

This unit starts in Topic 1 by looking at the brain structures and mechanisms involved in some motivational states. Some of the theories of motivation used in psychology are considered in Topic 2. The first two topics in the unit overlap to some extent. Brain mechanisms involved in motivational states also play important roles in theories of motivation, especially homeostatic drive theory. To help you understand these brain mechanisms, Topic 1 starts by introducing the concept of 'homeostasis'. This is followed by a discussion of the role of brain mechanisms in motivational states. Homeostasis is then discussed more fully in relation to theories of motivation in Topic 2.

The subject of Topic 3 is emotion, which is discussed from the perspective of brain structures. You will then go on to look at theoretical approaches to emotion, using physiological, psychological and combined models.

Simon
Green

Two important health-related issues in society today seem contradictory. On the one hand, there is an epidemic in Western society of obesity, and on the other hand, we have an apparent dramatic increase in eating disorders, such as anorexia nervosa and bulimia nervosa. The media is full of stories about eating disorders in young women and, increasingly, in young men, while criticizing the fast-food culture that is believed to be responsible for this recent upsurge in obesity.

Hunger, feeding behaviour and weight regulation have traditionally been the main subject for the physiological and psychological study of motivation. Many thousands of research studies have led to models of how we regulate food intake and body weight, but a key

test for them all is how well do they explain the life-threatening weight loss of anorexia and the increasing levels of obesity?

Before you start reading this unit, think about the following questions:

1 Are these conditions purely down to physiological problems in, for instance, hormone levels or brain mechanisms of weight regulation? Or do they involve more complicated interactions between physiology and psychology?

2 Do you think that people with anorexia suffer from deep-seated psychological problems? Does the obese person simply lack will power? Or are they both victims of their physiology?

KEY CONCEPTS

Homeostatic drive: motivated behaviour aimed at satisfying a physiological drive, such as hunger or thirst, and so maintaining homeostasis.

Non-homeostatic drive: behaviour that is aroused and directed, but does not appear to be associated with homeostatic drives. Examples in animals include curiosity and manipulation, and a range of complex human behaviours such as studying for A-levels.

Expectancy: refers to the ability of rewarding stimuli to 'pull' or 'elicit' behaviour on the basis of previous experience, and contrasts with the drive approach that sees motivated behaviour as 'pushed' by internal drives.

Needs: Maslow's term for human motives, ranging from basic physiological needs to aesthetic needs and self-actualization.

Emotion: a complex pattern of events, involving perception of a situation, appraisal of the situation as threatening or harmless, feeling towards the situation, and expression of emotion in terms of behavioural and physiological changes.

Cognitive labelling: the proposal that emotional states involve a combination of non-specific bodily arousal, and cognitive appraisal of the situation that labels the arousal as a particular emotion, e.g. anger, euphoria, fear.

HOMEOSTASIS

Claude Bernard (1856) was the first person to emphasize the importance to survival of the maintenance of a constant internal environment. The internal environment of the body consists of such systems as the oxygen content of the blood, the concentration of various nutrients (such as glucose), the water balance of the body and body temperature. All of these systems can only fluctuate within narrow limits if health and survival are to be maintained. The maintenance of a constant internal environment is called 'homeostasis'.

Homeostatic drive-reduction

As a system departs from the stable state – e.g. as we use energy or go out into the cold – the body tries to restore homeostatic equilibrium through physiological and behavioural mechanisms. For instance, if we have not eaten for some time, we develop a bodily requirement for food. As the body is made up of tissues, such as the liver, the skin and the brain, this requirement is often referred to as a 'tissue need'. This need leads to a drive to eat, and eating reduces the drive and restores homeostasis. This sequence is a simple example of behaviour that is motivated by a primary physiological drive, aroused by a tissue need. A whole class of motivated behaviours is represented by these 'homeostatic primary drives' (see Fig. 14.1).

Since homeostatic drives such as hunger and thirst seem straightforward, they have been the most frequently studied. Homeostatic drives represent the physiological approach to the study of motivation. The simple picture of a tissue deficiency, leading to a specific need, which in turn motivates the appropriate behaviour, is very appealing and many thousands of

experiments have been carried out to see if this is indeed the case.

Another advantage of hunger and thirst over more complex motivational states, such as ambition or curiosity, is that humans and non-human animals are likely to have mechanisms in common because we share the same basic physiology. Most studies have been undertaken on non-human animals, especially rats, and many factors have been shown to contribute to the control of, for instance, body weight and eating behaviour. These include peripheral (bodily) systems, such as the stomach and intestinal tract (referred to collectively as the 'gastrointestinal system'), and hormones such as insulin and leptin. Some of these factors will be discussed in Topic 2 when we consider the homeostatic drive theory of motivation. However, the most dramatic findings in relation to the control of motivational states have involved brain mechanisms.

Figure 14.1 >> *A simple model of motivation: homeostatic drive-reduction*

BRAIN STRUCTURES AND HUNGER

The hypothalamus and feeding centres

In 1942, Hetherington and Ranson demonstrated that lesions of part of the hypothalamus, called the 'ventromedial nucleus' (referred to as the VMH, standing for the ventromedial nucleus of the hypothalamus), caused dramatic overeating in rats, so that they became massively obese. A few years later, Anand and Brobeck (1951) showed that lesions of the lateral nucleus of the hypothalamus (LH) inhibited eating so that the rats lost weight. The findings of these two studies, and many others since, suggest that the hypothalamus contains two feeding centres:

- one in the **ventromedial nucleus** which normally stops feeding at the appropriate time – a **satiety centre**
- the other in the **lateral nucleus** which normally stimulates feeding – a **feeding centre**.

This has led to the dual-centre hypothalamic model of hunger and feeding, which has been accepted for many years.

Although these centres are obviously important in the control of feeding, they can only act if they know the state of the body's energy reserves, so that feeding is related to need. An important index of the body's energy reserves is the level of glucose in the blood.

The glucostat hypothesis

This hypothesis suggests that glucose is the key signal to the hypothalamus to begin or end feeding behaviour. The sugar, glucose, is one of the main products of carbohydrate digestion, and blood glucose levels have been extensively studied as a likely candidate for the regulation of food intake and the control of motivation to eat (Wickens 2000). While it is unlikely that changes in blood glucose occur fast enough to affect the size of an individual meal, they may certainly affect the feelings of hunger that develop between meals and so influence our motivation to seek food.

Levels of glucose in the blood are controlled by food intake and by the hormone, insulin, which is released from the pancreas gland. Insulin enables the conversion of glucose into fats and the storage of fats in fat storage cells called 'adipocytes'. Therefore, the levels of blood glucose are closely related to levels of insulin; if insulin levels are low, as in people with diabetes, less glucose is stored in cells and levels in the blood are high. However, when blood insulin rises, more glucose is stored and less circulates in the bloodstream. Artificial increases in blood glucose via injections can decrease food intake (Tordoff *et al.* 1982). Insulin levels are lowest at night, when appetite decreases, and higher during the day, causing lower blood glucose levels and increasing appetite (LeMagnen 1981). Effects of glucose on appetite depend on specialized receptors called 'glucoreceptors', found in the lining of blood vessels, in the liver and in the brain, especially the hypothalamus. In this way, the brain is constantly monitoring blood glucose levels. However, this neat relationship between appetite and glucose is probably not the full explanation. In normal people, levels of glucose in the blood do not vary dramatically, even after long periods without food. Part of homeostasis involves maintaining steady levels, so that if less is eaten, stored fats are converted to glucose in the bloodstream; if more sugar is taken in the diet, insulin activity increases to convert blood glucose into stored fats in cells.

Even when levels do change dramatically, there is usually little effect on appetite and feeding behaviour. This can occur in people with insulin-dependent diabetes. In this condition, insulin levels are very low, usually due to problems with the pancreas gland and, consequently, blood glucose levels can be very high. In extreme cases this can lead to hyperglycaemic coma, but significant changes in general appetite are not usually found. Also contradicting the glucostat idea is the observation that injections of glucose directly onto hypothalamic glucoreceptors do not inhibit feeding (Wickens 2000), which one would expect if glucose was an important signal.

Body weight set-point

Another influential idea has been the concept of 'body weight set-point'. This suggests that our feeding systems try to maintain our body weight around a target weight or set-point. The best index of body weight is the amount of fat stored in the adipocytes (fatty tissue), and Nisbett (1972) suggested that the hypothalamus monitors fat levels through sensory nerves and maintains them around a set level. Lesions to the hypothalamus shift this body weight set-point – VMH lesions raise the level, so that rats overeat and become obese, while LH lesions lower it, so that rats stop eating to reduce their body weight. Nisbett demonstrated that rats with lesions to the VMH did not overeat permanently, but reduced intake when their body weight reached a new higher set-point.

The body weight set-point seems to be determined by inherited factors and early nutritional experience. Nisbett's model implies that the obese human, for instance, is not showing weakness of will or self-indulgence, but simply working to maintain a high target weight. While this is undoubtedly true for some people, there are many other factors involved (see the panel on 'Calorific intake and health' below).

Calorific intake and health

According to the body weight set-point approach, if we 'listen' to our bodies, we should eat appropriately to our needs and maximize our physiological health. However, some interesting studies have complicated this picture. In 1986, Weindruch *et al.* reduced the calorific intake of groups of mice by 25%, 55% or 65%. They found that all levels of reduction significantly improved health and led to longer lives, and these benefits were proportional to the degree of calorific reduction. The group on the most restricted diet had lower levels of cancer, the most efficient immune responses and lived 67% longer than the control mice that ate as much as they liked. Improvements in health and longevity were not related to loss of body weight (which was not substantial even in the most restricted group).

These findings from non-human animals are supported by studies on the Japanese island of Okinawa. For various reasons, the population of Okinawa consumes significantly fewer calories on average than people in the rest of Japan do. Levels of all age-related diseases (cancer, heart disease, strokes) were substantially lower and the number of Okinawans living to over 100 was up to 40 times higher than for the rest of Japan (Kagawa 1978).

These findings imply that if we follow our homeostatic internal signals of hunger generated from the hypothalamus, we are not necessarily doing what is best for our body. Reducing our calorific intake even slightly could well have positive benefits for our health and life span.

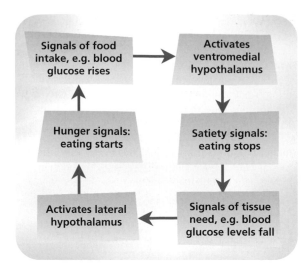

Figure 14.2 >> *Dual centre control of feeding: ventromedial hypothalamus (VMH) and lateral hypothalamus function as satiety and feeding centres*

Even in animals there is little direct evidence for this model. However, the impressive regulation of body weight in most people and in animals does support some kind of set-point, and Nisbett's ideas are the most convincing in this area (see Fig. 14.2). More recently, the discovery of leptin has helped to clarify the body's system for signalling body weight to the brain.

Leptin

Since the 1950s, a genetic mutation in mice has been known to lead to extreme obesity, with mice massively overeating. In 1994, Zhang *et al.* finally identified the cause. Mice with the mutation were not producing a protein called leptin. This is normally produced by the adipocytes (the fat storage cells) in proportion to the amount of fat they contain. It acts as a hormone, travelling via the bloodstream to the hypothalamus, where it acts to decrease food intake. This was confirmed by studies where leptin was injected into the obese mice lacking the leptin gene; food intake and body weight fell dramatically over a few weeks (Halaas *et al.* 1995). It seems likely that leptin may be the key chemical signal, telling the hypothalamus and its feeding regulation centres about the state of fat storage in the body.

Evaluation
the role of brain structures in hunger

(AO2)

- **Role of the hypothalamus** – There is convincing research evidence that centres in the hypothalamus are involved in hunger and feeding behaviour. In particular, the ventromedial hypothalamus appears to contain a satiety centre, while the lateral hypothalamus contains a feeding centre.

- **But what triggers the hypothalamus?** – It is still not certain what signals of the body's energy reserves the hypothalamus responds to.

- **Glucostat hypothesis** – There is some research support for the glucostat hypothesis. Glucoreceptors are found in the liver, blood vessels and in the hypothalamus, and injecting glucose into the bloodstream can decrease feeding. However, blood glucose levels do not normally vary very much and when they do, as in diabetes, feeding behaviour is often unaffected.

- **Body weight set-point** – Nisbett demonstrated that the overeating in rats after lesions to the VMH stops when body weight reaches a new higher set-point, supporting the idea that hypothalamic feeding centres regulate our body weight around a set-point, which is raised by VMH lesions. Research studies on the role of leptin suggest that it acts as a signal to the hypothalamus on the state of the body's fat reserves and body weight.

- **Role of psychological factors** – Emphasizing the roles of hypothalamic feeding and satiety centres ignores psychological factors in appetite and hunger. Our meals usually anticipate real hunger, and the taste, colour and smell of food affect the amount we eat. Studying brain structures alone will not provide a full explanation of hunger.

- **Difficulty in generalizing from non-human animals** – The vast majority of studies use non-human animals and the laboratory rat in particular. Although basic brain mechanisms appear similar, human feeding behaviour is far more complicated than that of rats, so we can only generalize to a limited extent from these studies.

BRAIN STRUCTURES AND THIRST

Like hunger, thirst represents a complicated interaction between the body's physiological systems and central control by brain structures. Regulation of the body's water content is absolutely basic to survival and involves several neural and hormonal systems.

Water is found both within cells ('intracellular') and outside cells ('extracellular'). The extracellular component, making up about 33 per cent of our water content, is divided into interstitial fluid, which surrounds and bathes all of the body's cells, and the blood plasma, which is that part of the blood which is neither the red nor the white blood cells.

Water contains dissolved substances, many of which are salts, including sodium chloride. The concentration of dissolved salts gives the solution what is called an 'osmotic pressure', with the pressure proportional to the concentration of salts. When two solutions are separated by a semi-permeable membrane (i.e. a barrier that allows water through, but not the dissolved salts), water passes from the solution with the lower osmotic pressure to the one with the higher pressure, until the pressures become equal. This is the position with regard to intracellular and extracellular water, because the cell membrane functions as a semi-permeable membrane. Drinking is aimed at maintaining the appropriate dynamic balance between the two water compartments.

Osmotic thirst

We usually lose water regularly through sweating, urination, breathing and evaporation through the mouth and through defecation. We replace water through drinking, while our diet may contain foods high in salts that can also affect osmotic pressure. If, through a combination of these effects, the osmotic pressure of the extracellular water compartment increases (through water loss and intake of salts), water will pass from the intracellular compartment through the semi-permeable cell membrane to try and equalize the pressures of intracellular and extracellular components. This also means that intracellular pressure will rise (less water, but the same salt content).

Although highly specialized, the brain's neurons are still cells of the body and they react in the same way to water loss. In the pre-optic area of the hypothalamus, a group of neurons function as 'osmoreceptors'. When their osmotic pressure rises through water loss, they react by directly stimulating drinking and the release of the anti-diuretic hormone (ADH) into the bloodstream through connections from the hypothalamus to the pituitary gland. ADH travels to the kidneys, where it acts on the kidney tubules to promote water recovery from the urine. So by these two effects – direct stimulation of drinking and water intake, and decreased water loss in the urine – the balance between intracellular and extracellular water compartments is restored.

Experimental studies have shown that injecting concentrated salt solutions into the pre-optic area of the hypothalamus stimulates drinking and the release of ADH from the pituitary gland. Injections of pure water, on the other hand, decrease drinking and ADH production. This demonstrates that the pre-optic osmoreceptors of the hypothalamus have a central role in controlling the body's water balance. Compared with hunger and feeding, where the brain needs a signal, such as leptin reflecting the body's energy reserves, we do not have to search for an indicator of water balance that signals the brain when to start drinking. This is because the pre-optic neurons of the hypothalamus react to water loss in the same way as all the other cells of the body.

Hypovolemic thirst

Thirst can also be produced by a sudden and dramatic loss of water from the extracellular compartment. This can be caused by haemorrhage (bleeding) through cuts or internal damage, or perhaps heavy menstrual flow. Besides water, dissolved salts are also lost. This is known as 'hypovolemic (low volume) thirst', and involves additional regulatory systems to those described above.

Low blood volume stimulates specialized pressure receptors, known as baroreceptors, in the walls of blood vessels. These send messages to the hypothalamus to stimulate drinking behaviour and to increase the release of ADH. Reductions in blood volume also stimulate the kidneys directly to release the hormone, renin, which is the starting point for a cascade of chemical events. Renin converts a large protein found in the blood, angiotensinogen, into angiotensin I. This in turn is rapidly converted into angiotensin II, which acts to constrict (narrow) blood vessels and therefore increases blood pressure. Angiotensin II also sustains the release of ADH, possibly by a direct action on the pre-optic area of the hypothalamus. Injection of angiotensin II into the pre-optic area also stimulates drinking behaviour, even in rats that have not been deprived of water (Epstein *et al.* 1970).

Aldosterone

Another control system also comes into play to deal with hypovolemic thirst. When salt levels fall, the cortex of the adrenal gland, which lies just above the kidneys, releases yet another hormone – aldosterone. This stimulates the kidneys to re-absorb salt from the urine, so together ADH and aldosterone reduce water and salt loss from the kidneys and help restore balance in the extracellular water compartment. It has been noted that hypovolemic thirst is associated with an increased appetite for salty foods, and this may be stimulated through the effects of aldosterone.

Acetylcholine and the cholinergic theory of drinking

Brain structures involved in thirst and the regulation of drinking focus on the pre-optic area of the hypothalamus. However, we also know that other brain areas and circuits may be involved. As long ago as 1962, Fisher and Coury found that injecting drugs which increased the activity of the neurotransmitter, acetylcholine, could produce drinking in non-deprived rats. The effective sites included the pre-optic area, but also covered areas in the limbic system (see p. 446). They concluded that drinking was controlled by a circuit of pathways within the limbic system that used acetylcholine as a neurotransmitter, and this has become known as the 'cholinergic theory of drinking'.

When do we drink?

Like eating, drinking usually anticipates states of thirst and, in fact, drinking is closely associated with meals; taking in water with food prevents sudden changes in osmotic pressure in the body, as the water dilutes the salts in the food. Drinking is also similar to hunger in that we often drink when there is no obvious physiological reason for it, such as an evening in the pub. So drinking, like eating, cannot always be explained using a simple homeostatic model.

Why can't we explain this kind of behaviour using the homeostatic model?

Your eating and drinking habits

Think about your own eating and drinking habits and whether these could be explained by the homeostatic model and the role of hypothalamic centres in feeding and drinking. Answer the following questions:

- When was the last time that you felt either very hungry or very thirsty? How often does this happen? Do you eat only when you feel hungry or do you tend to follow a set pattern?

- Have you eaten anything in the last few hours that you didn't really need?
- What was attractive about it – its look, its taste, its smell?
- If you eat chocolate, do you eat it for dietary reasons or because of the taste?
- Do you ever drink when you aren't thirsty? If so, why do you do this?

(AO2) Evaluation
the role of brain structures in thirst

- **Role of the hypothalamus** – Research studies are consistent in supporting a key role for the pre-optic area of the hypothalamus in controlling thirst and drinking behaviour. Injections of salt solutions into this area stimulate drinking, while injections of pure water stop drinking.

- **Simpler control mechanisms** – Control of drinking is more straightforward than control of feeding. Since only one substance – water – is involved, the brain mechanisms and the signals they respond to are better understood for thirst and drinking behaviour than for appetite and feeding behaviour.

- **Hypovolemic thirst** – Hormonal systems involved in hypovolemic thirst are more complicated than the control of osmotic thirst by the pre-optic area of the hypothalamus.

- **Role of acetylcholine as a neurotransmitter** – There is evidence that brain mechanisms associated with thirst and drinking are not limited to the hypothalamus, but also include circuits in the brain that use acetylcholine as a neurotransmitter.

- **Difficulty in generalizing from non-human animals** – Much of the work on brain mechanisms of thirst has involved non-human animals, so generalizations have to made with caution.

Brain structures and electrical self-stimulation of the brain

One of the simplest ideas behind motivated behaviour is that animals, including humans, are strongly motivated by rewards. From Skinner's rats pressing levers in Skinner boxes to obtain pellets of food, to people working overtime to earn more money, rewards are basic to many behaviours. An important contribution to our understanding of motivation would be if we could identify brain structures or pathways that were activated by rewarding stimuli.

In 1954, James Olds and Peter Milner were carrying out some studies on electrical stimulation of the brain in rats. They noticed that with one particular brain site, the rat would always move to the area of the cage where it was stimulated, as though the stimulation was rewarding. The stimulating electrode turned out to be in the septal area, which is part of the limbic system (see p. 446) and, in fact, it was not even the spot they had been aiming for! They then set up a Skinner box so that a rat could press the lever itself to deliver electric stimulation to the same area, and found that the animal would press the lever rapidly (up to 500 presses per minute) for hours on end. They called this phenomenon rewarding 'electrical self-stimulation of the brain' (ESB).

It turned out that electrical stimulation in many areas of the brain, including the septal area, amygdala and hypothalamus, led to high rates of ESB. It was clearly powerfully rewarding because hungry rats preferred it to feeding, and thirsty rats would press for ESB rather than drinking. Another feature was that ESB did not extinguish (see p. 441) in the way that hungry or thirsty rats eventually stop eating and drinking. Even though there was no obvious external reward, animals would continue to press the bar, sometimes only stopping when exhausted. This suggested that ESB was very different to everyday rewards, such as food and water, which can lead to highly motivated behaviour, but behaviour that stops when the animal is full or satiated.

Median forebrain bundle

Following up on the work of Olds and Milner, it turned out that one particular pathway in the brain contained most of the stimulation sites that led to high rates of ESB. This was the 'median forebrain bundle' (MFB), which is a network of nerve fibres in the brain, running through structures such as the septal area and the hypothalamus. The MFB has become known as the 'reward pathway' of the brain.

It seems, then, that the brain has a reward system, which gives rise to feelings of pleasure and satisfaction when stimulated. What may be happening is that whenever animals, including humans, experience pleasure, then the MFB is activated. The particular source of pleasure – eating when hungry, drinking, sex, alcohol, etc. – arouses its own control systems in the brain (such as the ventromedial and lateral hypothalamus for hunger), but also arouses the reward pathways of the MFB. The feelings of pleasure ensure that the behaviour is learned and repeated.

But what would happen if the reward pathways were activated independently of primary drives and rewards such as food and drink? As the activation is pleasurable, whatever led to it would be repeated, and since it was not linked to a primary drive such as hunger, it would not satiate as usually happens when we eat. This could be what is happening with ESB. The stimulating electrode is placed directly into the reward pathways, producing activity that is usually associated with feeding or drinking, but which in this case is independent of any other behaviour. As there is nothing to satiate, the behaviour is purely pleasurable and continues for as long as the animal has the strength to continue to press the bar.

Reward pathways and addictive behaviour

Reward pathways in the brain may also be involved in some of the most persistent human motivations – those involved in addictive behaviours. The neurons that make up the MFB use noradrenaline and especially dopamine as neurotransmitters, and some of the most potent drugs of abuse, such as ecstasy and cocaine, increase the activity of these neurotransmitters. If these drugs activate the reward systems of the brain directly, it would explain their pleasurable effects and the difficulty of breaking the habit. It also seems that other addictive drugs, such as heroin, indirectly increase dopamine activity in the brain's reward systems.

Although ESB is an artificial phenomenon, it has led to the discovery of reward pathways in the brain. These can provide a physiological explanation in terms of brain mechanisms for a range of motivated behaviours in animals and humans.

Evaluation
brain structures and ESB

- **Artificiality of ESB** – ESB is not an example of a naturally motivated behaviour. It is entirely artificial and seen only under experimental conditions, so using it to explain 'natural' behaviours, such as food seeking when hungry, must be done cautiously.

- **Characteristics of ESB** – ESB does not extinguish or satiate in the same way as natural behaviours do (for example, feeding when hungry or drinking when thirsty). Another difference is that ESB is a more powerful reward than food when hungry or water when thirsty, as is shown by the observation that when given the choice, hungry or thirsty animals prefer to press for ESB rather than eat or drink.

continued on next page

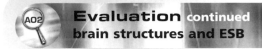
● *Reward pathways* – Research studies show that the brain pathways involved in ESB use neurotransmitters such as noradrenaline and dopamine. The same neurotransmitters are also stimulated by drugs of abuse such as ecstasy and cocaine; activation of reward pathways may

therefore explain the addictive properties of these drugs.

● *Difficulty in generalizing from non-human animals* – Almost all experimental studies of ESB have used non-human animals. Although we know that the same pathways exist in the human brain, there is only limited evidence for ESB in humans, so we have to be careful in explaining human behaviours, such as drug-taking, in terms of reward pathways in the brain.

✓ CHECK YOUR UNDERSTANDING

Check your understanding of the role of brain structures in motivational states by answering these questions. Try to do this from memory at first. You can check your answers by looking back through this first topic.

1 What is 'homeostasis'?

2 What do VMH and LH stand for?

3 Briefly describe the consequences of damage to the VMH and the LH.

4 In 100 words, outline the dual-centre model of feeding regulation.

5 Identify and give a brief account of three critical (AO2) points relating to the role of brain structures in hunger.

6 In 100 words, briefly describe the differences between hypovolemic and osmotic thirst.

7 What are osmoreceptors and where are they found?

8 Name two hormones involved in the regulation of drinking.

9 Outline the characteristics of ESB in 100 words.

10 Write 100 words outlining the main differences between ESB and natural everyday rewards.

REVISION SUMMARY

Having covered this topic you should be able to:

✓ provide a detailed description of the concept of homeostasis

✓ describe and evaluate theories relating to the role of brain structures (such as the hypothalamus) in hunger

✓ describe and evaluate research studies into the role of brain structures in hunger

✓ describe and evaluate theories relating to the role of brain structures (such as the hypothalamus) in thirst

✓ describe and evaluate research studies into the role of brain structures in thirst.

Below are some **possible examination questions** set on this topic, along with hints to help you understand and approach each question effectively:

1 Discuss research (theories **and/or** studies) relating to the role of brain structures in motivational states (e.g. hunger and thirst). (24 marks)

> Your answer must contain an equal amount of AO1 and AO2 – about 300 words of each. Finding AO2 in physiological psychology questions can be tricky, but you can do it either by evaluating a particular explanation or by looking at alternative explanations. The use of research evidence to support a particular explanation is crucial. Two examples of motivational states have been given in this question. These are given as prompts only – you do not have to cover both hunger and thirst. You could gain full marks if you dealt with one, with two or even with more motivational states. Examples are always taken from the specification. Note that, although the words 'structure' and 'mechanisms' can appear independently, you can include information relating to the latter in questions about the former (i.e. a brain structure works through brain mechanisms).

2 (a) Outline **two** theories relating to the role of brain structures in motivational states. (12 marks)
(b) Evaluate the theories that you have outlined in part (a) using research studies. (12 marks)

> The term 'theory' refers to a collection of related facts. The most straightforward theories would be the dual centre model of hypothalamic control of feeding, the role of the pre-optic area of the hypothalamus in thirst, and the theory that the median forebrain bundle is the reward pathway of the brain. However any *explanation* of the role of brain structures would be counted as a 'theory'. As two theories are required, the AO1 term 'outline' has been used instead of 'describe' (which suggests a greater level of detail). If you outline only one theory, there is a partial performance penalty of 8 marks in AO1. For part (b) you must also evaluate the two theories or incur the partial performance penalty for AO2 as well.

3 (a) Outline **one** theory relating to the role of brain structures in motivational states. (6 marks)
(b) Outline and evaluate research studies related to the theory you have outlined in part (a). (18 marks)

> Here, the AO1 term is again 'outline' because one theory is required for 6 marks, i.e. you have $7\frac{1}{2}$ minutes to write about 150 words on the one theory. In part (b,) there is some AO1 credit for the outline (AO1) of any research studies, but don't be seduced into providing lots of description because only one third of the marks for part (b) are AO1 marks. In this question you are required to evaluate the research studies (*not* the theory). You can do this by considering methodological strengths and limitations as well as what the studies tell us about the theory. Make sure that the studies you select are related to the theory you outlined in part (a).

4 Critically consider research studies relating to the role of brain structures in motivational states. (24 marks)

> The term 'critically consider' is an AO1+AO2 term. The AO1 component is clearly a description of two or more studies. It is probably unlikely that you will be able to describe two studies in sufficient detail for full marks but don't go to the other extreme and try to present a large number of studies, thus sacrificing breadth for depth. The 'depth-breadth trade-off' is an important consideration for good AO1 marks. Similarly, for high AO2 marks you must always elaborate your evaluative points.

5 (a) Describe **one** research study relating to the role of brain structures in motivational states. (6 marks)
(b) Describe **one** theory relating to the role of brain structures in motivational states. (6 marks)
(c) To what extent can motivational states be explained in terms of brain structures? (12 marks)

> The breakdown of this question is intended to help you structure your time effectively. In parts (a) and (b), you should present fairly detailed descriptions of one study and one theory. They do not have to be related to each other. The marks for part (c) are entirely AO2, so you must avoid any *descriptions* of research (theories or studies). Inevitably, you may have to provide some short descriptions for 'scene-setting', but the focus of your answer should be the *effective* use of this material. You might, for example look at research studies that indicate that brain structures are involved and then might consider methodological problems with these studies.

PHYSIOLOGICAL APPROACHES: HOMEOSTATIC DRIVES

As outlined earlier, the concept of homeostatic drives has been highly influential in developing models of motivation, and the best example of this approach is hunger. When we go without food for some hours, we feel hungry, we eat and the hunger drive disappears. The overall picture looks simple, but there are complications, even at this level. Our diet is made up of carbohydrates (such as sugar), proteins, fats and small amounts of trace elements and amino acids, vital to cellular function throughout the body. So, when we feel hungry, what do we feel hungry *for*? The most important need is for the foods we use for energy – carbohydrates and fats in particular. The energy content of these foods is measured in calories, and the best index of calorific intake is body weight, because calories that are taken in but not immediately used in cellular and muscular activity are stored as fat.

One of the most impressive aspects of food intake regulation is that body weight is usually maintained within fairly narrow limits, apart from the dynamic phases of growth and during pregnancy (although in the West, obesity is becoming a widespread problem). So, although we need a balanced diet, research has focused on the regulation of calorific intake and body weight, as described in the body weight set-point theory, outlined in Topic 1.

This regulation seems to anticipate needs because we take meals according to routines that are set by social and cultural patterns (breakfast, lunch and dinner). Again talking about relatively prosperous societies, we do not wait until we feel very hungry before eating. This anticipatory function is a departure from the simple homeostatic model. Meals themselves are usually short lasting, and certainly end before the food can have been fully absorbed with an effect on body weight. This last observation means that although body weight may be important in the long-term regulation of food intake, it does not decide the size of individual meals. There must be other factors that determine food intake in the short term, and these include the presence of food in the mouth, stomach and small intestine. They are jointly referred to as 'peripheral factors'.

Peripheral factors and the short-term regulation of food intake

Presence of food in the mouth

In one study, participants swallowed a rubber tube and could then press a button to inject a liquid diet directly into their stomach. After a few days, they established a regular intake that maintained their body weight, but they found the meals were unsatisfying and wanted to taste and chew the food (Spiegel 1973). This suggests that taste is an important feature, but not strictly necessary for regulation of meal size. This is supported by a study of sham-feeding using rats. Everything the rats swallowed passed out of the oesophagus (via a tube) before it could reach the stomach. The rats ate far more than they normally would, showing that the presence of food in the mouth is not itself sufficient to regulate intake (Antin *et al.* 1975).

Presence of food in the stomach

The study by Spiegel (1973) demonstrates efficient regulation of food injected directly into the stomach. The earliest suggestion that the stomach is central to food intake regulation was by Cannon (Cannon and Washburn 1912). Stomach contractions were recorded in humans, using a balloon swallowed by participants and then inflated so that contractions altered the air pressure of the balloon. The hunger pangs reported by the participants correlated with stomach contractions. Deutsch *et al.* (1978) carried out a more direct study with rats, using a reversible block of the passage between the stomach and the small intestine. Rats with the block in place still ate a normal-sized meal, even though food did not pass beyond the stomach. This demonstrates that signals of fullness (or 'satiety' as it is technically known) travel from the stomach to the brain, probably via the vagus nerve. The system is sensitive to the quality of food, as well as quantity, since the rats would eat smaller amounts of a high-calorie food, but larger amounts of a low-calorie food. Although the presence of food in the stomach is an important part of our regulatory apparatus, there is no evidence that people with substantial parts of their stomach removed, because of ulceration or cancer, suffer problems with food intake. There must, therefore, be alternative regulatory mechanisms.

Cholecystokinin (CCK)

Cholecystokinin (CCK) is a hormone released into the bloodstream from the duodenum (the part of the small intestine immediately following the stomach) in response to the presence of food in the duodenum. Injections of CCK have been found to reduce meal size in both rats and humans (Antin *et al.* 1978, Pi-Sunyer *et al.* 1982), and so it has been put forward as a satiety hormone. Intriguingly, CCK also functions as a synaptic neurotransmitter in the brain, and so it is tempting to see its effect on satiety and meal size as involving brain pathways. However, there is no direct evidence for this and it is more likely that CCK operates together with other factors such as the presence of food in the stomach (McHugh and Moran 1985).

The taste of food in the mouth, and the presence of food in the stomach and small intestine, all contribute in varying degrees to the regulation of food intake. After passing through the gastro-intestinal system, the products of digestion enter into the blood supply.

Homeostatic drive theory and brain structures

The basis of homeostatic drive theory is that a variety of signals from the body (such as the short-term and long-term control systems outlined above) keep the

brain informed about the physiological needs of the body. Topic 1 examined the role of brain structures in motivational states such as hunger. Signals from the peripheral bodily mechanisms described above, such as neural impulses from the mouth and stomach or CCK released into the bloodstream, travel to the brain where they influence brain structures such as the feeding and satiety centres in the hypothalamus. Homeostatic drive theory therefore involves both brain structures and peripheral mechanisms, but is essentially a fairly straightforward model of motivated behaviour (see Fig. 14.1 on p. 430).

Evaluation
homeostatic drive theory

- **Research into homeostatic drive theory** – By now, many thousands of research studies have uncovered the role of brain mechanisms and peripheral factors in the control of homeostatic drives such as hunger. Homeostatic drive theory provides a simple model of motivation that can account for much of the behaviour of non-human animals because hunger and thirst are key motivational states for them.

- **Difficulty in generalizing from non-human animals** – However, since most of these studies have been carried out on non-human animals, we have to be careful in generalizing the findings to humans.

- **Psychological motivations** – Although homeostatic drives are important, human behaviour involves more complex psychological motivations that cannot be explained using homeostatic drive theory.

- **When and how humans eat** – The simple view of homeostatic drive theory that behaviour is based on tissue need does not account for the fact that in humans meals usually anticipate need and are affected by social factors as well as the attractiveness of food.

- **Importance of sensory factors** – Rats will eat more of a pleasant-tasting new food (such as chocolate biscuits) and put on weight, showing that homeostasis can be overridden by sensory factors (taste) (Wickens 2000). Similarly, children will eat more Smarties if they are of different colours than if they are all the same colour (Rolls *et al.* 1982). This goes against homeostatic drive theory because it suggests that we are influenced by the characteristics of the food we eat and not just by our physiological needs.

- **Explaining excess food intake** – Increasing levels of obesity in the Western world suggest that food intake in humans is not entirely regulated by homeostatic drives. This fits with the two points above: the sight and taste of food influence our behaviour, and these can override physiological needs.

PSYCHOLOGICAL APPROACHES TO EXPLAINING MOTIVATION

The satisfaction of primary physiological drives such as hunger is probably the best-known example of motivated behaviour. In its simplest form, it applies to the satisfaction of physiological needs only. Humans lead complicated lives, though, full of complex psychological motivations, and a number of psychological theories have been developed to account for these.

Non-homeostatic drives and optimal arousal theory

Behaviour is not always obviously related to homeostasis, even in non-human animals. Monkeys prefer to watch a roomful of other monkeys rather than an empty room, and will do manipulative puzzles endlessly with no obvious external reward (Hebb 1958). Rats will learn to press the bar in a Skinner box (see p. 660) just to switch on a light (Tapp 1969). If we call

each of these behaviours a drive, we end up with long lists – curiosity, manipulative, exploratory drives, etc. – which do not really explain the behaviour. Rats run around a maze because they have an exploratory drive. How do we know? Because they run around mazes – the argument is totally circular.

To break out of this circularity, the concept of 'optimal arousal level' was introduced. This states that a major motivation for animals is to maintain an optimal level of arousal, which is neither too high nor too low. If they are under-aroused, they will seek stimulation to increase levels – for instance, by doing puzzles, exploring or playing. If they are over-aroused, they will avoid stimulation (Fowler 1965). See the panel below for a discussion of the work of Marvin Zuckerman, exploring aspects of the optimal arousal theory in relation to human motivation and personality.

Zuckerman's research into 'sensation seeking'

Although optimal arousal theory ignores the cognitive aspects of behaviour, and 'arousal' itself is hard to define precisely, it has been used to account for certain types of human personality. Marvin Zuckerman has developed a scale to assess an important personality characteristic which he called 'sensation seeking'. Aspects of sensation seeking include a liking for adventure and thrill seeking, and a very low boredom threshold. People high on the sensation-seeking scale look for ways to increase their arousal levels because their optimal arousal level is higher than in other people, so they are more motivated to take part in risky sports and other activities (Zuckerman 1994).

Zuckerman has also shown that this preference for arousing situations and stimuli extends to art and music. In one study, Zuckerman and colleagues (1993) asked participants to rate a series of paintings on the dimension of complexity. Participants who scored high on sensation seeking preferred more complex paintings, especially abstract ones, to placid pastoral scenes. Zuckerman argues that abstract paintings contain uncertainty and ambiguity, and because of this are more arousing than simple representational scenes.

Do people who take part in extreme sports have a high optimal arousal level?

Thus, optimal arousal theory can be a useful way of understanding some particular types of human personality and motivation.

A02 Evaluation
optimal arousal theory

- **A homeostatic approach** – This approach is similar to homeostatic drive theory, with animals seeking to maintain a constant level of arousal, and so it can explain, for example, bored monkeys doing puzzles.

- **Too simplistic?** – The theory is very general and even in non-human animals clearly ignores the particular demands of each situation. For instance, rats do not explore only out of curiosity. Tolman (1948) was the first to suggest that rats build a 'cognitive map' while they explore a maze. We now know that this 'spatial map' of the world is located in the hippocampus of the limbic system (O'Keefe and Nadel 1978). It seems clear that animals explore in order to find out about their environment, i.e. exploration has a cognitive function related to survival, and to account for it simply in terms of optimal arousal level overlooks its main purpose.

- **Inadequate explanation for human behaviour?** – Children play with toys. This also seems to fit optimal arousal theory because it does not appear to have any obvious purpose. But, again, it can be fitted into a picture of motor and cognitive development: the child is practising and learning skills that will be needed later in life (see, for instance, Piaget's stages of play and its role in cognitive development in Unit 18). To view play simply in general terms of arousal level ignores its most important aspects.

- **Is there a single 'arousal system' at all?** – The concept of 'arousal' itself has been questioned. Although the brain contains a network of neurons in the brainstem, known as the 'reticular activating system' (RAS), which was thought to be the main arousal system of the brain, we now know that activation and arousal of the brain involve many structures and pathways. Therefore the idea of a single 'arousal' system in the brain has largely been disregarded. However, optimal arousal theory has been used in models of some aspects of personality such as sensation seeking (see Zuckerman's research, above).

Expectancy theory

As mentioned earlier, the sight, smell and taste of food are important in deciding what we eat. On the whole, children and rats prefer chocolate biscuits to muesli, and rats will press bars for hours to obtain a non-nutritious but sweet-tasting saccharine solution (Valenstein 1967). Sight, smell and taste are capable of producing goal-directed behaviour, even though they do not lead to a balanced diet, while saccharine is rewarding because it has a sweet taste, even though it doesn't satisfy the primary drive of hunger.

Incentives

Stimuli, such as taste and smell, that can trigger goal-directed behaviour without requiring an internal physiological need for them are called 'incentives' and, as we shall see, play the central role in expectancy models of motivation.

Expectancy models are important in that they emphasize the ability of stimuli to 'pull' or elicit behaviour, rather than seeing behaviour as 'pushed' or driven by internal bodily states. Unfortunately, these models can be hard to disentangle from conventional drive-reduction approaches. Going to work is often quoted as an example of an expectancy approach: we go because work is there and we 'expect' certain rewards that then reinforce going to work. But some classic incentive studies, such as monkeys doing puzzles or rats pressing bars to turn lights on, do not involve clear-cut rewards. In any case, it is difficult to associate the 'reward' of a light coming on with a pay packet at the end of the week or rapid career progress. Complex human behaviours would seem to require complicated models, such as Maslow's hierarchy of needs which is discussed later in this section.

The most convincing models of the incentive or expectancy approach to motivation are based in non-human animals (Bolles 1967). The fundamental idea is that neutral stimuli acquire arousing and rewarding properties by association with primary rewards such as food. So the sight, taste and smell of food become 'incentives' through their association with food itself; exposure to the sight and smell of food leads to the expectation of the primary reward of food.

Persistence of responses

One feature of some incentive stimuli is that the behaviour does not 'extinguish' or fade away easily. If a rat is pressing a bar for nutritious food, responding reduces as the hunger drive is satisfied. If pressing is not rewarded with food, it extinguishes. Responding for saccharine does not reduce hunger, yet it can be very persistent (Valenstein 1967). One explanation of this is that incentives activate the reward pathways of the brain, described in the previous topic, producing powerful responses that do not extinguish.

Evaluation
incentive and expectancy approaches

- *Ability to explain human behaviour* – Expectancy theory can be used to explain human behaviours only in a very general way; we have learned from experience that going to work produces rewards such as wages and self-esteem, so the incentive of reward explains the motivation for going to work.

It still does not explain apparently 'pointless' behaviour, such as monkeys doing wire puzzles, or teenagers playing computer games.

- *Behaviour in non-human animals* – Systematic studies in non-human animals have shown how expectancy theory can explain responding for rewards that do not satisfy primary drives and so do not fall within classical homeostatic drive theory. But generalization to complex human motivations is almost impossible.

Maslow's hierarchy of needs

Maslow (1987) proposed that there are two sets of human needs. One set concerns basic survival needs such as those related to homeostasis, physiological needs and physical safety. The second set concerns 'self-actualization' – the realization of an individual's full potential, especially in relation to creativity and the use of intellect.

Maslow arranged the various needs in a hierarchy (see Fig. 14.3) because he stated that the basic survival needs had to be satisfied before you could ascend the hierarchy and begin to satisfy creative and intellectual drives. Also, the higher up the hierarchy you go, the more difficult it is to satisfy the needs, as they become psychological rather than physiological, and long term rather than short term. In fact, Maslow would argue that many of us never reach our full human potential, or self-actualize, and since his examples of successful self-actualizers include Einstein and Abraham Lincoln, this is not too surprising!

He associates 'peak experiences' with self-actualization. These are the moments when individuals are totally lost in themselves and are oblivious to other needs or to other people. Such moments are usually confined to the activity of the moment (work, sport, childbirth, etc.) and are difficult to reach consistently.

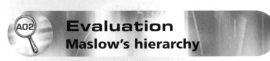

Self-actualization	Realizing one's full potential; 'peak experiences' and self-fulfilment.
Aesthetic needs	Love of beauty in art and nature, and the need for symmetry and order.
Cognitive needs	Desire for knowledge and understanding and the search for meaning.
Esteem needs	Desire for the respect of others and the need for self-respect through achievement and competence.
Love and belonging	Wish to be accepted and to belong, to affiliate with groups, to give and receive love.
Safety needs	Need to feel safe and secure from physical danger and anxieties.
Physiological needs	The basic drives of hunger, thirst, sex, sleep, and so on.

Figure 14.3 >> *Maslow's hierarchy of human needs*

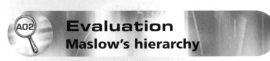

> ### A C T I V I T Y
>
> ## Your own motivation
>
> Pause for a moment to reflect on motivation in relation to your own life. Use the following questions to guide you:
>
> - Why are you studying A-levels?
> - Why are you studying psychology?
> - Are you motivated by short-term or long-term goals? Do you have a long-term plan that motivates you?

(AO2) Evaluation
Maslow's hierarchy

- ***Human emphasis*** – Maslow's theory has a uniquely human emphasis; only humans can self-actualize or engage in high-level cognitive and aesthetic activities. In this way, it is an advance on the largely animal-based physiological and reward-based models of motivation.

- ***A framework for discussion and understanding*** – Maslow's theory provides a framework for discussing the richness and complexity of human motivation that goes beyond homeostatic models.

It also provides the background to some humanistic approaches to understanding normal and abnormal behaviour.

- ***Are needs hierarchical?*** – There is no evidence that the needs operate as a strict hierarchy. In fact, it is a cliché that great artists like Van Gogh would paint rather than eat or earn the money to eat, and some activities such as pot-holing or mountain-climbing deliberately flirt with risk and danger.

- ***Lack of research evidence*** – There is little direct research evidence for the model; indeed, it is hard to imagine how one would collect such evidence.

A COMBINED APPROACH: HULL'S DRIVE-REDUCTION THEORY

Hull (1943) produced one of the grandest theories in the whole of psychology: a combination of physiological homeostatic drives (as described above) and psychological principles of learning, based on drive-reduction. His central belief is that all behaviour is motivated, and that all motivation originates in the satisfaction of homeostatic drives such as hunger, thirst and temperature control. Homeostatic drives are reduced by the appropriate stimulus (e.g. food, water or warmth). These stimuli serve to reinforce the behaviour that led to them, and the animal learns the behaviour because it is reinforced. Thus Hull's is a theory of motivation and learning through drive-reduction.

An obvious question is how such a theory could explain complex human behaviour. This requires the introduction of 'secondary reinforcers'. Imagine for a moment a baby being fed by its mother. The food she provides satisfies the homeostatic drive of hunger and is referred to as a 'primary reinforcer'. However, because of the constant association of the mother with food, she acquires reinforcing properties of her own, and becomes a secondary reinforcer to the baby. The child then learns to behave in ways that bring contact with the secondary reinforcer, i.e. Mum. It is then just a short step to seeing the mother's approval as an important reinforcer for behaviour. Although it may now seem silly to suggest that Alexander the Great's motivation for conquering the known world was a way of seeking his mother's approval, this view of motivation was taken seriously by psychologists for many years, and is still useful in the systematic study of learning in non-human animals.

Evaluation
Hull and drive-reduction

● **Role of secondary reinforcement** – Secondary reinforcement can be used to explain the research findings on expectation and incentive outlined above. Animals respond for rewards that do not satisfy primary drives (e.g. saccharine) because aspects of them, such as taste or smell, have in the past been associated with primary rewards such as nutritious food.

● **Over-emphasis on drive-reduction** – A weakness of Hull's theory is that he failed to address the complexity of human motivations (virtually all his work was undertaken on rats), placing too much emphasis on homeostatic drives and too little on higher cognitive processes. His prediction was that animals do not learn unless there are drives that are reduced through reinforcement. Rats will not learn their way through a maze unless they are, for instance, hungry and find food at the end. However, as early as 1932, Tolman had shown that rats learn mazes by developing cognitive maps without drive-reduction or reinforcement (Tolman 1948). We also now know that spatial learning in general is a highly developed cognitive ability in most animals and does not depend on drives and reinforcements (Olton 1976).

● **Limited view of psychological aspects** – Although Hull's is a combined approach, it had a strictly limited view of the psychological aspects of motivation. At the time he was working, psychology was dominated by Skinner's behaviourism, and cognitive psychology did not yet exist as a discipline. An ideal model of motivation would combine the complex psychological approach of Maslow with a study of underlying physiological and brain mechanisms, and we have not yet achieved this.

✓ CHECK YOUR UNDERSTANDING

Check your understanding of theories of motivation by answering these questions from memory. You can check your answers by looking back through Topic 2.

1 Name two peripheral factors involved in short-term regulation of food intake.

2 Write a 100-word précis of the motivational sequence involved in homeostatic drive theory.

3 Identify and give a brief account of four critical (AO2) points relating to homeostatic drive theory.

4 In 100 words, outline one behaviour that is better explained by optimal arousal theory than by homeostatic drive theory, and briefly describe one limitation of optimal arousal theory.

5 Outline the way incentives can lead to expectancies, and give one limitation of expectancy theory in 100 words.

6 Identify and give a brief account of two critical (AO2) points relating to Maslow's hierarchy of needs as an explanation of human motivation.

7 Write 150 words outlining the role of primary and secondary reinforcers in Hull's drive-reduction theory of motivation.

8 Identify and give a brief account of two critical (AO2) points relating to Hull's drive-reduction theory of motivation.

REVISION SUMMARY

Having covered this topic you should be able to describe and evaluate:

✓ homeostatic drive theory as a physiological model of motivation

✓ psychological models of motivation, including expectancy theory and the psychological approach of Maslow

✓ the drive-reduction theory of Hull as a combined physiological/psychological approach to motivation.

Below are some **possible examination questions** set on this topic, along with hints to help you understand and approach each question effectively:

1 (a) Outline and evaluate **one** physiological approach to explaining motivation (e.g. homeostatic drive theory). (12 marks)

(b) Outline and evaluate **one** psychological approach to explaining motivation (e.g. expectancy theory). (12 marks)

Parted questions such as this require very careful reading and even more careful planning. Clearly, you are required to write about two approaches, but one of these must be a physiological approach and the other a psychological approach of motivation. Note that the question does not ask for theories, but merely approaches. Second, you are asked to *outline* these two approaches. This involves a summary description rather than the more detailed description implied by terms such as 'describe'. Finally, you are also asked to evaluate your chosen approaches, the AO2 component of this question.

2 Critically consider **one** combined physiological/psychological approach to explaining motivation. (24 marks)

The specification names a third kind of approach to explaining motivation – those that combine physiological and psychological explanations. The example given in the specification is drive-reduction theory. Such examples are often included in exam questions as a prompt to what might form the basis of your answer. The problem is that some candidates feel such examples are *requirements* (which they aren't). In order to produce the right amount of material it helps to structure your answer. One way to do this is to divide your answer into 100-word 'chunks'. Six chunks would be sufficient for a good essay (as long as all of the material is focused on the question). Three chunks should be AO1 and three chunks AO2. An alternative approach is to produce 6 chunks, each with some AO1 and some AO2.

3 Discuss physiological approaches to explaining motivation. (24 marks)

This more general question poses a particular problem. You may know too much and be tempted to stuff it all into your 30 minutes. The consequence is that either you end up with too much AO1 content and too little AO2, or you provide many points of AO1 and AO2, but these lack detail and elaboration, both of which are important criteria for AO1 and AO2. The skill of selection is very important for good marks so limit yourself to doing a few things well rather than trying to display the breadth of your knowledge. You can use alternative approaches/theories as a form of commentary as long as such commentary is *sustained*.

4 Discuss **two or more** approaches to explaining motivation. (24 marks)

The question allows for 'two or more' approaches, but as you only have 30 minutes, two is usually enough. In 30 minutes, you would probably be able to write 600 words, so that's 300 on each approach, and that would be further divided into 150 words of AO1 and 150 words of AO2. If you cannot write that much for each theory, this question gives you the option of including a third approach. Do not waste valuable time on unnecessary introductions or conclusions. These often add little to the essay and time would be better spent plunging straight in.

5 (a) Discuss **one or more** theory related to the role of brain structures (e.g. hypothalamus) in motivational states. (12 marks)

(b) Discuss **one or more** psychological approach (e.g. expectancy theory) to explaining motivation. (12 marks)

This question illustrates the fact that it is 'legitimate' to combine topics from the same unit. So part (a) of this question relates to Topic 1 of this unit whereas part (b) relates to Topic 2. In both cases the phrase 'one or more' tells you that you can gain full marks if you only cover one theory or approach. However, if you feel that you cannot write enough on one explanation, you can opt for greater breadth and describe more than one explanation. This is probably unlikely because you have only $7\frac{1}{2}$ minutes to describe each theory/approach. It helps to practice producing $7\frac{1}{2}$-minute versions, as well as 15-minute versions (and even 3-minute versions!) of each theory before the exam.

WHAT IS EMOTION?

We all experience emotions and we all know what they are – fear, anger, love, sorrow, etc. We can work out that they have different aspects. We feel angry, we act angrily and our arousal level goes up – emotions involve subjective experience (the 'feeling'), behaviour and physiological changes. But can you define 'emotion'? Kleinginna and Kleinginna (1981) reviewed a variety of definitions and came up with a synthesis:

> << Emotion is a complex set of interactions among subjective and objective factors, mediated by neural (nervous) and hormonal systems which can (a) give rise to feelings of arousal, pleasure/displeasure; (b) generate cognitive processes; (c) activate widespread physiological adjustments to the arousal conditions; and (d) lead to behaviour that is often, but not always, expressive, goal-directed, and adaptive. >>

Besides being so general and therefore of not much practical use, there are problems in using this definition to compare, for example, anger and sorrow. Anger fits the definition quite well but does sorrow involve 'widespread physiological adjustments', and does it lead to behaviour that may be goal-directed and adaptive? Arnold (1960) suggested a more practical sequence of events in emotional situations:

- *perception* of the situation

- *appraisal* – an assessment of the situation as beneficial or potentially harmful

- *emotion* – a 'felt' tendency towards a beneficial stimulus or away from a harmful stimulus

- *expression* – physiological changes in the body associated with the emotion

- *action* – behavioural approach or withdrawal.

To make sense of research into emotion, psychologists have sensibly left the problem of a concise definition on the sidelines, and have concentrated on other, clearer questions. These involve the relationships between the subjective experience or feeling, the behaviour associated with the emotion along with physiological changes in the body, cognitive processes, such as perception and appraisal, and brain structures associated with emotion. We will start by looking at the long tradition of research investigating the role of brain structures.

We all know what emotion is – even if it is hard to define

THE ROLE OF BRAIN STRUCTURES IN EMOTIONAL BEHAVIOUR AND EXPERIENCE

As long ago as the 1920s and 1930s, lesion and stimulation studies in non-human animals had shown that extreme emotions, such as rage and aggression, were controlled from brain structures. Stimulation in sites such as the midbrain, hypothalamus and thalamus could produce threat and attack behaviour in cats (reviewed in Flynn 1976). Removal of the cerebral cortex led to 'decorticate rage', where aggressive behaviour was easily triggered by the mildest stimulus, showing that the behaviour was *organized* by systems outside the cortex, but that cortical structures *controlled* whether or not it was exhibited.

Kluver and Bucy demonstrated one of the most dramatic syndromes in 1939. They removed the temporal lobes in Rhesus monkeys and produced a pattern of behaviour that included extreme placidity (reduced fear and aggression), over-sexuality and 'orality' (a tendency to place everything they picked up in their mouths). The temporal lobes contain various structures, but follow-up work showed conclusively that the critical one for the Kluver-Bucy syndrome was the amygdala.

Eventually, Papez (1937) proposed a systematic model of brain structures and emotion. Papez was influenced by the ideas of Cannon and Bard (see p. 448) on the role of the hypothalamus in emotional expression (the observed behavioural and physiological signs of emotion) and their finding that the cortex was responsible for the subjective experience (emotional 'feeling'). Papez was also impressed by the heightened emotional behaviour of people with rabies (typically increased anger and rage); rabies is an infection that damages the hippocampus in particular.

Papez proposed that while the hypothalamus was responsible for emotional expression, emotional feeling involved the limbic system. This is a network of structures in the forebrain linked by neural pathways. It includes the hypothalamus, thalamus, hippocampus, septum and cingulate cortex (see Fig. 14.4). The amygdala has extensive connections with the limbic system and is often included with it (see panel below).

MacLean (1949) developed Papez's model, using the limbic system as one of three major divisions of the brain. The brainstem (the 'reptilian' brain according to MacLean) was responsible for essential physiological functions; the limbic brain (the 'old mammalian' brain) was involved in emotional feeling and behaviour; while the 'new mammalian' cortex looked after higher cognitive functions. The Papez-MacLean model of emotion has been very influential, with the limbic system still referred to as our emotional or 'feeling' system. However, while many studies have confirmed that damage or stimulation of limbic system structures affects emotions, there are many problems.

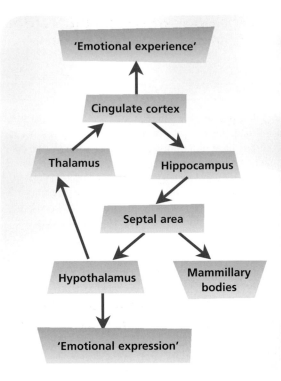

Figure 14.4 >> *The limbic system (formerly the Papez circuit)*

The amygdala and emotion

The Papez-Maclean limbic model of emotion has been popular for many years. More recently, the modern scanning techniques, described in Unit 12, have enabled researchers to look more closely at individual structures of the limbic system. In particular, the amygdala has become a focus for investigation. Research studies have shown that neuronal activity in the amygdala of monkeys and humans is selectively responsive to facial expressions such as anger, fear and happiness.

Morris *et al.* (1996) used human participants and PET scanning to assess amygdala activity in response to fearful or happy faces. They found that amygdala activity was selectively responsive to fearful faces, increasing with more intense expressions. In general, the amygdala is now seen as a central component of an emotion-processing system, involving other limbic structures and the frontal cortex. It has even been suggested that in some psychological disorders, such as psychopathy where emotional reactions are abnormal or totally absent, the amygdala may have been damaged during development of the brain (Mitchell and Blair 2000).

Evaluation
the limbic model of emotion

● *Research mainly on non-human animals* – Most of the experimental work has been done on non-human animals and therefore can only study emotional expression, i.e. the outward signs of emotion. They cannot be used to investigate emotional feeling, which is a vital part of the human experience of emotion.

● *Limited range of emotions* – As animals are used, the range of emotions studied is severely limited, usually to the most dramatic ones such as rage, fear and aggression.

● *Difficulty of generalizing* – The human brain is more highly evolved and complex than the brains of rats, cats and even monkeys. While our limbic system is certainly involved in emotion, it is unjustified to generalize directly from studies with non-human animals.

A2 Physiological Psychology

Applications of the limbic model of emotion: psychosurgery

Despite the problems of extrapolating to humans, the work of Papez, MacLean and others has been used to justify the use of brain surgery to treat so-called emotional disorders in humans. Up until the 1970s, lesions to the amygdala were used to try and reduce aggressive behaviour in adults and even children (Kiloh *et al.* 1974). Even more popular, in the 1940s, was the frontal lobotomy used to treat schizophrenia. Frontal lobe lesions had been shown to 'calm' chimpanzees, and so the frontal lobotomy was introduced as a method of tranquillizing schizophrenic patients, i.e. making them more manageable. There is no evidence that the operation improved the specific symptoms of schizophrenia and it largely disappeared, once the anti-psychotic drugs came into use in the 1950s.

As the ethical climate surrounding psychology and psychiatry changed during the 1960s and 1970s, it became clear that performing psychosurgery on either adults or children, who were often unable to give informed consent, was completely unethical. It was also often unjustified in terms of its effects, i.e. while it might calm patients, there could be side effects such as dramatic changes in personality. Although largely discredited, psychosurgery has not completely disappeared. It is sometimes a treatment of very last resort (after psychological therapies, drugs and electroconvulsive therapy have been tried) for disabling psychiatric conditions such as severe depression or obsessive-compulsive disorder. In 1999, the former child singing star, Lena Zavaroni, died from complications following psychosurgery. She had suffered for years from anorexia and depression.

PHYSIOLOGICAL APPROACHES TO EXPLAINING EMOTIONAL BEHAVIOUR AND EXPERIENCE

Brain structures clearly play a vital role in emotional expression and behaviour. There are, however, other research traditions which have emphasized the body's physiological and arousal systems, and have the advantage of studying emotions in humans. We now turn to these physiological theories.

James-Lange theory of emotion

Working independently, William James (1884) and a Danish psychologist named Lange (1885) put forward similar models of emotion, now known jointly as the 'James-Lange theory'. Their theory of emotion is 'counterintuitive', i.e. contrary to what common sense would suggest. Their idea was that the perception of an emotion-arousing stimulus (e.g. a hungry bear) leads to a behavioural response – probably running away. This response involves changes in the body's physiological systems (increased arousal in the autonomic nervous system and in skeletal muscles). The brain detects these physiological changes and interprets them as the emotion of fear. This can be summed up by the classic phrase – we do not run because we are scared, we are scared because we run (see Fig. 14.5).

Figure 14.5 >>
James-Lange model of emotion

This sequence of events goes against common sense, which would suggest that the perception and appraisal of the bear leads simultaneously to the feeling of fear and the response of running away. What the James-Lange theory is emphasizing is the central role of feedback to the brain of peripheral physiological arousal in generating emotional states, and it is on this particular aspect that it has been most heavily criticized.

Evaluation
the James-Lange theory

Cannon (1929) presented several major criticisms of the James-Lange theory of emotion:

- *Limited patterns of arousal* – If the emotion felt depends upon bodily arousal, then each separate emotion would have to be associated with a different pattern of arousal. Although extreme emotions, such as anger and fear, can be distinguished on the basis of physiological changes, usually such differences between emotions are subtle, if they exist at all.

- *Slowness of physiological changes* – Physiological changes occur too slowly, following perception of the stimulus, to account for the emotional feeling which occurs almost instantaneously.

continued on next page

- *Over-reliance on feedback* – Feedback from the body passes to the brain through the spinal cord. If the spinal cord is damaged, bodily changes and feedback are prevented, so there should be no emotional experience. Cannon quotes a study of a patient with spinal damage by Dana (1921) who reported a normal range of emotions. However, Hohmann (1966) reported on 25 such patients who did experience reductions in feelings of anger and fear, in line with predictions from the James-Lange theory.

- *Why doesn't exercise produce emotion?* – If bodily arousal was necessary and sufficient to produce emotion, then physical exercise or taking stimulant drugs should produce emotional feelings. Running up the stairs is not usually an emotional experience, but work on drugs is less clear cut. Cannon quotes a study by Maranon (1924), who injected participants with the drug adrenaline (known as epinephrine in the USA) which produces physiological arousal. None of the 210 participants felt real emotions, although 29 per cent reported that they felt 'as if' they were afraid or angry. Cannon concluded that the James-Lange theory was contradicted because the induced arousal did not produce real emotions as the theory predicted.

Cannon-Bard theory of emotional behaviour and experience

As an alternative to the James-Lange model, Cannon (1931) proposed a central theory of emotions (see Fig. 14.6). This theory proposes that peripheral arousal is unnecessary for emotional feelings. Incoming stimuli are processed through the thalamus in the brain. Messages then pass from the thalamus upwards to the cortex, which is where conscious emotional experience occurs, and messages are also sent downwards to the hypothalamus and then on to the body, producing physiological arousal and muscular activity. If the spinal cord is damaged, messages cannot reach the body from the brain and arousal does not occur, but messages still ascend from the thalamus to the cortex and so emotional feelings are preserved.

Figure 14.6 >>
Cannon-Bard's model of emotion

A COMBINED PHYSIOLOGICAL/PSYCHOLOGICAL APPROACH: COGNITIVE LABELLING THEORY

The Cannon-Bard theory did anticipate limbic models of emotion (see p. 446), but it also left unresolved the problem of whether bodily arousal played a role in emotional states. Remember that Maranon's participants experienced 'as if' emotional states, so the arousal induced by the injection of adrenaline did not just produce a pattern of generalized arousal, but led to specific reactions, even if they were not 'real' emotions. To try and clarify the situation, Schachter and Singer (1962) performed one of the most famous studies in psychology, one that led them to propose a combined theory of emotion.

Schachter and Singer (1962)

Schachter and Singer (1962) proposed that the debate about the role of arousal in emotional states had largely ignored the important role of cognitive factors. When we feel emotional, it is always *about* something, whether it is an external stimulus or internal thoughts

and memories. A crucial stage in any emotional experience is therefore cognitive appraisal, whereby a stimulus is perceived and evaluated.

Perception of the stimulus may also lead to bodily physiological arousal and, according to Schachter and Singer, it is the combination of arousal and cognitive appraisal that leads to the experience of emotion. For instance, if the sight of a grizzly bear produces the arousal, the cognitive appraisal of the situation leads us to interpret the arousal as the emotion of fear. If your brother dyeing your favourite T-shirt brown produces the arousal, cognitive appraisal leads to the interpretation of the arousal as the emotion of anger.

In Schachter and Singer's view, physiological arousal is necessary for emotional experience, but needs to be labelled or interpreted by cognitive appraisal of the situation. So they follow James and Lange in emphasizing the role of arousal, although they do not

Schachter and Singer's (1962) study of cognitive appraisal of bodily arousal

As in Maranon's study (see p. 448), adrenaline was used to produce a physiological arousal state, but Schachter and Singer deceived their male participants by telling them they were receiving a vitamin supplement called 'suproxin' as part of an experiment on vision. Participants given injections of adrenaline in the experimental group were either:

(a) told to expect the real physiological consequences such as increased heart-rate, dry mouth and palpitations

(b) misinformed about the physical effects of the injection

(c) left ignorant.

The experimental situation was manipulated in two ways:

● In the **'euphoria'** condition, accomplices of the experimenters acted in a manically happy way, flying paper aeroplanes and playing with balls of paper.

● In the **'anger'** condition, an accomplice of the experimenter became progressively more angry as he and the participant filled in a highly personal questionnaire ('Do members of your family require psychiatric care?').

There was also a control group receiving a non-active placebo, but which was otherwise treated in the same way as the experimental groups.

The emotional state of the participants was assessed using observers watching through one-way mirrors and by self-reports after the episodes with the accomplices, i.e. measures of emotional *behaviour* and emotional *experience*. The main predictions were:

● The group told to expect physiological arousal after the injection would have a cognitive explanation of their state, and would not need to explain it using the behaviour of the accomplices. This is similar to Maranon's study and changes in emotion would not be predicted.

● The group given the inactive placebo would not experience bodily arousal and therefore would have no arousal state to explain or label. They should not report changes in emotion.

● The group given adrenaline, but left ignorant as to the effects, would experience an unexplained state of bodily arousal. To interpret it, they would use cognitive appraisal of the environment; if they were with an accomplice behaving euphorically, they should label their state as euphoria, and if they were with an angry accomplice, they should label the state as anger.

The critical predictions Schachter and Singer make are that more emotional change should be seen in the adrenaline-ignorant group than in the placebo group, and that the emotion experienced would depend on which accomplice the participant was with. (The misinformed group was included for control reasons and will not be considered here.)

Schachter and Singer reported results in line with their predictions. Participants given no explanation for the arousing effects of the injection showed more emotional change than the placebo group, reacting more euphorically or angrily, in line with their accomplice's behaviour.

This seems a neat combination of the James-Lange and Cannon-Bard positions. Bodily arousal is necessary but not sufficient for emotion, which depends on an interaction between bodily arousal and the central processes of cognitive appraisal. Therefore, emotion is produced by a combination of peripheral and central factors.

There are, however, several problems with this classic study, summarized in the 'AO2 Evaluation' panel. Schachter and Singer's study does not, therefore, settle the dispute on the role of arousal and cognition in emotion. On the positive side, it did emphasize the major role of cognitive processes such as perception and appraisal.

propose that patterns of arousal vary between emotions. We feel different emotions because of cognitive labelling, and the same pattern of arousal can occur in different emotional states. If we see cognitive appraisal as based in the brain, Schachter and Singer are also emphasizing central mechanisms in emotion, so their position is a combination of the James-Lange bodily arousal theory and the Cannon-Bard central theory.

One clear prediction from the cognitive labelling theory is that if a state of unexplained bodily arousal is induced in participants, they will look around and try to explain it in terms of their environment. If this

cognitive appraisal involves an emotional element, then they will label their state of arousal as an emotional experience. This may sound similar to Maranon's experiment mentioned earlier, but don't forget that those people knew they had been injected with adrenaline, and so had a cognitive interpretation for their arousal state that did not involve emotions. Schachter and Singer intended to induce a completely unexpected and unexplained state of arousal, and then manipulate the environment to try and produce different emotional states. Read the Key research above.

Evaluation
Schachter and Singer's study

- *Emotion or simply imitation?* – The first statistical analyses produced significant differences between adrenaline-ignorant and placebo groups only for the observer ratings in the Anger condition. (Remember that there are four predicted differences, for observer ratings and self-reports in the two conditions of anger and euphoria.) When Schachter and Singer eliminated those participants in the adrenaline-ignorant group who they thought had worked out that the injection was responsible for their state of arousal, they found just one more significant difference, for observer ratings for the Euphoria condition. No significant differences were found for the self-report data on participants'

emotional feelings (observer ratings are of emotional behaviour). Therefore, adrenaline may simply make participants more likely to imitate an accomplice's behaviour, without changing the actual emotional state.

- *Lack of experimental control* – There was no assessment of participants' emotional state before the study, which may have interacted with the experimental manipulations.

- *Lack of validity* – Unexplained bodily arousal is an unusual state in real life, and so is drug-induced arousal. The study is far removed from natural emotions and this reduces its validity.

- *Findings not replicated* – Attempts to replicate the experiment (which for largely ethical reasons have been rare) have been unsuccessful (Marshall and Zimbardo 1979, Maslach 1979).

Explaining your reactions

You are walking home across the park late at night. You hear some footsteps some way behind you, but getting gradually closer. You feel a little scared. Your heart rate increases, the hairs prick up on the back of your neck and your hands start to feel clammy. You look around and see a park keeper coming to tell you that the park closes in ten minutes. You feel relieved, your heart rate falls and you relax.

Explain this sequence of events using:

1 a physiological theory of emotional behaviour and experience

2 a combined physiological/psychological approach to explaining emotional behaviour and experience.

Other researchers

The debate on the role of arousal and cognition in emotion continues, with some researchers taking extreme positions. Lazarus (1984), for instance, defines emotions as depending upon cognitive appraisal of the environment, while Zajonc (1984) proposes that cognitive processes and emotions can be independent. He gives the example of babies who can show emotions, such as fear and disgust, in the absence of high-level cognitive abilities. However, babies are scared or disgusted by something that they have sensed or perceived, and it seems to be splitting hairs to say that their emotions do not depend on some cognitive assessment of their environment.

Dutton and Aron (1974) reported a study they carried out on a suspension bridge study. An attractive female questioned male participants visiting a Canadian canyon about their reactions to the scenery. As part of the study, they were shown an ambiguous picture of a woman and asked to make up a story about her. The level of sexual imagery in the story was scored, and it was found that participants interviewed on a high

suspension bridge included more sexual imagery in their stories than those interviewed on a stable wooden bridge. The interpretation was that the bodily arousal produced by the fear and anxiety of being on the high suspension bridge had intensified the sexual attractiveness of the interviewer, and this was reflected in the stories. The conclusion to this study is that high levels of bodily arousal can intensify emotional states, giving some support to the position of Schachter and Singer (1962) that peripheral bodily arousal plays an important role in emotion.

Strongman (1987) draws the following conclusions:

- Bodily physiological arousal can be important, intensifying emotional experience in states such as fear and anger, but it is not necessary for all emotional experience. Emotions such as sadness occur in the absence of arousal.

- Cognitive processes such as perception and appraisal are basic and necessary for emotion.

- The vast range of human emotions means that simple models of the links between emotion, arousal and cognition are unrealistic.

Check your understanding of emotion by answering these questions. Try to do this from memory at first. You can check your answers by looking back through Topic 3.

1 List the stages of Arnold's model of reactions to emotional situations.

2 Describe two characteristics of the Kluver-Bucy syndrome; damage to which brain structure is responsible for the Kluver-Bucy syndrome?

3 Outline the main limitation of the limbic model of emotion.

4 In 100 words, briefly describe why the James-Lange theory of emotion is counterintuitive.

5 Identify and give a brief account of two critical (AO2) points relating to the James-Lange theory.

6 Summarize Cannon's conclusions concerning the role of peripheral physiological arousal in emotional states in 150 words.

7 Write 100 words outlining Schachter and Singer's views on the roles of cognitive labelling and peripheral arousal in emotional states.

8 Write 100 words summarizing the conclusions from Schachter and Singer's study.

9 Identify and give a brief account of two critical (AO2) points relating to the Schachter and Singer study.

10 Write 50 words summarizing Strongman's general conclusions on the roles of arousal and cognition in emotional states.

REVISION SUMMARY

Having covered this topic you should be able to:

✓ explain and evaluate the role of brain structures in emotional behaviour and experience

✓ describe the James-Lange physiological theory of emotion, and use Cannon's views to evaluate the theory

✓ describe Schachter and Singer's combined physiological/psychological cognitive labelling theory of emotion

✓ outline and evaluate Schachter and Singer's main research study.

✍ EXAMPLE EXAM QUESTIONS

Below are some **possible examination questions** set on this topic, along with hints to help you understand and approach each question effectively:

1 Discuss the role of brain structures in emotional behaviour **and/or** experience. (24 marks)

> As this question asks for brain structures in the plural, you should refer to more than one structure in your answer. The limbic system does not count as one structure, but is many structures as it includes the thalamus and hypothalamus, and has extensive connections to the amygdala. For the AO2 component of this question, you might offer a judgement of these explanations, e.g. 'While our limbic system is certainly involved in emotion, it is unjustified to extrapolate directly from studies with non-human animals'. Alternatively, you might examine the applications of an explanation, such as the use of the limbic model in justifying psychosurgery. Note that questions on emotion will not ask you to refer to research studies because this phrase doesn't appear in the specification under the heading of emotion (whereas it does appear in the topic of motivation).

2 (a) Describe the role of brain structures in emotional behaviour **and/or** experience. (12 marks)

(b) To what extent can emotional behaviour **and/or** experience be explained in terms of such brain structures? (12 marks)

The first half of this question matches the AO1 content of question 1. Any material included in part (a) that is commentary may be exported to part (b) (for the purpose of determining marks), but *only* if the material is relevant to the demands of part (b). The phrase 'to what extent' requires an AO2 response where you assess whether emotional behaviour and/or experience can be explained in terms of brain structures. You have to weigh up what you know about the evidence for brain structures against what you know about other explanations for emotion. There is no need for a conclusion in your answer but avoid any *description* of research (theory or studies) that you include.

3 (a) Outline and evaluate **one** physiological approach to explaining emotional behaviour **and/or** experience (e.g. James-Lange theory). (12 marks)

(b) Outline and evaluate **one** combined physiological/psychological approach to explaining emotional behaviour **and/or** experience (e.g. Schachter's cognitive labelling theory). (12 marks)

This is a straightforward question that requires careful time planning. Each part has 6 AO1 marks and 6 AO2 marks, so don't spend time describing theories or studies in great detail. The James-Lange theory is provided as an example but you don't have to use this theory, though it probably would be the best choice. If you wish to introduce the Cannon-Bard theory as evaluation, then use the theory as effective evaluation – don't just describe it as a second theory. For part (b) you are guided towards the cognitive labelling theory of Schachter and Singer. A description of this study would count towards your AO1 mark. Evaluation (AO2) can concentrate on problems with the study (see p. 450) and the failure of other researchers to replicate the findings.

4 Critically consider **one or more** physiological approach to explaining emotional behaviour. (24 marks)

All of the questions so far have referred to 'emotional behaviour and/or experience' in order to avoid making fine distinctions between what counts as behaviour and what counts as experience. In this question you are advised to ensure that the material presented does focus on behaviour rather than experience. This question also uses the wording 'one or more'; this tells you that one explanation would be enough for full marks, but if you don't feel you have enough to write about one approach, then you can introduce further approaches/theories.

5 Outline and evaluate **two** approaches to explaining emotional behaviour and experience. (24 marks)

This is similar to the previous questions, but puts slightly different demands on you. You can choose which approaches you outline and evaluate, and it is important that you select ones that allow you reasonable scope for evaluation. However, you must restrict your answer to *two* approaches only. More than this, and only the best two will be credited; less than two, and you incur a partial performance penalty. It would be legitimate, however, to group more than one theory under the heading of the 'physiological approach'. Thus, you could include both James-Lange and Cannon-Bard as one approach OR present these as two separate approaches.

UNIT SUMMARY

Topic 1: Brain mechanisms of motivation

- Behaviour linked to **homeostatic drives**, such as **hunger and thirst**, provide the simplest models of **motivation**.

- Research in these areas has identified **the role of brain structures in motivational states**, which centre on the **hypothalamus**.

- Rewarding electrical self-stimulation of the brain (ESB) led to the identification of reward pathways in the brain, in particular the median forebrain bundle (MFB). These pathways may explain the addictive properties of drugs of abuse.

Topic 2: Theories of motivation

- **Homeostatic drive theory** is a **physiological approach** to explaining simple motivational states such as hunger and thirst.

- Work in this area has identified the role of signals from the periphery in alerting feeding centres in the brain.

- **Psychological approaches to explaining motivation**, such as optimal arousal theory, have tried to account for non-homeostatic motivation, such as curiosity and exploration, but ignore the cognitive aspects of these behaviours.

- **Expectancy** and incentive theories emphasize the role of environmental stimuli in arousing and directing behaviour.

- Activation of reward pathways in the brain can explain incentive effects and also addiction to drugs of abuse.

- Hull's **drive-reduction theory combined physiological** and **psychological** approaches, but over-emphasized homeostatic drives and largely ignored cognitive aspects of motivation.

- Maslow tried to explain complex human motivations, but his theory lacks convincing experimental support, although he provides better descriptions of human behaviour than the physiological approach.

Topic 3: Emotion

- **Emotion** involves physiological changes, feelings and cognitive appraisals. Work with animals has identified the structures of the **limbic system** as central to basic emotional states.

- The **James-Lange theory** of emotions emphasized the role of bodily **physiological** changes. This theory was powerfully criticized by Cannon who proposed, instead, that emotion depended on brain structures such as the **thalamus** and **hypothalamus**.

- **Schachter and Singer** combined bodily arousal and central cognitive appraisal in their **cognitive labelling theory**. Although their main study is flawed, they correctly emphasized the importance of cognitive processes in emotional states.

- Human emotions are many and varied, and no single model is likely to explain all of them. Cognitive appraisal is central to emotional states, but the significance of physiological arousal varies from emotion to emotion.

FURTHER RESOURCES

Toates, F. (2001) *Biological Psychology*, London: Prentice-Hall.

Excellent and detailed coverage of homeostatic drives and models of emotion. It also explores the role of brain structures in motivation and emotion.

Rosenzweig, M.R., Leiman, A.L. and Breedlove, S.M. (1996) *Biological Psychology*, Sunderland, MA: Sinauer Associates.

Excellent coverage of homeostatic drives and models of emotion.

Strongman, K.T. (1996) *The Psychology of Emotion* (4th edn), Chichester: Wiley.

This text includes a range of useful material on theories of emotion.

Websites

www.vcu.edu/hasweb/psy/psy101/forsyth/zmoemo.htm

Developed by Professor Donelson Forsyth at Virginia University, this site has links to most aspects of the psychology of motivation and emotion.

http://emotion.salk.edu/Emotion/History/Hgeneral.html

Excellent coverage of the history and development of theories of emotion.

Unit 14 // Motivation and emotion

15
UNIT

ATTENTION &
Pattern
Recognition

PREVIEW

After you have read this unit, you should be able to describe and evaluate:

>> explanations of and research into focused attention, including early-selection and late-selection models

>> explanations of and research into divided attention, including controlled and automatic processing

>> explanations of and research into pattern recognition, including the role of biological mechanisms and of context, and theories of face recognition.

INTRODUCTION

In everyday speech, we use the word 'attention' to refer to several different kinds of mental activity. If you give your whole attention to something, such as taking an exam, you block out everything else that is going on around you. If you are waiting for an important telephone call, you will listen out attentively for the sound of the phone ringing. If you are speaking on the phone while standing in a noisy room, you will focus on the voice at the end of the line and ignore all the competing voices and sounds around you. There are certain familiar things in our environment to which we pay so little attention that we are scarcely aware of them, such as the weight of this book in your hands or the feel of clothes on your body. However, you can turn your attention to them if you choose to. An all-purpose definition of attention is that it is a focused concentration of mental activity, but attention is clearly not a unitary concept and psychologists do not agree on a definition. They have traditionally studied *focused* and *divided* attention separately, even though they are obviously related and the means of investigating them have been similar.

Once your attention has been directed at an incoming stimulus, you need to transform this raw and unprocessed information into something you can understand. This involves comparing the sensory input with information already stored in your long-term memory. Auditory pattern recognition occurs when, for example, you recognize a set of musical notes as a distinct melody, such as the opening bars of the National Anthem. In this unit, however, we will concentrate on visual pattern recognition. We are usually quite competent at distinguishing between various visual stimuli, but psychologists have not been able to explain this ability fully. Various theories have been proposed and we shall look at two of these – template theory and feature-detection theory. We shall then consider the role of the biological mechanisms that underpin pattern recognition, and also look at the effects of context on our interpretation of visual stimuli.

One particular type of pattern recognition that has interested psychologists is face recognition; the unit ends with a look at research in this area.

Jane
Willson

1   Sometimes, we can only perform well at a task if all other distractions are kept to a minimum. In an exam room, for example, any outside noise or activity may divert our attention and prevent us from concentrating. Why might we be distracted when taking an exam?

2   However, some people seem able to tackle attentional tasks in spite of noisy surroundings. Think of the Stock Exchange (see photo right), where quick thinking is required against a chaotic background of noise and activity. What do you think makes this possible?

3   Sometimes we find it quite easy to tackle two attentional tasks at once – making a cake and chatting to a friend, for example, or driving a car and listening to the radio. Why do you think we are able to do this?

4   What happens, though, if the circumstances change? What do we do, for example, if we are driving and see a child kicking a ball near the edge of the road or if there is a sudden downpour of rain?

Attention: a focused concentration of mental activity.

Focused or selective attention: the ability to focus on one thing at a time to the exclusion of other competing stimuli.

Divided attention: the ability to divide our attentional processes between more than one task.

Early-selection theories of attention: propose a filtering mechanism that selects some inputs and rejects others early on in the attentional process, before analysis for meaning occurs.

Late-selection models of attention: claim that both attended and unattended inputs are analysed for meaning before one input is selected and reaches consciousness.

Controlled (attentional) processing: a mental operation that is conscious, relatively slow and easily interrupted.

Automatic processing: a type of mental operation that is normally rapid, does not require conscious awareness, does not interfere with other mental activities and is usually a result of prolonged practice.

Action slip: a form of absentmindedness where a person performs an action that was not intended, caused by not paying attention to what is going on.

Pattern recognition: the process by which we transform and organize the raw information provided by our sensory receptors into a meaningful whole.

EARLY RESEARCH INTO FOCUSED ATTENTION

Focused or selective attention is the ability to focus on one thing at a time to the exclusion of other competing stimuli. Modern research on focused attention began in the 1950s and developed from a question raised by Colin Cherry (1953). He was interested in the answer to what he called 'the cocktail party problem', i.e. the ability to follow just one conversation when others are going on all around. Cherry devised an ingenious experimental technique called the 'dichotic listening task' (see panel right).

Studies by Cherry

Cherry (1953) carried out several studies investigating the so-called 'cocktail party effect' and reported some interesting findings:

- Participants seemed to recall very little about the message played to the unattended ear.
- They could recall no words from it.
- They did not know whether the message consisted of isolated words or continuous prose.
- They were not even aware that the language had switched from English to German.
- They did not usually notice if the message was played backwards.

However, participants clearly do not block the unattended ear completely. In Cherry's studies, they were able to notice:

- if the voice on the unattended ear changed from male to female

A dichotic listening task

Two simultaneous messages are played to the two ears via headphones. In an artificial replication of the cocktail party situation, participants are asked to pay attention to one of the inputs and ignore the other. Typically, the participant is asked to repeat back (shadow) the message heard in one ear.

- if the volume changed from loud to soft
- if the pitch changed from high to low
- if a pure musical tone replaced a human voice.

In other words, participants were able to recognize certain physical characteristics of the unattended message, but were oblivious to semantic aspects, i.e. the meaning of the words.

Background conversations

Mobile phone ring tones

Music

Thoughts

TV

Traffic noise

Evaluation (A02)
Cherry's research

- ***An important milestone*** – Cherry's studies represented an important milestone in attention research and provided the foundation for later theories. He was able to make use of the new multi-channel tape recorders that were becoming available at that time to provide controlled experimental conditions. He found that people cannot process two simultaneous auditory inputs for meaning although they can register physical properties of more than one input at a time.

- ***Later findings*** – However, not all experimental data confirmed this conclusion. Moray (1959) and later Wood and Cowan (1995), using more controlled conditions, found that 35 per cent of

participants would hear their own name if it were played on the unattended channel. This suggests that, in certain circumstances, people can pick out semantically important information from the other channel and switch their attention. For example, even if you are engaged in one conversation at a party, you are likely to hear your own name if it is mentioned in a nearby conversation. It also makes sense in evolutionary terms for us to be equipped with a mechanism which would allow us to switch our attention to something of greater importance, e.g. the sound of a predator approaching.

Therefore, any adequate theory of attention must be able to account for *both* these findings:

- our ability to focus on *one* stimulus input while blocking out most of the information from others
- our ability to *switch* attention to other messages if necessary.

EXPLANATIONS OF FOCUSED ATTENTION

The human brain is unable to analyse all the information that impinges on our senses, so all theories of selective attention include some mechanism/filter that selects certain inputs and rejects others. The filter is often seen as a bottleneck where parallel processing stops and serial processing begins. Attention theorists differ in their ideas about the precise location of the bottleneck.

Early-selection theories

Early-selection theories of attention propose a filtering mechanism that selects some inputs and rejects others early on in the attentional process, before analysis for meaning occurs.

Broadbent's filter model of selective attention

Broadbent (1954, 1958) proposed the first major theory of selective attention. He carried out his own investigations using a particular type of dichotic listening task called the 'split-span procedure' (see Key research below). On the basis of such findings, Broadbent reached the following conclusions:

- Two messages presented simultaneously to the two ears can be processed in parallel and gain access to a temporary staging post, which he called the 'sensory buffer store' (parallel processing).

- One of these messages is then selected on the basis of its physical properties and enters a filter mechanism. The other message waits its turn in the buffer. The buffer has a limited duration and material left there will be lost if it is not passed on quickly.

- The filter acts as a 'bottleneck' to prevent too much information flooding the attentional system. Beyond the filter is a limited-capacity processor that can only operate on inputs one at a time (serial processing). It is only at this stage that the input can be analysed for meaning.

These conclusions led Broadbent to produce the first comprehensive model of selective attention, in which he represented a sequence of processing stages in the form of a computer flow diagram, shown in Fig. 15.1 below. Using the computer as an analogy for human thinking processes is called the 'information-processing approach':

KEY RESEARCH >> FILTER MODEL OF ATTENTION

Broadbent's (1954) split-span procedure

Broadbent's split-span procedure involved participants recalling digits presented simultaneously in pairs, with one digit going to one ear and the other digit going to the other ear. Between the presentation of each pair of digits there was an interval of half a second. Following the presentation, participants were asked to recall the digits in one of two ways:

- 'pair by pair' – reporting the first pair of digits presented, then the second and finally the third
- 'ear by ear' – reporting the three digits heard by one ear followed by the three digits heard by the other ear.

Broadbent found that ear-by-ear reports were easier for participants, and produced more accurate responses, than pair-by-pair reports.

On the basis of these findings, Broadbent argued that the ears act as separate channels which can only be attended to one at a time. He suggested that in the pair-by-pair condition the participants had to switch between channels more often than in the ear-by-ear condition. Subsequently, Broadbent presented the first filter model of selective attention (see Fig. 15.1).

Figure 15.1 >> *Broadbent's (1958) filter model of selective attention*

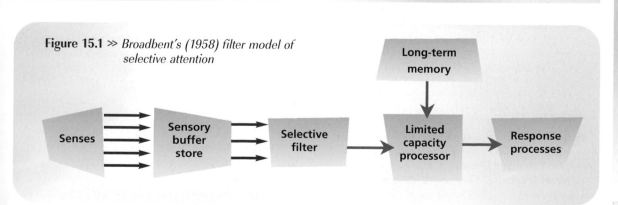

- The human brain, just like a computer, is required to handle large amounts of incoming information.
- These inputs frequently exceed the capacity of the brain (or computer) to process them effectively and so inputs have to be prioritized and processed selectively in order to avoid overload.

In Broadbent's model, each ear represents a separate channel and the brain can only fully process one channel at a time. This means that one of the two channels has to be selected for further processing. A key aspect of this model is that inputs are selected at the filter stage on the basis of physical properties. This idea will be easier to understand if you think of what happens in a noisy room full of people having separate conversations. In order to focus on what one person is saying, you are helped by:

- the distinctive sound of their voice (i.e. its pitch, rhythm and tone)
- the sound intensity (i.e. how loud or soft it is)
- the location of the sound (i.e. where the voice is coming from – you often tend to turn one ear towards the person who is speaking).

By attending to these physical properties of the person's speech, you can identify the conversation which you want to follow (i.e. process for meaning) and avoid being distracted by the semantic content of other conversations going on around you.

Evaluation
Broadbent's model

- *Use of the information-processing framework* – One advantage of this approach is that it can be tested experimentally and this has led to important further research.
- *Explanation of Cherry's findings* – The model fits with the idea that unattended input receives only minimal processing.
- *Explanation of Broadbent's findings from his split-span procedure* – If attention needs to be divided between the two ears in order to be able to monitor both messages at once, the filter can switch rapidly between channels on the basis of physical characteristics (in this case, the spatial location). The three items from one ear are reported back (shadowed), while the items from the second ear are held in the buffer. These latter items can only be reported when the filter switches to the other channel.
- *Semantic analysis of the unattended channel* – Moray (1959) found that listeners often recognized their own name if it was repeated on the unshadowed channel. This finding is incompatible with Broadbent's contention that recognition only occurs after selection on the basis of physical characteristics. Gray and Wedderburn (1960) used a variation of the split-span procedure in which they simultaneously presented material from two categories – digits and words. Participants had to report either ear

by ear or category by category. Gray and Wedderburn found that if the material in either ear was semantically related, as in 'Dear cousin Albert', participants reported this relationship as easily as they reported the ear-by-ear presentation. This finding created serious problems for Broadbent's model because it suggests that selection can occur on the basis of meaning.

- *Practice effect* – Underwood (1974) asked participants to shadow one message while an unrelated message was played to the non-shadowed ear. In addition, they were asked to detect particular digits that could be played to either ear. Novices at the task detected on average 8 per cent of the targets, but a highly practised participant was able to detect 67 per cent. This practice effect is difficult to accommodate within Broadbent's model.
- *What is a channel?* – The model has also been criticized because there is no precise definition of a channel. The notion of separate channels is easy to understand in the context of a dichotic listening task – each ear acts as a separate channel. However, it is not so clear what constitutes a channel in less artificial settings, such as listening to some singing on the radio and being able to pick out the words of the singer or the different instruments in the backing music.

It seems, then, that Broadbent's simple model of selective attention is unable to accommodate all the available experimental data.

Treisman's attenuator theory

Anne Treisman (1960) was interested in the findings from studies such as Moray's which suggested that there could be some breakthrough of content from the unattended channel. She set out to investigate how the meaning of auditory input might affect the selection

mechanism in a series of studies (see panel right). As a result of her findings, Treisman proposed an alternative model of attention. This revised model is shown in Fig. 15.2. Although Treisman had shown that breakthroughs from the unattended channel did sometimes occur during dichotic listening tasks, she also

Treisman's research (1960, 1964)

- In one of her experiments, Treisman used bilingual participants. They had to shadow a message in one ear, which was presented in English, while ignoring a message in the other ear, which was presented in the participant's second language, French. In fact, both messages had the same meaning, even though, of course, they sounded completely different. About 50 per cent of participants noticed that both messages were semantically identical, which suggests that the meaning of a message can be recognized prior to any focusing of attention.

- In another study, Treisman (1960) asked participants to shadow a story (story 1) in one ear and to ignore another story (story 2) which was being played into the other ear. During the shadowing task, story 1 was switched, without warning, to the other ear and story 2 ceased. A completely new story (story 3) replaced story 1 on the attended ear. Broadbent's model would predict that participants would have their filter tuned to the attended ear and would, therefore, have no awareness of the semantic content of the unattended channel. Accordingly, they would be expected to begin shadowing story 3 as soon as the switch was made. What participants actually did was to 'follow' story 1 by switching suddenly to shadowing the other ear. Treisman concluded that it is difficult to ignore the non-shadowed channel if it continues the meaningful content of the attended message.

- In a further series of studies, Treisman (1964) investigated factors affecting the ability to select one message on the basis of its content. She asked her participants to shadow one message and ignore the other. The shadowed message was always a passage read from a novel by a female voice. However, she varied the content of the unattended message, which was sometimes presented in the same female voice and sometimes not. The unattended message consisted variously of:

  - a passage from the same novel
  - a passage from a biochemical text
  - a passage in a foreign language
  - a set of nonsense syllables.

The ability of the participants to shadow the attended message was significantly affected by the content of the non-shadowed channel. Treisman's findings were as follows:

  - The most difficult condition for the participants was when both messages were passages from the same novel and read in the same female voice.

  - The more the non-shadowed message differed from the shadowed, both in semantic and physical terms, the easier the task became for the participants.

  - These findings are inconsistent with a filter that operates solely on the physical aspects of the input.

noted that they happen only occasionally and in certain circumstances. She believed that the filter selects one channel on the basis of physical properties and passes it on for semantic analysis. However, instead of blocking unattended channels completely, the filter allows them through in weakened (attenuated) form. For this reason, Treisman's theory is known as an 'attenuator model'. So, Broadbent's all-or-nothing filter is replaced in Treisman's model with a more flexible filter, which selects one input strongly, but lets others through in attenuated form. This means that *all* inputs gain access to the limited-capacity processor where semantic analysis takes place.

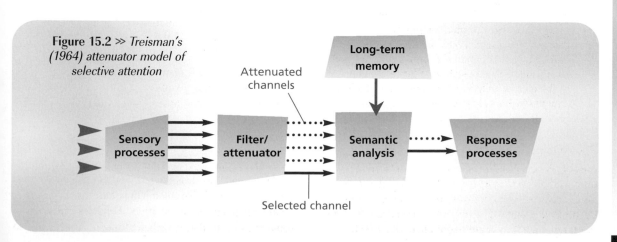

Figure 15.2 >> *Treisman's (1964) attenuator model of selective attention*

Attenuated channels

Long-term memory

Sensory processes **Filter/ attenuator** **Semantic analysis** **Response processes**

Selected channel

Another selection process then takes place – this time, on the basis of meaning.

Treisman proposed that the nervous system contains a collection of dictionary units which come into operation at the semantic analysis stage. Each dictionary unit corresponds to a single word and has a different recognition threshold depending on its salience to the individual. The threshold is the minimum intensity a word needs in order for its corresponding dictionary unit to be triggered. Words such as your own name, or words with potential survival value such as 'danger' probably have permanently low firing thresholds. However, many dictionary units will have fluctuating thresholds depending on their immediate relevance. For example, think of what happens when you listen to someone talking. The first words they speak will set up an expectation of what is to follow. If the sentence begins 'I heard an owl ...', you will expect the next word to be 'screeching' or 'hooting'. This expectation, based on your semantic knowledge, will prime the dictionary units for the expected words and so temporarily lower their firing threshold (see Fig. 15.3).

In a shadowing task, where participants are required to follow a message in the attended ear, breakthrough from the unattended channel is only likely to occur if that message contains words whose dictionary units have particularly low firing thresholds. In this case, even though the message is coming through in attenuated form, its dictionary unit will be triggered before that of the attended message and so will take precedence.

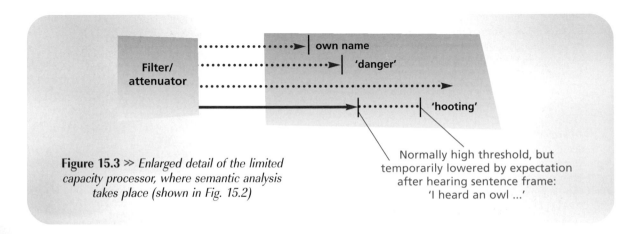

Figure 15.3 >> *Enlarged detail of the limited capacity processor, where semantic analysis takes place (shown in Fig. 15.2)*

Evaluation
Treisman's model

- *Flexibility* – Treisman's model, although similar to Broadbent's, differs in the flexibility of the selection mechanism. Her notion that selection takes place effectively in two stages accounts for much of the data that Broadbent could not explain. If unattended channels are not totally blocked, then attenuated information which is consistent with expectation (e.g. the continuation of the stories in Treisman's shadowing studies), or which is personally salient (e.g. the participant's name in Moray's 1959 study) will be recognized at the semantic analysis stage. The attenuator theory can successfully account for the breakthrough of certain unattended inputs.

- **Consistency with Cherry's findings** – Earlier studies showed that unattended inputs are not recognized. Treisman can explain this because,

most of the time, they do not come through at sufficient intensity to trigger their dictionary units.

- *Definition of attenuation* – One problem concerns the precise meaning of the term 'attenuation'. It is misleading to think of it as being a process akin to turning down the volume on a radio. Attenuation seems rather to involve a reduction in the amount of information that is passed on from the filter stage. Treisman has not specified exactly how this process works and, since attenuation is the key concept in her model, this lack of explanation is a major weakness.

- *Explanation of dictionary units* – It has also been suggested that Treisman's explanation of dictionary units is too vague and cannot account for the extensive semantic processing that would be needed, for example, to recognize that a French message on the unattended channel was a direct translation of the attended English message.

Late-selection models

Late-selection models of attention claim that both attended and unattended inputs are analysed for meaning before one input is selected and reaches consciousness.

Deutsch and Deutsch's model of selective attention

Deutsch and Deutsch (1963) were also interested in studies that demonstrated the breakthrough of information from the unattended channel, but they accounted for the semantic effects of the unattended message in a rather different way from Treisman. They argued that both attended and unattended inputs are *fully* analysed for meaning, and that it is only at this late stage that one input is selected and reaches conscious awareness. This means that the bottleneck occurs much later in the system than suggested by Broadbent. Selection at this point is said to depend on the salience or pertinence of the input (see Fig. 15.4).

Figure 15.4 >>
The Deutsch–Deutsch late-selection model of selective attention

Selected channel

Evaluation
Deutsch and Deutsch's model

- *Experimental support* – Lewis (1970) presented single words to participants in a shadowing task. Some words on the unattended channel were semantically related to those being shadowed while others were completely unrelated. After the experiment, participants were unable to recall anything from the unattended ear just as would be predicted by early-selection models. However, participants took longer to start shadowing a word on the attended channel if a semantically-related word was presented simultaneously in the other ear. This suggests, as the Deutsch–Deutsch model would predict, that unconscious semantic processing of the non-shadowed input slowed down the processing of the shadowed words.

- *Further experimental support* – Corteen and Wood (1972) and Corteen and Dunn (1973) conducted a series of studies making use of the galvanic skin response (GSR). GSR measures changes in skin resistance, which occur in response to heightened arousal or anxiety (see Key research on p. 462).

- *Methodological difficulties* – It has proved quite difficult to evaluate this theory because of the problem of demonstrating unconscious processing.

- *Alternative interpretations of the findings* – Treisman believed that she could explain all the above findings in terms of her attenuation theory. Treisman and Geffen (1967) challenged the late-selection theory with a study in which participants were required not only to shadow a message played to one ear, but also to tap their hand on the table when they heard particular target words on either channel. Treisman's own theory would predict much lower target recognition rates on the unattended ear because this input would only progress through the filter in attenuated form. The Deutsch–Deutsch model, on the other hand, would predict equal rates of target recognition for the two inputs, because there is supposed to be full semantic analysis of all incoming stimuli. Findings supported the Treisman model in that detection rates on the attended channel were 87 per cent compared to 8 per cent on the unattended channel.

- *Inefficient use of processing capacity* – Some critics (e.g. Johnston and Heinz – see Key research on p. 462) have suggested that it would be inefficient and uneconomical to analyse all inputs for meaning. It seems more likely that we only process inputs semantically if it is necessary to do so.

KEY RESEARCH >> UNCONSCIOUS PROCESSING

Corteen and Wood (1972), Corteen and Dunn (1973)

Corteen and colleagues conditioned participants to expect an electric shock every time they heard an example from a list of words pertaining to cities. The participants were then given a shadowing task to complete while measuring equipment was attached to the palms of their hands in order to record any GSR. Occasionally, one of the words from the list that had been associated with electric shock was played to the non-shadowed ear. In spite of the fact that participants denied recognizing any words from the non-shadowed ear, shock-associated words produced a GSR. In a variation of the study, participants were played some words into the non-shadowed ear, which had not appeared on the original list, but pertained to cities. These, too, provoked a GSR, suggesting that the unconscious processing of the non-shadowed channel could also involve semantic generalization.

KEY RESEARCH >> FLEXIBLE SELECTIVE ATTENTION

Johnston and Heinz (1978, 1979)

Johnston and Heinz (1978) proposed that attention may be focused at various stages of processing and that selection will occur as early as possible depending on the task's demands.

They tested this idea in a study (1979) where two words were presented simultaneously to participants over headphones. The task was to shadow certain target words, i.e. to repeat the target word every time it was heard on whichever channel. In one condition (high-sensory discriminability), the target words were always spoken in the same male voice while the non-target words were always spoken in a distinctive female voice. Thus, target and non-target items were always quite distinctive in physical terms even though participants did not know in which ear to expect them. In the second condition (low-sensory discriminability), both target and non-target words were spoken in the same male voice. Thus, the items could not be distinguished in physical terms.

Findings:

- Participants were more successful at shadowing in the high-discriminability condition,

presumably because they were simply listening out for the male voice (i.e. selecting on the basis of physical properties), and so were easily able to pick out the target items.

- However, in a subsequent unexpected recall task, participants in the low-discriminability condition were able to recall considerably more non-target items than participants in the high-discriminability condition. This suggests that non-target words needed to be more thoroughly processed in the low-discriminability condition. In the high-discriminability condition, non-target words could be selected out at an early stage of processing on the basis of physical properties. In the low-discriminability condition, target and non-target words were indistinguishable at the early stage, so non-target words could only be selected out once they had been recognized at a later stage of processing.

Conclusion:

- These findings support the view that the nature of the task determines the extent of processing and the point at which selection takes place.

Evaluation
Focused theories of attention

It soon became obvious that both early-selection and late-selection processes may be involved in selective attention. Johnston and Heinz (1978) put forward evidence suggesting that selective attention is more flexible than either the Treisman or the Deutsch–Deutsch model allows (see Key research opposite) Johnston and Heinz's explanation is certainly the most flexible one described so far and it does seem to account for much of the available data. However, as Styles (1997) has written:

<< It began to seem as if the bottleneck metaphor was wearing thin. As soon as the bottleneck can be moved around, or can be hypothesized to be located at either end or almost anywhere in the processing continuum, perhaps it ceases to be a bottleneck after all.>>

Researchers began to see that the concept of a single-channel processor was insufficient to explain attentional processes. Interest shifted to the idea of an attentional system limited not by structural constraints, but by the amount of processing resources available at any one time. We will look at such capacity-based models in the next topic.

✓ CHECK YOUR UNDERSTANDING

Check your understanding of focused attention by answering these questions. Try to do this from memory at first. You can check your answers by looking back through Topic 1.

1 What do you understand by the term 'focused attention'?

2 Briefly explain what is meant by a 'dichotic listening task'.

3 Outline Cherry's findings from his studies into the 'cocktail party effect'.

4 Draw a diagram and provide a brief explanation of Broadbent's filter model of attention.

5 Outline how the split-span procedure of Gray and Wedderburn differed from the one used by Broadbent and explain why their findings posed problems for Broadbent's model.

6 What are the similarities and differences between Broadbent's and Treisman's models?

7 Outline the findings from three studies and explain how they support Treisman's model.

8 Summarize the differences between early- and late-selection theories of focused attention.

9 Explain how the findings from Corteen and colleagues' study could be interpreted by
(a) the Deutsch–Deutsch model
(b) the Treisman model.

10 Construct a 300-word précis to outline and evaluate one late-selection model of focused attention.

REVISION SUMMARY

Having covered this topic, you should be able to:

✓ describe and evaluate early studies of focused (selective) attention, including those of Cherry

✓ describe and evaluate the early-selection models of focused attention of Broadbent and Treisman

✓ describe and evaluate the late-selection model of Deutsch and Deutsch

✓ describe and evaluate research studies related to these models

✓ use these studies effectively as AO2 commentary on each of the theories studied.

Unit 15 // Attention and pattern recognition

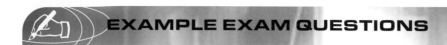

Below are some **possible examination questions** set on this topic, along with hints to help you understand and approach each question effectively:

1 Discuss studies of focused (selective) attention (e.g. Cherry). (24 marks)

The specification for this topic area refers to both studies and explanations, so you may be asked questions explicitly about one or the other, or both. As 'studies' is in the plural in this question, you must describe at least two studies and may, if you wish, discuss more than two studies. You don't need to present a large number of studies to attract high marks, as there are AO1 marks for detail as well as breadth. Similarly, there are AO2 marks for *elaboration* of any critical points you include, so it pays to spend time on detail and elaboration rather than throwing in undeveloped comments such as 'It was a lab study and therefore artificial'. What was artificial about it? Why is this a criticism? (See 'Innovative and effective AO2' on p. 937.) Here, an example is given in the question. Whenever examples are included in questions, they are taken from the specification. They are intended as guidance, but you don't have to write them – you are free to choose whatever relevant studies you wish, though Cherry's study would be an obvious one.

2 Critically consider **two or more** studies of focused (selective) attention. (24 marks)

The term 'critically consider' is an AO1+AO2 term (see Table 32.1 on p. 937), which means there is little difference between this and the previous question, except the phrase 'two or more' is used. This underlines the fact that a description (or probably just an outline) and evaluation of two studies would be sufficient for full marks, though more is acceptable. Remember the depth–breadth trade-off and don't try to include too much. Exam answers are not about writing everything you know, but about displaying a selection of the depth and breadth of your knowledge.

3 Outline and evaluate **two** explanations of focused attention (e.g. Broadbent, Deutsch and Deutsch). (24 marks)

In exam questions, the instruction 'describe' is used when asking for one explanation and 'outline' when asking for more than one. Presenting an *outline* of two explanations requires a précis of each one (just the most pertinent points), rather than the lengthier response if you were only asked for one explanation. This question can be conveniently divided into four 150-word 'chunks'. The first is the AO1 component of the first explanation and the second its corresponding AO2 component. This can then be repeated for the second explanation. If you only outline one explanation, there is a partial performance penalty (you can get a maximum of 8 out of 12 marks); the same applies to AO2 – if you only evaluate one explanation, your AO2 mark would be limited to 8 marks.

4 (a) Outline and evaluate **one** early-selection explanation of focused (selective) attention. (12 marks)
(b) Outline and evaluate **one** late-selection explanation of focused (selective) attention. (12 marks)

The mark split here is unusual as there are AO1 and AO2 marks in each part of the question (as indicated by 'outline and evaluate'). The particular explanations have been specified following the wording of the specification. Here, as in the question above, you are required to provide a shortened version of the explanations you have studied. In order to compose a good 6-mark version (about 150 words), you should practise reducing your longer version. For every explanation you need to have a long (12-mark version) and a précis of this (the 6-mark version) prepared in advance.

5 (a) Outline **one** explanation of focused (selective) attention. (6 marks)
(b) Outline and evaluate studies related to the explanation of focused (selective) attention that you described in part (a). (18 marks)

This question involves another unusual mark split. The AO1 marks are divided between parts (a) and (b). For part (a), you would use your 6-mark version of one explanation (early or late selection). In part (b), you need to outline two or more research studies, but don't be seduced into providing lots of descriptive detail of such studies because only one third of the marks for part (b) are AO1 marks. In this question you are also required to evaluate the research studies and not to evaluate the explanation (a mistake candidates often make). This can be done by considering methodological strengths and limitations as well as what the studies tell us about the theory. You must make sure that the studies you select are related to the explanation that you outlined in part (a).

Topic 2 >> Divided attention

Divided attention refers to the ability to divide our attentional processes between more than one task.

The bottleneck models we considered in Topic 1 all rest on the assumption that full attention can only be paid to one input channel at a time. However, in our everyday life, we know that we can often successfully divide our attention between two or more tasks. Try the activity below before you read on.

ACTIVITY

Doing several things at the same time

Think of some of the things you find easy to do at the same time. Now think of some of the things you find difficult to do at the same time. Are there any patterns of similarities and differences in the tasks you have identified? Is this pattern consistent or does it change as a result of other factors, such as how you are feeling at any particular time?

Examples might include driving and having a conversation, washing up and listening to the radio, listening to music and reading the newspaper, etc. However, there are some circumstances that prevent us from carrying out these activities simultaneously. For example, a driver will stop contributing to the conversation if something unexpected occurs, such as a flashing blue light appearing in the rear-view mirror, and learner drivers find it almost impossible to do anything other than concentrate on the driving task. There are also some activities which we seem never able to combine successfully – for example, reading a novel and simultaneously following a news broadcast on television. Such common-sense findings have led psychologists to suggest that there are various factors that can influence our ability to do more than one thing at a time.

Dual-task performance technique

The dual-task performance technique is the main way of investigating divided attention. Participants are given concurrent tasks and their performance is monitored. If performance on both tasks is as good as when each is performed singly, it suggests that the two tasks do not interfere with one another and that they are probably making use of distinct processing mechanisms. If performance on one or other of the two tasks is impaired, we can infer that the tasks do interfere with one another and are, therefore, competing for the same processing mechanisms.

RESEARCH STUDIES INTO DIVIDED ATTENTION

Effects of task similarity and competition

Allport *et al.* (1972) asked participants to shadow a continuous prose message played over headphones to both ears and, at the same time, to study a set of pictures depicting complex visual scenes, which were entirely unrelated to the content of the auditory message. In a later recognition task, participants were asked to identify these pictures from a larger set. There was no difference in the level of performance on the shadowing and the recognition task than when each of the tasks was performed singly. Allport and colleagues concluded that visual processing calls upon different processing mechanisms from those involved in monitoring auditory speech inputs.

In a second study, Allport *et al.* (1972) used participants who were all skilled piano players. They were asked to sight-read piano exam pieces while shadowing prose delivered at the rate of 150 words per minute. With very little practice, these participants were able to complete both tasks as competently and accurately as they could when asked to perform either of them separately. Again, the implication of these results is that the two tasks – in this study, processing speech and reading music – make use of different processing mechanisms. Allport and colleagues used the findings from such studies as evidence against a single channel for attentional processing.

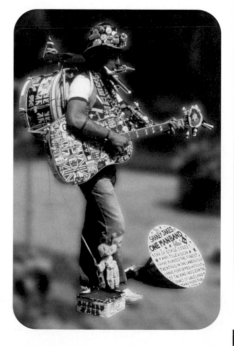

Is this a case of task similarity or task competition?

Unit 15 // Attention and pattern recognition

465

In another study, Shaffer (1975) demonstrated that tasks which call on the same types of processing, cannot be performed concurrently. A skilled typist was require to shadow an English prose message played over headphones to one ear while simultaneously typing a different English prose message played to the other ear. Her inability to carry out the two tasks simultaneously can be explained in terms of interference – both tasks make use of the auditory modality and so cannot be done in parallel. In a variation on this study, Shaffer asked the same typist to type a message presented aurally, while simultaneously reading aloud from a visually presented text. This, too, proved almost impossible, but the findings cannot be explained simply in terms of competition for the same modality. Audio typing depends on auditory input and motor output whereas reading aloud from written text requires visual input and articulatory output. On the face of it, then, it does not seem as if the same processing mechanisms are being used. The explanation for the interference between these two tasks seems to lie in the similarity of the tasks because they both require a response to the same kind of material, i.e. meaningful language.

Effects of practice

It seems likely that practice also may affect the ability to divide attention. Remember that Allport *et al.* (1972) and Shaffer (1975) used only highly-skilled practitioners – pianists and typists respectively – in their studies.

Spelke *et al.* (1976) conducted a study specifically to investigate the factor of practice. They persuaded two college students to spend five hours per week practising doing two tasks at once. They were required to read short stories while simultaneously writing down unrelated words which were dictated to them. The students found this very difficult at first and both tasks were performed poorly. However, after six weeks' regular practice, they were both able to read as quickly, and with the same level of comprehension, as when reading without dictation. However, although they could

accurately write down the dictated words, their subsequent recall was minimal. Spelke and colleagues then changed the dictation task, so that the students now had to write down the category to which the word belonged, instead of writing the dictated word. This was obviously a much more demanding task and the students' reading and writing performance suffered. Again, however, after several weeks training, the students were able to carry out the more difficult dictation task without any impairment in their reading comprehension. These findings suggest that learning and practice can affect the ability to divide attention.

The results of such a study should, however, be treated with some caution. The fact that only two participants took part makes any definitive interpretation difficult. It could be argued that students willing to give up approximately 12 weeks to such a project are likely to be fairly untypical in a number of ways. It is also unclear from this study what precise strategies were being learned to accomplish the tasks simultaneously. The findings could be explained either by the possibility that the participants had learned to switch rapidly between writing and listening, or by the possibility that the writing task had become so automatic, through practice, that it no longer required any attentional capacity.

It seems, then, that practice facilitates dual-task performance although it is not entirely clear how. Eysenck and Keane (1995) suggest three reasons why practice might have an effect:

- Participants may develop new strategies for performing each of the tasks, and so minimize task interference.

- The demands that a task makes on attentional or other central resources may be reduced as a function of practice.

- A task may initially require the use of several specific processing resources, but, with practice, may become more economical and rely on fewer resources.

EXPLANATIONS OF DIVIDED ATTENTION

Findings from studies using the dual-task performance technique have led to two different explanations of divided attention:

- capacity models
- modular theories.

Kahneman's capacity/ resource allocation model of divided attention

One of the best-known capacity models of attention was put forward by Kahneman (1973). This model is shown in Fig. 15.5.

It seems clear from research into divided attention that the human information processing system is limited in the number and complexity of tasks that can be effectively carried out at any one time. It also seems likely that various external variables can influence our ability to divide our attention. Revelle (1993) has reported on a number of factors, such as heat, noise, anxiety, motivation, lack of sleep, and personality, that affect performance on attentional tasks. Such findings are compatible with capacity or resource allocation models of attention. Instead of the structural bottleneck in information processing suggested by Broadbent, capacity theorists have

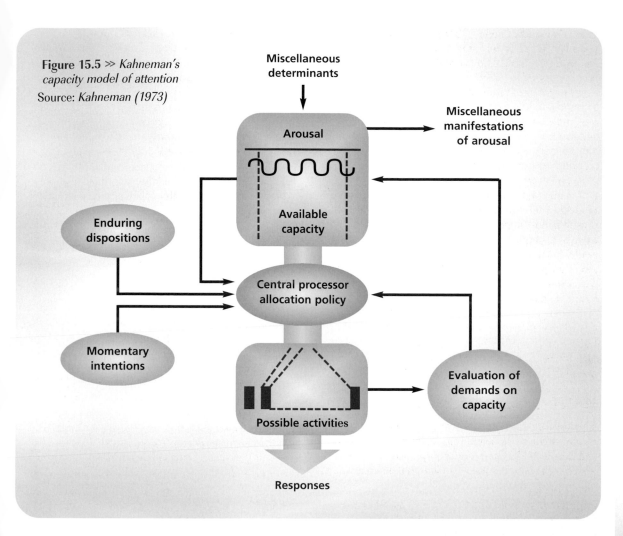

Figure 15.5 >> *Kahneman's capacity model of attention*
Source: *Kahneman (1973)*

Miscellaneous determinants

Miscellaneous manifestations of arousal

Arousal

Available capacity

Enduring dispositions

Central processor allocation policy

Momentary intentions

Possible activities

Evaluation of demands on capacity

Responses

proposed that we possess a pool of processing resources that we can allocate according to task demands and environmental factors. According to this approach, interferencc in the tasks will happen only if the demands of one, or both, of the tasks exceed the attentional capacity. This could occur at any stage in the processing and not at a fixed point (bottleneck) in the sequence.

Kahneman believes that attention is controlled by a central processor which coordinates and allocates a limited pool of resources. Although there is an overall limit on the total amount of attention available, the precise amount of attentional capacity can vary according to factors such as arousal. Kahneman's model also includes the concept of mental effort, which refers to the level of attentional processing required by a particular task.

The key characteristics of the model are as follows:

● The total amount of attention available is limited.

● Arousal levels can affect the total capacity – capacity increases with moderately high levels of arousal.

● More than one task can be performed at one time, provided that the combined mental effort required does not outweigh capacity.

● Some tasks require more mental effort than others. More difficult tasks require more mental effort.

● Practice can render some tasks automatic (e.g. driving) so that they require less mental effort.

● If the amount of mental effort required starts to exceed capacity, the central processor, which carries out constant monitoring, must determine which task takes precedence.

● In deciding between tasks, the central processor is affected by momentary intentions and enduring dispositions.

'Momentary intentions' are voluntary shifts in attention, such as deliberately paying attention to the right rather than the left ear in a dichotic listening task.

'Enduring dispositions' are responses to external stimuli, which are outside voluntary control, such as shifting your attention to a nearby conversation when your name is unexpectedly mentioned.

- *Flexibility* – Kahneman's model moved away from the structural limitations of the single channel models of attention and offered a more flexible account. For example, Kahneman could explain findings from dichotic listening tasks. He assumed that shadowing one of two inputs is a task that demands almost all of the available resources. There is very little attentional capacity left over to process the other channel in anything more than a superficial way. However, because of the effect of enduring dispositions, there is sometimes breakthrough from the non-shadowed message.

- *Dual-task studies* – Kahneman's model can also account for many of the dual-task study findings; tasks can be carried out concurrently provided the mental effort required for those tasks does not exceed the capacity of the available resources. For example, the model can account for the practice effect because practice allows us to economize on the attentional resources required.

- *Circularity* – The theory has been criticized for vagueness, notably by Allport (e.g. 1980). Allport believes that it is too easy to explain dual-task performance in terms of central capacity. In other words, if two tasks can be performed concurrently, it is because the tasks do not exceed the central capacity; if the tasks cannot be performed concurrently, it is because the combined effort required to accomplish them exceeds capacity. The problem here is that there is no independent definition of central processing capacity.

- *The role of arousal* – It is difficult to define arousal precisely. It is also a well-established finding that performance increases along with arousal up to an optimum point, after which further increases in arousal are associated with decrements in performance. This is known as the Yerkes–Dodson law (Yerkes and Dodson 1908). The Kahneman model, on the other hand, would predict a continued increase of performance with increased arousal.

- *The nature of the task* – Another prediction from the model is that the capacity required by a task will depend on the nature of that particular task, i.e. difficult tasks use up more capacity than simple tasks. Segal and Fusella (1970) gave participants the task of detecting a faint visual or auditory stimulus while simultaneously forming either a visual or auditory mental image. They found that the auditory imaging task impaired performance on the auditory signal detection task more than the visual imaging task did. Capacity theorists would explain this finding by saying that the auditory imaging task must, therefore, be more difficult than the visual imaging task. However, Segal and Fusella found that the auditory imaging task was less disruptive than the visual imaging task on a visual detection task. It seems that there is no difference in the inherent difficulty of the auditory or visual imaging tasks. The problems of concurrent performance seem to lie in the fact that similar tasks (i.e. tasks depending on the same modality) are competing for the same cognitive processors. This finding cannot be explained by Kahneman's capacity model.

Modular theories of divided attention

Allport (1980) has criticized the capacity models for their lack of explanatory power. Experimental data, such as that provided by Segal and Fusella above, led Allport to believe that the limitation on dual-task performance arose because the tasks were competing for the same processing mechanisms. He suggested that humans possess several different processing mechanisms or modules. Each of these is specialized for handling particular tasks and, although each module has limited capacity, there is no overriding, central processor. When tasks are similar (e.g. they both involve the auditory modality), they are assumed to be competing for the same module and so concurrent performance becomes difficult or even impossible. However, dissimilar tasks (e.g. shadowing speech involving auditory and articulatory modalities) and memorizing pictures (visual modality) can be combined with no decrement in performance because they use different modules and so are not in competition with one another for the same resource.

Evaluation
modular theories

● **Experimental support** – Various experiments that have looked at performance on concurrent tasks in the same and different modalities have shown support for the idea of different attentional modules.

● **Vagueness** – Allport has not specified the precise number of these modules, nor has he described their precise mode of functioning. The model can explain virtually any findings from divided attention research simply by postulating the addition of a further processing module. This kind of post hoc explanation is unsatisfactory.

● **Lack of coordination** – It is unclear how such a large number of independent modules could be coordinated to work effectively and efficiently in parallel.

RESEARCH INTO CONTROLLED AND AUTOMATIC PROCESSING

'Controlled (attentional) processing' is a mental operation that is conscious, relatively slow and easily interrupted.

'Automatic processing' is a type of mental operation that is normally rapid, does not require conscious awareness, does not interfere with other mental activities and is usually a result of prolonged practice. The idea of automatic processing is crucial to the notion of divided attention.

Some activities, such as riding a bike, although difficult to master in the first instance, become automatic with practice. Automatic processing is clearly helpful in carrying out everyday skills, but it is sometimes difficult to undo once learned.

Try the following activity before you read any further.

ACTIVITY

Counting Fs

Read the following sentence and count the number of Fs.

> FISH FINGERS ARE THE PRODUCT
> OF MANY YEARS OF DEVELOPMENT
> IN THE AREA OF FOOD PROCESSING.

You should have counted six Fs in the sentence. However, don't worry if you missed some because people often find tasks such as this quite difficult. People often miss the Fs in the word 'of', which occurs three times in the sentence. Try this out with friends and family.

Psychologists have investigated why this task might create problems for readers. People could be automatically converting the visual representation of letters into phonological representations. Therefore, the 'of's sound like 'ov's and people fail to detect the 'f's. Another explanation could be that, in reading, we automatically process frequently-occurring words, such as 'of', as whole units and find it difficult to focus on component letters.

Healy (1976) found support for this latter explanation when she asked participants to read a piece of English prose at normal reading speed while circling the letter 't' whenever it appeared in the passage. Participants were far more likely to detect the letter 't' in uncommon than common words. They were particularly likely to miss the 't' in 'the' which is the most common word in the English language. This suggests that our reading of high frequency words becomes automatic and that we recognize them as whole units rather than by their constituent letters.

The 'Stroop Effect' (Stroop 1935) is another example of the powerfully automatic nature of reading words and how this can interfere with other tasks. Stroop found that people have difficulty screening out meaningful information even when it is irrelevant to the task. He asked participants to read out a list of colour words (e.g. green, blue, red, yellow) printed in black ink. This is obviously a very simple task for skilled readers and presented no difficulties. He then presented a list of colour words printed in conflicting coloured inks (e.g. the word 'blue' printed in red) and asked participants to name the colour of the ink. This should also have been a simple colour-recognition task. However, participants took considerably longer to complete this second task than the straightforward reading task. It seems that words provoke an automatic reading response and, although conscious control can prevent this response being articulated aloud, there is a time delay while the correct response, i.e. ink naming, is activated.

Shiffrin and Schneider (1977), in their two-process theory, differentiated between controlled and automatic processes (see the panel at the top of p. 470).

Shiffrin and Schneider's (1977) studies of controlled and automatic processing

Shiffrin and Schneider (1977) reported a series of studies which explored the nature of automatic, or non-conscious, information processing. Their investigations led them to differentiate between two general modes of human information processing: controlled and automatic. They suggested that the two modes of processing have the following general features.

Controlled processing	Automatic processing
These processes are of limited capacity and require focused attention.	These processes are not hindered by capacity limitations.
These processes are serial in nature and, in line with single channel theories, each has to be dealt with singly.	These processes are fast, can operate in parallel and many processes can be active at any one time.
Tasks which are tackled using controlled processing can be learnt quickly and can be modified relatively easily.	Tasks only reach automatic status through considerable practice and are difficult to modify once learnt.
Controlled processes are usually consciously directed to a task.	Automatic processing usually takes place at a non-conscious level.
	Automatic processing is unavoidable; it always occurs when an appropriate stimulus is present.

Most of their studies were based on visual rather than auditory attention tasks. In a typical study, participants would be required to search for a fixed set of target items (e.g. the letters N, T and K) amongst a set of distractor items (e.g. the digits 1 to 9). In the first trials, target detection times depended on the number of distractors – the more distractors, the longer it took to find the targets. However, after considerable practice, search times became faster and appeared to become relatively independent of the number of distractors. Shiffrin and Schneider concluded that searching for targets begins as a serial search under conscious control, but that, after much practice, it becomes automatic. Poltrock *et al.* (1982) have found similar effects in an auditory detection task, suggesting that automatic and controlled processing may occur in modalities other than vision.

Evaluation
controlled and automatic processing

- *Useful concept* – The theoretical distinction between controlled and automatic processing has been useful and has stimulated further research.
- *Supporting experimental evidence* – The idea of parallel automatic processing and serial controlled processing is compatible with findings from many focused attention and dual-task studies.
- *Lack of explanatory power* – Shiffrin and Schneider claim that practice leads to automaticity, but they do not explain exactly how this is achieved. It could, for example, be that practice simply speeds up the processes needed to accomplish the task. Neisser (1976) believes that practice does not simply lead to a switch

from controlled to automatic processing, but involves the development of skill. This is similar to the idea of 'restructuring' proposed by Cheng (1985). She believes that practice allows the development of new and more efficient strategies for completing tasks.

- *Lack of clear distinction* – Another problem for the theory is that there seems to be no clear-cut distinction between automatic and controlled processes. Certain aspects of a task may be automatic whilst others may require attention. Making a cup of instant coffee, for example, involves mainly automatic processing, whereas preparing a three-course meal involves constant checking and monitoring even though some of the sub-processes, such as peeling the vegetables, may be automatic. This suggests that controlled and automatic processing operate on a continuum rather than as distinct, discrete entities.

SLIPS ASSOCIATED WITH AUTOMATIC PROCESSING

Reason's research into action slips

The term 'action slip' refers to a form of absentmindedness where a person performs an action that was not intended, caused by not paying attention to what is going on. Cognitive psychologists have used a number of techniques in their study of action slips. For example, questionnaires can be used to assess the frequency with which certain things are forgotten. Another method, which also relies on self-assessment, is the diary study technique.

Diary studies

In diary studies, participants are asked to keep daily records of the memory errors they make. One important diary study in this area was carried out by Reason (1979) – see Key research below.

KEY RESEARCH >> ACTION SLIPS

Reason's (1979) diary study of slips of action

Reason (1979) conducted a diary study in which 35 participants kept a diary record of their slips of action over a two-week period. The study revealed 400 errors and Reason divided them into five categories:

- *Storage failures* (40 per cent of total errors): forgetting that an action had already been performed and doing it again (e.g. putting the sugar in a cup of tea twice).
- *Test failures* (20 per cent of total errors): forgetting the goal of a sequence of actions and switching to a different goal (e.g. starting off making a cup of tea and ending up making a cup of coffee).
- *Sub-routine failures* (18 per cent of total errors): component actions of a sequence being omitted, or wrongly ordered (e.g. putting the boiling water in the tea pot without having put in the tea).
- *Discrimination failures* (11 per cent of the errors): confusing the objects involved in different actions (e.g. taking a fork instead of a spoon to stir your tea).
- *Programme assembly failures* (5 per cent of errors): wrongly combining actions from different sequences (e.g. opening a packet of tea and placing the wrapping in the teapot and the tea in the bin).

The remaining 6 per cent of errors were unclassifiable.

Commentary
diary studies

There are difficulties associated with diary studies:

- *Accuracy* – We cannot know how many slips have gone unreported – either because they were simply undetected, or because diarists were too embarrassed to record them. It is also possible that certain types of slip are more noticeable than others and are, therefore, more likely to be recorded.
- *Classification* – The distinctions between some of the categories are unclear, and so some of the slips may be wrongly classified. On the other hand, some slips, which have been classified together because of a superficial similarity, may reflect quite different underlying mechanisms. Grudin (1983) looked at videotapes of typists' fingers on keypads and noted any errors. The typists sometimes struck the wrong key which, on the face of it, would appear to be a single class of error. However, Grudin noted that, in some cases, the correct finger for one key slips onto an adjacent (wrong) key, whereas in other cases, the wrong key is struck by its own appropriate finger He concluded that the first error was due to faulty execution of the action, whereas the second error was due to faulty assignment of the finger. As Eysenck and Keane (1995) point out, we need more information than is available from diary studies to pick up such subtle differences in underlying mechanisms.

Laboratory study

Reason (1992) attempted to respond to some of the criticisms of diary studies by devising a technique to provoke action slips. He asked participants to respond as quickly as possible to a series of questions. In all cases, the most likely answer rhymed with 'oak'. (For example: 'What do we call a funny story?' = 'joke'; 'What is another word for cape?' = 'cloak'.) The last question was 'What do you call the white of an egg?' to which 85 per cent of the participants replied 'yolk' (the correct answer is in fact 'albumen'). Only 5 per cent of a control group, who were only given the last question, replied 'yolk'.

Although this is quite an ingenious technique, it does not seem to produce the kind of slips that are typical of those that occur in everyday situations.

Theories of action slips

Reason explained the error patterns by arguing that attentional processing works at three levels:

- a superficial level concerned with routine automatic tasks which require little conscious thought (the majority of errors seem to occur at this level)
- a deeper level of processing involving a realization that a routine is incorrect and that more attention and knowledge is required to correct the situation (errors can occur at this level if you misread a situation and then realize that your actions do not fit the current context)
- an even deeper level of processing in which you have to bring all your knowledge to bear and use all your conscious control to solve a problem (a further problem at this level is that by now you might have reached a critical point and fear or panic may not allow clear thinking).

Reason has used these ideas to look at disasters such as Chernobyl, and has concluded that, unless an understanding of the nature of human errors is allowed for in the design of new technology, these accidents are not only possible, but inevitable.

Dual-task limitations

A key finding from the Reason study is that the majority of errors seem to occur in highly practised, over-learned, routines. These action sequences often involve automatic processing and are carried out with little conscious monitoring. Automatic actions have the advantage of releasing attentional resources to be used in the performance of parallel activities, but they can also lead to errors. There is a tendency for a more commonly performed task to take over from one performed less often, particularly if both tasks share a component stage.

Slips of action often occur at junctions between stages when there can be a switch over to an incorrect procedure, e.g. walking or driving in the wrong direction because that is the way most often taken. In addition to these 'habit intrusions', people can also lose track of a sequence of actions, resulting in actions being repeated or omitted. Some people are more prone to these kinds of errors than others, and everyone finds that slips and lapses can increase with tiredness and stress.

Norman (1981) has proposed an explanation of attentional slips and lapses based directly on one of the most important theoretical ideas in cognitive psychology, known as schema theory.

Schema theory

The notion of schemas was first put forward by Bartlett (1932). Schemas can be thought of as organized sets of mental representations which incorporate all our knowledge of particular objects, concepts or events. According to schema theory, if the same incoming information is experienced repeatedly, it eventually becomes incorporated into a generalized schematic representation.

Schema theory attempts to explain how we organize knowledge from past experience to help us interpret, or guide, new information coming in from the senses. A good example of the influence of schemas in human information processing can be seen in a study by French and Richards (1993) (see Key research below).

KEY RESEARCH >> SCHEMAS IN INFORMATION PROCESSING

French and Richards' (1993) study of schema-driven attentional errors

In this experiment, French and Richards had three conditions.

- *Condition 1:* participants were shown a clock with roman numerals and asked to study the clock for one minute. After the time had elapsed, the clock was taken away and participants were then asked to draw the clock from memory.
- *Condition 2:* the same procedure was followed with the exception that participants were told they would be required to draw the clock from memory.
- *Condition 3:* the clock was left in full view of the participants and they were instructed merely to produce a drawn copy of the clock.

In the standard form of roman numerals, the number four is represented as IV, but on clocks with roman numerals the four is almost invariably represented as IIII. French and Richards found that in both the conditions in which participants had to draw the clock from memory, a significant majority reverted to the conventional IV notation. In Condition 3, however, all the participants used the correct IIII notation. French and Richards explained these results in terms of schema theory and the strong influence of schematic knowledge on the way people process information. In Conditions 1 and 2, the strong influence of schematic knowledge of roman numerals appeared to have affected participants' memory retrieval.

Norman's model of attentional slips and lapses

According to Norman's (1981) model of attentional slips and lapses, action sequences are controlled by schemas. He suggests that several schemas can be activated simultaneously and linked into related sets. The highest level, or parent schema, corresponds to the overall intention, or goal (e.g. going to school). Subordinate, or child, sub-schemas correspond to the component actions in the sequence (e.g. going to the bus stop, catching the bus, getting off the bus and walking to school). Each schema, or sub-schema, has its own activation level which is determined by both external (the current situation) and internal events (plans and intentions). Each schema also has a set of triggering conditions, and a given schema is activated if the activation level is sufficiently high and the current situation matches the triggering conditions. According to Norman, slips can occur as a result of:

- **Faulty specification** – when another schema has a higher level of activation than the one associated with the original intention. An example of faulty specification might be starting off going to visit an aunt you have not seen for some time and ending up around the corner at a friend's house which you visit more frequently.

- **Faulty triggering** – when the current situation, or context, triggers an alternative schema. An example of faulty triggering could be deciding to walk to school instead of catching the bus, but, as you are passing the bus stop, the bus arrives and before you have realized what you are doing, you are on the bus.

Evaluation
Norman's model

- **Useful explanation** – Norman's model provides a useful explanation of attentional slips and errors.
- **Everyday examples** – Most attention slips seem to occur in everyday, highly-practised activities, as would be predicted by the model, but it is not without problems.
- **Overlap of categories** – As with Reason's classifications, some errors do not fall neatly into either category and may result from a combination of factors (e.g. a combination of both faulty specification and faulty triggering).

- **Reliance on the concept of automatic vs controlled processing** – Schema theory relies heavily on the distinction between controlled and automatic processing and, as we have seen above, this is not yet fully understood. In particular, the factors that determine the mode of control in a given situation have not been clearly specified. Eysenck and Keane (1995) point out that the incidence of action slips is greater in relatively trivial activities than in activities that could have more serious consequences. They give circus performers as an example, whose routines are highly practised, but, because of their dangerous nature, these routines are rarely subject to attentional error. Current theories cannot provide an adequate explanation of such observations.

CHECK YOUR UNDERSTANDING

Check your understanding of divided attention by answering these questions from memory. You can check your answers by looking back through Topic 2.

1 What do you understand by the term 'divided attention'?

2 What is meant by the dual-task technique?

3 Draw a diagram and give a brief outline of Kahneman's capacity model of attention.

4 Identify two limitations of Kahneman's model and explain why these are a problem.

5 Outline the findings of one study that supports the modular theory of divided attention.

6 List three features of automatic processing and three features of controlled processing.

7 Name and give an example of each of the five categories of action slip identified by Reason.

8 Outline some of the problems involved with conducting research into action slips.

9 Summarize Norman's model of attentional slips.

REVISION SUMMARY

Having covered this topic, you should be able to describe and evaluate:

✓ Kahneman's capacity model and Allport's modular theory of divided attention

✓ research into controlled and automatic processing

✓ research into slips associated with automatic processing as AO2 commentary on each of the theories studied.

 EXAMPLE EXAM QUESTIONS

Below are some **possible examination questions** set on this topic, along with hints to help you understand and approach each question effectively:

1 Discuss **one or more** explanations of divided attention (e.g. Kahneman's capacity/resource allocation model). (24 marks)

> The way this question is worded means that you could write about only one explanation and still get full marks. The choice is yours. If you do cover two explanations, these do not have to be totally balanced for full marks. One explanation could be described and evaluated in slightly more detail. This means that, to cover all eventualities, you always need to have thorough knowledge of one explanation (which would allow you to earn up to 15 marks), a reduced version of this explanation (a 6/7-mark version) and a less thorough version of the second explanation (a 5/6-mark version).

2 (a) Outline **two** explanations of divided attention. (12 marks)
  (b) To what extent are the explanations of divided attention that you have outlined in part (a) supported by research studies? (12 marks)

> Part (a) is straightforward, although no credit would be given for using an explanation of focused attention. In part (b), you must present AO2 material ('To what extent' is an AO2 term). This means you must *use* your knowledge of research studies to consider whether they provide support for your chosen explanations. It might be useful to divide your response to part (b) into two sections, each of 150 words, one part related to each explanation. Then focus on *using* the research studies rather than describing them. Keep any description of the studies to a minimum, so as to maximize marks for commentary. The secret to effective use of research studies in your AO2 commentary is to focus on the *relationship* between explanation and study, and state the link. Why do psychologists carry out research in the first place? One important reason is to put theoretical assumptions to the test.

3 Discuss research (theories **and/or** studies) into automatic processing. (24 marks)

> The term 'research' refers to theories or studies, as indicated in this question. This means that you may describe either theories *or* studies *or* both, and should have a wealth of material to draw on for this answer. The danger is one of providing lots of breadth and very little detail/elaboration for both AO1 and AO2. The skill required here is *selectivity*. It may help to divide your response into 100-words chunks (remember that an answer is likely to be about 600 words in length). Each chunk might contain an outline of some research with appropriate commentary – 50 words of each to ensure balance. There is no need for an introduction or a conclusion.

4 Discuss research (theories **and/or** studies) into controlled and automatic processing. (24 marks)

> It is always vital to focus on the demands of each question. Here, the demands are that research is covered and this is related to both controlled *and* automatic processing. There should be a reasonable balance between the two 'halves' of the essay to achieve full marks, thus you might conveniently divide your answer into four chunks of 150 words: describe research on controlled processing and evaluate it, describe research on automatic processing and evaluate it.

Pattern recognition is the process by which we transform and organize the raw information provided by our sensory receptors into a meaningful whole.

Once our attention has been engaged by a stimulus, we need to be able to identify and make sense of it. This topic involves how we make sense of visual information. Look around you now. Whether you are in a classroom or at home, you are almost certainly surrounded by visual objects such as tables, chairs, books, pens, windows, doors, etc. Equally likely, you will have no difficulty in naming these objects and understanding their uses. Object recognition seems

such an effortless task that you may be wondering why it is a subject of interest for psychologists. In fact, object recognition is a rather more complex activity than it may at first seem. For example, you are able to identify a chair, even if it is partially obscured behind a table, is some distance from you, or is in shadow. Our ability to make sense of our visual environment regardless of such situational factors as lighting, angle and viewing distance, will be explored in more detail in the section on perceptual organization in Unit 16. For the moment, we will restrict discussion to the topic of pattern recognition.

EXPLANATIONS OF PATTERN RECOGNITION

Much of the research into pattern recognition has focused on how we identify two-dimensional patterns such as letters of the alphabet and digits. Consider the examples in Fig. 15.6. You will have no difficulty in recognizing all the shapes as the letter 'b', even though they are different in size, typeface and orientation. Any adequate theory of pattern recognition will need to be able to account for this ability to recognize the same overall pattern in spite of it being represented quite differently.

Template theory

This is the simplest kind of theory. It proposes the existence of a set of miniature templates (or copies) of

Figure 15.6 >> *Variations on the letter 'b'*

patterns which are stored in long-term memory and against which we match incoming information. When you see the letter 'b', for example, you compare it to your set of stored templates until you find the correct fit. Just as you have to find a piece of exactly the right shape to fit the available space in a jigsaw, so you have to find the correct match amongst your templates. So, the letter 'E' will not fit the template for 'F' because of the extra horizontal bar at the bottom.

Evaluation
template theories

(A02)

- *Practical applications* – Template matching works extremely well for computerized recognition systems, which depend on unambiguous identification of digits or symbols. It is the basis for barcode scanning in supermarkets and it is the way bank sorting systems recognize the distinctively shaped digits on the bottom of cheques. Forensic scientists also use it as a method of matching fingerprints.

- *Lack of efficiency* – The letters in Fig. 15.6 are all recognizable as the letter 'b', but they are certainly not identical in form. So, given the requirement for an exact match, we would have to assume that there is a separate template stored for every possible presentation of the letter 'b'. This would be very inefficient in storage terms and, even if such a huge set of templates were feasible, it does not explain how we are able to

recognize a letter 'b' for the first time in a typeface we have never actually seen before.

- *Orientation* – Another problem for the theory is its inability to account for the recognition of patterns viewed from non-standard angles. If you turn your textbook upside down and look at Fig. 15.6 again, you will still find it easy to recognize the letter 'b'. Jolicoeur and Landau (1984) found that humans require only 15 milliseconds of extra processing time to recognize rotated letters. It seems highly unlikely that we should have stored templates of rotated letters, so it is unclear from template theory how we are able to accomplish this task so quickly.

- *Complexity* – It is clear that there are problems for the theory even in accounting for the relatively simple task of letter and digit recognition. It is even more difficult for template-matching theory to account for our ability to make sense of the complex visual scenes that we encounter in everyday life.

Prototype theories

These theories are rather more flexible versions of the template-matching approach. A prototype is an abstract model stored in long-term memory, which embodies the most typical features of an object or pattern. When we see an object, we compare it to our set of prototypes and identify the stimulus as soon as we have a reasonably close match. Unlike original template-matching theory, the match does not have to be exact for recognition to occur. You may have a stored prototype for each of your teachers which includes details such as height, build, facial features, etc. However, if a teacher suddenly came into class wearing glasses for the first time, you would still be able to recognize them because the match would be close enough to your stored prototype for that person.

Evaluation
prototype theories

- *Flexibility* – Prototype-matching theory is more flexible and economical than the original template-matching theory and it can account for the ability to recognize different pictorial representations of the same basic shape.
- *Experimental support* – Several studies have shown that prototypes can be helpful in recognizing patterns such as geometric shapes (Posner and Keele 1968) and simple line drawings of faces (Reed 1972). Solso and McCarthy (1981) also demonstrated their importance in the recognition of police identikit pictures used for witness identification.
- *Storage* – The theory does not adequately explain how the prototypes are stored in memory.
- *Adequacy* – It does not explain how we are able to recognize objects that are partially obscured.

Feature-detection theories

An alternative explanation of pattern recognition can be found in feature-detection theories. According to these theories, we process images in terms of their basic constituent parts. In other words, we match features of a pattern to features stored in memory, rather than attempt to match a whole pattern to a template or prototype.

One of the first feature models was devised as a computer program by Selfridge (1959). It was called the 'Pandemonium model' because it was based on the metaphor of a hierarchy of demons, each with their own specific contributions to the pattern recognition task (see panel below).

Selfridge's (1959) Pandemonium model

Imagine being presented with the written letter 'E'. The image of this symbol will fall as a pattern of light on the retina where it will be passed on by an image or data demon to a set of feature or computational demons. Each feature demon has the task of looking out for a specific feature such as a straight vertical line, oblique line, continuous curve, acute angle, etc. If its particular feature is present in the visual image, the demon will 'shout'. The volume of the shouting is determined by the prominence of the feature. So, for example, the letter 'E' will provoke the demons responsible for horizontal lines and for right angles, which will shout more loudly than the vertical line demon because their features are more numerous. The shouting is relayed to the next layer of the hierarchy, where cognitive demons shout out possible matches for the combination of features that have been recognized by the feature demons. It is possible, at this stage, for cognitive demons to be shouting 'F', or even 'L', as well as 'E'. At the top of the hierarchy is the decision demon, which has the task of deciding, on the basis of the accumulated information and the volume of the shouting, which letter has the most matching features – in this case 'E'.

The notion of a crowd of demons shouting away inside our heads may seem bizarre, but Selfridge intended it only as a metaphor to represent some of the uncertainty contained in feature processing. Other formulations of feature theory do not make use of demons, but they all rest on the assumption that we recognize patterns by matching them against a set of distinctive features that we have stored in memory. Try the next activity before you read any further.

List 1	List 2
GCDROQ	IVEFXW
OQURCG	FWVYMN
QDOPUC	IWXNEV
COPQUG	MNWXIE
GCOUQP	VWXYMF
QOCUGD	FXWYIM
UGCOZQ	IVXNZM
QGUOPC	VWXMNI
CUODQG	WIYXMVF
CGQODU	IEVYWX
DUQOGC	VYWMNX
CQUGOD	MNWEFI
OCQPUR	XVYWMI
RPQOUC	WXNMIY
GUOCQP	YFEIVM

ACTIVITY

Feature-detection

Scan through Lists 1 and then 2 until you find the letter Z.

You probably found the letter 'Z' in list 1 more quickly than the one in list 2. See the 'Evaluation' below for an explanation of this.

(A02) Evaluation
feature-detection theories

- **Experimental support** – Neisser (1964) used arrays of letters similar to those in the activity above and asked participants to find certain target letters. He compared the time taken to detect the letter 'Z' when the surrounding letters consisted of straight lines and when the surrounding letters consisted of curved features. Target detection was faster in the second condition because the letter 'Z' has few features in common with the curved letters and so stands out more readily. Similar findings were presented by Gibson (1969) who found that participants take longer to decide whether letters such as 'P' and 'R' are different from one another than letters such as 'G' and 'M'. Garner (1979) found that decision speed increases as a consequence of the number of shared features of the letters. This lends support to the idea that some kind of stage-by-stage feature analysis process is taking place.

- **Biological evidence** – There is also some support for the feature models from biological studies carried out by Hubel and Wiesel (1959, 1962, 1979) (see Key research on p. 478).

- **Descriptive rather than explanatory** – One difficulty is that the theories simply list a set of features, but make no attempt to describe the relationship between features. For example, look at Fig. 15.7. All of the figures illustrated above meet the feature criteria for the capital letter 'T' – i.e. one vertical line, one horizontal line and two right angles – but none of them represent a real 'T'. We also need a structural description that gives information about the relationship between the features.

- **Relative importance of features** – The theory also fails to take into account that some features of a visual stimulus are more important than others.

- **Ignores effect of context** – An assumption of the feature model is that recognition of a pattern depends on analysis and synthesis. In other words, the visual system first identifies individual features of a stimulus and then combines these features to decide what the whole pattern represents. The model would, therefore, predict that complex patterns should take longer to identify than simple ones. Pomerantz (1981) showed that this is not always the case. He showed participants stimulus figures similar to those shown in Figs 15.8(a) and 15.8(b) and asked them, in each case, to pick the stimulus that was different from the others. Participants were faster to identify the odd one out in 15.8(b) even though these stimuli are more complex variations of the stimuli in 15.8(a). It seems that the provision of additional features in 15.8(b) – i.e. making the stimuli into familiar triangle figures – provided contextual cues that speeded up identification. We will explore the effects of context later in this section.

- **Lacks complexity** – Feature theory seems to provide a reasonable, if not complete, explanation of how we recognize simple patterns such as letters and digits. As with template and prototype theories, however, it is too simplistic to explain how we recognize more complex objects.

Figure 15.7 >> *Feature criteria of the capital letter 'T'*

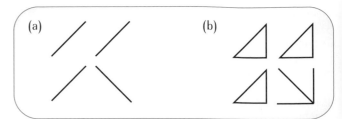

Figure 15.8 >> *Recognition of simple and complex patterns*

KEY RESEARCH >> PATTERN RECOGNITION

A study of biological mechanisms by Hubel and Wiesel (1962, 1979)

There are over 100 million neurons in the visual cortex – the area of the brain primarily responsible for the processing of visual information – and only the tiniest fraction of these have been systematically studied. Hubel and Wiesel undertook much of the pioneering work in this field in the late 1950s and they were awarded the Nobel Prize in 1981 for their research. Biological aspects of perception will be covered more thoroughly in Unit 16. We will focus here on biological research specifically relevant to pattern recognition.

Hubel and Wiesel (1962, 1979) inserted microelectrodes into various regions of the visual system in anaesthetized cats and monkeys. They then presented a variety of visual stimuli on a large screen in front of the animals and recorded signals detected by the microelectrodes. They found that the cortical neurons made no response to spots of light, but that they were most responsive to bar-like stimuli with specific orientations. They found three main types of cortical cells, each tuned to detecting the presence of particular features such as edges, light and dark areas, slits of light, orientation and direction of motion. These three types of cell were named simple, complex and hypercomplex cells.

● Simple cells respond selectively to lines, edges, bars and slits in specific retinal areas and at a particular orientation. Some simple cells respond best to a vertical stimulus, while others respond best to bars with horizontal or vertical orientations.

● Complex cells respond to similar stimuli, but respond best to moving lines in a particular direction of movement.

● Hypercomplex or end-stopped cells fire to bars of specific length or to moving corners and angles.

Since these cells identified by Hubel and Wiesel appear to respond differentially to specific features of the stimulus such as orientation, direction and movement, they are sometimes called feature-detectors.

The role of context

Bottom-up processing

Most of the theories we have looked at so far are based on the assumption that object recognition begins with the analysis of component parts. This kind of analysis of sensory inputs is known as *bottom-up processing*, a term which comes from the information-processing approach. This is based on the analogy of the human mind as a machine which manipulates information through a series of processing stages. Bottom-up processing, or data-driven processing, stresses the importance of the stimulus in pattern recognition. An example comes from the early work of Hubel and Wiesel (1962) (see Key research above). This research

indicated that the retinal image is analysed through layers of the cortex in increasingly complex ways until the output of the hypercomplex cells is integrated to form a whole perceptual representation of the visual stimulus. The idea, then, is that visual information is transmitted from the bottom level (i.e. initial sensory input) through a series of stages to the higher levels of analysis where information is synthesized.

Top-down processing

It is clear that physical properties, such as areas of light and shade, changes in direction and orientation, size and structural relationships, are important factors in the object-recognition process. However, there is another important contribution to object recognition that is

A2 Cognitive Psychology

called *top-down* or *conceptually driven processing*. According to this approach, the process of object recognition is guided primarily by expectations that are based on the context in which the stimulus is embedded, and on our knowledge about the world. In other words, we expect certain objects to be in certain locations and these expectations aid rapid object recognition. Have a go at the following activity before you read any further.

ACTIVITY

Reading recognition

Try reading the following fragmented sentence:

Sk-lled re-d-rs f-nd it e-sy to r-ad se-t-nc-s ev-n if t-ey a-e inco-pl-te.

You probably found it relatively easy to read the sentence above, even if it took slightly longer than reading a complete sentence. The fact that we can make sense of fragmented script suggests that reading cannot simply be a bottom-up processing task relying on stimulus information alone. According to Matlin (1998), the typical reader would need to make about 5,000 feature-detections a minute if reading involved identification of each component letter in terms of its distinctive features. This is obviously highly unlikely.

The idea that past experience and knowledge can influence perception was first put forward by Helmholtz in the nineteenth century, in the form of his *likelihood principle*, i.e. we will perceive the object which is most likely to occur in that particular situation. Palmer (1975) illustrated this principle by presenting participants with a picture of a familiar scene, such as a kitchen. He then very briefly flashed a drawing of an individual item onto the screen and asked participants to identify it. The rate of correct identification was 84

per cent for objects that might be expected from the context (e.g. a loaf of bread). However, performance fell to below 50 per cent for unexpected objects such as a letterbox. It seems that prior exposure to a kitchen scene primes recognition of associated objects.

A more recent formulation of the likelihood principle is to be found in Gregory's (1973) idea that perception is governed by *hypothesis testing*. Gregory believes that human perceivers act like intuitive scientists, i.e. they formulate and test hypotheses about the world. Sometimes these hypotheses are wrong and this can lead us to experience visual illusions (see Unit 16), but they can often help us to identify stimuli that are ambiguous or degraded. A good example is when we are able to decipher poor handwriting. Expectations arise from the context and allow hypotheses to be generated so that we can read quite degraded script provided it makes sense.

Try reading the sentence in Fig. 15.9. You should have no difficulty in deciphering that it says: 'Unfortunately the 5.00 pm class is cancelled today'.

Figure 15.9 >> *Handwriting sample*

However, if you now look closely, you will see that the '5' and the 's' at the end of 'class' are written in exactly the same way, the 'U' of 'Unfortunately' is the same as the 'll' of 'cancelled' and the 'cl' of 'class' is the same as the 'd' at the end of 'cancelled' – it is only the context that allows us to differentiate between them.

In practice, perception involves a combination of top-down and bottom-up processing.

RESEARCH STUDIES AND THEORIES OF FACE RECOGNITION

One of the most active, current research areas in pattern recognition concerns the perception of faces. Recognizing faces is very important for human social functioning. It can help us to form relationships, recognize a friend in a crowd and give us non-verbal cues about what a person is thinking and feeling.

All faces have eyes, nose and mouth placed in the same relative locations and yet we are able to identify thousands of different faces. Furthermore, we are able to recognize a particular face, e.g. the face of a best friend, regardless of the expression – angry, sad, amused, etc.

Research studies of face recognition

One of the most obvious ways of discriminating between faces seems to be on the basis of gender. Bruce *et al.* (1993) took photos of large numbers of men and women who were wearing swimming hats to conceal their hairstyles. The women wore no make-up and the men were closely shaven. In spite of the lack of obvious gender cues, observers were 96 per cent accurate in sorting the photos into appropriate gender piles.

According to many of the pattern recognition theories discussed earlier, analysis occurs in a bottom-up fashion. Psychologists have suggested that we might also recognize faces using a feature-detection approach, i.e. we might use information about individual features such as eye colour or mouth shape to build up a representation of the face. This approach is the basis of Identikit – a system used by some police forces to build up the face of a criminal on a feature-by-feature basis.

Bradshaw and Wallace (1971) used Identikit to construct pairs of faces that shared a number of features, but differed in others (see Fig. 15.10). Participants were asked to decide as quickly as possible whether pairs of faces were the same or different. The more differences there were between the two faces, the faster the judgements.

Bradshaw and Wallace (1971) concluded that participants were processing facial features independently and in serial fashion. Using sequential comparison of features, participants would encounter differences between the two faces sooner if there were several features that differed. However, these data can be interpreted differently. Sergent (1984) pointed out that the faces that differed in several features were also very different in terms of their overall configuration and that it may have been this factor which allowed participants to make speedy judgements. Sergent (1984) conducted her own study based on Identikit pictures and found that the faces were being processed in a holistic form, rather than as a set of independent features.

In another study, Young et al. (1987) supported the idea that we recognize faces by processing information about the overall configuration of the face, rather than by analysing individual features. They combined photos of the top half of one celebrity face with the bottom half of another. When the two halves were closely aligned to create a single face, participants experienced great difficulty in identifying the top half. This task became much easier when the two halves were misaligned or when the top half was presented in isolation. This seems to suggest that the close alignment in the first condition produced a novel configuration that interfered with recognition.

It seems likely that we process faces rather differently from other visual stimuli. Tanaka and Farah (1993) showed participants a set of six visual stimuli that included pictures of houses and pictures of faces. Once participants had become familiar with the items, they were given various recognition tests. For example, on some trials, they were asked to choose which of two face parts they had seen before, e.g. two noses. On other trials, they were asked to select which of two whole faces they had seen before. On these trials, the faces usually differed only by one feature, e.g. they had a different nose. There were similar trials showing pictures of whole houses or individual features, e.g. windows. Tanaka and Farah found that participants were far more accurate at recognizing facial features when they appeared in the context of a whole face, rather than in isolation. However, in the house trials, they were just as accurate for the house features presented in isolation, as for the house features appearing in the context of the whole house.

Yin (1969) found that recognition for faces is far superior to recognition for buildings, but that this superiority is reversed when the pictures are turned upside down. The explanation for such findings seems to be that normal recognition of upright faces depends on holistic processing, but that this configuration of facial features is lost when the face is turned upside down. Try the following activity to demonstrate this yourself.

(a) Starter face

(b) Different nose and chin

(c) Different nose, chin, mouth and hair

(d) Different nose, chin, mouth, eyes, brow and face lines

Figure 15.10 >> *Examples of faces similar to those used by Bradshaw and Wallace (1971). Face pairs were constructed showing differences in two, four or seven facial features*
Source: *Roth and Bruce (1995, p. 144)*

Upside-down facial recognition

Find a magazine, e.g. a TV guide, that contains lots of photos of famous people. Turn the magazine upside down and leaf through. How many celebrities are you able to identify? People who would be instantly recognizable in the upright position become much harder to identify.

Theories of face recognition

Bruce and Young (1986) have put forward an influential model of face recognition. Their model incorporated aspects of earlier formulations by Hay and Young (1982) and Ellis (1986) (see Fig. 15.11).

The model includes a number of different processing modules that are linked in sequence and in parallel.

- *Structural encoding* – separate stages of representation of the facial image.
- *Expression analysis* – drawing inferences about a person's emotional state from an analysis of their facial features.
- *Facial speech analysis* – making use of visual information from the face when deciphering speech. Bruce and Young sometimes refer to this as lip-reading.

- *Directed visual processing* – allows for certain kinds of face processing to occur without the necessity for recognizing the identity of the person, e.g. seeing whether or not the individual has a moustache.
- *Face recognition units* – stored structural descriptions of familiar faces.
- *Person identity nodes (PINs)* – provide personal details about an individual who is already known to the observer, e.g. their occupation or interests.
- *Name generation* – the name of the individual is stored separately from their other details.
- *Cognitive system* – this seems to hold additional information that might be of use in face recognition. For example, imagine you see someone in a local shop who looks like the Queen. The cognitive system would evaluate the likelihood of seeing her in such a context and save you from the potential embarrassment of misidentification. It also seems to play a part in determining which components of the system need to be activated.

Modifications to the Bruce and Young model

Burton *et al.* (1990) and Burton and Bruce (1993) have revised the original model and implemented aspects of it using an artificial intelligence model. The major differences in the new formulation are as follows:

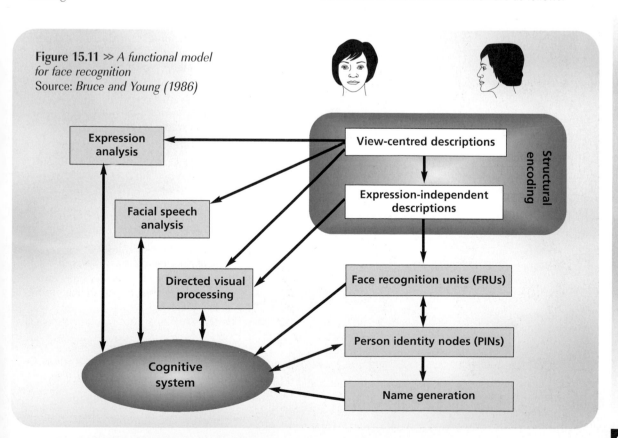

Figure 15.11 >> *A functional model for face recognition*
Source: *Bruce and Young (1986)*

- There is no separate store for names.
- Decisions about the familiarity of a particular face are made at the person-identity nodes, instead of at the face recognition units.
- The model has been made more precise and has been demonstrated in a computer simulation.

This model is being extended and updated and seems to provide plausible accounts of many aspects of face recognition. It cannot, however, account for the processes that allow new faces to be learned and for new identities to be stored in memory.

Progress in the field of face recognition research has been rapid over the past 10 years and it is likely that Bruce (1995) is correct when she predicts 'in only a few years time we should have several further pieces of the puzzle in place'.

Evaluation
theories of face recognition
(A02)

- *Empirical evidence* – There is considerable empirical evidence to support Bruce and Young's model that there are independent routes involved in processing facial expressions, facial speech and the identification of specific individuals. Much of the evidence comes from clinical studies of people with neurological defects that disrupt normal perception.
  - Young *et al.* (1993) investigated face perception in 34 ex-servicemen who had received missile wounds to the posterior regions of the brain. Some were selectively poor at familiar face recognition, whereas others only experienced difficulties in matching unfamiliar faces. Others found it difficult to decipher facial expressions accurately.

  - Sergent and Signoret (1992) conducted a study in which healthy individuals were given similar tasks to do while undergoing a PET scan. The three different activities were found to activate slightly different locations in the brain. These findings provide compelling evidence for the independence of these three functions.

- *Weak explanation* – The model has been influential and seems to account successfully for certain aspects of face recognition. However, some of the components in the model have been less well explained than others. In particular, the role of the cognitive system is not clearly specified. Bruce and Young (1986) have recognized this weakness and admitted that the cognitive system 'serves to catch all those aspects of processing not reflected in other components of our model'.

CHECK YOUR UNDERSTANDING

Check your understanding of pattern recognition by answering these questions. Try to do this from memory at first. You can check your answers by looking back through Topic 3.

1 What do you understand by the term 'pattern recognition'?

2 Explain how template theory accounts for pattern recognition.

3 Give one strength and one weakness of prototype theories.

4 Outline the findings of one study of target detection and explain how it supports feature-detection theory.

5 Summarize the role of biological mechanisms in pattern recognition.

6 Give a brief description and evaluation of feature-detection theories.

7 Outline how research has demonstrated the importance of context in pattern recognition.

8 Describe two studies of face recognition.

9 List the eight components of the face recognition model of Bruce and Young.

10 What are the main modifications made to the original model by Burton and Bruce?

REVISION SUMMARY

Having covered this topic, you should be able to describe and evaluate:

✓ template, prototype and feature-detection theories of pattern recognition

✓ the role of biological mechanisms and context in pattern recognition

✓ research studies and theories of face recognition.

EXAMPLE EXAM QUESTIONS

Below are some **possible examination questions** set on this topic, along with hints to help you understand and approach each question effectively:

1 Discuss explanations of pattern recognition (e.g. template and feature-detection theories). (24 marks)

> General questions such as this may appear a 'gift', but often cause problems because candidates have too much to write. The plural 'explanations' means that you must write about at least two explanations, but two would be enough for full marks. Many students try to write about too much in questions such as these and end up losing marks because their answers are not detailed enough.
>
> Two theories are suggested as examples in the question, but don't feel that you must do these theories – they are provided as examples only. For your AO2 commentary, two things are important. First it must be *effective* – it must be clear to the examiner what the point is you are trying to make: in what way is your commentary a positive or negative criticism? Second, it must be *elaborated* – which contributes to its effectiveness. Do not present one-line comments; you must justify any comments you make.

2 (a) Critically consider the role of biological mechanisms in pattern recognition. (12 marks)

    (b) Critically consider the role of context in pattern recognition. (12 marks)

> 'Critically consider' requires both AO1 and AO2, so your answer should neatly break down into four chunks of 150 words (answers for 30-minute questions should generally be about 600 words). The question focuses on the role of biological mechanism and the role of context, both of which are specified in the specification rather than being given as examples. This means that questions can be set explicitly on these, so you should be prepared for this kind of question.

3 (a) Describe **one** research study of face recognition. (6 marks)

    (b) Outline and evaluate **one** theory of face recognition. (18 marks)

> You are required to know about both research studies and theories related to face recognition, so questions 3, 4 and 5 are all legitimate. The split of marks given here should guide you as to how much time to allocate to each part of the question. In describing one research study, you might recall the divisions used at AS-level: aims, procedures, findings and conclusions. If you write a few sentences on each, you should build up the necessary detail for full marks.
>
> In part (b), the question focus changes to one theory, again 6 marks for describing this theory and then 12 marks for commentary. One way to provide commentary would be by alternative theories as evaluation, but this must be effective and sustained. It is not sufficient to say 'In contrast there is theory 2 …' and then merely offer a description of the second theory.

continued on next page

4 (a) Outline **two** theories of face recognition. (12 marks)
(b) Evaluate these theories of face recognition in terms of relevant research evidence. (12 marks)

> In part (a), it would be creditworthy to present modifications of the Bruce and Young theory as a separate theory, though you must make this explicitly clear. In order to avoid a partial performance penalty in part (b), you must make sure that you evaluate both theories separately or make clear that your comments apply to both theories.

5 Discuss research (theories **and/or** studies) into pattern recognition. (24 marks)

> This question combines both previous questions, though it would be acceptable to write about only one theory of face recognition because no plurality is given in the question. If you know enough about one theory, then this might be a good approach because you would ensure lots of detail. However, you may *describe* research studies as well to attract AO1 marks. Alternatively, such studies may be used as part of a sustained critical commentary, and other theories may be used in the same way. Both studies and theories may be AO1 or AO2 – the distinction between them lies in how the material is used.

UNIT SUMMARY

Topic 1: Focused attention

● In this unit, we have considered various aspects of attention. Early research in this field, initiated by **Cherry** (1953), concentrated particularly on **focused** or **selective attention**, whereby we focus on one input to the exclusion of all other competing inputs.

● **Broadbent** (1958) proposed an influential model of focused attention. This was a single channel, **early-selection** model in which one input was selected at a very early stage in the processing on the basis of physical properties and then passed on in serial fashion for semantic analysis.

● There were immediate challenges to the theory and **Treisman** (1964) put forward an attenuator model which proposed a more flexible filter (selector). One input is strongly selected but other inputs are allowed through in attenuated form.

● **Deutsch and Deutsch** (1963), in their so-called **late-selection model**, proposed that all inputs are fully analysed for meaning and that only then is a single input selected for conscious awareness.

● On balance, Treisman's early-selection theory seems better able to account for all the experimental data. During the 1970s, researchers began to see the limitations of the single channel models and started investigating the idea that attention is limited by capacity.

Topic 2: Divided attention

● It is clear that we are often able to divide our attention between tasks. Psychologists, using the dual-task performance technique, have investigated the circumstances under which this is possible, looking at factors such as task difficulty, task similarity and practice.

● One of the first theories put forward to explain **divided attention** was proposed by **Kahneman**. His **capacity resource allocation model** of attention rested on the assumption that the overall amount of attentional **resource** is limited. Factors such as arousal and mental effort can affect available capacity.

- Capacity theories are reasonably flexible, but they cannot satisfactorily account for all experimental findings.

- Modular theories, such as that proposed by Allport, can account for some of the findings that have proved incompatible with capacity theories. However, they are also criticized for being vague and descriptive rather than explanatory.

- Tasks seem to be easier to combine if one of them has become automatic. Shiffrin and Schneider (1977) have distinguished between **automatic** and **controlled processing**, although the distinction is not always entirely clear-cut.

- **Action slips**, which can sometimes occur during the course of carrying out a well-learned or **automatic** activity, have been investigated by a number of psychologists, including **Reason** (1979). There is currently no complete theoretical explanation of such errors, although Norman (1981) has proposed an explanation based on schema theory.

Topic 3: Pattern recognition

- There have been various theories of **pattern recognition** ranging from simple **template** matching to **feature-detection theories**.

- Feature-detection theories have received some support from **biological** research such as that carried out by **Hubel and Wiesel**. However, none of these theories provides a comprehensive account of human pattern recognition. They are based on **bottom-up processing** and do not account for the important effects of context and past experience (**top-down processing**).

- **Face recognition** is a special kind of pattern recognition that has attracted considerable research interest over the last few years. **Bruce and Young** have put forward an influential theory of **face recognition** that has been supported by a number of studies. However, it has not proved adequate and Burton and Bruce have made modifications. This formulation looks promising and has been shown to operate effectively in computer models. This is a rapidly developing field and new theories are likely to emerge in the near future.

FURTHER RESOURCES

Eysenck, M.W. and Keane, M.T. (2000) *Cognitive Psychology: A Student's Handbook* **(4th edn), Hove: Psychology Press.**

This is a good, all-round textbook on cognitive psychology. It has excellent sections on all the topics covered in this unit and, although aimed at undergraduates, the style is reasonably accessible and straightforward for A2-level students.

Styles, E.A. (1997) *The Psychology of Attention*, **Hove: Psychology Press.**

This is an excellent and comprehensive text on the field of attention. It is intended for undergraduates and contains some material that is beyond the scope of the A2-level specification. However, it is clearly written and the appropriate sections are quite accessible for students wishing to research the area in more detail.

Websites

www.richardgregory.org

Contains more information about Gregory's theory of hypothesis testing and the role of context in pattern recognition.

http://faculty.washington.edu/chudler/java/ready.html

Try the Stroop test for yourself.

Unit 15 // Attention and pattern recognition

16
UNIT

PERCEPTUAL PROCESSES &
Development

PREVIEW

After you have read this unit, you should be able to describe and evaluate:

>> the structure and function of the visual system and research into the nature of visual processing

>> theories of perceptual organization, including constructivist and direct theories, and their explanations of perceptual organization

>> explanations of perceptual development and studies of the development of perceptual abilities.

INTRODUCTION

Perception is an important area of study for psychologists because everything we know about the external world must first come in through our senses. The world around us is filled with people and objects which we can see, hear, touch, smell or taste. We receive this information as sensations arriving at sense organs in the body, such as the eyes, ears and nose. These sense organs contain sensory receptors which detect the physical properties of the world around us, such as light and sound, and pass this information to the brain and the central nervous system (CNS). This information is then converted through a number of processes into our perceptual experience of the world. Cognitive psychologists are interested in explaining the mental activity required to convert physical information from the environment into the psychological experience of perception. There has been a huge amount of research into perceptual processing, but most of it has concentrated on visual perception and that will be the focus of this unit.

Although perception occurs within the brain, our first contact with the external visual world is through our sense organs. It is, therefore, important to understand the physical make-up of the eye and visual pathways in the brain. We will look at the structure and function of the visual system and consider some of the research into the nature of visual information processing. We will then consider two rather different theories of perception. Gibson (e.g. 1979) first coined the term 'direct perception' to convey the idea that we pick up sufficient information from the visual environment to be able to form a conscious percept and that we do not need to make use of higher level cognitive processing in order to make sense of the visual world. An alternative view is called the constructivist approach (or 'intelligent perception'). According to this view, we often need to go beyond the information contained in the visual stimulus and use stored memories based on our previous experience to help us build or construct our conscious experience of the world. In particular, we will consider how these two approaches have helped us to understand the ways in which perception is organized.

The last section in this unit will focus on perceptual development and, in particular, on the nature–nurture debate, i.e. the question of whether adult perceptual skills are innate or develop as a result of learning through experience.

Jane
Willson

Motion agnosia

This is an account of a female patient who was admitted to hospital with damage to part of her cerebral cortex that is known to be associated with the perception of movement.

<< She had difficulty, for example, in pouring tea or coffee into a cup because the fluid appeared to be frozen, like a glacier. In addition, she could not stop pouring at the right time since she was unable to perceive the movement in the cup when the fluid rose. Furthermore, the patient complained of difficulties in following a dialogue because she could not see the movements of the face, and, especially, the mouth of the speaker. In a room where more than two people were walking she felt very insecure and unwell, and usually left the room immediately, because 'people were suddenly here or there but I have not seen them moving'. >> (Zihl *et al.* 1983, p. 315)

1 Read the description of motion agnosia. This shows how important the perception of motion is for everyday functioning. What other types of perception do you think are equally important?

2 Look at picture A and then at picture B. What do you see in picture B?

3 Now think how you would interpret picture B if you had been given a picture of a cat instead of an old lady in picture A. Why do you think you would see picture B differently?

A

B

KEY CONCEPTS

Constructivist theories: top-down (or concept-driven) theories that emphasize the need for several sources of information in order to construct our perception of the world. In addition, we need to use higher cognitive processes to interpret the information appropriately.

Direct theories: bottom-up (or data-driven) theories proposing that there is sufficient information in the sensory stimulus to allow us to make sense of our environment without the involvement of stored knowledge or problem-solving skills.

Nature–nurture debate: the controversy about the relative contributions of genetic factors (nature) versus environmental factors (nurture) in determining a person's characteristics and abilities.

Perceptual development: the systematic change of perceptual abilities and processes that develop as a result of maturation and experience.

Visual perception: the process by which we transform sensory information from the eyes to produce an experience of depth, distance, colour, etc.

Visual information processing: the transformation of a visual input into a meaningful perceptual experience.

Sensory adaptation: the ability of the sensory systems to adapt to a change in the environment.

The starting point for visual perception is light. Light is a narrow band of the electromagnetic spectrum with a wavelength of between 380 and 760 nanometers (1 nm is a billionth of a metre) which is visible to humans. Other types of electromagnetic energy, such as ultraviolet radiation, gamma rays and x-rays, are not visible to the human eye.

The reason that we are able to see various objects and people around us is that light is reflected from these things into our eyes. This reflected light is focused to create an image in the eye, which, in turn, causes electrical signals to trigger a chain of events in the brain which lead to conscious perception. Light falls on the back of the eyes as two small, upside-down, two-dimensional images, but what we actually 'see' is a coherent, colourful, three-dimensional world that is the right way up. We need to consider how this transformation occurs.

STRUCTURE AND FUNCTIONS OF THE VISUAL SYSTEM

The eye

Look at the cross-section of the eye in Fig. 16.1 before reading any further.

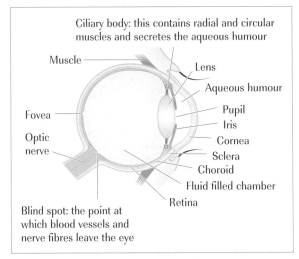

Ciliary body: this contains radial and circular muscles and secretes the aqueous humour

Muscle

Lens

Aqueous humour

Fovea

Pupil

Iris

Optic nerve

Cornea

Sclera

Choroid

Fluid filled chamber

Retina

Blind spot: the point at which blood vessels and nerve fibres leave the eye

Figure 16.1 >> *Cross-section through the eye*

The eye is an extremely delicate organ and, for protection, lies within a bony socket in the skull. It is protected externally by the eyelid which keeps out dust and dirt from the atmosphere and which closes in an automatic reflex action at the sudden approach of an object or movement towards the eye. The outer covering or 'white' of the eye is a strong elastic membrane called the sclera which is opaque and cannot admit light. The sclera bulges forward at the front of the eye to form a clear, domed window called the cornea. It is the first optically active element in the eye and its function is to gather and concentrate light reflected from objects in the environment. Because it has to remain completely transparent, the cornea cannot be nourished by blood vessels and so oxygen and nutrients are provided by a watery substance called the aqueous humour which fills the small chamber behind the cornea. Behind the chamber is a variable aperture – the pupil – which is controlled by a ring of coloured muscles called the iris. The colour of the iris seems to be determined genetically and can vary from blue, green, violet, brown to almost black. The function of the iris is to regulate the size of the pupil in response to external stimuli. Bright light will cause the pupil to constrict to as little as 2 mm in diameter, but, under dim light conditions, the pupil can dilate to up to 8 mm. This process of contraction and dilation occurs automatically and is not under conscious control.

The lens is situated directly behind the pupil and its function is to complete the process begun in the cornea of bringing light into focus on the *retina* at the back of the eye. The natural shape of the lens is spheroid, but, through a process called 'accommodation', it can change its shape to bring objects at various distances into focus. To focus on nearby objects, the lens becomes fatter and, to focus on more distant objects, the lens becomes thinner. Accommodation occurs automatically in adults, but does not seem possible for newborn infants whose focus appears fixed at about 19 cm (i.e. the approximate distance of the mother's face from the baby's during breastfeeding). Babies usually develop the ability to accommodate by about 8 weeks, but this ability declines with age. The lens loses elasticity as people grow older and they often become long-sighted (i.e. they have to hold a book at arm's length in order to be able to focus on the print) and they may need to wear corrective glasses. The lens has a slight yellow pigment which acts to screen out some of the ultraviolet light coming into the eye. This yellow tint becomes more pronounced with age and can affect experience of colour, particularly the distinction between blues and greens.

It is possible to focus on objects that are distant and close, but you cannot do both at the same time. In your normal everyday activities, the lens is constantly changing shape to focus on objects at different distances, and the process of accommodation works so quickly and efficiently that you probably feel that everything in the visual scene is in focus simultaneously. However, accommodation ceases to work when an object is too close to your face.

The retina

Light then passes through a large chamber filled with a jelly-like substance called 'vitreous humour' (which helps to maintain the spherical shape of the eye) and falls on the retina. The retina effectively works as a screen that covers most of the interior of the eye and it is here that light is changed or transduced into a neural response. It consists of three main layers of neural tissue:

- the outermost layers contain photoreceptors (light-sensitive cells)
- the middle layer contains bipolar cells (neurones)
- the third layer contains ganglion cells.

See Fig. 16.2 for a schematic diagram of the retina.

The photoreceptors consist of two different types of cell – rods and cones – and these appear to differ in both function and distribution. There are about 5 million cones in each retina and about 50,000 (i.e. about 1 per cent of the total number) are packed into the small central area called the fovea (Tyler 1997) (see Fig. 16.1). The fovea is a small depression at the centre of the retina no bigger than the size of this 'o', which is responsible for our most detailed and accurate vision. The other cones are in the peripheral retina where they are outnumbered by rods by a ratio of about 20 to 1. All 120 million rods are in the peripheral retina. Rods are believed to be responsible for vision under dim light conditions (scotopic system) and cones are responsible for vision under bright conditions (photopic system) and also for the experience of colour vision. Having these two different functional systems allows human observers to see over a wide range of light intensities.

The photoreceptor cells release neurotransmitter molecules to the bipolar cells which, in turn, connect to the ganglion cells. Axons from the ganglion cells then pass from the eye into the brain. The back-to-front

Figure 16.2 >> *Schematic diagram of the retina*

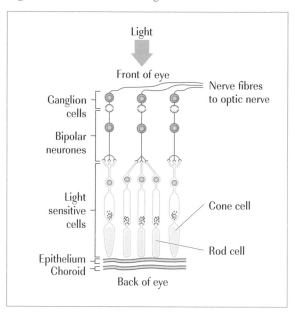

arrangement of the three cell layers in the retina (i.e. with the photoreceptors at the back facing away from the light) means that light has to pass through the other two layers first. This poses no problem because the bipolar and ganglion cells are transparent. The arrangement could, however, present a difficulty for the ganglion cell axons leaving the retina because the photoreceptors would block their exit. This problem is overcome by having a small area at the back of the retina which is completely free of photoreceptors, thus leaving a gap where one million ganglion cell fibres can leave the eye to form the optic nerve. However, the absence of photoreceptors at this point means that a blind spot is created. Now try the activity below.

Unit 16 // Perceptual processes and development

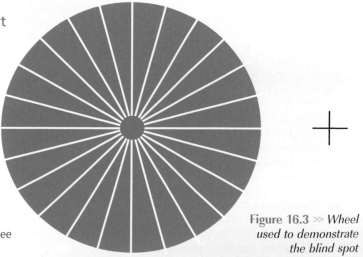

ACTIVITY

Demonstrating the blind spot

Hold the book out at arm's length in front of you. Close your right eye and focus with your left eye on the cross in Fig. 16.3. Gradually move the page towards you. At some point, the centre of the wheel will fall on your blind spot. You may need to do this several times before the centre disappears. However, once you locate your blind spot, you do not experience a void. The brain seems to 'fill in' the missing information and, according to Ramachandran (1992), you are likely to see the spokes of the wheel fill in the hole.

Figure 16.3 >> *Wheel used to demonstrate the blind spot*

We are not usually aware of the blind spot. This is partly because we have two eyes and so, if the image falls on the blind spot of one eye, it will be picked up by receptors in the other eye. We also seem to compensate for the blind spot – via some mechanism which is not yet fully understood – by 'filling in' the place from which the information has disappeared.

The visual pathways

The nerve impulses that travel along the optic nerve are no longer in the form of raw sense data because a great deal of neural processing has already taken place in the retina. The optic nerves from each eye come together at the base of the brain to form the optic chiasma (see Fig. 12.7 on p. 393).

The optic nerve fibres from the nasal retinas (the parts of the retina closest to the nose) cross to the opposite side of the brain at this point, while the fibres from the temporal retinas (the parts of the retina closest to the temples) continue on the same side of the brain. After they pass through the optic chiasm, the axons of the ganglion cells are called the optic tract. Most of the optic tract axons lead to the lateral geniculate nucleus

(LGN) which is part of the thalamus. Here they form optic radiations which lead to the primary visual cortex (or striate cortex) where additional processing is carried out. However, each module of the primary visual cortex only sees what is happening in one tiny section of the visual field. Information from these modules is combined in the visual association cortex so that we can experience whole objects and complete visual scenes. Once it arrives in the visual association cortex, the pathway diverges into two streams. These seem to have different functions:

- One terminates in the parietal lobe (the part of the brain just above the ears) and seems to provide information about visually guided movements. It probably allows people to detect the direction of moving targets, to judge the distance of approaching and retreating objects, and to reach out and grab objects.

- The other one terminates in the temporal lobe (the part of the brain beneath the temples) and seems to provide information about the nature of the thing being observed, i.e. whether it is dog, chair or carrot; if it is something to be welcomed or feared, etc.

Commentary

temporal lobe pathway and perception

A02

If either pathway is damaged, it causes severe problems for perception. Ramachandran and Blakeslee (1999) report on a study carried out by Kluver and Bucy (1939). They removed the pathway

in the temporal lobe from monkeys who were then able to walk around without bumping into one another or the walls of their cage (i.e. they still had spatial awareness), but who had real difficulties in recognizing objects and understanding their function. In the intact brain, these two pathways work in tandem and it is hard to separate out their contributions to the perceptual experience.

RESEARCH INTO VISUAL INFORMATION PROCESSING

It is clear from the previous section that the visual system is not a passive recipient of visual input, but that it actively transforms the original stimulus input into a meaningful perceptual experience. This is the process called 'visual information processing'.

Sensory adaptation

One characteristic of all the sensory systems is the ability to adapt to a change in the environment.

Sensory adaptation refers to a temporary decrease in sensitivity that occurs when a sensory system is exposed to a particular stimulus for a period of time and the temporary increase in sensitivity that occurs when a sensory system is not stimulated for a time. For example, if you dive into an unheated swimming pool, the water is likely to strike you as very cold at first, but after a while, your body adapts and you are said to have shifted to a new adaptation level. This means that you now have a new point of reference for cold/hot judgements. At this new adaptation level, an ice cube would now feel less cold on your skin than under normal conditions. Conversely, a cup with a hot drink would feel hotter in your hand than usual. However, once you get out of the pool and dry yourself off in the sun, your body will adapt to this warmer environment and so you will reach a different adaptation level.

Sensory adaptation appears to occur without conscious control and does not seem to depend on learning or experience. If you go back into the water after an hour of sunbathing, your body will go through the same process of adaptation and will take about the same length of time.

Sensory adaptation probably has evolutionary significance – once stimuli have been observed and recognized as posing no threat, they are of less significance for survival and need less attention. This means that sensory systems can be alert to changes in the environment.

Dark and light adaptation

One example of sensory adaptation in vision occurs when the visual system has to adjust to a sudden change in conditions from light to dark. Many motorists find driving in twilight conditions quite difficult because, although both rods and cones are operating, neither is operating at full effectiveness. It is even more difficult to cope if the change from light to darkness occurs more suddenly as, for example, when you go into a dark cinema from the brightly lit foyer. After a few minutes, your eyes become accustomed to the dark conditions (dark adaptation) and you are able to see other people in the cinema even though the lighting conditions have not changed. Similarly, if you come in from the dark into a bright room, you often squint or even shut your eyes briefly while they adjust to the change in light intensity. This is called light adaptation and usually occurs more quickly than dark adaptation.

Both kinds of photoreceptors contain photopigments, each of which consists of a molecule derived from vitamin A and a protein molecule. When struck by a particle of light (a photon), photopigments split into their two constituent molecules. This splitting marks the beginning of the process of transduction whereby light is changed into a neural response. Intact photopigments have a characteristic colour – for example, the photopigment rhodopsin is a pinkish-red. Once the action of light causes the photopigment to split, the colour breaks down and becomes bleached. The molecules rapidly recombine so that the photopigment is ready to be bleached again. Each photoreceptor cell contains thousands of molecules of photopigment, but the number of unbleached molecules present at any one moment depends on the relative rate at which they are being split by incoming photons and then re-combined. The number of bleached molecules increases the brighter the light because there are so many photons striking the photopigments. In very bright conditions, the rate of recombination of the molecules lags behind the rate of the bleaching process so that very few intact photopigment molecules remain. If you then go into a room with very dim levels of light, the likelihood of a photon striking an intact photopigment is very low. However, after a while, the regeneration of the photopigment overcomes the effects of the bleaching and the rods become full of unbleached rhodopsin so that incoming photons are much more likely to find an intact target. This is the process of dark adaptation.

Contrast processing

In order to be able to see clearly, it is important to have visual acuity, i.e. the ability to discern fine detail. However, visual acuity is not enough for excellent vision. It is also important to be able to detect brightness differences as well. Brightness is not an actual quantity of light intensity, but rather, our impression of light intensity. Visual contrast refers to the difference in brightness levels between adjoining areas. You can see this by looking at Fig. 16.4.

You probably experience the central square in (a) to be the brightest although all four central squares are actually exactly the same. The brightness of the light-green patch seems to depend on the difference between the contrasting regions so that it seems brighter the darker the background. This is known as the 'simultaneous lightness contrast'.

Figure 16.4 >> *Demonstration of the simultaneous lightness contrast*

(a)   (b)   (c)   (d)

Research into contrast processing

The physiological mechanism underlying simultaneous lightness contrast was first investigated by Hartline *et al.* (1956). They used the horseshoe crab because the make-up of its eye renders investigation easier than in the human eye. They monitored responses from a cell that is functionally similar to a human ganglion cell. Stimulation of the receptor attached to this cell caused increased activity in the cell, but this activity decreased if the researchers then illuminated another receptor located a short distance away. This suggested that illumination of neighbouring receptors inhibits the firing of the original receptor. They called this 'lateral inhibition' because its effects seem to be transmitted laterally, or sideways, across the retina. The amount of inhibition depends on the strength of stimulation any one receptor is receiving. The more a cell is stimulated and the closer it is to an adjacent cell, the more it will inhibit the activity of the other.

Commentary
contrast processing

This mechanism explains the simultaneous contrast effect experienced when looking at Fig. 16.4. The receptors exposed to the central square in (d) are illuminated by a light of moderate intensity while the receptors exposed to the surround in (d) are stimulated by light of high intensity. Since the receptors exposed to the surround are more intensely stimulated, they exert strong inhibition on the receptors exposed to the central square. This reduces their neural response rate and causes the central square to appear dimmer. The receptors exposed to the dark surround in (a) are not exposed to light of high intensity and so their inhibitory effect on their neighbouring cells is not strong. Since there is only minimal inhibition, the receptors exposed to the central square are not turned down so fiercely as for the square in (d) and so it is perceived to be brighter. So, even though the two central squares in (a) and (d) reflect exactly the same amount of light into our eyes, the differences in the amount of inhibition they receive from their surrounds make them seem to differ in terms of brightness.

Colour processing

In physical terms, what we refer to as colour should strictly speaking be termed 'hue', i.e. the wavelength of light reflected from an object. People with normal colour vision are able to see light waves of various hues within the visible electromagnetic spectrum. The shortest wavelengths we can see are violet (400 nm) and the longest are red (700 nm). Hue alone cannot explain all our experience of colour because saturation is also a factor. Saturation refers to the purity or richness of a colour, so that saturated hues seem to be vivid while desaturated hues look pastel or washed out. The average human observer can reliably discriminate among at least 200 different hues. We need to look at how this remarkable level of achievement comes about.

Trichromatic theory

An early theory of colour processing was proposed by Thomas Young in 1802 and then modified by the German physiologist von Helmholtz (1896). They believed that the human eye contains three kinds of colour receptor, each sensitive to a different hue (red, green and blue) and that the brain combines information from all three receptors and is thus able to synthesize any colour. Yellow, for example is produced when red and green receptors are stimulated simultaneously, while white is produced when all three receptor types are stimulated simultaneously (see Fig. 16.5). This is known as the 'trichromatic theory'.

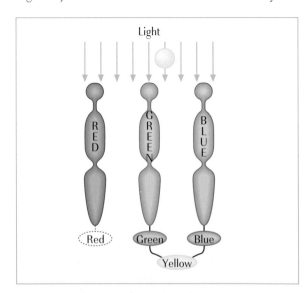

Figure 16.5 >> *The action of light on colour receptors, according to trichromatic theory*

A2 Cognitive Psychology

Commentary
trichromatic theory

AO2

● *Support for the theory* – There is some support for this theory and more recent studies have confirmed that there are three kinds of light-sensitive pigments in the cones. These do not correspond exactly to the Young–Helmholtz distinctions – one is primarily sensitive to wavelengths in the blue band, one is sensitive to green and the third is sensitive to the yellowish-red part of the spectrum – but they do confirm the existence of three types of cone.

● *A problem for the theory* – However, the Young–Helmholtz theory has not been able to account for some of the data from studies of colour-blindness. People with red/green colour-blindness have no difficulty in recognizing yellow, and yet trichromatic theory suggests that yellow perception is dependent on stimulation of red and green receptors.

Opponent process theory

Hering in 1870 tried to address the problems raised by the trichromatic theory. He believed that people tend to behave as if there are four and not three, primary colours and that yellow is seen alongside red, green and blue as a pure colour. This has been confirmed in later studies, e.g. Fuld *et al.* (1981). Hering noted that certain colour combinations, such as yellowish-blue or greenish-red are never reported and this led him to speculate that the four primary colours are arranged in opposing pairs. One opponent process would operate for red and green, while a separate opponent process would operate for yellow and blue. In other words, the activity of a single neuron would be increased by the presence of the colour red but decreased by green. Since it is impossible for a cell's activity to increase and decrease simultaneously, it would be impossible to experience reddish-green. This so-called *opponent process theory* of colour vision was later formalized by Hurvich and Jameson (1957) who also postulated a black–white opponent process to account for brightness perception.

Commentary
opponent process theory

AO2

● *Neurological support* – When Hering first proposed the opponent process theory, there was no neurological support for his hypothesis. It is now known that cells with this pattern of activity occur in the retinal ganglion cells and in cells within the lateral geniculate.

● *Afterimages* – Opponent process theory also accounts for the afterimage effect you experience if you stare at a coloured patch for a period of time and then look at a blank sheet of white paper. You will tend to see an afterimage of the same patch, but in its opponent colour.

● It seems that colour vision is at least a two-stage process incorporating elements of both these early theories. The retina contains three types of cones which respond differentially to lights of different wavelengths. Certain cells further along the visual system respond with a burst of impulses when stimulated by short wavelengths, but are inhibited when stimulated by long wavelengths, while, for other cells, it is the other way round. This suggests an opponent process operating at this level. It seems likely, in the future, that elements of the trichromatic and the opponent process theories will be synthesized to form a new, comprehensive theory of colour vision, but, as yet, there is no satisfactory complete explanation.

Feature processing

Brightness and colour are obviously important characteristics of human vision, but we also need to be able to detect contours in order to be able to recognize objects in our perceptual world. Contours can be curved or straight and can be oriented in various directions, e.g. vertical, horizontal, angled upwards, etc. Hubel and Wiesel (1959), who were pioneers in the field of single-cell recording studies in the brain, traced the path of neurons from the receptors in the retina through the ganglion cells and into the visual cortex. They identified several types of cell in the visual cortex which appear to respond to lines and edges of particular orientations. They called these simple cells, complex cells and hypercomplex cells. A simple cell responds to a line or straight edge in a particular orientation and which falls on a specific part of the retina. This cell will cease to fire if the line is tilted out of its orientation or is moved so that its image falls on a different part of the retina.

Complex cells also respond to a line in a particular orientation, but will continue to fire if the line moves (provided it maintains its orientation). Hypercomplex cells respond to lines in a particular orientation and of a particular length. Because these cells respond to particular lines and edges, they are called *feature detectors*. More recent research (e.g. DeValois and DeValois (1980), Shapley and Lennie (1985)) has found feature detectors that respond to corners and angles.

✓ CHECK YOUR UNDERSTANDING

Check your understanding of the visual system by answering these questions. Do it from memory at first. You can check your answers by looking back through Topic 1.

1 Explain briefly why light is vital to the visual process.

2 Draw and label a cross-section of the eye.

3 Write a brief description of the nature and function of each of the parts you have labelled in the diagram.

4 Identify two types of photoreceptor and explain what is the difference between them.

5 Explain why we all have a blind spot in each eye and suggest reasons why this does not usually cause us problems in our everyday life.

6 Describe the pathway of the optic nerve after it leaves the back of the eye.

7 Explain what is meant by the term 'sensory adaptation' and outline one everyday example of this.

8 Outline the findings and conclusions of a research study that has investigated contrast processing.

9 Identify one theory of colour processing and give a brief description of its main assumptions.

10 Identify three types of cell in the visual cortex which appear to respond to lines and edges.

REVISION SUMMARY

Having covered this topic you should be able to:

✓ describe the structure and functions of the visual system: the eye, retina and visual pathways

✓ describe and evaluate research into the nature of visual information processing: sensory adaptation, and the processing of contrast, colour and features.

✎ EXAMPLE EXAM QUESTIONS

Below are some **possible examination questions** set on this topic, along with hints to help you understand and approach each question effectively:

1 (a) Outline the structure and function of the eye, retina and visual pathways. (12 marks)
  (b) To what extent can these structures be used to explain perceptual processes? (12 marks)

You might think that there should be a partial performance penalty in part (a) of this question but, because there are so many different elements, it would be too difficult to administer (structure *and* function *and* eye *and* retina *and* visual pathways). The extent to which you are able to cover all aspects of the question will determine your mark. The term 'outline' is used to indicate that you may have a lot to do and therefore these will necessarily be done in less detail than if the term 'describe' was used. Part (b) is phrased in a way that should help you to produce appropriate material for AO2. 'To what extent' is an AO2 term, inviting you to consider the link between visual structures and *perception*. Perception is more than a record of sensory data. The data is summarized and meaning extracted; much of this is the outcome of cognitive processes such as expectations, but some of it is achieved in the eye. You may consider the relative contributions of all the components of the visual system in answering this part of the question (i.e. 'higher' and 'lower' processes).

2 Discuss the structure and function of the visual system. (24 marks)

> The AO1 part of the answer is very straightforward: 12 marks' worth of AO1 description. The AO2 part is more difficult – how do you evaluate the structure and function of the visual system? The answer is that you can use the same ideas as for any other question, e.g. consider advantages and disadvantages, comment on what happens when the system malfunctions, or report applications of this knowledge. All of these things assist our understanding of the *value* of the knowledge. Since the questions says structure *and* function, there would be a partial performance penalty for AO1 and AO2 if you only wrote about structure or function (maximum of 8 marks for AO1 and for AO2).

3 Describe and evaluate research into **two** forms of visual information processing (e.g. sensory adaptation and the processing of contrast, colour and features). (24 marks)

> In this question, four examples are given, but the question requires that you restrict your answer to only two (and remember they are only examples, not compulsory). If you write about more than two, only the best two will receive credit. The question contains the word 'research' which includes theories/explanations and/or studies. Avoid the danger of writing generally about visual perception, but instead focus on *research* and on *forms* of visual processing.

4 Discuss the nature of visual information processing. (24 marks)

> Broadly-worded questions such as this pose problems because you have to decide on the best direction to take. Again, it pays to decide on a structure to your answer and stick to it. Don't try to include everything you know on this topic, but only what is reasonable to write in 30 minutes and directly relevant to the question.

Topic 2 >> Perceptual organization

While appreciating the crucial contribution of physiological research, cognitive psychologists have been more interested in investigating the psychological processes involved in perception. In other words, how do we make sense of the myriad of visual stimuli that bombard the sensory system? How do we recognize objects and how do we understand the spatial relationships between them?

THEORIES OF VISUAL PERCEPTION

Theories of perception tend to fall into two categories:

● *direct theories* – which depend on bottom-up processing

● *constructivist theories* – which depend on top-down processing.

These terms derive from the information processing approach – a theoretical perspective within cognitive psychology in which the human mind is compared to a computer. According to this view, the human mind manipulates and transforms information through a series of processing stages. These can be represented schematically in flow diagrams which show the direction of the flow of information through the system (see Fig. 16.6).

Bottom-up and top-down processing are not mutually exclusive and it seems likely that we use both in our everyday life. The particular kind of processing used will probably depend on the nature of the visual stimulus.

Figure 16.6 >> *A simple flow diagram to represent processing stages*

| Input processes | → | Translation/storage processes | → | Output processes | → |

Unit 16 // Perceptual processes and development

Interaction of bottom-up and top-down processing (Palmer 1975)

Palmer (1975) carried out a study which demonstrates the way in which bottom-up and top-down processes interact. Look at Fig. 16.7(a). In themselves the drawings consist of little more than lines on the page. Palmer found that participants in his study were usually unable to recognize the objects depicted in them.

However, when he showed the participants the drawing shown in Fig. 16.7(b), they were easily able to identify the same 'squiggles' as facial features because they were embedded in a face. In Fig. 16.7(a), there is very little information available to us in the actual stimulus and there is no context to help us – we have to rely completely on bottom-up processing.
In Fig. 16.7(b), however, we can use both bottom-up and top-down processing – the facial features remain exactly the same (bottom-up), but now we have the context of a surrounding face (top-down) and so we have no difficulty in identifying the whole face and its constituent parts.

Figure 16.7 >> *Recognizing shapes in context*
Source: *Palmer (1975)*

Bottom-up and top-down processing

- *Bottom-up theories* are based on the assumption that the process of perception begins with the physical properties of visual stimuli, e.g. patterns of light reflected from objects in the environment. It is thought that there is sufficient information in the sensory stimulus to allow the individual to make sense of his or her environment without the involvement of stored knowledge or problem-solving skills. The incoming information triggers a response in the retina, which in turn triggers a response higher up in the visual pathways and so on. Bottom-up processing, then, is concerned with physiological processing from the senses, processed upwards in the direction of the cognitive system. Theories based on this are sometimes also known as 'data-driven' because the data (sensory input) received by the sensory receptors determines or 'drives' perception.

- *Top-down theories*, on the other hand, emphasize the involvement of context and prior knowledge in interpreting information derived from the sensory system. This approach stresses the importance of higher cognitive processing right from the beginning of the perceptual process. This kind of processing is also called 'concept-driven' processing because prior knowledge (stored mental concepts) determines (drives) the interpretation of the sensory data.

DIRECT THEORIES OF PERCEPTION

According to these theories, the array of information in our sensory receptors is all that we need in order to perceive and there is no necessity to call upon stored knowledge or past experience to mediate between sensory experience and perception.

Gibson's theory of direct perception

J.J. Gibson (e.g. 1979) is the best known champion of direct perception. He felt strongly that it was important to study perception in real-world environments instead of in the artificial surroundings of a laboratory. For this reason he sometimes referred to his theory as an 'ecological approach'. For example, during World War II, he was concerned with developing training programmes for pilots. One of the most difficult tasks for pilots is to land the plane; to accomplish this successfully, they require good depth perception. However, Gibson found that traditional training measures designed to help pilots make use of depth information were of little use. This finding led him to review contemporary ideas of perception and to formulate his own theory. Gibson's theory is complex and was developed over a period of more than 30 years, so we can only offer a simplified version here.

According to Goldstein (1999), the theory is based on four major assumptions:

- the pattern of light reaching the eye can be thought of as an optic array and contains all the information necessary for perception
- important information is provided by the movement of the observer
- the optic array contains invariant information, i.e. information that remains constant as the observer moves
- this invariant information leads directly to perception.

The optic array

Gibson believed that the starting point for perception is the structure of the light that reaches the observer. Light alone is insufficient for perception to occur.

To perceive objects, then, rather than blank nothingness, the light has to be structured by the presence of objects, surfaces and textures (the optic array). The structure is immensely complex because there are rays of light converging on the observer from every part of the surrounding environment and, furthermore, this structure will change every time the observer moves.

A person sitting at a desk can perceive the objects, surfaces and textures around them because of the way the light rays reaching them are structured by those objects, surfaces and textures. If the observer stands up, the structure of the light rays changes, so that the whole optic array is transformed, thus providing new information for the observer about the environment.

The importance of movement

The optic array changes as we move around. If you think about it, most of our perception occurs as we move relative to our environment. Even if we are not actually walking, running, driving, etc., we move our eyes and heads in order to observe things going on around us. Gibson was particularly interested in describing elements in the optic array that convey information to the moving observer. According to Gibson, this information remains invariant regardless of the movements of the observer.

Invariant information

There are various sources of invariant information available to the observer. We will look at three of these sources:

- *Texture gradient* is of fundamental importance in Gibson's theory. According to Gibson, our perceptual world is made up of surfaces of different textures, and these textures can be used to aid the perception of depth and orientation. A visual texture can be broadly defined as

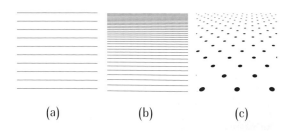

(a)   (b)   (c)

Figure 16.8 >> *Texture gradient*

a collection of objects in the visual field, and the gradient refers to the change in the relative size and compactness of these object elements. Look at Fig. 16.8. Figure 16.8(a) has a uniform texture and so appears like a representation of something flat like, for example, an upright garage door. In Fig. 16.8(b), however, the compacted lines at the top of the picture give the impression of depth, perhaps of some decking stretching out in front of us. There is an even stronger impression of depth when the gradient appears in both the horizontal and vertical placing of the object elements as in Fig. 16.8(c).

In addition to providing information about depth and distance, texture gradient also indicates the orientations of surfaces. Sudden changes in the texture often signal a change in the direction of a surface, e.g. a shift from floor to upright wall.

- *Horizon ratio* is another perceptual invariant and refers to the fact that all objects of the same height, whatever their distance from the observer, are cut by the horizon in the same ratio. Objects of different sizes, but at the same distance from the observer, however, have different horizon ratios – see Fig. 16.9. Although the size of the tree may become larger as an observer approaches it, the proportion of the tree that is above or below the horizon will remain the same.

- *Flow patterns* are created when objects in the visual environment flow past a moving observer. The nature of the flow provides information to the

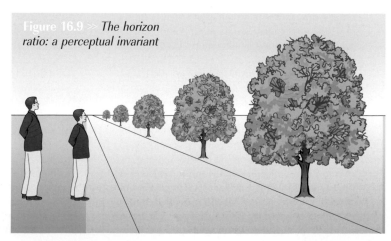

Figure 16.9 >> *The horizon ratio: a perceptual invariant*

observer about position and depth. Consider how it feels to be the driver or front passenger in a car going along a straight road like a motorway. You are faced with an expanding visual field in which elements that begin in the middle of the visual field pass around you as you move forward. For example, a motorway sign, first seen as a distant spot on the horizon, eventually passes to the left of you as you drive forward. If you sit in the back seat of the car and look out of the rear window, the situation will be reversed and you will be faced with a contracting flow field. So, the nature of the flow field – i.e. expanding or contracting – will provide information to the observer about whether they are moving forward or backwards. Looking out of the side window of a car will produce yet another type of optic flow pattern. Objects close to the observer, such as fence posts, appear to be moving very fast in a backwards direction, while objects further away (e.g. trees on the horizon) appear to be moving much more slowly and in a forwards direction (motion parallax). Gibson was particularly interested

in the role of optic flow patterns (OFPs) for pilots when landing aircraft. He believed that they provided unambiguous information about the direction, speed and altitude of the plane.

Recognizing objects

How is it, for example, that we know that the object we are looking at is something to eat, sit on, grasp, etc.? Gibson rejected the notion of top-down processing and suggested, instead, that the uses of objects are perceived directly. All objects in the world have behavioural significance for animals and humans. They offer (afford) certain responses to be made, so a door handle affords turning, a chair affords sitting, a bed affords lying down. The *affordance* of an object depends on the particular circumstances in which it is encountered. For example, a chair affords 'sitting down' if you are tired, but 'stepping on' if you want to reach a book on the top shelf. The same object can offer different affordances for different species. For example, a washing line affords hanging out clothes for a human, but perching for a bird.

Commentary
Gibson's theory

- *Stimulus for further research* – Gibson's theory has attracted considerable criticism, but it has stimulated useful debate in the field of visual perception. Greeno (1994), for example, has been developing an approach called *situation theory* which makes use of some of Gibson's ideas.

- *Research rooted in the real world* – Gibson has shown that traditional laboratory methods have underestimated the richness of information available in the stimulus input. In particular, he has shown how important it is to take into account the movement of the observer.

- *Practical applications* – Gibson's work with training programmes for pilots has already been mentioned and airports are now constructed with the best possible lighting and markings to enhance optical flow patterns for incoming pilots. Another practical application can be seen on approach roads to busy roundabouts where a set of parallel lines is painted on the road surface. The lines are painted closer and closer together as the road approaches the roundabout so that the driver gets the erroneous impression that they are accelerating. Without being given explicit instructions to do so, drivers tend to slow down automatically. As Hampson and Morris (1996) have pointed out, this traffic control technique changes perception by changing the structure of the perceived world, not by appealing to internal perceptual or cognitive mechanisms with a 'Reduce Speed' sign.

- *Biological evidence* – There has also been some support from studies which suggest that there may be some underlying physiological mechanisms which could account for certain aspects of direct perception. For example, neurons have been identified which learn from visual experience to perceive specific forms (Logothetis and Pauls 1995) and others have been identified which might account for our ability to perceive constancies (Tovee *et al.* 1994) (see p. 502 for psychological explanations of constancies).

- *Affordances* – The notion of affordance is seen as a weakness in Gibson's theory. Bruce and Green (1990) have suggested that the concept of affordance may be able to account for the visually guided behaviour of insects which have no need for a conceptual representation of the environment, but that this is an inadequate explanation for human perception. Humans function in an environment where knowledge about objects and their uses are influenced by cultural expectation and values.

- *Visual illusions* – Another difficulty for the theory concerns visual illusions (see p. 502). These are situations where an observer's perception of a stimulus does not correspond to the physical properties of the stimulus and so demonstrate that perception can sometimes be inaccurate. Gibson believed that studies based on the perception of illusions are carried out in highly artificial laboratory conditions and so have little relevance to real-life situations. However, in spite of the artificiality of some of the studies, visual illusions remain a phenomenon of perception which need to be explained and Gibson has been unable to provide an adequate account.

CONSTRUCTIVIST THEORIES

A much older, but still current, approach to perception is found in the constructivist theories. The theories are so called because of their emphasis on the combination of several sources of information required to build or construct our conscious perception of the visual world. They originated with the German psychologist, Helmholtz (1821–94), and survive in the work of researchers such as Rock (1983) and Gregory (1980). This approach equates perception with a logical process like reasoning. In addition to the information available in the sensory stimulus, we need to use higher cognitive processes to interpret it appropriately. Look at Fig. 15.9 on p. 479) and read the message. Then read the paragraphs around it, starting at 'Try reading the sentence in Fig. 15.9'.

You were not conscious of having to solve a problem when you read this sentence, but at some level, you were applying problem-solving strategies to this ambiguous piece of handwriting. So, you know that 'class' is an English word and, moreover, that it fits appropriately into this sentence frame. You also know that there is no such word as 'dass', so you automatically read the word correctly. According to constructivist theories, successful perception requires intelligence and reasoning in combining sensory information with knowledge based on previous experience. For this reason, it is sometimes referred to as 'intelligent perception'.

One aspect of intelligent perception is the concept of perceptual set identified by Allport (1955). This is a top-down activity involving the expectancies or predispositions that an observer brings to a perceptual situation and, for example, results in people seeing what they expect to see instead of what is actually there.

Gregory's theory of perception

Although a constructivist, Gregory acknowledges the contribution made by Gibson to our understanding of perception. In particular, he appreciated the importance of cues such as texture gradient and motion parallax.

However, he is not able to accept Gibson's key assertion that perception occurs directly without any intervention from higher cognitive processes. Gregory maintains that our perceptual representation of the world around us is much richer and more detailed than might be expected if we were simply relying on the information contained in the visual stimulus. We are often presented with degraded and ambiguous stimuli which lack detailed information and yet we usually manage to make sense of them.

Gregory suggests that we use visual stimuli as a starting point for making informed guesses about their meaning.

To illustrate this approach, look at the figure called the Necker cube in Fig. 16.10.

You will have no difficulty in identifying a cube, but, if you stare at it for long enough, you will find that the cube seems to pop in and out and you cannot stop it happening. Gregory explains this in terms of hypothesis testing. The figure is ambiguous, i.e. the small circle could be on the inside back wall of the cube or the bottom left-hand corner of the front face of the cube. In other words, the picture could depict a cube resting on a flat surface or a cube mounted against a wall. Gregory believes that we test first one hypothesis and then the other and, because there is no surrounding context to tell us which interpretation is correct, we switch between the two. In the real visual world, Gregory believes that there are usually enough contextual clues to remove ambiguity and to allow us to confirm a single hypothesis.

Figure 16.10 >>
The Necker cube

One of the consequences of the assumption that perception involves hypothesis testing is that we will sometimes make errors.

- *Intuitive appeal* – It seems clear that we often use top-down processes to help us make perceptual sense of our visual environment, particularly in ambiguous circumstances.
- *Experimental support* – Constructivist explanations are supported by many laboratory experiments.

- *Visual illusions* – Constructivist theories can account for perceptual errors more satisfactorily than direct theories.
- *Over-emphasis on errors* – There is an emphasis in constructivist theories on perceptual errors whereas, in fact, most people see the world accurately most of the time.
- *Persistence of illusions* – Certain illusions (e.g. the Müller-Lyer) persist even when we know that our eyes are being 'tricked'. It is difficult for constructivists to explain this.

continued on next page

● *Artificiality* – Gibson criticized the constructivist view because he felt that laboratory studies were highly artificial and did not reflect real-world perception. It is true that many of the studies that appear to support the constructivist position involve the presentation of ambiguous and fragmented information and presentations are extremely brief. Under these circumstances, it would be very difficult to rely on bottom-up processing. It could be, then, that the effects of context and experience are magnified in constructivist studies because of the nature of the stimulus material and that they may not be so important in our normal, rich visual environment.

● *Consistency* – We are remarkably accurate and consistent in our perceptions. If perception relies so heavily on hypothesis testing and making 'best guesses', we would be likely to make more mistakes than we do.

It seems likely that we use a combination of information from the sensory input and from our past experience and knowledge.

EXPLANATIONS OF PERCEPTUAL ORGANIZATION

Perception is clearly not a straightforward activity. In order to make sense of the complex visual information around us, we need to impose some form of organization on incoming stimuli. Both direct and constructivist theorists acknowledge the importance of organization but they explain it in rather different ways.

Depth perception

Imagine that you are looking out of the window at a busy road. You will have no difficulty in seeing one lamp-post as nearby and one on the other side of the road as being further away, nor of understanding that the space between the two has depth. How do we achieve this three-dimensional experience when the image falling on our retina is flat and two-dimensional? We have already seen how Gibson explained depth perception in terms of cues, such as texture gradient and motion parallax, picked up from the optic flow. Other psychologists have also seen the importance of cues and have identified a number of different types. Whereas direct perception theorists believe that these cues are picked up directly from the visual array, constructivists would suggest that they are learned through past experience with objects around us. It is likely that both views are tenable. It is possible, for example, that we have an innate ability to make use of depth cues, but that we learn through experience to use them more rapidly and efficiently.

Some depth cues are based on the fact that each eye receives a slightly different view of the scene in front of us. These are called 'binocular depth cues'. Other cues seem to be effective even when one eye is closed and these are called 'monocular cues'.

Binocular depth cues

Binocular depth cues include:

● *Convergence* – When you rotate your eyes so that the image of an object straight in front of you falls directly on the fovea, each eye has to turn inwards slightly. The closer the object, the more the eyes have to turn. Feedback from the eye muscles helps us to determine the distance of objects.

● *Binocular disparity* – This refers to the slight discrepancy in the viewpoint of each eye. The process by which these disparate views is merged into a single percept is called 'fusion'. The closer the object is to the viewer, the greater the disparity between the two images presented to each eye.

ACTIVITY

The process of fusion

Hold a pen with the tip pointing towards you and angled slightly downwards towards your nose. Now close each eye in turn and you will find that the pen seems to jump. With both eyes open, the image is fused and you see a pen straight ahead of you.

Monocular cues

There are several monocular cues and, because they are frequently used by artists to imply depth in paintings, they are also called 'pictorial cues'. They are listed below:

● *Overlap* – When one object partially blocks the view of another, the blocked object is perceived to be further away.

● *Linear perspective* – Parallel lines, such as those at the side of a road or a railway appear to converge in the distance.

● *Relative height* – Objects with their bases below the horizon are seen as more distant if they are higher in the visual plane (see, for example, the trees in Fig. 16.9); objects above the horizon are seen as more distant if they are lower in the visual field.

● *Relative size* – As an object moves further away, its retinal image diminishes in size. Smaller objects, therefore, are perceived to be further away.

- *Aerial perspective* – The image of a very distant object, e.g. a mountain in the distance, will appear slightly bluer in hue and less distinct than closer objects.

- *Shadowing* – Light usually travels in straight lines. This means that surfaces facing a light source will be relatively bright and surfaces away from the light source will be in shadow.

- *Texture gradient* – A change in the relative size and density of objects when viewed from different distances, e.g. pebbles on the beach look smaller and more closely packed the further away they are.

There is one further monocular depth cue, but this cannot be conveyed in pictures and so is not called a pictorial cue. Motion parallax is a cue that depends on movement. If you are sitting on a train looking out of the window, you will have the feeling that objects close to the track are moving very swiftly in the opposite direction, and that objects in the distance are moving much more slowly and in the same direction as you.

None of these cues are particularly strong on their own, but, in combination, they can provide powerful cues to depth and distance.

Perceiving movement

We take it for granted that we can perceive movement, so you probably cannot imagine what it would be like not to be able to do so. From the case study given in 'Getting you thinking' on p. 487, you can see just how important the perception of movement is for our everyday functioning, even though we take it for granted. Motion perception can also help us to draw inferences about form and pattern that cannot be picked up from static objects. Johannson (1975), for example, used actors dressed completely in black clothes and attached about ten small lights to key points on their bodies, e.g. wrists, ankles, elbows, hips.

(He called them 'point light walkers'.) He then filmed them in a darkened room so that only the lights were visible. When the actors remained stationary, observers reported seeing only a meaningless, two-dimensional pattern of lights. However, as soon as the actors began to walk or run, observers instantly recognized the movement as being produced by a moving person.

Gibson, as we have already seen, believed that environmental information provides the basis for perception. He identified two factors which are important in recognizing movement:

- *Local movement signal* – This occurs when a certain object moves in the environment while other objects remain stationary. Imagine that you are sitting on a quiet river-bank looking straight ahead at a house on the other side. A boat comes into view and sails past you, from left to right, providing a local movement signal by temporarily covering and uncovering parts of the distant (stationary) house. If you avert your attention from the house and start to follow the boat with your eyes, you will continue to receive a local movement signal. In this case, the crucial information for movement perception is still the local motion of the boat relative to its background. Although the boat will now remain as a stationary image on your retina, you will experience the background as moving from right to left. This means that the boat will continue to cover and uncover different parts of the background.

- *Global optic flow* – This occurs when the observer is moving – under these conditions, everything in the visual environment moves as well. Imagine that you get up from your seat by the river and start to walk along the towpath. The images of all the visual stimuli around you (e.g. trees, boats, houses) will slide across your retina. According to Gibson, this information tells you that it is you who are moving and not the stationary objects in the background.

Commentary
problems with perceiving movement

- *Gibson's explanation* of movement perception seems quite plausible in situations where the environmental background is clearly visible. However, he could not account for the fact that, under certain circumstances, human observers perceive movement when there is no physical motion of the target and no background information (apparent motion). The autokinetic effect is a powerful illusion in which observers, viewing a stationary point of light in a darkened room, erroneously believe that the light is moving.

- Another illusion of movement is the *phi phenomenon*, which occurs when two small, adjacent lights are alternately turned on and off in a darkened room. An observer will not be aware that one light is turned off and another is turned on. Instead, there will be a strong impression that a single light is on all the time and moving backwards and forwards between the two positions. This effect is often used in neon sign displays to convey the impression of movement. The existence of such illusions shows that the perception of movement cannot always occur as Gibson suggested.

continued on next page

- *Constructivist theorists* are better able to explain apparent movement. There are several studies which seem to support the idea of high-level cognitive processes being involved in the perception of apparent movement. For example,

Berbaum and Lenel (1983) showed that, if they placed an object in the path of the apparent movement, observers would perceive the movement as being deflected around the barrier. Shepard and Zare (1983) found that they could induce the perceived motion of a curved pathway if they first briefly flashed a curved path between two alternating stimuli, thereby setting up this expectation in observers.

Visual constancies

One remarkable aspect of perception is that our world remains stable in spite of the constantly changing image on our retinas as we move around, or dart our eyes about. If we took our retinal image at face value, objects and people would appear to shrink and grow as they moved towards or away from us; objects would change shape if we viewed them from different angles; and colours would alter in response to different levels of illumination. The fact that we do not experience such wild fluctuations depends on the perceptual constancies, that is, the tendency for objects to provide the same perceptual experience despite changes in the viewing conditions.

Size constancy

Size constancy is the perception that an object stays the same size regardless of the size of the image on the retina. The same object will provide differently sized retinal images depending on the distance of that object from the observer. If you are talking to a friend, for example, and she then walks away from you down the road, her image will become smaller and smaller on your retina as she moves further away. You do not, however, believe that she is shrinking.

- *Constructivist explanation* – size constancy depends on past experience and stored knowledge. We know from experience that people do not grow and shrink rapidly in the real world so, when our retinal image of a familiar person is very small, we infer that she is standing at a distance from us. If the image starts to grow, we infer that she must be walking towards us. The cue of familiarity is obviously important, but it cannot be the only explanation because size constancy also seems to operate with unfamiliar objects.
- *Direct theory explanation* – we also make use of the cue of relative size. In other words, we always judge the size of one object in the context of its surroundings. If you look at the phone as you go to answer it, you will find its retinal image gets larger as you walk towards it. However, the table on which it stands will also get larger as will the phone book lying next to it, so the ratio of the various objects remains constant. Thus, objects appear to stay the same as we

walk around because they maintain the same size relative to other objects around them. This fits in with Gibson's view that all the information necessary for size constancy was located within the stimulus. He believed that we make use of invariants such as texture gradient to judge the size of objects.

Shape constancy

Shape constancy is the ability to perceive objects as having a stable shape in spite of changes in orientation. Imagine looking at a door as someone opens it and comes into the room. The retinal image of the door will change from being a rectangle to a trapezoid as it swings open, and yet you will not think that the door is changing shape.

- *Constructivist explanation* – we depend on our past experience of doors opening and infer that it remains the same shape.
- *Direct theory explanation* – there is sufficient information in the background and in the unchanging texture elements on the door (wood-grain, panels, etc.), to recognize directly that we are looking at the same door. As usual, the direct theory has difficulty in accounting for perceptual errors (see 'Size constancy and shape constancy' on the right).

Visual illusions

We have seen in previous sections what complex mechanisms are involved in perception and yet, for most of the time, we maintain a remarkably stable view of the world and make very few perceptual errors. 'Veridical perception' is the term for perception which matches the physical situation. It occurs when viewing conditions are good and there is rich and detailed information available in the environment. However, under poor viewing conditions, e.g. bad lighting or adverse weather conditions, we can make mistakes. Most of the illusions that have been studied by psychologists are artificial ones that have been devised specifically for experimental purposes so that investigators can uncover some of the reasons why we might misperceive in real-life situations. Gregory (1978) has taken a particular interest in perceptual illusions and has identified four major categories:

Size constancy and shape constancy

Coren *et al.* (1999) give the following example of the close relationship between size and shape constancy, which is hard to explain in terms of direct perception. Look at the two shapes in Fig. 16.11 and consider the two box tops. Do you think they are the same shape? Now look at the two sides labelled (a) and (b). Which side is longer?

Now take a ruler and measure the two sides. You will probably be surprised to find that they are exactly the same length. If you were to trace the top of the box on the left and, after rotating it, place it on the top of the other box, you would also find that the shapes of the two tops were exactly the same.

Figure 16.11 >>
Shape constancy

Source: adapted from Coren *et al.* (1999, p. 338)

● *Ambiguous figures* – These can be interpreted in two equally plausible ways, e.g. the Necker cube (see p. 499). In the absence of any contextual information to reduce the ambiguity, the brain switches backwards and forwards between the two. In other words, the same input results in two different perceptions.

● *Paradoxical figures* – These look perfectly normal at first glance, but would be impossible to reproduce as a three-dimensional object, e.g. the Penrose triangle in Fig. 16.12.

Figure 16.12 >>
The Penrose triangle

● *Fictitious figures* – These are illusory figures which do not actually exist. In other words, we perceive a shape in the absence of appropriate sensory data. An example is the Kanizsa triangle in Fig. 16.13, where we 'see' a white triangle with its apex pointing upwards superimposed on another triangle with its apex pointing downwards. Each point of this illusory triangle appears to be obscuring a segment from each of three green 'circles'.

Figure 16.13 >>
The Kanizsa triangle

● *Distortions* – These appear to elicit a genuine misperception, e.g. the Müller-Lyer illusion where the two identical vertical lines appear to differ in length (see Fig. 16.14).

Figure 16.14 >>
The Müller-Lyer illusion with depth cues

The Müller-Lyer illusion explanations

The perceptual illusion which has probably attracted the most attention from researchers is the Müller-Lyer illusion, so we will focus on the various explanations which have been proposed to account for this.

Gregory has explained this in terms of 'misapplied size constancy'. In other words, we try to apply constancy mechanisms, which usually serve us well, in circumstances where it is not appropriate. Gregory has suggested that, at least in Western cultures, we are used to interpreting two-dimensional drawings as three-dimensional objects and that we attempt to do this when presented with the Müller-Lyer lines. He thinks that we 'see' the left-hand drawing as the inside corner of a room and the right-hand drawing as the outside corner of a building. Our retinal image of the two vertical lines is identical, but, because the inside corner appears to be more distant than the outside corner, we assume that the left-hand line is longer. It may seem unlikely to you that you should make this assumption about three-dimensional structures when you look at the Müller-Lyer illusion. Gregory, however, believes that this constancy scaling occurs unconsciously because of our ingrained, past experience in interpreting drawings. There is some evidence to support his view from cross-cultural studies (see p. 511), but not all psychologists have agreed with him.

Day (1990) has rejected the idea that we use depth information and has proposed an alternative explanation, which he has called 'conflicting cues theory'. He suggests that we use two separate cues when judging the length of lines like those in the Müller-Lyer illusion: (1) the actual length of the line, and (2) the overall length of the figure. In the Müller-Lyer illusion, the actual length of both the lines is the same, but the left-hand one is part of a considerably longer figure (i.e. the outward pointing fins make the overall length greater). Day believes that we try to integrate these two pieces of conflicting information by forming a compromise perception of length and deciding that the left-hand line is longer than the right-hand.

● *Illusions and misapplied constancy* – One challenge to Gregory's theory is that the illusion persists, even when the depth cues provided by the fins are lost as, for example, in Fig. 16.15.

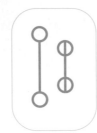

Figure 16.15 >> *The Müller-Lyer illusion without depth cues*

● *Illusions and ecological validity* – Gibson was unable to provide a satisfactory explanation for the experience of perceptual illusions. He dismissed laboratory studies of illusions as highly artificial and believed that they had little relevance in everyday viewing conditions.

There is, as yet, no satisfactory, single explanation for the experience of perceptual illusions and it seems likely that they occur as a result of a combination of factors.

CHECK YOUR UNDERSTANDING

Check your understanding of perceptual organization by answering these questions from memory. Check your answers by looking back through Topic 2.

1 What is meant by the terms 'bottom-up' and 'top-down' processing?

2 List four assumptions of Gibson's theory of direct perception.

3 Explain why Gibson believed that texture gradient was important for perception.

4 Give two strengths and two weaknesses of direct theories of perception.

5 Construct a descriptive 150-word précis of constructivist theories of perception.

6 Identify five monocular cues to depth perception and give a brief description of each.

7 Summarize Gibson's ideas about how we perceive movement.

8 Briefly outline what is meant by size constancy and explain how direct and constructivist theories differ in their explanation of this.

9 List four different types of visual illusion.

10 'Constructivist theories provide a satisfactory explanation of visual illusions.'

Construct a 300-word précis that considers this statement (150 words of AO1 and 150 words of effective AO2).

REVISION SUMMARY

Having covered this topic you should be able to:

✓ describe and evaluate constructivist and direct theories of perception

✓ describe and evaluate research relating to types of perceptual organization: depth, movement, constancies and illusions.

Below are some **possible examination questions** set on this topic, along with hints to help you understand and approach each question effectively:

1 Describe and evaluate **one** constructivist theory of visual perception (e.g. Gregory). (24 marks)

> The specification identifies two kinds of theory of visual perception: constructivist and direct. As these are both 'included' in the specification, questions may be explicitly asked about one or the other kind of theory, as here. The question requires that you focus on only one theory and gives an example (taken from the specification) to act as a prompt. When describing Gregory's theory, many candidates focus too much on visual illusions. This is creditworthy, but would at best be described as 'basic'. Make sure that you can provide a decent explanation of the theory itself. One way to do this is to select about 8 to 10 key descriptive points which you can elaborate on in the exam. That way, you will have enough to fill 15 minutes' worth of AO1 writing (about 300 words). Do the same for AO2 points – select enough to provide 300 words of commentary.

2 (a) Describe **one** direct theory of perception (e.g. Gibson). (12 marks)
  (b) Evaluate the direct theory of perception that you described in part (a). (12 marks)

> Here, the question is set explicitly on direct theories. Again, you need 15 minutes' worth of description for your one theory, and 15 minutes' worth of commentary. One of the ways to provide appropriate commentary is to use alternative theories. However, simply saying 'In contrast we might consider Gregory's theory ...' and then simply describing the alternative theory, does not in itself constitute AO2. You must continually compare and contrast the two theories, e.g. by considering strengths of one with limitations of the other. The other obvious route to offering commentary is through the use of research studies which support or challenge the theory, but if you do this, make sure you use the material as *effective* commentary.

3 Critically consider **one or more** theories of visual perception. (24 marks)

> Questions may be asked more generally about theories of visual perception, offering you the opportunity to decide which route will allow you to shine. 'One or more' means that you can get full marks either way – one theory or more than one theory. The only danger is that if you attempt to cover three or four theories, you inevitably lose time for detailed AO1 (an important AO1 criterion) and/or elaborated AO2. You might use your knowledge of other theories as sustained critical commentary.

4 (a) Outline and evaluate **one** constructivist theory of visual perception (e.g. Gregory). (12 marks)
  (b) Outline and evaluate **one** direct theory of visual perception (e.g. Gibson). (12 marks)

> This is yet another variation on the same theme, though you are required to do two theories and only one of each kind. The mark split in each part is 6 AO1 + 6 AO2 marks. The problem you may face is having to reduce your version of each theory to the time allocated – you have about 7 minutes to describe each theory, in which case it helps to be prepared with a précis of your 15-mark version (a selection of the most pertinent points).

5 Discuss explanations of perception organization (e.g. depth, movement, constancies and illusions). (24 marks)

> The wording of the specification means that you could be asked a general question about perceptual organization or could be asked how constructivist or direct theories explain perceptual organization. There is material in this unit about the examples of perceptual organization that are identified in this question. It might be useful to link the explanations to the different theories also presented in this topic. Such links could be used as a form of commentary when answering the question above, for example discussing how Gregory or Gibson might explain depth perception or certain visual illusions. It is also possible to provide commentary by considering applications of any explanation. Ideas for innovative and effective AO2 are given on pp. 937–40.

THE NATURE–NURTURE DEBATE

Psychologists have also been interested in finding out about the ways in which our perceptual skills develop. The nature–nurture question reflects a long-standing debate about the relative importance of innate and environmental factors in the acquisition of psychological abilities. As far as perception is concerned:

● The *extreme nativist* view holds that we are born with certain perceptual abilities which develop through a genetically programmed process of maturation and which owe nothing to learning.

● *Empiricists*, on the other hand, believe that we are born with only the most basic sensory capacity and that our perceptual abilities develop through experience and interaction with our environment.

It is unlikely that our acquisition of perceptual skills can be fully explained by either one of these extreme views. It seems much more likely that perceptual skills develop as a result of an interaction between innate and environmental factors.

INFANT STUDIES

The most direct method of investigating the nature–nurture debate is to observe human neonates (newborn infants). If perceptual abilities are inborn, they should be apparent in neonates. If perceptual skills are developed through learning and experience with the environment, they would be absent in young babies. However, this is not as easy to establish as it might at

first seem. Some of the difficulties of neonate research are given in the panel below.

As a result of using some of the techniques outlined in Table 16.1 (right), psychologists now know that babies have considerably more sophisticated perceptual skills than was previously thought. We will look at some of these abilities.

Difficulties of neonate research

- There are ethical and practical difficulties in obtaining permission from parents to run experiments with human neonates.

- It is difficult to attract the attention of young babies and even more difficult to hold it.

- Some abilities (see below) are not present at birth but emerge during the first few weeks of life. It can be difficult to disentangle the effects of maturation of the visual system from the effects of experience with the visual environment.

- Because of physical and cognitive constraints, babies produce only a limited range of observable behaviours. It seems relatively easy to show that a baby cannot do something, but it may simply be that babies do not have the behavioural repertoire to demonstrate all their abilities.

- Babies cannot understand instructions from the experimenter and cannot answer verbal questions.

- Psychologists have devised a number of experimental techniques to overcome some of these difficulties and these are outlined in Table 16.1 on p. 507.

Acuity and contrast

'Visual acuity' refers to the ability to perceive visual details and it is poorly developed at birth (Courage and Adams 1996). The level of acuity found in newborns seems to vary slightly with the technique used to measure it, but it is generally considered to be about 20/800 (i.e. the infant must view a stimulus from 20 feet in order to perceive it in the same detail as a normally sighted adult at 800 feet). However, it seems to develop rapidly over the first few months and reaches the adult level of 20/20 shortly after the age of 12 months (Haith 1990). Low acuity in infancy seems to be accounted for by physiological factors. Conel (1951),

for example, has demonstrated that the rapid development of neurons in the visual cortex, which occurs at the ages of 3 and 6 months, coincides with the parallel rapid development of visual acuity.

Infants are unable to perceive contrast in the same way that adults do and it has been estimated that the vision of 1-month-old infants is slightly worse than adult night vision (Pirchio *et al.* 1978). This can be explained in terms of the undeveloped fovea, which forces infants to rely mainly on their rod-dominant peripheral retina. However, in spite of the low acuity and poor contrast sensitivity, a 2-day-old infant can recognize its mother's face at close range (see opposite).

Table 16.1 >> Table of techniques used in neonate research

Technique	Description	Explanation
Preferential looking (PL)	The experimenter presents two distinctive visual stimuli together on a screen and monitors how long the baby looks at each of them.	If the baby looks at one for longer than at the other, the experimenter assumes that the baby can distinguish between them and has a preference for one over the other.
Eye-movement monitoring	The experimenter photographs babies' eye movements while they are viewing patterns on a screen.	If the infant appears only to focus on certain features of the stimulus, it suggests that the whole stimulus cannot be perceived.
Habituation	A single stimulus is presented to the infant, who will normally spend time looking at it. As time passes, the infant becomes familiar with it (habituates to it), loses interest and looks away. At this point, a new stimulus is presented.	If there is renewed interest in this novel stimulus, the experimenter infers that the infant has recognized that something has changed. This renewed interest is called 'dishabituation'.
Sucking rate	The infant is given a dummy to suck and the intensity of sucking is measured. Infants tend to suck at a faster rate if they are interested in something. Once the infant habituates to a stimulus, sucking rate declines.	If the sucking rate increases again when a novel stimulus is presented, it can be assumed that the infant is able to distinguish between the old and the new stimulus.
Conditioning	The baby is rewarded every time the baby's head turns towards a specific visual stimulus. The infant usually learns rapidly to respond to the visual stimulus.	If the baby continues to show a preference for this particular stimulus, even when it is embedded in an array of other visual stimuli, it is assumed that the baby can distinguish it.
Heart and breathing rate	Heart and/or breathing rate is/are measured for changes when various visual stimuli are presented.	If there are changes in rate when novel stimuli are presented, it is assumed that the baby can distinguish between them.
Positron-emission tomography (PET)	Electrodes are attached to the baby's scalp which detect electrical activity in the brain. Certain patterns known as VEPs occur in response to visual stimuli.	The experimenter can assume that the baby differentiates between two stimuli if each stimulus provokes a different pattern of VEPs.
Visually evoked potentials (VEPs) and functional magnetic resonance imaging (fMRI)	These are advanced techniques which allow mapping of brain function.	If different patterns of infant brain activity are recorded in response to different visual stimuli, it is assumed that the infant can distinguish between them.

Face recognition

Fantz (1961) conducted studies which seemed to demonstrate that face recognition was an innate ability. He presented 4-day to 6-month-old infants with stimuli similar to those in Fig. 16.16.

- Stimulus (a) is a representation of a human face
- Stimulus (b) depicts exactly the same black features, but not configured to look like a face.
- Stimulus (c) has the same amount of black shading, but presented as one solid block of colour.

Babies of all ages showed a slight, but distinctive preference for (a) over (b) and most of them paid little attention to stimulus (c). This suggested to Fantz that human babies possess an innate preference for human faces over other visual objects.

Figure 16.16 >>
Fantz's (1961) face stimuli

(a)   (b)   (c)

- Other researchers have criticized Fantz's conclusions saying that the stimuli were artificial and bore little resemblance to the real, animated and mobile faces that infants would encounter in the real world. Haith (1980) has suggested that infants in Fantz' study preferred stimulus (a) because it contained more contour than the other stimuli. This interpretation is reinforced by a study conducted by Flavell (1985) who found that babies, presented with faces and other stimuli with similar amounts of movement and contour, show no preference for faces.

- Whether or not babies have an innate preference for faces, it now seems that they are able to distinguish their mother's face at a very early stage. Walton and her colleagues (1992) videoed 12 faces of new mothers and then videoed 12 other women's faces which were matched in terms of hair and eye colour, complexion and hair-style. Neonates were then showed pairs of videos – one of their mother and one of the matched individual. By sucking on a dummy, babies as young as one day old were able to maintain the preferred video (of their mother) on the screen.

- It seems, then, that many perceptual abilities are present in the newborn baby or appear in the first weeks of life. It is highly likely that most of the abilities discussed above arise from maturational changes in the visual system and owe little to experience and learning. The distinction between innate and environmental factors is rather less clear-cut in the area of depth perception and the acquisition of the visual constancies.

Depth and distance perception

Depth perception is a complex skill. Babies need it from an early age in order to carry out what appear, on the surface, to be quite simple tasks, e.g. to reach out for a toy. Babies seem to be able to start making these kinds of judgements from the age of about 3 months and are often quite skilled by the age of about 6 to 7 months. This coincides with the time that many babies learn to crawl (Bornstein *et al.* 1992). The interesting question for psychologists is whether depth perception is innate or learned.

A classic experiment investigating this question was carried out by Gibson and Walk in 1960 (see the panel below).

The visual cliff experiment (Gibson and Walk 1960)

Gibson and Walk constructed a glass-topped table with two halves. One half of the table had glass covering a checkerboard design immediately below the glass, and the other half had the same design four feet below the glass. The depth cues from the apparatus gave the impression of a deep 'drop' (visual cliff) on one side of the table, even though the glass top continued, in reality, to provide a solid continuous surface. Gibson and Walk were unable to use infants under the age of 6 months because they needed to have babies who were independently mobile. They tested 36 babies by placing them individually on the 'shallow' side of the apparatus and encouraged them to crawl over the 'cliff' to the 'deep' side by having their mothers call to them. In spite of this encouragement from their mothers, most of the babies would not crawl over the perceived drop (see Fig. 16.17). Gibson and Walk concluded that depth perception is an innate ability.

Figure 16.17 >> *Gibson and Walk's (1960) 'visual cliff' study*

Commentary
infant perceptual development

- *Role of experience* – Critics argued that babies of 6 months could have learned this ability through experience. Gibson and Walk responded to these criticisms by repeating the experiment using newborn animals, which are independently mobile from birth. These animals refused to cross over the cliff and, if placed on the 'deep' side, showed signs of distress. This suggests that depth perception in such animal species is innate, but there are too many differences between humans and animals for us to be able to generalize this finding.

- *The visual cliff effect* – More convincing evidence came from a study by Campos and colleagues (1970). They compared the heart rates of 2-month-old babies when placed on the 'shallow' and the 'deep' side of the apparatus. Heart rates decreased slightly on the deep side suggesting that babies were able to make a distinction between the two sides. However, older babies (approx. 9 months) showed an increased heart rate when placed on the deep side, which is an indicator of anxiety. It may be that depth perception is innate since it can be demonstrated in such young babies, but that avoidance behaviour (i.e. recognizing the danger associated with certain situations) can only be learned through experience.

- *Infants and depth perception* – However, babies as young as 2 months have shown avoidance behaviour when a rather different technique is used to test depth perception. This technique involves showing babies a video of an object which appears to be moving towards them on a direct collision course. If depth perception is present, the babies should flinch, blink or move their head to one side. Such avoidance behaviour has been demonstrated in babies between 2 and 3 months (Yonas and Owsley 1987) suggesting that some awareness of depth perception is present in these very young babies.

- *Post-term babies* – An earlier study by Yonas (1981) lends weight to the nativist argument. He compared two groups of 6-week-old infants – one group of infants had been born on time, but the other group had been born four weeks late. The post-term babies were significantly more likely to respond to looming objects with an avoidance reaction than the normal-term babies, even though both groups had been exposed to environmental influences for the same time (i.e. six weeks).

- *Pictorial cues: learned or innate?* – The use of pictorial cues discussed on p. 500 appears to emerge rather later and probably means that they depend on experience with the environment rather than on physiological maturation. Granrud and Yonas (1985), for example, investigated infants' ability to perceive depth from the cue of overlap. They showed babies two-dimensional cardboard cut-outs like the ones in Fig. 16.18. Infants have a tendency to reach out for objects which seem nearer to them, so Granrud and Yonas reasoned that they were more likely to reach out for picture (a) (which has the impression of depth provided by overlap cues) than for either (b) or (c). This proved to be the case for 7-month-old babies, but not for 5-month-old babies, which suggests that the ability to use the pictorial cue of overlap emerges around the seventh month.

(a)

(b)

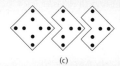
(c)

Figure 16.18 >> *Stimuli used in Granrud and Yonas' (1985) experiment*

Visual constancies

You will recall from the previous topic that constancies are an important means of maintaining a stable visual environment. The central question for developmental psychologists again concerns the nature–nurture debate. We will look at size and shape constancy since these are the ones which have attracted the most research interest.

Size and shape constancy

Bower (1965) conducted the classic study into size constancy in infants (see Key research on p. 510). Bower (1966) also investigated shape constancy and found that 2-month-old infants responded to a tilted rectangle as if it were the same as the original rectangle, even though a rectangle viewed from such an angle projects a trapezoid on to the retina. More recently, Slater and Morrison (1985) demonstrated shape constancy in newborn infants using the habituation method (see Table 16.1 on p. 507).

Babies seem to be able to match visual shapes to a shape that they have experienced through touch or feel. Kaye and Bower (1994) put one of two different types of dummy in the mouths of day-old infants. Once the baby started sucking, an image of the dummy would appear on a computer screen in front of the baby. If the

Bower's size constancy study (1965)

Bower conditioned nine infants between the ages of 40 and 60 days by rewarding them every time they turned their head in response to the presentation of a 30 cm cube placed 1 m away. The reward was a peek-a-boo response by an adult who popped up in front of the baby, smiled and tickled her and then disappeared from view again (see Fig. 16.19).

Once the baby had clearly learnt to respond to this particular cube, Bower introduced new stimuli:

Figure 16.19 >> *The set-up in Bower's (1965) study*

- the original 30 cm cube placed 3 m away from the infant (i.e. smaller retinal image than the original)
- a 90 cm cube placed 1 m away from the infant (i.e. larger retinal image than the original)
- a 90 cm cube placed 3 m away (i.e. same retinal image as the original).

Bower recorded the number of times the babies reacted with a conditioned response to the stimuli. The results are shown in the table below.

	Original stimulus	Test stimulus 1	Test stimulus 2	Test stimulus 3
Size	30 cm	Same – 30 cm	Different – 90 cm	Different – 90 cm
Distance	1 m	Different – 3 m	Same – 1 m	Different – 3 m
Retinal image		Different	Different	Same

Bower found, as he had predicted, that retinal size was not the crucial factor and that babies looked least at the stimulus which had the same retinal image, but which differed from the original both in terms of size and distance. He concluded that babies have innate size constancy.

Bower was interested in finding out what cues the babies were using in order to gauge the distance of the cubes. Several types of cue are known to assist in depth perception and these include texture gradient, motion parallax and retinal disparity (see pp. 497 and 501). Using three ingenious variations on his original experimental technique, Bower (1965) again tested nine infants for size constancy.

- condition 1: cues available = texture gradient and motion parallax

- condition 2: cues available = texture gradient
- condition 3: cues available = retinal disparity and texture gradient.

In condition 2, infants no longer seemed able to judge distance or the real size of the cubes, suggesting that texture gradient was not being used as a guide to distance. Performance in condition 1, however, was at the same level as in the original experiment where babies seemed to understand distance and size constancy. Since texture gradient did not seem to be an important cue, Bower concluded that they were relying on motion parallax. Performance in condition 3 was intermediate between the two other conditions, suggesting that retinal disparity was being used to a limited extent to judge distance.

Commentary
Bower's size constancy study

- On the basis of this series of experiments, Bower suggested that infants between the ages of 6 to 8 weeks have some degree of depth perception and size constancy and that this ability depends mainly on the cue of motion parallax. Retinal

disparity provides an additional but weaker cue and texture gradient is not yet being used.

- However, Bower's results have proved difficult to replicate and his conclusions have not been universally accepted by other psychologists. It is not easy to obtain a conditioned response in babies as young as this and their behaviour and body movements can often be misinterpreted.

baby paused in sucking, the dummy would disappear from the screen and be replaced by an image of the other dummy (which the baby had not experienced sucking). Once the baby started to suck again, the first dummy would reappear on the screen. In this way, the baby was able to control which image appeared on the screen. Babies consistently controlled their sucking to keep the image on the screen of the dummy in their mouth. This suggests that newborn infants are capable of sensing the shape of a dummy in their mouth and then generalizing this perception from the tactile to the visual modality. It is not clear what mechanism underlies this ability, but it seems clear that it is innate rather than learned.

Chimpanzees raised in the dark

Riesen (1965) reared chimpanzees in the dark and found that nerve cells in the retina and visual cortex began to atrophy. In order to avoid this destruction of nerve cells, Riesen conducted further studies in which he allowed chimpanzees and monkeys to experience some light stimulation by wearing translucent goggles from birth. At about 3 months, the animals could distinguish brightness and size like normal members of their species, but could not follow a moving object with their eyes or discriminate shapes.

Commentary
infant studies

A02

- It seems that both innate and learned factors have a role to play in the development of perceptual skills. With the development of ingenious experimental techniques, psychologists have been able to show that human infants possess remarkable perceptual abilities. Many of these are present at birth or appear in the first few weeks of life as the nervous system matures.

- However, there is also evidence that we need at least some minimal level of experience with the environment to develop our perceptual abilities to their full potential. Much of this evidence comes from studies carried out on non-human animals where animals are deprived of certain environmental stimuli (see panel above).

- It is difficult to generalize these findings to humans and it would clearly be unethical to carry out such studies on human neonates, but it does

suggest that perceptual abilities depend, to an extent, on interacting with the environment. This conclusion is supported by studies of children who have suffered deprivation for some reason or another. Dennis (1960) studied babies in Iranian orphanages who had been kept in highly impoverished environments with no stimulation or opportunity to move around. He found that these children showed major deficits in perceptual and motor skills.

- It seems, then, that both innate and learned factors are involved in perceptual development and psychologists have started to look beyond the nature–nurture debate. They are now beginning to ask how such factors are combined to produce a whole perceptual experience and what patterns of systematic change occur over time in the development of perceptual skills. One prominent researcher who has adopted this approach and has looked for patterns of change in children's development of perceptual strategies is Eleanor Gibson (e.g. Gibson 1969).

CROSS-CULTURAL STUDIES

Cross-cultural studies involve comparing the behaviours or abilities of people from different cultures.

We have seen how perception is shaped by an interaction of biological and environmental factors. Given that there appears to be at least some requirement for experience with the visual environment in order for the visual system to develop normally, psychologists and anthropologists have been interested in finding out the role of cultural background in the development of perceptual skills. People from different cultures may differ from one another in two important ways: biological and ecological.

- *Biological* differences depend on factors such as genetic inheritance, diet, disease patterns within the culture, etc. While such factors could influence

perceptual abilities, there has been little research interest in these areas.

- Researchers have been far more interested in *ecological* factors, such as local environment, cultural history and education. Do people who live in dense forest for example, develop different perceptual skills from people who live in open plains? Do people from cultural backgrounds with no tradition of drawing find it difficult to understand the pictorial cues found in paintings and drawings from other cultures?

Research on visual illusions

Much of the research in this area has centred on the experience of visual illusions (see pp. 502–4). See Key research on p. 512.

In a classic study, Segall *et al.* (1963, 1966) showed various straight-line illusions, including the Müller-Lyer illusion, to nearly 2,000 adult and child participants. There were 14 non-European groups, mostly from Africa, but also from the Philippines and three so-called European groups (actually from South Africa and North America).

The researchers found clear cultural differences: the European groups were considerably more susceptible to the Müller-Lyer illusion than the non-European groups. Segall and colleagues explain their findings in terms of the 'carpentered world hypothesis'. According to this hypothesis, many people live in an environment which is full of lines and angles and rectangular objects. Unless these objects are viewed from exactly the right angle, they will project a non-rectangular image onto the retina and yet we continue to perceive them as rectangular. Segall and colleagues believe that this tendency to

interpret trapezoid shapes on the retina is so pervasively reinforced in people who live in carpentered environments that it becomes automatic and unconscious from a very early age. People who live in environments with few straight lines and angles are less used to interpreting acute and obtuse angles on the retina as representations of right angles in the real world. When presented with a drawing of the Müller-Lyer illusion, the Europeans were likely to try to perceive it as a two-dimensional representation of a three-dimensional object. In other words they would interpret the drawings as, for example, the outside corner of a building and the inside corner of a room. Using misapplied size constancy, they would then perceive the apparently closer line to be shorter than the line that was apparently further away. The non-Europeans from non-carpentered environments were much more likely to take the drawing at face value.

Commentary
the carpentered world hypothesis

● *A biological explanation* – Pollack (1963), however, suggested that there might be a biological rather than environmental explanation for these findings. He had noted findings from several studies that susceptibility to the Müller-Lyer illusion declines with age. Since older people also experience increasing difficulty in detecting contours, Pollack hypothesized that there might be a functional relationship between these two abilities. Pollack and Silvar (1967) demonstrated that there was such a relationship – the harder people found it to detect contour, the less susceptible they were to the Müller-Lyer illusion. Silvar and Pollack (1967) then took this idea a stage further and demonstrated in a second study that there is a relationship between contour

detection and retinal pigmentation – the denser the pigmentation, the poorer the contour detection. Pollack suggested that retinal pigmentation, which may be denser in dark-skinned people, might have been responsible for the reduced susceptibility to the Müller-Lyer illusion found among the non-European samples in the study by Segall and colleagues. In other words, biological rather than cultural differences might be responsible for the different responses to visual illusions.

● *Support for Pollack* – There was some support for the Pollack hypothesis from Berry (1971) and Jahoda (1971), but both these studies have been criticized on methodological grounds.

● *Support for the environmental view* – However, Stewart (1973) conducted a well-controlled study which strongly challenged Pollack's hypothesis and, instead, provided support for the environmental view.

Research on size constancy

There is other evidence demonstrating that lack of experience with certain environmental depth cues can impair perceptual abilities such as size constancy. A well-known study by Turnbull (1961) illustrates this. He observed the behaviour of a group of Bambuti Pygmies who lived in dense forest. They have little opportunity to look far into the distance because their environment

is enclosed by trees and vegetation. Turnbull reported on a particular occasion when he accompanied his guide, Kenge, out of the forest for the first time in his life. On their journey, they crossed a broad, open plain and could see a herd of grazing buffalo a few miles way in the distance. The guide was puzzled and asked what kind of insects they were and laughed when he was told that they were buffalo. As they drove towards the herd in the car, Kenge seemed alarmed, although his anxiety disappeared once they had got very close and he could verify that they were indeed buffalo. However, he continued to be confused about what had happened and wondered how the buffalo had grown larger as they approached and whether some kind of witchcraft or trickery were involved.

This kind of report suggests that the environment we grow up in can influence the way in which we perceive new stimuli.

Research on two-dimensional drawings

Another area of cross-cultural research into perception has centred on the interpretation of two-dimensional drawings, pictures and photographs. In Western cultures, we are inundated with pictorial images in books, newspapers, television, etc., from a very early age. We usually have no difficulty in recognizing objects and in understanding the spatial relations between objects depicted in pictures and yet, pictures rarely reflect an accurate representation of the real-world scene – for example, they are flat, whereas the real world is three-dimensional and they are often in black and white. Some people (e.g. Gombrich 1972) have suggested that we can only understand and interpret pictures drawn according to Western artistic tradition because we are aware of a set of conventions agreed within that culture. If this were true, it would follow that people from other cultures would not readily be able to understand Western pictorial convention.

Hochberg and Brooks (1962) carried out a rather bold experiment on one of their own children. They shielded their son from any sort of pictures for the first 19 months of his life. They made sure that there were no pictures, magazines, newspapers or television in the child's vicinity. They even removed all the labels from tins and packages of food. At the end of this period, they showed him simple line drawings of everyday objects such as shoes. In spite of his restricted upbringing, the child had no difficulty in identifying all these objects. If we can generalize this finding, we can assume that the recognition of objects in pictures is not a learned convention. There is evidence from cross-cultural studies that individuals are able to recognize objects in pictures even if they have never seen examples of Western pictures before.

Hagen and Jones (1978) found that coloured photographs were readily understood by people who had never experienced pictures. It seems, however, that less realistic pictures, e.g. black and white photographs or line drawings present more problems.

Deregowski (1980) has collected a number of reports from anthropologists and missionaries which suggest that spontaneous object identification can be difficult under these circumstances. It should be noted that these findings derive from anecdotal evidence rather than from rigorously conducted scientific study. One report from a missionary working in Malawi tells of the initial puzzlement of local people when shown a line drawing of an ox and a dog. However, after carefully pointing out individual features such as the nose and ear of the dog and the horns and tail of the ox, recognition dawned. This suggests that object recognition can occur very quickly if attention is directed appropriately and so supports the idea that learning via prolonged exposure is unnecessary.

Hudson (1960, 1962) showed pictures containing various pictorial depth cues to groups of people in South Africa. Figure 16.20 shows an example of the type of picture he used.

Figure 16.20 >> *Picture used in Hudson's studies*
Source: *Deregowski (1972)*

In this picture, the cue of overlap tells us that the hunter and the antelope are standing in front of the rocks and are, therefore, closer to us. The cue of familiar size tells us that the elephant must be furthest away from us because, although it is casting a smaller image on our retina, we know that it is actually larger than either a man or an antelope. Hudson's technique was to ask observers first of all to name all the objects in the picture. Observers were then asked questions such as 'What is the man doing?' and 'What is closer to the man?' Results from Hudson's own study and from subsequent studies conducted in various parts of Africa reported by Deregowski (1980), indicated that non-Western observers had difficulty seeing pictorial depth. However, as Rock (1995) has commented, the cues are quite weak in this picture and, even for Westerners, there is likely to be some ambiguity.

There is some evidence that formal education using picture books and drawings can increase the ability to perceive depth in two-dimensional pictures (Pick 1987). Hagen and Jones (1978) have also demonstrated that certain cues, such as aerial perspective and texture gradient seem to enhance the ability to perceive depth in pictures. It may be the case that some pictorial cues are more helpful and familiar to non-Westerners than others. Non-Western cultures with no experience of pictures seem to find particular difficulty in perceiving implied movement in drawings. Look at the pictures in Fig. 16.21.

Figure 16.21 >> *Illustrations implying movement*

In these pictures, the artist has used a technique to imply movement that is familiar to Western observers from as young as 4 years of age. Duncan *et al.* (1973) showed a cartoon picture to a group of rural African children in which a boy's head was shown in three different positions to imply rapid movement of the head. The children did not understand the implied motion and several of them reported that the boy must be deformed. However, the ability to understand implied motion in line drawings is another skill that can be obtained through education, urbanization and exposure to pictures (Friedman and Stevenson 1980).

Evaluation
cross-cultural studies

- Cross-cultural studies have been important in trying to investigate the effects of physical environment and cultural background on perceptual abilities, but findings are often ambiguous and difficult to interpret. Some conclusions have been based on early observations by missionaries and anthropologists which were not conducted under controlled conditions. Later, more rigorous studies can still often be criticized for experimenter bias and for underestimating perceptual abilities.

- There has been very little empirical research in this area in recent years, but, as Segall *et al.* (1990) comment in a review of cross-cultural susceptibility to illusions: 'people perceive in ways that are shaped by the inferences they have learned to make in order to function most effectively in the particular ecological settings where they live ... we learn to perceive in the ways we need to perceive.' (p. 88)

- The issue of pictorial art is rather more complex. It is possible that the difficulties people from other cultures experience with Western art reflect aesthetic rather than perceptual factors. Hudson (reported in Deregowski 1972) asked groups of African adults and children who had not been exposed to Western culture to choose their preferred picture of an elephant from the two shown in Fig. 16.22. (b) shows a realistic, aerial view of an elephant as it would appear in a photograph taken from above. However, (a) was overwhelmingly the preferred choice in spite of its unnatural pose. Deregowski maintains that split drawings are preferred by children from all cultures, but that in Western societies, such preferences are suppressed. This is because

Figure 16.22 >> *Drawings of elephants used in Hudson's studies*

drawings using perspective cues convey more information than split drawings and so are thought to have more practical use.

- However, certain societies, where this preference has not been suppressed, have developed the split drawing technique to a high artistic level. It is possible, then, that initial puzzlement with Western-style drawings reflects unfamiliarity with the artistic convention rather than lack of perceptual ability.

- It seems, then, that the ability to identify objects does not depend on learning or cultural background. There may be more of a problem, however, in interpreting spatial relationships within two-dimensional pictures and this ability may well reflect different cultural conventions. Western artists have long made use of monocular pictorial cues (see p. 500) to imply three dimensions in their paintings. However, there is no binocular disparity between elements in the picture, and all objects require the same degree of accommodation and convergence. This means, as Pick (1987) points out, that, in order to perceive a flat, two-dimensional picture as a scene in three dimensions, we need to pay attention to some depth cues and ignore the absence of others. Perhaps people who have no experience of Western art will find it difficult to use pictorial cues in this way.

REVISION SUMMARY

Having covered this topic you should be able to describe and evaluate:

✓ explanations of perceptual development including the nature–nurture debate

✓ studies of perceptual abilities: visual acuity, tracking, colour vision, depth/distance perception and visual constancies

✓ infant and cross-cultural studies relating to perceptual development.

CHECK YOUR UNDERSTANDING

Check your understanding of perceptual development by answering these questions from memory. You can check your answers by looking back through Topic 3.

1 What do you understand by the term 'nature–nurture debate'?

2 Outline four difficulties involved in using human infants to investigate the development of perception.

3 Give a brief description of three experimental techniques used in human neonate research.

4 Explain why newborn babies do not have adult levels of visual acuity.

5 Outline the findings and conclusions of one study that has investigated depth perception in infants.

6 Describe research by Bower that has investigated size and shape constancy in infants.

7 Explain the difference between biological and ecological factors in cross-cultural research.

8 Summarize the findings and conclusions of cross-cultural research into visual illusions.

9 Evaluate the contribution of cross-cultural research to the nature–nurture debate in perception.

EXAMPLE EXAM QUESTIONS

Below are some **possible examination questions** set on this topic, along with hints to help you understand and approach each question effectively:

1 Discuss explanations of perceptual development. (24 marks)

> In this question, just two explanations would be fine and might even be preferable to trying to cover lots of explanations in limited time. It may be helpful to structure your answer carefully and write four 150-word paragraphs, one for the AO1 content of each explanation and one for the AO2 content of each explanation. You could base your answer on the nature–nurture debate and examine nature explanations and/or nurture explanations of perceptual development. Describing *studies* of perceptual development would not, on their own, constitute an explanation – you need to identify an explanation (e.g. 'the innate explanation') and then use a study as a means of explaining how perceptual abilities are inherited. Research studies can also be used as AO2 commentary as long as they are not simply described but there is some indication about what the study shows us.

2 Describe and evaluate studies of the development of perceptual abilities. (24 marks)

> In this question, 'studies' are the AO1 focus. AO2 can be achieved through looking at methodological flaws or strengths of the studies, or by suggesting what the studies can tell us more generally about perceptual development, or by contrasting the findings of one study with those from another. The description of studies would be AO1, but any contrasts would be AO2.

3 (a) Outline and evaluate **one** infant study of perceptual development. (12 marks)
   (b) Outline and evaluate **one** cross-cultural study of perceptual development. (12 marks)

The specification specifically mentions 'infant' and 'cross-cultural studies', which means that you can be asked to discuss such research, as in this question. This question has an unusual split of marks. In both parts there are 6 AO1 marks and 6 AO2 marks. For the 6 marks, you probably need to write about 150 words. Use your experience of writing 'APFCC' studies for AS-level and try presenting aims, procedures, findings and conclusions (for AO1), and criticisms (for AO2), when describing each study. The AO2 credit can be gained, for example, by considering methodological problems with the studies, or the implications of the findings for other theories or the nature–nurture debate.

4 (a) Outline **two or more** studies into the development of perceptual abilities. (12 marks)
   (b) To what extent do such studies contribute to the nature–nurture debate in perception? (12 marks)

This question is a variation on the previous question. Part (a) can be answered using the same two studies. You can describe more than two, if you wish, but two would be adequate for full marks. Part (b) requires the use of 'such' studies, which means that you are not limited to the studies that you have described in part (a). However, any *description* of studies in part (b) would not attract AO2 credit. Nor would any general evaluations of research studies, unless they shed light on the nature–nurture debate. For example, you might argue that one criticism of the Gibson and Walk study was that the conclusions reached were not valid – the infants were 6 months old and therefore the conclusion that depth perception is innate may not be justified. The question 'To what extent?' suggests that you need to present a conclusion but this is not required.

5 Discuss the nature–nurture debate as it relates to perceptual development. (24 marks)

The key words in this question are 'nature–nurture' and 'perception'. There are a number of ways to organize an answer. You can divide your essay into 'nature' and 'nurture', provide some evidence for each side of the debate and evaluate this evidence. Or you could examine a list of studies and for each comment upon what the study tells us about nature–nurture. Or you could present a more one-sided view of arguments for nature, and then use evidence and arguments for the nurture side of the debate as your AO2 content.

UNIT SUMMARY

Topic 1: The visual system

- In this unit, we have looked at various aspects of perception, starting with the **structure** and **functions** of the **visual system**.

- The **eye** is the sense organ for vision and it is here that the process of visual perception begins. Light enters the cornea from the environment and is brought into focus via the lens onto the screen at the back of the eye called the **retina**. This consists of a dense network of nerve cells responsible for transforming the incoming light energy into neural impulses. These impulses are then carried along the **visual pathways** to particular areas of the cortex for further processing and integration.

- **Sensory adaptation** is the process whereby we adapt to changes in the environment (e.g. light to dark conditions) and it has probably evolved for survival reasons.

- **Contrast processing** is the ability to differentiate between the brightness levels of adjoining areas. Two further perceptual abilities – **colour** and **feature processing** – both involve highly complex mechanisms, which are not yet fully understood.

Topic 2: Perceptual organization

- We considered two main types of theory of **perceptual organization**. **Gibson** proposed the **direct theory** of perception, which is based on the assumption that we 'pick up' information directly from the rich, detailed visual array that surrounds us, i.e. perception is a bottom-up process.

A2 Cognitive Psychology

- **Constructivist** theories, on the other hand, are based on 'top-down' processing. Theorists adopting this approach, e.g. **Gregory**, believe that our perceptual representation of the world is generally much richer and more detailed than could be expected if we were simply relying on information contained in the visual stimulus. They believe, instead, that information from the visual stimulus is combined, often unconsciously, with stored knowledge in a problem-solving approach to perception.

- Both theories have been influential, but both have been criticized in various ways. It seems likely that perception is a combination of 'top-down' and 'bottom-up' processing.

- We also considered some important aspects of **perceptual organization** which have been explained with varying degrees of success by both types of theory.

   - **Depth perception** is an important way in which we transform the two-dimensional image on our retina into our three-dimensional perceptual world.

   - It is also vital for normal perception that we are able to detect and interpret **movement** in the environment around us.

   - **Perceptual constancies** are a means of maintaining a stable perception, even though the images of objects and people are constantly sliding across our retina as we move around.

   - Finally, we considered some of the **visual illusions** which have been investigated by psychologists as a means of understanding normal perceptual processes.

Topic 3: Perceptual development

- One of the central issues in the area of perceptual development is the relative importance of innate and learned factors in the development of perceptual abilities (the **nature–nurture** debate).

- It seems that many perceptual abilities are present in human **neonates** from birth or emerge very shortly afterwards. This suggests that many aspects of perception depend on innate, maturational factors rather than on learning from the environment.

- The infant ability to perceive **depth and distance** and to apply **visual constancies** has also been investigated. It is less clear, in these areas, whether the skills are inborn or depend on experience.

- The methodological difficulties of studying human neonates make it difficult to draw firm conclusions. However, it seems likely that babies need to interact with the environment in order for their perceptual abilities to develop normally.

- Another way of investigating the relative importance of innate and environmental factors is to conduct **cross-cultural** studies. As with neonate research, there are certain methodological difficulties and it is not always easy to draw clear inferences. On the whole, evidence from cross-cultural research does seem to suggest that our geographical environment and cultural history may well affect our perception to some degree.

FURTHER RESOURCES

Carlson, N.R. (1998) *Physiology of Behaviour* (6th edn), Boston: Allyn & Bacon.

An up-to-date text aimed at undergraduates, but the sections on vision are fairly easy to understand and provide more detailed coverage of the visual system than is possible in this unit.

Eysenck, M. and Keane, M. (2000) *Cognitive Psychology: A Student's Handbook* (4th edn), Hove: Psychology Press.

A comprehensive text aimed mainly at undergraduates, containing readable and clear information on areas covered in Topics 2 and 3.

Rookes, P. and Willson, J. (2000) *Perception: Theory, Development and Organization,* London and New York: Routledge.

This text is aimed at A-level students and is written in a readable, accessible style.

Website

www.usask.ca/education/coursework/skaalid/theory/gestalt/gestalt.htm

To learn more about the Gestalt theory of perception.

Unit 16 // Perceptual processes and development

17
UNIT

LANGUAGE AND
Thought

PREVIEW

After you have read this unit, you should be able to describe and evaluate:

>> research into the relationship between language and thought

>> research relating to language acquisition

>> research into problem-solving and errors in reasoning.

INTRODUCTION

In this unit we will consider the nature of human language and thought, and look at some of the ways in which psychologists have sought to investigate these topics. Language is a highly complex system of communication based on words that have meaning. These words can be strung together according to a set of grammatical rules and used to create an infinite number of sentences. The flexibility, richness and complexity of human language sets it apart from other animal communication systems, but that very complexity poses an enormous challenge to psychologists attempting to explain the underlying processes of acquisition and everyday use.

Just as humans have developed a highly sophisticated system of languages, they have also outstripped other species in their ability to think and reason. All the processes involved in memory, attention and perception could legitimately be regarded as thought processes. However, when cognitive psychologists refer to thought, they usually mean particular types of goal-directed thinking, such as problem-solving, reasoning and decision-making, and so discussion will be limited to those areas in this unit.

The Hanuxoo of the Philippines have 92 names for rice. Why so many?

Jane
Willson

1 Why might the Hanuxoo of the Philippines have 92 names for rice? Could the way we think about (or value) things influence the way our language develops?

2 What happens when adults try to correct the language of young children? Read the transcripts of conversations on the right.

3 Two shops advertise meat using different approaches (see below). Which shop do you think will sell more meat? Why is this likely to be the case?

Child:	Want other one spoon, daddy.
Daddy:	You mean you want the other spoon.
Child:	Want other one spoon, please, daddy.
Daddy:	Can you say 'the other spoon'?
Child:	Other one spoon.
Daddy:	Say 'other'.
Child:	Other.
Daddy:	'Spoon'.
Child:	Spoon.
Daddy:	'Other spoon'.
Child:	Other spoon. Now give me other one spoon.

Source: Braine (1971)

Child:	Nobody don't like me.
Mother:	No, say 'Nobody likes me'.
Child:	Nobody don't like me.
	(This sequence is repeated **eight** times.)
Mother:	Now listen carefully, say 'NOBODY LIKES ME.'
Child:	Oh! Nobody don't like**s** me.

Source: McNeil (1966)

Adults often correct meaning rather than syntax:

Child:	Doggie (pointing at a horse)
Adult:	No, that's a horsie.

Source: Brown and Hanlon (1970)

90% LEAN MEAT

ONLY 10% FAT

KEY CONCEPTS

Linguistic relativity hypothesis: theory that the language we use is responsible for shaping our thoughts about the world. The *weak* version states that language *influences* thinking, whereas the *strong* version states that language *determines* the way we think.

Nativist theory: the proposition that children are biologically equipped to acquire language.

Language Acquisition Device (LAD): an innate mechanism that is programmed to recognize grammatical structure and therefore makes it easy for children to acquire language.

Gestalt approach: in problem-solving this refers to the need for structural understanding, i.e. the ability to understand how all parts of the problem fit together to meet the goal.

Means of representation: in problem-solving this refers to the way in which we construe and approach a problem.

Information-processing approach: a reference to the belief that the processing of sensory information takes place in a series of stages. In developmental psychology, this approach assumes that if adults think more successfully than children do, it is because they can process more information than children can.

Means–ends analysis: a problem-solving strategy that involves breaking problems down into their constituent parts, which are then solved in turn until the solution (goal) is reached.

Similarity or representative heuristic: rule of thumb that a particular instance will be similar to its prototype or stereotype.

Availability heuristic: a rule of thumb used to make decisions about frequencies of events based on how easily relevant examples can be remembered – a cognitive short cut.

This topic begins by looking at theoretical attempts to establish the links between language and thought. It then moves on to consider some of the social and cultural aspects of language use.

RESEARCH INTO THE RELATIONSHIP BETWEEN LANGUAGE AND THOUGHT

Behaviourists in the early part of this century believed that thought was nothing more than internalized language. Watson (1913), the founder of behaviourism, wrote that 'thought processes are really motor habits in the larynx'. It is certainly true that we often sub-vocalize when we are engaged in working out a problem – you are probably aware of this yourself when you are planning an essay. Early studies (e.g. Jacobsen 1932) appeared to confirm Watson's belief by detecting small movements in the throat muscles when participants were instructed to think. However, a later study (Smith *et al.* 1947) demonstrated in a rather dramatic way that thought *can* occur in the absence of sub-vocalization. Smith allowed himself to be injected with curare, a highly dangerous drug, which paralyses all the voluntary muscles in the body. After the effects of the drug had worn off, he reported that he had been able to think and to solve problems even though he had been completely incapable of moving any of the muscles in his speech apparatus.

It is clear, then, that there is more to thought than simply moving our vocal muscles and that language may not be essential for thought and problem-solving. Non-human animals can certainly undertake basic problem-solving activities without language and, in spite of considerable recent advances in teaching gorillas and chimpanzees human language (e.g. Savage-Rumbaugh and Lewin 1994), there is no convincing evidence that this language competence improves their performance on other cognitive tasks. However, it is wrong to conclude from animal studies that *all* thinking takes place independently of language. Animals can certainly solve problems without language, but their cognitive abilities are severely limited. Perhaps, as Harley (1995) suggests, language is a tool that sets us further apart from animals because it allows novel and more advanced types of thinking.

Psychologists are divided in their explanations of the relationship between language and thought. There are three main views:

- Language determines thought – the 'linguistic relativity hypothesis' or 'Sapir–Whorf hypothesis'.
- Cognitive development determines language development – Piaget's viewpoint.

- Language and thought begin independently, but become interdependent processes – Vygotsky's viewpoint.

There is a fourth position taken by Chomsky (1968), and latterly by Pinker (1994), that language and thought are independent processes, which is discussed in the section on language acquisition.

The linguistic relativity hypothesis

This focuses on the differences between languages and on the influence that languages have on the way native speakers think and perceive the world. This idea was first investigated by Edward Sapir (1921), who studied various North American languages and noted how their constructions differed both from one another and from English. He believed that differences in vocabulary and grammatical construction constrained (restricted) native speakers and influenced the way they perceived the world. Benjamin Whorf (1956) later conducted his own analysis of North American languages and drew a more radical conclusion than Sapir. He believed that the language we use is directly responsible for shaping our thoughts about the world.

The contention that language and thought are causally related (the 'linguistic relativity hypothesis') came to be known as the 'Sapir–Whorf hypothesis', even though the two men worked independently and had rather different views. Sapir suggested that language might *influence* thinking (the 'weak' version), whereas Whorf took the more extreme view that the language people speak *determines* the way they think about the world (the 'strong' version).

Both forms of the hypothesis are difficult to test, not least because the terms 'language' and 'thought' are not precisely defined. It has proved difficult to find unequivocal support for either the strong or weak form of this hypothesis because, even where cognitive differences are found in different language communities, it is impossible to isolate language as the only influence. Education, intelligence, age, experience and environment may all be contributory factors. Much of the evidence cited in support of the theory comes from observations that certain words and grammatical forms exist in some languages, but not in others.

Whorf's research

Whorf argued that each language imposes a particular world view on its native speakers. He noted that the Hopi have a single term to denote a flying object, whereas English distinguishes between birds, insects, planes, helicopters, etc. Similarly, he wrote that Inuit (Eskimo) people have several words for snow, whereas English has only one. The implicit assumption of Whorf's observations is that a huge choice of words allows native speakers to perceive and remember specialized categories of objects in a way that is impossible for native speakers of other languages that lack the appropriate vocabulary.

It was not only individual words that differentiated languages according to Whorf, but also their grammars. He translated passages of Apache language (for example, he stated that the sentence 'the boat is grounded on the beach' must be expressed in Apache as 'it is on the beach pointwise as an event of canoe motion') and concluded 'How utterly unlike our way of thinking!' (Whorf 1956).

Commentary
Whorf's hypothesis

Whorf's understanding of **vocabulary** and its role in thought has been criticized:

- **'The Great Eskimo Vocabulary Hoax'** – Pinker (1994) debunks what he calls 'the Great Eskimo Vocabulary Hoax' as follows: 'Contrary to popular belief, the Eskimos do not have more words for snow than do speakers of English ... One dictionary puts the figure at two. Counting generously, experts can come up with about a dozen, but by such standards English would not be far behind, with snow, sleet, slush, blizzard, avalanche, hail, hardpack, powder ...'

- **Need for linguistic labels** – It is an enormous inferential leap to assume that people are unable to conceptualize something in the absence of an appropriate linguistic label. A gardening expert, for example, has labels for sub-species of plants that most other people in the same language community do not need to know. These latter individuals, however, are just as capable of perceiving differences between the plants and could learn the labels if they chose to do so. Nor can we assume that the existence of a verbal label ensures complete understanding of a particular concept.

There are also real flaws with Whorf's analysis of **grammar** and Lenneberg and Roberts (1956) responded immediately to Whorf's paper with some major criticisms:

- **Assumed relationship between language and thought** – Whorf did not interview any Apaches in the course of his study and based all his assumptions about their world view on an analysis of their grammar. He believed that Apaches think differently because they speak differently, but he had no independent evidence of this. Whorf's argument is circular, i.e. he notes that a language is different from our own and, therefore, infers that speakers of that language think differently.

He then concludes that the differences in thinking stem from differences in the language. In fact, differences between languages prove *only* that languages differ. Without an independent measure of the thought patterns themselves, there is no evidence for a causal relationship between language and thought.

- **Method of translation** – Whorf translated Apache phrases literally into English, which inevitably sounds stilted. Mark Twain, an excellent German speaker, illustrated this by writing a literal English translation of a speech he gave in German. A small extract from the translation demonstrates the point: 'I would only the language method – the luxurious, elaborate construction compress, the eternal parenthesis suppress, do away with, annihilate; the introduction of more than thirteen subjects in one sentence forbid; the verb so far to the front pull that one it without a telescope discover can.' (from Brown 1958)

The language in this passage is constructed differently from English and a direct translation sounds ridiculous. If the passage had been translated sensitively into syntactically correct English, the ideas would have been perfectly comprehensible. Germans construct their sentences differently from English speakers, but this does not mean that they think differently.

- **Hopi ideas of time** – Whorf stated that the Hopi Indians had no words or grammatical forms to convey the idea of time or to express the concept of past and future. Whorf believed that this meant that the Hopi had no conception of time. However, the anthropologist Malotki (1983) found that the Hopi kept quite sophisticated records including methods of dating events and that they estimated time using the principle of the sundial. Moreover, Malotki demonstrated that the Hopi language contained vocabulary for units of time and also that the verbs could be changed to indicate past and future tenses.

Other research investigating the linguistic relativity hypothesis

Whorf's data are clearly unreliable and not based on rigorous research, so we need to consider whether there is any support for his theory from more controlled studies. While there is little evidence for Whorf's extreme version of the linguistic relativity hypothesis, there is some modest support for the weaker form. Research has been conducted in several areas:

● how verbal labels affect recall
● whether colour coding words affect colour discrimination
● bilingual participants and national stereotypes
● the cognitive effects of grammatical differences between languages.

The effect of verbal labels

In a classic experiment, Carmichael et al. (1932) looked at the effects of learning verbal labels on the recall of ambiguous line drawings (see Fig. 17.1). Results showed that the label that had been attached at the first presentation affected recall.

Research into the effects of labelling on colour perception

Brown and Lenneberg (1954) and Lantz and Stefflre (1964) found that people are better able to remember colour chips if they have a simple colour name (e.g. red, blue) rather than a composite name like 'bled'. Berlin and Kay (1969) found that languages differ in the number of terms they have for colours. Some languages only have two basic colour words but, where this is the case, the two terms always correspond to black and white. If there are three colour words, the third will be red, and so on. In other words, Berlin and Kay found that colour terms occur in different languages in a hierarchical form – it is only as the number of colour words increases, that less basic colours such as pink and grey are represented in the vocabulary. However, this does not mean that people have to have appropriate colour labels in order to distinguish between colours. Laws et al. (1995) showed that English speakers discriminate between shades of light and dark blue just as Russian speakers do, even though Russian, unlike English, has specific verbal labels for these shade variations. It seems likely that our ability to discriminate between colours depends on innate, biological factors rather than the language we speak.

Research using bilingual participants

There has been some research using bilingual participants to see whether the particular language they speak at any one time affects their thought patterns. Ervin-Tripp (1964) found that Japanese–American bilinguals given word association tests in Japanese produced responses that were typical of Japanese

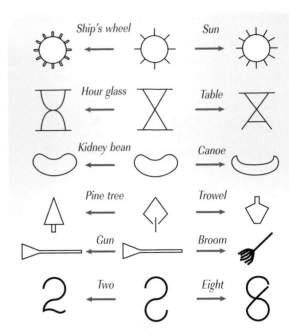

Figure 17.1 >> *Some examples of stimuli and responses showing the effect of verbal labels*
Source: *adapted from Carmichael* et al. *(1932)*

monolinguals. The same individuals, however, responded like American monolinguals when the test was in English. Although this appears to lend support for the Whorfian hypothesis, factors such as the nationality of the listener and the nature of the topics were also found to be influential, so language cannot be isolated as the causal factor.

A similar type of study was conducted by Hoffman et al. (1986), who gave English–Chinese bilingual participants descriptions of fictional individuals which were written in Chinese and English versions. These descriptions included characters that fitted with particular national stereotypes. For example, they included one type called in Chinese 'sh i gu'. This single word, for which there is no English equivalent, specifically describes a person who is, according to the researchers, 'worldly, experienced, socially skilful, devoted to his/her family and somewhat reserved'. Participants were then asked to write down their own interpretation of the passages they had just read. Findings showed that bilinguals using Chinese were more likely to recall Chinese stereotypes such as the 'sh i gu' character, and bilinguals using English were more likely to emphasize English stereotypes in their descriptions. This study suggests that language exerts some influence on the way people think about issues.

Research into the cognitive effects of grammatical differences

Attempts to investigate the possible effects of grammatical differences between languages have produced inconclusive evidence.

Carroll and Casagrande (1958) investigated the effect of a particular class of verbs in the Navaho language on the performance of cognitive tasks. In Navaho there are certain verbs that refer to handling (e.g. to carry) and the endings for these verbs must be changed depending on the form of the object being handled. (For example: 'hand over a piece of rope' (a long, thin, flexible object) = san*leh*; 'hand over a stick' (a long, rigid object) = san*tiih*, and so on. Navaho children have usually learned to use these forms appropriately by the age of 3 or 4 years. Since Navaho speakers have to pay attention to shape in this way, Carroll and Casagrande expected them to group objects according to form rather than to, say, colour. Their participants were Navaho children between the ages of 3 and 10 years, who were presented with two objects (e.g. a blue stick and a yellow piece of rope). They were then offered a third object (e.g. a blue rope) and asked to say which of the two original objects went best with the third one. All the children were at least partially bilingual so they were divided into Navaho-dominant and English-dominant groups. In line with the researchers' expectations, the Navaho-dominant children did, indeed, show a greater tendency to group according to form rather than colour. This would appear to support the weak Whorfian hypothesis, except that the results were confounded by some unexpected additional data from a control group of white American children who showed an even greater tendency to group by form than the Navaho-dominant children. This finding ran totally counter to experimental expectations. One possible explanation arises from what we know about Western children's normal cognitive development. Young children (3 to 6 years) tend to group objects more on the basis of colour rather than form, but, with increasing age, move towards form rather than colour. When the results of this experiment are analysed in terms of age, it can be seen that there is a greater tendency to group according to form as the age of the child increases, but that this increase begins earlier in the Navaho-dominant group. This suggests that the Navaho linguistic requirement to pay attention to form may facilitate the emergence of the ability to group by form, but does not actually cause it to happen. If this interpretation of the data is correct, it still provides only weak support for the linguistic relativity hypothesis.

Another example of research into the cognitive effects of different grammatical forms has been provided by Bloom (1981). He argued that because English speakers have a subjunctive mood, they find it easy to reason counter-factually (e.g. '*If* she had taken the bus, she *would have* arrived on time'). There is no subjunctive mood in Chinese and so Chinese speakers should find counter-factual reasoning more difficult. Bloom wrote some stories containing a series of events that would have happened if an original event had taken place: for example, 'Bier could not read Chinese, but if he had been able to do so, he would have discovered A.' He gave these stories to both Chinese and American students and asked them whether A had actually occurred. Bloom found that American students gave the correct answer 98 per cent of the time, but Chinese students got them right only 7 per cent of the time. He concluded that Chinese speakers find it difficult to understand counter-factual reasoning because of the constraints of their language. However, Au (1983) argued that Bloom's findings resulted from the unidiomatic nature of the Chinese versions of the stories. When Au repeated the experiment using more idiomatic Chinese, the Chinese students had no problems in answering the questions correctly. Liu (1985) also refuted Bloom's findings, arguing that such reasoning is possible in Chinese, but might take longer to formulate. While this casts doubt on the strong version of the linguistic relativity hypothesis, it does suggest that the facility within a language to express a concept in simple terms reduces processing time.

Evaluation
linguistic relativity hypothesis

- **Difficulty of isolating language differences from other factors** – The evidence from studies investigating the linguistic relativity hypothesis has sometimes been difficult to interpret because of the problem of disentangling the language component from other possible influences such as cultural factors.

- **Lack of objective evidence** – Whorf's own research has largely been discredited because of its subjective quality and there appears to be no convincing support for the strong version of the hypothesis.

- **Some support for the weak hypothesis** – There is some evidence for the weak version since language does seem to influence some habits of thought and also the facility and efficiency with which certain thoughts can be expressed, although research findings have not always been clear cut. You may have noticed that much of the research mentioned in this section is quite old and this reflects the fact that psychologists began to view the weak version of the hypothesis as too vague to be useful. There has, however, been some renewed interest in the idea of linguistic relativity. For example, Hunt and Agnoli (1991) have tried to explain the hypothesis in cognitive terms. They believe that there are bound to be significant, if slight, differences in the

continued on next page

performance and acquisition of cognitive tasks between speakers of different languages if an idea which is readily expressible in one language cannot be so easily expressed in the other. In their review of the Whorfian hypothesis, they cite examples that seem to support the idea of different cognitive styles arising from different language bases. Chinese, for example, has only 14 basic number terms (0 to 10, 100, 1000, and 10,000). All intervening numbers are expressed using combinations of those terms e.g. 12 = 10 and 2. However, English-speaking children have to learn special words for the numbers between 10 and 20 and Hunt and Agnoli contend that they take longer to learn to count in this 10-to-20 range than Chinese children.

- *Interaction between thought and vocabulary* – If causal links do exist between thought and language, they are likely to be bi-directional. We sometimes invent new words to meet a need and these new words, in turn, might come to affect the way we think. So, for example, 'chairperson' has been coined in order to provide a less gender-specific term than 'chairman', and those who introduced it hoped that its regular use would change views about gender roles. It seems that there is a constant interaction between thought and language within a cultural context. English, for example, is a dynamic language with new words and expressions being added all the time; it is also used extensively by people for whom it is not the native language. It has been estimated that English has a vocabulary that is three times greater than any other language and this gives rise to the scope for a greater range of expression. While this does not, of itself, guarantee more sophisticated levels of thought than are possible for speakers of less extensive languages, it may perhaps provide a more flexible tool for thinking.

- *Cognitive effects of grammatical differences* – It seems likely, then, that the properties of certain languages can have consequences for cognitive performance. Harley (1995) suggests, for example, that the lack of irregular words in languages such as Italian and Serbo-Croat have consequences for children learning to read, compared to children learning to read a language such as English, which has many irregular spellings. The study of dyslexia in other languages is still at quite an early stage, but it is likely to provide some important insights.

In summary, although there is no evidence for the strong version of the linguistic relativity hypothesis that language controls or determines thought, the weaker version of the hypothesis remains a useful concept.

Piaget and the cognition hypothesis

Unlike Whorf, who was concerned with differences between cultures, Piaget was interested in universal patterns that occur in all children's thought regardless of their native language. He saw language as just one type of symbolic function much like symbolic play and symbolic imagery. He believed that early language is egocentric and characterized by three distinct types of speech:

- *echolalia* – where children simply repeat utterances

- *monologues* – where children appear to be thinking out loud

- *collective monologues* – where two or more children give the appearance of engaging in dialogue, but are, in fact, simply producing monologues.

He recognized that language could have a facilitating effect on thinking, but that an understanding of underlying concepts was required *before* the appropriate verbal tag could be applied. Piaget's theory of cognitive development is explained in Unit 18. Here we will look briefly at research concerned with his 'cognition hypothesis', i.e. the idea that language requires some cognitive competence before it can develop.

For example, Piaget believed that children need to acquire 'object permanence' (the ability to understand that objects and people continue to exist even if they are not currently visible – see Unit 18 for a detailed explanation) before they can acquire language concepts such as nouns. He felt that this explained the fact that the vocabulary of children dramatically increases around the age of 18 months (i.e. when object permanence develops). There is some research (e.g. McCune-Nicolich 1981) which suggests that the child's use of relational words (e.g. 'no', 'down', 'gone') is related to the concept of object permanence. Tomasello and Farrar (1986) found that relational words such as 'up' and 'move' (relating to objects still present) are used before words such as 'all gone' (relating to objects which are absent from the visual field).

One way of testing the cognition hypothesis is to look at the development of children with learning difficulties. If Piaget is correct in assuming that language is dependent on cognitive competence, it would follow that children with learning difficulties should also show delayed or impaired language development. There is certainly evidence that spoken language is often delayed and limited in such children (Johnson and Ramsted 1983). However, this does not always have to be the case. Yamada (1990) has reported a case study of an individual known as 'Laura'. In spite of severe cognitive impairment and restricted short-term memory capacity, she is able to construct complex, grammatically correct sentences and complete other linguistic tasks, even though her overall language competence is not completely normal. Yamada suggests that such cases refute the idea that it is necessary to acquire certain cognitive concepts before language can develop.

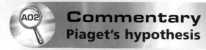

Commentary
Piaget's hypothesis

- **Relationship between language development and object permanence** – There seems to be little unequivocal evidence to support the cognition hypothesis. Children develop some limited language before they develop object permanence and the rapid expansion of vocabulary that takes place around the age of 18 months seems to have little direct relationship with the development of object permanence.

- **Play and imitation** – However, Bates *et al.* (1987) have suggested that language is delayed in children whose symbolic play and imitation are normally also delayed. They have also shown that children who are early to develop particular kinds of sequence-gesturing in their play (e.g. pouring pretend milk into a cup, drinking from it and then wiping their mouth) are also the first to start using two- and three-word sentences. Such findings have led Bloom (1993) to suggest, much as Piaget had many years before, that 'words a child hears from others will be learned if they connect with what the child is thinking and feeling'.

- **Children with learning difficulties** – Evidence from research on children with learning difficulties is mixed but, in general, lends support to the idea that language and thinking are separate, independent processes, rather than that cognition precedes language. Some psychologists believe that language training can actually improve performance on cognitive tasks, although Sinclair-de-Zwart (1969) showed that such training has only an indirect and temporary effect. Best (1973), however, found that deaf children were more likely to do well at cognitive tasks if they had a high level of competence in sign language. This suggests that their language ability facilitated their thinking.

According to Best (1973), deaf children are more likely to do well at cognitive tasks if they have a high level of competence in sign language

- **Lack of relevant research** – There is not much recent research on the cognition hypothesis and psychologists have tended to become more interested in looking at the social rather than cognitive factors that seem to affect language development (discussed in the next section).

Vygotsky and the interdependence of language and thought

A rather different view has been put forward by Vygotsky (1934). He believed that language and thinking have different roots and develop independently in infancy. At first, any attempts by an infant to use language are for social purposes and not linked to inner thoughts. Language at this stage is fairly basic and consists of vocalizations designed to attract attention. Thinking, which starts to develop during this same period, is also at a fairly basic level and occurs in the absence of language, i.e. it depends on images. Vygotsky suggested that around the age of 2 years, social speech and thought without language begin to merge and language starts to play a major role in the child's intellectual and social development. He believed that egocentric speech becomes internalized as inner speech and continues to play an important role in regulating and planning cognitive operations. In other words, unlike Piaget, he believed that cognitive development from this age is partly controlled by language. From the age of about 2 years, language has two functions:

- monitoring and directing thought
- communicating with other people.

At first, children find it difficult to disentangle these two functions and often engage in egocentric speech, i.e. they speak their thoughts aloud and do not always communicate effectively. By the age of approximately 7 years, the child has learned the distinction.

SOCIAL AND CULTURAL ASPECTS OF LANGUAGE USE

Language is a tool for social communication but, even within the same language-speaking community, individuals do not all speak in the same way. These differences within a particular language are called 'dialects' and are often seen as indicators of real or imagined differences in class, ethnic origin, religion or other aspects of life. Dialects usually arise when a particular group of individuals converse more amongst themselves than with people from the larger community outside the group. Profession, age, geography, social class and ethnic origin are all factors that can contribute to the use of dialect. Sometimes a single speaker will use a different dialect depending on the context. In Greece, for example, there are two forms of the Greek language – High Greek is used in formal settings (e.g. in courts of law, educational institutions, government offices) and Low Greek is used between friends and families.

Social aspects of language use

Basil Bernstein, a British sociologist, studied the differences between the language use of different social classes and concluded that these differences had 'cognitive consequences' (Bernstein 1971). In other words, he subscribed to the weak form of the linguistic relativity hypothesis. He made a distinction between 'restricted code' and 'elaborated code':

- *Restricted code* is a pattern of speech that uses fairly basic vocabulary and contains mainly concrete description. It can usually only be understood when set in context.

- *Elaborated code* is not context-bound and uses more complex grammatical structures and more abstract vocabulary.

Bernstein believed that working-class children use only restricted code whereas most middle-class children can use both, even though they have a greater tendency to adopt the elaborated. Hawkins (1973) asked 5-year-old children to tell a story depicted in a set of pictures. Middle-class children used elaborated code to link the events and people in the pictures and so were able to build up a coherent story that could be understood by listeners without reference to the pictures. Working-class children, on the other hand, were limited by restricted code and only listeners who had access to the pictures could understand their stories.

Bernstein believed that restricted code arises as a function of socialization within working-class family life. Status is defined in terms of age, gender and family relationship, and so there is no discussion or verbal elaboration to clarify roles. Because the father is in an unambiguous position of authority, he can give an order, e.g. 'Stop it', and will simply expect to be obeyed. In middle-class families, however, members tend to relate to one another more as individuals and the status of individuals within the family is much less clear cut. As a result, the meaning of communications has to be made much more explicit and there is often discussion and negotiation about decisions and rules, requiring a more elaborate form of language.

According to Bernstein, the class system restricts access to the elaborated code and, since most teachers are middle class, working-class children cannot understand or be understood by them properly, which exacerbates their problems at school. Bernstein believed that the use of a restricted code in working-class children was related to their low academic attainment compared to middle-class children.

'Now Tarquin, I want us to negotiate a reduction in these irrational rusk-rejection episodes'.

A2 Cognitive Psychology

Bernstein's conclusions have been the subject of considerable criticism, in particular by the American sociolinguist, William Labov (1970). Labov identified three major criticisms:

- Bernstein contended that the verbal IQ of working-class children was lower than their visuospatial IQ. However, verbal IQ is measured by tests of verbal analogy (e.g. 'toe is to foot as finger is to –') and verbal IQ, by this definition, seems to bear no

relation to the linguistic abilities which vary between elaborated and restricted code.

- Bernstein produced no evidence of a causal relationship between low academic achievement and the use of a restricted language code.

- Bernstein's methods for collecting data may have influenced the samples of language. He used middle-class researchers to collect samples from both working-class and middle-class children. The differences in the language samples collected may have reflected the working-class children's difficulty in relating to the interviewers.

Cultural aspects of language use

These criticisms of Bernstein are similar to those levelled at Whorf – namely that the differences he attributed to language might actually have arisen from differences in culture. There is little evidence that elaborated and restricted codes actually exist as separate entities. Bernstein did not record detailed transcripts to illustrate the two types of speech, and linguists such as Gordon (1981) regard his defining criteria for the two codes as unsatisfactory. There is also little evidence that different family types talk in distinctly different codes. Wells (1985), in a review of relevant research, found that most children of school age have been exposed to a similar range of syntax and language use. Tizard and Hughes (1984) found class differences in amounts of questioning, vocabulary, use of books and imaginative play in pre-school children, but the differences were not large and there were wider variations within classes than between them.

'Black English'

One of the most widespread non-standard dialects is that spoken by Black people, both in America and the

UK, and this has been another area of interest for sociolinguists. This dialect is commonly referred to as 'Black English', although researchers such as Labov (1972) prefer the term 'Black English Vernacular' (BEV). From a linguistic point of view, BEV does not vary significantly from Standard English. However, Labov (1970) has made an extensive study of the dialect and outlined some of the differences. Some of the grammatical rules are different so, for example, agreement between a subject and a verb is not always obligatory in BEV, e.g. 'She have a daughter' or 'They was going'. Similarly, BEV does not appear to have a past tense form for some strong verbs, e.g. 'come', 'see'. This is the kind of finding which might have led Whorf to conclude that speakers of BEV have no concept of the past. This would be a totally erroneous conclusion, however, because the tenses are negated differently: 'I don't see it' is the present tense while 'I ain't see it' is the past. In addition to certain syntactic differences, there are distinct vocabularies. Some BEV words such as 'rap' and 'right-on' have been appropriated by speakers of Standard English, but certain other terms remain distinctively BEV, e.g. 'crib' for house (Burling 1973).

Dialects

- *Racial differences or social class differences* – There has been a tendency to see ethnic dialects as somehow inferior and as evidence of a failure on the part of speakers to master the standard dialect. It is sometimes suggested that low academic achievement in black children is directly attributable to impoverished language skills. Some black children may, of course, experience problems in language development

just as some white children do, but it seems likely that poverty or other social factors retard many aspects of cognitive development. It is important, therefore, not to confuse racial differences with social class differences.

- *Method of collecting data* – Labov (1970) produced a critical analysis of some of the so-called deficits in children speaking BEV, and found that many instances of reported impoverished speech were caused by the method of collecting data.

continued on next page

AO2

Commentary continued
cultural aspects of language use

● **Misunderstood dialect differences** – Many examples of illogical speech from black children are simply misunderstood dialect differences. For example, the use of the double negative, e.g. 'He don't know nothing', is often cited as an example of poor logic in black children. In fact, the double negative is found in other standard languages such as Russian and Old English. Modern English is simply one of those languages that uses a single negative form. Both forms convey a precise meaning as long as the listener knows the underlying rules. It is simply wrong to assume that non-standard dialects are deficient grammatically.

Gender differences

● **Polite and rough speech** – There has also been some interest in the question of gender differences in language use. For example, in a study of Edinburgh schoolchildren, Romaine (1984) found that most children could differentiate between what he called 'polite' and 'rough' forms of speech, but that girls began to alter their speech patterns as they grew older. The girls used fewer non-standard forms than the boys did and their pronunciation and syntax were closer to 'polite' speech.

● **Content of speech** – Gender differences have also been found in the content of speech. Young adult males have been shown to talk more about their opinions, preferences and sources of personal pride whereas young women preferred to talk about their feelings and their fears (Rubin *et al.* 1980). Tannen (1990, 1993) believes that males and females have different goals for conversation – males prefer to inform whereas females prefer to consult – and that this can lead to serious misunderstandings between them, both in personal relationships and in the workplace.

● **Choice** – A number of studies have shown differences in the way that males and females use language, but it is clearly not the case that all men and women differ in their speech patterns. Nor is it likely that males and females are incapable of changing the way that they speak if they choose to. As Tannen (1995) herself says: 'If women and men talk *differently*, it is not because they can't talk any other way, but because they don't want to. Our ways of talking reflect the way we assume a good person talks – and we get our sense of how we should be a good person by observing the others we talk to *with whom we identify*.'

She illustrates this point with an anecdote from the anthropologist Keith Basso (1979), who spent most of his career working with the Western Apache. He recalls an occasion when he heard what sounded to him like a group of 'typical white men' conversing behind him. He turned to find that it was a group of young Apache men who told him that they were imitating 'white speech'. They were perfectly capable of doing this convincingly although they usually chose not to because they believed it was a shallow, insincere way to talk, and not their way.

✓ CHECK YOUR UNDERSTANDING

Check your understanding of language and culture by answering these questions from memory. You can check your answers by looking back through this first topic.

1 What do you understand by the term 'linguistic relativity hypothesis'?

2 Explain why it is difficult to test the linguistic relativity hypothesis.

3 Give two criticisms of Whorf's research into the Apache language.

4 Outline the findings and conclusions of two research studies that lend support to the weak version of the linguistic relativity hypothesis.

5 Briefly outline Piaget's view on the relationship between language and thought.

6 Outline Vygotsky's view of the relationship between language and thought.

7 Outline Labov's three main criticisms of Bernstein's work.

8 Explain what is meant by BEV and outline some of the differences between this and Standard English.

9 Outline some of the findings of research into gender and language.

10 Does language determine thought? Write a 300-word précis that answers this question (150 words of AO1 and 150 words of AO2).

REVISION SUMMARY

Having covered this topic you should be able to:

✓ describe and evaluate research into the relationship between language and thought, including the linguistic relativity hypothesis

✓ describe and evaluate investigations into social and cultural aspects of language use.

EXAMPLE EXAM QUESTIONS

Below are some **possible examination questions** set on this topic, along with hints to help you understand and approach each question effectively:

1 Discuss research (theories **and/or** studies) into the relationship between language and thought. (24 marks)

> The word 'research' in any question can refer to theories or studies. This leaves you with a decision about what to use for the AO1 focus of your answer. You could use explanations (theories) of the relationship between language and thought, such as the linguistic relativity hypothesis, or you could use studies, or both. It might be better (attract more marks) if you use either theories or studies as AO2. However, if you do use either of these as AO2 material, credit will only be awarded where they have been used as part of a *sustained* critical commentary, i.e. don't describe them, but use them to make critical points. Further ideas for innovative and effective AO2 can be found on pp. 937–9.

2 Critically consider the relationship between language and thought. (24 marks)

> The instruction 'critically consider' has the same meaning as 'discuss'. When answering broad questions such as this, the skill of selectivity is important. The more theories/studies you cover (increasing breadth), the less detail you can provide (decreasing depth). For high marks, depth and breadth must be in balance.

3 Describe and evaluate the linguistic relativity hypothesis. (24 marks)

> The specification refers specifically to this one explanation of the relationship between language and thought, which means that questions may explicity be asked about it. It would be acceptable to describe all forms of the hypothesis (e.g. weak and strong). One way to ensure that you have enough to write would be to identify about 8 to 10 key points which you can elaborate in order to be able to provide the 300 words necessary for AO1. You can do the same for AO2.

4 (a) Outline research (theories **and/or** studies) into the relationship between language and thought.
(12 marks)

(b) To what extent is language shaped by thought? (12 marks)

> In exam questions, the instruction 'describe' is used when asking for one theory and 'outline' when asking for more than one. Hence, in part (a), it is likely that you would write about more than one theory (although there is actually no requirement to). 'To what extent' is an AO2 instruction which requires you to use your knowledge to present *effective* critical commentary – for example, to consider whether studies of Eskimo language do or do not indicate that language affects thought. Part of your commentary might include the flaws in such research which challenge the validity of the conclusions.

5 Describe and evaluate research (theories **and/or** studies) into the social **and/or** cultural aspects of language use. (24 marks)

> In answering this question, you may use research by Bernstein and Labov, or any of the other research under the heading 'Social and cultural aspects of language use'. You could also use material from earlier in the unit provided that you stress the important role of social/cultural determinants. If you *describe* research studies for your AO1, then you may use theories as commentary or vice versa, but ensure that any AO2 material is *effectively* used.

Language acquisition is one of the most remarkable of human achievements. Clark (1991) has estimated that an average child has acquired a vocabulary of 14,000 to 15,000 words by the age of 6. In this topic you will look at the process of language acquisition and then consider various explanations of how language develops in children.

RESEARCH INTO THE PROCESS OF LANGUAGE ACQUISITION

Speech perception

Before a child can use language, the child needs to be able to discriminate between speech sounds. This is a more complex ability than you might at first imagine. The child has to distinguish, for example, not only the difference between the sounds of 'd' and 't', but also to recognize that a 't' spoken by a deep male voice is the same sound as a 't' spoken by a much higher-pitched voice. It has been demonstrated that this remarkable ability is present either right from birth or very soon afterwards (Bates *et al.* 1992). At first, babies seem

able to distinguish a whole range of speech sounds but, as they get older, they seem to 'tune in' more to the speech sounds of the native language to which they are continually exposed.

Speech production

Speech perception appears to be quite well developed in young infants, but in order to use language, babies need to be able to *produce* speech sounds. There are clear stages in language production, which seem to be universal (see Table 17.1 below).

Table 17.1 >> Stages of language acquisition

Age	Stage of development
From birth	>> Ability to show fine auditory discrimination between different speech sounds. >> Crying – carers are usually able to distinguish between different types of cry (e.g. hunger, pain).
Approx. 1 month to 2 months	>> Cooing – vocalizations consist of vowel sounds such as 'uuu' and 'aaa'. >> There is considerable variation in tone, volume and pitch.
Approx. 4 to 6 months	>> Babbling begins – consonants are now sounded, e.g. 'bababa', mamama', 'gagaga'. At first, babbling includes sounds not heard in the infant's native language. Deaf children babble in the same way as hearing children.
Approx. 9 months	>> Babbling sounds become mainly restricted to the sounds heard in the infant's native language. Similarly, the ability to discriminate speech sound becomes limited to those heard in the infant's native language. >> Babies appear able to understand the meaning of some words even though they cannot produce the words themselves.
Approx. 12 to 18 months	>> The first real words are uttered. At this one-word stage, children typically overgeneralize, e.g. use 'dog' for all animals. Vocabulary increases rapidly. >> This period is sometimes called the 'holophrastic' stage (McNeill 1970) – this means that babies use a single word to convey a much broader meaning, e.g. 'ball' accompanied by outstretched arms and cupped fingers may mean 'throw me the ball'.
Approx. 18 months	>> Babies start to produce basic two- and three-word sentences. Brown (1973) has called this the 'telegraphic' stage. Although sentences are constructed in the correct order, grammatical markers such as 'ed', 'ing' and 's' endings are often omitted.
Approx. 2.5 years onwards	>> Vocabulary rapidly increases and children master how to use grammatical markers. They develop a much more sophisticated grasp of syntax and begin to take account of pragmatic aspects of language.

Prelinguistic phase (birth to approx. 12 months)

During the pre-linguistic phase, babies appear to understand the meaning of words even though they cannot yet produce them. In other words, their receptive language outstrips their expressive language. Fenson et al. (1994) conducted a large-scale survey of mothers to find out about their babies' language comprehension. They found that 10-month-old babies could understand about 30 words, while 13-month-olds recognized as many as 100 words.

One-word stage (12 to 18 months approx.)

The first real words are usually uttered around the child's first birthday and tend to refer to people and objects (Clark 1993). Although children can vary tremendously in the rate at which they learn new words, Fenson et al. (1991) found, in a large-scale study, that the average rate was 12 words at 12 months, 179 words at 20 months and 380 words at 28 months. This explosion from about the age of 16 months may be due to several factors. Bates et al. (1992) have suggested that it is linked to rapid increases in synaptic connections in the brain. Another factor is what de Villiers and de Villiers (1992) have called 'fast mapping'. This is the ability to use context to make a reasonable guess about a word's meaning after just one or two exposures. This contrasts with the early period of acquisition (around 12 to 16 months) when a child typically learns words slowly and after many repetitions.

At the one-word stage, children typically overgeneralize (e.g. use the word 'daddy' for all men) and use holophrases (see Table 17.1).

Telegraphic speech (18 months to 2-and-a-half years approx.)

The first sentences are usually produced around the age of 18 months. These usually consist of only two or three words and are very simple. This is described as 'telegraphic speech' because it resembles the kind of abbreviated sentences used by adults when writing telegrams or short advertisements in the newspaper. Children at this stage do not use inflections (i.e. grammatical markers such as the plural 's', the verb endings 'ing' and 'ed', or auxiliary verbs such as 'be' and 'do'). So, young children are likely to say 'dog run' rather than 'the dog runs' or 'Mummy sing' rather than 'Mummy is singing'. However, children seem to master how to use such grammatical markers fairly quickly and, by the age of approximately 3-and-a-half years, can use endings such as 's', 'ing' and 'ed' appropriately (Kuczaj 1977).

Overregularization (2-and-a-half years onward)

Once children are able to use the regular forms of the plural and past tense, they tend to apply these regular forms inappropriately, e.g. 'goed' and 'sheeps'. This tendency is called 'overregularization', although Pinker (1990) has found that children who have learned the 'ed' rule make errors on fewer than 5 per cent of irregular verbs. His data show that children often produce a correct and an incorrect irregular verb in the same sentence, e.g. 'They went and singed in church.' This suggests that the common irregular verbs are mastered before ones that are heard more rarely.

Children also have to come to grips with syntax – the rules that govern word order, sentence structure and the relationship between words – when they start combining words. As with the acquisition of vocabulary, there seems to be a sudden and rapid expansion after a slow start. Fenson et al. (1994) have shown that there is a very high correlation between the size of a child's vocabulary and the complexity of its sentence structures. However, it is not yet clear whether a large vocabulary encourages syntactic competence or whether increased understanding of the rules of sentence construction allows for easier learning of new words. It could be that both increases are due to the growing capacity of the child's working memory.

Social rules of language

Another important aspect of language learning is 'pragmatics'. This refers to the social, rather than the grammatical, rules of language. For example, children have to learn quite early how to make requests in a socially acceptable way, e.g. 'can I?' and 'may I?'. Ervin-Tripp et al. (1990) have shown that children learn to phrase a question in a different way if the first attempt provokes no response. They also need to learn the conventions of turn-taking in a conversation. Children have to anticipate when their conversational partner is about to finish speaking and this seems to be a skill that develops with experience. McTear (1985) showed that 2-year-olds take on average 1.5 seconds to respond to a conversational partner whereas adults take only about 0.8 seconds. Children also seem to learn from an early age that they have to adapt their language to suit the listener. Four-year-olds use simpler language when they are talking to 2-year-olds than when they are chatting to an adult (Tomasello and Mannle 1985). An important aspect of adult conversation involves non-verbal communication such as smiling, head nodding and eye contact. Miller et al. (1985) recorded children talking to adults on various topics and noted the degree of non-verbal communication in the children. They found that the number of such gestures increased with the child's age, suggesting that children learn this aspect of conversation through experience.

Research has provided us with a reasonable if not complete picture of the way language develops in young children. A much greater challenge for psychologists has been to explain *how* language develops.

We will now look at some of the theories that have attempted to explain language acquisition.

EXPLANATIONS OF LANGUAGE DEVELOPMENT

We will consider three rather different types of explanation provided by:

● environmental theories
● nativist theories
● interactionist theories.

Environmental theories

Skinner's learning theory

The earliest attempts to explain language acquisition were largely founded on the common-sense notion that it was a relatively uncomplicated process dependent on imitation and reinforcement. A formal, learning theory of language acquisition based on this idea was put forward by Skinner (1957). He referred to language acquisition as 'verbal behaviour' because he believed that it was acquired by exactly the same mechanisms of

conditioning and reinforcement that governed all other aspects of human behaviour. According to this theory, infants, motivated by a survival need to communicate, begin by emitting random verbal sounds. If adults reinforce these (e.g. by smiling or nodding approval), the sounds will be repeated, but if they are not reinforced, they will extinguish. In addition, children sometimes use echoic responses, i.e. they simply try to imitate what they have heard and these imitations are also reinforced. Skinner called the verbal labels used to name objects or events 'tacts'. Through a process of selective reinforcement, adults gradually shape children's vocabulary and this shaping process continues as the child is rewarded for putting words together. A child may be given a drink in response to the word 'more', but will later be expected to ask for 'more juice, please'. Verbal behaviour based on requests and commands which are rewarded in this way are called 'mands'.

Commentary
Skinner's learning theory

This extreme form of learning theory has a number of serious flaws:

● Most children achieve language competence even though their environments are very different.

● Language seems to be learnt at roughly the same rate and in the same sequence, regardless of environment.

● Adults generally correct only truth and meaning in children's utterances, not syntax and, on the occasions when they do attempt to correct grammar, it usually has little effect.

● Certain words (e.g. 'no!') are clearly understood by children well before they try to produce the words themselves.

● The pattern of acquisition of irregular verb and noun forms does not occur as learning theory would predict. There is often a U-shaped development where performance begins well, becomes temporarily worse, and then improves again. It is as though the child has to learn the general rules and then learn exceptions to those rules (Kolota 1987).

● Children often produce new utterances that they have never heard before and Skinner's theory cannot account for this creativity.

Transcripts of child language

Much of the research into child language has been based on tapes and transcripts of children talking. This has produced a rich source of material and provided many insights into the pattern of language development. There are difficulties with this approach. It is important, for example, to note the context as well as just the words. When a child says, 'Mummy coat' it could mean 'That's mummy's coat', 'Mummy has put her coat on', 'Put your coat on, mummy', etc. An adequate description of the child's language would have to include the range of relationships being expressed. It is also important to obtain a large sample of speech in order to avoid hasty conclusions about a child's competence. Adam, a child studied extensively by Roger Brown (1973), often used the

expression 'just checking'. It would be tempting to conclude that he had acquired an understanding of how to use the morpheme 'ing'. However, it was clear from analysing many of his utterances that he never used 'ing' except in this phrase, so the likely explanation was that he had simply picked up the whole phrase by imitation. Similarly, it is too simplistic to assume that a child who regularly uses a particular word or construction is actually using it in the way an adult would. Young children, for example, often use the conjunction 'because', but mean 'and then', e.g. 'I fell off the swing because I hurt my leg'.

In spite of some of the difficulties of interpretation, child language transcripts (such as those on p. 519) have provided some useful insights.

Other environmental explanations

While Skinner's extreme view of language acquisition receives little support, there is some evidence that the type of language the child hears spoken does have an effect on development. Children who listen to more spoken language are known to develop vocabulary faster than those who hear less (Engel *et al.* 1975). It also seems that children whose carers use language responsively show more rapid language development (Olson *et al.* 1986). One particular type of parental language that has attracted interest is the use of 'motherese' (Snow 1994). This is a simplified way of talking to children using shorter, slower, clearly segmented speech which includes more repetition and redundancy than is usual in adult speech and is delivered in a higher pitch than normal adult language. The term is something of a misnomer since fathers and other adults use it too (Hladik and Edwards 1984) and even children themselves use it when talking to younger children (Shatz and Gelman 1973), so it is sometimes called 'child directed speech' (CDS) instead.

CDS gradually fades as the child gets older and levels of comprehension improve. The evidence concerning the role of CDS in language development is not entirely clear, but it seems likely that it is helpful, at least in the early stages. Certainly babies seem to like to listen to

ACTIVITY

Talking to children

Try to 'listen in' to a carer (usually, but not always, a mother) talking to a young child. A queue at a supermarket checkout is often a good location to do this if you have no other access to a young family. See if you notice anything about the tone, pitch, choice of words, sentence structure, and so on, that is different from language used between adults.

motherese and, from only a few days old, show a preference for it over normal adult speech (Cooper and Aslin 1994). CDS is found in most cultures even though Lieven (1994) has suggested that the style of the speech differs quite widely between language communities. The fact that some form of CDS is almost universal and that babies show a very early preference for it suggests that it has an important developmental function. Gleason and Ratner (1993) believe that the rhythm and simplicity of CDS serves to break speech down into major syntactic constituents so that it is more comprehensible to infants.

Commentary
environmental theories

- ● *Incomplete explanation* – While learning theory undoubtedly offers an explanation for certain aspects of language acquisition, such as pronunciation and understanding of word meanings, it is too simplistic to account for the complexity and rapidity of the achievement.

- ● *Role of CDS* – As far as CDS is concerned, it does not, on its own, explain the process of language acquisition since children who are not exposed to it still manage to learn a complex grammar, even if they do so at a slower rate. It seems reasonable to conclude that CDS is not necessary for language development, but that it might facilitate the process.

Nativist theories

Given that language development appears to follow a very similar pattern across cultures, it would seem likely that the ability is somehow 'wired in'. The best-known theorist to adopt this position is Chomsky (1957) although, more recently, the cognitive psychologist, Steven Pinker (1989, 1994) has also written in support of this view.

Language acquisition device (LAD)

Chomsky argued that children learn language by acquiring a set of rules or grammar. He maintained that this could not occur as a result of environmental exposure alone because much of what they hear spoken is 'degenerate output'. In other words, the adults surrounding them produce language which consists of false starts, hesitations, slips of the tongue and blurred

word boundaries. He also believed that language acquisition could not be dependent on intelligence or experience because it occurs at a time when the child is incapable of complex cognitions. Chomsky thought that children acquire language readily because they are biologically equipped to do so and possess an innate mechanism that is programmed to recognize grammatical structure. This 'language acquisition device' (LAD) is not specific to a particular language, but rather it sets limits on what is permissible in any language. Chomsky believes that there are linguistic universals that are features common to all languages, for example, phonological elements such as vowels and syllables and syntactic structures such as nouns, verbs and tenses. These similarities between languages exist at what Chomsky calls 'the deep structure' level, whereas differences between languages exist at 'surface structure' level (see the panel overleaf).

Deep and surface structures

Chomsky believed that we possess an innate understanding of grammar that allows us to distinguish between acceptable sentence structure and meaningless strings of words. One aspect of our grammar is a set of rewrite rules which enables us to analyse sentences into their lowest level constituents (e.g. noun phrases, verb phrases, nouns, verbs). A constituent is a unit of language that can be replaced with a single word without altering the basic grammatical structure of the sentence although it might alter the meaning. For example, in the sentence 'The friendly, little girl spoke to the grumpy, old woman', 'the friendly, little girl' is a constituent because it could be replaced with 'Emma' while 'the friendly, little' is not a constituent because it cannot be replaced by one word; 'spoke to the grumpy, old woman' can be replaced simply by 'spoke' so this, too, is a constituent, whereas 'to the' is not. We can use these constituents to generate novel sentences and to avoid producing non-sentences. However, this phrase-structure grammar alone cannot account for all our linguistic competence and in 1965 Chomsky revised his theory to include the concept of

transformational grammar, which converts deep structure (the underlying meaning of a sentence) into surface structure (the actual words that are written or spoken). Chomsky recognized that sentences could have different surface structures but similar deep structures. For example:

> The boy ate the apple.

> The apple was eaten by the boy.

On the other hand, sentences can have similar surface structures but quite different deep structures. For example:

> He is easy to please.

> He is eager to please.

Occasionally, a sentence can have one surface structure but two underlying deep structures (as in the case of an ambiguous sentence). For example:

> Teachers should stop drinking in classrooms.

Chomsky proposed that people use transformational rules to convert surface structure to deep structure when trying to understand language, and to convert deep structure into surface structure when producing language.

Principles and parameters theory (PPT)

Children have an innate ability to use transformational rules that allow them to transform deep structure into surface structure and vice versa. In Chomsky's early writings in the 1950s, the LAD was not described in any great detail and he replaced it later with the idea of 'a universal grammar'. This slightly revised formulation of Chomsky's original ideas has been termed

'principles and parameters theory' (PPT). Although all languages share many common features ('linguistic principles'), they can differ greatly in superficial ways ('parametric variation'). Children have to learn the particular details of their own native language; Chomsky (1981) calls this 'parameter setting'. In order to acquire language, children have to identify the correct parameter from a range of possibilities. There is, for example, only a limited range of ways in which languages allow questions to be formed. In other words, the universal grammar sets constraints on question formation and the child must pick the correct parameter within that innately specified range. This process has been likened to a set of switches that constrain the grammatical possibilities of language; exposure to a particular language will set the switches to a particular position.

Evidence for nativist theories

● *Creole* – Bickerton (1984), for example, has reported on pidgin and creole languages. Pidgin is a highly simplified form of English, which was originally developed in order to communicate with black slaves in areas such as the Caribbean. Creole, on the other hand, is a language that has become the native tongue of children of pidgin speakers. Creole languages are much richer semantically and syntactically than the original pidgin and seem to demonstrate that there is an innate drive to develop syntax even if it is not present in the language of one's parents. Pinker (1994) has shown that even hearing-impaired children develop a creole sign language if they are exposed to signing pidgin.

- *Specific language impairment* – Some support is emerging from the relatively new research field of genetic linguistics. Gopnik and Crago (1991) have found that specific language impairment (SLI) runs in families and their study of one British family has led geneticists to suggest that a single dominant

gene is involved. As Pinker (1994) points out, 'This single gene is not, repeat not, responsible for all the circuitry underlying grammar … Remember that a single defective component can bring a complex machine to a halt even when the machine needs many properly functioning parts to work.' However, this evidence does suggest that there is some pattern of genetically programmed events in the development of the brain that is specialized for the 'wiring-in' of language competence.

Commentary
nativist theories

Most of the arguments cited earlier against learning theory can be used *in support of* Chomsky's theory:

- Most children achieve language competence and progress through the same developmental stages of language regardless of their environment and culture.

- Adults rarely correct grammar and yet children rapidly develop accurate syntax.

- Children produce novel utterances that they have never heard before. Sometimes they are incorrect (e.g. 'he goed'), but they demonstrate an awareness of underlying grammatical rules.

The nativist view of language acquisition seems able to explain more aspects of the process than the learning theory account, but there are still a number of *criticisms*:

- Learning must play some part; otherwise, for example, children would not progress from saying 'gived' to 'gave'.

- Exposure to spoken language would seem a necessary prerequisite.

- Chomsky's theory largely ignores social and cognitive factors.

- There is some evidence (e.g. Akiyama 1984) that world languages are not as similar as Chomsky supposed.

- The slightly revised version of Chomsky's view – PPT – has been quite influential in providing a framework for the acquisition of language and an impetus for research, but it is subject to many of the same criticisms. In particular, it raises questions about how bilingual children are able to acquire two different languages to the same level of competence. As Messer (1999) has pointed out, it seems unlikely that the same parameter can be set in different positions for two different languages.

Interactionist theories

Most contemporary researchers have rejected the extreme forms of both the learning and the environmental approaches and have opted instead for an integrative view that stresses the role of innate factors *and* experience.

Cognitive theory

According to theorists such as Piaget, language is dependent on other cognitive and perceptual processes and follows the stages of cognitive development. His views are relevant to the issue of linguistic relativity and were covered earlier in the unit. We will just emphasize here that a feature of the cognitive approach is its emphasis on the child as an active learner. Flavell (1985) has suggested that children seem to be constantly formulating and testing hypotheses about the rules and properties of language.

The cognitive theory is not too far removed from the ideas of the nativist theorist, Slobin (1985). The difference centres mainly on whether the rules are innate or whether they arise from the child's active analysis and exploration of the environment.

Social interactionist theory

While accepting that certain biological and cognitive processes may be necessary for language development, social interactionists believe that these processes alone are not sufficient. They feel that the linguists' preoccupation with grammar obscures the main function of language, which is interpersonal communication. Bruner (1983) contrasted the idea of the LAD with that of the LASS ('language acquisition socialization system'). He believed that the mother–child relationship serves to develop important social skills, such as turn-taking and mutual gaze, which then play a part in conversational language.

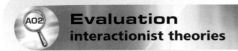

Evaluation
interactionist theories

Cognitive theory

● Children's rule-searching behaviour is apparent in other areas of development, not just language acquisition, and this lends weight to the argument that language learning is simply part of a wider cognitive process.

● There is little current research in this area, however; interest has focused more on the social interactionist approach.

Social interactionist theory

● Support for the necessity of exposure to language in a social context comes from studies of deprived children. Sachs *et al.* (1981) reported the case of 'Jim' whose parents were both deaf and unable to speak. Television provided his only exposure to spoken language up to the age of 3. Although he produced speech, it was grammatically idiosyncratic and poorly articulated, which suggests that exposure alone is insufficient – there must be some social interaction as well. It seems irrefutable that language development needs to occur in a social context to be completely effective.

● The social interactionist theory cannot, however, explain all the features of language acquisition.

CHECK YOUR UNDERSTANDING

Check your understanding of language acquisition by answering these questions. Try to do this from memory at first. You can check your answers by looking back through Topic 2.

1 Outline the stages of language development that occur in the pre-linguistic phase.

2 Suggest why there is a rapid increase in vocabulary from about 16 months.

3 What is meant by 'pragmatics' in the context of language acquisition?

4 Briefly outline Skinner's account of language acquisition.

5 Outline three problems with Skinner's theory.

6 Explain why CDS might be helpful in the process of language acquisition.

7 Outline the function of the LAD.

8 Explain briefly what is meant by 'transformational grammar'.

9 Outline two strengths and two weaknesses of Chomsky's theory.

10 'To what extent is language acquisition innate?'
Construct a 300-word précis that responds to this question.

REVISION SUMMARY

Having covered this topic you should be able to:

✓ describe and evaluate research into the process of language acquisition

✓ describe and evaluate environmental and nativist theories of language development.

A2 Cognitive Psychology

Below are some **possible examination questions** set on this topic, along with hints to help you understand and approach each question effectively:

1 Discuss research (explanations **and/or** studies) into the process of language acquisition. (24 marks)

> In some questions you are given the choice as to whether you wish to *describe* research studies (AO1) or to use research studies as *evaluation* (AO2). If you do the latter (use research studies as evaluation of theories), then you must ensure that they are presented as effective evaluation. Avoid the mistake of merely describing a study; in order to attract AO2 credit, you must clearly state the evaluative point you are making.

2 Describe and evaluate **one** environmental (e.g. learning) explanation of language development. (24 marks)

> You may be asked specifically about environmental and/or nativist theories, as these are given in the specification. This question cites learning theory as a hint to remind you what you might include. In this question you will only gain credit for description of one theory. If you know other environmental theories you may use these as evaluation, though it is more likely that you might wish to use your knowledge of nativist theory as evaluation. Remember that this will not gain any AO2 credit if you merely provide a linking sentence saying 'An alternative theory is …' and then proceed to *describe* the other theory. You must use another theory (or theories) as *sustained* critical commentary.

3 Describe and evaluate **one** nativist (e.g. Chomsky) explanation of language development. (24 marks)

> You may equally be asked for one nativist theory. Make sure that you can provide a decent explanation of each kind of theory – 12 marks' worth of AO1 and 12 marks' worth of AO2. One way to do this is to select about 8 to 10 key points and be able to elaborate these in the exam. This helps to ensure that you have enough to fill 15 minutes' worth of writing for each part (about 300 words).

4 (a) Outline and evaluate **one** environmental (e.g. learning) explanation of language development.
(12 marks)

(b) Outline and evaluate **one** nativist (e.g. Chomsky) explanation of language development. (12 marks)

> This question offers a different mark split, with 6 marks of AO1 and 6 marks of AO2 in each part. To answer this question effectively, you will need a précis version of each of your theories. You can prepare this before the exam, selecting the most pertinent points. This practice of preparing 15-minute and $7\frac{1}{2}$-minute AO1 versions of all theories (and the same for AO2) should also improve your understanding of the theories. This will be particularly useful here as many students find it hard to present coherent versions of Skinner and Chomsky's theories.

Topic 3 >> Problem-solving and decision-making

RESEARCH INTO PROBLEM-SOLVING STRATEGIES AND MEANS OF REPRESENTATION

Problem-solving is an everyday activity which is often taken for granted and yet it is a highly complex skill. It is used whenever we need to reach a goal that is not readily available. There is, for example, no problem to be solved in the equation $x = 5 + 2$, because this can be found in a single step (i.e. the goal is readily available). Real problem-solving involves greater complexity. Given the wide diversity of tasks that come under the heading of problem-solving – anything from solving the Northern Ireland situation to working out

the best route to an unfamiliar destination – it is not surprising that there is no single adequate theory to explain how we solve all our problems.

Means of representation

In order to be able to solve problems successfully, we need to understand the nature of the problem and how to represent or describe it. In other words, we need to know what information should be retrieved from long-term memory so that we can draw inferences and choose the appropriate operations to reach a solution. If we build up the wrong internal representation, we may reach an impasse and be unable to solve the problem. Try the following activity.

People find this problem hard because they build up a picture, or representation, of a scene taking place at night. If you realize that the man has been drinking during the day, the problem is easily solved. As you can see, the way you represent the problem has an enormous influence on your ability to solve it. You will read that the Gestalt psychologists saw 'restructuring' as an important way of representing the problem, whereas information-processing theorists believe that the sequential, heuristic, search techniques involved in means–ends analysis are the best way of representing the problem.

Matlin (1998) has suggested a number of different methods for representing problems, including symbols, lists, matrices, graphs and visual images. The key to successful problem-solving is choosing the means of representation which is most appropriate. The activity below contains two problems. Try to solve them before you look at the answers given at the end of the unit.

A number of theories have been put forward which suggest various strategies for problem-solving. One early theoretical account of problem-solving was offered by a group of German psychologists collectively known as the 'Gestalt School'.

The Gestalt approach to problem-solving

According to Gestalt psychologists, problem-solving requires 'structural understanding', i.e. the ability to understand how all the parts of the problem fit together to meet the goal. A key requirement is the reorganization of the different elements of the problem in such a way that the problem can be solved. Gestaltists believed that people often get stuck when they try to solve problems because they cannot change their problem-solving set, i.e. they cannot immediately see how to reorganize the elements in a novel way. Try the next activity before you read on.

Once given the clue provided in the answer, most people solve the problem quite quickly because they break free of their usual way of thinking about it. This new way of thinking is called 'insight' by the Gestaltists and is sometimes referred to as the 'aha! phenomenon' because the pieces of the problem suddenly fall into place after a period of intense thinking.

Research on Gestalt approach to problem-solving

Wolfgang Kohler (one of the founders of the Gestalt school of psychology) investigated insight in problem-solving in apes (see Key research below). The Gestaltists called this kind of thinking, which depends on creating a novel solution, 'productive thinking'. They contrasted this with 'reproductive' or 'trial and error' thinking, in which people simply reproduce old habits or behaviours.

Wertheimer (1945) reported on a study in which students were taught to solve a problem (finding the area of a parallelogram) using one or other of two teaching methods. One teaching method required the students to understand the structural relations in the figure, i.e. that the parallelogram could be rearranged as a rectangle by moving the triangular shape from one end of the figure to the other (see Fig. 17.2(a)). The students already knew how to find the area of a rectangle so they could easily find the area of the parallelogram once they had reorganized it. A second group of students were simply taught the formula required to solve the problem (see Fig. 17.2(b)). They, too, were able to apply this new knowledge and could calculate the area by using the formula. There was no difference in performance between the groups when given a series of similar problems. However, when asked to calculate the areas of unusual parallelograms or novel shapes ('transfer tasks'), the first group was successful whereas the second group typically said things like, 'We haven't covered that yet'.

This kind of finding suggests that people are more likely to be able to solve novel problems if they are able to reorganize them according to Gestalt principles. Gestalt studies are often criticized because of their lack of clear definitions and absence of statistical analysis. However, some support for Wertheimer's findings was provided by Hilgard *et al.* (1953), who undertook a more controlled study and found that the 'understanding' group performed significantly better on a series of transfer tasks than the 'rote-learning' group.

Dunker (1935), along with other Gestalt psychologists, believed that people often fail to think productively because they are locked into reproductive thinking habits. He referred to this inhibition as 'functional fixedness'. In a well-known study, he asked people to fix a candle to a wall so that it would not drip when lit.

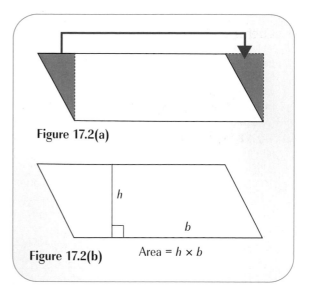

Figure 17.2(a)

Figure 17.2(b)   Area = $h \times b$

Each participant was given various objects including a candle and a box of drawing pins. The only successful solution was to empty the box, fix it to the wall with drawing pins, and stand the candle in it. However, Duncker found that few participants hit on this solution because they were 'fixated' on the usual function of the box (i.e. to hold pins) and, therefore, were unable to see it as a potential holder for the candle. Duncker found that participants were more likely to solve the problem when the box was presented separately and *not* as a container for pins.

More recently, researchers have cast doubt on the effectiveness of such hints. Weisberg *et al.* (1978) repeated Duncker's candle experiment, but preceded it with a word-pair memory test that included the pair 'candle–box'. Participants presented with the candle task were no more likely to solve it than people who had not previously undertaken the memory test, *unless* they were explicitly told beforehand that one of the word-pairs was relevant to the problem.

A related idea to functional fixedness is that of 'mental set', in which people get locked into a specific way of tackling problems that has been useful in the past, even when a solution could be reached in a simpler way. One well-known experiment on mental set was conducted by Luchins (1942) – see the panel on p. 540.

see the panel on p. 540.

KEY RESEARCH >> ANIMALS & PROBLEM-SOLVING

Insight in problem-solving (Kohler 1925)

Kohler spent some time during the First World War in Tenerife at an animal research station and published his findings on animals' problem-solving in 1925. A typical problem was to provide a caged chimpanzee with a stick, a number of crates and a banana hanging well out of reach from the ceiling. Typically, Kohler reported that the apes spent a long period of time in intense thinking, followed by a flash of insight that led them to pile the crates on top of one another in a series of steps and then climb up and hook down the banana with the stick.

Luchins' Water Jar Problem

Participants were asked to imagine that they had three jars A, B and C and an unlimited supply of water. For each problem, Luchins supplied a list of the capacities of all three jars and also specified a particular amount of water to be measured out. The task for the subjects was to use all or some of the jars to measure out the required (goal) amount of water. Try this yourself before reading any further.

The best way to solve Problem 1 is to fill Jar B and then remove from it one jarful using jar A and then two jarfuls using jar C. The first five problems are all solved best in this way and most people continue to apply this method for the whole exercise. However,

Problem	A	B	C	Goal
1	22	150	4	120
2	18	125	16	75
3	17	97	9	62
4	39	129	22	46
5	15	66	11	29
6	41	89	7	34

in this instance past experience works to the solver's disadvantage because, for Problem 6, there is a more direct method. It is easily solved by subtracting one jarful of C from A. Did you recognize this easier solution?

Evaluation
the Gestalt approach

- **Influence on later research** – Gestalt ideas have demonstrated that reproductive thinking is not sufficient for certain kinds of problem-solving and that past experiences can be detrimental when searching for novel solutions.
- **Improving problem-solving skills** – Their ideas stimulated research into ways of improving problem-solving skills and have practical applications.

- **Vague terminology** – The theory has been criticized, however, because some of the concepts, such as insight, are too vague to be testable.
- **Lack of experimental rigour** – Early research was often poorly controlled and did not provide a precise explanation of the processes that underlie productive thinking. Attempts to provide such explanations arose from research conducted within the information-processing framework, discussed in the next part of this topic.

The information-processing approach to problem-solving

The information-processing approach provides a common framework within which to study problem-solving. This approach arises from the work of Newell *et al.* (1958), which divides problems into a set of stages progressing from the original to the goal state. The stages involve:

- representing the problem
- selecting and implementing operators to tackle the problem
- evaluating progress to assess whether or not the goal state has been achieved.

These stages are flexible and allow the solver to go back to previous states or to set a series of sub-goals by which the final goal can be achieved. This approach has the advantage that it provides a broad framework that can then be elaborated to provide more detailed analysis of the specific processes involved in solving particular problems.

Computer modelling of problem-solving has developed from the information-processing approach and this has

proved useful in several ways – for example, by providing information about the nature of strategies, the importance of a knowledge base and the crucial nature of the representation stage in problem-solving. In 1972, Newell and Simon developed a computer program called the General Problem Solver (or GPS), in which they attempted to mimic the processes used by humans in tackling problems, including the means–ends analysis approach. The GPS was used extensively to study a number of different problems, but it was eventually discarded by Newell and Simon because it was not as applicable to human problem-solving as they had first assumed, particularly as far as tackling ill-defined problems was concerned.

Problem-solving strategies

Newell and Simon (1972) suggested that problem-solving consisted of searching through the 'problem space' which is made up of a number of linked 'states' leading to the 'goal state'. The solver crosses the problem space by using a range of 'permissible operators' that transform one state to another. One way of searching through the problem space which guarantees a solution is to use the algorithmic method.

I'm not sure replacing all our advisors with computers was such a good idea

What are the limitations of computer problem-solving programs?

ACTIVITY

Solving anagarams heuristically

Try solving the following anagram and think about the way you tackled it:

g w n i l k a

An algorithmic method would guarantee a solution but it is highly unlikely that you applied that method. The anagram has seven letters which means that there are 5040 possible permutations (i.e. $7 \times 6 \times 5 \times 4 \times 3 \times 2 \times 1$). It is more likely that you used a heuristic method. For example, you might have picked out 'ing' because you recognized this as a familiar combination found at the end of English words. You are then left with a much smaller problem space 'w l k a' and the solution 'walking' now becomes quite easy to find.

This involves a systematic random search in which all possible solutions are tried until the correct one is found. However, this approach can be time-consuming and inefficient, and it is more usual for human problem-solvers to adopt a 'heuristic' approach. This is a rule of thumb involving a selective search that looks only at those parts of the problem space that are most likely to produce a solution (see the activity above right).

Psychological research has focused more on heuristics than on algorithms, largely because we use heuristics far more frequently. There are several different kinds of heuristic strategies available to us. We will consider two: means–ends analysis and analogy strategy.

means–ends analysis

This heuristic is the main problem-solving strategy used in computer simulations of human thinking. It involves breaking a problem into a number of sub-problems which are solved in turn and which greatly reduce the difference between the original state and the goal state. In means–ends analysis, the solver always works on one goal at a time. If that goal is not directly achievable in one move, the solver must set a sub-goal that will remove the obstacles. At each stage the solver needs to ask the following questions:

- What is my goal?
- What obstacles are in my way?
- What operators are available to me for overcoming these obstacles?

Newell and Simon (1972) gave the following example of using means–ends analysis in everyday life.

> 'I want to take my son to nursery school. What's the difference between what I have and what I want? One of distance. What changes distance? An automobile. My automobile won't work. What is needed to make it work? A new battery. What has new batteries? An auto repair shop. I want the repair shop to put in a new battery: but the shop doesn't know I need one. What is the difficulty? One of communication. What allows communication? A telephone ... And so on.'

(A02) **Commentary**
means–ends analysis

- ***Use of sub-goals*** – Although this heuristic technique is widely used in computer simulations, the question arises whether humans establish such sub-goals in their problem-solving. There is certainly evidence that people pause at intervals during the problem and work out their strategy for the next few moves.

- ***Difference-reduction strategy*** – In dealing with certain problems, it is sometimes appropriate actually to increase the difference between the original state and the goal state by temporarily moving backwards. By focusing on the goal state alone, it is easy to ignore the crucial step needed to solve the problem. So, it is sometimes necessary temporarily to violate the difference-reduction strategy of the means–ends approach in order to reach a solution.

continued on next page

Unit 17 // Language and thought

Thomas (1974) found that solvers were often able to make a rapid jump to the goal state once they had realized this, which suggests that human problem-solvers do not always set as many sub-goals as a strict application of means–ends analysis would require.

- *Application* – means–ends analysis approach may well be a useful problem-solving strategy, particularly given the constraints of our working memory capacity (see Unit 1, Memory).
- *Solving ill-defined or multiple problems* – In real life, the problems we have to solve are often ill-defined and we are often faced with several problems that have to be solved simultaneously. The means–ends approach is less able to explain how we tackle this kind of situation.

Analogy strategy

Factors such as knowledge and experience affect both the way we represent problems and the way in which we solve them. In everyday life, problems are often poorly defined and novel, and we need to rely on existing knowledge and experience to find a solution. One heuristic that can be used in these circumstances is analogy. In other words, we use a solution to an earlier problem to help us solve a new one. Novick and Holyoak (1991) have suggested four processes that are required for successful problem-solving using analogies:

- Locating the appropriate analogical problem (source problem).
- Making the appropriate correspondence between parts of the source problem and parts of the target problem.
- Adapting the procedures that were helpful in the source problem.
- Developing an abstract schema for the whole class of problems that the source and target problems represent.

Commentary
the analogy strategy

- *Support from research into expert knowledge* – If these processes are prerequisites for the successful use of the analogy technique, it is, perhaps, not surprising that Novick (1988) found experts using analogies more frequently than novices. The superiority that Novick found for experts over novices has been demonstrated in several studies. Experts differ from novices in many ways – for example, their memory for task-related information, their knowledge base, their method of problem representation, their self-monitoring abilities, and their speed and efficiency.
- *Limitations in everyday use* – This would seem to be a useful approach, but research shows that problem-solvers frequently fail to notice a potential analogy and that, even when they do, they often make errors in their interpretation.

Evaluation
information-processing approach

- *Influence on problem-solving research* – This approach has been enormously influential in the field of problem-solving research. Newell amd Simon proposed a number of key concepts (e.g. heuristics) that have generated a huge body of research.
- *Failure to explain insight* – It is difficult, however, for this approach to explain how we solve some of the insight problems studied by the Gestalt psychologists.

RESEARCH IN DECISION-MAKING: PRACTICAL ISSUES

Other types of thinking such as judgement, reasoning and decision-making have interested psychologists. Decision-making is a particular kind of reasoning that involves making choices and sometimes taking risks.

Decision-making can be relatively simple, such as deciding whether to walk or catch the bus to school, or highly complex, as when a government has to decide between intervening in a war or remaining neutral.

Risk-taking behaviour in decision-making

Utility theory

Making any kind of decision usually involves weighing up the costs against the benefits. In most decisions, there is a degree of uncertainty or risk that the decision may be wrong. The decision-maker has to decide whether it is a risk worth taking.

Neumann and Morgenstern (1947) suggested that we work out the expected utility of each option using a simple equation:

$$\text{Expected utility} = \text{Probability of a particular outcome} \times \text{Utility of the outcome}$$

Imagine that you are trying to decide whether to buy a £5 lottery ticket which offers you a 1 in 100 chance of winning £250. The equation would work like this:

$$\underset{\text{(probability)}}{0.01} \times \underset{\substack{\text{(utility of} \\ \text{the outcome)}}}{£250} = \underset{\substack{\text{(expected} \\ \text{utility)}}}{£2.50}$$

In this case, you probably would not take the risk because the ticket is being sold for double its worth. However, this so-called 'utility theory', in which we seek to gain as much as we can of those things we value (i.e. to maximize utility), does not explain how we make more complex decisions where multiple factors have to be taken into account. In any case, research has shown that we do not always operate on the principle of maximizing utility when making decisions.

The framing effect

Carry out the following activity, which is based on an example used by Tversky and Kahneman (1987).

ACTIVITY

Making choices about risk

For each of the two choices below, select the option you prefer, (a) or (b).

- **Choice 1:** Assume that you are richer by £300 than you are today. You now have to choose between:
  (a) a sure gain of £100
  (b) 50 per cent chance of gaining £200 and 50 per cent chance of gaining nothing.

- **Choice 2:** Assume that you are richer by £500 than you are today. You have to choose between:
  (a) a sure loss of £100
  (b) 50 per cent chance of losing nothing and 50 per cent chance of losing £200.

If you think about this logically, both Choice 1 and Choice 2 are identical (i.e. the utilities are the same in both). In both cases, option (a) leaves you with £400 and option (b) gives you an even chance of either £300 or £500. There is no right or wrong answer – the option you choose simply reflects your willingness to take a risk. You would expect, then, that people opting for the first option in Choice 1 would also opt for the first one in Choice 2. However, Tversky and Kahneman found that most participants went for the first option in Choice 1, but the second option in Choice 2. In other words, they contradicted themselves by preferring the sure thing in Choice 1 and the risk in Choice 2.

Tversky and Kahneman explain this in terms of the 'framing' of the question (the way it is presented). In this case, people are influenced by the use of the negative word 'loss' in Choice 2 against the positive word 'gain' in Choice 1. When offered a sure gain, they seem to be averse to taking risks and prefer to hold on to what they have. When faced with a loss, they seem more ready to take a risk, presumably with the intention of trying to avoid or at least reduce the loss. The interesting point about these findings is not that people differ in their willingness to take risks – this is only to be expected given differing temperaments and circumstances – but that the *same* people differ in their risk-taking strategy depending on the language in which the risk is expressed.

You may think that the study described above is artificial and so cannot be a reliable indicator of how people make decisions in real life. However, the framing effect has been demonstrated in more realistic settings. For example, Johnson (1987) found that people are more likely to choose minced beef that is labelled 80 per cent lean rather than 20 per cent fat, and several studies (e.g. McNeil *et al.* 1982 and McNeil *et al.* 1988) have shown that the framing effect can also affect choice of medical treatment.

Errors in thinking about probability

It is wrong to assume that people are incapable of making reasoned decisions. Usually, the decision-making strategies available to us are perfectly adequate for handling a wide range of choices. However, people clearly do make errors of judgement and these tend to occur when they use a normally useful strategy in an inappropriate situation. (Note the parallels here with mental set and functional fixedness in problem-solving – see p. 539.) One type of strategy open to us is to use decision-making heuristics. When we make inappropriate decisions, it may be that we have tried to use these heuristics in situations that are beyond their range. We will look at three types of heuristic:

- the representativeness heuristic (similarity)
- the availability heuristic
- the anchoring and adjustment heuristic.

The representativeness heuristic (similarity)

This heuristic is based on the assumption that every instance of a particular category will resemble the prototype for that category (Pitz and Sachs 1984), i.e. it is based on similarity. For example, if people are given a description of someone and asked to decide whether that person is a librarian or an astronaut, they will base their decision on whether the description is typical of what they think librarians and astronauts are like. While this reliance on similarity and assumption of homogeneous categories can be helpful, it can also lead to error if the decision-maker ignores other factors such as sample size. One well-known error of this type is known as the gambler's fallacy – that a run of losses *must* be followed by a run of wins.

- *The gambler's fallacy* – Consider the following example. When a coin is tossed six times, which is the more likely sequence?

  - H T H T T H
  - H H H H H H

  Most people pick the first because they know that coin tossing usually produces heads and tails in random order and they think that the first sequence looks more random than the second. In fact, this is a fallacy; both sequences are equally probable. The coin itself has no memory and has no way of knowing that it is time for tails to come up. The likelihood of a tail on the next toss is 50:50, just as it is on every toss. The reason why most people choose the first sequence is based on inappropriate use of the representativeness heuristic. We know that, over a long series of coin tosses, a coin will produce equal numbers of heads and tails. We, therefore, assume that even a small number of tosses will show the same characteristics. In the example above, we believe that the first sequence is a more prototypical example of coin tosses than the second. Hill and Williamson (1998) have found that such biases are evident in the way people choose numbers for the Lotto. The tendency to choose numbers that have rarely come up before is an example of the gambler's fallacy.

- *The small sample fallacy* – Kahneman and Tversky (1972) have carried out a number of experimental studies to demonstrate the inappropriate use of the representativeness heuristic. One such is outlined in the activity below. Try it now before reading on.

Most people respond 'about the same', but this answer is statistically incorrect. We are given the information that 50 per cent of babies in the total population are boys. The larger the sample we have available, the more likely it is to be similar to the total population. On the other hand, a small sample is much less likely to be representative of the total population so the answer to this question should be (b). In this problem, people do not seem to take sample size into account. Most people do not intuitively understand this fundamental statistical concept, so misconceptions are not limited to naive participants. Tversky and Kahneman (1971) found that a group of experienced research psychologists could also be fooled by what the researchers called 'the law of small numbers', that is, the mistaken belief that the characteristics of small samples are likely to be the same as the characteristics of the wider population. This 'small-sample fallacy' can have important consequences. For example, it can lead to the selection of samples of inadequate size in research studies and thus lead to unwarranted, generalized conclusions. Hamilton and Sherman (1994) have shown that it can also lead to stereotyping where individuals form a detrimental view of a whole group of people, based on their impressions of just a small number of group members. However, it has been shown that people with experience of working out probabilities in particular areas (Kunda and Nisbett 1986) and people who have received training in small-sample theory (Fong *et al.* 1986) do not succumb to the small-number fallacy.

- *The base-rate fallacy* – Errors in thinking about probability may occur when people ignore information about the prior odds of a situation occurring, that is they tend to ignore how often the event actually happens in the population (see Key research on the next page).

The availability heuristic

It is not surprising that people make mistakes when estimating probability, because it is quite a difficult task. Sometimes people rely on the 'availability heuristic' to help them make decisions – they judge the frequency of an event by thinking of readily available examples of that event. If examples spring easily to mind, it is assumed that the event is more frequent

ACTIVITY

Assessing probability

A town has two hospitals. About 45 babies are born every day in the larger hospital whereas about 15 babies are born each day in the smaller hospital. Approximately 50 per cent of all babies born are boys. However, the exact percentage of babies who are boys

will vary from day to day. For a period of one year, both hospitals recorded the number of days on which more than 60 per cent of the babies born were boys. Which hospital do you think recorded more such days?

(a) the larger hospital

(b) the smaller hospital

(c) about the same.

Kahneman and Tversky (1973)

Kahneman and Tversky (1973) gave participants brief descriptions of five people and told them that the descriptions had been drawn randomly from a batch of 100. They gave half the participants the base rate information that the total group consisted of 70 lawyers and 30 engineers. The other half were told that the proportions were the other way round. Participants had to decide on the probability that the particular description they had been given was of a lawyer or an engineer. Some of the descriptions tallied with a picture of an individual which was similar to a general stereotype of an engineer, but quite dissimilar from a stereotype of a lawyer, e.g.:

<<Jack is a 45-year-old man. He is married and has four children. He is generally conservative, careful and ambitious. He shows no interest in political and social issues and spends most of his free time on his many hobbies, which include home carpentry, sailing and mathematical puzzles.>>

Participants from both base-rate groups responded to this description by suggesting that there was an approximately 90 per cent probability that this description was of an engineer. In other words, they ignored the base-rate information (70:30 or vice versa) and made their decision purely on the basis of representativeness. When they were presented with a completely neutral description, they estimated the probability of the person being an engineer to be 50 per cent whereas they should have estimated it in line with their given base-rates, i.e. either 70 or 30 per cent.

than if examples are hard to recall from memory. So, the availability of items determines our judgement of probability. The availability heuristic is often quite accurate, but it can lead to errors when jective availability does not match true, objective frequency.

Tversky and Kahneman (1973) asked people to assess whether there were more English words beginning with the letter k than having k as their third letter. Using the availability heuristic, most people say that words with an initial k are more common. It is much easier to think of words beginning with k (e.g. 'king', 'kettle') than words where k is the third letter (e.g. 'rake', 'like'). In fact, there are three times as many English words with k as the third letter than as the initial letter.

Studies like this can be criticized for artificiality. However, there are a number of other studies that suggest that people make errors based on the availability heuristic in real-life decisions. Weber *et al.* (1993), for example, have found that doctors are more likely to make a particular diagnosis if they have recently diagnosed a similar case. MacLeod and Campbell (1992) found that people who were encouraged to think about pleasant events from their past were more likely to expect good things to happen in the future than people who had been encouraged to recall unpleasant events. This could have implications for psychotherapy. There are also instances where people's judgements about the likelihood of events are influenced by the pattern of coverage in the media. Slovic *et al.* (1982) demonstrated that people significantly overestimated the frequency of death caused by such things as murder, road traffic accidents and fire, and significantly underestimated the number of deaths caused by stroke, asthma, tuberculosis and smallpox vaccination. These are all examples of availability bias and it seems that people rarely compensate for this even though they realize that there is a degree of media bias in reporting.

The anchoring and adjusting heuristic

The difficulty in setting aside faulty reasoning is evident in another kind of heuristic identified by Tversky and Kahneman (1973). The so-called 'anchoring and adjustment heuristic' refers to the tendency to make judgements by taking an initial value (anchor) and adjusting it (see the panel below).

The anchoring and adjustment heuristic

Tversky and Kahneman (1973) asked people to estimate the percentage of African nations in the United Nations (UN). Different groups were given arbitrary numbers such as 10 per cent or 65 per cent as a starting point and asked to say whether these figures were under– or overestimates. The mean estimates for groups given the above figures were 25 per cent and 45 per cent respectively. So, a number, which had no meaningful relationship to the original question, was used by participants as an anchor from which they then adjusted on the basis of their knowledge of information about UN nations. However, in almost all cases, participants were too conservative in their adjustments.

Unit 17 // Language and thought

Commentary
anchoring and adjusting heuristic

● **Influence of professional expertise** – There are potentially serious consequences of relying on the anchoring and adjustment heuristic in real life. Holtgrave *et al.* (1994) considered the task of risk assessors calculating the possibility of a disaster on a North Sea oil rig. Their risk estimate would be very skewed if they based their calculation on data from the Gulf of Mexico without adjusting for climatic and construction differences. However, Smith and Kida (1991) have shown that experts (in this case, accountants) are not significantly influenced by the anchoring and adjustment heuristic, and seem able to adjust their original estimates to accommodate new information.

● **Professionals influenced by anchors** – Northcraft and Neale (1987) asked estate agents to value a property based on a 10-page document giving details and pictures of the house, and also based on a tour. Some were given a guide price of approximately $66,000 and others were given a

price of about $84,000. Those given the lower anchor set their minimum acceptable price at $65,000, while those given the higher anchor set their minimum at $73,000. In this case, then, professional people were being influenced by the anchoring heuristic. Perhaps this reflects the fact that the housing market is rather volatile and that there are few objective criteria for pricing.

● **Limits on the influence of the anchoring heuristic** – Even when there is uncertainty, there appear to be limits on the influence of the anchoring heuristic. Chapman and Johnson (1994) have demonstrated that people are not influenced if the anchor is wildly implausible.

● **Reluctance of non-experts to adjust** – Although experts tend to be able to make appropriate adjustments in the light of new information, lay people are more likely to ignore new information. Shiloh (1994) has investigated the area of genetic counselling. People who seek advice about the risks of passing on familial disorders are more likely to base their final risk assessment on their own original estimates, without taking into account the information from the genetic counsellor.

Evaluation
heuristics and biases approach

● **Influential theory** – This approach, introduced by Kahneman and Tversky, has dominated the decision-making field for the last 30 years and has generated much research. It can explain many other research findings and is able to predict the outcome on a number of different tasks.

● **Practical applications** – The theory has been successfully applied in various real-life situations, e.g. to decision-making in business.

● **Pessimism** – The theory has been criticized for being overly pessimistic about our ability to make sensible decisions since it tends to emphasize our irrationality. Gigerenzer (1991) has shown that people are much better at making decisions when they are given better information about factors such as base rate.

CHECK YOUR UNDERSTANDING

Check your understanding of problem-solving and decision-making by answering these questions from memory, before checking your answers by looking over Topic 3.

1 Differentiate between the terms 'productive thinking' and 'reproductive thinking'.

2 Explain what Gestalt psychologists mean by 'insight'.

3 Briefly describe one study showing functional fixedness and one study showing mental set.

4 Give one strength and one weakness of the Gestalt explanation of problem-solving.

5 Identify the three stages of problem-solving described by Newell and Simon.

6 Differentiate between the algorithmic and the heuristic methods of problem-solving.

7 Give one strength and one weakness of the means–ends analysis approach to problem-solving.

8 Briefly explain what Kahneman and Tversky meant by the 'framing effect'.

9 Give brief descriptions of what is meant by: the availability heuristic, the representativeness heuristic and the anchoring heuristic.

10 'People are generally poor at decision-making'. Construct a 300-word précis that addresses this statement (150 words of AO1 and 150 words of effective AO2).

REVISION SUMMARY

Having covered this topic you should be able to:

✓ describe and evaluate research into problem-solving, including problem-solving strategies and means of representation

✓ describe and evaluate practical issues in research in decision-making, including risk-taking and errors in thinking about probability.

EXAMPLE EXAM QUESTIONS

Below are some **possible examination questions** set on this topic, along with hints to help you understand and approach each question effectively:

1 Describe and evaluate research (theories **and/or** studies) into problem-solving.   (24 marks)

> The specification provides examples of problem-solving, but these have not been included in this question, so it is up to you how you wish to answer it. In fact, when a similar question was set in one exam, some candidates wrote about problem-solving in dreams or problem-solving by non-human animals. Such responses are perfectly creditworthy but they generally fail to produce high marks because such answers do not focus on the particular demands of this question.

2 Discuss research into problem-solving strategies **and/or** means of representation (e.g. Gestalt approaches, means–ends analysis).   (24 marks)

> One way to tackle this question would be to structure your answer following the 'four-paragraph rule'. Write one descriptive paragraph about research (theory or studies) on problem-solving strategies and then one paragraph evaluating this research. Do the same for means of representation. If each paragraph is 150 words in length, your answer would be right for a 30-minute question.

3 Critically consider research (theories **and/or** studies) into decision-making.   (24 marks)

> There is no mention of 'studies' in the specification and so questions in this area tend to be of a general nature. Candidates fail to gain marks for a variety of reasons, such as material that is intended to be commentary (AO2) is not used effectively, but is only given at a descriptive level, or answers are not coherently structured and shaped to the question set – instead they are a mish-mash of everything learned under the heading of this topic. Candidates also throw away marks by wasting time writing introductions and conclusions which often repeat material credited elsewhere in the answer.

4 (a) Outline and evaluate research (theories **and/or** studies) into risk-taking behaviour.   (12 marks)
   (b) Outline and evaluate research (theories **and/or** studies) into errors in thinking about probability.   (12 marks)

> There are 6 AO1 marks and 6 AO2 marks in each part of this question. The term 'outline' indicates that the AO1 material need not be too detailed, given the time constraints. However, you must include some detail and so won't have time to write about more than two or three theories/studies at most. If you are not selective about this, you will limit the time available for the AO2 content.

5 Discuss practical issues relating to research (theories **and/or** studies) in decision-making.   (24 marks)

> Given the wording of the specification, this too would be a legitimate question. Don't be too put off by the phrase 'practical issues', as the material on pp. 542–4 of this unit would be perfectly acceptable insofar as they do address practical issues. A good answer to this question would emphasize the practical nature of such research.

Topic 1: Language and culture

- Interest in the **relationship between language and culture** stimulated research into the notion that language determines thought: the **linguistic relativity hypothesis** or the **Sapir–Whorf hypothesis**. There has been some support for the weak version of this, but even where differences in thinking can be demonstrated in different language communities, it is impossible to infer that language is the sole factor that distinguishes one group from another.

- Researchers such as **Bernstein** and **Labov** have been interested in the **social** and **cultural aspects** of language use. Bernstein investigated social class differences and described two distinct speech codes – restricted and elaborated. However, there is little evidence to support this distinction and more recent research suggests that all children of school age have been exposed to a similar range of language.

- Labov investigated Black English and found that, far from being an impoverished dialect, it has its own distinctive grammar and is capable of conveying a rich variety of meaning.

Topic 2: Language acquisition

- **Language acquisition** is a remarkable human achievement. Children appear to progress rapidly and in similar ways through a series of distinct stages in acquiring language: discriminating speech sounds, producing speech-like sounds, developing a vocabulary and acquiring syntactical competence.

- Psychologists have developed a good understanding of the way in which humans acquire language. There is less agreement about the precise mechanism whereby language develops. **Environmental theories** suggest that language is learned through the joint processes of reinforcement and imitation.

- **Nativist theories** appear to account for data which are inconsistent with the learning approach. Given that language development appears to follow a very similar pattern across cultures, **Chomsky** believed that language ability is somehow 'wired in', i.e. depends on innate mechanisms. The evidence for this approach is fairly strong but it fails to take into account various social and cognitive factors.

- There is not yet a complete theory of language acquisition which adequately accounts for all the data. It seems likely that learning, innate mechanisms, cognitive and social factors all contribute.

Topic 3: Problem-solving and decision-making

- **Problem-solving** is an everyday activity which appears simple, but actually involves quite complex skills. In order to be able to solve problems successfully, we need to understand the nature of the problem and be able to **represent** it appropriately.

- **Gestalt psychologists** believed that the various elements of a problem needed to be reorganized so that a solution would become clear. Their ideas have stimulated research, but concepts such as 'insight' have been seen as too vague and the lack of empirical support is seen as a weakness.

- The information-processing approach, a more testable account of problem-solving, argues that we adopt various heuristics, including **means–ends analysis**, to break problems down into stages which we solve systematically. Computer programs have been designed which effectively solve problems using these strategies – this does not mean that they accurately reflect the strategies used by humans.

- **Decision-making** usually involves weighing costs against benefits. This often involves an element of uncertainty or **risk**, and the decision-maker has to decide whether the risk is worth taking. The precise odds can be calculated using a mathematical formula, but this does not work for every type of decision and is not the most likely strategy for day-to-day decision-making. People are not entirely logical when they take risks, but are affected by such factors as the framing effect.

- In decision-making, as with problem-solving, it seems likely that we make use of heuristics. While such strategies usually help us to make decisions and judgements in our everyday life, they can let us down. It seems that people are particularly prone to making errors in **thinking about probability**. They tend to ignore important aspects of the situation (e.g. the prior odds of a situation occurring) and focus inappropriately on less important aspects, such as representativeness.

- Common **errors** in thinking about probability include the gambler's fallacy, the small sample fallacy, base-rate fallacy and inappropriate use of availability, similarity, anchoring and availabilty heuristics.

Garnham, A. and Oakhill, J. (1994) *Thinking and Reasoning*, **Oxford UK and Cambridge USA: Blackwell.**

Includes a wide range of research into all aspects of thinking and reasoning. It is aimed primarily at undergraduates, but the clear, lucid style will make it accessible to A-level students who would like to cover the topic in greater depth.

Harley, T.A. (2001) *The Psychology of Language: From Data to Theory* **(2nd edn), Hove: Psychology Press.**

A comprehensive and up-to-date account of the psychology of language. It is an undergraduate text, but it is accessible for A-level students who would like more detailed coverage.

Lund, N. (2003) *Language and Thought*, **Hove: Routledge.**

A clearly written text that covers all the topics in this unit – readily accessible for A-level students.

Mayer, R.E. (1992) *Thinking, Problem-solving, Cognition* **(2nd edn), New York: W.H. Freeman & Co.**

A clearly written text covering many aspects of thinking and reasoning. It goes well beyond the A-level syllabus but has good, relevant chapters with some clear examples and illustrations.

Website

www.lhs.berkeley.edu/Java/Tower/Tower.html

This shows an interactive version of the Tower of Hanoi problem often used to test the means–end analysis approach to problem solving

ANSWERS TO ACTIVITIES

Methods of representing problems, p. 538

There is no right way to solve these problems, but the following solutions are quick methods that guarantee a correct solution.

1 The best method here is to represent the problem using symbols. Let the symbol s represent Sarah and the symbol h represent Helen. The problem can then be translated into the following formula:

First sentence is translated to: $s = 2h - 10$

Second sentence is translated to: $s + 5 = h + 5 + 8$

Now you can substitute for s in the second equation: $2h - 10 + 5 = h + 5 + 8$

Therefore, you find that $h = 18$.

If you substitute this for h in the first equation, you find that $s = 26$.

You now have to translate the symbols back into words, i.e. Sarah is 26 and Helen is 18.

2 There is more than one way of solving this problem, but Schwartz (1971) found that people were most successful if they used a matrix method. This involves setting up a table like the one on the right and fitting in the information given.

Once you have put this information in, there are only two name spaces left in the matrix. One of these is someone with kidney problems, but we know that Susan has heart disease, so she can only be in Room 3. Kate must, therefore go into the remaining name space which means that she has kidney problems and is in Room 4.

Room	Disease	Name
1	Asthma	Emma
2	Appendicitis	Rachel
3		
4	Kidney problems	
5		Mary

The matchstick problem, p. 538

Most people take four sticks and form a square from them. They then make an X from the remaining two sticks and try to place them inside the square – see Fig. 17.3(a). However, this is not an acceptable solution because the diagonal sticks are not long enough to complete the triangles, which would in any case not be equilateral. It is necessary to reorganize the elements of the problem and think in three dimensions – see Fig. 17.3(b).

Figure 17.3(a)

Figure 17.3(b)

18
UNIT

COGNITIVE
Development

PREVIEW

After you have read this unit, you should be able to describe and evaluate:

>> how thinking develops in children using the theories of cognitive development by Piaget and Vygotsky

>> the practical application of these theories to education

>> the development of measured intelligence test performance, focusing on the role of genetics and cultural differences (such as race)

>> the development of moral understanding using, for example, the theories of Piaget and Kohlberg

>> the development of pro-social reasoning using, for example, Eisenberg's theory of pro-social development

>> the influence of gender and culture on moral/pro-social development.

INTRODUCTION

'Cognitive' is the word psychologists use to refer to mental activities. So 'cognitive development' is the study of how our mental activities develop. This includes mathematical skills, intelligence and even the way you think about right and wrong (moral development).

Topic 1 starts by looking at the development of thinking. Some psychologists believe that thought changes as children get older – that young children use quite a different sort of logic than adults and are less capable of abstract thought. This change happens as part of growing up in the same way that your body changes as you get older – your biology drives these changes. However, other psychologists believe that people around you (parents, teachers, and friends) teach you things and this drives forward your own development.

The question about whether change is biological or social (the influence of other people) is part of the 'nature–nurture' debate – a key debate in psychology. 'Nature' is the outcome of a person's biological or genetic make-up and 'nurture' refers to the environment, including physical and social experiences. In terms of the development of thinking, the nature–nurture debate asks to what extent our abilities to think (remember, solve problems, perceive and so on) are influenced more by nature or by nurture.

In terms of intelligence (the focus of Topic 2), the nature–nurture debate asks to what extent your intelligence is innate and unchangeable, or is due to your experiences and environment, such as what you eat and how many books you have at home!

Moral development, discussed in Topic 3, can also be thought of in terms of nature and nurture – your sense of right and wrong may be the same as a person living in China (i.e. universal and innate), or it may be different because your sense of right and wrong is based on your society's values (i.e. relative and learned). Thus one of the themes in this chapter, as in all developmental psychology, is about what factors have made you what you are.

Cara
Flanagan

1 Which of the two babies shown above would you prefer to cuddle? Which baby would make you smile back?

You probably chose the one who is smiling at you. Perhaps that baby was born with a sunny disposition? And this will mean that more people will smile at the baby and cuddle her. The more smiles and cuddles the baby gets, the happier she will be.

2 How do you think this might affect that baby's development? The baby started life with a sunny personality (nature) and this influences the environment she is in (nurture).

How could your experiences since infancy have affected your personality? Could they have affected your intelligence? Do you think that the way other people respond to you affects your behaviour?

3 What about twins? Do you know any identical twins? How much are their personalities alike, or how different? What things might have made them alike or different?

KEY CONCEPTS

Schema: a cluster of inter-related concepts that tell us about how things function in the world – a schema about television would include our knowledge about how they work and what sort of programmes they are likely to display.

Stage theory: a theory that describes development in terms of an invariant sequence of separate ability levels. At each stage, a child can do or think in a progressively more sophisticated (adult-like) way. This applies, for example, to cognitive or moral development. It is presumed that development from one stage to the next is related to biological maturation.

Nature and nurture: the question of what factors contribute to development. Nature refers to factors that are inherited and may be present at birth or may appear later in life as a consequence of maturation. Nurture refers to the influence of the environment, both physical and social. The result of environmental interactions is experience.

Genetics: we each inherit genes from our parents. Each gene is present in a pair, where one member of the pair has come from your mother and the other member has come from your father. Altogether each person has about 30,000 genes. The code carried on each gene affects many different behaviours and characteristics.

Heritability: refers to the proportion of the total variation in a given characteristic, in a given population, that can be attributed to genetic differences between members of that population. The importance of this concept, when considering the question of nature and nurture, is the extent to which differences in IQ are due to genetic factors.

People used to think that the difference between child and adult thinking was that children just knew less than adults, but psychologists have shown that it isn't just a matter of 'more', but of 'different'. The way that children think is different to the way that adults think, and the way younger children think is different from the way that older children think. But in what way is it different? Consider some examples:

● 'A sentence is a big word with holes in it.'

● 'A is greater than B, B is greater than C; therefore A is greater than C.'

● 'Mary didn't mean to hurt Anne; therefore she shouldn't be punished.'

These sentences illustrate the way younger and older children think. But if children think differently to adults, then how does child-like thought develop into more adult-like thought? Do adults just know more things and think faster?

PIAGET'S THEORY OF COGNITIVE DEVELOPMENT

Jean Piaget (1896–1980) is probably the best-known psychologist, after Sigmund Freud. He was born in Switzerland and initially trained as a zoologist – the first thing he published (at the age of 10) was on molluscs. His interest in cognitive development started when, in the early 1920s, he worked on some of the first intelligence tests. Piaget noticed that children of the same age tended to make similar kinds of errors on test questions. He thought that younger children might be following rather different logical rules from older children. Their errors were quite predictable and could, therefore, be described in terms of a *stage theory*. In other words, the errors made at certain ages formed a kind of stage of development, and these stages formed a sequence. Piaget suggested that children's thought changes *qualitatively* as they pass through the stages.

Thus there are two strands to Piaget's theory:

● An account of the *causes* of developmental changes (adaptation). We will begin by examining the causes.

● An account of *what changes* during development: the cognitive activities at each stage.

The causes of development and the stages of development are biologically driven, according to Piaget. They occur as a consequence of the maturation of innate forces and structures. Piaget acknowledged the role of experience in cognitive development, intertwining nurture with nature.

The structure of the intellect

Piaget (1926, 1954, 1960) noted that all babies are born with similar biological 'equipment' (Piaget used the term 'structures'). These biological structures were the senses, the brain and reflexes (such as sucking and grasping). At the start of life, an infant has a set of basic reflexes and also a set of innate schema. Piaget introduced the term 'schema' to mean a psychological structure that represented everything that the infant or child knew about an object or an action built up from basic reflexes. An example of an innate schema would be a mental representation of a human face – there is evidence that infants are born with an innate ability to

recognize faces (e.g. Fantz 1961). From birth onwards, the infant's schemas develop as a result of interactions with the environment. New experiences lead to new schemas being developed. For example, infants learn separate schemas for the faces of people they know.

What is the exact process by which schemas become more complex? Piaget proposed two ways in which this might happen:

● *assimilation* – the process of fitting new information and experiences into existing schemas

● *accommodation* – the process of changing the existing schemas when new information cannot be assimilated.

For example, a child may have the schema 'four legs, fur and wet nose (dog)'. Every new instance of a creature with the same characteristics is assimilated into this schema. However, one day someone uses the word 'cat' and this challenges the current schema. This new information cannot be assimilated into the existing schema; instead the child's schemas must alter to accommodate the new information and a new schema is formed.

Table 18.1 >> Piaget's stages of cognitive development

1	**The sensorimotor stage (0 to 2 years)**	The infant's knowledge is limited to what they can experience through their senses (sensory) and their attempts to coordinate this new knowledge with what they can do (motor).
2	**The pre-operational stage (2 to 7 years)**	The child can now use symbols (as in language), but their concepts are general (preconceptual), for example 'Daddy owns a blue car – therefore all blue cars are called "Daddy's car".' The child's reasoning is pre-operational (it lacks adult logic).
3	**The concrete operational stage (7 to 11 years)**	Children now use logical mental rules, but only in the context of concrete rather than abstract information. For example, they cannot cope with the problem 'Mary is taller than Susan, Susan is taller than Anne. Who is tallest?' unless the problem is presented using dolls (i.e. in concrete form).
4	**The formal operational stage (11+ years)**	Abstract and systematic thought becomes possible, as distinct from more random problem-solving methods.

Note that even though age ranges are given, these are not fixed – they are only guides. It is the sequence that is important. Children pass through all stages, though there is some debate as to whether everyone reaches the final stage of formal operations.

The driving force behind these changes or 'adaptation' is the principle of 'equilibration'. The intellect strives to maintain equilibrium or a sense of balance. If an experience cannot be assimilated into existing schemas then there is a state of imbalance. Cognitive development is the result of adaptation between the individual's existing schema and environmental 'demands' for change, such as new experiences which don't fit existing schema.

Stages in development

A new stage in development is reached when two things happen:

1 The child's brain has matured to a point of 'readiness'.

2 Some new information or experiences that cannot be assimilated challenge the child's thinking.

When the child is 'ready', new experiences will lead to a major reorganization of schemas, so that a new and qualitatively different stage of cognitive development is reached. Each stage is characterized by a coherent structure of principles that operate during that time. These stages are outlined in Table 18.1. We will look briefly at the empirical evidence related to each stage.

The sensorimotor stage

Piaget's descriptive account of the sensorimotor stage is based on his detailed observation of young infants, mainly his own three children. He suggested that early movements are uncoordinated. The infant in the cot comes to realize that the object waving back and forth in front of their eyes is in fact their own hand. They coordinate sensory information with motor information and construct new schemas. In total there are six sub-stages within the sensorimotor stage (reflexes, primary circular reactions, secondary circular reactions, coordination of schema, tertiary circular reactions and mental combinations). The concept of 'circular reactions' describes the infant's repetition of actions in order to learn new schemas.

One crucial development during the sensorimotor stage is that of 'object permanence' – the realization that objects continue to exist even when they cannot be seen. Up to about eight months, 'out of sight' seems to be 'out of mind', as babies do not search for objects that are hidden from view. By the age of one, object permanence is quite securely developed and infants will search for an object where it was last seen, expressing surprise if it is not there.

(A02) Commentary
the sensorimotor stage

● *Underestimating infants* – Not everyone, however, has accepted Piaget's claims about object permanence. For example, Bower (1981) showed that if an object disappeared behind a screen and then the screen was lifted, babies as young as five months would show surprise if the object was not there. This suggests that they did expect the object to be there. However, the issue is not so much at what age these changes occur, but *that* they occur and Bower's evidence merely suggests that Piaget may have underestimated what infants could do.

The pre-operational stage

This stage begins when the child is able to use symbols and most importantly language. Piaget named this stage pre-operational because the child is still unable to use operations. Operations are logical mental rules, such as rules of arithmetic. Pre-operational thought is guided more by external appearances than internal consistency or logic. This is not to say that children of this age are not using rules, but that their reasoning lacks logic.

Piaget divided the pre-operational stage into two sub-stages:

- the *preconceptual stage* – from 2 to 4 years
- the *intuitive stage* – from 4 to 7 years.

The term 'preconceptual' was used to describe the fact that the child does not yet have fully formed concepts – for example, a young child might call all men 'Daddy'. Another characteristic of children at this stage is 'animism' – a willingness to give lifelike qualities to inanimate things (e.g. 'The moon wants to hide behind the clouds').

The intuitive sub-stage describes the fact that children of this age base their knowledge on what they feel or sense is true, but they cannot explain the underlying principles. Piaget highlighted some fundamental weaknesses in pre-operational children's thought (see Table 18.2 below). Egocentrism is perhaps the most serious limitation in pre-operational children's thinking. The pre-operational child finds it hard to take on the perspective of another. Piaget's classic 'three mountains task' (see panel on the right) demonstrated such egocentrism.

Piaget's 'three mountains' task

The three mountains were differently coloured and could also be distinguished because there was snow on the top of one, a cross on the top of another, and a house on the top of the third (see Fig. 18.1). The child was asked to say what the doll could see.

Typically, pre-operational children said that the scene would look just the same as from their own viewpoint. This was the case wherever the doll was positioned.

Figure 18.1 >>
The set-up in Piaget's 'three mountains' task

Table 18.2 >> Some limitations in pre-operational thought

1	Egocentrism	This means viewing the world and thinking about it from one's own point of view and being unaware that others may have different points of view or thoughts.
2	Irreversibility	Reversible means 'can be returned to the original state'. For example, pouring liquid from one glass beaker to another can be reversed by simply pouring it back again. Pre-operational children lack this flexible reversibility of thought.
3	Centration	This refers to the pre-operational child's tendency to focus or centre attention on only one aspect of a task, and ignore other relevant aspects.

Commentary
pre-operational stage

- ***Relating the task to the children*** – This study has been challenged by other researchers who

claimed that the three mountains task did not relate to a child's everyday experiences and thus the child would not fully engage and fully utilize their cognitive skills. See Hughes's (1975) 'hiding' task described in the panel opposite.

Hughes's hiding from the policeman task

Hughes (1975) designed a similar test where a child was asked to hide a boy doll from two policemen (see Figure 18.2). This differed from the three mountains test because it was a more realistic task (hiding from someone else) and also Hughes conducted some practice sessions beforehand. The child participant was shown the walls with one policeman and a boy doll in various positions and asked whether the policeman could see the boy. If the child participant was wrong the errors were explained. Hughes found that 90 per cent of the children tested (aged 3-and-a-half to 5 years) could cope with the task, i.e. they were quite capable of taking another person's perspective when they understood the task.

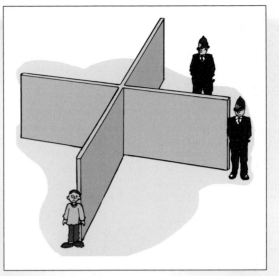

Figure 18.2 >> *The set-up in Hughes's 'hiding' task*

Concrete operational stage

At the concrete operational stage intuition is replaced by a use of logical rules. Yet children's understanding is still limited because it only deals with the actual 'concrete' world. Piaget thought concrete operational children had difficulty in considering ideas that were hypothetical or abstract. Two such important abilities associated with this stage are:

- *Seriation* – This cognitive operation allows the child to order a set of items in terms of dimensions like height, or width or both together. For example, when given a set of dolls of different heights, the child can arrange the dolls in order so that the tallest doll is at one end, followed by the second tallest doll and so on, down to the shortest doll at the other end of the row.

- *Transivity* – This is the ability to recognize logical relationships within a series. For example, if David is taller than John, and John is taller than Mike, then it follows logically that David is taller than Mike.

One of Piaget's most famous ways of assessing children's thinking was to present them with conservation tasks. 'Conservation' refers to the logical rule that quantity does not change even when a display is transformed. Figure 18.3 gives examples of the different types of tasks that Piaget used. To succeed at a task, a child must realize, for example, that the number of counters in a row does not change even when the row is more spaced out. Pre-operational children fail at this task because they cannot conserve quantity, whereas the concrete operational child comprehends the rule and applies it to this concrete situation.

Figure 18.3 >> *Examples of conservation involving number and volume*

Number:

Stage 1   Transformation   Stage 2

Volume:

Stage 1   Transformation   Stage 2

During Stage 1, the child agrees the initial equality of the critical attribute. This is followed by a transformation which destroys the visual similarity, yet does not affect the critical attribute (number, volume, etc.).

The child is again asked about the critical attribute. A child is classified as a 'conserver' if he or she affirms the equality of the critical attribute after the transformation has occurred.

- *Demand characteristics* – Rose and Blank (1974) criticized Piaget's methodology and suggested that Piaget's use of *two* questions might have confused younger children. In the original experiment the children were shown the first display and asked 'Are the two displays the same?', and then asked the same question after the transformation. A pre-operational child might think 'If the question is being asked again, even though nothing has changed, perhaps there is a different answer.' This is called a 'demand characteristic' because it leads the child to behave in a predictable way. Rose and Blank tried asking just one question, after the transformation, and found that pre-operational children could cope better. However, there were still age differences.

- *An alternative method* – Donaldson *et al.* (1978) raised a second criticism of the conservation tasks. They suggested that another demand characteristic

of Piaget's experiments was that the deliberate change of the display suggested to the child that the experimenter was looking for a different response. If the change was accidental, the children should focus more on the actual transformation. McGarrigle and Donaldson (1974) tested this by using a 'naughty teddy' glove puppet that 'accidentally' spread out one row of beads in the standard Piagetian conservation task. The children's ability to conserve was much improved compared to performance on Piaget's original version of the task.

- *Children distracted by 'naughty teddy'* – However, more recent research suggests that Donaldson may also have been mistaken. It is possible that the children were so absorbed in the 'naughty teddy' routine that they didn't actually notice the transformation. Moore and Frye (1986) tested this possibility by seeing how children would respond if the 'naughty teddy' removed or added a counter. The children answered that no change had taken place, despite the fact that this time there had been a change, suggesting that 'naughty teddy' was indeed a distraction.

Formal operational stage

Formal operational thinkers are capable of abstract and systematic thought. If children are asked to conduct an investigation, the concrete operational child will not usually have a systematic plan. In contrast, formal operational thinkers typically develop an overall plan. For example, when solving a problem they keep all the variables constant except one in order to determine its effect, and in this way systematically explore all the possibilities.

Piaget and Inhelder (1956) demonstrated this with the 'beaker problem'. Participants were given four beakers of colourless liquids and asked to find out which combination will produce a yellow liquid. The younger children tried all sorts of random combinations and may or may not have found the answer. The older children took a more systematic approach and systematically excluded possibilities until they found the correct solution. They used *abstract deductive reasoning*: forming a principle, deriving a hypothesis and testing this to confirm the hypothesis.

- *Is it really universal?* – The main criticism of this stage is that it may not be universal. Dasen (1994) claimed that only one third of adults ever reach this stage. When Wason and Shapiro (1971)

tested students using an abstract reasoning task they found that only 10 per cent could work out the solution but this rose to 62 per cent if the task was given in a concrete form. The fact that Piaget assumed that everyone reaches this abstract level of reasoning may be a reflection of his own experience of working with highly intelligent individuals and not be universally true.

- *Piaget underestimated the age at which children could do things* – This may be because he failed to distinguish between *competence* (what a child is capable of doing) and *performance* (how a child performs on a particular

task). Piaget's studies tested performance and then he assumed that a child who failed simply lacked the underlying cognitive structures that he believed were needed to succeed on that task. Subsequent research (such as those cited earlier) suggests that a child may have these competencies earlier than Piaget suggested.

continued on next page

- *Piaget's timetable of development is too prescriptive* – However, Piaget's theory is not only about age boundaries, but also about universal, qualitative, biologically regulated cognitive changes that occur during development. This is supported by cross-cultural research that has replicated Piaget's findings (e.g. Smith *et al.* 1998).

- *Practice should not improve performance* – If a person is not biologically ready to move on to the next stage then no amount of practice should get them there. However, there is evidence to suggest that practice can make a difference. For example, Bryant and Trabasso (1971) trained children under the age of 7 so that they could cope with using logical mental rules.

- *Piaget underplayed the role of language and social factors in cognitive development* – Piaget's views on the lack of influence of language were supported by an experiment by one of his co-workers, Sinclair-de-Zwart (1969). In an earlier

experiment she found that children who were non-conservers differed in terms of the language they used from children classed as conservers. Non-conservers mainly used absolute rather than comparative terms such as 'big' rather than 'larger'. They also used a single term for different dimensions such as 'small' to mean 'short', 'thin', or 'few'. These findings suggest that cognitive and linguistic development is tied together, but which comes first? In a further experiment, Sinclair-de-Zwart tried to teach appropriate verbal skills to the non-conservers. However, 90 per cent of these children were still unable to conserve. This supports Piaget's view that cognitive maturity is a prerequisite for linguistic development (see also Unit 17).

Despite the many shortcomings, the strengths of Piaget's approach and theory should not be overlooked. Piaget produced the first comprehensive theory of children's cognitive development. The theory has been more extensively developed than any other. It has changed our ideas about children and has had a general influence on educational practice. Like all good theories, it has also generated research.

VYGOTSKY'S THEORY OF COGNITIVE DEVELOPMENT

Vygotsky believed that cultural input was fundamental to development. Born in pre-Revolutionary Russia, Vygotsky, like Piaget, had a varied early career. Piaget and Vygotsky were contemporaries, though they never met. You should also note that many of the dates used to reference Vygotsky's work are after his death. This is because his research was only published in English after his death.

The influence of culture

Vygotsky (1934) suggested that the intellect consisted of *elementary* and *higher* mental functions. Elementary

functions are innate capacities such as attention and sensation. Vygotsky's view was that these will develop to a limited extent through experience, but cultural influences are required to transform them into higher mental functions, such as decision-making and comprehension of language. Without culture, an individual would not progress further than the elementary functions. When Vygotsky used the concept of 'culture', he was referring to the body of knowledge which is held by, for example, books and experts, and which is largely transmitted through language. Therefore, according to Vygotsky, cultural knowledge is the means by which cognitive development takes place.

- *Papua New Guinea counting systems* – If higher mental functions depend on cultural influences, then we would expect to find different higher mental functions in different cultures. Gredler (1992) recorded an example of this. Children in Papua New Guinea are taught a counting system which begins on the thumb of one hand and proceeds up the arm and down to the other fingers, ending at 29. This means that it is very difficult to add and subtract large numbers and thus limits mathematical calculations (a higher mental function) in that culture.

- *Language and animals* – Further evidence of the influence of culture is provided by research attempts to teach primates to use human language and other symbol systems (such as arithmetic). The most successful attempts have involved the use of enculturation. For example, Savage-Rumbaugh (1991) taught Bonobo chimpanzees to use human language as well as to use number and quantity concepts by immersing the chimpanzees in a human learning environment. In the wild the chimpanzees' elementary mental functions are not transformed to higher mental functions, but given appropriate cultural input they are able to develop some higher functions.

continued on next page

A02 **Commentary** continued
cultural influences

● *Availability of knowledge* – A final source of
evidence for the influence of culture comes from
research on IQ, which we will examine on p. 567.
This research shows that IQs in many different

countries have been steadily increasing in recent
decades. One explanation is improved diet but
another explanation is the general increase in
knowledge that surrounds children. More and
more books and vast amounts of information via
the internet enhance the culture that surrounds
today's children and contributes to the general
increase in IQ.

The process of cultural influence

In Piaget's theory we saw that the process of cognitive
development was driven by maturation and by the
experience of disequilibrium. In contrast, Vygotsky
argued that it is the influence of others that drives the
process of cognitive development; knowledge is *socially
constructed* and mediated by culturally derived sign
systems. We will examine the various concepts that
Vygotsky used to explain this.

The zone of proximal development (ZPD)

The ZPD is the distance between a child's current and
potential abilities at any moment in time. According to
Vygotsky, one's potential can only be achieved with the
guidance of others. Instruction 'wakens a whole series

of functions that are in a stage of maturation lying in
the zone of proximal development' (Vygotsky 1987,
p. 212). Ideally the 'other' will be sensitive to the
learner's current capabilities (the functions that are in
a stage of maturation) and thus can best guide the
learner through the ZPD (see the panel below).

This shows in what way the instructor (in this case the
child's mother) can be sensitive to the ZPD in order to
enhance the learning process. Vygotsky's predicted that
the greatest teaching input will occur at the *edge* of the
ZPD, the point at which the child can still cope.

Semiotic mediation

The process of cognitive development is *mediated* by
semiotics (i.e. language and other cultural symbols).
In other words, the symbols act as a medium through
which knowledge can be transmitted from others

McNaughton and Leyland (1990) – The ZPD and jigsaw puzzles

A study by McNaughton and Leyland (1990) demonstrates the
ZPD in action and also shows how sensitivity to the ZPD
enhances learning. McNaughton and Leyland (1990) arranged
for children to work with their mothers on solving a variety of
progressively more difficult jigsaw puzzles. They noted the
highest level of difficulty achieved by the children. A week
later the children returned and worked on new jigsaws, this
time unaided. The level of jigsaw difficulty reached was
lower for most children. The difference between the two
sessions enabled McNaughton and Leyland to define the
child's ZPD. The child's unaided performance indicated
their current *ability*, whereas aided performance represented
their potential *capability*.

Results

In observing the mothers working with their children, the
researchers found that there were three types of scaffolding
given by the mothers, which were related to task difficulty.
When the children were doing puzzles which were too easy
(below the child's ZPD), the mothers were mainly concerned
with keeping the child on task. At the second level (within the child's ZPD), the mothers focused at
helping the children solve the puzzle for themselves. At the third level (beyond the child's ZPD), the
emphasis was on completing the puzzle by whatever means. At this level the mother (expert) has
recognized that little or no learning will take place because it is beyond the child's capabilities, therefore
she takes over. At the level below, the mother guides learning through the use of 'shared meanings'.

(e.g. the experts instructing the child or 'culture' more widely) to the child. It is these symbols that enable the transformation to take place, turning the child's elementary abilities into more sophisticated, higher cognitive abilities. Semiotic mediation is a social process.

Commentary
social and individual planes

● **Self-regulation vs. regulation by another –** Various studies by Wertsch (1985) have shown how self-regulation increases with age and experience. In one study children under age 5

were observed while working on jigsaw puzzles with their mothers. Self-regulation was assessed by analyzing children's gazes – looking towards mother was taken to imply less self-regulation. Such gazes decreased with age. In another study children were again observed as they solved puzzles. As the session went on, and the children became more proficient, regulation was transferred from other to self.

The role of language

One of Vygotsky's central interests was in the relationship between language and thought, and this produced a set of developmental stages (see Table 18.3).

In Vygotsky's view, language and thought are separate functions in children under the age of two. Vocal activity, or pre-intellectual language, is a form of social interaction and emotional expression. At the same time, children use prelinguistic thought, mental activities such as problem-solving which do not use verbal operations. This is a period of practical intelligence, when elementary functions are developing. After the age of 2, the child begins to use external symbols or signs,

such as language or other cultural tools, to assist in problem-solving.

A young child will often talk out loud when solving problems, a kind of egocentric speech. After the age of 7, this self-talk becomes silent (inner speech) and differs in form from social speech. Inner dialogues are used as a means of self-regulation, to control one's cognitive processes. Learning has moved to the individual plane but continues to be mediated by language.

Throughout life, language serves a dual purpose: for thought and for social communication. Social processes shape language and also shape thought. (See Unit 17 for a discussion of the relationship between language and thought, including Vygotsky's views.)

Table 18.3 >> Vygotsky's stages of concept formation

1	Vague syncretic stage	Largely trial and error without understanding.
2	Complexes stage	Some appropriate strategies are used but the main attributes are not identified.
3	Potential concept stage	One attribute only (e.g. tall) can be dealt with at a time.
4	Mature concept stage	The child is able to deal with several attributes simultaneously (e.g. tall and square).

Commentary
role of language

● **Supporting studies –** Vygotsky supported his view of inner speech with a number of experimental studies. For example he deliberately introduced obstacles to a child's activity and found that inner speech increased dramatically (Vygotsky 1934). Laura Berk has conducted research related to inner speech, observing children's behaviour in the natural setting of school. Berk (1994) reported that children talked to themselves more when they

were faced with a difficult task, when working by themselves, or when a teacher was not available to help. Berk and Garvin (1984) studied inner speech in Appalachian children as well as middle class children, and found that Appalachian children's private speech developed at a slower pace than those who were middle-class. One reason that they found this to be true may come from the fact that middle-class parents talk to their children more often than Appalachian parents. This would also back up Vygotsky's theory that inner speech stems from social communication.

Stages in the development of thinking

Vygotsky's theory is not a 'stage theory' as such, though he did propose stages in the development of language and thought, as outlined above. He also proposed stages in the process of concept formation derived from a research study he conducted (Vygotsky 1987).

Children were given wooden blocks of varying height and shape, with each block labelled with a nonsense symbol (e.g. 'ZAT' was used to label tall and square blocks). The child's task was to work out what these labels meant. Vygotsky observed that children went through three stages before achieving mature concepts (see Table 18.4).

Table 18.4 >> The development of language and thought

Speech stage	Age	Function
>> *Pre-intellectual, social speech*	0–3	Language serves a social function. At the same time thought is prelinguistic.
>> *Egocentric speech*	3–7	Language is used to control one's own behaviour, but is often spoken aloud.
>> *Inner speech*	7+	Self-talk becomes silent. The child also uses speech for social purposes.

Evaluation
Vytgotksy's theory

- **Empirical support** – For many years there was very little empirical support for Vygotsky's theory, but this is now growing, as interest in the theory has increased. Part of the reason for the lack of empirical study is that the theory focuses on the *process* of cognitive development rather than the outcome, and this is harder to test.

- **Strengths and limitations** – Similarly, because empirical support for the theory has only slowly become available, there is limited negative criticism of it. On the positive side, the theory has found successful applications in education.

- **The role of biological and individual factors in cognitive development** – Vygotsky's theory may overemphasise the importance of social influences and underemphasize biological and individual factors in cognitive development. If social influences alone were necessary for cognitive development, then we would expect learning to be faster than it is.

Evaluation
comparing Piaget & Vygotsky

- **Individual versus social construction** – Piaget suggested that knowledge was something that a child creates from themselves (an individualist, Western approach). Vygotsky saw knowledge as a collaborative, social process (a collectivist approach). In other words, both approaches are constructivist – individual versus social construction.

- **The role of egocentric speech** – Piaget believed that development proceeds from the individual to the social world. Egocentric speech occurs because the child is unable to share the perspective of another. As a child grows older their speech moves away from being self- to other-oriented, a sign that they are able to adopt the perspectives of others. In contrast, Vygotsky suggested that development moves from the social to the individual plane where learning is internalised. Egocentric speech is the transition between social context and inner speech.

- **Development or learning, which comes first?** – Piaget suggested that development precedes learning, Vygotsky suggested that the opposite is true: learning comes first and this promotes development.

- **Scope for assisted learning** – Vygotsky's approach may be the more positive one because it offers more scope for assisting learning whereas, according to Piaget, one must wait.

- **Individual differences in learning** – The two approaches reflect cultural differences but also individual differences. Some learners may prefer more individually-directed learning whereas others benefit more from expert guidance.

Glassman (1999) argues that it is wrong to see Piaget and Vygotsky as opposites, that in fact the two theories are remarkably similar especially at their central core. Piaget focused on the natural laws of intellectual development while Vygotsky concentrated on the impact of social processes and culture. An integration of both views might therefore be highly productive.

PRACTICAL APPLICATIONS IN EDUCATION

The ultimate test of any theory is the extent to which it can inform practice. In the case of theories of cognitive development, the major application is to advise educational practice. The essential advice based on the theories examined is:

- Piaget claimed that children do not need to be taught. They learn because they are drawn into experiences. If a child is taught something prematurely that they could have discovered for themselves, this prevents them from ever completely understanding it. It is a child-centred approach.

- Vygotsky suggested that the desire to learn is an *outcome* of learning rather than being a prerequisite for learning. Vygotsky also felt that expert guidance is needed to move the child through the ZPD, and that without active intervention the child learns less. This is a more teacher-centred approach.

The educational methods derived from both theories have been called 'discovery learning' because, as we have seen, both theories are constructivist – they suggest that knowledge is constructed individually or socially (in contrast with the behaviourist idea that learning is passive). Thus learning is construction of knowledge i.e. discovery.

It is as well to remember that learning doesn't just take place at school, but also at home, with parents and siblings, and many of the applications considered below can be adapted for use either at home or in school.

Piaget's discovery learning

The first outcome of Piaget's theory for educational practice is the view that children learn by constructing their own knowledge when placed in novel situations. The teacher should provide materials and questions which moderately challenge current schemas, leading to disequilibrium, accommodation and the construction of new schemas. The teacher does not make the discrepancies explicit, but stands back and allows the child to work it out for him or herself. Peers are also important in presenting conflict and breaking down egocentrism.

A further outcome from Piaget's theory is linked with his view that logic is not an innate mental process, rather it is the outcome of cognitive development. Therefore logic, mathematics and science should be taught in primary schools because they will facilitate cognitive development. However, these concepts can only be taught when the child is 'ready' because otherwise the child won't fully understand them.

Another implication of Piaget's theory for the school curriculum is the use of concrete materials in teaching young children. He believed that it is vital for students to have the chance to manipulate concrete objects when they are first learning abstract principles. This philosophy underpinned the Nuffield Secondary Science project as well as the Montessori approach to teaching pre-school children.

Evaluation
Piaget's approach in education

- **Piaget and primary education in the UK** – Piaget's views on cognitive development had an enormous influence on education in the UK. The Plowden report, written in the 1960s recommended that primary education should move from being teacher-led to being child-centred and justified this change in terms of Piaget's view that learning is only truly successful when a child invents it for him or herself.

- **The importance of readiness** – Research is equivocal on the importance of readiness. Some research (e.g. Bryant and Trabasso, see p. 557) suggests that practice can improve performance when children appear not to be 'ready'. However, other studies have found no benefits from practice given to a child before he/she is ready. For example, Danner and Day (1977) coached students aged 10, 13 and 17 in three

formal operational tasks. The effects were limited with the younger participants, but very marked at 17 years, showing that training makes a difference, but only when it is given at an appropriate stage of development.

- **Criticisms relating to Piaget's theory** – These are equally relevant as criticisms of its application to education. Notably, the fact that his research often failed to explore alternative explanations for observed phenomena means that his insight into cognitive development is flawed. For example, in the object permanence experiments he failed to exclude the possibility that babies know the object still exists but simply can't do anything about it (Bryant 1995). Many (e.g. Modgil *et al.* 1983) feel that discovery activities in the classroom may actually reduce *real* learning because they reduce time that can be spent on content learning related to the basics (reading, writing, etc.). In addition, judging a child's stage of maturation may be beyond most teachers in terms of time available as well as skill.

Applying Piaget's theory to *education*

Sara Meadows is a Senior Lecturer in the Graduate School of Education of the University of Bristol. Her research started with Piaget and moved into analysis of the social bases of differences in cognitive development. She is currently working with the Children of the Nineties study.

Q **Piaget's theory has been around for over 70 years. What do you feel is its current status?**

A Piagetian theory was a tremendous intellectual achievement and has influenced the field in a remarkable way. His model of cognition being shaped by biological processes such as maturation and brain development, by internal intellectual processes such as assimilation and accommodation, and by environmental input, including influences from the social environment, was way ahead of any other at the time. It is still the model we have to work to, even if many current researchers choose to place the emphasis on other developmental processes. His account of cognitive structure is psychologically too rigid and does not deal adequately with the influence of context. More recent work looking at cognitive processes in a more experimental way lets us pinpoint where things are going wrong for children in real classrooms.

Q **What would you say are the main weaknesses of his theory of cognitive development?**

A For me, the first issue is false negatives. For example, he performed studies using the semi-structured interviews with under-7s. They made mistakes, appearing to come from incorrect beliefs about how quantity changed in the transformation. Piaget describes their errors, and then generalizes to a wide-ranging deficit in concrete operations for all children at this stage. But if you change the questions or the display a bit, or compare conservation with other cognitive operations, you get behaviour that often suggests that young children may understand more than we see in the standard Piagetian test.

The second weakness is partly a result of our selective attention to some parts of Piaget's work rather than others. Social interaction is included in the basic forces behind cognitive development, but most accounts of Piagetian theory emphasize the child's internally-generated struggle to understand and under-emphasize

what other people seek to teach the child. Once you start looking about children's lives in their families and in schools, you realize how pervasive and formative this teaching is, and how intertwined cognition and emotion are. This leads you towards something more like Vygotsky's theory.

Q **Piaget suggests that the mechanisms and stages of cognitive development are universal. Does this mean that the context of a child's development is less important?**

A If you emphasize 'universals', you don't develop research on individual differences, which can be what shows how important the context of the child is. If you are interested in the subtle variations between children in how they develop the whole range of cognitive skills and understanding, you focus on factors in their context, especially their social context. If you do interdisciplinary research – psychology with education and child health, for example – you can make great progress in establishing how the social and physical environment produces small improvements or deficits in development. We are looking at things like diet, mothers' mental health, parenting practices, family poverty, and how they are associated in facilitating or impairing children's development.

Sara Meadows

Q **Does Piaget's view of cognitive development have any relevance to modern day educational practices?**

A Piaget was very hostile about educational practices that involved children acting only as passive recipients of information, such as rote learning and recitation. When his theory first became known in the UK, it was used to justify much more child-centred approaches to education – learning through activities, respecting the child's own drive to work things out – and educational practice became more friendly, particularly in primary schools. There remains a lot of education which requires pupils to memorize and practise what they have been told or shown by the teacher. Sometimes this is the most efficient way to master a body of knowledge or a skill. But being a Piagetian child is probably more fun!

A2 Developmental Psychology

Vygotsky's discovery learning

Scaffolding

Vygotsky did not accept that teachers should wait for a child to be ready to learn and claimed that 'what a child can do with assistance today he/she can do by him/herself tomorrow'. The social context enables learning. This can be seen in the concept of 'scaffolding', a term coined by Wood *et al.* (1976) to describe the process whereby a more experienced 'other' (the expert) offers guidance as appropriate. The 'as appropriate' is crucial because there are times when the learner should be left to work independently but there are also times when progress requires assistance (a scaffold).

The study previously described by McNaughton and Leyland (1990) illustrates the process of scaffolding. Wood *et al.* (1976) conducted a similar study observing mothers and children (aged 4 to 5 years) working together. They found that the most efficient strategy was a combined approach of both general and specific instructions. When the learner runs into difficulty, the instructor gives specific instructions; when the learner is coping well only general encouragement is needed. The learner is given a scaffold by those more expert and the scaffold enables them to 'climb higher' i.e. achieve more. In time, we all learn to scaffold ourselves (self-instruction). The process of scaffolding is outlined in Table 18.5.

Collaborative learning

Vygotsky advocated cooperative group work: small groups of children working together and discussing what they are doing. Bennett and Dunne (1991) found that children who were engaged in cooperative group work were less competitive, less concerned with status and more likely to show evidence of logical thinking than those who worked alone (see panel below).

Peer tutoring

Peers can also be experts, and peer tutoring was seen by Vygotsky as an effective form of learning. Research has also found that peer tutoring may have greatest benefit for the more expert peer (Cloward 1967).

Table 18.5 >> The stages involved in scaffolding

1 *Recruitment* – gaining the child's interest

2 *Reduction of degrees of freedom* – breaking the task down into manageable steps

3 *Direction maintenance* – encouraging and motivating the child until they have become self-motivating

4 *Marking critical features* – drawing attention to aspects of the problem that will help further progress

5 *Demonstration* – the tutor finishes the task off so that the learner can imitate this back in a better form

---

Blaye *et al.* (1991) – The benefits of group problem-solving

A study by Blaye *et al.* (1991) shows the advantages that can come from children working in pairs. The study observed 11-year-olds, working either alone or in pairs, trying to solve difficult problems presented in the context of a computer adventure game. At first no children working on their own solved the problems and only a few of the pairs could manage, but by the second session this improved to 20 per cent and 50 per cent respectively. In the final session all children worked on their own. What was interesting was that over 70 per cent of children who had previously worked in pairs were successful compared with only 30 per cent of children who had previously worked individually. This shows that working together benefits both partners while working together and afterwards once separated.

Even in play, children can accomplish more in pairs!

- *Individual differences* – There are individual differences in the effectiveness of these techniques. For example, collaborative learning does not benefit all children equally. In the study by Blaye *et al.* some of the children working in pairs did not outperform those working alone.

- *The role of 'experts'* – Vygotsky's approach also relies on sensitivity from teachers and other 'experts' to recognize the limits of ZPD, and know when and how to respond. Skilful application of this approach may be an unrealistic goal.

- *The importance of social influences* – The current popularity of Vygotsky's work is at least in part due to its emphasis on the importance of social influences on education. He argued that it is educationally more valuable to know what children can do with some assistance, rather than what they can do unaided. This means that his theory offers the potential for making greater use of instructors. On the other hand, if Piaget is right, by using expert intervention we are stifling creativity and complete understanding.

- *A combined approach* – It may be most productive to combine both approaches. One science programme (CASE – cognitive acceleration through science education) has combined the Piagetian approach to setting situations that create cognitive conflict with the Vygotskian approach to collaborative learning to produce improved performance in experimental groups in maths, science and English (Adey and Shayer 1993).

CHECK YOUR UNDERSTANDING

Check your understanding of the development of thinking by answering these questions from memory. You can check your answers by looking back through Topic 1.

1 Write a very brief (no more than 200 words) explanation of the stages of development proposed by Piaget.

2 Piaget's theory is sometimes called an 'ages and stages theory'. Describe **one other** major feature of his theory.

3 What do you regard as the **two** most significant criticisms of Piaget's theory?

4 According to Piaget, what factors drive cognitive development?

5 According to Vygotsky, what factors drive cognitive development?

6 What was Vygotsky referring to by 'elementary mental functions'?

7 Explain how the 'zone of proximal development' is crucial to cognitive development.

8 Both Piaget and Vygotsky used the idea of 'egocentric speech'. Explain how their explanations differed.

9 List **three** educational recommendations derived from Piaget's theory.

10 What is 'scaffolding' and how does it relate to Vygotsky's theory?

REVISION SUMMARY

Having covered this topic, you should be able to:

✓ describe and evaluate Piaget's theory of cognitive development

✓ describe and evaluate Vygotsky's theory of cognitive development

✓ describe and evaluate the application of Piaget and Vygotsky's theories to education.

Below are some **possible examination questions** set on this topic, along with hints to help you understand and approach each question effectively:

1 Describe and evaluate Piaget's theory of cognitive development (24 marks)

> You are required to spend half your time describing Piaget's theory (15 minutes) and the other half evaluating it (15 minutes). In fact, you are not required to do this but the marks are allocated in such a way that you would be foolish doing otherwise. Many students fail to leave enough time for the evaluation. You should prepare a 15-minute description and 15-minute commentary before the exam so that you don't waste valuable exam time. This might involve selecting about eight key points for AO1 and the same for AO2.

2 (a) Outline Vygotsky's theory of cognitive development. (6 marks)
　　(b) Outline **one or more** applications of Vygotsky's theory of cognitive development. (6 marks)
　　(c) Evaluate this application/these applications of Vygotsky's theory of cognitive development. (12 marks)

> The instruction 'describe' is used when asking for one theory and 'outline' when asking for more than one or when the one theory is assigned 6 rather than the normal 12 marks. Both Piaget and Vygotsky's theories are specified in the specification rather than being provided as examples only and this means that questions may be set on those theories. You may be asked for a 12-minute version (as in question 1), or for a 6-minute version, as here. It may be helpful to produce a précis of your précis for each theory to get it down to a 6-minute version. Part (c) of this question is entirely AO2. One way to evaluate the *applications* is to consider the flaws in Vygotsky's theory. If the theory is flawed then the method derived from the theory may also be flawed.

3 Discuss **one or more** theories of cognitive development. (24 marks)

> This question offers you the choice about which theory to discuss and even offers the option of writing about more than one theory. The phrase 'one or more' means that you can gain full marks if you only cover one explanation. However, if you feel that you cannot write enough on one explanation you can opt for greater breadth and describe more than one explanation. You can always use other theories as a means of commentary. It is not enough, though, to say 'In contrast there is theory 2 …' and then merely offer a description of the second theory. Any features of the second theory that are introduced must be used as commentary and thus would be 'sustained'.

4 'Piaget's theory is often described as "ages and stages" but there is more to the theory than this.'
　　(a) Describe Piaget's theory of cognitive development. (12 marks)
　　(b) To what extent does Piaget's theory offer useful applications? (12 marks)

> The quotation is intended to offer you some help – in this case to remind you that a good description of Piaget's theory would consider more than the four stages. Here, you are not obliged to address the quotation. Part (b) of this question is all AO2 marks ('to what extent' is an AO2 term). The difficulty here will be to avoid writing any *descriptions* of applications (which would be AO1 material and not relevant to the AO1 part of this question) and focus only on the value of these applications. Some description may be necessary as 'scene-setting' but this should be kept to a minimum. Reference to research evidence would be very useful but, as in an earlier question, you can use criticisms of the theory as a means of evaluating the applications.

5 Discuss applications of theories of cognitive development (e.g. to education). (24 marks)

> The word 'application' is in the plural which means you must describe and evaluate more than one application in order to avoid the partial performance penalty (a maximum of 8 marks for AO1 and 8 marks for AO2). However, if you consider the application of more than one theory this would count as multiple applications, or you could write about education at home and in school. The example given in the question is taken from the specification to act as a reminder. Such examples sometimes unfortunately restrict candidates because they think that this is the only possible way to answer the question, and, in as in this case, one example appears to suggest that only one application is required – whereas the question requires two

You may be asking why this section is entitled 'the development of *measured* intelligence'. This neatly side steps the question 'what is intelligence?', which may be one of the most challenging questions in psychology. However, we need not concern ourselves with what intelligence is and instead will focus only on one aspect of intelligence – the intelligence test, and to what extent 'measured intelligence' is due to nature or nurture.

INTELLIGENCE TESTS

The issue of assessing children's intelligence was first tackled by Binet in 1905. The French government had asked Binet to develop a way of identifying pupils who needed special remedial education. Binet and his colleague Simon developed a test of 'general mental ability' consisting of a range of items which varied in difficulty. Binet and Simon determined at what age the average child would succeed with each item by giving the tests to many school children. In this way, they could then identify those pupils who were performing below average. (These were the tests that Piaget worked on when he noticed the consistent errors that children of certain ages were making.) Binet's developmental approach was so successful in predicting school performance that it became the basis for many other intelligence tests. The Stanford–Binet test is based on the original model and is still used today.

IQ

In many intelligence tests, the score is given as an 'intelligence quotient' (IQ). This score enables one individual's performance to be compared with the performance of others. It is called a 'quotient' because it used to be calculated by dividing test score by chronological age. This reflects the fact that 10-year-olds inevitably do better on an intelligence test than 6-year-olds because they are older not because they are more intelligent. Dividing by chronological age allowed

an adjustment to be made. Today most IQ scores are calculated using norms for different age groups. These norms are established by using the test with large groups of children.

Types of IQ test

No doubt you will have taken an intelligence test at some time in your life, even if you didn't realize it. Often IQ tests are given to groups although some of them require one-to-one testing. There are also different kinds of test items. Some are verbal items (e.g. choose the word which is opposite in meaning to the word in capital letters PARTISAN: (a) commoner, (b) neutral, (c) ascetic, (d) pacifier). Some are non-verbal, such as asking a child to arrange pictures in an order so they tell a story or Raven's Progressive Matrices (shown in Figure 18.4). Some non-verbal tests are called 'culture-fair' because people from all over the world should be just as able to understand them, whereas verbal tests or even telling a story with pictures may be tasks that simply wouldn't make sense to people outside a particular culture.

Figure 18.4 >>
An example of a culture-fair IQ test, Raven's Progressive Matrices. It is assumed that cultural background will not make this test easier or more difficult for anyone taking it because it is testing an innate, logical ability.

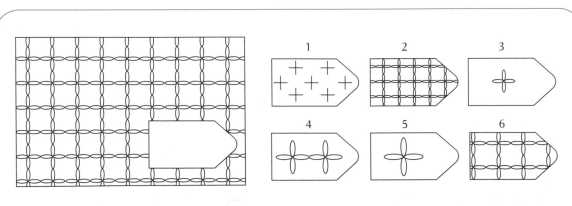

Which of the patterned shapes fits into the hole?

FACTORS THAT AFFECT INTELLIGENCE TEST PERFORMANCE

Is intelligence due to nature or nurture? At one time the nature-nurture debate in psychology (discussed on pp. 571–2) was viewed as a choice between nature or nurture, and the question was asked 'which of these influences is more responsible for IQ?' More recently psychologists have recognized the extent to which nature and nurture are interdependent. We will first of all examine evidence for nature and then for nurture, and finally look at research on the interdependence of these factors.

Nature: The role of genetics

If we want to discover what effects genetics have on IQ we need some way to control environmental and/or genetic factors to observe their independent influence.

Psychologists have done this using a variety of research designs including twin studies and other kinship studies, adoption studies and gene-mapping.

Twin studies

Twins provide an opportunity to conduct a natural experiment where either genetics or environment is constant or varied. Identical twins and non-identical twins (where the person is genetically the same or different) are studied, either reared together or apart (environment the same or different). Identical twins share the same genetic material and are monozygotic (MZ) – they come from the same egg (one zygote). Non-identical twins are as similar as any two siblings are because they came from two separate eggs (dizygotic, DZ).

Twin study by Shields (1962)

A classic study was conducted by Shields (1962) who, by advertising on the television, managed to find 44 pairs of MZ twins who had been reared apart. He found that these individuals had quite similar IQs (a correlation of 0.77). What was more surprising was that this correlation was similar to that of MZ twins reared together (0.76). This suggested that environment had very little influence on the development of their IQ and appears to support the view that genetic factors are of greater importance. This conclusion was further supported by the fact that correlations between DZ twins even reared together were significantly lower (0.51).

These monozygotic twins not only look alike – according to Shields (1962), their IQ will be virtually the same, too

Commentary
twin studies

- **Empirical support** – Major criticisms were levelled at Shields' research, most notably by Kamin (1977) who pointed out that, in reality, the twins had actually spent a substantial amount of time together. Therefore, they were not truly raised in different environments. However, subsequent, better controlled twin studies have found similar evidence. For example, the Swedish Adoption/Twin Study of Ageing (SATSA) (Pederson *et al.* 1992) has followed DZ and MZ twins, half of whom were separated before the age of one. The correlations obtained are similar to Shields' study: MZ twins reared together 0.80 and DZ twins reared apart 0.32.

- **Influences on monozygote twins** – A more fundamental criticism of twin studies is that they assume (1) that MZ twins are identical and that (2) twins reared together share the same environment. As regards MZ similarity, there is the problem of determining whether the twins were in fact identical. Research has found that, for a surprising number of twins, it appears that beliefs about identicalness were incorrect (Scarr and Carter-Saltzman 1979). As regards similar environments, psychologists now recognise the extent to which each individual creates his or her own *microenvironment*. The fact that twins grow up in the same home does not mean they share the same environment. Twins may have different friends or teachers, they also may have slightly different temperaments from birth. Different temperaments cause different responses from people in the environment and, in return, these may have an influence on the development of IQ.

Other kinship studies

Kinship studies show that the more closely individuals are related, the more similar their IQ, suggesting a genetic influence. Bouchard and McGue (1981) conducted a meta-analysis of many other studies and calculated for relatives living together a correlation of 0.86 for MZ twins, 0.60 for DZ twins, 0.47 for siblings, and 0.38 for parents and offspring.

Commentary
kinship studies

- **Comparison of data** – These findings indicate that genetic factors are at least partially responsible for differences in IQ scores. However, comparison of data between reared together and reared apart pairs shows considerable environmental effects. For example the correlation of MZ twins reared apart (0.72) is lower than that of MZ twins reared together (0.86). The correlation for DZ twins reared together (0.60) is higher than that for siblings reared together (0.47) – DZ twins and siblings are just as closely related but DZ twins would share a more similar environment then siblings because they are the same age, so that particular events (such as moving house) would affect them more similarly.

Adoption studies

Adoption studies allow researchers to compare the IQ correlations of children with both their biological and their adoptive parents, offering a different way of controlling genetics and environment. One large-scale study (the Texas adoption project, Horn 1983) showed that adopted children's IQ was more closely correlated with their biological than their adoptive mother (0.28 compared with 0.15) though the differences were small. However, the most interesting finding emerged many years later when the children's IQs were tested again. The correlation with the biological mother had increased and that with the adopted family had decreased (Plomin et al. 1988).

This increase in genetic influence can be explained in terms of something Scarr and McCartney (1983) call 'niche picking'. Genes influence each individual's particular likes and dislikes and, as we get older, each of us increasingly picks the experiences (environments) that we prefer. This means that genetically-related individuals tend to select more similar environments than non-genetically-related individuals and the environments have an effect on development. Loehlin et al. (1989) found that the adoptive siblings in the Texas adoption project had an IQ correlation of 0.26 at age 8 (lower than the figure from Bouchard and McGue) but this dropped to zero by age 18. This provides strong support for genetic influences which may be indirect (niche picking) and no environmental effect.

Commentary
adoption studies

- **Trans-racial adoption studies** – A possible challenge to this evidence comes from a transracial adoption study conducted by Scarr and Weinberg (1976). American Black children adopted by middle-class White families were found to have an average IQ of 106 at age 7 whereas similar children brought up in low-income biological Black families had an average IQ of 97. This would appear to support the influence of environment.

However, by age 17 the IQs of the adopted Black children had dropped to 97 (Weinberg et al 1992), again supporting the niche-picking hypothesis and eventual strength of genetic influences.

There is a note of caution regarding these results: a number of factors were not controlled and may have confounded the findings such as the fact that parental IQs were not known, adoption agencies may have selectively placed the children, the Black children were adopted at a late age and had previously been in care – all factors that may have affected their IQs.

Gene-mapping studies

Plomin has claimed to have identified the first gene related to intelligence, called IGF2R (see Chorney et al. 1998). Since many genes determine intelligence (i.e. it is polygenic), it is likely that high intelligence will be determined by having a variety of high quality genes. A person who has a lot of these 'plus genes' will have high IQ, whereas those who have a mixture of pluses and minuses would have average IQ. If, therefore, one compared the genes from individuals with high IQs ('super-brights') with those of average intelligence, one should be able to single out genes which are associated with brightness. This is what Plomin and his co-workers did and they found that IGF2R was present in 33 per cent of the 'super-brights', but in only 17 per cent of the average group. This one gene would only contribute a small amount to the individual's IQ, perhaps just 4 IQ points, but a series of pluses will add up to 'super-bright'. The fact that not all the super-brights had the gene is understandable because you only need a lot of the 'bright' genes to be bright – you don't need to have them all.

Nurture: Environmental and cultural factors

The 'environment' includes all the physical and social factors that surround a developing child, including culture and experience. The term 'culture' refers to the rules, morals and methods of interaction that bind a group of people and which are determined through the process of socialization. Socialization is achieved largely through parents, school and peers, as well as members of one's culture in general. IQ may be influenced by these individuals, as described in the following sections.

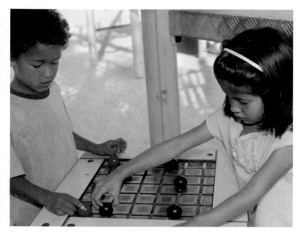

Strategy games that make children think about their decisions have been shown to improve IQ

Home background

The Rochester Longitudinal Study (Sameroff *et al.* 1993) has demonstrated the important factors in the home that contribute to a child's IQ (see Table 18.6). The study began in the 1970s and has followed several

> ### Table 18.6 >> Environmental factors affecting IQ scores
>
> 1 The mother has a history of mental illness.
> 2 The mother has serious anxiety.
> 3 The mother has rigid attitudes, beliefs and values about her child's development.
> 4 There are few positive interactions between mother and infant.
> 5 The main earner in the household has a semi-skilled job.
> 6 The mother did not go to High School.
> 7 The child is from a minority group.
> 8 The father does not live with the family.
> 9 The family has suffered more than 20 stressful events, such as divorce or separation, before the child was aged 4.
> 10 There are four or more children in the family.
>
> *Source:* Sameroff and Seifer (1983)

hundred children from birth to adolescence. The more of the factors that a child had, the lower their IQ. In fact, IQ decreased at a rate of about 4 IQ points per factor, and together the factors were found to account for almost half the variability in children's IQ scores.

Home background has also been explored by Caldwell and Bradley (1978) who have developed a checklist of items to use when gathering information about the quality of children's home environment, called the Home Observation for Measurement of the Environment (HOME). Bradley and Caldwell (1984) found that children who score well on pre-school IQ tests are generally from families who are emotionally responsive and involved with the child, provide appropriate play materials and opportunities to explore and learn, and expect their child to learn and achieve.

Commentary
home background

- *Rochester longitudinal study* – However, we again should note that these data are correlational. It may be that low parental IQ was the *cause* of the risk factors (e.g. 'mother did not go to High School') and also the cause of low IQ in the child (child inherited low IQ).

- Interestingly this correlation between HOME scores and IQ is lower for middle childhood,

possibly because by then children are spending time in other environments such as school but also because, as we saw earlier, genetic factors may be gaining in importance. In fact the influence of the home environment can also be explained in terms of genetic factors. The quality of the home environment is affected by parents' genes because intelligent parents (with high IQ genes) create a more enriching home environment (more books, richer language and so on). So home influences may be an example of how genetic factors *indirectly* affect the development of IQ.

Parental involvement

The 'culture of the home' includes the quality of language used. Hart and Risley (1995) conducted a long-term investigation of the verbal interactions between parents and children, analysing tape recordings taken during the children's first three years. All the children started speaking at about the same time, but by the age of three there were significant differences in vocabulary which were associated with home background. Children from professional families had about 1,100 words; children from working-class homes had 750 words; and those from families on welfare had just above 500 words. These differences were related to language use in parents. Hart and Risley identified five parental behaviours that were strongly related to vocabulary development in children. These were: using a wide vocabulary; high rates of approval; language with a high information content; asking children about things rather than being directive; and responding to children. Most importantly there was a correlation of 0.78 between IQ at age 3 and these parenting behaviours.

Compensatory programmes

Given that factors in the home environment may affect the development of measured intelligence it makes sense to offer children from disadvantaged backgrounds additional enrichment to boost their intelligence. If intelligence were entirely genetic, then such compensatory programmes should not be effective. Head Start is the name given to the largest enrichment programme that has ever been conducted. Begun in the 1960s This was sometimes accompanied by the extra provision of social services, medicine and nutritional advice, as well as involving the children's families in care and education. When children who had been involved in the pre-school programme entered school, they showed more advanced cognitive and social behaviour than children who were not involved in the programme (Lee *et al.* 1990). However, the initial positive effects disappeared in the years following entry, but later research showed a 'sleeper effect'. When the children were older they had higher arithmetic and reading skills, greater feelings of competence, and were more likely to go to college (Lazar and Darlington 1982).

Commentary
compensatory programmes

- **Head Start programme** – There have been some criticisms of the Head Start programme, however, such as the fact that the choice of the control groups of children was not strictly random. It is also worth noting that the outcome measures were also not IQ scores but other life-style signs of achievement.

The Flynn effect

All of the research examined so far indicates that the environment can significantly affect the development of measured IQ but perhaps one of the strongest arguments for cultural/environmental effects is the so-called 'Flynn effect', after James Flynn who has been studying IQ scores from all over the world for the last 60 years. In general, there have been increases of between 5 and 25 points per generation in all countries for which data exist (Flynn 1996). There are three possible explanations:

1 Human intelligence is evolving, but such a rapid development cannot be explained in terms of genetic change.

2 People are getting better at doing IQ tests because, for example we are more used to doing timed activities and more familiar with visually-based technologies. In other words, IQ is not actually changing.

3 Environmental factors are enabling individuals to reach the maximum level of their *reaction range*. The concept of a reaction range was introduced by Gottesman (1963) to describe how our genes provide us with a potential range for height, weight, creativity, intelligence and so on. The environments we experience determine the extent to which we reach the maximum of our own particular range. So, a good diet and education will maximize your genetic potential. This third explanation supports the view that IQ can be enhanced by environmental factors.

Commentary
the Flynn effect

- **The effect of dietary supplements** – The effects of diet have been indicated in many studies. For example, Benton and Cook (1991) found that when vitamin and mineral supplements were given to six-year-old children over a six-week period their IQs increased by an average of 7.6 points.

A subsequent study by Schoenthaler *et al.* (1999) found similar results but more interestingly also found that the variation in IQ scores was greater in the group who were given the supplements rather than those given a placebo. This suggests that the effect of the supplements was to stretch those who were underperforming but of course would have little effect on those already performing near their maximum, providing further support for the reaction range hypothesis.

Racial differences

The most controversial issue in this area of psychology is the extent to which differences in IQ can be related to race. Jensen (1969) sparked off an emotional and political controversy when he published results of research that showed that on average Black Americans scored 15 points below White Americans. He claimed that this showed that Black people were genetically inferior to White people. The study described earlier by Scarr and Weinberg (p. 568) supported such racial differences. In this study the Black children, despite being raised in middle-class environments ended up, at age 17 with IQs that were well below those for adopted White children.

Commentary
nature and nurture

● *Disentangling nature and nurture effects* – If the development of measured intelligence is like planting seeds in a rich or poor soil, then you can imagine that all the seeds in the good soil would be taller than those in the poor soil (see Fig. 18.5). Variations within similar environments are going to be due to genetic factors. However, it is not possible to make a simple statement about the influence of genetic or environmental factors because each assumes a different importance in different conditions. This point is illustrated in recent research by Turkheimer *et al.* (2003) who found that in poor children the contribution of genetic factors to their IQ was very low (heritability of 0.10) whereas the contribution of genetic factors to the IQs of wealthy children was very high (0.72). (Note that heritability refers to the proportion of the total variation in a given characteristic, in a given population, that can be attributed to genetic differences between members of that population). The fact that heritability rates for IQ are often high (around 50 per cent) may be due to the fact that middle-class samples are frequently tested.

● *Transgenerational effects* – There are other factors that complicate the nature–nurture picture. One of these is referred to as *transgenerational effects*. Research has found, for example, that Dutch women who had babies during the Second World War gave birth to normal-sized babies despite their impoverished living conditions. However, when their babies grew up and had children themselves these babies were very small. Such effects are now explained in terms of *epigenetic material* – non-genetic material that is transmitted across generations which is environmental in origin (Reik *et al.* 1993). This shows that apparently genetic effects are actually environmental. We have also seen that apparent environmental effects (home influences) may be genetic (indirect effects of parental genes).

● *Race differences in IQ* – Research on racial differences in IQ is extremely dangerous because of the potential support it gives to racist prejudices. But it is especially dangerous because it is flawed in a number of ways. First, the concept of 'race' is misleading. In reality, people with apparently similar biological heritage come from a range of different cultural backgrounds and experiences. Second, differences between Black and White children are often explained by environmental rather than genetic differences. For example, Brooks-Gunn *et al.* (1996) also found a 15-point IQ difference between Black and White children studied but also found that poverty and home environment accounted entirely for that difference. Tyler (1965) found that Black people from the northern parts of America did better than those from the southern states.

continued on next page

Figure 18.5 >>
If the same seeds are planted in two different environments, we find large average differences between the groups. The most logical explanation is that the differences are due to the environment. Within each group there are also differences. Since all group members share the same environment, the within-group differences must be due to genetic differences.
We can apply this to differences between different groups of people. A group of children living in a city slum will have a lower average IQ than those in middle-class suburbs. Within each of these groups there will be some variation, and this will be down to their genetic differences. The same principle can be applied to differences between racial groups.
Source: adapted from Colby *et al.* (1983)

Seeds

Between-group differences (cause: the soils in which the seeds were sown)

Within-group differences (cause: genetic variations in the seeds)

Unit 18 // Cognitive development

These differences must be due to environment, which in turn suggests that Black/White differences must also be environmental. Finally, most IQ tests are designed by middle-class Americans, i.e. they are *culture-biased*. It is likely that other social and ethnic groups will do less well. Williams (1972) designed BITCH (Black Intelligence Test of Cultural Homogeneity) to show that one could produce a test which would advantage Black American children, while White children would do less well by comparison. It seems clear that conclusions about innate racial differences are unlikely to be correct and, at best, can only serve to perpetuate extremely damaging prejudices.

● *Raising IQ or raising hopes?* – Hereditarians such as Herrnstein and Murray (1994) argue that because IQ has a significant genetic component then we are wasting resources trying to educate individuals beyond their potential. However, the research clearly shows that environmental enrichment matters a lot, especially to underprivileged individuals. The Perry Pre-school Project (Schweinhart *et al.* 1993) examined the lives of 123 African Americans born in poverty and at high risk of failing in school. From 1962–7, at ages 3 and 4, these children were randomly divided into a group who received a high-quality pre-school programme and a comparison group who received no pre-school programme. The enrichment group had significantly higher average achievement scores at age 14 and literacy scores at age 19 than the control group. Almost a third as many enrichment group members as control group members completed high school.

✓ CHECK YOUR UNDERSTANDING

Check your understanding of the development of measured intelligence by answering these questions from memory. Check your answers by looking back through Topic 2.

1 Describe **two** findings from Shields's study of twins.

2 Why are studies of twins reared apart problematic?

3 What can you conclude from studies of adopted children? (Identify at least **two** conclusions.)

4 What gene is linked with being super-bright?

5 List **three** factors in the home environment that have a beneficial effect on IQ.

6 What is the Flynn effect?

7 Outline **one** argument to support the nature position regarding the development of measured IQ.

8 Outline **one** argument to support the nurture position regarding the development of measured IQ.

9 What is 'heritability'?

10 Give **one** example of how genetic and environmental factors interact.

REVISION SUMMARY

Having covered this topic, you should be able to:

✓ describe and evaluate the role of genetics in the development of measured intelligence.

✓ describe and evaluate the role of cultural factors (such as race) in the development of measured intelligence.

✓ in general, critically consider what factors determine the development of measured intelligence.

Below are some **possible examination questions** set on this topic, along with hints to help you understand and approach each question effectively:

1 Describe and evaluate research (theories **and/or** studies) into the role of cultural differences in the development of intelligence test performance (e.g. race). (24 marks)

> When asked to consider research you may use theories (explanations) and/or studies as the AO1 or AO2 focus of your answer – or both! The difference lies in the way material is *used*. Any straightforward descriptions are credited as AO1, but if material (theory or study) is presented as commentary, then it becomes AO2. There are many other ways to provide commentary, such as considering methodological strengths or limitations, or implications of a theory. The question refers to 'the development of intelligence test performance'. For the purposes of answering questions on this topic you may assume that 'intelligence' is equivalent to 'intelligence test performance'. The question also says 'the role of cultural differences'. You may include many different things under the heading of 'cultural differences' such as the effects of home environment, dietary habits, enrichment programmes and so on – in short, anything that may be cultural in origin.

2 Critically consider the role of genetics in the development of intelligence test performance. (24 marks)

> 'Critically consider' is an AO1+AO2 term. In contrast with question 1, this question focuses on genetic factors. This means you must *describe* material related to the role of genetics but you may evaluate this material by considering the alternative view – that intelligence is affected by cultural or environmental differences. This means that must use the material differently from how you would for question 1. Here, you must describe genetic influences and related evidence, and may *use* research on cultural factors as one means of evaluation.

3 (a) Describe research (theories **and/or** studies) into cultural differences in measured intelligence. (12 marks)
   (b) To what extent does such research suggest that the development of measured intelligence can be explained by cultural factors? (12 marks)

> In most parted questions, the AO1 and AO2 content of the question are separated. In this case, you are asked to describe research on cultural differences in part (a), but then must use such research to argue about whether this provides an explanation for the development of measured intelligence. In part (b), you might use your knowledge of opposing views but must steer clear of *describing* such evidence, as this would not gain credit in an AO2 part of a question.

4 Discuss the development of measured intelligence. (24 marks)

> On some occasions, very general questions are set which may appear to be a gift, but there may be a sting in the tail. Given that you only have 30 minutes to answer this question, selection will be an important criterion in distinguishing good answers from weaker ones. You probably will not have time to include everything you know and so it is important to structure your response carefully. One way to do this would be to divide your essay into two 300-word chunks (600 words is about right for a 30-minute essay). In one half of you answer, you may deal with evidence for genetic factors and in the other half, deal with evidence for cultural/environmental factors. In each half you might describe a few studies (150 words) and offer commentary on each (150 words in total). One mistake that many candidates make is to spend time writing an introduction and a conclusion. Such 'extras' rarely attract much, if any, credit and are best avoided. Instead use your precious time to address the exact demands of the question.

5 Describe and evaluate research (theories **and/or** studies) into factors associated with the development of intelligence test performance. (24 marks)

> This question looks quite different from question 4, but the same answer would be acceptable. This shows how important it is to read the wording of questions carefully to ensure that you know exactly what is required. One extra word (such as 'cultural') could change the demands of the question and mean that you have to shape your material in a different way in order to attract good marks.

Unit 18 // Cognitive development

Moral development is concerned with the rules about the rightness and wrongness of certain behaviours and how people should behave towards each other. Moral behaviour is related to pro-social behaviour because both promote social relationships. Traditionally, psychologists have studied three aspects of moral development:

- how children *think* and *reason* about moral issues
- how children actually *behave* when required to exercise judgment
- how children *feel* about moral issues – for example, feelings of guilt.

Cognitive developmental theories, such as those of Piaget and Kohlberg, have looked at *thinking* and *reasoning* about moral issues. Some of the learning theories such as classical and operant conditioning, and social learning theories, have been concerned with actual moral *behaviour*, and the psychodynamic theories of Freud and Erikson have shed some light on *feelings* about ethical and moral matters. In this unit we are going to focus on the development of moral understanding.

PIAGET'S THEORY OF MORAL UNDERSTANDING

Moral understanding is a mental activity and therefore it is no surprise to find that Piaget (1932) applied his ideas on cognitive development to the specific area of moral development. Piaget's theory of the development of moral understanding followed similar principles to his stage theory of cognitive development, as you can see in Table 18.7 on p. 576. At each stage of the child's development, the way that they are able to think about right and wrong is related to their cognitive abilities generally. So, for example, pre-school children are likely to be 'premoral' because they cannot as yet use abstract rules and their egocentricity makes it hard for them to understand the intentions of others.

Piaget believed that equal-status contact with peers was critical in enabling the child to understand the perspective of others and develop socially and morally. When children go to nursery or to school for the first time, they begin to engage more in social situations without adult involvement. They have to learn to handle inevitable conflicts over who should have a turn first or what game to play. Because peers have equal status, they must work out a compromise between themselves in order to function as a group. In doing this they gradually begin to see that rules are social contracts achieved in relation to context. It is critical that adults are not involved because they would only serve to reinforce the child's respect for authority and inflexible rules.

Piaget's research studies

Piaget (1932) based his theory on two lines of investigation. First of all he observed groups of children aged between 3 and 12 playing games of marbles and asked them questions about the rules of the game. He found that the youngest children used no

rules at all. By the age of 5 the children were using rules, but these were seen as absolute law, fixed and unchangeable. Rules must also be obeyed, and failure to obey a rule automatically results in punishment ('imminent justice'), based on the idea that someone in authority instantly punishes wrongdoing. According to Piaget, this is the stage of 'heteronomous morality' or 'moral realism'. Children of 10 had moved on to the next stage of 'moral relativism' because of their greater cognitive maturity. They now realized that the rules could be changed, as long as everyone agreed. Piaget called this the stage of 'autonomous morality' or 'morality of reciprocity'. Children are now more flexible in their thinking and can adopt alternative ways of looking at things.

Piaget's second kind of investigation involved pairs of 'moral stories' (see 'Piaget's stories'). In each pair there was one story where the child had good intentions, but accidentally caused considerable damage, whereas in the other story there was less damage, but the child's intentions were also less good (the child behaved without due care and attention). Piaget asked children, 'Which of the characters was the naughtier and who should be punished the most?' Piaget was interested in the reasons the children gave for their answers rather than just the answers themselves, and whether it was the consequences or intentions that formed the basis for their moral judgement.

Children in the stage of moral realism focused on the *consequences* of the action rather than the *intent*. Older children were able to take intention into consideration when considering the morality of an action, thereby refraining from making judgments that are purely based on the outcome or *consequences* of an action.

Evaluation
Piaget's theory of moral development

Support

- *Armsby (1971)* – manipulated moral stories so that there was either a small amount of deliberate damage or a large amount of accidental damage. Younger children did take intention into account, but had difficulty weighing up the relative importance of value and intention, which meant that they ended up making judgements in terms of outcome alone, as Piaget had found. The conclusion must be that younger children rely *more* on consequences than intentions when judging right and wrong, but that moral behaviour does not follow a simple formula.

- *Cross-cultural support* – An important feature of Piaget's theory is his claim that the moral stages are innate and universal. This would lead us to expect cross-cultural support for his stages. Linaza (1984), for example, found the same sequence of development in Spanish children. However, we should note that where researchers have used the same research methods as Piaget, they might well find the same results because of the methodological flaws described above. Not all cross-cultural evidence has been as supportive.

- *The peer participation hypothesis* – Piaget also claimed that peer interaction would be important in the development of moral understanding, in the same way as he suggested that cognitive challenges lead to the accommodation of existing schemas. Moreover, he suggested that adult interaction would be less valuable. Kruger (1992) found support for the *peer participation hypothesis*. In this experiment, female participants (average age 8 years) were paired either with a friend of the same age or with their mother. Prior to the experiment, each girl was questioned to determine her stage of moral development. Then each pair was asked to reach an agreement about two moral stories. All individuals were again assessed on a moral reasoning task, and it was found that those girls working with peers showed a greater increase in moral maturity than those

working with their mothers. Presumably, the more appropriate discussions between peers assisted moral understanding, even within this short space of time.

Limitations

- *Moral rules and social-conventional rules* – Are games of marbles an appropriate test of morality? Turiel (1983) suggested that people do use social-conventional rules as a way of making moral judgments and therefore it would be reasonable to suggest a scheme of moral development based on the use and understanding of such rules. However, Turiel also pointed out that there are other social rules, such as those related to etiquette and games. Marbles would be an example of the latter and therefore not fully representative of moral behaviour.

- *Consequences and intentions* – The 'moral story' evidence has also been criticized. It is possible that the reason the younger children made judgments on the basis of consequences rather than intentions was because the consequences were much easier to identify. When intentions are made clearer, even younger children appear to be able to make decisions based on them. For example, Chandler *et al.* (1973) found that when the format of these stories was changed from a verbal to a videotaped presentation, then 6-year-olds recognized the intentions of the actor just as well as older children did. Likewise, Feldman *et al.* (1976) found that young children were able to make judgments based on intention when the intentions of the characters in the stories were evaluated separately from the outcomes, whereas in Piaget's original stories, the intent of the child was always confused with the consequences of the action.

- *The complexity of moral reasoning* – Overall, more recent research suggests that Piaget may have underestimated the complexity of moral reasoning. One reason for this is that children, today, are more advanced at an earlier age due to cultural changes such as those which have led to increased IQs (see p. 570).

KOHLBERG'S THEORY OF MORAL UNDERSTANDING

Both Piaget and Kohlberg's theories stem from the cognitive developmental area within psychology and have certain common characteristics:

- They suggest that moral development proceeds through a sequence of innately determined stages which follow an invariant sequence.

- Development occurs as a consequence of maturation but also through disequilibrium. Inconsistencies that

arise through experience challenge current thinking.

- Each stage is defined by the kind of thought (cognition) used to make moral judgments.

- They focus more on *how* people think rather than *what* they think.

- There is an underlying assumption that moral principles are linked to moral behaviour.

Table 18.7 >> Stages of moral development (Kohlberg 1976)

Level 1: Preconventional morality

Stage 1: Punishment and obedience orientation
The child decides what is wrong on the basis of what is punished. Obedience is not valued for its own sake; the child obeys because adults have superior power.

Stage 2: Individualism, instrumental purpose and exchange
The child follows rules when it is in his immediate interest. What is good is what brings pleasant results. Right is also what is fair, what is an equal exchange, a deal or an agreement.

Level 2: Conventional morality

Stage 3: Mutual interpersonal expectations, relationships and interpersonal conformity
The family or small group to whom the child belongs becomes important. Moral actions are those that live up to others' expectations. 'Being good' becomes important for its own sake, and the child generally values trust, loyalty, respect, gratitude and keeping mutual relationships.

Stage 4: Social system and conscience (law and order)
A shift in focus from family and close groups to the larger society. Good is fulfilling duties one has agreed to; laws are to be upheld except in extreme cases. Contributing to society is also seen as good.

Level 3: Principled or post-conventional morality

Stage 5: Social contract or utility and individual rights
Acting so as to achieve the 'greatest good for the greatest number'. The child is aware that there are different views and values, that values are relative. Laws and rules should be upheld in order to preserve the social order, but they can be changed. Still, there are some basic non-relative values, such as the importance of each person's life and liberty that should be upheld no matter what.

Stage 6: Universal ethical principles
The person develops and follows self-chosen ethical principles in determining what is right. Since laws usually conform to those principles, laws should be obeyed, but when there is a difference between law and conscience, conscience dominates. At this stage, the ethical principles followed are part of an articulated, integrated, carefully thought-out and consistently followed system of values and principles.

Lawrence Kohlberg's (1963) theory built on Piaget's ideas and extended them to cover adolescence and adulthood. Kohlberg's classification was more complex consisting of three levels of moral reasoning, sub-divided into six stages (see Table 18.7 above).

Kohlberg's research studies

The basis of Kohlberg's theory was research he conducted using a set of 10 moral dilemmas. Participants were asked a series of accompanying questions, which reflected the fact that in real life there often is no single 'correct' answer. The key factor is how people explain their decision rather than the decision itself. Kohlberg's first study using these dilemmas was cross-sectional, interviewing 72 boys aged between 10 and 16. Each interview lasted two hours. For each dilemma Kohlberg decided what stage of moral reasoning best described the individual's responses. For example, in the case of Heinz, a person might say that 'He should steal the drug for his wife because people would think he was bad if he let her

die'. This would be classed as Stage 3 because it shows a sense of living up to other people's expectations. Kohlberg found that each individual tended to have one dominant category of reasoning across all the dilemmas. In other words their reasoning on each dilemma might be at a different level, but overall they showed a tendency to one particular stage of reasoning. The resulting anaysis enabled Kohlberg to produce his classification scheme.

The original sample was followed for a further 26 years (Colby *et al.* 1983). The boys and men were tested six times in all, at three-yearly intervals, as shown in Fig. 18.6 above right.

At age 10 the children displayed mainly Stage 2 reasoning, but there were examples of Stages 1 and 3. By the age of 22, no one used Stage 1 reasoning, and Stages 3 and 4 were predominant. By the age of 36, and the end of the study, there was still very little evidence of Stage 5 reasoning (about 5 per cent).

In order to demonstrate that his moral stages were universal, Kohlberg (1969) studied the moral reasoning of children in other countries – Britain, Mexico, Taiwan, Turkey, USA and Yucatan – and found the same pattern of development. He also found that development tended to be slower in non-industrialized countries. Colby and Kohlberg (1987) reported longitudinal studies in Turkey and Israel that produced similar results.

Figure 18.6 >>
Use of Kohlberg's moral stages at ages 10 to 36 by male participants studied longitudinally over a 20-year period. Source: Gleitman (1991)

Evaluation
Kohlberg's theory of moral development

Support

● *Cross-cultural support* – Kohlberg's cross-cultural research was supported by Snarey *et al.* (1985), who examined 44 different cross-cultural studies conducted in 26 countries. All 44 studies found a progression from Stages 1 to 4 at about the same ages. However, very few studies found any Stage 5 reasoning and where it occurred it was likely to be in urban areas. Eckensberger (1983) reviewed over 50 studies again lending support to the invariant progression of Kohlberg's stages.

● *The importance of social interactions* – Like Piaget, Kohlberg felt that social interactions were important. Moral understanding develops not from being *told* what is right or wrong, but through experiencing situations that demand moral responses. In support of this Hartshorne and May (1928) found that children who attended Sunday school were less rather than more likely to be honest! More seriously, Berkowitz and Gibbs (1983) suggested that the key to moral progression lay in 'transactive interactions'. These are discussions where each participant engages in the discussion, such as saying 'Have you considered what would happen if ...?' This supports Kohlberg's view that cognitive challenges to one's current thoughts promote moral growth, *but* only if the person is 'cognitively ready'. Such considerations have also been applied to the teaching of moral education in school.

Limitations

● *How universal are 'universal ethical principles'?* – Stage 6 is probably a moral ideal rarely reached and the same is largely true for Stage 5. In fact,

Colby and Kohlberg (1987) performed a more careful analysis of the original data and found only 15 per cent reached Stage 5 and that there was no evidence whatsoever of Stage 6 judgments. Universal ethical principles (Stage 6) may characterize only a handful of people such as Martin Luther King or Gandhi, and even then it is probable that they do not function at this level in all areas of their lives. Nevertheless, Stage 6 represents the ideal state of moral development.

● *Gender bias* – Gilligan (who was Kohlberg's student) suggested that Kohlberg's theory was gender-biased. Kohlberg's theory is based on principles of justice whereas Gilligan argued that women operate quite a different sense of moral understanding to men, an 'ethic of care'. It is likely that Kohlberg's scheme was biased towards male morality because the early participants were all males. This bias might explain why Kohlberg claimed that women were less morally developed than males. Kohlberg believed that women's moral deficiency was a consequence of a life lived mainly within the home but it is more likely to have arisen because they were being measured using a male-created standard. Kohlberg's theory is therefore *androcentric* (a male-centered view) and *alpha-biased* (suggested a real and enduring difference between men and women).

● *Artificial dilemmas* – The dilemmas (like Piaget's stories) are rather artificial tests of morality understanding. They are perhaps tests of moral ideals. When people are questioned in real-life situations, their moral reasoning may reflect different criteria for making judgments. Gilligan (1982) interviewed women who were facing the dilemma of whether or not to have an abortion. The results produced a stage theory (described on p. 580) quite different to Kohlberg's, although this may be because the participants were women.

continued on next page

Unit 18 // Cognitive development

577

Evaluation continued
Kohlberg's theory of moral development

- *Cultural-bias* – Kohlberg's theory may only apply to our Western cultures. The cross-cultural evidence cited earlier appears to indicate that Kohlberg's stages are universal, but there is some question about whether people in other cultures could truly understand dilemmas drawn from

Western cultures. The dilemmas and Kohlberg's stage descriptions are typical of middle-class Western Europeans, i.e. a society where the needs of the individual are considered to be of greater importance than the needs of the community. In other cultures, meeting family obligations and submitting to the authority of elders is regarded as reflecting the highest of moral principles, and yet would be scored at lower levels according to Kohlberg's theory (Snarey *et al.* 1985).

EISENBERG'S THEORY OF PRO-SOCIAL REASONING

Both Piaget and Kohlberg overlook the strong emotional component in moral decisions, which is a part of the theory of 'pro-social' moral reasoning developed by Nancy Eisenberg (sometimes referred to as Eisenberg-Berg). This refers to that area of thinking concerned with helping or comforting others possibly at a personal cost (see also Unit 11 which discusses pro-social behaviour). Like Piaget and Kohlberg, Eisenberg believed that changes take place in moral reasoning in parallel with the maturation of general cognitive abilities.

According to Eisenberg *et al.* (1987) *empathy* is a key feature of the development of pro-social moral reasoning. Empathy is a person's ability to experience the emotions of another. One way to learn this is through taking on the roles of others and seeing the world through another's eyes. Children's games often involve the practice of these *role-taking skills* that may be vital to their moral development.

As empathy grows, children become capable of experiencing compassion or 'sympathetic distress'. There is a distinction between this cognitive understanding of the other person's condition and a younger child's more primitive empathetic distress displayed when they are with someone who is suffering. Cognitive awareness leads the child to go to the assistance of others, whereas distress on its own does not.

Eisenberg's research

Eisenberg also used dilemmas in her research. Her dilemmas focused on situations where there was conflict between the child's own needs and those of others, and were set in a context where the role of laws, rules, punishments or formal obligations were minimized. Each dilemma involved a situation where the central character has to decide whether or not to comfort someone when this pro-social act would be at some personal cost to the giver (i.e. to behave altruistically).

Eisenberg-Berg and Hand (1979) found that the responses of pre-school children to these stories tended to be 'hedonistic' and self-centred. For example,

they might say that Mary should go on to the party so she wouldn't miss out. In contrast, older children were better able to take the feelings of the other person into account. By adolescence, some of the children interviewed expressed the view that they would lose their own self-respect if they ignored the needs of the other person.

The same children were tested with various different dilemmas and, like Kohlberg, the researchers found that moral understanding was not consistent. For example, some pre-school children mentioned their own feelings as well as the needs of others, displaying the characteristics of their own level and some of the next level of pro-social moral development. When the children were tested a year and a half later, there was evidence of development – fewer hedonistic justifications and an increase in altruistic ones.

Eisenberg *et al.* (1983) started a longitudinal study that has followed a group of children from age 4 through to adolescence (Eisenberg *et al.* 1987, 1991) asking them questions about the stories. They have found continuing support for the stage or 'levels' theory outlined in Table 18.8 opposite.

'What are you doing?'

'I am seeing the world through Mary's eyes Miss, like Eisenberg told me to'

Table 18.8 >> Levels of pro-social reasoning (Eisenberg *et al.* 1983)

Level	Brief description	Age range
1 Hedonistic (self-centred)	Pro-social behaviour most likely when it will benefit self in some way	Pre-school and early primary
2 Needs oriented	Will consider needs of others, but not much evidence of sympathy or guilt	A few pre-schoolers, mainly primary
3 Approval oriented	Pro-social behaviour in return for approval and praise from others; understanding of what is appropriate	Primary and some secondary
4 Empathetic or transitional	Evidence of sympathy and guilt; vague reference to principles, duties and values	Older primary and secondary school pupils
5 Strongly internalized	Strong sense of internalized principles which are important to self-respect	A small number of secondary and perhaps a few primary

A further follow-up (Eisenberg *et al.* 1999) has found that those children who displayed spontaneous pro-social behaviour at age 5 years continued to behave in this way in early adulthood, showing that there are stable individual differences in pro-social behaviour that have their origins in early childhood.

Evaluation
Eisenberg's approach

● *Primitive and sympathetic distress* – The prediction that pro-social behaviour is motivated by 'sympathetic distress' but not by the more primitive distress shown by younger children is supported by research. For example, Caplan and Hay (1989) found that children aged between 3 and 5 were often upset by another child's distress, but rarely offered to help. The children said it was because an adult was available to help. This suggests that their cognitive interpretation was that, in times of distress, an adult will aid the victim. Older children come to realize that it doesn't have to be the adult.

● *Empathy and altruism* – The empathy-altruism hypothesis (Batson 1991) supports Eisenberg's view of pro-social behaviour, proposing that human altruism is motivated by experiencing the distress of another. However, Cialdini *et al.* (1982) have opposed this view, suggesting the negative state relief hypothesis – the view that we feel distressed when someone else is distressed and act in order to relieve our own distress. (See Unit 11, p. 352, for evidence relating to these views).

● *A different perspective on moral understanding* – Eisenberg's theory offers a different perspective on the development of moral understanding to that of Piaget and Kohlberg. It emphasizes the importance of emotional factors and focuses on pro-social reasoning rather than issues of wrongdoing. Nevertheless, there are strong parallels between this theory and Kohlberg's stage account, and therefore it can be seen as a broadening of Kohlberg's original approach (Bee 1995).

● *Practical relevance* – Eisenberg's approach can be adapted to give useful advice to parents, and others involved with children, about how to raise children who are helpful and altruistic. Examples include getting children doing helpful things, such as looking after pets and younger siblings, and giving toys away. It will be counterproductive if you have to force children to do these things (Bee 1995).

THE INFLUENCE OF GENDER AND CULTURAL VARIATIONS

Piaget and Kohlberg proposed that the development of moral understanding is driven by innate processes and is universal, therefore we would not expect to find gender or cultural variations. However, we have already seen that there is evidence to the contrary. The fact that culture is defined as the rules that bind together a group of people – their practices, attitudes, child-rearing methods and their morals – would lead us to expect morals to vary between different cultural groups and also between men and women who represent a kind of sub-culture.

Gender variations

Gilligan (1982) believed that Kohlberg's theory reflected a male view of morality and ignored the rather different view that women take towards moral issues: i.e. one concerned more with care than with justice. Gilligan compiled her own stage theory of moral development based on the interviews she conducted with women (see Table 18.9 below). These stages represent a morality of care as opposed to justice.

Gilligan created further evidence for gender differences in a later study (Gilligan and Attanucci 1988) where both men and women were rated on moral dilemmas. This study found that, *overall*, men favoured a justice orientation and women favoured a care orientation, though most people displayed elements of both moralities.

Gilligan et al. (1990) have explained why such gender differences may arise. They claim that women have a stronger sense of 'interconnectedness', relationships and intimacy. This interconnectedness arises during early development as a result of maternal attachment. Boys become independent from their mothers at an earlier age and develop 'separateness'. This means they have to coordinate the interactions of independent individuals earlier, leading them to become more concerned with issues of justice. Girls, however, because of their continued attachment to their mothers, are not as keenly aware of the demands of independent others and are, hence, less concerned with fairness as an issue.

Table 18.9 >> Gilligan's stages of moral development

Stage 1	Self-interest	Similar to Kohlberg's pre-conventional stage
Stage 2	Self-sacrifice	Conventional stage of caring for others and sacrificing one's own needs to achieve this
Stage 3	Integration	Post-conventional stage of 'non-violence', where individual tries to avoid hurting anyone and balances this against own needs

---

Evaluation
gender variations

Support

- *Eisenberg* et al. *(1987)* found gender differences similar to Gilligan's: girls between the ages of 10 and 12 tended to give more caring empathetic responses than boys of the same age. However, this may be because girls mature more quickly than boys, while boys catch up later in adolescence. It may also be a result of demand characteristics within the research (those features of an experiment which 'invite' particular behaviours from participants). Eisenberg and Lennon (1983) found that, when researchers were known to be looking at empathetic behaviour, women portrayed themselves in line with their stereotypically nurturant and empathetic role. When the aim of the study was less apparent, gender differences disappeared.

- *Garmon* et al. *(1996)* – Gilligan and Attanucci's findings have received some support from Garmon et al. They conducted a study testing 500 participants and found that females were more likely to refer to issues of care when judging moral dilemmas.

Limitations

- *Limited evidence of gender variations* – In general, however, research has found only small gender differences. In Walker's (1984) meta-analysis of 108 studies, there were only 8 clear indications of sex differences, but even in those cases, the effects were confounded by other sociological and scoring factors and the differences themselves were very small – less than half a stage.

- *Unrepresentative samples* – Sommers (2000) has attacked Gilligan's initial interviews, pointing out that they involved only a small sample of urban US women who were deciding whether to have an abortion or not. Such a small and biased sample can hardly constitute a sound basis for a universal stage theory of moral development.

- *Gender similarities in moral reasoning* – Garmon et al. and Gilligan and Attanucci found that there were large overlaps in the moral reasoning shown by men and women. Other research (e.g. Wark and Krebs 1996) has found that men and women, when reasoning about real-life dilemmas they have faced, use care- and justice-orientations equally.

continued on next page

Shaffer (2002) concludes that 'it is quite clear that the justice and care orientations are not sex-specific moralities as Gilligan had claimed.

Nevertheless, Gilligan's theory and the studies designed to test it have broadened our view of morality by illustrating that men and women often think about moral issues ... in terms of their responsibilities for the welfare of other people. Kohlberg emphasized only one way ... of thinking about right and wrong.'

Cultural variations

The idea of different moralities, suggested by Gilligan's research, is even more of an issue when considering different cultures – it makes sense that different cultural groups would develop different moralities in response to needs of their society. However, this is contrary to Kohlberg's claims that the principles of moral understanding were universal. Kohlberg cited evidence from Mexico, Turkey, India and Kenya that supported his findings (Colby and Kohlberg 1987).

Individualist versus collectivist cultures

You should be familiar with the distinction made between *individualist* and *collectivist* cultures. Individualist cultures, such as the US and UK, emphasise individual concerns and value *independence* rather than reliance on others. In contrast, many non-Western cultures, such as Israel and Japan are described as collectivist. Collectivist cultures are characterized by the extent to which things are shared – groups live and work together sharing tasks, belongings and valuing *inter*dependence.

It would be reasonable to expect differences between individualist and collectivist societies in terms of moral and pro-social attitudes, since morals are a way of governing social relationships. We would expect individualistic societies to be more competitive and collectivistic societies to be more altruistic. Indeed, Whiting and Whiting (1975) found that 100 per cent of Kenyan children (collectivist) behaved altruistically, whereas only 8 per cent of American (individualist) children did. Eisenberg and Mussen (1989) found that children living on Israeli kibbutzim (communal farming communities) were more cooperative than North Americans.

We would also expect collectivist societies to be more concerned with interpersonal moral orientations (Gilligan's ethic of care) rather than a justice orientation. Miller and Bershoff (1992) interviewed Americans and Asian Indians and found they differed in their attitudes to justice versus interpersonal rules. Consider the hypothetical case of Ben who is in Bombay and needs to get to San Francisco for his friend's wedding where he is to be best man. He has the ring for the wedding and must get home but has lost his ticket. His only two choices are (a) to steal someone else's ticket or (b) miss the wedding. The choice is between contravening the moral of justice (you should not steal) or care (you

should not let a friend down). Miller and Bershoff found that 84 per cent of Indians took option (b) whereas only 39 per cent of Americans selected this option. Different cultures give different priorities to interpersonal obligations.

Urban versus rural influences

Hedge and Yousif (1992) did not find differences in helpfulness when comparing individualist (British) and collectivist (Sudanese) people, but they did find urban and rural differences in both countries. It is possible that the individualist-collectivist distinction arises from a different dichotomy – rural versus urban human cultures. For example, Korte and Kerr (1975) found that stamped-addressed letters left lying in the street were more likely to be placed in a post box if the street was in a rural rather than an urban location. Korte and Ayvalioglu (1981) compared helpfulness between people in Turkish cities and towns, finding that willingness to change money, or agreeing to participate in a short interview was higher in small towns.

However, Kohlberg's focus was on the universality of moral principles rather than pro-social behaviour (helpfulness and altruism). Research has found differences with regard to moral principles. For example, Snarey and Keljo (1991) have found that post-conventional understanding occurs mainly in more developed, industrialised societies and is much less usual in rural communities. It may be that the complexity of urban societies demands greater moral sophistication. Such societies pose more conflicts for individuals and this, in turn would lead to further moral development. In contrast, people living in rural communities don't have the need or stimulation to move to 'higher' levels of development.

Different kinds of moralities

Moral transgressions involve breaking social rules. These rules can be separated into social conventions (people should not jump queues) and 'deeper' moral issues (you should not kill another person). It makes sense that the kind of moral rules that are social conventions would vary between cultures.

Shweder *et al.* (1987) interviewed children age 5 to 13 and adults in India and the US, asking them their views on violations of certain rules such as:

1 The day after his father died, the eldest son decided to have a haircut and eat a chicken.

2 A young woman was beaten by her husband because she went out to the cinema without his permission.

Indian interviewees rated the first as one of the most morally offensive acts whereas the second didn't rate at all, whereas the opposite was true for US interviewees who regard the first one as an arbitrary social convention. Indians regarded it as a universal moral rule and believed that it would be wrong to change it even if most others thought it should be changed. This shows that social conventional rules do vary between cultures,

and also that they can be perceived as high-level moral principles. Miller and Bershoff's study, described earlier showed that Indians see interpersonal morals as a post-coventional form of moral reasoning whereas Americans (in general) see justice as the highest level of moral development. What this shows us is that different cultures use different moralities.

The issue remains about whether there are any *universal* moral principles. Berry *et al*. (1992) report that there are more similarities than differences when you look at serious moral issues.

Commentary
cultural variations
(AO2)

● *Intra-cultural variations* – The individualist–collectivist dimension may be an oversimplification of reality. To say that one society is individualist or collectivist is to ignore variations within a culture. For example, Miller (1994) studied Indian Muslim and Indian Hindu students, finding that Muslims behaved in a collectivist way, whereas Hindu students behaved more like Americans, favouring an individualist perspective.

● *The equivalence of alternative moralities* – Caution needs to be exercised in suggesting that any one moral perspective is more advanced than another. In complex urban societies moral rules

may seem more complicated but this is merely because we are distracted by the complicated lives we lead in such societies. Moral rules develop as a means of coping with the social needs of a particular society, and can therefore be considered *relative* (i.e. important in that society) rather than *universal* (i.e. important in all societies).

● *Moral relativism or moral universalism?* – The main conclusion must fall on the side of *moral relativism,* though there is some evidence for *moral universalism.* This does not strictly follow Kohlberg's theory, whose own view of universalism was shaped, in part, by the Holocaust (the murder of European Jews by the Nazis in World War II). He felt it was vital to regard certain atrocities as universally wrong and not in any way dependent on context.

✓ CHECK YOUR UNDERSTANDING

Check your understanding of development of moral understanding by answering these questions. You can check your answers by looking back through Topic 3.

1 According to Piaget, what is the difference between heteronomous and autonomous morality?

2 What **two** kinds of research did Piaget conduct to assess childrens' moral understanding?

3 List as many similarities as you can between Piaget and Kohlberg's theories of moral development.

4 List the **six** stages of Kohlberg's theory and give a brief description of each.

5 What factor(s) may have led Kohlberg's theory to be gender-biased?

6 Identify **two** features of Eisenberg's approach that are different to Kohlberg's approach.

7 Write a short summary (about 150 words) of the stages proposed by Eisenberg. You should avoid presenting just a list of the stages.

8 What explanation did Gilligan present to explain why men and women may operate different moralities?

9 Name **one** study that supports Gilligan's views on gender differences and **one** study that doesn't support them.

10 Why might you expect there would be differences between individualist and collectivist societies in terms of their moral principles?

REVISION SUMMARY

Having covered this topic, you should be able to describe and evaluate:

✓ Piaget and Kohlberg's theories of moral understanding

✓ Eisenberg's theory of pro-social reasoning

✓ the influence of gender variations on the development of moral understanding, with particular reference to Gilligan's research in this area

✓ the influence of cultural variations on the development of moral understanding.

EXAMPLE EXAM QUESTIONS

Below are some **possible examination questions** set on this topic, along with hints to help you understand and approach each question effectively:

1 (a) Describe **one** theory of the development of moral understanding. (12 marks)
   (b) Evaluate the theory of moral understanding that you described in part (a). (12 marks)

> This is a straightforward question, but you must make sure that you allocate your time appropriately, spending the same amount of time on evaluation as on description. A 'good' description also involves a balance between depth and breadth – i.e. covering lots of aspects of the theory (breadth) but making sure you provide details of each aspect (depth) in order to display your understanding.

2 Critically consider **one or more** theories of the development of moral understanding. (24 marks)

> In this question you have been offered the choice of covering one theory or more than one. The theories do not need to be presented equally, nor do you have to provide equal evaluation of them. However, you must ensure that, overall, you have spent as much time on evaluation as on description. In order to achieve the appropriate balance it may help to have a plan in mind. You could either write 300 words on the theory (or theories) and then 300 words of commentary. Or divide the answer into 6 paragraphs of 100 words each, and do one paragraph AO1 followed by one AO2 and so on.

3 Describe and evaluate **one** theory of pro-social reasoning (e.g. Eisenberg). (24 marks)

> This part of the specification refers to theories of the development of moral understanding *and* of pro-social reasoning so you need to be prepared to answer both kinds of question. You could argue that Kohlberg's theory is a theory of pro-social reasoning but, in order to gain credit for this theory, you must justify its inclusion *and* ensure that you address the pro-social aspects of his theory. You can use your knowledge of alternative theories as a form of commentary, as long as you do *use* it in this way rather than simply describing it.

4 Critically consider the influence of gender **and/or** cultural variations on the development of moral understanding. (24 marks)

> Sometimes open-ended questions, such as this, pose more difficulties than the very narrow questions. Where do you begin? First you need to decide whether you know enough about gender or cultural variations to write for 30 minutes on one topic alone. You can attract full marks by doing this. If you decide to cover both gender and cultural variations then ensure you spend enough time describing key points for each *and* evaluating them.

5 (a) Describe **one** theory of moral understanding. (12 marks)
   (b) Evaluate the theory of moral understanding you described in part (a) in terms of the influence of gender variations. (12 marks)

> This is a repeat of question 1 – with a difference. This time you will not receive any marks for just evaluating your theory. You are directed to evaluate the theory with reference to gender variations *alone*. This is a rather narrow topic, but it serves to warn you that any area of the specification can 'legitimately' be used in a question.

Topic 1: Development of thinking

- **Piaget's theory** suggests that there are two strands to cognitive development: what causes change to occur and what actually changes. The process is mainly biological (determined by maturation) but is also influenced by experience.

- **Development is caused** because the intellect strives to maintain **equilibration**. New experiences that fit with existing schemas are assimilated, whereas those that create disequilbrium necessitate accommodation. **Development proceeds through stages** during which cognitive activities change.

- Piaget's theory has generated much research, most of it aimed to highlight the **flaws in his research methods and theory**. Studies have shown that his techniques lacked realism and may have confused children so that their performance did not reflect their true competence.

- **Vygotsky's theory** centred on the **social construction** of knowledge and the role of experts, language and culture. Innate mental structures (**elementary functions**) will not develop much without cultural input. Development is **caused** by experts leading a child through his/her **zone of proximal development**, from current capabilities to potential capabilities. Learning takes place on a **social plane** first, and then is internalized. This is reflected in a change from **egocentric** to **inner speech**. Concept formation proceeds through stages.

- Vygotsky's theory is being researched more as it is becoming more popular, especially in its applications to education. Vygotsky may have **overemphasized social factors**.

- There are both **differences of emphasis** (e.g. in the role of language, individual versus social construction) and **considerable overlap** (e.g. in the importance of experience and the construction of knowledge) between the theories.

- Theories of cognitive development can be **applied to education**, emphasizing individual (Piaget) or social (Vygotsky) learning. **Piaget's theory** also emphasized the importance of **readiness** and the need to use stage-appropriate materials. **Vygotsky's approach** underlies the use of **scaffolding**. **Collaborative learning** and **peer tutoring** are also important.

- The **CASE** programme has successfully combined both approaches.

Topic 2: Development of measured intelligence

- Intelligence is measured using **IQ tests**. These are tests that purport to be '**culture-fair**'.

- Studies of **twins, relatives and adopted children** are natural experiments which permit genetic and/or environmental factors to be controlled. Identical twins reared apart or together have **very similar IQs**. However, both genetics and environment may not be well controlled in these studies.

- Kinship studies show a reasonable **environmental contribution** to IQ. A surprise finding from adoption studies is that adopted children's **IQs become more similar to their biological parents** as they get older, which may be explained in terms of **niche picking**.

- Research suggests that **super-bright** individuals are more likely to have the **IGF2R gene**, this is likely to be one of many genes that contribute to high IQ.

- **Cultural influences** on IQ include the home environment, which may also be an example of **indirect genetic influence**. **Compensatory programmes** indicate that environmental enrichment does affect achievement and IQ.

- Perhaps the strongest argument for environmental influence on IQ is based on using the concept of **reaction** range to explain the **Flynn effect**, supported by evidence from studies of the **effects of diet** on IQ.

- Research that offers a genetic explanation for **racial differences** in IQ is flawed in a number of ways. For example, it ignores alternative explanations for and the **culture-bias** of IQ tests.

- Attempts to make simple statements about genetic and cultural/environmental influences ignore the fact that **genetic influences vary depending on the quality of the environment**. In addition, many apparent genetic effects may be environmental (e.g. the **transgenerational effect**) or vice versa (e.g. **indirect genetic effects** in the home).

Topic 3: Development of moral understanding

- **Piaget** produced a cognitive developmental stage theory related to his theory of cognitive development. Children progress through **moral** realism to **moral relativism** using **heteronomous** and **autonomous** morals respectively. The theory has been supported by other research, e.g. looking at the **peer participation hypothesis**. However, **criticisms** have been made of the stories.

- **Kohlberg's theory** has much in common with Piaget but extended it to older age groups. The theory was based on research using **moral dilemmas** with American boys, who were re-interviewed 26 years later, though few reached Stage 6. **Cross-cultural studies** supported the findings.

- Other researchers have reported similar findings however, in general, the moral dilemmas are rather **artificial** producing a theory of doubtful validity which is both **gender** and **culture biased** (justice rather than care/interpersonal dimension).

- An alternative way of looking at moral development has been investigated by **Eisenberg** in her theory of **pro-social reasoning**, which focuses on the importance of **empathy** which grows out of **role-taking skills**. Eisenberg developed **pro-social dilemmas** more appropriate for young children and found consistent developmental changes. Other research (studies and theories) suggests that **sympathetic distress** does motivate helping behaviour.

- **Gender and cultural differences** are important considerations in relation to moral understanding. **Gilligan** highlighted the difference between the **ethics of caring** and of **justice**. She portrayed women as having a 'different voice' towards moral issues. However, research **has not supported this male/female distinction** though it has recognized the idea of different moralities.

- **Individualistic** and **collectivistic** societies are likely to have different views of pro-social and moral principles, and vary in the extent to which they use an **ethic of care** or **justice**, though some variation may be due to **rural/urban** differences.

FURTHER RESOURCES

Bryant, P. (1995) 'Jean Piaget', in R. Fuller (ed.) *Seven Pioneers of Psychology*, London: Routledge.

A useful explanation and evaluation of Piaget.

Donaldson, M. (1978) *Children's Minds*, London: Fontana.

A classic critique of Piaget.

Durkin, K. (1995) *Developmental Social Psychology*, Oxford: Blackwell.

A really excellent text with detailed units on moral development.

Mooney, C.G. (2000) *Theories of Childhood: An Introduction to Dewey, Montessori, Erikson, Piaget and Vygotsky*, St Paul, MN: Redleaf Press.

Brief and straightforward descriptions with a focus on educational practice.

Shaffer, D.R. (2002) *Developmental Psychology* (6th edn), Belmont, CA: Wadsworth/Thomson Learning.

An American textbook, providing a slightly different perspective.

Smith, P.K., Cowie, H. and Blades, M. (2003) *Understanding Children's Development* (5th edn), Oxford: Blackwell.

The latest edition of this standard developmental text includes a nice feature of studies reported in detail.

Websites

www.theatlantic.com/issues/2000/08/letters.htm

Gilligan and Sommers: debating the gender research.

http://digital.library.upenn.edu/women/montessori/method/method.html

To find out more about the Montessori method.

www.piaget.org/index.html

The website of the Piaget Society.

http://danny.oz.au/communities/anthro-l/debates/race-iq/

Race and IQ debate.

www.marxists.org/archive/vygotsky/

Information on Vygotsky – you can read some of his works.

SOCIAL AND PERSONALITY
Development

PREVIEW

After you have read this unit, you should be able to describe and evaluate:

>> psychodynamic explanations of personality development, including Freud's theory of personality

>> social learning explanations of personality development, including Bandura and Walter's theory and Mischel's situationalist perspective

>> explanations of the development of gender identity and gender roles in terms of social learning and social cognitive theories, and Kohlberg's gender consistency and gender schema theories

>> research into social development in adolescence, including the formation of identity

>> research into relationships with peers and parents during adolescence

>> cultural differences in adolescent behaviour.

INTRODUCTION

The common thread running through this unit is social development. We are going to explain human behaviour from the social developmental perspective. 'Social' refers to any situation involving two or more members of the same species. In terms of social development, this means we are going to focus on those aspects of development which affect our social relationships, and which are also affected by our social relationships. These include relationships with friends and peers; siblings, parents and grandparents; teachers; and other members of our community including pop stars, people on television and authors of books.

The development of personality, gender and adolescence all involve an interaction between nature and nurture. We are born with certain elements of our character predetermined, but probably the greater contribution to our adult personalities comes from life experiences, especially social experiences. Topic 1 examines theories that explain how social factors influence personality development. In Topic 2, we move on to look at gender development. Genes determine the sex of boys and girls, which is a biological fact. However, the extent to which an individual behaves in a masculine or feminine manner is a feature of their gender, rather than of their sex, and gender is related to their social experiences and cultural influences.

In Topic 3 we focus on adolescence – a stage of development which is triggered by biology in the form of puberty. There are major psychological changes at this time and many of these can be related to social factors. We can see the influence of these factors by looking at cultural variations in adolescence.

Cara
Flanagan

1 Look at the photo on the right. 'She's got bags of *personality*.' But what does it mean 'personality'? Do some people have more personality than others? Is personality something you are born with, or do you acquire it through your childhood? Does it go on developing even when you are old?

2 Is your gender part of your personality? How important is it to you that you are a boy or a girl? Do you think everyone thinks the same way about their gender?

3 Do your parents affect how your personality develops? Do they make you more pessimistic? Or more cautious? Or more generous?

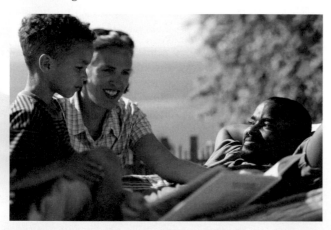

4 How do your friends or peers affect your personality development? Do they affect your gender development? Who teaches you how to behave like a boy or a girl?

5 What are the main influences on adolescent behaviour? Is it your biology (your genes), or parents, or peers? Are adolescents troubled? And if they are, who is their source of comfort?

KEY CONCEPTS

Nature and nurture: the question of what factors contribute to development. Nature refers to factors that are inherited and may be present at birth or may appear later in life as a consequence of maturation. Nurture refers to the influence of the environment, both physical and social. The result of environmental interactions is experience.

Culture: the rules, customs, morals, ways of interacting, child-rearing practices and so on shared by a group of people. Such attitudes and practices bind the group of people together. They are learned through the process of socialization.

Social development: acquiring social behaviours, i.e. any behaviours that assist relationships with other members of one's species. This includes the abilities to form relationships, to cooperate with others and to conform, and also involves the process of socialization.

Socialization: the process by which an individual acquires the attitudes, beliefs, values, social skills and so on that enable them to become a part of a particular social group.

Gender: refers to one's sense of being male or female, whereas 'sex' refers to the biological category of male or female. For most people their sex and their gender are the same. Gender gives rise to a gender identity ('I am masculine'/'I am feminine') and to following expected behaviours for that gender (gender-role behaviours).

WHAT IS PERSONALITY?

'Personality' is a term we all use. You might describe someone as being 'clever but with no personality', meaning that they lack certain socially attractive qualities. Psychologists use the term in a more formal sense and have tried to identify the key characteristics of the concept:

- Personality refers to a *characteristic set of behaviours,* attitudes, interests and capabilities.

- These characteristics are relatively *stable* – a 'kind' person is someone who generally behaves in a kind manner.

- These characteristics are useful for *predicting future behaviour* – we have expectations that a kind person will behave in a kind fashion.

- These characteristics have some *coherence* – we don't just possess a list of characteristics, but they all combine somehow into a 'personality'.

- Personality is an *individual difference* – it is a means of distinguishing between people.

Psychologists have presented various theories to explain the development of personality. We will look first at a psychodynamic explanation and then at two social learning theory approaches.

THE PSYCHODYNAMIC APPROACH

A psychodynamic explanation is one which tries to explain what drives or motivates development (hence the use of the word 'dynamic'). Many psychological explanations of development aim to identify what causes behaviour, but few of them look of the dynamics of this cause. The best-known psychodynamic approach is Freud's psychoanalytic theory. He suggested that the individual is driven to satisfy biological urges and these motives cause us to interact with the environment in certain ways, so that early experience plays a critical role. As we will see, biological drives and early experience are the cornerstones of Freud's theory.

Freud's personality theory

Sigmund Freud's training in medicine and interest in neurology led him to develop his ideas about the causation and treatment of neurotic (or psychological) illnesses. Until then, it was thought that neurotic illnesses had physical causes. Freud proposed a radical new theory and therapy; 'psychoanalytic theory' describes the development of personality, and 'psychoanalysis' is the therapy derived from psychoanalytic theory.

The first year of life

In the early months of life, an infant's behaviour is driven by the 'pleasure principle'. This means that infants do things that produce pleasure or gratification, and avoid pain. In Freudian terms, it is not the infant that is motivated in this way, but rather it is the part of the infant's personality called the 'id', the primitive, instinctive part of the personality that demands immediate satisfaction.

During development, the individual seeks gratification through different organs of the body. In the first year, the focus is on the mouth and pleasure is gained by eating and sucking. Therefore this stage of development is called the 'oral stage'. This drive for oral satisfaction

would clearly be a useful drive for a young infant, directing its attention towards gaining food.

Thus we have the three strands of Freud's personality theory (1920): the driving force (pleasure), the personality structure (the id), and the organ-focus (on the mouth). As children get older, they pass through other stages, each of which focuses on a different organ. These so-called 'psychosexual stages' are discussed later and summarized in Table 19.1, p. 590.

Other personality structures

In addition to the id, there is the 'ego', or 'I' (the term Freud used). The ego develops during the first two years of life as a consequence of the infant's experiences of the world. The force that motivates the ego is the 'reality principle', which makes the child accommodate to the demands of the environment. The ego is equivalent to our rational mind, which must modify the demands of the id.

The superego (or 'above-I') emerges around the age of 5. This embodies the child's conscience and sense of right and wrong. Freud proposed that children enter the phallic stage around the age of 3. At this time their id derives satisfaction from the genital region, in the same way that the young infant gained pleasure from its mouth. This coincides with the age when children are first becoming aware of their gender, and also aware of a three-way conflict between themselves and their parents. Initially, the child rejects the same-gender parent and the opposite-gender parent becomes the love-object. This conflict is resolved differently in boys and girls:

- In boys it is called the 'Oedipus conflict' (after the Greek myth concerning Oedipus who fell in love with his mother and killed his father). A young boy sees his father as a rival for his mother's love and wishes him dead, thus creating anxiety and guilt, which is reduced when the boy comes to identify with his father.

- Freud suggested that during the genital stage, girls come to recognize that they don't have a penis and blame their mother for this. The girl's father now becomes her love-object and she substitutes her 'penis envy' with a wish to have a child, leading to a kind of resolution.

In both sexes, resolution leads to identification with the same-gender parent, which results in their taking on the attitudes and ideas of that parent, including their notions of right and wrong. Thus the superego is born. Freud concluded that girls never develop quite as strong a sense of justice as boys because they do not experience quite as strong a resolution of their genital conflicts.

Handling conflict

The id, ego and superego are inevitably in conflict. Conflicts are perhaps most common between the id and the superego, because the id's demands for instant gratification clash with the superego's moral standards. Conflicts cause the individual to experience anxiety. In order to reduce this anxiety, the ego uses 'defence mechanisms'. These ego defences are unconscious and are a key dynamic of the personality.

For example, a small child does something wrong, such as spilling milk all over the sofa. In order to 'defend their ego', they may deal with this event by repressing it – forgetting that it happened – so that when their mother asks what happened, the child genuinely says 'I don't know'. As well as repressing, the child might project and blame the mother for spilling the milk, deny guilt, adopt a highly self-righteous attitude towards others who spill their milk or intellectualize the accident by informing the mother about the effects of gravity!

In the long term, ego defences may cause abnormal personality development because they exert pressure through unconsciously motivated behaviour. Freud's case history of Anna O. illustrates this (see panel below).

The notion of the unconscious was another key element of Freud's theory. He proposed that there are three levels of the mind:

- The *conscious* consists of those thoughts that are currently the focus of attention.
- The *preconscious* consists of information and ideas that could be retrieved easily from memory and brought into consciousness.
- The *unconscious* consists of information that is either very hard or almost impossible to bring into conscious awareness.

Stages of psychosexual development

Table 19.1 overleaf shows the five stages of psychosexual development. Freud believed that an individual's 'libido' or sexual drive is fixated on a part of the body during particular periods of a child's life. The 'choice' of body region is related to phases of development. The mouth is important in the early months, the anal region becomes important during toilet training, and the genitals are an obvious focus during gender identity development.

Freud's use of the term 'sexual' may be misleading. He did not mean that the satisfaction is sexual in the adult sense of the word, but more as a source of physical pleasure – 'sensual' perhaps rather than 'sexual'.

If a child experiences severe problems or excessive pleasure at any stage of development, this leads to 'fixation', i.e. the individual's libido becomes attached to that stage. Later in life, when in a stressful situation, an adult tends to 'regress' (move back) to the psychosexual stage on which they had previously fixated. The result would be that they behave as they would have done at that age. Freud described various personality traits that are the result of early fixations. These are also shown in Table 19.1.

Summary of the main points of Freud's theory

Freud proposed that the dynamics of personality development come from several sources:

- Pleasure and reality principles drive the id and ego.
- The libido motivates the individual to focus on specific body regions during stages of development.
- Conflict between personality structures creates ego defences, leading to personality characteristics.

The case of Anna O.

Anna O. sought help from Freud because she developed various physical disorders which had no physical cause – some paralysis of the limbs and extreme nausea when she tried to eat. During one session with Freud, Anna recalled an occasion when she was with her governess and how that lady's little dog, which she hated, had drunk out of a glass. At the time she remained silent, but in therapy she expressed her anger and then suddenly drank a large amount of water. From there on she had no trouble drinking. Her other symptoms also disappeared after she was able to describe other thoughts and feelings that had been repressed. Freud concluded that such thoughts had been relegated to her unconscious mind, where they continued to influence her behaviour. She could only deal with these thoughts if they were brought back into consciousness.

Table 19.1 >> Freud's psychosexual stages and their consequences

Stage in development	Description	Personality structure	Fixations	Effects on adult personality
The oral stage (0–18 months)	The infant's main source of pleasure is the mouth.	The id	Fixations may be caused by insufficient breastfeeding or too much pleasure at the breast.	The oral receptive personality is very trusting and dependent on others whereas the oral aggressive personality is dominating. Orally fixated individuals may seek gratification through smoking, thumb-sucking and pencil chewing.
The anal stage (18–36 months)	Pleasure is derived from expelling and/or withholding faeces.	The ego	Fixations may be caused by strict toilet training, or by intense pleasure associated with, for example, smearing faeces on the wall.	The anal-retentive character wants to make a terrible mess and therefore builds up defences against this, such as being very orderly, rigid and hating waste. Other associated traits include stinginess, punctuality, possessiveness. The anal-expulsive character is very generous and may also be creative and productive.
The phallic stage (3–6 years)	Children focus on their genitals and on the opposite-gender parent. Resolution is by identifying with the same-gender parent.	The superego	Fixations are caused by a lack of identification with an adult.	A fixation at this stage results in the phallic personality type who is self-assured, vain and impulsive. Conflicts may result in homosexuality, authority problems, and rejection of appropriate gender roles.
Latency stage	Little development takes place. Boys and girls do not interact much.			
The genital stage (Puberty)	The main source of pleasure is again the genitals. Focus is also on the development of independence.		If some issues remain unresolved, the individual can't shift focus from their immediate needs to larger responsibilities involving others.	

- Early fixations result in further enduring personality traits.
- Adult personality is the product of early experience and is motivated by unconscious ego defences.

Freud did not intend the idea of personality structures (id, ego and superego) to suggest real entities; 'he was not literally dividing the mind into three parts, but describing the *experience* of being pulled in different directions by conflicting influences' (Jarvis 2000).

Also, Freud did not intend the five stages of psycho-sexual development to be seen as abrupt transitions.

Empirical evidence

A theory is based on empirical data (observations made in the real world). Freud's empirical data were the observations he made of patients undergoing psychoanalysis. He never made any notes during a therapeutic session, feeling that any lack of attention during therapy would interfere with its progress. He believed that he would be able to record all the important details afterwards. His expectations and selective recall may have introduced bias into these notes. Freud recorded only a few case histories, such as Anna O. described earlier. Another case study, Little Hans (Freud 1909), documented the Oedipus conflict in a little boy. Hans resented his father and little sister because they were in competition with him for his mother's affections. The anxieties aroused by such resentment were projected elsewhere, creating a phobia for horses which disappeared when Hans was able to acknowledge his feelings of resentment. At the same time, he identified with his father and ceased to desire his mother – thus demonstrating the processes Freud predicted would occur in the phallic stage of development

There is other evidence that supports some aspects of Freud's research. The concept of repression is of interest to memory researchers. One line of evidence comes from the study of 'repressors', e.g. Myers and Brewin (1994). They tested the personalities of a number of people and identified various sub-groups in terms of their trait anxiety (how likely one is to become anxious) and defensiveness (the tendency to protect oneself from anxiety). Repressors are low on trait anxiety and high on defensiveness, i.e. they lack anxiety but are very defensive – it may well be that their low anxiety is due to effective ego defence. Myers and Brewin found that repressors took much longer to recall negative childhood memories than other personality types. This suggests that there is a link between the personality type and the tendency to suppress anxiety-provoking memories. Furthermore, Myers and Brewin found that the 'repressors' actually reported *more* painful memories, which suggests that individuals with anxiety-provoking memories are more likely to repress such memories.

Another area of cognitive psychology that has drawn on Freud's ideas is that of 'perceptual defence' – the concept that things are likely to be ignored if they are unpleasant or emotionally threatening. McGinnies (1949) demonstrated this in a classic study where participants were shown lists of words. The presentation time for each word was increased until the participant was able to identify the word correctly. McGinnies found that emotionally threatening words, such as 'raped' and 'penis', required longer exposure time than words such as 'apple' and 'dance'.

Research in all of these areas tends to lack objectivity. It is an interpretation of the facts from one particular perspective – that of the psychoanalyst.

(A02) Evaluation
Freud's theory

Strengths

- *Theoretical merits* – Freud's theory remains one of the most pervasive theories in psychology, and beyond. Hall and Lindzey (1970) put this down to the fact that Freud's conception of human nature was both 'broad and deep'. The use of picturesque language and mythological allusions gives his work an exciting literary quality, and the fact that he was not a rigorous scientist is balanced by the meticulous observations he made.

- *Accounts for rationality and irrationality* – Jarvis (2000) identifies the most significant feature of Freudian theory as the notion that the human personality has more than one aspect: '... we reveal this when we say things like 'part of me wants to do it, but part of me is afraid to...'.' Freud's introduction of the unconscious permits us to explain how someone can be both rational and irrational, and this can account for many aspects of behaviour, such as the fact that people predict they will behave in one way and actually do something quite different.

Limitations

- *Based on the study of abnormal individuals* – This can perhaps be justified in that one of the main applications of personality theory is in the treatment of abnormality. However, the theory may not be appropriate as an explanation of normal personality development.

- *Based on a limited sample* – Freud's subjects were White, Viennese, middle-class individuals who were mainly neurotic women. It is unlikely that we can generalize from this to all human nature. For example, Freud's overemphasis on sex may be due to the fact that he wrote at a time of great sexual repression. This may have caused sex

to be something that *was* repressed in many minds at that time, but may not apply to development now or in other cultures.

- *Problems of recollection* – Freud studied adults and based his theory of childhood on the *recollections* of childhood. This is not likely to be reliable given what we know about the accuracy of memory over long periods of time and the influences of emotional factors on memory.

- *Lack of falsifiability* – Falsifiability is an important criterion for any scientific theory. Theories should generate hypotheses that can be tested to see if they are true or false. If this is not possible, then you cannot 'prove' a theory's validity. Freud's account of personality permitted him to place interpretations on behaviour which could not be shown to be wrong. For example, he would argue that a person behaved in a certain way because of something that happened in infancy. If the person agreed, this showed Freud was right. If the person disagreed, Freud could argue that this shows that the patient was repressing certain experiences.

- *Overemphasis of sexual influences* – Subsequent psychologists, called neo-Freudians, have adapted Freud's theory to try to incorporate social influences and address the rather unreasonable way that he dealt with women. To some extent, these later theories are re-interpretations of what Freud meant. For instance, Lacan (1966) suggested penis envy was envy of the penis only insofar as the penis is a symbol of male dominance. This was a reasonable conclusion in nineteenth-century society, but may be less true in our age of more equal opportunity.

- *Development ends in adolescence* – Another neo-Freudian, Erik Erikson, presented a stage theory that covered the whole lifespan and is another example of the psychodynamic approach to personality development (see p. 606 and pp. 621–2).

THE SOCIAL LEARNING APPROACH

Learning theory and social learning theory

Learning theory is based on the principles of classical and operant conditioning. The development of personality is probably best explained in terms of the latter: any behaviour that results in a rewarding consequence is more likely to be repeated in the future. Rewards reinforce the probability of that behaviour being repeated. Punishments decrease future probabilities.

This can explain how any behaviour is acquired, including the behaviour we are interested in – the acquisition of personality characteristics. For example, individuals might acquire the personality trait of friendliness because they are rewarded when displaying such behaviour (operant conditioning).

However, Albert Bandura felt that learning theory was not sufficient to explain *all learning*; it would simply take too long to learn everything through trial and error, reward and punishment. He formulated an extension of learning theory, which would incorporate the social context. He suggested that reinforcement or punishment could take place *indirectly*. If an individual sees someone else being rewarded, they are likely to imitate that behaviour. This is called 'vicarious reinforcement'.

Bandura's classic studies using the Bobo doll (see Unit 11, p. 341) showed that children do acquire new behaviours by imitating the behaviour of others. Simply watching the behaviour of another *may* lead to the imitation of that behaviour. This is made more likely if the observer identifies with the model (e.g. they are the same gender or age), or if the model possesses desirable qualities (e.g. they are a TV personality), and if the model is rewarded or praised for their actions.

This element of reward highlights the difference between learning and performance. A child may *learn* a new behaviour simply through observation. However, the behaviour will only be repeated *if* there is an expectation of a reward and *if* the child possesses appropriate skills. Subsequent repeating of the behaviour occurs only *if* the behaviour turns out to be rewarding for the child (direct reinforcement). If the behaviour doesn't produce rewards, then the behaviour will not be repeated. Thus social learning relies on observation, vicarious reinforcement and imitation, and, finally, is maintained through direct reinforcement.

Bandura's personality theory

Bandura (Bandura and Walters 1963) developed a theory of personality development based on the principles of social learning theory. According to this view, *all* aspects of personality are learned. A child may learn novel behaviours through direct or indirect reinforcement, or through punishment. Punishment reduces the probability that a behaviour will be repeated. Subsequently, personality characteristics that are in the child's repertoire may be strengthened or weakened depending on whether the child is directly or indirectly rewarded or punished.

Demonstrating social modelling

Bandura's Bobo studies are given as evidence that specific behaviours are learned through observation and vicarious reinforcement, and also that general aggressiveness is learned in this way. In one study, Bandura (1965) also demonstrated the difference between learning and performance. If children were offered rewards after the observation of a model, then they repeated the model's behaviour even if they had originally seen the model punished. This shows that what is learned is (a) a behaviour and (b) the expectation of reward or punishment. The latter affects the likelihood of a behaviour being repeated.

In another study, Walters and Thomas (1963) demonstrated how someone will learn to *reduce* rather than produce a behaviour. In this experiment, participants were paired with experimental confederates and told to give the learner a shock following each error that was made on a learning task. After each error, the participant was given the opportunity to select the level of shock to use for the next trial. Prior to the experiment all participants had been shown a film. Those participants who watched a violent scene were found to select higher shock intensities than those who watched a non-violent movie scene. Bandura and Walters explained this in terms of 'disinhibition'. The participants observed socially unacceptable behaviour in the film and this *weakened* the pro-social behaviours they had previously learned.

Reciprocal determination and self-efficacy

To explain personality development further, Bandura (1977) introduced two important concepts:

- *Reciprocal determinism* – Both learning theory and social learning theory portray the individual as being controlled by their environment. Things happen to the individual, which increase or decrease the likelihood of any future behaviour. However, Bandura recognized that learning is not merely passive – it is reciprocal. As the individual acts, this changes the environment, thus affecting subsequent behaviour. For example, if you watch your mother baking a cake and then start to imitate her, this modifies her behaviour and subsequently affects you. Individuals are also capable of reinforcing themselves. They are capable of making their own choices and this ultimately affects what they imitate.

- *Self-efficacy* – Bandura (1977) claimed that a person's sense of their own effectiveness (or 'efficacy') influences what they ultimately achieve. If you believe that you cannot jump over a two-metre hurdle, this will affect the way you approach the task and thus what you achieve. Your sense of self-efficacy is an important personality trait. It is derived from both direct and indirect experience. In the case of direct experience, your own successes and failures alter future expectations of success. However, this can be artificially manipulated as in the case of some training programmes used with gymnasts. It was found that if they were shown edited films of their performance such that they only saw the best bits, this led to improved performance (Feltz 1982). Other research has shown how self-efficacy can be increased indirectly. Schunk (1983) observed how primary school children who were told that their friends had done well on a maths test did better than those who were not told this.

A person's sense of their own effectiveness can influence what they achieve ...

Evaluation
Bandura's theory

Strengths

- *Well supported by research evidence* – Bandura's theory consists of testable propositions (unlike Freud's theory) which means that the validity of the concepts can be demonstrated.

- *Applications* – This is a powerful explanation of behaviour and has generated useful applications. For example, the concept of self-efficacy is widely applied in health psychology to provide a means to improve the likelihood that people will follow doctor's orders.

Limitations

- *Methodological problems* – Research has generally been conducted in contrived laboratory environments, which do not represent the complexities of real life. Bandura responded to such criticisms by showing children a film of a live clown being beaten by a model; when given the opportunity, these children did then imitate the behaviour with a real clown. Even so, such behaviour may be the effect of *demand characteristics* in an experimental situation. In real life, our behaviour is affected by a variety of factors. Such studies also focus on short-term

effects and may not demonstrate how longer-term behaviours are learned.

- *Lack of detail and cohesiveness* – Social learning theory has never been very successful because it lacks detail and cohesiveness as an account of personality development. It is rather sketchy on the details of *how* we influence our environment and make choices. There is no doubt that social learning explains aspects of personality development, but usually as an addition to other perspectives.

- *Alternative perspectives* – One alternative perspective is the biological perspective, which is omitted from the social learning account. Freud's theory had a biological element to it, but Hans Eysenck's (1963) 'type theory' was even more rooted in biology. He suggested that the three main personality dimensions – introvert/extrovert, neurotic/stable, and normality/psychoticism – are based in biology. Extroverts have been found to have lower cortical arousal than introverts, which means that their brains operate at a generally lower level of arousal. Thomas and Chess (1980) demonstrated that babies are born with certain characteristic patterns of emotional response or temperament which develop in childhood, and these traits tend to endure throughout life. Temperament interacts with life experience to produce adult personality.

Mischel's situationalist perspective

The situationalist view is a departure from all personality theories because it suggests that personality is not an enduring trait. At the very core of all personality theories is the notion that the traits we possess are lasting and in some way these traits have unity. Walter Mischel (1968)

made the radical suggestion that personality is not consistent at all. He argued that, in reality, people are only consistent in the *same situations*, and their behaviour varies from one situation to another. You might be shy in class but quite the opposite when alone with your friends. In other words, behavioural differences are due more to situational rather than individual dispositional differences.

Mischel pointed out that the reason we may think that personality is consistent is because we tend to see people in similar situations, and offer excuses for occasional lapses. One advantage of Mischel's theory, therefore, is that it can explain personality inconsistency.

A further reason why we think of personality as being consistent is because that is the way our minds are organized. The notion of consistency is a useful tool for organizing our perceptions about others and ourselves, and it allows us to be able to make predictions about subsequent behaviour. We all intuitively recognize the situational element whenever we say, 'She is never late except when her children are ill'. However, Mischel suggests that this is a 'personality paradox', because we think that we and others have consistent personalities but this is not true.

Behaviour specificity

Mischel used the term 'behaviour specificity' to describe how the choice of how to behave is determined by the specific situation in which a person finds themselves. It is determined by past experiences of reward and punishment. Certain behaviours are rewarded in certain situations but not in other situations, so that the probabilities are altered from situation to situation. Mischel's theory is an example of the social learning approach because it suggests that we learn through *selective* reinforcement – we learn that certain behaviours are most appropriate or successful in certain situations. This leads us to behave in the same way in those situations, but not in the same way in other situations.

This is similar to the concept of 'context-dependent learning' (or retrieval): things that are learned in one situation are more easily remembered when the circumstances are the same.

Demonstrating situationalism

Read the Key research below. Mischel and Peake's findings have been criticized in various ways. For example, is it reasonable to assume that the trait of conscientiousness is the same across these different situations? Perhaps the most important criticism concerns 'aggregation'. Epstein (1979) pointed out that Mischel had made the mistake of using moment-to-moment correlations – observing one behaviour on one occasion and seeing if it was similar on one other occasion. Such correlations are inevitably low because so many factors may cause our behaviour to vary from one occasion to another. However, if you aggregate or average observations, correlations increase. Epstein demonstrated this by collecting data from students about their moods over a period of a month. On each day he obtained two scores: one for positive feelings and one for negative feelings. He compared scores on any two days and found a correlation of 0.20, but when he averaged scores on all the odd numbered days and all the even numbered days, the correlation rose to 0.80. The same calculations have been done with Mischel and Peake's original data and the figure for temporal stability (consistency across time) rose to 0.65, and cross-situational consistency rose to 0.13.

Other studies have found similar levels of consistency. For example, Fleeson (2001) rated students on the 'big five personality factors': openness to experience, conscientiousness, agreeableness, extroversion and neuroticism (there is considerable evidence that these five factors – OCEAN – are the major traits in personality). In this study the students carried palm pilots around and regularly reported their behaviours and feelings. Fleeson found very high correlations for the aggregation scores (over 0.87) and lower rates for moment-to-moment scores (see Table 19.2 below).

Table 19.2 >> Correlations found for cross-situational behaviours (Fleeson 2001)

	O	C	E	A	N
Moment-to-moment	0.54	0.28	0.29	0.48	0.36
Aggregated scores	0.94	0.87	0.90	0.94	0.90

KEY RESEARCH >> SOCIAL LEARNING APPROACH

Mischel and Peake's Carleton study (1982)

Mischel and Peake (1982) conducted the Carleton study where friends, family and strangers were asked to rate the behaviour of 63 students in various situations. The observers were asked to focus on friendliness and conscientiousness (class attendance, study-session attendance, room neatness, personal-appearance neatness, etc.) over a semester. When comparing how people behaved in the same situation across time, they found a correlation of 0.29. In other words, one student would be recorded as punctual for class on three out of ten occasions, but not on the other seven that were recorded). However, the correlation for cross-situational consistency was even lower, it was 0.08. In other words, there was almost no relationship between conscientiousness in different situations, such as class attendance and room neatness. Based on this and other personality research, Mischel (1968) concluded 'there is no personality'.

This suggests high cross-situational consistency. This is consistent with the definition of traits as tendencies that influence behaviour in many situations but not all the time. Hence, findings like these challenge Mischel's claim that 'personality does not exist'.

Interactions between person variables and the situation

Mischel (1973) introduced a second strand to his theory: 'person variables'. These include the following:

1 *Competencies* – skills, problem-solving strategies, concepts about the world, based on experiences

2 *Encoding strategies and personal constructs* – attentional strategies (what you pay attention to)

and individual schemas (how you categorize and interpret the world)

3 *Expectancies* – expectancies based on past experiences with similar situations ('if I do this, then I can expect that')

4 *Subjective values* – one's own personal values

5 *Self-regulatory systems and plans* – using past experience to determine future goals and plans.

Person variables are not traits; they are beliefs, values and information-processing strategies specific to a person. Person variables determine how a person will respond to a situation and explain individual differences. Person variables develop as a consequence of previous experience, i.e. they are learned.

Evaluation
Mischel's situationalist perspective

Limitations

● *Social learning accounts deny free will* – Situationalism suggests that we are controlled by situations, though subsequent formulations indicate how the products of reinforcement (person variables) affect future behaviour.

● *People are actually more consistent* – Subsequent research, such as Epstein's and Fleeson's described above, suggests that people are actually more consistent in their behaviour than Mischel had original proposed. This suggests that personality traits *do* influence behaviour.

Strengths

● *Telling it like it is* – Mischel's research correctly challenged the trait-only view of personality, and

promoted the idea that biology and learning interact with situations to produce behaviour.

● *A combined approach* – Mischel and Shoda (1998) suggest that it is possible to combine situationalism with consistency. People are consistent in their situational differences, i.e. you may be shy in a large group of strangers but not with your friends. You always behave in a particular way in particular situations – thus you are consistent, but also exhibit behavioural specificity.

● *Consistency versus situationalism* – The issue of consistency versus situationalism may be resolved by recognizing that the influence of the situation varies depending on circumstances. Buss (1989) proposed that situational factors will be strong in situations which are novel, formal, brief and where there is little choice about how to behave. In situations which are more informal, longer in duration and where one is more free to act according to personal inclination, then dispositional factors will outweigh situational factors.

✓ CHECK YOUR UNDERSTANDING

Check your understanding of personality development by answering these questions from memory. You can check your answers by looking back through the first topic.

1 Explain how the id and ego interact and influence adult personality.

2 Name Freud's stages of psychosexual development.

3 Name two personality types identified by Freud and explain how each might have developed.

4 Briefly describe one of Freud's case studies (in no more than 50 words).

5 Describe one other piece of evidence that can be used to support Freud's account of personality development.

6 Under what conditions do rewards increase the likelihood that a behaviour will be repeated?

7 Explain the concepts of 'reciprocal determinism' and 'self-efficacy'.

8 Describe one criticism of the social learning approach to explaining personality development.

9 Why was Mischel's theory called 'situationalism'?

10 Name at least two of the person variables identified by Mischel.

REVISION SUMMARY

Having covered this topic you should be able to:

✓ describe and evaluate Freud's theory of personality

✓ describe and evaluate Bandura and Walter's social learning theory of personality

✓ describe and evaluate Mischel's situationalist perspective.

EXAMPLE EXAM QUESTIONS

Below are some **possible examination questions** set on this topic, along with hints to help you understand and approach each question effectively:

1 (a) Outline **two** explanations of personality development. (12 marks)

(b) Evaluate the **two** explanations of personality development that you outlined in part (a). (12 marks)

> When required to provide two explanations, there is a partial performance penalty if you only describe one theory (maximum of 8 out of 12 marks for AO1) and/or only evaluate one theory (maximum of 8 out of 12 marks for AO2). However, there is not a requirement that both theories are described in balance. You may receive up to 8 marks AO1 and 8 marks AO2 for the first theory, so might spend two-thirds of your time in both parts of the question on this theory. In general, most candidates know one theory better than the other, so this division of marks is helpful.

2 Critically consider **one or more** social learning approach to the development of personality. (24 marks)

> 'Critically consider' requires you to do AO1 and AO2. Covering one theory would be enough for full marks, but if you feel that you cannot write enough on one explanation, you can opt for greater breadth and describe more than one. In this question, you would not receive any credit for Freud's theory (because social learning approaches have been specified) *unless* you explicitly use this theory to comment on the social learning approach, e.g. by highlighting similarities or differences.

3 'Personality is often defined as the stable characteristics of a person that endure over time and across different situations.'

Discuss different accounts of personality development. (24 marks)

> Some questions include a quotation, as in this case. You do not have to discuss the quotation – it is there merely to provide you with some ideas. You must discuss (describe and evaluate) more than one explanation in order to avoid the partial performance penalty, but other than that there are no restrictions on how to answer this question. The most obvious ways to present evaluative material would be through the use of research studies and/or contrasts with other theories. If you do use research studies, remember that marks are awarded on the extent to which such studies are *used* as commentary. Description should be kept to the minimum and focus should be on the conclusions and what they tell us about the theories.

4 (a) Outline and evaluate **one** theory of personality development based on the psychodynamic approach. (12 marks)

(b) Outline and evaluate **one** theory of personality development based on the social learning approach. (12 marks)

> It is possible that a question will combine both kinds of theory, requiring a short description and evaluation of each. The term 'outline' indicates that a summary description is appropriate for 6 marks of AO1. There is no equivalent 'outline' term for the AO2 content, but this too should be reduced in comparison with a 12-mark answer. In order to perform well on such questions, it is useful to practise writing very short answers that appropriately summarize the material, e.g. a $7\frac{1}{2}$-minute version of Freud's theory and a $7\frac{1}{2}$-minute version evaluating this (because 12 marks is equivalent to 15 minutes of examination time).

WHAT IS GENDER?

Sex is a biological fact. You are born as a male or female. Gender refers to the psychological characteristics associated with being male or female. Your 'gender identity' is a fundamental part of your self-concept: 'I am a boy' or 'I am a girl'. Gender identity generates gender behaviour – behaving like a boy or a girl. But such behaviour depends on knowledge of 'gender roles'. A gender role is a set of expectations that prescribe how males and females should think, act and feel. In this topic we look at how children develop gender identity and their knowledge of gender roles.

There are various approaches to explaining gender development, which are not mutually exclusive. The ultimate account is likely to be a mix of:

- the effects of socialization, i.e. your parents and your culture – this is *social learning theory*
- the changes in the way a child thinks – this is the *cognitive-developmental approach*
- biological factors – this includes the *psychoanalytic* and *evolutionary* approaches.

In this topic we will focus on social explanations of gender development: social learning theory and cognitive-developmental theories.

SOCIAL LEARNING THEORY

We can apply the basic principles of social learning theory to an understanding of how gender is learned – through direct and indirect reinforcement.

Direct reinforcement

Influence of parents

Children learn gender-appropriate and gender-inappropriate behaviours through the application of reward and punishment. For example, parents may encourage more traditional feminine behaviour in their daughter by saying, 'You do look pretty when you wear a dress, instead of jeans', or discourage the same in their sons, 'You look like a girl in that shirt'.

Much direct reinforcement is unconscious, as illustrated by the following experiment. Smith and Lloyd (1978)

videotaped women playing with a 4-month-old baby. The baby was dressed either as a boy or a girl and was introduced with an appropriate name. There were seven toys present:

- a squeaky hammer and stuffed rabbit in trousers (masculine)
- a doll and squeaky Bambi (feminine)
- a squeaky pig, a ball and a rattle (neutral).

They found that each woman's choice of toy varied with the perceived gender of the infant. The women also responded differently to gross motor activity from boys than girls. In other words, the women were reinforcing gender stereotypes (which include information about gender roles), probably with very little conscious thought.

A02 **Commentary**
Smith and Lloyd's study

- *Demand characteristics* – It is possible that the women behaved in the way they did as a

demand characteristic of the experiment – they had only the one clue to guide their behaviour, which was the apparent gender of the infant. In real life, parents' behaviour will be affected by many other factors and thus people might behave in a less stereotyped fashion.

The influence of peers

Peers are also important in this process of direct gender-behaviour reinforcement. Lamb and Roopnarine (1979) observed a group of nursery schoolchildren and found that the children generally reinforced peers for gender-appropriate play (by giving them more attention or imitating them) and were quick to criticize gender-inappropriate play.

Indirect or vicarious reinforcement

You may learn gender-appropriate behaviour by being rewarded or punished yourself (as we have just seen), but you can also learn it vicariously by observing other people being rewarded or punished for their feminine or masculine activity. The media is a very potent source of such indirect reinforcement.

The influence of the media

Gender stereotypes portrayed in the media have a powerful influence on all of us, but especially on children who are acquiring their gender concepts. A stereotype is a fixed, often simplistic picture of a group of people. Cultural attitudes are communicated through stereotypes; for example, the image of a woman doing the washing-up is a stereotype that communicates an expectation about gender roles in our society. Our society has many persistent gender stereotypes (a typical male is assertive, independent, good at maths; a typical female is dependent, relatively passive, good at verbal tasks). Stereotypes that are rewarded are more likely to be imitated, but even in the absence of rewards, a stereotype can act as a model.

Evidence on the effects of media stereotypes comes from Williams (1985) (see panel below).

Williams' Notel/Multitel experiment (1985)

Williams recorded the effects of television in an unusual natural experiment. The residents of a small Canadian town were going to receive television for the first time. He called the town 'Notel' and used a control town nearby ('Multitel') to assess the impact of TV on local behaviour. Behaviour was observed over a period of two years. One of the findings was that the Notel children's gender-role attitudes became more traditional and gender stereotyped. Williams suggested that American television portrays men and women in traditional roles and this influenced the gender-role attitudes of the children. He felt that the effects of television were stronger in developing countries where children have relatively less information to influence their attitudes, whereas children in the developed world would be less influenced by television stereotypes.

Leary et al. (1982) found that children who watched television frequently were more likely to hold stereotypical ideas about gender and more likely to conform to gender-role preferences of a culturally appropriate nature. The fact that these data are correlational means that we cannot be sure whether the TV programmes made the children more gender-stereotyped or that gender-stereotyped children watch more TV.

Other studies have looked at stereotypes in children's books. For example, Crabb and Bielawski (1994) compared children's books from 1938 and 1989 in terms of how they represented the way men and women use equipment such as washing machines, lawn mowers, and so on, and found relatively little change.

Social cognitive theory

The social learning approach traditionally portrays the child as a passive part of the process, whereas there is evidence that individual motivation, self-regulation and cognitive processes play a crucial role in gender-identity development, as we shall see in the cognitive-developmental accounts which follow. Taking the example mentioned earlier, if 'looking pretty' does not matter to the girl in question, then rewarding her for such behaviour will have no effect.

Recently, Bandura and colleagues have adapted traditional social learning theory to allow for the mediating effect of cognitive and motivational factors. This development is called 'social cognitive theory' (Bussey and Bandura 1992). This theory re-integrates the factors discussed above, suggesting that gender development arises from three sources of influence:

- *Modelling in the immediate environment* – Children acquire their knowledge of gender stereotypes from observing others.

- *Enactive experience* – As soon as a child begins to perform gender-related behaviours (enactive representation of their knowledge of gender stereotypes), their behaviour is selectively reinforced. This is an important part of the theory because it explains why boys and girls do not imitate opposite-sex behaviours despite being exposed to them. Selective reinforcement from others creates 'outcome expectancies' for the individual. It is these outcome expectancies that form the cognitive part of the theory.

- *Direct tuition* – Parents reinforce gender behaviours through direct tuition, e.g. telling children what behaviours or activities are appropriate. Fathers are even more likely to encourage appropriate behaviours and discourage inappropriate behaviours (Leve and Fagot 1997).

The crucial factor is the child's ability to regulate their own activities according to the rules relating to gender-appropriate behaviour. This indicates a shift from parental control over this process to a more independent self-evaluation of how children themselves feel when engaged in either gender-appropriate or cross-gender play. Bussey and Bandura demonstrated this in a study of pre-schoolers (Bussey and Bandura 1992). The children were asked to decide whether they would feel 'real great' or 'real awful' if they played with a variety of same-gender or opposite-gender toys. By the age of 4, boys felt great about playing with dump trucks and robots, but were not comfortable with kitchen sets and baby dolls. Girls showed the opposite preferences. Bussey and Bandura concluded that children learn early in life that there are sanctions against cross-gender behaviour, and they start to regulate their own behaviour accordingly.

● *Avoiding demand characteristics* – These results were particularly interesting because the researchers had arranged things so the children thought they were registering their responses anonymously. This means that the results cannot be explained easily in terms of demand characteristics, i.e. that they chose the toys because they thought they were expected to.

Evaluation
social learning theory

Strengths

● *Reducing gender-role stereotypes* – Insights from social cognitive theory can be used to help reduce gender-role stereotypes. 'Counter-conditioning' or 'counter-stereotyping' refers to attempts to present children with non-traditional stereotypes, such as female doctors or men looking after children. The effectiveness of attempts may be low because of real-life experience; when children are exposed to stereotypes which contradict what they see on television, they will be most affected by their direct experience. Counter-conditioning may also lack effectiveness because people feel more comfortable with information that confirms their stereotypes. This is called a 'confirmatory bias' – the tendency to recall information consistent with stereotypes.

● *Explains cultural differences* – Whiting and Edwards (1988) examined 11 different cultures and concluded that 'we are the company we keep'. This view of 'cultural determinism' can only be explained in terms of different child-rearing practices and different cultural attitudes. However, there is also evidence for 'cultural relativism', the view that some gender behaviours are universal. This view is especially supported by evolutionary psychologists who argue that different male and female gender-role behaviours exist as a consequence of adaptive pressure. The essential principle is that any behaviour which increases an individual's survival and reproduction is desirable and 'adaptive'. Any gender behaviour that promotes survival is likely to be retained in an animal's repertoire.

Limitations

● *Alternative perspectives* – Research has demonstrated the importance of biological factors in gender-role development, which means that social learning theory is not a sufficient explanation of gender-role development *on its own*.

When are attempts at 'counter-stereotyping' most successful?

● *Conflicting evidence* – Some evidence conflicts with the empirical data outlined above. For example, Jacklin and Maccoby's (1978) study found that boys and girls are not treated differently in terms of the kinds of gender reinforcements they receive. Also, Smith and Daglish (1977) found that parents who exhibited more gender-stereotypical behaviour (i.e. behaved in a particularly masculine or feminine fashion) did not necessarily have children who were equally gender-stereotyped, whereas social learning theory would predict such a link.

● *Artificial research* – Research evidence is largely removed from natural situations (Katz 1987) and overlooks the fact that children may actually pay little attention to adult models of gender behaviour, especially when they are young.

● *Adevelopmental* – This theory does not explain why children's behaviour changes as they get older, yet there is much evidence to demonstrate that this is the case, as we will see when looking at cognitive-developmental theories.

Unit 19 // Social and personality development

COGNITIVE-DEVELOPMENTAL THEORIES

You may be familiar with some cognitive-developmental theories from other units in this book, especially Unit 18, which explored Piaget's theory of cognitive development. The cognitive-developmental approach focuses on how children's thinking changes as they get older. Most importantly, these changes are regarded as a consequence of maturation, which means that they are universal. This approach produces a stage theory, where the ages identified may not be crucial, but the sequence of development is. Maturation leads young children to be able to think about gender in different ways. This means that children can only acquire gender concepts when they have reached an appropriate age and are 'ready' to acquire this knowledge.

The two theories examined below differ in one main respect. Kohlberg proposed that learning about gender-appropriate behaviour can only take place after a child recognizes that gender is a constant. According to Kohlberg this happens around the age of 7. In contrast, Martin and Halverson proposed that this happens at a much earlier age (about 3); as soon as a child knows what gender they are, they begin to collect information about what constitutes gender-appropriate behaviour.

Kohlberg also suggested a child had developed a gender identity by the age of 3, but this rather superficial understanding of gender (based on physical characteristics only) did not, in his view, lead to the formation of gender stereotypes. (In social cognitive theory stereotypes are learned first and early, and then enactive experience leads to selective reinforcement.)

Kohlberg's gender consistency theory

Kohlberg (1966) proposed a stage theory of gender identity and gender-role development (see Table 19.3). He suggests that children go through each of the stages described in the table, in order to develop an understanding of gender. The stages of development are related to Piaget's outline of cognitive development in general (see pp. 552–7). For example, children are not able to acquire gender consistency until they are able to understand the principle of 'conservation' (that things do not change even if they appear to look different). This happens around the age of 7. It is not surprising that Kohlberg predicted this, simply because the same logic is involved. The child has to be able to infer that something remains the same, although it *looks* different. Once a child can think consistently of their gender, this leads them to *identify* with members of the same gender and actively seek information about gender-appropriate behaviour. In other words, they further their gender development.

Empirical support

Slaby and Frey (1975) conducted research with children. If children over the age of 2 are shown a picture of a young boy and girl and asked 'Which one are you?', they can give an appropriate response. This is the stage of 'gender identity', the recognition of being a boy or a girl. The next stage is 'gender stability'. Slaby and Frey asked children, 'Were you a little boy or a little girl when you were a baby?' and 'When you grow up, will you be a mummy or a daddy?'. Children do not recognize that their gender is stable until they are about 3 or 4 years old.

The final stage is 'gender constancy'. Slaby and Frey showed pre-school children a film with men on one side and women on the other. Those children who had previously been rated as having greater gender consistency watched more same-gender models. This shows that children at this stage of development are more focused on same-gender models who will provide them with information about gender-appropriate behaviour. It also suggests that gender consistency is the cause, rather than the effect, of identification.

Table 19.3 >> Kohlberg's stages in the development of gender identity

Approx. age	Stage of understanding of gender	Description
2–3 years	Gender identity	The child recognizes that he/she is a boy or a girl.
3–7 years	Gender stability	Awareness that gender is fixed. The child accepts that males remain male and females remain female. Little boys no longer think they might grow up to be a mummy and little girls give up their hopes of becoming Batman.
7–12 years	Gender consistency	Children recognize that superficial changes in appearance or activities do not alter gender. Even when a girl wears jeans or plays football, or when a boy has long hair or a burning interest in needlepoint, the child's gender remains constant.

Source: Kohlberg (1966), cited in Hetherington and Parke (1993, p. 547)

- *Ages and stages* – As with all stage theories, there is some disagreement about the actual ages when these changes take place, although the sequence is not contested. Age discrepancies may be due to the methods used to test the children's understanding. For example, when pre-school children were shown *drawings* where gender-inappropriate changes in hairstyle or dress have been made, very few of them were able to recognize that gender remains the same despite the changes (Emmerlich *et al.* 1977). However, if they were shown *photographs* of real children, first in the nude with sexual anatomy visible, and then dressed in gender-inappropriate clothing, almost half the 3- to 5-year-olds knew that the child's gender had not changed (Bem 1989). An additional finding is that when pre-schoolers are asked whether they themselves would change gender if they wore gender-inappropriate dress, almost all of them realized that they would remain the same (Martin and Halverson 1983). It seems that children grasp this concept earlier when applied to themselves, than when applied to others (Wehren and DeLisi 1983).

- *Universal sequence of development* – The sequence of gender development appears to be universal. Munroe *et al.* (1984) observed the same sequence of identity, stability and constancy in children of many different cultures. This suggests that the sequence is biologically controlled (the view that cognitive-developmental theorists take) because people in different cultures will have different social experiences.

- *Conflicting evidence* – Evidence from Martin and Little (1990) suggests that Kohlberg was wrong in suggesting that children do not begin collecting information about appropriate gender role behaviour before they achieve constancy. Martin and Little (1990) measured gender concepts, sex-typed preferences and stereotyped knowledge in children aged 3 to 5. Gender concept measures included ability to identify and to discriminate the sexes, understanding gender group membership, temporal stability of gender, and gender consistency over situational changes. Martin and Little found that pre-school children had only very rudimentary gender understanding, yet they had strong gender stereotypes about what boys and girls were permitted to do, i.e. they had already collected information about gender-appropriate behaviour. Thus, only rudimentary gender understanding is needed before children learn about sex stereotypes and show strong sex-typed preferences for peers or toys.

Gender schema theory

Martin and Halverson's (1983) alternative cognitive-developmental approach differs from Kohlberg insofar as they suggested that children are motivated to begin to acquire knowledge about their gender at a much younger age. In Kohlberg's theory, children must recognize the permanence of gender before they can begin to imitate same-gender models. In gender schema theory, rigid, early gender identity is the starting place for gender development, at about the age of 3. Children then begin searching for rules or 'schemas' which will help them make sense of the world around them. The term 'schema' refers to 'concept clusters' that a child acquires in relation to the world. Gender schema are 'theories' about how men and women should behave which help children both to organize and to interpret their experience. It is the *readiness* to categorize gender information that drives the development of gender.

Empirical support

This theory would lead us to expect children to have a greater interest in schemas related to their own gender, called 'in-group schemas', and less interest in 'out-group schemas', because gender identity motivates them to find out about gender-appropriate behaviour. This has been demonstrated in various studies. For example, Martin *et al.* (1995) showed toys to children aged 4 to 5 years old. The children were told that the toys were either for boys or for girls. Later they were asked whether they and other boys or girls would like to play with the toys. The answers were always related to the gender information provided at the start, so that a boy who was told that a magnet was a 'boy toy' said that he would like to play with this and so would other boys, whereas a boy who was told a magnet was a 'girl toy' would say he wouldn't like to play with it but girls would.

Further support for the importance of in-group schemas is related to how such schemas affect the processing of information. Liben and Signorella (1993) showed young children pictures of adults engaged in stereotypical opposite-gender activity (such as a male nurse). They found that the children disregarded the information, missed the point or forgot it completely, insisting that the nurse was a woman. This supports the notion that children only notice information that is consistent with their existing stereotypes and underlines the importance of stereotypes in acquiring further knowledge. This is again the 'confirmatory bias'.

A02

Evaluation
gender schema theory

- *The persistence of stereotypes* – Gender schema theory explains how gender stereotypes persist because people are more likely to remember information that is consistent with their schemas and to forget or distort gender-inconsistent information.

- *Research support* – Further support comes from the evidence that children are more receptive to same-gender reinforcement. A key feature of the gender schema approach is that it explains why boys are not influenced by female teachers or influenced by men trying to reinforce feminine-type behaviours – it is because the children are actively processing the information consistent with their gender schema. Only this view can explain how children who are exposed to a multiplicity of stereotypes, select the ones appropriate for them. Empirical support for this comes from Fagot (1985) who showed that teachers tend to reinforce 'feminine' behaviours in both boys and girls, such as quiet, sedentary activities. However, both display different behaviours, suggesting that the boys' gender schema overrides the reinforcement.

- *Gender awareness and gender-typed behaviour* – Research has failed to find anything but very weak connections between gender awareness and gender-typed behaviour (Bee 1999), whereas gender schema theory would predict a close relationship. Strong differences between boys and girls have also been found, with girls tending to have more flexible gender concepts and a greater tendency to engage in opposite-gender activities (Archer 1989). Such findings are not consistent with the theory.

- *Resolving contradictions* – Stangor and Ruble (1989) suggest a way to resolve the apparent contradiction between the two theories. Gender schemas and gender consistency may represent different and complementary processes that occur during development. They suggest that gender schema has two separate aspects:

1 The schema contains knowledge about gender-appropriate differences in such areas as activities, behaviours and attire. Such knowledge is acquired early and facilitates memory about gender schema.

2 The schema encompasses the degree to which the knowledge is used to guide behaviour, i.e. how motivated a child is to repeat certain behaviours.

Why do you think girls have a greater tendency to engage in 'opposite-gender' activities?

ACTIVITY

Understanding gender-stereotyped behaviours

Work with a partner and write a list of gender-stereotyped behaviours – things that girls would do but boys wouldn't do, and vice versa. Collect these in your class and ask everyone to anonymously rate how likely they would be to engage in each of the activities. Girls should score 1 for each girl activity ticked and 0 for any boy activities; boys score 1 for boy activities and 0 for girl activities.

How rigid are you and your classmates in terms of gender-stereotyped behaviour?

COMPARING THEORIES OF GENDER DEVELOPMENT

All three theories suggest ways that children take an active role in their gender development, though social cognitive theory still includes the passive effects of selective reinforcement. Each theory suggests a different place for gender identity as shown in the summary table (Table 19.4). Cognitive-developmental theories suggest a sequence of development, whereas

social cognitive theory is largely adevelopmental (gender learning is the same at all ages).

All three theories emphasize the role of social factors, while biological factors are largely overlooked, except that cognitive-developmental theories do include the influence of maturational factors. There is strong evidence that biological factors do have some role in

A2 Developmental Psychology

Table 19.4 >> Comparing the theories of gender development

Bussey and Bandura	→ stereotypes (direct and indirect reinforcement) → enactive experience → selective reinforcement	*Gender behaviour is the cause of gender identity: 'I'm treated like a boy so I must be one.'*
Kohlberg	→ identity (age 3) → stability → constancy (age 7) → acquire knowledge about gender-appropriate behaviour	*Gender consistency is the cause of gender identity: 'My gender isn't going to change so I should start behaving like a boy.'*
Martin and Halverson	→ identity (age 3) → acquire in-group/out-group schema	*Gender consistency is the effect of gender identity: 'I'm a boy so I should find out about how boys are supposed to behave.'*

gender-role behaviour, as suggested earlier with reference to evolutionary psychology. There is also evidence to support the role of hormones.

The influence of hormones

Females who are exposed to male hormones during pre-natal development show more masculine behaviours. Beach (1974) found that female dogs that were exposed perinatally to male hormones were subsequently likely to urinate in the manner of males. Similarly, Young *et al.* (1964) found that female

monkeys exposed to male hormones during the critical pre-natal period were more likely to engage in rough-and-tumble play in their early years. There is also some evidence for the same effects on human behaviour. At one time, mothers who were liable to miscarry were treated with male hormones to prevent this. This treatment was stopped when it became apparent that the mothers gave birth to genetic females with male genitals. The girls received corrective surgery, but appeared to behave in a more tomboyish fashion when assessed later in childhood (Money and Ehrhardt 1972).

✔ CHECK YOUR UNDERSTANDING

Check your understanding of the development of thinking by answering these questions. Try to do this from memory at first. You can check your answers by looking back through Topic 2.

1 Briefly describe one piece of evidence that shows how the media influences gender development.

2 What was the main way that Bandura's social cognitive theory differed from the original social learning theory explanation for gender development?

3 According the social cognitive theory, what are the three main influences on gender development?

4 List the three stages proposed by Kohlberg.

5 Outline **one** study that supports Kohlberg's theory.

6 What is the main difference between Kohlberg's theory and gender schema theory?

7 Briefly describe the study which suggests that Kohlberg was wrong.

8 What are 'gender schemas'?

9 Outline **one** study that supports gender schema theory.

10 Outline **one** similarity and **one** difference between social learning approaches and cognitive-developmental approaches to explaining gender development.

REVISION SUMMARY

Having covered this topic you should be able to:

✓ understand how gender identity and gender roles develop

✓ describe and evaluate social learning theories of gender development (social learning theory and social cognitive theory)

✓ describe and evaluate cognitive-developmental theories of the development of gender development (Kohlberg's gender consistency theory and gender schema theory)

✓ consider the similarities and differences between each approach.

EXAMPLE EXAM QUESTIONS

Below are some **possible examination questions** set on this topic, along with hints to help you understand and approach each question effectively:

1 Outline and evaluate **two** explanations of the development of gender roles. (24 marks)

> The term 'outline' has been used for the AO1 segment of this question because two explanations are required and you would not have time to present both in detail. You may count 'cognitive-developmental' as one explanation and include Kohlberg's theory and gender schema theory as part of one explanation, or you could present these as two separate explanations. Note that this question is limited to gender roles only, so you must make sure that your explanations make reference to this and not to gender identity. Always shape your knowledge to the requirements of the question you are answering.

2 Critically consider **two or more** explanations of gender development (e.g. social learning theories, cognitive-developmental theories, gender schema theory). (24 marks)

> This is a slight variation on the previous question. First of all you are offered the option of writing about as many explanations as you wish. The phrase 'two or more' tells you that two explanations are sufficient for full marks. The examples are given to prompt you – you don't have to write about all of them. In this question, the more general phrase 'gender development' has been used rather than either gender roles or gender identity, which makes life simpler.

3 Discuss psychological research (explanations **and/or** studies) into the factors that influence gender roles. (24 marks)

> 'Discuss' requires both description (AO1) and evaluation (AO2). In this essay there is no reference to any specific number of explanations or indeed to any explanations/theories. Instead the term 'research' is used. 'Research' is equivalent to either theories or studies (as indicated in the question), so you can describe any explanations or any studies, or both. You need to be careful to indicate how the theories or studies are being used – what is AO1 and what is AO2. A study that is used for evaluation should be introduced by saying, for example, 'This is supported by a study ...' You should then focus on what the findings/conclusions tell us and then might, for example, consider whether methodological flaws challenge the validity of the conclusions.

4 (a) Describe **one** explanation of the development of gender roles. (12 marks)
(b) To what extent is the explanation of the development of gender roles that you described in part (a) supported by research studies? (12 marks)

> In parted questions, material may be 'exported' to a different part of the answer (for the purpose of determining marks) if it is not relevant. This means that if you included evaluation in part (a), that material might be exported but, in this case, only if it concerned research studies. Some candidates fail to part their answers to parted questions and the danger is that they fail to notice the particular requirements of part (b).

WHAT IS ADOLESCENCE?

Adolescence is a transitional period between childhood and adulthood. *Biologically*, this period begins when the individual enters puberty and ends on reaching sexual maturity. *Psychologically*, there are a number of levels on which the individual makes the transition to adulthood (e.g. social, emotional and cognitive) which do not have clear beginnings and ends.

There are many questions about adolescence:

- What psychological development takes place during adolescence, especially in terms of identity?
- Is adolescence necessarily a time of conflict?
- What relationships are important during adolescence?
- To what extent are there cultural differences?

SOCIAL DEVELOPMENT IN ADOLESCENCE

Unit 18 describes how children's minds develop as they get older. Piaget reported an important biological change about the time of puberty, namely that the child moves from the stage of concrete operations to the stage of formal operations, and becomes capable of abstract thinking and systematic rational thought. Such intellectual changes have many important consequences: they enable the adolescent to reach a higher level of moral development and become more critical in their thinking, tackling more complex academic subjects. These changes also enable adolescents to think in new ways about themselves.

Development of autonomy

Earlier in this unit, we saw that Freud identified puberty and adolescence as the *genital stage*, when a child focuses again on genitals but also on the development of independence. Blos (1967) took up Freud's ideas and suggested that adolescence was like a second period of 'individuation'. The first period of individuation took place when the infant became a self-reliant toddler. In adolescence, the individual is again achieving independence ('re-individuation'). Adolescents may typically overreact to parental authority and be at pains to assert their individuality. This separation from parents, according to Blos, results in an emotional emptiness that is satisfied by group experiences. The

ACTIVITY

Your experience of adolescence

Reflect on your own adolescence. In what way do you feel that adolescence has been different to childhood in terms of:

- the degree of closeness or conflict you have experienced with parents
- your relationships with other family members
- your relationships with peers?

What would you regard as you main 'task' during this period of psychological development? Is it becoming independent, deciding about your future, establishing an identity, or something else?

striving for independence may also lead to regression to more childlike behaviour, which Blos regarded as a healthy and necessary response. Regression may be to a more infantile state in order to receive substitute parenting, or regression may take the form of hero worship that can act as a substitute parent. Blos also believed that rebellion was important as a means of ego defence in order to prevent adolescents becoming dependent on their parents again.

Commentary
Blos' concept of deindividuation

- *Independent but connected?* – The notion that independence is part of healthy adolescent development may be an oversimplification. More recent research suggests that autonomy develops best when it is accompanied by continuing attachment to parents – independence and *connectedness* leading to healthy development.

'Connectedness' does not mean dependence but describes how independence can only occur when an individual continues to have a *secure base*, in the same way that infant exploration is related to a secure base and secure attachment (Ainsworth *et al.* 1970). Adolescents who are securely attached to their parents have greater self-esteem, better emotional adjustment, are less likely to engage in problem behaviours and are physically healthier (Cooper *et al.* 1998).

Development of identity

Adolescence is traditionally seen as a time of identity formation. Prior to adolescence the child has established a sense of identity, but this is challenged by the physical changes of puberty, increasing independence and the child's new intellectual abilities.

Erikson's account of psychosocial development

Erikson (1968) described the period from age 12 to 18 as one of 'identity versus role confusion'. This period of development is one of the eight stages that people go through in their development (see p. 621 for an outline of all eight stages). Erikson's theory was derived from Freud's notion that at various stages in life an individual is presented with a conflict, which must be resolved successfully for healthy psychological development to occur. Erikson (1968) suggested that these conflicts were psycho*social* rather than Freud's psycho*sexual* crises – resolving social rather than physical conflicts. During adolescence the crisis to be resolved is the conflict between *identity* and *role confusion*. If the crisis is resolved, the outcome is 'a subjective sense of an invigorating sameness and continuity' (Erikson 1968, p. 19). This enables an individual to cope well with the demands of life and, importantly, to be able to form adult relationships. If the crisis is not resolved, the result is identity confusion, when an adolescent remains uncertain and unable to make commitments to life choices. Erikson identified four kinds of behaviour related to identity confusion:

- *Negative identity* – Adopting an extreme identity, such as taking on the role of a delinquent or a drug-abuser, provides some sense of control and independence from others.
- *Intimacy* – The adolescent avoids intimacy because of fear of losing their own fragile sense of identity. This may result in isolation or the formation of stereotyped relationships, such as the kind of popstar worship characteristic of some teenagers.
- *Time perspective* – The role-confused adolescent avoids making plans for the future because such plans mean thinking about the future and the complexities of being an adult, all of which provoke feelings of anxiety.
- *Industry* – Adolescents find it difficult to get their level of 'industry' right. They either compulsively overwork or they find it hard to concentrate.

During the stage of adolescence, role confusion is healthy. The adolescent considers different roles: what job do I want to do, what religious and political beliefs should I hold, and so on. During this period of 'confusion', Erikson proposed that an adolescent will experience a 'psychosocial moratorium', i.e. a temporary suspension of activity. Adolescents would use this time to adopt certain attitudes or occupations temporarily in order to decide which suited them best. Role sampling is a way of establishing one's own identity, the dominant task for this age group. Resolution of this role confusion results in formation of an adult identity.

Evaluation
Erikson's psychosocial theory

Support for Erikson's theory

- *Empirical support* – There is some empirical support for Erikson's theory, most notably Marcia's research reported below. Erikson's theory was based on his own experiences as a psychoanalyst working with adolescents and adults. He also based his developmental ideas on extensive interviews with Dakota Indians.

- *Adolescence as crisis* – Further support comes from research which suggests that adolescents are in a state of crisis. For example, Smith and Crawford (1986) found that more than 60 per cent of students in secondary school reported having suicidal thoughts. However, other research (see below) suggests that adolescence is not a time of crisis.

Challenges to Erikson's theory

- *Androcentrism* – The theory is androcentric, written by a man and more applicable to male behaviour. It portrays male values of independence, autonomy and achievement as 'healthy', and ignores female values such as mutuality and interdependence. Erikson also suggested a gender difference for male and female development – female identity depends on finding a partner first, whereas for males, identity precedes relationship development. This difference may reflect women's roles 40 years ago rather than a universal difference in development.

- *Eurocentrism* – Identity development is important in individualist societies (such as the UK) but may be unimportant in collectivist groups that emphasize the importance of 'we' rather than 'I'. In addition, Kroger (1996) suggests that identity and role choice only occur in industrialized societies where there are choices.

- *Historical bias* – Erikson's conception that identity formation is related to role decisions may be dated. The notion of finding a 'job for life' may be less true today than it was 40 years ago.

- *Adolescence is not a time of turmoil* – Evidence discussed below suggests that adolescence is not necessarily a time of stress and conflict. It may be that this 'turmoil' view of adolescence (and all development) was because Erikson's theory was based on life histories of abnormal individuals.

Marcia's theory

Erikson's ideas were largely theoretical and others, such as Marcia (1966), have reformulated them so they could be tested empirically. For a description of Marcia's research, read the Key research panel below.

Marcia's research into adolescent identity (1966)

Marcia tested Erikson's ideas by interviewing adolescents, asking them about their 'identity status' in areas such as occupation, religion, politics and attitudes about sex. For example, he would ask: 'Have you ever had any doubts about your religious beliefs?' He then analysed the answers and decided that they could basically be placed in one of four categories or 'identity statuses':

- *Identity diffusion or confusion* – In this stage the individual hasn't even started to think about the issues. They might respond, 'My parents are churchgoers but I've never given it any thought'.

- *Identity foreclosure* – An individual in this stage has prematurely formed an opinion which is not based on individual consideration. For example, they may have unquestioningly taken on conventional attitudes as a means of avoiding the uncertainties of thinking for themselves.

- *Identity moratorium* – This is similar to Erikson's concept of a stage when decisions about identity are put on hold while the adolescent may 'try on' various possibilities.

- *Identity achievement* – This occurs when an adolescent has been through the period of confusion or crisis, and achieved their own identity. For example, 'I've thought a lot about alternative religions and feel most in tune with the far Eastern beliefs'. This is seen as the most mature status.

The most likely route for an adolescent would be to start at identity diffusion, to proceed to moratorium, possibly via foreclosure, and to end with identity achievement. However, the four statuses are not necessarily sequential – some adolescents may skip certain stages, though Marcia found that moratorium appears to be a prerequisite for identity achievement. Marcia (1980) argued that adolescent identity formation involves both crisis and commitment. Crisis occurs through having to re-evaluate previous choices and values. Commitment happens after this re-evaluation, when the individual takes on a set of roles and ideologies. The four stages of adolescent development can be categorized in terms of commitment and crisis (see Table 19.5 below).

Table 19.5 >> Four identity statuses proposed by Marcia (1980)

	High degree of crisis	Low degree of crisis
High degree of commitment to a particular role or value	**Identity achievement status** (crisis is past)	**Foreclosure status** (crisis not gone through, but commitment made)
Low degree of commitment to a particular role or value	**Moratorium status** (in the midst of the crisis and no commitment made)	**Identity diffusion status** (not in crisis and no commitment made, perhaps because in pre- or post-crisis)

Evaluation
Marcia's approach

- *An empirical theory* – Marcia's intention was to provide a stage theory that could be empirically investigated, and many researchers have done this. Meilman (1979) looked at 12- to 24-year-old males and found that the percentage of individuals rated as identity achievers rose steadily after the age of 15. However, at age 24 only 50 per cent were classed as identity achievers, which means that a lot of people had not resolved this stage.

continued on next page

- *Research support* – Marcia's identity statuses were further supported by Waterman (1985), who used data from several cross-sectional studies of 11- to 21-year-olds. He found a decrease in diffusion status and an increase in identity achievement with age. Moratorium was quite uncommon at all ages, and a total of 33 per cent were in foreclosure. Identity achievement occurred somewhat later than Erikson predicted, but this is probably explained by the fact that most of the participants studied were college students who tend to postpone adult status.

- *Historical bias* – A study by Waterman and Waterman (1975) found that there may be cohort effects, in other words that people during particular historical periods behave differently. They studied fathers and sons and found that the sons were mainly classed as identity moratorium or identity diffusion, whereas the fathers were in identity foreclosure. It is possible that the fathers, who grew up in the pre-war period, were encouraged to achieve this kind of adult identity. This suggests a flaw in both Erikson's and Marcia's theories – that they are relevant to a historical period and a particular culture.

- *Oversimplification* – The idea of a single identity may be an oversimplification. Archer (1982) used Marcia's interview technique and found that only 5 per cent of those interviewed were classed in the same identity status for occupational choice, gender role, religious values and political ideology; 90 per cent were in two or three different stages across all four areas. For example, someone might be in 'identity confusion' as regards their sexual attitudes, but be in 'identity achievement' in terms of their occupational choice. This suggests that Marcia and Erikson's views offer an oversimplified account of a more complex picture.

Storm and stress

Erikson described adolescence as a time of conflict – but then he suggested that every stage of development involved conflict. The view that adolescence is a period of 'storm and stress' or *'Sturm und Drang'* stems from the writings of various 19th-century German writers such as Goethe. This idea was taken on by G. Stanley Hall (1904), one of the founders of developmental psychology. He suggested that during adolescence a child must experience the turbulent history of the human race in order to reach maturity. This so-called 'recapitulation theory' has little real foundation. Nevertheless, Hall's adaptation of the 'storm and stress' concept has had a lasting influence on both popular culture and psychological theories.

Adolescence is stressful

As already mentioned, Smith and Crawford (1986) found a high rate of suicidal thoughts in adolescents, suggesting that they were experiencing a high level of inner turmoil. This was supported by the Chicago study (Csikszentmihalyi and Larson 1984) which collected data about 75 American high-school students by contacting them at frequent intervals using pagers. Each time, the teenagers had to record their mood and other information. The Chicago study found that adolescent experiences are marked by frequent and drastic mood changes, some of which occur within very short periods of time. They suggested that the mood swings were a consequence of the never-ending conflict between the goals and rules of society and the instincts, values and habits of the adolescent.

Cross-cultural evidence

It is possible that the experience of 'storm and stress' is due to cultural pressures rather simply a natural part of the process of reaching psychological maturity. Studies of adolescence in other cultures suggest that 'storm and stress' are not the norm all over the world. Margaret Mead's classic book, *Coming of Age in Samoa* (1928), described how boys and girls growing up on the South Sea island of Samoa experienced a relatively easy passage from childhood to adulthood. She noted that, in that culture, sexuality was dealt with in an open, casual manner and children were therefore spared the guilt, anxiety and confusion that many Western children experience. She suggested that the turmoil that some adolescents experience may be due to the pressures of growing up in an industrialized society where they are faced with a large choice of opportunities and decisions. In a small, rural community there are very few choices to be made and this may explain why there is no identity crisis. Mead's advice was that we should recognize the stress that is caused by life choices and prepare adolescents more carefully.

Bronfenbrenner (1974) compared child-rearing patterns in the USSR and the USA, and found that Russian adolescents showed more pro-social behaviour and less of the antisocial behaviour common in the American adolescents. One reason for this finding could be that Russian youths had more opportunities to integrate with adult society early on, whereas the American youths tended to be segregated and discouraged from entering adulthood. The greater degree of conflict shown by the American youths could, therefore, have resulted from the development of a youth sub-culture distinguishing itself from adults by adopting a different set of values and norms.

Evaluation
Storm and stress in adolescence

- *What causes storm and stress?* – This research supports the view that it is Western culture that creates conflicts for adolescents. The conclusion appears to be that 'storm and stress', where it does occur in any society, may be due to the way adults handle adolescence rather than as a consequence of the stage of transition itself.
- *Accuracy of cross-cultural research* – We have to be cautious when considering cross-cultural research because it is prone to many difficulties. Freeman (1983) criticized Mead's conclusions, arguing that she was not sufficiently closely involved with the Samoan people and that she saw only what she wanted to see. He argued that she may not have established sufficient trust with the Samoan people to expect total honesty from them. For example, one woman told Freeman that she had not been honest with Mead about her sexual experiences. It is hard to know whether Mead or Freeman provides the more accurate account. Mead studied women, while Freeman's research was based on studying males. In addition, these two studies took place at different times – the influence of Western ideas on the Samoans from Christian missionaries and American air-base staff might have brought about change.

Explaining adolescent turmoil

It appears that some adolescents experience an emotionally difficult time during adolescence, but this is certainly less true for adolescents in other cultures and it also is not true of all adolescents in Western culture. A classic study by Rutter *et al.* (1976) reported that adolescent turmoil was rare. The Isle of Wight study involved over 2,000 14-/15-year-olds and their parents and teachers. The general picture was one of good relationships between parents and their teenage children with growing mutual trust and appreciation. Clinical depression was rarely found, although 1 in 5 reported often feeling miserable or depressed, leading Rutter and colleagues to query whether adolescence is any different from other stages of life in this respect. To test this idea, the incidence of psychiatric disorder in a group of 10-year-olds was compared with that in 14-/15-year-olds and this showed only a modest increase in the teenagers (from about 11 per cent of 10-year-olds to 13 per cent of 14-/15-year-olds).

Rutter and colleagues concluded that adolescent turmoil does exist but its importance has probably been overestimated in the past.

Coleman (1974) has attempted to explain the conflicting findings about adolescence. Adolescents have a number of issues to deal with: changing physical appearance, increase in sexual feelings, desire for friendships, increasing autonomy and so on. Such issues are in addition to those that individuals face at any age, such as parents who separate, illness, and problems in personal relationships. This means that adolescents have more issues to cope with than at other ages but, as long as there are only a few issues at any one time, the adolescent can 'focus' on these issues and is able to cope. Thus Coleman called his theory 'focal theory'. Coleman did not agree with Erikson that crisis and conflict were inevitable and healthy, but they are more likely in adolescence than at other times because of the additional issues that have to be dealt with.

Evaluation
focal theory

- *Research support* – Coleman supported his theory with research (Coleman and Hendry 1990). A large group of adolescents (800 boys and girls aged 11 to 17 years old) were questioned about topics which were anxiety provoking, such as self-image, being alone, occupational choice, and peer, sexual and parental relationships. The results showed that each issue seemed to have a different distribution curve, peaking in importance over a particular age. Concerns about peer relations, for example, peaked earlier than occupational choice. In addition, some adolescents came to these issues earlier than normal, and others experienced them later. The coincidence of a number of important issues all peaking at once could cause problems, but generally, adolescents navigate carefully through this stage of life, choosing whether to engage with particular issues immediately or later.

continued on next page

- *Practical applications* – Coleman's theory has clear practical applications related to dealing with adolescent stress. Troubled adolescents might be advised to reduce the number of issues they are currently coping with and to focus on a few at a time.

- *Storm and stress?* – If Coleman is right, then why is the 'storm and stress' view perpetuated? One reason may be that some psychological theories have been developed by psychiatrists who have based their ideas on the biased samples of troubled adolescents with whom they

worked. A second reason may be 'media amplification'. Certain adolescent behaviours, such as vandalism and drug taking, are often reported sensationally in the media and this creates an exaggerated picture of the problem in the eyes of the general public.

- *Alternative explanation* – Eccles *et al.* (1993) suggested that the reason many adolescents experience stress is because of the mismatch between their developing needs and the opportunities afforded to them by their social environments. Indeed, in some Western cultures, adolescents would appear to be held in a state of moratorium by laws that block access to the adult world, such as the minimum school-leaving age and minimum voting age.

RELATIONSHIPS IN ADOLESCENCE

There are many sources of social influence during adolescence, such as the media, parents and peers. One view of adolescent social development is that it is a time of transition from 'parent orientation' to 'peer orientation'. Traditionally, adolescence is seen as a time of becoming independent from parents and experiencing conflicts with them and authority figures.

Relationships with parents

Autonomy

The traditional view of adolescence, as discussed earlier, was one of growing independence from parents, whereas more recent research indicates an important role for parents in the development of autonomy. Connectedness and secure attachment promote healthy development in both infancy and adolescence. Further support for this comes from a study by Apter (1990) who studied 65 mother–daughter pairs in the US and the UK, and found that most of the adolescent girls said that the person they felt closest to was their mother. They might have minor quarrels, but these might be best understood as attempts to change the power balance of the parent–child relationship from a one-sided one of parental authority to a more equal adult relationship.

Identity

Waterman (1982) reviewed a number of studies that looked at the relationship between parenting styles and identity development. He concluded that domineering parenting is associated with identity foreclosure, whereas moratorium and identity achievement are connected with a more warm, democratic style. Noller and Callan (1991) suggested that this is because democratic parents impose less rigid moral standards which allow their children to explore alternative identities. A strong sense of connectedness has also

been related to the development of identity. Connectedness provides a warm, secure base for exploration. Archer and Waterman (1994) found that when connectedness is weak, adolescents often display an identity confusion status.

Conflict

The traditional view of adolescence is one of conflict with parents. Research suggests that conflict is at its highest in early adolescence, but decreases with age (Santrock 2001). Most of the conflict appears to be related to the normal, everyday events of family life, such as household chores, family rules, personal habits and family obligations, whereas conflicts about major issues such as sex, drugs, religion and politics are much less frequent during the early years of adolescence. Montemayor (1982) found that, on average, adolescents had one argument every three days for 11 minutes. The fact that conflicts are mainly 'mild' supports the 'healthy' nature of adolescent–parent rows as a means of achieving individuation.

Many studies report that conflicts are more likely between mothers and their daughters. For example, Laursen (1995) reported that most adolescent conflicts were with mothers followed by friends, romantic partners and fathers. This may be explained by the fact that boys become independent from their mothers at an early age whereas girls have an 'interconnectedness' with their mothers (Gilligan *et al.* 1990).

Although not necessarily the cause of adolescent–parent conflict, adolescents' relationships with their parents are certainly affected by parenting style. Baumrind (1991) suggested that there are two key dimensions to parenting styles: responsiveness and demandingness. *Authoritative* parenting, which is a combination of consistent parental responsiveness and demandingness, has been linked by many studies with social competence, positive emotional adjustment, higher school performance and overall maturity in childhood and adolescence. In contrast, parents whose style is permissive, authoritarian, neglectful or

indifferent may encounter conflicts when their children enter adolescence (Steinberg and Morris 2001). However, this may be a cultural matter, as studies of adolescence in India show low levels of conflict despite highly authoritarian parenting (Larson 1999).

A02

Evaluation
research into relationships with parents

- *Oversimplification of family relationships –* Studies that relate parenting styles to adolescent behaviour oversimplify complex family relationships. No parent uses one single parenting style, though one style may dominate. 'Adaptive' parenting may be the best strategy, where a parent responds to different situations with permissiveness, authoritativeness and authoritarianism as appropriate (Santrock 2001).

- *A two-way process –* Parents are also socialized by their adolescent children. The parent–adolescent relationship is a two-way relationship. Parents benefit from their relationships with adolescent offspring. For example, Montemayor *et al.* (1993) found mid-life stress in fathers was negatively correlated with

quality of interaction between them and their adolescent children.

- *Parental conflict –* Conflict may be created by parents rather than adolescents. Parents are also stressed by the experience of having adolescent children. Benin (1997) found that marital dissatisfaction was higher when offspring were adolescents rather than children or adults. Parental stress may lead to parent–adolescent conflicts. Furthermore, the ethological view, relating human behaviour to animal behaviour, suggests that adolescence is a time when children should be 'kicked out of the nest'. There may be an innate drive in parents to sever ties and create conflict with their adolescent children.

- *Gender and cultural differences –* Parental relationships have been found to be more important for boys than girls (Frey and Rothlisberger 1996). In other cultures, such as India, adolescents continue to have closer and more subordinate relationships with parents (Larsen 1999).

Relationships with peers

In adolescence, peer relationships assume a major role. Frey and Rothlisberger (1996) found that adolescents had twice as many relationships with peers than family. During childhood, friendships are important but, in adolescence, these become deeper and take on extra importance in relation to the 'psychological tasks' facing adolescents, such as autonomy and independence. In childhood, relationships with parents were stronger but now peers take over.

Peer relationships are different to relationships with parents. Piaget (1932) argued that parent–child relationships consist of unilateral control whereas peer relationships are more egalitarian. Children conform to parents' rules and regulations because parents have authority and greater knowledge. Peers evolve standards of behaviour that are mutually acceptable.

Autonomy

Blos (1967) offered an explanation for the importance of the peer group. He suggested that peers provide a 'way-station' on the road to achieving separation and individuation because they help the adolescent to avoid feelings of loneliness without having to make any commitment. Kirchler *et al.* (1991) have pointed out that adolescents who do not develop peer relationships and who stick to their families may have trouble establishing their autonomy and engaging in adult

relationships. The peer group in adolescence can therefore be seen to play an important role.

Steinberg and Silverberg (1986) suggest that the security of peer acceptance provides adolescents with the necessary confidence to break away from parental dependence. In a study of American 10- to 16-year-olds, Steinberg and Silverberg found that as autonomy increased, peer involvement also increased and was strongest between the ages of 11 and 13. This would seem to support Blos, although Ryan and Lynch (1989) suggest that the findings could be interpreted differently. It could be that those children who engage most in peer relations are doing so because they have failed to get adequate emotional satisfaction at home.

Peer friendships provide warmth and support, i.e. peers become attachment figures who provide a secure base for independent exploration. In later adolescence, attachments change again, this time from peer attachments, which require little commitment, to more intimate 'romantic' relationships. Erikson claimed that such romantic relationships were only possible if the individual has successfully resolved their identity crisis.

Identity

Erikson (1968) suggested that peers are important for healthy identity development because they allow adolescents to explore different ideologies, test their ability to form intimate relationships with others and help them to relinquish their psychological dependence on parents. Peers also provide adolescents with a means of knowing themselves. Self-knowledge comes through seeing oneself in the reactions of others (Cooley 1902) and in making comparisons with others. Many self-concepts are comparative terms, such as 'tall' or 'clever', and therefore require standards to be set by others.

A part of adolescent peer relationships is the formation of 'cliques', a small group of friends who interact frequently. Cliques are important for the development of identity because they provide an adolescent with a 'group' or 'social identity' (Coleman 1961). Each of us has a number of social identities (the football team you support, the town you live in, the A levels you have chosen, etc.). Each of these identities influences our personal identity and affects our self-esteem. For example, if your football team wins, it makes you feel good. Brown and Lohr (1987) assessed self-esteem in students in one US high school, finding that those individuals who did not belong to any clique had the lowest self-esteem, whereas those in the most popular cliques (the 'jocks' and the 'socials' – sporty types and those leading social activities) had the highest self-esteem. However, it may be that low self-esteem is a reason why some adolescents did not join a clique rather than being caused by non-clique membership.

Conflict and peer conformity

A common stereotype of adolescents is that they behave in an anti-social manner. Parents fear that their adolescent children will be led by peer group pressure into drug-taking, crime and rebellion. Adolescents do identify with their peers and there are strong pressures to conform to peer pressure, for good reasons. Peers provide both informational and normative social influence (see Unit 5, p. 157). Physical changes in early adolescence and increasing interest in the opposite sex mean that adolescents want to know the 'right' way to present themselves. Adolescents also want to behave in ways that will make them liked by same- and opposite-sex peers.

Berndt (1979) conducted a classic study of peer conformity with American adolescents. He asked them questions about the likelihood of conformity in particular situations and found that, in general, conformity was greater for pro-social behaviour rather than anti-social behaviour. From early to mid-adolescence (about the age of 15), there is an increase in anti-social conformity but this then declines. Peer conformity probably declines in later adolescence because there is a growing focus on individual identity and individual romantic attachments, so interest in the peer group wanes.

Evaluation
research into relationships with peers

- *Lack of research support* – The stereotype of peer conformity is not supported by all research (Hartup 1983), and autonomy is an important part of adolescent development.

- *Peers may have a negative effect on development* – Adolescents who are actively disliked (rejected) by their peers or those who are friendless but not disliked (neglected) often have serious problems later in life, such as mental health and criminal problems. In some cases, rejected/neglected adolescents are quite aggressive and this is associated with delinquency (Kupersmidt and Coie 1990).

- *Parents and peers are not two different worlds* – Parents' choice of where to live means that they contribute to selecting who

their children's friends will be. Parents also give advice about peer relationships. Gauze (1994) found that adolescents talked to mothers rather than fathers about peer relationships. Also, good relationships with parents are fundamental for good relationships with peers. Adolescents who are securely attached to parents are also securely attached to peers (Armsden and Greenberg 1984).

- *Individual differences* – Fuligni and Eccles (1993) questioned nearly 2,000 11-year-olds, and found that peer orientation was higher in adolescents who rated their parents as more authoritarian and where adolescents felt they had few opportunities to be involved in decision-making. Adolescents who experience a democratic parenting style may rely less on their peers. Also, adolescents who lack emotional support at home may be more dependent on peers (Ryan and Lynch 1989).

CULTURAL DIFFERENCES IN ADOLESCENT BEHAVIOUR

If we took a strictly biological approach, we would expect the experience of adolescence to be universal. It isn't. The decade between 10 and 20 is a time of many changes or transitions in our culture – leaving school,

getting a job, going to university, leaving home, experiencing love and/or sex for the first time – this suggests that the experience of adolescence needs to be explained in terms of more than biology alone.

Autonomy

Jensen (1999) reviewed research on adolescence and concluded that some of the difficulties reported during adolescence might be related to living in an *individualist* society – a type of culture which values individual needs and independence. The quest for autonomy and independence might be unique to individualist societies as contrasted with *collectivist* societies, where individuals share tasks, belongings and income, and value interdependence. In a collectivist society such as Japan, *dependence* rather than independence is regarded as a central part of becoming an adult (Doi 1973). Gilani (1995) compared Asian and White British families, looking at family relationships with teenage daughters (examples of collectivist and individualist societies respectively). In Asian families, the wishes of the parents came first; girls were expected to conform to family values rather than establish independence.

In some cultures, relationships with parents remain strong. For example, in Italy, where family is more important than in the US, Claes (1998) found that family relationships remained strong in adolescents, whereas friends played a more important role for Canadian youths. Belgian teenagers were intermediate between the two extremes. These findings highlight the importance of cultural values in adolescent experiences.

Identity

Individualist versus collectivist cultures

Identity may also be unique to individualist societies. In Western cultures, group identities contribute to individual (self) identity. In contrast, in Chinese culture, individual identity ('the little me') is sacrificed for group identity ('the big me') (Dien 1983). In China, successful development is related to interdependence between group and individual identity.

Urban versus rural cultures

Life in a contemporary Western culture provides adolescents with many choices which are not available in non-industrialized, more rural communities. Tupuola (1993) interviewed youths born in Samoa who had come to live in New Zealand. The youths said that the concept of adolescence was completely new to them. In Samoa, there were no choices available about their adult identity. Adult roles are decided by the wider community and a child becomes an adult when they are regarded as mature. The transition from child to adult appears to become more delayed the more pluralized and fragmented a society becomes (Chisholm and Hurrelmann 1995), presumably because choices become greater and less clearly defined in more complex societies.

Difficulties with identity formation may be particularly problematic for youths in inner cities who often have little job choice and where the jobs that are available are not very desirable. This, together with a lack of community standards, leads youths to turn to illegal activities or not working or both (Wilson 1987), all of which makes identity achievement difficult. The existence of such cultural differences means that Marcia's outline of identity development cannot be universally applied.

Ethnic minorities

Identity has many components, including ethnicity. Identity formation may be especially difficult for adolescents belonging to ethnic minorities. For many of them it is the first time they have consciously become aware of their ethnicity. Phinney (1996) defined ethnic identity as 'an enduring, basic aspect of the self that includes a sense of membership in an ethnic group and the attitudes and feelings related to that membership'.

Berry (1997) proposed that there are four routes that can be taken by members of ethnic minorities:

- *assimilation* – identifying with dominant culture and rejecting ethnic origins
- *integration* – identifying with both dominant and ethnic cultures
- *separation* – focus exclusively on ethnic culture and reject dominant culture
- *marginality* – remain on fringes of both cultures.

Research has found that integration is associated with better adjustment in adolescents (White and Burke 1987). Another study found that those ethnic minority college students who had resolved issues related to ethnicity had higher self-esteem than those who didn't (Phinney and Alipuria 1990). However, there are many barriers to resolving ethnicity. For example, there is often a lack of suitable ethnic role models, and ethnic minority groups are often portrayed negatively, both of which make it difficult for an adolescent to resolve their ethnic identity. In fact, they may feel they have to distance themselves from their ethnic origins and thus delay their identity achievement.

Conflict

We have already considered cross-cultural research related to the question of whether 'storm and stress' is a universal adolescent experience. The answer appears to be no. It may be that conflict is avoided because adolescence is a brief transitional period, if it occurs at all. In many non-industrialized rural communities, individuals move fairly abruptly from child to adult, a transition marked by 'rites of passage'. These rites are often quite dramatic and endowed with religious meaning. They make it clear that the child is now an adult, in contrast to Western cultures, where this transitional period is a stage of limbo and the individual is not allowed to be a child but is not given the status of an adult.

Historical change

The concept of culture can include historical as well as group differences. Shaffer (1993) claimed that adolescence is an 'invention' of the twentieth century. He argued that when it became illegal to employ children, this created a new section of the population, an 'adolescent peer culture', which was isolated from those who were younger and older. Until this time, there was no 'adolescent' phase. It was G. Stanley Hall, writing at the beginning of the twentieth century, who first identified this period of development. According to Gross (1996), the concept of a 'teenager' is even more recent, being coined in the 1950s. Adolescence is therefore historically a new conception, as well as being culturally specific.

Evaluation
cultural differences

- *The importance of cross-cultural research* – Cross-cultural research is important because it shows us to what extent social context affects adolescent development. Cultural values, such as individualism versus collectivism, have a major impact on adolescent development. This cultural influence is not surprising since adolescents are being socialized into becoming members of their society.

- *Problems with cross-cultural research* – In the past, studies of people in non-Western cultures were conducted by Western psychologists, who may have had difficulty understanding local people and may have recorded biased observations based on preconceived expectations. More recently, this situation has improved as more research is done by indigenous psychologists, who are better able to understand the populations they are studying. Nevertheless there are always sampling issues for any research and also there is the question of the extent to which people present themselves to psychologists (or anthropologists) so they appear as the psychologists want them to appear. Furthermore, psychologists may use tests and other measurement tools developed for Western participants, which are not appropriate for others.

- *Minimizing cultural differences* – Exposure to the universal culture of American media (television and internet) may reduce cultural differences. TV and the internet are establishing a universal and fairly American culture for today's adolescents. Programmes such as *Friends* and *Buffy the Vampire Slayer* create a new set of adolescent norms and values.

✓ CHECK YOUR UNDERSTANDING

Check your understanding of adolescence by answering these questions from memory at first. You can check your answers by looking back through Topic 3.

1   In what way is 'connectedness' important for healthy psychological development in adolescence?

2   According to Erikson, what conflict do adolescents have to resolve and what are the possible outcomes?

3   Identify three criticisms of Erikson's theory.

4   How is Marcia's research related to Erikson's theory?

5   Name Marcia's four identity statuses.

6   Outline the main principle of Coleman's focal theory.

7   What parenting style is linked to positive emotional adjustment and social competence in adolescents?

8   At what point in adolescence is peer conformity greatest?

9   What is 'ethnic identity' and what is the best way for ethnic minority adolescents to resolve their identity crisis?

10 In what kind of culture are you most likely to find that adolescents seek independence and personal identity?

REVISION SUMMARY

Having covered this topic you should be able to describe and evaluate:

✓ research into social development in adolescence (autonomy, dealing with crises and Coleman's focal theory)

✓ research into the formation of identity (Erikson and Marcia)

✓ research into relationships with parents during adolescence

✓ research into relationships with peers during adolescence

✓ cultural differences in adolescent behaviour.

 EXAMPLE EXAM QUESTIONS

Below are some **possible examination questions** set on this topic, along with hints to help you understand and approach each question effectively:

1 Discuss research (theories **and/or** studies) into social development in adolescence. (24 marks)

'Discuss' requires you to describe research and to evaluate it. You are permitted to consider theories (such as Erikson's) or studies (such as Marcia's) or both. It is possible to use the same theories or studies as description or evaluation, but you must use them differently. For example, you might describe Erikson's theory (AO1) and then use Marcia's study as a means of assessing (AO2) the validity of Erikson's theory. If you describe Marcia's research this will count as AO1.

2 Describe and evaluate research (theories **and/or** studies) into relationships with parents **and/or** peers during adolescence. (24 marks)

The focus of this question is again on research, but this time specifically into relationships between adolescents and parents and/or peers. Most candidates will discuss both kinds of research because they don't feel they know enough about one or the other. However, there is always the danger that you end up giving lots of information about a number of studies, but little detail about any of them. For top marks, detail and breadth should be balanced (the 'depth–breadth trade-off'), so it is important not simply to list all the studies you know, but perhaps only cover some of them, giving yourself sufficient time to provide detail and evaluate them.

3 (a) Describe research (theories **and/or** studies) into social development in adolescence. (12 marks)

(b) Assess the effects that relationships with parents and peers have on adolescent development. (12 marks)

This question combines elements of questions 1 and 2. For the AO1 part of the question, you are required to describe research into social development, as before. For the second half of the question, the AO2 part, you are required to *assess* the effects of parents and peers on adolescent development. This means you will gain no credit for *describing* any research but must *use* your knowledge of such research to comment on how both parents *and* peers affect adolescent development. For example, you might say that parents are important in providing a secure base for connectedness.

4 Critically consider research (theories **and/or** studies) into cultural differences in adolescent behaviour. (24 marks)

'Critically consider' is an AO1+AO2 term (see Table 32.1 on p. 937) which means you should describe research and also evaluate it. This evaluation may be done by drawing conclusions from any theory or study. Or you may comment upon methodological problems with cross-cultural research. Or you might consider the implications of a particular study for theories about adolescence, such as recognizing that adolescence is not seen as a time of turmoil in all cultures.

5 (a) Outline research (theories and/or studies) into social development in adolescence. (12 marks)

   (b) To what extent are there cultural differences in adolescent development? (12 marks)

> This question begins with an AO1 part focused on research into social development. The AO1 term 'outline' has been used instead of 'describe', which means that full marks will be given for a summary description of more than one theory or study, rather than one well-detailed one. In part (b), AO2 marks are awarded for a consideration of cultural differences. As this part of the question is AO2 only ('To what extent' is an AO2 term) you must avoid descriptions of any studies and aim to use your knowledge effectively to present an informed opinion about cultural differences in adolescence.

UNIT SUMMARY

Topic 1: Personality development

- **Freud's theory** of personality (**psychoanalysis**) concerns how **personality structures** (id, ego, superego) and **psychosexual stages** lead to adult personality traits. Conflicts between personality structures lead to **ego defences** (e.g. repression) and **unconsciously** motivated behaviour.

- Freud's theory is based on **biased case histories** of abnormal individuals (European, neurotic, largely female). There is some **experimental support** for concepts such as repression.

- The **social learning approach** emphasizes the importance of social interactions and reinforcement. Behaviours are acquired through observation, vicarious reinforcement and imitation, and are maintained through direct reinforcement.

- **Bandura's personality theory** is supported by research studies which show the effects of imitation (including disinhibition). Bandura further developed the theory to include reciprocal determinism and self-efficacy, both concepts which explain how the individual plays an active role in their own personality development.

- **Mischel's situationalist theory** proposed that personality is not consistent – any consistency only occurs because people tend to be in similar situations. We learn behaviours through selective reinforcement (behavioural specificity). Mischel's findings have been challenged, as subsequent studies have found much greater consistency when scores are aggregated.

Topic 2: Gender development

- The development of **gender identity** and of **understanding gender roles** can be explained in terms of social and biological factors.

- **Social learning theory** suggests that children learn gender identity and gender roles either from direct reinforcement (e.g. parents) or from observation and vicarious reinforcement (e.g. media).

- Social learning theory was further developed into **social cognitive theory**, a theory that emphasizes modelling (observing gender behaviour), enactive experience (selective reinforcement and self-regulation) and direct tuition (direct reinforcement).

- Social learning theory and social cognitive theory explain **cultural differences** but overlook **biological determinants**.

- **Cognitive-developmental theories** suggest that children's thinking about gender changes as a consequence of **maturation** and thus follows a fixed sequence.

- **Kohlberg** proposed that gender identity (physical characteristics) and gender stability (stable across time) come first and finally gender constancy (consistency across time and situations, about age 7), at which point children identify with members of their own gender and only then seek information about gender-appropriate behaviour.

- **Martin and Halverson** propose that such active seeking about gender information (**schemas**) starts at age 3, as soon as a child recognizes its own gender. It is possible that the contradiction between these two theories occurs because **gender schema theory** focuses on acquiring schemas (memory processes) whereas **Kohlberg** focuses on performance (motivational factors).

Topic 3: Adolescence

- **Psychoanalytic psychologists** (Freud, Blos) propose that adolescence is a second period of individuation, a time to establish autonomy from parents and rebel. However, healthy development may be related to connectedness as well as independence.

- **Erikson**, a neo-Freudian, proposed that in adolescence, the conflict between **identity and role confusion** must be resolved order to cope with the demands of adult life and adult relationships. **Marcia** developed a set of **identity statuses** in order to investigate Erikson's theory further: diffusion, foreclosure, moratorium and achievement. Both Erikson and Marcia's research may be oversimplified, androcentric, Eurocentric and historically biased.

- The view that adolescence is a time of **storm and stress** is supported by some Western research but not found in other cultures, suggesting that Western culture creates stress.

- Relationships with **parents** are important in adolescence, though probably less so than with **peers**. Warm, democratic **parenting styles** are important for identity development; **authoritative parenting** is associated with reduced conflicts and healthy development.

- Relationships with **peers** act as a way-station and secure base for achieving autonomy and independence. Peers also help **identity formation** through exploring different ideologies (Erikson), social comparison and group identities (**cliques**).

- Autonomy is important in **individualist cultures**; dependence on families is common in **collectivist societies** and those where family values are strong. Ethnic minority adolescents have to consider their **ethnic identity** for healthy development; **integration** with dominant and ethnic cultures is best. **Conflict** may be reduced in non-Western cultures because the transition between childhood and adulthood is short and marked by an abrupt **rite of passage**.

FURTHER RESOURCES

Coleman, J.C. and Hendry, L.B. (1999) *The Nature of Adolescence* (3rd edn), London: Routledge.

Part of the Routledge series on 'adolescence and society' edited by John Coleman. Full of fairly up-to-date research on all areas of adolescence.

Hall, C.S., Lindzey, G. and Campbell, J.B. (1997) *Theories of Personality*, New York: John Wiley.

This latest revision of a classic textbook on personality theory includes some excellent descriptions of relevant research, although much more detail than is required for A-level studies.

Santrock, J.W. (2001) *Adolescence* (8th edn), Boston: McGraw Hill.

American textbook on adolescence. Vast amount of research with many interesting and useful features and summaries.

Smith, P.K., Cowie, H. and Blades, M. (1998) *Understanding Children's Development* (3rd edn), Oxford: Blackwell.

This clearly written text contains some useful material on gender development and adolescence.

Websites

http://intropsych.mcmaster.ca/psych2b3/general/links.html

Links to sites related to various personality theories.

www.emory.edu/EDUCATION/mfp/effpage.html

Links to many aspects of Bandura's work, such as social cognitive theory and self-efficacy.

www.freud.org.uk/

The Freud museum site with some background theory and useful links.

www.mead2001.org/default.htm

Details of Margaret Mead's cross-cultural research.

20 UNIT

Adulthood

PREVIEW

After you have read this unit, you should be able to describe and evaluate:

>> theories of development in early and middle adulthood

>> evidence for the existence of crises and transitions in early and middle adulthood

>> research into family and relationships in adulthood, including factors associated with marriage (or partnering), divorce and parenthood

>> research into cognitive changes in late adulthood.

INTRODUCTION

In a song for his son, John Lennon wrote 'Life is what happens to you while you're busy making other plans' and Woody Allen once remarked 'Life is hard and then you die'. Until the latter half of the 20th century, psychologists had little more to say about development over the entire course of life than this. Adulthood, in particular, which for many of us could last for over 50 years, was relatively ignored. In fact, Levinson (1978) remarked that adulthood was 'one of the best kept secrets in our society' (p. ix). Now we can ignore it no longer. This unit takes adulthood as its main theme and presents a selection of the existing theories and research in this increasingly complex area.

We all realize that psychological development does not stop once we reach adulthood. However, compared to the well-defined milestones of our growing-up years, we may be rather vague about what to expect next. Early and middle adulthood are times of immense change (sometimes even crisis) and adjustment. Our increasing openness about and preoccupation with this feeds the scriptwriters of such long-running series as *Coronation Street, Friends* and *Hollyoaks*. Through these, we can experience at second hand the growing pains of adults at various life stages. As we watch the characters cope with the demands of marriage/partnering, parenthood, divorce and bereavement (often at unusual ages and stages, for dramatic effect), it is evident that, as in reality, one size does not fit all. Our individual life-courses may have some similarities, but they are also unique. Thus, understanding this lengthy stage of unpredictable development, and its associated challenges, provides a unique test of psychologists' research skills.

The mass media constantly remind us that we live in an ageing society. As life expectancy increases, the life style of the elderly is changing. With improvements in living conditions and health care, people can expect not only to live longer but also to provide for themselves for longer. There are ongoing discussions about the adequacy of existing and future pensions to support people in an extended retirement, especially if retirement is taken early. At the same time, there are concerns about loss of skills from the workforce in cases where elderly people, with a wealth of experience, are expected or forced to retire at a particular age. As the population ages, the value placed on a self-sufficient, skilled, elderly workforce is likely to increase and retirement age is likely to become more flexible. Psychologists are well placed to investigate cognitive changes in those people who work into late adulthood. This knowledge can inform us about how to cope with the nature and needs of an ageing population.

Alison Wadeley

Doting grandparents? Actually, the baby is this couple's first child

Playing with their younger brother? No, this couple became parents in their teens

Neugarten (1968) referred to a 'social clock', by which she meant that we have stereotypical ideas about the 'right' time to do things in our lives such as become parents. The couple in the photograph on the left have become parents for the first time later in life, whereas the couple on the right are still barely into adulthood. Compared to a couple who become parents in their twenties, consider the following issues:

1 The arrival of the couples' first babies marks a transition to parenthood. For many new parents this is a crisis requiring enormous adjustment. How might such adjustment differ for these two couples? Consider the experience of fathers and mothers separately as well as that of the couple.

2 Assuming the 'social clock' is otherwise on time for these couples, what other life events might they be dealing with at the same time as learning to be parents? How might these differ between the couples?

3 When these two babies become adults, what stage will their parents have reached and how might this affect the young adults' own adulthood?

Adulthood: the period when one has matured or grown to full size and strength. May be arbitrarily defined in the UK as the period between 16 or 18 years, and death.

Activity theory: proposition that individuals prefer to remain active and productive in later life, even resisting disengagement from society – contrasts with social disengagement theory.

Social disengagement theory: proposition that healthy ageing is a gradual and mutual process of separation between individuals and their social roles and interests.

Psychosocial theory: the view that personality continues to develop throughout adulthood, with an emphasis on social forces as important in shaping personality.

Selectivity theory: proposition that focuses on the way in which social relationships, and the needs they fulfil, change with age.

Crystallized intelligence: the ability to store and manipulate learned information.

Fluid intelligence: a general, problem-solving ability that we bring to bear on novel or unfamiliar problems.

Terminal drop: the notion that there is little decline in intellectual functioning until about the last five years of life.

This topic looks at three stage theories of adult personality development. The focus of attention will be on early and middle adulthood, roughly spanning the ages of 20 to 60, but we will at times need to draw in earlier and later stages of development so that the context in which each stage occurs is clear. After clarifying some important terminology, we will consider some of the general methodological problems faced in studying adulthood.

ADULTHOOD, AGEING AND METHODOLOGICAL ISSUES

What is adulthood?

A general definition of the term 'adulthood' is 'to have matured or to have grown to full size and strength'. In psychology, some theorists have focused their definitions on specific aspects of development. Freud, for example, thought that adults were in the 'genital stage' of personality development (see Unit 19, p. 590), while Piaget suggested that adults had reached the 'formal operational stage' of intellectual development (see Unit 18, p. 553). Others prefer more general definitions. To them, adulthood is not an unchanging state or even just a steady decline to death. Baltes and Baltes (1990), for example, prefer to see adulthood as a time of, often positive, development and change with gains and losses along the way. This development and change occurs on many different fronts and these work together to affect the whole person (see 'Transitions to adulthood' below).

Types of ageing

Ageing measured in terms of time (e.g. in years) is known as 'chronological' age and so starts from the moment of conception, but this type of ageing becomes a less useful concept for understanding development once we have matured. There are three additional types:

- *biological ageing* – changes in bodily functions and in bodily tissues and organs
- *psychological ageing* – mental reactions to growing older and how one sees oneself
- *social ageing* – how individuals relate to society as they grow older. Neugarten (1968) used the term 'social clock' to describe society's timetable mapping out what we should do at different times of life (e.g. have children, retire). Successful social ageing may depend on whether we are in time with the social clock, as well as on whether society reveres or rejects its older members.

These four types of ageing may synchronize with each other or be out of step; either way, they exert an important influence on how we cope with adulthood.

Transitions to adulthood

How do we know when someone has reached adulthood? Many cultures mark the onset of puberty in recognition that childhood is drawing to a close and the transition to adulthood has begun. Many tribal and village cultures have highly ritualized procedures, e.g. following girls' first menstrual period or attainment of a particular age. The role of the adolescent may then change quite markedly. In certain religions there may be ceremonies such as the Jewish bar mitzvah (for boys) or Christian confirmation (for either sex) but the roles played by these adolescents may not change in any perceptible way. In the UK, there is a variety of legally defined transitions which adolescents make according to age, e.g. the right to marry, to vote, to buy and consume alcohol and cigarettes, to drive or leave school. The eighteenth birthday is often a critical point, but in the absence of clear guidelines, adulthood in many western cultures is conferred imperceptibly.

Ageing encompasses psychological and social aspects as well as biological

Research designs for studying ageing

The usual way of studying age-related changes is to employ either a longitudinal or cross-sectional research design. The first of these repeatedly studies the *same* group at different points in time, whilst the second studies a number of *different* age groups all at the same time. They answer the same research questions about the effects of ageing, but in different ways.

A central problem in cross-sectional research is in controlling, or accounting for, cohort differences, whereas longitudinal studies are especially affected by the historical time of testing. A cohort consists of a group of individuals, or 'generation', who were born during the same time interval and who will, therefore, age together. Each cohort is of a specific size and will generally decline in number, usually with a shift to there being more females (who tend to outlive males). A cohort occupies a unique historical niche. Think of the impact of the motor car, World Wars I and II, television, the contraceptive pill and advances in communications and information technology. Any conclusions we try to draw about adult development must always be evaluated in the light of the historical context of the cohort. Try the following activity.

ACTIVITY

Your cohort

Spend a few minutes listing the main social, cultural, historical and other influences on people born in the same year as you. If you can, compare your list with those of people from other cohorts.

Types of theory

Using these methods, some psychologists have succeeded in formulating developmental theories of the entire lifespan whilst others have focused on specific stages or phases of life, such as old age. Still others have chosen to approach adulthood through studying reactions to the kinds of life events that many adults experience, such as marrying or becoming a parent; Neugarten (1980) advocates this latter approach. As we will see, stage theories of adult personality development have the disadvantage of playing down individual differences. The life-events approach does overcome this drawback to some extent. The strengths and weaknesses of different approaches need to be borne in mind when assessing research findings and the theories that arise from them.

THEORIES OF ADULT DEVELOPMENT

Erikson's 'Eight ages of man'

Psychosocial development

Erikson (1980) agreed with Sigmund Freud's psychoanalytic theory that personality developed in stages and that it consisted of an id, ego and superego, but he disagreed that personality was largely laid down in childhood. Instead, he thought that it continued to develop throughout adulthood. He also saw social forces as far more important in shaping personality then sexual ones (hence his approach is known as a 'psychosocial' theory of personality development). In addition, Erikson's theory is more flexible than Freud's, in that he saw greater possibilities for change.

Stages of development

Erikson saw personality development as advancing through eight invariant stages (see Table 20.1) rather like sensitive periods, in that certain aspects of personality development are best dealt with at particular stages in life. Problems not resolved earlier on can still be revisited later in life and worked through more positively. On the other hand, healthy development can be undone by later experiences. Each stage, which is roughly age related, presents the individual with a specific psychosocial 'crisis' to be worked through. This means that the individual faces, and must resolve, a series of psychological conflicts relating to their interactions with others in increasingly wider social settings.

We will consider just two stages of adult development here but, by doing this, we only have a part of the picture.

Early adulthood

In early adulthood, between about 20 and 30 years of age, the first major psychosocial crisis is that of 'intimacy versus isolation'. The individual's main task is to develop close, meaningful, caring relationships with others and to avoid the isolation that may result from failing to do so. By the time they enter this stage, the individual needs to have navigated successfully through the previous stage of 'identity versus role confusion' and to have established a relatively firm and enduring identity. Without this sense of clarity about who we are, we risk becoming isolated and unable to share ourselves fully with someone else.

Middle adulthood

In middle adulthood, between about 30 and 60 years of age, the crisis to be resolved is that of 'generativity versus stagnation'. 'Generativity' refers to the consequent need to be productive, creative and caring about others, while 'stagnation' refers to a sense of pointlessness, frustration and preoccupation with oneself. A feeling of stagnation may lie behind the 'midlife crisis', when an adult may feel their current life pattern has little purpose or meaning.

Table 20.1 >> Erikson's (1980) psychosocial stages of personality development

Approximate age	Quality to be developed	Social focus	Virtue
0 to 1 year (infancy)	Basic trust vs mistrust	Maternal person	Hope (an optimistic trust that the world will meet one's needs)
2 to 3 years (early childhood)	Autonomy vs shame and doubt	Parental persons	Will (the ability to exercise self-restraint and choice)
4 to 5 years (play age)	Initiative vs guilt	Basic family	Purpose (a sense of goal-directedness)
6 to 12 years (school age)	Industry vs inferiority	Neighbourhood, school	Competence (a sense of confidence in one's own abilities)
13 to 18 years	Identity vs role confusion	Peer groups	Fidelity (the ability freely to pledge loyalty to others)
19 to 25 years	Intimacy vs isolation	Friendships	Love (both romantic and erotic and including the ability to commit oneself to others and maintain the commitment through degrees of compromise and self-denial)
26 to 40 years	Generativity vs stagnation	The household	Care (a sense that certain things in life have meaning and importance, leading one to be productive in life)
41 years +	Ego integrity vs despair	Humankind	Wisdom (a sense that life has been worthwhile, arrived at by integrating the outcomes of previous stages)

Evaluation
Erikson's theory

- **Development as a lifelong process** – Erikson has been very influential in establishing the lifespan approach to human development. His theory has emphasized how development is a lifelong process rather than something that largely terminates in adolescence (the Freudian view).

- **High face validity** – The theory has face validity because it appeals to intuition and common experience, at least in a traditional pattern of adulthood. Unlike many psychological theories that represent development in an abstract manner, Erikson's theory describes aspects of adult development that would be recognized by most adults, particularly those in Western cultures.

- **The importance of social influences** – Erikson has shown the importance of social influences in personality development, although some see this as a weakness, since successful development is not just restricted to those who conform to the social clock and is still possible in individuals who are 'out of step' with society's expectations.

- **Difficulty of testing the theory** – There are some problems with testing a theory such as Erikson's. We would have to depend on extensive self-report, clinical interviews and questionnaires with all their attendant problems. In addition, many of Erikson's ideas are difficult to put into a testable form. These problems mean that there is a lack of sound empirical evidence for the theory.

- **Relevance to contemporary life styles** – People's life experiences differ so much that the three adult goals of intimacy, generativity and ego integrity may not necessarily be achieved in an orderly fashion, if at all. Today, adults are faced with a more uncertain future as concepts such as 'marriage for life' or 'a job for life' change, making it harder to achieve intimacy through marriage or identity through work. There is also an increasing tendency for adults to delay commitment to an intimate relationship and to delay having children. A possible consequence of this is that they may well be dealing with all three adult goals simultaneously. This does not necessarily invalidate Erikson's ideas, but it does highlight the influence of the historical niche in which they were developed.

Levinson's 'Seasons of a man's life' (Levinson 1978)

In 1969, Levinson selected a sample of 40 men, aged from 35 to 45 years, from a variety of occupational groups. Over a period of two to three months, each participant had between five and ten biographical interviews each lasting one to two hours.

A central idea in this theory is the 'life structure' defined as the 'underlying pattern or design of a person's life at any given time' (1978, p. 41). The life structure changes over the lifespan and we build it primarily around our relationships and work. Using transcriptions of the detailed interview

material, Levinson was able to illustrate that the life structure evolves through a series of alternating stable ('structure building') and transitional ('structure changing' or 'crisis') phases. These he called 'the seasons of a man's life'. An outline of these stages and approximate ages is given in Fig. 20.1. The lifespan is seen as covering four eras of pre-, early, middle and late adulthood, each with specific tasks to be mastered. Where the eras overlap, we experience transitions lasting roughly five years.

Daniel Levinson's 'Seasons of a man's life'

Start this section by reading the Key research above.

Early adulthood

- *Pre-adulthood (0 to 17 years)* – This is the foundation for the period of early adulthood. In this phase, the individual grows from dependent baby to early and more independent adulthood.

- *Early adult transition (18 to 22 years)* – As with future transitions, this stage is a time of reappraisal. It involves separating oneself from pre-adulthood by continuing to move towards all kinds of independence e.g. financial, emotional. The individual is able to explore some of life's possibilities in terms of, say, occupational choice and personal identity without yet making firm commitments. A life structure in which to live as an adult will begin to appear but this structure is fairly fluid as different options are explored. Young adults also begin to develop life 'dreams' (possibly influenced by more experienced and, perhaps older, mentors) that start to guide them and give them a sense of direction and purpose.

- *Early adulthood (22 to 40 years)* – This can be one of the most dynamic, challenging and stressful periods of adult life. Initially, individuals forge firmer links between themselves and the adult world. Possibilities are still being explored, but this is the time to make some choices and commitments to begin to give life more structure (although it is important still to leave open possibilities for change). It may now be possible to fulfil some of the 'dreams' of youth, perhaps establishing a home and family, qualifying in one's chosen career and finding a way to balance them all.

Levinson believed that many of his interviewees experienced a crisis that he called 'age 30 transition', taking the end of the third decade as an

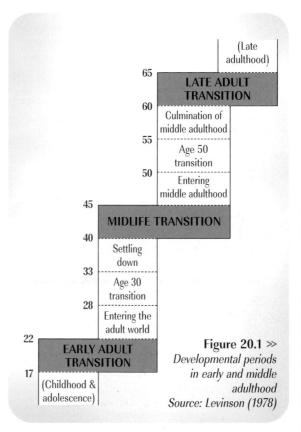

Figure 20.1 >>
Developmental periods in early and middle adulthood
Source: Levinson (1978)

inescapable signal that life is passing by. For some, but not all, this means experiencing doubts about the wisdom of existing plans and decisions, reassessing them and possibly changing them before it is too late. After this, the individual will hopefully settle down, decide on a few key choices, find a 'niche' in the adult world and, from its security, continue to grow through contributing constructively to aspects of personal, home and working life. The later part of this phase has been dubbed 'becoming one's own man' or 'BOOM'.

Middle adulthood

- *Midlife transition (40 to 45 years)* – The sense of passing time and one's own mortality become even more pressing as the physical signs of ageing become more obvious and as the deaths of older relatives and one's contemporaries occur. Initial dreams and plans may or may not be realized, and for some (not all) this can be a period of 'midlife crisis', in which changes must be made in order to avoid extreme disappointment. In this transition, however, BOOM is completed and, with luck, individuals emerge from it wiser and able to be more loving, caring and reflective, rather than isolated and stagnated.

- *Middle adulthood (45 to 60 years)* – During this stage, illusions of immortality and eternal youth will usually disappear. It is a time to build on choices and decisions made during the midlife transition. For some this may mean a new occupation, perhaps new key relationships. For others, the change may be more subtle such that the existing occupation and relationships remain, but the person's attitude to them changes. Typically, adults in this stage are less inward looking and are more concerned with the generations that follow. They have the power, authority and wisdom to make an important and lasting impact on the world and others around them. In a small way, this could mean acting as a mentor to others or becoming more of a family person. On a larger scale, the individual could become involved in community or even global issues. For many people, successful progress through this era could make it one of the most satisfying, positive and productive phases of life.

Late adulthood

These stages of development are followed by the *late adult transition (60 to 65 years)*, in which the signs of physical decline become increasingly obvious and the individual becomes 'old' in the eyes of their culture.

Evaluation
Levinson's work

- *Lack of quantitative data* – There are few quantitative data to support the ideas of Levinson because the information collected was in the form of clinical interview reports. Some would see this as a strength because of the richness of the qualitative data. Others regard it as a weakness.

- *Limited sample size* – Most of the interviewees in the study had not reached the age of 45. In fact, information was only gathered for 15 participants after the age of 45. Consequently, the evidence for

Late adulthood (65 years to the end of life) follows. A final acceptance that life is finite is unavoidable. Again for some, this is a time of crisis, for others a period of calm and reflection.

Research into Levinson's theory

A key feature of Levinson's theory is the concept of the structure-changing, midlife transition or crisis – an idea that has essential validity for some, especially those following the traditional pattern of adult life. Levinson even viewed this crisis as necessary and inevitable. He claimed that 80 per cent of his sample had experienced a moderate or severe crisis in midlife and that those who had not were likely to pay the price later.

Durkin (1995) questions whether the inevitable ups and downs of life are particularly acute in midlife and concludes that they are not. In fact, some studies (e.g. Farrell and Rosenberg 1981) showed that only about 12 per cent of people experience midlife as unusually critical and that most experience it as positive. Findings such as these emphasize how varied people's life courses are and how important the coincidence of any stage of life with other events is. For example, at midlife, some adults are emptying the nest of children, whilst others might have a 'crowded nest' full of offspring unwilling or unable to move out. Still other adults might become parents for the first time or start a second family.

Levinson's original work was androcentric ('male-centred'), prompting others to ask whether the findings for men have relevance for women. Roberts and Newton (1987) reported on studies involving female interviewers and 39 female interviewees. Although women's lives appeared to be more complex than men's, some broad similarities in development were found. Early adulthood involved transition, with age 30 being particularly critical. The concept of a 'dream' was also central for females, but often involved the success of their husband and family relationships rather than their own personal career. There is also evidence for 'seasons' in women's lives, but an important difference is that their investment in others as part of their lives' dreams puts them at greater risk of disappointment.

the later eras is sketchy, being based on a very small group of adults.

- *A narrow sample* – The original sample studied by Levinson was limited in age and occupational background, as well as being all male. Although further research has been carried out, there is still a need for further work involving females and across cultures.

- *Importance of the sociocultural and historical setting* – Levinson's theory highlights the importance of taking into account the sociocultural and historical setting when describing adult development. These are important influences that had largely been ignored by earlier theorists.

Gould's 'Evolution of adult consciousness' (Gould 1978, 1980)

Gould's (1978, 1980) ideas stem from his work as a psychiatrist. They are based on medical students' ratings of taped therapy sessions from which a questionnaire was devised. This questionnaire was sent to 524 white, middle-class 16- to 50-year-olds who were not clinical patients. From their responses, Gould identified seven age-related stages of adult development. He proposed that, as we move through these stages, we progress from childhood to adult consciousness and we do this by facing and leaving behind major false emotional assumptions. While we hold these assumptions (shown in Table 20.2), they give us an illusion of safety and serve to protect us from anxiety, which is why giving them up can be both difficult and painful. Gould thought that our 40s could be a particularly challenging period because the passing of time and a greater sense of our own mortality make facing our false assumptions all the more pressing.

Roger Gould's 'Evolution of adult consciousness'

Early adulthood

During the stage of late teens to early 20s, there is usually a sense that the family we grew up with is still there for us, although this may not be overtly acknowledged. It acts as both a trap and a safety net from which we can contemplate a seemingly limitless future, stretching ahead and full of flexibility and possibilities. As the 20s progress, we develop a sense of ourselves as increasingly self-reliant and independent. At first, we tend to feel that there is some kind of direction and purpose but, later, there is a realisation that our ideas might actually be quite vague or even stereotypical. As a consequence, later in this decade, we will need to face these uncertainties and begin to consolidate our plans and make some firm choices. By the end of this decade, a much clearer idea of our life pattern should be developing.

In our 30s and 40s, our sense of time begins to change as we realize the inevitability of growing older in a time span that is increasingly real and limited. Time becomes finite and the sense of our own mortality becomes more compelling. Life is still full of possibilities but, because time is limited, and few of us can do all we would like, priorities must be set and compromises and choices made. For some this might entail a radical adjustment of how we spend our time.

Middle adulthood

By the time we are in our 50s, we should have given up our illusions of dependency, limitless time and immortality and developed what Gould calls a sense of 'me' and a feeling of autonomy – that 'I own myself'. There is a contact with one's 'inner core', which gives us a sense of meaning and the personal strength to deal with whatever life still has to bring. We should have dealt with the separation anxiety of childhood, freed ourselves from illusions of absolute safety and learned to stand alone. Individuals who do not reach this stage may feel rootless and that life lacks meaning.

By this stage we should realize that we are creators of our own lives and are not constrained by the false assumptions of earlier stages in life. An important factor in this is the changed sense of time with age. Before young adulthood, the future is nebulous and there is a sense of time stretching endlessly ahead. As we progress through life, we should have a sense of moving along a fairly well defined timeline, especially if we have chosen a particular career path. By our 30s and 40s, there is a growing sense that time is not unlimited and that choices must be made. This increasing urgency is also fuelled by a sense of our own mortality, so that what we do with the available time matters more and more. The modern phenomenon called 'downshifting' provides some anecdotal evidence for this. Downshifters are people who, in midlife, find themselves leading a pressurized life style with long working hours and many demands on time. They make a conscious choice to simplify their life style and settle for less in monetary terms in order to improve their quality of life.

In what ways is 'downshifting' a response to changing priorities of middle adulthood?

Age in years	False assumption and its components
Late teens to early 20s	I will always belong to my parents and believe in their world.
	● If I get any more independent, it will be a disaster.
	● I can only see the world through my parents' assumptions.
	● Only they can guarantee my safety.
	● They must be my only family.
	● I don't own my body.
20s	Doing it my parents' way with willpower and perseverance will probably bring results. But when I am too frustrated, confused or tired, or am simply unable to cope, my parents will step in and show me the way.
	● Rewards will come automatically if we do what we are supposed to do.
	● There is only one right way to do things.
	● My loved ones are able to do for me what I haven't been able to do for myself.
	● Rationality, commitment and effort will always prevail over other forces.
Late 20s to early 30s	Life is simple and controllable. There are no significant coexisting contradictory forces within me.
	● What I know intellectually, I know emotionally.
	● I am not like my parents in ways I don't want to be. I can see the reality of those close to me quite clearly.
	● Threats to my security aren't real.
Mid-30s to 50	There is no evil in me or death in the world. The sinister has been expelled.
	● My work (for men) or my relationship with men (for women) grants me immunity from death and danger.
	● There is no life beyond this family.
	● I am innocent.

Evaluation
Gould's theory

● **Restricted sample** – Gould's theory is based on the evaluations of taped patient interviews from only eight medical students. Their relatively inexperienced evaluations were then used as a basis for the questionnaire and this calls its validity into question. The 524 questionnaire respondents were white, middle-class adults, which tells us little about other adult groups. Gould's theory, cannot, therefore be considered a *universal* theory of adult development.

● **Lack of reliability** – There were no attempts to assess the reliability of the questionnaire. Reliability is a fundamental requirement in psychological questionnaires, as it demonstrates that a particular measure will measure something *consistently*. A lack of reliability means that such consistency can only be assumed.

● **Life after 60** – The detail about life after 60 is sketchy, but this is hardly surprising given the age range of Gould's questionnaire respondents (medical students and 16- to 50-year-old respondents).

Transitions and crises in adulthood

The theories of adulthood described so far are all based on research evidence for stages, transitions, crisis and adjustment. Although they differed methodologically, all of them uncovered what they believed to be recognizable developmental processes in adulthood. They described these using different terminology, but there is still general agreement about the overall pattern of adulthood (e.g. finding an identity in adolescence, establishing intimacy, making career choices, becoming generative and, finally, looking for a meaning to life and facing death). The forces behind these trends differ in each theory, but they share an emphasis on phases or stages that all adults can expect to move through with varying degrees of success.

Another area of agreement is in the concept of particularly difficult phases worthy of the term 'crisis':

- Erikson's theory, constructed over decades and based on clinical observations and cross-cultural comparisons, sees every developmental stage of life as involving the needed to face and resolve a crisis.

- Levinson's work, based on depth interviewing, revealed 'age 30 transition' and midlife as being particularly challenging.

- Gould's findings, based on questionnaires and clinical insight, illustrated the difficulty many people have with letting go of false assumptions.

More recent evidence for transitions and crises in adulthood comes from a number of sources. Research by Sangiuliano (1978, cited in Bee and Mitchell 1984) pointed out differences in timing for men and women, where women tended to achieve intimacy before

identity. Women seemed to commit themselves to family responsibilities at first, but by middle age, were able to attend to identity development. For men, the achievement of identity through work came earlier. This traditional pattern may still hold in certain pockets of society, but there is strong evidence that women's work patterns are changing (Office for National Statistics 1999) and this will alter their opportunities for ego development.

Of particular interest is the way in which changing life styles have meant that the timing of the challenges of adulthood is often not in tune with the stereotypical 'social clock'. Such 'out-of-time' transitions have been examined in a book entitled *New Passages* by Sheehy (1996). She suggests that in the industrialized world, people are increasingly able to choose when to engage with particular challenges. Progress in contraception and fertility treatments, for example, have allowed us to choose when and if to have children. Economic changes have enabled us more choice in who looks after them. Marrying at any life stage, or not at all, is increasingly acceptable. Divorce no longer carries the stigma that was in evidence in the last century. Plastic surgery is more openly admitted to as people strive to maintain their youth in the many ways currently available.

Evaluation
stage theories of adult development

These approaches offer a much-needed framework for understanding the alleged crises and transitions of adulthood, but there are important limitations:

- *Research methods* – In each case there are some doubts about the soundness of the research on which the ideas are based, particularly with regard to the number and type of participants used and the methods of data collection.

- *Emphasis on crisis* – Some critics think there is a rather negative overemphasis on crisis, particularly in midlife, and that this could be because of the nature of the cohorts used.

- *Generalizability* – We cannot be sure how well the three approaches apply to different individuals, societies and cohorts. Possible

variation within these is well worth further investigation. Future research needs to take into account the impact of sociocultural, socioeconomic and gender differences on the development and life experiences of adults.

- *Other age-related changes* – We must also remember that the changes described in these theories go on against a background of many other age-related changes (e.g. physiological and cognitive/intellectual) that individuals have to cope with at the same time. (Cognitive changes are considered later in this unit. For a discussion of other changes, see Bee 1998 or Berk 1998.)

- *Life stages or life events?* – Some researchers think that there is little convincing evidence for *stages* in adult development and prefer instead to focus on specific life *events* that affect many adults and which could be considered critical. We will return to this in the next topic.

REVISION SUMMARY

Having covered this topic you should be able to describe and evaluate:

✓ theories of early and middle adulthood proposed by Erikson, Levinson and Gould

✓ evidence for the existence of crises and transitions in early and middle adulthood.

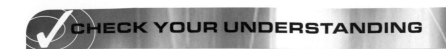

✓ CHECK YOUR UNDERSTANDING

Check your understanding of the theories of early and middle adulthood by answering these questions from memory. Check your answers by looking back through Topic 1.

1 What age ranges are generally said to cover 'early' and 'middle adulthood'?

2 Identify the methods used by Erikson, Levinson and Gould in their studies of adulthood.

3 For each theory, name and identify the ages and names of the stages relating to early and middle adulthood.

4 For each theory, write a 150-word précis of the key characteristics of early and middle adulthood.

5 Make three critical points for each of the three theories.*

6 What evidence is there that we experience transition and crisis in the three theories outlined here? Construct a 300-word response to this question.

7 Make three points that could be used to evaluate (i.e. AO2) the worth of evidence of transition and crisis.*

* Remember that general material relating to defining ageing and methodological difficulties are all relevant here.

✍ EXAMPLE EXAM QUESTIONS

Typical examination questions on this topic include the following:

1 Discuss **one** theory of development in early and middle adulthood. (24 marks)

> In this question, which asks you to focus on just one theory, the problem might be having enough material to fill a 30-minute answer. It is useful to practise producing a 15-minute description of each theory, selecting eight to ten points that can be elaborated in the exam. This ensures that you have enough to write and can give a rounded version of your theory. The instruction is to write about 'early and middle adulthood'; this does not mean you have to write about both, but tells you that either or both approaches are acceptable.

2 Outline and evaluate **one or more** theories of development in early and middle adulthood (e.g. Levinson, Gould). (24 marks)

> The term 'outline' indicates the need for a slightly less detailed AO1 response than would be the case with the instruction 'describe'. The main decision here is whether to restrict your answer to just *one* theory, or to write about more than one. It really is your decision, but you don't lose marks by just using one theory. If you don't feel that you have enough material with just one theory, then go for more than one. The examples are provided as a prompt and do not mean that you must cover *both* theories named or, indeed, *either* theory. Remember that theories can be used as critical commentary as long as they are *used* in this way and not just linked by saying 'A contrasting approach is …' and then give a description of another theory. In such cases this would only attract AO1 credit.

3 Critically consider **two** theories of development in early and middle adulthood. (24 marks)

> This is virtually the same question as question 2 except that here you don't have to make a decision about how many theories to write about, as that decision has already been made for you. In questions such as this, a *précis* is required of each of two theories. It pays you, therefore, to be very strategic with your use of time. This essay could conveniently be broken down into four 'mini-essays', each one of about 150 words or $7\frac{1}{2}$ minutes (outline one theory, evaluate it, outline second theory, evaluate it). If you only outline one theory, there is a partial performance penalty of a maximum of 8 marks out of 12 for AO1. The same is true if you only evaluate one theory (a maximum of 8 marks out of 12 for AO2). This weighting of marks means that, if two theories are required, you can get full marks even if the two theories are not presented in balance. It is almost as if there are 16 marks for theory 1 and 8 marks for theory 2.

4 (a) Outline **two** theories of development in early and middle adulthood. (12 marks)

    (b) To what extent does evidence support the existence of crises and transitions in adult development? (12 marks)

> In this question you can use the same AO1 material as in the previous question, but different AO2 material. Note that you are not *always* asked to evaluate material you have described. This is a case in point and shows you how important it is to focus on the exact demands of a question – instead of just writing a prepared answer on two theories, you must read what is required for part (b) and answer this separately. The AO2 component of this question requires you to assess the extent to which there are crises and transitions in adult development. It isn't enough to merely *describe* such crises and transitions, but you should use this material as AO2 commentary. This might include assessing the research support (or otherwise) for crises and transitions, assessing the implications of such phases of development and so on.

5 Discuss evidence for the existence of crises and transitions in adult development. (24 marks)

> The part (b) of question 4 could be expanded to an essay question in its own right, as given here for question 5, albeit probably a tough question. It does mean that the descriptions of any crises or transitions would now be creditworthy, which in a way makes your task easier. However, do not make the mistake of outlining a whole theory. You must restrict your discussion to those points from any theory that are relevant. Commentary should always be coherently elaborated, which means, for example, stating the point you are making, explaining why it is a positive or negative criticism and also justifying it (see 'Innovative and effective AO2' on p. 937 for further details).

Topic 2 >> Family and relationships in adulthood

Bearing in mind the many variables that can affect how individuals react to life events, can we make any general statements about the effects of specific life events? To address this question, this topic focuses on three key events affecting many adults – marriage (or partnering), parenthood and divorce. Two further events, retirement and bereavement, are considered later in the unit.

The Social Readjustment Rating Scale (SRRS)

One major attempt to classify and measure the effects of life events was made by Holmes and Rahe (1967). They studied 5,000 patient records and listed 43 life events that had occurred in the months preceding illness. With the help of 100 judges, who rated each event in terms of how much change it would entail, they developed the Social Readjustment Rating Scale (SRRS). On this scale, each event has a value indicating 'life change units' or LCUs, where 'death of a spouse' has the highest rating (100) and 'minor violations of the law' has the lowest (11). Marriage has a rating of 50, divorce is 73 and pregnancy 39. A copy of the complete SRRS is included in Unit 3, p. 89.

MARRIAGE (OR PARTNERING)

Marital trends

Western-style, voluntary, heterosexual marriage is only one of several forms of adult intimate living arrangement and, according to figures from the Office for National Statistics (2003), it is in decline. In 2000, there were 180,000 first-time marriages, but this is less than half the number recorded in 1970 when first-time UK marriages peaked. In 1997, there were 9,000 fewer marriages than in 1996, the lowest rate since 1917. In 2000, there were 306,000 marriages in total, a 2 per cent increase from 1999 (ONS 2003). Not surprisingly, there is a corresponding increase in cohabitation, but the most common reason for cohabitation ending is still marriage. In spite of the relatively high risk of divorce or separation, many people still opt for marriage or some other form of long-term, partnered, living arrangement and most psychological research is still focused on marriage. What can it tell us about why people marry and what they can expect from marriage? Try the activity on the right.

Why marry?

On a practical level, marriage fulfils basic needs for companionship and security. It is an overt sign of adult status and provides a legitimate unit within which to rear children. In Erikson's (1980) terms, marriage is one way to solve the psychosocial crisis of intimacy versus isolation. Through making a commitment to another person, we develop the ego quality of being able to love (even if this means some self-denial and compromise) and avoid emotional isolation. With time, the initial passionate and erotic love that can draw two people together may deepen into a more profound and secure attachment that stands the test of time and the inevitable rough patches in life.

Marital satisfaction

In terms of marital satisfaction, some relationships clearly wear better than others. To try to understand why, psychologists have studied the quality of marital relationships at different stages in the marriage and come up with conflicting views. One of the more persistent findings (Bee 1998) concerns the 'U-shaped' curve of marital satisfaction which occurs because satisfaction, which is at its highest before children are born, declines after marriage, reaches a low when children are at school, and rises to peak in retirement.

Cohabitation

With respect to partnering, Bee (1994) cautions that we should not treat married people who have never cohabited with cohabitees as if they are equivalent. Cohabitees who do go on to marry are more likely to be dissatisfied with their marriage and to divorce later on and Bee thinks that this is because they differ in important ways from married people. She suggest that cohabitees tend to be less traditional in their attitudes and more challenging of the status quo and this, perhaps, is why they are more likely to terminate an unsatisfactory marriage.

Cross-cultural comparisons of marriage

Comparisons of marital satisfaction in men and women persistently show that Western women are less satisfied with their marriages than men (e.g. Schumm *et al.* 1998). In a comparison of American and Japanese spouses, Kamo (1993) discovered that the quality of marital interactions was regarded as important in both cultures. However, he also found that age and satisfaction were negatively related in the USA, but not in Japan, and that husband's income mattered more for Japanese wives than for American wives.

In a study of 11 cultures (India, Pakistan, Thailand, Mexico, Brazil, Japan, Hong Kong, the Philippines, Australia, England and the US), Levine *et al.* (1995) reported that, in cultures which emphasize individualism, greater importance was assigned to love in marriage than was the case in collectivist cultures. They also found that love mattered in cultures with higher standards of living, higher marriage and divorce rates, and lower fertility rates.

Marital status, gender difference and mental health

The benefits of marriage

With regard to the link between marital status and health, Bee (1998) showed that, compared with never-married individuals, married people enjoy better physical health and markedly better mental health. Single men are worst off in these respects and married men fare best, with married and single women falling between these two extremes. Argyle and Henderson (1985) argue that it is the quality of the relationship that seems to contribute most to this effect – a close confiding relationship matters more than simply living in the same house or having a sexual relationship. One reason why marriage seems to favour men could be that women are better confidantes for their husbands than their husbands are for them. In other respects, in spite of changes in attitudes towards women's role, marriage for them may be less satisfactory, not only because of possibly greater domestic and work role conflict, but also because the arrival of children requires a relatively greater adjustment for women than it does for most men.

Berk (1998) and Bee (1994) summarize a number of factors that correlate with marital quality and stability, including length of courtship, similar family background, higher social class, approval from friends and family, stable marital patterns in extended family, effective communication, and secure financial and employment status. These are correlational, however, so offer no guarantee of marital success!

PARENTHOOD

Parenthood, like other life events, can be both stressful and rewarding. Unlike some other life events, such as marriage, it is irrevocable. In our culture, there may be little preparation for parenthood and little support, other than from a number of, often contradictory, child-care books. Increasingly, children in the UK are being born outside marriage – in 2001, this was true for 40 per cent of all births, compared to 25 per cent in 1988, but over 80 per cent of these births were registered by both parents, with three-quarters of these registrations showing that parents shared the same address (*Social Trends* 2003). This leaves substantial numbers of parents coping with lone parenthood with widely varying degrees of support from others.

Stages of parenthood

Within marriage, the arrival of children is typically associated with the early years. At that time there may be additional pressures such as low income and high job pressure while the parents establish themselves at work. By the time the children are at school, parents may find themselves under the greatest pressure in their career (especially if they are competing with keen, younger, childless colleagues who are also cheaper to employ). Parents with adolescent children seemed to be under even greater strain. Bee (1994) reported that the happiest parents were young couples with few financial pressures. In spite of this, 80 to 90 per cent of couples with children said they were very happy and that parenthood had improved their relationship. This was especially true just before the 'empty nest' phase when children were about to be launched into the adult world. For many parents, the 'empty nest' phase was particularly good, being marked by an increase in energy and zest for life and much satisfaction in the adult offspring.

Cultural differences in parenthood

The arrival of a child is also one of the most abrupt transitions experienced by adults in the Western world regardless of whether they are partnered or single. Contrast this with a Mexican American family ritual, *La cuarentena* (see panel right). In less well-developed cultures, such as that of the Amazonian Penare Indians or the nomadic Wodabe of Western Sudan, newborns are welcomed into a tight system of social support where parents are not isolated in their new role.

Western parenthood calls for major readjustments in life style and is accompanied by practical issues, such as general fatigue, as well as physical changes (for the mother) and the emotional changes that accompany coming to terms with suddenly being entirely responsible for a helpless and vulnerable baby. Within couples, the roles of the new father and mother may

La cuarentena

In certain regions of Mexico, a special period of 40 days called *la cuarentena*, is observed after the birth of a child. This does not involve isolation, as in true 'quarantine', but is a time when grandmothers, friends or mothers-in-law play a central role, not only helping with household chores, but also acting as the primary caregivers. The father generally participates very little. However, mothers are usually positive about this and protect the male's image. This opinion may be influenced by the financial help that males provide but also by the belief that men do not know how to participate in the child-rearing process. This culturally prescribed pattern of behaviour helps to ease both the mother and the father into their new roles as parents, as well as aiding the recovery of the mother after birth and the survival of her infant.

initially become more traditional and polarized, and the pre-parenthood balance and quality of the relationship will probably never return. This pattern seems to be generally true in developed Western culture. Nickel *et al.* (1995), for example, showed a general decrease in marital satisfaction after the birth of children in Germany, the USA, Austria and Korea.

In non-Western cultures, on the other hand, where parenthood is highly valued and the extended family is supportive, the decline in satisfaction levels is less marked (Berk 1998). Whatever the circumstances, parenthood exerts a powerful pull. Turner and Helms (1983) suggest a number of reasons why adults choose parenthood:

- *ego expansion* – a sense of importance and purpose
- *creativity* – a sense of achievement (or what Erikson would call successful resolution of the generativity crisis)
- *status and conformity satisfaction* – fulfilling the expectations of your culture
- *control and authority* – over your dependants
- *love and affection* – both given and received
- *happiness and security* – through the creation of a stable family unit.

These remain remarkably consistent across cultures, although Barnes (1995) adds that, in some cultures, the child's ability to work and/or contribute to the family's income is critical.

Parenthood and gender roles

How is the impact of parenthood on women and men different? Sadly, traditional male–female roles appear to hinder both genders in their capacity as parents. Women still carry the brunt of domestic and parenting tasks even when both partners work outside the home (Berk 1998), and the adjustments they are required to make are considerably greater. Women also have to battle with idealized ideas about 'mother love' and 'maternal instinct' and the 'good mother's role', and these may be difficult to reconcile with other needs such as career fulfilment. Those who have established identities outside motherhood may find a constant conflict of interests between career and parenting, while those who immerse themselves in motherhood may have identity problems when the children become less dependent or leave home.

Men may initially be more involved in practical aspects of child care, and just as immersed in their newborns as women, but they are typically less well prepared for parenthood and may feel left out or unequal to meeting the demands of being provider, household help and nurturer. Both sexes have to adjust to sharing their time and affection differently within the family but, initially, this can be harder for the father, particularly if he is less involved in the daily care of the infant. Indeed, some studies (e.g. Terry et al. 1991) show that marital satisfaction after transition to parenthood is greater when the woman perceives that her spouse is contributing fairly to the performance of household tasks. A Scandinavian study (Olsson et al. 1998) found that new parents agreed that the metaphor of the spider's web described the tension in their changed relationship – the mother is the spider carrying the baby on her back, and the father only enters the web on her terms. Levine (1976) suggests that the roles need to be redefined and revitalized so that more of the satisfactions of parenthood are open to men and women (as well as more of the strains).

DIVORCE

Next to the death of a spouse, divorce is the most difficult life crisis we are ever likely to experience. Bee (1998) notes that divorce is more likely in those:

- who marry younger or older than average
- who are childless
- whose parents had an unhappy marriage
- who married because of an unplanned pregnancy.

Overall, the divorce rate in the UK is high. The number of divorces more than trebled between 1968 and 2000 (Office for National Statistics 2003). Figures from 1996 show that 9 per cent of marriages ended within the first three years, peaking at 28 per cent between five and nine years (Office for National Statistics 1999). Durkin (1995) suggests that increasing freedom to enter into or terminate relationships in general has led to higher and idealized expectations of the married relationship and what it is required to provide in terms of exclusivity, fulfilment and love. For example, both partners expect to fulfil their life's dreams (Levinson 1978) and if their marriage is only allowing one of them to do that, it may be at risk.

On the positive side, divorce can be good for you. It may mark the end of a long period of unhappiness and lack of personal growth but, even if the eventual outcome is good, divorce is nearly always traumatic and the weight of the evidence suggests that a long and difficult period of coping and adjustment is necessary. Bohannon (1970) suggested six stages in the divorce process:

1 **Emotional** – The marriage collapses, there is conflict and antagonism.

2 **Legal** – The marriage contract is dissolved.

3 **Economic** – Decisions are made over money and property.

4 **Co-parental** – Custody of and access to children is decided.

5 **Community** – Relationships with friends and family are adjusted.

6 **Psychic** – There is adjustment to singlehood and autonomy is regained.

Stages in the divorce process

Each of the stages may be accompanied by a conflicting range of emotions including pervasive feelings of failure, ambivalence towards the partner, grief, relief, loneliness and excitement. There may be greater anxiety, loss of self-esteem, reduced productivity at work and greater vulnerability to mental and physical illness. In a review of relevant research, Gottman (1998) links divorce with an increased incidence of physical illness, suicide, violence, homicide, suppressed immunity and mortality from diseases.

For both men and women, disorganization is a feature of the year following divorce. Both men and women experience a drop in income, but women generally seem to suffer more financially from a divorce, especially if they assumed their major role would be as a home-maker, or if they took a career break in order to rear children and their earnings fell behind. Indeed, employed women seem to suffer less loss of self-esteem and distress than women without a clear work identity (Bisagni and Eckenrode 1995). There is some evidence (e.g. Berk 1998) that divorcees over the age of 50 find adjustment harder than do younger ones. The older age group seems to feel they have fewer options open to them and find their social life is more difficult. Older men in particular have difficulty envisaging what the future would hold.

Parents and children in divorce

Divorcees with children have to deal with their own distress as well as that of their children. In addition, they have to take sole responsibility for discipline and may find it hard to be consistent, so the children's behaviour may deteriorate.

Another great source of conflict concerns access rights to children. Whilst Berk (1998) points out that divorce is never 'good for the children', she says that its effects are less likely to cause serious, long-term damage if there is frequent and satisfactory contact between the child and both parents, coupled with a minimum disruption to the child's life style and daily routine. Naturally, children of different ages react differently to divorce, and understanding this can help parents to cope better with both the child's unhappiness and their own worries about the child's unhappiness.

There is also some evidence that boys become more unruly following divorce and that their schoolwork suffers more than it does for girls, possibly because they receive less overt emotional support (Berk 1998). Some parents cope by arranging for their families to become 'blended', i.e. where step and biological parents both take responsibility for the children's welfare. Difficult though this can be, it does help to maintain contact between divorced parents and their children and lessen the pressure on both.

Cultural differences and similarities in divorce

Existing research does seem to show that at least two years of turmoil is extremely likely following divorce. For adults, divorce-related disorganization tends to decline after two years depending on the degree of financial pressure, number and age of children, and the emotional support available. Interestingly, in a study of

Do you believe that divorce is 'never good for the children' (Berk 1998)?

divorcees in Israeli kibbutzim, Kaffman (1993) found that, because of their relatively collectivist, non-materialistic and simple life style, the legal, parenting and economic obstacles that usually exacerbate stress in divorce in more individualistic and materialistic cultures were relatively minor considerations. This meant that life after divorce held fewer sources of conflict for them than it did for non-kibbutz dwellers. What remained for kibbutz dwellers to deal with was something Kaffman called the 'authentic emotional divorce'. However, when he compared the emotional impact of divorce on kibbutz and non-kibbutz dwellers, he found that it was similar in both samples, pointing to what he calls 'the ubiquitousness of the human experience' (p. 117). In other words, divorce feels pretty much the same to everyone regardless of the practical and material issues that accompany it.

Evaluation
life events research

- **Cross-sectional or longitudinal research?** – The advantages of one tend to be the disadvantages of the other, e.g. participant attrition, which occurs more in longitudinal research, is less problematic in cross-sectional research but has to be weighed against greater variation between participants in the latter. For example, findings about marriages and marital satisfaction tend to be based on the cross-sectional method and, as times goes on, unsatisfactory marriages may have ended and consequently been lost from the samples of 'older' marriages. This would lead to an artificial impression of growing satisfaction with time.

- **Increasing the quality of research** – People marry, divorce, enter parenthood and experience bereavement at varying stages of life. The context of these events is, therefore, difficult to control and a host of unaccounted-for influences could affect the quality of research into these. This is no reason to give up! One solution is for researchers to study specifically chosen ('purposive') samples of people who share certain characteristics, and choose their research method with care. A method such as depth interviewing on relatively smaller samples yields rich data that may be limited in generalizability, but if that were combined with more superficial survey data on larger samples, a more complete picture would emerge.

continued on next page

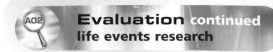

- *Qualitative or quantitative research?* – Research methods in the life events research discussed here tend to be more qualitative than quantitative in nature. This is not a problem in itself if the chosen method is appropriate and the research is well done. What is more problematic is in meeting what researchers call 'criteria for adequacy'. Traditionally, in quantitative research, these have revolved around validity and reliability, and a host of statistical techniques for establishing them. Qualitative data in the form of simple percentages or text have to assessed in different ways, e.g. replicability in quantitative research is matched in qualitative research by providing an 'audit trail' whereby researchers' claims can be traced back to original data; objectivity in quantitative research is matched by confirmability in qualitative research, in which other sources of or angles on an issue might be called in to verify a claim. There is some disagreement amongst psychologists about just how adequate such qualitative criteria are.

- *The value of qualitative data* – Marriage, divorce and parenting (or the absence of them) are issues that are central to many people's lives and often full of emotional charge. Participants are therefore, likely to frame their accounts of their experiences to researchers in many different ways depending on factors to do with themselves, the research method, the researcher and the relationship between them. Qualitative researchers are probably better placed than most to recognise this, but others, not so persuaded, would question the general value of information that is apparently so fluid.

- *Ethical issues in life events research* – The relatively greater emphasis on qualitative

methods also raises ethical issues as, in some cases, application of the standard guidelines for research might fall short of protecting participants sufficiently. For example, in some kinds of quantitative research, it might be possible to obtain fully informed consent beforehand, but in some qualitative methods such as interviewing, it is not always possible to know beforehand what information might emerge or whether participants will feel they have disclosed too much or be upset by confronting difficult issues.

- *Gender and cultural bias* – With regard to gender and culture, the validity of findings about differences in life events can be called into question. This is not only because there are general difficulties with developing adequate measures of the impact of life events, but also because the criteria for judging such things vary both within and between genders and cultures. The findings described in the relevant sections above show this clearly. Cultures other than the 'home' one may be based on quite different value systems, e.g. about the ideal timing of life events and their meaning, and this will affect how people judge their impact.

- *Inappropriate measures* – Measuring instruments developed in one culture or by one gender and imported into another run the risk of a being a 'poor fit'. Berry (1969) called instruments developed within and suitable for particular cultures 'emics'. Instruments that can be applied to any culture are called 'etics' (see p. 821). A problem arises if an instrument assumed to be an etic is really an emic, but is imposed on another culture. An example of this might be to take a measure devised to test heterosexual marriages and impose it on same-sex relationships. Another less obvious example would be of a researcher who had never been a parent devising a measure to test feelings about parenthood.

REVISION SUMMARY

Having covered this topic, you should be able to:

✓ describe and evaluate research into factors associated with effects on the individual of marriage/partnering, parenthood and divorce

✓ describe research into factors associated with gender and cultural differences in the effects of marriage/partnering, parenthood and divorce.

Check your understanding of the effects of life events by answering these questions. Try to do this from memory at first. You can check your answers by looking back through Topic 2.

1 Western-style heterosexual marriage is just one form of living arrangement. What other kinds of living arrangement are there?

2 Give three reasons why people may opt for marriage.

3 How might cohabitees differ from married couples who have never cohabited?

4 In 150 words, explain why marital satisfaction often follows a 'U-shaped curve.

5 Describe three findings about cross-cultural or gender differences in marital satisfaction.

6 Give three reasons why people might choose to become parents.

7 In no more than 150 words, explain Kaffman's (1993) findings about divorce in kibbutz and non-kibbutz dwellers.

8 Summarize three general methodological problems that challenge the validity of life events research.

9 Summarize one general methodological problem that psychologists face when conducting life events research comparing genders or cultures.

EXAMPLE EXAM QUESTIONS

Typical examination questions on this topic include the following.

1 Discuss research (theories **and/or** studies) into factors associated with marriage (or partnering). (24 marks)

> The term 'discuss' gives you the chance to write a more discursive response to the question. Your AO1 material would be a description of research into factors associated with marriage, but your AO2 material could include any of the evaluative points included on pp. 633–4. We have included nearly 1000 words of possible AO2 material, but you will only get the chance to use about one-third of this. Don't try to write a bit about everything and thus reduce the amount of coherent elaboration you demonstrate (an important AO2 criterion and something that makes your AO2 more *effective*).

2 Discuss research (theories **and/or** studies) into factors associated with divorce **and/or** parenthood. (24 marks)

> This is similar to question 1 except that the life events are different, *and* you have the choice of either discussing research on *two* life events (divorce *and* parenthood), or just choosing one of these. Remember that you don't have to write about more than one life event if you feel you have enough material on either divorce or parenthood alone. One of the dangers in trying to cover both is that you end up with less detail and elaboration for each – the more breadth, the less depth (the 'depth–breadth trade-off'). Always try to get a good balance in these.

3 (a) Outline research (theories **and/or** studies) into factors associated with marriage and divorce. (12 marks)
  (b) To what extent are there gender **and/or** cultural differences in the effects of marriage and divorce on the individual? (12 marks)

> Here, you are instructed to write about *two* life events (marriage *and* divorce). For the AO2 component of this question, it isn't enough to merely *describe* gender and cultural differences, but you should use this material as AO2 commentary. This might include assessing the research support (or otherwise) for gender and cultural differences and so on. There is a lot to cover in this question, so you need to be very careful in how you apportion your time. Even though part (b) asks 'To what extent ...?' you are not required to reach a conclusion. There is never special credit in any question for a conclusion and often candidates merely repeat material they have already presented and thus gain no further credit.

4 Discuss research (theories **and/or** studies) relating to gender differences in **two** aspects of adult relationships (e.g. marriage, divorce, parenthood). (24 marks)

> In this question, AO1 credit will be given to any description of the way that men and women differ in adult relationships. The use of the general phrase 'adult relationships' means that it would be creditworthy to consider material from other areas of the specification, such as research on relationship formation or dissolution. Commentary can be provided through the use of research studies (as long as they are used effectively and not merely described) or, if you are evaluating research studies, then you might consider the validity of the conclusions from such research (e.g. if the methodology is flawed, then the conclusions may not be justified).

5 Critically consider research (theories **and/or** studies) into relationships in adulthood. (24 marks)

> A rather general question such as this poses its own problems. You may have too much to write about and thus your answer lacks structure and selectivity. You should impose your own structure. You might for example, divide your essay into two kinds of relationships (e.g. marriage and divorce) and write 300 words about each (150 words on AO1 and 150 words on AO2). Alternatively, you could list relevant research studies and for each provide some details plus some commentary. If you write 100 words of AO1+AO2 for each, then six studies should be sufficient for full marks.

Topic 3 >> Late adulthood

The increase in life expectancy means that late adulthood may span three, or even four, decades. Researchers in this field typically divide later life into three phases:

1 **young old** – 60 to 69 years of age

2 **middle-aged old** – 70 to 79 years of age

3 **old old** – 80 to 89 (or more) years of age.

Unlike other phases of adulthood, these stages have not yet been as clearly delineated. Instead, there are theories that cover the whole period recognizing that physical changes inevitably accompany old age at some time and that these will be somewhat limiting.

Two theories of successful ageing are described here, emphasizing the social context of ageing in later life. In comparing these theories, it will become obvious that there is some value in each of them, but no one theory is sufficient on its own. People vary considerably in how they want to spend their later years and in how much control they have over this. In fact, successful ageing would appear to result from achieving a balance that suits the individual concerned.

We should also consider many other variables (such as health, income, place of residence, sense of control, social support systems, marital status and family) when assessing a person's life satisfaction. The related critical life event of retirement is also considered in this context. We then go on to consider possible cognitive changes in later life and finish with a consideration of the impact of one further critical life event, bereavement.

EXPLANATIONS OF ADJUSTMENT TO OLD AGE

Social disengagement theory

Social disengagement theory (Cumming and Henry 1961) sees ageing as a gradual and mutual process of separation between individuals and their social roles and interests. As people age, their activity levels tend to decrease and they may become freer of family and work responsibilities. This is a natural, and often positive, process whereby, in later life, the ageing person becomes more reflective and self-sufficient and less absorbed in other people and events. They generally bring this about themselves, but other events, such as loss of spouse and retirement, also encourage disengagement to happen. Cumming and Henry described three phases in the process of disengagement as people move towards the end of their lives:

1 There is *shrinkage of life space* brought about by fewer interactions with others and the relinquishing of some of our roles.

2 There is *increased individuality*, as the individual becomes more flexible in the way in which the remaining roles are expressed.

3 There is *acceptance* of these life changes. This is not meant to imply that the individual is resigned to disengagement. Instead, acceptance leads to the person becoming more inward and self-reliant as though preparing for death.

Of course, this is a culturally specific view in which society is seen as withdrawing itself from the person. In some tribal and village cultures, and in more developed countries such as China, elders may become pivotal in the life of the community and valued for their wisdom and advice. The problems with this theory must, therefore, be considered in the light of cultural differences:

- *Disengagers and reorganizers* – People who apparently disengage may simply be embracing a life style that they prefer but were prevented from adopting before. This has to do with personality rather than advancing age. In a follow-up study of some of the original sample of Cumming and

Henry (1961), Havighurst *et al.* (1968) identified different personality types. There were some called *disengaged* whose activity, but not contentment levels, had fallen. By contrast there were *reorganizers*, whose activity levels had not dropped; they had simply changed.

- *Quality not quantity* – People may disengage from a wider social circle, but replace a larger number of superficial contacts with a smaller number of high-quality, more rewarding contacts (see the account of selectivity theory below).

- *Cohort effects* – There may be a cohort effect that gives a false impression of disengagement. Later generations of elderly people may be healthier, more financially secure, generally better catered for socially and so have greater choice. If this proves to be the case, 'disengagement' may disappear (Bromley 1988).

Activity (re-engagement) theory

Havighurst and colleagues' activity theory (1968) directly challenges the notion of disengagement in old age. There are plenty of examples of people who do not welcome or expect disengagement and are unhappy when social forces require them to. This calls into question whether disengagement really is 'natural' and inevitable, or even 'accepted', as stated in Cumming and Henry's last stage. Essentially, health and financial factors permitting, individuals may strongly resist disengagement, preferring to remain active and productive in later life. Old age is thus more like an extension of middle adulthood. Those who remain

actively, socially engaged are often happier than those not so engaged. Unfortunately, ingrained ageism, and the way the elderly are stereotypically viewed in Western cultures, create social barriers that can make continued engagement difficult. Some disengagement is inevitable (e.g. through children leaving home, statutory retirement, reduction in income, loss of loved ones and changes in physical capabilities), but the individual is less likely to be demoralized if they are well prepared and have plenty of substitute activities and companions. The quality of these activities is also important for life satisfaction. Activities that simply maintain the frequency of social contact are a poor substitute for roles and relationships that are meaningful and worthwhile to the individual.

- *Cultural differences* – As with disengagement theory, it is important to remember the cultural context of activity theory. There are many cultures in which the elderly are fully integrated rather than marginalized. Disengagement is not an issue because the experience and wisdom of the elders is respected and valued regardless of any physical limitations that may be present.

- *Occupational re-engagement* – Bond *et al.* (1993) observed that activity theory might underestimate the importance Western culture places on being economically productive and that it was, perhaps, over-optimistic about the ability of older people to remain engaged in the eyes of others once they had lost their main

employment. However, anxieties about the adequacy of pensions and the need to retain older workers in employment has led some companies to recruit actively from older age groups (e.g. the DIY chain B&Q).

- *Selectivity theory* – A newer approach called 'selectivity theory' (Field and Minkler 1988; Lang and Carstensen 1994) focuses on the way in which social relationships, and the needs they fulfil, change with age. In our younger years, we may select relationships, not just for companionship, but also for guidance, information and affirmation. Older people appear to disengage from unrewarding relationships and engage or re-engage with those that are primarily emotionally supportive and pleasant. This theory suggests that, at least in an ideal world, individuals can find a balance that works for them.

EFFECTS OF RETIREMENT

Retirement in the Western world is a relatively modern creation, made possible by the promise of at least some financial support (in the form of pensions) for those who are retired, although the traditional concept of a 'job for life' until the age of 65 is also changing rapidly. Changes in the nature of work and in the working patterns of men and women mean that cohort effects are particularly relevant when considering research about retirement. Both men and women now retire at a variety of ages and for different reasons. For many, the transition to retirement is abrupt, whilst for others it is blurred as they disengage gradually from work or become 'unretired–retired' having never completely stopped working at all.

As health care and longevity improve, many of us can anticipate long years of retirement, but is this always a welcome prospect? In a cross-cultural study, Gee and Baillie (1999) questioned 183 Australian and British men and women in employment who were aged 40 and over about their expectations for retirement. Their main finding was that most participants regarded retirement optimistically as a 'new beginning', but expected to undertake some active preparation to help them to adapt to the changes they would have to face. Research bears out their intuition that retirement is not so much a single event as a process of adaptation. For example,

Atchley (1982, 1988) identified five periods of adjustment that people who retire in the traditional sense, but not all, may experience to varying degrees:

- **Honeymoon period** – A period of relative enjoyment and euphoria (more common for voluntary retirees who are financially secure). There may be a feeling of being on holiday and of being able to busy oneself with things that there was no time for while at work. Extensive travel and/or house moves are possible.
- **Rest and relaxation period** – A time to rest and take stock after the initial activity of the honeymoon phase.
- **Disenchantment period** – A period thought to affect only a small proportion of retirees. Expectations may have been unrealistic or unmet because of bereavement and/or physical and mental health problems. Support may be reduced if social networks have been disrupted.
- **Reorientation period** – Another opportunity to take stock and adjust expectations in line with the more clearly understood reality of the situation.
- **Routine period** – A stable and satisfying routine is established giving structure and meaning to retirement.

AO2 Evaluation
studies of retirement

- **Individual differences** – Findings such as Atchley's, while informing potential retirees of what they could expect, do not apply to everyone. Schaie and Willis (1991) comment that most people adjust well to retirement, but that problems are least likely among those who retired voluntarily and who enjoy financial security and good health. Furthermore, people who report high personal involvement in their jobs, or whose leisure time is unsatisfactory, feel the greatest disruption to their lives following retirement; some of these will cope by retaining a foothold in their occupation for as long as possible.
- **Problems of adjustment** – Those who do not judge their self-worth primarily in terms of their job, and who engage in a variety of activities outside their work, tend to adjust to retirement more easily. Particular problems of adjustment may be apparent for couples whose pre-retirement relationship conformed to the stereotypical domesticated woman/working man pattern. In these cases, although both need to

adjust to the changed situation, the male may have more to do in adapting to a domain which is more familiar to, and dominated by, his partner.
- **Research support** – An Australian study by Sharpley and Layton (1998) supports some of these ideas. They questioned 349 males and 385 females, aged between 44 and 90 years old, for the first five years after retirement from full-time work. A key finding was that men and women who had retired voluntarily were significantly less anxious, depressed and stressed than those who had retired because of ill health or redundancy. Furthermore, with regard to physical health, males who retired earlier fared better than later retirees, but no such pattern emerged for women.
- **Easing the effects** – A better understanding of this particular life event has led to the recognition that it can be made easier to manage if pre-retirement education is given. Importantly, Sharpley and Layton's findings suggested that pre-retirement education which addressed social, health, personal, relationship and, of course, financial aspects of the retirement could help to reduce some of the psychological distress which is sometimes part of this phase of life. In this respect, forewarned is forearmed.

COGNITIVE PROCESSING CHANGES IN ADULTHOOD

While it is true that certain diseases associated with ageing can lead to a reduction in cognitive functioning, the rather negative stereotype of inevitable intellectual decline in late adulthood is something of a myth.

Intelligence in late adulthood

Care should also be taken over what is meant by 'intellectual ability'. Psychologists generally agree that 'intelligence' is multi-faceted. For example, a distinction can be drawn between 'crystallized' and 'fluid' intelligence. Crystallized intelligence is 'the ability to store and manipulate learned information' (Durkin 1995, p. 645), while fluid intelligence is a general, problem-solving ability that we bring to bear on novel or unfamiliar problems. Baltes and Baltes (1990) claim that crystallized intelligence increases with age, but that there is a general decline in fluid intelligence. This difference could quite simply be accounted for by practice. Crystallized intelligence is maintained on a daily basis while fluid intelligence may be more frequently exercised in younger people.

Some evidence suggests that older people generally perform less well on tasks that require mental processing speed which are a feature of many well-established intelligence tests. Berk (1998) suggests that this could be due to deterioration in neural networks as neurons in the brain die. Alternatively, information is lost as an ageing system takes longer to move it through the various processing stages, or it may simply be a question of how practised a person is. This could affect any intelligence (and memory) test which incorporates mental speed into its scoring procedures.

Memory in late adulthood

A further aspect of a negative stereotype about older people is that their memories become unreliable but, as with intelligence, we need to define the term with care, as there are many different kinds of memory. Typically, tests of recall show a decline with age, while tests of recognition show no such decline. Older adults may recall lists less efficiently than younger ones, although they can often recall the gist of a passage of prose equally well. Older adults may process certain information less deeply than younger ones, but training in memory strategies can eliminate this difference (Schaie and Willis 1991). An example of research in this area is a study by Laursen (1997) involving 711 participants from four cohorts born in 1922, 1932, 1942 and 1952 and followed up over 11 years between 1982 and 1994. Laursen found a decline in:

- **non-verbal** learning and memory
- **retention** of verbal memory
- **concentration** and **reaction time**, which could underpin performance on other tests.

Analysis of the data led Laursen to the general conclusion that such abilities become more scattered with age such that there is more variability in older generations than in younger ones. However, this study also underlines the problems inherent in such research. For example, Laursen began with over 1,000 participants, but lost over 300. The greatest loss of participants (attrition) was found among those with only primary schooling and low social status, and among the oldest participants. The sample that remained, although large, was inevitably self-selected. This could account for the apparent increase in variability of participants' abilities.

(see the panel overleaf)

Evaluation
research into cognitive changes in late adulthood
(AO2)

- **Compensating for age-related changes** – A decline in processing speed may be accounted for by the fact that older people have more experience than younger ones and may be able to consider more, and more complex, strategies for solving a problem (e.g. Stuart-Hamilton 2000). In certain cases, this might enable them to arrive at a better solution, albeit more slowly.

- **Cohort effects** – When we compare mental abilities in different generations, we must take account of their different educational experiences. Younger people may be more familiar with being tested in particular ways and so have developed strategies that help them to succeed. Younger people may also be more recently practised. However, Schaie and Hertzog (1983) showed that both age and cohort effects matter in tests of mental ability. They compared Americans born in different decades and found differences for age and cohort effects were equally strong.

- **Cultural attitudes to ageing** – Cultural context may help to shape the way in which research questions are framed. In China, government ministers in their 70s might be regarded as youngsters and prone to hot-headedness, whereas in the UK or USA they might be seen as wiser, but stereotyped as being prone to senility (Durkin 1995). Levy and Langer (1994) found that a person's *own* attitudes towards ageing can affect specific cognitive tasks (see the panel overleaf).

- **The 'terminal drop'** – Bee (1998) points out that there is little decline in intellectual functioning until about the last five years of life (a phenomenon referred to as the 'terminal drop'). Because each cohort contains more and more people within this range (we live in an ageing society), it looks as if the whole cohort is declining intellectually.

The stereotype that intellectual capacities decline with age may be, at least partly, in the mind. Levy and Langer (1994) investigated the impact of negative stereotypes about ageing on memory. Their participants were drawn from three groups:

- hearing American adults
- Americans with profound hearing disability
- Chinese adults.

They further sub-divided the groups into younger (15- to 30-year-old) and older (59- to 91-year-old) participants. They reasoned that hearing-disabled Americans would be insulated from dominant cultural messages about ageing and that the Chinese participants would also be protected from negative stereotypes as a result of the veneration enjoyed by elderly Chinese people. They measured participants' memory on a series of tests. They also recorded participants' stereotypical views about the elderly.

Is age-associated memory loss actually a culture-associated phenomenon?

They found that the Chinese and hearing-disabled Americans had more positive stereotypes about the elderly. In addition, elderly participants in these two groups out-performed the elderly hearing American group on the memory tasks. Also, the correlation between performance and attitude in the elderly was positive while in younger participants it was negative. These findings point to the role of psychological factors, as well as age-associated physiological ones, in determining cognitive ability.

COPING WITH BEREAVEMENT

The term 'bereavement' describes the objective event of the death of someone who is personally significant to us in some way. 'Grieving' refers to the many emotions and physical reactions that people experience after such a loss, and 'mourning' to how grief is expressed. Mourning is both public and private, behavioural and psychological, and different according to the context in which it occurs. In a nutshell, mourning is what we do in order to cope with the grief that follows bereavement.

Research into coping with bereavement

Bereavement is an almost universal experience. Very few of us make it through life without experiencing it at some time. What is strikingly *different*, according to researchers, is *how* people mourn. Patterns of mourning do not reflect fundamental differences between people. Instead, they would appear to be different ways of expressing the same thing in a way which fits a culture's particular needs at particular times in their history (see the panel on p. 642).

Stroebe and Stroebe (1987) comment that, whatever form mourning rituals take, 'following culturally prescribed rituals aids recovery from bereavement'. There are two major ways in which this might occur.

Mourning rituals activate social support

Mourning rituals allow the bereaved to call on practical support from others. They may also activate social

support networks which could assist people in coming to terms with their loss.

A social network that can fulfil these social functions is the 'convoy' (Kahn and Antonucci 1980). This consists of friends, family and others who accompany us through life providing psychological and practical support. Evidence suggests that people who lack a convoy are more prone to illness, emotional disturbance and death after bereavement but people with a complete convoy that meets their needs cope with bereavement more effectively. Littlewood (1992) gives one example of this. In 1966 in Aberfan, 116 school children and 28 adults lost their lives when a coal-waste tip engulfed a school and neighbouring buildings. Littlewood suggests that close community and family ties were one reason why the residents of Aberfan coped with relatively little outside help.

Mourning rituals allow time for healing

Mourning allows us time for the process of acceptance and recovery. Elizabeth Kübler-Ross's (1969) clinical interviews with terminally ill and dying people enabled her to formulate a stage theory of dying (see Table 20.3). In such cases, it appears that mourning can begin before the death itself, possibly even with the help of the dying person. This has become known as 'anticipatory grief'. Table 20.3 also outlines Fulton's (1970) four stages of grieving in the person facing bereavement and Collin Murray-Parkes's (1972) description of stages of coping following bereavement.

Stages of dying (Kübler-Ross 1969)

>> Denial	The person resists facing death and may seek other professional opinions or reassurance from religion.
>> Anger	The person asks 'Why me?' and may feel hostile, resentful and envious of others. There may also be a strong feeling of frustration over unfinished business.
>> Bargaining	When 'Why me?' is not answered, bargains may be struck with God or fate. Many bargains will be made and broken.
>> Depression	Denial becomes impossible. Hospitalization may be necessary. There may be physical deterioration and a great sense of loss as well as guilt and worry about letting others down.
>> Acceptance	In this 'final rest before the long journey', the dying person may feel devoid of feelings, weak and resolute, although not happy.

Stages of grieving in the person facing bereavement (Fulton 1970)

>> Depression	Accompanied by extreme upset and anticipatory grief.
>> Heightened concern	For the ill person, accompanied by the need to deal with unfinished business and discuss things. Caring well for them can help to obviate guilt when they die.
>> Rehearsals for the death	Developing coping strategies.
>> Adjustment	New coping strategies along with those developed at the third stage can help here.

Stages of grieving after the death has occurred (Murray-Parkes 1972)

>> Initial response	Shock, disbelief, extreme sorrow, numbness, coldness and emptiness.
>> Coping	Anxiety and fear about breaking down completely. The person may turn to tranquillizers, sleeping pills or alcohol, and may show a number of physical and psychological symptoms. These will become more sporadic in the first year or so.
>> Intermediate phase	Characterized by obsessional reviews ('I could have done more'), trying to explain the loss ('It was God's will') and searching for the presence of the deceased through reminiscing and revisiting certain places.
>> Recovery phase	In about the second year, a more positive attitude may develop, even pride at having survived the crisis and grown through it.

ACTIVITY

Highs and lows of life

Ask people of different ages to identify the three major highs and three major lows of their lives to date. Deliberately leave the question open ended. Ask each person to mark on a diagram the extent to which they saw each event as positive or negative, and how much change was involved.

1 Do people mention the kinds of life event listed in the SRRS (see p. 89)?

2 What kind of events might be indicated by the crosses A, B and C?

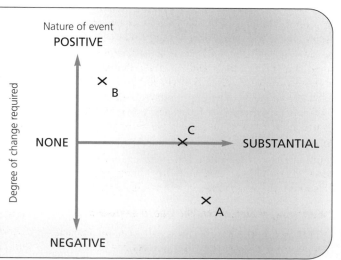

Mourning rituals across cultures

Within cultures, differing religious beliefs and ideas about the afterlife also affect the pattern of mourning. A striking contrast in recent times is provided by the Muslim and Church of England ceremonies following the deaths of Dodi Al Fayed and Princess Diana in 1997. Dodi's faith dictated that the funeral should take place within 24 hours of his death. Diana's was a much lengthier affair.

The Hopi Indians of Arizona fear and dislike the dead. They do their best, through ritual, to break the bonds between the living and the dead. Funerals are short and perfunctory and, afterwards, the bereaved work hard to forget. For the Kota of southern India, expressions of grief are more protracted. Shortly after death, a 'green' funeral is held while the loss is still 'fresh'. This is followed by a 'dry' funeral, which takes place at annual intervals, lasts for 11 days and includes remembrance of others who have died in the previous year. Further expressions of grief are encouraged as various rituals are enacted but, at the end of this phase, the sombre mood ends abruptly to be replaced by an atmosphere of celebration. There are more rituals (including sexual intercourse for the widowed, preferably with a sibling of the dead person), all intended to return the bereaved to normal life.

In Japanese Shintoism and in Buddhism, the dead become ancestors. Small shrines, or altars, in Japanese homes allow continued contact with ancestors and provide a place where food, drink and treats can be left for them. Christians also believe in the afterlife and see no harm in commemorating the dead in various ways. Some people believe that dying is simply a point in the continuous cycle of life and death that affects all living organisms and that the dead should not be embalmed but simply returned to the earth in biodegradable coffins thus causing as little contamination as possible.

In what ways are mourning rituals important for the bereaved?

Commentary
cultural differences in coping with bereavement

● **The practicalities of mourning and bereavement** – The stage theories proposed by Kübler-Ross, Fulton and Murray-Parkes are based on Western culture, in which the medical profession is powerful. Such findings are not necessarily applicable to other cultures, especially those where death may be more commonplace or where views of health and illness are not based on the medical model. In wealthier, developed countries, medical advances mean that most of us can hope to live long and healthy lives and to die of old age. However, where day-to-day survival is not assured, a period of non-productivity is a luxury, so a swift recovery and return to everyday life are essential. Around the world, the form of mourning is, to a large extent, shaped by such practicalities.

● **Mourning rituals and mourners' needs** – In the wealthier Western world, where survival is relatively more assured, we can take time over mourning. The close match between the mourning rituals in some of these cultures and the stages described by Kübler-Ross and others offer indirect but strong support for their findings in such contexts. Orthodox Jewish customs, for example, seem to fit the proposed stages particularly well and consist of structured rituals and phases of mourning that can last up to a year. This is a clear example of the timing and nature of mourning rituals being allowed to evolve to match mourners' needs.

● **The effectiveness of mourning in different cultures** – Research into cultural differences in coping with bereavement has enabled researchers to compare the effectiveness of patterns of mourning. Secularized cultures are particularly poor at providing clear guidelines about mourning. Orthodox Jews, on the other hand, encourage the ritualized expression of grief over time and this is thought to be therapeutic. Contrast this with the indigenous American Maya Indians whose mourning period is limited to just four days. Comparisons like these lead us to greater understanding of how to protect people from the worst effects of bereavement and achieve the best possible outcome in terms of their health and wellbeing.

A2 Developmental Psychology

✓ CHECK YOUR UNDERSTANDING

Check your understanding of late adulthood by answering these questions from memory at first. Check your answers by looking back through Topic 3.

1 Précis the main points of disengagement theory and activity theory in 150 words each.

2 In what ways might these theories be able to co-exist?

3 Name the five periods of adjustment to retirement proposed by Atchley (1982, 1988).

4 Identify three individual differences that might affect responses to retirement.

5 In 150 words, outline research findings into either intelligence or retirement in late adulthood (AO1), and in a further 150 words,

make three evaluative (AO2) points about them.

6 Outline the four stages of grieving upon bereavement suggested by Murray-Parkes (1972).

7 What two major social functions do mourning rituals fulfil?

8 Using cross-cultural research to illustrate your answer, explain how different beliefs about the meaning of death shape mourning rituals.

REVISION SUMMARY

Having covered this topic, you should be able to:

✓ describe and evaluate disengagement theory and activity theory as explanations of adjustment to old age

✓ describe and evaluate research into the impact of retirement

✓ describe and evaluate studies into cognitive changes in late adulthood

✓ describe research into bereavement and be able to evaluate these from a cross-cultural perspective.

✎ EXAMPLE EXAM QUESTIONS

Typical examination questions on this topic include the following.

1 Outline and evaluate **two** explanations of adjustment to old age. (24 marks)

> In 'outline' questions such as this, a *précis* is required of each of two explanations. It pays you, therefore, to be very strategic with your use of time. This essay could conveniently be broken down into four 'mini-essays', each one of about 150 words or $7\frac{1}{2}$ minutes. Writing a précis is not as easy as it sounds, so you need to *practise* before you try it for real in the exam. A good précis should contain the gist of an explanation but also some degree of detail.

2 Discuss research (explanations **and/or** studies) related to the effects of retirement. (24 marks)

> You could use the material presented on p. 638 for the main part of the AO1 component of your answer, but research in this area is constantly giving us new insights into the effects of retirement, so it pays you to search the Internet and add a couple of studies of your own. This makes the material more personal, more meaningful and therefore more *memorable*.

Unit 20 // Adulthood

643

3 Discuss research (theories **and/or** studies) into cognitive changes in late adulthood.   (24 marks)

> The term 'discuss' requires both AO1 description and AO2 commentary (analysis and evaluation). The AO1 content is quite straightforward, and would probably include a description of research into intelligence and memory changes in late adulthood. Although you can plan your answer in any way you want, it would be easy to construct two 150-word descriptive accounts of these two areas to form the AO1 component of your answer. For the AO2 component, we have included four evaluative points in this unit (see p. 639). Each of these could be represented in your answer *or* you could use the Internet to find a study for yourself that you feel *supports* or *challenges* the AO1 points, and use this to replace (or in addition to) these AO2 points.

4 (a) Describe research (theories **and/or** studies) into how people cope with bereavement.   (12 marks)
   (b) To what extent are there cultural differences in the way that people cope with bereavement?
   (12 marks)

> The AO1 component of this question would be a description of how people cope with bereavement (part (a) of the question). The AO2 component of this question requires you to assess the extent to which there are cultural differences in the way that people cope with bereavement. As always, it isn't enough to merely *describe* these cultural differences, but you should use this material as AO2 commentary, i.e. what do such differences tell us about behaviour and these theories?

5 (a) Outline and evaluate research (theories **and/or** studies) into cognitive changes in late adulthood.
   (12 marks)
   (b) Outline and evaluate research (theories **and/or** studies) into how people cope with bereavement.
   (12 marks)

> In this question, there is an unusual mark split with 6 marks of AO1 and 6 marks of AO2 in each part of the question. It may appear to be a generous question as it gives you lots of choice about what to write, but this brings its own difficulties, because you might find you have rather too much to write for the AO1 component of each part of the question and thus restrict the AO2 content – as a result you would reduce your overall mark. It will pay to structure your answer quite strictly and stick to the word allocations (150 words for each outline and 150 words for each evaluation). Remember that you can always use a study as AO2 instead of AO1.

UNIT SUMMARY

Topic 1: Early and middle adulthood

- Psychologists have taken a variety of approaches to studying the relatively neglected area of lifespan psychology. Some have produced overarching theories, while others focus on particular stages of life or on specific life events.

- The study of the lifespan is dogged by methodological difficulties, especially those concerning **cohort effects** and the inherent problems associated with **cross-sectional** or **longitudinal** research.

- **Theories of development in early and middle adulthood** proposed by **Erikson**, **Levinson** and **Gould** offer different views of the nature of these phases of life. All three theories are built on research evidence that suggests that important transitions occur during adulthood.

- They also acknowledge the **existence of crises in adulthood**, which require that adjustments are made, but which vary in the relative emphasis placed upon these. Some critics argue that adulthood is no more critical than any other life phase, while others question whether 'crisis' is an artefact created by cohort effects.

Topic 2: Family and relationships in adulthood

- The impact of the three life events of **marriage (or partnering), parenthood** and **divorce** are commonly experienced during early and middle adulthood.

- There are gender and cultural differences in the nature and **effects of such events on the individual**, although all seem to require considerable adjustment. The timing of these life events within the lifespan and their co-occurrence with other events are additional factors that can affect their impact.

Topic 3: Cognitive changes in late adulthood

- **Explanations of adjustment to old age** offer differing views about the social forces operating in the later phases of life. Some individuals seem to disengage (**social disengagement theory**), while others prefer to remain active. Selectivity theory suggests that as we grow older, we simply become more particular about who and what we choose to engage or disengage with (health and circumstances permitting).

- Studies of **cognitive changes in late adulthood** yield mixed results depending on the type of ability being measured. In some cases there appears to be a decline associated with age, but these can be explained in many ways, including neurophysiological degeneration, changes in strategies, or even changes in a person's beliefs about their abilities.

- **The effects of retirement** are becoming increasingly nebulous as more and more people retire early and/or keep aspects of their working life going.

- **Coping with bereavement** is regarded as one of the most distressing life events of all. Although some of the immediate emotional reactions seem to be universal, there are **cultural differences** in patterns of coping which seem to serve the same basic purpose of allowing grief to take its course and to activate social support systems.

- **Kübler-Ross's** pioneering work into how people who are terminally ill or dying cope with their impending death has helped in understanding and supporting both the person who is dying and their bereaved relatives.

FURTHER RESOURCES

Bee, H. (2001) *Lifespan Development* **(3nd edn), New York: Longman.**

A very readable survey of psychological development from birth to death.

Berk, L.E. (1998) *Development through the Lifespan*, **London: Allyn & Bacon.**

An interactive text covering lifespan development and which features case studies of real people and much useful information on cultural issues.

Durkin, K. (1995) *Developmental Social Psychology*, **Oxford: Blackwell.**

An excellent, detailed, general text focusing on lifespan developmental psychology.

Website

www.nlm.nih.gov/medlineplus/bereavement.html

An interesting collection of resources on the topic of bereavement in both adults and children.

21
UNIT

DETERMINANTS OF
Animal
Behaviour

PREVIEW

After you have read this unit, you should be able to describe and evaluate:

>> evolutionary explanations of at least two types of non-human behaviour, including at least two biological explanations of apparent altruism

>> classical (Pavlovian) conditioning and its role in the behaviour of non-human animals

>> operant conditioning and its role in the behaviour of non-human animals

>> explanations and research studies relating to the role of social learning in the behaviour of non-human animals

>> evidence for intelligence in non-human animals, including self-recognition, theory of mind and social intelligence.

INTRODUCTION

It is useful to make clear right from the start that the question of whether genetics (nature) or learning (nurture) underlies any given behaviour is essentially meaningless. Any behaviour, however simple or complex, has an element of both inheritance and learning about it. The only point of debate is concerning the relative importance of the contributions of phylogeny and ontogeny to a specific behaviour. 'Phylogeny' refers to the inheritance of species-specific behaviour patterns, e.g. the arching of a cat's back when it is threatened. 'Ontogeny' refers to behaviour acquired during the lifetime of the individual which is not shared with every member of the species. For instance, some cats learn how to open doors by pulling downwards on the handle. Similarly, some blue tits learn how to tear into the caps of milk bottles left on the doorstep. Whenever a behaviour is seen in all members of a species, the strength of inheritance is clear. However, the occurrence of a behaviour in just one or two individuals does not necessarily mean it is '100 per cent learned'. This is because some forms of behaviour are only slight modifications of natural forms. For instance, the opening of the milk-bottle top by blue tits involves similar actions to those they use when stripping the bark from trees to reach insects underneath. The influence of inheritance in this case is still very strong. As we shall see, disentangling the contribution of nature and nurture with respect to animal behaviour is not as straightforward as we might like to think.

Darwin's theory of evolution, including the processes of natural selection and survival of the fittest, is considered in Topic 1 in order to examine evolutionary explanations of animal behaviour. Biological explanations of apparent altruism are also discussed because Darwin was puzzled by the fairly widespread incidence of apparently altruistic behaviour in the animal world when, according to his theory, an animal should behave selfishly in order to increase its fitness and reproductive success. In Topic 2, you will examine the principles of classical (Pavlovian) conditioning and operant conditioning and evaluate their role in determining animal behaviour. In the final topic of this unit, you will explore the intriguing issue of whether animals living in social groups learn from each other, and also the evidence for the very challenging concept of intelligence in non-human animals.

Mike
Cardwell

From wolf to family pet – what characteristics of its wild ancestors led to the development of the modern-day domesticated dog?

Next time you look at your dog, don't just think of it as the lovable family pet, but the end product of thousands of years of selective pressure. But how exactly did dogs' association with humans lead to their evolution from their wild wolf ancestors? Natural selection would have played a key role in this process. Wild dogs that were less cautious around people may have

begun to live near humans, scavenging scraps from early human settlements. Natural selection would have then led to the gradual emergence of dogs that did not fear humans and could live in close proximity to them. Artificial selection by humans may have further shaped their evolution because dogs with traits desired by humans would have been better cared for, and would have been more likely to survive and breed. You will read more about domestication in the panel on p. 648, 'The domestication of the fox'.

Altruism: an animal is said to be engaging in altruistic behaviour when by so doing it increases the survival chances of another animal whilst decreasing its own. The term apparent altruism refers to the fact that such behaviours are frequently selfish when viewed from another level.

Classical conditioning: a form of learning where a neutral stimulus is paired with a stimulus that already produces a response, such that over time, the neutral stimulus also produces that response.

Evolution: the change over successive generations in the genetic make-up of a particular group or species, as a result of natural and sexual selection.

Fitness: a measurement of the number of offspring left behind by an individual compared to the number of offspring left behind by other members of the same species.

Intelligence: an underlying ability which enables an individual to adapt and function effectively within a given environment.

Kin selection: animals are more likely to show cooperation and altruism towards close genetic relations. The closer the genetic relationship, the greater the likelihood of help, and therefore the greater the likelihood of these relatives surviving and reproducing.

Natural selection: animals that are well adapted to their environment will leave behind more offspring than those who are less well adapted.

Operant conditioning: an explanation of learning that sees the consequences of a behaviour as being of vital importance to the future appearance of that behaviour.

Sexual selection: individuals possess features which make them attractive to members of the opposite sex (intrasexual selection) or help them compete with members of the same sex for access to mates (intersexual selection).

Social learning: a form of learning in which people learn by observing and imitating the behaviour of others

<<I have called this principle, by which each slight variation, if useful, is preserved, by the term Natural Selection.>> (Charles Darwin 1859)

Darwin's theory of evolution has four main parts:

- Organisms have *changed over time*. Those living today are different from those that have lived in the past. The world is not constant, but changing, and organisms must constantly adapt to these changes.

- All organisms are derived from *common ancestors*. Over time, populations split into different species that are related because of this common ancestry. This explains the similarities of organisms that are classified together – they are similar because of shared traits inherited from their common ancestors.

- *Change is gradual and slow*, taking place over a long period of time (this belief has been challenged by the view that evolution takes place through a process of rapid change and long periods of stability (stasis), known as 'punctuated equilibrium').

- The mechanism by which this change takes place is known as '*natural selection*' – a process that occurs over successive generations.

Darwin's theory of the process of evolution was shaped by his observations of the selective breeding of domesticated animals, as well as by his field studies of natural selection. Species of horse, cattle, dogs and other household pets have been bred in order to emphasize certain features which humans either exploit or else find aesthetically pleasing. For instance, horses bred for racing are lighter, leaner and weaker than those bred for farm work, which are tougher, stronger, have more stamina and are less 'temperamental'. Many dogs and cats have features that are the result of hundreds of generations of selective breeding. These features may be physical (such as long ears, thick coat, large eyes or drooping jaw) or behavioural (such as running ability, a placid or aggressive temperament, or hunting ability). These diverse breeds possess such qualities as a result of humans systematically mating females with males over many generations in order to produce the most exaggerated forms of the required characteristics. The different breeds become genetically altered from the original, and this is the basis of the 'purity' (i.e. pedigree) of each breed.

The domestication of the fox

Belyaev and his team designed a selective-breeding programme to reproduce a single major factor, a strong selection pressure for tameness. Starting in 1959 with 130 foxes, they allowed only the tamest animals to breed over many generations. If they were vicious, they didn't join the experimental population. If they showed slight fear and friendliness, they did. To ensure that their tameness resulted from genetic selections, the scientists didn't train the foxes and their contact with humans was limited to brief behavioural tests. Now, 40 years and 45,000 foxes later, the changes are dramatic. The current crop of foxes are friendly, playful and eager to please – they compete for the attention of humans and show very little aggression. Physical changes mirror those in other domestic animals like dogs. The foxes display a variety of coat colours, and many have floppy ears. Corticosteroid levels, which are involved with the fear and stress responses, have halved and then halved again. Serotonin, the neurotransmitter associated with 'calmness', has risen substantially compared with the wild fox (Trut 1999), and generally the 'foxes' show more in common with the domestic dog than the ancestral fox.

Darwin himself became a keen breeder of pigeons in order to study the process by which this type of selection is achieved. He believed that the means by which evolution brings about changes in appearance and behaviour of species is similar to the selective breeding of animals that he witnessed first hand.

The pressures on animals that happen in a natural environment bring about adaptations, i.e. those individuals having the best means of overcoming an extreme circumstance (such as climatic change, floods, predation or competition for scarce resources) are those that are most likely to survive.

NATURAL SELECTION

The logic behind the process of natural selection is as follows (see also Fig. 21.1):

1 All organisms are capable of 'overreproducing'. If all the offspring that organisms were able to produce were to survive and reproduce, they would very quickly overpopulate the planet.

2 As a result, there is a 'struggle' to survive and reproduce, in which only some individuals succeed in leaving offspring.

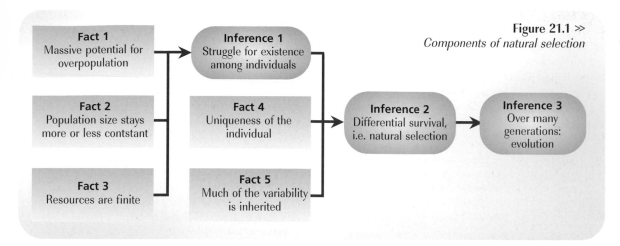

Figure 21.1 >>
Components of natural selection

Fact 1
Massive potential for overpopulation

Fact 2
Population size stays more or less contstant

Fact 3
Resources are finite

Inference 1
Struggle for existence among individuals

Fact 4
Uniqueness of the individual

Fact 5
Much of the variability is inherited

Inference 2
Differential survival, i.e. natural selection

Inference 3
Over many generations: evolution

3 Organisms show variation in characteristics that influence their success in this struggle for existence.

4 Offspring tend to resemble their parents, particularly in terms of those characteristics that influence success in the struggle to survive and reproduce.

5 Organisms that possess certain traits that enable them to survive and reproduce will contribute disproportionately to the offspring that make up the next generation.

6 Because offspring resemble their parents, the population in the next generation will contain a higher proportion of individuals that possess whatever adaptation enabled their parents to survive and reproduce.

Natural selection will only occur if there is some inheritable variation for the trait in question and if there is differential survival and reproduction associated with the possession of that trait. For example, some individuals are faster than others because of differences in their genes. If their predators, however, were that much faster, then speed differences in the prey species would make little difference to their survival and so evolution of that trait would not take place (for example, if cheetahs hunted snails). Natural selection can only occur among existing variations in a population. It may well be advantageous for polar bears to have white noses, but as the genes for white noses do not exist in the existing population of polar bears, this development cannot happen. Variants do not arise because they are needed, rather they arise by random processes that are governed by the laws of genetics.

Survival of the fittest

The idea that evolution is a process of selecting out the weakest and least competitive animals, often referred to as 'the survival of the fittest', is usually thought to be all that Darwin had to say. In fact, the very expression 'survival of the fittest' was not even written by Darwin himself, but by a political economist called Herbert Spencer, when advocating the 'naturalness' of market-

place economics. Darwin regarded physical endurance as only one quality that animals must show in their struggle to survive.

In Darwin's theory, 'fitness' is not a quality that individuals possess, such as muscular physique, physical durability or a state of good health. Bodily strength and physical fitness do not in themselves guarantee the survival of individuals in an evolutionary sense, however useful these qualities may be in competition with other members of the same species ('conspecifics') for scarce resources. In terms of evolution, fitness is linked with reproductive success. It is individuals who leave the most surviving offspring who have the greatest chance of evolutionary success. Darwin took for granted that differential reproductive success was at the centre of the process of evolution. In addition to differences in the relative success of individuals to reproduce, are the fitness and survival prospects of their offspring ('fecundity').

Natural selection in action

Why do young animals cry so much?

From a bird's first squawk to a newborn baby's cry, helpless offspring have evolved many extravagant ways of demanding attention that parents find difficult to ignore. Indeed, the displays of most offspring seem far more extravagant and ostentatious than necessary to elicit attention from parents already eager to protect and feed their own. So why hasn't evolution programmed helpless young to seek parental care with less extravagant sounds and gestures? Trivers (1974) suggested that, because the offspring of most animals share only half their genes with each parent, each individual must try to maximize the presence of its own genes in succeeding generations. Exaggerated indications of need, with each offspring trying to secure more than its fair share of parental resources, would increase the likelihood of survival and so would be favoured by natural selection. The result would be a selective process leading to more and more ostentatious demands by offspring.

Such extravagant displays are not without their costs. Noise and activity may attract predators, and also use up valuable energy. McCarty (1996) measured oxygen consumption in chicks and found that when they begged, their metabolic rates increased dramatically – in tree swallows, this was by as much as 42 per cent. An additional explanation is that such costly displays may have evolved because they also reveal an offspring's health and vigour (Furlow 2000), indicating that that offspring is worth investing in. In conditions where food and parental energy are limited, it may not pay for a parent to invest equally in all its young if some have little chance of surviving to reproductive age. Furlow suggests that one way which parents could 'force' offspring to reveal how healthy they are compared with their siblings would be to refuse to invest, at least initially, until the young have performed some costly and energy-sapping task.

Evaluation
evolutionary explanations of animal behaviour
(A02)

- *Ultimate or proximate causes?* – Gould (1984) claims that evolutionary explanations of behaviour (i.e. explaining a behaviour in terms of its *ultimate* cause) can often be ignored because explanations in terms of immediate developmental or physiological causes (i.e. *proximate* explanations) make them unnecessary. He argues that it is more appropriate to explain how a particular behaviour came into being through the animal's developmental process, or how that behaviour is controlled by its physiological mechanisms, than it is to attempt to explain why natural selection resulted in the spread of that characteristic.

- *Nature or nurture?* – What exactly *is* inherited in animal behaviour? Clearly, genes do affect behaviour, but all animals develop within some sort of environment, and it would be impossible to test whether behaviour would develop in the same way in completely different environments. The fact that members of the same species demonstrate the same behaviour does not exclude the possibility that all members of a species share common learning experiences. Simple 'nature/nurture' or 'instinctive/learned' dichotomies have now been abandoned. Nowadays, psychologists are more interested in investigating what does or does not affect behavioural development, and how genetic and environmental factors *interact*.

- *Natural selection and sexual selection* – Some characteristics of animals seem to have nothing whatsoever to do with survival; in fact, many would appear to impede survival, making it questionable to think that evolution could have produced such features. The most obvious example is the peacock's tail, which is clearly a major investment in terms of energy, but does not appear to contribute to survival ability. A credible explanation for the peacock's magnificent tail is that it serves to gain advantages in sexual reproduction by attracting mates. Those males with the larger and more gorgeous trains will have greater mating success, leaving greater numbers of descendants who are also endowed with large, attractive trains. So, despite being a physical burden, a large and spectacular train enables the peacock to be selected by the peahen as her mate. As long as the females continue to find long-tailed males the most attractive, evolution will ensure that tail length (or any other sexually selected feature) will prevail. The basis of this sexual selection is discussed in detail in Unit 23 (see p. 702).

- *The problem of altruism* – The behaviour of social insects, where individuals behave suicidally by attacking large and aggressive intruders to their nest or hive, initially seems inexplicable in terms of natural selection. Individuals who pay any cost (calculated in terms of reducing their reproductive potential) for the benefit of others should receive such a heavy penalty in evolutionary terms that such behaviour would be strongly selected against. This would ultimately lead to extinction, i.e. there would be no descendants left of individuals who acted in this way. Compare this with others acting selfishly. They would pay no costs, obtain most benefits, and thereby gain more reproductive potential. In short, selfishness should rapidly outrun altruism in the evolutionary race. The existence, in social insect societies, of castes which forego reproductive effort altogether is a particular challenge to Darwin's (1859) version of the theory; these individuals (such as worker honeybees) spend their entire lives caring for the brood of others, usually the single queen of the colony.

- *Levels of selection* – Part of the problem was that Darwin's reasoning was occurring at the wrong 'level', i.e. he believed that individuals live to reproduce. It is more accurate to consider evolution in terms of the transmission of life's units (i.e. genes) from one generation to the next. Darwin's 'problem' of the caste system of social insects can be explained in this way. Among these social insects, the high degree of genetic relatedness among sisters means that it is more productive (in terms of increased fitness) for them to help each other than it would be to have their own offspring.

BIOLOGICAL EXPLANATIONS OF APPARENT ALTRUISM

Darwin was puzzled by the prevalence of apparently altruistic behaviour in the animal world. The point is that in any given circumstance an animal ought (i.e. 'ought' in terms of increasing its fitness, or reproductive success) to behave selfishly. The reason for this is that altruism, in comparison with a strategy that is selfish, would be less successful and therefore would not evolve in competition with non-altruism. In the section that follows, we examine a number of explanations for altruism in animals that offer a very different picture of the benefits of such behaviour. We shall see that what *appears* completely altruistic at one level, is often quite selfish at another, leading to the use of the term 'apparent altruism'.

Kin selection theory

Darwin's paradox was resolved by the work of Hamilton (1963, 1964) who showed in his kin selection theory that evolution does not operate directly on individual organisms, but on their genetic make-up. In other words, any one individual may pass on genes to future generations, not just by means of their *own* reproductive success, but also by facilitating the reproductive potential of their relatives (who, of course, share some genetic material). In theory, the closer this genetic relationship is, the greater the cooperation and altruism each should show towards the other. Hamilton used the term 'inclusive fitness' to describe the effect of genetic relatedness in determining how individuals would behave altruistically towards one another. For example, Sherman (1981) showed that in Belding's ground squirrel, the females who are close relatives (such as mother–daughter or sister–sister) not only display little antagonism to each another, but also often actively help each other in defending their young from attack by predators or intruders. Related females were seen to give alarm calls at the sight of a predator to warn one another – a behaviour observed only when they were in one another's company; they remained silent at other times.

Altruism can be defined as an act of helping which increases the (reproductive) fitness of the individual who is helped, at some cost to the fitness of the helper. The *cost* of helping is essential to this definition, in understanding both the helper's contribution, as well as the important gain made by being helped. In both cases, the essential cost and benefit is fitness or reproductive success, i.e. the total contribution made to the gene pool by an individual, their own offspring and those succoured by all those individuals to whom they are genetically related. Helping a close relative or one of their offspring can, therefore, be considered an example of a selfish commitment to maximizing this inclusive fitness. But altruism is not confined to acts of helping between related individuals. Before reading any further, complete the activity above right.

ACTIVITY

Apparent altruism in animals

Consider the following examples of apparent altruism in animals. What reasons can you suggest to explain why these apparently altruistic behaviours occur?

● A lamb becomes alarmed by the sight of a dog and rushes to its mother who allows it to suckle.

● A juvenile male chimpanzee wrestles with a larger male but their play turns more aggressive. A second young male intervenes, and both chase off the larger male.

● A grouper fish remains motionless with its mouth agape while a tiny fish swims in and out of its mouth collecting morsels of food from inside.

● An ant returning to its nest after eating encounters a beetle grub near the entrance. The larva prods at the ant's mouth parts, and receives a meal of regurgitated food.

According to the definition given above, each of the behaviours listed in the activity qualifies as altruism, though the costs and benefits to helper and those helped are not the same throughout.

Kin recognition and selection

It might seem 'natural' for a parent to care for its young by providing food and protection. Clearly, there are common interests between two related individuals, and in this case, the mother will usually place herself between the dog and her lamb. The lamb's alarm response of suckling enables her to achieve this. But the lamb is also allowed to suckle from the mother even without the dog being there, and this is also altruistic since it is costly by depleting her own food reserves. Though the lamb may be at a stage when it can graze successfully for itself, the mother still does not reject its suckling, especially when the lamb is in a state of alarm (such as caused by seeing the dog). However, any lamb straying away from its mother will obtain no help from other mothers in the same field. However hard the lamb may try, other mothers will only offer protection and milk to their own lambs. They recognize their own offspring by a combination of sound and body smell.

Mechanisms of kin recognition

This form of altruism is based on kinship, i.e. individuals act favourably towards others to whom they are related.

But, without a language to express relationship, how could animals 'know' they are related? The exact way in which animals come to favour their relatives over non-relatives has raised some controversy (Grafen 1982, 1990), but there are a number of mechanisms by which this could occur (Stuart 1991). Two examples are:

- *spatial proximity* – family groups stay together
- *phenotype matching* – related individuals have certain characteristics such as smell, appearance or behaviour in common.

In gregarious species that spend time with non-relatives (such as in the case of lambs playing together), kin recognition becomes important. In species where the young have a period of dependency (often referred to as 'infancy'), the parents and young often form early 'bonds', in which each learns to recognize the other by some feature such as odour or visual cues. Farmers often exploit this 'natural' mechanism when a ewe dies giving birth. The farmer brings the surviving lamb to a ewe who has herself just lambed. In the minutes after giving birth herself, the foster mother is allowed to sniff and lick the second lamb as if it were her own. After just a few minutes together they will act as mother and offspring for life.

Evaluation
kin selection explanations of apparent altruism
(A02)

- *Research support* – Evidence for the importance of phenotype matching in kin selection comes from studies of Belding's ground squirrels. Because females may mate with more than one male, litters may contain both full siblings and half siblings. It is possible for researchers to ascertain this by DNA tests, and this can be matched to the pattern of altruism shown by the offspring. Females raised with full and half sisters consistently show more altruistic behaviour (e.g. defence against predators and in territorial disputes) towards their full sisters than their half sisters (Holmes and Sherman 1982).

- *Major Histocompatibility Complex* – Studies of mate choice in different strains of inbred mice have supported the claim that genetically similar individuals share distinctive odours that serve to trigger altruistic behaviour and also prevent inbreeding. These strains differ mainly in a group of genes called the 'Major Histocompatibility Complex' (MHC). These genes are responsible for the recognition of tissue as 'self' or 'not self'. The MHC differs in mice that are otherwise genetically identical. Male mice prefer to mate with females of a different MHC, based on the ability to discriminate female odours (Boyse *et al.* 1991).

- *The importance of kin selection* – There are a number of reasons why it is important for an individual to respond differently to kin and non-kin:

  – Parents who fail to recognize their own offspring would waste resources on another's young. This does sometimes occur in what is known as 'brood parasitism', discussed shortly.

  – If the young are to be protected by the parent, they will need to recognize one another quickly so that help can be provided.

  – Related individuals who collaborate are more likely to fend off aggression from others who are non-relatives.

  – On reaching sexual maturity, individuals must avoid mating with relatives to ensure diversity of genetic material between generations. Inbreeding itself is believed to have disadvantages that would affect the fitness of offspring.

- *Degree of relatedness* – This raises the question of whether the *exact* relatedness between individuals matters in this argument, i.e. does it matter whether an individual is helping a sister or a cousin? The answer is 'yes'. Helping a distant relative has much less benefit, in terms of inclusive fitness, than does helping a sibling (brother or sister). Any measure of relatedness is also an inverse measure of 'unrelatedness'. For instance, stating that you share half your genes with one parent means that half of the genes are not shared, i.e. are unrelated. With a distant relative, the majority of your genes are not common to you both. In fact, any relationship more distant than a sibling relationship means that you have much more unshared than shared genetic material.

Reciprocal altruism

Trivers (1971) proposed this explanation for apparently altruistic behaviour. Trivers argued that one animal might show altruistic behaviour towards another if the recipient of this favour reciprocated some time in the future. This can be seen as a 'loan' that will be repaid on some future occasion. In the activity on p. 651, the behaviour of the second young chimp could be explained in this way. Such reciprocating arrangements are not unusual in the animal kingdom. For instance, Wilkinson (1984) found that unrelated vampire bats regurgitate food for one another on their return to the nesting site. While in many instances the recipient of the meal was a relative of the regurgitating individual, often they were not. However, the unrelated animals were usually roosting neighbours of the altruist, and Wilkinson went on to demonstrate experimentally that the exchanges taking place between unrelated individuals were reciprocated.

Dealing with cheats: the 'tit for tat' strategy

In such a social climate, it could be argued that a cheating strategy (i.e. taking a favour but not returning it) would gain more than an honest one. But within the community of vampire bats, the cost of being denied a meal having once cheated is very high because a hungry bat rarely survives on cold nights.

Trivers was aware of the possibilities of cheating in such arrangements and suggested that reciprocal altruism would only evolve in species where individuals could recognize each other and apply sanctions to those who refused to reciprocate. But if cheating is so potentially profitable for an individual, why is it not more common? Axelrod and Hamilton (1981) put forward a very simple explanation that would reward cooperation and discourage defection. The 'tit-for-tat' strategy called for one animal to cooperate with another (in this case, to display altruistic behaviour to another) who would then return the favour. If one party simply returns whatever happened in the previous interaction between the two animals, cooperation would be met with cooperation, defection with return defection. In this way, a cooperative alliance could be formed between two animals that would jointly benefit both.

A02   **Evaluation**
reciprocal altruism

- *Fitting the facts* – According to Manning and Dawkins (1998), the example of the vampire bats, described earlier, would fit nicely into this model of reciprocal altruism for the following reasons:
  - These bats return to the same roost day after day and associate with other individuals over long periods, remembering benefits given and received. This means that they are able to detect cheating in bats that do not reciprocate.
  - Bats are sensitive to whether another individual is starving or well fed, and are able to help a starving bat without too much cost to themselves. A starving bat loses weight at a much higher rate than a well-fed bat, so giving of a blood meal provides the recipient with more time until starvation than the donor loses.
  - Failing to obtain a feed can happen to any of the bats, so all bats benefit from the 'insurance policy' of being fed by others in times of need.

- *Delayed reciprocal altruism* – A problem with this explanation concerns the time period between giving and receiving. As a result, the term 'delayed reciprocal altruism' is often used. Until the altruist has been repaid, the altruist has gained nothing. In fact, it is worse off than if it had done nothing. This may well explain why documented cases of reciprocal altruism are rare (Manning and Dawkins 1998). It is more common to find examples of immediate mutual cooperation between animals.

Other explanations of apparent altruism

Mutualism (or return effects)

Some cooperative relationships may even involve individuals from differing species. For example, the cleaner fish survives by removing skin parasites from other fish, or, in the case of the grouper fish (see activity, p. 651), food particles which could harbour bacteria inside the mouth of the host fish. The grouper not only refrains from eating the small fish, but occasionally closes its mouth with it inside when danger looms to threaten the safety of its small companion.

Sometimes individuals will cooperate and help one another because they can achieve more as a team than by working alone. For instance, lionesses will hunt together in bringing down other large mammals which they could not tackle safely alone. Having killed the prey, the lionesses will then share it, though not necessarily equally (Caraco and Wolf 1975).

Some mutualistic relationships involve human beings and animals. The greater honeyguide has such a relationship with humans in parts of Africa. This bird leads people to honeybee hives (Grier and Burk 1992). When the humans break into the hive to get the honey, they leave bee larvae and wax which the birds consume. The humans and birds have developed, through evolution or learning, elaborate interspecific (i.e. 'between-different-species') communication signals. A three-year field study by Isack and Reyer (1989) confirmed the validity of this relationship. They found that when guided by these birds, the Boran people of Kenya were able to find hives much more quickly than when they were unguided.

Induced (or manipulated) altruism

Some strategies that solicit help from others can be regarded as ploys, which are aimed at cheating. This 'induced altruism' is sometimes referred to as 'manipulated' or 'social parasitism'. Such behaviour would include the laying of eggs in another bird's nest ('brood parasitism'). This is practised by the cuckoo (see p. 654) and a number of other species. Another example is the beetle grub 'begging' for food from the passing ant; Hölldobler (1971) found that the larva of the *Atemelles* beetle mimics the begging behaviour of ants in order to obtain food from passing workers. Wickler (1968) found similar examples of deception in *Aspidontus* – a fish that looks like the cleaner fish (*Labroides*). However, rather than clean the host fish, *Aspidontus* individuals approach it and then bite into its flesh, swimming away with a morsel of food.

The cost of recognition

The European cuckoo lays its eggs in the nests of other birds. When the young cuckoo hatches, it pushes the eggs of the host bird out of the nest. In this way it monopolizes the parental effort of the host bird while reducing the reproductive success of the host to zero.

Cuckoos' eggs are very good mimics of their host's eggs, with cuckoos 'specializing' in different host species and laying eggs that closely resemble those of the host. The host thus faces a problem. If the host bird rejects one egg from its nest, it may break others in the process and there is always the possibility that it may be rejecting one of its own eggs. When the potential for parasitism is high, however, the benefits of rejecting eggs outweighs the costs, and host birds should discriminate more strongly against possible 'deviant' eggs. Exposing reed warblers to a stuffed cuckoo on the edge of their nest increases the likelihood that they will reject a model cuckoo egg (Davies *et al.* 1996).

Why do host birds not reject the cuckoo after it has been born? This supposes that the parent bird knows what its offspring should look like in the first place. On average, birds that accept any offspring in

The European cuckoo – a clear case of manipulated altruism within the animal kingdom

the nest have more reproductive success overall compared to birds that learn what their offspring look like from the first brood and reject in the future any offspring that look different (Lotem 1993). In the case of the cuckoo, any host bird that was parasitized might learn to accept cuckoos and reject any future young of its own. This is clearly not in the host bird's best interests. This is one occasion where learning is more costly than not learning.

Evaluation
alternative explanations of apparent altruism

- *Mutualism* – Mutualistic relationships between animals and humans are relatively rare, but can be explained without resorting to a truly altruistic explanation. There are two main benefits of the greater honeyguide's relationship with humans. First, they have much greater access to hives with human help and, second, the use of smoke to

clear the hives reduces the chances of the birds being stung by the bees.

- *Why does manipulated altruism work?* – What looks like altruism on the part of the host animal is actually manipulation and deception on the part of the recipient (see 'The cost of recognition' panel above). Recent research suggests that the cuckoo chick even mimics the begging calls of the host's chicks and even sounds like more than one chick to encourage the host to feed it more (Moksnes and Røskaft 1995).

✓ CHECK YOUR UNDERSTANDING

Check your understanding of evolutionary explanations of animal behaviour by answering these questions. Check your answers by looking back through Topic 1.

1 What are the four main components of Darwin's theory of evolution?

2 What are the six points that constitute the logic of natural selection?

3 People often misunderstand the concept of 'survival of the fittest'. In 100 words, provide a summary of this concept that would clear up any misconceptions about its real meaning.

4 How did Darwin explain the 'problem' of the peacock's tail?

5 The fact that some social insects give up their reproductive opportunities to help genetic relatives appears to pose a problem for Darwin's theory of evolution through natural selection. How is this behaviour explained in a way that remains consistent with basic Darwinian principles?

continued

6 What is 'apparent altruism'?

7 Construct a descriptive 150-word précis of kin selection theory as an explanation of altruism.

8 Identify three critical (i.e. AO2) points relating to kin selection theory as an explanation of

the formation of relationships, and explain in what way these support the theory.

9 Construct a descriptive 150-word précis of reciprocal altruism.

10 In what ways does the behaviour of vampire bats support the idea of reciprocal altruism?

REVISION SUMMARY

Having covered this topic, you should be able to:

✓ explain the logic behind the process of natural selection

✓ describe and evaluate evolutionary explanations of at least two types of animal behaviour

✓ describe and evaluate at least two biological explanations of apparent altruism.

EXAMPLE EXAM QUESTIONS

Below are some **possible examination questions** set on this topic, along with hints to help you understand and approach each question effectively:

1 Discuss evolutionary explanations of the behaviour of non-human animals. (24 marks)

> The term 'discuss' allows for a wide-ranging response to this question. The AO1 component is clearly a description of evolutionary explanations of animal behaviour, but the AO2 can include criticisms, research support, implications, etc. It is quite acceptable to include material on altruism in your answer, but you should try to cover other behaviours as well to establish a *breadth* in your response. Note also that the question asks for evolutionary explanations of *behaviour* rather than explanations of physical characteristics, so keep the latter to a minimum.

2 Critically consider **two** evolutionary explanations of the behaviour of non-human animals. (24 marks)

> This is a variation on question 1. 'Critically consider' is an AO1+AO2 term (see Unit 32, p. 937). The number of explanations has been specified, so here you must restrict your answer to only two. If you present only one, there is a partial performance penalty (max. 8 marks for AO1 and 8 marks for AO2). If you present *more than* two explanations, then only the best two will receive credit. Natural selection can count as one explanation, and sexual selection or kin selection could count as the second. Note that in all of these questions the explanations must relate to *non-human animals*.

3 Outline and evaluate **two** biological explanations for apparent altruism in non-human animals. (24 marks)

> Questions such as this can be difficult to answer in 30 minutes, as there are four distinct 'chunks'. However, this gives you a ready-made structure to your essay. If we 'deconstruct' this essay title, we get the following (using kin selection and reciprocal altruism as the two chosen explanations):
>
> ● outline description of one biological explanation for apparent altruism (e.g. kin selection) – this should take $7\frac{1}{2}$ minutes of writing time and be approximately 150 words in length (30-minute essays are, on average, about 600 words in length).
> ● evaluation of kin selection as an explanation for apparent altruism – $7\frac{1}{2}$ minutes (approx 150 words)
> ● outline description of second explanation (e.g. reciprocal altruism) – $7\frac{1}{2}$ minutes (approx 150 words)
> ● evaluation of reciprocal altruism as an explanation for apparent altruism – $7\frac{1}{2}$ minutes and approximately 150 words.

4 (a) Outline biological explanations for apparent altruism in non-human animals. (12 marks)
   (b) To what extent can apparent altruism in non-human animals be explained using such biological explanations? (12 marks)

> In part (a), the term 'outline' indicates that your descriptions need not be in great detail. In part (b), the term 'such' means that you can use explanations other than those given in part (a). For your AO2, you might consider whether the evidence that supports one of your explanations does indicate that a particular biological explanation is valid. Or, if there are flaws in such evidence, then you might conclude that it does not provide support. Or you might consider alternative explanations, and their research evidence and decide whether they offer an equally good explanation.

Topic 2 >> Classical and operant conditioning

CLASSICAL (PAVLOVIAN) CONDITIONING

Classical conditioning was first described in detail by the Russian physiologist, Ivan Pavlov (1927). Pavlov was investigating the salivatory reflex in dogs; this response occurs automatically when food is placed on the animal's tongue. He observed that his animals salivated not just in response to this stimulus (which is the basic reflex action itself), but also in response to anything else that regularly coincided with the feeding routine, such as the presence of the food dish, or the person who regularly fed them. All animals are born with a number of reflexes, which may be either simple, such as a constriction of the pupil of the eye when strong light is seen, or complex, such as the righting reflex of the cat when it falls to the ground. The whole point about natural reflexes like these is that:

● they are innate, i.e. they are present in the animal at, or soon after, birth
● they are triggered consistently and automatically by the occurrence of one kind of stimulus
● once such a response is triggered, it is not normally altered for its duration by subsequent events
● experience does little to alter the time course or pattern of the response.

Acquisition

In a typical classical conditioning experiment, the researcher selects one naturally occurring reflex of an animal and then deliberately and consistently presents an artificial stimulus (i.e. one which does not normally trigger the reflex itself) prior to the natural stimulus (the one which does normally trigger that reflex). Imagine for the purpose of this description that this artificial stimulus is the sound of a buzzer.

Pavlov used terminology to define different components of the procedure involved. The natural stimulus for any reflex (e.g. food touching the tongue, in the case of salivation) is referred to as an 'unconditioned stimulus' (UCS), where the term 'conditioning' may be regarded as 'training'. An unconditioned stimulus is one that produces a response that is innate, or 'untrained'.

When our eyes blink when an object approaches them at speed, this is not a trained response but one that we are born with. When the reflex is described as an 'unconditioned response' (UCR), it means it occurs after an unconditioned stimulus. Before training takes place, the artificial stimulus is referred to as the 'neutral stimulus' (NS), and after training it is referred to as a 'conditioned stimulus' (CS).

At the start, the NS does *not* bring about a reflex response by itself, but after many pairings of the NS and UCS, the situation changes. The animal's salivation reflex begins at the onset of the buzzer and now occurs even though the dog's tongue is not stimulated. The NS has now acquired the ability to produce the response in question and is now a CS (see Fig. 21.2). Pavlov realized that the salivation, which occurs in response to the buzzer, still has the properties of a reflex, but now happens as a learned response. Furthermore, the range of stimuli which can act as a CS seemed potentially infinite – this can be anything audible, visible, tactile or of any sensory modality which the participant (in this case, the dog) can detect.

Before conditioning

Food (UCS) → Salivation (UCR)

Buzzer (NS) → No response

During conditioning

Buzzer (NS) + Food (UCS) → Salivation (UCR)

After conditioning

Buzzer (CS) → Salivation (CR)

Figure 21.2 >> *The process of classical conditioning*

A2 Comparative psychology

Table 21.1 >> Conditioning outcomes of different time intervals between the NS & the UCS	
Time interval between NS and UCS	**Conditioning outcomes**
>> *Standard (forward) pairing*– NS precedes UCS but overlaps with it	Conditioning effects are strong with this pairing
	Response elicited by UCS extends backwards as it becomes associated with NS
>> *Delayed pairing* – NS precedes UCS	As above, but the longer the delay, the weaker the strength of conditioning
>> *Simultaneous pairing* – NS and UCS occur together	Conditioning tends to fail – NS ca　　　　　d to *predict* the onset of the UCS
>> *Backward pairing* – UCS precedes NS	Conditioning tends to be ineffective – as UCS has already elicited a response, therefore the response is not dependent on a relationship between NS and UCS

Timing

The precise timing of the NS(CS)–UCS pairing has a considerable influence on whether the NS will become a reliable CS, leading to a predictable CR. As we have seen, a dog initially only salivates when presented with the food (UCS), but gradually the buzzer (NS) begins to elicit salivation, and after a number of trials the dog salivates as soon as it hears the buzzer. The relative timing of this period between the onset of the NS and the UCS is crucial to the success of conditioning (see Table 21.1).

Extinction and spontaneous recovery

Innate reflexes are almost permanent features of the animal's behavioural repertoire, however young or old the animal may be, and they show little or no change over the lifespan. Pavlov examined the nature of the conditioned reflex to compare it with these aspects of the UCR. Unlike the UCR, he found that the CR is 'labile', i.e. it does not become permanently established as a response. On the contrary, the CR does not last very long after the removal of the UCS. So, for instance,

Figure 21.3 >> *Extinction of CR when UCS is no longer paired with CS*

although the dog may have been trained to salivate to the buzzer sound, if the buzzer is continually sounded without being followed by the food stimulus, then salivation to the buzzer rapidly diminishes. This dying out of the CR when the CS is no longer paired with the UCS is referred to as the process of 'extinction'. Figure 21.3 shows what happens when the trials proceed as with training, except that the UCS no longer follows the presentation of the CS. However, Pavlov found that extinction is not like a process of forgetting. The unique thing about a CR that has become extinct is that it is always liable to reappear suddenly, under the right conditions. This sudden reappearance is referred to as 'spontaneous recovery', and there are two main situations that can bring this about:

● a postponement of training (i.e. a time lapse between one extinction trial and another), which is sufficient to reinstate the CR

● the participant being startled (e.g. any sudden event, such as loud noise, which occurs during the process of extinction training may bring back the CR, however briefly).

There is another reason to question whether extinction is analogous to forgetting. When the participant is retrained, using the original CS–UCS pairings, the CR is quickly reinstated. This reinstatement occurs much faster than the original conditioning, which implies that the CR was not really 'lost'. To explain this process of response extinction, Pavlov described the CR as being inhibited, much like the energy that may be maintained in a coil spring by keeping your hand pressed down on it. When the inhibition is removed, the response returns (using the metaphor of the coil spring, it rebounds into shape when your hand pressure is removed).

It is as if the nervous system has the property of being able to hold back a learned response until some 'releasing' event takes place. What was known about the generally inhibitory action of the cerebral cortex (described in Unit 12) suggested to Pavlov, and other neurophysiologists of his time, that much of the brain in complex animals was designed for suppressing learned responses until the occasion was right for 'release'.

Stimulus generalization

Pavlov also introduced the term 'stimulus generalization' to describe what happens when a stimulus is presented which is similar to the CS, but not identical to it. For instance, if conditioned to salivate at the sound of one buzzer, will the response occur when a different buzzer sound is played? The more similar the new buzzer is to the CS, the greater the similarity between the responses to this new sound and to the original one. When plotted graphically, the effect is a bell-shaped curve, illustrated in Fig. 21.4. So, despite the fact that conditioning involved the use of only one stimulus (CS), the response itself may be generalized to others. Where people experience a strong fear (phobia) of one stimulus, such as a spider, this may be generalized to other similar insects.

Figure 21.4 >> *Generalization of CR to stimuli similar to CS*

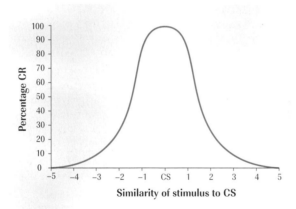

Stimulus discrimination

In contrast to generalized responses, Pavlov found that conditioning can bring about discrimination of response to the CS. When discrimination occurs, only the CS can evoke the learned reflex, i.e. the typically generalized responses to other similar stimuli are absent. During the original conditioning, where the CS–UCS pairings were made, there needs to be a number of occasions when other stimuli, similar to the CS, are introduced. These other stimuli, however, are never paired with the UCS. The outcome of discrimination training is that the response that is conditioned to the CS is highly specific to it. For example, during the procedure to condition a dog to salivate (CR) to a black square (CS+), a grey square (CS–) is introduced intermittently. However, the grey square is never paired with food (UCS). Initially, the dog will sometimes salivate to the grey square, but gradually it will learn to discriminate between the two squares and will only salivate (CR) when the black square (CS+) is presented.

Pavlov reported that if such training persists, so that the distinction between stimuli is so fine that the participant's senses are hardly able to detect them, a condition of 'experimental neurosis' might arise. For example, self-immolation may occur, where the animal may bite its own paws during the procedure. Taken to this degree, discrimination training has the potential to inflict psychological distress on the participant.

Higher-order conditioning

It is possible to condition a second neutral stimulus (NS) by pairing it with an already established CS; this procedure is known as 'higher-order conditioning' (or 'second-order conditioning'). Suppose a dog has learned to salivate to the sound of a buzzer; a bell can be rung just before the buzzer. With repeated pairings of the bell and buzzer, the dog may learn to salivate to the sound of the bell, although the bell will elicit less salivation than the buzzer.

The role of classical conditioning in animal behaviour

The importance of classical conditioning to animals lies primarily in their ability to learn that one thing (the CS) predicts the occurrence of something else (the UCS). In Topic 1, we discussed how animal behaviour might be influenced by evolutionary factors. Therefore, it makes sense to examine classical conditioning from this perspective. One possibility is that the display of conditional responses (CRs) in some way gives animals a selective advantage.

Foraging and hunting behaviour

In their foraging behaviour, animals may learn that certain tastes will be followed by illness, whereas others have more beneficial consequences. The importance of the relationship between the CS and CR in feeding was demonstrated dramatically in a conditioned taste-aversion study by Garcia *et al.* (1977). In a taste-aversion study, an animal is conditioned to avoid a particular food that has been associated with some painful outcome or toxic reaction. The animal learns to avoid that food because of a conditioned aversion response to its smell or taste (Reber 1995). In the study by Garcia and colleagues, coyotes and wolves were made ill by feeding them mutton wrapped in raw sheep hide and laced with a toxic substance, lithium chloride. By allowing the animals to approach live sheep the effects of this conditioning episode were tested. Rather than attacking the sheep as they normally would, the coyotes sniffed their quarry and turned away, some of them retching. The wolves initially charged the sheep and made oral contact on their flanks, but then immediately released their prey. During the next half hour, the sheep became increasingly dominant and the wolves withdrew like submissive pups (Garcia *et al.* 1977). These responses are evidence that the CS (the taste and smell of sheep) paired with illness was sufficient to change the behaviour (CR) of the predators towards their prey. In the natural world, learning to avoid food that makes you ill is a valuable lesson.

Behaviour towards conspecifics

Research with male blue gourami fish lends some support to the prediction that animals that change their behaviour in response to CS have a selective advantage. In one study by Hollis (1984), male gouramis were trained to expect an aggressive encounter with another male, following the lighting of a red panel on the side of their tank. The fish showed evidence of having learned the relationship between the CS (red light) and the UCS (rival male's arrival) by beginning their aggressive display during the CS. When control males (who had not been conditioned to the CS) and conditioned males were allowed to fight each other, the conditioned males directed more bites, showed more aggressive displays and invariably won.

In many species, males who hold territories behave aggressively towards any animal approaching their territory, even females. Mating would be facilitated if males could anticipate the approach of a female and inhibit aggression towards her (Shettleworth 1998). Using techniques similar to the experiment described earlier, Hollis (1990) found that conditioned males directed fewer bites and more courtship behaviour towards a test female than did the controls. More importantly, this behaviour translates into greatly enhanced reproductive success. Conditioned males fathered, on average, over 1,000 young, whereas the control males (where the CS had not been paired with a female) fathered, on average, less than 100 young (Hollis *et al.* 1997).

Evaluation
classical conditioning

Insights from classical conditioning research have led to striking discoveries about animal behaviour. The appealing simplicity of Pavlov's views have come under attack as psychologists have discovered certain limitations of the generality of findings relating to classical conditioning (Zimbardo *et al.* 1995).

● *Biological preparedness* – Different animals face different challenges in order to survive in their particular ecological niche. As a result, different species may well have different capabilities for learning in a given situation. Therefore, we might expect some relationships between CS and UCS to be more difficult for some species to learn than for others. To accommodate this possibility, Seligman (1970) proposed the concept of 'preparedness':

– Animals are '*prepared*' to learn associations that are significant in terms of their survival needs.

– Animals are '*unprepared*' to learn associations that are not significant in this respect.

– Animals are '*contraprepared*' to learn any association that in some way runs contrary to any naturally occurring behavioural predisposition.

● *Taste-aversion learning* – This is an example of an association for which animals might be biologically prepared. As discussed earlier, research on taste-aversion learning poses particular problems for Pavlovian conditioning. You may recall that an animal may eat poisoned food, and later become ill (but survive). After just one experience, and despite a long interval between the CS (tasting the food) and UCS (becoming ill), the animal learns to avoid all foods with that taste.

What's more, this learned association is remarkably resistant to extinction. This form of learning challenges the assumptions of Pavlov's view of classical conditioning in three ways:

– *Number of trials*: classical conditioning is a gradual process, requiring many associations between the NS and the UCS. In taste-aversion, learning takes place after just one trial; this phenomenon is known as 'one-trial learning'.

– *Delay between NS and UCS*: the longer the delay between the neutral stimulus (NS) and the UCS, the less likely a learned association will develop between the two. In taste-aversion, conditioning takes place despite several hours between the two.

– *Extinction*: in classical conditioning, the withdrawal of the UCS means that extinction sets in rapidly. Yet in taste-aversion, the time period before extinction is prolonged way beyond what we would normally expect.

● *How universal is classical conditioning?* – It is clear that species differ in terms of their motives, motor and cognitive capacities, and certainly in the degree to which their natural style of life depends on learning. We must, therefore, be cautious about generalizing from one species to another. Each species' genetic make-up places limitations on their learning abilities. These biological constraints suggest that the principles of classical conditioning cannot be universally applied across all species or all situations. Some aspects of classical conditioning clearly depend on the way an animal is genetically predisposed toward stimuli in its environment. What any organism can and cannot readily learn appears to be as much a product of its evolutionary history as its learning opportunities.

OPERANT CONDITIONING

>>Operant conditioning ... resembles a hundred
million years of natural selection or a thousand years
of the evolution of a culture compressed into a very
short period of time.>> (Skinner 1981, p. 502)

Although the title of 'founding father of behaviour
analysis' is attributed to B.F. Skinner (following the
publication, in 1938, of his book *The Behaviour of
Organisms*), the roots of this approach go back at least
to the 19th century. Skinner acknowledged the
influence of Thorndike on his early work, especially
Thorndike's (1911) description of a 'law of effect'. The
'law of positive effect' states that any behaviour that
leads to a positive outcome, such as a successful
solution to a problem or a state of 'satisfaction' in the
organism, will tend to be retained and repeated in
future. The increasing frequency of this behaviour by an
organism will be reinforced by each further successful
outcome that behaviour brings about.

Reinforcement

In terms of Thorndike's 'law of positive effect', the
outcome of a behaviour will strengthen (or 'reinforce')
that behaviour. In Thorndike's view, behaviour is
reinforced and maintained by its consequences.
Therefore, any behaviour that fails to bring about a
successful outcome will not be reinforced and should
not appear as often when the animal is placed in
similar circumstances. Thorndike demonstrated the
law of effect by giving animals problems to solve. For
instance, a cat placed in a box from which it could
escape only by operating a latch, would eventually
learn to do this. Before learning the successful
strategy, the cat would have tried numerous other
unsuccessful behaviours, such as scratching and
biting, and these would not have brought about its
escape. Escape is itself a reinforcing outcome for the
action of operating the latch and so when returned to
the box again, the latch would become the focus of
the cat's behaviour and actions directed towards it
would be those most in evidence.

The Skinner box

Skinner devised an easier measurement technique for
investigating how reinforcement acts upon behaviour.
The Skinner box was designed by him to reward the
participant, not by allowing escape, but by providing
food pellets. In this circumstance, the animal (usually a
rat or a pigeon) would initially only show escape-
seeking behaviour in the box. However, one of these
actions, such as pressing downward on a lever, would
trigger a food reinforcer (see photo above right).

This action would bring about reinforcement in the
form of a food pellet delivered automatically from the
hopper. This is much the same mechanism that
delivers a chocolate bar from a machine when a coin

is inserted. In the Skinner box, the participant's
actions are easily (and automatically) recorded by
measuring the number of food items obtained in a
given interval of time. For instance, if 25 pellets of
food were dispensed from the hopper in the first hour,
and 150 in the second hour, then the threefold
increase in the participant's response rate is easy to
monitor and record.

Many interesting insights have been gained about how
reinforcement comes to control a subject's responses
using the Skinner box arrangement. For instance, the
delivery of one food item for every lever press might
seem to be the optimal way of ensuring the response is
learned and maintained. But that is not what Skinner
discovered. He demonstrated that reinforcement exerts
subtle (but nonetheless predictable) effects on
behaviour depending on how the reinforcer is made
dependent upon the response.

The importance of timing

As in classical conditioning, the time interval between
two elements of the conditioning process (in this case
the response and the reinforcer) is crucial. If the
reinforcer follows immediately after the response,
conditioning is more effective than if they are separated
by a delay (Pearce 1997). This does not mean that
conditioning is impossible when this time interval is
extended. Lattal and Gleeson (1990) showed that the
rate of lever pressing in rats increased steadily over 20
sessions of training, even when the delay between
response and reinforcer was as long as 30 seconds.

Schedules of reinforcement

If a food reinforcer is not dispensed for every single
response (e.g. lever press), but is arranged according to
a predetermined 'schedule', such as one food pellet for
every fifth lever press, then different response patterns
arise, depending on the exact relationship between
response and reinforcement.

There are four ways in which reinforcement may be scheduled:

- as a *ratio of the number of responses* such as the 1:5 example above

- as a result of a *time-base* or *time-interval* criterion – for instance, this might mean the delivery of a food pellet at the end of, say, one minute *provided that the subject has responded in that interval* (and not otherwise).

In addition to the above two forms of schedule, in which reinforcement may occur by either a time- or response-based criterion, reinforcement may also be applied in either a fixed or variable schedule.

- A *fixed schedule* dispenses reinforcement on a reliable basis, e.g. in a 1:5 fixed-ratio (FR5) schedule, the reinforcer is delivered after every fifth lever press. Similarly, a fixed-interval schedule of one minute (FI1) will deliver reinforcement at the end of every minute, as long as the participant has made the required response (e.g. lever pressing) in that time.

- *Variable schedules* dispense food on an erratic basis, e.g. a variable ratio schedule of 1:5 (VR5) will deliver food *on average* once every five responses, but during any one trial that number may vary from 5. Only over a large number of trials will the schedule be seen to have averaged one reinforcer per five responses. On a variable interval schedule of one minute (VI1), the interval is varied around the period of one minute, although this interval alters from trial to trial, so that only over the long run does the one minute average become apparent.

Some schedules, such as a low-fixed ratio, tend to bring about rapid initial learning of the required response, but the response rate itself does not accelerate as rapidly as it does with, say, a variable-interval schedule. The 'extinction' rates also differ markedly between schedules, i.e. extinction being the rate at which the conditioned response (such as lever-pressing in the Skinner box) diminishes in frequency when the reinforcement is stopped altogether. Typically, a subject working on a VI schedule which has a relatively long interval will maintain their response rate far longer than will a participant working on one of the fixed-schedule types (i.e. FR or FI).

Because the above schedules all reinforce the participant for some, but not all, of their responses, they are usually referred to as 'partial reinforcement', to distinguish them from 'continuous reinforcement' (CRF), in which reinforcement is dispensed after every correct response. Typically, CRF schedules will produce rapid initial learning, a slower overall response rate, and rapid extinction. By comparison, partial reinforcement schedules generally produce slower initial learning, faster overall response rate, and slower extinction rates, though each of the four forms of partial schedule will

vary in their effects on these aspects of learning, as indicated above.

Punishment and negative reinforcement

Thorndike's original work also includes a 'law of negative effect'. By this he meant that if a participant's actions led to unwanted or unpleasant outcomes (what he called 'annoyers'), then those actions would diminish over time, i.e. the subject would become less likely on future occasions to repeat those actions. However, as Thorndike himself found, this association between a particular behaviour and negative consequences is less clear cut than that. One reason for this is that unpleasant outcomes may arise in a variety of ways, such as from:

- a failure to obtain a reward which was an expected consequence of some action the participant carried out

- a failure to avoid an unpleasant stimulus by taking appropriate avoiding action

- a direct consequence of the action itself.

For instance, a cat may be lying behind a door when it hears the rattle of keys outside. If the cat remains behind the door when it opens, it would be hurt. The cat's inaction brings about a negative consequence – had the cat moved in response to hearing the rattle of keys, it would not have been hurt. On subsequent occasions the sound of keys may be sufficient to prompt the cat into moving from the area. This key sound leads to avoidance behaviour. This is an example of 'negative reinforcement' in that failure to make the correct response will lead to an unpleasant outcome, whereas making the correct response (moving out of the way) will lead to a desirable outcome (i.e. not getting hurt).

Consider another situation where a dog is reaching up to a table by leaning against a stool, and the stool overturns under its weight. Pain is experienced this time as a consequence of the dog's actions, rather than inaction, and has the effect of *punishing* the behaviour that preceded it.

Negative reinforcement has generally been regarded as being more effective than punishment in bringing about learning because it aims to activate a desired response rather than to deactivate an unwanted one. Part of the problem with attempting to eradicate an undesirable behaviour is that it does not necessarily follow that a desired one will arise in its place. For instance, having learned not to reach up to the table by leaning against the stool, the dog may then embark on an even more risky or undesirable behaviour, such as jumping straight onto the table. There is also the view that punishment fails to do more than just suppress a behaviour while the punishing agent is present – a view that has tended to prevail in institutions such as prisons, where constant vigilance is required.

In negative reinforcement procedures, the participant has actively to avoid the unpleasant event. The event itself, say, a mild electric shock delivered to the feet in a Skinner box, has its onset signalled by the occurrence of a warning event such as a light or a buzzer. The shock is an aversive event and the participant will soon learn to avoid it if possible, in much the same way as learning to obtain food or water by pressing a lever. The activity required of pressing the lever when, say, the buzzer plays, enables the participant to avoid the shock altogether. Failure to respond appropriately to the buzzer will bring about the aversive event. In a 'Sidman avoidance' schedule, the participant is placed in a box that has two compartments. Shortly after the warning, the participant has to move from one section of the box to another in order to avoid the aversive event (hence the name 'shuttle box' is sometimes used to describe this apparatus). See Table 21.2 for a summary of the different types of reinforcement.

The key question, which negative reinforcement poses, is what is the reinforcer? For instance, when the participant responds to the lever in order to obtain a pellet, the reinforcement is the food item itself. But in negative-reinforcement procedures, the outcome is the avoidance of, rather than contact with, something. Some behaviourists reasoned that reinforcement of both positive and negative types acts on 'drive reduction' mechanisms. A 'drive' is like a biological instinct – for instance, the experience of hunger is accompanied by a drive or motivation to find food in order to satisfy that hunger. To experience fear when expecting a shock to happen motivates or 'drives' the response of seeking safety in order to reduce that fear.

However, when it is impossible to escape an electric shock in a shuttle box, the participant soon stops trying to avoid the shocks at all, but will also be less likely to learn an avoidance routine in future situations where an electric shock (or any other aversive event) *is* avoidable.

This situation has become known as 'learned helplessness' (Seligman 1975).

The role of operant conditioning in animal behaviour

The selective advantage of flexibility through learning

Unpredictable environmental changes during an animal's lifetime cannot be anticipated by pre-programmed forms of behaviour. The individual animal must rely upon its own resources in adapting to any such changes. The ability to modify behaviour in the light of unpredictable environmental changes is clearly a sign of intelligence, and gives such animals a clear selective advantage. Although most of the work on operant conditioning has taken place in the laboratory, there are also examples of natural behaviour that utilize the principles of operant conditioning.

Mating preferences

An example of operant conditioning 'in action' comes from a study of the mating behaviour of cowbirds. Cowbirds are brood parasites and so young males do not hear the songs of adults of their species during the early part of their life. West and King (1988) studied the origins of two geographical 'accents' in cowbirds in the USA. They discovered that rather than being less complex, the songs of males reared in isolation were more complex than males reared normally. Male cowbirds appear to have the elements of both dialects, but through the process of operant conditioning, narrow down their song pattern so that it matches the 'preference' of the local females. When the male sings particular elements from his repertoire, the female responds with a brief 'wing-stroking' display, similar to the copulation invitation found in many types of nesting birds. The male responds by increasing the frequency with which he produces the rewarded elements of his song, eliminating those that have no effect on the female.

Table 21.2 >> Types of reinforcement

	Primary reinforcer (unlearned)	Secondary reinforcer (learned by classical conditioning)
>> *Positive reinforcement* (presentation increases preceding response)	e.g. food, water	e.g. praise, money
>> *Negative reinforcement* (removal increases preceding response)	e.g. removal of pain	e.g. removal of feared stimulus (e.g. a light that signals onset of electric shock)

Note: both positive and negative reinforcement, by definition, always increase the probability of the response that precedes them. Punishment, on the other hand, has the opposite effect, decreasing the probability of the response that precedes it.

Evaluation
operant conditioning

● *Instinctive drift* – The principles of operant conditioning have been used in many different experimental settings and in many different applications, often with spectacular success. But how universal is operant conditioning, and can we truly teach anything to anyone using these techniques? Breland and Breland (1951) used operant conditioning techniques to train animals of many different species to perform a diverse range of behaviours. The Brelands believed that the principles of operant conditioning derived from laboratory research could be applied successfully to the control of animal behaviour outside the laboratory. After their training, however, some of the Brelands' animals no longer performed the 'tricks' they had learned using operant conditioning techniques. For example, a racoon was trained to pick up coins and put them in a 'piggy' bank for food reinforcement. The racoon eventually refused to give up the coins, rubbing them together in its paws, and 'dipping' them into the piggy bank before taking them out again. This is not surprising if we consider the fact that this is how racoons behave naturally, rubbing crayfish together to remove their shells and then washing them. The Brelands believed that even after conditioning, behaviours drift back towards instinct after a time. They called this process 'instinctive drift' (Breland and Breland 1951). The racoon's behaviour could not be explained by the simple relationship between stimulus – behaviour – consequence, but was understandable if we consider the species-specific behaviour tendencies of racoons. These tendencies override the temporary changes that are brought about by operant conditioning – the animals' inherited behaviour pattern was incompatible with the operant conditioning task (Zimbardo *et al.* 1995).

● *The incompatibility of responses* – Attempts to teach totally arbitrary responses in the laboratory (such as bar-pressing in rats or disc-pecking in pigeons) may fail because these arbitrary responses are incompatible with the consummatory responses related to the animals' motivational state (e.g. the hungry racoon 'washing' the coins). In this case, the required operant response of releasing the coins (to obtain food as reinforcement) is incompatible with the classically conditioned response of rubbing them together as if they were food.

● *Operant or classical conditioning?* – One of the main assumptions of operant conditioning is that the consequences of a behaviour determine the likelihood of its future occurrence. Pigeons have been trained to peck a small illuminated disc on the wall of a Skinner box to obtain the reward of food. The delivery of food was contingent on the response of pecking the illuminated disc. However, if the disc is merely illuminated for a few seconds prior to the delivery of food, regardless of the pigeons' behaviour, the birds end up pecking the disc as vigorously as they would if their pecking behaviour had previously been reinforced. However, the relationship is simply one between the stimulus and the reinforcer, with the response of the pigeon being irrelevant to the delivery of the food. The classically conditioned association between light and food is sufficient to generate the high rate of pecking behaviour, the pigeons' consummatory response to food. This has led some people to conclude that classical conditioning is responsible for much of what researchers have been recording as operant behaviour (Mackintosh 1981).

✓ CHECK YOUR UNDERSTANDING

Check your understanding of classical and operant conditioning by answering these questions. You can check your answers by looking back through Topic 2.

1 Identify six key characteristics of classical conditioning that you would include in a précis of this theory.

2 Using the same six characteristics, write approximately 25 words on each.

3 Using the same six characteristics, expand this to 50 words on each.

4 Identify two ways in which classical conditioning has been used to explain the behaviour of non-human animals.

5 Identify three critical (i.e. AO2) points relating to classical conditioning as an explanation of

animal behaviour, and explain *why* these pose problems for the theory.

6 Identify six key characteristics of operant conditioning that you would include in a précis.

7 Identify two ways in which operant conditioning has been used to explain the behaviour of non-human animals. Explain why the acquisition of behaviour through operant conditioning is advantageous in each case.

8 Identify three critical (i.e. AO2) points relating to operant conditioning as an explanation of animal behaviour.

REVISION SUMMARY

Having covered this topic, you should be able to:

✓ describe and evaluate the nature of classical (Pavlovian) conditioning

✓ assess the role of classical conditioning in the behaviour of non-human animals

✓ describe and evaluate the nature of operant conditioning

✓ assess the role of operant conditioning in the behaviour of non-human animals.

EXAMPLE EXAM QUESTIONS

Below are some **possible examination questions** set on this topic, along with hints to help you understand and approach each question effectively:

1 Describe and evaluate the nature of classical conditioning.   (24 marks)

> This straightforward question can be answered with a description of the nature of classical conditioning (e.g. relationship between CS and UCS, the importance of timing, stimulus generalization, etc.). The AO2 component could include discussion of the biological constraints in classical conditioning, the role of cognition, or even the role of classical conditioning in the natural behaviour of animals. With questions on classical (and operant) conditioning, there is potentially a massive amount of procedural detail that you could describe, but you only have 15 minutes (= 300 words) to do it. It will help to prepare, in advance, a version of the appropriate length by selecting about 8 to 10 key points on classical conditioning. You can then expand on these in the exam to make up your 300 words.

2 Describe and evaluate the nature of operant conditioning.   (24 marks)

> This is the mirror image of question 1, but this time it covers operant conditioning. Make sure you understand the difference between the two, and make sure that you only include material related to operant conditioning in your answer. You could introduce classical conditioning as a form of commentary but only if you avoid *describing* it and simply draw on the features which provide some useful contrasts. Note that this question does not specify 'non-human animals' and so you could refer to operant conditioning in humans, e.g. its use as a successful therapy, because this illustrates the value of operant conditioning as an explanation of behaviour.

3 (a) Outline the nature of classical and operant conditioning.   (12 marks)
     (b) Assess the role of **either** classical **or** operant conditioning in the behaviour of non-human animals.
                                                                                                        (12 marks)

> What is required in part (a) is a précis of both classical and operant conditioning, i.e. a selection of the most pertinent points to produce a $7\frac{1}{2}$-minute version of each. Part (b) requires you to choose *one* of these explanations and show how it has been used to explain the behaviour of non-human animals. Try to draw your examples from outside the laboratory (because you are considering the *role* of conditioning, something not well demonstrated by lab experiments), and remember to focus on AO2 commentary in your answer rather just describing research in this area (which would gain only minimal marks). Note that in part (b) of this question 'non-human' animal behaviour is specified and therefore there would be no credit for anything based on human behaviour.

4 'Non-human animal behaviour can be explained entirely using the concepts of classical and operant conditioning'.
Critically consider the role of classical and operant conditioning in the behaviour of non-human animals.
                                                                                                        (24 marks)

> Questions may sometimes contain a quotation, but unless the question specifically says 'with reference to the quotation', you do not need to address it. The quotation is intended to raise some issues or point you in a useful direction. 'Critically consider' is an AO1 + AO2 term (see Table 32.1, p. 937). A useful way of dealing with such general questions is to divide the content into paragraphs – four paragraphs of 150 words each. Don't waste time on an introduction or a conclusion.

In Topic 2, we concentrated on what animals could learn on their own. However, as many animals live in groups, it would benefit them to be able to copy what other members of the group have learned through trial and error (Pearce 1997). Copying others may lead an individual animal to avoid poisonous food, or choose a nutritious food item, or, possibly, learn how to avoid predators by observing the behaviour of other animals in the group. Social learning clearly has great potential, but is it widespread among animals?

EXPLANATIONS AND RESEARCH STUDIES OF SOCIAL LEARNING

Imitation

If a problem is particularly difficult to solve, it might take animals a long time to come up with the solution. Once they have done that, however, it would benefit other members of their species to be able to imitate the behaviour of the successful animal. Imitation would, theoretically, be of great value to many different species. Evidence for imitation in non-human species is, however, relatively rare. From her work on imitation in rats, Hayes (1993) suggested that the difference between imitation and other forms of social learning lay in what the animal learned as a result of its observations. Non-imitative social learning involves learning about a particular stimulus or event (e.g. that a particular food is good to eat), whereas imitation involves an animal learning about specific responses or behaviours. It implies that the animal understands, as a result of observing another, that a particular behaviour or action has a specific relationship with an outcome.

There have been many experiments designed to explore imitation in non-human species. Bugnyar and Huber (1997) studied marmosets that were required either to push or pull a pendulum door in order to get a food reward inside a box. After they had learned these behaviours, the researchers exposed 'observer' monkeys to one of the two behaviours for one daily session over a period of three days. None of the observer monkeys imitated the specific strategies for getting the reward that they had been observing, although they were able to acquire some simple motor skills as a result of observing the other monkeys.

A field study of rehabilitated orang-utans in Borneo provided some evidence of imitation in a more natural setting (Russon and Galdikas 1995), although instances of imitative behaviour were comparatively rare. Where imitation did take place, the researchers noted a preference for models with whom the observer had an established relationship. For hand-reared orang-utans, this preference was for human models, and this preference gradually transferred to other orang-utans as these relationships developed. Status was also important, with subordinate animals seeming to imitate dominant animals.

Evaluation
imitation as social learning

- **Imitation in chimpanzees** – A study that provided clear evidence for imitation was carried out by Nagell *et al.* (1993). They investigated the abilities of chimpanzees reared by their mothers, 'enculturated' chimpanzees (i.e. raised in close contact with humans) and children. These three groups were tested on simple, complex and delayed imitative tasks using a human model. For the simple and complex tasks, mother-reared chimps performed more poorly than both the enculturated chimpanzees and the human children. In the delayed task, however, where there was a 48-hour time period between the demonstration and the opportunity to imitate, the enculturated chimpanzee group outperformed the other two groups.

- **Imitation or stimulus enhancement?** – One of the most famous examples of apparent imitation in animals is the incidence of washing sweet potatoes seen in Japanese macaque monkeys. A colony of macaques on Koshima Island was fed with sweet potatoes and, in 1953, a young female, Imo, was first seen taking her sand-covered potato to the stream and washing it before eating. This habit spread quickly to other members of the colony, apparently a clear case of imitative behaviour. There are reasons, however, for believing that such behaviour does not involve imitation. Nagell *et al.* (1993) have suggested that the spread of this habit is more likely to be due to 'stimulus enhancement', i.e. as a result of watching another animal, the observer's attention is drawn towards whatever they are doing. The attention of a naive monkey may be drawn to a potato when it sees another monkey pick one up. The naive monkey may pick up its own potato, and for social reasons follow the first monkey into the water, thus learning by accident the benefits of placing the potato in the water. The advantage of this explanation, however contrived, is that it relies on processes already known to exist, rather than suggesting that such animals are willing imitators (Pearce 1997).

Foraging

Norwegian rats (*rattus norvegicus*, the common laboratory rat) will eat almost anything that does not poison them (Shettleworth 1998). This means that young rats have lots of potential food to learn about, which is vital if they are to know what foods they may eat safely. When the young rats leave the nest to forage, they prefer to go where other rats are feeding or have recently been feeding. Combined with a preference for familiar flavours, this ensures that they eat only what will not harm them. Research by Galef and Wigmore (1983) tested the feeding preferences of rats exposed to the food preferences of other rats. They paired rats together in cages, and fed them normal laboratory rat food. They then removed one of each pair (the 'demonstrator') who was put in another cage, deprived of food for 24 hours, then fed *either* cinnamon-flavoured or cocoa-flavoured food. Each demonstrator was then returned to its previous companion (the 'observer' rat) and the two were allowed to interact for 15 minutes. The demonstrator rat was then removed again, and for the next 24 hours, the observer rat had a choice of two bowls of food, cinnamon and cocoa flavoured. The observer rat showed a distinct preference for whatever food the demonstrator rat had been fed on. These findings suggest that a rat colony could serve as a centre where rats could exchange information about nearby food sources. Rats behave in a way that facilitates this type of learning because when they meet they engage in mouth-to-mouth contact and sniffing.

Evaluation
social learning in foraging

AO2

Why do blue tits peck the tops off milk bottles?
An intriguing example of behaviour that we have already encountered in this unit is the removal of milk bottle tops by blue tits, which then feed off the thick layer of cream at the top of the bottle. This bottle-opening behaviour became common in localized areas of Britain, rather than being found more randomly spread across the country as a whole. This suggested that the behaviour was being culturally transmitted, i.e. being transferred from one bird to another. However, there are other explanations for this phenomenon that do not require the process of social learning:

- The act of tearing and pecking at a bottle top is clearly not imitation because pecking and tearing at bark are an important part of the blue tits' natural foraging behaviour (Shettleworth 1998).
- Blue tits that encountered open bottles (the results of another bird's work) would come to associate the opened bottle with food. Coming across an unopened bottle, they would engage in food-related behaviours such as pecking and tearing, which would then be reinforced (Hinde and Fisher 1951).

How did blue tits first discover the cream at the top of a bottle of milk?

Why these birds began opening the bottles in the first place is a mystery. Sherry and Galef (1990) reported that caged birds who had never experienced milk bottles before were unlikely to open a foil-covered container of cream when in isolation. However, if they could see another bird in an adjacent cage they would begin to peck at the foil until they were eventually able to open it. The reasons for this effect are not clear, but it is possible that the sight of the other bird reduced fear or in some way encouraged foraging responses (Pearce 1997). What is clear, however, is that this skill is unlikely to have been learned through imitation.

Do animals teach others?

To be classified as 'teacher', an animal has to modify its behaviour in some way when in the presence of naive individuals, so as to facilitate their learning (Caro and Hauser 1992). The teacher will incur some short-term cost, but for teaching to evolve, the teacher should reap some benefit in the long term, perhaps in terms of increased inclusive fitness. In a number of species, adults can be observed apparently teaching their young what foods to eat, or how to catch them. Domestic cats will first bring back dead birds and mice (prey that are usually difficult to catch) to the nest and present them to the kittens. Later, the mother will bring back live prey and allow the kittens to play with it. Finally, the kittens are able to capture prey by themselves without any help from the mother. In this example, there is an immediate cost to the mother of delayed feeding while the inexperienced offspring interact clumsily with the prey she has brought (sometimes the prey escapes and is lost). However, this also has two potential advantages:

- She will be able to reduce the time she has to spend finding food for her offspring, as they quickly become more efficient foragers.
- In the longer term, the offspring may increase her inclusive fitness by becoming more efficient foragers and producing more grandchildren for the teacher.

There is also evidence of certain aspects of tool-use in chimpanzees being 'taught' in this way. Boesch (1991) observed hundreds of cases where chimpanzee mothers 'stimulated' or 'facilitated' their infants' coula nut-

cracking behaviour. Stimulation consisted of leaving a stone 'hammer' near an 'anvil' block, and facilitation involved providing both hammers and nuts for infants at or near the anvils. Although stimulation and facilitation were fairly common, direct teaching was less common. In two cases observed by Boesch, however, chimpanzee mothers actively intervened when their infants were unsuccessful at breaking open the nuts. In these cases, the mother positioned either the nut or the hammer correctly for the infant.

A02 **Evaluation**
animals teaching each other

What is the teacher's intention?
In contrast to Boesch's findings, there was no evidence found of either teaching or imitative learning in chimpanzees in another part of West Africa (Inoue-Nakamura and Matsuzawa 1997). Although there is some evidence of animals behaving in a way that is

instructional to their offspring, it is not clear that it is the mothers' *intention* to teach their offspring. There are two particular problems in trying to ascertain whether the mother does intend to teach her offspring. First, it is virtually impossible for us to assess the mother's intention. Second, there is little evidence that the mothers understand what knowledge another animal possesses, a capacity referred to as having a 'theory of mind'.

INTELLIGENCE IN NON-HUMAN ANIMALS

Animal intelligence is a notoriously difficult concept. It may be seen as a hierarchy of learning processes, with habituation, the most basic form of learning, being shared by all species. More advanced animals have acquired the ability to learn by association (classical and operant conditioning), complex learning abilities such as problem-solving and learning sets, and finally, the acquisition of language (considered unique to humans). However, many comparative psychologists criticize this view of intelligence as being unacceptably narrow. If intelligence is seen as the ability to solve problems that have ecological relevance in the animal's

own environment, then all species must be seen as equally intelligent in their own ways.

There has been much interest in species differences in self-recognition and theory of mind, although the relevance of such cognitive abilities to animals is still uncertain. Intelligence may simply be a product of brain size, which presents humans and the cetaceans (marine mammals) as among the most intelligent species. Relative brain size (i.e. brain size relative to body size) is considered to be a better indicator of animal intelligence, although such a view also has problems (see 'The intelligence of cetaceans' below).

The intelligence of cetaceans

It is widely believed that whales and other cetaceans (such as dolphins and porpoises) are highly intelligent. The basis for this belief appears to be partly the size and complex surface appearance of cetacean brains (Klinowska 1994). The brain of a mature male sperm whale does weigh in at a whopping 7.8 kg (compared to the human equivalent of 1.5 kg), but as a percentage of brain size to body weight, the sperm whale returns a miserly 0.02%. The degree of convolutions (or folds) of the cerebral cortex has also been seen as an indicator of intelligence. Ridgway (1986) provides evidence that bottlenose dolphins have a much higher degree of folding than humans, but the neocortex of cetacean brains is relatively thin (about half that of humans), giving an average dolphin neocortical volume that is about 80 per cent that of humans.

Dolphin brains are still relatively large – so is that an indication of high intelligence? Crick and Mitchison's (1983) theory of dream sleep may provide an alternative explanation for such large brains. They propose that REM sleep (see Unit 13, p. 411) acts to remove undesirable interactions in networks of cells in the cerebral cortex. They call this process 'reverse learning'. Animals that cannot use this system must have another way to avoid overloading the neural network, e.g. by having bigger brains. The spiny anteater and dolphins are the only mammals so far tested which do not have REM sleep (Mukhametov 1984), and they have disproportionately large brains. If we follow this line of reasoning, spiny anteaters and dolphins have large brains because they cannot dream.

continued on next page

The behaviour of dolphins and other cetaceans is also cited as evidence of high intelligence. Many of us have been amazed by the performance of captive dolphins and killer whales in marine parks, but many other animals, from elephants to fleas, can achieve such feats. The complexity of cetacean 'societies' is also quoted as evidence for a highly intelligent species, but ants and bees have highly complex societies and are not usually described as 'intelligent' because of this. Although we still know little about the cetaceans' 'sophisticated communication abilities', they appear to be extremely rudimentary compared with the sophistication of human language. Although cetaceans appear able to communicate information about 'what', 'where' and 'who', there is no substantive evidence that they can transmit information about 'when', 'how' or 'why' (Gaskin 1982).

Self-recognition

The ability to recognize oneself in a mirror is usually seen as reflecting a state of self-awareness in animals, although even human beings need some practice at using mirrors. Congenitally blind people who have had their sight restored and young children who have never seen a mirror before behave as though they are seeing another person the first time they are confronted by their own reflection in a mirror. This reaction, however, is quickly replaced by self-recognition (Povinelli *et al.* 1993). Gallup (1970) first demonstrated that chimpanzees were able to recognize themselves in a mirror. After they were accustomed to using mirrors (chimpanzees typically use them to inspect their anal-genital area and other 'hidden' parts of their bodies), they were anaesthetized and a red mark placed on their foreheads and ears. After recovering from the anaesthetic, none of the subjects showed any interest in the marks until they saw themselves in a mirror, whereupon they touched the red marks on their own faces. The chimpanzees appeared to be using the mirror to direct responses towards their own body. Although there is still some debate about what the mark test really does indicate in terms of cognitive abilities, the data overwhelmingly support a division on performance on this task, with the great apes and humans on one side and all other species on the other side.

The reason why some animals demonstrate self-recognition of themselves in mirrors and others do not is unclear. One suggestion is that self-recognition is confined to those species that can make use of information provided by mirrors. However, studies by Pepperberg *et al.* (1995) with parrots and Povinelli (1989) with elephants, have shown that some species can use mirrors but show no evidence of self-recognition.

A different explanation comes from Gallup (1983), who believes that the use of mirrors for self-recognition depends on self-awareness. A chimpanzee is presumed to be able to use a mirror to locate a red spot on its forehead because it is self-aware, i.e. it knows it is looking at its own reflection.

Evaluation
self-recognition

- *Lack of research support* – The view that animals have self-recognition is not shared by all researchers. Heyes (1998) argues that there is little reliable evidence that any non-human primates are able to use a mirror to derive information about their own bodies, and even if there were, that this would not indicate the possession of a self-concept or any other aspect of self-awareness.

- *An alternative explanation: the 'anaesthetic artefact hypothesis'* – As mentioned above, in the original procedures carried out by Gallup (1970), animals with some experience of mirrors are anaesthetized and marked on their forehead with red dye. Several hours later, the number of times that the animal touches the marks on its head is measured, first in the absence of the mirror and then with the mirror present. Chimpanzees typically touch the marked areas of their head more in the mirror condition than when there is no mirror. Heyes suggests an alternative explanation for this finding – the 'anaesthetic artefact hypothesis'. In the mirror-present condition (which occurs second), the animals would have had time to recover from the anaesthetic, therefore would be more active than in the previous, mirror-absent condition (Heyes 1998).

- *Self-recognition or self-awareness?* – Even if there were evidence that some primates did have the capacity implied by mirror self-recognition tasks, it would not, according to Heyes (1995), imply that the animal was 'self-aware'. To use a mirror as a source of information about its own body, an animal must be able to distinguish sensory inputs resulting from its own body and those inputs originating elsewhere. If an animal could learn that when it is standing in front of a mirror, the input it receives correlates with inputs from its own body, it might be said to possess a 'body concept'. The humble pigeon can learn to use a mirror to detect paper dots attached to its feathers (Epstein *et al.* 1981), yet few would argue that pigeons possess a self-concept or are self-aware.

Theory of mind

Human beings possess a 'theory of mind' which we use to explain our behaviour by referring to mental states (e.g. 'I made that mistake because I was tired'). Our theory of mind not only allows us to explain our own behaviour, but also to make inferences about the intentions, desires, knowledge and states of mind of other animals (Pearce 1997). Premack and Woodruff (1978) were the first researchers to investigate the possibility of a theory of mind in chimpanzees experimentally. They presented Sarah, an adult female chimpanzee, with a series of videotape sequences showing a human experiencing some sort of 'problem'. In one sequence, the human was seen shivering violently while standing next to an unplugged heater. As each video reached the point where the human would be likely to come up with a solution, the tape was stopped. Sarah was then given several photographs and was required to choose one. In the example given, Sarah chose the photograph with the heater plugged in, inferring, we presume, that heat would thus be provided and the human would be warm.

As a result of this original research study, Premack and Woodruff asked the question whether chimpanzees, and other apes, really do have a 'theory of mind'. Two kinds of research evidence have been used to address this question.

Deception

If an animal can understand that the actions of other animals can be influenced by the knowledge that they have, this leads us to the intriguing possibility that one animal might deliberately manipulate the information that the second animal receives. Woodruff and Premack (1979) tested this possibility in a study designed to see if chimpanzees were capable of deception. In this study, chimpanzees, studied individually, observed a laboratory trainer hiding some food under one of two containers. The chimpanzee was then placed where it could see the two containers but could not reach them. Another trainer then came into the room, and (depending on the condition) would either help the chimpanzee get the food if the animal pointed at the right container (the 'cooperative trainer' condition) or keep it for himself (the 'competitive assistant' condition). Some of the chimpanzees were able to earn food under both conditions, suggesting that they had learned to direct the 'competitive' trainer to the wrong container, thus keeping the food in the other container for themselves. If the chimpanzees *knew* that the trainer would act on their false information, this would clearly be evidence for a theory of mind. This would be understandable because in times of food shortage, it would benefit animals living in social groups (such as chimpanzees) to be secretive about food so that it would not be stolen by another member of the group (Pearce 1997).

Attributions to others

A simpler way of assessing whether chimpanzees have a theory of mind is to test whether they are capable of attributing knowledge to another animal. Povinelli *et al.* (1990) explored this possibility with a study designed to see if chimpanzees could understand the very different knowledge states of *seeing* and *knowing*. In this study, two experimenters were initially present with a chimpanzee. One of the experimenters left the room and while they were out of the room, the second experimenter hid some food under one of four cups behind a low screen. The chimpanzee could see that food was being hidden under one of the cups, but could not see which cup it was. When the absent experimenter returned, both experimenters pointed to a cup. The experimenter who had hidden the food (the 'knower') always pointed to the right cup, but the other experimenter (the 'guesser') always pointed to a wrong cup. Four of the five chimpanzees tested were eventually able to choose the right cup reliably on the basis of this information.

Evaluation
theory of mind evidence

- **Deception** – Findings such as Woodruff and Premack's are intriguing, but a complicated line of reasoning would be required for such behaviour to be a product of a 'theory of mind'. First, the animals must understand that the trainer intended to steal the food. Second, they must understand that it is possible to give false information about the location of the food by pointing to the wrong container. Finally, they must believe that this knowledge would hinder the assistant in his search for the hidden food. There is little evidence that apes are capable of such sophisticated reasoning, and Premack and Woodruff's findings are more easily explained in terms of learned discrimination between different responses and their outcomes. In other words, when one trainer is in the room, pointing at the right container becomes associated with the reward.

- **Attributions to others** – There are two interpretations of Povinelli's findings. The interpretation that is consistent with a theory of mind explanation is that the chimpanzees were able to attribute knowledge to the assistant who had stayed in the room and knew that the assistant who had left the room lacked this knowledge. An alternative explanation is that the chimpanzees had learned a much simpler rule,

continued on next page

i.e. that picking the person who had stayed in the room leads to a reward whilst picking the other person does not lead to a reward. Modifications to the design of this experiment – for example, having the 'guesser' stay in the room with his head in a bag

– have produced ambiguous results and have led Heyes (1998) to conclude that although these arguments are plausible, they are based on fairly weak experimental evidence. To assume that chimpanzees must possess a theory of mind, simply because they are developmentally close to young children is an assumption that has yet to be supported by reliable evidence.

Social intelligence

Another aspect of intelligence may also be how animals solve social problems as well as physical problems, a form of intelligence that social psychologists call 'social cognition'. Primates that form large and stable social groups are assumed to have the most highly developed social cognition of all animals. Repeated interactions over a prolonged period allow these animals to learn each other's identity and to build up altruistic or antagonistic relationships. According to evolutionary psychologists, reasoning ability evolved largely out of the need to detect cheaters in social relationships (i.e. that animals that take the benefits of a social relationship must also pay a cost).

Observations of vervet monkeys suggest that they know a great deal about their social world, but are less impressive in their understanding of their physical world (Cheney and Seyfarth 1990). For example, vervets appear to know many of the characteristics of their own and neighbouring groups, such as their voices, their relationships and where they might be found. In contrast, their knowledge of aspects of their physical environment is considerably less detailed. For example, leopards and snakes are two common vervet predators. However, although vervets react to the presence of these predators, they appear unable to recognize the signs that such dangers are nearby (e.g. a dead antelope over a tree or snake trails in the dust). This fairly simple example of 'learning by association' might be expected in an 'intelligent' species, yet is absent in vervet monkeys.

Machiavellian intelligence

A particular variant of social intelligence is the 'Machiavellian intelligence' hypothesis (Byrne and Whiten 1988). The main claim of this hypothesis is that the intelligence of primates is primarily an adaptation to the special complexities of primate social life. This was in sharp contrast to the view that animal intelligence was a response to non-social environmental problems such as finding food. Why is this called 'Machiavellian' intelligence? Primates often act as if they were following the advice that Niccolo Machiavelli offered to 16th-century Italian politicians to enable them to manipulate their social competitors (Machiavelli 1532, cited in de Waal 1982). Although many animal species are social without being particularly intelligent, primate societies are characterized by their complexity. An aspect of this social complexity is the formation of alliances that change with circumstance and over time. Relationships in primate societies are frequently manipulative and sometimes deceptive at quite sophisticated levels. For example, dominant male chimpanzees will rarely share food with those that they see as rivals, but do share with those not perceived to be a threat and with those who are allies in the power-struggle (Nishida *et al.* 1992). An individual may also use behavioural tactics to manipulate those who are not allies or relatives into giving help. An example of such manipulation would be evident where another animal's attention is diverted either towards or away from something in a way that would profit the deceiver (Byrne 1995).

Evaluation
social intelligence

- *Selective pressures* – An important prediction of the social intelligence hypothesis is that greater social intellect in some individuals will exert selection pressures on others, so that over evolutionary time there will be an 'arms race' of social intelligence within a particular species.

- *The advantages of coalitions* – The ultimate goal of animal behaviour is selfish in the face of natural selection, but animals may sometimes profit more from cooperation than from competition. Primate

coalitions are a good example of the advantages of cooperation, in that they enable an individual animal to achieve something (such as an important resource or access to a mate) that it would otherwise be unable to achieve.

- *Brain size and Machiavellian intelligence* – One way of testing the Machiavellian hypothesis is to examine the relative brain size across different species. Research (e.g. Dunbar 1995) has shown that the best predictors of increased brain size do not appear to be the environmental complexity faced by a species (e.g. the size of their home range), but rather the size of the social group (an indicator of social complexity).

Check your understanding of social learning in non-human animals by answering these questions. Check your answers by looking back through Topic 3.

1. What, according to Heyes (1993), is the main difference between imitative and non-imitative social learning?

2. Construct a descriptive 150-word précis of imitation as an explanation of social learning in non-human animals.

3. Identify two evaluative (i.e. AO2) points relating to imitation as an explanation of social learning in non-human animals, and explain what this tells us about the role of imitation in social learning.

4. Briefly explain the relationships between social learning and foraging.

5. How do blue tits learn to peck the tops off milk bottles?

6. Briefly review the evidence for animals teaching each other. Do you feel the evidence is convincing for this phenomenon?

7. Identify three critical (i.e. AO2) points relating to self-recognition in non-human animals, and explain *why* these pose problems for the view that animals are self-aware.

8. Prepare a 150-word analysis of evidence for and against the idea that non-humans can practise deception.

9. What is the 'Machiavellian intelligence hypothesis'?

10. Identify and explain two pieces of evidence that might support the existence of Machiavellian intelligence.

REVISION SUMMARY

Having covered this topic, you should be able to:

✓ describe and evaluate explanations relating to the role of social learning in the behaviour of non-human animals

✓ describe and evaluate research studies in the areas of imitation, foraging and teaching others and which relate to the role of social learning in the behaviour in non-human animals

✓ use these studies effectively as AO2 commentary on each of the explanations studied

✓ describe and evaluate evidence for intelligence in non-human animals, including self-recognition, theory of mind and social intelligence.

EXAMPLE EXAM QUESTIONS

Below are some **possible examination questions** set on this topic, along with hints to help you understand and approach each question effectively:

1. Outline and evaluate **two or more** explanations relating to the role of social learning in the behaviour of non-human animals (e.g. foraging, hunting in groups, imitation). (24 marks)

> The use of the instruction 'two or more' is meant to open up this question to those who feel less able to fill a 30-minute response with just two explanations. If you are confident that you can offer a detailed and suitably critical discussion of just two explanations, then stick to that. Offering more than two may just mean watering down your answer so that your AO1 is less detailed and your AO2 lacks elaboration. This is called the 'depth-breadth trade-off', as you inevitably sacrifice depth (both detail in AO1 and elaboration in AO2) if you try to cover many different explanations (breadth). Ultimately though, the choice is yours. The examples given in this question are merely hints about what you *could* use, not what you *must* use, so do not be drawn into covering them all.

2 (a) Outline **one or more** explanations relating to the role of social learning in the behaviour of non-human animals. (12 marks)

 (b) Evaluate the explanations relating to the role of social learning in the behaviour of non-human animals you described in (a) in terms of relevant research studies. (12 marks)

> In part (a), writing about only one explanation is enough for full marks, but you can cover more than one if you prefer. In part (b), the form of commentary has been specified ('in terms of relevant research studies'), so you must to shape your response to these demands. Here, it is not sufficient to *describe* the research studies, you must provide an evaluation of your chosen explanations *using* those research studies.

3 Describe and evaluate research (explanations and/or studies) relating to the role of social learning in the behaviour of non-human animals. (24 marks)

> You could respond to this question in exactly the same way as question 2 above. Alternatively, you could offer a more general commentary on your chosen explanations *or* you could restrict yourself completely to research studies as AO1 and commentary on these studies as AO2. Whichever route you take, you will need both AO1 and AO2 in your answer. It makes sense, therefore, to use your research studies only as AO2. There are many ways of providing AO2, as described in the section on 'Innovative and effective AO2' on p. 937.

4 (a) Describe **one** research study relating to the role of social learning in the behaviour of non-human animals. (6 marks)

 (b) Discuss explanations relating to the role of social learning in the behaviour of non-human animals. (18 marks)

> For this topic, questions may specifically be asked about research studies, as they are mentioned in the specification. For part (a), 6 AO1 marks are available for just one study. You can draw on your experience of writing 'APFCC' studies for AS-level and achieve the required detail by presenting aims, procedures, findings and conclusions when describing the study. Part (b) is worth 18 marks, consisting of 6 marks AO1 for any outline of explanations and 12 marks for the commentary. This mark split should be reflected in the way you organize your answer: 18 marks is about 450 words, so if you outline two explanations, that means about 75 words each, followed by 150 words of commentary for each. The commentary may include research studies as long as they are used effectively.

UNIT SUMMARY

Topic 1: Evolutionary explanations of animal behaviour

- **Animal behaviour** evolves through the process of natural selection. However, not all behaviour has evolved because it confers an adaptive advantage on animals. The essence of Darwin's theory of evolution is that organisms attempt to maximize their reproductive output. **Evolutionary explanations of behaviour** are now seen as occurring not to benefit individual animals, but to benefit the gene pool.

- Animals sometimes behave in **apparently altruistic** ways that increase the reproductive fitness of the individual that is helped at some cost to the helper. However, there may be a **biological explanation** for this. As a result of this self-sacrificing behaviour, animals may increase their inclusive fitness and are therefore displaying selfishness at a genetic level (kin selection).

- In reciprocal altruism, animals may help one another, but have the favour returned sometime in the future. Some animals will cooperate and help one another because as a team they can achieve more than by working alone.

Topic 2: Classical and operant conditioning

● In **classical conditioning**, a naturally occurring reflex (the UCS–UCR reflex) is associated with another stimulus (the CS) that is not typically capable of producing the response in question. Following consistent association with the UCS, the new stimulus is able to trigger the original behaviour (CR). If the CS is no longer paired with the UCS, however, the CR is extinguished. The CR might reappear under certain conditions in a procedure known as spontaneous recovery.

● When a stimulus is presented which is similar to the CS, the response might generalize to it, depending on the degree of similarity. If other stimuli are never paired with the UCS, however, the organism will discriminate between them and only respond to the original CS.

● **Operant conditioning** refers to learning that is dependent on the outcome of a behaviour. If behaviour is reinforced in some way, that behaviour will reappear more frequently in the future. This reinforcement may be positive (a pleasant event) or negative (avoiding or escaping from an unpleasant event).

● Reinforcement can also be presented in various schedules. These might be continuous or partial. Continuous reinforcement schedules produce more rapid initial learning but also more rapid extinction rates. Partial reinforcement results in slower extinction rates. If a behaviour produces unpleasant consequences (punishment), it is less likely to be produced in the future.

Topic 3: Social learning in non-human animals

● Many animals live in groups. Therefore, it would benefit them to be able to copy what other members of the group have learned. **Imitation** would, theoretically, be of considerable value to many different species, yet evidence for imitation in non-human species is relatively rare.

● Some animals learn about **foraging** and preferred food sources by associating with members of the same species (conspecifics).

● **Animal intelligence**, a difficult concept, may be seen as a hierarchy of learning processes, with the most basic forms of learning being shared by all species and 'higher' levels being associated with the more 'intelligent' species.

● There has been considerable comparative interest in **social learning in non-human animals**, especially species differences in **self-recognition** and **theory of mind**, although the relevance of such cognitive abilities to animals is still unclear.

● **Intelligence** may also be seen as a product of how animals solve social as well as physical problems, with recent research suggesting that some primate species possess **Machiavellian intelligence**.

FURTHER RESOURCES

Alcock, J. (2001) *Animal Behaviour: An Evolutionary Approach*, **Sunderland, MA: Sinaur Publishing.**

A comprehensive introduction to evolutionary explanations of animal behaviour, with excellent detailed descriptions of studies.

Manning, A. and Dawkins, M.S. (1998) *An Introduction to Animal Behaviour* **(5th edn), Cambridge: Cambridge University Press.**

A very readable and beautifully illustrated text.

Pearce, J.M. (1997) *Animal Learning and Cognition* **(2nd edn), Hove: Psychology Press.**

A comprehensive account of all aspects of animal learning (described in this unit) and animal cognition (described in Unit 22).

Websites

www.behavior.org/
The Cambridge Center for Behavioural Studies – information resources about the practical applications of behavioural technology.

www.kli.ac.at/theorylab/
The Konrad Lorenz Institute for Evolution and Cognition Research theory laboratory.

www.uwc.edu/OperantCon/
An interactive web exercise was created to help students understand operant conditioning.

www.dogmanners.com/conditioning.html
This site uses conditioning principles to help you teach your pooch good manners!

Unit 21 // Determinants of animal behaviour

22
UNIT

ANIMAL
Cognition

PREVIEW

After you have read this unit, you should be able to:

>> describe and evaluate explanations and research studies into animal navigation, including homing and navigation

>> discuss the use of visual, auditory and olfactory signalling systems in non-human animals

>> describe and evaluate explanations of the use of different signalling systems in non-human animals

>> describe and evaluate research studies into animal language

>> describe and evaluate explanations and research into memory in non-human animals

>> explain the importance of memory in navigation and foraging behaviour.

INTRODUCTION

Our interest in the cognitive abilities of animals may be fuelled partly by academic interest, but also it is born out of a sense of wonder about our natural world. Anecdotes about amazing feats of domestic pets, the spectacular navigational skills of homing pigeons or the haunting song of the humpback whale have all contributed to the belief that animals may be a lot smarter than we perhaps imagine. The study of animal cognition is one way we can apply the principles of scientific psychology to this fascinating area of animal behaviour.

To move between parts of their habitat (sub-habitats) efficiently and safely, animals must travel the right distance, in the right direction and at the right time (Waterman 1989). Navigation enables animals to find their way from one place to another. A good navigator must be able to sense direction, distance and time. Sometimes this is over vast distances, as in the migration of the Arctic tern from the Antarctic half way around the world to its feeding grounds on the coast of Greenland. Sometimes this is more localized, with animals trying to find their way back home after a morning's foraging for food. Some animals navigate by sight, some use the sun and the stars as a celestial 'map', and some, such as whales, follow the contours of coastlines. Some animals use senses that are very different from ours, as in the case of echolocation in dolphins. In Topic 1, you will explore various explanations of animal navigation, including homing behaviour and migration, and consider research studies into animal navigation.

Animal communication and human language have fundamental differences in both their structure and also their function. The intriguing possibility that non-humans might be able to learn human language has led to a flurry of research projects which have explored the linguistic capacities of chimpanzees, gorillas, dolphins and even parrots. The claim that these animals are demonstrating language is one of the most hotly contested assertions in comparative psychology and is discussed in Topic 2, along with a number of different signalling systems used by non-human animals.

The study of animal memory is concerned with how information acquired at one time can influence behaviour in the future. In species that store food in order to retrieve it at a later date, a good spatial memory is vital. If we establish that animals can, indeed, retain information about past events, then we begin to ask questions about the sort of information they might retain, how much they might be able to remember, and for how long. In the final topic of this unit, we consider various explanations of memory in non-human animals and some of the research that has been undertaken on this fascinating subject.

Mike
Cardwell

The animals in the two photos – the parrot and the grey squirrels, two very different species – possess impressive cognitive skills.

Parrots display a rudimentary ability to use human language and the grey squirrel is able to retrieve nuts that it buried months earlier. How do you think that these non-human animals achieve these feats? What about others, such as racing pigeons that are able to find their way back to their home roosts after long, tiring journeys? Are these activities as impressive as they seem?

In this unit, we will examine some of the evidence that suggests that non-human animals have many of the same skills that we traditionally attribute only to our own species.

KEY CONCEPTS

Communication: occurs when one animal (the signaller) performs an action that in turn causes some voluntary change of behaviour in another animal (the receiver) as a result of their perception of that signal.

Foraging: the different ways that animals are able to satisfy their nutritional requirements (e.g. grazing, predation, scavenging).

Homing: the ability of animals to navigate towards a target that is usually their home range.

Language: an agreed set of symbols and rules that enable us to convey meaning and converse with others who share the same language.

Memory: a mental function by which animals can retain and retrieve information about events that have happened in the past.

Migration: a term usually used to describe the mass movement of members of a species from one location to another.

Natural animal language: characteristics of animal communication patterns that satisfy at least some of the criteria for human language.

Navigation: true navigation is the ability to reach a goal regardless of starting point. This is contrasted with simple compass orientation, which involves always heading in one specific compass direction regardless of the 'correct' direction.

Spatial memory: the ability of an animal to form a mental image or 'map' of a familiar area or home range.

HOMING BEHAVIOUR

A fundamental distinction between plant and animal life is the ability to move at will around the environment. Most plant life acts like a chemical factory, making up and breaking down chemicals into nutrients and waste products, and using one of a number of reproductive mechanisms to germinate and reproduce. Animals tend to move around in search of food (foraging), whether obtained from plants or other animal life. Some animal species build or otherwise manufacture a home (e.g. a nest, burrow or shelter) that they use more than once. They not only need to have some way of remembering where the home is, but also need to have some form of navigational or direction-finding protocol for locating it from a distance. The means by which animals locate their home range from afar can be very impressive, with some species able to do so as part of a migratory pattern which may take them many thousands of miles each year (MacFarland 1993). The albatross is able to home successfully after trips of around 4,000 miles!

Animals have a variety of different strategies for homing:

- the use of landmarks
- homing using true navigation
- use of the sun compass
- use of magnetic cues.

The use of landmarks

Tinbergen and Kruyt (1938) demonstrated how the digger wasp uses the main features around its burrow to locate its home when returning from a foraging flight. The wasp makes its home by burrowing a short distance into soft dirt and, just before leaving each time, makes a hovering flight overhead, as if 'taking in' any changes in the environment near the burrow entrance. Tinbergen and Kruyt carried out an ingenious experiment by altering the position of landmarks (pine cones they had placed themselves) after the wasp had flown out of sight. When the resident wasp returned, it was deceived by the new placement of cones into searching for its burrow entrance in entirely the wrong place.

The impressive ability of pigeons to find their home loft after release is largely dependent on their ability to learn prominent landmarks in the area. If they are released within sight of these landmarks, they can use them to find their way home. When they are released from more distant locations, their journey times improve with successive journeys, suggesting an increasing reliance on landmarks, as they become more familiar with their terrain (Pearce 1997).

(A02) **Evaluation**
the use of landmarks in
navigation

- *Not only landmarks* – There are good reasons for not believing that pigeons make exclusive use of landmarks for navigation. Pigeons that are taken a considerable distance from their home

loft are still able to find their way home, despite the fact that they have never seen any of the landmarks before. In other words, in the absence of familiar landmarks, pigeons appear to be capable of 'true navigation' (see below), not just finding their way home from a familiar starting point, as in the case of the digger wasp described earlier. They must use at least one other form of navigation.

Homing using true navigation

Perdeck (1967) carried out an ingenious experiment to test whether birds are capable of true navigation (i.e. have the ability to reach their goal regardless of their starting point), or simply show a compass orientation (always heading in one specific compass direction, regardless of the 'correct' direction). He captured *young* starlings on their annual migration from their breeding grounds around the Baltic Sea to their wintering sites in southern England, Belgium and northern France. After tagging the birds, they were then taken by aeroplane to

Switzerland, where they were released. After release, the birds continued on the same heading as before (southwest) despite the fact they had been displaced by nearly 500 miles from their original route! Instead of ending up in southern England, many of the birds arrived in northern Spain (see right-hand picture in Fig. 22.1). Interestingly, adult birds that were captured and released in the same way compensated for the displacement and headed northwest – the proper direction for their usual wintering grounds. It appears that the juveniles were relying on compass orientation and the adults on true navigation.

Figure 22.1 >> *Results of experiment to detect whether birds use compass orientation or true navigation*

Evaluation
homing using true
navigation explanations

● *'Map-and-compass' components* – The theory of true navigation in pigeons has been unanimously supported by the research literature, and is often referred to as 'map-and-compass' navigation. It is so called because in order to find its way home, the pigeon must be able to work out its map position, and then from this position must orient itself in the home direction using some sort of compass mechanism. The evidence seems to suggest that the map component is based on olfactory, magnetic and visual cues, while the compass sense appears to be guided by the sun and magnetic information (Wallraff 1990).

The sun compass

It has long been believed that pigeons use the position of the sun to help them navigate. Kramer (1952) trained pigeons to locate food, using the sun as a directional cue. When he deflected the image of the sun with mirrors, he found that the orientation of the birds shifted to accommodate this. The sun compass is assumed to operate in the following way. When a pigeon is released, it observes the position of the sun and compares it with its internal body clock. If a pigeon is released at noon (according to its body clock), it would expect the sun to be directly overhead. If the sun appears to be lower in the sky, then the pigeon should be able to compute the direction it should take to return to its home loft. This is a complex calculation, but clock-shifting experiments suggest it is not beyond the capabilities of pigeons.

An animal's internal clock is set according to the light–dark cycle (see Unit 13). If pigeons are kept in an artificial environment with a light–dark cycle that is out of sync with the external light–dark cycle, it should be possible to alter the birds' internal clock and hence the accuracy of the sun compass. In a typical clock-shift experiment, the birds are kept in conditions where the lights might be switched on at midnight and off at midday, with all external cues removed. After a few days, it is possible to have shifted the birds' internal clock forward 6 hours (dawn is actually at 6 a.m., but the birds' internal clock tells them it is midday). If a bird is then released at 9 a.m., its internal clock tells it that it is actually 3 p.m.; this leads the bird to infer that the sun should be in the southwest (where it *should* be at 3 p.m.), whereas it is actually in the southeast. The bird should then make its computations based on this information, and fly at right angles to the actual direction home. A number of experiments (e.g. Keeton 1969) have confirmed these predictions, confirming the importance of the sun compass in homing in pigeons.

Commentary
the sun compass explanation

● *Sun compass navigation in monarch butterflies* – Every year, monarch butterflies fly about 3,500 kilometres from their breeding grounds in Canada to a site in Mexico where they spend the winter. Some researchers have suggested that monarch butterflies maintain their course using either the sun or the earth's magnetic field or, possibly, both. A study by Mouritsen and Frost (2002) provides convincing support for the importance of the sun in this amazing journey, showing that monarch butterflies use the relative position of the sun at a particular time of day to set their course (see Key research below).

● *Sun compass navigation in pigeons* – Keeton (1969) also suggested that pigeons must use another system apart from the sun compass to determine directional information. For example, on overcast days when the sun is not visible, pigeons are still able to home successfully. Interestingly, he found that clock-shifted pigeons deviated from normal pigeons only on sunny days. On overcast days, however, both clock-shifted and normal pigeons homed successfully and there appeared to be no difference in performance between the two groups. From this finding, Keeton concluded that the sun is only used for directional information when it is visible, but at other times pigeons must make use of another secondary compass sense.

KEY RESEARCH >> ANIMAL NAVIGATION

sun compass navigation in monarch butterflies (Mouritsen and Frost 2002)

Mouritsen and Frost tethered butterflies in a specially built flight simulator that used airflow from underneath to simulate hours of flying without influencing the way the butterflies headed. The monarch butterflies reliably chose a southwesterly path, whereas 'jet-lagged' butterflies (whose day–night cycles had been experimentally shifted six hours in either direction) were tricked into setting a course 90 degrees from normal. This indicates that they steer according to where they think the sun *should* be at a given time of day. Additionally, the butterflies did not respond to changes in a magnetic field, which has been proposed as a potential navigational mechanism for cloudy days. The researchers suggest that monarch butterflies are using patterns of polarized light visible through the clouds.

Monarch butterflies are able to navigate using patterns of light from the sun, even on cloudy days

Magnetic cues

The core of the earth gives off a magnetic field, with magnetic energy going from the South Pole and re-entering at the North Pole. Evidence suggests that some animals can navigate by detecting the strength of the magnetic field and the angle at which the field meets the earth (Lohmann and Lohmann 1996), which are distinct for each spot on the globe. How the brain processes this information is still unclear, although some species do have specific brain areas that respond to this magnetic information. Walker *et al.* (2002) proposed that animals might be able to detect magnetic field information because of specialized nerve cells ('magnetoreceptors') that react to different characteristics of the magnetic field. These might be thought of as an internal compass, such that the 'needle' of the compass moves with the changing magnetic field. When the needle is displaced, it can trigger the activation of other cells that help the animal sense where to direct its movements.

The Key research panel opposite give details of research into the way that two very different creatures might use magnetic cues.

Pigeons (Keeton 1971)

Keeton (1971) suggested that pigeons might have the ability to detect the earth's magnetic field. To investigate this possibility, he glued small magnets onto the heads of the birds and then released them from unfamiliar sites. The magnets disrupted any detection of the magnetic field of the earth, and should, therefore, have made successful homing impossible on overcast days. As predicted, he found that these birds had no difficulty homing on sunny days, but were unable to find their way back to their home loft on overcast days. Keeton concluded that pigeons appear to use two compass systems during navigation. The primary system relies on the position of the sun, and the secondary system on the earth's magnetic field. Keeton also found that young, inexperienced pigeons were often disorientated when wearing the magnets, even in sunny conditions. He suggested that this was an indication that the magnetic compass was innate, and was used to calibrate the sun compass as a result of homing experience. Inexperienced birds were unable to use the information provided by the sun because of their inexperience and could not use the earth's magnetic field because of the magnet.

The Caribbean spiny lobster

Experts on the Caribbean spiny lobster have recorded occasional tales of its superior navigation over long distances. Research by Boles and Lohmann (2003) has now confirmed this. Their experiments suggest that the lobsters manage their remarkable feat by sensing their location within the magnetic field of the earth. These lobsters normally live in the western Atlantic Ocean between Bermuda and Brazil. To investigate whether they have a homing ability, the researchers caught more than 100 lobsters in different locations and transported them for about an hour in various ways to a test site. They kept the lobsters in opaque, rope-suspended compartments. On reaching the test sites, researchers blindfolded each lobster by applying removable caps to fit over their eyestalks and tethered the animal in a tank with a slippery floor. The lobster then moved in a direction close to its homeward bearing.

Commentary
magnetic cues explanation

● *Lack of research support for pigeon navigation using magnetic cues* – Attempts to train pigeons to respond to a change in the magnetic field have failed. These experiments are based on the assumption that if pigeons can detect a change in the magnetic field, it should be possible to train them to respond to such a change. Kreithen (1975) tested 97 pigeons for their ability to detect changes in the magnetic field, using a classically conditioned increase in heart rate as the conditioned response (see Unit 21 for an explanation of classical conditioning). The birds were first exposed to an experimentally induced change in the magnetic field followed by a weak electric shock that caused the pigeon's heart rate to increase. After several trials, if the bird was able to detect a change in the magnetic field, it would be able to anticipate the electric shock after sensing the change in the magnetic field, and its heart rate would increase. No such response was found. Although this might indicate some problem with the laboratory method, a more likely explanation is that the pigeon was unable to sense such changes.

● *Evidence from false field studies* – To explore what cues the lobsters might be using, and support the idea that spiny lobsters really were using magnetic cues for navigation, Boles and Lohmann (2003) placed each lobster into a device that recreated the magnetic field of a different location. When in a field that mimicked conditions 400 kilometres north of their home, the lobsters walked south, and those in a false southern field walked north.

MIGRATION

Migration is a generic term that usually describes the mass movement of members of a species from one location to another. The trigger for this behaviour may be seasonal changes in weather, air temperature or day length, or in response to fluctuations in the environment, such as food supply. For instance, wildebeest on the African savannah move towards rain when they sense it during the dry season. They seem to be able to read the signs, such as darkened clouds or cool winds emanating from the direction of the rains.

The distance over which animals migrate may range from one to two metres (e.g. the vertical movements of zooplankton in a lake, moving to different depths according to time of day) to several thousand miles, such as the albatross or the monarch butterfly. Usually these are return migrations, but not always. For instance, adult Atlantic salmon migrate from the Sargasso Sea (South Atlantic) to the lakes and rivers of Europe where they themselves were spawned. After spawning near the site of their own birthplace, they die, leaving the next generation to fight their way along the freshwater pathways back to the sea.

Birds that migrate over large distances are able to use a range of environmental cues to guide them, such as the smell of the sea while following a continental coastline, the sight of mountains or other landmarks, or by using the earth's magnetic field. The use of such landmarks is not confined to migratory journeys, however, since many animals utilize knowledge of their environment (a so-called 'cognitive map') to navigate during their daily forays from home.

The migration of birds

When the terrain allows it, birds often migrate in stages. Their overall migration may, therefore, be made up of a series of relatively short steps punctuated by rest stops. These are necessary to replenish the body resources needed to travel such long distances. Most small songbirds stop to feed each day during their migration, with their migratory flights normally taking place at night. If they are crossing a large body of water or desert, these birds may fly for a full 24 hours at a time. Other birds (such as storks) make use of the rising air currents to make long flights during the day. Birds that soar, such as the stork, depend on thermal updrafts for their migration and appear reluctant to fly over water if they cannot see land on the other side because of the absence of the rising warm air necessary to soar.

Birds migrating for the first time frequently travel without more experienced adults. As the first-time migrators leave either before or after the adults, they cannot guide their navigation. There is evidence that experienced birds are better able to navigate direct routes than juveniles and therefore reach their destination first. Successful navigation also depends on the effects of wind and weather. Computer modelling has shown that birds migrating from North America to the Eastern Caribbean islands or to South America in the autumn may be aided by strong, seasonal prevailing winds. Shortly after a strong cold front with its brisk northwest winds, birds head southeast out to sea in great numbers. If they fly at their most efficient sustained speed, they generally make landfall in three to four days. This model indicates that in such instances, successful navigation would not require a precise compass heading, nor a specific place of leaving, nor even a specific altitude or air speed. As

ACTIVITY

Learning about birds and migration

If you live close to a Wildfowl and Wetlands trust site (such as Slimbridge in Gloucestershire or Welney in Norfolk) try to visit between October and December to see the migrating Bewick swans at the end of their 4,000-kilometres migration from Arctic Russia.

long as typical weather conditions prevail, a high degree of success would be expected without any elaborate navigational control. Without the right weather pattern, however, mass disaster would occur. Weather is, of course, notoriously unpredictable, but it does have some major reliable features that can be exploited in migration. The steady westerly gales that blow at high southerly latitudes propel the wandering albatross around the world in its yearly circuit. Between 30° and 60° north of the equator, southwesterly winds prevail, while northwesterly winds blow between 30° and 60° south (Waterman 1989).

Aquatic migration

Many aquatic animals migrate over vast distances. In the Bahamas, spiny lobsters that spend the summer in shallow water move during the autumn to deeper water. They typically form a 'queue' of up to 60 individuals, and walk to their new home, perhaps 50 to 60 kilometres away. The queuing may serve to reduce the drag of the water on each individual, and thus save energy. Adult wool-handed crabs live in rivers such as the Yangtze and the Rhine, but migrate downstream as far as 1,200 kilometres to release their eggs in the sea.

Navigating underwater is quite different from navigating in air because of the extremely poor visibility and the underwater currents. Visual piloting is therefore of limited usefulness underwater. Many species do have well-developed visual systems, however, and these must be primarily important for prey detection, and to a lesser extent for orientation and navigation. Visual functioning in the absence of daylight is also possible because of 'bioluminescence' (the production of light by organisms themselves), which is widespread in the sea.

Water currents are in many ways similar to winds. They are generally much slower than winds, but then swimming is much slower than flying. As winds can help or hinder the migration of birds, so currents can help or hinder the migration of aquatic organisms. Winds and tides supply most of the energy for ocean currents although, typically, currents reach only about 2 per cent of the driving wind's speed (Waterman 1989).

The migration of salmon

One of the most closely studied migrating fish is the salmon. Typically, immature fish descend from the streams in which they were born, to spend part of their life at sea. This urge to migrate varies according to the species. In some salmon species, it is rare; in others, it is common. In the first phase of migration, the juvenile salmon live in fresh water. At the right time, these juveniles swim downstream towards the sea. For some species, this is days after their birth; in others (such as the Atlantic salmon), this can be as long as seven years after their birth. During the one to five years that salmon spend in the ocean, they feed extensively and achieve most of their growth. During this second phase, they must find food and avoid predators.

In the third phase, salmon return as adults to the mouths of their native rivers. The different populations sort themselves out and navigate successfully to their own home stream. In the fourth phase, the salmon must swim against the current (for some, a distance of 4,000 kilometres), often ascending a long river. At every fork in the river, the fish must make the correct navigational decision. It seems certain that chemical cues are used to recognize both the home estuary and also the precise spawning area. This hypothesis is supported by research carried out by Wisby and Hasler who plugged the noses of salmon that then homed less accurately than untreated controls (cited in Harden-Jones 1968). The results of this experiment are shown in Table 22.1 below.

The navigation of these fish is clearly tied to specific geographical objectives, because individual fish return exactly to their parents' spawning site. Breeding experiments clearly show that precise navigation depends on both genetic factors and juvenile learning.

Table 22.1 >> Results of Wisby and Hammer's research into salmon migration

Stream of origin		Number released	Number recaptured		The figures show the numbers of coho salmon released and later recaptured in two rivers in Washington state, with and without their olfactory sense impaired
			Issaquah	East Fork	
>> Issaquah	Controls	121	46	0	
	Nose plugged	145	39	12	
>> East Fork	Controls	38	8	19	
	Nose plugged	38	16	3	

Commentary
migration

- **Exploit the best breeding or feeding conditions** – Though such migration may seem rather a pointless activity, the benefits are usually that the individuals exploit the best breeding or feeding conditions in both places. In latitudes at some distance from the equator, climate, food or other resources fluctuate greatly with the seasons. For example, southern latitudes experience much better winter weather than we have in Europe and, during our summer, much of the southern latitudes are covered in snow and ice. By moving south, insectivores (insect eaters) and frugivores (fruit eaters) are able to find food that they would never be able to find in a harsh, winter environment. Many of the birds that stay in the north forage on seeds which remain available throughout the winter. Northern summers also tend to have much longer days for birds to forage. Tropical days tend to be around 12 hours long, whereas days in a northern summer may be as long as 16 hours. This is particularly important during the breeding season when parent birds have to feed nestlings that will increase to 50 times their hatching weight in 13 days.

- **Reducing predation pressures** – Another advantage of migration is that it diminishes at least some of the predatory pressures on migratory species. Predators that specialize in hunting one particular bird species cannot evolve because their prey are not around as a food source full time.

- **To migrate or not migrate** – The impetus to migrate may not be a decision left to individual animals – the so-called 'migration instinct' can markedly affect an animal's behaviour at the close of a season. On the other hand, many individuals of bird species seem to decide not to migrate in a given year, although, of course, no 'reasoning' is implied here. The response not to migrate may simply be one where the environmental cues have not been sufficiently strong to trigger the behaviour seen in others of the species.

Check your understanding of animal navigation by answering these questions. Do it from memory at first. You can check your answers by looking back through Topic 1.

1 Identify three ways in which animals might navigate.

2 Construct a 100-word précis of the sun compass explanation of navigation.

3 How do monarch butterflies navigate using the sun? How does this research affect the status of the sun-compass explanation?

4 How do animals make use of the earth's magnetic field in their navigation?

5 Why is the Caribbean spiny lobster significant for a magnetic cues explanation of navigation?

6 Identify two evaluative points relating to the magnetic cues explanation, and suggest how these contribute to its status as an explanation of animal navigation.

7 Construct a descriptive 150-word précis of the migration of birds, and a descriptive 150-word précis of aquatic migration.

8 Identify three benefits of migration.

REVISION SUMMARY

Having covered this topic you should be able to:

✓ describe at least two explanations of animal navigation, including homing behaviour and migration

✓ describe and evaluate research studies into animal navigation, including homing and migration

✓ use research studies effectively as AO2 commentary on each of the explanations of animal navigation studied.

✎ EXAMPLE EXAM QUESTIONS

Below are some **possible examination questions** set on this topic, along with hints to help you understand and approach each question effectively:

1 Outline and evaluate **two or more** explanations of animal navigation. (24 marks)

> Questions such as this can be hard to answer in 30 minutes, as there are (at least) four distinct 'chunks'. This division can, however, be useful to you when planning your response, as it gives you a ready-made structure to your essay. Try to spend 15 minutes on the AO1 component of your essay and 15 minutes on AO2. Be careful, too, to evaluate each 'explanation' that you outline. One way of illustrating the strengths and limitations of a particular explanation is to examine the balance of research evidence that either supports or challenges its assumptions. For example, although there is research evidence to support the claim that pigeons make extensive use of the sun compass in their homing, there is also evidence that they must be using another navigational system as well.

2 Critically consider research (explanations **and/or** studies) into homing **and** migration (24 marks)

> 'Critically consider' is an AO1+AO2 term. The AO1 component is a description (or just an outline) of research. You have the choice of describing explanations or studies. If you decide to describe explanations, using research studies as AO2, then be sure to use the studies as effective evaluation rather than describing them (in which case they would receive no AO2 credit). There is a discussion about 'Innovative and effective AO2' on p. 937. Note that you must describe and evaluate *both* homing *and* migration. If you cover only one of these, there would be a partial performance penalty.

3 (a) Outline **two** explanations of homing in animal navigation. (12 marks)

(b) Evaluate the explanations of homing in animal navigation that you described in part (a) in terms of relevant research studies. (12 marks)

> In contrast with question 1, here you are restricted to just two explanations – if you cover more than two, then credit is given to the best two. In part (b), there are specific instructions about how to present your AO2 commentary – 'in terms of relevant research studies'. Both explanations must receive this treatment, otherwise you would be demonstrating 'partial performance', and would lose marks. When questions are parted, an examiner may 'export' material from one part to another when determining marks, but this is not a good thing to rely on because material is not always creditworthy, as is the case here. Always carefully shape your response to the particular demands of the question.

4 Discuss research studies of animal navigation. (24 marks)

> Given the wording of the specification, a question could be set that was restricted to research studies only, as here. You may consider homing or migration or both, or any other example of animal navigation. You do have to consider at least two research studies and evaluate at least two in order to avoid the partial performance penalty. One effective way to evaluate research studies is to consider methodological flaws: how do such flaws (or strengths) affect the validity of the conclusions? Elaboration is an important AO2 criterion, which means stating your criticism and then explaining it. You can also comment on research studies by considering the implications of such studies for explaining navigation or considering the applications of such knowledge. Finally, you could also contrast studies as a means of attracting AO2 marks.

Topic 2 >> Animal communication and language

SIGNALLING SYSTEMS IN NON-HUMAN ANIMALS

Language is a system of communication in which messages are conveyed between people. But are the elements of human language present in other species? The question of whether language is unique to humans remains controversial.

The ability of humans to use spoken language stems from the fact that our brain is designed in important and unique ways for dealing with auditory communication within a given frequency range corresponding to the human voice (about 1 to 5 kHz). There have been numerous attempts to teach animals to understand human language, but the most productive approach to studying animal communication has been to try to learn the secrets of how *their* communication systems work.

Communication channels

Any communication system involves a signaller and a receiver. The means by which signals are communicated depends partly on the properties of the mode through which the signal is transmitted. For instance, the fabulous display of the peacock is both visual and auditory (the feathers make a fluttering sound during full display), but the

effectiveness of colour and movement depends upon the peahen (as receiver) attending to the peacock at the time. To bring about, or to retain, her interest in him, the peacock often has to strut around in front of her or encircle her in order to intercept her gaze whenever she turns away.

The female, in this instance, is able to some extent to ignore the visual information provided by the male. But other forms of communication are less easily switched on and off by the receiver. For instance, the bellowing sound made by a band of howler monkeys as they patrol the boundary of their territory echoes around the South American forests like a foghorn. Only a very deaf individual would fail to receive the warning message from such a troupe.

Ants use a chemical signal to communicate sources of food. For instance, the fire ant scout lays a scent trail that excites workers to follow it, eventually leading them towards the food source. In their turn, workers lay their own scent trails so as to maintain the 'pathway' until that food supply has been exhausted. We can now look at each of these 'channels' of communication in more detail.

Visual communication

The evolution of visual signals

Many communication systems become 'ritualized' during evolution, i.e. the behaviour may become rigidly automatic and takes on a new function from that for which it was originally designed. For instance, during courtship, the mandarin drake uses its bill to tap against the brightly coloured markings on its wing tips. This gesture is believed to originate from a preening movement, but now serves to impress the female by emphasizing its wing markings.

Many visual displays are ritualized like this, particularly those occurring during courtship and conflict encounters. A ritualized display is one where two or more members of the same species (sometimes referred to as 'conspecifics') engage in stereotypical sequences of action, each one's responses serving as a stimulus or trigger for the further responses of the other.

Visual signals in courtship and mating

Such ritualization in behaviour sequences serves to 'tune in' each individual to the responsiveness of the other. During courtship rituals, this process enables 'sexual selection' to occur (described in Unit 23), where individuals are able to assess the qualities of the other. The stereotypical behaviour patterns that occur during visual displays also serve to prevent crossbreeding between closely related species. The appropriate responses to any one behaviour in such a sequence would only be made by a conspecific, with individuals of other species making no such response. Hybrids arising from crossbreeding are rarely as viable as purebred offspring and so are costly errors for parents wanting to ensure the perpetuation of their genes.

Visual signals in conflict situations

In conflict situations, too, ritualized bouts enable visual signalling to precede actual combat. This enables an opponent to withdraw when they make the assessment that the other is bigger or stronger than themselves. To learn of this after a fight has started may prove immensely costly, adding injury to defeat.

Visual signals in parental behaviour

Tinbergen and Perdeck (1950) discuss a well-known example of visual communication. They carried out some ingenious experiments, which demonstrated that the orange spot on the mandible of the herring gull bill serves as a 'target' for the chick's pecking. When the chick pecks at this spot, it triggers the adult to regurgitate food into the nest for the young to eat.

Advantages

Grier and Burk (1992) identify a number of advantages and disadvantages of visual communication.

- *Speed* – Visual communication may be transmitted instantaneously (as in the arching of a cat's back or the flash of bright plumage).
- *Volume* – It can carry a large amount of information (about sex, status, breeding condition and so on).
- *Direction* – It is highly directional, permitting the source to be detected easily.
- *Effort* – Some aspects, such as body colouration, are permanent. After the initial expenditure of energy to produce them, they require little further energy to maintain. (The use of visual displays, however, such as the courtship display of the peacock, may involve a considerable amount of energy to bring them to the attention of others.)

Disadvantages

- *Distance* – Visual communication cannot be used over great distances, being limited by obstructions (such as dense undergrowth, poor visibility or the limited visual acuity of the receiver).
- *Light* – It requires light or the production of light and is, therefore, of little use in the dark. As we saw in Topic 1 when we discussed migration, some animals are capable of generating their own light by a process known as bioluminescence.

An honest signalling system

A good reason for the evolution of stereotypical, ritualized behaviour patterns is that they create a system which is difficult to infiltrate or exploit by others. A system which is hard to counterfeit is less open to outsiders or cheats to exploit – a process referred to as 'dishonest signalling' (Zahavi 1979).

Auditory communication

The nature of auditory signals

Sound signals are potentially capable of immense variety. They can be varied in terms of pitch, loudness and timing. Humpback whales, for example, span the whole range of human hearing (and probably beyond), resembling a deep rumbling cathedral organ at one end of the scale and a piercing bat's squeak at the other (Dawkins 1981). The song of the humpback whale is so loud that other whales on the far side of the world could, theoretically at least, hear it.

Bird song

Singing appears to serve two main functions in birds:
- defending territories
- attracting females to mate.

The mobbing call found in many species of songbird is used to attract companions to help in harassing a predator that may pose a potential threat. You may well have heard a blackbird using such a call in the presence of a neighbourhood cat. The alarm calls of many species share the same acoustic properties, thus making it difficult to detect the exact location of the caller. This makes a lot of sense, as calling in the presence of a predator might attract unwanted attention and act as a beacon for the predator. Dawkins (1981) suggests that alarm calls signal 'Danger', rather than 'Danger over here', for just that reason.

Auditory signals in reproductive behaviour

The songs of male birds may also stimulate female reproductive behaviour. Female canaries that are played recordings of the artificially reduced repertories of male canaries tend to build nests at a lower rate (Kroodsma, cited in Ridley 1995). Males in polygamous species tend to have more complex songs than males in monogamous species, suggesting that as competition is greater in polygamous species, females use complexity of song as an important criterion for mate selection.

(A02) Commentary
advantages and disadvantages of auditory communication

Advantages

- *Penetration* – Auditory signals can go around obstacles and through dense vegetation, and can be used in the dark.
- *Speed* – Auditory signals are much quicker to transmit than chemical signals.
- *Flexibility and complexity* – Auditory communication is much more flexible than other types of signal and allows for longer and more complex messages. Many monkey species (such as the titi monkeys and gibbons) produce long and complex 'songs' made up of much smaller elements. These can be used for courtship and to give information about sex, rank and even 'marital status' (Cowlishaw 1992).

Disadvantages

- *Interference* – Sound is subject to interference (e.g. from other elements of the acoustic environment) and attenuation (fading with distance).
- *Use of energy resources* – A major disadvantage of auditory signals is that they require considerable energy to produce and must be produced repeatedly. This means they are often easy for predators to 'overhear'.

Source: Grier and Burk (1992)

Chemical communication

Pheromones

Chemical signals ('pheromones') are particularly well developed in insects and mammals. Some chemical signals are very short lived, highly volatile and have low molecular weights, such as the chemicals used by ants to signal alarm. If these signals were not short lived, it would be impossible to change the signal quickly in the event of a new danger. These signals disperse quickly over localized ranges, but are virtually undetectable after a minute or so. Many moths use chemical signals to attract mates, while the silkworm moth's receivers are so sensitive to the airborne chemical message that just one or two molecules are enough to trigger a response.

Territory marking

On the other hand, some other chemical signals are extremely long lasting. This has the tremendous advantage of allowing the signal to persist in the absence of the signaller. Territory markers need to be persistent for just this reason and therefore require a fairly high molecular weight (Manning and Dawkins 1998). If the territory is fairly small, scent markers are placed along the territorial boundary. If the territory is large and it is impossible to keep the boundary fully scented, pheromones and faeces are deposited at strategic points within the territory to inform others that the territory is occupied.

(A02) Commentary
advantages and disadvantages of chemical communication

Advantages

- *Penetration* – It transmits through darkness and around obstacles (useful for nocturnal species).

- *Range* – It has the greatest potential range (sharks are known to detect the smell of blood from many kilometres away).
- *Permanence* – It may be stable and long lasting, as in the boundary marking of territorial animals, and may be transmitted 'into the future', so that the signaller does not have to be always present.

continued on next page

Unit 22 // Animal cognition

Commentary continued
advantages and disadvantages of chemical communication

● *Privacy* – Chemical signals are relatively 'private': receivers need specific receptors to receive them, making it hard for predators to 'eavesdrop'.

Disadvantages

● *Slowness* – Chemical signals may be slow to transmit (the larger the molecule, the slower the transmission).

● *Rate of fading* – Chemical signals may fade too quickly or may not fade quickly enough, and so interfere with subsequent messages.

Deception in communication

In some encounters between pairs of animals, individuals may engage in disputes that could escalate into actual combat. In such a case, one or both individuals may initially signal their determination to fight in order to bluff the other that they mean serious business. Conversely, a weakening in the resolve to fight may be 'leaked' in their body language, signalling to the other that victory is about to be conceded. Under such circumstances, the message may be either reliable (an 'honest' signal) or deceptive. For instance, an individual hoping to win a dispute by any means (short of actual combat) may rely heavily on bluff, perhaps by appearing to be stronger or more aggressive than they actually are. This strategy will involve dishonest signalling to the opponent.

Animals may also signal dishonestly when faced with a predator. For instance, many prey species inflate their body or 'stand tall' when threatened, in order to look like formidable opposition. On the other hand, appearing carefree in front of an opponent or predator may also send a useful signal. For example, Thompson's gazelles show a pronounced escape gait known as 'stotting' or 'pronking', in which they leap by 'bouncing' along on all four legs one metre or two into the air (see photo).

The whole countenance of a gazelle while stotting seems to be one of nonchalance, or even arrogance. This behaviour appears in the presence of some, but not all, of its many predators. Most of the big cats that prey upon gazelle are able to catch them if the chase is over a short distance. Gazelles, not surprisingly, do not stott in front of a big cat. However, when pack predators (such as African hunting dogs) approach, stotting is seen in many of the herd members. It is believed that this gait signals to the predator that this individual is both strong and fast and, therefore,

The unique 'pronking' gait used by Thompson's gazelles when under threat is thought to confuse predators

unlikely to be caught if chased. This interpretation is based on the observation that few of the stotting gazelles are singled out by the dogs, implying that stotting is a clear signal of an individual's ability to escape (Fitzgibbon and Fanshawe 1988). However, it is by no means clear whether all the stotting males are signalling honestly.

Sometimes a signal to a predator may take the form of outright bluff, as occurs when a crane or a partridge feigns a broken wing in order to lead a predator, such as a fox, away from the location of their nest. Interest in deceitfulness in animal communication has been stimulated by the controversy over whether animals have conscious awareness (Griffin 1984, 1991). Some argue that in order to deceive others, an individual must have a 'Machiavellian' intent to fool them (Byrne and Whiten 1988). In plain language, animals able to 'lie' must presume that those they are deceiving have 'minds' that can be misled (see Unit 21 for a discussion of 'theory of mind' in non-human animals).

ANIMAL LANGUAGE

One of the most provocative debates over recent years has been about whether language is an ability unique to humans. Research evidence from studies of chimpanzees and gorillas has begun to challenge this assumption of language being 'species-specific'. The debate has been looked upon with amusement by some scientists and with intense emotion by others. At this point, it would make sense to have a look at what is

actually *meant* by language. This then gives us some criteria against which to assess whether, in fact, these researchers have succeeded in teaching language *per se*, or some other non-linguistic behaviour. One of the first major attempts to construct criteria for language were the 'design features' of language published by Hockett (1959). Hockett's sixteen features that define 'language' are outlined in Table 22.2.

A2 Comparative Psychology

Table 22.2 >> Hockett's design features of language

1   *Vocal/auditory* – Sounds are transmitted from one person to another.

2   *Broadcast/directional* – Sounds are 'broad' cast, although the listener can determine the direction of their origin.

3   *Rapid fading* – The signal fades away rapidly.

4   *Total feedback* – Speakers can hear what they themselves are saying.

5   *Interchangeability* – A sender can receive signals as well as transmit.

6   *Specialization* – Language has a special communication function – it is not a by-product of some other behaviour.

7   *Semanticity* – Language has meaning.

8   *Arbitrariness* – The use of arbitrary units (e.g. words) means that they do not need to resemble physically the event they represent.

9   *Traditional transmission* – Language can be passed from one generation to the next.

10   *Learnability* – New forms of language can be learnt.

11   *Discreteness* – Language can be organized into discrete units (e.g. words) and the meaning of a communication determined by the organization of these units (e.g. sentences).

12   *Duality of patterning* – Language has more than one level of organization. Speech sounds can be organized into words and words can be organized into sentences.

13   *Displacement* – The speaker is able to refer to things that are not present in space (e.g. out of sight) or time (e.g. yesterday).

14   *Productivity* – A language user can produce an infinite variety of novel utterances.

15   *Prevarication* – Language can be used to deceive, to talk about things that are not true.

16   *Reflexiveness* – Language enables users to talk about themselves, to describe their own experiences.

Dance language of the honeybee

The waggle dance

Language clearly includes the ability to speak of things that are not present or that have not yet happened. This immediately appears to rule out just about all animal language. Or does it? Lindauer (1955) and von Frisch (1967) studied the remarkable communication system in honeybees, known as 'dance language'. Honeybee scouts scour the countryside around the hive looking for sources of nectar. When one scout locates a source, it will return to the hive and engage in a 'waggle dance'. This signals to the workers both the direction (within ±25 degrees) and the distance (within ±15 per cent) of the source of nectar from the hive. This dance is thought to provide information – via sight, sound, vibration and odour – about the quality and location of the food, and is effective even when danced in the hive in darkness. The waggle dance system is used not just for conveying information about food sources, but is also used in other circumstances. For instance, during a swarm, when a new colony is founded, the dancers seem to convey information about possible sites for establishing the new hive.

Interpreting dance language

A number of commentators have suggested that the bees are merely responding automatically to the stimulus of movement and sounds produced by the returning scouts, but there is evidence that the workers make decisions about whether or not to follow up the information they are provided with. For instance, Gould (1986, 1992) led a captive scout to a nectar source he had placed in a boat in the middle of a lake, and then released the bee. Despite the scout's dancing on returning to the hive, very few workers left the hive to investigate. Not only do bees dislike flying over water, but the prospect of finding food in the middle of a lake must seem remote. This seems a reasonable deduction because, when Gould next took the captive scout fully across the lake to the opposite shore, the scout was able to recruit workers by the waggle dance when it returned to the hive. The basis of the honeybee's dance is believed to be far more complex than was first thought, since it contains a number of interacting signals (Kirchner and Towne 1994).

(A02) **Commentary**
the role of dance language in bees

● *Communicating displacement* – Research on the dance language of bees appears to challenge one of the most basic assumptions of language, that non-humans are unable to show the ability to 'talk' of things that are removed in time or space in their communication (this is known as 'displacement').

NATURAL ANIMAL LANGUAGE

Language and the human/non-human divide

There is a traditional belief that humans are unique organisms. However, with Darwinian theory, the idea that there is some sort of massive evolutionary discontinuity that separates us from other animals has become more questionable. Attempts to identify uniquely human behavioural traits have focused on a number of issues, including the incidence of tool use, the killing of conspecifics and the possession of language. Since the first two of these have been documented in a number of non-human species, language has become the major focus of research.

Language depends on a complex package of cognitive and anatomical features – so much so that it would seem to be the exception to the otherwise clear pattern of continuity between humans and other animals, particularly the higher primates. It is, however, possible to isolate the different functional attributes of language (e.g. Hockett 1960) and then search for these in the cognitive and communicative abilities of other animals. Any such research is immediately faced with a considerable challenge: the lack of a common communication system between the human researchers and the animal they are studying.

Approaches to the study of animal language

Beginning in the 1960s, a series of projects has documented the behaviour of chimpanzees and marine mammals that have been trained to respond to sign language or to arbitrary symbols, often in complex sentences. This kind of research has revealed much about the cognitive abilities of animals and particularly about their ability to solve logical problems. We will focus on this approach to the study of animal language in Topic 3.

A second approach has been to focus on the natural communicative systems of non-human animals. A major goal of this approach is to determine whether the signals employed by other species have evolved properties in common with human language. Research in this area has searched for three types of cognitive ability:

- Are animals, like humans, able to partition the structure of sound into discrete categories (i.e. words)?
- Can animal signals be reasonably considered to describe external objects or environmental events?
- Does the production of animal signals indicate a sensitivity to the presence of appropriate receivers?

Research in these three areas has revealed that the parallels between animal communication and human language are more extensive than is commonly supposed.

The categorical perception of sounds

When human beings are presented with tape-recorded syllables made up of single consonant–vowel combinations (such as 'da' or 'ta'), they are reliably able to detect where one ends and the other begins. This ability, known as 'categorical perception', involves two aspects:

- the perceptual exaggeration of differences among items that fall into different categories (e.g. 'da' and 'ta')
- the minimization of differences among items that fall into the same category (e.g. 'da' and 'daa').

This ability to perceive such phonemes categorically is generally believed to indicate our possession of a specialized decoder, i.e. a cognitive device that has evolved for processing speech sounds. We might, therefore, expect the categorical perception of phonemes such as 'da' and 'ta' to be uniquely human. This appears not to be the case. Experiments using chinchillas have shown that they are able to discriminate between sounds in much the same way as humans, i.e. they are able to recognize 'phonetic boundaries' between different speech categories (Kuhl 1981). If it is not unique to humans, perhaps this is an ability that might be unique to mammals? This has also been shown not to be the case, with budgerigars also able to be trained to learn the 'da' and 'ta' categories and discriminate accurately between them when presented with novel examples (Dooling et al. 1987).

The referential nature of animal signals

Until recently, there was little reason to believe that animal signals might be 'referential', i.e. that they might provide information about the event that elicited the signal. The first evidence to challenge this assumption came from studying vervet monkeys in Amboseli National Park in Kenya. Vervets live in social groups and have a large vocal repertoire that includes a variety of calls used in social interactions and several types of alarm calls (see the Key research opposite). Vervets are not the only primates that have this ability. Ring-tailed lemurs give different types of alarm calls in response to predators in the air and those on the ground. Playback experiments involving tape-recorded calls have shown that different types of call produce qualitatively different and adaptive responses in conspecifics (Macedonia 1990).

Cheney and Seyfarth (1990) recorded the sounds made by vervet monkeys in response to the sight of an eagle, leopard and snake. The grunting noises they produce in these situations seem all the same to the untrained human ear. But during playback of these same sounds to the monkeys, it was found that their responses were appropriate to the signal being sent (Seyfarth and Cheney 1992). For instance, vocal signals made when a leopard was seen caused the vervets to run up trees – a sanctuary beyond the reach of any big cat. Playback of the vocalizations made in the presence of a snake caused them to rear up on their hind limbs and stare around them into the undergrowth from where a snake might approach. Vocalizations made in response to an eagle caused the vervets to rush into thicket, a place where a large-winged bird could not enter. There is also evidence that vervet monkeys respond to the alarm calls emitted by starlings, a warning sound which may also be in response to the approach of an eagle (Hauser 1988). In detail, an eagle call sounds like a two-syllable cough, whereas a snake evokes a chuttering sound from the vervets.

The leopard call is also found to be different when made by males and females. The male gives a loud bark whereas the female gives a high-pitched 'chirrup' when a leopard is seen.

The social context of animal signals

Audience effect

Animal signalling is generally assumed to be essentially 'reflexive' – that is, when a stimulus sufficient to elicit anti-predator behaviour is presented (e.g. a hawk to a chicken), then alarm calls will necessarily be produced (Evans and Marler 1995). Bickerton (1990) suggests that the capacity to control the production of vocal signals independently of other reactions to a stimulus is an essential element in the evolution of language. Research by Gyger et al. (1986), however, was the first to challenge this assumption. Male chickens were confined in a wire cage, with a second cage next to them on the floor. The male chickens were presented with a hawk stimulus in the presence of a female chicken, a female bobwhite quail or an empty cage. The male chickens gave significantly more alarm calls with the hen present, than with either the bobwhite quail or the empty cage. This selective calling is referred to as an example of 'audience effect', and casts doubt on the claim that animal signals are purely reflexive.

Vocal interaction

Non-human animals have also shown an ability to engage in vocal interactions that are precisely timed, with duets being the most striking example. In some species, there is evidence of 'turn-taking' reminiscent of that which occurs during human conversations, suggesting that there are rules determining when call production is appropriate (Chaiken 1990). Experiments using interactive playbacks have demonstrated that birds (McGregor et al. 1992) and frogs (Schwartz 1991) are sensitive to the timing relationship between their signals and those that are broadcast to them.

Vocal learning

Further parallels between animal communication and human language are suggested by studies of song-learning in birds, which reveal the existence of a sensitive period early in life and the importance of auditory feedback (Marler 1991). Song-learning therefore provides evidence of transmission from one generation to the next (Hockett's language criterion of 'traditional transmission'). This vocal learning process also gives rise to geographical variation in structure, similar to linguistic dialects. In addition, anatomically distinct regions on one side of the brain control the production of learned song, as in human speech. Research with primates, especially the Japanese macaque, has shown an enhanced ability to discriminate species-specific calls when they are presented to the right ear (and hence the left hemisphere).

A02 Commentary
natural animal language research

● *No one species has all these characteristics –* Although there are extensive parallels between the functional properties of animal communication and those of human language, there are no animal signalling systems that have all the characteristics just described. For example, there is no evidence of vocal learning in non-human primates.

continued on next page

Commentary continued
natural animal language research

● *Can animals describe abstract items or use grammar?* – Animal calls that have been studied to date appear to provide information about the approach of potential predators (Seyfarth and Cheney 1980) or the discovery of food. There is no evidence, however, that animals are capable of describing abstract concepts, nor evidence that animal calls have anything that corresponds to the grammatical items (e.g. big, over, many) that allow humans to encode information about relative properties, such as size, position and number, as well as indicating tense.

● *Lack of language rules* – The most dramatic contrast between animal communication and human language is provided by the rules of language (known as 'syntax'). The rule-based nature of grammar gives rise to the property of 'productivity' (Hockett 1960) – the ability to generate an almost infinite variety of meaningful new utterances using a relatively small set of basic components. Despite the extraordinary flexibility that productivity provides, studies of animal signals provide no evidence of the evolution of such an ability in non-human species.

TEACHING LANGUAGE TO ANIMALS

There have been many different research projects that have attempted to demonstrate language ability in non-human species and these have taken one of two major approaches. Some researchers, such as Gardner and Gardner (1969) in their work with the female chimpanzee, Washoe, have attempted to teach a form of sign language, known as American Sign Language (ASL), used in the USA by some people who are born deaf. Patterson (1978) took this same approach with her gorilla, Koko, as did Terrace *et al.* (1979) with their chimpanzee, Nim (an abbreviated form of its full name, Neam Chimpsky – not totally unlike the name of a famous psycholinguist, Noam Chomsky!).

Washoe and Koko

Gardner and Gardner (1969) taught Washoe how to use ASL. The Gardners used a variety of techniques, such as moulding Washoe's hands into the correct shape for a particular sign, modelling the sign themselves and reinforcing her whenever she used an appropriate sign. Washoe showed herself to be a very able pupil. The Gardners devised a number of procedures to test whether she was using signs accurately or in a more random manner. In one situation, Washoe was shown a series of pictures and was required to respond with the appropriate signs. She signed correctly in 72 per cent of the trials.

Washoe showed other evidence of Hockett's design criteria for language. When a small doll was placed in her drinking cup, Washoe made the signs for 'Baby in my cup'. In this way she was demonstrating Hockett's criterion of productivity, in that she was combining signs to produce a novel sentence. There was even evidence of displacement (see p. 687) in her signing, as she would occasionally refer to things that were not physically present (Gardner and Gardner 1969). Patterson (1979) also found evidence of displacement when she 'conversed' with Koko, the gorilla. In the following sequence, Penny Patterson and Koko are 'discussing' an incident that had happened some days earlier, in which Koko had bitten Patterson.

Patterson:	What did you do to Penny?
Koko:	Bite.
Patterson:	You admit it?
Koko:	Sorry, bite, scratch. Wrong bite.
Patterson:	Why bite?
Koko:	Because mad.
Patterson:	Why mad?
Koko:	Don't know.

ACTIVITY

Finding out about Koko

Pay a visit to the Gorilla Foundation at **www.koko.org/** to find out more about Koko. This site includes a range of fascinating materials, including some artwork produced by Koko and other gorillas, as well as videos and an online book written by Penny Patterson about her work with Koko.

Kanzi

An alternative approach to the study of ape language has been to use external objects such as keyboards and plastic signs that are associated with words. After the association is learned, the researcher can note the ape's ability to use the symbol in an appropriate and spontaneous manner. An impressive example of this approach has been in Sue Savage-Rumbaugh's work with a pygmy chimpanzee called Kanzi (see Key research opposite).

teaching Kanzi to communicate (Savage-Rumbaugh 1988)

One of the most exciting research projects in the area of ape language has been that carried out with Kanzi, a pygmy chimpanzee (or bonobo) by Savage-Rumbaugh and her colleagues (Savage-Rumbaugh 1988). Kanzi was born in captivity in Atlanta in 1980. Right from the start, the project was designed with all the criticisms from previous ape studies in mind, so that the same criticisms could not be made about Kanzi's language abilities. For example, all the work was video-taped, and there were other careful control procedures to rule out any unconscious cueing from Kanzi's trainers.

Kanzi can communicate with his trainers by touching a symbol on a keyboard, which in turn is connected to a speech synthesizer so that the appropriate word is produced. To communicate with Kanzi, his trainers can use spoken English. In her 1988 publication concerning Kanzi's progress, Savage-Rumbaugh claimed that he had responded correctly 100 per cent of the time to 109 out of 194 spoken test words, and 75 per cent to another 40 test words. He also responded appropriately to 105 out of 107 action-object sentences ('Kanzi, go get me a coke'). Kanzi also appears to have some syntactic ability, since he responds differently to a word depending on the way it is used in a sentence.

Unlike many of the earlier studies in this area which concentrated solely on the production of language, research with Kanzi has also focused on the comprehension of language. Is this ape acquiring language? Savage-Rumbaugh believes that he is.

Kanzi's impressive linguistic performance (which is seen as equivalent to that of a 2-year-old child) suggests a possible species difference between bonobos and chimpanzees that somehow predisposes bonobos to language more than chimpanzees. Savage-Rumbaugh (1986) discovered, for example, that like young children, Kanzi was able to acquire many of his English comprehension skills through observation, just as young children typically comprehend much more than they can produce. Although other bonobos have been studied and appear to have a greater propensity to acquire comprehension of spoken English than chimpanzees (Rumbaugh *et al.* 1994), the reasons for this difference are not clear.

Commentary
A02 attempts to teach language to animals

● *Nim Chimpsky (Terrace 1979)* – The greatest setback to this type of research came with the publication, in 1979, of the results of Terrace's investigation with the chimpanzee, Nim. Not only did Terrace find that Nim's linguistic abilities were far short of a child of equivalent age (for example, he seemed unable to move beyond two-word utterances), but also Nim seemed less interested in initiating conversation than in copying the signs made by his trainers. From films of other signing chimps, Terrace was able to show that they were also simply responding to the signs made by their trainers, rather than using language spontaneously. Even Terrace's claims about Washoe's famous 'Baby in my cup' phrase could have been produced as a response to signs made immediately before by Washoe's trainers. Terrace suggested that what appeared to be sentence construction by chimpanzees, such as Washoe, may well be a result of the apes responding to subtle and unconscious cueing by the trainers (Terrace *et al.* 1979).

● *Response to Terrace's criticisms* – Responding to Terrace's criticisms, researchers such as Roger Fouts have claimed that Terrace's own failures with Nim could be attributed to the use of untrained and incompetent volunteers in Nim's training. Nim's environment was undoubtedly quite different from those of the other signing chimps, and possibly not as conducive to learning. Fouts believed that Terrace had drilled Nim by the application of operant conditioning and, as a result, Nim had become passive and inactive, producing only those behaviours that had previously been reinforced, rather than spontaneously generating new utterances. Claims that Washoe was merely responding to unconscious social cueing are also contradicted by the many successful double-blind experiments carried out by Gardner and Gardner (1989).

Evaluation
is it really language?

● *Animal language as associative learning* – Part of the controversy surrounding attempts to teach language to animals seems to revolve around whether these animals really demonstrate linguistic competence (i.e. show evidence of syntax, reference and so on), or whether they are merely showing the product of conditioning (see Unit 21). Shettleworth (1998) suggests this is paradoxical. While the experience of conditioning procedures is increasingly being said to lead to complex and subtle representations of the world, it is proposed that interpreting an animal's communicative behaviour as being the result of associative learning somehow robs it of any interesting cognitive content.

● *The social context of language* – Many of the criticisms of these ape studies focus on the fact that they do not demonstrate some, or all, of the features that are found in human language. Perhaps this is the wrong way to go about this type of evaluation. Reynolds (1981) argues that we should evaluate a species' linguistic competence in the light of its other cognitive and behavioural

capacities. Terrace's claim that apes are not really inclined to comment spontaneously on conversation topics introduced by others, says Reynolds, is consistent with other aspects of ape behaviour. In their use of tools and in other social behaviours, chimpanzees and other apes rarely show evidence of the coordination of individual actions to produce a common product. The fact that their sign language also lacks these features does not, therefore, seem surprising. These discrepancies do not prove that chimpanzees and gorillas lack language, but rather that they lack language as it is used by human beings in their everyday social interactions.

● *Quantitative or qualitative differences?* – Whether the difference between humans and non-humans in the use of language is a quantitative or qualitative divide is not clear. What is clear, however, is that human language is much more than the type of language displayed by apes and other animals. Human language has shaped our species and is an integral part of our consciousness. We might ask whether it is profitable to attempt to teach animals to use a language system for which they are not adapted. Perhaps a more profitable approach might be to learn more about the communication systems that animals use.

CHECK YOUR UNDERSTANDING

Check your understanding of animal communication and language by answering these questions from memory. Check your answers by looking back through Topic 2.

1 Construct a 150-word précis describing three ways that non-human animals use visual signals.

2 Identify two advantages and two disadvantages of visual communication.

3 What are the functions of birdsong?

4 Identify two advantages and two disadvantages of auditory communication.

5 Identify two advantages and two disadvantages of olfactory communication.

6 Identify five of Hockett's 'design features' of language.

7 Summarize research into natural animal language into a descriptive 300-word précis.

8 In 150 words, construct an argument to discount the claim that animals are capable of language.

9 What were Terrace's main criticisms of earlier attempts to teach language to chimpanzees?

10 Identify three critical (i.e. AO2) points relating to attempts to teach language to animals, and explain in what way these influence our understanding of this area.

REVISION SUMMARY

Having covered this topic you should be able to describe and evaluate:

✓ explanations of at least two types of signalling system used by non-human animals

✓ research studies of animal language.

A2 Comparative Psychology

692

Below are some **possible examination questions** set on this topic, along with hints to help you understand and approach each question effectively:

1 Outline and evaluate the use of **two** different signalling systems used by non-human animals (e.g. visual, auditory, olfactory communication). (24 marks)

In exam questions, the instruction 'describe' is used when asking for one theory and 'outline' when asking for more than one. Here, you are asked to write about just two signalling systems. These could be based on two different modalities, such as vision and sound, or could be based on two different species, such as whales and monkeys. Remember the examples in the question are just that, examples. Three different examples are given in the question, but that doesn't mean you must do all three – if you did, only the best two would receive credit. In any case, you don't have to use any of the examples suggested, although you would be well advised not to include examples of animal language since this has somewhat tenuous relevance in this context.

2 Discuss explanations of the use of different signalling systems used by non-human animals. (24 marks)

This is question 1 in a slightly different form. In this question, you must address 'explanations', i.e. *explain* how different animals use their signals or how different modalities are used. A definition is a rather two-dimensional description, whereas an explanation brings a definition to life so that your audience understands what is going on. In other words, include details on how and why the signals are used. The term 'explanations' can be interpreted rather loosely here (i.e. it doesn't have to be a formal explanation provided by a named psychologist), but it appears in the question because it is in the specification. In this question, no numbers are included to limit the scope of your answer, so the danger is that you end up writing too much AO1, leaving insufficient time and space for AO2.

3 Critically consider research studies of animal language. (24 marks)

In this tempting, but broad, question, it is essential to be selective and choose perhaps three or four studies that you feel you can both précis (i.e. outline) and evaluate in equal measures. A précis is a careful selection of the key features of a study (or theory). Remember that evaluation does not have to be directed at specific studies, but may be more generally focused on a particular area of research (e.g. studies of natural animal language). In a 30-minute response, you *could* précis four studies at 75 words each, and then make four or five critical points as your AO2 component.

4 (a) Outline **two or more** research studies of animal language. (12 marks)

(b) To what extent do such studies provide conclusive evidence that non-humans possess the ability to use language? (12 marks)

Part (a) is the AO1 component and is essentially the same as in question 3. In both questions a minimum of two studies are required. If you wrote about only one, you would incur a partial performance penalty for AO1. In part (b), you are not required to evaluate your research studies. You need to be careful that you are doing more than just criticizing research studies, but are assessing whether these do provide some degree of 'proof' that animals do or do not possess the ability to use language. Don't be afraid to state explicitly what you are trying to demonstrate with the studies you mention, e.g. why do they support the claim you are making?

5 (a) Outline **one** research study of animal language. (6 marks)

(b) Discuss explanations of different signalling systems in non-human animals. (18 marks)

This rather awkward question could be set because 'research studies' are part of this topic area. Part (a) is fairly straightforward as long as you can assemble sufficient detail. In part (b), you need to be careful that you provide sufficient evaluation and not too much description, as there are only 6 remaining AO1 marks and 12 AO2 marks. You also need to be careful to switch hats and discuss explanations of signalling systems (as for question 2) and not explanations of animal language.

In order for learning to occur, information must be retained from one occasion to the next – that is, it must be remembered. The study of memory in non-human animals poses particular problems for the researcher because they cannot be asked what they remember. Researchers must therefore find other ways of testing this. As in the study of human participants, we must keep in mind the distinction between performance on a task and the proposed cognitive mechanisms that underlie that performance. Two areas in particular have attracted a great deal of attention, and also controversy. These are:

- the use of memory in navigation (especially the proposition that somehow animals can construct and remember a cognitive map of their immediate area)
- the relationship between spatial memory and the specialist behaviour of birds that cache food.

MEMORY AND NAVIGATION

Honeybees and other nesting animals face the problem of finding their way between nest sites and distant feeding sites. To set and maintain their course, animals must first determine their position relative to their goal, and then choose the appropriate direction of travel, using features of the environment that are detectable at their starting point and along the way. For insects moving about a large foraging range, an important source of navigational information appears to be celestial cues (the sun and sun-linked patterns of polarized light). These celestial cues provide a true compass for insects and so compensate for the sun's movement relative to other landmarks on the ground. If the sun's position is to be used effectively for navigation, bees must be able to compare the position of the sun and their inbuilt time sense (which is determined by the light–dark cycle, described in Unit 13). Research studies (e.g. Dyer and Dickinson 1994) have suggested that bees are equipped with an innate template that charts the sun's position throughout the day, and that this is modified by further experience.

The importance of landmarks in navigation has been covered in a previous section, but it is worth looking again at some of the earlier research. You may recall how digger wasps use landmarks (such as rows of trees) near the nest to guide their final approach (Tinbergen and Kruyt 1938). Baerends (1941) also studied digger wasps, and found that they also use landmarks to set a homeward course when neither the nest nor its environs can be seen.

A02 Commentary
digger wasps' navigation

- *Finding an explanation* – Baerends proposed a relatively simple explanation for the digger wasp's abilities. As the wasp travels through the environment, it memorizes the sequence of visual images that lead it to food and back again. When a homing wasp finds itself on one of these routes, it compares what it sees with what it has previously memorized and sets an appropriate course. Baerends found that wasps were able to learn more than one route connecting their nest to other parts of their habitat, but were unable to connect these up into a more global spatial representation of the different routes. This view was challenged in the 1980s with the suggestion that honeybees do form such cognitive 'maps' that chart the relative positions of familiar locations (Gould 1986).

Cognitive mapping

The ability to learn a relationship among widely separated sites would certainly be impressive because it implies that an animal could memorize spatial relationships simply as a result of its movement through the environment. It would be difficult enough to 'draw' a picture mentally of the landscape from directly above it, but just imagine how difficult this would be if one were the size of a bee and flying at the height of only a few metres above ground.

Experienced bees appear to be able to use both landmarks and celestial cues independently to obtain directional and positional information during flight. That is, they can use the sun as a celestial compass to find their way even when in unfamiliar terrain, and by using landmarks they can find their way even on cloudy days. Whether bees can use a memorized relationship between landmarks and the celestial compass for navigation is less clear. The ability to exploit a memorized relationship between landmarks and celestial cues would be particularly useful when landmarks provide ambiguous information by themselves (e.g. encountering a landmark that has similar aspects from all sides). However, according to Dyer (1996), bees have a very limited ability to exploit the relationship between celestial cues and large-scale features of their environment for navigation. This suggests that they lack the ability to organize their memory of large-scale landmarks in the way proposed by Gould (1986).

Commentary
bees' navigation

● *An undemanding system* – The apparent simplicity of the bee's spatial memory may well be advantageous because it imposes low computational demands on an animal whose capacity for processing information is presumably constrained by its small nervous system.

● *Rapid learning* – These simple representational systems may have another advantage, in that they may allow more rapid learning of useful navigational information than mechanisms that encode more complex representations of the environment (Dyer 1996). Mechanisms that allow the rapid development of spatial memory would clearly be highly advantageous for a species that collects food for only about ten days before it dies.

Evaluation
the role of memory in navigation

● *Evidence for cognitive-mapping ability* – The suggestion that bees and other insects possess cognitive maps has been more or less discarded, but the view that mammals might have cognitive-mapping abilities has been harder to address. There is considerable evidence that mammals process and store large amounts of information about the environment, but their ability to demonstrate more global 'view-from-above' navigation has not been demonstrated in the wild. When a wild mammal shows its ability to navigate straight to a goal within its home range, it is not possible to assess whether it has relied on a cognitive map or some simpler orientation mechanism (Benhamou 1996).

● *Evidence for memory in migratory birds* – In some species of birds, a substantial proportion of individuals return to the same breeding, wintering and stop-over sites in successive years. Observation suggests that migrants such as Bewick swan (see photo) have evolved special cognitive abilities that enable them to accomplish these feats. Mettke-Hofmann and Gwinner (2003) provided supporting evidence showing that memory of a particular feeding site persisted for at

Many migratory birds, such as the Bewick swan, return to exactly the same feeding grounds, year after year

least 12 months in a long-distance migrant, whereas a closely related non-migrant species could remember such a site for only two weeks. They suggested that the migratory lifestyle has therefore influenced the learning and memorizing capacities of migratory birds. These results are consistent with previous neuro-anatomical results from the same two species, reporting an increase in the relative size of the hippocampus (a crucial region in the brain for processing spatial information) from the first to the second year of life in the migrant species, but not in the non-migrant species (Healy *et al.* 1996).

MEMORY AND FORAGING

Food storing

Food-storing birds have the ability to retrieve food that they have hidden over many hundreds of square metres after various periods of time. Some species can even successfully retrieve food stored the season before. In order to accomplish this impressive feat, food-storing species would need to possess a large spatial memory capacity, or at least it would need to be larger than that of non-food-storing species. Research has generally demonstrated this fact (e.g. Hampton and Shettleworth 1996). It has also been shown that food-storing species tend to remember spatial cues with greater accuracy than non-spatial cues, and that the increased memory capacity necessary for this behaviour has a neuro-anatomical representation. A general hypothesis that would explain this is that the selective pressure of filling a food-storing niche within a given ecosystem caused the food-storing species of birds to evolve specialized brain structures that would give them the necessary memory ability (Clayton and Krebs 1995).

The most impressive of the food-storing species is Clark's nutcracker. These birds collect many thousands of pine seeds every autumn and bury them in shallow holes (caches). Each cache is made by using their bill to create a small hole and then depositing a few seeds in the hole and covering them with soil. The seeds are retrieved throughout the winter and spring. The birds are believed to store the caches in over 3,000 different locations. Balda and Kamil (1992) allowed captive birds to form caches in a large room with suitable holes drilled in the floor. The birds were then excluded from the room for varying periods. Even after periods as long as 40 weeks, the birds sought out the correct locations far better than by chance. Close relations of food-storing species (such as the great tit or the jackdaw) tend to store very little, if any, food. Interestingly,

these species also perform less well in tasks involving spatial memory (Manning and Dawkins 1998).

Neuro-anatomical correlates of spatial memory

This difference in spatial memory has a neuro-anatomical correlate in that the hippocampus (a part of the brain thought to be significant in learning and memory) is larger in food-storing species of birds than in their non-food-storing relatives (Krebs *et al.* 1989). Similar differences in the relative size of the hippocampus have been found between mammals that hold territories (and therefore require a good spatial memory), such as the gibbon, and those that do not (Sherry *et al.* 1992). This type of comparison, which tries to relate brain proportions in different species, is not without problems, as we cannot be certain that we are comparing like with like. However, there has been rapid co-evolution of brain and behaviour in food-storing species and there is some evidence of the same type of specialization in mammals as well.

AO2 Commentary
memory and foraging

● *Spatial memory as an evolved adaptation* – Studies have shown that nectar-feeding birds learn more easily to avoid a location where they have recently fed, than to return to such a location within a short period of time. This has been interpreted as evidence of an evolved adaptation to the fact that nectar is a depleting resource, i.e. a certain time period is necessary for nectar stocks in a particular location to recover. Burke and Fulham (2003) tested this in captive-reared regent honeyeaters. The birds generally avoided successful feeding locations after a short retention interval (10 minutes), but returned to these locations after a long retention interval (three

hours). This behaviour is in line with the replenishment rate of the flowers exploited by this species in the wild, even though the particular individuals tested were born and reared in captivity (Burke and Fulham 2003).

● *An evolutionary explanation of food-storing behaviour* – An evolutionary explanation of the relationship between memory and foraging behaviour requires the relationship between spatial memory and food-storing behaviour to be evident in other species as well. The prediction that food-storing species have better spatial memory than other species has been tested with other birds and with titmice, but the pattern of results has not been consistent with the proposition that spatial memory varies with dependence on stored food (Shettleworth 1995).

REVISION SUMMARY

Having covered this topic you should be able to:

✓ describe and evaluate at least two explanations of memory in non-human animals

✓ describe and evaluate research studies related to these explanations

✓ use these studies effectively as AO2 commentary on each of the explanations studied

✓ discuss the importance of memory in both navigation and foraging behaviour.

Check your understanding of memory in non-human animals by answering these questions from memory. Check your answers by looking back through Topic 3.

1 What is a cognitive map?

2 How does Baerends (1941) explain the navigational abilities of the digger wasp?

3 Briefly summarize the work of Mettke-Hofmann and Gwinner on memory in migratory birds. Why is their research so significant?

4 What specific memory requirements are necessary for food-storing species?

5 What is the neuro-anatomical evidence for spatial memory?

6 Outline two AO2 points relating to the relationship between memory and foraging. Do these support or challenge the view that this is an evolutionary adaptation?

7 What particular skills are demonstrated by the following species?
  – digger wasps
  – migratory birds such as Bewick swans
  – Clark's nutcracker
  – regent honeyeaters

8 Construct a descriptive 150-word précis of the relationship between memory and navigation.

9 Construct a descriptive 150-word précis of the relationship between memory and foraging.

10 In 300 words, evaluate the importance of memory in animal behaviour.

EXAMPLE EXAM QUESTIONS

Below are some **possible examination questions** set on this topic, along with hints to help you understand and approach each question effectively:

1 Describe and evaluate research (explanations **and/or** studies) of memory in non-human animals. (24 marks)

This question allows you to choose which of three options you might take in response. You could describe and evaluate *explanations* of memory in non-human animals, *research studies* of memory in non-human animals, or combine both in your answer. Whichever route you take, you *must* remember that you will need both AO1 and AO2 in your answer. If you choose to include both explanations *and* studies, it makes sense to use your research studies as AO2. This would require more than just a *description* of relevant research studies; it requires an evaluation of your chosen explanations *using* those research studies.

2 Critically consider explanations of memory in non-human animals. (24 marks)

In this question, your choice is limited – you must provide explanations as your AO2 content. Since 'explanations' is in the plural, you also must provide at least two of these. You can always use other explanations as further AO2 (in addition to, for example, research studies as AO2). However, when using alternative explanations as AO2, it is not sufficient to offer a linking phrase such as 'In contrast there is another explanation …' and then merely offer a description of the other explanation. Each feature of an alternative explanation that is introduced must be linked to the explanations you are commenting on and thus the commentary would be 'sustained'.

3 (a) Outline **one** explanation of memory in non-human animals. (6 marks)
   (b) Outline and evaluate research studies related to the explanations of memory in non-human animals that you described in part (a). (18 marks)

Here, part (a) has 6 AO1 marks and part (b) has 6 AO1 marks plus 12 AO2 marks, as indicated by the instructions that have been used. It is important to follow this allocation of marks when planning and writing your answer. So, you might write 150 words for part (a) – an outline of one explanation. Then write a total of 150 words describing relevant research studies and 300 words evaluating these. You must focus on evaluating the studies and not the theories, as that is what is required by the question. The research studies must also be related to your explanation in part (a).

4 Discuss the importance of memory in navigation **and/or** foraging behaviour.　　　(24 marks)

> The term 'discuss' allows for a much more discursive and wide-ranging response to this question. The AO1 component is clearly a description of research into the role of memory in navigation and/or foraging, but the AO2 can include criticisms, research support, implications, etc., provided these are *used* as part of your AO2 commentary on this research. Note that the question suggests you can write about memory in navigation *and/or* foraging. There are two important points to make about this. First, the choice of whether you write about *both* navigation *and* foraging is entirely yours. You do not get more marks by including both. Second, you *must* write about the importance of memory in these areas, not just write about navigation or foraging without this context. Always shape your response to the demands of any question.

5 Discuss research (explanations **and/or** studies) of memory in foraging behaviour in non-human animals.　　　(24 marks)

> In this question, you need to have 15 minutes' worth of description and 15 minutes' worth of evaluation on foraging behaviour alone. You also need the same for navigation in case that topic comes up in an exam question. On the positive side, there is no focus in this question on 'the importance of memory'. However, this does not mean you should simply write anything you can think of related to foraging. Good answers will be well structured (an important marking criterion). Plan each paragraph of your essay to ensure good coverage of research and to ensure balanced AO1 and AO2. You might do six paragraphs each of 100 words: three AO1 and three AO2. Alternatively, do a bit of AO1 and a bit of AO2 in each paragraph.

UNIT SUMMARY

Topic 1: Animal navigation

● The **homing** ability of animals has been the focus of considerable debate. Some animals are able to home using landmarks, whereas others (such as pigeons) appear to be capable of true navigation.

● Pigeons make use of the sun as a primary navigational aid, but on overcast days when the sun is not visible, they may switch to a secondary system, such as the use of a magnetic sense. There is some disagreement over whether pigeons make use of olfactory information in their homing behaviour, although this is generally accepted to be of key importance in the migratory behaviour of salmon.

● Animals **migrate** from one location to another for a variety of reasons, such as seasonal changes or fluctuations in the food supply. The benefits of migration are that individuals exploit the best breeding or feeding conditions in both locations. Many migrating birds make use of the prevailing winds in their migration, whereas others use the thermal air currents.

Topic 2: Animal communication and language

● **Communication** occurs when one animal (the signaller) signals to another (the receiver) in such a way that it changes the behaviour of the receiver in some way. The environment and lifestyle of an animal determine the type of sensory channel that it most often uses.

● **Non-human animals use a number of different signalling systems**. **Visual communication** is often instantaneous, requiring little energy and containing a large amount of information (especially for mating). However, visual signals can only be transmitted at close range. **Auditory communication** can be used in the dark and travels long distances, but it uses up a lot of energy and can be intercepted. **Chemical** and **olfactory communication** has the greatest range and is private; it is often used for marking territory.

- **Signals** have frequently become ritualized over time so that their current function has little in common with their original function. Deceptive communications have the advantage of manipulating the behaviour of another animal to the signaller's advantage.

- Debates over whether animals possess **language** have focused primarily on studies of apes. In **studies of natural animal language** (in vervet monkeys, for example), the discovery that ape language is deficient compared to human language is seen as a characteristic of the general behaviour of the species, rather than as a deficiency in the ability to learn and use some form of language.

- Early attempts to teach language using sign language – for example, with Washoe and Nim – have been criticized because of the possibility of methodological weaknesses in the testing procedures. Later research, particularly with Kanzi, has produced more convincing evidence that apes do, in fact, have the ability both to produce and understand some form of language.

Topic 3: Memory in non-human animals

- The study of **memory in non-human animals** has failed to demonstrate that either insects, such as honeybees, or mammals, show evidence of utilizing a cognitive map. Research on honeybees has shown that they are able to use a sun compass and the information provided by terrestrial landmarks to **navigate**, but they are unable to integrate information from both of these to provide a more global representation of their habitat.

- Research on **foraging** has shown that birds that are keen food-storers also tend to have well-developed **spatial memories**. The behavioural specialization of these species appears to be reflected in the neural specialization that accompanies it. Birds that are skilled at **food caching** and retrieval tend to have relatively more neurons in the hippocampus, an area of the brain that has important functions in learning and memory.

FURTHER RESOURCES

Pearce, J.M. (1997) *Animal Learning and Cognition*: *An Introduction* (2nd edn), Hove: Psychology Press.

This book provides an accessible introduction to research that is highly relevant to this unit.

Shettleworth, S.J. (1998) *Cognition, Evolution and Behaviour*, New York: Oxford University Press.

A fairly advanced text, but a wonderfully comprehensive account of research in this area.

Websites

www.cccturtle.org/

The migration-tracking program of sea turtles enables you to track your favourite turtle on its annual migration!

www.dolphin-institute.com/

Based in Hawaii, the Dolphin Institute is dedicated to dolphins and whales through education, research and conservation.

www.santafe.edu/~johnson/articles.chimp.html

An article on the chimpanzee language debate in the *New York Times*.

http://friendsofwashoe.org/research/projwashoe.htm

A site dedicated to the Washoe project.

www.koko.org

A site dedicated to Project Koko and the Gorilla Language Project.

www.monarchwatch.org

This site focuses on research and education on the monarch butterfly, including migration.

www.pigeon.psy.tufts.edu/peoplef.htm

Find out more about research on animal cognition, especially in relation to pigeons.

23
UNIT

EVOLUTIONARY EXPLANATIONS OF
Human Behaviour

PREVIEW

After you have read this unit, you should be able to describe and evaluate:

>> explanations of the relationship between sexual selection and human reproductive behaviour, including evolutionary explanations of sex differences in parental investment

>> evolutionary explanations of human mental disorders, including depression and anxiety disorders

>> explanations and research studies of the evolutionary factors in the development of human intelligence, including the relationship between brain size and intelligence.

INTRODUCTION

In his groundbreaking book entitled *The Origin of Species*, first published in 1859, Charles Darwin argued that all species evolve gradually through the process of 'natural selection', whereby only those characteristics or traits that conferred some advantage to an organism would be selected. Those that conferred no advantage, or in some way inhibited an organism's chances of survival, would die out. A summary of the process of natural selection is given in the panel on the opposite page.

This view presents a problem. Many characteristics appear to give no advantage to the individual that possesses them. In fact, some characteristics, such as mental disorders, appear directly to threaten their viability. This is not the problem that it may at first appear. Rather than focusing on contemporary explanations for a particular behaviour (referred to as 'proximate' explanations), evolutionary psychologists focus more on how these behaviours might have been adaptive in our ancestral past (what is known as an 'ultimate' explanation). The modern human mind has evolved in response to the specific problems faced by our ancestors hundreds of thousands of years ago. Something that appears to confer no particular advantage today (such as depression or jealousy) may well have given our ancestors an advantage in the struggle for survival.

In this unit, we examine some of the different ways in which our ancestral past has shaped the way we are today. In Topic 1, we focus on evolutionary explanations of sexual selection and reproductive behaviour in humans, including sex differences in parental investment in their offspring. Then, in the second topic, we will consider evolutionary explanations of three mental disorders – depression, anxiety disorders and schizophrenia. Finally, in Topic 3, we go on to explore possible evolutionary factors in the development of human intelligence, including the relationship between brain size and intelligence.

Mike Cardwell

Evolutionary explanations of behaviour are concerned with how and why particular behaviours might have evolved among our ancestors. However, they are notoriously difficult to prove or disprove. Despite this, it is possible to construct evolutionary explanations for all kinds of behaviours, and then design a simple investigation to test the theory. What, for example, would be an evolutionary explanation for the following behaviours:

● bulimia nervosa
● xenophobia (a fear of foreigners or strangers – see photo)
● conformity.

It is fascinating to work out for yourself how and why such behaviours might have evolved among our ancestors in the first place.

EEA (Environment of Evolutionary Adaptiveness): the environment to which a species is adapted and the set of selection pressures that operated at that time, generally regarded as a period between 10,000 and 5 million years ago.

Fitness: a measurement of the number of offspring left behind by an individual compared to the number of offspring left behind by other members of the same species.

Inclusive fitness: a measurement of an individual's own fitness, plus their effect on the reproductive success of genetic relatives.

Intelligence: an underlying ability which enables an individual to adapt and function effectively within a given environment.

Natural selection: the process whereby animals that are well adapted to their environment will leave behind more offspring than those animals who are less well adapted.

Sexual selection: the process that favours individuals possessing features that make them attractive to members of the opposite sex (known as 'intrasexual selection') or help them compete with members of the same sex for access to mates ('intersexual selection').

Natural selection

Natural selection is a mechanism of evolution that assumes that environmental conditions determine how well particular characteristics (or traits) help the survival and reproduction of an organism (for example, by enabling them to be better at finding food or defending themselves against predators). Organisms that possess these traits are more successful and therefore pass on their genes more readily, whereas organisms lacking these traits are likely to be less successful and may die before reproducing. Provided environmental conditions remain the same, these beneficial traits will continue to be adaptive and will, over time, become more common within the gene pool for a given population. However, in the long term, environments *do* change, and so if successive generations did not develop adaptations which allowed them to survive and reproduce, species would simply die out.

Natural selection, therefore, provides a mechanism by which a species can continually adapt to changes in their environmental niche.

Darwin summarized the basic principles of natural selection as follows:

1 *If* there are organisms that reproduce, and
2 *If* offspring inherit traits from their parents, and
3 *If* there is variability of traits, and
4 *If* the environment cannot support all members of a growing population,
5 *Then* those members of the population with less-adaptive traits (determined by the environment) will die out, and
6 *Then* those members of the population who possess the favoured traits will produce more offspring than those less well adapted, with the result that the composition of the population is changed.

SEXUAL SELECTION AND HUMAN REPRODUCTIVE BEHAVIOUR

In addition to natural selection (outlined in the Introduction), Darwin also suggested that species also evolve through 'sexual selection', the view that competition for mates between individuals of the same sex affects the evolution of certain traits. An example of sexual selection operating over time is the relative hairlessness of human beings compared with the other great apes. The accepted explanation for this phenomenon has been that hairlessness enabled our ancestors to keep cool through sweating (an adaptation that would have occurred through 'natural selection'). However, more recently, Pagel and Bodmer (2003) have put forward the theory that hairlessness would have allowed humans to 'advertise' their reduced susceptibility to parasitic infection (hairless skin is much easier to keep clean), and this trait therefore became desirable in a mate (i.e. it would have been a consequence of sexual selection). The greater loss of body hair in women would have resulted from stronger sexual selection pressures from men to women.

The nature of sexual selection

The strange case of the peacock's tail

Darwin's idea of natural selection was that animals should end up with physical and behavioural characteristics that allow them to perform well in competition with their rivals. Therefore, most features of plants and animals should have some adaptive function in the struggle for existence. Nature should allow no extravagance or waste. So what about the peacock's tail? It does not help a peacock to fly any faster or better. Also, the elaborate plumage of the peacock makes him more conspicuous to predators, and the piercing calls that he makes to attract females also informs predators of his whereabouts. As one of the principles of natural selection was to promote anti-predator adaptations, the peacock's tail should have been eliminated by natural selection long before now. In contrast, the tail of the peahen is far more modest and sensible, and her overall colouration is less gaudy and ostentatious than that of the male.

Sexual selection and reproductive success

Darwin provided the answer to the seeming paradox of the peacock's tail in his book entitled *Descent of Man and Selection in Relation to Sex*, which was published in 1871. Here he explained that the force of sexual selection complements the force of natural selection. Therefore, individuals possess features that make them attractive to members of the opposite sex or help them to compete with members of the same sex for mates. Viewed from this perspective, we are better able to explain the gaudy and cumbersome tail of the peacock

– it is a consequence of female choice. If a particular characteristic becomes established as a universal preference among females, then males who possess the best examples of that characteristic will have greater reproductive success. As a result, there is selective pressure on males to produce brighter and more dramatic tails. If natural selection is survival of the fittest, then sexual selection could be described as 'survival of the sexiest'. This is as true of humans as it is of other species. Studies of human mate preference (e.g. Buss 1999) have shown how men from a wide range of cultures find the classic hourglass shape of young women particularly attractive. This makes sense when applying sexual selection theory since this shape is an indicator of fertility in women (Workman and Reader 2004). This is the basic premise of the theory of sexual selection – any trait that increases the reproductive success of an individual will become more and more exaggerated over evolutionary time.

Intrasexual and intersexual selection

There are two important types of sexual selection – intrasexual and intersexual (see Fig. 23.1). Where conditions favour 'polygyny' (more than one partner), males must compete with other males, and this leads to 'intrasexual' selection ('intra' meaning within). On the other hand, a female investing heavily in offspring, or only capable of raising a few offspring in a season or lifetime, needs to make sure that she has made the right choice. There will probably be no shortage of males, but the implications of a wrong choice for the female are more serious than for the male, who may be seeking other partners anyway. Females under these conditions can afford to be choosy. This leads to 'intersexual' selection ('inter' meaning between). Among humans, both males and females have a highly developed sense of male and female beauty. Both sexes are discriminating in their choice of partners, and this

Figure 23.1 >> *Inter- and intrasexual selection*

aesthetic sensibility is consistent with a high degree of maternal and paternal investment. It serves to remind us of the fact that, although in principle a human male could desert his mate and continue to impregnate other women, human infants need prolonged periods of care from both parents. This means that if a male wishes to ensure the survival of his offspring, he needs to stay around and perform his share of caring and nurturing.

The origins of mate choice

Mate choice is a product of mate preferences formed in the 'environment of evolutionary adaptiveness' (EEA). Our ancestors evolved neural adaptations that favoured mating with those individuals possessing particular traits (such as relative hairlessness). Mate choice among modern-day humans operates by rejecting some potential mates and accepting or soliciting others. But why did these mechanisms for mate choice evolve in the first place? The fundamental principle of mate choice is that it pays to be choosy because the genetic quality of your mate will determine half the genetic quality of your offspring. By forming a joint genetic venture with a high-quality mate, one's genes are much more likely to be passed on (Miller 1998). Some of the main criteria of mate selection are described below.

Selection for indicators

One of the most important criteria is the characteristic preferences for indicators of viability (likelihood of survival) and fertility (likelihood of reproduction) in a potential mate. These can take many forms because almost any perceivable bodily or behavioural trait can serve as an indicator, revealing information about age, health, strength, dominance, disease resistance, etc. Returning to the example of the peacock's tail, peacocks with inferior tails tend to get eaten more often by predators (Petrie 1992), so tail quality probably reflects some underlying physiological, heritable quality that correlates with the ability to escape predators. As a result, females are more likely to choose males on the basis of tail quality, and so males have an incentive to display large, healthy tails as vigorously as possible (Petrie *et al.* 1991). These indicators reveal traits that might be passed on to offspring (selection for 'good genes'), as well as the

likelihood that the mate will survive to provide for, protect and support their offspring (selection for 'good parents'). Indicators are also subject to the 'handicap principle', i.e. they must be costly to produce in order to be reliable because if not, they can be faked too easily (Zahavi 1991).

Selection for provisioning

Females can gain benefits from mate choice if they favour those males that offer gifts. Evidence of the importance of male provisioning in sexual selection can be seen in male insects giving nuptial gifts such as caught prey, male birds building nests and sex-for-meat exchanges in humans (Fisher 1992). Male provisioning is useful to females because it increases their resource budget and so eases the burden (in terms of nutrition and energy expenditure) of producing eggs, pregnancy and feeding the young (Workman and Reader 2004). In modern-day, polygynous hunter-gatherer societies, the best hunters have the most wives and are also more likely to have extra-marital affairs (Hill and Kaplan 1988).

Selection for mental characteristics

Human brain size has tripled over the last two million years, resulting in the evolution of phenomenal mental capacities, many of which might be attributable to sexual selection. A particular characteristic of human beings is our love of novelty (known as 'neophilia'). Before the arrival of television and computers, our ancestors would have had to amuse each other and neophilia would have led to ever-more creative displays from potential mates. This would explain many of the characteristics that are universally and uniquely developed in humans, such as music, art and humour, all of which are highly valued during mate choice (Miller 1998). The gradual evolution of language was also important in the process of selecting a mate because it gave potential mates a unique window into each other's minds.

The consequences of sexual selection in humans

The pressures of intersexual and intrasexual selection have led to a number of consequences for human 'morphology' (i.e. physical characteristics) and behaviour. Human bodies in particular reveal a wide range of criteria used by our male and female ancestors when choosing a mate. They also tell us a lot about the selective pressures faced by our ancestors in the EEA.

Facial preferences

The human face plays an important role when choosing a mate, but why are some types of face considered more attractive than others? The evolutionary view is that human facial attractiveness is linked to the advertisement of 'good genes'. Individuals who possess attractive facial features are preferred as mates, partly because of the potential benefits from passing on these attractive characteristics to offspring.

Research has revealed that 'averageness' (how closely a face resembles the majority of other faces within a population) is attractive because individuals with 'average' faces are considered less likely to carry harmful genetic mutations (Little and Hancock 2002). Research has also shown that females are attracted to male faces with 'masculine' facial characteristics such as a large jaw and prominent cheekbones (Grammer and Thornhill 1994). These characteristics arise as a result of the actions of male sex hormones, such as testosterone, but may also be a handicap because testosterone is also known to suppress the immune system. As a result, only 'healthy' individuals can afford to produce these masculine traits, indicating their dominance and the strength of their immune system to females who are then more likely to select them as possible mates (Thornhill and Gangestad 1999).

Males also have clear facial preferences, preferring females with more child-like faces, including large eyes, small noses and full lips. These characteristics indicate youth and fertility, making them more attractive as potential mates (Thornhill and Gangestad 1993).

Human genitalia and sexual selection

Evolutionists speculate that the relatively large size of the human penis (between five and six inches, compared to three inches for chimpanzees, and half that for gorillas) may have been to frighten other males (intersexual selection), or to attract females or enhance

their pleasure (intrasexual selection). Because a longer penis would give a female pleasure, female choice might have been a factor driving penis length to extremes among primates (Small 1993). Perhaps the best hypothesis is that a longer penis delivers sperm more closely to the eggs. According to Margulis and Sagan (1991), in primate species, 'the male with the longest penis delivered his sperm more safely' in females who mated with several males. The structure of the female clitoris probably did not evolve as a direct result of male mate choice, but clitoral orgasm does have two important roles in sexual selection:

- Baker and Bellis (1995) suggest that the function of human female orgasm may be to produce vaginal and uterine contractions, which serve to suck sperm into the uterus, thereby increasing the likelihood of fertilization by males who are sexually exciting (and therefore of high quality). Because it can be hard to achieve clitoral orgasm, this would reinforce sex only with those males who provide emotional warmth and willingness to provide the right kinds of sexual stimulation (Miller 1998).

- Orgasms may also serve, through clear tactile, visual and auditory signals, as a fairly reliable indicator of female sexual satisfaction and fidelity. Some aspects of female orgasm may therefore have evolved through sexual selection to promote male certainty of paternity and, as a result, male protection and investment (Miller 1998).

Evaluation
evolutionary influences on human morphology

- *Evidence for evolutionary influences on facial preferences* – Differential interest in attractive adult female faces emerges early in the first year of infancy; this implies that the preference for attractive faces is more likely to be an evolved response than a learned behaviour (Langlois *et al.* 1987). There is also a significant degree of cross-cultural agreement in ratings of facial attractiveness (Perrett *et al.* 1994). Taken together, this evidence disproves the argument that criteria of facial attractiveness are determined by cultural conventions.

- *Facial preferences and women's menstrual cycles* – Women's preferences for attractive faces are not static, but change according to their position in the menstrual cycle. Penton-Voak *et al.* (1999) found evidence that women are attracted

to more masculine-looking men during the most fertile time of their menstrual cycle and showed a preference for more feminine-looking faces during their less fertile times. This may indicate that a less masculine-looking man may make a better long-term partner (being seen as kinder and more cooperative), but that women benefit from being unfaithful in order to produce the strongest, healthiest children as a result of a quick fling with a more masculine-looking man.

- *Explaining size differences between male and female genitalia* – A small, relatively hidden and quite hard-to-stimulate clitoris would have provided females with a useful way of assessing sexual stimulation by males. A larger and more 'obvious' clitoris that could have been effectively stimulated by almost any tactile contact, however inept, would have made its female bearer less able to judge the relative stimulation capabilities of different males. As a result, she might have mated with less sexually competent males and produced less sexually competent sons (Miller 1994).

Sperm competition

The mate selection process does not end when copulation (the act of sexual reproduction) begins. In many species, females mate with more than one male during a breeding season, so 'sperm competition' is an

important factor in determining which male is successful in fertilizing her egg. Seen from this perspective, males do not compete for females, they compete for fertilizations. As a result of this competition, males have evolved larger penises and larger testicles, larger ejaculates and faster-swimming sperm. Among primates, testicle size tends to increase with the intensity of sperm competition across different species (Harcourt and Harvey 1984). For example, female chimpanzees are highly promiscuous and so male chimpanzees have evolved large testicles in an effort to increase their chances in the 'reproductive lottery'. When a female chimpanzee is sexually receptive, she is attended by a number of males, many of whom she will mate with. The male with the biggest testicles is more likely to be successful in fertilizing the

female because he will produce the most sperm. Gorillas, on the other hand, live in groups usually consisting of one adult male and two to three adult females. When a female is ready to mate, just one male mates with her. The male gorilla can therefore afford to have tiny testes (relative to body size) because the only sperm attempting to fertilize the female's egg are his own. By comparison, male humans have medium-sized testicles, suggesting that females in the EEA were moderately promiscuous (Baker and Bellis 1995).

Evaluation
sperm competition

● *Ethnic differences* – Harvey and May (1989) have suggested that ethnic differences in testicle size may reflect adaptive differences in mating strategies within different populations. Measurements made during autopsy showed that testicle size in two Chinese samples was approximately half the size of testicles in a Danish

sample, whereas differences in body size only made a small contribution to these values.

● *Evolutionary psychology is not the answer to everything* – Nicolson (1999) believes we have overemphasized the relevance of evolutionary factors. She argues that this is not actually how people really live and choose partners – decisions are more likely to be made on a whole range of issues. She suggests, therefore, that evolutionary influences on human reproductive behaviour are most probably lost in today's social context.

EVOLUTIONARY EXPLANATIONS OF SEX DIFFERENCES IN PARENTAL INVESTMENT

Parental investment theory

Over 100 years after Darwin first proposed the mechanism of sexual selection, Robert Trivers suggested that choosiness in females is a direct result of the fact that they invest more in their offspring than males do. Trivers (1972) defined parental investment as 'any investment by the parent in an individual offspring that increases the offspring's chance of surviving (and hence reproductive success) at the cost of the parent's ability to invest in other offspring'. In most species, males and females do not invest equally. Female investment tends to be far greater because female gametes (eggs) are less numerous and more costly to produce than male gametes (sperm). A female can only have a limited number of offspring, whereas a male can (potentially) have a virtually unlimited number. As a result of this asymmetry, the sex that invests least will compete over access to the sex that invests most, and the sex that invests most will have more to lose by a poor match and so will be choosier over the choice of partner.

Maternal investment

Females usually put more time and effort into the rearing process. The human mother must carry the developing embryo and foetus to full term (nine months), and even after birth, the infants of early humans would have been completely dependent on their mother's milk for up to two years. In addition, the gradual increase in brain size over the last two million years has resulted in a more difficult childbirth (due to the enlargement of the skull). To compensate for this difficulty, childbirth occurred earlier in development,

and human infants were born relatively immature compared to other animals. Whereas the young of most other species became independent in a matter of months, humans remained dependent on their parents until at least their teenage years. But why was the majority of post-natal care carried out by the mother rather than the father? As women breast-fed infants, they were obliged to care for small children, but evolutionists also suggest that part of the greater parental investment of females could be explained because they were more certain that they were the mothers as a result of internal fertilization in mammals.

Paternal investment

Human males can opt out of parental investment in a way that females cannot. By expending a relatively large part of their reproductive effort on courtship and mating, males of most species can afford to devote comparatively little to parental care (Daly and Wilson 1978). Males do not have the same degree of certainty concerning their paternity of offspring, and determining fatherhood may be tricky in promiscuous mating arrangements (see 'Sperm competition' above). The great vulnerability for men is that they may use up valuable resources raising children who are not their own (this is known as 'cuckoldry'). The possibility of sexual infidelity posed different adaptive problems for males and females. For a man, an unfaithful mate meant that he risked investing in offspring that were not his own. For a woman, an unfaithful mate may have led to the diversion of resources away from her and the family. Buss (1995) suggested that sexual jealousy might have evolved as a solution to these problems.

Because of the risk of cuckoldry, men are more jealous of the sexual act itself, whereas women are more concerned about the shift in emotional focus (and consequent loss of resources) towards another woman.

Parental investment and mating behaviour

Trivers concluded that because of the differential investment of males and females, the optimum number of offspring for each parent would be different. In the case of many mammals, a low-investing male will have the potential to sire more offspring than a single female could produce. A male will therefore increase his reproductive success by increasing the number of his copulations. Clutton-Brock and Vincent (1991) have suggested that a fruitful way of understanding mating behaviours is to focus on the potential offspring production rate of males and females. These authors suggest that it is important to identify whether it is men or women who are acting as a 'reproductive bottleneck' for the other. It is their involvement in gestation and nurturing that places limitations on the reproductive output of females in mammals.

Humans are a special case in point. Although the range of possible parental investment by a male ranges from near zero (if the male deserts) to equal or more than that of the female, a male is capable of siring more offspring than a single female could bear. With this in mind, it is probably true to say that among humans, the limiting factor in reproduction is marginally with the female. This by itself would predict competition between males over access to females – one of the defining features of sexual selection in humans. The male's best strategy to optimize his reproductive success would be to divert more effort into mating than to parenting; in other words to pursue polygyny. A female, on the other hand, will be more disposed towards monogamy (just one partner) since success, as she sees it, is not the number of times she is impregnated, but the level of resources she is able to access to support gestation and nurture. The law in Western countries prescribes monogamy, but this may not be the ancestral system to which we are adapted.

Cultural distribution of mating systems

A broad overview of different human societies reveals that in many, the sexual behaviour observed departs from the monogamy advocated in a legal sense in most Western cultures. Figure 23.2 shows that the most common mating system found in traditional cultures is polygyny. It is also instructive to examine hunter-gathering societies, since for most of our time on this planet humans have lived in this mode of existence. Studies, such as those by Howell (1979) on the !Kung-San people, tend to reveal a pattern of mild polygyny. Food supply and the role of hunting in obtaining food are important factors in understanding the mating strategies of hunter-gatherers. It is likely that a foraging way of life, never really sustained a high degree of polygyny. There are two fairly simple reasons for this:

- Hunting animals is risky and needs a combination of cooperation and luck. Hunting is generally carried out by males, while the cooperation needed means that male rivalry must be kept within strict limits. Following a kill, the meat must be shared between all those that helped as well as other unsuccessful groups. If a high degree of polygyny prevailed, sexual rivalry would militate against such sharing.

- Even if there were a surplus after sharing, meat is difficult to store. It is therefore hard to see how, in a foraging culture, sufficient resources could ever be accumulated by one man to support a sizeable harem. Predictably, in the few hunter-gathering societies left, only mild polygyny is seen.

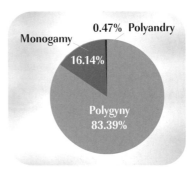

Figure 23.2 >> *Human mating systems in traditional cultures prior to Western influence. Source: Smith (1984)*

Monogamy 16.14% · 0.47% Polyandry · Polygyny 83.39%

KEY RESEARCH >> GENDER DIFFERENCES IN PARENTAL INVESTMENT

investing in stepchildren (Andersson *et al.* 1999)

Andersson and colleagues looked at the willingness of men to pay for their children's college education as a means of assessing paternal investment strategies. Men were most willing to pay for their own child when they were still living with the child's mother. A surprising finding was that men did not discriminate financially between a child who was born to a current partner from a previous relationship and their own child from a previous relationship. This is puzzling because a man is genetically related to the latter child, but is only the stepfather of the former child. How can we explain this using parental investment theory? A man may invest less in his children from previous failed relationships because he may not be sure that he is the true father. However, he may invest in a stepchild of his current partner in order to convince the mother that he is a 'good provider' and so promote future mating possibilities.

Polyandry (more than one male partner at a time) amongst humans is very rare. It seems that males and females linked polyandrously would appear to gain little. From the female's perspective, sperm from one male is sufficient to fertilize all her eggs, so why bother to mate with more than one male? From the male perspective, it is even worse; if a male is forced to supply some parental care, then the last thing he should want is to share his mate with another male and face the prospect of rearing offspring that are not his own.

Evaluation
evolutionary explanations of gender differences in parental investment

- *Males do help out* – The fact that human infants are born in a relatively immature and helpless state means that they need almost constant attention for a large part of their development. One way that females can reduce the burden of prolonged maternal care is by forming long-lasting pair bonds with male partners who are prepared to help provide for the offspring. It is, therefore, in the interest of the male to impress females with their potential skills as carers and show their value as a potential mate.

- *Willing fathers* – According to parental investment theory, males are more likely to share resources with children who they know are their own, and are less likely to share with those with whom they do not share a blood relationship. However, a study by Anderson *et al.* (1999) suggests that this is an oversimplification of paternal investment (see Key research opposite).

- *Sexual jealousy* – Research by Buss *et al.* (1992) found that male students showed more distress (measured by the galvanic skin response, or GSR, an objective measure of emotional arousal) when asked to imagine sexual infidelity of their partner, whereas female students showed more concern about emotional infidelity. Although this supports parental investment predictions about male and female concerns, Harris (2003) questions whether such gender differences are an adaptive response. She has discovered that men respond with greater arousal to any sexual imagery, regardless of its context, suggesting that such gender differences are more likely to be a product of social learning than of evolutionary history.

CHECK YOUR UNDERSTANDING

Check your understanding of human reproductive behaviour by answering these questions from memory. Check your answers by looking back through this first topic.

1 What is the difference between natural selection and sexual selection? Give an example of each.

2 Identify three criteria used in mate selection, and construct a 100-word précis for each.

3 Why might 'masculine' facial features be considered a handicap for males having them?

4 What, according to Penton-Voak and colleagues, is the relationship between menstruation and female preference for male facial characteristics?

5 Gorillas, humans, chimpanzees – which has the largest-sized testicles (relative to body size) and why?

6 Why, according to parental investment theory, are there sex differences in parental investment?

7 Why, from an evolutionary perspective, would males sometimes invest in their offspring and sometimes not?

8 Distinguish between polygyny, polygamy, polyandry, monogamy and promiscuity.

REVISION SUMMARY

Having covered this topic you should be able to:

✓ describe the relationship between sexual selection and human reproductive behaviour

✓ evaluate the evidence relating to evolutionary explanations of the relationship between sexual selection and human reproductive behaviour

✓ outline evolutionary explanations of sex differences in parental investment

✓ evaluate the evidence relating to evolutionary explanations of sex differences in parental investment.

The evolutionary *perspective*

Lance Workman is Principal Lecturer in Psychology at Bath Spa University College. Lance regularly works in the media appearing on radio, television and in national newspapers explaining and discussing psychological principles. During the 1990s he presented his own series, 'Mind Matters', on BBC Radio Wales. In 2004, he co-authored Evolutionary Psychology *with Will Reader of Sheffield Hallam University.*

Q By accepting an evolutionary perspective on human reproductive behaviour, does this imply that we are 'prisoners of our genes' and that other influences play no part?

A Absolutely not. Although this accusation of 'genetic determinism' is sometimes aimed at evolutionary psychologists, our approach is very much an interactionist one. We propose that genes are an important ingredient in determining behaviour, but that all behaviour is a result of an interaction between the genes that we inherit and input from the environment. Take the male preference for an hour-glass figure in a potential female mate. This preference has been documented in a wide range of cultures (Buss 1999) suggesting a genetic influence. Superimposed onto this, however, is a great deal of cross-cultural variability in the male preference for plump versus thin body types (Symons 1979). This has to be related to environmental input.

Lance Workman

Q If modern-day behaviour is an adaptation to pressures in the EEA, does that mean that all aspects of human reproductive behaviour, such as rape, sexual infidelity and paedophilia are in some way 'adaptive'?

A Relating reproductive behaviour to the EEA is always a sensitive area. The important point here is that we should avoid mixing up arguments that concern how we feel people should behave morally with arguments concerning strategies to boost inclusive fitness. Thornhill and Palmer (2000), for example, have argued that rape may be adaptive in that some sexually aggressive men might have used it as a strategy to pass on their genes (albeit not consciously). Such an argument has incensed some people, who see it as a justification for rape. Arguing that a behaviour pattern

might be adaptive, however, tells us nothing about the morality of that behaviour. I do think, however, there are some sexual acts that people commit today that are clearly not adaptive. Paedophilia, for example, is probably better explained by abnormal psychology than by evolution.

Q Does the relatively high proportion of males and females who are in homosexual relationships threaten the idea that human sexual behaviour is linked to increased reproductive fitness?

A In his book *The Selfish Gene*, Richard Dawkins (1976) tells of a letter he once received from a critic of evolutionary theory who suggested that the existence of homosexuality disproves the theory of natural selection. Exclusive homosexual behaviour certainly appears to reduce reproductive fitness. There are, however, at least four ways in which homosexual behaviour can be explained without abandoning inclusive fitness theory. First, homosexual behaviour may be functionally maladaptive in that it may be a result of 'abnormal' developmental processes. Second, it may be maladaptive to the individual but adaptive to the parents who use manipulation in order to maximize production of grandchildren via other offspring. Third, it may be a phase that individuals pass through prior to becoming reproductively active. Finally, it might be adaptive in that individuals may increase their inclusive fitness indirectly via kin selection (i.e. investing in nephews and nieces). You might not be convinced by these arguments, but the point is that all of them can be tested. As a new approach, the problem that evolutionary psychologists face lies in devising predictions that don't support more than one of these explanations or that might not be better explained by other approaches.

Below are some **possible examination questions** set on this topic, along with hints to help you understand and approach each question effectively:

1 Discuss the relationship between sexual selection and human reproductive behaviour.   (24 marks)

> This is a very open-ended question. This is a good thing because you could potentially draw on *any* of the material in the preceding pages for your response. It also lets you determine the structure of your answer, but out of all the material you have available, what *do* you choose for a 30-minute response? It is important, therefore, to plan this essay very carefully. Be *selective*, and remember the need to balance the AO1 and AO2 material in your essay.

2 (a) Outline the relationship between sexual selection and human reproductive behaviour.   (12 marks)

  (b) To what extent can human reproductive behaviour be explained by evolutionary explanations? (12 marks)

> This question covers the same ground as question 1 but specifies the AO2 component. It is often difficult to separate AO1 from AO2 in this topic area. One way is to consider: 'What does this research tell us?' In part (b), you need to reflect on whether evolutionary explanations do or do not explain human reproductive behaviour. What are the flaws in the arguments (e.g. they are based on research with non-human animals, people can think whereas animals don't)? What are the alternative explanations? Questions that say 'to what extent' (an AO2 term) do not require a conclusion.

3 Discuss **one or more** evolutionary explanations of sex differences in parental investment. (24 marks)

> 'Discuss' means you have to include AO1 description and AO2 evaluation in equal measures. You only need about 300 words in an appropriate combination of depth *and* breadth, so aim to make about six points, each of about 50 words. You are also given the choice of whether to restrict your answer to just *one* explanation, or to include more than one. Trivers' parental investment theory underlies much of the material in this section, so whether this counts as one binding explanation or whether the material you choose is from many smaller explanations is of academic interest only. Finally, you need to restrict yourself to explanations of 'sex differences in parental investment', so think carefully about material you include.

4 Outline and evaluate evolutionary explanations of parental investment.   (24 marks)

> It would be legitimate to have a question like number 3 but without the 'sex differences', as in this question. How might your answer to this question differ from your answer for question 3? You could present the same answer to question 4, but the same isn't true in reverse. The key thing is to shape your answer carefully to the question set, rather than lazily presenting an essay you prepared earlier.

Topic 2 >> Evolutionary explanations of mental disorders

Evolutionary psychology makes an important distinction between ultimate and proximate causes for behaviour:

● **Ultimate** causes require an understanding of the contribution of a particular trait to the reproductive fitness of an organism in its original (i.e. its ancestral) environment.

● **Proximate** causes are the sum of all the biological processes (e.g. genetics, biochemical factors) that directly produce that phenomenon.

Some psychological disorders have only proximate causes (such as the gene mutation involved in Huntington's disease, a hereditary disease that develops in adulthood) and others have a much longer history. Some disorders (such as anxiety and depression) may represent an extreme expression of normal human traits, whereas others may be the product of misplaced psychological strategies. In such cases, the search for the ultimate cause of a mental disorder is essential for a full understanding of that disorder (Abed 2000). In this topic we examine three such disorders – depression, anxiety disorders and schizophrenia – in an attempt to understand why they evolved in the first place, and also why they persist despite being maladaptive for the individuals who are afflicted by them.

DEPRESSION

Depression is an affective state that is emotionally painful, as well as affecting concentration, reducing the pleasure to be had from routine activities, such as eating and sex, and causing changes in the pattern of social interaction. There can be no doubt, one might feel, that such a disorder is maladaptive. Some evolutionary psychologists have begun to question the assumption that depression is always maladaptive, suggesting instead that it evolved to fit more adaptive functions. There are several reasons why this may be the case:

1 Unlike many other mental disorders, depression appears to be a universal disorder (Nesse and Williams 1994). Its incidence in most societies is high, with a lifetime risk estimated to be about 20 per cent (Kessler *et al.* 1994).

2 The prevalence of depression is not restricted to modern, industrialized societies, but is also evident in traditional societies such as the !Kung-San of Southern Africa (Howell 1979).

3 An adaptionist explanation of depression argues that genes for depression would not have evolved unless they conferred net benefits in some way. There is no doubt that depression is costly for the person suffering from depression, but adaptionist theories stress that depression may well have had a beneficial effect that outweighed these costs.

The two theories below offer possible ways that depression may have evolved as an adaptive response, thus providing important benefits that justified its continued expression in the gene pool.

Evaluation
social competition hypothesis

● **Depression as a yielding signal** – An important contribution of this theory is that it suggests that the real value of depression may be because it acts as a signal that the loser has actually yielded to the winner, and this helps restore social harmony. The object of this strategy is, therefore, damage limitation. This view is supported by clinical evidence of episodes of depression that have been triggered by social

The social navigation hypothesis

The social navigation hypothesis (SNH) suggests that depression evolved to perform two complementary social problem-solving functions (Watson and Andrews 2002):

● It focuses limited cognitive resources on planning ways out of complex social problems; this is known as the 'social rumination function'.

The social competition hypothesis

Price *et al.* (1994) propose that depression is an adaptive response for the person who loses any conflict over position or status within a group. It forces the loser of such a conflict to:

● cease competing with the winner
● accept the fact that they have lost
● signal their submission to stop further conflict.

According to this theory, such a response is adaptive because it helps the individual adjust to the fact that they have lost and must now occupy a subordinate position in the dominance hierarchy. It prevents the loser from risking further injury by continuing the conflict and preserves the stability of the social group. In defeat, an involuntary process comes into operation which both prevents the individual from continuing to compete and reduces their level of aspiration. This process results in the loss of energy, depressed mood and loss of confidence – all typical characteristics of depression.

When humans interact, the question of dominance may not arise initially. However, after working or living in close proximity for some time, conflict may arise, perhaps over leadership of the group or over access to resources (such as promotion). Over the course of time, the depressive response may also become triggered by other situations that do not necessarily involve the loss of rank, but involve a loss of some other sort (perhaps the ending of a close relationship). In such circumstances, a response that has been selected by natural selection because it *is* adaptive is activated in situations that make it psychologically maladaptive.

competition and resolved by reconciliation (Brown *et al.* 1995).

● **Is depression an adaptation?** – Nesse (2000) believes that some aspects of depression may be adaptive because they inhibit dangerous or wasteful temptations to challenge authority, as predicted by the social competition hypothesis. Despite this, it is essential to emphasize that many depressions are disease states caused by emotional problems or through brain dysfunction. The fact that some aspects of depression may be useful should not distract us from the fact that depression can be a very serious medical problem.

● It provides an honest signal of need and some partners will be willing to help, particularly if they feel that an improvement in the individual's fitness is worth the sacrifice that they are making – the 'social motivation function'.

The social rumination function of depression

Social situations that have the greatest risk of triggering a depressive episode (such as divorce or unemployment) place considerable cognitive demands on the individual. Since such events are difficult to deal with, it pays the individual to shut down involvement in other interests or activities in order to focus more closely on these situations in an attempt to resolve them. In particular, the SNH draws attention to the anhedonia (loss of pleasure in previously enjoyed activities) that is a key characteristic of depression. As a result of this displaced cognitive effort, the SNH proposes that depression is associated with an enhanced analysis of social information. People suffering from depression pay closer attention to social information and process it more extensively than other people (Gannon *et al.* 1994). People who do not have depression tend to exhibit a 'self-serving bias' (SSB), in which they attribute their successes to their ability, and their failures to chance or to a lack of effort. People suffering from depression, on the other hand, display a 'depressive attributional style' (DAS), where they are less likely to attribute their successes to ability, or their failures to chance or lack of effort. There is evidence to suggest that the SSB offers a distorted view of reality and that the DAS may be more accurate (Ackermann and DeRubeis 1991).

The social motivation function of depression

Because depression is costly, it serves as an honest display of need to those with whom the person with depression shares their life. Other social partners may not see it as being in their interests to help, even though they are aware of this indication of need.

Perhaps the most important adaptive function of depression is that the many personal costs suffered by the individual (e.g. fatigue, lack of motivation) impose costs on all their close social partners. Others may have an investment in the normal activities of the person with depression (e.g. they may rely on the person financially) and so may have their own reproductive fitness threatened in some way if the illness continues. When the mental mechanisms that underlie depression are activated, they cause the person with depression to engage in what Watson and Andrews (2002) refer to as unintentional 'fitness extortion'. This type of extortionary depression ('help me or else you will also lose out') can elicit help from partners who perceive that it is better to help than to continue to suffer the rising 'costs' of the other person's depressive episode. As a result, depression may be designed to motivate the entire social network of partners, as the person with depression 'navigates' through the difficulties associated with their current social problems.

ACTIVITY

The potential adaptiveness of depression

Read the symptoms for unipolar depression in Table 25.1 on p. 766. In what ways might each of these symptoms be adaptive today and/or in the EEA?

Evaluation
the social navigation hypothesis

- **Displaced cognitive effort** – Evidence supporting the view that depression serves a social rumination function comes from studies (e.g. Hartlage *et al.* 1993) showing that people with depression exhibit diminished performance on cognitively demanding tasks of a non-social or abstract nature (e.g. intelligence tests, memory tasks). This is to be expected if their cognitive efforts are focused elsewhere.

- **Suicide as a signal of need** – Evidence supporting the view that depression serves a motivational function comes from studies that have found that suicide attempts generally stop when relationships improve (Hawton and Fagg 1992). An attempted suicide could inform partners about the individual's level of need. Under the extortion hypothesis, such attempts impose a risk of loss on all those with an

interest in that individual's continued existence. To serve this motivational function, those who attempt suicide should survive, yet they get greater motivational 'power' by incurring a greater risk of death. As a result, the person with depression trades the risk of death against the possible benefits of motivating close social partners to help them (Watson and Andrews 2002).

- **Anti-depressant medication** – An implication of the SNH is that anti-depressant medications may handicap a depressed individual's ability to control their social environment, which could therefore hinder their attempts to make significant improvements to the quality of their life. If the SNH is correct, claim Watson and Andrews, any therapeutic approaches designed to reduce suffering may be irresponsible since they mask the functions of a potentially adaptive depression. They suggest, therefore, that drugs should not be given unless the *cause* of the depression is also addressed.

ANXIETY DISORDERS

Anxiety is often useful. A bit of anxiety before an exam may persuade you to revise more thoroughly. Anxiety in the face of danger, such as walking through a field with a bull in it, may ensure you keep your distance or, more sensibly, avoid the field altogether. At this point, it is important to distinguish between fears and phobias. Fears are natural human emotions that bear some relationship to the source of danger. Phobias are fears wildly out of proportion to the actual hazards faced. Fears are adaptive whereas phobias can lead to maladaptive behaviour.

If fear and moderate anxiety represent evolved responses, then it could be argued that some of our innermost and recurring fears represent ancestral memories of hazards encountered in the EEA. Fear of the dark, for example, is clearly understandable in these terms – humans are more vulnerable at night from attack by predators with better night vision or from humans with ill intent. Table 23.1 shows how we could, in principle, map specific fears to the adaptive memory they represent.

The fears shown in Table 23.1 are ingrained to some degree in the human psyche. It is significant that more city dwellers go to psychiatrists with excessive fears of snakes and strangers, than with fears of cars or electrical sockets (Buss 1999). Yet for modern, urban humans, electricity and cars represent statistically a far greater risk than snakes or strangers.

Table 23.1 >> Types of fear and their adaptive origin

Type of fear	Adaptive origin
>> *Fear of snakes*	Poisonous snakes have been a threat to primates and hominids for the last few million years.
>> *Fear of heights (Acrophobia)*	Humans are relatively large animals and falling has always posed a grave danger. Significantly, acrophobia usually provokes a freezing reaction, making it less likely that a person will fall.
>> *Claustrophobia*	In a small confined space humans are vulnerable since escape is difficult.
>> *Stranger anxiety (Xenophobia)*	Harm from unfamiliar humans, especially males has always been seen as a potential threat.
>> *Agoraphobia*	Risks lie beyond the familiar territory of the home.

Biological fears also have a social dimension. Given our history as social animals, it is not surprising that some social circumstances also evoke a specific fear response. This response can be shown when children are suddenly faced with an unknown adult and begin to cry. It is likely that infanticide was a real risk for our primate ancestors. In polygynous mating groups of several animal species, when the dominant male is displaced by another, the new male sets about killing the infants fathered by his previous rival. This has the effect of bringing the females back into heat and also ensuring that neither he nor his new mate waste energy on raising infants that are not his own. This brutal side of our past may have left its mark on humans today. Daly and Wilson (1988) found that the risk of infanticide for a stepchild is 100 times higher than for a child with natural parents. The fearful and often tearful reaction of a 1-year-old child when a strange male approaches may be a remnant of our brutal past. In fact, such a reaction has been reported in a number of cultures (Smith 1979).

The evolution of fears and phobias

Preparedness

Rather than inherit rigid behavioural responses to specific situations that may well change over time, a more flexible arrangement would be to have an innate readiness to learn about dangerous situations. Seligman's concept of 'preparedness' accounts for this. According to Seligman (1970), animals, including humans, are biologically prepared to learn rapidly an association between particular, potentially life-threatening stimuli and fear and, once learned, this association is difficult to extinguish. What is inherited, therefore, is not a fixed fear of certain things, but the predisposition to form certain associations rather than others. Most phobias are focused on a small number of fear-inducing stimuli, such as snakes and spiders, or situations such as heights or closed spaces. These fears all appear to have evolutionary significance, in that each would have represented a survival threat to our ancestors. The theory of biological preparedness

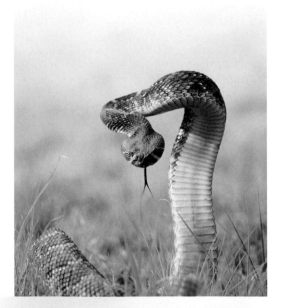

assumes that most feared objects (such as snakes and spiders) are those which had been particularly hazardous for our ancestors. The selection pressures generated by these hazardous stimuli have therefore resulted in the evolution of predispositions to associate these stimuli with traumatic consequences. Since the venom of some snakes and spiders is lethal, it is assumed that this was the selection factor that generated a biological predisposition to associate such stimuli with fearful consequences (Davey 1994).

Evaluation
the preparedness explanation

● *Evidence from animal studies* – Some of the most convincing evidence for biological preparedness has come from studies of the observational learning of fear of snakes in primates. Cook and Mineka (1989) got laboratory-bred monkeys to look at a video of a wild-reared monkey behaving fearfully in the presence of a variety of stimuli. They discovered that monkeys that had never seen a snake before would rapidly acquire an intense fear, when shown a toy snake, after they had watched a wild-reared monkey behaving fearfully. However, the same monkeys did not become fearful towards less 'snake-like' stimuli (such as a toy rabbit), but did acquire fear to stimuli, such as toy crocodiles, which resemble snakes more closely. Since these monkeys had never seen a snake, crocodile or toy rabbit before,

it seems very likely that the difference in their reaction to toy snakes versus toy rabbits is a result of evolutionary factors rather than learning.

● *Cultural differences* – Explaining phobic fears in terms of biological preparedness assumes that all members of a species would share such predispositions. There are, however, distinct cultural differences. For example, fear of spiders may not be a universal phenomenon, and may be restricted to Europeans and their descendants (Davey 1994). In many areas of Africa, the spider is revered as a wise creature and its dwelling places are cleaned and protected by the local people (Renner 1990). In many areas of the world, spiders are frequently eaten as a delicacy, including those that are most lethal to humans (Bristowe 1945). Many cultures consider spiders to be symbols of good fortune rather than fear. For example, it is common practice in Egypt to place a spider in the bed of a newly married couple (Bristowe 1958).

Obsessive-compulsive disorder

Abed and de Pauw (1999) offer an evolutionary explanation for obsessive-compulsive disorder (OCD). They argue that OCD is an accentuated version of an adaptive strategy that enhanced the reproductive fitness of those ancestral humans who possessed this trait compared with those who did not. This view is supported by the observation that unwanted intrusive thoughts and compulsive rituals are universal phenomena across cultures (Osborn 1998). This theory assumes the existence of a modular configuration for the human mind. The 'modular mind' consists of a number of specific systems that have evolved to carry out specific tasks that would have been selected because of their contribution to inclusive fitness.

Obsessional phenomena are involuntary thought processes that stimulate strong aversive emotional states (such as fear and disgust) associated with particular objects or events. Abed and de Pauw suggest that the brain system that generates these phenomena (the 'Involuntary Risk Scenario Generating System' or IRSGS) allows the individual to develop behavioural strategies to avoid harm, without experiencing the risks involved in real-life dangers.

The adaptive function of this system is that it saves the individual organism from having to experience physical and social dangers in real life, producing the same learning response in complete physical safety. The ability of some organisms to learn to avoid common dangers without the need to experience them in real life would have provided a clear advantage on the individuals who possessed this trait over those who did not. This would have led to obsessional traits becoming widespread within the population. However, extreme expressions of this trait would be maladaptive and so reduce reproductive fitness (Abed and de Pauw 1999).

AO2 **Evaluation** the evolutionary explanation of OCD

● **OCD is pervasive and universal** – The evolutionary explanation of OCD assumes that obsessions and compulsions are the consequence of a psychological adaptation that the majority of humans possess. This is consistent with research findings that the majority of the population experience unwanted, intrusive thoughts at some time during their lives (Osborn 1998), as well as the finding that OCDs appear to occur universally across cultures (Rapoport and Fiske 1998).

● **Gender differences** – Surveys of the incidence of OCD among males and females have shown that slightly more females than males suffer from the disorder (Weissman 1998). Research has consistently found that females engage in risk-taking behaviour less frequently than males (Browne 1998), so such a finding would be consistent with Abed and de Pauw's hypothesis. Research has also shown gender differences in the age of onset of OCD, with males showing a higher prevalence before puberty and females more commonly affected after puberty (Penn et al. 1997). Abed and de Pauw suggest that females were exposed to increased risks within the ancestral environment following puberty, which could have led to the increased activity of the IRSGS and greater incidence of OCD.

SCHIZOPHRENIA

Schizophrenia is almost certainly a disorder with a strong genetic component (see Unit 25). There is evidence that it runs in families and that concordance rates for monozygotic twins (twins who are genetically identical) are far higher than for dizygotic twins (sharing 50 per cent of their genes in common) (Torrey et al. 1994). The possibility that schizophrenia is an ancient disorder that originated in our ancestors' time is given further support by the fact that schizophrenia is found in even the most remote ethnic groups. Australian Aborigines became isolated from the rest of human kind about 60,000 years ago, yet schizophrenia has been observed in this group (Torrey 1987). As a result, evolutionary forces have shaped schizophrenia over a very long time. But why did it originate in the first place? Some evolutionary explanations see it as a disadvantageous by-product of normal brain evolution, whereas others see it as an evolutionary advantageous condition. The former view is reflected in the first explanation below (schizophrenia and language), and the latter in the second explanation (the group-splitting hypothesis).

Schizophrenia and language

For a genetic disorder such as schizophrenia to persist, it must be balanced by some substantial advantage, such as language. Crow (2000) suggested that schizophrenia and language may have a common evolutionary origin, both resulting from a sudden genetic change that took place over 150,000 years ago. The result of this genetic mutation would have affected foetal brain development so that one hemisphere of the brain developed faster than the other, causing the two hemispheres to develop with some degree of independence. A side effect of this was an inevitable variation in the degree of cerebral asymmetry. The brain is normally asymmetrical, bulging at the right front and at the back left, yet evidence from post-mortems (Zaidel 1999) shows that the brains of people with schizophrenia tend to be much more symmetrical.

Unlike the other apes, humans have an overwhelming preference for right-handedness, a preference that may arise from the same developmental mechanisms that produce left-hemisphere language processing in the majority of people. People with schizophrenia are less strongly right-handed than the rest of the population, and children who go on to develop schizophrenia are more likely to be ambidextrous (Francks et al. 2003).

Schizophrenia is also characterized by a number of problems relating to language and thought. People with schizophrenia may feel that their thoughts are being controlled by others, that their thoughts are being broadcast, or that their own thoughts are the voices of others. Each of these symptoms represents a failure to distinguish between thought and speech, or between one's own ideas and the ideas of others. Crow argues that these symptoms represent disruptions of the normal relationship between the right and left hemispheres.

● **The wider problems of schizophrenia** – This view suggests that schizophrenia is linked closely to language dysfunction. Although it is true that schizophrenia can and does cause disordered language, the disorder also impacts heavily on social behaviours. Furthermore, delusions and auditory hallucinations are commonly experienced in the context of normal syntax (i.e. they are grammatically correct) (Polimeni and Reiss 2003).

● **Punctuated equilibria** – In order to explain how schizophrenia and language evolved rapidly, perhaps even as the result of a single gene, Crow (2000) makes use of the idea of 'punctuated equilibria'. This theory of evolution proposes that changes can occur very quickly, with long periods of little change in between. Not only does this theory disregard observations of symbol use in other primates (Savage-Rumbaugh and Fields 2000), but also the evidence that language most likely evolved gradually over several million years (Deacon 1997).

The group-splitting hypothesis

Stevens and Price (2000) have proposed a novel hypothesis for the persistence of schizophrenia. They suggest that schizoid personalities have previously performed the valuable function of dividing tribal communities when they become too large. All such groups have their optimum size. As the size of a group increases, so more eyes and brains become available to watch out for predators and to find food. However, beyond a certain group size, negative effects begin to outweigh the disadvantages. Although food may be more easily spotted, there are also more mouths to feed and the share for each is therefore reduced. This means that the group must travel a greater distance to find a sufficient quantity of food. As the travel distance increases, so does the energy used in finding food and so do the risks from predators. It follows that as a group grows in size through reproduction, or the

movement in of outsiders, there comes a point when the optimum group size is exceeded and fission (i.e. splitting the group) will increase the fitness of each individual. Schizophrenia, therefore, is an adaptation whose function is to facilitate group splitting. This would be achieved by the formation of a sub-group under a charismatic leader, who, because of their psychotic thinking, can separate themselves from the dogma of the main group and create a new community with a new world view (Stevens and Price 2000). Stevens and Price maintain that it is the symptoms of a schizoid personality (such as mood changes, bizarre beliefs, hallucinations and delusions of grandeur) that would have induced others, who were already feeling discontented by the conditions in a group that was beginning to exceed its optimum size, to follow and form a new community. Such traits, argue Stevens and Price, are frequently found in charismatic leaders such as Adolph Hitler and Joan of Arc.

● **Schizophrenia and shamanism** – Polimeni and Reiss (2002) offer an alternative to the group-splitting hypothesis. They propose that schizophrenia may be linked to 'shamanism'. The shaman is a central charismatic figure within a tribal community. They are frequently associated with supernatural qualities that transcend human nature, with the ability to speak to spirits and perform magic. Schizophrenia could have enhanced a shaman's ability to perform religious ceremonies. Such ceremonies are universally observed in all cultures, and religious-based delusions are also common in schizophrenia (Brewerton 1994). Rather than the schizophrenic behaviour of charismatic individuals being used

to split communities, as suggested by the group-splitting hypothesis, Polimeni and Reiss suggest that schizophrenic symptoms in some individuals may well have reflected an ancient, and important, form of behavioural specialization.

● **Genetic advantages** – Nesse (1999) takes issue with the claim that the benefits of a disorder such as schizophrenia necessarily lie with the disorder itself – in this case, its effects on cognitive and emotional systems. Rather, he suggests that those with the gene, *but without the disorder*, may experience the benefits of a genetically based disorder. The benefits may have nothing to do with the changed mental life of a person with schizophrenia but may, for example, guard against infection. The test, argues Nesse, is to examine the relatives of people with schizophrenia for traits that would somehow have been advantageous in our ancestral environment.

Unit 23 // Evolutionary explanations of human behaviour

Check your understanding of evolutionary explanations of mental disorders by answering from memory. Check your answers by looking back through Topic 2.

1 What is the difference between 'ultimate' and 'proximate' explanations of mental disorders?

2 What two pieces of evidence led evolutionary psychologists to believe that depression might have originally had an adaptive function?

3 Write a 150-word précis of the social navigation hypothesis explanation for depression.

4 Why might therapeutic intervention for depression have detrimental effects for the person with depression?

5 Why do you think the following four fears might have been adaptive in the ancestral environment: snakes, heights, the dark, closed spaces?

6 Identify two evaluative points relating to the preparedness explanation, and suggest how these contribute to its status as an explanation of the evolution of phobias.

7 Construct a 150-word précis of the evolutionary explanation for OCD.

8 What is the significance of Australian Aborigines and other isolated ethnic groups in determining the origins of schizophrenia?

9 Construct a descriptive 150-word précis of the relationship between the evolution of language and the emergence of schizophrenia.

10 What are 'shamans' and in what way might they be linked to schizophrenia?

REVISION SUMMARY

Having covered this topic you should be able to describe and evaluate:

✓ two evolutionary explanations of depression: the social competition hypothesis and the social navigation hypothesis

✓ two evolutionary explanations of anxiety disorders: the preparedness explanation of fears and phobias and an evolutionary explanation of OCD

✓ two evolutionary explanations of schizophrenia: the schizophrenia and language hypothesis, and the group-splitting hypothesis.

EXAMPLE EXAM QUESTIONS

Below are some **possible examination questions** set on this topic, along with hints to help you understand and approach each question effectively:

1 Outline and evaluate evolutionary explanations of **two** human mental disorders.   (24 marks)

> You have 30 minutes to answer this question and there are four distinct parts to it (two outlines and two evaluations). The question is open-ended, in that it doesn't dictate which mental disorders you should cover. So, you can cover depression and schizophrenia, anxiety disorders and depression, anxiety disorders and schizophrenia, or even two different types of anxiety disorder (phobias and OCD). However, you must restrict your descriptions to *evolutionary* explanations of your chosen disorders. You might use other, non-evolutionary explanations as commentary. There is a partial performance penalty for candidates who only describe one explanation (maximum of 8 marks for AO1). The same applies to your evaluation.

2 (a) Outline and evaluate **one** explanation of depression from an evolutionary perspective. (12 marks)
   (b) Outline and evaluate **one** explanation of anxiety disorders from an evolutionary perspective.
   (12 marks)

> This could be answered in more or less the same way as question 1 (if you had chosen depression and anxiety disorders). There is a subtle difference between the two questions. In question 1, you were not limited in terms of the *number* of evolutionary explanations provided you covered two mental disorders, but in this question you are. Each part of the question asks you to outline and evaluate just *one* explanation of the disorder specified in that part of the question. So for example, you would choose between the social competition hypothesis and the social navigation hypothesis for the first part of the question. Note that the words 'from an evolutionary perspective' remind you that the question requires more than just a general account of the disorders identified.

3 Critically consider evolutionary explanations of depression (e.g. unipolar and bipolar disorder). (24 marks)

> As both depression and anxiety disorders are in the specification, they may form the basis of an entire question. Two examples are given for depression in the specification and in this question. Examples are there to help you, but you are not obliged to cover them. Here, for example, if you can write enough about unipolar depression, then that would be perfectly acceptable for full marks (without writing about bipolar disorder). Note the plural 'explanations', though – this means that you do need to consider more than one explanation.

4 Critically consider evolutionary explanations of **one or more** anxiety disorders. (24 marks)

> This is the alternative version of question 3, this time focusing on anxiety disorders. No examples are listed in the specification, so none are given in the question. In order to provide effective explanations, it may be a good idea to practise producing précis of the explanations covered in this unit.

Topic 3 >> Evolution of intelligence

THE RELATIONSHIP BETWEEN BRAIN SIZE AND INTELLIGENCE

Brain size in humans and other mammals

Since the 19th century, there have been numerous attempts to establish which features of the human brain, if any, confer upon humans their unique qualities. It is tempting to think that we simply have bigger brains than other mammals, but even a cursory examination of the evidence rules this out. Elephants have brains four times the size of our own and there are species of whales with brains five times larger than the average human brain. We should expect this of course – larger bodies need larger brains to operate them. If brain size were the most important indication of intelligence, we would expect the world to be governed by elephants rather than humans! The next step would be to compare the relative size of brains among mammals (i.e. brain mass/body mass). The results are not particularly helpful – primates such as the mouse lemur, which has a relative brain size of 3 per cent compared to 2 per cent for humans, now outclass us.

A more accurate idea of the intelligence of different species can be gained by considering actual brain size relative to *expected* brain size for a particular body mass. If we divide the 'actual' brain mass of a species by its 'expected' brain size, this gives us the 'encephalization quotient' (EQ) for that species. An EQ of more than 1.0 would indicate a brain size greater than might be predicted for the body size of that species, which in turn might indicate greater intelligence. An EQ of less than 1.0 would indicate a brain size smaller than might be expected for that body size, and therefore a less intelligent species. With a score of 7, humans have the highest EQ of any animal, with primates scoring around 2.34 and dolphins about 4.5 (Jerison 1973). Some values for the great apes and early hominids are shown in Table 23.2.

Table 23.2 >> Body weights, brain weights and encephalization quotients for selected apes and hominids

Species	Body weight (g)	Brain weight (g)	Jerison EQ
>> Orang-utan (Pongo pygmaeus)	53,000	413	2.35
>> Gorilla (Gorilla gorilla)	126,500	506	1.61
>> Common chimp (Pan troglodytes)	36,350	410	3.01
>> Homo habilis	40,500	631	4.30
>> Homo erectus	58,600	826	4.40
>> Homo sapiens	60,000	1250	6.55

The problems of large brains

Metabolically speaking, the human brain is an expensive organ. Although it represents only 2 per cent of body mass, the brain uses about 20 per cent of basal metabolic rate in humans and about 10 per cent in other primates. Viewed from an adaptationist position, unless large brains substantially contributed to evolutionary fitness (i.e. increased survival of genes through successive generations), they would not have evolved (Rushton 1995). Exactly why we developed such large brains is a disputed subject. For about 1.5 million years, the brain remained at about 750 cc, but then doubled to its present volume in the last half a million years. This rapid growth has led some, such as Miller (1996), to suggest that a sexual selection process must have been at work that favoured increased intelligence in potential mates. Whatever the cause, an increase in brain size posed at least two problems for early hominids:

● how to obtain enough nourishment to support energetically expensive neural tissue
● how to give birth to human babies with large heads.

The first problem was probably solved by an earlier switch to a meat-eating diet about two million years ago. The second problem was solved by bringing about what is, in effect, the premature birth of all human babies. One way to squeeze a large-brained infant through a pelvic canal is to allow the brain to continue to grow after birth. In non-human primates, the rate of brain growth slows relative to body growth after birth. Non-human primate mothers have a relatively easy time and birth is usually over in a few minutes. Human mothers can experience many hours of childbirth pains and the brain of the infant still continues to grow at pre-birth rates for about another 13 months. Measured in terms of brain weight development, if we were like other primates, a full term for a human pregnancy would be about 21 months, by which time the head of the infant would be too large to pass through the pelvic canal. As in so many other ways, natural selection has forced a compromise between the benefits of bipedalism (walking on two legs, which requires a small pelvis) and the risks to mother and child during and after childbirth. Human infants are born, effectively, 12 months premature.

Evolutionary factors in the brain size/intelligence relationship

Given the problems of big brains, why is the human brain so large? Many anthropologists believe that our brain is larger than that of other primates because our ancestors were faced with a dramatic climate shift that changed their environment. As their world became drier and changed from tropical rain forest to grassland, our ancestors had to adapt to this new environment. A key factor in this adaptation was a brain that could support walking upright, as well as developing new food-gathering techniques.

The primate life style

Anthropologists believe that the primate life style acted as a selective pressure that drove the development of larger brains. Compared to animals that forage on grass or leaves ('folivores'), early humans had to develop skilled movements that allowed them to climb trees for fruit, or to hunt and trap animals. They also had to develop cognitive maps of the environment to help them find preferred sources of food, as well as learn seasonal changes in food sources and animal migratory patterns. Each of these complex skills would have required the evolution of new brain regions or the development of more cells within existing regions.

Gender differences – the 'man-as-hunter' hypothesis

Are male and female brains different in size? Examining data gathered from autopsies, Ankney (1992) discovered that the brains of European–American men were heavier than the brains of European–American women, and the brains of African-American men were heavier than the brains of African–American women. Does this indicate differences in intelligence between males and females? Research indicates that men and women perform about the same on general measures of intelligence. However, there are fairly consistent sex differences in specific cognitive skills. Males tend to show an advantage in visuo-spatial abilities, such as aiming at stationary or moving targets, as well as throwing and intercepting projectiles (Kimura 1992).

Males also perform better than females in navigation. Many of these abilities would have been important for survival when humans lived in hunter-gatherer societies, where males navigated unfamiliar terrain while hunting, and females foraged nearby areas to gather food. The differing roles of men and women during human evolution may therefore have contributed to the differential development of their brains. Ankney (1995) argued that selection for hunting abilities (requiring skills such as targeting ability and navigation) would have led to relatively larger brains in men in order to process spatial information. Therefore, the 'man-as-hunter' hypothesis, proposed by Washburn and Lancaster (1968), places the selective pressure for the evolution of the brain solidly in the male, who hunted, rather than the female, who did not.

Racial differences – the 'out-of-Africa' hypothesis

Beals *et al.* (1984) analysed about 20,000 skulls from around the world and found that East Asians averaged cranial volumes of 1,415 cm^3, whereas Europeans averaged 1,362 cm^3 and Africans 1,268 cm^3. Differences in cranial capacity suggest differences in brain size between the three populations. Rushton

(1995) has suggested an evolutionary hypothesis for such differences. Modern humans are generally regarded as having their origins on the hot African savannah (the EEA) some 200,000 years ago, with an African/non-African split about 110,000 years ago, and a European/East Asian split about 40,000 years ago (Stringer and Andrews 1988). Evolutionary selection pressures were different on the savannah, where Africans evolved, compared to the cold Arctic where East Asians evolved. Rushton argues that the further north these populations migrated, the more they encountered cognitively demanding problems such as gathering and storing food, finding shelter and raising children during prolonged winters.

Innovation, social learning and tool use

Reader and Laland (2002) have suggested a new approach to the brain size/intelligence relationship in primates. They searched the major primate journals for evidence of innovation (displaying novel solutions to environmental or social problems), social learning (the acquisition of information from others) and tool use. The frequency of such behaviours would provide a measure of the behavioural flexibility of a species. This, in turn, would be an ecologically relevant measure of intelligence. After gathering data on innovation, social learning and tool use from 116 primate species, Reader and Laland found that the frequency of all three behaviours was significantly correlated with brain size.

(AO2) Evaluation
the brain size/intelligence relationship

● **Limitations of encephalization as a measure of intelligence** – Although the notion of an EQ offers a more meaningful indication of brain size relative to body size, it has proved difficult to establish a strong correlation between EQ and intelligence. One of the main problems with the EQ is that animals vary considerably in their body and brain weights at different times of the year and at different periods of life, making it hard to estimate an accurate brain-to-body ratio. Some animals appear to have a low EQ, but they may not actually be unintelligent. Animals who feed on cellulose (grass, leaves, bark, etc.) have a tough time digesting this and therefore need an extensive digestive tract to break down this material. This suggests that folivores, such as cows, may not have a smaller brain for their body size, but larger bodies for their brain size.

● **The 'man-as-hunter' hypothesis** – This hypothesis largely neglected the role of the female in the evolutionary process, in favour of selective pressures acting almost exclusively on

male hunters. However, anthropological evidence from many traditional societies has shown that food gathering by females is, and was, more nutritionally important for these groups (Zihlmann and Tanner 1978).

● **Racial differences** – The case for racial differences in brain size is based on estimates of measures of cranial capacity. Such estimates are not without problems, and may have different validity for men and women. For example, Willerman *et al.* (1992) found a significant correlation between brain size and head perimeter for women, but not for men. Likewise, Reed and Jensen (1993) report an average cranial capacity of 1,550 cm^3 for a high IQ group (124 to 136) and 1,549 cm^3 for a low IQ group (87 to 111), a difference of only 1 cm^3! Although population differences between racial groups in relation to intelligence have yet to be established with any degree of certainty, there are many other possible explanations for such differences that have nothing to do with overall differences in brain size. Among East Asians, for example, intelligence is culturally valued, a fact that by itself could explain data that show higher intelligence levels for this group.

continued on next page

● *Language and the use of technology* –
Increases in the size of primate brains have come
despite the fact that brain tissue is metabolically
very costly (Harvey *et al.* 1987). What selective
pressures have overcome these costs? When the
question is applied to humans, answers typically
refer to the adaptive advantages of technology
(initially, stone tools) and language. But monkeys
and apes use only rudimentary tools and lack

language entirely, yet their brains are significantly
larger than those of similar-sized mammals. Some
other selective pressures must be at work.

● *We are not alone* – Progressively larger brains
have evolved in all primates, not just humans.
Reader and Laland's (2002) research challenges
the view that large brains arose predominantly
because of the unique problems faced during
human evolution. They suggest that intellectual
accomplishments specific to human beings, such
as language use, may have played a smaller role
in the evolution of our sizeable brains than has
often previously been thought.

EVOLUTIONARY FACTORS IN THE DEVELOPMENT OF HUMAN INTELLIGENCE

If brain size alone does not offer the answer to the
origins of human intelligence, what other factors might
have led to the huge leap from our animal ancestors
to modern-day cognition? One suggestion is that the
ever-changing demands of the environment created a
selective pressure for high intelligence among our
ancestors, particularly in terms of the challenge of
finding food. In contrast to this 'ecological'
explanation of the evolution of human intelligence,
others suggest that primate brains (including those of
humans) evolved primarily to deal with social
problems. Primates live in relatively large groups,
where survival and reproductive success depends on
the ability to manipulate others within a complex web
of kinship and dominance relations.

Ecological theories of intelligence

Foraging

The need for our ancestors to hunt and forage for food
had a number of consequences for the evolution of
intelligence. These included the need for superior
memory and navigational abilities (to enable efficient
food exploitation and return to the home range), as well
as the development of tools to hunt and carve up prey.
There was also a need to develop social and
communicative skills as groups of hunters/gatherers are
always more successful than individuals. A small group
of hunter-gatherers might obtain far more food than they
could eat at the time, but which could be distributed
amongst kin and non-kin, requiring the development of
cooperation and social exchange mechanisms.

As early hominids moved from plant-eating to fruit-
and meat-eating, their teeth became smaller and their
brains increased in size. Comparative brain size is
closely related to diet with folivores having smaller
brains, with proportionally less neocortex relative to

body size, than frugivores (fruit eaters). Dunbar (1992)
suggested that the evolution of intelligence among
frugivores indicated an increased cognitive demand to
monitor a widely dispersed food supply. Frugivores
must remember the location of their food supply,
evaluate the ripeness of fruits, develop a harvesting
plan and decide how they will survive in the
meantime. Foliovores, on the other hand, have much
smaller home ranges and therefore can more easily
monitor food availability. Consequently, there is less
pressure for larger brains and the development of
complex cognitive abilities.

Extracting food and tool use

Some food is not immediately obvious and must first
be extracted before being eaten. Opening nuts or
extracting termites requires the use of extractive tools.
The chimpanzee, for example, must use tools for just
that purpose. Boesche *et al.* (2002) studied
chimpanzees in the remote West-African rainforest
where they found evidence that chimps use stones
and branches as hammers to crack open different
types of nuts when foraging. Many of the stone by-
products of chimpanzee nut-cracking are similar to
those found in early human archaeological sites in
East Africa. The nomadic !Kung-San of the Kalahari
traditionally lived by hunting and gathering in one of
the most challenging desert environments on earth.
Despite the hostility of their environment, they
survived for thousands of years. The !Kung-San use
highly elaborate tools, whereas less successful groups,
such as the Tasmanian Aborigines, only used very
simple tools. From such evidence, we might conclude
that groups who have evolved sophisticated tool use
are more successful and that the development of
foraging which involves extracting food and the use
of tools require intelligence in both human and
non-human species.

Evaluation
**ecological explanations of
the evolution of intelligence**

● *Foraging advantages versus problems of a
large brain* – If large brains give animals
significant advantages when it comes to finding
food, why don't all species have large and
complex brains? Animals with large brains are
relatively rare, probably because of the 'costs'
involved. A large brain is extremely demanding in
terms of energy and must compete with other
body organs for scarce resources. A large brain
takes a long time to mature, which means that
infants are heavily dependent on their parents for
longer, and this limits the rate at which an
individual can reproduce.

● *Extractive foraging: a cause or a consequence
of intelligence?* – Parker and Gibson (1979)
argue that many mammals forage extractively (e.g.
opening nuts, probing for nectar), but there is
little evidence of a systematic relationship with
their general intelligence. Parker and Gibson
suggest that the crucial distinction is an
ecological one. Specialist extractive foraging on
one type of food that is available all year round
(such as cockle shells for herring gulls) promotes
tool use of a relatively 'unintelligent' nature. For
omnivores (animals that eat all kinds of food),
such as the higher primates, foods that are
available seasonally and which necessitate the
use of extractive foraging, require more intelligent
tool use. Their theory does not see tool use as a
cause of intelligence in higher primates, but as a
consequence. Intelligent species could adapt to
the ecological pressures of seasonally available
food by developing appropriate tools, whereas
less intelligent species had no need to do so.

● *Intelligence comes at a cost* – Although the
change from eating vegetation and fruit to eating
fish and meat led to improvements in brain
function, this may also have had a side effect – the
increasing incidence of schizophrenic behaviours
(Horrobin 1998). Horrobin proposes that the
biochemical changes resulting from these dietary
changes increased brain size, improved neural
connectivity and led to creative intelligence, but
also produced a series of disordered behaviour
patterns such as paranoia and mild sociopathy.
These were kept in check by sufficient dietary
levels of the essential fatty acids, which modern
diets tend to replace with saturated fatty acids. As
levels of essential fatty acids have dropped in the
modern diet, the very behaviours that led to the
development of human intelligence are expressed
in the more extreme behaviours of schizophrenia
and manic depression.

Social theories of intelligence

The Machiavellian intelligence hypothesis

In recent years, there have emerged several related
hypotheses that suggest that it may be the demands of
the social world, rather than the problem of finding
food, that have been the main determinant of the
growth in primate intelligence. Whiten and Byrne (1988)
developed these theories and labelled them together as
the 'Machiavellian intelligence hypothesis', named after
the Renaissance politician and author, Nicolo
Machiavelli. The main idea of the Machiavellian
intelligence hypothesis is that primate intelligence allows
an individual to serve their own interests by interacting
with others, either cooperatively or manipulatively,
without disturbing the overall social cohesion of the
group. This view of intelligence suggests that individuals
who are able to use and exploit others in their social
group without causing aggression would be able to
increase their reproductive fitness.

In complex social groups, power is often determined
not by outright strength, but rather by the cultivation of
alliances with other individuals. One way in which
individuals within a group can cultivate an alliance is
through mutual grooming. Grooming involves one
individual picking through the fur of another, removing
bits of plant material, fleas or scabs. There is now
general agreement that grooming serves a more subtle
and sophisticated function than simple fur hygiene.
Pairs of primates who regularly groom each other are
more likely to provide assistance to each other when
one is threatened, than non-grooming partners. The
larger the social group, the more important these
alliances are and, consequently, the more time animals
spend in selective grooming.

What functions does grooming serve apart from simple hygiene?

Alliances can be maintained in several ways. Alpha-male chimpanzees rarely share food with other animals that they see as rivals, but do share with those who they do not see as a threat and with those who are allies in the power struggle (Nishida *et al.* 1992). Harcourt (1992) suggests that although other animals form alliances, only the catarrhine primates (such as apes and humans) cultivate alliances on the basis of an individual's ability to provide useful help in the future. As groups become larger and more complex, this characteristic becomes essential for the survival of the individual animal and so spreads quickly amongst the population.

Among social living animals, individuals may also use tactical deception to manipulate other animals into giving help. Byrne and Whiten (1985) define tactical deception as 'acts from the normal repertoire of the agent, deployed such that another individual is likely to misinterpret what the acts signify, to the advantage of the agent'. The following example illustrates this concept. A juvenile baboon watched a larger, adult female digging up a corm. These are highly nutritious but difficult to dig up from the hard ground, particularly for a juvenile. The watching juvenile screamed loudly, with the result that his mother appeared and chased away the adult female (Byrne 1995). This ability to understand and plan deception in behaviour appears to be restricted to the great apes, although other primates appear able to learn such tactics from watching others.

Meat-sharing

For our ancestors in the EEA, meat was an important source of saturated fat. This was vital for survival and yet was not readily available in early human environments. An anthropologist, Craig Stanford, studied chimpanzees in Tanzania's Gombe National Park and found that they face the same problems today. After coming close to starvation for much of the year, when they do manage to kill a colobus monkey (their main prey), they go straight for the fattiest parts – the brains and bone marrow – rather than the tender, nutritious flesh. Because of the importance of meat for early humans, Stanford believed that it was this strategic sharing of meat that paved the way for human intelligence. Not only could meat be used to forge and maintain alliances, but it could also be used to persuade females to mate. In his observations of chimpanzees at Gombe, Stanford observed that lower-ranking males frequently traded meat for mating privileges, which led to his 'meat-for-sex' hypothesis (Stanford 1999). Stanford also noted that when begging for meat, swollen females (i.e. those 'in oestrus' and therefore sexually receptive) had more success than non-swollen females. Stanford believed that strategic meat-sharing required considerable cognitive abilities because males must be able to recognize individuals with whom they had previously shared meat, as well as keep a 'running scorecard' of debts, credits and relationships that may stretch over a period of many years.

Evaluation
social explanations of the evolution of intelligence

- *Neorcortex size and group size* – To test the Machiavellian theory of neocortex enlargement, Dunbar (1993) plotted the ratio of the volume of neocortex to the rest of the brain against various measures of environmental complexity and also against group size. The results were fairly conclusive. He found no relationship between neocortex volume and environmental complexity, but a strong correlation between the size of the neocortex and group size. Dunbar's work is important because it supports the theory that the complexity of the human cortex is due more to the demands of our social environment than the demands of our physical environment.

- *Forming alliances* – Harcourt (1992) found evidence that primates differ from most other species in at least one measure of the complexity of social interaction – patterns of alliances. Alliances occur in many species, but only primates form strategic alliances, soliciting support from some individuals more than from

others. If primates are, in fact, unique in forming strategic alliances, and if this requires knowledge of the relations that exist among others, then the social competition found in large groups offers an explanation for the unusually large brains of primates unrelated to tools or language.

- *The meat-sharing hypothesis* – Hill and Kaplan (1988) found evidence to support the 'meat-for-sex' hypothesis in human beings among hunter-gatherer societies such as the Ache people of Paraguay. Among the Ache of Paraguay, plant food and insect grubs are not shared outside the nuclear family, although meat is. Skilled hunters are rewarded not only with the majority of the hunting spoils, but also with disproportionate sexual favours from women, who often directly exchange sex for meat.

- *The sharing under pressure hypothesis* – This hypothesis, put forward by Wrangham (1975), offers a simple alternative to the idea that males trade meat for sex or to forge alliances. A male in possession of meat must expend a lot of energy defending his kill from others. An animal that does not share expends energy chasing others away and must leave his kill to do so, thus risking theft by scavengers. By sharing with others, he can eat without interruption.

Check your understanding of the evolution of intelligence by answering these questions from memory. You can check your answers by looking back through Topic 3.

1 Explain how you would calculate the encephalization quotient (EQ) of any given species.

2 Identify two problems of having large brains for our human ancestors.

3 What is the 'man-as-hunter' hypothesis?

4 Why, according to the 'out-of-Africa' hypothesis, did East Asians develop larger brains than Europeans?

5 Identify three criticisms of the brain size/intelligence relationship, and prepare a brief summary of each.

6 Why does foraging place a greater cognitive demand on frugivores than it does on folivores?

7 What is the 'Machiavellian intelligence' hypothesis?

8 Briefly outline two ways in which primates show evidence of 'social' intelligence?

9 What is the significance of meat in the evolution of intelligence?

10 Identify two criticisms of social explanations of the evolution of intelligence, and briefly explain why these are significant in the evaluation of this perspective.

REVISION SUMMARY

Having covered this topic you should be able to describe and evaluate:

✓ evolutionary factors affecting the relationship between brain size and intelligence

✓ evolutionary factors in the development of human intelligence, including ecological theories and social theories.

EXAMPLE EXAM QUESTIONS

Below are some **possible examination questions** set on this topic, along with hints to help you understand and approach each question effectively:

1 Discuss the relationship between brain size and intelligence. (24 marks)

For this question, you can draw on any of the material in the first part of this topic *as well as* some selected parts of the latter part. For example, you could include Dunbar's analysis of neocortex size compared to group size and social intelligence (p. 722). When choosing what to include, it is best to include descriptive material for which you have the corresponding AO2 material. To receive really high marks, you need to balance breadth and depth, so be selective. A good plan might be to choose six AO1 points (at 50 words each) and six AO2 points (also at 50 words each).

2 (a) Describe the relationship between brain size and intelligence. (12 marks)
  (b) Assess the relationship between brain size and intelligence. (12 marks)

Sometimes questions are parted in an effort to help you construct your answer. In this case this is exactly the same question as question 1 except you are required to separate your AO1 and AO2. In parted questions, material that is 'peripherally relevant' or 'irrelevant' to one part of the question but would earn marks in the other part, is then 'exported' (when determining marks) to that part. However, it is much better to retain a clear focus on the demands of the question.

3 Critically consider the evolution of intelligence. (24 marks)

> The demands of this broad question are similar to the questions above, except that here the focus is on the evolution of intelligence. You may find the AO2 content quite challenging. When writing AO2, the two main criteria to bear in mind are that it must be *effective* and must be *elaborated* to attract high marks. An example of effective commentary is to introduce a relevant piece of research evidence *accompanied* by a statement of what this evidence shows us (e.g. 'This study shows that brain size is not always related to intelligence'). Elaboration involves making an additional statement of some sort, such as a qualification ('but most research has found a correlation' or 'but correlational evidence doesn't show cause and effect').

4 Discuss the development of intelligence from an evolutionary perspective. (24 marks)

> This final example has been included as a further variation of what is essentially the same question! One thing this shows you is that, in this topic area, you have rather less work to do than in other areas because there are not many questions that can be asked – you have every opportunity to produce the perfect answer!

UNIT SUMMARY

Topic 1: Human reproductive behaviour

● Darwin argued that all species gradually evolve through the process of **natural selection**. Organisms possessing traits that enable them to survive and reproduce are more successful and pass on their genes more readily; organisms lacking these traits are less successful and may die before reproducing.

● Darwin believed that the force of **sexual selection** complements the force of natural selection. Individuals possess features that make them attractive to members of the opposite sex or help them compete with members of the same sex for access to mates. Any trait that increases the reproductive success of an individual will become more exaggerated over evolutionary time through sexual selection.

● Among the most important criteria for mate choice in any species are the characteristic preferences for **indicators of viability** (likelihood of survival) and **fertility** (likelihood of reproduction).

● The pressures imposed by **intersexual** and **intrasexual selection** have led to a number of consequences for human morphology and behaviour, including faces and genitalia.

● Morphological comparisons across different species tell us something about reproductive strategies adopted by our ancestors in the EEA. Such comparisons suggest that females in the EEA were moderately promiscuous compared with other primates.

● Trivers highlighted **sex differences in parental investment** and suggested that choosiness in females is a direct result of their greater investment in their offspring. As a result of this asymmetry in parental investment, males tend to compete over access to females, whereas females have more to lose by a poor match and so will be choosier over their choice of partner.

● Men are more jealous of the sexual act itself, whereas women are more concerned about the shift in emotional focus (and the consequent loss of resources) towards another woman.

Topic 2: Evolutionary explanations of mental disorders

● Some evolutionary psychologists question the assumption that depression is always maladaptive, suggesting instead that it evolved to fit more adaptive functions. **Evolutionary explanations of depression** suggest that it may have had a beneficial effect that outweighed its costs.

● The **social competition** hypothesis proposes that depression is an adaptive response for the individual who loses any conflict over position or status within a group. The purpose of the depression is to prevent the loser from risking further injury by continuing the conflict and thus preserve the relative stability of the social group.

- The **social navigation** hypothesis suggests that depression focuses limited cognitive resources on planning ways out of complex social problems and, because depression is 'costly', it serves as an honest display of need to those with whom the person with depression shares their life.

- Rather than inherit rigid behavioural responses to specific situations (which may well change over time), it is more appropriate for individuals to have an innate readiness to learn about dangerous situations. Seligman's concept of **preparedness** accounts for this.

- The adaptive function of anxiety disorders is that they save the individual organism from having to experience physical and social dangers in real life, producing the same learning response in total physical safety.

- Some evolutionary explanations regard schizophrenia as a disadvantageous by-product of normal brain evolution (its co-evolution with language), whereas others see it as advantageous in evolutionary terms (schizoid personalities divide tribal communities when they become too large).

Topic 3: Evolution of intelligence

- A reasonably accurate idea of the intelligence of different species can be gained by considering actual brain size relative to expected brain size for a particular body mass (known as the **encephalization quotient** or EQ).

- Metabolically speaking, the human brain is an 'expensive' organ. From an adaptationist position, the brain would not have evolved unless large brains contributed substantially to evolutionary fitness. Many anthropologists believe that human brains became larger because of changes in the life style of primates or the selective pressures of hunting.

- More recently, researchers have established a significant correlation between brain size and a species' behavioural flexibility across 116 primate species, demonstrating that animals with larger brains are able to cope with their environment in a more adaptive and efficient way.

- **Ecological theories** of intelligence stress that the foraging needs of our ancestors had a number of consequences for the evolution of **human intelligence**. These included the need for superior memory and navigational abilities, as well as the development of tools to hunt and carve up prey.

- **Social explanations** of intelligence claim that primate brains evolved primarily to deal with social problems. Primates live in relatively large groups where survival and reproductive success depends on their ability to manipulate others within a complex web of kinship and dominance relations.

FURTHER RESOURCES

Cartwright, J. (2000) *Evolution and Human Behaviour*, Basingstoke: Macmillan.

Workman, L. and Reader, W. (2004) *Evolutionary Psychology*, **Cambridge: Cambridge University Press.**

These two texts deal with most of the topics in this unit.

Stevens, A. and Price, J. (2000) *Evolutionary Psychiatry: A New Beginning* (2nd edn), **London: Routledge.**

One of the few books that deals specifically with the evolution of human mental disorders.

Websites

www.evoyage.com/

A useful starting point for many useful sites on various aspects of the evolution of human behaviour.

www.anth.ucsb.edu/projects/human/evpsychfaq.html

FAQs relating to evolutionary psychology.

http://human-nature.com/ep/

Gives you access to *Evolutionary Psychology*, a free online journal of evolutionary psychology – definitely a resource for the serious student who is seeking to impress!

24 UNIT

ISSUES IN THE CLASSIFICATION AND DIAGNOSIS OF Psychological Abnormality

PREVIEW

After you have read this unit, you should be able to:

>> describe and evaluate the ICD and DSM classificatory systems

>> compare and contrast ICD and DSM as alternative approaches to the classification of psychological abnormality

>> describe and evaluate research into the reliability and validity of classification and diagnosis

>> describe case studies of Multiple-Personality Disorder (Dissociative Identity Disorder)

>> describe and evaluate research into Multiple-Personality Disorder as a spontaneous or iatrogenic phenomenon

>> describe case studies of culture-bound syndromes

>> discuss arguments for and against the existence of culture-bound syndromes.

INTRODUCTION

Unlike medical diagnoses of physical disorders, the classification of mental illness has always attracted criticism. One of the main problems lies in determining where we draw the line between 'normal' behaviour that may be a little eccentric, and 'abnormal' behaviour that requires psychiatric intervention. There are several different ways of defining 'abnormality', including statistical infrequency, deviation from social norms, behavioural dysfunction and unexpectedness of a person's responses. Each of these has limitations. When bereaved, for example, we may all behave in ways that suggest we are – at least for a period – acting in a 'dysfunctional' manner (perhaps becoming withdrawn). A lottery win may also lead to 'statistically infrequent' behaviour (perhaps spending vast sums of money and appearing elated for lengthy periods). However, given the circumstances, neither of these responses would be sufficient for a diagnosis of mental illness.

As a result, psychiatrists, clinical psychologists and other mental health workers use a combination of these factors when making their diagnoses of mental illness. In order to identify serious abnormality, psychiatrists have devised classification systems that allow them to distinguish between transient mood and behavioural changes due to circumstances and serious long-term mental health problems. In Topic 1, we examine the two most widely used systems for the classification and diagnosis of serious mental illness and evaluate their reliability and validity. In Topic 2, we go on to discuss four case studies of Multiple-Personality Disorder (also known as 'Dissociative Identity Disorder'), as well as research into Multiple-Personality Disorder in order to examine the evidence for it being spontaneous or manufactured by the therapist ('iatrogenic'). The final topic focuses on culture-bound syndromes and considers the arguments for and against their existence.

Lance Workman
Paul Humphreys
Roger Cocks
Pamela Prentice

Comer (2004, p. 107) defines a classification system as 'a list of disorders, along with descriptions of symptoms and guidelines for making appropriate diagnosis'. Consider the questions below and then discuss your answers with another psychology student:

1 What do you think are the main advantages of using a classification system of psychological abnormality? Consider this from the perspective of: (a) individuals experiencing some form of mental disorder, and (b) health professionals such as psychiatrists and clinical psychologists.

2 What are the main limitations of using a classification system of psychological abnormality?

3 How would you check that a classification system accurately described each of the categories of psychological abnormality included within it, i.e. that it was valid?

4 How would you check that a classification system was reliable? For example, how could you be sure that different psychiatrists would arrive at the same diagnosis when presented with a person with the same cluster of symptoms?

5 Apart from the limitations inherent in any classification system of psychological abnormality, why do you think that mistakes are sometimes made when diagnosing mental disorders?

ICD (The International Classification of Diseases and Related Health Problems): the classification system for medical and mental health problems that is used by the World Health Organization (WHO).

DSM (The Diagnostic and Statistical Manual of Mental Disorders): the classification and diagnosis system developed by the American Psychiatric Association.

Sociogenic hypothesis: the argument that poorer people in society are placed under the greatest stress and that this, in turn, makes mental illness more likely.

Social-selection theory: the argument that people who suffer from schizophrenia become

or remain poor because they are unable to function effectively.

Dissociative disorders: disorders that involve changes in memory for personal events.

Multiple-Personality Disorder/Dissociative Identity Disorder (DID): a form of dissociative disorder whereby a person appears to develop two or more separate personalities.

Iatrogenic disorder: a disorder that has been unintentionally produced by a clinician.

Spontaneous disorder: a disorder that is 'real' as opposed to being induced by a therapist.

Culture-bound syndromes (CBSs): locality-specific patterns of aberrant behaviour and experience.

Topic 1 >> Classificatory systems

Classification systems are needed for the purpose of treatment and for research. It can also be comforting to an individual and their family to be able to identify what their problem is and give it a name. Any classification system relies on the symptoms that an individual displays. However, just as in a physical illness, such as flu, symptoms tend to cluster together, so most classification systems of mental disorder focus on syndromes (i.e. clusters of symptoms that tend to occur together). However, there is not always a perfect fit between the symptoms displayed by an individual and those identified for a particular diagnostic category, such as schizophrenia.

TWO MAJOR CLASSIFICATION SYSTEMS

The two systems currently used to classify psychological abnormality are the *International Classification of Diseases and Related Health Problems* (ICD) and the *Diagnostic and Statistical Manual of Mental Disorders* (DSM). These classification systems are constantly being revised – mental disorders are added, deleted and reorganized in the light of new research evidence. We will look at each of these in turn.

Unit 24 // Classification & diagnosis of psychological abnormality

First, though, it is worth clarifying terminology and, in particular, the distinction between classification and diagnosis:

- **Classification** is what, for example, botanists do when they differentiate between types of flowers (roses as distinct from orchids) and variations within those categories (e.g. different kinds of roses). Classification is deciding what schizophrenia is (as opposed to depression, for example) and what the characteristics of the different types of schizophrenia are.

- **Diagnosis** is when botanists look at one particular flower and decide that its characteristics identify it as a rose (as opposed to a tulip, etc.). In the field of mental health, diagnosis is the clinical judgement that a particular person is suffering, for example, from schizophrenia.

The ICD

The ICD classification system dates back to 1893, with the publication of the *Bertillon Classification or International List of Causes of Death*. The current edition, ICD-10, published in 1992 by the World Health Organization (WHO), is a large work consisting of three volumes and over 2,000 pages. The primary function of the ICD is to make it easier to collect and report general health statistics. Mental disorders were not included until the sixth revision in 1952 (ICD-6).

The main purpose of any classification system, and the ICD in particular, is to gain agreement on a universal definition for specific disorders or syndromes. This helps to ensure that whenever research is carried out on a disorder with a particular set of symptoms, the disorder can be universally recognized. Without agreed definitions and labels, it would be difficult for researchers and clinicians to communicate effectively. ICD-10 identifies 11 general categories of mental disorders, listed in Table 24.1.

The DSM

While the primary purpose of ICD is the classification of disorders, the DSM classification system has an additional purpose of assisting clinicians to *diagnose* a person's problem as a particular disorder. Clinicians can also use the available information on a given disorder to decide on the most appropriate course of treatment.

The American Psychiatric Association first published the *Diagnostic and Statistical Manual of Mental Disorders* (DSM-I) in 1952. DSM-I and DSM-II (published in 1968) caused a great deal of debate amongst clinicians because there was a lack of consensus over the precise listing of disorders (Davison *et al.* 2004). DSM-III (published in 1980) included many more disorders than its predecessors. The current version, DSM-IV, was developed in 1994 and a 'text revision' – DSM-IV-TR – was published in

> ### Table 24.1 >> The 11 categories of mental disorder in ICD-10
>
> >> organic, including symptomatic, mental disorders (e.g. dementia in Alzheimer's disease)
>
> >> mental and behavioural disorders due to psychoactive substance abuse (e.g. those arising from alcohol abuse)
>
> >> schizophrenia, schizotypal and delusional disorders
>
> >> mood (affective) disorders (e.g. recurrent depressive disorder)
>
> >> neurotic, stress-related and somatoform disorders (e.g. anxiety disorders)
>
> >> behavioural syndromes associated with physiological disturbances and physical factors (e.g. anorexia nervosa)
>
> >> disorders of adult personality and behaviour (e.g. paranoia)
>
> >> mental retardation
>
> >> disorders of psychological development (e.g. childhood autism)
>
> >> behavioural emotional disorders with onset usually occurring in childhood or adolescence (e.g. conduct disorders)
>
> >> mental disorders not specified elsewhere.

June 2000. As with ICD, it is based on the assumption that symptoms can be grouped together to form a specific mental disorder. DSM-IV-TR lists around 400 such disorders covering clinical disorders, personality disorders and mental retardation. DSM-III saw the first use of multi-axial classification, which is used to rate an individual on five separate dimensions (or axes) that may affect functioning. The five axes of DSM-IV-TR are shown in Table 24.2.

For most individuals with a mental health problem, there will be a diagnosis either on Axis I or Axis II, but some individuals will be classified on both. When a clinician works through the axes, they can paint an increasingly accurate picture of an individual client.

DSM-IV defines a mental disorder as:

> '... a clinically significant behavioral or psychological syndrome or pattern that occurs in an individual and that is associated with present distress (e.g. a painful symptom) or disability (i.e. impairment in one or more important areas of functioning) or with a significantly increased risk of suffering death, pain, disability or an important loss of freedom.'

Table 24.2 >> Multi-axial assessment in DSM-IV-TR

>> **Axis 1: Major clinical syndromes** – This includes all mental disorders such as schizophrenia, mood disorders, anxiety disorders and dissociative disorders.

>> **Axis 2: Personality disorders and mental retardation** – This includes personality disorders, such as anti-social personality disorder, histrionic personality disorder and narcissistic personality disorder, as well as problems of intellectual development.

>> **Axis 3: General medical conditions** – This includes medical problems that can lead to symptoms of an Axis 1 or an Axis 2 disorder (e.g. cirrhosis of the liver).

>> **Axis 4: Psychosocial and environmental problems** – This includes events that have occurred during the past year, which again may have an impact on diagnosis (e.g. divorce or loss of job).

>> **Axis 5: Global Assessment of Functioning scale** – This scale is used to rate an individual's ability to function psychologically, socially and in terms of occupation on a scale of from 1 to 100. A score above 90 would indicate a person is in a very good state of mental functioning; a score of 70 would suggest some mild symptoms, whilst a score as low as 30 would suggest a number of very serious problems. A person who scores less than 10 on this scale would present a persistent danger of seriously hurting self or others and/or be unable to maintain minimal personal hygiene. (See also Unit 4, p. 121.)

However, devising systems to classify and diagnose different forms of mental disorder is quite challenging.

<< Botanists would never have advanced their field without a clear taxonomy for classifying plants. Mere 'plant' and 'not plant' would not be very fruitful. So, too, we need to have a system that allows us to identify the different types of disorders which fall under the rubric of 'abnormality'.>> (SUNYB2 1999)

Requirements for a robust classification system

Any robust classification system must satisfy the following criteria (SUNYB2 1999):

- It should provide an ***exhaustive system*** that includes *all* types of abnormal behaviour.

- The classificatory categories should be ***mutually exclusive***, i.e. the boundaries between different categories should not be 'fuzzy' and it should, therefore, be clear what disorder(s) a particular person is suffering from.

- It should be ***valid*** – see the panel below.

- It should be ***reliable***, that is, each time a classification system is used, it should produce the same outcome. More specifically, the consistency with which clinicians agree on a diagnosis for a particular set of symptoms is known as 'inter-rater reliability'. For DSM and ICD to be reliable, those using it must be able to agree when a person should or should not be given a particular diagnosis.

Three types of validity (Davison *et al.* 2004)

Davison and colleagues identify three types of validity in relation to classification systems:

- ***Content validity*** is achieved when a measure adequately samples the problem of interest. So, in the DSM, for example, if an interview is used to determine where a person should be placed on Axis 1 and/or Axis 2, it will have good content validity if the questions asked really do find out about the symptoms listed on these two axes.

- ***Criterion validity*** is achieved when a measurement is associated in a predicted way with another measurement. We might, for example, expect to find that most people with schizophrenia are also likely to have difficulties in personal relationships.

- ***Construct validity*** is met when ratings on an assessment, such as the ICD, relate to other variables in a way that theory would predict. This is quite a complicated concept to grasp. A concrete example might be that the diagnosis of a mood disorder, such as depression, will be supported by self-reported behavioural problems and by clinical observations, since both of these would be predicted by the diagnosis.

- *Are the categories of mental illness real and meaningful?* – One has to assume that the categories of mental illness are 'real' and exist 'out there', and that each disorder is a distinct entity. However, it may be that they are simply perceptual categories that we impose on the world to make it orderly and enable us to understand it better, i.e. they may merely be 'figments of scientists' imaginations!' (SUNYB2 1999).

- *When description become diagnosis* – It is important to appreciate that terms used in psychology, including those used in clinical psychology, have a variety of meanings and can refer to different things. When using terms such as 'anxiety' or 'depression', how confident can we be that we are talking about the same thing? These are inevitably subjective judgements. There is, therefore, a real possibility that: 'the words we use to describe people, such as anxious, depressed and so on, were meant for just that, to describe them. However, there is the danger that those terms will be turned around to explain people's behaviour: "Why does she act that way?", "Because she is depressed". The description becomes the explanation – a circular and thus meaningless explanation is set up. The description is used to explain itself!' (SUNYB2 1999, pp. 7–8)

- *Overinclusion and 'pathologizing' problems* – Since it was first published in 1952, the DSM classification system has been extended with each new edition and encompasses increasingly large numbers of individuals. Comer (2004) suggests that as high a proportion as 48 per cent of the adult population of the USA might qualify for a diagnosis on the DSM. Is it really possible that half of a nation's people have a classifiable mental health problem? Clearly, people who hear voices and believe that they are someone that they

obviously are not are likely to be suffering from a serious mental health problem. But, do the quite large mood changes that some women experience with their monthly menstrual cycle, for example, really constitute the category of pre-menstrual dysphoric disorder? This new category was added to the DSM classification in 1994. Many would argue that women who suffer most from monthly mood swings are merely at the extremes of the normal distribution and that the inclusion of such a category might 'pathologize' women who suffer from pre-menstrual syndrome, leading to stereotyping of such women as having 'raging hormones' (Comer 2004). Likewise, where, in DSM, do we draw the line between maintaining a strictly controlled diet and having an eating disorder, such as anorexia nervosa? Interestingly, one way in which ICD-10 differs from DSM-IV-TR is that ICD-10 devotes less attention to eating disorders and to sexual disorders than DSM-IV-TR. One reason for this might be that eating disorders and sexual disorders appear to be more common in the USA, where the DSM system is developed, than in other cultures (Andrews *et al.* 1999).

- *Improved specificity?* – In contrast to the criticisms of 'overinclusion' above, some clinicians found when using DSM-IV-TR and ICD-10, that previous editions did not spell out the criteria for inclusion clearly enough, leading to misdiagnosis (Oltmanns and Emery 2004). In addition to inclusion criteria, DSM-IV-TR contains *exclusion* criteria, which means that some specific diagnoses may be ruled out under certain conditions. An example of this is obsessive-compulsive disorder (OCD). If the obsessions (such as recurrent thoughts and impulses) and the compulsive tendencies (such as repetitive hand-washing) only occur when a person with alcohol problems is drunk, then the diagnosis of OCD should not be made. Hence, clinicians who modified the DSM system would argue that its precision has been improved.

RESEARCH INTO THE RELIABILITY AND VALIDITY OF CLASSIFICATION AND DIAGNOSIS

As we saw earlier, reliability is the extent to which a classification system repeatedly produces the same outcome. More specifically in relation to mental health workers, inter-rater reliability is the extent to which two independent clinicians agree about the diagnosis of a person with mental health problems (Davison *et al.* 2004). Psychiatric diagnosis is frequently regarded as being notoriously unreliable. Studies have shown that even very experienced psychiatrists may only agree about 50 per cent of the time (Spitzer and Williams 1985).

The impact of Rosenhan's classic research study

In the 1960s and 70s, there was some concern that psychiatrists gave a diagnosis of schizophrenia too readily. There was even greater concern that many people were being admitted to mental hospitals when they were not mentally ill and, once admitted, they were detained and given treatment without their informed consent. This assertion was supported by Rosenhan (1973) – see Key research opposite.

on being sane in insane places (Rosenhan 1973)

In the early 1970s, David Rosenhan carried out a classic study which led, in part, to the development of a new edition of the DSM. Nine healthy people presented themselves at different psychiatric hospitals and said that they were hearing voices saying things like 'empty' and 'thud'. All were admitted and all, except one, were diagnosed as suffering from schizophrenia. The 'pseudopatients' consisted of three psychologists (including Rosenhan and another, Martin Seligman, who was to become a famous psychologist), a paediatrician, a psychiatrist, a psychology graduate student, a housewife and a painter (eight in all as one of the pseudopatients was later excluded due to falsifying details). Apart from changing their names and jobs, all other information given to the clinicians at the hospitals thereafter was true. As soon as they were admitted to psychiatric wards, all eight stopped simulating any symptoms of abnormality.

The pseudopatients were never detected and were eventually discharged with the diagnosis of schizophrenia in remission. Length of hospitalization ranged from 7 to 52 days (average 19). Perhaps most interesting, though, is the fact that several fellow patients (35 out of 118 in the first three hospitalizations, when detailed records were kept by the pseudopatients) 'detected their sanity'. One said, 'You're not crazy. You're a journalist, or a professor (referring to the constant note-taking by the pseudopatients). You're checking up on the hospital.'

On the basis of what happened in each of these cases, Rosenhan suggested that psychiatrists are unable to determine who is sane and who is insane. Rosenhan's study made a deep impact on the classification of mental illness and was taken into account in tightening up the guidelines for diagnosis of schizophrenia under the DSM system. But is it fair to accuse psychiatrists of being unable to determine who is mentally ill or well on the basis of this study? Hearing voices is *the* most common symptom of schizophrenia (Davison *et al.* 2004) and all of the pseudopatients reported that this was the problem they were having. Also, we need to consider the difficult position that the clinicians were placed in, since the repercussions of sending someone away who might be seriously mentally ill are likely to be much worse than the repercussions of admitting someone into hospital who turns out to be mentally well.

In addition to problems of reliability, Rosenhan's (1973) study also raises questions about the validity of the DSM. Validity refers to how well a measuring instrument really measures what it is designed to measure. Unlike physical health problems, validity is always going to be a problem for diagnoses of mental health problems. A person suffering from flu will have quite specific symptoms, such as a raised temperature and aches and pains. Moreover the flu virus can be physically detected. A person diagnosed as suffering from schizophrenia, however, may or may not exhibit paranoia, they may or may not hear voices, and in either event no pathogen will be detected. So validity for mental illness is less direct than for physical illness. Construct validity (see p. 729) is determined for schizophrenia by observing the extent to which a person who is given this diagnosis then behaves in a way that would be predicted. Criterion validity may be verified if the sufferer has similar associated problems to others with the same diagnosis and, as is generally the case, they may also have difficulty forming relationships. In Rosenhan's study, for example, the behaviour of the pseudopatients was not abnormal once they had gained admission to the hospitals and so their diagnosis was low on validity (despite this they were all detained for some time). In contrast to this low level of validity, for the diagnosis of Rosenhan's pseudopatients, the reliability of the diagnoses was high since nearly all were given the diagnosis of schizophrenia. This demonstrates that a diagnosis may be high in reliability and low in validity at the same time.

With each new edition of the DSM, attempts are made to improve both the reliability and validity of the diagnostic criteria. The current version is considered to have reliability and validity for most of its anxiety disorder and mood categories (Brown *et al.* 2001). In contrast, its validity for some other classes, such as personality disorders, has been questioned, as has the validity of Axis 5 (Global Assessment of Functioning) (Moos *et al.* 2000).

The Composite International Diagnostic Interview

An attempt to improve both the reliability and the validity of the DSM is the Composite International Diagnostic Interview (CIDI), developed in Australia by Andrews and Peters (1997). Patients/clients work through a highly structured interview, using a computer program (currently CIDI 2.1), working either on their own or with an assistant. They answer a range of questions about psychological disorders, and their responses to these are used to determine which questions from the pool they are subsequently asked and which are omitted. If sufficient symptoms are endorsed and they occur in certain patterns or clusters, a clinical diagnosis is made. All of this is carried out automatically by the computer program.

- *A more acceptable method* – A study by Griest *et al.* (1987) shows that patients who took part in the study found this method of analysis and diagnosis acceptable. Indeed, many reported that they felt *more* comfortable answering the questions on a computer than in a face-to-face interview situation. Many reported that it provided them with an opportunity to reveal

symptoms about which they had never been asked before.

- *High reliability and validity* – Andrews and Peters (1997) report that both reliability and validity are high and concluded that the CIDI 'provides the opportunity for improving diagnostic accuracy in routine clinical practice. This computerized interview could be used in psychiatry as laboratory tests are used in other branches of medicine. Improved diagnostic accuracy should lead to better treatment and thus, to more effective patient outcomes.'

Bias in the diagnosis of mental disorders

In addition to Rosenhan's (1973) study and the work of Andrews and Peters (1997) outlined above, research into the effects of social class, ethnicity and gender also illustrate problems of reliability and validity in relation to the diagnosis of psychological abnormality. Accusations have been made by a number of people, including Fernando (1991), Rack (1982) and Ussher (1992), that there are biases in diagnosis. We will conclude this topic by examining some relevant evidence, which suggests that social class, race and gender have a significant bearing on the likelihood of someone being diagnosed as mentally ill.

Social class

Umbenhauer and DeWitte (1978) investigated the effects of social class on the attitudes of mental health professionals. They found that upper-class people received more favourable clinical judgements and were

more likely to be offered psychotherapy than working-class people. Johnstone (1989) highlighted a number of studies which showed that regardless of symptoms, more serious diagnoses were given to working-class people. In particular, persons from lower socio-economic classes were more frequently diagnosed as suffering from schizophrenia than those from the higher classes (Keith *et al.* 1991, Davison *et al.* 2004). They were also more likely to spend longer periods in hospital and to have a poorer prognosis. Working-class patients were more likely to be prescribed physical treatments, such as electroconvulsive therapy (ECT) and drugs, and less likely to be offered psychotherapy.

Johnstone (1989) suggested that health professionals justify giving more physical treatments to patients of low socio-economic class by claiming that working-class people were less able to benefit from verbal therapies because they were less articulate. She concluded that working-class patients, who experienced the most social and economic hardship, ended up receiving 'disabling' rather than 'empowering' psychiatric treatments.

- *Social class and self-esteem* – Although there are robust findings with regard to the relationship between social class and mental illness, some researchers have suggested that this relationship is not straightforward. Pilgrim and Rogers (1993) see mental illness, and in particular depression, as being a secondary effect of coming from a lower social class. They suggest that a lack of self-esteem resulting from the vulnerability related to unemployment is an important predictive factor in the development of mental illness. If this is the case, then it may not simply be a matter of being labelled more frequently as mentally ill because a person comes from a lower social class. Rather, self-knowledge of one's position in society and the

possible consequences of this may make real mental illness far more likely.

- *Sociogenic hypothesis or social-selection theory* – In addition to the arguments of Pilgrim and Rogers, two alternative theories have been proposed to explain the relationship between schizophrenia and social class. The sociogenic theory suggests that poorer people in society are placed under the greatest stress and that this, in turn, makes mental illness more likely (Susser *et al.* 1996). In contrast, the social-selection theory proposes that people who suffer from schizophrenia become or remain poor because they are unable to function effectively (Munk and Mortensen 1992). This latter argument therefore reverses the direction of causation by suggesting that people who develop mental illness then exhibit a downward drift in society (Davison *et al.* 2004).

Ethnicity

Fernando (1988) claims that stereotyped ideas about race are inherent in British psychiatry. For example, there are stereotypes of Black violence and the belief that Black people cannot 'use' help and are not, therefore, suitable for open hospitals. Table 24.3 lists some British research on ethnicity and mental health.

Research has shown that the compulsory detaining of African-Caribbean patients in secure hospitals is higher than for any other group. Ineichen *et al.* (1984) examined hospital admissions in Bristol and found that non-White groups (West Indians plus other non-Whites) accounted for 32 out of 89 compulsory admissions (i.e. 36 per cent), but only 30 out of 175 voluntary admissions (17 per cent). In a survey conducted by McGovern and Cope (1987) on hospital-detained psychotic patients in Birmingham, it was found that two-thirds were African-Caribbean (both migrants and British born), whilst the remaining one-third were White and Asian.

Table 24.3 >> Research studies on ethnicity and mental health (Fernando 1988, p. 74)

1 Over-diagnosis of schizophrenia in:

>> West Indian and Asian immigrant in-patients (Cochrane 1977, Carpenter and Brockington 1980, Dean et al. 1981)

>> patients of West Indian ethnicity admitted compulsorily in Bristol (Harrison et al. 1984) and in Birmingham (McGovern and Cope 1987).

2 Excess of compulsory admission of:

>> patients of West Indian ethnicity in Bristol (Harrison et al. 1984) and in Birmingham (McGovern and Cope 1987).

3 Excessive transfer to locked wards of:

>> West Indian, Indian and African patients (Bolton 1984).

4 Excessive admission of 'offender patients' of:

>> people of West Indian ethnicity in Birmingham (McGovern and Cope 1987).

5 Overuse of ECT for:

>> Asian in-patients in Leicester (Shaikh 1985)

>> Black immigrant patients in East London (Littlewood and Cross 1980).

Commentary
diagnosis in relation to ethnicity

● *Western bias?* – Cochrane and Sashidharan (1995) point out that there is a common assumption that the behaviours of the White population are normative and any deviation from this by another ethnic group reveals some racial or cultural pathology. Conversely, as Rack (1982) points out, if a member of a minority ethnic group exhibits a set of symptoms that is similar to that of a White British-born patient, then they are assumed to be suffering from the same disorder, which may not actually be the case. For example, within the culture of one ethnic group, it might be regarded as normal to see or hear a deceased relative during bereavement. Under DSM-IV-TR criteria, this behaviour might be misdiagnosed as a symptom of a psychotic disorder. Cochrane and Sashidharan (1995) suggest that practitioners are almost forced into assuming that mental illnesses, such as schizophrenia, depression and neurosis, which are commonly found in European patients, are also found in non-European patients.

● *Behaving differently to survive* – According to Sue and Sue (1999), many members of minority groups may adopt responses that help them to survive in what to them is a hostile society. African-Americans, for example, may appear suspicious or mistrustful to White clinicians because of previous negative encounters with the White majority. Such responses may be labelled as paranoia and make the diagnosis of a mental illness more likely, even though they are really acting in an adaptive way that they feel helps them to survive in that particular society.

● *Do cultures really differ in their symptomology of mental illness?* – There is some evidence from cross-cultural surveys that there is cultural variability in the symptoms that people present to their general practitioners (GPs). Ulusahin *et al.* (1994), for example, found that Turkish outpatients exhibited more somatic symptoms, such as insomnia and hypochondria, than British outpatients. Furthermore, prevalence rates of depression are now known to vary quite considerably between different cultures. Compton *et al.* (1991) have found much higher rates of depression in Western countries than in Taiwan and Hong Kong. This might be taken as evidence that ethnicity directly affects rates of mental illness. Alternatively, ethnicity might only be indirectly related to mental illness, since different cultures might have different coping strategies.

Gender

Mental health statistics indicate that certain mental disorders are diagnosed more frequently in men, while others are diagnosed more frequently in women (Davison *et al.* 2004). It has been suggested that this can be explained through biological differences. However, those who argue that the differences merely reflect stereotyped judgements among mental health professionals have challenged this view (Caplan 1995).

Broverman *et al.* (1981) thought that since certain behavioural characteristics have traditionally been ascribed to either male or female gender, it is likely that clinical diagnosis of mental disorders will reflect these distinctions. In an important study, they found that clinicians have different concepts of health for men and women, and that these differences do tend to parallel the common gender-role stereotypes in our society. They asked 46 male and 33 female mental health professionals (clinically trained psychologists, psychiatrists and social workers) to rate the characteristics of the healthy man, the healthy woman and the healthy adult. They found that the healthy adult and the healthy man were rated in a similar way as assertive, decisive and relatively independent. The healthy woman was regarded as more submissive, dependent and emotional than the healthy man.

In the light of their findings, Broverman and colleagues suggest that a double standard of mental health exists within clinical diagnosis, with certain behavioural characteristics thought to be pathological in members of one gender, but not in the opposite gender.

Worell and Remer (1992) claim that sexism can occur in assessment and diagnosis of patients in four ways:

1 *Disregarding environmental context* – Assessment and diagnosis focus mainly on traits and behaviours of the individual without due regard to the environmental context, such as poverty, patriarchy and powerlessness. Judgements are made without taking into account the person's response to the environment. Consequently, if the clinician holds strong, stereotypical views on gender roles, behaviour can either be dismissed as an overreaction or regarded as abnormal or pathological.

2 *Differential diagnosis based on gender* – If female and male clients present the same symptoms, but different diagnoses are made, then gender bias is occurring. This is most likely to happen if symptoms mirror traditional gender-role stereotypes and if diagnostic classifications use descriptions such as 'dependent' or 'submissive', which are more likely to be associated with a female stereotype.

3 *Therapist misjudgement* – Because of sex-role stereotyping, therapists may have preconceived ideas about particular symptoms and may therefore perceive those symptoms more readily in either males or females. Because people are often unaware that they hold stereotypical beliefs, therapists may be unaware that they are making these assumptions.

4 *Theoretical orientation gender bias* – Diagnosis is often made on the basis of the therapist's own theoretical orientation. If that orientation is gender-biased, then it is more likely that the assessment made by the therapist will also be biased.

(A02) Commentary
diagnosis in relation to gender

● *Gender roles and mental health?* – It is generally believed that health consists of good adjustment to one's environment. Men and women are trained from birth to fulfil different social roles, and so healthy adjustment for a woman is to accept the behavioural norms for her gender, even though these behaviours may be considered less healthy for the generalized healthy adult. If the 'adjustment' notion of health were accepted, then it would be maladaptive for a woman to exhibit characteristics that are considered to be 'healthy' for men, but not women. One of the dangers of mental health professionals adopting the adjustment view of health is that they then actively reinforce and perpetuate gender-role stereotypes (Nolen-Hoeksema 2002).

● *Diagnosing the person or the situation?* – Nolen-Hoeksema (1995, 2002) points out that women's experience in Western culture predisposes them to depression, and clinicians are therefore diagnosing a *situation* rather than a *person*. Cochrane (1995) explains that depression can be related to the long-term effects of child abuse and also to gender-role socialization, which produces increased female vulnerability. He points out the adverse effects on women of power relationships and gender discrimination. Despite the vast amount of evidence that relates women's depression to sociocultural factors, many clinicians continue to ignore environmental circumstances and convey the message that the problem lies in the person's illness (Johnstone 1989, Nolen-Hoeksema 2002). Johnstone believes that this also applies to men. She points out that unemployed men have a high rate of psychiatric breakdown. By labelling the problem as a mental disorder, the person has the stigma of a psychiatric label and the problem is viewed only in individual terms, rather than in the wider social and political context.

continued on next page

● *Gender bias in DSM classification* – Gender differences are particularly marked in the prevalence rates for specific personality disorders (see Table 24.4). This differential diagnosis may reflect gender bias in the diagnostic system, rather than actual differences. In a study by Hamilton *et al.* (1986), clinicians were given client descriptions consistent with the symptoms of histrionic personality disorder (see Table 24.4), which has

traditionally been diagnosed more frequently in women than in men. In these descriptions, the gender of the client was varied, but the symptoms were identical. Clinicians consistently rated female clients as more histrionic than males, suggesting that at least some clinicians do demonstrate gender bias in their diagnoses. Narcissistic personality disorder (see Table 24.4), on the other hand, is diagnosed more frequently in males. The diagnostic symptom criteria in DSM-IV-TR list behaviours that reflect stereotypical male gender roles much more than female – for example, 'shows arrogance', 'has a sense of entitlement', 'has a grandiose sense of self-importance'.

Table 24.4 >> DSM-IV diagnostic description for personality disorders more prevalent in males or females

>> **Histrionic personality disorder** *(diagnosed more frequently in females)* A pervasive pattern of excessive emotionality and attention seeking.	>> **Narcissistic personality disorder** *(diagnosed more frequently in males)* A pervasive pattern of grandiosity (in fantasy or behaviour), need for admiration and lack of empathy.
>> **Dependent personality disorder** *(diagnosed more frequently in females)* A pervasive and excessive need to be taken care of that leads to submissive and clinging behaviour and fears of separation.	>> **Obsessive-compulsive personality disorder** *(diagnosed more frequently in males)* A pervasive pattern of preoccupation with orderliness, perfectionism and mental and interpersonal control, at the expense of flexibility, openness and efficiency.

✓ CHECK YOUR UNDERSTANDING

Check your understanding of classificatory systems by answering these questions from memory. You can check your answers by looking back through Topic 1.

1 What is the main purpose of a classification system?

2 Outline the main differences between classification and diagnosis.

3 Prepare a 150-word précis of (a) ICD-10 and (b) DSM-IV-TR.

4 Summarize the main similarities and differences between the ICD and the DSM.

5 List the four criteria that any robust classification system should satisfy.

6 Describe in less than 150 words the three forms of validity that a classification system should have.

7 On what grounds might the DSM-IV-TR category of 'pre-menstrual dysphoric disorder' be criticized?

8 Outline two evaluative points in relation to Rosenhan's study – 'Being sane in insane places'.

9 What, according to Broverman and colleagues (1981), is the danger of mental health professionals adopting the view that mental health consists of good adjustment to one's environment?

10 In what four ways did Worell and Remer (1992) claim that sexism could occur in assessment and diagnosis?

REVISION SUMMARY

Having covered this topic, you should be able to:

✓ outline the main purpose of any classification system

✓ distinguish between classification and diagnosis

✓ describe the current version of the ICD classification system

✓ describe the current version of the DSM system of classification and diagnosis

✓ discuss the concepts of reliability and validity in relation to the classification and diagnosis of psychological abnormality

✓ describe and evaluate research into the reliability and validity of classification and diagnosis, including research into the effect of race, social class and gender.

EXAMPLE EXAM QUESTIONS

Below are some **possible examination questions** set on this topic, along with hints to help you understand and approach each question effectively:

1 (a) Outline ICD and DSM. (15 marks)

(b) To what extent are these classificatory systems reliable **and/or** valid? (15 marks)

> You have 40 minutes in total to answer this question, so should allocate about 10 minutes (about 200 words) to each outline (800 words is about right for a 40-minute question). If you only do one of them, there would be a partial performance penalty of a maximum of 9 marks for AO1. In fact, you are not required to present both DSM and ICD in balance. There is a 9/6 mark split, with up to 9 marks for one classificatory system and 6 marks for the other. Part (b) of this question starts with the phrase 'to what extent', indicating an AO2 response. The trick is to avoid *describing* any material and instead to focus on *using* your knowledge to construct a response. So, you might argue that the ICD is reliable because research has found a fair degree of agreement in diagnosis. In contrast, you could look at evidence against this view. You must consider both classificatory systems, but you do not have to consider both reliability *and* validity (because of the phrase 'and/or').

2 (a) Outline **two** classificatory systems. (15 marks)

(b) Evaluate **one** of the classificatory systems that you have described in part (a). (15 marks)

> In this question, the two classificatory systems are not specified, so you could consider others. It always pays to plan responses in advance of the exam and prepare a 15-mark version of each (for questions requiring just one of these) and also a $7\frac{1}{2}$-mark version (for questions such as this). The longer version is a précis of the material on pp. 727–9, selecting the most important points and ensuring a broad coverage of the different features of the systems rather than just a list of the categories. The $7\frac{1}{2}$-mark version is a précis of the précis. For your AO2 in part (b), you can again evaluate the classificatory systems in terms of reliability and validity, and might prepare a plan for this. In total, you should write about 400 words, giving 200 words on each of the reliability and validity of your chosen system.

3 'Reliability and validity are major concerns for classificatory systems such as the DSM and ICD'.

With reference to the quotation above, discuss issues that it raises. (30 marks)

> Quotations are more common on AQA Module 5 questions because of the 'synopticity' criterion (see Unit 32, p. 940). Questions are set to elicit synopticity because they ask you to consider several different approaches or issues. Here, you are asked to consider the issues in the quotations: two different issues in two different classificatory systems (representing two different approaches). Don't overlook the AO2 component of the essay ('discuss' invites a discursive approach consisting of AO1 and AO2). In this essay you can choose to *describe* research on reliability and validity or use it as evaluation. If you do the former, then you can evaluate the methodology or implications of such research. You could also describe ICD and DSM, and evaluate them in terms of reliability and validity.

4 'Psychologists don't always agree on the diagnosis made of a particular patient, especially if the patient comes from a different culture to the psychologist.'

Critically consider research into the reliability and validity of classification and diagnosis (e.g. Rosenhan). (30 marks)

Here, there is no requirement to address the quotation, which is there to provide some ideas about what to write. In this question, descriptions of classificatory systems would *not* be creditworthy (whereas they were for question 3) as you have been asked to describe and evaluate research into reliability and validity. Remember that 'research' can be taken to refer to theories or studies.

5 Compare and contrast ICD and DSM. (30 marks)

'Compare and contrast' is an AO1+AO2 term (see Table 32.1, p. 937). The simplest route to take here is to outline ICD and DSM for the AO1 component, and then consider similarities and differences for your AO2. This 'consider' may involve a description of such similarities and differences, or a commentary on them – such as the implications of any differences or the desirability of any similarities. Alternatively, you could describe the similarities and differences as AO1 and evaluate/comment upon these as AO2.

Topic 2 >> Multiple-Personality Disorder (Dissociative Identity Disorder)

As the case studies in this topic illustrate, one of the most interesting examples of mental disorder is what, until recently, was called 'Multiple-Personality Disorder' (MPD) and is now referred to as 'Dissociative Identity Disorder' (DID). The film *Sybil* documents one intriguing case. If you have not seen this film, try to get hold of a copy. We will examine what underlies this disorder and examine the argument that it is *iatrogenic* (i.e. induced unintentionally by therapeutic practice) rather than *spontaneous*.

CASE STUDIES OF DID

Four short case studies are included in this topic to help you understand some of the features associated with DID. We start with descriptions of Eve and George (Case studies 1 and 2 respectively), with descriptions of Sybil and Ken following later.

Case study 1: The three faces of Eve

Of all the personalities typical of DID, the most famous is probably *The Three Faces of Eve*, described in a book by Thigpen and Cleckey (1957) and also made into a film. Eve was a mother within a troubled marriage who sought psychotherapy. During therapy she complained of hearing an imaginary voice. Although she had blackouts, these did not disturb her. During therapy, the authors of the book describe the birth of a new personality: 'after a tense moment of silence, there was a quick reckless smile and in a bright voice that sparkled, she said "Hi there, Doc!".' A new personality emerged, Eve Black, a happy-go-lucky, flirtatious woman, who did not like Eve White, the mother and primary personality. During therapy a third personality, Jane, revealed herself. Hypnosis was used to reconcile the characters. The therapist tried to allow one character, the calmer Jane, to dominate, and treatment ended with one character in control. This character was like Jane, but she labelled herself Evelyn White. 'Chris Sizemoore' was Eve's real name. Historically, psychologists believed that Multiple-Personality Disorder usually involved two or three sub-personalities, but according to the American Psychiatric Association, the average is nearer 15 and, although Eve had three faces, she claimed that she had 22 personalities, but they always appeared in groups of three. In a book that she wrote after her therapy was complete, she insisted that her identities were not a result of role-play or mood, but were separate identities with different appetites, handwriting, skills, IQ, facial expressions and dress codes.

As can be seen in the case study of Eve, a person with DID displays two or more distinct personalities, often called 'sub-personalities', each with a unique set of behaviours, emotions and thoughts. At any given time, one of the sub-personalities dominates the person's consciousness and interactions with other people.

Case study 2: George

George lost his short-term memory and it was a strange experience seeing him and then meeting him again, just five minutes later, when he behaved as if the first meeting had not occurred. The sheer bewilderment on his face as he tried to cope in this new, but alien, world signified the importance of the loss. One feature of his behaviour concerned the battle to order and sequence events in his life by attempting to make a written diary to keep track of the happenings in his life. Without the continuity that memory brings to us, life would lack coherence and meaning. We would not have a sense of who we are without our memory. Our expectations, values and goals in life could not possibly develop without memory. People with dissociative disorders are described in the DSM-IV-TR as having an alteration in the integrative functions of consciousness, identity or motor behaviour. 'Dissociation refers to a disruption in memory where a separation of one part of a person's identity from another occurs.' The disruption referred to occurs in the absence of an identifiable physical cause.

What is DID?

Dissociative disorders consist of a cluster of problems that involve changes in a person's personal memory, sense of identity or consciousness. Individuals suffering from a dissociative disorder may take on a new identity and wander away from their home for a period of time.

The DSM-IV-TR distinguishes four major sub-types of dissociative disorders:

1 *dissociative amnesia* – where individuals are unable to recall important personal information

2 *dissociative fugue* – a dreamlike, altered state of consciousness

3 *Dissociative Identity Disorder* – see below

4 *depersonalization disorder* – where a person's self-perception is altered in a disconcerting way.

All of the above, except depersonalization disorder, involve important personal events that cannot be recalled or where one's current identity is lost. This is why Multiple-Personality Disorder is now called Dissociative Identity Disorder in the DSM-IV-TR, as it signals the commonalities with other conditions. Since DSM-IV-TR now uses the term Dissociative Identity Disorder, this is the term we will use in this topic.

Alters (ego states)

We may all feel that our mood and behaviour varies to some extent from time to time. Despite this variability, we are recognizable as ourselves to our friends and family. In the case of DID (MPD), however, two or more separate identities appear to inhabit an individual's mind. In order to be diagnosed as suffering from DID under current DSM guidelines, an individual must have at least two separate modes of internal state and response. These are called 'alters' (ego states). They should exist independently of each other and each must be in control at different times. Finally, for a diagnosis of DID, there must be gaps in the personal memory of the alters with regard to other alters. In extreme cases, one alter may have no access to the memories of another alter and might not even be aware of the existence of the latter. People diagnosed with DID typically reveal between two and four alters, but during treatment it is not uncommon for even more to emerge (Davison *et al.* 2004).

THEORETICAL EXPLANATIONS OF DID

Psychodynamic explanation

Repression is one of the defence mechanisms described by Freud as part of his theory of human motivation (see Unit 19, p. 588). The purpose of defence mechanisms is to prevent anxiety by stopping painful thoughts and memories from reaching a person's consciousness. We all employ such defences, but in some cases the process results in the application of the defence repression in an extreme way that prevents normal functioning. This is one explanation of dissociative amnesia and dissociative fugue. Psychodynamic theorists suggest that hurtful experiences, such as a parent's extreme reaction to expressions of id impulses, especially unacceptable infantile sexual desires in the Oedipal stage, can lead to massive repression where a person unconsciously blocks the memory of emotionally charged situations.

In DID, individuals are seen by psychodynamic theorists as using the different identities to cope by escaping elsewhere. Theorists also point to extremely traumatic childhood experiences, especially childhood abuse, as being central to the occurrence of DID. Schreiber (1973) illustrates this vividly in the case of 'Sybil' (see Case study 3). Sybil's mother took delight in suspending her upside down from the ceiling and filling her bladder with cold water through an enema. According to psychodynamic theorists, children such as Sybil fear for their existence in what seems to them a cruel and dangerous world. Their only escape is to live in the world of another person, thus making them an observer from afar. Sybil's therapist, Dr Wilbur, described Sybil as looking for rescue from those around her, but after recognizing the futility of this search, she turned inwards in order to escape among her multiple personalities.

Case study 3: Sybil

In the 1980s, Sybil became a well-known example of someone suffering from DID. It was clear to most observers that Sybil was troubled and eager for help. She was not, however, aware of her identities/personalities until her therapist introduced her to them. In a *Horizon* programme broadcast on BBC television in 1999, clips of the film *Sybil* were shown to illustrate that the therapist tries quite hard to convince her that the personalities exist. *Horizon* then interviews Professor Hubert Spiegel, who explains his doubts about the authenticity of DID as a genuine disorder. He describes how, when Dr Wilbur needed to be out of town, she had asked Professor Spiegel to stand in as a locum. In therapy, Sybil was reported to have asked Professor Spiegel: 'Do you want me to be Helen?' He replied that it was not necessary, but if she wanted to, then she should feel free to do so. Sybil replied that if it was not necessary, she would prefer not to. He got the impression that she was being cued to live experiences as she recalled them, but as if she was someone else. With Professor Spiegel, however, she did not experience alters (separate identities/personalities). The *Horizon* programme makers suggested that Dr Wilbur was the answer to Sybil's willingness to please. At the time DID was almost unknown as a condition, yet almost overnight most therapists had clients with DID on their couches. Professor Spiegel called the clinics 'training schools', where therapists learned to uncover DIDs. This would fit well with a behavioural reinforcement view of DID.

Commentary
the psychodynamic explanation for DID

● *Abuse as a causal factor?* – There is some evidence to support the role of abuse. Kluft (1984) suggests that there have been instances of physical and/or sexual abuse in 97 per cent of cases.

However, DIDs are regarded as relatively rare in comparison to the known incidence of child abuse. In fact, fewer than 100 cases had been reported prior to 1970. We should bear in mind, however, that there has been a huge increase in DID to over 1,000 cases reported by the mid-1980s. We might ask has there been a corresponding increase in child abuse during this period? If so, this might be taken as providing some support for Kluft's view.

Behavioural explanation

Behaviourists suggest that the basis of DID is an acquired response learned through the mechanism of operant conditioning, with the reinforcement being the relief from anxiety that occurs when one's mind drifts to more neutral subjects (Casey 2001). In this respect, the behavioural view is similar to the psychodynamic view, where the central elements are trauma and anxiety avoidance. Behaviourists, however, believe that dissociations occur by chance and that subtle reinforcement processes are essential in order to keep the person unaware that the personality is using dissociation as a means of escape. Again, evidence is based largely on case studies.

Commentary
the behavioural explanation for DID

● *Can DID be learned?* – Comer (2004) points out that behavioural theory does not explain why more people do not develop DID, given that there are far more cases of abuse in children than there are DIDs. However, this criticism might reflect an outdated view of learning, where all stimuli are assumed to have an equal ability to elicit responses in all people. On the evidence of researchers such as Seligman (1971), one could explain the selective nature of DID as a predisposition in the genetic make-up of some individuals to respond in particular ways. Seligman has also used this approach to explain the selective nature of phobias.

● *Learning and emotional states* – Bower (1990) demonstrated that a person's particular mental state can affect their learning and memory. In the case of DIDs, experiences occurring in a dissociated state are more likely to be remembered in that state. Somehow, and this is not yet fully understood, different states represent different levels of arousal, so that memories acquired at one level of arousal will be forgotten in another level of arousal. Clusters of distinct memories develop and these are the sub-personalities. This seems plausible because it explains how personality transitions occur rapidly and in stressful circumstances, because large changes in arousal levels can occur in such circumstances. However, theorists do not agree on the relationship between arousal and memory.

Hypnosis and self-hypnosis

Some people believe that some form of self-hypnosis could induce people to forget unpleasant events. Since people suffering for DID are known to be particularly susceptible to hypnosis (Comer 2004), self-hypnosis has also been used to explain DID. Those supporting such explanations suggest that children are highly suggestible and that in traumatic circumstances, children would escape to fulfil a wish to be someone else. Others have suggested that whilst using hypnosis to treat psychological problems, therapists might have unwittingly created the 'alters' that sufferers of DID report (see below, Cohen 1995). There are, however, too many puzzles about the nature of hypnosis to be certain about its relationship with DID.

Commentary
the hypnosis explanation for DID

● *What is hypnosis?* – When someone is hypnotized, they appear to experience loss of control over their responses and become very open to suggestion. Within psychology, however, there is disagreement about whether hypnosis is a special trance-like state or whether it can be explained by normal social, attentional and cognitive processes (Barnier 2002). If the former is the case, then anybody who is susceptible to hypnosis might arguably become susceptible to the special state of DID. If the latter is the case, then this would suggest that DID is merely a social role that people take on due to expectations. Clearly, like DID itself, the status of hypnosis remains an unresolved issue in psychology.

● *Can hypnosis explain DID?* – Whether hypnosis is a special trance-like state or a role that people play, the question still has to be asked about whether it can explain the existence of DID? Despite claims that it can (Cohen 1995), a survey by Coons (1989) found that most DID patients had never been hypnotized. So, even if hypnosis does play some role in DID, this is unlikely to be the major explanation for it. This, of course, still leaves the possibility of self-hypnosis.

RESEARCH INTO DID AS A SPONTANEOUS OR IATROGENIC PHENOMENON

The explanations of DID in the theories discussed above are not particularly convincing, but despite this it has not been extensively investigated experimentally. In fact, it has been treated with scepticism by some researchers in the field.

According to Lilienfield *et al.* (1999), there are two views of the nature of DID:

● The *post-traumatic model (PTM)* regards DID as a distinct condition, best conceptualized as a defensive response to early trauma, as in the case of Sybil (see p. 739). To cope with the pain, individuals divide their experience into separate personalities and this allows the person to pretend that the abuse is happening to someone else. In this model, DID is viewed as a spontaneous disorder.

● The *sociocognitive model (SCM)*, on the other hand, sees both iatrogenic and sociocultural factors as playing a role in DID. To quote Lilienfield and colleagues, DID may be seen as 'a syndrome that consists of rule-governed and goal-directed experiences, and displays of multiple enactment that have been created, legitimized and maintained by social reinforcement ... these are synthesized by drawing on a wide variety of sources including broadcast media, cues provided by therapists, personal experiences and observations of individuals who have enacted multiple identities'.

DID as an iatrogenic phenomenon

When DID is described as an iatrogenic disorder, this implies that it has been induced unintentionally by therapeutic practice (Casey 2001, Comer 2004). The therapists create multiple identities or personalities by suggesting their existence during therapy or eliciting them by hypnotic suggestion (discussed above). By looking for such identities/personalities, the therapist is believed to reinforce certain patterns of behaviour by becoming more interested when their clients exhibit symptoms of dissociation.

A form of role-play?

Spanos (1994) suggests that DID is created by role-play. He argues that patients are influenced by their therapist's goals and expectations, rather like an actor who loses all sense of perspective and eventually believes that the role he is playing is real. In Spanos' (1985) study, undergraduate students role-played second personalities. This was done so well that the personalities being acted out even scored differently on a personality test, indicating that when the situation demands it, people can adopt another personality. This only indicates that convincing role-play is possible and not that DID is no more than role-play.

Case study 4: Ken Bianchi

Davison and Neale (1997) report on the case of Ken Bianchi, the hillside strangler, who attempted a defence of insanity for his killings. The court decided he was faking DID to avoid punishment. During the trial, Spanos (1985), who was highly sceptical of the existence of DID, managed to elicit another personality in Ken during a pre-trial meeting. In the interview the therapist said, 'I've talked to Ken, but I think there is another part of Ken that I have not spoken to'. Eventually Steve emerged. Steve hated Ken for being nice and Steve admitted that he murdered a number of women. The jury however remained unconvinced.

A North American diagnostic fad?

Gleaves (1996) notes that although the disorder occurs in other cultures, it is extremely rare in Europe and Japan, leading some, such as Mersky (1992), to suggest that it is merely a North American 'diagnostic fad'

Evaluation
DID as a spontaneous or iatrogenic disorder

- **Can iatrogenic factors alone explain DID?** – Gleaves (1996) criticizes the SCM, arguing that no disorder can be due solely to iatrogenic factors. Although iatrogenic factors may be a common cause of DID, the disorder can also occur spontaneously in their absence. For instance, DID occurs in societies where the involvement of mental health professionals is minimal. Individual differences in personality may therefore operate alongside personal and sociocultural factors to predispose people to DID. For example, a study by Scroppo et al. (1998) suggests that people suffering from DID showed increased imaginative activity, a reduced ability to integrate mental contents, a complex and driven cognitive style, and a highly unconventional view of reality. So, even supporters of the SCM do not deny that 'much of the psychopathological raw material from which DID is sculpted exists prior to professional intervention' (Lilienfield et al. 1999). In other words, iatrogenesis may contribute to DID, but no more so than many other social influences.

- **Shaped during therapy or spontaneous?** – Case study 4 illustrates concerns about DID presenting itself as a response simply because it is rewarding to do so (i.e. Bianchi's attempt to use it in his defence). Gleaves (1996) suggests that this is a key assumption behind the sociocultural model. However, it is recognized that in some instances

caused by the power of suggestion. Writing in the *Journal of Abnormal and Social Psychology*, Thigpen and Cleckey (1954) also admit that the relatively few cases reported – for example, those mentioned by William James (1890) and by Morton Prince (1906) – were treated sceptically by psychologists. McDougal (1908) is reported to have suggested that such cases may have been 'moulded in their development to a degree that cannot be determined'. This was said because the therapy was mostly based on hypnosis.

DID as a spontaneous phenomenon

DID can also occur spontaneously in the absence of iatrogenic factors. Thigpen and Cleckey (1957) seemed totally convinced by the 'three faces' of Eve (p. 737): 'A thousand alterations of manner, gesture, expression, posture, of nuances in reflex or instinctive reaction, of glance, of eyebrow tilting and eye movement all argued that this could only be another woman ... We think it unlikely that someone consciously acting could over a period of months avoid even one telling error or imperfection. But it is not impossible.'

DID may be feigned in order to avoid responsibility for criminal actions or to attract attention. Such problems have fuelled debates about its existence. Supporters of the SCM claim that there is confusion about the existence and causes of mental illness. Those arguing for the SCM do not claim that DID is not a 'real' phenomenon, in the sense that there are individuals who show all the signs of DID. They do, however, wonder if the condition is best described as a response to trauma (the idea behind the post-traumatic model) or as a 'socially influenced product that unfolds largely in response to the shaping influences of therapeutic practices, culturally based scripts, and social expectations' (Lilienfield et al. 1999).

- **Are the patterns of abnormality consistent between suffers of DID?** – Sceptics maintain that iatrogenesis is one of the main reasons for the reported increase in numbers and believe that DID patients do not really share any underlying causes or psychological processes that one would expect to see in any 'real' mental disorder (Cohen 1995). Alternatively, those who believe that dissociation occurs because of the results of severe trauma highlight other factors, such as more rigorous diagnostic criteria and wider awareness of DID, to account for the increase in numbers. In a study of 21 DID patients and 21 non-DID patients, Scroppo et al. (1998) reported that the DID patients demonstrated fairly consistent patterns of behaviour in a number of different areas and also showed a distinctive and theoretically consistent set of perceptual and cognitive characteristics that clearly differentiated them from the non-DID participants.

Commentary
the increase in reported cases of DID

The diagnosis of DID has been on the increase for 30 years. This raises the question of whether it is really becoming far more common or whether clinicians are simply diagnosing it more frequently?

● *Tightening up the DSM?* – Changes to the DSM criteria may have had an impact on DID diagnosis. Early editions of the DSM led to the diagnosis of schizophrenia for individuals with a wide range of abnormal patterns of behaviour, possibly including sufferers of DID (Turkington and Harris 2001). Under the increasingly more strict criteria for schizophrenia that were developed and used in more recent editions of the DSM, fewer individuals with mental health problems are now diagnosed with schizophrenia. Given that the symptoms of DID overlap with those of schizophrenia (for

example, problems of identity) the growth in cases of DID may well be a direct result of the reduction in the numbers being diagnosed with schizophrenia (Comer 2004).

● *Differences in acceptance of DID between the USA and the UK* – Although rates of reported cases of DID have soared in recent years, the vast majority of this increase has been due to diagnosis in the USA. David Cohen, writing in the *New Scientist* in 1995, describes a survey of 1200 American doctors of whom 70 per cent stated they believed in the diagnosis of DID and had each seen at least one case. Only 12 per cent did not believe in the diagnosis. By contrast, Cohen found that a large proportion of British psychiatrists saw the condition as being contrived. If this is the case, then the increase may be largely due to a different interpretation of the DSM system of classification and diagnosis in the USA, when compared with clinicians working in the UK.

ACTIVITY

Arguments relating to DID

<< Dissociative identity disorder is best understood as an iatrogenic phenomenon. >>

Prepare a list of arguments in support of this statement and then prepare arguments to challenge this statement. On balance, do you feel that there is more evidence to support or refute this claim?

CHECK YOUR UNDERSTANDING

Check your understanding of Multiple-Personality Disorder [Dissociative Identity Disorder] by answering these questions. Check your answers by looking back through Topic 2.

1 Describe what is meant by the terms 'iatrogenic' and 'spontaneous' in the context of Dissociative Identity Disorder (DID)?

2 List and briefly describe the four major sub-types of dissociative disorder.

3 Describe two case studies of DID, and identify any similarities and differences between them.

4 According to psychodynamic theory, which defence mechanism plays a major role in DID and how does it operate?

5 Prepare a descriptive summary of the behavioural explanation for DID in around 100 words and then identify two critical (i.e. AO2) points relating to this explanation.

6 What, according to Lilienfield *et al.* (1999), are the two views of the nature of DID?

7 What name is given to the explanation for DID as 'a syndrome created, legitimized and maintained by social reinforcement ... [and] synthesized by drawing on a wide variety of sources'?

8 Describe the post-traumatic model of DID.

9 Construct a 150-word précis evaluating the claim that DID might be an iatrogenic disorder and a summary of the evidence that could be used to present a case to counter the claim that DID might be an iatrogenic disorder?

10 Briefly discuss the relationship between abuse and DID.

REVISION SUMMARY

Having covered this topic, you should be able to:

✓ describe four case studies of Dissociative Identity Disorder

✓ discuss three possible causes of Dissociative Identity Disorder and evaluate the evidence to support these different theoretical explanations of DID

✓ describe and evaluate the evidence for and against Dissociative Identity Disorder as an iatrogenic phenomenon

✓ describe and evaluate the evidence for and against Dissociative Identity Disorder as a spontaneous phenomenon.

EXAMPLE EXAM QUESTIONS

Below are some **possible examination questions** set on this topic, along with hints to help you understand and approach each question effectively:

1 Critically consider whether Multiple-Personality Disorder (Dissociative Identity Disorder) is an iatrogenic or spontaneous phenomenon. (30 marks)

> As with all exam questions, you need to identify the AO1 (descriptive) content and the AO2 (commentary) content. Here, you could further divide your essay into an 'iatrogenic' part and a 'spontaneous' part. So, in one quarter of the answer (about 200 words, 10 minutes of writing) you may describe the evidence for iatrogenesis. In the second half you should comment on this evidence, e.g. considering the validity of the evidence. The final two parts of the essay will look at the evidence for spontaneity and then commentary on this. This is only one possible plan.

2 'Case studies of Multiple-Personality Disorder, such as those of Eve by Thigpen and Cleckley, suggest that this is a spontaneous phenomenon.'

With reference to the quotation above, discuss the causes of Multiple-Personality Disorder (Dissociative Identity Disorder). (30 marks)

> Sometimes, questions require that you address the quotation in your answer, as here. The quotation is written in such a way as to provide ideas about how you might answer the question. In this case one case study is suggested (an example from the specification), but you do not have to discuss this study. You do, however, need to discuss some case studies and consider whether they do or do not suggest that MPD is a spontaneous disorder. The penalty for *not* addressing the quotation is a maximum of 9 marks for AO2. AO2 evaluation may be achieved by referring to other research evidence. In order to attract AO2 credit, this must be *used* as effective critical commentary not simply described. This means that you have to be explicit about what the evidence demonstrates. You may also, as part of your critical commentary, consider flaws in the studies that might challenge the validity of the conclusions.

3 (a) Outline **two or more** case studies of Multiple-Personality Disorder (Dissociative Identity Disorder). (15 marks)

(b) To what extent have case studies, such as those described in part (a), led us to believe that Multiple-Personality Disorder (Dissociative Identity Disorder) is iatrogenic? (12 marks)

> Both the AO1 and AO2 parts of this question are clearly specified. 'Case studies' are identified in the specification in relation to MPD and so you are expected to know the details of at least two. If you only describe one, there would be a partial performance penalty in both halves of this question. Part (b) of this question focuses on iatrogenesis alone. You can use your arguments for and against spontaneous explanations but only insofar as you do *use* them as part of an effective and *sustained* commentary on iatrogenesis. Your focus at all times must be on 'what does this tell us about iatrogenic causes?'.

continued on next page

4 Compare and contrast case studies of Multiple-Personality Disorder (Dissociative Identity Disorder). (30 marks)

> The term 'compare and contrast' is explained in full on p. 937. The easiest way to answer this question would be to describe case studies (minimum two) for the AO1 component and, for the AO2 component, to identify any similarities and differences between them. Such similarities/differences may be along the lines of spontaneous versus iatrogenic causation or could relate to the validity of the studies, the number of 'alters' involved, or even possible gender or culture differences.

Topic 3 >> Culture-bound syndromes

Imagine you are a psychiatrist working in East Asia and a man is referred to you because he believes his penis is retracting into his abdomen and that if it is allowed to do so, it will kill him. He shows signs of intense anxiety and consistently holds on to his penis in order to stop it from disappearing into his body. You carry out a number of tests and find that you can rule out schizophrenia or obsessive-compulsive disorder. You take down DSM-IV-TR from your bookshelf in an attempt to find some other possible diagnosis. The problem is that it doesn't give you any guidance on this problem. Despite this, the man is demonstrating a problem that is not uncommon in his culture. It's called 'koro' and is one of a large number of culture-bound syndromes (CBSs) (Hallak *et al.* 2000; see Table 24.5 and Case study 3 on p. 747).

Although both the ICD and DSM aim to be universal and scientific, such culture-bound syndromes do not fit comfortably into them. Although the DSM now lists 25 CBSs, it does not provide any criteria for them (Carlson *et al.* 2000). In fact, CBSs raise a serious challenge to both of these classification systems. In this topic, we will look at what CBSs are, including a categorization system and some examples of CBSs currently recognized. Finally, we will examine the crucial question of whether CBSs really are 'unique ways of being mad' (Gross 2001), or whether they are merely localized manifestations of illnesses listed in the DSM/ICD.

A DEFINITION OF CULTURE-BOUND SYNDROMES

The ICD-10 states that CBSs share two main features:

- They are not easily accommodated by the categories in established and internationally used psychiatric classifications.

- They were first described in, and subsequently closely associated with, a particular population or cultural area.

DSM-IV-TR defines CBSs as 'locality-specific patterns of aberrant behaviour and troubling experience that may or may not be linked to a specific DSM-IV diagnostic category. Many of these patterns are indigenously considered to be "illnesses", or at least afflictions, and most have local names' (p. 898). The term 'indigenous' is central to the concept of the CBS. Kim and Berry (1993) define it as developing within a culture (i.e. is not 'imported') and serving a function for that culture. So, for example, Coca Cola is consumed internationally, but is indigenous only to the USA.

The DSM definition of CBSs is not, however, without its problems. Humphreys (1999) highlights the following issues:

- 'Locality-specific patterns' – several CBSs are found across quite a large number of cultures; does this then weaken their right to be called CBSs?

- 'Aberrant' – whose criteria are used to judge what is considered to be aberrant?

- 'Troubling' – to whom?

- 'Indigenously considered to be an illness' – does this mean that, if the local people do not consider it to be an illness but rather view it as acceptable, 'normal' behaviour, then it does not count as a CBS?

- What may appear to outsiders to be 'aberrant behaviour and troubling experiences' may be quite logical in the context of a particular culture (see the example of *pa-feng* in Table 24.5).

Closely related to the concept of CBSs is that of 'folk illness', and the way in which a folk illness is treated through folk medicine (Neff undated). These, too, are concepts of illness, which are held by localized (indigenous) groups of people. Bell's (1999) *Folk Illness Glossary*, for example, includes five CBSs out of a total of 21 illnesses. The principal difference between the two is that the majority of folk illnesses do not relate to mental disorders, but to what Pfeiffer (1982) refers to as 'concrete' illnesses. So, for example, *Masuk angin*, found in Indonesia, means 'wind enters' and refers to bloated stomach, and is believed to result from standing in windy places and staying out after dark.

Table 24.5 >> Examples of culture-bound syndromes by geographical area

East Asia

China

>> *Koro* – The belief that the penis (or, more rarely, the vulva or nipples) is retracting into the body and that when it is fully retracted, death will result. Panic attempts to keep the penis from retracting can lead to severe physical damage. Koro occasionally occurs in local epidemics. Also found in Assam and Thailand. Found in isolated cases in the USA and Europe.

>> *Pa-feng* – A phobic fear of the wind. Sufferers fear an excess of *yin* (negative energy) from exposure to the wind and wrap up in warm clothing and eat hot foods.

>> *Shenkui* – Anxiety or panic symptoms. Symptoms include dizziness, backache, fatigue, general weakness, insomnia, frequent dreams and sexual dysfunction. The condition is attributed to excessive semen loss from frequent intercourse, masturbation or nocturnal emission. The men fear semen loss because it represents the loss of their vital essence.

Japan

>> *Imu* – Imitative behaviour (usually amongst women) that seems beyond control. Movements and speech are copied and individuals in this state are compliant to commands to do things that they ordinarily would not (for example, uttering obscenities).

>> *Shinkeishitsu* – A syndrome marked by obsessions, perfectionism, ambivalence and social withdrawal.

>> *Taijin kyofusho* – Intense fear that one's body, body parts or bodily functions are displeasing, embarrassing or offensive to other people.

South and Southeast Asia

India

>> *Dhat* or *jiryan* – Semen-loss syndrome (see *shenkui*, China)*.

Indonesia

>> *Latah* (see *imu*, Japan)* – Also occurs in Malaysia where it is more frequent in middle-aged women.

Malaysia

>> *Amok* – Usually found in males. A period of brooding followed by short-duration, wild, aggressive behaviour, in which there are outbursts of violent, aggressive, destructive and even homicidal behaviour. (The term 'running amok' is in common usage in the West.)

>> *Koro* (see China)*

Sri Lanka

>> *Sukra prameha* – Semen-loss syndrome (see *shenkui*, China)*

The Mediterranean

Greece

>> *Nerva* – Distress. It refers to a general state of vulnerability to stressful life experiences. There are many symptoms including emotional distress, headaches, irritability, digestive and sleep disturbances, nervousness, an inability to concentrate and tingling sensations.

Spain

>> *Mal de ojo* – The 'evil eye'. Occurs as a common form of disease, misfortune and social disruption throughout the Mediterranean, Latin America and the Muslim world.

Latin America

>> *Bilis or colera* – Part of a general Latin American form of distress and explanation of physical or mental illness as a result of extreme emotion, which upsets the humours (described in terms of hot and cold). Bilis and colera specifically implicate anger in the cause of illness.

>> *Mal de pelea* (Puerto Rico) (see *amok*, Malaysia)*

>> *Mal do ojo* (see Spain)*

>> *Nervios* (similar to *nerva*, Greece)*

Native Americans, Arctic and Polynesia

>> *Cafard/cathard* (Polynesia) (see *amok*, Malaysia)*

>> *Iich'aa* (Navaho) (see *amok*, Malaysia)*

>> *Kuru* (New Guinea) – A progressive psychosis and dementia indigenous to cannibalistic tribes in the region. It results from an aberrant protein that is capable of replicating itself by deforming other proteins in the brain. It has been identified with a form of Creuzfeldt-Jacob Disease (CJD).

>> *Windigo or witiko* (Algonkian Indians, Northeast USA; Eastern Canada) (see Case study 2, p. 747)

USA and Western Europe

>> *Anorexia nervosa* – Severe restriction of food intake, associated with morbid fear of obesity. Other methods may also be used to lose weight, including excessive exercise. May overlap with bulimia nervosa.

>> *Bulimia nervosa* – Binge eating followed by purging through self-induced vomiting, laxatives or diuretics. A morbid fear of obesity; may overlap with anorexia nervosa.

> ** Indicates similarity of symptoms, although they may not be identical.*

Looking for patterns

There is a danger that we may regard CBSs merely as a list of exotic or quaint illnesses that occur in far-away places. This would undervalue their significance entirely. We should bear in mind that CBSs also exist in Western countries, although they may not appear to be labelled as such on either ICD-10 or the DSM-IV-TR. Examples of this are anorexia nervosa and bulimia nervosa, both of which are largely restricted to Western cultures (Comer 2004). We need to view CBSs in the light of what patterns of similarities and difference we can detect. Pfeiffer (1982) argues that it is impossible to have a single classificatory category called CBSs (in the way that the ICD-10 has neurotic disorders and personality disorders, for example). This is because they are too diverse and, perhaps most importantly, only make sense in terms of the values of the cultures within which they occur.

Despite this, we can still try to impose some form of organization on them. One of the most prolific writers on CBSs in recent times, Timothy Hall (1998a, 1998b, 1998c, 1998d) categorizes CBSs in the following way (Hall 1998a):

1 a psychiatric illness (not organically caused) which is locally recognized as an illness and which does not match a recognized Western category (e.g. *amok**).

2 a psychiatric illness (not organically caused) which is locally recognized as an illness and resembles a Western category, but may lack some symptoms that are regarded as important in many cultures (e.g. *taijin kyofusho**).

3 a psychiatric illness not yet recognized in the West (e.g. *kuru**).

4 a psychiatric illness (which may or may not be organically caused) that is found in many cultures, but is only regarded as an illness in one or a few (e.g. *koro**).

5 culturally accepted forms of illness which would not be regarded as acceptable in mainstream Western medicine (e.g. *mal de ojo**).

6 a syndrome supposedly occurring in a given culture, but which does not in fact exist (e.g. *windigo***) which is used to justify the expulsion or execution of an outcast in the same way that witchcraft was.

* These specific CBSs are described in Table 24.5.
** Windigo is described in Case study 2 on p. 747.

THREE CASE STUDIES OF SYNDROMES APPARENTLY BOUND BY CULTURE

Where in the world do they exist?

Hall offers a number of categorizations of CBSs: (a) alphabetically, (b) by symptoms and (c) by geographical locality. Since we are exploring whether or not psychiatric illnesses can be classified globally, the examples of CBSs in Table 24.5 are listed in terms of where they are found in the world. This arrangement also emphasizes that CBSs exist in North America and in Western Europe (the homeland of the DSM and the ICD).

The descriptions of specific CBSs in Table 24.5 are taken from DSM-IV (pp. 845–9), Berry *et al.* (1992), Hall (1998b, 1998d) and Humphreys (1999). A total of 36 different CBSs have been identified across the world. When preparing for the A-level exam, you would only need to refer to a small sample of these to illustrate your answers.

Case study 1: Dibuk ak Suut and *latah*

Dibuk ak Suut is a Malaysian woman who, following a fright, will sometimes enter a trance-like state. During this trance she is likely to shout out offensive phrases and may also mimic the behaviour of those around her. However, despite her swearing, she is quite compliant and will obey commands from others during this trance. On recovery from the trance she will generally feel embarrassed by her vulgarity and apologize profusely. This strange behaviour is known as *latah* in Malaysia and is similar to *Imu* found in Japan (Osborne 2001). *Latah* nearly always occurs in middle-aged women of Malay and Javanese origin. It is one of the CBSs now recognized by DSM-IV-TR (as are those described in Case studies 2 and 3 opposite).

Despite its recognition in DSM-IV-TR, *latah* remains a controversial CBS. Robert Bartholomew (1994) described how, after marrying into a Malay family, he would often observed *latah* in his female inlaws, but only when there was a sizeable audience. He also noted that these middle-aged women appeared to be incapable of going into this state when they were holding a baby or doing some other activity which might have lead to someone becoming harmed. Following numerous personal observations, Bartholomew eventually became convinced that *latah* was a self-induced act performed by those who desire attention.

A2 Individual Differences

Case study 2: Red Bear and *windigo*

Red Bear was a member of the Algonquin native American hunters. One day, having returned some days previously from a failed hunting expedition, he suddenly sat bolt upright and stared at his wife lying next to him. He had just awoken from a dream of *windigo* – a mythical monster with a heart of ice. He felt cold and yet he sweated profusely. As he looked at his wife, she appeared to turn into a wild deer. Red Bear drew his knife and plunged it into his wife again and again, believing that she was the prey he had been hunting. On hearing the screams of his wife, Red Bear's kinsmen rushed into his wigwam where the body lay limp. Outraged they dragged him outside and killed him swiftly (Comer 2004).

Red Bear was suffering from a condition known to afflict native Americans in the northern USA and Eastern Canada called *windigo* (or sometimes *witiko*). The disorder was considered to be due to being bewitched by a giant supernatural monster, which made them want to commit murder and devour their victims. Although windigo is well documented for native American tribes in the north, in most cases it appears to involve desires which are not actually carried through. Fortunately, it is very rare for a tribesman like Red Bear actually to kill a member of his household. This might be taken as evidence that the desire to kill and cannibalize others may not be as powerful as reported and, unlike others who generally experience windigo, perhaps Red Bear was suffering from a serious mental illness (Comer 2004).

Case study 3: H.K.F. and *shook yong*

H.K.F. was a 34-year-old Chinese man who had an unusual experience while visiting a cinema. During the film he felt the need to urinate and went to the gents toilet in the foyer. As he was urinating, he suddenly began to lose feeling in the genital area and the notion that his penis was going to retract into his body occurred to him. His penis appeared to be getting smaller and this made him feel extremely anxious. For the next 30 minutes he sat on the floor holding his penis so that it wouldn't disappear into his abdomen. Finally, this feeling began to disappear and he was able to leave the cinema. H.K.F. went to see a medical expert who prescribed him with some pills. The doctor reassured H.K.F. that the idea of a man's penis disappearing into his body was a social myth and that it couldn't really happen. Following his doctor's reassurance no further attacks occurred.

This belief that a penis can disappear into a man's body is called *shook yong* in China and *koro* in Malaysia and has also been given the name 'genital retraction syndrome'. Although it generally occurs in individual cases, there are also accounts of it taking hold of hundreds or even thousands of men at the same time, in which case it may be seen as an epidemic (Leng 1985). Despite these accounts, we should bear in mind that for such a widely reported and powerful disorder, all it took for H.K.F. was a little reassurance from his doctor to stop *shook yong* returning.

ARGUMENTS FOR AND AGAINST THE EXISTENCE OF CULTURE-BOUND SYNDROMES

Do CBSs exist at all?

This is the first, and perhaps most important, question to ask. The list in Table 24.5 would seem to suggest that they do exist. However, increasingly, some may have become historical 'curiosities' as the world has shrunk due to technological developments, especially those relating to travel and communication. In particular, we should point to what has been called the Americanization of the world, i.e. the increasing influence of American culture in the world today. Pfeiffer (1982, p. 216) argues:

<<The universal spread of technical civilization and of the scientific medicine pertaining to it, has caused the disappearance of well-defined syndromes that are specific to a certain culture ... This does not mean, however, that the dimensions of cultural influence ... have lost their meaning.

They have merely become harder to recognize now that the contrast between folk medicine and scientific medicine is missing.>>

The answer to our first question would appear to be that CBSs *do* exist, although several may be harder to find now than, say, 50 years ago. Furthermore, as noted above, the 'Americanization of the world' might bring with it new CBSs, such as eating disorders.

Can CBSs be classified?

Another key question to raise is whether the CBSs are really 'unique ways of being mad', or whether they could be assimilated within those classificatory and diagnostic clusters of, for example, the DSM. The ICD-10 states:

<<The status of these disorders is controversial: many researchers argue that they differ only in

degree from disorders already included in existing psychiatric classifications, such as anxiety disorders and reactions to stress, and that they are therefore best regarded as local variations of disorders that have long been recognized. Their exclusive occurrence in specific population or cultural areas has also been questioned.>>
(Unit V(F), p. 1)

However, before we can begin to address this second question, there is an even more fundamental one that we must ask which is – are the CBSs classifiable at all? Certainly, they are not classifiable as a single, coherent entity, as both Arieti and Meth (1959) and Pfeiffer (1982) have convincingly argued. CBSs are far too dissimilar and can only be fully understood when viewed through the values of the different cultures in which they are used to make sense of certain symptoms. However, Hall (1998c) argues that we should not merely regard the 36 CBSs as different entities, as many of them share common symptoms or characteristics.

Universal or culturally relative?

If CBSs cannot be accommodated within a single individual category, can the various forms of CBSs be accommodated in the DSM and ICD classification and diagnostic systems? In examining cross-cultural analysis of psychopathology, Berry *et al.* (1992) argue that three positions can be taken in relation to abnormalities, mental disorders, etc. These are:

● *absolute* – unchanging in terms of origin, symptoms, etc. in all cultures studied

● *universal* – found in all cultures, but affected by cultural influences in terms of what brings them out, what forms they take, etc.

● *culturally relative* – unique to some cultures and understandable only in terms of values and concepts held within those cultures.

Since CBSs clearly do not fit the 'absolute' position, do they fit either the second or third categories listed above? Are they mental disorders which are found in most, if not all, cultures, but which are triggered by different factors in different cultures and take somewhat different 'forms'? Or are they really unique to certain cultures? A chief supporter for the 'universal' view is Pow-Meng Yap (1974) who argues as follows:

● Human mental disorders are broad, spanning all cultures, i.e. are 'supracultural'. So, for example, the dopamine hypothesis has been put forward as a biopsychological explanation for schizophrenia (see Unit 25). Thus, it could be argued that symptoms emerge from within the individual and these symptoms cluster together to form discrete categories of mental illnesses. This was precisely the starting point of contemporary psychiatry in the early work of Kraeplin in the late 19th century.

● Comparative psychiatry aims to establish common links across cultures in a similar manner to the way in which comparative psychology explores links between behaviours in different species. CBSs are seen as culturally-specific expressions of common human problems and disorders that are addressed by the ICD and DSM. For example, Yap (1974) believes that *latah* is a local cultural expression of 'primary fear reaction', *amok* is a 'rage reaction' and *windigo* is a 'possession state'.

● *Why CBSs might not be 'at home' in the DSM?* – Pfeiffer argues that CBSs must be viewed at the level of the individual culture, rather than from the vantage point of Washington DC, the home of the American Psychological Association, because they are specific in the following four aspects:

   1 Cultures differ in those things that place people under unbearable stress; in one culture it may be work and status; in another, family relations.

   2 Different cultures allow and ban certain expressions and behaviours. What might be permitted as a culturally acceptable release mechanism in certain cultures may not be allowed in others.

   3 We may have culture-specific interpretations – a behaviour is one thing, but what we take it to mean and what sense we make of it, is entirely another. Think how certain women were 'discovered' to be witches because of culturally specific interpretations of their behaviour (Ussher 1992).

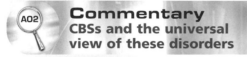

Commentary
CBSs and the universal view of these disorders

● *Supracultural or specific to cultures?* – Pfeiffer (1982) argues against the supracultural position on CBSs. He agrees with Yap (1974) that the manifestations of illnesses, i.e. the human behaviours, may indeed be 'a universally human character', but argues that this is only one part of the issue. His view is that the diagnostic and classificatory systems of the Western world are so qualitatively different in nature to the folk illnesses and medicines specific to particular cultures that they cannot be integrated except by distortion. He writes: 'The attempt to bring the culture-bound syndromes into a psychiatric diagnostic system is doomed to failure because the symptoms in the two spheres are selected and ordered from qualitatively disparate points of view.'

continued on next page

A2 Individual Differences

Commentary continued
**CBSs and the universal view
of these disorders**

4 We have not explored the variety of culture-specific ways of treating disorders, but folk medicine is a good example of the ways in which indigenous peoples treat their illnesses.

So, if CBSs are a form of folk illness to be treated by folk medicine, then they are qualitatively inconsistent with the aims and purposes of the ICD and the DSM.

CHECK YOUR UNDERSTANDING

Check your understanding of culture-bound syndromes by answering these questions from memory. You can check your answers by looking back through Topic 3.

1 What is a culture-bound syndrome (CBS) and what two features do CBSs share?

2 How does the DSM define a CBS? Identify two problems with this definition of a CBS.

3 Why, according to Pfeiffer (1982), is it impossible to have a single classificatory category called 'culture-bound syndromes'?

4 Who has devised a category system for CBSs?

5 Some researchers believe that CBSs are found in all cultures, but that the form they take depends on cultural influences. What name is given to this view and by whom?

6 What four reasons did Pfeiffer (1982) give in support of the view that CBSs are unique to some cultures?

7 Prepare a 150-word précis of the evidence *for* the existence of CBSs?

8 Prepare a 150-word précis of the evidence *against* the existence of CBSs?

REVISION SUMMARY

Having covered this topic, you should be able to:

✔ describe what is meant by the term 'culture-bound syndromes' and outline some examples

✔ describe three case studies of syndromes apparently bound by culture

✔ discuss the arguments for and against the existence of CBSs.

EXAMPLE EXAM QUESTIONS

Below are some **possible examination questions** set on this topic, along with hints to help you understand and approach each question effectively:

1 Discuss case studies of syndromes apparently bound by culture.   (30 marks)

This is a generous question which most candidates should find easily accessible. One danger may lie in over-enthusiasm about describing case studies (a minimum of two is required for full marks) and a consequent loss of time available for AO2 material. Always aim to provide an equal amount of AO1 and AO2. One way to assist this is to prepare précis versions of material that you are likely to have to use. For example, you might reduce each case study to about 100 words of description and 100 words of evaluation. This would permit you to present about four case studies in an exam answer (as 40-minute answers are about 800 words). Such breadth is an important criterion for the marks you receive.

continued on next page

2 (a) Outline **two or more** case studies of syndromes apparently bound by culture (e.g. Koro, Dhat). (15 marks)

(b) To what extent have case studies, such as those described in part (a), led us to believe that some syndromes are bound by culture? (15 marks)

> Part (a) might contain the same descriptive material as you used for question 1. If you feel that you know two case studies in enough detail, you can restrict your answer to just these two. This will not limit you in part (b) because it only says 'such as' which means you can refer to other case studies. Examples of two culture-bound syndromes are provided because these are the ones given in the specification. Remember that you do not have to address these particular examples, but make sure that you do describe case studies rather than the culture-bound syndromes.

3 'One of the major criticisms of classificatory systems is that they have, until recently, ignored the influence of culture and existence of culture-bound syndromes'.

With reference to the issues such as those in the quotation above, critically consider the existence of culture-bound syndromes. (30 marks)

> Here, there is no requirement to address the quotation. The quotation is intended to suggest that you might draw on material relating to classificatory systems (the subject of Topic 1). Questions may be set spanning more than one topic within any unit. There is no directive to use case studies in your answer, though you might refer to them as part of the AO2 content of your answer. Take care, if using these as AO2, not to spend too much time *describing* them but focus on using them as effective AO2.

4 Discuss arguments **for** the existence of culture-bound syndromes. (30 marks)

> You may be asked to discuss either the arguments for the existence of culture-bound syndromes, or those against. Much of the same material can be used in both essays, except you must clearly shape your answer to the particular question set. For this question, AO1 marks are given for any arguments *for* the case. This may include reference to case studies or descriptions of particular culture-bound syndromes. Your commentary may include arguments *against* their existence but only if such arguments have been placed next to, and comment on, an argument *for* culture-bound syndromes.

UNIT SUMMARY

Topic 1: Classificatory systems

● The **ICD** and the **DSM** offer clinical means of **classifying** and diagnosing **psychological abnormality**. The ICD is a classification tool, whereas the DSM enables the clinician to classify and diagnose. The World Health Organization in Europe produces the ICD and the American Psychiatric Association in the USA produces the DSM. Both the ICD and DSM are regularly revised.

● The ICD consists of 11 categories of mental disorder, including mood (affective) disorders, behavioural syndromes and mental retardation. Assessment on the DSM involves five axes: clinical disorders; personality disorders and mental retardation; general medical conditions; psychosocial and environmental problems; and the Global Assessment of Functioning scale.

● It is important to carry out **research into the reliability** and **validity** of the **classification and diagnosis** of mental disorders. **Rosenhan's** (1973) classic research study is an example of such research. Davison *et al.* (2004) suggest that three types of validity are important when assessing any classification system – content validity, criterion validity and construct validity. The Composite International Diagnostic Interview (or CIDI), that involves patients answering a series of computer-generated questions, seems promising in terms of both improved validity and reliability.

● There is also considerable empirical evidence to suggest that there is **diagnostic bias** relating to race, class and gender. For example, there is evidence of overdiagnosis of schizophrenia in West Indian, immigrant in-patients in Britain. Worell and Remer (1992) suggest that gender can influence diagnosis in four ways: disregarding the environmental context, differential diagnosis based on gender, therapists' misjudgements, and therapists' orientation that may be gender biased.

Topic 2: Multiple-Personality Disorder (Dissociative Identity Disorder)

● **Dissociative identity disorder** (or **Multiple-Personality Disorder**, as it used to be more commonly known) is illustrated by the **case studies** of George, Eve (documented by **Thigpen and Cleckey** 1957), Sybil and Ken. It has, however, been subject to few experimental investigations. In 1970, only 100 cases had been reported, but by the mid-1980s this had risen to well over 1,000. Mersky (1992) argues that many of these cases are **iatrogenic** (i.e. they have been manufactured by the therapist) rather than being **spontaneous** (i.e. a real condition).

● A number of explanations for Dissociative Identity Disorder (DID) have been put forward, including a psychodynamic explanation, a behavioural explanation and self-hypnosis. Two views of DID have become dominant – the **post-traumatic model (PTM)** and the **sociocognitive model (SCM)**. SCM gives a larger role to iatrogenesis than does the PTM. The results of a study carried out by Scroppo *et al.* (1998) suggest that DID is associated with genuine, distinctive and theoretically coherent psychological processes.

Topic 3: Culture-bound syndromes

● **Culture-bound syndromes** (CBSs) are included in the latest editions of both the ICD and DSM: 36 CBSs (e.g. **koro, dhat**) have currently been identified and described. They are often listed by the geographical region in the world where they occur.

● The **existence of CBSs** offers a clear illustration of the importance of cultural factors in psychiatric classification and diagnosis. However, Pfeiffer (1982) argues that it is not possible to have a single classificatory system because CBSs are too diverse and only make sense within their cultural setting.

● There are **arguments for and against the existence of culture-bound syndromes**, i.e. whether they have the same clinical status as other pathologies listed in the ICD and DSM or are merely 'exotic' manifestations of pathologies that are already included. The former position is supported by Pfeiffer (1982), whilst Yap (1974) advocates the latter position. Hall (1999) argues that many CBSs do not fit easily into the Western classificatory and diagnostic systems and are qualitatively inconsistent with the aims and purposes of the ICD and DSM (i.e. a scientific and universal approach).

FURTHER RESOURCES

Caplan, P.J. (1995) *They Say You're Crazy: How the World's Most Powerful Psychiatrists Decide Who's Normal*, Reading: MA: Addison-Wesley.

A controversial look at how clinicians make diagnoses.

Nolen-Hoeksema, S. (1990) *Sex differences in Depression*, Stanford: Stanford University Press.

A very readable account of why women are more frequently diagnosed as suffering from mental illness and, in particular, depression than men.

Davison, G.C., Neale, J.M. and Kring, A.M. (2004) *Abnormal Psychology* (9th edn), Chichester: Wiley.

An up-to-date account of the history, causes and classification of mental illness.

Websites

www.worthpublishers.com/comer

A series of multiple-choice questions on mental illness.

http://weber.ucsd.edu/~thall/cbs_intro.html
and
http://weber.ucsd.edu/~thall/cbs_frame.html

These two sites provide an introduction to, and descriptions of, culture-bound syndromes.

http://weber.ucsd.edu/~thall/cbs_koro.html

A description of koro – an Asian CBS.

UNIT 25

Psychopathology

PREVIEW

After you have read this unit, you should be able to:

>> describe the clinical characteristics of schizophrenia

>> describe and evaluate biological and psychological explanations of schizophrenia

>> describe the clinical characteristics of depression

>> describe and evaluate biological and psychological explanations of depression

>> describe the clinical characteristics of anxiety disorders, including phobias and obsessive–compulsive disorder

>> describe and evaluate biological and psychological explanations of anxiety disorders.

INTRODUCTION

Psychopathology is the study of psychological or mental disorders. Modern diagnostic systems distinguish between many different kinds of mental disorder, but in this unit we will consider three major types: schizophrenia, depression and anxiety disorders.

A number of different explanations for mental disorders have been proposed and researched, and these tend to be split into two major groupings.

- The first represents the *medical model*, which views mental disorders as an 'illness' or a 'disease'. Research in this field examines whether the mental disorder can be explained by neurological damage to the brain or by a dysfunction in the action of neurotransmitters (brain chemicals). In addition, the medical model seeks to establish whether particular mental disorders are inherited through genetic predisposition.

- The second grouping represents the view that mental disorders are problems caused by *psychological dysfunction*, relating to the interaction between individuals and their environment. These explanations include views based on learning theory, cognitive–behavioural theories, psychodynamic theories and social learning theories. In addition, there is a theory known as the 'diathesis-stress model', which examines the interaction of social factors with other vulnerability factors.

You will find that some explanations seem plausible for certain disorders, but not for others. As yet, no one cause (aetiology) has been accepted as the complete explanation for any single mental disorder, and an open mind on a combination of aetiologies seems more appropriate.

Jane Willson

1 What is the most likely emotion that you would feel in each of the situations shown in the pictures?

2 How might you show your emotion?

It is natural to experience strong emotions at events such as these. For example, to feel sad at a funeral or nervous when giving a talk in public is understandable and appropriate.

3 How would you react if someone started laughing out loud at the funeral? Or started mumbling incoherently while giving their talk?

Mental disorders can distort normal emotional responses.

People suffering from schizophrenia may experience inappropriate affect (feeling/emotion), such as crying at a joke or laughing at a funeral.

Someone with depression may experience an exaggerated grief response to loss or bereavement or fail to experience pleasure even about 'good' events such as collecting a degree at an awards ceremony.

While it is perfectly normal to feel anxious when facing a challenging, new situation, those who suffer from anxiety disorders experience irrational responses, e.g. extreme anxiety when eating in a restaurant or speaking in public.

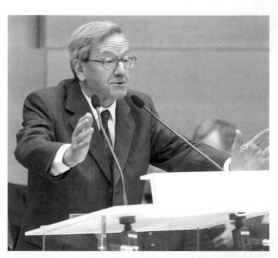

Schizophrenia: a serious mental disorder characterized by severe disruptions in psychological functioning and a loss of contact with reality.

Depression (unipolar disorder): a type of mood disorder where the person experiences feelings of great sadness, worthlessness and guilt, and finds the challenges of life overwhelming.

Bipolar depression (manic-depressive disorder): a mood disorder characterized by extremes of mania and depression.

Reactive depression: a reaction to stressful events outside ourselves, such as the death of someone close, redundancy or failing exams.

Endogenous depression: thought to arise from within the person, independent of external events.

Learned helplessness: a psychological state produced as a result of being exposed to

uncontrollable events. Observed in people who give up trying to cope because previous attempts have been frustrated and led to failure.

Anxiety disorder: the most common of adult mental disorders, characterized by severe anxiety. Phobias are probably the most familiar of these disorders.

Phobia: a type of anxiety disorder where there is a persistent and unreasonable fear of an object or situation.

Preparedness: species-specific, biological predisposition to fear certain potentially dangerous stimuli, dating back to our ancestors.

Obsessive–compulsive disorder (OCD): an anxiety disorder in which the individual is plagued with uncontrollable thoughts (obsessions) and performs seemingly senseless rituals (compulsive behaviours).

Unit 25 // Psychopathology

WHAT IS SCHIZOPHRENIA?

Schizophrenia is the condition most often associated with the term 'madness'. The earliest clear descriptions of this disorder date from the end of the 18th century, but it was not until 1911 that the Swiss physician, Eugen Bleuler first coined the term 'schizophrenia'. Although the word literally means 'split mind', Bleuler was not referring to a split personality, but to a disorder associated with disconnected thought processes and a loss of contact with reality. Since that time, the term schizophrenia has been used widely and indiscriminately so that, by the 1950s, it had been reduced to an overarching label for any kind of severe mental disorder. This led to low reliability in diagnosis,

which, in turn, meant that research into the underlying causes and into effective treatments was hampered. Clinicians came to realize that they needed to agree on a common, operational definition of schizophrenia if any progress was to be made. There is still no universally agreed definition and there are different sets of criteria that are used for diagnosis and research purposes, e.g. the St. Louis criteria, the Research Diagnostic Criteria, DSM-IV and ICD-10. Although these criteria share many similarities, the lack of consensus about schizophrenia highlights the point that definitions of mental disorders are fairly arbitrary and liable to change according to prevailing influences.

CLINICAL CHARACTERISTICS

In most countries across the world, the lifetime risk of being diagnosed with schizophrenia is 1 per cent. The onset of the disorder usually occurs between the ages of 15 and 45. It is equally common in males and females but it usually occurs in males 4 to 5 years earlier than in females. There is a distinction between acute and chronic onset schizophrenia.

- In *chronic onset*, there is often an insidious change in an apparently normal young person who gradually starts to lose drive and motivation and to drift away from friends. After months, or even years of this deterioration, more obvious signs of disturbance, such as delusional ideas or hallucinations, appear.

- In *acute onset*, these more obvious signs can appear quite suddenly, usually after a stressful event, and the individual shows very disturbed behaviour within a few days.

People who have been diagnosed with schizophrenia will not all display the same behaviour, so the major classification systems include lists of symptoms only some of which need to be present before a diagnosis can be made. See the panel at the top of the next page for the symptoms listed by ICD-10.

Sub-types of schizophrenia

Many researchers believe that schizophrenia is not a single disorder and have suggested various sub-types. ICD-10 distinguishes between seven different sub-types, whereas DSM identifies only five. The sub-types and their characteristics are as follows:

- *Paranoid schizophrenia* – Delusions and/or halluci-nations are the predominant characteristics. Negative symptoms such as flattening of affect and poverty of speech are less apparent than in other types.

- *Hebephrenic schizophrenia* (called Disorganized schizophrenia in DSM-IV) – Behaviour is aimless and disorganized and speech is rambling and incoherent. There is marked flattening and inappropriateness of affect.

- *Catatonic schizophrenia* – Psychomotor abnormality is the central characteristic of this sub-type. Individuals sometimes adopt strange postures or flail their limbs around in an uncontrolled fashion. They often show negativism where they resist all instructions or attempts to move them.

- *Undifferentiated schizophrenia* – This is a sort of general category where individuals are placed who have insufficient symptoms for any of the sub-types or so many symptoms that they do not neatly fit into any category.

- *Post-schizophrenic depression* (not in DSM-IV) – Criteria for schizophrenia have been met in the last 12 months but are not currently present. Depressive symptoms are prolonged and severe.

- *Residual schizophrenia* – Criteria for schizophrenia have been met in the past but are not met at the present time. However, there have been many signs of negative symptoms throughout the previous 12 months.

- *Simple schizophrenia* (not in DSM-IV) – There is slow but progressive development (over a period of at least a year) of social withdrawal, apathy, poverty of speech and marked decline in scholastic/ occupational performance. In all cases (apart from simple schizophrenia), the general criteria for a diagnosis of schizophrenia must be met as well as the specific criteria for each sub-type. Two case studies of different sub-types of schizophrenia are described in the panel opposite.

ICD-10: Symptoms of schizophrenia

In ICD-10, the following groups of symptoms are considered important. There is a minimum requirement for at least one of the signs and symptoms listed under 1 or two of those listed under 2 to be present for a period of at least one month.

1 [a] *Thought control*

– *Thought withdrawal* – thoughts are extracted from the person's mind

– *Thought insertion* – unwelcome thoughts are inserted into the person's mind

– *Thought broadcast* – private thoughts become accessible to other people.

[b] *Delusions of control, influence and passivity* – A delusion is a distorted belief. The individual does not feel in control of their own thoughts, feelings and will.

[c] *Hallucinatory voices* – These are voices that do not exist, but that feel real to the person hearing them. The content of the voices is very variable but often takes the form of a running commentary on the person's behaviour.

[d] *Other persistent delusions* – These are distorted beliefs that are culturally inappropriate or involve impossible powers and capabilities.

2 [a] *Persistent hallucinations* – These are distorted perceptions arising from any of the senses and may be accompanied by delusions.

[b] *Incoherent or irrelevant speech* – This arises when the train of thought is disrupted and the person's speech is so jumbled that it becomes meaningless. Neologisms (made-up words) are often inserted into the conversation that make little sense to anyone else.

[c] *Catatonic behaviour* – This refers to unusual body movements and includes the adoption of odd postures, uncontrolled limb movements and, sometimes, complete frozen immobility.

[d] *Negative symptoms* – These are the less florid symptoms associated with schizophrenia, and include apathy and a general lack of drive and motivation. Speech often conveys little meaning and is often repetitive. The individual shows flat affect, i.e. displays little emotional response to what is going on around them and speaks in a monotonous, expressionless tone. When emotion is displayed, it can be inappropriate, e.g. laughing at bad news or crying at a joke, and there can be sudden mood swings.

Case studies of schizophrenia

Catatonic schizophrenia

Maria is a 19-year-old college student who has been psychiatrically hospitalized for more than a month. For days before her admission, and for the weeks she has been in the hospital, Maria has been mute. Rigidly posturing her body and staring at the ceiling, she spends most of the day in a trance-like state that seems impenetrable. Her family and college friends are mystified. In trying to sort out why and when she began showing such odd behaviour, the only incident that could be recalled was Maria's ranting and raving, just prior to going into the catatonic state, that one of her lecturers was a 'demon'.

Paranoid schizophrenia

Esther is a 31-year-old unmarried woman who lives with her elderly mother. A belief that the outside world is filled with radio waves that will insert evil thoughts into her head keeps Esther from leaving the house. The windows in her bedroom are 'protected' with aluminium foil that 'deflects the radio waves'. She often hears voices that comment on these radio signals.

Source: Halgin and Whitbourne (1993)

In practice, most British psychiatrists use the overarching category of schizophrenia and only make use of the sub-types for individuals who fit their criteria exactly. Crow (1980), however, made a further distinction:

- *Type I syndrome* – an acute disorder characterized by positive symptoms (hallucinations, delusions and thought disorder)

- *Type II syndrome* – a chronic disorder characterized by negative symptoms such as flattening of affect, apathy and poverty of speech.

There are problems with this typology because people do not always fit neatly into one or other category. However, it remains a useful distinction because, as you will see in the next section, the two types may have different underlying causes.

BIOLOGICAL EXPLANATIONS OF SCHIZOPHRENIA

The causes of schizophrenia are not fully understood, and it seems likely that the disorder arises from an interaction of various contributory factors. However, there is strong evidence that biological factors have an important part to play.

Genetic explanation for schizophrenia

It has been known for a long time that schizophrenia runs in families. This could be because families share the same disadvantaged environment, but research evidence suggests that genetic factors are important. This evidence comes from three major sources:

- family studies
- twin studies
- adoption studies.

Evidence from family studies

First-degree relatives (parents, siblings and offspring) share an average of 50 per cent of their genes, and second-degree relatives share approximately 25 per cent. To investigate genetic transmission of schizophrenia, studies compare rates of schizophrenia in relatives of diagnosed cases compared to relatives of controls. There is now a considerable body of evidence that suggests that the closer the biological relationship, the greater the risk of developing schizophrenia or a related psychotic disorder. For example, Kendler *et al.* (1985) have shown that first-degree relatives of those with schizophrenia are 18 times more at risk than the general population. Family studies are often inconclusive because they are conducted retrospectively, in that they are comparing a cross section of people who have already been diagnosed. A prospective (longitudinal)

study can provide more reliable data and a number of large-scale projects have been undertaken in different parts of the world (see Key research below).

Evidence from twin studies

Twin studies offer another way of establishing genetic links, by comparing the difference in concordance rates (i.e. the likelihood of both twins being affected with the disorder) for identical (MZ) and fraternal (DZ) twins. Both share the same environment, but only the MZ twins have identical genetic make-up. Many studies have been conducted and they all show a much higher concordance rate in MZ than in DZ twins. To separate out genetics conclusively from the environment, researchers have sought out MZ twins reared apart where at least one twin has been diagnosed with schizophrenia. Obviously, they are few in number and an added problem is that one of the reasons for separation may have been a problem in the family. Gottesman and Shields (1982) used the Maudsley twin register and found 58 per cent (seven out of twelve MZ twin pairs reared apart) were concordant for schizophrenia. If the genetic hypothesis is correct, then the offspring of a non-affected discordant MZ twin should still be high-risk. A study by Fischer (1971) found that 9.4 per cent of such offspring developed schizophrenia, which is a much higher incidence than in the general population (approximately 1 per cent). A study in London using the Maudsley Twin Register by Cardno *et al.* (1999) found a 40 per cent concordance rate in MZ twins, compared to 5.3 per cent in DZ twins.

However, even in the rare cases where MZ twins are reared apart, they still share the same environment in the womb before birth, so the contribution of environmental factors cannot be entirely discounted.

the Copenhagen High-Risk Study (Kety *et al.* 1962)

This study was carried out in Denmark and began in 1962. Kety and colleagues identified 207 offspring of mothers diagnosed with schizophrenia along with a matched control of 104 children with 'healthy' mothers (low-risk). The children were aged between 10 and 18 years at the start of the study and were matched on age, gender, parental socio-economic status and urban/rural residence. Follow-up of the children was conducted in 1974 and in 1989. Results published by Parnas *et al.* (1993) strongly support a familial link with two psychotic disorders:

- Schizophrenia was diagnosed in 16.2 per cent of the high-risk group compared to 1.9 per cent in the low-risk group.

- Schizotypal personality disorder was diagnosed in 18.8 per cent of the high-risk group compared to 5.0 per cent in the low-risk group.

Combining the figures for the two disorders, the percentages are 35 per cent high-risk, compared to 6.9 per cent low-risk.

Another prospective study with offspring of patients with schizophrenia – the New York High-Risk Project – has reported similar findings at a 25-year follow-up (Erlennmeyer-Kimling *et al.* 1997). The main difficulty with family studies is that they cannot differentiate between genetic and environmental influences because the individuals share the same environment.

Evidence from adoption studies

A more effective way of separating out the effects of environmental and genetic factors is to look at adopted children who later develop schizophrenia and compare them with their biological and adoptive parents. The *Finnish Adoption study*, which Tienari began in 1969, identified adopted-away offspring of biological mothers who had been diagnosed with schizophrenia (112 index cases), plus a matched control group of 135 adopted-away offspring of mothers who had not been diagnosed with any mental disorder. Adoptees ranged from 5 to 7 years at the start of the study and all had been separated from their mother before the age of 4. The study reported that 7 per cent of the index adoptees developed schizophrenia, compared to 1.5 per cent of the controls (Tienari *et al.* 1987).

The Danish Adoption Study, reported by Kety *et al.* (1994), taking a national sample from across Denmark, found high rates of diagnosis for chronic schizophrenia in adoptees whose biological parents had the same diagnosis, even though they had been adopted by 'healthy' parents.

The data provided by these prospective studies have, so far, indicated a strong genetic link for schizophrenia. A major problem in these longitudinal studies, however, is that diagnostic criteria for schizophrenia are continually being updated and changed.

Twin, adoption and family studies continue to provide reliable evidence that the degree of risk increases with the degree of genetic relatedness (see Fig. 25.1). However, no twin study has yet shown 100 per cent concordance in MZ twins, which would provide the most conclusive evidence for genetic links alone.

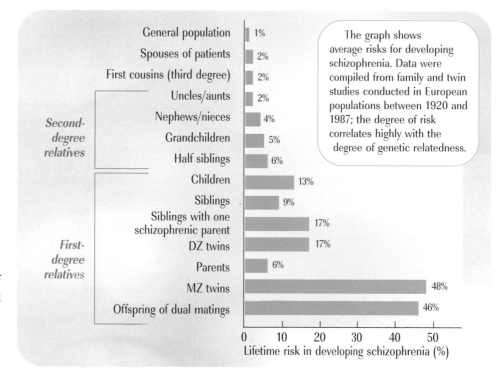

Figure 25.1 >> Genetic risk of developing schizophrenia

Source: Zimbardo *et al.* (1995)

The graph shows average risks for developing schizophrenia. Data were compiled from family and twin studies conducted in European populations between 1920 and 1987; the degree of risk correlates highly with the degree of genetic relatedness.

Evaluation
genetic explanation of schizophrenia

- *Research evidence* – There is now very strong evidence, particularly from adoption studies, that genetics are a clear risk factor for schizophrenia.
- *Degree of risk* – Although studies have clearly shown that the risk of schizophrenia is increased if close relatives have been diagnosed with the disorder, the chances are never 100 per cent.

Even if a MZ twin has the disorder, the risk for the other twin is less than 50 per cent. This suggests that genetics cannot offer a complete explanation.

- *Search for relevant genes* – Studies conducted so far do not tell us which genes might be important for the transmission of schizophrenia. Without knowing which precise genes are involved, it is impossible to understand the underlying mechanisms that lead from the genetic risk to the symptoms of the disorder. The search for specific genes continues.

Biochemical explanations of schizophrenia

If genetic factors are important, they are likely to work by exerting an influence on the hardware of the brain. In other words, structural or biochemical abnormalities should be detectable in the brains of those diagnosed with schizophrenia. In particular, research interest has focused on the action of certain neurotransmitters or chemical messengers.

The dopamine hypothesis

Interest in the neurotransmitter dopamine arose when it was found that phenothiazines (neuroleptic, anti-psychotic drugs which reduce the symptoms of schizophrenia) work by inhibiting dopamine activity and that L-dopa (a synthetic dopamine-releasing drug) can induce symptoms resembling acute schizophrenia in non-psychotic people.

Studies of drugs like amphetamines and LSD, which are known to have an effect on the dopaminergic system, have provided further support. These drugs can induce states very similar to acute schizophrenia in healthy individuals and can exacerbate symptoms in people who are already vulnerable. In a study by Randrup and Munkvad (1966), behaviour similar to that found in those suffering from schizophrenia was induced in rats by administering amphetamines. The effects were then reversed by neuroleptic drugs.

Further support for the dopamine hypothesis comes from post-mortems of patients with schizophrenia. These have revealed a specific increase of dopamine in the left amygdala (Falkai et al. 1988) and increased dopamine receptor density in the caudate nucleus putamen (Owen et al. 1978).

Given the findings from post-mortems, and assuming that dopamine is the important factor in the action of anti-psychotic drugs, then it would be expected that dopamine metabolism is abnormal in patients with schizophrenia. With the development of PET scans, metabolic activity can now be monitored in live brains. PET scan research conducted by Wong et al. (1986) revealed that dopamine receptor density in the caudate nuclei is indeed greater in those with schizophrenia than in controls. However, this has not been supported in some subsequent studies.

A02 Evaluation
the dopamine hypothesis

- *Support for the hypothesis* – Current available evidence supports some form of the dopamine hypothesis. Excess dopamine activity has been clearly demonstrated in certain individuals with schizophrenia, particularly those displaying positive symptoms. Drugs alleviate positive symptoms, but are not so effective with negative symptoms.

- *Effect of different drugs on different sub-types* – It is possible that the inconclusive findings in dopamine studies merely reflect the two sub-types of schizophrenia (Type I and Type II). Amphetamines (known to affect the dopaminergic system) worsen positive symptoms associated with acute schizophrenia and lessen negative symptoms associated with chronic schizophrenia, whilst phenothiazines (anti-psychotic drugs) alleviate positive symptoms, but are not so effective at lessening negative symptoms.

- *Cause or effect?* – Unfortunately, neither post-mortems nor PET scans can reveal whether increased dopaminergic activity causes schizophrenia, or whether schizophrenia interferes with dopamine metabolism.

- *Role of dopamine in other disorders* – Dopamine is unlikely to be the only factor in schizophrenia because it has also been implicated in mania and a number of other mental disorders which have quite different symptoms. Each of these disorders is alleviated by quite different drugs, yet the main evidence for the dopamine link in schizophrenia is the effectiveness of phenothiazines in alleviating symptoms.

Neuroanatomical explanations

Recent advances in technology have enabled the medical profession to examine the live brains of people with schizophrenia. Magnetic resonance imaging (MRI) has been a tremendous breakthrough because it provides a picture of the living brain. MRI studies show quite definite structural abnormalities in the brains of many patients with schizophrenia.

Evidence for neuroanatomical explanations

Brown et al. (1986) found decreased brain weight and enlarged ventricles, which are the cavities in the brain that hold cerebrospinal fluid. Flaum et al. (1995) also found enlarged ventricles, along with smaller thalamic, hippocampal and superior temporal volumes. Buchsbaum (1990) found abnormalities in the frontal and pre-frontal cortex, the basal ganglia, the hippocampus and the amygdala. As more MRI studies are being undertaken, more abnormalities are being identified.

Structural abnormalities have been found more often in those with negative/chronic symptoms, rather than positive/acute symptoms, lending support to the belief that there are two types of schizophrenia: Type I (acute) and Type II (chronic). An argument against this is that many people with acute symptoms of schizophrenia later go on to develop chronic symptoms, which could indicate a further degeneration of the brain rather than two distinct types of schizophrenia.

The critical period for the onset of schizophrenia is not usually before adolescence. Therefore, if brain abnormalities precede the onset of clinical symptoms, this would confirm the view that schizophrenia is a developmental disorder. Weinberger (1988) claims that, despite much research, the evidence is still inconclusive as to whether there are progressive structural brain changes prior to the initial onset of schizophrenia or whether they follow the onset of clinical symptoms.

One of the main problems in trying to understand the causal direction is that, so far, brain imaging in relation to schizophrenia has mainly been restricted to people who have already been diagnosed. A study of teenage monkeys by Castner et al. (1998) may shed some light on this debate. They subjected the monkeys to brain-damaging X-rays during fetal development and found that they showed no ill effects during childhood, compared to the control group, but at puberty they developed symptoms of schizophrenia, such as hallucinations. There are, of course, ethical issues associated with animal research of this kind.

Evaluation
the neuroanatomical explanation

● *Conflicting findings about structural abnormalities* – Whilst MRI studies appear to provide conclusive evidence of structural abnormalities, it is worth noting that they do not always agree on the regions of the brain affected. For example, Flaum et al. (1995) found no abnormalities in the temporal lobe regions, whereas Woodruff et al. (1997) found quite

significant reductions in the temporal lobe, compared with control.

● *Structural abnormalities as cause or effect?* – Because most studies using MRI techniques have been carried out on people already diagnosed with schizophrenia, it is not clear whether structural abnormalities predispose to schizophrenia, or whether the onset of clinical symptoms cause structural changes.

● *Types of study* – Prospective studies, which could shed light on the direction of causality have been carried out only on animals and it is difficult to generalize such findings to humans.

Pregnancy and birth factors as explanations for schizophrenia

Other avenues of research have been explored for alternatives to the genetic view of schizophrenia as a developmental disorder. Since the late 1920s, it has been noticed that an overwhelmingly high proportion of people diagnosed with schizophrenia were born in the winter and early spring (Hope-Simpson 1981). Bradbury and Miller (1985) conducted a review of the evidence and found that this was borne out in most countries in the northern hemisphere. A recent study in England and Wales shows that this has remained consistent over the latter half of this century (Procopio and Marriott 1998). In southern hemisphere countries, a high proportion of those diagnosed with schizophrenia were born in July to September (i.e. their winter months).

Viral infections during pregnancy

A number of viral infections, such as measles, scarlet fever, polio, diphtheria and pneumonia and, in particular, the virus Influenza A, have been suggested as an explanation (Torrey et al. 1988, Torrey et al. 1996). Influenza A is most prevalent in the winter and, if implicated in some way, could explain the high proportion of winter births in those diagnosed with

schizophrenia. The suggestion is that if the mother is infected during pregnancy there is pre-birth exposure to the Influenza A virus. It is thought that the 25- to 30-week foetus is most vulnerable because of accelerated growth in the cerebral cortex at this time (Mednick et al. 1988). It is hypothesized that the viral infection enters the brain and gestates until it is activated by hormonal changes in puberty. Alternatively, there may be a gradual degeneration of the brain which eventually becomes so severe that symptoms of schizophrenia emerge.

Further support for the viral hypothesis comes from the observation that, throughout history, peaks in schizophrenia diagnosis have corresponded with major flu epidemics (Torrey et al. 1988).

Birth complications

There is now quite convincing evidence for both structural abnormalities and neurochemical abnormalities in the brains of people with schizophrenia, but there are conflicting views as to whether these abnormalities result from a genetic defect or from birth complications leading to brain damage. A longitudinal study by Dalman et al. (1999) found significant links between birth complications and later development of schizophrenia, with pre-eclampsia being the most significant risk factor.

● *Methodological problems* – Although the evidence relating to viral infections is suggestive, there are some problems. For example, studies such as those of Torrey were based on correlational data and so caution should be observed when attempting to infer causation. The data are also based on DSM-II diagnostic criteria for schizophrenia, which included a broader diagnostic range of patients than DSM-III onwards.

● *Genetic predisposition* – Torrey *et al.* (1988) claimed that the link between viral infection and schizophrenia only occurs in those who are already genetically predisposed. If that were the case, however, 100 per cent concordance would be expected in MZ twins and perhaps in DZ twins, because they are in the uterus together and are both therefore exposed to the same viruses.

● *Birth complications as sole cause?* – It is unlikely that birth complications like pre-eclampsia could be the sole cause of schizophrenia, because this is a common problem and not all such infants go on to develop schizophrenia.

Diathesis-stress model explanation for schizophrenia

Although it has been well established that biological factors are important in explaining the origins of schizophrenia, it is clear that environmental influences also have a part to play. One explanation that links biological vulnerability to environmental stressors is the 'diathesis-stress model'. The reasoning behind this theory is that certain individuals have a constitutional predisposition to the disorder, but will only go on to develop schizophrenia if they are exposed to stressful situations. The predisposition may be genetic and/or the result of illnesses or damage early in life. Stressful events in the environment, such as major life events, traumatic experiences, or dysfunctional families, may then act as a 'trigger' in a high-risk individual (see Fig. 25.2).

Support for the 'diathesis-stress' model also comes from prospective longitudinal studies. Even though such studies have provided compelling support for the importance of genetic factors, they have also shown that schizophrenia did not always develop in those thought to be genetically vulnerable. This led researchers back to the environment in the search for precipitating factors.

The Finnish Adoption Study undertaken by Tienari (1987) investigated environmental factors by assessing the quality of parenting through a battery of tests and interviews. All of the reported cases of schizophrenia occurred in families rated as 'disturbed'. Furthermore, where the rearing environments were rated as 'healthy' in the high-risk sample, the occurrence of schizophrenia was well below general population rates. However, this cannot be seen as evidence for a purely environmental aetiology because low-risk children from 'disturbed' families did not develop schizophrenia.

The Israeli High Risk Study (Marcus 1987) investigated environmental factors by assessing the parents on hostility, inconsistency and over-involvement. All the reported cases of schizophrenia had poor parenting ratings. However, all of these cases also showed signs of neuropsychological abnormalities at the time of initial assessment (13 years previously), which raises the question of whether these abnormalities had influenced the parent–child interaction.

These studies are ongoing and many of the children have not yet passed through the critical period for the onset of schizophrenia. However, the evidence so far strongly supports the diathesis-stress model.

Figure 25.2 ≫ *Diathesis-stress model*

Diathesis/vulnerability factor
(individual stress-tolerance thresholds)

Person A
(high threshold)

Person B
(medium threshold)

Person C
(low threshold)

Degree of environmental stress

When environmental stressors (illustrated by the shaded arrows) penetrate the tolerance threshold for an individual, this results in physical or mental symptoms (illustrated by the darker shaded areas).

● A small number of stressors, such as minor ailments or failing a driving test, may penetrate the stress tolerance of person C (who has a low threshold).

● Additional stressors may penetrate the stress tolerance threshold of both person C and person B (who has a medium threshold).

● The cumulative effect of many stressors, or one significant or life-threatening event, may penetrate the stress-tolerance threshold of persons C and B and even of person A (who has a high threshold).

PSYCHOLOGICAL EXPLANATIONS OF SCHIZOPHRENIA

Family relationships

In the past 50 years, there has been some interest in the idea that disturbed patterns of communication within families might be a factor in the development of schizophrenia. The term 'schizophrenogenic families' (coined by Fromm-Reichmann 1948) was used to describe families with high emotional tension, with many secrets, close alliances and conspiracies. Bateson *et al.* (1956) suggested the 'double-bind hypothesis', where children are given conflicting messages from parents who express care, yet at the same time appear critical. It was thought that this led to confusion, self-doubt and eventual withdrawal. Lidz *et al.* (1965) coined the term 'marital schism' to explain an abnormal family pattern where discord between parents was associated with schizophrenia in offspring. Such theories were based on methodologically flawed studies. For example, they did not include control groups and used poorly operationalized definitions of schizophrenia. One major problem was that families were studied retrospectively, long after the person's mental disorder may have affected the family system. Living with someone who is suffering from schizophrenia is difficult and distressing for the whole family. Routines are disrupted, often with one parent having to give up paid employment to care for the person. As families struggle to cope with schizophrenia, to suggest that they have caused the disorder is unhelpful, if not highly destructive.

Expressed emotion

By the mid-1970s, psychologists had become more interested in the part the family might play in the *course*, rather than the *cause*, of schizophrenia. Unfortunately, there is quite a high risk that someone who has had one episode of schizophrenia will experience another one. This means that it is possible to set up prospective studies to investigate the degree of relapse in people who have already been diagnosed.

Research relating to expressed emotion

Vaughn and Leff, working at the Medical Research Council in London, published a paper in 1976 suggesting that the extent of expressed emotion within a family was a strong predictor of relapse rates among discharged patients. Their research was stimulated by an earlier study by Brown (1972) showing that patients with schizophrenia who returned to homes where a high level of emotion was expressed (high EE) – such as hostility, criticism, over-involvement and over-concern – showed a greater tendency to relapse than those returning to low-EE homes. Vaughn and Leff (1976) found similar results, with 51 per cent relapse in those in high-EE homes and only 13 per cent relapse in those in low-EE homes. Vaughn and Leff included in their study the amount of time spent in face-to-face contact with relatives after discharge and found that relapse rates increased as face-to-face contact increased with high-EE relatives. The study also included data on whether or not the patient was on medication and it was found that the relapse rate increased to 92 per cent in high-EE homes with increased contact coupled with no medication. However, no study has since replicated these particular results relating to medication.

Twenty years on, EE has now become a well-established 'maintenance' model of schizophrenia and many prospective studies have been conducted which support the expressed-emotion hypothesis across many cultures. So well accepted has this model become that treatment programmes for schizophrenia usually include education and training for family members in controlling levels of EE.

What part might the family play in the course of schizophrenia?

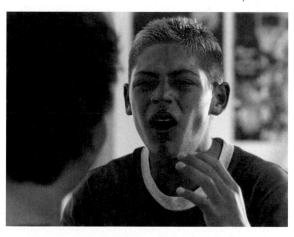

Evaluation

(A02) role of family and expressed emotion

- *Relapse rates and estrangement from the family* – Despite the widely held acceptance of the EE model, it is not without its critics. Many patients with schizophrenia are either estranged from their families or have minimal contact, and yet there is no evidence that such people are less prone to relapse (Goldstein 1988). There is no reason why this should negate the model, however, because presumably any social involvement could be regarded as high or low EE. Research may focus more on families simply because they are usually the first and most frequent point of contact for those with schizophrenia.

continued on next page

● *High EE and abnormalities in the patient* –
It should also be remembered that relationships
within the family work both ways and there is
some evidence that certain aspects of high-EE

behaviour are associated with abnormalities in the
patient (Miklowitz *et al.* 1983).

● *High EE as a response to living with*
schizophrenia – It has been found that high EE
is less common in the families of first-episode
patients than in those with frequent
re-admissions. This suggests that high EE may
well develop as a response to the burdens of
living with schizophrenia.

Cognitive explanations of schizophrenia

Schizophrenia is characterized by profound thought
disturbance. Cognitive psychologists suggest that
disturbed thinking processes are the *cause* rather than
the *consequence* of schizophrenia. Much cognitive
research has focused on the role of attention in
schizophrenia. It is thought that the mechanisms that
operate in normal brains to filter and process incoming
stimuli are somehow defective in the brains of people
with schizophrenia. Most people are able to focus
attention selectively. It is suggested that people with
schizophrenia cannot filter information in this way and
they simply let in too much irrelevant information. This
means that they are inundated by external stimuli which
they are unable to interpret appropriately and so they
experience the world very differently from the rest of
us. Such ideas are supported by evidence that shows
that some people with schizophrenia are poor at
laboratory tasks which require them to pay attention to
some stimuli, but to ignore others.

Physiological abnormality and cognitive malfunction

Cognitive psychologists believe that there are almost
certainly physiological abnormalities associated with
schizophrenia and that these lead to cognitive
malfunctioning. Explanations that relate underlying
biological impairments to psychotic symptoms are often
referred to as 'neuropsychological theories'.

One such hypothesis has been proposed by Hemsley
(1993) who suggested that the central deficit in
schizophrenia is a breakdown in the relationship
between information that has already been stored in
memory and new, incoming sensory information.
Packages of information stored in our memories as
schemas influence the way we interpret later events.
For example, if we go out to eat in a restaurant, we
know from past experiences what to expect and,
therefore, know which aspects of the current situation
need our attention and which we can take for granted.
Such processing normally occurs very quickly and
without conscious awareness. Hemsley suggests that
this processing breaks down in schizophrenia and that
schemas are not activated. As a result, people with

schizophrenia are subjected to sensory overload and do
not know which aspects of a situation to attend to and
which to ignore. This means that superficial incidents
might be seen as highly relevant and significant (e.g. a
conversation at the next table is interpreted as being
personally relevant) and could explain symptoms such
as delusions. Hemsley further suggests that internal
thoughts are sometimes not recognized as arising from
memory and so are attributed to an external source and
experienced as auditory hallucinations.

Frith's model (1992) was an attempt to explain the
onset and maintenance of some of the positive
symptoms of schizophrenia. His idea is that people with
schizophrenia are cognitively impaired in that they are
unable to distinguish between actions that are brought
about by external forces and those that are generated
internally. He believes that most of the symptoms of
schizophrenia·can be explained in terms of deficits in
three cognitive processes:

● inability to generate willed action

● inability to monitor willed action

● inability to monitor the beliefs and intentions of
others.

Frith suggests that these three processes are all part of a
general mechanism which he calls 'meta-representation'.
This is the mechanism which allows us to be aware of
our goals and our intentions and to understand the
beliefs and intentions of others. According to Frith, faulty
operation of this mechanism is due to a functional
disconnection between frontal areas of the brain
concerned with action and more posterior areas of the
brain that control perception. He has produced some
evidence for his ideas by detecting changes in cerebral
blood flow in the brains of people with schizophrenia
when engaged in specific cognitive tasks.

Genetic links

Cognitive psychologists are attempting to find evidence
for genetic links by examining whether malfunctioning
cognitive processing is a family trait. Park *et al.* (1995)
identified working memory deficits in people with
schizophrenia and in their first-degree non-schizophrenic
relatives, a study that has been supported by Faraone *et*
al. (1999), who also found impairments in auditory
attention. Faraone and colleagues claim that these

memory and attention impairments are a manifestation of the genetic predisposition to schizophrenia and are even bold enough to claim that these are the cause of schizophrenia. They admit, however, that their data cannot explain why some relatives do not develop schizophrenia, even though they have the predisposing genes. They suggest that further work is needed to establish whether some people have a low 'dose' of the genes, or, alternatively, whether they have not been exposed to any environmental agents that may trigger the disorder. Cannon *et al.* (1994b), who also identified verbal memory and attention, but not visual memory deficits, in people with schizophrenia and their non-schizophrenic siblings, suggested that the mediating factors that determine the expression of these genes are birth complications.

- *Scope of cognitive theories* – Cognitive theories in themselves do not really explain the causes of schizophrenia. They simply describe some of the symptoms of the disorder in cognitive terms. In order to explain the origins of schizophrenia, they need to be combined with the biological model (see the neuropsychological and genetic explanations outlined previously).

- *Explaining symptoms* – Cognitive theories may not be able to offer a full explanation of schizophrenia, but they may help to explain the origins of particular symptoms (e.g. hallucinations and delusions).

- *Why doesn't brain injury always lead to mental disorder?* – Cognitive impairments can result from brain injury resulting from, say, a stroke or an accident, but these rarely result in a mental disorder.

- *A genetic origin?* – Cognitive impairments thought to have a genetic origin have, however, been implicated in a number of different mental disorders, e.g. Attention Deficit Hyperactivity Disorder. As an explanation for schizophrenia, this is a new area of research and, as yet, it is not possible to evaluate the validity of such a link.

- *Hemsley's model* – Hemsley has tried to link his cognitive model to an underlying neurological system, in particular to the hippocampus and related brain structures. There is currently very little clear-cut empirical evidence, but there has been some promising research with animals offering tentative support for his ideas.

- *Frith's theory* – Frith's theory has provided a comprehensive framework for explaining many of the symptoms of schizophrenia. However, research support is far from conclusive and the theory is still regarded as speculative. Some critics regard his theory as too reductionist in that it fails to take into account the role of environmental factors.

CHECK YOUR UNDERSTANDING

Check your understanding of the characteristics of and explanations for schizophrenia by answering these questions. Check your answers by looking back through Topic 1.

1 Briefly explain the difference between acute and chronic onset schizophrenia.

2 Outline the clinical characteristics of schizophrenia.

3 Explain the distinction between Type I and Type II syndrome.

4 Outline the procedures and findings of the Copenhagen High-Risk Study.

5 Explain why adoption studies provide the most effective way of investigating genetic influences in schizophrenia.

6 Briefly outline the dopamine hypothesis, and identify one strength and one weakness of the theory.

7 Outline the diathesis-stress model of schizophrenia.

8 Explain briefly how families might affect the course of schizophrenia.

9 Explain the possible role of cognitive deficits in the origin of schizophrenia.

10 Is schizophrenia primarily caused by biological factors? Construct a 300-word précis that answers this question.

Research into
schizophrenia

*Professor **Paul Harrison** qualified from Oxford University in medicine in 1985 and then trained in psychiatry. He returned in 1991 to set up a laboratory to investigate the molecular neurobiology of psychiatric disorders, and is currently professor in the Department of Psychiatry.*

Q **Schizophrenia is generally regarded as a disorder with physical origins. Does that suggest that psychological factors are unimportant in its development?**

A Evidence does seem to show that physical factors are more important than psychological ones in causing schizophrenia. Previously it had been thought that psychological factors such as parental characteristics and family social environment were important. However, this has not been borne out by research. Indeed, adoption studies show that the family in which a child is brought up in makes little, if any, difference to that child's risk of developing schizophrenia. On the other hand, psychological factors undoubtedly influence the course of the illness; that is, the chances of a patient with schizophrenia relapsing and becoming ill again are affected by how the people around them (particularly their family members) behave. Psychological factors may also play a part in determining when the symptoms begin and how they manifest themselves.

So, the answer to the question is 'yes and no': psychological factors are relatively unimportant in the underlying causes of the illness, but they are important in determining what happens after it has begun.

Q **How close are we to finding a genetic cause for schizophrenia?**

A One of the few certainties about the cause of schizophrenia is that it is largely genetic. About three quarters of a person's risk for schizophrenia is in their genes, the rest coming from environmental factors. This makes schizophrenia – perhaps surprisingly – more 'genetic' than many other diseases. However, it has been very difficult to find the gene or genes responsible. There are many reasons for this, the most important probably being simply that there is not one crucial gene but lots of little genes each of which play only a minor role. This

Paul Harrison

makes them difficult for researchers to find. At last progress is being made, and since 2001 about six of these schizophrenia risk genes have been found. The strongest evidence is for a gene called Neuregulin. It is important to emphasize that neither Neuregulin nor any other gene make it inevitable that a person gets schizophrenia, it is just that different forms of these genes affect an individual's risk of this happening.

Q **Has research found evidence for a particular type of brain dysfunction that might be linked to schizophrenia?**

A Diagnosing schizophrenia is difficult, since it is based on patterns of symptoms which a psychiatrist or other health professional has to discover from what a person says and does. There is no absolute diagnostic test like, for example, measuring a blood sugar level to diagnose diabetes. Hence researchers continue to try and discover the central or 'core' abnormalities, which really characterize schizophrenia.

At the moment, there are two neuropsychological areas of interest. The first is attentional deficits. Second, and possibly related to the attentional problems, patients have abnormalities of working memory, apparent when trying to problem solve or do similar tasks. These difficulties are associated with abnormal functioning of the frontal lobes.

Q **Is schizophrenia one disorder or several disorders with different origins?**

A Because there remain so many unanswered questions about the causes of schizophrenia, it is still not known whether it is one illness or several. Neither is it clear where, or if, a boundary should be drawn between schizophrenia and bipolar disorder (manic depression) – or even from normal extremes of mental experience. For the time being, most researchers assume that schizophrenia is a single and discrete disorder, in part because it makes research easier!

REVISION SUMMARY

Having covered this topic, you should be able to:

✓ describe the clinical characteristics of schizophrenia

✓ describe and evaluate biological explanations (including evidence) of schizophrenia

✓ describe and evaluate psychological explanations (including evidence) of schizophrenia.

EXAMPLE EXAM QUESTIONS

Below are some **possible examination questions** set on this topic, along with hints to help you understand and approach each question effectively:

1 Discuss **two or more** explanations of schizophrenia. (30 marks)

> This question does not specify the particular explanations required, so you can do any two biological explanations or psychological explanations, or a mixture of the two. You can also, if you wish, discuss more than two explanations if you feel you do not know enough about two to fill a whole essay. However, if you write about lots of different explanations, this inevitably squeezes the time available for detail of each explanation (an important AO1 criterion) and also time available for AO2. Make sure you focus on explaining, e.g. explaining how genes may lead to schizophrenia, rather than just offering descriptions of research evidence (such as concordance studies). Such studies do offer a partial explanation, but might equally provide good AO2.

2 Critically consider **two or more** biological explanations of schizophrenia. (30 marks)

> The term 'critically consider' is an AO1+AO2 term (see Table 32.1, p. 937). The AO1 component is clearly a description (or probably just an outline) of two or more explanations. This time you are restricted to just biological explanations. Of course, you can use psychological explanations as a form of commentary but proceed with caution. There is no credit for any *description* of these psychological explanations, but any contrasts that can be made would receive credit. This means doing more than saying '…in contrast there are behavioural explanations which say the cause is environmental'. Spell out what this means and thus provide *elaboration* of your commentary.

3 Critically consider **two or more** psychological explanations of schizophrenia (e.g. social and family relationships). (30 marks)

> An obvious alternative is to be asked to describe and evaluate *psychological* explanations. The same comments as made above apply here. Dangers to avoid in all of these questions is providing too general critiques of the approach (i.e. of the biological or psychological approach), or simply describing treatments instead of using such applications as AO2 commentary (you could argue that a positive criticism of any explanation is its successful application). In this question, examples have been added, taken from the specification. Remember, they are things you could include, not things you must include.

4 (a) Outline **two** clinical characteristics of schizophrenia. (5 marks)
  (b) Discuss **two or more** explanations of schizophrenia. (25 marks)

> Here, pay attention to the split of marks. For part (a), there are only 5 marks available which means you should spend a proportionate amount of time on the question – about 6 minutes or 120 words (a 40-minute essay is typically 800 words). If you write a lot more than this, you will still only receive 5 marks and you will reduce the time you can spend building up credit in other parts of the question. There is also no credit for coverage of more than two characteristics, though you could group a number of characteristics under the broader headings of positive and negative symptoms, which would then count as two characteristics. In part (b), there are 10 further marks for AO1 and 15 marks for AO2, which should be reflected in the time you spend on each. You might choose your explanations on the basis of those for which you are best able to offer effective evaluation.

WHAT IS DEPRESSION?

We all feel depressed from time to time and this is quite normal. Usually, it is short-lived and does not interfere too much with our everyday functioning; we carry on going to work, school or college, even though we might not feel much like socializing. This is not depression in the clinical sense. Clinical depression is when everyday functioning is seriously impaired. Depression often co-exists with other psychological problems and many people diagnosed with depression also meet the DSM and/or ICD criteria for at least one other disorder.

Depression is an 'affective' (mood) disorder, characterized by feelings of sadness and a general withdrawal from those around us. The degree of impairment varies and can range from mild to severe, such that it causes an inability to feed or dress or maintain personal hygiene. Depression can be so serious that it leads to suicide.

The term 'unipolar' distinguishes the mental disorder of depression from the quite different disorder of manic-depression, which is known as a 'bipolar' disorder because of the two extremes of mania and depression. This topic is concerned only with depression: a unipolar disorder.

Depression is one of the most common types of psychological abnormality and can occur at any age. Onset most commonly occurs between the ages of 20 and 50, but recent epidemiological studies suggest that the incidence of major depressive disorder is increasing in people younger than 20. A robust finding is that women are twice as likely to be diagnosed with depression than men. While some of this difference might be due to diagnostic practice, it also seems to reflect hormonal differences and the differing psychosocial stressors for men and women.

CLINICAL CHARACTERISTICS

It has long been thought that there are two discrete categories of depression – 'reactive' and 'endogenous' – with quite different aetiologies:

● *Reactive depression*, as the term implies, is a reaction to stressful events outside ourselves, such as the death of someone close, redundancy or failing exams.

● *Endogenous depression* is thought to arise from within the person, independent of external events.

Whilst reactive depression can range from mild to quite serious, endogenous depression is usually very severe. Although the categories of reactive and endogenous are in common use by clinicians, they are not contained in either ICD-10 or DSM-IV , which only serves to emphasize the difficulties associated with classification and diagnosis.

DSM-IV lists two sub-types of depressive disorder, 'major depressive disorder' (MDD), which is severe but can be short-lived, and 'dysthymic disorder' (DD), which may be less severe but is more chronic, i.e. it has a longer duration. If the depressive episode has lasted for two consecutive years with less than two months without symptoms, then dysthymic disorder is diagnosed. Major depression can become a psychotic illness when very severe, with symptoms such as delusions or hallucinations. Table 25.1 lists some of the main symptoms of depression.

Table 25.1 >> Symptoms of depression

Cognitive	Behavioural	Emotional	Physical
>> Low self-esteem	>> Decrease in sexual activity	>> Sadness	>> Loss of weight
>> Guilt	>> Loss of appetite	>> Irritability	>> Loss of energy
>> Self-dislike	>> Disordered sleep patterns	>> Apathy (no interest or pleasure in activities)	>> Aches and pains
>> Loss of libido (no interest in sex)	>> Poor care of self and others		>> Sleep disturbance
>> Negative thoughts	>> Suicide attempts		>> Menstrual changes
>> Suicidal thoughts			
>> Poor memory			
>> Lack of ability to think and concentrate			

BIOLOGICAL EXPLANATIONS OF DEPRESSION

There are several factors that suggest biological mechanisms may play a part in depression:

- The symptoms of depression include physical changes (e.g. sleep and appetite disturbance, weight change, fatigue, lack of energy).
- There is great similarity in the symptoms across cultures, races, gender and ages.
- Depression runs in families (although this could be due to a shared environment).
- Anti-depressant medication can be successful in treating depression (although this does not in itself prove an underlying biological cause).
- Certain drugs used to treat other conditions can induce the symptoms of depression in non-depressed individuals.

Genetic explanations

Depression seems to run in families and a number of studies have shown an increased risk for depression in first-degree relatives of people with unipolar depression. Research into the influence of genetics has been carried out in the form of family, twin and adoption studies.

- *Evidence from family studies* – Gershon (1990) reviewed ten family studies and found that the rates of unipolar depression in first-degree relatives ranged between 7 per cent and 30 per cent, which is considerably higher than in the general population. However, it is not clear whether this is due to genetic influence or to a shared environment, and family studies often show inconclusive results. DSM-IV states that there is a high incidence of unipolar depression in the offspring of those with

bipolar (manic) depression. However, that may be a reaction to living with a parent with manic-depression.

- *Evidence from twin studies* – There have been a number of twin studies comparing MZ (identical twins) with DZ (fraternal) twins, although these, too, cannot easily separate out the effects of genetics and the environment. McGuffin *et al.* (1996) found 46 per cent concordance in MZ twins compared to 20 per cent in DZ twins in a total of 109 twin pairs, with no evidence of the effect of shared environment. However, Bierut *et al.* (1999) carried out a study of 2,662 twin pairs in Australia and, although they reported a hereditability factor of between 36 and 44 per cent, they claimed that environmental factors played a larger role.

- *Evidence from adoption studies* – Adoption studies provide the best way of disentangling genetic factors from environmental, since they look at depressed people who have been adopted at an early age and brought up away from the influence of their families. Most of these studies have shown an increased risk in the biological relatives of people with depression rather than in the adopted relatives. Wender *et al.* (1986), for example, found that biological relatives were eight times more likely to have depression than adoptive relatives.

One way of trying to resolve some of the problems with genetic research is to locate a particular gene that is present in all cases of depression. Studies exploring genetic patterns in families with bipolar disorder have been quite promising, but it has proved much more difficult with unipolar disorder and it seems unlikely that a single gene will ever be identified.

A02 **Evaluation**
genetic explanations

- *Genes or environment?* – Whilst there appears to be some degree of genetic evidence for depression, in most cases those diagnosed share the same environment, which means it may equally be a learned behaviour.
- *Risk factor only* – Although the risk for depression seems to be increased for MZ twins, the chances have never been shown to be

100 per cent. Genetics seem to be a risk factor for depression but not the whole explanation.

- *Predisposing factor* – There may be a genetic component operating as a predisposing factor, with additional precipitating causes.
- *Genetic uncertainty* – Even if genetic factors do play a part in the origins of unipolar depression, it is not yet clear what the precise mechanism is that is transmitted. Without knowing the specific genes involved, it is impossible to understand how they code for biological structures and functions that produce the symptoms of depression.

Biochemical explanations of depression

The role of neurotransmitters

The biochemical theory of depression emerged in the 1950s, when it was discovered that a certain class of

drugs, known as tricyclic drugs, was effective in treating depression. These are known to work by increasing the availability of a group of neurotransmitters in the brain called 'monoamines'. These neurotransmitters, especially serotonin, noradrenaline and dopamine, are important in the functioning of the limbic system in the brain, which plays a significant role in the regulation of drives such as appetite, and in the control of emotion.

It is thought that tricyclic drugs increase noradrenergic function, which is thought to be reduced in people with depression, but so far there is no conclusive evidence to support such a view. Post-mortems of depressed patients have not revealed any abnormality of noradrenaline concentration (Cooper 1988). However, there is some support from findings relating to the drug reserpine, which is known to act by reducing the availability of noradrenaline. When this drug is administered to patients to reduce high blood pressure, it can have the unwanted side effect of producing depressive symptoms and suicidal tendencies.

Serotonin serves to modulate neural activity and is thought to regulate emotional reactions. If the level of serotonin is too low, then it allows wild fluctuations in other neural activity, producing symptoms of depression. The drug Prozac, which has been found to be an effective anti-depressant works by increasing availability of serotonin in the brain, but does not seem to have any effect on noradrenaline. However, it cannot be ruled out that the serotonin levels fluctuate as a result of decreased motor activity in a state of depression. Advances in technology have enabled healthcare professionals to measure the action of neurotransmitters through PET scans. Mann *et al.* (1996) found impaired serotonergic transmission in people with depression.

Dopamine is thought to be especially involved in depression in old age, because the dopamine content of the brain diminishes considerably over the age of 45. However, the synthetic drug L-dopa (which replicates the action of dopamine) has no specific anti-depressant effect.

The role of hormones

Another biological explanation has emerged from endocrinology. Levels of the hormone cortisol are found to be high in those suffering from depression and techniques known to suppress cortisol secretion have been found to be successful in depressive patients (Carroll 1982). This suggests that there is overactivity in the hypothalamic-pituitary-adrenal cortex. However, this may be due to the stress of being ill, because increased cortisol secretion is a function of the stress response. A study by Nemeroff *et al.* (1992), however, has shown that there is marked adrenal gland enlargement in those suffering from major depression, which is not found in controls.

Endocrine (hormonal) changes could account for depression relating to pre-menstrual, post-natal and menopausal phases. These types of depression can be very serious indeed, leading to suicide attempts. In the case of post-natal depression, psychotic elements often appear, such as fantasies and loss of contact with reality. Some mothers with severe post-natal depression may harm or even kill their newborn child. Cooper (1988),

however, found little difference between the number of women suffering from depression immediately after childbirth and a control group of non-pregnant women of a similar age. Pre-menstrual depression occurs in the week prior to menstruation and 25 per cent of women are affected, although most are not of diagnosable severity. An oestrogen–progesterone imbalance has been suggested (Dalton 1964), oestrogen levels being too high and progesterone levels too low. At menopause, oestrogen levels drop. Hormone replacement therapy appears to be reasonably effective for treating many (but not all) women who suffer from menopausal depression. Both oestrogen and progesterone increase greatly during pregnancy and then fall rapidly after childbirth, which may account for post-natal depression. However, research evidence for these hormone-imbalance theories is inconclusive (Clare 1985).

Nevertheless, if hormonal changes are not implicated, then it is difficult to explain why these depressive states occur more frequently during periods of hormonal change. One of the problems in trying to ascertain hormonal links with depression is that there are invariably social changes occurring at the same time. A possible explanation is that hormonal changes interact with a genetic predisposition to depression, together with excessive tiredness and a stressful domestic situation.

Seasonal Affective Disorder (SAD)

Depression can be seasonal: that is, the person suffers a regular period of depression at a specific time of year. Winter depression is the most common. One explanation is that this relates to changes in the number of daylight hours and that either the person is not exposed to enough natural light, or they are adversely affected by too much artificial light. Special daylight light bulbs can now be purchased and appear to be effective for those suffering from this type of depression (see Unit 13, p. 405).

Attempts have been made to ascertain the reason for SAD and there is some evidence for links with brain chemicals, particularly seratonin and noradrenaline. It has been found that treatment with anti-depressant drugs which contain serotonin are effective, whereas those drugs containing noradrenaline have no effect (Lam *et al.* 1996). They concluded that SAD may be related to serotonergic mechanisms. However, the relationship cannot be causal because treatment does not cure the problem, which returns when drug treatment is ceased. Perhaps there is a genetic component. Although not a great deal of research has yet been conducted, some evidence is emerging for a genetic predisposition. For example, Madden *et al.* (1996) report a significant genetic influence in winter-pattern SAD. Their data were collected from 4,639 adult twins in Australia via a mailed questionnaire. However, it has been found that people do not always answer such questionnaires truthfully.

Evaluation
biochemical explanations

- *Role of neurotransmitters* – There is a considerable body of evidence that supports the role of certain neurotransmitters in unipolar depression. However, theories based on excess or deficit of such chemicals in the brain are too simple. For example, anti-depressant drugs have an immediate effect on increasing neurotransmitter availability, but typically take several weeks to have a significant effect on mood.

- *Delayed effects of anti-depressants* – Much of the evidence implicating noradrenaline comes from observations of the effects of reserpine and of anti-depressant drugs. However, these drugs do not simply affect levels of noradrenaline – it, may, therefore, be other properties of these drugs that relate to depression and not their reaction with noradrenaline.

- *Isolating cause and effect* – It is difficult to disentangle cause and effect in many of the studies. It may be that depression causes biochemical changes rather than the other way round.

- *Impairment of the stress-response system* – Abnormal levels and regulation of cortisol have suggested that depression may be related to impairment of the stress-response system. However, such irregularities are not found in all people with depression and are sometimes found in people with other kinds of mental disorder.

- *Role of female hormones* – Females are more likely to be diagnosed with depression than males and female hormones have been suggested as a reason for this difference. However, evidence for their importance in depression is weak. For example, only a small minority of women suffer from severe post-natal depression, so this is not an inevitable response to hormonal changes.

- *Biological factors as predisposing factor* – There is no definitive evidence of biological features as the cause of depression, although there is a lot of support for the idea that they are a contributory factor. It is likely they predispose people to depression, but that environmental triggers are required before the disorder emerges.

PSYCHOLOGICAL EXPLANATIONS OF DEPRESSION

Psychodynamic explanations

The Freudian psychoanalytic view relates depression in adulthood to the individual's early relationship with parents. Hostile feelings towards parent(s), it is claimed, are redirected towards the self in the form of self-accusation or self-hatred. These feelings may arise from a lack of love and care, support and safety, or from child abuse. In general terms, the psychodynamic view sees the repression of early trauma re-emerging in adulthood in the form of an anxiety disorder or depression. The case study of Robert (see panel right) is an example of the longer-term effects of early trauma.

In his theory of 'attachment and separation', John Bowlby (1973) suggested that separation from or loss of the mother in early childhood could result in severe depression in adulthood. Support for this view comes from carefully conducted studies by Hinde (1977), who examined the effects of separating infant rhesus monkeys from their mother. These monkeys (both mother and child) very quickly displayed behaviours similar to the symptoms of depression in humans. However, Paykel (1981) subsequently reviewed 14 studies and found the evidence inconclusive because seven studies supported the hypothesis and seven did not support the hypothesis. It should also be borne in mind that it may be unwise to use studies of primates to support aetiological theories of disorders in humans.

Case study of Robert

Robert is in his early twenties and suffers from severe clinical depression. He was a small, thin child and from the start of junior school he was bullied by a group of boys. Pleas to his parents and to the school did not resolve the problem and he became more and more withdrawn. He felt abandoned and learned not to trust anyone.

His fear of being bullied also became an obsession and he began to ruminate in his head almost all of the time: for example, 'Will the bullies be waiting round the corner?', 'What would happen if I took another route?', 'Will I be able to escape?' These ruminations completely took over his thoughts and became an integral part of his personality, such that as an adult he now cannot cease to ruminate upon every single aspect of daily activity. These ruminations, together with his inability to trust others, are at the root of his depression.

- *Difficult to test* – It is difficult to test Freud's ideas empirically because it is impossible to demonstrate unconscious motivations.

- *Presence of anger* – There is some evidence that people with depression show more anger than non-depressed people, but findings have been inconsistent. In any case, the studies have been unable to show that this anger is directed inwards.

- *Effect of loss of parent* – There is some evidence that the loss of a parent in childhood is associated with later depression. However, such loss affects the environment in which the child lives as well as the child's psychological functioning. It might be that the social and financial hardships that such loss might entail create a vulnerability to depression.

Behavioural explanations of depression

Learning theory

Lewinsohn (1974) suggested that depression is caused by a reduction in positive reinforcement. For example, if someone experiences a bereavement or loses a job, there may be less opportunity for enjoying pleasant experiences and receiving positive reinforcement. Depression may then occur. There is a secondary gain, in that the depressive behaviour may be positively reinforced by others in the form of sympathy or concern. However, this cannot explain why the depression continues long after sympathy from others has waned.

Learned helplessness

Seligman (1974) proposed a behavioural theory of 'learned helplessness' to explain reactive depression.

In the course of investigating the effects of Pavlovian fear conditioning in dogs, Seligman found that, after being placed in an inescapable and unavoidable stressful situation, the dog failed to initiate escape behaviour in another stressful situation where escape was possible. Seligman suggested that people are generally able to influence many aspects of their environment, but sometimes things just happen, irrespective of their own behaviour. If this occurs too often, then people lose their motivation and just give up, because they have learned that they are unable to influence situations (that is, they have learned they are helpless).

Maier and Seligman (1976) tested this theory with humans. They subjected people to inescapable noise or shocks, and found that they later failed to escape from similar situations where escape was possible.

- *Not a complete explanation* – Like many behavioural theories, learned helplessness is seen to be inadequate as a complete explanation because it does not take account of cognitive processes.

- *Inconsistent findings* – Findings of learned helplessness in humans have not always been replicated. Some studies showed that helplessness actually facilitated subsequent performance (Wortman and Brehm 1975).

Cognitive–behavioural explanations of depression

In view of the inadequacy of the learned helplessness account, Seligman later reformulated his theory in cognitive, attributional terms calling this the 'hopelessness theory of depression' (Abramson *et al.* 1978). Hopelessness has been identified as one of the core characteristics of depression, particularly in suicide. Beck, who had previously used the term 'hopelessness' to describe a system of expectancies held by a person about their future, developed a 'Hopelessness Scale' used to measure and quantify levels of hopelessness (Beck *et al.* 1974). The hopelessness theory suggested that when people experience failure, they usually try and attribute the failure to a cause. Causal explanations operate on three dimensions of judgement:

- *internal–external* – personal or environmental
- *stable–unstable* – always so or just on this occasion
- *global–specific* – all-encompassing or specific to this situation.

A 'maladaptive attributional' style would involve attributing all negative events to internal, stable, global causes because these causal explanations tend to lead to negative expectations, which in turn can lead to symptoms of depression (see Fig. 25.3). Research in

support of the hopelessness theory comes from studies using the 'Attributional Style Questionnaire', devised by Seligman (1974), which gives scores for internality, stability and globality of an individual's expectations. A study on grade aspirations in college students, showed that most of those with poor results were depressed after the exams. Two days later, however, those who made unstable, specific attributions about their failure had recovered, whereas those who had made stable, global attributions remained depressed.

Figure 25.3 >> *An example of attributional judgements leading to depression*

Bad event	→	Causal explanation	→	Attributions and expectations	→	Symptoms
e.g. poor performance on psychology paper		internal stable global		e.g. 'I am stupid (internal), and I will never (stable) succeed at anything (global).'		hopelessness, leading to depression

(AO2) Evaluation
cognitive–behavioural explanations

- *Research subjects* – Most of Seligman's studies were conducted on college students, rather than on clinically depressed patients.

- *Perception of control* – One of the key elements of the hopelessness theory is that depressed people believe they have little control over their lives. Ford and Neale (1985), however, found that depressed students did not underestimate their degree of control.

- *Hopelessness as cause or effect?* – It is not clear whether hopelessness is a cause of depression, or whether it is a side effect of becoming depressed. If it is the cause, then it would have to precede the onset of depression. A five-year longitudinal study of children by Nolen-Hoeksema *et al.* (1992) found no connection between attributional style and depression in young children. However, they did find a

connection as the children grew older, suggesting that attributional styles may develop over a number of years.

- *Hopelessness expectancy* – Abramson *et al.* (1989) further reformulated their theory of hopelessness, to include the role of expectancy. They outlined a sequence of events which they claimed leads to hopelessness. This begins with a negative event which interacts with the person's already-held negative schemas, and a stable and global attribution is made about why the event occurred. These beliefs lead to 'hopelessness expectancy' for the future, which then results in depression. Abramson and colleagues have even suggested 'hopelessness depression' as a sub-type of depression. DeVellis and Blalock (1992), in a longitudinal study of 57 adults, tested the claim that hopelessness expectancy is a sufficient cause for depression. They found support for the link between expectancy and depression, but as a moderating, rather than mediating factor, i.e. it does not by itself cause the depression, merely the degree.

Beck's cognitive theory of depression

Beck (1967), although trained as a psychoanalyst, was struck by the negative thinking shown by depressed clients and developed his own explanation.

He suggested that depression is the result of negative thinking and catastrophizing, which he called 'cognitive errors'. Beck (1991) maintained that there are three components to depression, which he called the 'cognitive triad':

1 negative views of the *self* as worthless and helpless

2 negative views of the *world* as full of obstacles and a negative view of one's ongoing experience of the world

3 negative views about the *future* as continuing in much the same way.

As these three components interact, they interfere with normal cognitive processing, leading to impairments in perception, memory and problem-solving abilities, with the person becoming completely obsessed with negative thoughts. These thoughts arise spontaneously and are not a result of conscious intention. Not surprisingly, constant exposure to these faulty cognitions can lead to depression.

Negative self-schemas

In addition to this triad of negative cognitions, Beck believed that depression-prone individuals develop a 'negative self-schema'. They possess a set of beliefs and expectations about themselves that are essentially negative and pessimistic. Beck claimed that negative schemas may be acquired in childhood as a result of traumatic events and/or negative treatment. Experiences that might contribute to negative schemas include:

- death of a parent or sibling
- parental rejection, criticism, overprotection, neglect or abuse
- bullying at school or exclusion from peer group.

Gotlib and Macleod (1997) have supported the idea that negative schemas are deep-seated belief systems which develop early in life as the result of a series of negative events.

Cognitive distortions

People with negative self-schemas become prone to making logical errors in their thinking and they tend to focus selectively on certain aspects of a situation while ignoring equally relevant information. Beck referred to these logical errors as 'cognitive distortions' and they include the following:

- *Arbitrary inference* – Drawing conclusions on the basis of insufficient or irrelevant evidence: for example, thinking you are worthless because an open-air concert you were going to see has been rained off.

- *Selective abstraction* – Focusing on a single aspect of a situation and ignoring others: for example, you feel responsible for your team losing a football match even though you are just one of the players on the field.

- *Overgeneralization* – Making a sweeping conclusion on the basis of a single event: for example, you get a D for an exam when you normally get straight As and you, therefore, think you are stupid.

- *Magnification and minimization* – Exaggerating or underplaying the significance of an event: for example, you scrape a bit of paintwork on your car and, therefore, see yourself as a totally awful driver; you get praised by your teachers for an excellent term's work, but you see this as trivial.

- *Personalization* – attributing the negative feelings of others to yourself. For example, your teacher looks really cross when she comes into the room, so she must be cross with you.

Personality types

Beck has adapted his theory over time and one important modification concerns personality differences. He thought that there are individual differences that determine the types of event that can trigger depressive episodes. For example, he identified the 'sociotropic personality' type, where a person bases their self-esteem on the approval and regard of others. For this kind of person, a perceived snub from a colleague, neighbour, boss, etc., might be enough to instigate depressive thoughts. The 'autonomous personality' type, on the other hand, would react badly to a situation where their sense of achievement or independence has been challenged, e.g. losing a game of tennis or having a decision overruled at work.

Evaluation
cognitive explanations

- *Stimulus for research* – Cognitive explanations of depression have stimulated a huge amount of research into the disorder over the last few decades and contributed greatly to our understanding.

- *Therapeutic use* – The cognitive model has given rise to cognitive–behavioural therapies, which have been found to be very helpful in alleviating the symptoms of depression.

- *Studies into negative thinking* – There have been hundreds of studies which have investigated whether depressed people actually think more negatively than non-depressed people (see Gotlib and Hammen (1994) for a review). On the whole, such studies have shown strong evidence for higher levels of negative thinking in depressed people.

- *Causal or correlational?* – Although studies have demonstrated high levels of negative thinking in depressed individuals, they are based mainly on correlational data. It is difficult to determine whether the negative thinking is causal.

continued on next page

- *Does negative thinking precede depression?* – There have been very few studies to investigate whether negative thinking precedes the onset of depression. The few longitudinal studies that have been reported do not show that cognitive vulnerability is a predictor of depression.

- *Negative thinking as consequence of depression* – If negative thinking is a vulnerability factor in depression, it would be expected that depressed people would show more dysfunctional self-schemas than non-depressed people, even if they are not currently depressed. In other words, the vulnerability would be present even in the absence of current depressive symptoms and would, therefore, increase the risk of future episodes. However, numerous studies (reviewed by Segal and Ingram 1994) that have compared non-depressed and recovered depressed patients have found no difference on a variety of cognitive vulnerability measures. This suggests that negative thinking is a consequence of having depression rather than a causal factor.

- *Cognitive factors as part of an integrative model* – Some critics have suggested that the focus on internal cognitive processes as the main trigger for depressive episodes is too simplistic and ignores the influence of external factors such as family relationships and work pressures. It is likely that depression can only be fully explained by an integrative model combining cognitive factors with biological, social, environmental and developmental aspects of the disorder.

Diathesis-stress model

It seems clear that no single explanation can account for depression; it is much more likely that various contributory factors interact to bring about the disorder. According to the diathesis-stress model, underlying predispositions, such as a genetic vulnerability, childhood loss or patterns of negative thinking, can give rise to depressive symptoms only if activated by stressors in the environment. There is considerable evidence that links stressful events such as bereavement, unemployment, divorce and serious illness to the onset of depression.

The role of stressful life events in triggering depression

Precipitating and vulnerability factors

In 1978, Brown and Harris published a very influential book, entitled *The Social Origins of Depression*, the result of a major study of depression among housewives in Camberwell, London. Brown and Harris identified two types of *precipitating factors* for depression:

- severe life events
- long-term difficulties.

These factors came into play when the person also experienced 'vulnerability factors', such as lack of paid employment outside the home, two or more children under the age of five, early loss of mother and, especially, the lack of a close confiding relationship. Further research into depression among working-class mothers is shown in the panel on p. 774.

'Lock and key' hypothesis

Parker *et al.* (1998) propose a 'lock and key' hypothesis of depression, which posits that early adverse experiences establish locks that are activated by keys mirroring the earlier adverse experience. These, in turn, induce depression. They interviewed 270 severely clinically depressed patients and found 'lock and key' links in almost one-third of their sample (see Table 25.2 for examples). These cases were predominantly in the endogenous category of diagnosis, with the remaining two-thirds being predominantly diagnosed with 'reactive' depression, suggesting that the 'lock and key' hypothesis relates to those with more severe chronic depression.

Table 25.2 >> Examples of patients' 'lock and key' links to depression (Parker *et al.* 1998)

Lock	Key
>> Death of both parents when 11; children split up and fostered out	>> Loss of job and loss of identity
>> Forced into boarding school at young age – no choice	>> Triple bypass operation – no choice
>> Mother left, put into orphanage	>> Marital separation, husband left
>> Two siblings died as children	>> Son married, Crohn's disease diagnosed
>> Physical and sexual abuse by father	>> Physical illness

Depression among working-class mothers

Brown and Harris (1978) originally identified people who were already depressed. However, they have continued to research their life-events theory to incorporate early-life experiences. They conducted a study in Islington with 404 working-class women who were single mothers living in an inner-city area. An eight-year follow-up (Brown and Harris 1993) found:

- Early-life experience was a strong predictor of adult depression.

- The most significant childhood adversities were parental indifference and physical or sexual abuse.

- Early loss of mother was not significant unless it increased the chances of negative experiences.

A prospective study by Bifulco *et al.* (1998) confirmed these findings. They gathered data on 105 working-class mothers with vulnerability factors (e.g. negative close relationships, and adverse early-life experiences), but who were not depressed. They found:

- Over a period of 14 months, 37 per cent of these women became depressed and, of these, two-thirds had experienced childhood neglect or abuse.

Why do you think early-life experience might be a strong predictor of adult depression?

- Early loss of a parent was not significant, provided that subsequent care had been good, which does not support Bowlby's theory of the effects of early separation mentioned above.

Gender differences

Veijola *et al.* (1998) conducted a study on gender differences in adult depression and found that adverse early-life experiences predisposed females to depression in adulthood, especially sexual and physical abuse. They only found a weak association between parental loss, through death or divorce, and adult depression. They found no significant relationship between early-life experience and adult depression in males and suggested that, in males, early adverse experiences were more likely to be expressed in anti-social personality and alcoholism.

Evaluation
role of stressful life events

- *Support for life-events theory* – The life-events theory has received a great deal of support and is now incorporated into the DSM diagnostic criteria under Axis IV, where social and environmental circumstances are assessed.

- *Not a complete explanation* – The theory does not explain why many patients do not report critical life events at the onset of their depression or why many people have ongoing psychosocial stressors yet do not become clinically depressed.

- *Life events as triggering factors* – The diathesis-stress model provides a way of integrating the life events theory to some of the other explanations outlined in Topic 2. Life events may be triggering factors that interact with vulnerability factors such as a genetic predisposition, personality factors or adverse early-life experience.

REVISION SUMMARY

Having covered this topic, you should be able to:

✓ describe the clinical characteristics of depression

✓ describe and evaluate biological explanations (including evidence) of depression

✓ describe and evaluate psychological explanations (including evidence) of depression.

CHECK YOUR UNDERSTANDING

Check your understanding of the characteristics of and explanations for depression from memory. You can check your answers by looking back through Topic 2.

1 What is the difference between 'reactive' and 'endogenous' depression?

2 Outline the main clinical characteristics of unipolar depression.

3 Give three reasons why biological factors might be important in understanding the origins of depression.

4 Briefly outline the role of neurotransmitters in depression.

5 Outline two strengths and two weaknesses of biological explanations of depression.

6 Outline Freud's theory of depression.

7 Explain what is meant by 'learned helplessness theory' and explain how this is different from the 'hopelessness theory'.

8 Outline Beck's theory of depression.

9 What role might stressful life events have in the origins of depression?

10 Consider the view that depression is caused by psychological factors. Construct a 300-word précis that answers this question.

EXAMPLE EXAM QUESTIONS

Below are some **possible examination questions** set on this topic, along with hints to help you understand and approach each question effectively:

1 'The biological approach tells us all we need to know about depression.'
   With reference to the quotation above discuss the issue that it raises.   (30 marks)

> As a general rule, when there is a quotation, your task is to answer the *question* and not the quotation, even if you are required to address it. Here, the quotation makes the claim that biological explanations are sufficient for understanding depression. Do you agree? A good answer will consider the arguments/evidence for biological explanations and the flaws in these explanations. For AO2, you might consider the rival claims of psychological explanations, though there would be no credit for simply describing psychological explanations. Your focus should be on the *value* of such alternative explanations. Why might they be better? Note that, despite the fact that the quotation starts with the phrase 'the biological approach', there is little credit here for descriptions of the biological approach in general. Your answer must focus on the biological approach as applied to depression.

2 (a) Outline **two or more** biological explanations of depression.   (15 marks)
   (b) To what extent are such explanations supported by research evidence?   (15 marks)

> The *content* of your answer may be similar to your answer to 1 above though the *shape* of your answer should be different to demonstrate your focus on this particular question. In part (a), you must cover a minimum of two explanations, but would get credit for as many explanations as you have time for. Remember the depth-breadth trade off when describing a number of different explanations. In part (b), the 'such' means that you are not limited to evaluating explanations covered in part (a). Here, you are required to use research evidence as evaluation, but *not* to describe such evidence. You may have to supply some brief descriptions as 'scene-setting' but keep them as short as possible. You might consider the value of opposing evidence, i.e. related to psychological explanations, though such evidence needs to be handled carefully.

3 Critically consider psychological explanations of depression (e.g. learned helplessness).   (30 marks)

> Here, the plural 'explanations' means that you must provide a minimum of two explanations, or incur a partial performance penalty (maximum of 9 marks for AO1 and the same for AO2). One example is given in this question, but this doesn't mean that you have to cover only one explanation (or indeed cover the one mentioned), but it might help you think of appropriate explanations.

continued on next page

4 (a) Outline **two or more** clinical characteristics of depression. (5 marks)

(b) Discuss **two or more** explanations of depression. (25 marks)

> Some of the AO1 marks for this question have been set aside for a list of two or more clinical characteristics. Do not go overboard and write everything you know as there are only 5 marks available. Two reasonably detailed characteristics would be enough for 5 marks. In part (b), you should balance your AO1 and AO2 material appropriately for 10 AO1 marks and 15 AO2 marks. For 10 AO1 marks (about 240 words), you might hope to cover three explanations. To prepare for this, you might précis the explanations in this topic so you can include the most pertinent points. You can also prepare a précis of appropriate commentary. These are like 'modules' that can be fitted into exam questions as appropriate.

5 Compare and contrast **one** biological explanation of depression and **one** psychological explanation of depression. (30 marks)

> The 'compare and contrast' questions cause candidates greatest problems, but they shouldn't. You are given credit for a description of both biological and psychological explanations. You might divide your answer into four 200-word components – one chunk on your biological explanation, one on your psychological explanation, one chunk describing/commenting on similarities and one chunk on doing the same for differences. These chunks do not have to be exactly equal but they would ensure that you focus on the exact requirements of this question.

Topic 3 >> Anxiety disorders

WHAT ARE ANXIETY DISORDERS?

Fear and anxiety are complex reactions to a threat or danger. We react to fearful situations on several levels:

- *emotionally* – we experience a sense of panic and alarm

- *cognitively* – we worry about what will happen and often anticipate dire consequences

- *physiologically* – we show many involuntary physiological responses such as dry mouth, palpitations, tensed muscles, perspiration etc.

- *behaviourally* – we show a tendency either to freeze or to run away.

These are perfectly normal reactions in the face of a threatening stimulus. They are helpful to us because they allow us to anticipate impending danger and take action to deal with it. Such reactions only lead to anxiety disorders when they are out of all proportion to the threat posed or when they exist in the absence of any obvious danger.

DSM-IV lists several disorders characterized by excessive fear and anxiety. In this section, we will look at two of them:

- phobias

- obsessive–compulsive disorder.

PHOBIAS

What are phobias?

Phobias are classified as anxiety disorders in DSM-IV and are the most common of all anxiety disorders. We all have aversions to certain things or situations, which can make us feel a little squeamish or anxious – or even fearful – when we encounter them. This is quite normal. It is only when the aversion becomes an excessive and unreasonable fear that it is classified as a phobia. Even then many people adapt their life in order to avoid or cope with their extreme fears. When someone cannot do this, however, and the fear or anxiety becomes so severe that it interferes with their life so much that their behaviour becomes dysfunctional, then the phobia is classified as a mental disorder. Phobias are often accompanied by fainting and mild depression.

Phobias have been categorized into three main types:

- specific (isolated) phobias

- social phobias

- agoraphobia.

A2 Individual Differences

Onset appears to be earliest for animal phobias, followed by other specific phobias and social phobia, with the latest onset being for agoraphobia (Kendler *et al.* 1992a). The likelihood of a person developing a phobia during their lifetime is 11.3 per cent for specific phobias, 13.3 per cent for social phobia and 6.7 per cent for agoraphobia (Magee *et al.* 1996), and females outnumber males by two to one (Eaton *et al.* 1991).

Clinical characteristics of phobias

Specific (isolated) phobias

As the term implies, these are fears relating to something specific. Earlier versions of DSM, prior to DSM-IV (1994), called these 'simple' phobias, although they are far from simple. When the person encounters the feared object, they show an immediate fear response. They will often anticipate situations where the phobic object might be encountered and will go to great lengths to avoid it. People with specific phobias usually recognize that their fears are irrational and exaggerated, but this does not help them to deal with their anxiety. Four major sub-types of specific phobia have been identified:

- *Animal type* – e.g. fear of spiders (arachnophobia), dogs (cynophobia), cats (ailurophobia)
- *Situational type* – e.g. fear of flying (aerophobia), enclosed spaces (claustrophobia)
- *Natural environment type* – e.g. fear of heights (acrophobia), water (hydrophobia)
- *Blood-injection-injury type* – e.g. fear of blood (hematophobia), injections (trypanophobia).

There is also a fifth category of 'other' for those that do not fit one of the four major types. With the increase in air travel, fear of flying is becoming one of the most common phobias and many airlines now offer therapy programmes based on systematic desensitization (see Unit 26, p. 799). Specific phobias that begin in childhood often disappear without treatment. However, if they persist into or begin in adulthood, they usually only disappear in response to some kind of therapeutic intervention.

Social phobia

Social phobia is an excessive fear of social situations. Most people are nervous about public speaking, but someone with a social phobia is afraid of any activity performed in public, such as eating in public or going into a public lavatory. It has been suggested that social phobia is merely a case of excessive shyness, but this is not so because, for example, there are many actors and athletes who perform in public yet are excessively shy, and their shyness does not usually extend to, say, eating in public. This kind of phobia is different from specific phobias in that the phobic object is not the situation per se, i.e. being in a restaurant or a public lavatory;

the fear is rather of the possibility of embarrassment or humiliation in front of other people. The age of onset tends to be around 15 years and is most prevalent in people aged 18 to 29 years. If the phobia is severe, it is often accompanied by depression or substance abuse.

Agoraphobia

Agoraphobia is a fear of public places. It is especially debilitating because it can result in people being afraid to go out of their home, meaning they are unable to go to work or even shop for provisions. For these reasons it is thought to be the most serious of all phobias. Many people with agoraphobia are also prone to panic attacks when they venture into public places. Agoraphobia is closely associated with 'panic disorder', as people with panic disorder fear public places because they are likely to induce a panic attack. Indeed, DSM-IV classifies two types of panic disorder: with and without agoraphobia. However, agoraphobia can continue even if the person has not had a panic attack in years. Onset of agoraphobia is generally in early adulthood and is most common in females. Again, it differs from specific phobias in that it is not the shop or the workplace itself that induces the fear reaction; the fear is focused on the inability to escape from the situation.

Case study of a phobia

Eddie had always been terrified of travelling in cars and had managed to avoid this for most of her life by using buses or trains. For some reason she was not afraid to travel by these methods.

Eddie finished her degree and got a good job with an advertising agency. They told her she would need to drive in order to visit clients and would have access to the pool car. Eddie knew she would have to overcome her fear and arranged driving lessons. To her surprise she did not find this as frightening as she had expected and passed on the second attempt. The first time she used the pool car, however, she tried to reverse out of a parking space and hit the adjacent car, doing considerable damage to both cars. The car park attendant told her the other car belonged to the Managing Director. Eddie lost her nerve and went straight home, resigning from her job immediately.

After that Eddie stayed at home, refusing to go out socially or to find another job, even one which did not involve driving. Eddie was referred for treatment by her general practitioner (GP). She knew that her recent anxiety was related to the car accident, but she had no idea why she had been terrified of cars since she was a young child. She could not recall a car accident in her past.

Biological explanations of phobic anxiety disorders

Genetic explanations

Fear and anxiety have evolutionary advantages for survival, because they trigger our 'fight-or-flight' mechanisms, i.e. the release of certain brain chemicals which give us a spurt of energy in threatening or dangerous situations either to attack or to escape faster. We know, therefore, that fear and anxiety are part of the genetic make-up of many species, including humans. However, not all humans develop such extreme fears that they become phobias and most phobias are related to things which are not potentially harmful. Genetic research, therefore, is attempting to establish whether there is a familial genetic link – whether the tendency to develop phobias is hereditary. Research into phobias has focused mainly on family studies with first-degree relatives (parents, children, siblings) and, in a few studies, with second-degree relatives (aunts, uncles, nieces, nephews). There has been a small number of twin studies and virtually no adoption studies.

Family history studies

These have focused mainly on agoraphobia:

- A study by Solyom *et al.* (1974) of 47 phobic patients found a family history of psychiatric disorder in 45 per cent of the cases (with 30 per cent of their mothers having phobias), in contrast to only 19 per cent in families of a non-phobic control group of patients.
- Noyes *et al.* (1986) found a higher-than-normal rate of agoraphobia (11.6 per cent) and panic disorder (17.3 per cent) in first-degree relatives, using the family interview method.
- Another family interview study by Fyer *et al.* (1990) of 49 first-degree relatives of people with a specific phobia found that 31 per cent of relatives were also diagnosed with phobias, but only two people had the same type.
- Reich and Yates (1988) found a 6.6 per cent rate for relatives of people with social phobia compared with 2.2 per cent in controls. When categorizing people into those with animal-types of phobias and those with non-animal types of phobias, they found a much higher frequency of the same type of phobia in relatives compared with controls.

Twin studies

- A twin study by Slater and Shields (1969) found 41 per cent concordance in 17 MZ twin pairs versus 4 per cent in 28 DZ twin pairs, for any type of anxiety disorder.
- A more recent study conducted by Torgersen (1983) found 31 per cent concordance in 13 MZ twin pairs for panic disorder and agoraphobia versus zero concordance in 16 DZ twin pairs, although none of the concordant twins shared the same phobia.
- Kendler *et al.* (1992a) interviewed 722 female twins with a lifetime history of phobia. They found that MZ twins have significantly lower concordance rates for agoraphobia than DZ twins, which goes against the genetic hypothesis, although they suggest it may reflect a protective effect of the close emotional bond between MZ twins. For specific phobias they found that a shared environment was a much more likely explanation than genetic.

Evaluation
genetic explanations

- *Family studies* – Most of the family studies show that the relatives of those with phobias are more likely to suffer phobias themselves compared with relatives of non-phobic controls. However, there are methodological difficulties with family studies, the main problem being that in most instances family members share the same environment and could equally therefore have learnt the behaviour.

- *Twin studies* – Twin studies offer more reliable data to test the genetic hypothesis, but unfortunately very few have been conducted. Adoption studies would provide more convincing evidence, but such studies have been sparse.
- *Role of genetic factors* – There is some evidence for genetic factors in the development of phobias. However, this is more likely to be a tendency to inherit a physiological predisposition towards anxiety in general, rather than being a predisposition specific to phobias.

Biochemical explanations of phobias

Research indicates that people who develop phobias are those who generally maintain a high level of physiological arousal which makes them particularly sensitive to their external environment. One suggestion is that phobias arise because of a dysfunction in neurones that inhibit anxiety. GABA is a neurotransmitter which is automatically released in response to high levels of arousal. It binds to receptors on excited neurones, which underlie the experience of anxiety, and inhibits their activity. This produces a reduction of arousal levels and, therefore, a decrease in experienced anxiety. Evidence to support this idea comes from studies of people treated with benzodiazepines such as valium and librium. These drugs work like GABA by binding to neuroreceptors and decreasing arousal and experienced anxiety.

Evaluation
biochemical explanation

- *Low levels of GABA activity* – There is some evidence to support the idea that anxious people have unusually low levels of GABA activity.

- *Effect of benzodiazepines* – There is some evidence for the anxiety-reducing effects of benzodiazepines in adults, but the effects seem to be short term. In children, benzodiazepines produce only marginally better relief than placebos (chemically inert substances).

Psychological explanations

Psychodynamic explanations of phobias

The psychodynamic view is that the anxiety expressed towards an object or situation is a displacement of internal underlying anxiety. The psychoanalytic view (Freudian) is that phobias are associated with unconscious sexual fears (or 'id' impulses) and that they operate through the defence mechanisms of repression and displacement. The original source of the fear is repressed into the unconscious and the fear is then displaced onto some other person, object or situation. Thus the fear appears to be irrational because there is no conscious explanation for it. Freud's theory of phobias rests on his 1909 case study of a boy named Little Hans who developed a fear of horses (Freud 1909). Freud believed that the boy's phobia was directly related to his unconscious fear of his father, associated with the Oedipal phase.

Bowlby (1973) suggested that phobias can be explained by his theory of 'attachment and separation' (see Unit 2). For instance, agoraphobia is said to relate to a fear of losing someone to whom the person has become attached (most often the mother). He maintained that the origins lie with 'separation anxiety' in early childhood, particularly where parents are overprotective.

Evaluation
psychodynamic explanations

- *Freud's reliance on case studies* – Freud's theory is based almost entirely on case studies and there is no direct evidence to support his ideas.

- *Link between phobias and 'strict' cultures* – Although there is no empirical evidence to support Freud's theory directly, cross-cultural studies (e.g. Whiting 1966) do indicate that anxieties and phobias are more common in cultures characterized by strict upbringing and punishment.

- *No evidence of symptom substitution* – The theory predicts that the phobia can only be treated by uncovering the real, underlying fear – simply removing the overt fear will result in 'symptom substitution', i.e. the development of another displaced fear. However, when phobias are removed, e.g. by behavioural treatments, there is no evidence of symptom substitution.

- *Inconsistent evidence for Bowlby's theory* – The evidence for Bowlby's theory with regard to phobias is inconsistent. For example, Parker (1979) found that being overprotected during early childhood correlated with the development of social phobias later on. On the other hand, the development of agoraphobia was found to correlate with having parents who had tended to display a lack of affection. Many studies indicate no relationship at all between parental rearing styles and types of anxiety disorders.

The behavioural (conditioning) explanation for phobias

This explanation proposes that first a panic attack occurs in response, for instance, to being trapped in a lift. This results in an association being established between anxiety and that lift (classical conditioning). Subsequently, this anxiety becomes generalized to all lifts. Consequently, the person will actively avoid using lifts in the future. Avoidance of lifts is further reinforced by the reduction in anxiety experienced when the person adopts alternative strategies, such as using the stairs (operant conditioning).

● *Support for conditioning explanation* – The conditioning explanation for phobias has been extensively researched and is supported by early studies on humans and animals that would now be regarded as unethical. In a now classic study, Watson and Rayner (1920) apparently conditioned a 10-month-old boy, named Little Albert, into developing a phobia towards a white rat, using classical conditioning techniques.

● *Support for behavioural explanations not replicated* – Although there has been considerable support for the behavioural explanation of phobias, more recent studies have failed to replicate their findings. Munjack (1984) took a group of people with driving phobia and found that only 50 per cent of them had actually had a frightening experience in a car. In addition, 50 per cent of the *control group* in Munjack's study who did not have a phobia had had a frightening experience in a car, many of these involving an accident. The behavioural explanation cannot account for such individual differences.

● *Selectivity of phobias* – If phobias are simply learned through classical conditioning, it should be possible to develop a phobia for virtually anything. In fact, phobias are quite selective.

ACTIVITY

Objects of phobias

Look at the various things shown above. Which of these do you think are most likely to be the objects of phobia. Why might this be so?

Research into preparedness (Ohman *et al.* 1976)

Ohman and colleagues conditioned fear in a group of volunteer students using various prepared and unprepared stimuli. In the prepared condition, participants were shown pictures of snakes or spiders (i.e. stimuli that are potentially dangerous) whereas in the unprepared condition, they were shown pictures of houses, faces or flowers. Presentations of the pictures were paired with a brief, but painful electric shock in both conditions. Ohman and colleagues' findings were as follows:

● Fear conditioning occurred rapidly in the prepared condition after only one pairing.

● It took approximately five pairings to condition a fear response in the unprepared condition.

The conclusion is that humans are more likely to learn a fear response to potentially dangerous things than to neutral objects.

Preparedness theory

The recognition that some phobic reactions are more common than others has prompted the suggestion that there is species-specific, biological predisposition to fear certain stimuli, dating back to our ancestors. This was researched by Seligman (1971) who proposed the concept of biological 'preparedness': all species are innately 'prepared' to avoid certain stimuli because they are potentially dangerous. A classic study by Garcia and Koelling (1966) showed that rats could easily be conditioned to avoid life-threatening stimuli, such as shocks or toxic liquids, but not to avoid stimuli which carried no adverse consequences, such as flashing lights. Human phobias, such as fear of the dark or fear of heights, are consistent with this theory. See the panel above for an example of a study of preparedness.

Evaluation
preparedness theory explanation

● *Explains some phobias, but not others* – Preparedness theory can account for the fact that certain objects and situations are more likely to induce phobic reactions than others. However, it is possible to develop phobias of things like buttons and feathers, although these are much rarer; it is more difficult for the theory to explain them.

● *Explains irrationality of phobias* – Preparedness theory also accounts for the irrationality of phobias, i.e. the fact that phobias persist in the face of logical argument. In Ohman's study, for example, the participants were assured at the end of the experiment that no more shocks would be delivered. The conditioned fear to the neutral items extinguished immediately, but the conditioned fear to the prepared stimuli was much more resistant to extinction.

● *Explains ease of developing phobias* – It suggests why people can develop a phobia without any memory of a traumatic event. There is evidence that prepared fear conditioning can be acquired with the minimum contact with the feared stimulus. Mineka *et al.* (1984), for example, found that rhesus monkeys developed a persistent phobia for snakes after brief exposures to the sight of their parents behaving fearfully in the presence of a toy snake.

● *Does not explain individual differences* – It does not explain why there are such wide individual differences in the tendency to acquire phobias.

● *What is the real fear?* – Further criticism of the theory of 'biological preparedness' comes from a study by McNally and Steketee (1985). They found that in 91 per cent of cases of snake and spider phobias, the cause for concern was not a fear of being harmed, but rather a fear of having a panic attack. The exception was dog phobias, where most people were afraid of being bitten.

Social learning theory

The ease with which certain phobias can develop could equally be accounted for in terms of social learning, that is, modelling our behaviour on others and, in particular, on our parents. If certain stimuli are potentially dangerous, then from an early age we observe others avoiding these. In the same way, we also learn that certain stimuli are commonly avoided within a given culture. This could explain apparent phobias for stimuli that are not necessarily life-threatening – for example, snakes and large spiders, most of which are not dangerous. Bandura and Rosenthal (1966) asked participants to watch someone (actually a confederate of the experimenters) who appeared to be receiving a painful electric shock every time a buzzer sounded. After witnessing this, the participants themselves showed a fear response when they heard the buzzer even though they had never directly experienced the shocks.

Evaluation
social learning theory explanation

● *Inconsistency in the development of phobias* – Many people who seek treatment for phobias do not have experience of witnessing their fear in others. Similarly, many people who have been exposed to phobic models do not go on to develop phobias themselves.

● *Social learning as part explanation* – There is evidence that vicarious learning can lead to phobic reactions, but it cannot provide a complete explanation.

Cognitive–behavioural explanations

The cognitive–behavioural explanation for phobias extends the behavioural view of the conditioning of physiological reflexes to the cognitive domain of 'thinking'. Leading theorists in this field, such as Albert Ellis (1962) and Aaron Beck (1963), suggest that catastrophic thoughts and irrational beliefs contribute to the development of a phobia. For example, an experience of feeling 'hemmed in' in a crowded lift might be maintained later on by thoughts and beliefs such as 'I might suffocate if I were trapped in a lift'. This then turns into a fear of lifts, which is then generalized to other similar situations, resulting in the onset of claustrophobia. Therefore, it is not only an initial exposure to a fearful situation that initiates the phobia; rather it is also the person's irrational thoughts about the future possibility of a fearful situation.

According to Beck, people with phobias have a belief system whereby they know at a rational level that danger is minimal, yet they also truly believe that their feared object or situation will cause them physical or psychological harm. Beck *et al.* (1985) found that danger beliefs are activated when the person is in close proximity to the phobic stimuli, but at a distance they may state that the probability of harm is almost zero. The 'odds' then gradually change as the person comes closer and the sense of danger increases until they are actually in the feared situation, when the fear becomes 100 per cent. Beck and colleagues (1985) also found that people with phobias are more preoccupied with their 'fear of fear' than the actual object or situation itself.

Williams *et al.* (1997) examined this concept by subjecting people with agoraphobia to a hierarchy of increasingly scary tasks, while monitoring their thoughts throughout. Their results supported Beck and colleagues, in that participants' statements, which were tape-recorded, were mainly a preoccupation with their current anxiety rather than their safety.

Negative self-appraisal appears to be a key feature in social phobia, together with a sense of perfectionism. A study by Bieling and Alden (1997) found that people with social phobia scored significantly higher than controls on perfectionism and had lowered perceptions of their social ability.

Evaluation
cognitive–behavioural explanations

- *Research support* – The cognitive–behavioural explanation has found considerable support from numerous studies.

- *Explains susceptibility to phobias* – It can explain why certain people are more prone to develop phobias than others.

- *Success of therapy* – Cognitive–behavioural therapy is very effective in reducing phobic anxiety, although this in itself does not verify the underlying theory.

- *Irrational thoughts as cause or symptom?* – It is difficult to ascertain whether irrational thoughts are the cause of phobias, or merely a symptom of the disorder.

Diathesis-stress model explanation of phobias

As with the other disorders considered in this unit, the diathesis-stress model suggests an interaction between vulnerability factors and triggering events. Major life events have long been regarded as a major contributing factor in all anxiety disorders, including phobias. Holmes and Rahe (1967) explained the cumulative effects of major life events, and the work of Kobasa (1979) highlighted the effects of everyday minor hassles (see Unit 3). Kleiner and Marshall (1987) found that in a group of agoraphobics, 84 per cent had experienced family problems prior to the onset of their first panic attack and this finding has been confirmed by a number of other studies. However, the difficulty with the life-events theory is that many people who experience the most adverse life events do not develop an anxiety disorder.

The diathesis-stress model proposes an interaction between various factors and may explain individual differences in susceptibility to stress. It is suggested that we all have our own individual tolerance thresholds which form a predisposition to stress; this is known as our 'diathesis' or 'vulnerability' factor. The origin of this predisposition to vulnerability is not certain. It may be genetically inherited or it may be acquired through early experience; explanations include psychodynamic, behavioural and cognitive ones. The interaction between this vulnerability factor and the degree of life stress a person encounters (major life events and/or minor hassles) is thought to determine the likelihood that anxiety will reach a degree where it becomes dysfunctional, and from this phobias may develop.

There is some evidence to support the behavioural view of conditioning and, indeed, many people with specific phobias do report a fearful experience as the onset of the phobia. However, many people have a similar experience and do not develop a phobia, which suggests that other vulnerability factors play a part and lends support for the diathesis-stress model.

The vulnerability factor is the key to the aetiology of phobias. This could be a physiological vulnerability, or a deeper underlying problem expressing itself in a phobia or in negative ways of thinking. However, we all have fears and anxieties; they only become a mental disorder when they are so extreme that the person's life has become dysfunctional.

OBSESSIVE–COMPULSIVE DISORDER (OCD)

Most of us have obsessional thoughts at times, often related to fears, and on occasions have a compulsion or impulse to act in ways that are strange and out of character. Most of us have certain ritualistic or routine ways of doing things, such as always putting on our clothes in a particular order and many of us have certain superstitious beliefs. For someone with 'obsessive–compulsive disorder' (OCD), these are so invasive and taken to such an extreme, and are accompanied by such severe anxiety, that the person cannot function effectively in their daily life. OCD is probably the most severe of all anxiety disorders and is one of the most difficult to treat.

- *Obsessions* are persistent and recurrent thoughts, images, beliefs and impulses which enter the mind apparently uninvited and which cannot be removed.

- The *compulsive* element of OCD is the irresistible urge to carry out repetitive acts ritualistically in order to ward off some imagined dire consequence.

Clinical characteristics of OCD

- People with OCD are generally aware that their obsessional thoughts and behaviours are illogical, but they are powerless to overcome them. Often they attempt to hide them from others.
- People with OCD suffer severe anxiety, which is thought to precipitate the symptoms. However, the obsessions and compulsions do not appear to alleviate the initial anxiety, rather they create additional anxieties as a consequence.
- People with OCD also tend to suffer from severe depression, which is an understandable reaction.

The age of onset for OCD is usually in late teens and early twenties, and it affects around 2 per cent of the population (American Psychiatric Association 1994). The disorder seems to occur equally in men and women, although women are more likely than men to have compulsions that involve cleaning. Some examples of obsessive–compulsive behaviours are given below:

- *Obsessional cleanliness* – An obsession with dirt and contamination leads to compulsive behaviours such as repeated hand-washing, whereby a person can scrub their hands raw. There is also continual scrubbing and bleaching of surroundings, especially sinks, toilets and doorknobs.
- *Compulsive rituals* – These are specific ways or orders of doing things that are totally fixed and rigid, yet accompanied by an urge to resist.
- *Obsessional doubts* – These are usually related to safety concerns: for example, doubting whether they have switched off the gas hob or locked the door when leaving the house.
- *Compulsive checking* – This follows on from obsessional doubts. Here, the person will have a compulsion to check and double-check continually and is often unable to leave the house because they cannot stop checking.
- *Obsessional ruminations* – These are internal debates which are endlessly reviewed, the person presenting arguments for and against even the simplest of actions.
- *Obsessional impulses* – These are strong urges to perform acts of an embarrassing, dangerous or violent nature, such as jumping in front of a car or blaspheming in church.

A02 Evaluation
biological explanations

- *Genetics or environment?* – Although there is some evidence that OCD can be passed on genetically, studies have found it difficult to disentangle the effects of genetics from those of shared environment.

Biological explanations of OCD

Genetic explanations

There is tentative evidence to support OCD as a genetically inherited disorder. Family history studies report a prevalence of up to 10 per cent in first-degree relatives (e.g. Carey and Gottesman 1981), while twin studies (e.g. Hoaker and Schnurr 1980) indicate a concordance rate of between 50 and 60 per cent. In all these studies, however, people shared the same environment, suggesting that environmental factors might have a strong influence. It has been suggested (e.g. Rapoport 1989) that obsessions and compulsions result from fixed action patterns in the brain that have evolutionary significance for survival. In stressful and dangerous situations, certain action patterns are triggered, but most people cease to perform actions when their purpose has been completed. For people with OCD, the fixed action patterns are inappropriately triggered by their own perceptions of danger.

Biochemical explanations

Some researchers believe that OCD results from a deficiency of serotonin or a malfunction in serotonin metabolism. Support for the biochemical explanation comes from the effectiveness of medication – in particular, drugs which inhibit the re-uptake of the neurotransmitter serotonin, which have been found beneficial for up to 60 per cent of patients with OCD (Zohar *et al.* 1996). However, they seem to provide only partial alleviation of the symptoms, which recur when medication is ceased (Lydiard *et al.* 1996), indicating that medication is not a cure.

Neuroanatomical explanations

Rapoport and Wise (1988) have suggested that OCD arises from a structural dysfunction in the central nervous system (CNS), probably in the basal ganglia. Support for this idea comes from the finding that OCD frequently occurs in people with disorders such as Huntington's chorea, Parkinson's disease and Tourette syndrome which are known to involve basal ganglia pathology. Also Rapoport *et al.* (1994) have reported that surgery which disconnects the basal ganglia from the frontal cortex brings relief in severe cases of OCD.

- *Inconsistent findings regarding serotonin* – Studies on the role of serotonin in OCD have yielded inconsistent findings. Much of the evidence is flawed and studies have not included controls to rule out the possibility that anti-depressant drugs bring relief because they alleviate the symptoms of depression that frequently accompany OCD.

continued on next page

Evaluation continued
biological explanations

● *Effectiveness of psychological therapy* – There is strong evidence that psychological therapy alone can be very successful in treating OCD and it is difficult to account for this within the serotonin hypothesis.

● *Possible dysfunction in the basal ganglia* – Neuro-imaging techniques have enabled researchers to study the basal ganglia of people with OCD. Unfortunately, results have been inconsistent. For example, Aylward *et al.* (1996) found no differences between OCD patients and matched control participants.

Psychological explanations of OCD

Given the lack of consistent findings from studies investigating the biological causes of OCD, it seems likely that psychological factors may be more important.

Psychodynamic explanation

Freud believed that OCD stems from a fixation at the anal stage of development. The child has to accept the will of the parents and be neat and clean when its natural preference is to be messy and aggressive. When these natural impulses are particularly strong and parental restrictions are too strict, development is arrested and so the issues related to this stage become issues in adulthood as well. However, because this takes place at an unconscious level, the adult really believes that they are concerned with keeping themselves clean. Psychoanalysts think that OCD is most likely to occur in people who are anally fixated and thus show anal personality characteristics. Such people are excessively neat, orderly and punctual.

Behavioural explanations

The behavioural explanation is that OCD is an extreme form of 'learned avoidance' behaviour. An initial event is associated with anxiety or fear; avoidance behaviour initially alleviates this fear, subsequently becoming a conditioned response.

Cognitive–behavioural explanations

According to the cognitive view, the disorder is a consequence of faulty and irrational ways of thinking taken to an absolute extreme. Specific environmental stimuli are paired at some time with anxiety-provoking thoughts and these stimuli, therefore, become conditioned. These stimuli trigger obsessional thoughts, and compulsive rituals are then used to try and neutralize them. According to Rachman and Hodges (1987), some people are more susceptible to developing obsessive thoughts. Vulnerability factors include genetically determined hyper-arousability, depressed mood and poor socialization experiences.

Evaluation
psychological explanations of OCD

Psychodynamic explanation

● *Hard to test* – It is difficult to test the idea of unconscious motivation experimentally.

● *Importance of obsessive personality style* – There is evidence of an obsessive personality style. However, such people do not seem any more likely to be diagnosed with OCD than anyone else (Peterson 1992).

Behavioural explanations

● *Flaw in the argument* – The behavioural explanation falls down in that the symptoms of OCD, such as avoidance behaviour, themselves create anxiety; it is hard to argue that people learn these responses in order to reduce fear.

● *Effectiveness of behavioural therapies* – The behavioural view is supported by the effectiveness of behavioural therapies (see Unit 26), such as graded exposure and flooding. Studies, such as the one by Baxter *et al.* (1992) and Schwartz *et al.* (1996), have found that behavioural therapies not only reduce symptoms of OCD, but also bring about changes in biochemical activity. Marks (1981) found behavioural therapy to be very effective in treating obsessive cleaning and checking behaviour, but not so effective for obsessional thoughts.

Cognitive–behavioural explanations

● *Lack of evidence* – There is little evidence to suggest that OCD is the result of socialization.

● *Effectiveness of cognitive–behavioural therapies* – Cognitive–behavioural therapies (see Unit 26) have been shown to be reasonably effective in treating OCD (e.g. Emmelkamp *et al.* 1988).

● *No long-term solution* – Neither medication nor psychological therapies, however, appear to offer a long-term solution to OCD, and it remains a very difficult disorder to understand and treat effectively.

Check your understanding of anxiety disorders by answering these questions. Check your answers by looking back through Topic 3.

1 What distinguishes a normal fear from a phobic reaction?

2 What are the three main categories of phobias?

3 What are the main clinical characteristics of phobias?

4 Briefly outline the case for a genetic predisposition to phobias.

5 Briefly outline the GABA hypothesis.

6 Briefly outline the psychodynamic view of phobias and give two weaknesses of this approach.

7 Explain what is meant by 'learned helplessness' and give a brief evaluation of this theory.

8 Outline the main clinical characteristics of OCD.

9 Give a brief outline and evaluation of biological explanations of OCD.

10 Consider the view that anxiety disorders are caused by psychological factors.

REVISION SUMMARY

Having covered this topic, you should be able to:

✓ describe the clinical characteristics of one disorder (phobias or obsessive–compulsive disorder (OCD))

✓ describe and evaluate biological explanations (including evidence) of the chosen disorder

✓ describe and evaluate psychological explanations (including evidence) of the chosen disorder.

EXAMPLE EXAM QUESTIONS

Below are some **possible examination questions** set on this topic, along with hints to help you understand and approach each question effectively:

1 (a) Outline **two or more** clinical characteristics of **one** anxiety disorder. (5 marks)

(b) Critically consider biological explanations of the anxiety disorder that you described in part (a). (25 marks)

The specification requires that you study one anxiety disorder which can be of your choosing. Questions will always focus on only one disorder and you will gain no credit for covering more than one, unless you introduce this as effective critical commentary. In this question, you have 5 marks for a brief outline of clinical characteristics. Do not include these in any essay unless specifically required to do so. In part (b), you must focus on biological explanations only. Evaluation may be in terms of research evidence, though AO2 credit will be for the *use* of such material not its description. Other ways to gain AO2 credit would be to consider any methodological flaws and the extent to which these challenge the validity of the studies. You might also consider applications of this knowledge, though *descriptions* of therapies would not be creditworthy.

2 (a) Outline and evaluate **one** explanation of **one** anxiety disorder. (10 marks)

(b) Outline and evaluate **two or more** explanations of depression. (20 marks)

This is probably an unlikely question but has been included to make two points. One is that it is legitimate to combine topics within one unit, as has been done here. Second it is always vital to pay attention to the split of marks as a guide to how you should spend your time. In part (a), there are 10 marks for one explanation (which can be biological or psychological). You have about 7 minutes to describe your explanation and the same for the evaluation (about 120 words for each). In part (b), if you provide two explanations then you have the same constraints here.

continued on next page

3 Critically consider the evidence for biological explanations of **one** anxiety disorder. (30 marks)

> The specification includes the phrase 'including the evidence on which [explanations] are based'. This means that you could be asked a question such as this which requires a description of the evidence as AO1, rather than a description of the explanation, and then commentary on the evidence as AO2. Take great care that you do not simply present your prepared essay on biological explanations which would receive limited credit, depending on the extent to which evidence was described and evaluated. You could be asked this same question about schizophrenia or depression.

4 'The strength of biological explanations is the increasing research evidence now available in relation to anxiety disorders.'
With reference to the quotation, discuss biological explanations of **one** anxiety disorder. (30 marks)

> Here, you are required to address the quotation as part of your answer. It is intended to be slightly challenging. Has there been increasing evidence? What evidence is there? How good is it? Note that the question requires that you discuss *explanations* not evidence. You must always answer the question, and refer to the quotation as appropriate. In this case it should help your AO2 commentary.

5 Compare and contrast **two or more** explanations of **one** anxiety disorder. (30 marks)

> Here, you are not required to compare and contrast one biological and one psychological explanation, but to compare and contrast *any two* explanations. You could even extend the scope of your essay by including a third explanation to describe and compare/contrast. As with question 5 on p. 776, divide your response into an appropriate number of chunks.

UNIT SUMMARY

- This unit has looked at different types of mental disorders: **schizophrenia, unipolar depression and anxiety disorders.** There are many explanations, both psychological and physiological, of the causes of specific disorders and some have been supported by **empirical evidence** more strongly than others. However, this does not inevitably make these explanations more correct.

- **Schizophrenia** is a serious mental disorder characterized by severe disruptions in psychological functioning and a loss of contact with reality.

- **Depression (unipolar disorder)** is a type of mood disorder where the person experiences feelings of great sadness, worthlessness and guilt. In extreme cases, it can lead to suicide.

- **Anxiety disorders** include a range of conditions characterized by excessive and inappropriate anxiety or fear. **Phobias** are a common form of anxiety disorder where the individual experiences fear of an object or situation which is out of all proportion to the actual danger posed. **Obsessive–compulsive disorder (OCD)** is an anxiety disorder where the individual is plagued with uncontrollable thoughts (obsessions) and performs seemingly pointless rituals (compulsions).

- There is no single explanation that can adequately account for any of the major disorders. However, explanations have been offered by **biological** and **psychological** models which all have strengths and weaknesses.

- **Twin, adoption** and **family studies** continue to provide strong, although not yet conclusive, evidence for a genetic link with schizophrenia. There is some evidence for a **genetic link** with unipolar depression, although this has not been firmly established. Evidence for a genetic link with the anxiety disorders is fairly weak. It may be that there is a genetic tendency in some individuals to be more sensitive to the environment and, as such, more susceptible to certain types of mental disorder, such as depression and anxiety.

- A **genetic predisposition** merely predisposes someone to developing a disorder, i.e. they are more or less at risk depending upon the degree of relatedness; it does *not* mean that someone who is at risk will automatically develop the disorder.

- **Neurological research** has highlighted possible **structural brain abnormalities** linked with schizophrenia, which could be due to a genetic defect, or caused through brain complications or viral infections. The structural abnormalities could even be caused by having schizophrenia, since it is still not clear whether they precede the onset of the disorder or develop as a consequence.

- There is no clear-cut evidence for structural brain abnormalities in depression and anxiety disorders, such as phobias, although structural dysfunction in the basal ganglia has been implicated in OCD. Some of the cognitive explanations suggest that the cognitive impairments associated with some of these disorders might be linked to underlying brain abnormalities.

- There is evidence for **biochemical involvement** in both schizophrenia and depression and, to a lesser extent in the anxiety disorders, although it is still not clear whether this is causal, or simply a physical symptom of the disorder.

- There is very little evidence for **social/psychological explanations of** schizophrenia, other than levels of expressed emotion, which could act as a trigger or affect the length of remission between acute episodes. The **psychodynamic and behavioural** approaches offer plausible psychological explanations of depression and phobias and OCD, but not for schizophrenia. **Cognitive models** have been put forward as explanations for all the disorders and they have stimulated much interest. However, many of these theories remain rather speculative as they lack sound empirical support.

- The **diathesis-stress model** offers an explanation which accounts for individual differences, by suggesting a predisposition to vulnerability which interacts with environmental factors, such as stressful life events.

FURTHER RESOURCES

Carlson, N.R. (1998) *Physiology of Behaviour* (6th edn), Boston: Allyn & Bacon.

An excellent text on physiological psychology aimed at undergraduates, but the sections on vision are fairly easy to understand and provide more detailed coverage of the visual system than is possible in this unit.

Comer, R.J. (2004) *Abnormal Psychology* (5th edn), New York: Freeman.

Davison, G.C. and Neale, J.M. (2003) *Abnormal Psychology* (9th edn), New York: John Wiley.

These two books both provide readable, comprehensive accounts of the disorders discussed in this unit.

Oltmanns, T.F., Neale, J.M. and Davison, G.C. (1995) *Case Studies in Abnormal Psychology* (6th edn), New York: John Wiley.

This book provides extended, detailed case studies to illustrate mental disorders.

Websites

www.artvt.com/expressed_emotion.htm

A short, but highly readable essay from the Harvard Medical School on expressed emotion and the schizophrenic patient.

www.mentalhealth.com/main.html

A major source of information about all aspects of mental health, and links to other relevant sites.

www.schizophrenia.com/

A non-profit-making information, support and education centre focused specifically on schizophrenia.

www.schizophrenia.com/newsletter/buckets/hypo.html

This site has lots of recent news updates on research findings on schizophrenia.

Unit 25 // Psychopathology

26 UNIT

TREATING
Mental
Disorders

PREVIEW

After you have read this unit, you should be able to:

>> describe and evaluate biological (somatic) therapies, including the use and mode of action of chemotherapy, ECT and psychosurgery

>> understand issues surrounding the use of such therapies (e.g. appropriateness and effectiveness)

>> describe and evaluate behavioural therapies, including the use and mode of action of therapies based on classical and operant conditioning

>> understand issues surrounding the use of such therapies (e.g. appropriateness and effectiveness)

>> describe and evaluate alternatives to biological and behavioural therapies, including psychodynamic therapies and cognitive–behavioural therapies (CBTs)

>> understand issues surrounding the use of such therapies (e.g. appropriateness and effectiveness).

INTRODUCTION

A therapy is a deliberate intervention designed to treat mental disorders either by effecting a complete cure or by making the symptoms more manageable. A number of different therapies and treatments for mental disorders will be outlined, each one based on a particular theoretical orientation regarding the basis of human nature and the causes of psychological problems. You will already be familiar with these orientations or models of mental disorder from your AS-level studies into individual differences (see Unit 4); you may wish to refresh yourself on these before starting this unit, as this background knowledge is essential to an understanding of therapies.

This unit will explain the use and mode of action of each type of treatment, followed by an account of attempts made to assess the effectiveness and appropriateness of the treatment. There are considerable ethical and practical issues involved with therapy and intervention and these have important implications for all of those involved in mental health, whether recipients or practitioners. Some of these points will be considered in the context of each type of therapy. There are, however, some important general issues surrounding the use of therapies. These are described on p. 790 and we recommend that you start by reading about these and also come back to them later on as you evaluate the various types of therapy.

Jane
Willson

1 In the past restraints such as straitjackets were used to control mentally ill patients. Nowadays we use different methods to treat mental illness. But is drug therapy just a chemical straitjacket?

2 When might therapies be used as means of control?

3 Read the excerpt from the BBC news report on the right. Do you think that people suffering from mental disorders should ever be compelled to undergo therapy?

Sword attacker's release condemned

A parishioner at a church where a schizophrenic man attacked the congregation with a samurai sword has condemned his early release from a secure mental hospital ... One of the seven people who over-powered and disarmed [the attacker] has grave concerns about his release ... [saying] his release made him as much a risk to himself as to the public. 'He could, tomorrow, just flatly refuse to take his medication and we are back to square one,' he said.

Source: BBC news report, 29 June 2002 (news.bbc.co.uk)

KEY CONCEPTS

Therapy: a systematic intervention to help people overcome their psychological difficulties.

Biological (somatic) therapies: an approach to the treatment of mental disorders that relies on the use of physical or chemical methods.

Chemotherapy: treatment by using drugs.

Electroconvulsive therapy (ECT): a treatment involving passing an electrical current through the brain by the application of between 70 and 130 volts which induces a convulsion or epileptic seizure.

Psychosurgery: cutting brain tissue in order to alleviate the symptoms of severe psychological disorder.

Behavioural therapies: therapeutic techniques of changing behaviour that are based on the principles of classical conditioning. The term 'behaviour modification' is more usually used for techniques derived from operant conditioning.

Cognitive–behavioural therapies: techniques that involve helping clients to identify their negative, irrational thoughts and to replace these with more positive, rational ways of thinking.

Psychodynamic therapies: treatments that help clients to uncover past traumatic events and the conflicts that have resulted from them. These conflicts can then be resolved so that the client is able to restore an adaptive level of functioning.

IMPORTANT GENERAL ISSUES SURROUNDING THE USE OF THERAPY FOR MENTAL DISORDERS

All therapies, from whichever theoretical orientation, are intended to alleviate suffering and to restore normality. Therapy can be expensive, time-consuming, and, in certain cases, harrowing and uncomfortable for the recipient. The chosen therapy must have a likely chance of success, i.e. it should be appropriate for that particular individual and effectively bring about a change for the better in their condition. Research is an important way of establishing which therapies are effective and for which disorders. However, there are many problems associated with research in this area which means that conclusions should be drawn with caution. Here are a few points for you to consider when you are evaluating research studies:

- *Operational definitions* – In order to carry out meaningful research, the investigator must precisely define and measure the concepts under investigation. A concrete measure of an abstract concept is called an 'operational definition'. If, for example, the research concerns depression, some agreed definition of what is meant by depression must be established. Researchers in the field of abnormal psychology often use the current diagnostic manuals such as DSM-IV and ICD-10 to provide operational definitions. However, these manuals are not totally reliable and decisions based on their criteria could lead to inclusion of participants in the research sample who have widely differing symptoms. For example, it is possible to diagnose two people with schizophrenia even though they might exhibit very different behaviours. Treatment outcomes for these different types of schizophrenia might vary. We know, for example, that positive symptoms (see Unit 25, p. 755) are alleviated by neuroleptic drugs, but that negative symptoms show little improvement in response to drug therapy. The research sample used to investigate treatment outcomes must, therefore, be recruited according to strict operational definitions otherwise the results will be misleading.

- *Allocation to treatment groups* – Ideally, participants should be allocated randomly to the different conditions of an experiment, so that there is no room for bias. This means that, in treatment outcome research, the group in the new treatment condition should not differ significantly from the group in the control condition. Truly random allocation can only occur with the consent of the patients and of their supervising doctor and, in practice, this rarely happens. Severely disturbed patients are often unwilling to take part in clinical trials and doctors are often reluctant to assign older patients or those with very acute symptoms to experimental groups. This means that the results of the research will not give an accurate picture of the effectiveness or appropriateness of the treatment.

- *The role of the therapist* – Research into a specific form of treatment is often instigated and carried out by people who are particularly skilled or committed to that type of therapy. It is known that the personal characteristics of the individual therapist can be important in the efficacy of a particular treatment. Factors such as skill, experience, age, gender, culture and even attractiveness have all been shown to affect treatment outcomes. It is, therefore, possible that promising results obtained in such research studies may not hold good when the treatment is used in everyday practice where the therapist may be more of a generalist and not as skilled in or committed to that particular therapy.

- *The effects of existing treatments* – Participants involved in treatment outcome research have often already had some form of therapy for their disorder. It is important to ensure that the effects of the original treatment do not then confound the results of the research into the new treatment. For example, some drug therapies can affect levels of concentration and arousal. This means that they might be less responsive to a therapy such as REBT than they would be if they were drug free. It is important, therefore, to stop medication in all patients some time before they take part in research into an alternative therapy. However, for obvious ethical and practical reasons, this rarely happens.

- *Placebo effect* – There is an argument that therapy produces beneficial effects simply because attention is given to the patient and an expectation of success is created when treatment is offered (the placebo effect). By this reasoning, the specific type of therapy offered should be unimportant. In order to rule out this possibility, most well-controlled treatment outcome research includes a placebo group. For example, in a drug trial, the control group would receive an inert substance packaged and presented in exactly the same way as the real drug of interest and, in double-blind designs, neither the participants nor the doctors would know which group was receiving the genuine medication. If the drug group shows significantly greater improvement than the placebo group, it can be fairly confidently concluded that the effect is due to the pharmacological rather than the psychological properties of the drug. It is more difficult to control for the placebo effect when assessing psychological treatments such as CBT or psychodynamic therapy, where it is hard to find a truly inert substitute. It is also virtually impossible to carry out a double-blind design with these types of therapy. There is a further complication when comparing treatment and placebo groups. This is the phenomenon known as 'spontaneous remission', where people simply recover over the course of time without any type of therapeutic intervention. The precise reasons for this are not known, but it has been estimated to occur in 30 to 60 per cent of cases (Bergin and Lambert 1978).

- *The concept of cure* – It is difficult to determine the criteria for deciding whether a particular treatment has been effective or not, because the concept of a 'cure' for mental disorders is hard to establish. For example, is a person with schizophrenia 'cured' if the major, psychotic symptoms are kept under control by drugs even though the symptoms may well return if the drugs are discontinued? Is someone with a rat phobia only 'cured' if they start keeping rats as pets or is it enough for them to show less anxiety about rats than they did before? A related problem is the issue of time. Some therapies take considerably longer than others to take effect. At what point should the measure of effectiveness take place?

Biological treatments arise from the medical model of abnormal behaviour: mental disorder is an illness which results mainly from a biochemical imbalance. Biological treatments are designed to redress this imbalance, through the administration of chemical drugs, electroconvulsive therapy (ECT) and, in rare cases, psychosurgery. The term 'somatic' is often used to describe biological therapies, somatic meaning 'related to the body'. Many people who are experiencing psychological problems or who show disturbed behaviour patterns go for help to their family doctor. This means that the first line of treatment offered is usually medical. Somatic therapies can be used for a whole range of psychological disorders from mild anxiety to schizophrenia. They aim to alter abnormal behaviours by intervening directly in bodily processes.

USE AND MODE OF ACTION OF CHEMOTHERAPY

Since the 1950s, the use of drugs in the treatment of mental disorders has been widespread and they account annually for a large proportion of NHS prescriptions. The main types of drug used fall into the following categories:

- anti-anxiety drugs
- anti-depressant drugs
- anti-psychotic drugs.
- anti-manic drugs
- stimulants

These so-called 'psychoactive drugs' work by affecting the nervous system. Neurons communicate with one another via a number of different chemical messengers (neurotransmitters) (see Unit 12, p. 377).

There are many different types of neurotransmitter, but the main ones are:

- dopamine
- serotonin
- noradrenaline (norepinephrine).
- acetylcholine
- GABA

The psychoactive drugs work in various ways, but essentially they serve either to increase or decrease the amount of available neurotransmitter.

Anti-anxiety drugs

These consist of a class of drugs called 'benzodiazepines' and are minor tranquillizers designed to reduce levels of anxiety. Benzodiazepines such as Librium and Valium were introduced in the 1950s and 1960s and soon became the most prescribed drugs in the world. They were taken up eagerly by GPs because they offered an apparently safe way to alleviate anxieties in patients. They did not lead to fatality when taken in overdose, unlike opioids, such as morphine and laudanum. These had been the only drugs previously available and doctors were loath to prescribe them because of the dangers of addiction, severe side effects, overdose and potential fatality. The benzodiazepines are sedatives which inhibit the nervous system and produce muscle relaxation and an overall calming effect.

Evaluation
the use of anti-anxiety drugs

- **Effective in reducing symptoms** – Benzodiazepines have been found to be effective in reducing symptoms of anxiety and panic. Gelernter et al. (1991) found them to be more effective than a placebo for social phobia and Lecrubier et al. (1997) found that around 60 per cent of patients with panic disorder remained free of panic while on medication.

- **Dangers of dependence** – These new drugs offered an easy solution for GPs who could write a prescription rather than engage in counselling (for which few GPs are trained). Unfortunately, benzodiazepines did not prove to be a magic solution, because they created dependence on the drug, sometimes for years. The frequency and willingness with which GPs prescribed benzodiazepines in the 1960s/70s has led to the recent development of self-help groups for people trying to overcome long-term dependence. Most GPs now restrict such drugs to short courses.

- **Tolerance** – Benzodiazepines also create tolerance, so that the dosage needs to be increased over time to produce the same effects.

- **Withdrawal** – Dependence leads to physical withdrawal symptoms, such as tremors and insomnia. However, Linden et al. (1998) found that neither the dosage nor length of treatment were major factors in dependence. When patients were asked to take a three-week drug holiday programme, withdrawal occurred before the programme began, indicating that the dependency was psychological, not physical.

- **Treating the symptoms not the cause** – One of the main problems with anti-anxiety drugs is that they do not treat the cause of the anxiety. This is illustrated by the statistic that there is around a 90 per cent relapse rate when benzodiazepine medication is ceased (Fyer et al. 1987).

Anti-depressant drugs

These drugs are designed to enhance the mood of people with depression and to reduce panic in people with anxiety disorders. They affect the availability of serotonin and noradrenaline which are the neurotransmitters thought to be implicated in depression. The main anti-depressants are monoamine-oxidase inhibitors (MAOIs), tricyclics (TCAs) and selective serotonin re-uptake inhibitors (SSRIs).

Monoamine-oxidase inhibitors (MAOIs)

The first MAOI was Iproniazid. Its anti-depressant effect was discovered by accident when it was tried as a new drug for tuberculosis and found to induce euphoria. MAOIs block the action of the enzyme that breaks down noradrenaline and serotoni, so increasing the availability of these neurotransmitters in the nervous system.

Tricyclics (TCAs)

Tricyclics, such as Tofranil, operate in a similar way to MAOIs, but are milder anti-depressants and, although they are slower acting, have fewer severe side effects.

Selective serotonin re-uptake inhibitors (SSRIs)

The SSRIs, such as Prozac, inhibit the re-uptake of serotonin and thus make more of this neurotransmitter available. More recently, the natural herb hypericum, commonly known as St John's Wort, has been found in clinical trials to have anti-depressant qualities with very few side effects (Holden 1997). It is thought that the herb alters serotonin function in some way.

Commentary
the use of anti-depressants

- **Effective in reducing symptoms** – Anti-depressants have been tested in trials with placebos and found to be effective in reducing symptoms of severe depression in around 65 to 75 per cent of cases, compared to around 33 per cent for placebos (e.g. Prien 1988).

- **Comparing effectiveness and side effects of MAOIs and TCAs** – Spiegel (1989) found that around 65 per cent of depressed patients improved with tricyclics, although there are potential side effects, the most serious being cardiac problems. MAOIs are equally effective, but require dietary restrictions and can interact dangerously with other drugs such as cold remedies. Tricyclics are prescribed more often since they are milder anti-depressants and, although slower acting, have fewer severe side effects. MAOIs are still prescribed, but only with extreme caution. A study by Jarrett *et al.* (1999) found that MAOIs were much more effective than tricyclics for severe depression and Thase *et al.* (1991) claimed that they might be the only recourse for treating depressive episodes in bipolar disorder.

- **Prozac, the wonder drug?** – Prozac was hailed as a 'wonder drug' when it was first introduced in the late 1980s and is currently the most frequently prescribed of all anti-depressants. However, it has recently become a media target because there have been so many anecdotal reports of serious side effects, including a preoccupation with violence and suicide (Steiner 1991).

- **Use with older and younger people** – Anti-depressants are less effective with children, but are very effective with older people, although with more side effects.

Anti-psychotic drugs

These are the neuroleptic drugs used in the treatment of schizophrenia and other psychotic disorders. Neuroleptics are major tranquillizers, the most notable being 'phenothiazines', which sedate the person and improve symptoms of psychosis, such as delusions and hallucinations. Before phenothiazines were introduced in the 1950s, schizophrenia was considered untreatable and patients were interned in mental institutions. As Rosenhan and Seligman (1995) vividly explain, the back wards of mental hospitals were called 'snake pits', filled with inmates who were unreachable or mutely catatonic, or were wild with delusions and straitjacketed, or were 'giggling out' unrelated words. All previous attempts to treat schizophrenia, such as insulin shock, ECT and drugs, had failed.

Commentary
the use of anti-psychotic drugs

- **Effective in treating symptoms of schizophrenia** – Anti-psychotic drugs have provided a breakthrough in treating the symptoms of schizophrenia. They produce a calming effect and a reduction in psychotic symptoms such as delusions and hallucinations and motor disorders. However, they seem to have little effect on the negative symptoms such as social withdrawal and apathy.

continued on next page

- *Compliance and care in the community* – The American Psychiatric Association (APA) (1997) reports that phenothiazines are effective with 60 per cent of patients, enabling many to live a reasonably normal life in the community. Community care, however, has proved inadequate for many people with schizophrenia, one problem being poor compliance with medication. Research indicates that if anti-psychotic drugs are stopped abruptly, then symptoms recur (Davis *et al.* 1993). This has led to the 'revolving door syndrome' of continual discharge into the community and re-admission into hospital.

- *Side effects of phenothiazines* – It is estimated that around 7 per cent of people diagnosed with schizophrenia refuse to take phenothiazines (Hoge *et al.* 1990), perhaps because they have considerable side effects. One is the development of symptoms similar to those found in Parkinson's disease, such as stiffness, immobility and tremors. In its most serious form, this leads to a condition called 'tardive dyskinesia', which includes uncontrollable, sucking and smacking of the lips and facial tics. It is thought that phenothiazines destroy a part of the brain. This occurs in around 30 per cent of those taking the drug and the risk increases with prolonged usage (Gualtieri 1991).

- *Newer neuroleptics (e.g. Clozapine)* – A note of optimism is that newer types of neuroleptics, such as Clozapine and Risperidone are reported to have far fewer side effects (APA 1997). Research has also shown that Clozapine can have therapeutic effects in patients who have not responded to other anti-psychotic drugs. However, other studies (e.g. Umbricht and Kane 1996) have found side effects that may be potentially life threatening. One is its effect on white cell production and subsequent damage to the immune system. Other drugs then have to be administered to counteract this effect and regular blood tests are necessary. This makes the treatment very expensive and limits its availability.

- *Important role in treatment* – Despite side effects, drugs continue to be the main form of treatment for psychotic disorders because other forms of therapy, such as psychotherapy, have traditionally been thought to have little effect.

Anti-manic drugs

These drugs are used to control mania in those suffering from bipolar disorder. They were discovered through the work of John Cade, an Australian physician, who tested a lithium preparation on manic patients and found that their manic euphoria had calmed within a few days. By the 1970s, lithium carbonate had become the routine treatment for manic-depression.

- *Effective in reducing symptoms of manic-depression* – These drugs have been found to be effective for around 80 per cent of patients with manic-depression (Rosenhan and Seligman 1995). Prior to their introduction, 15 per cent of manic-depressives committed suicide and a large proportion were unable to function properly in daily life because of their extreme mood swings.

- *Disadvantages and side effects* – Many patients are loath to take medication because they like being in a euphoric state (Johnson *et al.* 1989) and because lithium carbonate has side effects. It is toxic and can lead to gastro-intestinal and cardiac problems – even death. Another problem is that if a person starts on lithium and then discontinues it, its future use can increase the risk of manic-depressive episodes (Suppes *et al.* 1991).

- *Danger of relapse* – Although lithium has been found to be effective for mania, studies (e.g. Gitlin *et al.* 1995, in a five-year prospective study) indicate that around 70 per cent of people relapse while on medication.

Stimulants

The most widely used stimulant drugs are the amphetamines, which increase alertness and elevate mood. Ritalin, a closely-related compound, is used mainly for the treatment of children diagnosed with attention deficit/hyperactivity disorder (ADHD). It may seem contradictory, but the effect of this stimulant drug is to reduce hyperactivity and increase the attention span in such children. Children who are prescribed Ritalin are often kept on the drug until adolescence when, for reasons that are not fully understood, hyperactivity tends to diminish.

Unit 26 // Treating mental disorders

Commentary
the use of stimulants

● *Effectiveness in reducing hyperactivity in children* – There is evidence that hyperactivity reduces in children given Ritalin. Whalen *et al.* (1989) found that such children are viewed more positively by their peers once on medication.

● *Effectiveness in treatment of adults* – There is also evidence that Ritalin is effective in treating adults where the condition has persisted from childhood (Spencer *et al.* 1995).

● *Side effects* – There are side effects such as insomnia, loss of appetite and reduced growth rate. 'Drug holidays', where the drugs are temporarily withdrawn, can be useful as a way of minimizing side effects and monitoring behaviour to see whether medication is still required.

● *Controversy over diagnosis of ADHD* – The diagnosis of ADHD is a controversial one and not all clinicians agree that it is a valid diagnostic category. There are important ethical considerations involved in prescribing powerful drugs for children, particularly when the diagnosis is not universally accepted.

Evaluation
the use of drugs

● *Use of drugs to control* – There has traditionally been a good deal of criticism levelled at the use of chemotherapy for psychological problems, particularly in mental institutions where patients have no choice. Are they administered to alleviate suffering in the patient, or to sedate patients so they are more compliant with institutional regimes? As a result of such criticism, there has recently been greater emphasis on voluntary agreement and the right to refuse treatment.

● *Dangers of the right to refuse* – There are two sides to this debate: the right to refuse versus the consequences of non-compliance. For example, some patients with schizophrenia can be dangerous to themselves or others. Their symptoms are kept under control with anti-psychotic drugs. Ensuring that such patients stay on their regime of drugs was not too difficult in the days of mental institutions, but in the current climate of civil rights and care in the community, this is not so straightforward. Issues of compliance with medication have become high profile after some innocent bystanders have been attacked by schizophrenia outpatients (see 'Getting you thinking...', on p. 789).

● *Dangers of inaccurate prescription* – Compliance with medication can have adverse effects if drugs have not been accurately prescribed. For example, neuroleptic drugs can produce the symptoms of schizophrenia in people without a psychotic disorder (see 'It was the drugs that made me mad' opposite).

● *Treating the symptoms, not the cause* – It has now become clear that drugs do not necessarily offer a long-term cure, because in many cases symptoms recur when the drugs are no longer taken. It is believed by many psychologists that biochemical imbalance is the result of, rather than the cause of, mental disorders. This leads to the claim that drugs merely treat the symptoms (e.g. the anxiety or depression), but do not address the cause of the problem (e.g. why the person is anxious or depressed). Consequently, they can only provide short-term alleviation.

● *Costs versus benefits* – Given that there are also numerous side effects from drugs, it is arguable whether the benefits could ever outweigh the costs, particularly if the initial problems still remain. Many people, however, prefer drugs. This may be because taking medicine is a familiar activity, whereas psychological treatment is unfamiliar territory.

● *Combining drugs and psychological treatment* – For psychological therapies to be effective, clients or patients must have some insight, that is, they must recognize that they have a problem. Some people suffering from chronic psychotic disorders have little or no insight and so psychological treatment is difficult. With the assistance of phenothiazines, which reduce psychotic symptoms such as delusions and hallucinations, psychotic patients can become 'more available' to psychological therapies, such as insight therapies and family therapy. Short courses of anti-depressant drugs can be worthwhile in cases of severe clinical depression, because without these drugs, patients often have no motivation to engage in psychological treatment. Anti-depressants may even be essential as a first line of treatment for severe clinical depression, because of the high risk of suicide. These examples illustrate ways that somatic treatment and psychological treatment can work together, rather than as alternative forms of treatment.

USE AND MODE OF ACTION OF ELECTROCONVULSIVE THERAPY (ECT)

This controversial form of treatment developed from the mistaken idea that schizophrenia was incompatible with epilepsy. It was thought that schizophrenia could be alleviated by artificially inducing epileptic seizures. Initially, seizures were induced by giving patients insulin. However, this proved to be extremely unreliable since it was difficult to judge the correct dosage and the side effects were very unpleasant. In 1938, Cerletti and Bini tested the technique of applying electric shocks to the brain in order to induce seizures. In the couple of decades following the introduction of this technique, ECT was widely used for a broad range of psychiatric disorders. The original procedure involved passing very high currents of electricity across both hemispheres of the brain and was known to lead to severe memory loss, speech disorders and irreversible brain damage. Its use declined significantly with the arrival of the new psychoactive drugs in the 1950s. The decline was partly as a result of bad publicity because ECT was seen as a barbaric and punitive treatment that caused serious side effects. However, it soon became clear that the new drugs did not offer a complete solution and interest revived in ECT.

Modern techniques are much more humane and the patient is given muscle relaxants and a short-acting anaesthetic before ECT begins. The standard procedure is unilateral and involves administering a current of between 70 and 130 volts to the temple of one side of the head for between half a second to five seconds. This usually induces convulsions for a brief period after which the patient comes round from the anaesthetic with no recollection of the treatment. Usually a course of approximately six sessions will be given over a period of a few weeks.

ECT is ineffective in reducing the psychotic symptoms of schizophrenia, but has been found to be very effective in alleviating severe depression in some people. It works much more rapidly than anti-depressant drugs and hence is often the treatment of choice for patients who are severely depressed and a suicide risk. In spite of its effectiveness, the precise mechanism underlying its therapeutic action is not understood. It seems likely that ECT increases the levels of available noradrenaline, but it is such an invasive technique that it is difficult to isolate the element that brings about therapeutic change.

Evaluation
the use of ECT

● *A controversial treatment* – ECT is controversial, not least because the medical profession is still unsure of how it works – an analogy has been drawn with banging the side of the television set to make it work (Heather 1976).

● *Effective in treating severe depression* – ECT has been successful in treating severe depression in patients where all other methods have failed

and many argue that this is sufficient justification for its use, especially if it prevents suicide. It is a quick form of treatment, in contrast to drugs or psychological therapies, and Klerman (1988) maintains that ECT may be the optimal treatment for severe depression.

● *Success rate* – Studies indicate that 60 to 70 per cent of patients improve with ECT (e.g. Sackeim 1988), although a large proportion of these become depressed again the following year (Sackeim *et al.* 1993).

continued on next page

- *After other treatments have failed* – ECT should only be administered if anti-depressant drugs have no effect and if there is a risk that the person will commit suicide. However, it has been found that the relapse rate is high if it is followed by the same ineffective anti-depressant drugs (Sackeim *et al.* 1990). With acute mania, ECT has been found to be effective in around 80 per cent of people who had not responded to medication (Mukherjee *et al.* 1994).

- *Side effects* – When ECT was first introduced, there were dangerous side effects, such as bone fractures, memory loss and confusion. There are no detectable changes in brain structure with the newer procedure and, as the technique is continually improved, side effects are being reduced. Studies examining cognitive side effects have confirmed this. For example, Devanand *et al.* (1994) found no evidence of long-term memory loss or any other longer-term cognitive changes.

- *Nature of the treatment* – Although techniques are improving, the decline in the use of ECT continues. As Comer (1995) argues, applying an electrical current to the brain is a frightening and forceful form of intervention. Even with the newer techniques there are still side effects, especially with repeated use. Effective anti-depressant drugs now provide a more attractive alternative.

- *Consent and control* – Nowadays, ECT requires consent from the patient or a close relative. However, ECT has a history of abuse, being used as a means of punishing or controlling people in mental hospitals. Some people have received hundreds of ECT treatments.

USE AND MODE OF ACTION OF PSYCHOSURGERY

Psychosurgery is an extreme form of biological treatment since it involves the destruction or removal of neural tissue in the brain. The first modern psychosurgery technique was the 'pre-frontal lobotomy', developed in the 1930s by Egas Moniz, a Portuguese neurologist, as a cure for schizophrenia. This is a fairly drastic surgical procedure involving the destruction of fibres connecting the higher thought centres of the frontal cortex with the lower centres of the brain. Moniz claimed high rates of success using this procedure and it was taken up enthusiastically by surgeons in other parts of the world. It is estimated that about 40,000 to 50,000 operations were carried out in the USA and about 10,000 in the UK between the late 1930s and the early 1950s. Although originally intended to alleviate the symptoms of schizophrenia, these operations were also carried out on people with depression and, sometimes, on people with personality or anxiety disorders. In spite of Moniz's claims, there was no evidence that the lobotomy provided an effective form of treatment. Many patients did indeed calm down and could even be discharged from hospitals, but the re-admission rate was high and significant detrimental effects were found such as withdrawal, stupors, seizures and even death. With the introduction of the psychoactive drugs in the 1950s, the lobotomy was largely abandoned.

Psychosurgery today

Nowadays, psychosurgery is performed only in extreme cases when all other forms of treatment have failed and where, because of the disorder, the person is likely to cause harm to themselves or to others. Modern surgical procedures are much more sophisticated and involve considerably less damage to neural tissue. A more recent procedure is the 'cingulotomy', where a tiny cut is made in the cingulum nerve fibres, using an electrode needle which is guided by magnetic resonance imaging.

AO2   **Commentary**
the use of psychosurgery

- *A last resort* – Psychosurgery continues to be regarded as the most controversial of all treatments for mental disorders. The modern procedures are less invasive, but there are still dangers and this kind of treatment should only be offered as a last resort. However, according to Beck and Cowley (1990), the procedure can be beneficial in some cases of severe anxiety, depression and obsessive–compulsive disorders.

- *A controversial treatment* – Psychosurgery has come under attack more than any other treatment for mental disorders. Comer (1995) explains that it was performed on tens of thousands of people in the 1950s as a response to overcrowding in mental institutions and the absence of effective treatments for many serious mental disorders. There was also concern in the USA about the suspected use of psychosurgery to control perpetrators of violent crimes. The lobotomy also became a civil rights issue with claims that it was being used as a means of silencing political activists and of controlling difficult mental patients in institutions.

continued on next page

A2 Individual Differences

● *Informed consent* – Certain people, including children, those with learning impairments and people with psychotic disorders, may not be able to give informed consent for treatment. For this reason, it has been possible for clinicians to administer biological treatments, in the form of medication, ECT and even psychosurgery, without informed consent. This is particularly so in the case of someone who has been detained under sectioning laws and where treatment is usually decided by the consultant psychiatrist. However, the Mental Health Act for England and Wales 1983 states that the patient's consent is now required for psychosurgery, along with a second opinion by an independent doctor.

CHECK YOUR UNDERSTANDING

Check your understanding of biological therapies by answering these questions from memory. You can check your answers by looking back through Topic 1.

1 What is meant by the term 'somatic therapy'?

2 Identify the five main types of drug used in the treatment of mental disorders.

3 Explain briefly how psychoactive drugs take their effect in the brain.

4 Give two advantages and two disadvantages of using benzodiazepines in the treatment of anxiety disorders.

5 Identify the three major types of anti-depressant.

6 Give two advantages and two disadvantages of using anti-psychotic drugs to treat schizophrenia.

7 Briefly outline three ethical issues concerning the use of drugs to treat mental disorders.

8 Give a brief outline of the use and mode of action of ECT.

9 Give a brief outline of the use and mode of action of psychosurgery.

10 Discuss some of the issues surrounding the use of somatic therapies (e.g. appropriateness and effectiveness).

REVISION SUMMARY

Having covered this topic, you should be able to describe and evaluate:

✓ the use and mode of action of: chemotherapy, ECT and psychosurgery

✓ issues surrounding the use of: chemotherapy, ECT and psychosurgery.

EXAMPLE EXAM QUESTIONS

Below are some **possible examination questions** set on this topic, along with hints to help you understand and approach each question effectively:

1 Critically consider biological (somatic) therapies. *(30 marks)*

> The terms 'critically consider' allows you great scope about what to include in this answer. You need to present at least two biological methods (because 'therapies' is plural), otherwise you would incur a partial performance penalty for AO1 and AO2 (maximum of 9 marks for each skill). The description of these therapies would form the AO1 part of your answer and AO2 would be any commentary. This might involve any research evidence or other means of considering the effectiveness of these methods. You can also consider ethical issues, consequences, or implications.

2 (a) Outline the use **and** mode of action of chemotherapy **and** ECT. (15 marks)

(b) Evaluate the use of chemotherapy and ECT with reference to issues surrounding their use
(e.g. appropriateness and effectiveness). (15 marks)

> In part (a), two of the therapies in the specification have been specified so you would get no marks for psychosurgery and partial performance marks for only chemotherapy or ECT. The two therapies do not have to be provided in equal detail though a reasonable balance is desirable. In order to have enough to write (and also to avoid having too much to write), it is worth practising writing a 7-minute version of each, a kind of précis. Note that the question also says 'use and mode of action' (words taken from the specification), so make sure for each therapy that you do consider both how it is used and how it works. In part (b), you must evaluate the therapies but this time, in contrast with question 1, the form that this evaluation must take is specified, i.e. only in terms of appropriateness and effectiveness.

3 'There is considerable evidence to show how effective biological therapies are, however they may not be appropriate and also raise ethical problems.'

Discuss issues relating to the use of biological therapies, such as those raised in the quotation. (30 marks)

> In AQA Module 5, quotations are often included as a way of increasing the breadth and synopticity of candidate's answers. Synopticity is explained on pp. 939–40. In some cases you are required to address the quotation, but here the phrase 'such as' tells you that the quotation is included to provide some useful prompts about what you *might* include in your answer, not what you *must* include. It is vital to answer the question and not the quotation. The question *does not* require a description of any therapy; it requires a description of the issues, and then AO2 is a commentary on this. AO2 may be achieved, for example, by providing comments about any studies that demonstrate effectiveness (were such studies valid?) or analysing whether ethical issues are criticisms of the methods.

4 (a) Outline and evaluate chemotherapy. (10 marks)

(b) Outline and evaluate ECT. (10 marks)

(c) Outline and evaluate psychotherapy. (10 marks)

> Questions are written in a way that should help you in forming your answers. This is a straightforward question asking you to outline and evaluate the three kinds of biological therapy. One problem you may face is having too much to write at least for some of these therapies so that something gets squeezed out – either one method is given in less detail, or the amount of AO2 is restricted, or you have less time for one of your other questions. Any of these would restrict your final mark.

Topic 2 >> Behavioural therapies

Behavioural therapies emerged in the 1950s and are a logical extension to behaviourism as applied to the field of psychopathology. The main assumption of the behavioural view is that abnormal behaviour is acquired in the same way as normal behaviour, through the principles of classical and operant conditioning, and through modelling. Behavioural therapists, therefore, suggest that maladaptive behaviours can be unlearned and replaced with new, more desirable behaviours. The therapy is usually targeted at specific, well-delineated anxiety disorders such as phobias and compulsions.

USE AND MODE OF ACTION OF BEHAVIOURAL THERAPIES

Over the past 30 or 40 years, a number of therapeutic techniques have been developed with the overall aim of encouraging adaptive strategies to enable the person to function more effectively in the environment. The first stage in behavioural therapy is a 'functional analysis'. The aim of this is to:

- assess the person's level of functioning
- identify the antecedents to maladaptive responses (i.e. what came before)
- decide upon the most appropriate treatment techniques.

Behavioural therapies based on classical conditioning

Systematic desensitization

'Systematic desensitization' (devised by Wolpe 1958) is a technique developed specifically to counter-condition fears, phobias and anxieties. Counter-conditioning is a process whereby a fearful reaction is replaced by another emotional response that is incompatible with fear. This is usually achieved by teaching the individual deep muscle relaxation techniques. The therapist then works with the client to compile a hierarchical list of feared situations, starting with those that arouse minimal anxiety, progressing to those that are the most frightening. After this preliminary training, the desensitization procedure can begin. Muscular relaxation is induced and the client is then asked to visualize the situation associated with the least anxiety-provoking item in the hierarchy. After several repetitions without anxiety, the treatment continues by repeating the process for every rung in the hierarchy. The client can indicate a feeling of anxiety at any stage in the process, usually by raising their hand. The therapist will then immediately stop the visualization, recreate the relaxation state and then return to the item again. Treatment is complete when the client is able to work through the entire hierarchy without anxiety. This technique can be conducted either *'in vitro'* (through imagined imagery) or *'in vivo'* (in real-life).

ACTIVITY

Tackling fears

In pairs or small groups, think about a specific fear that one of you has. Write down a hierarchy of graded exposure in line with systematic desensitization, starting with the least fearful situation relating to the specific fear, through a number of systematic steps of increasing fearfulness, and ending with the most frightening situation.

Flooding

Research into the effectiveness of systematic desensitization has shown that visualization can occasionally bring about therapeutic change even without relaxation. This finding has led to the development of an extinction treatment called 'flooding'. Flooding involves exposing clients to a phobic object in a non-graded manner with no attempt to reduce prior anxiety. For ethical and practical reasons, this technique is conducted mainly *in vitro* (also known as 'implosion therapy') after the therapist has first ensured that the person is in good physical health. Typically, the client is placed alone in the phobic situation, for example, in an enclosed space in the case of claustrophobia, and is required to remain there until there is a marked decrease in anxiety. In implosion therapy, the client would be asked to imagine themselves in such a situation. Physiologically, it is not possible to maintain a state of high anxiety for a very long period, and so eventually it will subside. This can take about an hour and it is important not to remove the person from the feared situation too early. If this happens, the person will be released when anxiety is still high and this will merely serve to reinforce the original fear. In the initial stages of the treatment, anxiety is very high, but it will reduce fairly quickly as emotional exhaustion and/or habituation set in and the client realizes that they are still safe and that nothing dreadful has happened to them. Thus the fear should be extinguished.

Aversion therapy

'Aversion therapy' is a technique based on classical conditioning, developed to deal with habits and addictions such as smoking, alcoholism or drug addiction. The therapist attempts to remove unwanted behaviours by associating them with unpleasant or aversive stimuli. For example, in the case of smoking the taste of tobacco might be paired with a feeling of nausea, for example by inserting a nausea-inducing substance into cigarettes. The major problem with this technique is that it is doubtful that aversion will continue once the negative pairing has been discontinued. As with the other therapies based on classical conditioning, there is a variation in which the unpleasant consequences are imagined rather than experienced in reality. In this case, therapy is called 'covert sensitization'.

Hey, I think you've got the wrong idea about 'flooding'!

- *Effective treatment for anxiety disorders and addictions* – Behavioural therapies based on classical conditioning are more appropriate for certain disorders than others. For example, they are effective methods of treatment for anxiety disorders such as phobias and post-traumatic stress disorder, and for addictions. However, they are not regarded as suitable for psychotic disorders such as schizophrenia.

- *Relatively quick* – Behavioural therapies are widely adopted by clinical psychologists within the NHS and are relatively quick, usually taking just a few months, in contrast to psychodynamic therapies that usually last several years.

- *High success rate* – The efficacy of behavioural techniques has been shown to be quite high: McGrath *et al.* (1990) found systematic desensitization effective for around 75 per cent of people with specific phobias. In their review, Barlow and Lehman (1996) reported that for specific phobias, graded exposure (systematic desensitization) was very effective and the preferred choice of patients. They also reported that for blood-injection-injury types of phobias, 90 per cent of patients were cured in around five sessions of graded exposure.

- *Single-session success* – Ost *et al.* (1991) conducted a study where the whole hierarchy of feared stimuli were presented in a single session over several hours to 20 patients with spider phobias. They found that, no matter how severe the phobia, 90 per cent were much improved or completely recovered at a four-year follow-up. Of course, it should be borne in mind that reported recovery might not have been a direct consequence of the one session of behavioural therapy received four years earlier.

- *Treating agoraphobia* – Agoraphobia is one of the most difficult phobias to treat, yet systematic desensitization has helped improve between 60 and 80 per cent of cases (Craske and Barlow 1993). However, improvements are shown to be only partial and in 50 per cent of cases relapses occur.

- *In vitro vs in vivo* – There is some evidence to suggest that not all behavioural therapies are equally effective. For example, *in vivo* techniques are found to be more effective for specific phobias than *in vitro* (Menzies and Clarke 1993).

- *Combining treatments* – Behaviour therapies are sometimes used in conjunction with other therapies. A number of studies comparing different types of therapy have found systematic desensitization to be equally effective for phobias when administered alone, or in combination with other treatments, such as medication or cognitive–behavioural therapy (e.g. Burke *et al.* 1997). However, a study by Beurs *et al.* (1995) of 96 patients found that systematic desensitization combined with medication was the most effective treatment for panic disorder with agoraphobia.

- *Symptom substitution?* – Critics of behavioural methods point out that quite often people with phobias have no recollection of any traumatic experience involving the object of their fear. Psychoanalytic theorists (see later in this unit) claim that this is because the phobia is merely a symptom, a signal from the unconscious that something is wrong. They claim that removing the phobia through behavioural techniques will simply result in a new phobia emerging because the treatment does not resolve the underlying conflict. However, there is no evidence that such symptom substitution occurs after behavioural therapy.

- *Unpredictable effects of therapy* – When agreeing to a particular therapy, patients and to some degree even therapists, cannot always anticipate what may occur during the course of therapy. This has been a major criticism of behavioural therapies, in particular the technique of 'flooding'. Even when conducted *in vitro* rather than *in vivo*, there may be dangerous consequences such as hyperventilation, raised blood pressure or heart attacks. Flooding, therefore, should not be undertaken without adequate training and proper medical supervision. Aversion therapy has also come under attack because it breaches ethical guidelines in its use of induced pain or nausea as aversive stimuli.

Behavioural therapies based on operant conditioning

Therapies based on operant conditioning aim to change behaviours through a process called 'behaviour modification'. Because these techniques depend on monitoring behaviour across a number of situations, they are less suited to therapy sessions than the techniques based on classical conditioning. In practice, behaviour modification techniques are usually used in institutions such as schools, mental hospitals and prisons, where the behaviour of individuals can be monitored consistently and systematically over time.

Token economy

Token economy is a behaviour modification programme based on Skinner's (1953) principle of behaviour shaping through positive reinforcement. It has been applied extensively in institutions, mainly with psychotic patients and with people who have severe learning difficulties. People in institutions sometimes neglect personal hygiene or develop anti-social eating habits. As a reward for carrying out target behaviours, such as washing, dressing, eating with cutlery, etc., the person receives rewards in the form of tokens, which can be collected and exchanged for goods, outings or privileges.

Social skills training

Social skills training is based on Bandura's (1969) 'social learning theory', an extension of operant conditioning, to include learning through observing and modelling the behaviour of others. According to social learning theory, phobias can develop through observing those fears in significant others and modelling behaviour upon those observations. Originally, Bandura applied the concept of 'modelling' as a treatment for phobias, but more recently, modelling has been applied widely in social skills training, particularly for developing assertiveness and interpersonal skills. The technique involves behaviour rehearsal and feedback. People are encouraged to practise appropriate responses to replace maladaptive responses in the safety of a role-play situation. Skills training is thought to be particularly helpful for people with low self-esteem, for those who are anxious in social situations and for those who are often exploited by others.

Evaluation
techniques based on operant conditioning

- **Cure or social programming?** – Programmes of behaviour modification, such as token economy, are accused of not offering a cure for mental disorders; they are merely intended to enable patients to 'fit' better into their social world. For example, chronic psychiatric patients often have no motivation to maintain personal hygiene, but by earning for washing, brushing hair, etc., they can gain some dignity. The natural rewards that will eventually replace the tokens are that others will be more sympathetic towards them.

- **Effectiveness of token economy** – Token economy has been widely adopted in psychiatric institutions with psychotic patients and found to be very effective in reducing inappropriate behaviour (Emmelkamp 1994). It has been suggested, however, that the so-called 'success' of this therapy may have more to do with its requirement for closer interaction between patient and nurse, suggesting that it is the attention that is therapeutic rather than the technique.

- **Increased involvement of care professionals** – Behavioural modification techniques have provided an opportunity for nursing staff to become far more involved in treatment, which may have increased their investment in helping the patient.

- **Effectiveness of modelling in treating phobias** – Bandura and Menlove (1968) and Bandura et al. (1969) have provided evidence to support the effectiveness of using modelling in the treatment of phobias. In clinical studies of nursery children with dog phobias and adults with snake phobias, they claimed a 90 per cent success rate.

- **Criticisms of token economy** – Token economy has been widely administered in institutions, but has been open to criticism with regard to the choice of goals, which may actually go against the patient's wishes. Whenever goals are imposed by others, then desirable behaviour is inevitably influenced by personal or institutional bias, even when the goal is truly believed to be for the client's own good. One of the major criticisms of token economy is that, in order to be effective, important reinforcements need to be controlled, which may violate basic human rights, such as restrictions on food, privacy and freedom of movement. Comer (1995) explains that boundaries have now been set on basic rights that clinicians cannot violate, but this may reduce the impact of token economy programmes. One of the saddest consequences of token economy programmes is that people become dependent on the regime and find it very difficult to think for themselves when outside the institutional setting. This has been the case with many people who have recently found themselves back in the community after prolonged institutional care.

REVISION SUMMARY

Having covered this topic, you should be able to describe and evaluate:

✓ the use and mode of action of therapies based on classical conditioning and on operant conditioning

✓ issues surrounding the use of therapies based on classical conditioning and on operant conditioning.

✓ CHECK YOUR UNDERSTANDING

Check your understanding of the nature of behavioural therapies by answering the following questions from memory. Check your answers by looking back through Topic 2.

1 Briefly outline the basic goal of therapy according to behavioural therapists.

2 Identify three different types of therapy based on classical conditioning.

3 Explain the difference between '*in vivo*' and '*in vitro*' therapy.

4 Explain why you think that therapies based on classical conditioning are so widely used.

5 Give a brief account of two pieces of research that have shown behavioural therapies to be effective.

6 Identify two ethical issues concerning the use of therapies based on classical conditioning.

7 Explain why techniques based on operant conditioning are more suitable for use in institutional settings than in individual therapy.

8 What is meant by 'social skills training'?

9 Outline what is meant by 'token economy' programmes, and give one strength and one weakness of this kind of therapy.

10 Discuss some of the issues surrounding the use of behavioural therapies (e.g. appropriateness and effectiveness).

✎ EXAMPLE EXAM QUESTIONS

Below are some **possible examination questions** set on this topic, along with hints to help you understand and approach each question effectively:

1 Compare and contrast therapies derived from the biological (somatic) **and** behavioural models of abnormality in the treatment of mental disorders. (30 marks)

> The question is not as hard as it might seem at first glance. One route to answering it is to describe (AO1) both kinds of therapy and then to consider similarities and differences (AO2). A slightly harder route would be to describe similarities and differences (AO1) and comment on these similarities or differences (AO2). If you take the simpler route, you can structure your answer quite simply: one quarter of your time (10 minutes, 200 words) should be a description of one or more biological therapies. A further quarter should be a description of one or more behavioural therapies. The third quarter of your answer would be on the similarities and the final quarter on differences. These need not be in balance, but you do need both to compare (similarities) and to contrast (look at differences).

2 Discuss issues surrounding the use of behavioural therapies (e.g. flooding, token economies). (30 marks)

> Questions such as this require great care. A quick glance might lead you to start writing your 'behavioural therapies' essay, but that's not the question and would result in low marks. The question requires you to describe the *issues* related to these therapies not the therapies themselves. Some examples are provided just to make it clear which group of therapies are being referred to. The AO2 element requires you to comment on the issues not the therapies.

3 (a) Outline behavioural therapies based on classical (e.g. flooding) **and** operant (e.g. token economies) conditioning. (15 marks)
  (b) Assess the therapies you described in part (a) in terms of issues (e.g. appropriateness and effectiveness) surrounding their use. (15 marks)

> The specification requires you to study therapies based on classical and operant conditioning, which means you might be asked about both in a question. Here, you must provide at least one example of each, or else incur a partial performance penalty. The examples given offer some help in doing this. You may only have time to write about one of each, but can do more if you have not got enough material for 10 minutes' worth of description on therapies derived from each type of conditioning. In part (b), you must evaluate the therapies in terms of issues surrounding their use. The examples given in the specification are provided as hints, but other issues are equally creditworthy, e.g. ethics.

4 (a) Outline **one or more** therapies based on classical conditioning. (5 marks)

(b) Outline **one or more** therapies based on operant conditioning. (5 marks)

(c) Discuss issues surrounding the use of such therapies. (20 marks)

This is a slight variation on question 3. This time the descriptions of classical and operant conditioning are worth 10 instead of 15 marks and thus time should be allocated appropriately. It also means that 5 AO1 marks are included in part (c) and that's why the instruction used is 'discuss'. Part (c) obviously involves considerably more evaluation, so your focus should largely be on commentary on the issues rather than a description of such issues, as was required in question 2.

Topic 3 >> Alternatives to biological and behavioural therapies

USE AND MODE OF ACTION OF COGNITIVE–BEHAVIOURAL THERAPIES

Cognitive–behavioural therapies began in the 1960s. Albert Ellis (1962) founded 'rational-emotive therapy' (RET) which he subsequently renamed 'rational-emotive-behaviour therapy' (REBT). Aaron Beck (1976) developed a cognitive therapy for depression and Donald Meichenbaum (1975) developed a CBT for stress management. The rationale for CBT is that thoughts (cognitions) interact with, and have an enormous influence on, emotions and behaviour. When these thoughts are persistently negative and irrational, they can result in maladaptive behaviour.

Aims of CBT

The aim of CBT is to help the client to identify their negative, irrational thoughts and to replace these with more positive, rational ways of thinking. A therapy session includes both *cognitive* and *behavioural* elements, with homework between sessions.

● *Cognitive element* – The therapist encourages the client to become aware of beliefs which contribute to anxiety or depression, or are associated with a general dysfunction in daily life. This involves direct questioning, such as: 'Tell me what you think about ...'. The therapist does not comment upon the client's beliefs, but instead they are treated as hypotheses and examined for validity. Diagrams (such as the ABC model in Fig. 26.1) can be used to help the client understand better where their faulty cognitions are leading them.

● *Behavioural element* – The therapist and client decide together how the client's beliefs can be reality-tested through experimentation, either as role-play or as homework assignments. The aim is that by actively testing out possibilities, clients will themselves come to recognize the consequences of their faulty cognitions. The therapist and client then work together to set new goals for the client in order that more realistic and rational beliefs are

incorporated into ways of thinking. These are usually in graded stages of difficulty so that clients can build upon their own success.

Figure 26.1 >> *An example of the ABC model in action*
Source: Prentice (1995), adapted from Ellis (1991)

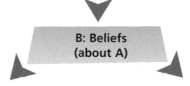

A: Activating event

Linda gets a low mark in her mock exam for A level psychology.

B: Beliefs (about A)

Rational thoughts	**Irrational thoughts**
Linda tells herself that she could have done better, but did not put in enough revision.	Linda tells herself that she should have done well and this means she will fail in her final exams.

C: Consequences (of B)

Desirable emotions	**Undesirable emotions**
Linda feels disappointed with her own efforts	Linda feels that she must be awful at psychology.

Desirable behaviour	**Undesirable behaviour**
Linda resolves to put in more effort for her final exams.	Linda decides to give up college.

Ellis and REBT

Ellis (1962) maintained that people can become habituated to their disturbed thoughts and this results in problems such as anxiety and depression. Ellis (1991) devised the ABC model (see Fig. 26.1) to illustrate how irrational, self-defeating thoughts can lead to maladaptive behaviour.

ACTIVITY

An activating event

Think about a recent activating event (A). Did you follow the rational or the irrational route, as illustrated in Fig. 26.1?

(A02) Commentary
REBT

- *Use and effectiveness of REBT* – Ellis (1980) maintains that REBT is appropriate for any kind of psychological problem, such as anxiety disorders, sexual problems and depression, but not for severe mental disturbance, where the person cannot be treated with talking therapies. He maintains that REBT helps clients to 'cure' themselves in an elegant way because it can be incorporated into their way of life.

- *Research into the effectiveness of REBT* – Haaga and Davison (1989) found REBT to be effective for anger, aggression, depression and anti-social behaviour, although not as effective as systematic desensitization in reducing anxiety. Engels *et al.* (1993) examined quantitative data from 28 controlled studies which showed REBT to be superior to placebo and no treatment, but only equally effective when compared with systematic desensitization or combination therapies (those combining REBT with some form of behaviour therapy). A more recent appraisal by Haaga and Davison (1993) suggests that there are difficulties in evaluating the effectiveness of REBT because of the difficulty in defining and measuring 'irrational beliefs'.

Beck, cognitive therapy and depression

Beck's work has centred mainly on depression. He devised the 'Beck Depression Inventory', which is an assessment scale for depression, and from this many more have been devised, such as the 'Suicide Intent Scale'. These scales have been widely adopted by clinical psychologists to monitor depression in clients, and employed by researchers for outcome studies. Beck has subsequently applied his techniques to phobias and anxieties (Beck *et al.* 1985) and to personality disorders (Beck *et al.* 1990). The concept of irrational beliefs has been tested and supported empirically (e.g. Beck 1991).

Meichenbaum's stress-inoculation model

Meichenbaum (1972), a cognitive–behavioural theorist, suggested that it is not a situation itself which causes anxiety, but the negative way that we talk to ourselves in relation to the situation. Meichenbaum developed 'stress inoculation therapy' (SIT), which he also called 'self-instructional training' (again SIT). This therapy has been extensively developed within stress management training and has been widely adopted in industry (see panel opposite and pp. 104–5).

Meichenbaum (1975) evaluated his model with anxious college students before exams. He compared his own cognitive modification methods with traditional systematic desensitization, plus a third group of waiting list controls. Students were given eight therapy sessions, evaluated through test performance and self-reports obtained immediately after treatment and at a one-month follow-up. The cognitive modification methods were found to be the most effective, followed by systematic desensitization. Those in the control condition showed no reduction in anxiety.

Use of CBT with schizophrenia

In the main, cognitive–behavioural therapies are thought to be appropriate only for those who have developed good problem-solving skills and are capable of gaining reasonable insight into their problems. However, both Beck and Meichenbaum see a role for CBT with psychotic patients. Hole *et al.* (1979) worked with chronic schizophrenia patients encouraging them to reality-test their delusions, and they found that in half of the patients they could reduce the pervasive nature of delusions. One of the major symptoms of acute schizophrenia is 'inner speech' and this is usually of a controlling nature (telling the person what to do). Meichenbaum and Cameron (1973) developed a programme wherein patients are trained to develop more adaptive controlling statements in their 'inner speech'.

Cognitive–behavioural techniques for schizophrenia are continually being developed and refined (e.g. Kingdon and Turkington 1994) and although they do not offer a cure for schizophrenia, they are effective in 'normalizing' symptoms.

Meichenbaum's 'stress-inoculation therapy'

Meichenbaum's 'stress-inoculation therapy' is based upon the belief we are often unaware of the negative way that we talk to ourselves and it is this, rather than a given situation itself, that causes anxiety. Negative self-speech, or what Meichenbaum calls 'self-defeating internal dialogue', such as anticipating failure and minimizing strengths, creates anxiety, which in turn produces a self-fulfilling prophesy, because high levels of anxiety lead to poor performance. The aim of stress management training is to redirect self-speech into something more positive and confidence building. The Meichenbaum Model consists of three phases:

Phase 1: Identifying the problem

This first phase is often called the 'educational phase', the aim being to identify and examine faulty internal dialogues that lead to inadequate behaviour, e.g. 'In the exams I will forget everything I know', leads to 'I will forget, therefore I am going to fail'. This in turn leads to maladaptive behaviour, e.g. dizziness, fainting, mental blanks, which then leads to a self-fulfilling prophesy of failure.

Phase 2: Acquiring coping skills

The aim now is to examine these self-defeating dialogues for validity (it is usually found that negative statements are rarely based in reality). The next step is to restructure thinking by converting these negative self-dialogues into positive self-statements – what Meichenbaum calls 'preparation statements', e.g. 'I'm going to do better than I thought' or 'I've coped with situations like this before'.

Phase 3: Practising coping responses

Having devised a number of preparation statements, the final phase is to practise these continually until they become automatic and replace the previous self-defeating dialogues.

I'll never manage this

KEY RESEARCH >> COGNITIVE–BEHAVIOURAL THERAPY

comparing CBT and systematic desensitization (graded exposure)

Burke *et al.* (1997) tested two groups of females with agoraphobia, balanced for age, severity and duration of the phobia, and the presence of panic. One group was given the cognitive rationale for graded exposure, with prior CBT when they were taught to identify and challenge negative thoughts; the other group was given only a behavioural rationale. Each group was given ten sessions, and was assessed at the end of the sessions and six months later. Burke and colleagues found:

- Both groups had improved equally, with no significant difference six months after treatment.

- They concluded that CBT does not add to the effectiveness of graded exposure in the treatment of agoraphobia.

- However, the sample size was very small – they started with 39 people and 13 dropped out.

- Burke and colleagues themselves also point out that a six-month follow-up may not have been long enough to test whether CBT is more effective in preventing relapse.

Beurs *et al.* (1995) conducted a similar study with people diagnosed with agoraphobia. They found that CBT combined with graded exposure was not superior to graded exposure alone. Although CBT was found to be effective in a number of comparative studies, it has not been found to add to the effectiveness of behavioural treatments for phobic disorders. It should be borne in mind, however, that these studies did not test CBT alone versus graded exposure alone.

- *Advantages* – Like the older behavioural therapies, cognitive–behavioural therapies are structured, with clear goals and measurable outcomes. They are increasingly becoming the most widely employed therapy by clinical psychologists in the National Health Service, not least because they are short term and economic.

- *Appeal of CBT* – CBT appeals to clients who find insight therapies (which delve into inner emotional conflicts) too threatening. Although subject to the criticism that it does not address underlying causes, CBT attempts to empower clients by educating them into self-help strategies. Despite this, many clients do become dependent upon their therapist.

- *Use and effectiveness of CBT* – CBT is thought to be particularly effective for depression and anxiety disorders, and sexual problems. It has also been widely employed in stress management. A number of studies have compared this therapy with traditional chemotherapy (anti-depressant drugs) in the treatment of major depression. Some have found CBT to be more effective (e.g. Seligman *et al.* 1979) whilst others have not. Most studies find both types of therapy equally effective although, of course, CBT has no physical side effects.

- *Use of CBT in people with depression* – In studies on depression, CBT has been found to be equally or more effective than drugs (e.g. Hollon *et al.* 1992). Long-term follow-up studies have also shown that the relapse rate is lower in those who received CBT (Evans *et al.* 1992). A study by Brent *et al.* (1997) with 107 adolescents diagnosed with major depression, compared individual CBT, systematic behaviour, family therapy and individual supportive therapy. They found CBT to be the most effective, with a more rapid and complete treatment response. Brent and colleagues felt that

the rapidity of improvement was an important factor because a significant proportion of severely depressed adolescents commit suicide in their first episode of depression. They also view rapidity as an economic advantage for both patients and the health service.

- *Use of CBT in treating phobias* – In a review of behavioural versus CBT for anxiety disorders, Barlow and Lehman (1996) found CBT to be more effective for generalized anxiety disorder and social phobia, but behavioural therapy was found to be more effective for specific phobias and obsessive-compulsive disorder. However, a study by Thorpe and Salkovskis (1997) reported significant improvements in patients with spider phobia after just one session of CBT compared to no therapy.

- *Graded exposure vs CBT* – A number of studies have compared graded exposure treatment (systematic desensitization) with CBT and graded exposure combined. Burke *et al.* (1997) hypothesized that graded exposure would be more effective if the rationale was presented in cognitive terms (i.e. as an opportunity to challenge negative thoughts), rather than in strictly behavioural terms. See Key research box for an account of Burke and colleagues' findings.

- *Use of CBT with schizophrenia* – As described earlier, CBT is also being developed for use with schizophrenics.

- *Difficulty in evaluating therapies* – A difficulty in assessing the effectiveness of therapy for depression, according to Senra and Polaino (1998), is the measurement scale used to monitor the effects of treatment. They assessed 52 patients suffering from major depression with the Beck Depression Inventory, the Hamilton Rating Scale and the Zung Self-Rating Depression Scale (Beck *et al.* 1961, Hamilton 1960 and Zung 1965, respectively). They found different measures of improvement, depending on which scale they used, illustrating the difficulty of evaluating a therapy.

Research on CBT and drug therapy

A study by Jarrett *et al.* (1999) found CBT and MAOI anti-depressant drugs to be equally effective with 108 patients with severe depression in a 10-week trial. Hollon *et al.* (1992) found no difference between CBT and treatment with tricyclics (anti-depressant drugs) with 107 patients over a 12-week trial. They also found no difference between CBT alone and CBT combined with anti-depressant drugs. Hollon and colleagues claimed that relapse often occurs when people cease medication; however, with CBT the effect is maintained beyond the termination of therapy. They point out, however, that only about 40 per cent of those who begin treatment – either drugs or psychological therapy – will complete it. One of the difficulties with studies of this kind is that they are generally undertaken with small samples and over too short a period of time to assess the longer-term effectiveness. Another difficulty is that a control group (no treatment) is essential and these people often exert their right to withdraw in order to seek treatment themselves.

USE AND MODE OF ACTION OF PSYCHODYNAMIC THERAPIES

Psychoanalysis

Psychoanalysis was first introduced by Freud at the beginning of the 20th century. The aim of psychodynamic therapy is not to 'cure' the patient's psychological problems in the same way that the medical profession might hope to find a cure for cancer. Psychoanalysts do not aim simply to remove the symptoms of mental disturbance, because this will not tackle the underlying problem – indeed, it might make the situation worse by creating a different set of symptoms (symptom substitution). Rather, the aim is to enable the person to cope better with inner emotional conflicts that are causing disturbance. The purpose of therapy is to uncover unconscious conflicts and anxieties that have their origins in the past, in order to gain insight into the causes of psychological disturbance. After bringing these conflicts into consciousness, the client is encouraged to work through them by examining and dealing with them in the safety of the consulting room, and, in so doing, release the power they exert over behaviour – a process known as 'catharsis'. An important aspect of this is that confusing or traumatic childhood experiences can be better understood with the benefit of adult knowledge.

In psychodynamic therapy, a variety of techniques are employed to facilitate the process of catharsis, including the following:

- **Free association** – The client is asked to recline on a chair or couch (with the therapist out of sight) and allow the free flow of feelings, thoughts or images. As these come to mind, clients express them in words, without censorship. The analyst must listen, suspending their own values and judgements and interrupting from time to time to ask the client to reflect upon the significance of associations. The reasoning is that associations should arise from, and therefore reflect, internal dynamic conflict.

- **Word association** – The client is read a list of words one at a time and asked to reply with whatever comes instantly to mind. The analyst pays particular attention to unusual responses, hesitations and mental blanks, which may indicate repression.

- **Dream analysis** – Freud believed that our unconscious drives are expressed uncensored in dreams, although they are disguised in symbolic form in order to protect the conscious mind. The role of the analyst is to help the client interpret the significance of their dreams. In Freudian psychoanalysis, dreams are interpreted as wish-fulfilment, usually of a sexual or aggressive nature. In Adlerian therapy, dreams are viewed as an attempt to avoid feelings of inferiority, the most common dreams being of flying or falling. In Jungian analysis, dreams are an attempt to solve particular problems or to anticipate the future.

- **Transference** – This occurs when the client redirects feelings (e.g. of hostility) towards the therapist, that are unconsciously directed towards a significant person in their life (usually a parent), but which have been censored from the conscious mind. Transference is important because it indicates that repressed conflict is coming very close to conscious awareness. Transference must occur naturally, however, and the therapist must neither encourage nor prevent it. The aim is to identify the source (person) of the transference and the circumstances surrounding the repression.

- **Projective tests** – There are many types of projective test, the most well-known being the Rorschach Ink Blot and the Thematic Apperception Test. The client is asked to describe what they see in the ink blot or to tell a story around the picture. These are used as tools to uncover recurrent themes that may reveal the unconscious needs and motives of the person.

(A02) **Evaluation
the use of psychodynamic
therapies**

- **Timescale of therapy** – Psychodynamic therapy is generally conducted over a number of years, which makes it expensive. However, more modern, brief psychodynamic therapies have emerged where the focus has been much more on current, rather than past, concerns and these can produce some quick improvements in functioning. Such newer brief therapies have made this type of therapy more affordable.

- **Suitability for use with different disorders** – Psychodynamic therapy is not the treatment of choice for all psychological disorders. It has been regarded as appropriate for psychological problems traditionally labelled as 'neuroses', such as anxiety disorders, depression and eating disorders, although its use may be limited with depression. Comer (1995) cites the American Psychiatric Association's concern about 'transference' with patients suffering from depression, because of their tendency towards extreme dependency on important people in their lives. Comer also points out that psychodynamic techniques may be detrimental to the treatment of obsessive–compulsive disorder, because 'free association' may inadvertently increase the person's tendency to ruminate and over-interpret.

continued on next page

Evaluation continued
the use of psychodynamic therapies

Psychodynamic therapy was traditionally believed to be of little benefit for patients with schizophrenia, because their loss of contact with reality would prevent them from using insight therapy. With the introduction of phenothiazines, however, patients with schizophrenia can now be much more 'available' to psychotherapy and it has been shown to be beneficial (Boker 1992).

- **Does psychotherapy actually work?** – Probably the most-quoted indictment against psychodynamic therapy came from Eysenck (1952) who claimed that it simply does not work. However, other studies have been more supportive (see Key research opposite).

- **Issues in evaluating the effectiveness of psychotherapy** – Corsini and Wedding (1995) claim that, depending on the criteria involved, 'cures' range from 30 to 60 per cent. The concept of 'cure' is, however, inappropriate, and Bolger (1989) makes the point that much of the evaluative research is based on the medical model of problem behaviour that assumes that a psychological disorder follows a course similar to that of a disease. It is now generally accepted that there are methodological difficulties in evaluating the effectiveness of psychodynamic therapy. It generally spans several years and the point at which it is assessed may be crucial to a measurement of efficacy. Corsini and Wedding (1995) also explain that there are too many variables involved to enable a controlled and statistically valid outcome study. Comparisons may be made between symptoms at the beginning and termination of treatment, but during the course of therapy, other complications may arise as a direct result of insight during therapy. Because treatment is over such a long period, there may also be other factors occurring in the client's life during the course of therapy which impact upon the outcome. Effectiveness is a subjective concept, measurable only by the extent to which clients feel that their condition has improved. Freud himself was quite modest about the therapeutic claims of psychoanalysis (Freud 1937).

- **Danger of emotional harm** – Criticism has been levelled at psychodynamic therapies in relation to emotional rather than physical harm (as with medical treatments). For example, a psychoanalyst may guide a client towards an insight that may prove emotionally distressing, yet is necessary for recovery from their current problem. The distress surrounding the new insight may prove to be greater than the distress of the current problem. Psychotherapists abiding by a professional code of ethics should warn their clients of this danger before engaging in therapy, and therapists should never work beyond their competence in dealing with what may arise in therapy. Recovered memories of child abuse have been the subject of much debate and legal wrangling over the past few years, in discussions of what has become known as 'false memory syndrome' (see panel below). Supporters of false memory syndrome (FMS) have suggested that a client may succumb to the belief because the suggestions come from an authority figure. Toon *et al.* (1996) report that FMS supporters accuse therapists in private practice of even inducing false memories for financial gain, because the therapy will take longer. Toon and colleagues point out, however, that there is no clear-cut evidence, as yet, to demonstrate the existence of therapist-induced false memories.

False memory syndrome (FMS)

Many patients claim to have uncovered traumatic memories during therapeutic sessions. The debate over whether such memories are accurate representations of events that have happened in childhood is one of modern psychology's most contentious issues. Critics have cast doubt on their validity on two counts:

1 They point to the somewhat bizarre or unlikely nature of many of the recollections.

2 They question the use of techniques such as suggestion and hypnotic regression to extract these memories.

The consequences of either side of the FMS argument pose ethical problems for the therapist:

1 If these are *false* memories (often about sexual abuse), then there is concern over the consequences of parents being falsely accused of abusing their children.

2 If these are *true* memories, there may be harmful effects on the people abused in childhood in not being believed (Andrews *et al.* 1995).

A further ethical issue is now emerging as a direct result of the proliferation of media articles on FMS over the past few years. These have created a climate of disbelief about the credibility of disclosures of child sexual abuse to the extent that adult survivors are now discouraged from disclosing and seeking help for themselves (Toon *et al.* 1996).

Eysenck's (1952) critique of the effectiveness of psychotherapy

Eysenck (1952) reviewed two outcome studies, incorporating waiting-list controls, which showed that 66 per cent of the control group improved spontaneously, whereas only 44 per cent of psychoanalysis patients improved. He concluded that psychoanalysis did not work.

However, not everyone agreed with Eysenck's conclusions. In a review of the original data, Bergin (1971) reported that patients in one of the control groups were in fact hospitalized and those in the other group were being treated by their GP. He also found that by selecting different outcome criteria, improvement in the psychoanalysis group increased

to 83 per cent and the control groups dropped to 30 per cent.

Eysenck, however, was still defending his attack on psychotherapy in an interview in 1996 with Colin Feltham at Sheffield Hallam University (Feltham 1996). Eysenck referred to a meta-analysis published in 1991 (40 years after his initial indictment) conducted by Svartberg and Stiles. (Meta-analysis is a statistical technique for combining the data from a number of experiments.) In 19 studies comparing psychoanalysis with no treatment, no difference was found in outcome one year after the end of treatment. Eysenck said: 'Clearly there was no evidence that psychoanalysis or psychotherapy did any good'.

research support for psychotherapy (Thase *et al.* 1997, Mufson *et al.* 1999)

A meta-analysis of six studies with a total of 595 patients diagnosed with major depressive disorder, conducted by Thase *et al.* (1997), examined the effectiveness of psychotherapy combined with pharmacological treatment (anti-depressants) compared to psychotherapy alone. They report that, over a 12-week period, with less severe patients, there was no significant difference in the outcome of psychotherapy with or without additional medication (37 per cent versus 48 per cent showing a marked improvement in their clinical condition), indicating that improvement was due to psychotherapy alone. However, with more severe patients, the combined psychotherapy and medication patients showed a much greater improvement than with psychotherapy alone (25 per cent versus 43 per cent). This suggests

that if the disorder is more severe, it is advisable to combine medication with therapy.

Mufson *et al.* (1999) conducted a 12-week clinical trial with 48 adolescents diagnosed with major depression, aged between 12 and 18 years and randomly assigned to a psychotherapy group or a control group (with no therapy, but fortnightly assessment of functioning). After 12 weeks there was a notably greater decrease in depressive symptoms and increase in social functioning and problem-solving skills in 75 per cent of the psychotherapy group compared to 46 per cent of the control group.

It should be borne in mind, however, that both the above studies were conducted over a 12-week period. It may not be possible to test the effectiveness of psychotherapy over such a short period.

Psychodrama

<<Psychodrama is a group therapy technique that calls for group members to act out dramatic roles as if they were participating in an improvised play in which they express their feelings and thoughts, explore new behaviours and attitudes, and empathize with the feelings and perspectives of others.>> (Comer 1996)

Psychodrama was developed by J.L. Moreno in the early 1920s. Moreno was a psychiatrist working in Vienna at the same time as Sigmund Freud. However, he rejected Freud's methods of psychoanalysis for two main reasons:

● He believed that people could be better helped through groupwork, rather than one-to-one therapy.
● He believed that therapy should be an active experience rather than based on talking alone.

Moreno observed the therapeutic effects of role-playing within children's play and believed this could be extended to adults through drama. Problems and anxieties can be expressed or 'acted out' in a role-play situation within the safety of an understanding and supportive therapy group. (Incidentally, Moreno coined the terms 'roles' and 'role-play'.) Moreno believed that:

- Every human being is an actor, performing their own personal drama. He gave as an example that of women playing many roles, such as wife, mother, sister, daughter, nurse and teacher.

- A psychologically healthy person can switch roles easily, but problems emerge when people are rigidly fixed within a specific role or when one role dominates the person.

- Everyone was capable of being their own saviour.

In 1922, Moreno began to combine professional theatre with therapy by presenting personal dramas on stage, where the actors would improvise roles and a psychodrama would emerge. The purpose was that people in the audience, as well as the actors, could engage with the drama in a therapeutic way.

Although Moreno lived close to Freud in Vienna, they met only once when Moreno attended a lecture by Freud. On this occasion Freud asked him about his work and Moreno replied: 'Well Dr Freud, I start where you leave off. You meet people in the artificial setting of your office; I meet them on the street and in their homes ... You analyse their dreams; I try to give them the courage to dream again.' (Moreno 1970, p.6).

Moreno moved to the USA in 1925 and founded the Moreno Institute, where he developed psychodrama further into a structured therapy. It was not until 1965, however, that the first set of rules for psychodrama were published and this was by his wife Zerka (Moreno 1965). Psychodrama takes place within a group setting and group sizes vary, but are usually between 10 and 15 people. A single session can span several hours. One member of the group will elect to play out a chosen scenario, or drama, from a problem area in their life.

Everyone in the group will then be assigned a role from the following:

- **The director** – the therapist trained in the use and techniques of psychodrama. This person directs the drama, including the preparation and planning. The director will monitor the drama as it unfolds, intervene where necessary to change the direction or focus, offer clarification and provide a summary at the end. The director can also facilitate the playing-out of a future event.

- **The protagonist** – the volunteer who is electing to play out their drama. The director can at any point ask the protagonist to engage in a soliloquy where they are asked to think out loud.

- **The auxiliary egos** – significant people within the drama, such as a parent or spouse. The protagonist chooses the actors for these roles from within the group. At any point the director can ask the protagonist to move into the role of one of the auxiliary egos in order to experience the drama from that perspective.

- **The double** – the inner voice of the protagonist whose role is to move the action to a deeper level in order to enable the protagonist to access their unconscious. The double will mirror the actions and words of the protagonist, who can then observe aspects of their own self of which they had previously been unaware.

- **The audience** – the remaining members of the group. Their role is to observe and give feedback in general discussion at the end. They are also able to benefit therapeutically from the experience by themselves identifying with the emerging drama.

Evaluation
the use of psychodrama

- *Effectiveness in coming to terms with past events* – Psychodrama is a powerful therapy and the experience can be traumatic, which is why every member of the group must be sensitive and supportive. Claims have been made for its effectiveness in coming to terms with unresolved events in the past, such as re-experiencing a childhood trauma or coming to terms with the loss of a significant person.

- *Other applications of psychodrama* – Psychodrama is also useful in testing out scenarios involving people whom it would be difficult to address in real life, and for learning new skills and ways of interacting with others. Karp (1995) found psychodrama effective for people with psychosomatic disorders. Hugh (1998) cites Dayton (1994), who also found it helpful for people with addictions, in order for them to explore emerging situations better.

- *Challenges and difficulties* – There are some people who might find it hard to engage in role-play with an audience and would not wish to explore their problems in such a dramatic and public way. As Davies (1993) explained, psychodrama is not a panacea and requires a great deal of risk-taking, and so many people may prefer the safer, more traditional, one-to-one psychotherapies.

- *Value of working in a group* – Moreno's work precipitated the wider use of groupwork within therapy, though often without the drama element. The value of working through problems within a supportive group is widely recognized. These include self-help groups and facilitated groups for specific problems, such as for addictions or eating disorders. Another area of use is with specific groups of people such as abusers or victims of abuse. Working with those who share the same experience helps them feel less alone, or 'different', and enables them to address their problems more readily and openly.

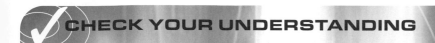

CHECK YOUR UNDERSTANDING

Check your understanding of the nature of alternative therapies by answering these questions from memory. You can check your answers by looking back through Topic 3.

1 Identify three different types of cognitive–behavioural therapy.

2 Explain briefly how the ABC model (part of REBT) works.

3 Outline two strengths and two weaknesses of CBT.

4 With reference to research, outline how CBT compares with chemotherapy as an effective treatment for depression.

5 What is the principal aim of psychoanalysis?

6 Describe three techniques used in psychoanalysis.

7 Outline the procedures involved in psychodrama.

8 How does Moreno's psychodrama therapy differ from Freudian psychoanalysis?

9 Discuss some of the issues surrounding the use of cognitive–behavioural therapies (e.g. appropriateness and effectiveness).

10 Discuss some of the issues surrounding the use of psychodynamic therapies (e.g. appropriateness and effectiveness).

REVISION SUMMARY

Having covered this topic, you should be able to describe and evaluate:

✓ the use and mode of action of either psychodynamic-based or cognitive–behavioural therapies

✓ issues surrounding the use of either psychodynamic-based or cognitive–behavioural therapies.

EXAMPLE EXAM QUESTIONS

Below are some **possible examination questions** set on this topic, along with hints to help you understand and approach each question effectively:

1 (a) Describe **one** therapy derived from **either** a psychodynamic **or** a cognitive–behavioural model of abnormality. (15 marks)

(b) Assess the therapy you described in part (a) in terms of **two or more** issues (e.g. appropriateness and effectiveness) surrounding its use. (15 marks)

All questions in this topic area must give you a choice between the psychodynamic or cognitive–behavioural models of abnormality. Don't ever write about both, as only one will receive credit (the one that is best in terms of marks). In this question you must also only describe one therapy from your chosen model. In part (b), you are required to provide commentary on the therapy presented in part (a). The form of this commentary has been specified, i.e. it must be in terms of at least two issues surrounding the use of the therapy (e.g. appropriateness and effectiveness). Marks will only be awarded to the extent that this is commentary rather than description.

2 Discuss issues surrounding the use of **one or more** therapies derived from **either** the psychodynamic **or** cognitive–behavioural model of abnormality. (30 marks)

There is a critical difference between this question and the previous one. It is not simply an alternative way of wording the previous question because there is no longer credit for a description of the therapies. This time you must describe the issues and then evaluate them. The issues should be related to the use of the therapies rather than to the therapies themselves. An essay that is generally related to ethics would not gain any credit. In addition, you are offered the opportunity of presenting more than one therapy from your chosen model. This is useful if you feel you do not have enough material to write for 40 minutes on one therapy (though you should be prepared for this).

Unit 26 // Treating mental disorders

3 'There are many methods of therapy for patients to chose from – those derived from the biological, behavioural, psychodynamic or cognitive–behavioural approaches.'

Critically consider **one** therapy used to treat mental disorders. (30 marks)

> The concept of 'one therapy' could be interpreted in a generic way as 'behavioural therapy' and thus you might include several therapies under this superordinate category. However, in order for this to be creditworthy you must make it clear that this is one therapy otherwise the examiner will see it as several therapies and only credit the best one.

4 Compare and contrast **two** therapies used to treat mental disorders. (30 marks)

> In this question it is up to you which therapies you choose, which permits you to choose two therapies that are significantly different in order to produce good material for the similarities and differences part of your answer. Do ensure that you compare/contrast the therapies and do not simply make general comparisons between approaches.

UNIT SUMMARY

General comments

- Each of the therapies outlined in this unit offers quite different methods of treatment for mental disorders, based upon their respective model of abnormality.

- When we evaluate any therapy for mental disorders, there are several issues to bear in mind:
  - how we operationalize a given mental disorder
  - problems in allocating patients to treatment groups
  - to what extent the personal qualities of the therapist might influence outcomes
  - the effects of existing treatments on how a patient responds to therapy
  - the placebo effect
  - how we define 'cure'.

Topic 1: Biological (somatic) therapies

- **Biological (somatic) treatments** address physical symptoms of mental disorder. The most frequently used biological treatment is **chemotherapy**, where drugs are prescribed to redress biochemical imbalance. Drugs are reasonably effective in the short term, although there are numerous adverse side effects and they usually act solely on symptoms without addressing the underlying causes of the disorder. Drugs have been developed to treat anxiety, depression, schizophrenia, mania and ADHD. Dependence can be created if drugs are taken over a long period of time.

- With severe depression, **ECT** has been found to be effective for some patients, but again there are adverse side effects.

- **Psychosurgery** continues to be regarded as a controversial and extreme form of therapy, even with the newer procedure of cingulotomy, largely because it involves permanent damage to the neural tissue.

Topic 2: Behavioural therapies

- **Behavioural therapies** attempt to identify maladaptive learning and to modify it into more adaptive behavioural strategies.

- Techniques based on the principles of **classical conditioning**, such as systematic desensitization, are thought to be effective for phobias.

● Behaviour-modification programmes (based on the principles of **operant conditioning**) have been subjected to ethical scrutiny on the grounds that the goals are set by the institution and may not serve the interests of the recipient. Token economy programmes may result in people becoming dependent on the regime and finding it difficult to cope outside the institution.

Topic 3: Alternatives to biological and behavioural therapies

● **Cognitive–behavioural therapies** (CBTs) extend the behavioural model to the realms of thinking and attempt to replace distorted irrational thoughts with more rational ways of thinking. They have been found effective for coping with anxiety and social phobia. Beck's CBT has been found to be more effective than any other therapy for depression. To date, however, CBTs are of limited use in treating psychotic disorders.

● **Psychodynamic (insight) therapies** (such as psychoanalysis and psychodrama) attempt to uncover unconscious anxieties and conflicts in order to disable their power over behaviour. Although their success is difficult to test empirically, they are thought to be effective for certain disorders, such as anxiety and depression.

● Some therapies are easier than others to test for **effectiveness**, but this does not necessarily mean that they are more effective. Many therapists nowadays take an eclectic approach. They are trained in a number of different therapies and draw on whichever they feel to be most **appropriate** for a particular client.

● Since therapists deal with people who are disturbed and distressed, this inevitably raises **ethical issues**, including consent and the protection of patients/clients on treatment programmes.

FURTHER RESOURCES

Corsini, R.J. and Wedding, D. (1995) *Current Psychotherapies* **(5th edn), Illinois: FE Peacock Publishers.**

An American text which covers traditional, along with more recent, theories and applications of therapy.

Dryden, W. (1996) *Individual Therapy: A Handbook***, Milton Keynes: Open University Press.**

A British text with a unit for each therapy written by different authors. Written in a clear style that is interesting and informative.

Nelson-Jones, R. (1995) *The Theory and Practice of Counselling* **(2nd edn), London: Cassell.**

This text provides well-written accounts of a variety of theories and how they are developed in practice. Self-assessment questions are included.

Websites

www.rethink.org

Site for Rethink, formerly the National Schizophrenia Fellowship. It offers advice and support to people with severe mental illness.

http://www.epub.org.br/cm/history_i.htm

History of neurosciences – includes two excellent articles on the history of psychosurgery and the history of shock therapy (lots of pictures!).

http://apsa.org/

The American Psychoanalytic Association – a huge and informative site that is even interactive!

http://www.antipsychiatry.org

A comprehensive site full of articles criticizing the use of traditional psychiatric techniques.

www.pe2000.com/desens-what.htm

Explains how you can systematically desensitize yourself to overcome a phobia!

www.apsa.org/pubinfo/about.htm

This site from the American Psychoanalytic Association provides a straightforward description of the psychoanalytic process.

27
UNIT

ISSUES IN
Psychology

PREVIEW

After you have read this unit, you should be able to describe and evaluate:

>> gender bias in psychological research (theories and studies)

>> cultural bias in psychological research (theories and studies)

>> ethical issues involved in psychological investigations using human participants, including the ethics of socially sensitive research

>> the constraints on the use of non-human animals in psychological investigations

>> ethical and scientific arguments for and against the use of non-human animals in psychological investigations.

INTRODUCTION

The aim of this unit is to consider the major issues that concern psychologists. Some of these issues should be familiar to you from your AS-level studies, e.g. the issue of balancing participants' rights against the needs of researchers (ethical issues). Socially sensitive research poses special ethical difficulties for research psychologists. For example, research into gender differences or race often carries significant consequences, not only for those who take part in the research, but also for members of the social groups they represent. Psychologists need to be aware that their research can be manipulated and exploited for bad as well as good purposes. Ethical issues also include the use of non-human animals, especially as there are strong moves to recognize equal rights for some non-human animals and humans. The decision about whether or not to use non-human animals in research concerns more than ethics. There is also the question of whether findings from research are *relevant*.

Two other major issues are considered in this unit: gender and cultural bias. A survey of psychology studies in the 1980s found that the majority used psychology students as their participants – and these were mainly American, male undergraduates. There is no problem with this if we believe that men and women are not different in their beliefs, attitudes, drives and so on. Equally there is no problem if we believe that students do not differ from the general population or we believe that Americans are the same as people from other cultural groups. However, what is clear is that psychology as we know it is largely a record of American, undergraduate male behaviour. That's a major issue.

There is a secondary aim of this unit. It is intended to *summarize* what you have studied through your course. This unit covers part of the AQA specification section headed 'Perspectives'. Perspectives are 'general views' or an overview. Through your study of psychology you may have noticed certain concepts keep being repeated. For example, 'cultural bias', 'ethical issues', 'determinism' or 'social learning theory'. These are the threads that run through the specification. Some of these threads are collectively called 'issues', some are 'debates' and some are 'approaches'. In this unit, and the two following, issues, debates and approaches are discussed. In each case the substantive *content* of the unit is drawn from things you may have studied through your psychology course (such as Kohlberg's theory of moral development). The aim of the unit is to draw on your existing knowledge and offer a *structure* for understanding the issues, debates or approaches.

Cara
Flanagan

Consider the story in each photograph. What issues does each of these photos raise?

1 This shows the 'learner' confederate in Milgram's obedience study, covered in detail in Unit 5, pp. 171–5. What is it that made Milgram's experiments so controversial?

2 In Harlow's study of attachment, infant monkeys were 'raised' by wire mothers – one with a bottle and one covered in cloth (see Unit 2, p. 53). What issues does this research raise about the treatment of non-human animals?

Bias: a leaning in a particular direction, a systematic distortion in one's attitudes and beliefs based on prejudices or pre-existing ideas.

Gender: the psychological element of a person's sex; masculinity and femininity as distinct from the biological category of male and female.

Alpha bias: the tendency of some theories and research to assume real and enduring differences between men and women, e.g. by overvaluing or devaluing women.

Beta bias: the tendency of some theories and research to ignore or minimize differences between men and women.

Culture: the beliefs and customs that a group of people share, such as child-rearing practices.

Ethnocentrism: the term used to describe the belief in the superiority of one's own ethnic and cultural group.

Ethics: that which is deemed right or wrong in terms of human behaviour. Ethics are the moral principles used by a group of professionals, such as doctors, solicitors or psychologists.

Socially sensitive research: any research that may have direct social consequences for those taking part in the study or the class of people who are represented.

Topic 1 >> Gender bias

Beliefs about gender

1 Write five comparative statements about women and five comparative statements about men, such as 'Women are kinder than men', 'Men are more intelligent than women'. To what extent do you think these represent *real* differences or are *exaggerations* of real differences?

2 Now write some more statements: this time about ways in which men and women are the same, such as 'Men and women are equally interested in food'. To what extent do you think your statements have *minimized* differences between men and women? Did you make statements that aren't quite true? Do you think that in fact men and women do differ on your identified characteristics?

Gender bias is not new. For centuries people have held biased assumptions about the differences between the sexes. Aristotle suggested that women's inferiority was biologically based. 'We should look upon the female,' he said, 'as being a deformity.' In Aristotle's philosophical writings, women are portrayed as not possessing fully developed rationality. Men, therefore, must both rule them and be responsible for them.

What is new is an understanding of the effects of such biases on our perceptions of reality. We perceive that there are differences between men and women, for example that women are kinder than men or men are more intelligent than women. But such gender differences may not be true, they may be a product of the way we construct theories. This means that what we observe as differences may not, in reality, exist.

Hare-Mustin and Marecek (1988) propose that our stereotypes of gender (and also culture, age, class, etc.) are 'social constructions' of reality and these constructions lead to two types of bias in psychological research: theories that exaggerate the differences between men and women, and those which ignore them. Hare-Mustin and Marecek describe these as 'alpha bias' and 'beta bias' respectively.

Alpha bias

Alpha-biased theories assume that there are real and enduring differences between men and women. Sometimes alpha-biased theories heighten the value of women, as in Chodorow's conception of women as more relational and caring (Chodorow 1978), while sometimes they are used to devalue women. Within sociobiology, for example, differences in male and female behaviour may be attributed to genetic determinism. Thus, male social dominance or sexual promiscuity might be seen as a product of their evolutionary history.

Beta bias

Beta-biased theories ignore or minimize sex differences. They do this either by ignoring questions about the lives of women, or by assuming that findings from studies of males apply equally well to females. Such approaches – at best misguided, at worst arrogant – have resulted in what is essentially an 'androcentric' view of human behaviour (i.e. 'based on and concerning males'), rather than offering insights into what is essentially one half of the human race. There are also rare examples of 'estrocentrism' in psychology – a bias towards females.

(A02) Commentary
gender bias and social construction

Feminist psychology

The strong androcentric bias of psychological research, reflecting the power of males in our society, has led some psychologists to develop an alternative force – feminist psychology. The main aims are to:

- *Challenge androcentric generalizations* – Highlight instances where statements are made about human behaviour which are really only relevant to male behaviour (and probably Western, middle-class male behaviour).

- *Challenge pathologization of female behaviour* – Avoid the situation where female behaviours are seen as abnormal, which leads us to judge female behaviour as pathological ('ill'). For example, 'premenstrual syndrome' is seen as an unhealthy and undesirable state rather than simply a facet of normal behaviour.

- *Challenge biological explanations of differences* – Avoid explanations that suggest that gender differences are biological because they perpetuate the idea that such behaviours are inevitable and universal. It may be that gender differences are in part biological but they are also socially constructed. A psychology that finds such differences is perpetuating stereotypes.

Real differences

- *Physiological and psychological differences* – There are real differences between men and women. There are obvious physical differences and there are also some well-documented psychological differences. For example, Maccoby and Jacklin (1974) reviewed a large number of gender studies and concluded that girls have a superior verbal ability whereas boys are better at spatial tasks. It is possible that such differences are due to the effects of hormones on the developing prenatal brain. Hormones may also explain why men are more aggressive than women (the male hormone testosterone is associated with increased aggressiveness).

- *Debatable differences* – There are a range of other findings which are more debatable. For example, Maccoby and Jacklin also found that boys have better mathematical abilities. This superiority may occur because boys are expected to do better and such expectations lead to improved performance.

- *So are there differences or not?* – Hare-Mustin and Maracek suggest that, before being able to answer this question, one must consider the extent to which any research is biased. Only then can we disentangle 'truth' from the way psychological research has found it.

GENDER BIAS IN PSYCHOLOGICAL THEORIES

Alpha-biased theories

A particular theory may exaggerate the differences between men and women from either an androcentric (male-centred) or estrocentric (female-centred) view. An example of each is described below.

- *Androcentrism* – Freud's theory of psychoanalysis (see Unit 19, pp. 588–91) took male behaviour as the standard for all human behaviour and described female behaviour as a deviation from that standard. This is particularly clear when considering Freud's description of the genital stage of development (see p. 590).

- *Estrocentrism* – Gilligan's (1982) theory of moral development was developed as a response to the theory proposed by Kohlberg (see below). She argued that women have a 'different moral voice' from men; they discuss the world and make judgements using different criteria, such as interpersonal concerns and caring rather than justice and logic, which are male principles. Re-read Unit 18, p. 580 for an overview of her theory.

Evaluation
alpha-biased theories

- *Freud and androcentrism* – Williams (1987) argues that Freud's theory is not alpha-biased. He did not claim that innate factors make men and women different, but rather that social context transforms biological factors into mental representations and these create differences. Thus Freud explained the differences he observed in terms of mental or social representations – women inevitably envy the male penis because it represents male dominance.

- *Gilligan and estrocentrism* – Gilligan's theory has not been supported by other research. For example Walker's (1984) meta-analysis of 108 studies found only eight clear indications of gender differences. Hare-Mustin and Maracek (1988) offer a further criticism. They point out that the suggestion that women are inherently more concerned with caring than men closes off a different and important explanation for the gender difference in terms of social construction. It may be that female caringness is a necessary trait for those placed in subordinate positions in order to suppress their anger and placate those in authority over them.

Beta-biased theories

There appear to be two kinds of beta-biased theories. In both cases, the theories assume that men and women are the same, i.e. such theories minimize gender differences. One kind of beta-biased theory attempts to provide a 'unisex' view of human behaviour. The second type are those theories based on research with one gender and then proclaimed as a universal theory of human behaviour.

Unisex theories

One example of a 'unisex theory' is Bem's (1976) theory of psychological androgyny. She proposes that the psychologically 'best' or most healthy state is one of androgyny, where both men and women are free to select whatever personality traits they wish. Thus they can integrate masculine and feminine qualities appropriate to their individual temperament rather than being constrained by stereotypes. However, Hare-Mustin and Maracek point out that this assumes that masculine and feminine qualities are equivalent, whereas even Bem acknowledges that masculine qualities are regarded as more adaptive and thus to be more highly valued. This means that the theory of androgyny overlooks the social context in which choices are made.

Hare-Mustin and Maracek provide a second example of this kind of beta bias: family systems theory

(Minuchin 1974). Family systems theory is used to explain the development of anorexia in one family member as a consequence of interactions within the family. However, different gender orientations are ignored. It is a neutered representation of family life (Libow 1985).

Theories based on research with one gender

Hare-Mustin and Maracek (1988) say that prior to the 1970s, most generalizations that psychologists made were based on observations of male behaviour; male experience was assumed to represent all experience. The classic example of this is Kohlberg's (1963) theory of the development of moral understanding (see Unit 18, pp. 575–8). Kohlberg used moral dilemmas to find out about how people made moral decisions, and then used the answers to classify the stage or level of moral reasoning that a person had reached. This led him to develop an age-related theory of moral development which he claimed would be universal. However, the sample he used to develop the stage theory was one entirely of boys and solely American boys. Not surprisingly, when Kohlberg came to assess women using his moral dilemmas (which were androcentric) and classifying them with his stage theory (based on male responses), the women were found to be inferior.

Evaluation
gender bias in psychological theories

- *Positive consequences of alpha bias* – Alpha bias has at least had the benefit that it has led some theorists (e.g. Gilligan) to assert the worth of certain 'feminine' qualities (they may not be truly feminine but are possessed by most women), which counters the devaluation of women (Hare-Mustin and Maracek 1988). Alpha bias has also led to a healthy criticism of cultural values that extol certain 'male' qualities such as aggression, self-interest and individualism, assuming that these are desirable, adaptive and universal.

- *Differences within the genders* – A focus on differences between genders, even when the differences favour women, implies similarity *within* each gender. Saying that women value interpersonal relationships and men value abstract justice ignores the many ways in which women differ from each other and men differ from each other.

- *Positive consequences of beta bias* – Beta bias makes people see men and women as the same, which has led to their equal treatment in legal terms and also in terms of equal access to, for instance, education and employment. However, a focus on similarities between genders has had the disadvantage of drawing attention away from women's special needs and the differences in power between men and women.

- *Negative consequences of beta bias* – All of these theories *appear* to be gender neutral while really being gender-biased. Beta bias is an apparently egalitarian position, but it results in major misrepresentations of one or both genders. Perhaps more importantly, it results in creating and/or sustaining prejudices.

Bias-free theories

There are a number of ways that psychological theories can avoid biases. Worell and Remer (1992) offer four criteria by which theories might be evaluated in order to overcome the often detrimental models of women that develop from more traditional non-feminist models. They argue that theories should be:

- *Gender-free* – View men and women as similar in their psychological make-up; avoid sexist and stereotyped concepts.

- *Flexible* – Use ideas that can apply equally to individuals or groups of any age, race, gender or sexual orientation. Such theories emphasize within-sex differences in behaviour, as well as between-sex differences. They thereby offer a range of satisfying and fulfilling life styles for both men and women, rather than devaluing one or the other as less mature, incomplete or unhealthy due to some preconceived notions of what might be considered normal or healthy.

- *Interactionist* – Recognize the interaction between a range of individual-centred factors (including affective, cognitive and behavioural factors) and those which are more environmental (other people, institutions, etc.). Interactionist theories would recognize multiple influences on a person's behaviour and accept that an individual could not be properly understood without consideration of all relevant factors. Gender is thus seen as only one contributing factor in a person's behaviour.

- *Lifespan* – Assume that behaviour changes at any time during an individual's lifetime, rather than being restricted to specific periods that exert powerful influences on later behaviour. When applied to gender-related behaviour, such theories suggest that these behaviours are not fixed in people but may always be open to change. Individuals develop within a particular social-historical environment and, as such, experience a range of influences specific to that time, but nevertheless remain capable of choice and thus self-determined change.

GENDER BIAS IN PSYCHOLOGICAL STUDIES

Bias in the research process

There are certain aspects of the way studies are conducted which make it inevitable that the findings of such studies will be biased. Denmark *et al.* (1988) suggests that gender bias is found at all stages of the research process, including:

- *Question formation* – Gross (2003) points out that topics that are studied in psychological research often reflect the prevalent gender stereotypes of the culture. For example, leadership is often defined by researchers in terms of dominance, aggression and other characteristics that are stereotyped as typically 'male'.

- *Research design* – The experimental approach is a 'masculine' approach based on logic and rationality rather than the 'feminine' characteristics of caring and relatedness.

- *Research methods* – Rosenthal (1966) found that male researchers were more pleasant, friendly, honest and encouraging with female than with male participants, leading Rosenthal (1966) to conclude: 'male and female subjects may, psychologically, simply not be in the same experiment at all'. This could explain why some studies discover gender differences that are not really there.
- *Selection of research participants* – Psychologists have typically developed theories from white, male undergraduates. This is then represented as 'human behaviour' (Fine and Gordon 1989).
- *Inappropriate conclusions* – Findings based on one sex are applied to both, as in the case of the theories discussed above.
- *Publication bias* – There is a strong trend in all areas of science for journals to publish only those studies that produce positive findings. In gender research, this means that studies that find gender differences are more likely to be published than those that find no differences, thus exaggerating the difference and producing an alpha bias (Tavris 1993).

Alpha-biased studies

Evolutionary psychology has been accused of an alpha bias and the studies used to support this theory fall under the umbrella of the same criticism. The basis of the argument is that males and females face different problems in order to ensure reproductive success. Males produce many sperm at little physiological cost, and so those males who mate frequently with the most fertile females will be most successful. Females produce few eggs and make a larger physiological investment in each. Females who mate with males who assist with some of the reproductive burdens will be most successful. The genes of those males and females who are successful will be perpetuated.

Derived from this argument are a range of expectations about male and female human behaviour. For example, we would expect men to seek physical attractiveness and youth as signs of fertility and for women to seek men with resources who would thus be good providers. We would also expect men and women to advertise themselves differently (men advertise resources and women advertise attractiveness). A number of studies have looked at personal ads for male and female partners and supported this hypothesis (e.g. Dunbar 1995).

Such research is an example of gender bias in the way the research question is asked and the research is designed. It is possible that if such 'lonely-hearts' advertisements were analysed without any preconceived expectations about what might be found, then other categories would emerge which did not demonstrate a gender difference.

Beta-biased studies

The classic studies of social influence that were part of your AS-level studies (e.g. Asch, Zimbardo, Milgram) involved no women. This was not done because the researchers wished to find about how men behaved. They wanted to find out how people behaved and *assumed* that studies conducted with men could be generalized to men and women. In fact, some of the social influence research did involve women. Hofling *et al.* (1966) studied female nurses, but this was still an example of beta bias because the findings were generalized to all human behaviour.

Milgram did later study obedience in women and found that obedience rates were equally high as those for men, as Hofling and colleagues had found. However, an Australian study found that women were much less obedient than men (16 per cent rather than 40 per cent), though this contradictory finding may be due to the fact that in Milgram's study, females gave males electric shocks, whereas in the Australian study, females were required to shock other females.

Evaluation
gender bias in psychological studies

- *Gender bias in action* – Many of the points raised earlier as commentary on gender bias in psychological theories apply to gender bias in psychological studies. Traditional psychological research has presented women in an unfavourable and unrealistic way because of both alpha bias and beta bias. Theories written by men and studies conducted by men have exaggerated gender differences (an alpha bias). Studies using male samples that are generalised to explain all human behaviour (a beta bias) misrepresent women and may result in a view of female behaviour as inferior, abnormal and even pathological.
- *More constructive approaches* – Both psychology and society are in the process of learning how to think more constructively about gender roles. We may never be able to extricate the 'true' effects of sex (based on biological factors) from those of gender (based on social factors), but we can be aware of the biases that distort what we think is reality.

Check your understanding of gender bias by answering these questions from memory. You can check your answers by looking back through Topic 1.

1 Which term is used to describe a theory that minimizes differences between men and women?

2 Give **one** example of an alpha-biased theory.

3 Give **one** positive consequence and **one** negative consequence of beta-biased theories.

4 Describe **one** criterion that could lead to a bias-free theory.

5 Describe **two** ways in which the research process is gender-biased.

REVISION SUMMARY

Having covered this topic, you should be able to describe and evaluate:

✓ different kinds of gender bias

✓ gender bias in psychological theories

✓ gender bias in psychological studies.

EXAMPLE EXAM QUESTIONS

Below are some **possible examination questions** set on this topic, along with hints to help you understand and approach each question effectively:

1 Discuss **two or more** examples of gender bias in psychological theories. (30 marks)

'Discuss' requires you to describe and evaluate examples of gender bias. The discussion must specifically relate to gender bias in the theories and not be a more global evaluation of the theories themselves. Note also that you are asked for 'two or more'. This means that two examples (such as alpha bias and beta bias) would be sufficient for full marks but further examples (e.g. androcentricism) would also be creditworthy. If you present only one example of gender bias this would mean a partial performance penalty. The same applies if you only present one theory as 'theories' is in the plural.

2 Discuss **two or more** psychological theories in terms of their gender bias. (30 marks)

There's a subtle but important difference between this question and question 1. This time the focus of your answer should be on theories instead of gender bias. You may ultimately use the same material but this time you must shape your answer to this question. In other words you should focus on the theories but not provide a description and evaluation of these theories, only focus on the gender bias aspects of the theory both for the description and evaluation. Synopticity is achieved because you have considered at least two theories (see pp. 939–40).

3 (a) 'Many theories have been criticized for showing gender biases (such as alpha bias, beta bias and androcentrism). If such criticisms are true then the value of the theories should be seriously questioned.'

Discuss gender bias in psychology, with reference to issues such as those raised by the quotation above. (30 marks)

Some questions require that you address the quotation whereas this question says 'with reference to issues *such* as those raised in the quotation' which means that the quotation is there to provide you with possible ideas about what to discuss but there is no requirement to address these issues. If the question had been 'with reference to the issues raised in the quotation' you would need to analyse what issues are in the quotation (criticisms made of theories, whether these are true and whether they do devalue the theories) and make sure you specifically address these in your answer.

A2 Perspectives

4 (a) Describe **one** example of gender bias in psychology.   (5 marks)
   (b) Evaluate **two or more** psychological theories in terms of their gender bias.   (25 marks)

Only one example is required in part (a) which means that 10 AO1 marks have been 'moved' to part (b). Now you will get credit for description of the theories though there are more AO2 marks in this part of the question so you must still focus on commentary. Only commentary related to gender bias would be creditworthy.

Topic 2 >> Cultural bias

WHAT IS CULTURAL BIAS?

What do we mean by culture? 'Culture refers to the collective programming of the mind which distinguishes members of one group from another' (Hofstede 1980). The term 'culture' does not refer to the group of people, but the beliefs, attitudes, child-rearing practices and so on that a group of people share.

Cultural bias can affect psychological theories and studies in a similar way to the effect of gender bias. Hare-Mustin and Maracek (1988) proposed that the same alpha and beta biases apply to culture as well as gender. In fact, it can be argued that gender is an example of a culture insofar as males and females display different beliefs, attitudes, practices and so on. More correctly, gender should be seen as a 'sub-cultural' group – a group of people within a dominant culture who share many of the cultural characteristics of that culture, but also have some distinctive characteristics of their own.

Ethnocentrism and eurocentrism

Probably the most significant cultural bias is 'ethnocentrism', the effect that one's own cultural perspective has on one's perceptions of other cultures. Our own cultural perspective (beliefs, attitudes etc.) is taken as the standard by which we measure other cultures and this inevitably leads one to see one's own cultural practices as superior. 'Eurocentrism' is the most dominant form of bias because people from Europe/America dominate the world. In psychology, Eurocentrism is dominant because most psychologists are European/American. Their theories are taken to be universal descriptions of human behaviour whereas they are clearly culturally biased.

Individual–collectivism

Individualist cultures are those where an individual's identity is more defined by personal achievement and

independence. In a collectivist culture, identity is defined by collective achievement and interdependence. Many psychological explanations are individualist because of their Eurocentric bias. Individualism also tends to co-vary with urban, post-industrial societies whereas collectivism relates to rural, non-industrialized societies.

The emic–etic distinction

Another kind of cultural bias that affects psychology can be described in terms of emics and etics (Pike 1967).

- *Etic* analyses of behaviour focus on the universals of human behaviour. For example, 'phonetics' is the general study of vocal sounds. In an etic approach, the observer uses the rules, beliefs, categories of an alien culture rather than those of the native culture being studied.
- *Emic* analysis of behaviour focus on the varied ways in which activities and development are observed in any specific cultural setting. For example, 'phonemics' is the study of sounds used in a specific language. In an emic approach, the observer attempts to understand a culture by learning the rules, beliefs and so on of a culture from within the culture's own logic system.

The etic approach is inevitably biased because it means ignoring the cultural context of any behaviour and observing it from a position outside the culture. The observers are inevitably influenced by their own culture and therefore make biased judgements of behaviour in other cultures.

Historical bias

The concept of culture can apply to historical comparisons as well as national or ethnic ones. The culture of Britain in the 1950s varies considerably to that of the early 21st century. Theories developed 50 years ago may well not apply to human behaviour today.

Commentary
cultural biases

Howitt and Owusu-Bempah (1994) argue that 'we have a moral obligation to challenge cultural bias, otherwise we are "guilty of complicity".' What ways are there to combat the biases identified above? Two possibilities are:

● *Cultural relativism* – the recognition that there are no universal standards for behaviour but that all behaviours are relative to the cultural context in which they originate

● *Abandoning the etic approach* because it is inevitably biased – all research should be conducted from an emic perspective.

A further issue is raised by Smith and Bond (1998). They point out that there are dangers in attempting to distinguish one culture from another. In doing so, we are attempting to draw definitive lines in terms of what is generally a characteristic in one culture but not, perhaps, a characteristic of another. There are two major problems with this:

● Behaviour differences between any two countries may also be found between different sub-cultures within the same country.

● We assume that cultures are free from conflict and dissent in the behaviour of their members. It is clear that within any culture, there will be a great deal of divergence in the experiences of individuals that make up that culture.

CULTURAL BIAS IN PSYCHOLOGICAL THEORIES

ACTIVITY

Spotting cultural bias

Think about the theories that you have studied so far in your psychology course. Try to identify at least two theories that are culturally biased and explain in what way they are biased and how this affects the way they explain human behaviour.

Are there other, less biased theories that can explain the target behaviours of these theories?

A selection of theories are described below, each as examples of one kind of bias. Most of the theories

could equally well be placed in several other categories. For example, Kohlberg's theory is beta-biased and also an example of an individualist and of the etic approach.

Beta bias

Any theory based on research conducted with one cultural group that is then presented as a theory of *all* human behaviour is beta-biased – it minimizes or ignores cultural differences. Kohlberg's theory of the development of moral reasoning is beta-biased in terms of culture as well as gender. Kohlberg proposed that his developmental stages are driven by biological changes in cognitive maturity which thus must be universal. That is, all individuals, regardless of culture, would experience the same developmental processes at about the same ages.

Commentary
beta bias in terms of culture

● *Support for Kohlberg's theory* – There is evidence from cross-cultural studies that Kohlberg's stages are universal. For example, Snarey et al. (1985) examined 44 different studies conducted in 26 countries that all found a progression from Stages 1 to 4 at about the same ages as Kohlberg found in the US.

● *... but not at 'higher' levels* – However, the same may not apply to the higher stages of moral development (Stages 5 and 6) because the highest moral principles are more typical of urban, individualist, middle-class Western Europeans, i.e. a society where the needs of the individual are considered more important than those of the community. In other cultures, meeting family

obligations and submitting to the authority of elders are regarded as reflecting the highest of moral principles, and yet would be scored at lower levels according to Kohlberg's theory.

● *Higher or just different?* – Indeed Snarey and Keljo (1991) have found that post-conventional understanding occurs mainly in more developed, industrialized societies and is much less usual in rural communities. It may be that the complexity of urban societies demands greater moral sophistication. Such societies pose more conflicts for individuals and this, in turn, would lead to further moral development. In contrast, people living in rural communities don't have the need or stimulation to move to 'higher' levels of development. This is not to say that one group are superior, but that there are differences related to cultural background.

Ethnocentric and Eurocentric

One approach to explaining the formation and maintenance of relationships are the so-called 'economic theories' of interpersonal attraction, such as social exchange theory and equity theory. For a description of these, see Unit 10, pp. 313–6.

Economic theories of relationships are mainly based on US students – a fairly narrow part of one particular culture. Such theories probably only apply to

North American middle-class individuals in short-term relationships – a very specific sub-culture. Studies of European students (Gergen *et al.* 1980) showed a preference for equality rather than equity. Moghaddam *et al.* (1993) suggest that North American relationships are predominantly individualist, voluntary (determined by family) and temporary (most relationships have the option of being ended if desired). Conversely, non-Western relationships are often collective, obligatory and permanent.

Commentary
economic theories of relationships

● *Ethnocentric* – The economic theories are ethnocentric because they are written from one cultural perspective and imply that it is psychologically healthier to have choice in

relationships. They also imply some sense of moral superiority in people who have the option of being able to assert their individual rights rather than following duty.

● *Historically biased* – Moghaddam (1998) further suggests that equity theory is *historically* biased as it was developed during the 1970s when psychology was influenced by the cognitive approach to explaining behaviour.

Etic approach

Mental illness is diagnosed using DSM (Diagnostic Statistical Manual) or ICD (International Standard of Classification of Diseases). Both are used with individuals regardless of their cultural background, assuming that the behaviours of the dominant white culture is the standard which should be applied to all

people (Cochrane and Sashidharan 1995). For example, hearing voices is regarded as a symptom of schizophrenia in some cultures, whereas it is regarded as normal behaviour in others. This misapplication of norms from one culture to another may explain why African-Caribbean immigrants in the UK are seven times more likely than white people to be diagnosed as schizophrenic (Cochrane and Sashidharan 1995).

Commentary
etic approach

● *Alternative explanations* – There are alternative explanations for cultural differences in diagnosis. For example, it may be that immigrants experience

higher levels of stress (from living in a strange place, being exposed to prejudice, etc.), which leads to more mental illness. However, this is not supported by the evidence that immigrants from South Asia, who presumably experience equal stress, are not differentially diagnosed to white people (Cochrane 1983).

Historical bias

Psychodynamic theories have been criticized for their historical bias. Freud's overemphasis on sex may be due to the fact that he wrote at a time of great sexual repression, which may not apply to development now or in other cultures. Subsequent Freudians (or neo-Freudians) played down the role of sexual motivation

though even then they, in turn, have been accused of historical bias. For example Erikson (a neo-Freudian) proposed that identity formation is related to role decisions but this may be related to a historical period when people did seek a single role or 'job for life', but this may be less true today than it was 40 years ago.

Evaluation
cultural bias in psychological theories

Various comments have already been made in relation to individual psychological theories (see

Commentary boxes on previous pages). Many of the points are relevant to all of the theories discussed, e.g. the issue that differentiation between cultures in terms of individualism or collectivism masks differences *within* cultures. In addition you might consider some other points:

continued on next page

- *How is culture operationalized?* – Simply using country of origin as an indication of culture assumes that all the people in one country belong to the same culture. Using race or ethnicity as a representation of an individual's belief system may similarly be mistaken.

- *Does ethnocentricity imply superiority?* – It doesn't necessarily follow that an ethnocentric position has to be one of superiority/inferiority. It is possible to recognize differences as nothing more than differences. Other forms of bias, such as Afrocentrism (centred on individuals of Black African descent), can redress the balance by providing alternative perspectives which remind us that biases may go unrecognized.

CULTURAL BIAS IN PSYCHOLOGICAL STUDIES

Bias in the research process

Cross-cultural research

Research is conducted to test universal theories by repeating the same tests in different cultural contexts, for example Snarey and colleagues' studies of moral development described earlier, or replications of Milgram's obedience studies. Findings from the latter have ranged from 16 per cent obedience, in female students in Australia (Kilham and Mann 1974), to 92 per cent, in Holland (Meeus and Raaijmakers 1986). Differences may be attributed to different cultural behaviours, but it is also possible that differences are due to a lack of equivalence in the procedures. Smith and Bond (1998) suggest the following problems that may arise:

- *Translation* – Participants are instructed by spoken or written word, and their verbal or written responses often constitute the main findings of the research. These instructions and responses must be faithfully translated for the purposes of comparison.

- *Manipulation of variables* – The operationalization of variables and the impact of any manipulation must be the same in each cultural group studied. For example, the expression of happiness might be different in different groups, and the impact of a specific independent variable (such as an insult) might be dramatically different depending on the way it is interpreted by those involved in the study.

- *Participants* – Although these may be taken from similar social groups (university students, schoolchildren, etc.), they may have quite different social backgrounds and experiences in different cultural groups. To gain access to a university in some cultures, for example, does not involve the same criteria as it does in the West.

Biases in sampling

The main bias lies in a researcher's choice of experimental participants. Almost all American and British research is carried out on members of the researchers' own culture. This bias is clearly seen in an analysis of introductory psychology text books by Smith and Bond (1993). They found that in one standard American textbook (Baron and Byrne 1991), 94 per cent of the studies referred to were American, and in one British textbook (Hewstone *et al.* 1988), 68 per cent of the cited studies were also American.

In fact, research populations are even more restricted than this. Sears (1985) reported that 82 per cent of research studies used undergraduates as the participants in psychology studies and 51 per cent were psychology students. This suggests that a considerable amount of psychology is based on middle-class, academic, young adults who are most often male. Psychology findings are not only unrepresentative on a global scale, but also within Western culture.

The imposed etics

One way of overcoming the problem of restricted sampling is to encourage research which uses participants from other cultures. However, this may lead to another source of bias. A researcher is likely to use a method or technique that has been developed by Western psychology, such as using an American IQ test to assess intelligence. This means that the researcher is taking an emic (a perspective from their 'home' culture) and using it as the basis for a comparison between the two cultures – an 'imposed etic' (Berry 1969). This imposed etic makes the assumption that whatever measures have been used in one cultural context (in this case the USA), will have the same meaning when applied in a different cultural context. This is unlikely to be true.

For example, Takahashi (1990) conducted a study of Japanese infants and found that the infants responded quite differently in the Strange Situation from how American infants behave. The Japanese infants were much more disturbed after being left alone. This may be due to the fact that Japanese infants experience much less separation – they are almost never left alone. Hence, the behaviours observed were reactions to extreme stress, not the original aim of the Strange Situation. Thus using the Strange Situation (an imposed etic) with Japanese infants was not comparable to using it with American infants.

Commentary
cultural bias in psychological studies

There are some possible solutions to the problems identified above.

● *A derived etic approach* – Berry (1969) suggested that participants could be observed in their natural environment, to learn about their culture specific traditions, before the studies are executed. This would enable researchers to take a more emic viewpoint and design their research more appropriately.

● *Ethnography* – This is an approach used by anthropologists where reports are collected from different cultural contexts containing information about patterns of behaviour, dynamics, institutions and so on. A collection of such reports can be used to produce a larger picture of human behaviour.

● *Indigenous psychologies* – The growth of psychology and psychological research in different countries around the world means that we will become more enlightened about how people in different cultures behave. According to Yamagishi (2002), there are now more social psychologists working in Asia than in Europe.

 CHECK YOUR UNDERSTANDING

Check your understanding of cultural bias by answering these questions from memory. You can check your answers by looking back through Topic 2.

1 Distinguish between emic and etic approaches in psychology.

2 Aside from the emic–etic distinction, identify **two** other kinds of cultural bias in psychology.

3 Give an example of a psychological theory that represents an individualist perspective, and explain in what way it is individualist.

4 Outline **two** reasons why cross-cultural research may lack validity.

5 What is an 'imposed etic'?

REVISION SUMMARY

Having covered this topic, you should be able to describe and evaluate:

✓ different kinds of cultural bias

✓ cultural bias in psychological theories

✓ cultural bias in psychological studies.

 EXAMPLE EXAM QUESTIONS

Below are some **possible examination questions** set on this topic, along with hints to help you understand and approach each question effectively:

1 'Many psychological theories are based on research with "Western" participants but accepted as explanations of human behaviour. We probably haven't begun to understand the effects that such generalizations have had on modern life.'

Discuss cultural bias in psychology, with reference to the issues raised by the quotation above. (30 marks)

> In this question you are required to address the issues raised in the quotation or a partial performance penalty will be applied to your AO2 mark (this means a ceiling of 9 marks for AO2). Your first task, therefore, is to identify the issues in the quotation. If you wish, you can make these explicit in the opening paragraph of your answer ('The issues in the quotation are …') and then use these issues to organize your answer.

2 Critically consider **two or more** examples of cultural bias in psychological research (theories **and/or** studies). (30 marks)

> 'Critically consider' is an AO1+AO2 term, which means that you should both describe and evaluate the two or more examples. Your description should focus on your chosen examples of cultural bias and you should *use* the research as a way of elaborating the examples. Your evaluation should again be of the cultural bias in the research. The 'two or more' means that two examples are enough, but you can discuss more than two – so it is two examples in detail (depth rather than breadth) or more examples in less detail (breadth rather than depth). Note that 'research' can be broadly interpreted – not just theories and studies but the process of conducting research, as we have done in this unit.

3 (a) Explain the issue of cultural bias. (5 marks)
   (b) Discuss **two or more** examples of cultural bias in psychological theories. (25 marks)

> This question is parted unevenly. The term 'explain' in part (a) is an AO1 term requiring a brief explanation of why cultural bias is an issue. In part (b), the term 'discuss' is an AO1+AO2 term. There are only 10 marks remaining for the AO1 part of this question, so you should devote slightly more energy (and time) to the evaluation. Again, steer away from any general evaluation of your theories and focus on the cultural bias in the theory when offering evaluation. As there is credit for synopticity in all of these questions it is always desirable to base your answer in as many different kinds of theories as possible – without trying to do too many and thus reduce the detail given for each.

4 Discuss cultural bias in psychological research (theories **and/or** studies). (30 marks)

> It pays to organize an answer to a more general question such as this. You might decide to discuss cultural bias in two theories. In this case, you can divide your essay into four chunks: describe and evaluate theory 1 (200 + 200 words, as essays in 40 minutes contain about 800 words) and then describe and evaluate theory 2. Here, AO1 is a description of theories (or studies) in terms of their cultural bias and AO2 is a commentary on the bias, e.g. in the form of a discussion of the implications and ways to overcome the problems.

Topic 3 >> Ethical issues with human participants

ACTIVITY

Ethical issues

1 Think back to your AS course. List all of the ethical issues that you recall studying.

2 Draw up a list of some of the 'key studies' you covered at AS level. Give each study a rating on a scale of 1 to 10 where 1 is not ethical at all and 10 is very ethical.

3 What criteria did you use to make your judgements?

'Morals' concern what is acceptable or right in terms of human behaviour. 'Ethics' are a set of moral principles used by a group of professionals. Ethical *issues* arise in psychological research when there are conflicts between the rights of participants and the needs of researchers in conducting valid investigations. Ethical

guidelines have been developed as one way of dealing with ethical issues. There are other ways to deal with the ethical issues that arise when planning and conducting research, such as the use of ethical committees and the decision to stop a study earlier than planned.

The distinction between ethics and morality

There may at first appear to be no clear-cut distinction between the terms 'ethics' and 'morality', and indeed, many writers use these terms interchangeably. We can, however, make a useful distinction between the terms if we use the term 'ethics' to refer to professional, work-related issues, and the term 'morality' in the more personal context of living one's own life (Jones 1999). Work can be viewed as a rule-governed and disciplined activity designed to accomplish some specific task. The overriding value which penetrates the entire activity of work is called 'competence'. Historically, the role of ethics has been to help promote and maintain

A2 Perspectives

competence in a particular discipline or activity. Ethics thus fosters the wellbeing of a particular line of work such as medicine, law or psychology. What these three disciplines have in common is that they contain the three basic elements necessary in order for ethics to have a role:

1 They require the acquisition of *specialized knowledge*.

2 They have *standards of competence*.

3 They have well-defined *sets of practices* that allow the knowledge and standards of competence to be utilized.

One consequence of these qualities is that professions tend to produce a body of rules to promote the long-term welfare of the work. These rules are called 'ethics'. The main ethical issues that concern psychologists are considered below.

Deception

Deception involves withholding information or misleading research participants. Psychologists use deception in research studies because participants' behaviour may be altered by their expectations about how they should behave in a study and this would invalidate the research findings. The *issue* is one of weighing the need for deception against the potential harm to a participant. The potential harm to participants ranges from the distrust that such practices create in participants (and thus their unwillingness to participate in future studies) to actual psychological or physical harm experienced without having had the chance to decline to participate.

Resolving the issue of deception

The issue can be resolved in various ways:

- Certain situations can be identified where deception is acceptable, such as when the deception is minor or where there is no potential for harm (such as memory experiments).

- Certain situations can be identified where deception is *not* acceptable, such as when an investigation is trivial in nature or when the potential harm to participants is large.

- Participants may be offered debriefing and the right to withhold their data.

- Passive deception may be more acceptable than active deception. There is a difference between withholding certain research details and deliberately misleading participants about the purpose of the research.

A02
Commentary
deception

- *Informed consent* – Probably the most serious consequence of deception is that it removes the ability of participants to give their fully informed consent to take part in an investigation. If we don't tell participants everything that is going on, then how can they really make a fully informed decision about whether they should take part? This does create dilemmas for the researcher, especially since complete openness may decrease the effectiveness of the investigation.

- *Other consequences of deception* – Baumrind (1985) suggests that the use of deception may decrease the number of naive participants available for future research, and may reduce support for psychological research in general (e.g. in the media and within the general population).

- *Alternatives to deception* – We may, for example, take a random sample of the population to be studied and introduce them to the research design, including knowledge of the deception to be used. If they agree that, knowing the true aim of the investigation, they would still have given their voluntary informed consent, then we may presume that they represent the views of the rest of their population group. This is called 'presumptive consent'.

- *Does deception actually work?* – Kimmel (1996) suggests that in order for deception to be effective, the level of naiveté among participants should be high, the experimental procedure should not produce cues that might be interpreted by participants as indicating that deception is taking place and participants' suspiciousness of deception should not alter the experimental effect. It may be that many participants don't fully believe the deception used by a researcher.

Informed consent

The essence of informed consent is that participants can agree or refuse to participate in the light of *comprehensive* information about the nature and purpose of the research. Homan (1991) suggests that there are two issues implied in the 'informed' part of informed consent and two involved in the 'consent' part.

'Informed'

To be *informed* means that:

- all pertinent aspects of what is to happen and what *might* happen are *disclosed* to the participant

- and that the participants should also be able to *understand* this information.

Epstein and Lasagna (1969) discovered that only one third of participants volunteering for an experiment really understood what was involved. Even if researchers have sought and obtained informed consent, that does not guarantee that participants really do understand what they have let themselves in for. As Schuler (1982) points out, many designs are unintelligible to professional colleagues, let alone participants! Another problem is the requirement for the researcher to point out any likely benefits and risks of participation. Researchers are not always able to predict accurately the risks of taking part in a study.

'Consent'

To give *consent* means that:

- the participant must be *competent* to make a rational and mature judgement
- the agreement to participate should be *voluntary*, free from coercion and undue influence.

Some participants may initially give their consent to take part in a study, but if they later realize that they would like to withdraw that consent (for whatever reason), they should be free to do so, even if they have previously accepted payment for their participation. The issues of consent and withdrawal may appear compromised by the payment of participants. After all, we live in a society where people who accept payment are seen as entering into a contract to provide services. If a shopkeeper changed his mind about handing over your groceries after he had taken your money, you would be justifiably aggrieved.

Issues surrounding informed consent

It benefits psychological researchers to be open and honest in their research, as this is more likely to generate public respect and support than more secretive practices. Even those researchers who claim to have obtained informed consent may sometimes be selective in how much they have told their participants. The issue is not between telling the truth and telling lies, but about where one draws the line in deciding how much information is sufficient (Homan 1991). A general rule is that the greater the risk, the more meticulous should be the operation of informing potential participants (Homan 1991).

The issue of informed consent is slightly different when we consider research that takes place in more naturalistic settings (i.e. field research). The major obstacle to obtaining informed consent here is that it is often simply not feasible (Kimmel 1996). Kelman (in Kimmel 1996) says: 'In one sense field experiments are more problematic than lab experiments for the reason that in a lab experiment at least the person knows that he or she is coming for an experiment.'

In situations where behaviour is public (such as in shopping malls and at football matches) and where the procedures used do not significantly affect participants' lives or pose any risk for them, then informed consent is cumbersome and unnecessary (Kimmel 1996). In such situations, obtaining informed consent may be seen as ethically and methodologically undesirable *provided* other measures have been taken to safeguard the interests of the participants (e.g. to ensure their anonymity and to minimize invasions of privacy).

Commentary
alternatives to fully informed consent

If it is not feasible to obtain fully informed consent, one alternative is not to conduct the research study. Other alternatives include:

- *Debriefing* – Participants are fully informed after the study has taken place and given the option to

withhold their data. However this cannot wipe away any bad experiences. (See also Unit 5, p. 183.)

- *Presumptive consent* (as outlined above) and *prior general consent* – Prospective participants are informed that *sometimes* participants are misinformed about the true purpose of the study and asked to give consent without knowing whether their study will involve deception. (See also Unit 5, p. 182.)

Privacy

Privacy is a central issue in field research where people are frequently unaware that they are acting as research participants. Four dimensions are used to determine where a particular piece of research lies on the privacy continuum, and therefore how acceptable observation is under such circumstances.

- *How public the setting is* – People can less reasonably expect privacy in shopping malls or football grounds than in the private settings of their own homes.

- *The publicness of the person* – Public personalities are regularly subject to observation and reporting that would be considered an invasion of privacy for a less public individual.
- *The degree of anonymity provided* – Privacy is maintained when the link between an individual and the information obtained is severed.
- *The nature of the information disclosed* – Certain information (e.g. about sexual practices or benefit fraud) is considered more sensitive and poses a greater risk to participants than other information.

Psychological and physical harm

In some ways deception is an example of psychological harm. No research participant should leave a research study in a different state from the one at the beginning of the study. No participant should feel humiliated, embarrassed or with a lowered sense of self-esteem. However, in many studies, such outcomes are possible if not inevitable. Again the issue is to balance the researchers' needs against the participants' right not to be harmed. A certain degree of potential harm or risk is considered to be acceptable *if* it is no greater than the risks participants might be expected to face in their everyday lives. Thus a modicum of stress is reasonable, as in the case of the Strange Situation study by Ainsworth and Bell (1970).

One of the problems with risk assessment is that it is difficult to assess risks or harm before conducting a study. In many studies, the amount of distress displayed by participants was not anticipated. In such situations, researchers may deal with unexpected distress by stopping a study early.

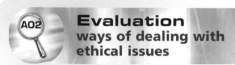

Evaluation
ways of dealing with ethical issues

The 'AO2 Commentary' panels on the preceding pages outline some of these ways that ethical issues may be resolved. There are a few other general comments to make here.

- *Costs and benefits* – Ethical issues are largely resolved by weighing costs against benefits, for example the costs to participants or costs to research validity against the importance of the research. However, in reality there are many problems with this. As already noted, it is not always possible to calculate costs beforehand. It is also difficult to decide which costs to consider – there are costs to the participant, costs to the research process and costs to society at large (which we will consider later, in the section on socially sensitive research). Cost–benefit analyses tend to ignore the rights of individual participants in favour of practical considerations. Baumrind (1975) has pointed out that cost–benefit analyses appear to raise as many ethical dilemmas as they are supposed to solve.

- *Hidden ethical issues* – Techniques such as prior general consent and presumptive consent may not be real alternatives either because they raise further ethical issues (passive dishonesty to participants, invalidating the research process by altering participants to possible deception).

- *Debriefing alone may not be enough* – The use of debriefing does not address all issues. For example, participants may not listen to the debriefing because they wish to go home or they may not believe that the researcher is telling the truth – having been given false feedback in an experiment about an intelligence score they may think they researcher is only trying to make them feel better and that the score was correct.

- *Ethical guidelines have problems* – For example they lead the individual researcher to feel absolved of responsibility for ethical decisions. Guidelines leave the responsibility with someone else and remove the need for individuals to think for themselves.

- *Other ways to deal with ethical issues* – For example, institutions involved in research have ethical committees (institutional review boards – IRBs). These are composed of lay and professional members who consider the costs and benefits of proposed research and assess proposed steps to protect participants. Punishment is also used to enforce ethical guidelines. Psychologists who contravene ethical codes may be disbarred from their professional association.

ETHICAL ISSUES IN PSYCHOLOGICAL INVESTIGATIONS WITH HUMAN PARTICIPANTS

This part of the specification is also concerned with *synoptic* topics, i.e. those drawn from across the specification. Therefore it follows that you should use your knowledge from other areas of psychology when discussing ethical issues (as well as when discussing gender and cultural bias and the use of non-human animals in research). You may use studies from the AS course as well as those from your A2 course, though AS studies should be treated with greater sophistication than they were when studied at AS. Tables 27.1 and 27.2 identify a range of possible studies. One study in particular, Milgram's obedience study, has attracted a number of ethical comments so we will examine this in detail below.

Milgram's obedience research

Deception and lack of informed consent

Milgram's studies of obedience are covered in detail in Unit 5, pp. 171–5 and 184–6. For Milgram, deception was a necessary part of his research design. Without it, participants would have behaved differently. There is support for and against this belief. Prior to the study, Milgram asked a group of students how they thought participants would respond. They estimated that less than 3 per cent would go to the maximum level. This suggests that, if participants knew it was fake, they would behave as the students predicted. This was borne out in a study by Mixon (1972), who conducted a replication of Milgram's research. Read the panel 'Alternatives to using deception' on p. 183.

Commentary
justifications for Milgram's research

Milgram's use of deception may be further justified by looking at the circumstances when deception is considered to be acceptable:

- **If the effects of deception were unanticipated** – Milgram (1974) argued that he could not predict how the participants would behave as previous information suggested that most people would not obey.
- **Where the potential for harm is minimal** – As he believed that most participants would not obey, Milgram expected that psychological harm would be minimal. In any case it is arguable as to how

Harm

Baumrind (1964) accused Milgram of showing insufficient respect for his participants. The participants trembled, stuttered and sweated; one even reportedly had a full blown seizure. As well as such short-term effects, Darley (1992) has suggested that there are possible harmful long-term effects. The evil that is latent in all of us might have been activated by participation in this investigation and thus participants' behaviour subsequent to the study might have been altered in an undesirable way. Milgram (1974) acknowledges that once the investigation was under way it became clear that some participants would go all the way and experience stress. At that point he did wonder if he should abandon the study but he says that

Evaluation
Milgram's obedience research

Milgram's research has been both harshly criticized and highly praised. Milgram (1974) suggested that the ethical disapproval was actually related to the findings, not the procedures, i.e. the horror was that people could behave like that and this was turned into a

On the other hand one might question whether participants actually believed in the deception. If they didn't believe in the deception, then it was not necessary. Orne and Holland (1968) claim that Milgram's participants basically knew the shocks were not real because it wouldn't make sense for such an extreme amount of harm to be inflicted on the learner in a mere learning experiment (see the panel 'Experimental (internal) validity' on p. 175).

much harm the participants did experience (see below).

- **If the research is non-trivial** – Many psychologists regard Milgram's study as extremely important. Elms (1972) called it the 'most morally significant research in psychology'. Even it isn't of this level of importance, it was not trivial research; Milgram started from the view that more crimes are committed against humanity in the name of obedience than in the name of rebellion.
- **If there is adequate debriefing** – After the study was completed Milgram performed a variety of debriefing tasks. Participants were introduced to the 'learner' so they could see that all was well. They were all interviewed about their experiences and sent documents about the findings of the study. Some were interviewed a year later.

there was no indication of any injury and that 'momentary excitement was not the same as harm'.

It is difficult to produce evidence to counter Darley's criticism but Milgram did argue, to the contrary, that there were actually benefits from his research for the participants. When sent a questionnaire, 74 per cent of the participants said they had learned something of personal importance from taking part. One participant wrote to Milgram later saying that what he had learned from the experiment was an insight into *why* he had behaved in this way, and that he was later able to apply this understanding to his decision to register as a conscientious objector (he did not want to be placed in a position where he might have to obey orders with which he disagreed).

horror about the way he treated his participants. We can ask some final questions about the research:

- **Could the same findings be produced without the deception?** – Probably not.
- **Were the findings important?** – Were they *sufficiently* important to justify the short and long-term effects? Psychologists are divided in their answers to these questions.

continued on next page

Evaluation continued
Milgram's obedience research

● *Did Milgram create an 'obedience alibi'?* – Mandel (1998) claimed that Milgram's research oversimplified the processes of obedience.

Milgram produced evidence that certain situational factors (such as proximity to a victim) and certain psychological processes (such as agentic shift) lead to destructive obedience. Mandel says this is not borne out by real-life studies of obedience and thus Milgram, in his research, created an alibi for all those people who mindlessly obey (see p. 174).

Other investigations

Tables 27.1 and 27.2 summarize details of studies across the AS and A2 specifications respectively. Note that there are many examples of *good* practice, as well as cases where psychologists have been criticized.

Table 27.1 >> Ethical issues in psychological investigations (AS study areas)

AS studies	Ethical issues	Attempts to deal with issues
>> Curtiss (1977) Genie was isolated through her childhood and then studied intensively by psychologists interested in the effects of privation on development. (See Unit 2, p. 64)	In 1979, Genie's mother Irene filed a case against the psychologists, claiming that they had subjected Genie to 'extreme, unreasonable and outrageous intensive testing, experimentation, and observation ... under conditions of duress and servitude'. In short, performing unethical human experimentations (Rymer 1993).	The case was settled by Curtiss giving the proceeds from a book to Genie ($8,000). One of the psychologists commented: 'It turned out that Genie, who had been so terribly abused, was exploited all over again, just by a different set of characters, of which I'm sorry to say I was one.' (Rymer 1993)
>> Zimbardo *et al.* (1973) Stanford prison study. Students given roles as either guard or prisoner in a mock prison at Stanford University. (See Unit 5, pp. 162–3 and 186–7)	The guards became brutal, harassing the prisoners by making them perform offensive tasks such as cleaning toilets with their bare hands. The prisoners felt humiliated, some of them became anxious and depressed, and asked for early release. The importance of this study has been challenged as it did little to change prison environments, which had been the aim of the study.	The study was designed with special attention to ethical issues. Fully informed consent was obtained except for 'prisoners' being arrested at home. However, Zimbardo thought that withholding this kind of procedural detail was justifiable given the nature of the study. The study was stopped prematurely. Participants were thoroughly debriefed both after the study and a year later.

Table 27.2 >> Ethical issues in psychological investigations (A2 study areas)

A2 studies	Ethical issues	Attempts to deal with issues
A2 Social psychology **>> Piliavin *et al.* (1969)** The 'subway Samaritan study' investigated how willing people are to help in an emergency situation. During a seven-and-a-half minute journey on a busy New York subway train, a 'victim' collapsed on the floor of the train and remained there until someone helped. (See Unit 11, p. 356.)	Such a staged emergency poses risks for unsuspecting bystanders. Some may be distressed from seeing someone collapse and could even suffer a heart attack; others might be injured in a rush to help the victim. Those who do not help may feel guilty afterwards for not helping (Kimmel 1996). Such research causes people to become cynical and rationalize their anti-social behaviour (Baumrind 1977).	It was not possible to debrief participants as this was a field experiment. The researchers did not address any ethical issues in their report. *continued on next page*

Table 27.2 >> Ethical issues in psychological investigations (A2 study areas) continued

A2 studies	Ethical issues	Attempts to deal with issues
A2 Physiological psychology **>> Schachter and Singer (1962)** Emotional experience may be a mixture of physiological arousal and cognitive cues. This hypothesis was tested by giving adrenaline to some participants. They were told it was a new vitamin, given to them as part of an experiment on vision. Some participants were warned that they might experience the real effects of adrenaline. (See Unit 14, p. 449.)	All participants were deceived, including the control group who were given a placebo instead of adrenaline (epinephrine). Those who did receive adrenaline had not provided consent.	Participants were given health checks beforehand and debriefed afterwards. Adrenaline is a natural substance that we are all exposed to on a daily basis, so could be presumed to be something no greater than normal experience and thus not objectionable.
A2 Cognitive psychology **>> Bower et al. (1970)** In this study, perceptual development (size constancy) was assessed in infants by seeing whether they showed a defensive response to approaching objects. The infants were less than 2 weeks old.	The fact that a defensive response was what was being studied should lead researchers to predict that this activity might be quite distressing for infants. In one condition, where the moving object approached very near to the infants, the effect was violent upset.	The experiment was immediately abandoned.
A2 Developmental psychology **>> Bandura et al. (1963)** The main evidence for social learning theory is from the studies of children (aged 3 to 6 years) observing an adult behaving aggressively to the Bobo doll. (See Unit 11, p. 341.)	The hypothesis for this research is that children will acquire certain behaviours through observation of models. Thus the children were being conditioned to become more aggressive.	There is no mention of ethical concerns in the article reporting this study, although it was conducted before Milgram's research, when psychologists were less alert about ethical issues, though there were ethical guidelines.
A2 Individual differences **>> Kirsch et al. (2002)** This meta-analysis looked at the findings from nearly 40 studies comparing anti-depressants with placebos, concluding that patients who got placebos fared almost as well as those getting real drugs.	Depressed patients assigned to placebo conditions think they are being treated physiologically but are getting nothing. They are deprived of treatment that is proposed as beneficial and, in addition, there is an increased risk of suicide and attempted suicide in participants who are placed in placebo groups (Khan and Khan 2000). This has lead psychiatrists to feel increasingly uneasy about the use of placebos in drug trials.	Drug effectiveness can be assessed by comparing patients using two different kinds of drugs, though this does not provide information about pharmacological vs psychological effects.

THE ETHICS OF SOCIALLY SENSITIVE RESEARCH

Social psychologists such as the late Stanley Milgram have an ethical responsibility to society as a whole, and we might argue that they would not be fulfilling that responsibility if they did not carry out socially important research to the best of their ability. We will now consider this idea of socially important research and the particular ethical issues that arise.

What is socially sensitive research?

Trying to define anything in psychology creates problems and 'socially sensitive research' is no

different. Indeed, rather than trying to isolate certain research areas as being potentially more sensitive than others, we might argue that all research is potentially 'socially' sensitive. In fact, few textbooks use this term at all, although many acknowledge the special problems that social researchers face in their work. Sieber and Stanley (1988) offer the following definition of 'socially sensitive research': '... studies in which there are potential social consequences or implications, either directly for the participants in research or the class of individuals represented by the research.' (Sieber and Stanley 1988, p. 49)

The essence of this definition is that much of what we study in psychology has a *social* impact. The potential for that is greater with some investigations than others. For example, it is hard to imagine the social impact of research into perceptual illusions or short-term memory. Research about the genetic basis of criminality, on the other hand, can have profound social consequences (compulsory genetic testing, imprisonment of genetically influenced criminals, and so on). One of the problems of any research that comes under this definition is that it is likely to attract a good deal of attention, not only from other psychologists, but also from the media and the public (Wadeley *et al.* 1997). Whilst this is not necessarily a bad thing, given that the results of psychological research should be more available to a wider audience, it does mean that a wider (and sometimes ill-informed) population are led to think that certain behaviours are normal or understandable.

We could avoid the controversies associated with this kind of research by restricting our research interests to areas that attract little attention from the media and from peers outside our area of interest. However, this raises equally important ethical issues because topics or groups of people are *not* being studied and as a result unfair treatment and prejudice may continue.

Examples of socially sensitive research

The sort of research that would come under the heading of 'socially sensitive research' includes research into sexual orientation, racial differences, gender-related abilities and mental illness. Not only does this type of research have implications for the people that take part, but also for the wider social group that they represent. Some of the ethical issues that arise in such research are listed below:

- *Privacy* – During the research process, a skilled investigator may extract more information from participants than they intended to give. Some research (e.g. into AIDS) may lead to social policies that are an invasion of people's private lives (e.g. through compulsory antibody testing/quarantine).

- *Confidentiality* – In some areas of research, questions may reveal information of a sensitive nature (such as sexual habits or drug use). In such situations confidentiality is paramount. Otherwise, participants would be less willing to divulge this information in the future and further research in this area would be compromised.

- *Sound and valid methodology* – Some of the controversies that arise from socially sensitive research can be attributed to poorly designed or executed studies or inappropriate interpretations of the findings. Although other scientists may be aware of these problems, the media and the public may not, and thus poor studies might shape important social policy.

- *Justice and equitable treatment* – All participants must be treated in an equitable manner and resources which are vital to the participants' well-being (e.g. educational opportunities) must not be withheld from one group whilst being available to another. Likewise, ideas that create prejudicial treatment of one sector of society are seen as unfair and therefore unacceptable. Freud's ideas of the 'deficient' nature of women were instrumental in the treatment of women as second-class citizens in the early part of this century.

- *Scientific freedom* – It is the role of the researcher to carry out scientific research. This freedom to pursue scientific research is balanced against the obligation to protect those who take part or the sectors of society that they represent. Censorship of scientific activity is generally regarded as unacceptable, but some careful monitoring of the research process is seen as necessary.

Gay and lesbian relationships

Research in this area is likely to be alpha- or beta-biased – that is, differences between homosexuals and heterosexuals are minimized (beta bias) or exaggerated (alpha bias). Early research on homosexuality tended to be alpha-biased, demonstrating that homosexual relationships followed similar patterns to heterosexual ones. However, Kitzinger and Coyle (1995) described this as 'liberal humanism' – a movement that attempted to show that homosexuals were not abnormal.

However, such research and its findings ignores the particular difficulties faced by homosexuals, such as family support for their relationships. Thus subsequent research has tended to be more beta-biased, recognizing the ways that homosexual relationships *differ* from heterosexual ones. For example, research by Nard (1992) suggests that, unlike heterosexual couples, lesbians and gay men are more likely to remain friends after a relationship has finished (see Unit 10, p. 330).

Intelligence and race

Jensen wrote an article in 1969 that stated that research showed that intelligence was inherited and that the 15-point difference in IQs of black and white Americans was at least partially genetic. This sparked off an emotional and political controversy which was re-ignited by Herrnstein and Murray's book *The Bell Curve* (1994). This also claimed that IQ is largely genetic and that societies waste resources trying to educate individuals beyond their innate potential.

Eating disorders

One issue that can arise with socially sensitive research is that the participants might be vulnerable and distressed or might have a number of unresolved conflicts, and might not be fully in control of the interview. In the research process, the skilled researcher may extract more information from the participant that they intended to disclose (Sieber and Stanley 1988). This applies to research into eating disorders.

● *Differences within same-sex relationships*
  – One problem with alpha bias is that this
  approach tends to ignore differences *within* any
  group, promoting the view that homosexual
  relationships differ from heterosexual ones and
  are similar to each other, thus glossing over the
  differences between gay and lesbian relationships.
  There is research into such differences, e.g. into
  personal ads in newspapers and contact
  magazines described in Unit 10, p. 329, which
  identified the different qualities sought by gay
  men and lesbians in a potential partner
  (Davidson 1991, Huston and Schwartz 1995).

● *Social effect of gay and lesbian research* – In
  general, research on gay and lesbian relationships
  has been increasingly beneficial to a wider
  understanding of such relationships, increasing
  tolerance and reducing prejudice. The simple fact
  that such relationships are studied signals a
  greater value placed on such relationships, which
  has an effect on attitudes generally.

● *Implications of research into race and
  intelligence* – One implication of this debate
  is that disadvantaged children (racially or
  economically disadvantaged) should not be
  offered enrichment programmes. While it is
  generally agreed that there is a significant genetic
  component in IQ (see evidence on p. 567), this
  does not mean that environmental factors have no
  importance – though that is the implication. In
  fact, research has shown that environmental
  factors have the largest influence on
  disadvantaged children. Studies conducted with
  middle-class children show inherited influences
  are predominant – but this is because, when
  environmental factors are cranked up to maximum,
  then genetic factors are the only possible factor
  that will affect variation (Turkheimer *et al.* 2003).
  In contrast, for disadvantaged children, IQ
  variation is much more related to environmental
  differences (such as poor diet or low educational
  attainment of parents).

● *Importance of research into eating disorders* –
  Despite the need to treat participants with the
  greatest sensitivity, such research is important in
  educating the public about the prevalence and
  causes of eating disorders.

● *Hanged if you do and hanged if you don't* –
  Ignoring these important areas of research would
  amount to an abdication of what Aronson (1999)
  refers to as the 'social responsibilities' of the
  psychological researcher.

● *Ethics of research versus ethics of socially
  sensitive research* – Are the needs of society
  more important than the needs of the individual?
  Aronson (1999) suggests that psychologists face a
  particularly difficult dilemma when their wider
  responsibility to society conflicts with their more
  specific responsibilities to each individual research
  participant. This conflict is greatest when the
  issues under investigation are issues of great
  social importance. The more important the issue
  and the more potential benefit a study might have

for society, the more likely it is that the individual
participant may experience some degree of
discomfort or anxiety. Perhaps we are too short-
sighted in condemning research for the more
immediate impact that it has on the people that
take part. Longer-term social issues should be
carefully weighed against the more usual concern
with shorter-term individual rights.

● *Use of ethical guidelines* – Ethical guidelines
  are essential, but the problem with them is that
  they are largely focused on the immediate needs
  of research participants and may not deal with
  all the possible ways in which research may inflict
  harm on a group of people or section of society.
  The Canadian Psychological Association
  (1991), for example, advises its members to
  'analyse likely short-term, ongoing and long-term
  risks and benefits of each course of action on
  the individual(s)/group(s) involved or likely to
  be affected'.

REVISION SUMMARY

Having covered this topic, you should be able to describe and evaluate:

✓ ethical issues in research using human participants

✓ the ethical issues in psychological investigations using human participants

✓ the ethics of socially sensitive research.

Socially sensitive
research

*Professor **Joan Sieber** is a psychologist at California State University, Hayward, who specializes in culturally sensitive methods of research and research ethics. She is the author of eight books and numerous other publications, including software and encyclopedia entries, on ethical problem-solving in social and behavioural research.*

Q What do you mean by 'socially sensitive research'?

A Socially sensitive research potentially poses some threat for the researchers or the researched due to some aspect of the data collection, holding or dissemination. Many research topics are potentially sensitive, but the actual sensitivity lies in the social context of the research. The main risk is breach of confidentiality, which, in turn can lead to many kinds of harms: physical, emotional or psychological (e.g. stress), legal (e.g. prosecution for illegal acts), social (e.g. stigma), and economic (e.g. loss of employment).

Q Could you give some examples of research that would be considered 'socially sensitive'?

A (1) Research on domestic violence may involve many kinds of risks: the abuser may learn of the research and, in anger, harm the subject or the researcher; the victim may experience severe distress at recounting experiences of being abused; the data may be subpoenaed in an investigation of the abuser's trail of misdeeds towards others.

(2) Smoking-cessation research programmes for teenagers are sensitive because most teens smoke unbeknown to their parents. Research on minors cannot ordinarily be conducted without parental permission, but if such permission is to be sought, most teens would be unwilling to enter the programme. (A waiver of parental permission is generally permissible under these conditions, however, offering a solution to this problem.)

(3) Research on injection drug users who may be HIV+ is sensitive in many respects: the subjects may not want to be identified either as drug users or as HIV+, and must be approached via trusted gatekeepers and in ways that do not jeopardize the relationship of the gatekeeper to the subjects. Drug users typically insist on being paid for participation and have no way to cash cheques, yet the researcher who enters the street environment with a pocket full of cash is in peril.

Joan Sieber

Q How should psychology respond to the special problems posed by socially sensitive research?

A The following situations describe two contexts in which researchers successfully interviewed injection drug users who are HIV+. (1) The researcher studied outpatient drug abuse patients at a community clinic. All arrangements were made through the clinic – which had established a relationship with these patients based on mutual trust and respect. The team of researchers agreed to abide by all clinic rules and to share their research findings with the clinic (with subjects' permission).

(2) A researcher interviewed prostitutes, some of whom were injection drug users and carried sexually-transmitted diseases. To do this, the researcher established a relationship with an outreach programme that gave prostitutes food, medical service, counselling, and assistance in leaving 'the life'. To become part of this team, the researcher had to commit considerable time simply working in the van as one of the trusted outreach individuals. The research role was explained to the prostitutes, and those who were willing to be interviewed about their safe-sex practices, life style and plans for the future were recruited for the research.

Q Should researchers simply avoid research in socially sensitive areas, or would that be an abdication of their responsibility as scientists?

A To shy away from all socially sensitive research topics is to fail to study socially important issues. However, socially sensitive research is not casually entered into. Such topics require that the researcher invest the time and effort to gain a deep understanding of the persons to be studied and the context in which they live. Much planning is required and the researcher must make a considerable commitment to serving those they seek to study. Socially sensitive research is not for the faint of heart. It requires a level of effort and commitment far beyond what most research methodology textbooks ever mention.

Check your understanding of ethical issues with human participants by answering these questions. Check your answers by looking back through Topic 3.

1 In what way is 'informed consent' an 'ethical issue', whereas debriefing is not an ethical issue?

2 Psychologists resolve ethical issues by using ethical guidelines. Name **two** other ways of resolving ethical issues.

3 Under what circumstances might psychological harm be acceptable in a research study?

4 Outline Mandel's criticism of Milgram's research.

5 Briefly explain what is meant by 'socially sensitive research'.

 EXAMPLE EXAM QUESTIONS

Below are some **possible examination questions** set on this topic, along with hints to help you understand and approach each question effectively:

1 Discuss ethical issues relating to **two or more** psychological investigations that have involved human participants. (30 marks)

> 'Discuss' is a term requiring you to describe and evaluate. The 'two or more' indicates that if you only consider two investigations, this is enough. Alternatively, you may discuss more than two investigations, but there will be a trade off between the number of investigations (breadth) and the detail you can provide (depth). The 'details' required are about ethical issues. Do not make the mistake of describing the investigations themselves, but only information relating to the ethical issues arising in the investigations. Your evaluation (AO2) should also be related to ethical issues as opposed to other points of commentary you might make about the studies. However, any synoptic points (e.g. about gender bias, determinism, nature/nurture) would be credited.

2 (a) Outline ethical issues in psychological investigations that have involved human participants. (15 marks)
(b) Evaluate the ethical issues in psychological investigations that you identified in part (a). (15 marks)

> This question is split into an AO1 and AO2 component to help you separate AO1 and AO2 and encourage you to present equal amounts as appropriate to the mark allocation. In part (b), you should only evaluate the issues raised in part (a). Here, it is the issues that should be evaluated and not the psychological investigations. In questions such as this, many candidates go no further than Milgram and Zimbardo, and if they do, their essay still focuses on social influence research alone. In this unit we have included other areas of research to encourage you to think more widely about ethical issues in all areas of psychological investigation.

3 'Psychologists consider ethical issues when designing research in term of both short- and long-term costs for both the participants *and* their groups. They should also consider the possibility that *not* conducting the research may be equally harmful.'
Discuss ethical issues in psychology, with reference to the issues raised in the quotation. (30 marks)

> In this question, you are required to address the quotation (or incur a penalty to your AO2 mark of a maximum of 9 marks). In this case it would be creditworthy to discuss both ethical issues and socially sensitive research – in fact, the quotation directs you to include both. It will probably be easier to discuss the issues with reference to particular studies. The quotation is intended to help you and so it may be a good starting point to identify the issues in the quotation (of which there are many) and address each of these in turn, thus providing a useful structure to your answer. You might divide your 800-word response (about right for a 40-minute question) into a suitable number of paragraphs for each issue in the quotation and a commentary upon the issue.

THE USE OF NON-HUMAN ANIMALS IN PSYCHOLOGICAL INVESTIGATIONS

Non-human animals have been used in many different kinds of psychological investigation. We will begin this topic with a short review of such studies. This review is a brief sample of a wide range of other studies that have been covered in this book. You should easily be able to supplement this list with examples of your own.

Laboratory experiments

Harlow's monkeys

Harlow's original interest lay in research about learning. He needed monkeys for these experiments and wished to reduce disease in the monkeys by raising them in his own laboratory away from their mothers. He noticed that the motherless monkeys formed strong attachments to pieces of cloth in their cages, leading him to wonder whether contact comfort rather than feeding was critical for attachment to develop. To test this, Harlow and Harlow (1962) isolated young monkeys with surrogate wire mothers. In one study the wire mothers blasted the monkeys with strong jets of air and metal spikes pushed the monkeys away (to test the effects of abusive mothering). However, the most significant ethical issue raised in this study was the lasting effects on all of the monkeys. They become 'maladjusted' as adults, they had difficulties in reproductive relationships and were poor parents. See also Unit 2, p. 53.

Skinner box

Skinner (1938) devised a technique to investigate how reinforcement acts on behaviour. A rat is placed in a Skinner box (see Unit 21, p. 660) and receives reinforcement when a lever is pressed. The outcome is that the rat learns a new response – lever-pressing. Skinner conducted similar experiments with pigeons. As a result of these experiments, Skinner devised general laws of learning that were also applied to humans.

Field experiments

Animal language

In some field studies the experimental nature of the work may not be immediately apparent, i.e. the study may appear to be observational whereas in fact some manipulation of the environment was undertaken. For example, Seyfarth and Cheney (1992) recorded the use of different alarm calls in vervet monkeys. They tested the monkeys' understanding of these alarm calls by using *playback* and were thus able to demonstrate a causal link between the vocalization and a monkey's response. It is possible that monkeys may habituate to hearing these calls in the absence of a predator, and this may put the animals in danger should they fail to respond to alarm calls involving real predators.

Teaching human language to non-human animals

Studies by Gardner and Gardner (1969) and Savage-Rumbaugh (1988) have recorded their attempts to teach primates to use human language. In these studies primates such as Washoe and Kanzi have been immersed in human culture as a means of teaching them language. Washoe was brought up by the Gardners at home and communicated with using sign language; Kanzi and other Bonobo chimps were also taught to use language (lexigrams) in the course of every day life. Thus they weren't simply rewarded for using language but enculturated by their human researchers. Some of the primates in these studies have continued to be cared for by research foundations, but this hasn't been true of all primates in such research programmes.

Naturalistic observations

Social learning and sweet potatoes

One of the most famous examples of imitation in non-human animals is the incidence of sweet potato washing in Japanese macaque monkeys. Researchers studying the monkeys tried to bring them into the open by placing sweet potatoes along the beach. One monkey named Imo by the researchers began to wash the sand off of her sweet potatoes in the water instead of brushing it off with her hand as the other macaques did. Over time, this behaviour spread to other members of the troop and was passed on from generation to generation (Kawai 1965).

Dance of honey bees

Von Frisch (1967) recording the remarkable dance used by honeybees to communicate the location of a source of nectar to other bees in the hive. The 'waggle dance' communicates the direction and distance of the source. Werner (1964) further studied communication in bees, recording their dance with a camera and a tape recorder. He found that the duration of the sounds made by the bees was equivalent to the distance to the source.

● *Physical or psychological harm* – Laboratory experiments involving non-human animals do not always involve harm, as in the case of the behaviourist experiments. Field experiments may appear to be potentially less dangerous but may actually cause as much harm to animal participants as laboratory experiments. By their very nature, field experiments alter the natural environment of the animal in some way. This tampering with nature in order to understand it places great responsibilities on the researcher to ensure that the disruptive effects of any manipulation are kept to a minimum. Cuthill (1991), in an analysis of over 930 research papers published in the journal *Animal Behaviour* between the years 1986 and 1990, calculated that 46 per cent were field studies of which one third involved experimental manipulations.

● *The importance of research* – As with research with human participants it is important to weigh any harm to non-human animal participants against the benefits for humans (and possibly non-human participants). Harlow's research with monkeys has made a significant contribution to our understanding of behaviour. Prior to this research no one believed that comfort alone might be of such importance. Indeed the long-term effects of the experiment were surprising.

● *Humane treatment of non-human animal participants* – Humane treatment is most importantly to do with their care during and after an experiment. Careless and insensitive handling usually causes more harm than the experimental procedures themselves. The legislation that regulates animal research focuses on this aspect of the research as much as on the procedures used in the experiment, as we will see in the next section.

CONSTRAINTS ON THE USE OF NON-HUMAN ANIMALS IN RESEARCH

Legislation

The use of non-human animals in research is regulated by legislation, the Animals (Scientific Procedures) Act (1986). This Act is mainly concerned with the regulation of animals used in commercial research, such as for testing drugs and cosmetics, and in research related to genetic engineering. The use of animals in psychological research is a relatively minor issue but one covered by the same regulations. The main points of the Act are described in Table 27.3.

● *Effectiveness of the Act* – The number of live animal experiments in Great Britain has halved since the 1970s, however BUAV (The British Union for the Abolition of Vivisection) claim that the Act is not working effectively to protect animals (BUAV 2003) . They state that the decline in the number of animals used in experiments has been slowed down and thus the Animals (Scientific Procedures) Act must be reviewed. There is currently a review in relation to Regulatory Toxicology and Safety Evaluation Studies.

No research using live animals may be conducted until a licence has been granted by the Home Office. In a recent proposed revision to the act (Home Office 2003), the Home Office endorses its commitment to the 3Rs proposed by Russell and Birch (1959), that is, where possible, to:

● *refine* the experimental procedures to minimize suffering
● *reduce* the number of animals used to the minimum required to support sound risk assessments to protect humans, animals and the environment
● *replace* the use of animals, for example, by *in vitro* methods.

Code of conduct

The British Psychological Society, similar to other professional organizations around the world, produces a code of conduct for psychologists in relation to the use of non-human animals in psychological research. Any psychologists contravening such principles may be struck off the professional register.

The main points of the BPS code in relation to research with non-human animals are:

● *Legislation* – Psychologists must conform to current legislation.
● *Choice of species* – Should be suited to research purpose and the psychologist should be aware of the animal's previous experience.

- *Number of animals* – The smallest number should be used.

- *Procedures* – Any procedure that may cause pain should be carefully evaluated and alternatives considered. Regulation of food intake (e.g. for conditioning experiments) may be considered to be harmful and researchers should consider an animal's normal food intake and metabolic requirements. Investigators studying animals in the field should minimize interference.

- *Other issues* – Researchers should also be concerned with the procurement of animals (always from reputable suppliers), housing and animal care, final disposal, and the use of animals in teaching.

Developing criteria for assessing research on animals

If we are to find an acceptable way of using animals in research, what kinds of criteria, over and above those covered by the Animals Act (1986) (outlined earlier), should be considered? In 1986, Professor Patrick Bateson, Secretary of the Ethical Committee of the Association for the Study of Animal Behaviour, proposed a system based on three criteria that would enable researchers to evaluate research with non-human animals, referred to as 'Bateson's decision cube' (see Fig. 27.1).

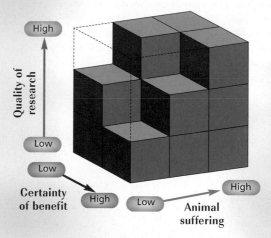

Figure 27.1 >> *Bateson's decision cube*

A cube for deciding whether a research project should proceed (clear space) or it should not (solid space) (from Bateson 1986). The most obvious case for proceeding is when the amount of suffering is negligible, the quality of the research is high and the benefit is certain. At the other extreme, the clearest case where research should not be done is when the suffering is likely to be great, and the quality of the work and the benefit uncertain.

Quality of the research

Although determining the quality of research may appear to be very subjective, there is actually a great deal of agreement among psychologists about what constitutes high-quality research. The difficulties of obtaining research funding, together with the sheer expense of animal research, means that institutional committees are likely to award research grants only to animal research of the highest quality (in terms of design and procedures).

Degree of animal suffering

It is, of course, difficult to put oneself inside the mind of an animal and assess the degree to which a particular animal is or is not suffering as a result of the procedures to which we expose it. Some animals when threatened by danger remain rigid and silent because that is the safest thing to do. We may not recognize such behaviour as being a state of stress. As we increase our knowledge of how animals behave, we become more aware of what is and what is not likely to be stressful for a particular species.

Certainty of benefit

In the minds of many, if not most, people great human suffering is felt to be worse than the possibility of moderate discomfort inflicted on an animal in the course of research. The funding of high-quality psychological research may not always be seen in that light by its critics. It is difficult to predict exactly what the benefits of such research might be to the lives of humans and other animals. One example of this is research conducted on Alzheimer's disease (see panel right). There is no known cure, but investigations using rats and monkeys allow us to begin to understand how certain brain circuits may function. You might like to ask yourself whether, in such cases, the ends really can justify the means.

Alzheimer's disease

One of the major social problems of the 21st century will be the increasing numbers of old people. A proportion of these will suffer from senile dementia, the commonest form of which is Alzheimer's disease. In its severest form, Alzheimer's produces severe memory loss, confusion, loss of the sense of self-identity, and double incontinence. Caring for sufferers is usually a family affair, 24 hours a day every day of the year, and involves watching your husband or wife, father or mother, degenerating in front of you.

There is as yet no cure for Alzheimer's disease ... We know from the brain changes seen at post-mortem that there is a particular pattern of damage to brain circuits, and we know from animal studies that these circuits are also involved in memory in rats and monkeys ... this model of Alzheimer's disease is being used to develop possible treatments. These include new drugs to restore brain function, and the use of grafts of brain cells to replace cells that have died. ... Animal research is also helping to reveal the biochemical abnormalities responsible for producing the brain damage.

There are encouraging signs that a treatment for Alzheimer's disease may emerge, which will have depended absolutely on the use of animal testing for its development. If successful, it would have a dramatic impact, improving the quality of life for both those with Alzheimer's and those who would otherwise sacrifice their lives in caring for them. Is this potential benefit sufficient to justify the use of animals in psychological research?

Source: Green (1994)

Evaluation
the Bateson decision cube

● **Benefits of the model** – This model provides an indication of when animal research may be tolerated and when it can not. It is also obvious that certain levels of animal suffering cannot be tolerated regardless of the quality of the research or the probability of benefit. The model would also permit research which has no direct benefit, yet was of high scientific quality and involved little animal suffering.

The effectiveness of a model such as that proposed by Bateson depends on any evaluation of quality, benefit and suffering being accurate. This is not as straightforward as it might appear.

● **Evaluating the quality of the research** – This should pose little problem to the scientist who should be aware of whether research is high quality or not. All research applications are routinely assessed along these lines.

● **Measuring animal suffering** – Different species react differently to stress, and these reactions may be very different to those that cause human beings to react in an avoidant manner. Dawkins (1985) suggests that three factors can be used to measure animal suffering: an animal's state of physical health, signs of stress and the animal's behaviour.

● **Evaluating the potential benefits of the research** – This is a more difficult judgement to make. The aims of a particular piece of research should go beyond what is essentially curiosity and delve into gaining a real understanding.

ARGUMENTS FOR THE USE OF NON-HUMAN ANIMALS

Arguments both for and against the use of non-human animals can be separated into *ethical* and *scientific* arguments. Ethical arguments concern what is right or wrong, whereas scientific arguments concern usefulness (i.e. how much can we find out from using non-human animals in research).

Ethical arguments

Ethical arguments in favour of using animals are listed below. The AO2 Commentary box that follows lists some counterarguments to each point.

1 Easing human suffering

'We are morally obliged to use animals to ease human suffering' – This is probably the most well developed of the pro-animal research arguments. Evolution has placed human beings 'on top' of the phylogenetic tree, so it is natural for us to make use of 'lower animals' for our own ends. If, by using animals, we can ease human suffering, then we are morally obliged to do so.

2 Human, not animal, rights

'Animals don't have rights' – Rights arise as a result of implicit contracts between members of society, and imply duties. Animals have no such responsibilities, cannot reciprocate and therefore have no rights.

3 Human, not animal, feelings

'Animals do not have the same feelings as humans' – The traditional defence of the use of non-human animals (for whatever purposes) has centred around the philosophical notion that humans and non-humans can be differentiated, in that non-humans do not possess a soul and so are not capable of moral choice – or, indeed, any other feelings and emotions that are peculiarly human.

4 Protection through legislation

'Animal welfare is protected by legislation' – There are strict laws (e.g. the 1986 Use of Animals Act) and codes of conduct (e.g. guidelines produced by the British Psychological Society) that protect animals that are used in research.

5 Using less invasive methods

'Modern methods are less invasive' – A number of less invasive procedures have been developed and are being used in animal research. This minimizes animal suffering and provides a moral justification for animal research.

Commentary
ethical arguments: some counterarguments

1 *An obligation to ease human suffering* – This is known as the 'naturalistic fallacy'. Natural history may well have provided us with an understanding of why our morals have evolved into their present form, but we can *transcend* our nature. Not using other species for our own ends may be seen as the next step in that evolution. This position is also still open to criticism from those who argue that the pro-animal research lobby has a tendency to overemphasize the benefits and play down the suffering that produced those benefits.

2 *Animal rights?* – Animals have rights by virtue of their 'inherent value'. These rights include the right to be treated with respect and not to be harmed. The traditional scientific position on animal research treats animals as 'renewable resources' rather than as organisms of value whose rights we must respect. If we fail to recognize the rights of other species, we would be violating the principle of respect. Furthermore, some humans, such as infants and the mentally ill, might not be able to fulfil their obligations to society, but are not denied rights within it.

3 *Animals' feelings and emotions?* – Increasing research evidence shows that animals are, in fact, capable of experiencing a whole range of emotions and feelings. For example, one recent study found that fish do feel pain (Sneddon *et al.* 2003). Despite such research, the view of animals as 'mechanical systems' or 'renewable resources' is a hard one to shake off.

4 *Legislative protections* – Most ethical guidelines are based on a 'costs–benefits' model, where the recipients of costs (i.e. the animals) and benefits (i.e. humans) tend to be different, and which ignore the substantive rights of animals in favour of practical, utilitarian considerations.

5 *Using less invasive methods* – If researchers were not allowed to use animals in research, they would have to develop other techniques (such as clinical and epidemiological studies) to take the place of animal research. CT, PET and MRI scans, and in-depth computer modelling are among the modern approaches that are available as real alternatives to animal research. If we were to adopt a model based on animal 'rights', then animals would have the right not to be used by humans for research *regardless* of how 'non-invasive' the research procedures or how potentially beneficial the consequences for human beings.

Unit 27 // Issues in psychology

Scientific arguments

Scientific arguments in favour of using animals are listed below. Again, the AO2 Commentary box that follows lists some counterarguments to each point.

1 Usefulness of the research

'Non-human animal research is useful' – The use of animals in such research is usually justified to the public because it contributes directly to the relief of human suffering. Developing a cure for a disease such as cancer or Alzheimer's disease can offset much of the terrible physical, social and economic suffering that inevitably accompanies such conditions.

2 Studying animals for their own right

'Animals may be studied simply because they are fascinating in their own right' – The development of 'ethology' (the study of behaviour in its natural environment) has arisen for this very reason.

3 Greater control and objectivity

'Animals offer the opportunity for greater control and objectivity in research procedures' – Much of behaviourist theory was established using animal studies for just this reason. Objectivity is more easily attained with non-human than human animals, simply because it is difficult to remain completely objective when studying our own species. We may have expectations, biases and stereotypes of members of our own species that are not as evident when we work with another species.

4 When research on humans is not possible

'We may use animals when we can't use humans' – Animals have been exposed to various procedures and events that would simply not be possible with human beings. Harlow's deprivation work with rhesus monkeys (described earlier) could not have been carried out on humans. Often the need to establish cause-and-effect relationships in psychological research involves participants in procedures that they would not consent to take part in.

Human beings and non-human animals have sufficient of their physiology and evolutionary past in common to justify conclusions drawn from the one being applied to the other. Behaviourists such as Skinner saw sufficient similarity between rats and humans to warrant a special interest in rats as research subjects.

Commentary
scientific arguments: some counterarguments

1 *Useful research?* – Contributions to the relief of human suffering have often been accomplished at considerable expense in terms of animal suffering. Adopting a costs–benefits analysis of individual research projects should ensure that the costs (in terms of animal suffering) and the benefits (in terms of significant medical and scientific advancements) are predictable, but neither of these is certain before a study starts. By calculating the benefits to humankind, but the costs to animals, we might be committing 'speciesism' (see next page).

2 *Studying animals for their own right* – Even field studies may involve ethical concerns, as described earlier.

3 *Greater control and objectivity* – In some circumstances, such as behaviourist research, there is little harm to the animal participants though simply being looked after in captivity and conditioned for trivial purposes may be unacceptable. The BPS code of conduct mentions the possibilities that rewards, deprivation and aversive stimuli may be harmful to animals.

4 *When research on humans is not possible* – This raises the moral question of why we might expose animals to research procedures that we could not justify with human participants. This question is considered in the next section.

ARGUMENTS AGAINST THE USE OF NON-HUMAN ANIMALS

<< Even granting that we [humans] face greater harm than laboratory animals presently endure if ... research on these animals is stopped, the animal rights view will not be satisfied with anything less than total abolition. >>

<< If abandoning animal research means that there are some things we cannot learn, then so be it ... We have no basic right ... not to be harmed by those natural diseases we are heir to. >> (Regan 1983)

Ethical arguments

We may take an extreme ethical stance over the issue of animal research, contending that pain or distress is never justifiable in animal research, regardless of the benefits to humankind. This position owes much to the work of people such as Peter Singer and Tom Regan (Regan and Singer 1976).

Animal rights (Regan 1983)

The fundamental belief of the animal rights position is that all animals have rights that are based on their *inherent value*. These rights include the right to be treated with respect and not to be harmed. A consequence of this position is that animals have the right not to be used by humans for research regardless of any potential benefits for humans that might arise from such research.

The traditional scientific position on animal research, claim proponents of this position, treats animals as 'renewable resources' rather than as organisms of value whose rights we must respect. If we fail to recognize the rights of other species, according to this argument, we would be violating the principle of respect.

Tom Regan, a champion of this position, believes that we cannot justify animal research by quoting benefits for human beings or even improvements to research conditions. Unlike the utilitarian position, animal research would not be tolerated under any conditions. Cost–benefit considerations are insufficient justification for animal research. Regan claims that current legislation does not go far enough in protecting the subjects of animal research. What is needed, he claims, is not larger, cleaner cages, but empty cages (Regan 1983).

The utilitarian argument: Speciesism (Singer 1975)

The main focus of the utilitarian argument is that what is ethically acceptable is that which produces the greatest pleasure and happiness (relative to pain and suffering) for the greatest number of people. According to this argument no one person's happiness is more important than any other's. Peter Singer's book *Animal Liberation*, published in 1975, extends this utilitarian argument to include all sentient (capable of sensation) creatures. His 'principle of equality' holds that *all* such creatures have an equal interest in avoiding pain and suffering.

Consistent with this principle of equality is the belief that we have no moral basis for elevating the interests of one species (e.g. humans) over those of other species. To do so would be to commit 'speciesism', which is logically parallel to other forms of discrimination such as racism and sexism. Speciesism, according to Singer, is the result of a prejudiced attitude, which sets the interests of our own species above those of other species.

Research on animals might be permitted under some circumstances, but only when the potential benefits of the research are high and the research could not be carried out using human subjects.

Commentary
the animal rights position

● *Counterargument* – In defence of the use of animals in research, the British Association for the Advancement of Science produced a Declaration on Animals in Research (1990), which includes the statement:

'Continued research involving animals is essential for the conquest of many unsolved medical problems, such as cancer, AIDS, other infectious diseases, and genetic, developmental, neurological and psychiatric conditions.'

Scientific arguments

The essence of a scientific argument against the use of animals is that animal experiments would tell us nothing of any value about human behaviour because of the dissimilarities between humans and non-humans. Whilst it is true that some research is carried out on animals to discover facts about animals, the majority of animal studies in psychology are comparative, i.e. animals are being used because they may give us important insights into human behaviour.

If animals are to be used to tell us something about human behaviour, then it follows that there should be sufficient similarity between the brains and behaviour of humans and non-human animals. If this were not so, then the ethical case for studying animals to gain insights into human behaviour would be very weak indeed. Critics of animal research often assert that these assumed similarities just do not exist.

Commentary
scientific arguments against animal research

● *Counterargument* – Green (1994) argues otherwise: the basic physiology of the brain and nervous systems of all mammals is essentially the same. Although the human brain might be more highly developed, its similarity to the brains of non-human mammals is far greater than critics of this approach would have us believe. Similarly, the basic classifications of behaviour (affective, cognitive and motivational) are evident in all mammalian species.

Check your understanding of cultural bias by answering these questions from memory. You can check your answers by looking back through Topic 4.

1 What were the '3 Rs' proposed by Russell and Birch (1959)?

2 Briefly outline **two** of the guidelines in the Animals (Scientific Procedures) Act (1986).

3 Identify **three** arguments for the use of non-human animals.

4 Explain Singer's concept of speciesism.

5 What position did Regan take with regard to animal research?

REVISION SUMMARY

Having covered this topic, you should be able to describe and evaluate:

✓ the use of non-human animals in psychological investigations

✓ the constraints on the use of non-human animals in psychological investigations

✓ arguments (both ethical and scientific) *for* and *against* the use of non-human animals in psychological investigations

EXAMPLE EXAM QUESTIONS

Below are some **possible examination questions** set on this topic, along with hints to help you understand and approach each question effectively:

1 Critically consider the use of non-human animals in psychological investigations. (30 marks)

> Many students feel passionately about this topic, but it is important to resist the temptation to present an emotional argument. In order to attract credit in an exam question, you must provide well-informed statements about the use of animals. There is no requirement for a balanced answer, but an informed answer is likely to include some arguments from both sides of the debate. Some candidates think that arguments *for* the use of non-human animals will count as AO1 and arguments *against* their use will count as AO2. Any arguments (for or against) that are simply *described* count as AO1. As always, AO2 credit is awarded for the extent to which such material has been used effectively. A common error is to describe the investigations themselves. Such descriptions gain no credit except for some minimal marks as 'scene-setting'.

2 (a) Outline the use of non-human animals in psychological investigations. (15 marks)
  (b) To what extent can such use of non-human animals in psychological investigations be justified? (15 marks)

> Both questions 1 and 2 contain the wording 'use of' which means that it is important focus to how the animals were *used* in investigations rather than, for example, the methodology flaws in the investigations. In part (b) of this question, 'to what extent' is an AO2 term which indicates that you must comment on the extent to which such investigations can be justified. You do not have to limit this to ethical issues. The use of the term 'such' means that you are not limited to the investigations outlined in part (a). Since the question is 'to what extent' it suggests that some kind of conclusion is required. You are not required to present a conclusion but this would be creditworthy as long as it is not merely a repetition of the points you have already made.

3 Critically consider the constraints on the use of non-human animals in psychological investigations. (30 marks)

This would be a legitimate question given the wording of the specification, which says 'the use of non-human animals in psychological investigations, including constraints on their use'. The word 'including' means that the topic can form a specified part of a question. We have covered the constraints on the use of non-human animals in this unit. Take care to focus on their use in psychological investigations as distinct from, for example, medical research or the cosmetics industry. Commentary can be achieved by considering the success of such constraints or looking at alternatives, as well as problems imposing constraints and other advantages or disadvantages.

4 Describe and evaluate the case **for** the use of non-human animals in psychological research. (30 marks)

In the exam you may well be asked to present one side or the other side. In such cases you may use the opposing side of the debate as your AO2 content. So, in this question you would present arguments *for* the use of non-human animals as the AO1 content and the arguments *against* as the AO2 content. However, you must ensure that you use the arguments 'against' in an *effective* manner – i.e. use the arguments against as a means of evaluating the arguments for. A useful strategy might be to separate the scientific and ethical arguments. This would help planning your answer – by dividing it in half (400 words each) and dividing each half into half again – you need 200 words on *describing* the scientific arguments for the use of non-human animals, 200 words *evaluating* this, and then the same for ethical arguments.

UNIT SUMMARY

Topic 1: Gender bias

- **Alpha-biased theories** assume that there are real and enduring differences between men and women, and may heighten or reduce the value of women. **Beta-biased theories** ignore or minimize sex differences because they are based on the findings of research with male participants (**androcentric**) which are then generalized to all behaviour.

- **Feminist psychology** aims to redress the imbalance created by androcentric biases in psychological research so that gender stereotypes are not perpetuated. There are some **real psychological differences** though these may be obscured by bias in the research process.

- Alpha and beta bias have **positive and negative consequences**. Alpha bias has led to an appreciation of the worth of feminine qualities but also implies similarities within genders. Beta bias leads to equal treatment of men and women but draws attention away from the special needs of women.

- **Aspects of the research process** lead to gender bias, for example biased question formation, research design (which is masculine), research methodology (treating women differently), selection of participants (males only), formulation of conclusions (apply male data to all behaviour) and publication bias (studies published that do find differences).

- **Alpha bias** can be found in the hypotheses produced from **evolutionary theory**. Social influence studies are examples of **beta bias**.

Topic 2: Cultural bias

- **Ethnocentrism** results in using one's own culture as a standard by which to measure other cultures. **Eurocentrism** occurs in psychological research because most psychologists are European/American.

- Cultural bias also arises because psychologists conduct **etic studies** of behaviour (observer uses categories of an alien culture to study a native culture) rather than **emic studies** (observer attempts to understand native culture and use appropriate research methods). Cultural bias may also arise from **historical bias**, and may be **alpha-biased** or **beta-biased**.

- The problem of cultural bias may be dealt with by appreciating **cultural relativism** and abandoning the **etic approach** and using a **derived etic approach** instead. There are problems with making **cross-cultural comparisons**, such as assuming that all people belonging to the same culture *all* share the same beliefs.

- **Kohlberg's theory of moral development** is an example of **beta bias** and his stages may not be universal; moral development in urban individualist societies may be more complex because such societies are more complex.

- **Cross-cultural studies** are used to test universal theories but may not be valid because, for example, instructions are misunderstood or participants used in different cultures are not equivalent.

- There is cultural bias in **sampling methods**. Psychological studies tend to use a restricted range of participants (American, male psychology students) resulting in culturally biased theories.

- The use of **imposed etics** in psychological studies results in culturally biased theories. This may be overcome by using a derived etic approach, using ethnography and encouraging indigenous psychologies.

Topic 3: Ethical issues with human participants

- **Ethical issues** arise when there are conflicts between the rights of participants and the needs of researchers in conducting valid investigations.

- **Deception** is necessary to avoid participants' expectations altering their behaviour; this must be set against the cost – possible harm to participants without having a chance to decline to participate. Deception may be **acceptable** under certain circumstances, but there are **consequences**, including lack of informed consent and reduced participation in psychological research.

- Lack of **informed consent** in field studies may be dealt with by safeguarding the participants' interests. In laboratory studies **debriefing** and the **right to withhold data** can be used to compensate for a lack of informed consent. **Prior general consent** is another alternative.

- **Privacy** can be assessed with reference to how public the setting is, the publicness of the person, anonymity provided, and nature of information disclosed.

- **Psychological and physical harm** is **difficult to assess** prior to a study, but such studies can always be stopped. Risks should be no greater than experienced in **everyday life**.

- Milgram's use of deception in his obedience research can be **justified** because the effects were unanticipated, he believed there was little harm, the research was important and there was adequate debriefing. However, was the deception **believable**?

- **Milgram** was accused of causing both psychological and physical **harm** to his participants, with **short-** and **long-term effects**. Milgram judged that the harm was momentary and participants reported having benefited from taking part in the study in the longer term.

- **Socially sensitive research** refers to studies in which there are **potential social consequences or implications**. Such research should not be stopped because of the problems raised but needs careful consideration. Ethical guidelines are focused on the needs of **individual participants** rather than **wider social consequences**.

- **Gay and lesbian research** is one example of socially sensitive research. Despite exaggeration of differences between homosexuals and heterosexuals (alpha bias) and masking differences within groups (due to alpha bias), such research has led to a wider understanding of such relationships.

- Research on the link between **intelligence and race** ignores the fact that for some people environmental enrichment does make a difference, even if IQ is largely genetic. Such research has serious political implications. Research on **eating disorders** is also socially sensitive.

Topic 4: The use of non-human animals

- Non-human animals have been studied in both **laboratory** and **field experiments**.

- Field experiments may cause as much **harm** as laboratory experiments because behaviour is permanently changed. Benefits of non-human animal research may outweigh the costs). Harm may come from insensitive handling rather than any experimental manipulation.

- The use of non-human animals in research is regulated by the **Animals (Scientific Procedures) Act** (1986). The Home Office endorses the principles of the 3 Rs: refine, reduce, replace. The BPS have produced a code of conduct for the use of animals in psychological research.

- **Bateson**'s **decision cube** offers three criteria for evaluating the acceptability of research with non-human animals: quality of research, degree of suffering and certainty of benefit.

- The **ethical arguments for** the use of non-human animals include: we have a **moral obligation** to use animals to ease human suffering; animals don't have rights because they have no responsibilities; animals don't have feelings; animals are protected by legislation; and some methods are less invasive.

- The **scientific arguments for** the use of non-human animals include: animal research is useful for understanding human behaviour and for understanding animal behaviour; experiments with animals can be more highly controlled; animals may be used when we can't use humans.

- The **ethical arguments against** the use of non-human animals include Singer's utilitarian argument and Regan's view of animal rights.

- The **scientific arguments against** the use of non-human animals include the view that research with non-human animals can tell us nothing of value about humans.

FURTHER RESOURCES

Berry, J.W., Poortinga, Y.H., Segall, M.H. and Dasen, P.R. (2002) *Cross Cultural Psychology: Research and Applications* **(2nd edn), Cambridge, MA: Cambridge University Press.**

Comprehensive overview of cross-cultural research in psychology.

Hare-Mustin, R.T. and Marecek, J. (1988) 'The meaning of difference: gender theory, post-modernism, and psychology', *American Psychologist,* **43, pp.455–64.**

Clear explanation of alpha and beta bias. Original journal articles can be obtained through the British Library document supply centre by giving the full reference to your local library.

Kimmel, A.J. (1996) *Ethical Issues in Behavioural Research: A Survey,* **Cambridge, MA: Blackwell.**

A comprehensive account of the ethical issues of psychological research with non-human and human participants.

Sieber, J.E. and Stanley, B. (1988) 'Ethical and professional dimensions of socially sensitive research', *American Psychologist,* **43(1), pp. 49–55.**

Well worth reading. A detailed account of the issues of socially sensitive research as well as ways of dealing with these issues.

Websites

www.vanguard.edu/faculty/ddegelman/amoe baweb/index.cfm?doc_id=2416

Ethical issues in therapy and research, with many useful links.

http://www.bps.org.uk/documents/Code.pdf

British Psychological Society code of conduct for conducting research with human participant and animals.

www.homeoffice.gov.uk/docs2/ regtoxicologydraftrevision4_03.html

Revised draft of the Animals Act (1986).

DEBATES IN
Psychology

After you have read this unit, you should be able to describe and evaluate:

>> arguments for and against free will and determinism, and assumptions made about each in psychological research

>> arguments for and against reductionist explanations, and examples of reductionism in psychological theory and research

>> definitions and varieties of science, and the development of psychology as a separate discipline

>> arguments for and against the claim that psychology is a science

>> definitions of nature and nurture, and the history of the nature–nurture debate

>> assumptions made about nature and nurture in psychological theory and research, and different views regarding the relationship between nature and nurture.

INTRODUCTION

The term 'debates' suggest some disagreement or contrasting opinion. People conduct public debates in order to help others crystallize their own views on topics such as whether the age of consent should be lowered, whether capital punishment should be reintroduced in the UK or whether sports injuries should be treated free on the NHS. On any topic, you may be able to think of a few arguments to support your own opinion, but you need to be aware of the possible counterarguments. In public debates, the person or persons proposing the motion will present a series of arguments and evidence to support their position. The opposing side must be ready with counterarguments and counterevidence in order to sway the audience and help them see the flaws of the proposer's arguments, assumptions and conclusions. In many debates there are no 'right' answers, the aim is to arrive at a better understanding of the issues involved in order to hold a more informed opinion.

The debates around free will versus determinism, reductionism versus holism, and nature versus nurture have a long history in psychology and philosophy. Few psychologists adhere rigidly to only one side in these debates, ignoring blindly all arguments offered by the other point of view. Increasingly, psychologists seem to be resolving these issues by adopting a more interactionist approach. The debate over whether psychology is – or should even try to be – a science is still a contentious issue, one that gets to the very heart of what psychology is about and how it should conduct its investigations.

Cara
Flanagan

Which is better – an orange or an apple?

'But then you can cut an orange up and eat it from the skin.'

'It is easier to eat an apple because oranges are hard to peel and make your fingers sticky.'

'You can do that with an apple. Apples are crisp and tasty.'

'That is purely subjective and, anyway, some apples are disappointingly soft and sour.'

'The same can be said of oranges – some are all dried up. You can't grow oranges in this country unless you have special conditions.'

'Apples can be bruised easily.'

'You can make orange juice from oranges. And more people drink orange juice.'

'You can make cider from apples.'

'Oranges have vitamin C which prevents colds and scurvy.'

'Apples are good for your health: "an apple a day keeps the doctor away".'

If you like working out arguments for and against, then you'll enjoy the debates!
By listening to opposing views you can make up your own mind.

KEY CONCEPTS

Debate: a discussion where two (or more) contrasting points of view are presented; a formalized system of logical argument.

Free will: the philosophical doctrine that individuals are capable of making their own choices, i.e. can be self-determining and free from coercion.

Determinism: the philosophical doctrine that an individual's behaviour is shaped or controlled by internal or external forces rather than an individual's will to do something.

Mind–body problem: the problem of determining the relationship between the physical realm (the body) and the mental realm (the mind).

Nature: those aspects of behaviour that are inherited. Nature does not simply refer to abilities present at birth but to any ability determined by genes, including those that appear through maturation.

Nurture: aspects of behaviour that are acquired through experience, i.e. learned from interactions with the physical and social environment.

Reductionism: the act of breaking complex phenomena down into more simple components. A belief in reductionism implies that this is preferable because complex phenomena are best understood in terms of a simpler level of explanation.

Science: a body of knowledge, or a method of study devoted to developing this body of knowledge, gained through systematized observation and experimentation.

THE FREE WILL/DETERMINISM DEBATE IN PSYCHOLOGY

Exercising your own free will?

List various things that you have done today (behaviours, activities and so on). For each one, try to identify how that behaviour might have been determined by some internal or external factor (e.g. hormones, genes, another person, past experiences).

Can you think of any things that you freely chose to do?

If you can think of any examples – think again, were they truly free choices or were they selected from a limited range of possibilities?

Free will

The idea that we are able to have some choice in how we act is fundamental to most common-sense theories of psychology. The notion of 'free will' allows us to separate out what is clearly the intention of an individual from what has been caused by some internal or external event. Free will assumes that we are free to choose our behaviour, in other words we are self-determining. It does not mean that behaviour is random, but that we are freed from the causal influences of past events (such as instinct or of our past reinforcement history).

Determinism

The determinist approach proposes that all behaviour is determined and thus predictable. Some approaches in psychology see the source of this determinism as being *outside* the individual, a position known as 'environmental determinism'. Others see it as coming from *inside* the organism, e.g. in the form of unconscious motivation or genetic determinism – a position known as 'biological determinism'. The position you take on this issue will have an important effect on the way that you explain human nature.

A02   **Commentary**
reconciling free will and
determinism

The idea of free will is inconsistent with the opposite idea of determinism, because under the latter view of human behaviour, individuals act as a result of some prior cause. Part of the scientific perspective in psychology is a belief in this causal determinism. Free will, therefore, would appear to be incompatible with the goals of scientific psychology. This is not, however, necessarily the case as the following potential resolutions indicate:

● *Proximate and ultimate goals* – The concept of 'will' refers to the idea that people make decisions about the goals they are seeking to achieve. Such goals or *ultimate* aims of behaviour (e.g. getting an A-level, finding a birthday present for a friend) are then translated into our current or *proximate* thoughts and actions. For example, if I decide that I want to learn to play the piano, I might buy a piano, seek out a piano teacher and start practising. All these actions are clearly the product of conscious planning (i.e. my free will), but are *determined* by my final goal, that of being able to play the piano. Indeed, anyone who knew of my intention to learn the piano could probably predict my proximate actions. Thus the concept of free will is compatible with a wider view of determinism.

● *Soft determinism* – William James, in the 19th century, coined this phrase to describe the fact that behaviour can be separated in mental and physical activities. Mental activities are subject to free will whereas physical states are determined. Thus, both free will and determinism are possible, if one accepts this dualist position (that mental and physical events are separate).

● *Liberal determinism* – There have been other attempts to define a softer kind of determinism. For example, Heather (1976) suggested a version which has been called 'liberal determinism', the view that behaviour is determined to the extent that people act consistently with their character. It is easier to reconcile this view of determinism with the idea of free will, because the liberal version allows for choice (free will) within a range of options (determined).

● *Free from coercion* – Others take the view that free will, simply means free from coercion. Giving money to someone with a collecting tin is seen as free will, whereas if the same act was carried out at gun point it is determined. In fact, both acts are determined, but the latter is not 'free' because the behaviour is the result of coercion.

ARGUMENTS FOR AND AGAINST FREE WILL AND DETERMINISM

The arguments presented below are fairly interchangeable – the arguments *for* free will can be turned around so that they are arguments *against* determinism; arguments *against* free will are also arguments *for* determinism. Equally, the commentary (AO2 points) on arguments *for* free will are also arguments *against* free will and thus are arguments *for* determinism!

Arguments *for* free will

1 The psychological argument

'People have a subjective sense of free will' – Most people feel that they possess free will and are able, at any time, to make free choices. Dr Johnson, in the 18th century, said 'We know our will is free, and there's an end on't'.

2 The ethical argument

'In order to expect moral responsibility, one must accept the concept of free will' – If an individual's behaviour is determined by forces beyond the individual's control, then the individual cannot be held responsible for their actions. However, our laws insist that adults do have individual responsibility for their actions and so have free will.

AO2 Commentary
arguments for free will

1 The psychological argument

- *Feeling free* – Simply *feeling* that you are free does not mean this is true. Skinner claimed that free will was an illusion – we think we are free, but that is because we are not aware of how our behaviour is determined by reinforcement. Freud also thought that free will was an illusion. Freud claimed that most of the causes of our behaviour are largely hidden from us and unconscious; we may think we are acting freely, but in fact our behaviour is determined by unconscious forces and is predictable.

- *A tenable proposition* – On the other hand, Valentine (1982) claims that this subjective sense of free will is a tenable proposition. It is something that can be studied and thus shown to be true. For example, attitudes towards free will

have been found to increase with age and also are more common in *individualist* cultures where personal responsibility receives greater emphasis.

2 The ethical argument

- *Morals as determined behaviour* – It may be possible to behave in a moral fashion without having moral responsibility. For example, behaviourists suggest that moral behaviour is learned largely through punishment or the threat of punishment. There is no individual responsibility because good or bad behaviour is determined by external forces.

- *A range of choices* – It may not be free will *per se*, but the range of accessible choices that determines our moral responsibility. We can be held responsible as long as we have a range of choices to choose from, even if those choices are predetermined. Free will only requires that choices exist.

Arguments *against* free will

1 Difficulty in specifying free will

The notion of free will implies that there is something doing the 'willing', something that is mental rather than physical. Besides trying to establish what might do the willing, there is the further question of how mental states might interact with physical states – in other words, how it is that thinking about moving one's foot results in the nervous and muscular activity required. 'Materialists' believe that only physical states exist, whereas 'dualists' believe that there are separate mental and physical states.

2 Inconsistency with science

The notion of current events being determined by something in the past is fundamental to scientific psychology. We might argue that discovering the determinants of behaviour is the ultimate goal of psychology. When we speak of the determinants of an action, we are implying that the action has been caused by some specific past event. Indeed, the essence of the experimental method in psychology is that we measure a behaviour before and after an experimental procedure in order to explore the relationship between cause and effect. However, if human behaviour is governed by free will, then there is no causality to be discovered.

1 *Difficulty in specifying free will* – From a materialist perspective, we may gain insight into the location of free will by considering mental illnesses, such as schizophrenia, or other illness, such as Huntingdon's disease, where patients lack voluntary control or the ability to initiate activity. Such deficits have been associated with the *limbic system*, a fact which is further supported by research with non-human animals where the removal of the limbic system stops the animal being able to initiate activity (Ridley 2003).

Arguments *for* determinism

1 Success of science in investigating human behaviour

Scientific investigations of human behaviour have produced valid knowledge which can be applied to the real world. For example, research into stress and cardiovascular illness has shown how psychological states influence physical health and what steps may be taken to reduce such stress (e.g. Friedman and Rosenman 1974).

2 Predictability of people's behaviour

The same argument that was presented for free will, can also be made for determinism: we have a subjective sense that the psychological world, like the physical

2 *Inconsistency with science* – Modern science no longer upholds the view that the world is predictable; it is best described as 'probabilistic' (Dennett 2003). Heisenberg's 'uncertainty principle' (1927) suggests that the behaviour of subatomic particles cannot be systematically predicted, i.e. one cannot make statements about causal relationships that will always be true. However, O'Connor (1971) concludes that 'the findings of quantum mechanics do not offer any clear and indisputable evidence in favour of free will'. In other words, the fact that indeterminism has been found in physics does not mean that there is free will.

world, is predictable, which suggests that behaviour *is* caused in a lawful way. People believe in their own predictability and the predictability of others. For example, we know ourselves to be generous or mean with money and expect to behave in a similar way in the future. Similarly, we expect that a person who has previously been generous will continue to behave that way in the future.

3 Will as a determined, physical activity

If the 'will' has a physical basis then it too is determined. It is possible to locate free will within a determinist framework. If the will is an outcome of brain activity (as suggested above), then it is subject to the same influences as all other physical activities, i.e. genetic influences, hormones, nerves and so on.

1 *Science's lack of success* – Psychological research which may appear to have discovered cause-and-effect relationships in the laboratory may, in fact, not be applicable in the real world. Such charges have been made against, for example, Milgram's (1963) study of obedience. Scientific investigations tend to oversimplify complex behaviours so that the findings are meaningless in relation to real life. Later in this unit, we will look at arguments against reductionism and against psychology as a science, both of which suggest that scientific research may not always be an appropriate way to understand human behaviour.

2 *Are people unpredictable?* – Mischel's theory of personality (1968, see p. 593) proposed that people do not have a consistent personality,

which would appear to challenge the claim that personality is predictable. He argued that, in reality, people are only consistent in the *same situations*, and their behaviour varies from one situation to another. You might be shy in class but quite the opposite when alone with your friends. However, research (e.g. Fleeson 2001, see p. 594) has found that people are actually highly consistent even across situations, thus supporting our subjective sense of predictability and also supporting the notion of causality in human behaviour – if people are predictable, then their behaviour must be caused in a lawful way, i.e. is determined.

3 *Volition or free will?* – Some people question whether volition or being able to initiate activity (which has been related to regions of the brain) is the same as free will. Volition implies the power of choice, whereas free will is something more than this – a capacity to make any choice in a fashion that could not be predicted.

Arguments *against* determinism

1 Determinism is not falsifiable

Theories should generate hypotheses that can be tested to see if they are true or false. If this is not possible, then you cannot 'prove' a theory's validity. The question of whether all behaviour can be explained within a determinist framework receives the reply that as yet this is not possible, but that one day it might be possible to explain all human behaviour in terms of causal relationships. However, this argument is not falsifiable; it is simply a matter of faith that theoretically we could predict all behaviour.

2 The ethical argument

The same ethical argument discussed earlier *for* free will can be used *against* determinism. If our actions are merely the product of some past event or of our biological 'programming', then we cannot be held responsible for our behaviours. This is a view that has concerned many psychologists and politicians, and is illustrated by the feature in the panel below.

'The DNA made me do it, M'lud ...'

<< What is the evidence linking biology to crime? A widely cited piece of research (van Dusen *et al.* 1983) is a Danish study of 14,427 people adopted as children by unrelated families. The theory is that if the biological parents have a heritable predisposition to crime, they might transmit these characteristics to their offspring. The research showed that as the 'criminality' of the biological parent increases from having no convictions on court records to three or more convictions, the proportion of adopted sons who are subsequently convicted themselves steadily increases from about 13 per cent to 25 per cent. This genetic predisposition is apparently for property crimes rather than violent crimes, and it is difficult to see how there could be a 'gene for theft'. Moreover, the findings are not clearly duplicated by a similar Swedish adoption study.

<< The first problem with studies linking biology and crime is that most simply fail to demonstrate an association between the two, let alone a meaningful cause. The second flaw is that where a link is made, it is quite illegitimate to extrapolate these results to the population at large, even if the claims are hedged with qualifications about biology only 'predisposing' individuals to crime. The consequences of arguing that crime has a genetic component can only be authoritarian. The legal and moral implications are likely to be greater calls for authorities to contain and control those deemed to be genetically unfit or dangerous. >>

Toby Andrew, *The Independent*, 23 January 1996

Commentary
arguments against determinism

1 *Determinism is falsifiable* – Valentine (1982) suggests that in fact determinism *is* falsifiable because it has been falsified by the uncertainty principle (see opposite)! Thus the proof that determinism is not true demonstrates that at least it can be falsified.

2 *Ethical counterargument* – As we have seen, a morally responsible sense of free will can be created by and exist even in an entirely causal world.

Evaluation
free will and determinism

● *The meaning of 'free will'* – The debate revolves around the question of what free will is taken to mean. Absolute free will means that behaviour is not determined in any lawful way. If this is the accepted definition, then, as Valentine concludes, 'determinism seems to have the edge in this difficult debate [but] it is not without problems either. There are difficulties in identifying it with predictability, and a number of discoveries show there are distinct limitations to its completeness' (p.19).

● *Free will in a determinist framework* – If one accepts that free will means free to make choices from a range of possibilities or being free from coercion, then it is possible to see free will within a determinist framework. Thus, we can investigate moral responsibility, decision-making, goal-selection and so on because people are self-determining.

FREE WILL AND DETERMINISM IN PSYCHOLOGICAL THEORY AND RESEARCH

Another way to present arguments *for* determinism is to consider whether determinist approaches in psychology have been successful. Thus, the examples below can be included as part of your arguments *for* determinism; and in some cases the limitations of such approaches can be viewed as arguments *against* determinism (or arguments *for* free will). Similarly, the success of free will approaches can be used as an argument *for* free will.

You are not, of course, restricted to the approaches that we have covered in this section, but you can use any approach or theory that you feel presents a clear position on the free will or determinism debate. For example, Hull's homeostatic drive theory of motivation (see p. 442) suggests that human motives are the product of biological forces and the social competition theory of depression (p. 710) presents an evolutionary perspective on depression that explains this as an adaptive and inevitable response to loss of status.

The psychodynamic approach

In his psychoanalytic theory, Freud believed that we are controlled by unconscious forces over which we have no control and of which we are largely unaware. An essential part of this theory is a belief in 'psychic determinism' – the view that events do not occur by chance, but are purposeful, being related to unconscious processes. This view of humans as being unable to choose their course of action was in stark contrast to the dominant belief of the 19th century that we were rational, thinking beings, fully in control of our own actions. Because of this control by internal forces, and the belief that any perceived freedom of choice is in fact illusory, this theory is also an example of 'biological determinism' (see Unit 19 for more about the psychodynamic approach).

Commentary
the psychodynamic approach

- *Successful therapeutic application* – The assumptions of psychoanalysis have been applied to the treatment of abnormal behaviour, using the method also called psychoanalysis. This method has been widely used and found to be successful with certain types of people and with certain types of disorder. Older reviews presented a rather unfavourable view of psychoanalysis (e.g. Eysenck 1952), whereas others (e.g. Bergin 1971) have found that the majority of patients undergoing psychoanalysis have benefited from such therapy. Such success supports the determinist explanation offered for the development of human behaviour. However, the fact that psychoanalysis is successful may be due to factors other than the correctness of the explanation offered; it may be the warmth of the therapist–patient interaction which permits a patient to become more self-accepting.

- *The theory lacks falsifiability* – Freud's account of personality permitted him to place interpretations on behaviour which could not be shown to be wrong. For example, he would argue that a person behaved in a certain way because of something that happened in infancy. If the person agreed, this showed Freud was right. If the person disagreed, Freud could argue that this shows that the patient was repressing certain experiences.

- *Overemphasis on sexual influences as determinants of behaviour* – Subsequent psychologists, called neo-Freudians, have adapted Freud's theory to try to incorporate social influences and address the rather unreasonable way that he dealt with women.

The behaviourist approach

Behaviourists believe that our behaviour is a product of the reinforcement provided by the environment. Within our own reinforcement history, we have been conditioned into behaving in specific ways. Although most of us accept that such conditioning clearly takes place, we still cling to the belief that we are free to plan our own actions. Skinner (1971) suggested that most human beings somehow believe that we are both free to choose and are controlled at the same time. For behaviourists, however, the position is much clearer: we have *no* freedom to choose our actions. They are determined by factors in our environment which, directly or indirectly, mould our behaviour. This approach is an example of 'environmental determinism'.

Commentary
the behaviourist approach

- *Successful therapeutic application* – The assumptions of behaviourism have also been applied to the treatment of abnormal behaviour, e.g. systematic desensitization and token economy (see Unit 26, pp. 799–801). One ethical criticism made of such therapies is that they are manipulative – the therapist determines suitable goals for the patient and manipulates the patient's behaviour through conditioning to reach these goals. Such manipulation is based on a determinist view of behaviour.

- *Behaviourist explanations are reductionist* – They reduce complex behaviour to a series of stimulus–response units that respond to reinforcement. This explanation may be suitable for non-human animal behaviour but is less relevant to most human behaviours, which have multiple determinants and where the ability to think about choices (free will) matters. Hence, the behaviourist approach in psychology has limited application to real-world behaviour.

- *Bandura's notion of reciprocal determinism* – This addresses some of the failings of the behaviourist approach. Both learning theory and social learning theory portray the individual as being controlled by their environment. Things happen to the individual, which increase or decrease the likelihood of any future behaviour. However, Bandura suggested that individuals are controlled by – but are also in control of – their environment. As the individual acts, this changes the environment, thus affecting subsequent behaviour. For example, if you watch your mother baking a cake and then start to imitate her, this modifies her behaviour and subsequently affects you. Individuals are capable of making their own choices and this ultimately affects what they imitate.

The cognitive approach

The cognitive approach in psychology assumes that behaviour can be explained in terms of cognitive processes, most importantly in terms of the way we *think* about our behaviour, but also in terms of perceptions, memory and language. This might appear to be an approach that exemplifies free will because of the emphasis on thinking. For example, the cognitive approach to explaining mental illness suggests that maladaptive and irrational thinking, which takes place without full awareness, leads to a distorted view of reality. Treatment, therefore, involves learning to think in a different and more rational way, and learning to be self-determining, a feature of free will.

Commentary
the cognitive approach

- *Successful therapeutic application* – The assumptions of the cognitive approach have also led to successful therapies (see cognitive–behavioural therapies described on pp. 803–6). Despite such therapies ultimately being related to self-determination, they are quite directive. The therapist challenges the patient's current thinking and trains the patient to think more rationally. In this way, the therapy is not related to free will.

- *The cognitive approach is also deterministic* – Another example of the cognitive approach is the use of the concept 'schema'. A schema is a set of interrelated concepts, a representation of previous experiences. These schema create expectations about the world which *determine* our perceptions and behaviours. In this way, the cognitive approach is also deterministic.

The humanistic approach

The humanistic approach is the antithesis of the previous approaches. Humanistic psychologists believe that human beings are free to plan their own actions and, ultimately, their own destiny. People are seen as struggling to grow and to make difficult decisions that will profoundly affect their lives (Rogers 1974). As a result of these decisions, each of us becomes unique and responsible for our own behaviour. 'Self-actualization' is one of the key concepts of the humanistic approach, the idea that we each have many different potentials (intellectual, athletic, artistic) and we constantly strive to fulfil them. According to Jahoda's (1958) view of ideal mental health, mental health problems occur when we are prevented from fulfilling our true potential. The concept of self-actualization was used by Jahoda and also by Maslow (1954) in his theory of motivation. He agreed with Hull's view that human behaviour is driven foremost by biological needs, but once these have been satisfied, other motives become important, with the need for self-actualization at the top of the hierarchy (see pp. 441–2).

● *Humanistic therapies* such as Rogers' person-centred therapy are based on the assumption of free will. The therapist helps clients to exercise free will in such a way as to maximize the rewards in their lives. Person-centred therapy, or counselling, has been enormously popular in the last 50 years in the treatment of many forms of less serious mental disturbance.

● *The humanistic approach is culturally biased* – Individualist societies are more concerned with independence than *inter*dependence, and individuals are more concerned with self- rather than group-goals. The humanistic view of self-determination and self-actualization is more relevant to individualist societies, whereas behaviour of members of collectivist societies is more determined by group needs.

CHECK YOUR UNDERSTANDING

Check your understanding of free will and determinism by answering these questions from memory. You can check your answers by looking back through Topic 1.

1 Briefly explain why free will is seen as the opposite to determinism.

2 Distinguish between 'proximate' and 'ultimate' causes of behaviour.

3 How can moral responsibility be explained within a determinist framework?

4 Outline **two** arguments *for* determinism.

5 Explain what is meant by 'environmental determinism'.

REVISION SUMMARY

Having covered this topic you should be able to describe and evaluate:

✓ the concepts of free will and determinism and the conflict between them

✓ arguments for and against free will

✓ arguments for and against determinism

✓ assumptions about free will and determinism in psychological theory and research.

EXAMPLE EXAM QUESTIONS

Below are some **possible examination questions** set on this topic, along with hints to help you understand and approach each question effectively:

1 (a) Explain what is meant by the terms 'free will' and 'determinism'. (5 marks)
(b) Discuss free will and determinism in **two** psychological theories. (25 marks)

The division of the marks in this question is unequal. In every question there are 15 AO1 marks and 15 AO2 marks. Here, some of the AO1 marks are in part (a) and the rest are allocated to part (b). Part (a) starts with the term 'explain', which tells you that it is an AO1 part. Part (b) uses the term 'discuss', which is a combination of AO1 and AO2. With 5 AO1 marks assigned to part (a), there are only 10 AO1 marks in part (b) and so your answer to part (b) needs to have more AO2-type material.

2 Discuss the free will and determinism debate with reference to **two or more** psychological theories **and/or** studies. (30 marks)

> Here, there are no marks for explaining the terms free will and determinism, so don't waste valuable time doing that. In this question you have the option of including more than two theories/studies if you feel you do not have enough to write about just two. Beware, though, the more you try to cover, the less time you have for detail and elaboration which are important AO1/AO2 criteria respectively.

3 Critically consider determinism in psychological research (theories **and/or** studies). (30 marks)

> A question could be set on either free will or determinism, as here. It is up to you to shape your answer accordingly, i.e. free will material will only be relevant to AO2 and then only if used effectively as part of critical commentary. You need to impose your own structure on this question. For example, you may divide your answer into four chunks, each of 200 words (800 words is about right for a 40-minute essay): 200 words about one theory and 200 words evaluating this, and the same for a second theory. Alternatively, you could write 135 words of description for each of three theories.

4 Critically consider arguments *for* determinism in psychology. (30 marks)

> The term 'critically consider' is an AO1+AO2 term requiring you to describe and evaluate arguments for determinism. You can use arguments *against* determinism (as well as those *for* free will) as commentary, but they must be used *effectively* in order to gain credit. For example, you may present an argument for determinism and then present an argument against determinism as a relevant piece of commentary, then present another argument for and an appropriate counterargument, and so on.

Topic 2 >> Reductionism

REDUCTIONISM AS A FORM OF EXPLANATION

One of the notable developments in scientific thinking in the behavioural sciences has been the notion that the simplest explanations of events are generally the best. A supporter of this view was C. Lloyd Morgan (1852–1936). Morgan's law of parsimony states that we have no need to explain behaviour in terms of complex psychological processes when it can be explained adequately in terms of much simpler processes.

This tendency to simplify explanations is one form of reductionism, 'reduction in explanations'. An alternative kind of reductionism is called 'methodological reductionism' or 'reductionism in methodology'. This refers to the use of reductionism as a method of investigating phenomena. In order to demonstrate causal links, a researcher reduces behaviour to a set of simple variables – the independent and dependent variables – which can be controlled and measured.

There are other forms of reductionism, such as 'theoretical reductionism', which is the view that theories from different disciplines can be related to each other and reduced to one all-embracing explanation of the world.

ARGUMENTS FOR AND AGAINST REDUCTIONIST EXPLANATIONS

Arguments *for* reductionism

1 Reductionism as a scientific approach

'Reductionism has worked well in other sciences' – Scientific research is reductionist and has led to many important discoveries that have enabled people to control and predict their world better. For example, knowledge about how various metals respond to stress has enabled people to build bridges. Reductionism creates the possibility of a fully scientific psychology, where we might be able to understand completely the causes of behaviour. As we have already noted, breaking complex behaviours down to smaller units permits us to discover causal relationships.

2 Appropriate for certain levels of explanation

Rose (1997) has distinguished between different levels of explanation, each of which has a valid contribution to make. The lowest level is the molecular (physics), followed by the intra-cellular level (biochemistry), then parts of individuals (physiology), behaviour of individuals (psychology) and, ultimately, the behaviour of groups (sociology). We can explain any particular behaviour at all these different levels. For example, mental illness can be explained in physiological terms (the behaviour of neurotransmitters at a synapse), in terms of the psyche (e.g. reinforcement) or in terms of social systems (e.g. family relationships).

Rose uses the example of five biologists trying to explain why a frog jumped into the water. The physiological psychologist explains that the frog senses a snake and its brain sends signals to the muscles to jump. The second biologist (an ethologist) says that to understand the frog's behaviour we need to look at goals – in this case to avoid being eaten. The third biologist is more interested in development and suggests that the behaviour can be best understood by looking at how it developed, the elements of nature and nurture that have contributed to why it jumped. A fourth biologist argues from an evolutionary point of view that one should explain a behaviour in terms of ultimate rather than proximate causation, i.e. its adaptive function as opposed to its immediate effect. Finally, the fifth biologist, a biochemist, says they have all missed the point. The behaviour occurred because of the biochemical properties of the muscles.

3 Reductionist explanations are successful

Later in this unit we will consider some reductionist explanations in psychology, together with their criticisms. Such explanations can be presented as part of an argument for reductionism.

A02 Commentary
arguments for reductionism

1 *Reductionism as a scientific approach* – Methodological reductionism may be appropriate for the physical sciences, but less appropriate when explaining behaviour that is more complex. Complex systems may not behave predictably, i.e. as a simple summation of the constituent parts. This was the view of 'Gestalt' psychologists, who argued that the whole is more than the sum of its parts. This 'holist' approach can also be seen in 'connectionist' (or neural) networks, a more current model for memory than the rather linear and reductionist multi-store model (part of your AS studies). The connectionist model of memory is based on the fact that the brain consists of an interconnected network of neurons, each neuron connected on average to 10,000 other neurons. The behaviour of such an interconnected network is not a simple sum of the individual links. Networking permits new properties to emerge such that the system as a whole has properties that do not belong to the parts.

2 *Levels of explanation* – Rose (1997) suggests that biologists need all five types of explanation and no one explanation is 'correct'; it all depends on what kind of explanation is required. However, the problem is knowing which kind of explanation to select. Selecting the wrong level may prevent a truer understanding of a behaviour. For example, the use of an antidepressant to treat depression may miss the *real* causes of a person's depression (e.g. a family problem).

If it were possible to link the different levels of explanation, there would be less of a problem when choosing one explanation rather than another. There are some examples in psychology where links between levels of explanation have been found, such as understanding that learning through conditioning can be equated to certain neurochemical changes in the brain (Kandel 1979), thus linking the psychological and physiological levels. In general, however, such links are not possible because of the essential conflict between mental and physical state – called the *mind–body problem*.

Arguments *against* reductionism

1 Erroneous explanations of behaviour

Methodological reductionism aims to make the study of behaviour more accessible by reducing the variables. The findings of such experimental research may not apply to other settings because key variables have been altered by being simplified. For example, memory research often involves learning nonsense syllables or word lists, a simplification of real-world memory tasks. Such variables are used because they permit easy study. However, the findings are mistakenly generalized to memory in general. If memory is studied in the 'real world', findings may be quite different. For example, experiments have found little evidence for long-term memory, but when Bahrick *et al.* (1975) studied recall of yearbook photographs – data which was meaningful to participants – they found good evidence for long-term recall (see Unit 1, p. 11).

2 Inappropriate for psychology

A second argument against reductionism is that reductionist goals are inappropriate for psychology. Humanistic psychologists (such as Rogers and Maslow) believe that it does not make sense to study reductionist accounts of human behaviour. They promote the view of 'emergence', that higher-level descriptions and understandings cannot be derived from lower-level ones. For example, Laing (1965) claimed that it is entirely inappropriate to see schizophrenia as a complex physical–chemical system that has gone wrong. The disorder only makes sense when studied at the level of the experience, and treatment should target this level of explanation.

Commentary
arguments against reductionism

1 *The value of different explanations* – It would be wrong to simply dismiss all studies conducted under artificial circumstances as being ungeneralizable. Often such research is important as a part of greater understanding. However, it is critical to recognize the limitations of such studies.

2 *Inappropriate for psychology* – This holist view would appear to be supported by the relatively modest success achieved by drug therapies in the treatments of mental illness (see pp. 791–5).

3 Appropriate only for certain kinds of question

Reductionist explanations may be appropriate only for certain kinds of question. Valentine (1992) suggests that physiological explanations focus on structures whereas holist explanations are more concerned with process. For example, when studying stress, it might be appropriate to consider physiological systems because one is studying structures; stress *management*, on the other hand, is more concerned with process and so holist approaches are more appropriate.

If physical–chemical explanations were appropriate, we should see far fewer individual differences and much higher success rates. However, the humanistic view would lead us to using more psychological treatments and these too do not have universal success.

3 *Appropriate only for certain kinds of question* – Higher-level explanations lack predictive power. It is more difficult to frame cause-and-effect predictions unless one reduces complex behaviours to simpler ones. In the next topic, we will consider the question of whether psychology is a science, which involves further consideration of the value of higher- versus lower-level explanations.

REDUCTIONISM IN PSYCHOLOGICAL THEORY & RESEARCH

Physiological reductionism

Because human beings are biological organisms, it should be possible to reduce even complex behaviours to their constituent neurophysiological components. There is a clear advantage to this, as it leads to the application of concise and concrete concepts, which are then susceptible to scientific methods of research (Wadeley *et al.* 1997). For example, scientists interested in the causes of schizophrenia (see Unit 25) have found evidence that excess activity of the biochemical neurotransmitter dopamine is a characteristic of schizophrenia. Evidence for the importance of dopamine in schizophrenia comes, in part, from the discovery that antipsychotic drugs that reduce dopamine activity in the brain may also reduce the symptoms of the disorder. This discovery has led to the hope that schizophrenia might be eradicated by controlling the brain chemistry of schizophrenics by the administration of antipsychotic drugs. Such a 'biochemical' theory of schizophrenia would effectively de-emphasize the importance of environmental factors in the development of the disorder.

Evaluation
physiological reductionism

● *Multiple causes of schizophrenia* – Most theorists agree that schizophrenia is probably 'caused' by a combination of factors. Genetic and biological factors may establish a predisposition to develop the disorder; psychological factors such as stress help to bring it to fruition; other psychological and sociocultural factors, such as individual misinterpretations or societal labelling, help maintain or worsen the symptoms.

● *Proximate and ultimate causes* – Examples such as schizophrenia show us that complex phenomena cannot easily be explained simply by reference to a physiological imbalance. The influence of these brain chemicals is indisputable, but to argue that they *cause* schizophrenia is to neglect all other potential influences in the course of this disorder. It may well be that, for example, stress is the *ultimate* (or original) cause of the disorder, which then creates physiological imbalances – the *proximate* (or here-and-now) cause.

Evolutionary reductionism

One of the most important influences on Western thought has been Darwin's theory of evolution, which offered a reductionist explanation of the complex living phenomena in our world. All this had come about, he argued, through the principles of natural selection (see Unit 21). Together with the principles of Mendelian genetics (unknown to Darwin), this provided a way of explaining how species change and how such variety is possible within the natural world. Behaviours that can be shown to arise from genetic factors must have some 'survival value'. It is possible that many human behaviours have also evolved because of their survival value, or more generally, their ability to increase an individual's opportunities for passing on their genes.

Evolutionary theory also claims that species have a point of 'common origin' – that is, differences between species are not seen as *qualitative* (i.e. implying differences in kind) but rather as *quantitative*, in that different species have evolved further than others along the evolutionary path. If, it is supposed, the forces of evolution work in the same way for all species, then it makes sense that we must share a number of natural processes with other species. Based on this idea of evolutionary continuity, behaviourists have chosen to study simpler species in order to understand more about these processes. This, suggest Slife and Williams (1995), provides the justification for studying non-human species and then generalizing to human beings.

A02 Evaluation
evolutionary reductionism

● *Drawing unwarranted conclusions about cause and effect* – We commonly think of our biology as affecting the way we experience the world, but the opposite may also be true. There are many studies that have shown how a stimulating environment can change the structure of an animal's brain (a concept known as 'neural plasticity'). The suggestion that an efficient brain is the *result* of superior performance rather than the cause of it is supported in research by Haier *et al.* (1992). In this study, participants who were allowed to play a computer game for a period of several weeks showed a slower glucose metabolism rate (i.e. they

were more neurologically efficient) than a control group who did not play the computer game.

● *Exaggerating the power of genes* – When we read about the role of genetics in a particular behaviour, we might assume that genes are the cause and the *only* cause. Even the words that we use to describe genetic influence, such as 'control' and 'determine' imply an inevitability that may not actually exist (Tavris and Wade 1995). Wilson (1978) argues that genes hold culture on a leash, but the problem, according to Gould (1987) is in determining the length of the leash. If it is only a foot long, then society has very little room to manoeuvre and change, but if the leash is ten feet long, biology would only establish a broad range of possibilities. This is a debate we will return to later, when we consider nature and nurture.

✓ CHECK YOUR UNDERSTANDING

Check your understanding of reductionism by answering these questions from memory. You can check your answers by looking back through Topic 2.

1 Explain what is meant by 'methodological reductionism'.

2 Name **two** arguments *for* reductionism.

3 For each of these arguments, briefly describe **one** counterargument.

4 Why can't one reduce everything to physiological influences?

5 In what way is the evolutionary approach reductionist?

REVISION SUMMARY

Having covered this topic you should be able to describe and evaluate:

✓ kinds of reductionist explanation

✓ arguments *for* and *against* reductionism

✓ examples of reductionism in psychological theory and research.

Below are some **possible examination questions** set on this topic, along with hints to help you understand and approach each question effectively:

1 (a) Explain what is meant by reductionism. (5 marks)
   (b) Discuss examples of reductionism in **two** psychological theories. (25 marks)

> Part (a) is AO1 and straightforward, so long as you make sure you write an amount appropriate for 5 marks (about 120 words). Part (b) contains a further 10 marks for AO1 and 15 marks for AO2. Select any two theories and then use these theories as the context for discussing as many examples of reductionism as you like. If you write about more than two theories, only the best two will be credited. Here, credit will only be given to description and evaluation that involves examples of reductionism in the context of theories. As this question is given credit for synopticity, it pays to select theories from different areas of psychology, so you might select, say, the psychological explanation of schizophrenia and the neurobiological theory of dreams.

2 'Some psychologists believe that reductionism has led to major advances in psychology whereas others see reductionism as a threat to true understanding of human behaviour.'

With reference to the issues raised in the quotation, discuss reductionism in psychological research (theory and/or studies). (30 marks)

> The quotation is intended to be helpful and remind you that reductionism can be a positive and a negative process. The question requires you to address both of these issues in your answer (if you don't, you will incur a partial performance penalty of a maximum of 9 marks for AO2). These issues are especially relevant to your commentary as you may assess the reductionism in your chosen theories/studies by considering whether this is a strength and/or limitation for the theory/study.

3 Discuss reductionism with reference to **two or more** psychological theories. (30 marks)

> In this question, discussing two theories will be sufficient to attract full marks, but if you feel that you don't know enough about two theories, then you can consider others. However, it is best to avoid discussing lots of theories. The highest marks are given to answers that show evidence of depth *and* breadth. There are two ways to structure your answer. First, you could describe and evaluate theories, using these to illustrate points about reductionism. The second approach would be to make a point about reductionism and illustrate this with reference to a psychological theory.

4 Critically consider arguments **against** reductionist explanations in psychology. (30 marks)

> 'Critically consider' is an AO1+AO2 term which requires you to *describe* arguments against reductionism. This could include examples of psychological theory/research which illustrate how reductionist explanations are unsuccessful or problematic. If such examples are used as a means of commenting on an argument, then they would attract AO2 credit, whereas if they are presented as the argument itself then they would receive AO1 credit.

Topic 3 >> Psychology as a science

DEFINITIONS AND VARIETIES OF SCIENCE

What is science? This may seem a fairly trivial question. We all know what science is, but what does it really mean to describe something as 'scientific', and can psychology really be considered scientific in the same way that the natural sciences are considered scientific?

The Latin root of the word 'science' literally means 'knowledge'. Science can, therefore, be seen as

concerned with what we *know* to be true, rather than what we *believe* to be true. Hence, we see science as an important way of distinguishing what is true and real from what is not. In the modern use of the term, science is often seen both as a body of knowledge that we accept as trustworthy, and as the method for attaining that knowledge (i.e. the *scientific method*).

The characteristics of science

Probably the most fundamental characteristic of science is its reliance on 'empirical methods' of observation and investigation, i.e. observation through sensory experience rather than a reliance on thoughts and ideas. All scientific ideas must, at some point, be subjected to empirical investigation through careful observation of perceivable events or phenomena. Science has emerged as a trusted approach to the acquisition of knowledge because of this reliance on sensory or direct experience. This does not mean, however, that science is purely empirical in nature. For science to 'make sense', it is necessary to explain the results of empirical observation. That means constructing theories, which in turn can be tested and refined through further empirical observation. These phases of science can be distinguished in the cycle of scientific enquiry shown in Fig. 28.1.

Slife and Williams (1995) identify a number of further attributes that characterize science.

- Scientific observation is made under *objective* conditions. In other words, observation is not influenced by factors such as bias or expectation or the particular cultural values of the scientist.
- Scientific observation takes place under *controlled* conditions, often in the context of the experiment.
- Science involves making *predictions* about what is expected to happen under specified conditions. In this way, the scientist is able to *validate* or *falsify* whatever theory or hypothesis led to the observations being made. This ability to control

Figure 28.1 ≫ *The cycle of scientific enquiry*

and predict behaviour in experimental settings gives us the expectation that we will also be able to control and predict behaviour in real-life settings. It is this expectation that drives psychology towards science as a chosen route to knowledge, and towards the establishment of a *technology* of behaviour.

- Scientific investigations are open to public scrutiny, i.e. the methods and results of scientific investigations are there for all to see and to check. Confidence in results is increased when investigations can be *replicated,* and the results repeated.

A02 Commentary
characteristics of science

- *A culture-specific account* – The account of science outlined above is a culture-specific one. It is specific to Western culture as well as to a

historical period (as considered further below). Other approaches in the past and present are systematic but lack the empirical approach that characterizes Western science. For example, Greek cosmology was a systematic form of investigation but not one that we would regard as scientific (Valentine 1992).

Varieties of science

Science as knowledge or as method

One way to characterize science is as a body of knowledge that explains the nature of the world. Viewed from this perspective, scientific knowledge has two main characteristics:

- Scientific explanations reject, and are preferred to, other explanations of naturally occurring phenomena (such as magic or other supernatural explanations).
- Scientific explanations are often stated as laws or general principles about the relationship between different events. Because of the regularity of the

way in which these events occur together, it then becomes possible to control and predict them.

A second way of characterizing science is to see it as a method of studying phenomena. Scientific investigation involves empirical observation and the development of theories, which, in turn, are constantly tested and refined in the light of further observation.

Hard and soft science

'Hard' sciences, such as physics and chemistry, are those that lend themselves more to reductionist approaches and experiments. People involved in 'soft' sciences, such as psychology and sociology, attempt to use the determinist and reductionist approaches of the hard sciences, but, because of the subject matter, cannot conduct research with the same kind of rigour as in the hard sciences.

Induction and deduction

We have already discussed the fact that there are two ways to discover knowledge about the world: empirical testing ('deduction') and theory construction ('induction'). Philosophers of the 19th century and earlier used inductive techniques. They made observations of the world around them and then produced general statements about the world (called 'natural laws') on the basis of the observations or facts. Induction is reasoning from the particular to the general, as shown in Fig. 28.1. Karl Popper (1959) suggested that this form of gaining knowledge could

never be used to demonstrate the truth of knowledge. Knowledge could be verified, but never falsified. For example, no amount of observing white swans can ever demonstrate that there are only white swans, whereas one observation of a black swan leads to the certainty that the natural law ('there are only white swans') is false. Popper's principle of *falsification* lead to the process of *deductive* science.

Natural laws or theories are proposed as an outcome of induction. Such theories produce hypotheses which can be tested through experiments. The outcome of an experiment leads a researcher to retain or reject the null hypothesis and thus accept or refine the theory that generated the hypothesis. This process of gaining knowledge is called *deduction*, reasoning from the general to the particular.

Commentary
varieties of science

- *Soft sciences* – Such lack of rigour may make 'soft' sciences less scientific, but this doesn't mean they are unscientific, because they continue to embrace the aims of scientific research, i.e. objectivity, replicability and so on.

- *Paradigms and the evolution of science* – Thomas Kuhn (1962) astonished the scientific community by arguing that the logical view of science (induction or deduction) did not actually represent how science evolves. He claimed that scientists generally collect data that fits with the accepted assumptions of that science. Thus, scientists seek to find confirming instances of their hypotheses rather than disconfirming instances. This is supported by the idea of a 'publication bias' – research that supports a popular position is more likely to be published,

or more likely to be conducted in the first place, than research which disconfirms dominant views (Dickersin 1990). Kuhn used the term 'paradigm' to describe this dominant view. He defined a paradigm as 'a shared set of assumptions about the subject matter of a discipline and the methods appropriate to its study'. According to Kuhn, this tendency to confirm existing beliefs does not continue without challenge and, at points in the history of science, the dominant view is overthrown by a minority position which has gradually changed the *zeitgeist*. One example of this is the Copernican revolution in the 16th century, when the dominant view that the earth was the centre of the universe was overthrown by the astronomer Copernicus. So, according to Kuhn, scientific discoveries occur through revolution or paradigm shift, rather than steady logical development. In fact, Kuhn's view in itself was a paradigm shift in terms of how we view the process of science.

THE DEVELOPMENT OF PSYCHOLOGY AS A SEPARATE DISCIPLINE

The *science* of psychology has a fairly short history – just over 100 years. Prior to that, psychology had been considered simply a branch of philosophy. The German physiologist and psychologist Wilhelm Wundt founded the first laboratory for experimental psychology in Leipzig in 1879. Wundt stressed the use of scientific methods in psychology, particularly 'introspection' (the process by which a person looks inward at their own mental processes to gain insight into how they work). Although the value of introspective reports was dubious, this approach did stress the need for precise subjective observations that contrasted with the poorly controlled observations of earlier studies in related fields.

There were those psychologists who felt that psychology would never be accepted as a science

unless it employed methods more objective than introspectionism. Such views led to the development of behaviourism by Watson in his 1913 paper *Psychology as a Behaviourist Views It*. At about the same time as behaviourism was developing in America, 'Gestalt psychology' developed in Germany (see p. 538). This initially had relatively little influence on American psychology, during the time when behaviourism was dominant. However, in the 1950s, when behaviourism was in decline, the Gestalt movement had its influence on American psychology. Simon (1992) reflected that the development of cognitive psychology in the 1950s could be seen as a combination of Gestalt and behaviourist ideas – focusing on perception and problem-solving.

● *Early theorists* – Despite the fact that most textbooks proclaim Wundt's introspectionism as the starting point of psychology, there is some dissent. Jones and Elcock (2001) point out that *experimental* psychology may have originated with

Wundt, but he actually contributed very little to the *theoretical* development of psychology. Jones and Elcock point to other theoretical origins of psychology, such as Darwin's theory of evolution and Galton's (1888) study of the correlation between brain size and intellectual abilities. Such theories and studies contributed more to the social and intellectual climate underlying the growth of modern psychology.

ARGUMENTS FOR AND AGAINST PSYCHOLOGY AS A SCIENCE

Arguments *for* the claim that psychology is a science

1 Psychologists use scientific methods

When viewed from this perspective, it is clear that psychology probably *does* qualify as a science, because scientific methods are the preferred method of investigation for most psychologists. Indeed, the laboratory experiment has probably become the dominant mode of investigation in psychology, offering

the psychologist opportunities for control and prediction that are absent in less 'scientific' methods.

2 Some levels of psychology are scientific

As we saw in the section on reductionism, psychology embraces explanations at different levels ranging from the physical to the sociological. One could make a lesser claim that at least *some* levels of psychology are scientific, such as research into the neurobiology of dreaming or of mental illness.

Commentary
arguments for psychology as a science

1 *Low validity of psychology's scientific methods* – Psychologists may use the scientific method but such research has been criticized in terms of a lack of both internal and external validity. As regards internal validity, many findings have been criticized because of 'demand characteristics' operating in the study. A demand characteristic is a feature of an experiment that invites predictable responses from participants so that they do not behave as they normally would; they are cued to behave in a particular way by the experimental conditions. Examples from your AS studies include Asch's study of conformity (1956) and Milgram's study of obedience (1963). These studies have also been criticized for low external validity. For example, Asch's study involved conformity on a relatively trivial topic (length of lines) and this may

not tell us much about conformity in other settings (low ecological validity). Therefore, we might conclude that psychologists may use scientific methods but the results of such investigations are relatively meaningless.

2 *Many levels, no paradigm?* – There is one main difficulty with this approach. It runs counter to the argument that psychology has a paradigm. Kuhn claimed that the paradigm was the key feature of any science – what characterizes any science is a shared set of assumptions and a shared methodology. If psychology consists of different levels or kinds of explanation, some of which are more scientific than others, then it cannot claim to have a paradigm. Thus, while some levels of psychology are scientific, psychology as a whole cannot claim to be a science. On the other hand, we might equally point to Rose's description of five biologists and the frog (p. 858). His view of biology was one of a number of different paradigms.

Arguments *against* psychology as a science

1 Science is determinist

The basis of the scientific approach is that behaviour is predictable: there are cause-and-effect relationships which can be discovered and these explain human behaviour. However, as we have seen, the determinist

view raises difficulties for free will and moral responsibility, which might lead us to reject the scientific approach as a way to investigate human behaviour.

2 Science is reductionist

To carry out a scientific test, we must be able to observe whatever it is we are investigating. This may seem a straightforward requirement, but it is not always so. For example, there are many events (such as motivation or fear) that we cannot observe directly. Instead, we observe something else that we feel represents the thing we are really interested in. For example, we may choose to define or *operationalize* fear in terms of some physiological change (such as pupil dilation), or motivation in terms of questionnaire responses.

3 Objectivity is not possible

We saw earlier that objectivity was an important characteristic of scientific enquiry. By that we mean that there is an assumption that any subjective influences (such as the values and expectations of the investigator) are excluded from the investigation. In this way, we can be sure that the results are not distorted because of the subjectivity of the investigator. There are many difficulties with objectivity in psychology, for example 'observer bias' – when a researcher observes behaviour, such observations are inevitably affected by the observer's expectations. Interviewer bias and experimenter bias lead to changes in participants' behaviour as a consequence of a researchers' expectations.

4 Psychology does not have a paradigm

According to Kuhn, all scientific knowledge emerges from within a specific set of influences (the paradigm), and these lead scientists to think about a problem in their own special way. The intention of studying any particular science is to become indoctrinated into its paradigm. It is questionable as to whether psychology does have a paradigm and indeed whether it is actually possible ever to establish a paradigm in psychology. Kuhn argued that psychology was in a state of 'pre-science', never having developed a paradigm.

Commentary
arguments against psychology as a science

1 *Science is not necessarily determinist* – The section on determinism showed us that there are ways to incorporate the concept of free will within a determinist framework (see p. 850) and also that there is regularity in human behaviour. In addition, the physical sciences no longer subscribe to a purely determinist framework and thus psychology is in step with other sciences.

2 *Problems with the reductionist approach* – The trouble with operational definitions is that they are not necessarily measurements of the thing we were originally interested in. The consequence of this is that psychologists often explore the relationship between two things (e.g. fear and motivation) without ever being able to measure either of these directly. Instead, as is the case with many investigations in psychology, our observations are always one step removed from the phenomenon (e.g. fear) that we are really interested in studying. The result is that psychologists end up measuring something different from their intended phenomena and reach false conclusions.

3 *Objectivity is not possible in any science* – The same problems over objectivity occur even in the physical sciences, not just psychology. Heisenberg's uncertainty principle (see p. 852) is derived from the observation that the simple act of measuring a sub-atomic particle changes the behaviour of that particle. Thus, true objectivity can only be an ideal for scientific research. The concept of science as being objective is also challenged by those who point out that science is as much a social activity as a mechanical application of correct procedures (Jones and Elcock 2001). The work of scientists is influenced by prevailing social attitudes (which influence the shape and structure of knowledge) and the day-to-day activities of scientists are affected by everyday human concerns (being liked by colleagues, getting promotion, and so on). This area of study is called the 'sociology of scientific knowledge' (SSK).

4 *Paradigms in psychology* – There are three possible counterarguments:

– Psychology may not have one single paradigm but then neither does biology, as we have already noted. Psychology has a number of mini-paradigms, such as behaviourism, psychoanalysis, the cognitive approach, and so on. As we will see in Unit 29, each of these paradigms or approaches has a common set of assumptions and a specific form of methodology.

– We can argue that psychology has had dominant paradigms through its history. Behaviourism was dominant in the first half of the 19th century, but was then superseded by the cognitive approach. Today the evolutionary approach is in ascendancy.

– We may criticize Kuhn's concept of paradigms in science. Some scientists (or philosophers of science) see this position as being rather extreme. For example, Lakatos (1970) suggested that these views are not appropriate. Instead, Lakatos proposed that science is a historically evolving body of knowledge that pursues thematic lines of enquiry. There is a succession of theories that are linked by a hard core of assumptions. Theories are tested and revised as a consequence of new discoveries and thus science is essentially a rational process. This description of science fits psychology.

Alternative views on the science–psychology relationship

We have been exploring the issue whether psychology might be considered to be a science, but this ignores an equally important question as to whether it *should* be scientific. It should be clear that some aspects of human behaviour might be more accessible than others to this type of empirical proof. For example, it may be a fairly straightforward endeavour to explore mundane issues such as the short-term memory span using scientific methods. However, psychology is concerned with human behaviour in all its richness and complexity, and scientific methods may not be the best route to investigate this area.

Slife and Williams (1995) present three positions on whether a science of human behaviour is possible or even desirable.

● *The need for empirical validation* – All theories should be subject to rigorous tests to show that they are internally consistent (i.e. make sense) and that they can explain a wide range of events consistent with the predictions of the theory. It is also important that the claims of a particular theory can be demonstrated through actual, observable behaviour.

● *The value of qualitative methods* – The study of human experience requires the use of different methods from those used in the study of the natural world. Scientists studying humans would place a great deal of importance on the experience of their participants as a way of understanding their behaviour. The use of *qualitative* methods in research avoids the measurement and quantification of behaviour, allowing participants to describe their own experiences within their own linguistic style. The role of the qualitative researcher would be to question, describe and interpret this experience. Examples of qualitative research include discourse analysis and ethnographic methods (see p. 825).

● *The need for a variety of research methods* – The study of human behaviour and experience requires 'methodological pluralism'. Researchers attempt to make sense of the world around them, and must make their choice of method based on the nature of the problem they are investigating. All methods open the door to knowledge in one way, but close it in another. On the basis of this, no one method might be considered superior to another.

CHECK YOUR UNDERSTANDING

Check your understanding of psychology as a science by answering these questions from memory. You can check your answers by looking back through Topic 3.

1 Give a brief definition of science (about 100 words).

2 Distinguish between 'induction' and 'deduction'.

3 Name **two** varieties of science.

4 One argument for psychology as a science is that psychologists use the scientific method. What counterargument could you present?

5 Explain what Kuhn meant by a 'paradigm'.

REVISION SUMMARY

Having covered this topic you should be able to describe and evaluate:

✓ definitions and varieties of science

✓ the development of science as a separate discipline

✓ arguments *for* the claim that psychology is a science

✓ arguments *against* the claim that psychology is a science.

EXAMPLE EXAM QUESTIONS

Below are some **possible examination questions** set on this topic, along with hints to help you understand and approach each question effectively:

1 Critically consider whether psychology is a science. (30 marks)

This essay covers the whole of this topic – it would be relevant to consider the question of what is meant by 'science', to consider arguments for psychology as a science and use arguments against as AO2 counterpoints (or vice versa), and/or finally to consider whether the goals of science are appropriate to psychology. You might organize your answer around the criteria for science and consider how well this applies to psychology, or examine different branches of psychology (e.g. those associated with Skinner and Freud). The main challenge will be one of selection.

2 (a) Explain what is meant by the term 'science'. (5 marks)
(b) Outline the development of psychology as a separate discipline. (10 marks)
(c) To what extent can psychology be considered to be a science? (15 marks)

The AO1 content of this question is in parts (a) and (b). Part (c) is entirely AO2 and here you must focus on considering the question rather than describing the arguments – a subtle difference! You might state that psychology is a science because it uses the scientific method. This gives you a platform from which you can make various evaluative comments such as: 'for example, there are many controlled laboratory experiments conducted in psychology ... (giving some examples) ... however, it is debatable whether such research actually tells us much about human behaviour in the real world'. These comments will form the AO2 content of your answer.

3 'Some psychologists feel that scientific methods are inappropriate to the study of humans because human behaviour is complex and cannot be reduced to simple causal relationships.'
Discuss arguments **for** the claim that psychology is a science, with reference to issues raised in the quotation. (30 marks)

The question requires that you address the issues in the quotation (if you don't, the penalty is that you are restricted to 9 marks for AO2). The intention of the quotation is to provide a few issues to 'kick against' when considering the arguments *for* psychology as a science. All arguments *for* psychology as a science will be credited as AO1 and all arguments *against* will be counted as AO2 *provided* that the arguments against are presented as counterpoints to the AO1 arguments.

4 (a) Describe arguments **against** the claim the psychology is a science. (15 marks)
(b) Evaluate the arguments **against** the claim the psychology is a science that you presented in part (a). (15 marks)

This question has been parted to help you focus on the AO2 element. This doesn't mean that you can simply describe the arguments *for* psychology as a science in part (b), but you must express them as arguments against the arguments you described in part (a). Start sentences with phrases such as 'The view that psychologists use the experimental technique is flawed because ...' and then present your evidence to show that it is flawed. Other AO2 approaches include considering applications or implications of the debate, or its relationship to other debates, such as reductionism versus holism. The science debate is also related to the free will/determinism debate.

Topic 4 >> Nature and nurture

DEFINITIONS OF NATURE AND NURTURE

The 'nature–nurture debate' is one of the standard debates in psychology and a central concern to psychologists, particularly in developmental psychology. What is it that has made each of us into what we are today? What elements of your physical and mental being can be explained in terms of your *nature* or physical being? And what elements are due to 'nurture' – the social and physical *environment* that has surrounded you?

- *Nature* – This refers to all those characteristics and abilities that are determined by your genes. This is not the same as the characteristics you are born with, because these may have been determined by your pre-natal environment. In addition, some genetic characteristics only appear later in development as a result of the process of maturation. Supporters of the 'nature' view have also been called 'hereditarians' or 'nativists'.

- *Nurture* – This refers to the influences of experience, i.e. what is learned through interacting with both the physical and social environment. Supporters of the 'nurture' view are 'empiricists', holding the view that all knowledge is gained through experience. You may be familiar with the term 'empirical research', where data is collected through sensory experience rather than a reliance on thoughts and ideas.

The nature–nurture debate used to be described as 'nature *versus* nurture' as if either one or the other could be given as the sole explanation for human development. However, it has been clear for some time that neither nature nor nurture can on their own provide complete explanations. All characteristics are a product of nature *and* nurture. Psychologist Donald Hebb used the analogy of the length and width of a rectangle – neither can be said to contribute more to the area of the rectangle, they are both important. The same is true of nature and nurture.

ACTIVITY

Nature and nurture in psychology

Begin this topic by writing three lists: one called 'nature', one called 'nurture' and one called 'nature and nurture'. In each list record all the theories or explanations that you have studied which would fit under the heading. For example, any genetic explanations belong in the nature list, behaviourism is an example of the nurture approach, and the diathesis-stress model emphasizes the role of both nature *and* nurture.

THE HISTORY OF THE NATURE–NURTURE DEBATE

Philosophical views

Although Sir Francis Galton first used the phrase 'Nature versus Nurture' in 1874, this debate has been going on much longer. The Greek philosopher Plato argued that the role of nurture was less than most people believed. According to Plato, children begin life with knowledge already present within them; they do not learn anything new but merely recollect knowledge that has previously lain dormant.

In the 17th century, the French philosopher René Descartes also claimed that people possess certain inborn ideas that enduringly underpin their approach to the world. These ideas can be contrasted with those of Descartes' English contemporary John Locke, who argued that there are no innate ideas. Locke was described as an 'empirical philosopher' who believed that the mind at birth was a 'blank slate'.

Early days of psychology

In the early days of psychology (around the turn of the 20th century), there was an almost inevitable tension between those who favoured a view of behaviour as a product of heredity (nature) and those who favoured the greater influence of environment (nurture). In order for the new science of psychology to be useful, it would have to have applications to everyday living. If behaviour was to be changed for the better, it made sense that only environmental intervention would accomplish this. This was the view increasingly championed by the behaviourists. However, the dominant view of human behaviour at the time was fundamentally hereditarian, seeing it as a product of biological influences and therefore implying that environmental influences were, at best, limited.

Learning and instinct

Midway through the last century, there were two dominant schools of thought concerning human behaviour:

- American *behaviourists*, as a result of extensive laboratory work with animals, concluded that all behaviour was the product of trial-and-error learning, i.e. nurture. What's more, this process was considered to be so universal that differences between species were regarded as irrelevant: learning applied to all species, including humans (de Waal 1999).

- In contrast to this extreme environmentalist position, the *ethological* school in Europe focused on natural behaviour. According to this position, animals are born with a number of 'fixed-action patterns' that are little changed by the environment. These fixed-action patterns are the result of evolutionary adaptations. We do not need to learn how to laugh or cry; these are innate signals, universally used and understood.

Although behaviourists accepted that evolution had some relevance in human behaviour, this was merely to acknowledge the continuity between humans and other animals. Humans shared a great deal with other animals, which made the study of the latter both understandable and justifiable. As Skinner bluntly put it: 'Pigeon, rat, monkey, which is which? It doesn't matter.'

● *Evolutionary diversity: a problem for behaviourists* – Although evolution implies continuity between species, it also implies diversity, each animal being adapted to a specific way of life in a specific environment (de Waal 1999). Behaviourists were gradually forced to adopt some of the ideas of evolutionary biology, especially with the discovery that learning is not the same for all species and across all species (see Breland and Breland, p. 663). Animals are specialized learners,

and will more easily learn associations that are important for survival.

● *Behavioural traits: a problem for ethologists* – Ethologists also ran into problems explaining some aspects of animal and human behaviour. Behavioural traits, such as the inhibition of aggression, or altruistic behaviour, were seen as being 'for the benefit of the species'. This may well be true, but animals are inclined to inhibit aggression or display altruistic behaviour for more fundamentally selfish reasons. These early ideas have now been replaced by theories of how an action benefits the animals concerned *and* its genetic relatives (known as 'kin selection', see p. 651).

ASSUMPTIONS MADE ABOUT NATURE AND NURTURE IN PSYCHOLOGICAL RESEARCH

Nature

Evolutionary explanations of human behaviour exemplify the nature approach in psychology. The main assumption underlying this approach is that any particular behaviour has evolved because of its survival value, or more generally, its ability to increase an individual's opportunities for passing on their genes. For example, Bowlby (1969) suggested that attachment behaviours are displayed because they ensure the survival of an infant and the perpetuation of the

parents' genes. This 'survival value' is further increased because attachment has implications for later relationship formation which will ultimately promote successful reproduction.

There are numerous other examples of behaviours that can be explained using the evolutionary approach. One other example from your AS studies is the explanation of stress as an adaptive response to environmental pressures. Animals born without such responses quickly die.

AO2 **Commentary**
assumptions about nature

● *Environmental influences in Bowlby's attachment theory* – Bowlby's explanation of attachment does not ignore environmental influences, as is generally true for evolutionary

explanations. In the case of attachment theory, Bowlby proposed that infants become most strongly attached to the caregiver who responds most sensitively to the infant's needs. The *experience* of sensitive caregiving leads a child to develop expectations that others will be equally sensitive, so that they tend to form adult relationships that are enduring and trusting.

Nurture

The behaviourist approach, most particularly radical behaviourism, is the clearest example of the nurture position in psychology. Watson, the 'father' of behaviourism famously said:

'Give me a dozen healthy infants and my own specified world to bring them up in, and I'll guarantee to take anyone at random and train him to become any kind of specialist I might select: doctor, lawyer, artist, merchant-chief, and yes, beggar and thief, regardless of his talents, penchants, tendencies, abilities, vocations and race of his ancestors.' (Watson 1913)

Behaviourists believe that all behaviour is the result of learning through classical or operant conditioning. Neo-behaviourists include social learning. Probably the best known social learning explanation is of aggression, derived from Bandura's studies using the Bobo doll (see Unit 11, p. 341). Social learning theory proposes that much of what we learn is through observation and indirect reinforcement. This provides us with models of how to behave. However, such behaviour only becomes part of an individual's behavioural repertoire through direct reinforcement – when a behaviour is imitated, it receives direct reinforcement (or not).

● *The genetic basis of learning* – Behaviourist accounts are all in terms of learning, but even learning itself has a genetic basis, as we have already noted – simply the ability to learn relies on appropriate neural mechanisms. For example, research has found that mutant fruit flies missing a crucial gene can not be conditioned (Quinn *et al.* 1979). Furthermore, it can be argued that Skinner's concept of reinforcement depends on an *instinctive* propensity to be reinforced by the pleasure resulting from having a drive met.

Nature and nurture

There are many areas in psychology where you can find examples of the nature–nurture debate. The examples you choose to use in any examination question will depend to a large extent on the topics you have studied. In this section we have focused on three obvious examples but other possibilities include interpersonal attraction, aggression, emotion, language, gender and mental illness (biological vs psychological explanations).

Perception

The extreme *nativist* view holds that we are born with certain perceptual abilities which develop through a genetically programmed process of maturation and which owe nothing to learning. *Empiricists*, on the other hand, believe that we are born with only the most basic sensory capacity and that our perceptual abilities develop through experience and interaction with our environment. It is unlikely that our acquisition of perceptual skills can be fully explained by either one of these extreme views. It seems much more likely that perceptual skills develop as a result of an interaction between innate and environmental factors, as supported by studies of infant perceptual development and cross-cultural research (see Unit 16).

One piece of research in particular illustrates how nature and nurture interact. Blakemore and Cooper (1970) placed kittens in a cylinder where they could only see either vertical or horizontal lines from the time they were first able to open their eyes. The kittens wore a cuff around their neck so they were not exposed to lines of any other orientation. At the age of 5 months they were finally allowed to see the real world and appeared to be virtually blind to objects whose orientation was perpendicular to the ones they were exposed to, for example kittens raised with vertical lines tripped over ropes stretched in front of them. This can be explained in terms of an earlier discovery by Hubel and Wiesel (1959), who identified several types of cell in the visual cortex which appear to respond to lines and edges of particular orientations. When the kittens' visual cortex was examined, it was found that the cells that usually respond to horizontal lines were absent in the vertically-lined reared kittens. The innate biological system (visual cortex) had been altered through experience.

Piaget's theory of cognitive development

Piaget's theory (see Unit 18) is significant in two respects:

● It bridges the gap between 'nature' and 'nurture', by arguing that biologically given structures unfold when placed in a nurturing environment.

● Piaget proposed four mechanisms of cognitive development (maturation, experience, social transmission and equilibration) through which the environment interacts with the internal structures of the individual. In Piaget's theory, the individual is the main focus, whereas the role of the environment is merely to facilitate the automatic unfolding of biological, cognitive structures. What was particularly significant about this theory, in terms of its position in the nature–nurture debate, was that it emphasized the potential that was available to all children with the right environmental events to bring it about.

Intelligence

Until the middle of the 20th century, intelligence was widely regarded as mainly biologically determined. The 'amount' of intelligence possessed by an individual was present at birth and would remain the same throughout life, regardless of experience or training (the nature view). This perspective led to the belief that it was intelligence that gave individuals their potential for life success. If intelligence, and hence potential, was inherited, there seemed little one could do for individuals of low intelligence. A different perspective, the origins of which stretch back as far as the 17th century, proposed that intelligence was largely a product of experience and was, within limits, completely malleable (the nurture view).

In the early 1950s, the predominant view concerning the origins of intelligence had shifted from the 'nature' to the 'nurture' side of the argument. Supporters of this view put forward arguments that intelligence was not genetically determined, but was due to the nature of an individual's experience. It was argued that intelligence was particularly malleable in early childhood. This led to the development of a number of compensatory education programmes, such as the *Head Start* programme in the USA, which were part of a wider 'War on Poverty' initiative.

Commentary
nature and nurture

- *Perception* – Blakemore and Cooper's work illustrates 'neural plasticity' – the ability of the nervous system to adapt to the environment. Such plasticity combined with neural specialization makes good evolutionary sense. It is advantageous for an animal's brain at birth to have certain hard-wired capacities, such as the ability to respond to lines of certain orientations. At the same time, it is advantageous for the brain to adapt to environmental conditions and 'specialize' in the directions required by the environment so that the nervous system can be used efficiently.

- *Vygotsky: a contrast to Piaget* – Vygotsky (see Unit 18) presented an account of cognitive development that contrasts with Piaget's theory. According to Vygotsky, cognitive development occurs largely as a consequence of social influences (nurture). A child is born with innate elementary mental functions (attention and sensation), which are transformed into higher mental functions through cultural influences such as language and the influence of 'experts' (people with greater knowledge). This account also combines elements of nature and nurture, but places much more emphasis on the latter.

- *The intelligence debate* – In Unit 18, evidence for and against nature and nurture is reviewed. The conclusion is that it is not possible to make a simple statement about the influence of genetic or environmental (cultural) factors, because each assumes a different importance in different conditions. This is illustrated in recent research by Turkheimer *et al.* (2003); they found that in poor children the contribution of genetic factors to their IQ was very low (heritability of 0.10), whereas the contribution of genetic factors to the IQs of wealthy children was very high (0.72). (Note that 'heritability' is not the same as 'correlation'. Heritability refers to the proportion of the total variation in a given characteristic, in a given population, that can be attributed to genetic differences.)

Evaluation
methodological difficulties in the nature–nurture debate

- *Manipulation variables* – There is no agreement about how we might define or measure the environment in which a person grows up. There are no standard units of environment by which we might compare one environment against another. At best, the efforts to manipulate environmental variables focus on gross dimensions; at worst, the efforts to define and manipulate the environment are laden with value judgements about good and bad environments that have minimal empirical support (Horowitz 1993).

- *Animal research and human behaviour* – Researchers using animals have, for obvious reasons, been much more successful in defining and manipulating environmental variables. This kind of research emphasizes that much of behavioural development that was taken to be 'innate' (and therefore effectively unalterable) is subject to environmental influence. Trying to understand how such environmental variables would affect human behavioural development is a much more complex issue. This difficulty becomes most pronounced at the cultural level, yet it is probably at the level of cultural influences that the most powerful and subtle environmental variables may well operate (Horowitz 1993).

DIFFERENT VIEWS REGARDING THE RELATIONSHIP BETWEEN NATURE AND NURTURE

Gene–environment interactions

Genes may not only influence behaviour, they may also influence the environment itself. In other words, our experiences may be influenced in part by our genetic make-up – people may react differently to us because of some inherited aspect of our personality. Likewise, we may choose certain experiences because they fit best with our innate preferences. Research has suggested three types of gene–environment relationships (Azar 1997).

- A *passive* relationship between genes and environment may occur because parents transmit genes that promote a certain trait and also construct the rearing environment. For example, if we assume that musical ability is genetic, then musically gifted children may be assumed to have parents who are musically inclined and who provide both the genes and the environment that promote the development of musical ability.

- An *evocative* relationship between genes and environment may occur because genetically distinct individuals may evoke different reactions in those around them. For example, a musically gifted child may be chosen for special training and opportunities by teachers or may produce reactions of awe from their peers.

- An *active* relationship between genes and environment may occur because individuals actively select experiences that fit in with their genetically influenced preferences. For example, musically gifted children may seek out musical friends and opportunities.

Reaction range

An alternative, but not mutually exclusive, view of gene–environment interactions was formulated by Gottesman (1963). He argued that experience does affect development of any particular skill or ability, *but* this is inevitably limited by our biological endowment.

For example, your adult height is affected by the quality of food you eat through childhood. However, even if you had the best possible diet, you would not grow beyond the height laid down by your genes. Genes do not determine development precisely, but establish a reaction range within which development occurs. The same 'genotype' (the genes an individual possesses) determines different 'phenotypes' (an individual's observable characteristics as an expression of their genes) depending on life experiences.

Nature via nurture

There are many other ways to consider gene–environment interaction, but the most recent understanding has been called 'nature via nurture' (Ridley 2003). Our understanding of how genes behave has led scientists to realize that genes don't simply interact with the environment, but they are *activated* by experience. This switching is performed by tiny stretches of DNA called 'promoters'. Our bodies have hundreds of these, which both switch genes on and turn them off. Some of these promoters are affected by our environments. This latter process, therefore, explains how nurture has such a profound impact on the individual, because it influences living organisms via their genes. Ridley suggests that the nature versus nurture debate is akin to debating whether a cake comes from the recipe or the ingredients. Genes are the recipe for life and the environment influences how the genes will be expressed.

Commentary
nature via nurture

- *Genetics and free will* – An interesting extension of this new understanding is that genetic

explanations, which have always been regarded as determinist explanations, can now be reframed as examples of free will. Genes are not our hard-wired masters, but 'the epitome of sensitivity, the means by which creatures can be flexible, the very servants of experience'.

CHECK YOUR UNDERSTANDING

Check your understanding of nature and nurture by answering these questions from memory. You can check your answers by looking back through Topic 4.

1 Define the terms 'nature' and 'nurture'.

2 Identify **two** developments in the history of the nature–nurture debate.

3 Give **two** examples of nurture in psychological research.

4 Use the example of Piaget's theory to explain how nature and nurture each contribute to behaviour.

5 Outline **three** kinds of gene–environment interaction.

REVISION SUMMARY

Having covered this topic you should be able to describe and evaluate:

✓ the terms 'nature' and 'nurture'

✓ the history of the nature–nurture debate

✓ the assumptions made about nature and nurture in psychological research

✓ the different views regarding the relationship between nature and nurture.

EXAMPLE EXAM QUESTIONS

Below are some **possible examination questions** set on this topic, along with hints to help you understand and approach each question effectively:

1 (a) Explain what is meant by the nature–nurture debate. (5 marks)

(b) Discuss **two or more** examples of the nature–nurture debate in psychology. (25 marks)

Part (a) of this question is AO1 requiring a brief explanation of the terms, which can be done through the use of examples. In part (b), there are 10 AO1 marks and 15 AO2 marks. You can gain full credit by considering only two examples, but you are permitted to describe more than two. The danger in providing too many examples is that none of them is described in enough detail for good marks. You should also take care to focus on the nature and/or nurture aspects of your examples rather than engaging in a general description and evaluation. It is always possible to offer commentary on nature examples by making contrast with nurture examples (and vice versa).

2 (a) Outline what is meant by the 'nature–nurture' debate. (5 marks)

(b) Discuss psychological research in terms of its contribution to the nature–nurture debate. (25 marks)

This is a similar question to question 1. Part (a) requires the same answer and poses the same problem – that you may spend too much time for only 5 marks. You should write about 120 words for part (a). Even an extra sentence for part (b) may earn more marks. In part (b), the focus is on *research* rather than examples of the debate in psychology. Avoid the danger of focusing on the general principles of the debate or focusing too much on the theories/studies without relating their discussion to the nature–nurture debate.

3 (a) Outline the history of the nature–nurture debate. (15 marks)

(b) To what extent can behaviour be explained by nature alone? (15 marks)

In this question the AO1 and AO2 marks have been separated into parts (a) and (b). For part (a), you could include material as described on pp. 868–9, or could include any description of nature–nurture topics as long as there is a sense of historical development in the description. For part (b), you must focus on commentary and thus *use* examples to offer an answer to the question posed.

4 Discuss the history of the nature–nurture debate in psychological research. (30 marks)

It would be legitimate to ask a question solely about the history of the debate. The AO1 content would be the same as in question 3. You can gain AO2 credit by offering any comments on your historical outline, such as the implications or consequences for the development of psychology. You might also consider the consequences outside psychology, for example the effects of early intelligence research on people's lives – the hereditarian position had important effects.

5 Discuss different views regarding the relationship between nature and nurture (e.g. gene–environment interaction). (30 marks)

The example in this question is given as a reminder about what might constitute appropriate material. This does not mean you have to limit your discussion to gene–environment interaction or even include this in your discussion. The thing to focus on is discussing the *relationship* between nature and nurture rather than describing examples of nature or nurture separately.

Unit 28 // Debates in psychology

Topic 1: Free will and determinism

- **Free will** is self-determination not randomness. **Determinism** refers to internal or external causes of behaviour which make behaviour predictable.

- Science is determinist but can be reconciled with the free will position if one considers **proximate and ultimate goals** – the latter are subject to free will. Free will and determinism can also be reconciled through soft determinism or liberal determinism or being free from coercion.

- **Arguments *for* free will** include our subjective sense of free will and the need to account for moral responsibility.

- **Arguments *against* free will** include the problem of what does the 'willing' and of reconciling free will with the scientific approach.

- **Arguments *for* determinism** include the success of science in investigating human behaviour, our subjective sense of human predictability and being able to equate free will with brain activity.

- **Arguments *against* determinism** include the impossibility of falsifying determinism (but it has been falsified) and the implications for moral responsibility.

- Examples of the determinist approach in psychology include the **psychodynamic approach** (psychic and biological determinism) and the **behavioural approach** (environmental determinism, reciprocal determinism). Determinism is supported by the success of **psychotherapies** derived from these approaches, but each approach has limitations as well.

- The **cognitive** approach is an example of free will and is also determinist (schemas). The **humanistic** approach exemplifies free will, assuming that people are ultimately driven by self-actualization. Humanistic psychology and free will may apply more to individualist societies.

Topic 2: Reductionism

- One form of reductionism is '**reductionism in explanations**', such as Morgan's law of parsimony. Other forms include methodological reductionism and theoretical reductionism.

- **Arguments *for* reductionism** include: the usefulness of reductionism in other sciences; appropriateness for some levels of explanation; the success of some reductionist explanations.

- **Arguments *against* reductionism** include the following: reductionism leads to erroneous explanations because behaviours are oversimplified; the goals of reductionism are inappropriate for psychology because human behaviour is complex; it may be that reductionist explanations are only appropriate for certain kinds of question (structure rather than process).

- **Examples of the reductionist approach** in psychology include: physiological explanations and evolutionary explanations.

Topic 3: Psychology as a science

- '**Science**' means 'knowledge' as distinct from belief. It also refers to the method of gaining such knowledge through empirical methods. Science is also characterized as being objective, controlled, falsifiable and replicable.

- There are different **varieties of science**, such as the body of the knowledge (theories) or the method by which it is obtained; hard and soft science; and induction and deduction.

- The development of **psychology as a separate discipline** began with Wundt's laboratory for experimental psychology where he used introspectionism. Behaviourists sought to develop a more scientific discipline led by Watson. At the same time Gestalt psychology was developing in Germany. Other theoretical origins have been identified, such as Darwin's theory of evolution.

- **Arguments *for* psychology as a science** include the fact that psychologists do use scientific methods or at least some levels of psychology are scientific, such as neurobiological research.

- **Arguments *against* psychology as a science** include the following: science is determinist and is also reductionist (resulting in false conclusions); objectivity may not be possible in psychology; psychology may be a pre-science without a paradigm (but it may have mini-paradigms).

● There is also the question as to whether psychology **should be scientific**. There is a need for empirical validation, but psychology may require the use of different methods than those used in the hard sciences (such as qualitative methods) or, even better, a mixture of different methods.

Topic 4: Nature and nurture

● **Nature** is inherited (though not necessarily present at birth); **nurture** is the influence of experience and the social and physical environment.

● The **history of the nature–nurture debate** can be traced from the Greek philosopher Plato (a nativist) to the 17th-century philosophers Descartes (nativist) and Locke (empiricist) to early psychologists in the 19th century who were mainly hereditarians (e.g. Galton). In the early 20th century, behaviourism dominated psychology with its empiricist views. Ethology, popular in the mid-20th century, proposed the importance of inherited fixed-action patterns. In reality, no approach (e.g. behaviourism or ethology) is completely nurture or nature.

● Examples of **assumptions about nature** in psychological research include **evolutionary explanations**, such as Bowlby's theory of attachment and models of stress. Such theories acknowledge the influence of nurture.

● Examples of **assumptions about nurture** in psychological research include behaviourist accounts of attachment and mental illness and social-learning accounts of gender and aggression. However, learning itself is inherited.

● Examples of **assumptions about nature and nurture** in psychological research include perception, Piaget's theory of cognitive development and intelligence.

● There are **methodological difficulties** in investigating nature–nurture because it is difficult to be objective about what constitutes good and bad environments.

● There are **different views regarding the relationship** between nature and nurture, such as considering gene–environment interactions (which may be passive, evocative or active), reaction range and the extent to which genes are activated by experience (nature via nurture).

FURTHER RESOURCES

Slife, B.D. and Williams, R.N. (1995) *What's Behind the Research? Discovering Hidden Assumptions in the Behavioural Sciences*, Thousand Oaks: Sage.

> A clearly written and authoritative text that covers most of the issues in this unit.

Dennett, D. (2003) *Freedom Evolves*, London, Allen Lane.

> Dennett argues that free will is not incompatible with determinism, but has evolved as a special characteristic of humans.

Jones, D. and Elcock, J. (2001) *History and Theories of Psychology: A Critical Perspective*, London: Hodder.

> A comprehensive look at how psychology has been shaped by ideas from different disciplines.

Ridley, M. (2003) *Nature via Nurture*, London: Fourth Estate.

> An up-to-date, wide-ranging and accessible look at research on nature and nurture.

Valentine, E.R. (1992) *Conceptual Issues in Psychology* (2nd edn), London: Routledge.

> A summary of the major approaches and controversies in psychology.

Websites

www.bbsonline.org/documents/a/00/00/04/88/ bbs00000488-00/bbs.rose.html

> A précis of Steven Rose's book *Lifelines: Biology, Freedom, Determinism*.

www.channel4.com/science/microsites/S/ science/life/biog_galton.html

> The life story of Sir Francis Galton.

www.sfu.ca/~dant/projects/psyc100/de_waal_ nature_nurture.pdf

> A pdf version of the article by deWaal (1999) cited in the text, 'The end of nature versus nurture'.

APPROACHES IN
Psychology

INTRODUCTION

When sitting in the bath trying to think of a reason not to get out, we are sometimes moved to consider the great questions of life: Who am I? What's it all for? How did I come to be like this? These questions have been the cause of many discussions since people first had the ability to think. They are the big questions that psychology sets out to answer, and although much of the psychological research you read about appears to be quite detailed and narrow, the ultimate aim is to discover more about who and what we are.

Psychologists offer many different explanations for human behaviour and experience. The type of explanation depends upon the approach (perspective) adopted by the psychologist. Inevitably this means that we sometimes come across different explanations for the same event. This does not mean that only one explanation is right and all the rest are wrong, but rather that the explanations are affected by the context (approach) used.

In psychology, there are a number of contrasting contexts in which we choose to view people. Each one of them adds to our overall understanding of what makes people behave and experience the world in the way that they do, but none of these contexts is able to give us the whole story. These contexts are sometimes referred to as 'perspectives' or 'approaches' or 'paradigms'. Whatever we choose to call them, they are made up of the same components:

● a set of assumptions or key concepts about the basic influences on behaviour and experience

● a metaphor (or story) about how people operate or function

● evidence that supports the metaphor and adds to our overall understanding of people

● a general method of investigating the validity of the assumptions and/or metaphor.

The approaches outlined in this unit are different from each other and you may wonder how such different approaches can exist within the same subject. However, two things unite them: their subject matter (the behaviour and experience of individual people) and their attempts to obtain evidence systematically in order to enhance our understanding of human beings.

We will consider five of the traditional approaches used by psychologists. They focus on different aspects of behaviour and experience:

● what we *are made of* (the *physiological* approach)

● how we *evolved* (the *evolutionary* approach)

● what we *feel* (the *psychodynamic* approach)

● what we *do* (the *behavioural* approach)

● what we *think* (the *cognitive* approach).

Cara
Flanagan

'Oh to be young and in love! It gives your heart palpitations'.

'I wonder what they are thinking'.

'Lovers don't think – it's unconscious desires that drive their behaviour'.

Like these three women, people look at the same thing and see something different. It's the same with psychologists. They have characteristic ways of looking at behaviour.

An approach is a *paradigm*. But what is a 'paradigm'? It is the essence of what a thing is, the idealized example. If you look at all the examples of a 'tree' on the right, you can see they all differ, but there is an essence to what a tree is – that's the paradigm. The same is true in psychology. There are many physiological explanations and theories, but underlying this is a shared set of assumptions about the subject matter of a discipline and the methods appropriate to its study.

KEY CONCEPTS

Approaches: the term 'approach' in psychology refers to what was once called a 'school of thought' – a group of psychologists who share a common way of thinking about things and share characteristic methods for studying phenomena.

Methodology: a way of conducting research in order to verify theories and explanations.

Behavioural approach: the view that one need go no further than what is observable when trying to explain behaviour and that all behaviour can be explained in terms of learning and the environment (i.e. nurture rather than nature).

Biological approach: the view that behaviour can be explained in terms of physical factors, either physiological, genetic or evolutionary.

Cognitive approach: cognitive psychologists are interested in how mental processes affect behaviour, likening the mind to an information-processing machine.

Evolutionary approach: behaviours can be explained in terms of the principles of natural selection, i.e. any behaviour that is adaptive is more likely to be perpetuated in future generations. Selection is made at the level of the genes.

Physiological approach: explaining behaviour in terms of the body systems, such as nerves and hormones.

Psychodynamic approach: any approach that emphasizes the dynamics of behaviour, i.e. the forces that motivate it. This approach is associated with psychoanalytic theories.

Topic 1 >> The physiological approach

The main assumption of the physiological approach is that all behaviour can be explained in terms of bodily activity. Physiological explanations belong under the heading of 'biological explanations', i.e. explanations based on the study of living organisms. Evolutionary explanations are also biological and are discussed in Topic 2.

THE PHYSIOLOGICAL METAPHOR

Physiological psychology explores human behaviour and experience by looking at people as if they are biological machines. This idea has some value because it is clear that our physiology affects our behaviour and experience. On a simple level, we know that certain foodstuffs such as coffee or alcoholic drinks will affect the way we see the world and the way we behave. Also, it has been known for a long time that damage to the brain and nervous system can have an effect on behaviour and experience. Therefore, the structure and biochemistry of the nervous system are two important aspects of physiological psychology. However, the real issue is *how much* our biology affects our behaviour and experience and to what extent other factors intervene.

KEY CONCEPTS OF THE PHYSIOLOGICAL APPROACH

Bodily activity can be described using a variety of key concepts. It may be helpful to divide these into two of the major systems of the body:

- the *central nervous system* (CNS), which consists of the brain and spinal cord
- the *autonomic nervous system* (ANS) which controls the release of hormones.

Both of these systems explain how you behave. The CNS provides rapid responses; the ANS is slightly slower and governs behaviours that are largely outside conscious control (they are automatic).

The central nervous system (CNS)

A summary of this systems is given below. Topic 1 of Unit 12 goes into this system in more detail.

Brain organization

The brain is divided into two hemispheres. Some research has suggested that the two hemispheres have different characteristics. For example, the left hemisphere, which usually contains the language centres, is generally more verbal, whereas the right hemisphere is more involved with visuo-spatial processing and emotion. Sperry (1985) proposed that the left hemisphere usually processes information in an analytic or logical fashion, whereas the right hemisphere processes information in a synthetic fashion (holistically). Such suggestions have led to the notion that there are right-brained and left-brained people, those who prefer one style of thinking rather than another – intuitive/creative/subjective (right-brained) or rational/deductive/objective (left-brained).

The brain is also divided into lobes, each associated with different activities. For example, the frontal lobe contains the motor cortex (responsible for fine movement) and the pre-frontal cortex (responsible for forward planning and goal-directed behaviour as well as working memory). The cortex is the thin layer of grey matter that covers the surface of the brain. Deeper inside the brain are many important sub-cortical structures such as the limbic system (the centre for emotions) and the hypothalamus (which regulates the autonomic nervous system). Olds and Milner (1954) identified a specific region in the hypothalamus (the pleasure centre) which may be used to explain reinforcement – when an animal's behaviour is reinforced this part of the brain is activated producing a sensation of pleasure. The same sensation can be created by directly stimulating this part of the brain.

Many aspects of human behaviour can be explained in terms of such localized areas of the brain. For example, a study of London taxi drivers showed that an area of the hippocampus was active when the drivers recalled their routes around the capital, and that this area was bigger than in controls – this is not because they were born this way but because their hippocampi had responded to increased use (Maguire *et al.* 2000). When certain regions of the brain are damaged, they lead to characteristic behaviours. For example, Wernicke and Broca studied patients with localized brain damage permitting them to demonstrate the function of specific language centres (Unit 12, p. 380).

Brain chemistry: Neurotransmitters

The last 30 years have seen a dramatic growth in our knowledge about the way that chemicals affect our behaviour and experience. The centre of the action is the synapse, the gap between nerve cells that is bridged by the release and uptake of neurotransmitters (see Unit 12, p. 377). It has been found, for example, that morphine and other opium-based drugs attach themselves to specific receptor sites at some synapses. They are able to do this because they resemble one class of neurotransmitters called 'endorphins' (Snyder 1984). Opiates and endorphins block pain pathways.

Other important neurotransmitters include serotonin, dopamine and noradrenaline (norepinephrine). There are a relatively small number of neurotransmitters, but they have a wide range of effects because these effects vary depending on the neuron they are acting on.

- Low levels of *serotonin* in the brain lead to abnormal behaviours, such as depression, suicide, impulsive aggression, alcoholism, sexual deviance and explosive rage. High levels of serotonin have been associated with obsessive compulsion, fearfulness, lack of self-confidence and shyness.

- *Dopamine* affects brain processes that control movement, emotional response and the ability to experience pleasure and pain. It may be that this link with pleasure explains dopamine's role in addictions to things such as drugs, sex and chocolate. Dopamine may be 'the master molecule of addiction' which creates intense feelings from any enjoyable activity (Volkow *et al.* 1997). High levels of dopamine have also been linked to hallucinations and schizophrenia (see Unit 25, p. 758).

The autonomic nervous system (ANS)

The ANS has two branches:
- the *parasympathetic* division – which governs the resting state
- the *sympathetic* division – which is associated with bodily arousal, when heart rate and blood pressure

increase, fats and carbohydrates are mobilized, and activity in the digestive system slows down. This bodily arousal ('fight or flight') takes place when adrenaline and noradrenaline are produced by the adrenal medulla which itself is activated by the hypothalamus. Adrenaline and noradrenaline are hormones as well as neurotransmitters.

Hormones

The ANS produces its effects through direct neural stimulation or by stimulating the release of hormones from endocrine glands (such as the adrenal and pineal glands). Hormones are biochemical substances which are released into the bloodstream and have a profound effect on target organs and on behaviour. They are present in very small quantities and individual molecules have a very short life, so their effects quickly disappear if not secreted continuously.

There are a large number of other hormones. For example:

- melatonin is released by the pineal gland and acts on the brainstem sleep mechanisms to help synchronize the phases of sleep and activity
- testosterone is released in the testicles and may influence aggressiveness
- oxytocin is released by the pituitary gland and affects milk production and female orgasms.

Some hormones are released as a response to external stimuli, such as the pineal gland responding to reduced daylight. Other hormones follow a circadian rhythm, with one peak and one trough every 24 hours. For example, levels of cortisol rise about an hour before you wake up and contribute to your feelings of awakeness or arousal. The female hormones oestrogen and progesterone vary according to an infradian rhythm, governed by the pituitary gland. Research suggests that women experience increased aggressiveness prior to menstruation (pre-menstrual syndrome, Floody 1968).

Pheromones

There are substances similar to hormones, called pheromones, which are released by one individual and affect the behaviour of another individual of the same species. One study showed that women's menstrual cycles become synchronized if the sweat from one women (which contains these chemical pheromones) was transferred to another (Russell *et al.* 1980).

ACTIVITY

Explaining your behaviour in physiological terms

At this very minute, what aspects of your behaviour could you explain using physiological concepts?

Evaluation
the physiological approach

- *Determinist* – A completely physiological view of human behaviour suggests that we are not capable of self-determination (free will) and are ruled by predictable bodily functions. On the positive side, such an approach lends itself to scientific investigation, which also assumes determinist relationships between variables – everything has a cause and an effect.

- *Reductionist* – One way to understand complex behaviours is to break them down to smaller units, thus allowing us to discover causal relationships. Rose (1997) suggests that there are many different levels of explanation with the physiological level at the opposite end to the sociological (explaining behaviour in terms of social groups). There are advantages in each level of explanation. However, the problem is knowing which kind of explanation to select. Selecting the wrong level may prevent a truer understanding of a behaviour. For example, the use of an anti-depressant to treat depression may miss the *real* causes of a person's depression (e.g. a family problem). Thus reductionism has both advantages and disadvantages.

- *The mind–body problem* – One of the main problems with the 'lower' levels of explanation is

that they suggest that all behaviour can be reduced to physical activity (the body) and deny the existence of separate mental states (the mind). Ryle (1949) described the mind as nothing more than a 'ghost in the machine'. Others (e.g. 'dualists') believe in separate mental states and the possibility that such mental states can control physical states (and vice versa).

- *Individual and cultural differences* – Physiological explanations can explain individual differences, such as differences between men and women and differences due to abnormal development. However, physiological explanations can't explain why people respond differently to the same drugs, nor why they react differently to stress situations. Nor can they explain cultural differences. In fact, much of the research on human physiology has been conducted with male undergraduates and mistakenly generalized to all people. For instance, the human stress response was assumed to be universal whereas it is now recognized that not all people respond in this way.

- *Physiological explanations have useful applications* – Understanding how the body works has led to many therapeutic interventions such as giving insulin to diabetics and treating mental illness with drugs. However, arguably such treatments have not been that successful (see Unit 26, pp. 791–5).

METHODOLOGY USED BY THE PHYSIOLOGICAL APPROACH

A wide variety of methods are used to study physiological explanations, such as laboratory and natural experiments (described and evaluated on pp. 885 and 892–3) and case studies of brain-damaged individuals (see pp. 888–9). Such methods may involve the use of techniques to measure hormone levels or brain activity. Methods used to investigate brain function can be broadly divided into invasive and non-invasive techniques. These techniques are briefly outlined here (for fuller information, see Unit 12).

Invasive techniques of studying the brain

Invasive techniques involve direct interference with the brain.

- *Electrical stimulation* is one of the oldest techniques. Thin wire electrodes can be implanted in the brain and used to stimulate brain neurons artificially in order to investigate their effects on behaviour. For example, Penfield (1958) stimulated the temporal lobe in humans and some individuals reported experiencing vivid memories from their childhood.

- *Chemical stimulation* involves administering drugs that either stimulate a post-synaptic receptor (stimulants or agonists) or, by combining with the receptor, inactivate it (blockers or antagonists). We can then relate the effects of the drug on behaviour to their effects on synaptic neurotransmitters, and so increase our understanding of the functions of brain neurons and their neurotransmitters. So, if we wish to investigate the role of dopamine synapses in behaviour, we can give animals drugs that specifically stimulate or block dopamine receptors. By observing the behavioural effects, we can then draw some conclusions about what the dopamine system may be doing.

- A third possibility is the physical destruction of brain tissue by *ablation* and *lesioning*. Thousands of experiments have been done using these techniques with non-human animals. Early experiments involved rather primitive needlepoints or knife cuts. Nowadays, localized areas of damage, or 'lesions', are usually produced using thin wire electrodes. A current is passed through which heats the tip of the electrode and the heat creates a small sphere of destruction around the tip. Psychosurgery, which continues on a small scale today (see Unit 26, p. 796), also involves making lesions.

As well as systematic damage in non-human animals, we can also study accidental damage in humans. Brain tumours, strokes, car crashes and other accidents can all damage brain tissue and produce effects on behaviour that can be studied systematically.

Non-invasive techniques of studying the brain

Non-invasive techniques do not involve direct interference with the brain, but instead record electrical activity from the skull surface or create images of the brain using a variety of scanners.

Recording electrical activity

The electroencephalograph (EEG) records the electrical activity of billions of cortical neurons, using a number of small metal electrodes on the surface of the skull. The EEG can be synchronized with a recognizable and repeated waveform, or desynchronized with an apparently random pattern of waves and spikes. It also has a frequency or number of waves or spikes per second (measured as 'hertz'). Certain patterns correlate highly with behavioural states. For example, alertness and activity produce a fast, desynchronized EEG, while drowsiness leads to a synchronized pattern called the 'alpha rhythm', with a frequency of 8 to 12 hertz.

Besides behavioural states, event-related potentials (ERPs) can also be recorded using the EEG. ERPs can be used to investigate the rapid processing underlying, for instance, selective attention. By presenting sequences of stimuli and recording the responses in different areas of the brain, we can generate models of where in the brain different aspects of attention and perception occur.

Scanning and imaging

Brain scanning and imaging have become the main sources of information on human brain function since the relevant technology was developed in the early 1970s.

- **Functional magnetic resonance imaging** (fMRI scanning) involves placing the head in a powerful magnetic field and bombarding the brain with radio waves. Molecules in the brain vibrate in response to the radio waves and emit radio waves of their own which are used to build up a very accurate three-dimensional picture of brain structures.

- **Positron emission tomography** (PET scanning) involves injecting radioactive glucose into the bloodstream. The parts of the brain that are more active take up more glucose and emit more radioactivity; a computer is used to provide an activity map of the brain. This procedure can be used to identify, for instance, those parts of the brain which are most active during speech, or problem-solving, or recognizing faces, etc. This ability to correlate activity in different brain areas with psychological functions makes PET scanning the most useful of current computer-based techniques.

Evaluation
methodology used by the physiological approach

For an evaluation of experiments, see pp. 885 and 893. For evaluation of case studies, see pp. 888–9.

- **Invasive techniques mainly involve non-human animals** – In some cases, such as research on the visual system, work on non-human primates has been largely confirmed by studies of humans with damage to the visual cortex. However, in the area of cognitive functions, such as memory, planning and problem-solving, our abilities are so different from other animals that generalizing such findings is far less justified.

- **Difficulty of linking effects of brain damage to area of brain damaged** – Lesion and ablation studies mistakenly assume that the effects of brain damage can be identified with the area of brain damaged. All neurons are part of intricate circuits and so lesion effects are never restricted to the site of damage. Interpreting the findings of such studies can therefore be very difficult. However, lesion studies in non-human animals and the study of brain-damaged humans have contributed enormously to our understanding of brain function.

- **Difficulty of interpreting EEG records** – It is difficult to interpret EEG records because we do not know how the electrical activity of populations of neurons combines to form the overall EEG recording.

- **Using scanning to view the living brain** – We can use scanning techniques to investigate the human brain in living participants, looking at structure as well as function. This eliminates the ethical problems of using non-human animals and practical issues such as generalizing from animals to humans.

- **Practical problems with scanning techniques** – PET, MRI and fMRI scanners involve recording over long periods (usually hours) with the participant's head enclosed in the tube-like scanning machine. Procedures are highly technical, expensive and time-consuming.

Check your understanding of the physiological approach by answering these questions from memory. You can check your answers by looking back through this first topic.

1 Briefly outline the organization of the human brain.

2 Describe the effects of **two** neurotransmitters.

3 What is the difference between a neurotransmitter and a hormone?

4 Describe the effects of **two** hormones.

5 Identify **one** method/technique used to investigate physiological explanations and outline **two** criticisms of this method.

REVISION SUMMARY

Having covered this topic you should be able to:

✓ describe and evaluate the key concepts of the physiological approach

✓ describe and evaluate the key methods used by the physiological approach.

Topic 2 >> The evolutionary approach

The biological approach includes both physiological and evolutionary explanations, each of which can be considered as an 'approach' in its own right as each has a set of core assumptions and a unique approach to investigating the explanations.

If you had to pick one scientific idea that has had the greatest effect on modern thought, then you might well pick the theory of evolution. This has transformed the way we look at ourselves and continues to exert an influence on psychology, particularly with the growing interest in genetic explanations of behaviour. You might be encouraged to discover that the author of the theory, Charles Darwin, did not do very well at school, and in his autobiography he said of his education that 'Nothing could have been worse for the development of my mind ...' (Darwin 1869, p. 27). Darwin eventually recovered from his schooling and wrote *The Origin of Species*, published in 1859. The book presented an argument for the development of species over time through the process of natural selection.

THE EVOLUTIONARY METAPHOR

The evolutionary metaphor is that we are just slightly more complex animals, and that our behaviour has developed in the same way that our bodies have. The features that have been most 'fit' (adaptive to the environment) have been passed on. The evolutionary account views human behaviour in the context of general animal behaviour. It also explains our behaviour as having a biological cause, and suggests we are what we are because that is the way evolution shaped it, i.e. *determined* it. The evolutionary account also suggests that differences between people are largely due to genetic variation.

KEY CONCEPTS OF THE EVOLUTIONARY APPROACH

Natural selection

According to Darwin's (1859) account of evolution, natural selection is the way that species change over time and become increasingly more adapted to their environment, i.e. possess characteristics that promote their survival and reproduction in that environment. The key features of this are:

- Individuals have unique genetic characteristics (including the way we behave).
- Some individuals survive and breed while others die before they breed.
- The genetic characteristics of the survivors are retained.
- The genetic characteristics of those who do not breed are lost.

What this means is that the characteristics that enable some individuals to survive and reproduce are likely to be passed on to the next generation. The species then develops through a process of selective breeding – 'selection' occurs through 'selective pressures' exerted by the social and physical environment. Characteristics that do not 'fit' the environment are not 'selected', and so those that do fit are passively selected. Note that it is the characteristics that are selected, not the individuals or the species. (For a more detailed explanation, see pp. 701–5).

Sexual selection

Darwin recognized that the principle of natural selection could not explain all behaviour. For example, it could not explain why some animals possess characteristics that appear to threaten their survival, such as the peacock's bright and lengthy train. It does not help the animal to fly faster or better and, in fact, would actually appear to threaten, rather than enhance, an individual's survival. According to the principles of natural selection, such a characteristic should not continue. Darwin (1871) proposed that the force of natural selection is complemented by the force of sexual selection: individuals possess features that make them attractive to the opposite sex or that help them compete with members of the same sex for access to mates. These features mean that the possessor breeds successfully, whereas those individuals without the features are less successful. Thus, traits that are solely concerned with increasing reproductive success are naturally selected and are retained.

In general, it is the males of any species that possess sexually selected traits (males and females of the same species often have different forms). This is because females are generally the selectors and so males that possess attractive traits are more successful in reproduction. The reason that females are selectors is because females produce relatively few eggs at a greater physiological cost than sperm. Those females who take greatest care with each reproduction are the most successful in the long term, whereas males, who produce thousands of sperm, do best by mating as often as possible.

Kin selection

The issue of altruism also presents a major problem for the theory of natural selection. Any behaviour that is selfless should not be naturally selected because it does not promote the possessor's survival. Darwin couldn't explain this, but sociobiologists (who seek to explain the evolution of social behaviours such as altruism in terms of adaptiveness) have provided an answer. Hamilton (1963) argued that natural selection does not operate directly on individuals but upon their genetic make-up. This means that an individual may pass on their genes to future generations not just by means of their own reproductive success, but also by facilitating the reproductive success of genetic relatives, such as caring for the offspring of close relatives, since they share a significant number of one's genes. The phrase the 'selfish gene' (Dawkins 1976) describes the fact that it is genes that are the driving force behind evolution. Hamilton used the phrase 'inclusive fitness' to describe an individual's own fitness plus their effect on the fitness of any relative. The biologist J.B.S. Haldane once quipped: 'Would I lay down my life to save my brother? No, but I would to save two brothers or eight cousins.' The reasoning behind Haldane's calculation is that you only share 50 per cent of your genes with a brother, and 12.5 per cent with a cousin, so you would have to save enough relatives to at least break even.

Mental modules

Cosmides and Tooby (1987) took the argument a step further. They proposed that human behaviour was not directly related to genes, but that underlying psychological mechanisms or 'mental modules' are. These genetically determined modules evolved at some time in our ancestral past in response to the selective pressures operating at that time. Mental modules evolved in the same way that complex physical structures (such as the eye) evolved. This 'ancestral past' of behavioural evolution is called the 'environmental of evolutionary adaptation' (EEA), which, in terms of human evolution, occurred some 35,000 to 3 million years ago. This approach to understanding human behaviour has been called 'evolutionary psychology' – the view that the way to understand a particular behaviour is to understand what natural selection designed it to do.

One example of this approach is the rank theory of depression, which proposes that depression is an adaptive response to losing rank in a status conflict (see p. 710). Loss triggers a 'yielding sub-routine'. The response is adaptive because it helps the individual adjust to the fact that they have lost and must now adopt a subordinate position in the dominance hierarchy. It also shows the winner that they have really won and should cease conflict with no further damage to the loser. In modern humans, when this mental module is activated in situations of loss, the response may not be adaptive, but this evolutionary explanation can help us understand the 'ultimate' cause of the behaviour, i.e. the underlying reason for the response as distinct from the 'proximate' cause (which is loss).

Evaluation
the evolutionary approach

- *Reductionist and determinist* – In the same way that physiological explanations might be regarded as oversimplification, evolutionary explanations can be accused of the same thing. They suggest that complex behaviours have a single guiding principle – adaptiveness. Such explanations are also determinist because they propose that behaviour is genetically determined by past environments and that current behaviours are not subject to free will.

- *Difficult to falsify* – The concept of adaptiveness can be applied to many behaviours and is difficult to prove or disprove. Popper (see p. 863) argued that it should be possible to disprove any explanation, otherwise we have no way of establishing the validity of the explanation. There is some experimental evidence to support the process of natural selection, such as Kettlewell's (1955) study of how moths adapted to the new post-industrial environment in England. Within a short space of time, a species that had been light-coloured became dark in coloration presumably because they were less likely to be eaten on trees blackened by smoke from the new industries. However, this is a natural experiment and thus causal conclusions are not justified.

- *Based on research with non-human animals* – Darwinians and sociobiologists present a range of examples from the animal world to support their argument, though it is difficult to see the similarity between, for example, wasp society and human society. It is also worth noting that they offer relatively few examples of mammal behaviour to support their theory. Human behaviour is affected by many other factors, such as emotion and thought.

- *Has human evolution stopped?* – If mental modules were as rigidly defined as evolutionary psychologists claim, then humans would be in dire straits, as it suggests that we no longer adapt to changing environmental conditions. In fact, many scientists believe that humans are continuing to evolve physically and psychologically and the rate of human evolution has been dramatically faster than for any of our close relatives (see Wills 1999).

- *Advantages of the evolutionary approach* – One important strength of this approach is that it considers ultimate rather than proximate causes, and thus may lead to more valid ways of treating apparently maladaptive behaviours by understanding their adaptive significance. For example, evolutionary psychiatrists propose that the way to treat depression is to understand the ultimate problem (the individual's yielding behaviour), rather than focus on the proximate problem (the feeling of being depressed).

ACTIVITY

Explaining our behaviour in evolutionary terms

Try to use the evolutionary approach to explain some aspect of human behaviour. For example, you might have observed that newborn babies have a very strong grip. If they ever get hold of your hair, you certainly know about it. This gripping behaviour might well have had some advantage when mothers carried young animals around. Those who managed to hold on to her body hair were more likely to survive than those who did not manage to.

What about our anxiety/fear responses, or our delight in dancing, or our pleasure in good food? How might the evolutionary approach attempt to explain why older men marry younger women more often than older women marry younger men? Indeed, could the evolutionary approach explain why people are more disapproving of the latter kind of relationships?

METHODOLOGY USED BY THE EVOLUTIONARY APPROACH

Demonstrating genetic causes

The basis of any evolutionary argument is that the target behaviour is inherited. The process of natural selection (and sexual selection and kin selection) applies only to behaviours that have a genetic basis. Therefore, one way to investigate such explanations is to demonstrate whether or not the behaviour has a genetic cause. The most common way to demonstrate genetic cause is through the use of kinship studies – to look at twins, adopted children and their biological and non-biological relatives, or simply to study related individuals. For example, the genetic basis of IQ has been investigated by comparing the IQs of identical twins (it should be the same even when reared apart).

One can also compare identical and non-identical twins. Identical twins should have a greater concordance for any behaviour than non-identical twins (who share only 50 per cent of their genes). Studies have also been done of adopted children, comparing their IQs with those of biological parents and adopted parents and/or siblings. Finally, research has considered whether there is increasing similarity in IQ the more closely related two individuals are (for example, siblings share 25 per cent of their genes, parents and children share 50 per cent of their genes).

'Gene mapping' is a different approach to studying genetic causes. Analysis of chromosomes from different individuals allows researchers to discover the genes certain individuals have in common. So, if one looked at the chromosomes from highly intelligent children and compared these with the genes of less intelligent children, one might discover whether certain genes were present in one group rather than another.

Experiments

As described earlier, it is possible to conduct natural experiments, utilizing conditions where environmental conditions vary naturally, such as degree of relatedness (the independent variable) to observe the effect that this has on characteristics that may be inherited, such as IQ (the dependent variable). There have also been attempts to conduct field experiments to test the predictions of evolutionary theory, though these invariably involve non-human animals. For example, Andersson (1982) cut the tails of male widow birds and replaced them with tails of varying lengths to see which birds were preferred by females – the females

preferred those with longer tails, thus supporting the hypothesis that females prefer males with exaggerated characteristics (see Unit 23, p. 702).

Observations and surveys

It is possible to investigate human behaviour using observational methods. For example, one study by Dunbar (1995) investigated the prediction arising from evolutionary theory that women should seek men with resources and advertise their attractiveness, and vice versa for men. An analysis of 'lonely hearts' advertisements supported this hypothesis (see Unit 10, p. 310). Human behaviour can also be investigated using surveys – asking people about their preferences or behaviour. Buss (1999) conducted a survey of men and women in 37 different cultures, again finding that the predictions arising from evolutionary theory were supported (see Unit 23, p. 702).

Cross-cultural studies

Buss' study is an example of another method or technique used to investigate evolutionary explanations – cross-cultural studies. The human behaviours that have evolved through selective pressure should be the same all over the world. Therefore, if we study people in different cultures, we should not find differences. Such research has been used to support, for example, attachment theory – parents and infants in different cultures were studied and it was found that attachment behaviours were relatively similar all over the world which suggests that this is an innate and adaptive behaviour (Van Ijzendoorn and Kroonenberg 1988).

Evaluation
methodology used by the evolutionary approach

- **Concordance studies do not demonstrate cause-and-effect relationships** – Such studies are natural experiments where the independent variable is genetic closeness and the dependent variable is the target behaviour. As participants have not been randomly allocated to conditions, we cannot conclude that the IV caused the DV. There may be other factors to explain similarity, such as the fact that parents have an influence on an offspring's environment (passive gene–environment interactions) so that genes have only indirectly affected behaviour.

- **Experiments are reductionist** – When operationalizing independent and dependent variables, complex behaviours are reduced to something simpler. This means that the behaviours studied may not truly represent complex natural

behaviours and thus the findings from experimental studies cannot be generalized to the real world.

- **Observational studies and surveys are subject to bias** – Observational studies and surveys enable researchers to collect rich data, but are subject to problems such as 'social desirability bias' (the tendency of interviewees to provide answers which put them in a good light), 'interviewer bias' (to provide answers they think the interviewer wishes to hear) or 'observer bias' (observations are affected by expectations).

- **Cross-cultural research involves the use of an imposed etic** – A questionnaire or psychological test or procedure that is developed in one culture is likely to have a different meaning when used in another culture. Therefore, the behaviours measured in different cultures are not comparable and may in fact be meaningless. The use of such techniques is called an 'imposed etic' (see p. 824).

Check your understanding of the evolutionary approach by answering these questions from memory. You can check your answers by looking back through Topic 2.

1 What is the difference between natural selection and sexual selection?
2 What are 'selective pressures'?
3 In what way is a gene 'selfish'?
4 Explain what the EEA is.
5 Explain **one** strength of evolutionary explanations.

REVISION SUMMARY

Having covered this topic you should be able to:

✔ describe and evaluate the key concepts of the evolutionary approach

✔ describe and evaluate the key methods used by the evolutionary approach.

Topic 3 >> The psychodynamic approach

When people are asked to name the most famous figure in the history of psychology, they usually come up with the name of Sigmund Freud. Freud's approach to understanding human behaviour, known as 'psychoanalysis', has had a profound effect within psychology, yet his approach is one of many that share some common assumptions, whilst differing fundamentally in others. Contemporaries of Freud, such as Carl Jung and Alfred Adler, despite being inspired by Freudian theory, emphasized different issues in human development and experience. All of these theories are described as 'psychodynamic' because of their emphasis on the factors that *motivate* behaviour, i.e. the 'dynamics' of behaviour.

THE PSYCHODYNAMIC METAPHOR

Freud's ideas about the mind have been likened to an iceberg with the area above water being the conscious mind and the part under the water the unconscious mind (see Fig. 29.1). In this image, the id lurks below the surface of conscious awareness and cannot be seen (i.e. we are not aware of its influence). As with an iceberg, the majority of the mass of the mind (and hence its greatest potential influence) is under the surface. This analogy should not be overworked, but it does illustrate the relationship between consciousness and Freud's three aspects of the mind.

Another metaphor used to describe the psychoanalytic explanation of how the mind works is that of a dramatic conflict between different forces struggling for control. The best-known example of this is Freud's account of the Oedipal conflict (see Unit 19, p. 588).

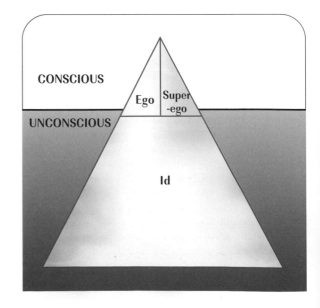

Figure 29.1 >> *The iceberg representation of the human mind*

KEY CONCEPTS OF THE PSYCHODYNAMIC APPROACH

The structure of the mind

Freud believed that the human mind had both conscious and unconscious areas. The unconscious part of the mind was seen as being dominated by the 'id', a primitive part of the personality that pursues only pleasure and gratification. The id is not concerned with social rules but only with self-gratification and is driven by the 'pleasure principle'. This disregard for the consequences of a behaviour is referred to as 'primary process thinking'. The second area is the 'ego', which dominates the conscious mind. This is the part of our mind that is in contact with the outside world, the part that considers the consequences of an action and thus carries out 'secondary process thinking'. The ego is driven by the 'reality principle'.

The third part of the mind is the 'superego'. This develops as we become more aware of the rules and conventions of society and, specifically, of our parents, around the age of 4. It contains our social conscience, and through the experience of guilt and anxiety when we do something wrong, it guides us towards socially acceptable behaviour. According to Freud, the ego and the superego dwell largely in the conscious mind, while the id is in the unconscious area of our mind.

Drives and ego defences

According to Freud, we have two drives or instincts: sex and aggression. Everything we do is motivated by one of these two drives.

- *Sex*, also called 'Eros' or the 'life force', represents our drive to live, prosper and produce offspring.
- *Aggression*, also called 'Thanatos' or the 'death force', represents our need to stay alive and stave off threats to our existence, our power, and our prosperity.

When the sexual instinct is high, the id demands gratification and determines to carry out behaviours that will result in sexual (or sensual) gratification. In most civilized societies, however, sexual gratification is not something that can be achieved without a consideration of social morality. The superego may, therefore, *oppose* gratification with the result that the ego is caught between two conflicting demands: the id demands immediate gratification, while the superego demands conformity to the moral conventions of the society. The ego struggles to maintain a balance between these conflicting demands, and is helped by ego defences. Such defences deal with the anxiety created by conflict. For example, 'repression' places anxieties into the unconscious, while 'regression' deals with anxiety by returning to an earlier, safer stage of development. Other ego defences are described in Unit 4 on p. 131 and in Unit 19 on p. 589.

Ego defences are not necessarily unhealthy – in fact, the lack of such defences may lead to problems in life. However, we sometimes employ the defences at the wrong time or overuse them, which can be equally destructive.

Psychosexual developmental stages

Another of the key aspects of Freud's theory is the claim that people move through a series of developmental stages (described in Table 19.1 on p. 590). Each of the stages is characterized by a focus on a different region of the body. Freud believed that an individual's 'libido' or sexual drive is fixated on a part of the body during particular periods of a child's life. The 'choice' of body region is related to phases of development; the mouth is important in the early months, the anal region becomes important during toilet training, and the genitals are an obvious focus during gender identity development.

If we do not receive the right amount of gratification, receiving either too much or too little, we become 'fixated' in a particular stage – that is, we continue to have the same demand for gratification that we had at that stage throughout the rest of our life. This condition is thought to produce a variety of 'neurotic behaviours' depending on the type of fixation. Freud believed that to deal with fixation at any particular stage (the 'fixation point'), we must go back, or 'regress', to that stage and resolve the issues that led to the fixation.

Personality types

Such fixations also lead to characteristic adult 'personality types':

- The *oral receptive character* has been overgratified during the oral stage, leading to a preoccupation with oral activities. This type of personality may have a stronger tendency to smoke, drink alcohol, overeat or bite their nails. In terms of personality, these individuals may become overly dependent upon others, gullible and perpetual followers.
- The *oral aggressive* character has been undergratified during the oral stage and, like the oral receptive character, has a preoccupation with oral activities, but tends to be pessimistic and aggressive.
- The *anal expulsive character* has been overgratified during the anal stage, and tends to be messy and disorganized.
- The *anal retentive character* has been undergratified during the anal stage, resulting in an obsession with cleanliness, perfection, and control.
- A *fixation during the phallic stage* could result in sexual deviancies (both overindulging and avoidance), and weak or confused sexual identity.

- *The theory of psychoanalysis lacks empirical support* – This is largely because the concepts are not falsifiable (i.e. cannot be demonstrated to be wrong – they can be made to fit most sets of data). There is, however, support for some of the concepts, such as repression, and a limited amount of support for personality types. There has also been support for the importance of early childhood experiences in later development; for example, research by Hazan and Shaver (1987) showed a link between secure attachment in childhood and later romantic experiences.

- *Determinist and reductionist* – The objection to determinist accounts is that they suggest that individuals have no ability to be self-determining. Reductionism tends to oversimplify complex behaviours, which may prevent us from investigating more complex and possibly more useful explanations, e.g. considering social and cultural influences. On the other hand, reductionist

explanations may help us understand certain basic processes in behaviour.

- *Overemphasizes sexual influences* – Such factors may have been important in nineteenth-century society, but are less applicable today. Subsequent psychodynamic theories (such as Erikson's) gave more weight to social influences.

- *Recognition of influences of which we are not aware* – Psychoanalysis made a large contribution to our understanding of unconscious motivations and the importance of childhood experiences in adult behaviour.

- *Accounts for rationality and irrationality* – Jarvis (2000) identifies the most significant feature of Freudian theory as the notion that the human personality has more than one aspect: '… we reveal this when we say things like "part of me wants to do it, but part of me is afraid to…".' Freud's introduction of the unconscious permits us to explain how someone can be both rational and irrational, and this can account for many aspects of behaviour, such as the fact that people predict they will behave in one way and actually do something quite different.

METHODOLOGY USED BY THE PSYCHODYNAMIC APPROACH

Case studies

Freud supported his theory of personality by providing case histories of patients and indicating how the patient's behaviour and experience could be explained using the concepts of psychoanalysis. In the same way, we can support any psychoanalytic explanation of behaviour using interviews with individuals to understand their motives more clearly and demonstrate the validity of the explanation. Freud used several techniques to enable unconscious thoughts to be revealed, such as free association and dream analysis. See p. 807 for a description of further techniques.

- *Free association* – A client is asked to lie on a couch with the therapist out of sight, and to allow the free flow of feelings, thoughts and images. The client expresses these without any censorship while the therapist listens objectively. The therapist may interrupt from time to time to ask for more elaboration or ask the client to comment on the

personal significance of any associations. Associations should arise from, and therefore reflect, internal dynamic conflicts.

- *Dream analysis* – Since Freud believed that our unconscious thoughts are expressed uncensored in our dreams, it follows that discussions of dream content may be a way to access the unconscious mind. However, in dreams the true meaning (the actual or 'latent' content) is disguised in order to protect the conscious mind and so the therapist has to attempt to understand the symbolic form ('manifest' content) of the dream.

Experiments

In Unit 19, we reviewed several experiments that have investigated Freud's explanations, such as those on repression and on oral personalities. Freud endorsed the notion of a scientific approach and thus the use of experiments is in keeping with this approach.

Evaluation
methodology used by the psychodynamic approach

Some of the strengths and weaknesses of the experimental method are reviewed in the next topic, so we will focus on case studies here.

- *Case studies provide rich data and are more 'true to life'* – Conducting a case study permits an investigator to ask far-ranging questions during the course of more than one interview. This means that the interviewer can adjust the questions in response to previous answers.

continued on next page

Evaluation continued
methodology used by the psychodynamic approach

The answers provide a complex picture of human behaviour and experience which may better represent real life as compared to more reductionist experimental methods of research.

● *Interviewer's expectations may affect participant's recollections* – An interviewer may (unconsciously) pursue lines of enquiry based on their own expectations, leading a participant to provide certain answers. Face-to-face interviews may also place more pressure on interviewees to provide socially desirable answers or to try to

please the interviewer by giving the answers they want. In fact Freud's patients did report that they didn't always believe his interpretations but went along with them because *he* believed in them so earnestly (Storr 1989).

● *Hard to generalize from small samples* – Case studies are likely to draw on the unique experiences of only a few individuals because they are concerned with unusual behaviours (and therefore ones that are less usually encountered) and/or because of the in-depth nature of the method. It is difficult to make generalizations about other people on the basis of such particular cases, each with a unique set of circumstances.

ACTIVITY

Explaining our behaviour in psychodynamic terms

Consider the following psychoanalytic explanation of behaviour. Sarah is painfully shy and has a severe stutter. Inevitably, this means that she avoids social occasions because of the anxiety that is aroused when she even thinks of talking to a few people. She read a psychoanalytic account of the causes of stuttering that suggests that it arises in the anal stage of development (Freud 1901). According to Freud, adult stuttering develops in childhood as a result of a conflict between the wish to defecate symbolically on one's parents (and authority figures generally) by using hostile words, and a simultaneous fear of retaliation that causes the stutterer to hold the

fecal-orientated words inside. Other psychoanalysts have proposed a more general view that stuttering could be a conflict developed at the same time as speech is developing, around the age of 2. A child experiences a desire to be independent while at the same time wishing to remain completely dependent. Stuttering develops as a conflict between wanting to talk (and grow up) and wanting not to talk (and thus remain a baby) (Knapp 1997).

How might you investigate whether either explanation is valid? *Do not* try to cure Sarah (though this may be one result of your investigation) – your task is to try to decide if this explanation is right.

CHECK YOUR UNDERSTANDING

Check your understanding of the psychodynamic approach by answering these questions from memory. You can check your answers by looking back through Topic 3.

1 Briefly provide a short précis of Freud's structure of the personality.

2 According to Freud, what forces motivate our behaviour?

3 List the stages of psychosexual development.

4 What happens if an individual is overgratified during any of these stages?

5 Identify and explain **one** criticism that can be made of psychodynamic explanations.

Topic 4 >> The behavioural approach

Behaviourism was one of the great intellectual movements of the twentieth century and it continues to have a far-reaching effect on the way that we see ourselves and the ways that we deal with people.

The term 'behaviourism' was first used by John B. Watson in a paper written in 1913, in which he outlined a plan for the conduct of psychology that was to dominate the subject for the next 50 years.

THE BEHAVIOURAL METAPHOR

The behaviourists believed that we can understand an animal or a person by thinking of it as a machine, and looking at what goes into the machine or 'black box' ('stimulus' or 'inputs') and measuring what comes out ('responses' or 'outputs'). They are only concerned with the behaviours that we can observe rather than any activity going on inside the machine. In this view, animals and people respond in the same way and are like puppets who respond to stimuli with no more control than one has over a reflex action such as a knee jerk. Put like this, the approach sounds harsh and simplistic, but it has led to a number of effective applications, such as therapies for treating mental disorders, classroom management techniques and teaching strategies.

KEY CONCEPTS OF THE BEHAVIOURAL APPROACH

Learning theory

The basic principles of learning theory are described in Unit 21. A brief reminder of the essential concepts is provided below.

Classical conditioning

Classical conditioning describes how we learn through 'association'; the association of two things (one 'old' and one 'new') that occur together means that the new stimulus acquires the properties of the old one. The 'old' stimulus, such as the smell of bacon frying, produces a reflex response of salivation. The response is produced with no thought, nor can it be controlled: it is automatic. If a 'new' stimulus occurs at the same time as the 'old' one on a number of occasions, an association between the two will be formed. For example, if every time bacon is fried, you hear certain sizzling sounds (the sounds of bacon frying), these two stimuli become associated so that the 'neutral stimulus' (the sound) takes on the properties of the 'unconditioned stimulus' (the smell). The neutral stimulus now becomes a 'conditioned stimulus' and will produce the 'unconditioned response' (the salivation) if heard at another time when there is no bacon being fried. The sound is now a conditioned stimulus.

A classic study by Watson and Rayner (1920) illustrates how humans can acquire emotional responses through conditioning (see Unit 4, p. 134, the case of 'Little Albert').

Operant conditioning

Operant conditioning describes how we learn through reinforcement. The likelihood that a behaviour is repeated is increased or decreased through experience. Again, this change of behaviour is produced without thought or control. An animal operates in its environment. From time to time, a particular behaviour results in a reward – for example, by biting a piece of fruit, hunger is satisfied and it is tasty. The fact that this is rewarding means the behaviour is likely to be repeated. Each time the same action is repeated and rewarded, the behaviour becomes increasingly likely. If, however, you bite into a piece of fruit that tastes nasty, this will decrease the probability of repetition. Through reward and punishment, behaviours are learned or unlearned (behaviours are stamped in or out). Skinner (1938) described this as the ABC of behaviour:

Antecedent → Behaviour → Consequence

It is the *consequences* of any particular behaviour that determine the likelihood that it will be repeated.

Rewards are also called 'reinforcers'. Positive reinforcement occurs when the reward is pleasant. Negative reinforcement is also pleasant, but as a consequence of escaping from something that was unpleasant! The frequency of rewards affects the success of conditioning. Such 'schedules of reinforcement' include partial and continuous schedules each of which is effective in particular circumstances. For example, continuous reinforcement schedules (CRF) induce rapid initial learning and rapid extinction, whereas the opposite is true of partial reinforcement schedules (see p. 661 for further detail).

Shaping

It is difficult to see how complex behaviours might be learned through this process, but the fact is that animal trainers do use the principles of operant conditioning to teach complex activities. For example, Skinner was able to demonstrate that he could train pigeons how to operate the guidance system of missiles. He achieved this using the process of 'shaping'. The animal is initially rewarded for quite simple behaviours, but gradually the rewards are reserved for behaviours that are closer and closer to the target behaviour.

Generalization, discrimination and extinction

Things that are learned may be generalized to other, similar situations. This applies to both classical conditioning and operant conditioning. For example, having learned a conditioned response to the sound of frying, one might salivate to all similar sounds. However, if subsequent experience produces no further association (sound of frying but no smell of bacon), then the learned response will become extinguished *unless* that special sizzling sound continues to be linked to the smell of bacon whereas other frying sounds have no associated smell. In this case one learns to *discriminate* between different stimuli.

SOCIAL LEARNING THEORY

Direct and indirect reinforcement

Bandura (1965) recognized that learning theory could only explain a limited amount of what we learn because classical and operant conditioning rely on *direct experience*. Animals also learn *indirectly* by observing the behaviours of others and imitating it. Social learning theorists emphasize that for behaviour to be imitated, it must be seen to be rewarding in some way, i.e. it is *reinforced*. The term 'vicarious reinforcement' describes how we experience reinforcement indirectly. The likelihood of a person imitating another person's behaviour is determined by:

- their previous experiences of that behaviour – both their own and that of others
- the degree to which their own similar behaviour was successful in the past
- the current likelihood of whether this behaviour will be rewarded or punished.

This means that memory is involved, a concept that was alien to learning theorists who believed that there was no need to look further than what goes into the machine and what comes out. Social learning theory is sometimes referred to as 'neo-behaviourism' because it is a kind of 'new behaviourism' – one that includes mental concepts. According to social learning theory, we observe others and store representations of behaviour. If a behaviour is imitated, then it may or may not receive *direct* reinforcement. This determines the extent to which the behaviour becomes part of an individual's repertoire.

Reciprocal determinism

This account of social learning (learning from other people) is determinist – your current behaviour is a product of past reinforcement experience. Bandura introduced the concept of 'reciprocal determinism' to express how individuals do exert some control over their development. As the individual acts, this changes the environment, thus affecting subsequent behaviour. For example, if you watch your mother baking a cake and then start to imitate her, this modifies her behaviour and subsequently affects you. Individuals are also capable of reinforcing themselves. They are capable of making their own choices and this ultimately affects what they imitate.

Self-efficacy

Bandura (1977) also claimed that a person may influence their reinforcement experiences as a consequence of 'self-efficacy' – their sense of their own effectiveness (or efficacy) which influences what they ultimately achieve. If you believe that you cannot jump over a two-metre hurdle, this will affect the way you approach the task and thus what you achieve. Your sense of self-efficacy is an important personality trait. It is derived from both direct and indirect experience. In the case of direct experience, your own successes and failures alter future expectations of success. You may also learn indirectly by watching others' successes and failures and applying this knowledge to your self-expectations.

Evaluation
the behavioural approach

- *Learning theory is based on research with non-human animals and is reductionist* – Learning theory suggests that all behaviour can be reduced to stimulus–response units. This may be true for the behaviour of non-human animals and learning theory may account for some complex behaviours. However, it cannot provide a complete explanation of human behaviour, which often has multiple influences, such as emotion and thought. Social learning theory provides a richer explanation of behaviour, but still excludes influences such as emotion.

- *Research is conducted in contrived laboratory environments* – As a result, such research is not seen as representing the complexities of real life. Laboratory-based studies also focus on short-term effects and may not demonstrate how longer-term behaviours are learned.

- *Learning theory is determinist and suggests that people have no free will* – This has implications for moral responsibility and self-

responsibility in general (this is discussed on p. 851). Learning theory is also focused on *environmental determinism* suggesting that only nurture and not nature can explain the development of behaviour. This assumption ignores the fact that learning itself is inherited and varies from species to species. For example, there is evidence that animals are born with a predisposition to learn certain fears more rapidly (see 'biological preparedness' on p. 659).

- *Learning theory can explain individual differences* – On the positive side, environmental determinism can explain why people are different (due to different reinforcement experiences).

- *It is a scientific approach* – Reductionism can also be a strength because it permits variables to be operationalized and experiments conducted to test explanations. Broadbent (1961) argued that behaviourism was the best approach for rational advance in psychology.

- *Social learning theory includes social influences* – As a result, it is able to explain the influence of cultural as well as individual differences.

ACTIVITY

Explaining our behaviour in behavioural terms

Behaviourists attempt to explain all behaviour in terms of association, reinforcement and punishment. We could reasonably explain how we learn to ride a bicycle in terms of trial and error: we get on a bike and try a range of activities, persisting with those that work and excluding those that don't. Can we use this type of explanation for a range of other behaviours?

Try and give a behavioural explanation for the following:

1 learning to swim
2 solving a mathematical problem
3 painting a picture
4 chatting up a boyfriend or girlfriend
5 becoming hooked on computer games.

METHODOLOGY USED BY THE BEHAVIOURAL APPROACH

Laboratory experiments

Behaviourists use laboratory experiments as the method to investigate their explanations. This fits with their view that behaviour can be reduced to simple units. Experimental design is covered as part of your AS-level studies (see Unit 6). It involves identifying one or more independent variables (the variables that the experimenter will manipulate) and dependent variable(s) (the behaviours to be measured). For example, if one wished to investigate whether helping behaviour was caused by reinforcement, the independent variable would be reinforcement and the dependent variable would be helping behaviour. The next step would be to

'operationalize' these variables. For example, reinforcement could be operationalized as spoken praise or a smile or some physical reward. Helping behaviour could be operationalized in terms of how much litter some school children collected (with or without reward).

A hypothesis could then be written based on these variables and a method decided on to test the hypothesis (such as repeated measures or independent groups). It might also be necessary to identify and control any possible extraneous variables. Other design decisions include what sampling technique to use, how to deal with any ethical issues and how to analyse the data.

A2 Perspectives

Research with non-human animals

Behaviourists argue that all animals have a 'common origin', as demonstrated by evolutionary theory, and so different species are seen to differ only in terms of quantity. They all consist of the same building blocks but 'higher animals' have more of these. An essential belief within behaviourism is the fact that all organisms learn and behave in essentially the same way, and so the processes of learning and conditioning must be the same in all species. These means that one is justified in investigating human behaviour by studying simpler species in order to understand more about these processes in a more basic form.

Evaluation
methodology used by the behavioural approach

- **The scientific, experimental approach is reductionist** – In order to conduct experiments one needs to operationalize behaviours and this results in studying something that may be different to the thing we were originally interested in. The consequence of this is that psychologists may reach false conclusions. In other words, experiments lack 'external validity' and the findings may not generalize to situations and/or participants outside the experiment.

- **Experiments also lack internal validity** – Experimental findings may lack validity because the participants' behaviour was affected by the experimenter's expectations (experimental bias) or demand characteristics in the experiment. There also may be confounding variables that were not controlled.

- **There are strengths to the experimental approach** – The experimental method is designed to be objective and controlled so that we can make statements about cause-and-effect relationships, which is not possible when using other methods of research. Experiments can also be replicated as a way of verifying the findings.

- **Studies of non-human animal behaviour may not generalize to human behaviour** – Even though all animals are composed of the same materials (e.g. nervous systems), the way these systems behave is quite different. Complex systems may not behave predictably, i.e. as a simple summation of the constituent parts. New properties emerge in complex systems such that the system as a whole has properties that do not belong to the parts.

- **Ethical issues with human participants** – Behavioural experiments involve reinforcing target behaviours in participants, thus leading to the establishment of new future behaviours. One of the guiding principles in research ethics is that participants should leave a study in the same condition as when they started, but this is not the case if new behaviours have been reinforced.

CHECK YOUR UNDERSTANDING

Check your understanding of the behavioural approach by answering these questions from memory. You can check your answers by looking back through Topic 4.

1 Describe **one** key assumption of behaviourism.

2 Explain how classical and operant conditioning differ.

3 What is 'shaping'?

4 Write an outline of social learning theory in 100 words.

5 Identify and explain **two** criticisms of laboratory experiments.

REVISION SUMMARY

Having covered this topic you should be able to:

✓ describe and evaluate the key concepts of the behavioural approach

✓ describe and evaluate the key methods used by the behavioural approach.

Topic 5 >> The cognitive approach

The cognitive approach is probably the dominant approach in modern psychology. It looks at how mental processes affect our behaviour, processes such as perception, memory, problem-solving and language. The approach became popular in psychology departments once the problems with the behavioural approach could not be ignored any longer. The behaviourists viewed the mind of people as a 'black box', studying what went into the box (stimuli) and what came out (responses), but not paying attention to what went on inside. As we all know, a lot goes on inside our heads and much of our behaviour can be affected by mental events. As such, the cognitive approach is really neo-behavioural, or to put it in other words, is a reworking of the ideas of Watson and Skinner, but with a twist. Cognitive psychology as an approach views people as being like machines although acknowledging that the machinery is very complicated.

THE COGNITIVE METAPHOR

Cognitive psychologists explain behaviour in terms of how the mind operates, and the working of the mind is seen as being similar to a machine or computer. The approach looks at the inputs (the stimuli) to the machine and the outputs (what it does), as well as the various processes that occur between input and output. It views these processes as mechanistic.

The metaphor used by the cognitive approach has changed with the development of machine technology. In the 1950s and 60s, the information-processing models tried to model human thought processes on a telephone exchange (e.g. Broadbent 1958). The arrival of the microchip made this metaphor redundant and cognitive psychologists now model the human mind on the most complex technology available to date – the computer. Increasingly advanced computers have moved from using parallel processing to using interconnected networks. An interesting feature of such networks is that their behaviour cannot be simply predicted from the behaviour of the individual parts and thus such networks can be seen as examples of 'holism'.

> ### ACTIVITY
>
> ## Humans and computers
>
> But what are the similarities and differences between people and computers? Make a list of some cognitive activities and consider how they are similar and different in people and computers. For example, you might think about how a person's culture or mood could affect their ability to think or remember.

KEY CONCEPTS OF THE COGNITIVE APPROACH

Mental and perceptual set

Problem-solving

Behaviourists focused on trial-and-error learning as a way to explain problem-solving. However, 'Gestalt psychologists' (in the first half of the 20th century) recognized that there was more to problem-solving than this. They suggested that problem-solving requires 'structural understanding', the ability to understand how all the parts of the problem fit together to meet the goal. A key requirement is the reorganization of the different elements of the problem in such a way that the problem can be solved. However, people often get stuck when they try to solve problems because they cannot change their problem-solving or 'mental set' (also called 'functional fixedness'). Once given a clue, most people solve the problem quite quickly because they break free of their usual way of thinking about it.

Perception

The concept of 'perceptual set' is similar to mental set. According to constructivist theories, successful perception involves combining sensory information with knowledge based on previous experience. This 'intelligent perception' applies, for example, to how you learn to see depth as well as how you interpret the words you read (knowing that 'read' is an English word). We have expectations about what we are likely to encounter and this sometimes leads us to make mistakes. When shown the symbols TAI3LE, we tend to read this as 'table' because the digits are interpreted as letters because of expectations created by the context, a perceptual set.

Schema, stereotypes and social representations

Memory

Bartlett's theory of reconstructive memory differed from later information-processing models (e.g. the multi-store model) because it incorporated the influence of expectations or 'schemas' on memory. Schemas are knowledge packages which are built through experience with the world and which also embody cultural expectations. Bartlett's (1932) famous 'War of the Ghosts' research showed participant's recall of unfamiliar information is affected by cultural knowledge.

Other research has explored the effects of stereotypes on memory. Stereotypes are 'mental short cuts' that help us process information more quickly but which also lead to errors and prejudices. For example, Cohen (1981) showed how people recalled different information about a woman in a video depending on whether they were told beforehand that the woman was a librarian or a waitress. Such labels conjure up expectations about a person and influence what we 'see' and later recall. People tend to remember information that is consistent with stereotypes.

Language

Stereotypes are often communicated through the words we use. For example, using the term 'chairperson' instead of 'chairman' affects the stereotypes we have about a person in that position. It is questionable as to whether language merely shapes our thinking or actually *determines* it, e.g. whether people who speak in different languages actually think in different ways because of the language they use. There is evidence to suggest there are some differences. For example, the Chinese have fewer words for numbers, which may mean that they can count more quickly (see Unit 17 for a discussion of language and thought).

Thinking may affect language as well as language affecting thinking. Learning new concepts enables the learner to acquire new vocabularies because they become capable of making the finer discriminations necessary (thought affects language). The classic example is referred to as the 'Great Eskimo Vocabulary Hoax' – the claim that Inuit people (Eskimos) have a large vocabulary of words for snow which thus enables them to make finer distinctions (language affects thought). However, the same could be argued in reverse – it is their wider experience of snow which leads them to develop and be able to use all these words (thought affects language). In any case, Pinker (1994) claims there are as many words for snow in English (see p. 521 for a further discussion).

Social cognition

Social cognition refers to the area of social psychology that is concerned with how people think about other people or groups of people. This field shares many similarities with cognitive psychology (e.g. studying stereotyping), but there is an assumption that the way in which we think about other people (i.e. our *social* world) differs in important ways to the way in which we think about the physical world. One area of interest is the attribution of causality – seeking explanations for our own behaviour and the behaviour of others. Different theorists have attempted to unravel the rules that we use to make causal attributions about each other's behaviour. This is not as clear cut as it might at first appear, as much of our attributional thinking is biased, e.g. the 'self-serving bias' or the 'fundamental attribution bias' (see Unit 9, p. 278).

In recent years, social psychology has moved away from the laboratory to an exploration of the truly *social* aspects of human behaviour. 'Social representations theory' is our attempt to discover how common-sense representations of the world become so widely spread and shared by most members of a culture. Social representations are similar to schemas, but operate at a more collective level and can be used, for example, to explain patterns of health and illness (see p. 283).

Maladaptive thinking

Cognitive–behavioural therapies suggest that psychological problems arise because individuals have developed maladaptive ways of thinking. The problem only exists in the way that a person thinks about their problem; in other psychological models, the problem is an entity in itself. In order to treat such disorders, therefore, clients need to be challenged about their maladaptive and irrational thoughts. Ellis (1962) called this 'faulty thinking' and developed rational emotive behaviour therapy (REBT) as a way to help people 'cure' themselves. Beck (1963) proposed that depression occurred as a consequence of three kinds of negative thoughts: views about oneself, about the world and about the future (the cognitive triad).

Evaluation
the cognitive approach

- *Lack of evidence for abstract concepts such as memory* – It is clear that we are able to record information, store it and recall it at a later date, but there is no evidence that we have a 'thing' called a memory. The same criticisms apply to all cognitive concepts – they may be 'reifications', i.e. attempts to make abstract concepts into a thing. The danger is that the 'thing' becomes real and prevents a truer understanding of the underlying processes

(as is the case with Freud's concepts of the 'id', 'ego' and so on).

- *It is a scientific approach* – Despite the fact that many of the concepts of cognitive psychology are abstract and unobservable, the approach lends itself to testable hypotheses. This scientific approach is both a strength and a limitation. It is a strength because it permits theories to be tested, falsified and adapted in response to new findings. It is limited insofar as it reduces behaviour to something quite different to real life and thus the findings cannot always be generalized.

continued on next page

Evaluation continued
the cognitive approach

● *Social and cultural factors often ignored* – Some cognitive psychologists have shown the importance of these variables (e.g. Bartlett and the social cognition approach), but they do not form part of the general debate in cognitive psychology. A recent review of mainstream British psychology journals (Banyard and Hunt 2000) found that very few articles considered issues of culture, social class or sexual orientation. This is not to say that these variables will affect all research issues in cognitive psychology, but it is not reasonable to assume they will affect none of them.

● *Is the brain like a computer?* – If the brain can be legitimately conceived of as a computer, then it should be possible eventually to build a computer that does what a human brain can do. Turing (1950) suggested that one could test this by asking a person to communicate with two 'people' hidden from view: one a real person, the other a computer program. If the participant cannot reliably identify which is the computer and which is the person, then the computer program has passed the test and can be said to be able to think and understand like a person. Tests have shown that under certain circumstances computers can pass the 'Turing test' (Searle 1980), but it is clear that their use of rather unintelligent pattern-matching strategies in no sense amounts to understanding. Therefore, to date, the computer metaphor remains an inadequate way of modelling human cognitive processes.

METHODOLOGY USED BY THE COGNITIVE APPROACH

Research today in cognitive psychology is largely conducted using laboratory experiments. These are discussed on p. 893. In some areas of cognitive psychology, case studies of brain-damaged individuals are used to allow us to understand how the physiology of the brain relates to cognitive behaviours. For example the study of HM (Milner 1966) showed that the hippocampus was implicated in short-term memory, thus supporting the idea of separate memory stores.

More recently, imaging studies such as PET scans have been used to study brain activity. For example, Squire *et al.* (1992) used PET scans to show that blood flow in the right hippocampus was higher when participants were engaged in cued recall task rather than a word-completion task. This shows that different kinds of memory may be governed by different areas of the brain, thus tying aspects of cognitive processing to a physical state.

Evaluation
methodology used by
the cognitive approach

All the methods described here have already been evaluated in this unit. Experiments are discussed on pp. 885 and 893, case studies on pp. 888–9 and scanning techniques on p. 881.

CHECK YOUR UNDERSTANDING

Check your understanding of the cognitive approach by answering these questions from memory. You can check your answers by looking back through Topic 5.

1 What is the key assumption of the cognitive approach?

2 How does mental set affect problem-solving?

3 Define the terms 'schema' and 'stereotype'.

4 Explain the difference between a schema and a social representation.

5 Give **one** limitation of scanning techniques.

REVISION SUMMARY

Having covered this topic you should be able to:

✔ describe and evaluate the key concepts of the cognitive approach

✔ describe and evaluate the key methods used by the cognitive approach.

The Approaches question is different from all other questions set in the A-level exam. It consists of a short piece of stimulus material (a description of a behaviour) plus a set of four questions. The question parts are the same in every exam – it is only the stimulus material that varies. You might, for example, be given the following piece of stimulus material, followed by the invariable set of questions listed below:

> There are so many events that people celebrate throughout the year: Christmas, New Year, Easter, Halloween, Bonfire night and so on, as well as more personal celebrations such as birthdays and wedding anniversaries. And it's the same the world over – not always the same festivals but often ones that are very similar. It appears to be a universal phenomenon that people like to celebrate public and personal events.
>
> **(a)** Describe how **two** approaches might try to explain the universal celebration of public and personal events. (6 + 6 marks)
>
> **(b)** Assess **one** of these explanations for the universal celebration of public and personal events in terms of its strengths and limitations. (6 marks)
>
> **(c)** How would **one** of these approaches investigate the universal celebration of public and personal events? (6 marks)
>
> **(d)** Evaluate the use of this method of investigating universal celebration of public and personal events. (6 marks)

In fact, in each exam you will be given two pieces of stimulus material to select from. When answering the question parts, bear the following tips in mind:

● In all parts of the question, you must ensure that your answer is *contextualized*, i.e. relates to the stimulus material rather than being a description or evaluation of the approach or methodology in general.

● You have 40 minutes in total to answer this question, which is worth 30 marks. This means just about $7\frac{1}{2}$ minutes for every 6 marks, probably enough time to write about 150 words – this length answer will be enough for full marks *provided* that your 150 words are focused on the stimulus material.

● For part (a), select two approaches that you can elaborate, i.e. present a multi-dimensional explanation of the target behaviour. You need to do more than saying, for example, 'people might do it because they are imitating others'. Why are they imitating others? Why might they imitate this particular behaviour rather than other behaviours? And so on.

● For part (b), select one of the approaches from (a), and give at least one strength and one limitation. You may not have time to do much more than two of each because it is vital that you elaborate these criticisms, i.e. do not just give one-line comments such as 'the approach is reductionist' but explain in what way it is reductionist and why this is a strength or limitation.

● For part (c), you may continue working with the same approach as selected for part (b) or use the other of the approaches described in part (a). It might be helpful to think of your explanation in (a) as a hypothesis – write down a statement of what you believe to be true, and then try to think of some way of conducting a study that could see whether your hypothesis is true. *But* remember to choose a method of investigation that is appropriate to the approach and is plausible. You might include many different aspects of the procedures, such as how you might operationalize the IV and DV, how you might select the sample, what questions you might ask if you are conducting a questionnaire or what stimulus material you might use if it is an experiment. You might also consider how you would deal with ethical issues.

● For part (d) you should evaluate your answer to part (b). There is no requirement in this part to include both strengths and limitations, but, again, you do have to ensure that your answer is contextualized and not just a list of the general strengths and limitations of, for example, experiments or questionnaires. As with all parts of this question, your task is to *use* your knowledge of approaches and methodology in psychology to explain and investigate the behaviour identified.

Topic 1: The physiological approach

- The physiological **metaphor** is that people are **biological machines** and that bodily activity can explain behaviour and experience.

- The **central nervous system** and **autonomic nervous system** are two important components of physiological explanations. We can consider **brain organization** (e.g. laterality, left versus right brain, localization) and **brain chemistry** (**neurotransmitters** such as endorphins, serotonin and dopamine).

- Physiological accounts are **determinist** and **reductionist**. Such approaches lend themselves to **scientific research**, but they may prevent a truer understanding of behaviour and question the existence of the **mind** (the 'mind–body' problem). Physiological explanations can explain some, but not all, **individual differences** and they cannot explain **cultural differences**.

- Physiological investigations involve the use of **experiments** and **case studies of brain-damaged individuals** using techniques to record brain activity. Invasive techniques include **electrical** and **chemical stimulation**, **ablation** and **lesioning**. Non-invasive techniques include **EEG** and **ERPs**, **MRI** and **PET scans**.

- Most of such research is done with **non-human animals**, creating problems **generalizing** this to human behaviour.

Topic 2: The evolutionary approach

- The evolutionary **metaphor** is that both physical and psychological characteristics have evolved in all animals in the same way – features most fit (**adaptive to the environment**) have been passed on.

- The key concepts to explain this process are **natural selection** and **selection pressure**. **Sexual selection** and **kin selection** explain certain paradoxes such as the peacock's tail and altruism. Evolutionary psychology suggests that **mental modules** evolved during the EEA and continue to explain our behaviour.

- Evolutionary explanations are **determinist** and **reductionist**, difficult to **falsify** and **based on research with non-human animals.** On the plus side, evolutionary explanations explore **ultimate** rather than **proximate** causes, which may lead to better therapies.

- Research into the **genetic basis** of behaviour looks at similarities between **kin**. **Gene-mapping** studies are also conducted. **Field experiments** with non-human animals have been used to test evolutionary predictions.

- Concordance studies do not demonstrate **cause-and-effect relationships**. Experiments are **reductionist**. Observational studies and surveys provide **rich data** but are subject to **bias** (e.g. social desirability bias). Cross-cultural research involves the use of an **imposed etic**.

Topic 3: The psychodynamic approach

- The psychodynamic **metaphor** is that the human mind is like an iceberg with the majority of the mind below the surface of conscious activity.

- The mind is divided into **unconscious** and **conscious** areas, and into the **id**, **ego** and **superego**. The id is ruled by the **pleasure principle** whereas the ego is governed by the **reality principle**.

- The theory of psychoanalysis generally **lacks empirical support** and is **not falsifiable**. It is a determinist and **reductionist** account, and overemphasizes **sexual influences**. It does acknowledge **unconscious** motivation, the influence of **childhood** experiences and both **rational and irrational** behaviour.

- **Case studies** are one way to assess the validity of a psychoanalytic explanation, using techniques such as **free association** and **dream analysis** to access unconscious thoughts. Case studies provide **rich data** and are more '**true to life**', but suffer from effects such as **interviewer bias**.

Topic 4: The behavioural approach

- The behavioural **metaphor** is that a person is like a **black box** and we should be concerned only with what goes in and comes out (observable behaviours).

- **Learning theory** explains how new behaviours are acquired through **classical** and **operant conditioning**, through **association** and **reinforcement** respectively. **Punishment** and **schedules of reinforcement** affect learning too. **Shaping** explains how complex behaviours are acquired. Other important concepts include **generalization**, **discrimination** and **extinction**.

- Learning theory is based on research with **non-human animals** and is **reductionist**. Even social learning theory **excludes influences** such as emotion. Research is conducted in **contrived laboratory environments** focusing on short-term effects. Learning theory is an example of **environmental determinism** and largely ignores innate factors. However, learning and social learning theory can explain **individual and cultural differences**, and they are **scientific**.

- The **experimental approach** is **reductionist** so that findings may lack **external validity**. They also may lack **internal validity**, e.g. because of demand characteristics. However, experiments can be **objective** and lead to justifiable **causal conclusions**.

Topic 5: The cognitive approach

- The cognitive **metaphor** is that the working of the mind is seen as similar to a **machine or computer**, with inputs and outputs and the **mechanistic** processes that occur in between.

- **Problem-solving** behaviour can be explained in terms of **mental set** (similar to **perceptual** set). Perception is in part determined by **expectations** which may lead us to make mistakes. **Memory** is affected by **schema** (cultural knowledge) and by **stereotypes** (mental short cuts). **Language** (and the stereotypes it conveys) may determine thought or merely shape it; thinking also affects language. Social behaviour can be explained in terms of **attribution theory** and **biases**, and **social representations**, all of which involve cognitive processes. Abnormal behaviour has been explained in terms of **maladaptive thinking**.

- The **abstract concepts** used by the cognitive approach are **reifications** and cannot be demonstrated. This approach is **scientific** (both a strength and a limitation). Cognitive explanations often **ignore social** and **cultural factors**. There is no evidence to suggest that the **mind is like a computer** (the Turing test).

- Cognitive explanations are investigated using **laboratory experiments**, **case studies** of brain-damaged individuals and **imaging techniques** to relate cognitive processing to brain activity.

FURTHER RESOURCES

Glassman, W.E. (2000) *Approaches to Psychology* (3rd edn), Buckingham: Open University Press.

An account of five major approaches: biological, behaviourist, cognitive, psychodynamic and humanistic, and the assumptions, methods and theories associated with each.

Miller, G.A. (1966) *Psychology: The Science of Mental Life*, Harmondsworth: Penguin.

A classic introductory text giving an interesting account of the history of psychological ideas and with brief biographies of major figures.

Wadeley, A., Malim, T. and Birch, A. (1997) *Perspectives in Psychology*, (2nd edn), Basingstoke: Macmillan.

Covers approaches, debates, methods at a level appropriate for students.

Eysenck, M.W. (1994) *Perspectives on Psychology*, Hove, Sussex: Psychology Press.

Part of a series called 'Principles of Psychology' written for A-level students and undergraduates. Brief coverage of the major approaches plus chapters on controversies such as reductionism.

Websites

www.ryerson.ca/~glassman/approach.html

Website maintained by William Glassman, associated with his book 'Approaches to Psychology'.

www.psych.ucsb.edu/research/cep/

Centre for evolutionary psychology with a primer on evolutionary psychology and an interview with Leda Cosmides.

www.anth.ucsb.edu/projects/human/ evpsychfaq.html

Evolutionary psychology FAQs. Answers to all your questions.

www.freud.org.uk/

The Freud museum site with some background theory and useful links.

http://psych.athabascau.ca/html/Behaviorism/

A tutorial on behaviourism with questions on the text (which are checked).

Unit 29 // Approaches in psychology

30
UNIT

Coursework

PREVIEW

After you have read this unit, you should be able to:

>> plan a piece of psychology coursework and write a project brief

>> appreciate the ethical issues that must be considered when undertaking psychology coursework

>> organize and present your coursework in a clear and concise way

>> write up a coursework report.

INTRODUCTION

The aim of this unit is to enable you to gain maximum benefit from your psychology coursework. The purpose of coursework is to give you experience of designing a study, collecting and analysing data, and writing a report. Undertaking coursework should also enable you to apply and gain a better understanding of some of the important concepts that you have learned about during your A-level course. For A2 Module 6 of AQA Psychology Specification A, you are required to submit a project brief and the report of one psychological investigation. This can be either an experimental or non-experimental study, but you must use inferential statistics to analyse your results, i.e. you are required to apply an inferential statistical test to the data you collect and interpret your findings.

Your research method must be selected from one of the following:

● laboratory, field or natural experiment

● survey

● observational study

● correlational research.

The psychological investigation you conduct for your coursework must be supervised by a teacher or lecturer and must focus on a topic from the AQA AS or A2 Psychology Specification A, subject to practical and ethical constraints. It should be a replication or variation of a previous study, rather than original research. You are allowed to work in small groups (of no more than four students), but you *must* write your own project brief and your own report of the investigation.

The coursework accounts for 15 per cent of your final mark, so is worth doing well. This means that you should allow plenty of time to plan and carry out your investigation, analyse the data and write your report.

You may wish to ask your teacher/lecturer, parent/guardian or others for help with your coursework. This is fine as long as the report you produce is your own work. However, you must acknowledge *all* sources of help that you receive while carrying out your coursework investigation.

Graham Davies

THE PROJECT BRIEF

Before you carry out your investigation, you must complete a project brief. The purpose of this is to help you clarify your thinking and plan your coursework efficiently. It is important to submit your project brief to your teacher or lecturer for comment, as this may help you to improve it and undertake a better study. Your teacher/lecturer needs to give their approval for your planned project *before* you begin to collect any data.

How the project brief is marked

Your project brief is marked as part of your coursework assessment and needs to include all the items listed in Table 30.1. A maximum of 12 marks can be awarded as indicated in the middle column of the table. The right-hand column directs you to relevant parts of this book.

Table 30.1 >> Items to include in your project brief

Item	Marks available	Relevant sections
>> A clear statement of the aim of the research and the experimental/alternative hypotheses	Assessed as part of the coursework report	Unit 7, pp. 216–17
>> Explanation of why a directional or non-directional experimental/alternative hypothesis has been selected	*1 mark*	Unit 7, p. 217
>> Identification of the research method (experimental – laboratory, field or natural experiment – or non-experimental – correlational analysis, naturalistic observation, questionnaire survey or interview) and, if appropriate, the design used	*1 mark*	Unit 6, pp. 195–211 Unit 7, pp. 218–224
>> Explanation of the advantages and disadvantages of your chosen research method/design	*2 marks*	Unit 6, pp. 195–211 Unit 7, pp. 218–228
>> Identification of potential sources of bias in the investigation (e.g. order effects, researcher bias) and any possible confounding variables	*2 marks*	Unit 7, pp. 218–229
>> Explanation of plans for dealing with the potential sources of bias and confounding variables you have identified	*2 marks*	Unit 7, pp. 218–229
>> A clear statement of the minimum level of statistical significance to be reached before the experimental/alternative hypothesis will be retained	*1 mark*	Unit 31, pp. 916–7
>> Discussion of any relevant ethical issues and an explanation of the steps taken to deal with any such issues arising from the study	*3 marks*	Unit 5, pp. 181–91 Unit 6, pp. 195–211 Unit 27, pp. 826–36

ETHICAL ISSUES

You will already have considered ethical issues in your AS-level psychology course (see Unit 5). They are discussed further here because they arise whenever psychological research is carried out. You should also look back at Unit 27. It is essential that you consider ethical issues carefully when planning your coursework and *before* you carry it out. You will therefore need to address relevant ethical issues in your project brief. Any work that you carry out for your psychology coursework *must* be on a topic checked and approved by your examination centre *before* you start work on it. If you go ahead without this approval, the examination centre may refuse to accept your report for marking. Ask your teacher or lecturer for advice. A summary of the ethical guidelines for research with human participants, published by the

British Psychological Society in 2000 (BPS 2000), is given in Unit 5 (see pp. 188–9). You should remind yourself of the key issues in relation to the following:

- informed consent
- the use of deception
- the importance of debriefing
- the right to withdraw from an investigation
- confidentiality
- the protection of participants
- respecting privacy when carrying out observational research.

The key ethical issues are outlined in Table 30.2.

ACTIVITY

Ethical issues

Read through the list of ethical issues in Table 30.2 now and check that you understand why each is important. How might each issue relate to the psychological investigation that you are planning?

If you do not fully understand any of these issues, please consult your teacher or lecturer for advice before you start your coursework.

<<Psychological research can be fun, but it should not be carried out just for fun.>> (Association for the Teaching of Psychology 1992)

Some psychological research can be fun to do, but may have an impact on participants' rights or feelings that is unjustifiable (e.g. in terms of potential discomfort or embarrassment). Research that has been carried out in the past by qualified psychologists is not automatically appropriate for A-level psychology students' coursework. For example, research on bystander behaviour, conformity or personal space is likely to involve levels of deception or discomfort that make such work inappropriate for your coursework. Psychology offers many fascinating possibilities for studies that do not involve deception or physical or psychological discomfort.

You should not exploit others simply for your own interests. It is particularly important that you consider the rights of those who may not be in a position to give their fully informed consent, such as older people, those with special needs and people who are mentally ill. Children are another vulnerable group – if you are studying them, you must obtain informed consent from their parents and it is also polite to ask the children themselves. Remember that you will need to prepare a simple and jargon-free way of doing this, including a very clear description of what the study involves so that potential participants know exactly what would be expected of them. Sometimes, the fact that the investigator debriefs the participants is seen as

Table 30.2 >> Ethical considerations when carrying out psychological research

General issues

>> Should the study be carried out at all?

>> Is it being carried out in the most ethical way?

>> Do the ends justify the means?

>> What are the 'costs' and 'benefits' of the work?

Consent

>> Informed consent should be given by participants wherever possible.

>> Deception of participants should be avoided.

>> Debriefing of participants should take place.

>> Participants have the right to withdraw from an investigation at any time.

>> Participants completing an investigation have the right to refuse the use of their data.

>> Participants may see a researcher as being in a position of power, so pressure should not be placed on people to continue to take part when they do not wish to do so.

>> Right to privacy should be respected.

>> Some participants may not be in a position to give informed consent themselves (these include children, some elderly people and those with special needs).

Conduct

>> Safety of self, those in the investigator's care and others the investigator comes into contact with must be maintained at all times.

>> Physiological and psychological discomfort to others should be avoided.

>> Act within the law.

>> Do not copy data, copyright materials or other people's wording.

>> Participants should leave the research situation in at least as good a psychological state as they entered it.

Competence

>> Researchers should be sufficiently qualified to carry out the work undertaken.

Confidentiality

>> Maintain confidentiality of data at all times.

>> Do not name participants (numbers or pseudonyms may be used).

Source: Davies (1994)

removing any risks that result from deception. You need to think carefully about this – deception can sometimes be an issue within the debriefing process, e.g. when a participant asks 'How did I do?', as in the cartoon.

If you feel that answering a question such as this honestly might upset participants, then you should not undertake the study in the first place.

The following two scenarios could easily arise from a psychological investigation, so how would *you* feel if...

● ... you are a parent and are with your children in a park. You notice someone watching your children closely and making notes on their behaviour.

● ... you carry out a survey involving questions on activities such as under-age drinking or the taking of illegal drugs. A legitimate authority (e.g. a head teacher, college principal or the police) then questions you about your sources of information. In such circumstances you have no legal right to keep your participants' identities confidential.

Before carrying out any psychological investigation, including your A-level coursework, you should ask yourself the questions in the panel below. If you have any doubts about any ethical aspect of your investigation, you should *not* go ahead with it.

Questions to ask before carrying out investigations

● Should I be conducting this kind of study at all?
● What is the most ethical way of carrying it out?
● Am I sufficiently competent to carry it out?
● Have I told participants everything they need and would expect to know before taking part?
● Have they willingly agreed to take part?
● How do I ensure that all research records are confidential and anonymous, and will remain so?
● How do I ensure that my research is carried out professionally and in a way that protects the rights of those involved?

Source: ATP (1992)

Topic 2 >> The coursework report

Once you have carried out your study, the final stage is to write the report. This topic provides detailed guidance on how to organize and present your coursework report, including what to include under the various headings.

ORGANIZING AND PRESENTING YOUR REPORT

The maximum length for your coursework report is 2,000 words (excluding the project brief, any tables, graphs, charts, the list of references and any appendices). You will need to plan your report carefully and be selective about what you include – conciseness is very important when writing your report. Reports that are too long will be penalized.

Your report should be submitted on A4 paper in a plastic document file. Avoid using bulky ring files, paper clips or plastic wallets from which the work has to be removed before it can be read, as most moderators dislike these!

The write-up of your investigation needs to be organized and produced in an appropriate style for a scientific report. There is no single correct way of doing this, but the approach outlined in this unit is one that is widely used. The following tips may be useful:

● Avoid using the first person singular or plural (i.e. 'I' or 'we'). Many students comment that they find it easier to write reports using the third person in the passive voice (i.e. 'An investigation was carried out' rather than 'I carried out an investigation').

● Always write in the past tense. Your coursework is reporting what has taken place, rather than what you are about to do. If you don't use the past tense, you may find yourself stringing together phrases such as 'The participants were about to have been able to have been ...'

- Label every piece of paper associated with a particular investigation with the report title; if you do not do this, it can be difficult to work out later which pages are relevant.

- Write your report as soon as you have completed the investigation – it is much harder if you leave it and return to it later.

- Allow plenty of time to write your report – it will probably take longer than you think, and rushed work often leads to careless mistakes. Don't forget

that credit is given to the quality of your written expression as well as the content.

When drafting your coursework report, you are strongly advised to refer to the assessment criteria for the project brief (a maximum of 12 marks) and the report (a maximum of 48 marks) which is included towards the end of AQA Psychology A-level Specification A (available on the AQA website at **www.aqa.org.uk**). The written guidance will enable you to identify what you need to do to achieve a good mark for each section and maximize your overall mark for your coursework.

WRITING UP A COURSEWORK REPORT

When writing your report, remember that it is being written for someone who is unfamiliar with the investigation you have carried out. However, the reader should be able to replicate your work from the description you provide. Therefore, when you have finished your report, give it to someone else to read and ask them whether they could replicate your study exactly.

You are not required to type your report, but using a word-processor can make it easier to draft and redraft your work so that what you submit for marking is your very best effort. You are permitted to hand in an early draft to your teacher or lecturer and should use their feedback when preparing the final draft. Word-processing can also help to ensure that your report is legible and well presented. Your report should be sub-divided into the following sections.

Title

The title should provide a clear indication of the focus of the study. However, selecting an informative title isn't always as easy as it seems. Avoid a general title that gives the reader little information on the nature of the investigation (e.g. 'A study of short-term memory'). At the same time, avoid a title that is too long and complicated (e.g. 'A study to investigate gender differences in self-reported health behaviours and stress levels of a group of 14- to 16-year-old young people who attend a large, inner-city comprehensive school').

A useful way of thinking about a title is to consider the key variables involved in the investigation – for example, 'The relationship between health and stress levels' or 'The effect of visual imagery on short-term memory encoding'.

Abstract

The aim of writing an abstract is to provide a clear and concise summary of the entire investigation in about 150 words, so that someone new to the topic being investigated can gain an idea of what actually happened. The abstract of a journal article, for example, should enable readers to decide whether or not the rest of the article is likely to be of interest.

Although an abstract should not be more than one or two paragraphs, it needs to be written carefully using

full sentences – composing an abstract is a skill that needs to be practised in order to do it well. Within this short section you should provide information on:

- the background idea of the investigation, including the previous research that it was based on

- the aim of the investigation and the experimental/alternative hypotheses tested

- a brief description of the research method used and, if appropriate, the design (e.g. repeated measures design)

- the sample of participants and the setting

- a brief description of the findings, including the statistical tests used, the statistical significance of the results and how the findings were interpreted

- any conclusions drawn and any key limitations or implications identified of the study.

Given the short length of an abstract you can only write a sentence or two on each of the above points. Although the abstract will appear at the beginning of the report, you will almost certainly find it easier to write it after you have completed the rest of your report because it summarizes the entire investigation.

Introduction, aim(s) and hypotheses

The introduction section should be around 600 words and should provide a clear rationale for the investigation that you have undertaken. It should provide support for your study using the psychological literature (this means research published in books and journal articles), including relevant previous research and background material. It should end with a clear statement of the aim of your investigation and the experimental/alternative hypotheses tested.

Your writing should progress smoothly and avoid any sudden changes in direction. Coolican (1999) provides a helpful way of thinking about this process, suggesting that the introduction to a report should be like a funnel – see Fig. 30.1(a).

A good way to start the introduction is to outline briefly in broad terms the area that you are investigating. Then continue with a discussion of two or three previous research studies relating to the topic in question. The key point here is to make sure that the research you include is focused on the topic being investigated. Do not regard the introduction as an opportunity to write a general essay on the area concerned. Try not to fall into the trap of writing absolutely everything that you can find on the topic – if you produce an introduction that is far too long, you cannot obtain full marks for this section. Remember that the introduction should be regarded as a logical 'funnelling' process – as you write it, you move closer and closer to the specific focus of your own investigation. So, you should end this part of your introduction with a description of the research that is closest to the area you are investigating.

Always ensure that you use your own words. It is all too easy to copy sentences written by someone else which you feel are particularly well expressed and use them in your report. Unacknowledged use of text from books, journal articles or other media is regarded as plagiarism, so take care never to use other people's words without proper credit. If you cannot put another person's written ideas into your own words, you can present it as a verbatim quotation, using quotation marks and identifying the source of the original text, but take care not to use too many direct quotations.

Once you have reviewed previous, relevant research, you then need to present the rationale behind your own investigation. How did your ideas develop from the previous research? Why did you consider this an interesting area for further investigation? This should

Phew, that's the Introduction cracked

lead into a clear statement of the aim of your study and the experimental/alternative hypotheses investigated; these should be written in an operationalized form (i.e. one that is precisely testable). A common problem with the phrasing of hypotheses in coursework reports is that they often read more like general aims rather than testable statements (see Unit 7, pp. 216–17, for further guidance on this).

If you re-read your introduction, you should be able to see a logical flow of ideas from the research topic through the aim of the investigation to the hypotheses tested.

Figure 30.1(a) »
Coolican's concept of the introduction as a funnel compared to some less successful approaches, e.g. Fig. 30.1(b) and (c) below

Start with the general psychological subject area. Discuss theory and research work which is relevant to the research topic. Move from the general area to the particular hypotheses to be tested via a coherent and logical argument as to why specific predictions have been made. State the specific **HYPOTHESIS**

Figure 30.1(b) »

Sometimes, however, the general topic area remains broad and the discussion is not focused specifically on the research topic in question. There is no real attempt to formulate the hypotheses and a sudden break in continuity occurs before the specific hypothesis is stated.

Another approach which fails to achieve the funnelling down achieved in Fig. 30.1(a) is one in which general information on the research area in question occurs in various places throughout the introduction. Research studies on the area of interest are included, but not presented in a logical order, which makes the development of ideas hard to follow. Again, a break in continuity occurs before the specific hypothesis is stated.

Figure 30.1(c) »

Some students prefer to include the aim of the study and hypotheses as a separate section, rather than at the end of the introduction. Select whichever approach suits you best.

Method

In the method section (approximately 400 words) you will need to describe precisely how your investigation was carried out. A key aim to keep in mind here is *replicability* – if you give your report to someone unfamiliar with the investigation concerned, they should be able to replicate it exactly after reading your description. You may find it easier to write this section by dividing it into sub-sections. There is no single correct way of doing this – what follows is a common, 'tried-and-tested' format. Each sub-section may consist of only one or two paragraphs.

Design

Here you will need to state the research method used (e.g. naturalistic observation or experiment). To achieve high marks you need to elaborate this and justify why this method was used. You should then outline and justify the actual design used. For example, if your report is based on an experiment using a repeated measures design, you might briefly outline what the experimental conditions were and state why this design was used in preference to an independent measures design. Mention such things as the number of participants per group or how many trials the participants undertook. This is also the place to tell the reader what the key variables were. For example, in an experiment it is useful to report the independent and dependent variables here, being careful to avoid vague descriptions.

Participants

Here you should state the number of participants you used and describe where they were tested or observed. You might also report demographic details, such as age or gender, but only if these are relevant to your investigation. You should also state the sampling method used to select your participants, together with the population from which they were drawn. A common misconception here concerns random samples (see Unit 7, pp. 219 and 228). Remember that neither selecting every tenth person nor using anyone that is available is a random technique (although either may result in a representative sample), as every participant does not stand an equal chance of selection. Don't forget to state how your participants were allocated to different groups or conditions, if appropriate.

Apparatus/materials

The actual title of this sub-section can be varied to meet the needs of your investigation (e.g. it may involve materials but no apparatus as such). This is a sub-section where students sometimes do not do themselves full justice. Here you should report the details of any apparatus or materials used. If materials are in written form, such as a questionnaire, include a copy in an appendix at the end of your report. You might also find it helpful to refer to lists of stimulus material or score sheets here – it is vital to include the latter as this helps to ensure that the investigation is fully replicable. However, don't include trivial details, such as makes of pens or pencils, and remember that you do not need to include every single response sheet or questionnaire – a specimen included in an appendix is sufficient.

If you designed your own stimulus material, you should explain how you did this. For example, 'A list of 20 randomly generated sequences of four lower-case letters was prepared, taking care not to include any meaningful sequences of letters (see Appendix 1)'.

Procedure

The procedure is the place to report exactly how the investigation was carried out. Once again, the key issue is replicability. If, for example, you are carrying out an observational study, you will need to report it in such a way that someone else could carry out a similar study after reading your description. If it is an experiment, then you will need to say what the participants had to do. If you test each participant individually, you will probably find it easier to report the procedure for one participant and then state that this procedure was repeated x times. Include any standardized instructions to participants here. (You may prefer to present these as an appendix at the end of your report, but if you do this, remember to refer to them here in the procedure section.)

Results

Coursework assessors are often surprised by the indifferent quality of the results sections when compared to other sections of reports. Results sections often appear to have had less time and effort spent on them. Again, there is no single correct way of writing up this section. Alternative approaches are possible, all of which can earn you full marks, so adopt the way that suits you best. For example, some students divide their material into two sections, headed 'Results' and 'Treatment of results', whereas others prefer to use a single section headed 'Results'.

Organization

Whichever approach you decide to adopt, it is important to organize your results section in such a way as to present a logical flow of information to the reader. The best A-level students guide the reader through the various elements of the results, which greatly improves the accessibility of this section. As with the rest of your report, write clearly and concisely, and assume that the assessor is unfamiliar with the study you have undertaken.

First, decide what information you are going to present in the results section, and what you are going to place in an appendix. Items best placed in an appendix are those that interrupt the flow of the text, such as tables of raw data, specimen score sheets, completed questionnaires or statistical computations. They should, however, be mentioned in this section – it is good practice for every appendix to be referred to at a relevant point in the text.

The results section might include the following:

- a statement of how data have been obtained – for example, how questionnaires or observational studies have been scored; students frequently omit this, which means that it is difficult to achieve full marks for replicability
- reference to a table containing the raw data which should be included as an appendix to the report – for example, 'A table showing the numbers of words recalled correctly by participants in the visual imagery and random list conditions can be found in Appendix 2'
- a summary table of the results – this table should also be referred to in the text of the results section
- reference to any graphs and/or charts which have been used to summarize the data
- the full reasons for choosing the inferential statistical test(s) you used to analyse the data
- the results of the application of any statistical test(s).

A summary table might include appropriate descriptive statistics. For example, relevant measures of central tendency (such as the mean or median) or of dispersion (e.g. the range or standard deviation) can often be used to summarize the data. Select the measures that are most appropriate for your investigation and remember to state what these statistics actually tell us about the data.

A well-presented graph or chart can add greatly to the clarity of reporting your findings. An appropriate technique for a particular investigation might be a scattergraph (in a study involving correlational analysis), a bar chart, histogram or frequency polygon, although many students use other specialized techniques that are appropriate in the context of the investigation concerned. The key factor is to think carefully about your requirements before you begin to prepare your illustrations. Unfortunately, students often include beautifully drawn graphs or charts that are not relevant to the original aims and hypotheses of the investigation. The use of computer-drawn graphics can sometimes be a problem here. Simply because an impressive-looking graph can be produced on a computer does not guarantee that it is an appropriate technique to present your data. Two things that you should try to avoid are:

- graphs or charts with 'Participant number' on their x-axes – these rarely show useful information, and can sometimes lead to bizarre interpretations (e.g. 'participant 7.8 recalled 9.1 words'!)

- unnecessary repetition – you are unlikely to gain additional marks for presenting the same information in several different ways (e.g. in a pie chart, frequency polygon and histogram), so choose the method that you think presents the information most clearly.

Since the aim of using graphics is to add to the clarity (and quality) of your results, your graphs or charts should show something that can be related directly to the aims and hypotheses of your investigation. For example, they might compare the distributions of scores in the different conditions of an experiment, or show the relationship between sets of data being correlated. Always include a comment in the text on what a particular graph or chart actually shows.

The best coursework reports provide reasoned explanations for the choice of any inferential statistical test, with students basing their reasons for selection on the nature of the data they have obtained and on what they are trying to demonstrate from its application. State whether an analysis aims to find a difference, correlation or association, and comment on the nature of the data obtained (e.g. whether the statistical test treats the data as being at a nominal, ordinal, interval or ratio level of measurement). Do not include your detailed statistical calculations in the results section; they can be referred to here, but the actual calculations should always be presented in an appendix.

You must report the outcome of any inferential statistical test you have used. It is important here that you have adopted an appropriate minimum level of statistical significance, and reported the level of statistical significance actually achieved and your conclusion regarding the significance of the results. Was your null hypothesis rejected or retained at your chosen level of significance? When reporting the results of your statistical test(s), you may find it helpful to adapt the phrases used with the worked examples of statistical tests in Unit 31.

Presentation of results

Care taken in the presentation of the results section can be rewarding. When drawing graphs or charts, it is helpful to use a sharp pencil or an appropriate pen (not a 'blobby' ball-point or felt-tip pen). Alternatively, if you know that this is one of your weak areas, use computer-generated graphics. Don't forget to include a title for each graph, chart or table which makes it immediately clear what the illustration is showing, without having to refer to the text. For example, 'results' or 'data' would be insufficient. 'Table showing the mean number of words recalled in the imagery and random list conditions' would be far more informative. Some students head their tables with terms such as 'Condition A' or 'Condition B', but this does not make it easy for the reader to understand what this means, so always ensure that you describe each condition.

All graphs, charts and tables need to be clearly and accurately labelled. You should ensure that, for example, headings of columns of data and labels on axes of graphs are meaningful, with the relevant units of measurement stated wherever appropriate. It is helpful to number graphs, charts and tables so that they can be referred to more easily in the text. See Unit 7 for further guidance.

Discussion

The discussion section is worth 25 per cent of the overall marks for your coursework report. With careful planning and by sequencing your ideas logically, it is possible to maximize your marks. Try and answer the following six questions in this section, in no more than 600 words.

1 Explanation of findings – what do your results actually mean?

Ideally, this first part of the discussion section will follow on logically from the end of the results section. In fact, a good way to start the discussion is to state your main findings and how these relate to the aim and hypotheses that you proposed at the start of your study. This is also the place to discuss, if necessary, any unexpected results, e.g. any atypical data that may have affected the outcome of your study. Be careful when interpreting your findings; always keep in mind the nature of your sample of participants and take care not to generalize your results inappropriately.

2 Relationship to background research – how do your results fit in with previous research?

In the introduction, you will have discussed background research or theory relevant to the investigation that you carried out. In the discussion, you should now consider the ways in which your research findings support, or fail to support, previous research. It is not sufficient merely to state that 'the results support the findings of research by ...'. Instead you should go on to compare the data obtained from previous investigations with those from your own study, discussing the main similarities or differences. It is important to be selective when deciding what to include. If you have written an introduction that is suitably selective, this should benefit you here, as you will be linking your results to those from previous research or relevant theory.

If, however, your results do not fit in with those obtained from any previous research, then this is the place to suggest possible reasons why this might be. You may need to examine any differences in methods carefully here in order to do this well.

Remember that you should not need to introduce background studies into the discussion section that have not been mentioned previously in the introduction. If you find that you are doing this, then your selection of studies in the introduction may need revising. Also, avoid making statements that are demonstrably untrue

– statements claiming, for example, that your results 'prove the work of Smith to be wrong'. No single, small-scale investigation can claim to disprove the work of another researcher.

3 What are the methodological limitations of your study?

This is your opportunity to evaluate constructively the method you have used in your study. It is important that you confine your discussion here to factors that really are likely to have affected the outcome and not descend into insignificant detail. The possible effects of any serious design weaknesses should be addressed here – for example, a failure to counterbalance in a repeated measures design or problems with observer reliability in a naturalistic observational study. Try to avoid potentially trivial points, such as using a random sample instead of an opportunist one (when this is unlikely to have affected the results anyway), using more participants (when an adequate number were used in the original study), or minor issues such as time of day, light levels or room temperature. These should only be mentioned if you really feel that they may have genuinely affected your results.

4 If you did the investigation again, how could you improve it?

You now have the opportunity to suggest how the problems that you have identified could be overcome if you were to undertake the investigation again. The suggestions that you make here should be both practical and ethical.

5 What are the wider implications of your results?

This is your opportunity to step back and assess the wider practical and/or theoretical implications of your findings. You might also review any ethical issues that arose in your investigation. It is difficult to give precise guidance here as the implications are often specific to a particular study, but you might consider whether, for example, there are implications for society, education, specific psychological theories or equal opportunities policies.

6 What are your suggestions for further research?

You should now suggest some possible ideas for follow-up studies. Given your findings, where could you go from here? What suggestions for future research could you make? How would you carry this out? Avoid simply stating the general area that might be investigated, but rather try and go a bit further by suggesting the research method or design that might be used to achieve your proposal.

Conclusion

Although it is not credited separately, it is useful to provide a conclusion section that summarizes briefly your main findings. These should be described without the use of statistical notation.

References

Your list of references should be presented in alphabetical order by author name in a section at the end of your report, in the same way as the references at the end of this textbook. This allows readers to locate and follow up any of your references if they want to. As you prepare your report, it is a good idea to make a careful note of the details of every book, journal article or other source that you refer to. This will save time later when you may have forgotten where you found particular information that you want to include.

You need to provide full references for:

● all studies that you have quoted in your coursework report

● any books, journals, Internet sites or other sources of information from which you obtained information

● any computer packages that you have used.

For a book reference you need to give the author (including the initials), date of publication, *title of the book*, edition number (if there is more than one edition), place of publication and publisher. For example:

Coolican, H. (1999) *Research Methods and Statistics in Psychology* (3rd edition), London: Hodder and Stoughton.

References for journal articles should provide the author and title of the article, *name of the journal concerned*, volume number and relevant page numbers. For example:

Stroebe, M., van Vliet, T., Hewstone, M. and Willis, H. (2002) 'Homesickness among students in two cultures: antecedents and consequences', *British Journal of Psychology*, 93, pp. 147–168.

You may need to give the reference for an article in a book that has been edited by someone else.

This should be presented as follows:

Vernon, P.A., Wicket, J.C., Bazana, P.G. and Stelmack, R.M. (2000) 'The neuropsychology and psychophysiology of human intelligence', in R.J. Sternberg (editor) *Handbook of Intelligence*, New York: Cambridge University Press.

As you can see from the examples above, there are strict conventions about how to present references:

● Titles of books and journals are normally italicized (or underlined if you are writing by hand).

● Titles of articles or chapters in books are in Roman (ordinary) letters, but are placed inside quotation marks. These can be either single or double marks – it's up to you to choose, but once you have made your choice, use the same kind of quotation marks throughout.

● You can choose whether or not to include full stops after an author's initials. Again, be consistent – either put them all in or none at all.

● Internet sites should be referenced by giving the address of the site concerned, the title of the material obtained, and the date you accessed it.

Appendices

An appendix is the appropriate location for any material that interrupts the readability of your report, such as stimulus materials, diagrams of research layouts, tally charts from observational studies, specimen questionnaire surveys, tables of raw data or statistical calculations. Do not, however, treat them as a store for rough notes – remember that everything you include in your report will be marked. If you are including specimen response sheets or questionnaires, you will not need to include every single copy – an example is sufficient. Material in the appendices is not included in the word length for your report.

Final checks

When you have finished writing your report, you should do the following:

● Carefully check that you have included everything necessary and have not exceeded the maximum length of 2,000 words. The checklist in the unit summary will help you to do this (see pp. 910–11).

● Check the expression of your ideas, including the spelling carefully. Remember, marks are awarded for the quality of written language in your report.

● Complete a candidate record form and attach it securely to the front of your report.

● Add your completed project brief.

● Remember to photocopy your report if you are likely to want to look at it again before you have completed your course. This is a good idea anyway as the exam board sometimes retains reports for grading and archive purposes.

Checklist: A-level psychology coursework

This checklist is designed to help you maximize your marks for coursework, based on experimental research or correlational analysis. You can also adapt it for use with an observational or survey study. Create your own master copy which you can use for your own coursework (and any practice reports you produce). Not every question will apply to every study; check with your teacher if you are in doubt.

Name:

Title of practical work:

Project brief

Have you:

- [ ] stated the aim of the research clearly and the experimental/alternative hypotheses?
- [ ] explained why a directional or non-directional hypothesis has been selected?
- [ ] identified your chosen research method and, if appropriate, the design used and explained why this research method/design has been selected?
- [ ] identified the advantages and disadvantages of your chosen research method/design?
- [ ] identified possible sources of bias and any possible confounding variables?
- [ ] stated the procedures to be used to deal with potential sources of bias and any possible confounding variables?
- [ ] stated the minimum level of statistical significance to be reached before the experimental/alternative hypothesis will be retained?
- [ ] identified any relevant ethical issues and outlined your strategy for dealing with these?

Abstract (summary)

Have you stated:

- [ ] the topic area studied, including relevant previous research?
- [ ] the aim/hypothesis?
- [ ] brief details of the research method used and, if appropriate, the design?
- [ ] the sample of participants and the setting?
- [ ] the principal findings?
- [ ] the main implications of your findings?

Introduction, aim and hypotheses

Have you:

- [ ] stated the general area of your study?
- [ ] referred to carefully selected, relevant background studies?
- [ ] reported your reasons for studying this topic?
- [ ] clearly stated the aim of your study?
- [ ] precisely stated: (a) the experimental/alternative hypothesis and (b) the null hypothesis?
- [ ] stated whether the experimental/alternative hypotheses are directional or non-directional?
- [ ] explained how you arrived at the aim and hypotheses?
- [ ] organized your introduction in a logical way?

Method

Have you:

- [ ] divided this section into appropriate sub-sections?

Have you stated:

- [ ] the design used?
- [ ] the nature of any experimental groups/conditions?
- [ ] the nature of any control groups/conditions?
- [ ] the independent variable (IV) and the dependent variable (DV) or the variables to be correlated?
- [ ] the minimum level of statistical significance you will accept?
- [ ] the total number of participants?
- [ ] the population from which the participants were drawn?
- [ ] how participants were selected/sampled?
- [ ] how participants were allocated to experimental groups/conditions?
- [ ] relevant characteristics of participants, e.g. age range, gender, educational background?
- [ ] details of all apparatus and materials used?
- [ ] any standardized instructions given to participants?
- [ ] the procedure followed in such a way that someone else could replicate it precisely using your description?

Results

Have you:

- [ ] provided a summary table of the results?
- [ ] provided titles for all graphs, charts and data tables?
- [ ] labelled all axes and columns of your graphs, charts and data tables?
- [ ] used appropriate descriptive/inferential statistical techniques?

continued on next page

☐ stated full reasons why a particular statistical test was selected to analyse your data?

☐ reported accurately and appropriately the observed and critical values for any inferential statistical test you have used?

☐ reported your level of statistical significance?

☐ reported the outcome of your study in terms of the hypotheses tested?

Discussion

Have you stated:

☐ the results that you obtained?

Have you discussed:

☐ what your results mean in terms of your aim/hypotheses?

☐ your findings with reference to the studies included in your introduction?

☐ the limitations of your study?

☐ how improvements could be made to the study if it were to be done again?

☐ any wider implications of your findings?

☐ suggestions for follow-up studies?

Conclusion

Have you:

☐ briefly summarized your main findings?

References

Have you:

☐ provided full references for all sources used and quoted by name?

☐ presented all your references using a conventional and consistent style?

Appendices

Have you:

☐ provided copies of such things as stimulus materials and experimental layouts that are referred to in the text but not included elsewhere?

☐ provided a table of raw data?

☐ included specimen statistical calculations?

☐ provided appropriate titles and labelling for all appendices?

Presentation

Have you:

☐ written your report in a concise, scientific style?

☐ structured your report logically into sections/sub-sections?

☐ avoided unnecessary repetition or removed irrelevant information?

☐ provided a contents page and numbered all your pages?

☐ presented your report in such a way that someone else could precisely replicate the study from the description in your report?

☐ referred to all the graphs, charts and data tables in the text of your report?

☐ acknowledged all sources of help with your coursework?

FURTHER RESOURCES

British Psychological Society (2000) *Code of Conduct, Ethical Principles and Guidelines,* **Leicester: British Psychological Society.**
Available on the Internet at **www.bps.org.uk**
These sets of ethical guidelines are essential reading for any student undertaking psychology coursework.

Coolican, H. (1999) *Research Methods and Statistics in Psychology* **(3rd edn), London: Hodder & Stoughton.**

Coolican, H. (1996) *Introduction to Research Methods and Statistics in Psychology* **(2nd edn), London: Hodder & Stoughton.**
Two valuable reference texts, giving detailed information on the research methods that you are likely to be using in your coursework.

Searle, A. (1999) *Introducing Research and Data in Psychology,* **London: Routledge.**
This book is intended to provide a user-friendly introduction for those who find research methods and statistics daunting.

AQA assessment criteria
The assessment criteria for the project brief and the coursework report are included in the Psychology A-level specification, available on the AQA website at **www.aqa.org.uk**.

Website

www.theatp.org/ATP_Publications.html
The text of the ATP's *Guide to Ethics for Students of Psychology at Pre-degree Level.*

STATISTICAL ANALYSIS FOR Coursework

Graham
Davies

PREVIEW

After you have read this unit, you should be able to:

>> calculate a standard deviation

>> discuss the use of inferential statistics

>> understand the concept of statistical significance

>> use some of the inferential statistical tests which may be employed to analyse your coursework data, including:

- tests of difference (Mann-Whitney U Test, Wilcoxon Matched Pairs Signed Ranks Test, Sign Test)
- a test of correlation (Spearman's Rank Order Correlation Coefficient)
- a test of association (Chi-squared Test).

INTRODUCTION

This unit will look at some of the ways in which you can statistically analyse the data you collect when carrying out your coursework. You have already met some of the descriptive statistical techniques for data analysis when you completed the research methods component of your AS-level course. There you considered a range of descriptive statistical techniques, including three measures of central tendency (the mean, median and mode), three measures of dispersion (the range, the interquartile range and the standard deviation) and the preparation of graphs, histograms, bar charts, frequency polygons and scattergraphs. Look back at Unit 7 if you need to refresh your memory about any of these.

This unit will show you how to calculate the most important of the measures of dispersion – the standard deviation.

The concept of statistical significance will be introduced and you will be shown how to calculate some of the inferential statistical tests that you might wish to use to analyse and draw conclusions from your coursework data.

KEY CONCEPTS

Descriptive statistics: techniques used to describe or characterize obtained data.

Inferential statistics: the techniques (tests) used to analyse the data from samples to enable us to infer or draw conclusions about the population from which the sample is drawn.

Standard deviation: a statistical measure of the variation from the mean in a set of scores.

Statistical significance: a conclusion drawn from the data collected in a research study that the results are unlikely to have been caused by chance, and can therefore be attributed to the particular relationship under study.

Level of significance: the cut-off point used by researchers to determine whether a particular set of data differs from that which would be expected if only chance factors were operating.

Unit 7 describes how measures of dispersion enable us to examine the variability within data sets and help us to understand the extent to which scores in a given set of data are similar to or very different from each other. The standard deviation is one such measure of dispersion; it measures the variability (i.e. of the typical deviation) of a given sample of scores from its mean. The standard deviation was described in Unit 7, so you can refresh your memory by re-reading the relevant section (see p. 239). Before calculating the standard deviation, you need to remember that for it to be an accurate measure, you require data that are approximately normally distributed (see the panel on p. 237 of Unit 7). You also require data that are measured on an interval scale or ratio scale. Levels of measurement are an important concept in statistics (see the panel on p. 914 for a description of four levels of measurement).

Calculating the standard deviation involves working out the deviation of all the individual values in the sample of data concerned from the sample mean – in other words, we have to find the differences between each of these individual values and their mean.

The standard deviation can be calculated using either Formula 1 or Formula 2 in Fig. 31.1. This is the first time in this book that you have encountered statistical formulae. If you do not like maths, please don't panic! The calculations involved are simple, and remember that you will not be asked to carry out any statistical calculations under examination conditions. Computer statistical packages will calculate standard deviation for you, as will most scientific calculators, but it is important to learn how to use them so that you can analyse and interpret your own coursework data appropriately.

The statistical symbols used in these two formulae form part of a standard notation that will occur elsewhere, so it is worth the effort to get to know what these symbols mean.

Which formula to use

We will now look at when to use the two different formulae. In order to explain this, we need to refer to the concepts of population and sample.

- A *population* is a group of people that share a given set of characteristics about which a researcher wishes to draw conclusions (for example, all students registered for A-level psychology in a given year).

- A *sample* is a sub-set of a population, sharing the same characteristics of the population despite its smaller size (see also pp. 228–9 of Unit 7).

Which formula you use depends on whether you are working with data from a whole population or from a sample:

- *Formula 1* is used to calculate the standard deviation of values from a population where the whole population has been sampled. For example, we may be interested in, say, the data obtained from a particular psychology class and do not wish to say anything about any larger population.

- *Formula 2* is used to calculate the standard deviation of values from a sample that constitutes part of a total population that you wish to say something about. This formula gives you an estimate of the standard deviation of the population – the difference between the two formulae allows for any sampling errors. It is most likely that you will need to use Formula 2, since psychologists are often interested in making inferences about a wider population.

A specimen calculation, using Formula 2, is shown in Fig. 31.2. Notice that the formula involves squaring values – the function of this is to remove any minus signs (remember that when you multiply a minus value by a minus value the result is a positive value). Later in the calculation, a square root is used to restore the original units of measurement. The interpretation of a standard deviation value was introduced in Unit 7 (see p. 239).

Figure 31.1 >>
Formulae used for calculating standard deviation

Formula 1: $\quad S = \sqrt{\dfrac{\Sigma d^2}{N}}$

Formula 2: $\quad s = \sqrt{\dfrac{\Sigma d^2}{N-1}}$

where:

S or s = standard deviation (the statistic we are aiming to calculate)

$\sqrt{}$ = square root

Σ = sum of (i.e. add up) (The symbol Σ is pronounced 'sigma'.)

d^2 = the squared deviation of each value from the mean

N = the number of scores

In addition, knowing the standard deviation of a given sample of data allows us to calculate a standard score (also known as a 'z score'), which is the number of standard deviations a given value is away from its mean.

Once a standard score is known, then it is possible to calculate the proportion of individuals between that standard score and the mean (see Appendix 1 at the end of this unit for an explanation and an example).

Levels of measurement

The quantitative measurements that psychologists obtain from their research investigations can be made at different levels of measurement. These vary in terms of their precision and in how they can be used. The four most common levels of measurement will be discussed here.

● *The nominal level* – Nominal data provide the weakest level of measurement available to the psychologist, and are sometimes referred to as 'categorized' or 'frequency count' data. Data can be allocated into categories by counting frequency of occurrence within particular categories. An example might be the placing of research participants into categories based on their gender and the frequency with which they interpret a stimulus in different ways. For example:

	Interpretation A	Interpretation B
Female	25	15
Male	20	20

● *The ordinal level* – Ordinal data are capable of being placed into rank order (i.e. from highest value to lowest value or vice versa). This means the researcher can meaningfully compare scores with each other, although the extent of meaningful comparison is limited. It is possible to state that one value is higher than another, but it is not possible to assume more than this. For example, it is reasonable to assume that if children's helpfulness is rated on an eleven-point scale (with high numbers = high helpfulness), a child with a rating of 10 has been observed as being more helpful than a child with a rating of 5. However, it is unreasonable to conclude that the child with a rating of 10 is twice as helpful as the one with a rating of 5, as the points on such a rating scale are at intervals which are (or may be) arbitrary or unequal. It is impossible to tell precisely how much the points on the scale really differ, i.e. we cannot say that the difference between ratings of 1 and 2 and ratings of 9 and 10 are exactly equal. The most that we can achieve is the relative ranking of the children concerned.

● *Interval levels* and *ratio levels* – The interval and ratio levels of measurement are more precise –

they consist of data which are measured in fixed units with equal distances between all the points on the scale concerned (e.g. the difference between 10°C and 11°C is the same as the difference between 20°C and 21°C). The key difference between interval and ratio scales lies in how zero values can be interpreted. Well-known examples of the interval level of measurement include temperature measured in degrees Centigrade (C) or degrees Farenheit (F). In both these cases 0 degrees is not meaningful because neither 0°C nor 0°F can be interpreted as a baseline for no temperature. Minus values are possible, and proportions are meaningless if calculated with zero as the baseline.

Ratio scales provide the strongest level of measurement of those discussed here, and on such scales zero really does provide a baseline which can be used for calculating proportions. Examples of data measured on ratio scales are distance in centimetres and time in seconds.

There is debate between statisticians about the interpretation of these levels of measurement. For example, some people treat numbers of words recalled in a memory task as interval data, whereas others treat such data as ordinal on the grounds that all words are not equally easy to recall. This raises the important point that data do not arrive with a label signifying the level of measurement attached to them – the researcher needs to decide the appropriate level at which data are to be treated.

For example, let us assume we have a series of times, such as the times taken for rats to run a particular maze (all times are in seconds):

20 28 29 30 30 31 34 40 42 44 46 47

These data consist of times – fixed units of measurement which we could treat, correctly, as being on a ratio scale. However, we could allocate rank orders to these scores, thereby treating the data as being on an ordinal scale. Alternatively, we could group the scores into categories such as 'number of rats running the maze in less than 40 seconds' and 'number of rats taking 40 seconds or more to run the maze'. In this case, we are now treating the data as nominal.

Figure 31.2 >> *Calculation of the standard deviation (using Formula 2)*

Task

Calculate the standard deviation of the following data: 85 86 94 95 96 107 108 108 109 112

These data could represent, for example, the psychology test scores of a sample of 10 students.

Procedure

1 Calculate the mean of the data.   Mean $= \dfrac{85 + 86 + 94 + 95 + 96 + 107 + 108 + 108 + 109 + 112}{10} = \dfrac{1000}{10} = 100$

2 Place your data into the first column of a table organized as follows:

Psychology test scores	d	d^2
85	−15	225
86	−14	196
94	−6	36
95	−5	25
96	−4	16
107	7	49
108	8	64
108	8	64
109	9	81
112	12	144
		$\Sigma d^2 = 900$

3 Find the difference (d) between each of the values in the table and the mean (see d column in table left).

4 Square all the values of d (see d^2 column in table left).

5 Find the sum of all the values of d^2 (see Σd^2 left).

   $\Sigma d^2 = 900$

6 Substitute in the formula: $s = \sqrt{\dfrac{\Sigma d^2}{N-1}}$

   $s = \sqrt{\dfrac{900}{10-1}}$ $s = \sqrt{\dfrac{900}{9}}$

   $s = \sqrt{100}$ $s = 10$

CHECK YOUR UNDERSTANDING

Check your understanding of how to calcuate the standard deviation by answering these questions from memory. Check your answers by looking back through Topic 1.

1 A psychologist measures the motivation of a group of A-level students on a scale of 0 to 100 using an ordinal level of measurement. Person A has a score of 50 and Person B a score of 25. Can the psychologist claim that Person A is twice as motivated as Person B? Give reasons for your answer.

2 To calculate a standard deviation, what levels of measurement are needed:

   (a) nominal   (b) ordinal   (c) interval   (d) ratio?

3 Define what is meant by:

   (a) a population   (b) a sample?

4 A psychologist is interested in investigating the academic achievement of younger (those aged up to 19) and more mature students sitting A-level Biology in the UK (i.e. those aged 20 and over). She invites all those registered in England with the AQA Exam Board to participate in the study. Is this study based on a population or a sample?

5 Which is the most powerful measure of dispersion available to a researcher?

6 A psychologist measured the length of time in seconds and milliseconds that 12 young people took to solve a complex problem. Each person was tested twice, using two problems of a similar level of difficulty. Condition A required the participants not to have drunk any alcohol for at least 24 hours. For Condition B, each individual was required to drink three units of alcohol one hour before the test.

   (a) What level of measurement are the scores?

   (b) The standard deviation for Condition A is smaller than for Condition B; what does this tell us about the variability within the two data sets?

7 You have been asked to calculate the standard deviation for a sample that constitutes part of a total population that you wish to say something about. Would you use Formula 1 or Formula 2 to calculate the standard deviation?

REVISION SUMMARY

Having covered this topic you should be able to:

✓ describe four levels of measurement – nominal, ordinal, interval and ratio – and give examples of each

✓ state what levels of measurement are needed in order to calculate a standard deviation

✓ explain when it is appropriate to use Formula 1 and when to use Formula 2 to calculate a standard deviation

✓ calculate a standard deviation.

Topic 2 >> Inferential statistics

Describing data in the ways outlined in Unit 7 are not the only statistical techniques available to a researcher. The use of inferential statistics enables a researcher to draw conclusions about the wider population from which a particular sample has been drawn. By using such inferential techniques, the researcher can, on the basis of data obtained from a particular sample, make statements of probability about the likelihood of obtaining a particular set of results by chance. Through such statements, reasoned conclusions can be reached by the researcher as to whether a null hypothesis can be retained or rejected, and following on from this, whether an alternative hypothesis may be accepted.

STATISTICAL SIGNIFICANCE

The concept of statistical significance is central to inferential statistics. A 'statistically significant' result is one that is unlikely to have occurred through chance. In practice, we can never be 100 per cent certain that chance has not played a part. However, when the likelihood of obtained results having occurred through chance is only small, then researchers will prefer to reject the null hypothesis and accept the alternative hypothesis.

Level of significance

How do we know when to reject a null hypothesis and when to retain it? The answer to this question lies in the concept of 'level of significance'. This can be defined as an arbitrary value used as a criterion for ascertaining whether a particular set of data differs from that which would be expected if only chance factors were operating.

Significance levels may be written as percentages or decimals. For example:

● The *5% level of significance* can also be written as $p = 0.05$ (where p = the probability of the results being due to chance).

● The *1% level of significance* can also be written as $p = 0.01$.

Be careful that you do not mix up the different ways of expressing levels of significance; a common error is to add a percentage symbol onto the end of a decimal version (e.g. $p = 0.05\%$ is a very different value to

$p = 0.05$). In practice, the normal way of expressing significance levels is to use the symbol ≤, which means 'less than or equal to'. Thus, for example, the expression $p \leq 0.05$ refers to achieving a significance level of at least 5%, i.e. the probability of results such as these occurring through chance is no greater than 0.05 (or 5%).

While the choice of significance level is largely arbitrary, the 5% level of significance is usually regarded as being the minimum acceptable for deciding that results are statistically significant. If the 5% level of significance is achieved (i.e. $p \leq 0.05$), this means that the likelihood of the results obtained having occurred through chance is 1 in 20 or less (i.e. such results are likely to occur 5% or less of the time). When this level of significance is used in experimental research, we are stating that any difference between sets of scores is so large that it is unlikely to have arisen due to chance. The researcher will conclude that the results are unlikely to have occurred because the null hypothesis is true and, provided some other unwanted variable has not intervened, that the results are due to the effects of the manipulated independent variable. The alternative hypothesis can therefore be accepted.

The 5% level of significance is by no means the only one that is used by psychologists. Occasionally, less stringent levels (such as 10%) are employed, but it is sometimes important that more stringent levels of statistical significance are used, such as when we need to be even more certain that the results obtained are not due to chance.

More stringent levels of significance are likely to be needed when a 5% risk of results occurring through chance would be unacceptable. Such a situation might be where harm might occur to participants as a result – for example, in some medical research. Examples of more stringent levels include the 1% level of significance (or $p \leq 0.01$), where the null hypothesis would only be rejected if the likelihood of the results obtained occurring through chance is 1% or less. Even more stringent levels are the 0.5% ($p \leq 0.005$) or 0.1% ($p \leq 0.001$).

Type I and Type II errors

Why has the 5% level of significance become the one that is typically adopted by psychologists? The 5% significance level represents a reasonable balance between the chances of making a Type I error and a Type II error.

- A *Type I error* is said to occur when a null hypothesis is rejected when in fact it is true, and the likelihood of making such an error is equal to the level of significance employed. For example, at $p \leq 0.05$ the risk of making a Type I error is 1 in 20 or less. This type of error can occur when an insufficiently stringent significance level is adopted.

- A *Type II error* occurs when a null hypothesis is retained when in fact it is false, i.e. there is a failure to detect a difference or relationship that is really there. This can occur when significance levels are too stringent.

It is often considered preferable to run a higher risk of making a Type II error rather than make a Type I error, because it is better scientific practice to err on the side of caution.

If you used a 10% level of significance, you would be more likely to make a Type I error. You would reject the null hypothesis if the likelihood of results such as these occurring through chance were 10% or less. If you used a 1% level of significance, a Type II error would be more likely, as the null hypothesis would be rejected only if you were at least 99% certain that the results obtained were not due to chance.

USING AND INTERPRETING INFERENTIAL STATISTICAL TESTS

In order to obtain the probability level of a particular set of results occurring through chance, you need to select and apply an appropriate inferential statistical test. To do this, you need to know the answers to certain questions concerning the nature of the data obtained (see 'Selecting a statistical test' below).

These questions concern whether data are being tested for differences, relationships or associations, the level of measurement of the data and the design of the study. Look back at the panel on p. 914 if you need to remind yourself about levels of measurement and at Unit 7 for information on different experimental designs.

Selecting a statistical test

The following table shows the factors involved in choosing the correct statistical test.

Level of measurement	Two sample tests of difference		Two sample tests of correlation
	Independent data	*Related data*	
Nominal	Chi-squared Test for Independent Samples (χ^2) (see p. 919)	Sign Test (see p. 922)	—
Ordinal, interval or ratio	Mann-Whitney U Test (see p. 918)	Wilcoxon Matched Pairs Signed Ranks Test (see p. 921)	Spearman's Rank Order Correlation Coefficient (r_s) (p. 923)

THE MANN-WHITNEY U TEST

The Mann-Whitney U Test is a test of difference that is suitable for use with data gathered from two independent groups (an independent groups design). It can be used when at least an ordinal level of measurement has been achieved. It can therefore be used with data on an interval or ratio level of measurement that are converted to an ordinal level for the purposes of the test. Two versions of this test will be discussed here. The first is used when the larger of the two samples under investigation contains no more than 20 observations or when the size of each sample is equal, with up to a maximum of 20 observations in each. (See Unit 7 for information about an independent groups design and the panel on p. 914 for a discussion of levels of measurement.)

Specimen calculation using the formula for small observations

Below is a specimen calculation of the Mann-Whitney U Test (where there are no more than 20 observations in each condition), using data obtained from a memory experiment (see data below).

1 Place the data to be analysed into the appropriate columns of a table drawn up in a similar way to the one shown.

2 Rank the data, from the lowest value (allocated rank 1) to the highest value (rank N). *Notice that both data sets are ranked in a single sequence and that the ranks are shared for any scores that are the same.*

See Appendix 2 for how to rank your data.

3 Calculate the sum of the ranks for the smaller of the two samples and call this value T. If both samples contain the same number of observations, calculate the sum of the ranks for either sample.

In the example $T = 47$.

4 Substitute in the following formula:

$$U = N_1 N_2 + \frac{N_1(N_1 + 1)}{2} - T$$

Here,

U = the observed (i.e. the calculated) value of the Mann-Whitney statistic.

N_1 = the number of values in the smaller sample (or in the sample for which the sum of the ranks has been calculated if both are the same size).

N_2 = the number of values in the larger sample (or in the sample for which the sum of the ranks has not been calculated if both are the same size).

Here, $U = (9 \times 10) + \frac{9 \times (9 + 1)}{2} - 47$

$U = 90 + \frac{90}{2} - 47$

$U = 90 + 45 - 47 = 88$

$U = 88$. This is the observed value of U.

5 Substitute in the following formula:

$U' = N_1 N_2 - U$

Here, $U' = (9 \times 10) - 88$

$U' = 90 - 88$

$U' = 2$.

This is the observed value of U'.

	Condition 1			Condition 2		
Participant no.	*No. of words recalled (control condition)*	*Rank order*		*Participant no.*	*No. of words recalled (experimental condition)*	*Rank order*
1	7	2		10	20	19
2	6	1		11	14	11
3	8	3.5		12	14	11
4	12	8		13	18	17
5	9	5		14	15	13
6	14	11		15	17	16
7	8	3.5		16	13	9
8	11	7		17	16	14.5
9	10	6		18	19	18
				19	16	14.5

47 =
Σ ranks for Condition 1 (Σ = sum of)

6 Select the smaller value of U and U'. In this example, U' has the smaller value of 2. Whichever is the smallest value becomes the value of U.

7 Consult the table in Appendix 3 to obtain the critical values of U; a critical value of U is the maximum value of U that is significant at a given level of significance. (Statistical significance is discussed earlier in this unit.) In order to obtain this you need to know:

(a) the values of N_1 and N_2 (in this case 9 and 10 respectively)

(b) whether a one-tailed or two-tailed test is required (in this case, let us assume a one-tailed test).

(The concept of directional and non-directional hypotheses is discussed in Unit 7.)

Take the smaller of the observed values of U and U'. In this case the smaller is U', which = 2. If this value is equal to or less than the critical value for a given level of significance, the null hypothesis can be rejected. (Levels of significance are discussed on p. 916. Null and alternative hypotheses are discussed in Unit 7.)

A minimum significance level of $p \leq 0.05$ will be assumed in this case. From Appendix 3, Table 4, the critical value of U for $N_1 = 9$ and $N_2 = 10$ for a one-tailed test at $p = 0.05$ is 24. As the observed value of U (2) is less than the critical value (24),

the probability of these results occurring through chance is less than 5% ($p < 0.05$).

In this case, the null hypothesis could be rejected in favour of the alternative hypothesis.

Note: If the observed value had been greater than the critical value, then the probability of these results occurring through chance would have been greater than 5%. In this case, the null hypothesis would not have been rejected.

Formula for large observations

The formula for the calculation of the Mann-Whitney U Test where one or more of the samples has more than 20 observations is shown below:

$$z = \frac{U - \dfrac{N_1 N_2}{2}}{\sqrt{\left(\left[\dfrac{N_1 N_2}{N(N-1)}\right] \times \left[\dfrac{N^3 - N}{12} - \Sigma T\right]\right)}}$$

This formula provides the researcher with a z score. (See Appendix 1 for how to interpret z scores.)

THE CHI-SQUARED TEST FOR INDEPENDENT SAMPLES (χ^2)

The Chi-squared Test for Independent Samples (χ^2) is a test of association for use with data gathered from independent samples that are measured at a nominal level in the form of frequencies. It tests for differences by examining the association that exists between data categorized into rows and columns. It compares observed frequencies (those actually obtained) with expected frequencies (the average frequencies which would be observed if the null hypothesis were true). (See the panel on p. 914 for a discussion of levels of measurement and Unit 7 for a discussion of the null hypothesis.)

You need to be aware of some of the limitations on the use of the Chi-squared Test:

● The Chi-squared Test should only be used in situations where each observation is included in one category only. No overlap between categories is permissible.

● The observations used in the test must be actual frequencies of occurrence. Data such as averages, percentages or proportions should not be used.

● No individual participant should contribute more than one unit to a category. An exception to this is where all data relate to the same participant.

● The probability of making a Type I error is increased when there are expected frequencies of less than 5, especially when the total sample size is small (i.e. less than 20). It is, however, possible to employ the Chi-squared Test in such situations, although the potential for error increases with very small samples or an increase in the number of expected frequencies less than 5. This potential problem can be minimized by the use of a larger sample size. (Type I errors are discussed earlier in this unit.)

Specimen calculation

What follows is a specimen calculation of the Chi-squared Test for Independent Samples, using data from an investigation into children's thinking.

1 Place the observed values to be analysed into the appropriate boxes of a table drawn up in a similar way to the table shown on the next page. This kind of table is called a 'contingency table'; in this case it is a 2 × 2 contingency table since there are two rows and two columns of data. Other numbers of rows and columns are possible using this same test (e.g. 2 × 3).

	No. of children able to solve problem	No. of children unable to solve problem	Row total
4-year-old children	Cell 1 8	Cell 2 12	RT1 20
5-year-old children	Cell 3 17	Cell 4 3	RT2 20
Column total	CT1 25	CT2 15	GT 40

where RT1 and RT2 are row totals, CT1 and CT2 are column totals and GT is the grand total.

2 Calculate the expected frequency for each cell, using the formula:

$$\text{Expected frequency } (E) = \frac{RT \times CT}{GT}$$

For Cell 1: $\dfrac{E = 20 \times 25}{40} = \dfrac{500}{40} = 12.5$

For Cell 2: $\dfrac{E = 20 \times 15}{40} = \dfrac{300}{40} = 7.5$

For Cell 3: $\dfrac{E = 20 \times 25}{40} = \dfrac{500}{40} = 12.5$

For Cell 4: $\dfrac{E = 20 \times 15}{40} = \dfrac{300}{40} = 7.5$

3 Subtract the expected frequency (E) from the observed frequency (O) for each cell:

Cell 1: $O - E = 8 - 12.5 = -4.5$
Cell 2: $O - E = 12 - 7.5 = 4.5$
Cell 3: $O - E = 17 - 12.5 = 4.5$
Cell 4: $O - E = 3 - 7.5 = -4.5$

4 Calculate $(O - E)^2$ for each cell:

Cell 1: $-4.5^2 = 20.25$
Cell 2: $4.5^2 = 20.25$
Cell 3: $4.5^2 = 20.25$
Cell 4: $-4.5^2 = 20.25$

5 Calculate $\dfrac{(O - E)^2}{E}$ for each cell:

Cell 1: $20.25 \div 12.5 = 1.62$
Cell 2: $20.25 \div 7.5 = 2.7$
Cell 3: $20.25 \div 12.5 = 1.62$
Cell 4: $20.25 \div 7.5 = 2.7$

6 Add the answers to stage 5 to obtain the observed value of χ^2:

$$1.62 + 2.7 + 1.62 + 2.7 = 8.64.$$

This is the observed value of χ^2.

Note: Stages 2 to 6 can be represented by the following formula:

$$\chi^2 = \sum \left(\frac{(O - E)^2}{E} \right)$$

7 Calculate the number of degrees of freedom using the formula:

Degrees of freedom (df)
= (No. of rows − 1) (No. of columns − 1)

(Degrees of freedom are the number of cell values that are free to vary, given that row totals and column totals are known.)

In the example above:

$df = (2 - 1)(2 - 1)$
$df = 1.$

8 Consult the table in Appendix 4 to obtain the critical values of χ^2; a critical value of χ^2 is the minimum value of χ^2 that is significant at a given level of significance. (Statistical significance is discussed earlier in this unit on p. 916.) In order to obtain this you need to know:

(a) the number of degrees of freedom (in this case $df = 1$)

(b) whether a one-tailed test or two-tailed test is required.

You should note that a one-tailed test should only be employed with a 2 × 1 contingency table and a directional hypothesis. (Directional and non-directional hypotheses are discussed in Unit 7.)

If the observed value of χ^2 is equal to or greater than the critical value for a given level of significance, the null hypothesis can be rejected. (Levels of significance are discussed on p. 916; null and alternative hypotheses are discussed in Unit 7.)

A minimum significance level of $p \leq 0.05$ will be assumed in this case. From Appendix 4, the critical value of χ^2 for $df = 1$ and a two-tailed test at $p = 0.05$ is 3.84. As the observed value of χ^2 (8.64) is greater than the critical value (3.84), the likelihood of these results occurring through chance is less than 5% ($p < 0.05$). In this case, the null hypothesis could be rejected in favour of the alternative hypothesis.

Note: If the observed value had been less than the critical value, then the probability of results such as these occurring through chance would have been greater than 5%. In this case, the null hypothesis would not have been rejected.

THE WILCOXON MATCHED PAIRS SIGNED RANKS TEST

The Wilcoxon Matched Pairs Signed Ranks Test is a test of difference, suitable for use with data gathered from a repeated measures design. It can be used when data are at least an ordinal level of measurement. It can therefore be used with data on an interval or ratio level of measurement that are converted to an ordinal level for the purposes of the test. Two versions of this test will be discussed here. The first is used when there is a maximum of 25 pairs of observations (see specimen calculation below). (See Unit 7 for a discussion of a repeated measures design, and the panel on p. 914 for a discussion of levels of measurement.)

Specimen calculation for smaller observations

Below is a specimen calculation of the Wilcoxon Matched Pairs Signed Ranks Test where there is a maximum of 25 pairs of observations, using data obtained from a memory experiment.

1 Place the data to be analysed into the appropriate columns of a table drawn up in a similar way to that in the table, which represents the data obtained from a memory experiment.

2 Calculate the difference between each pair of scores (see the 'Difference' column in the table below). Note that it is essential that the direction of any differences is recorded.

3 Rank the data in the difference column, from the lowest value (allocated rank 1) to the highest value (rank N). Notice that:

(a) any zero differences are disregarded

(b) positive and negative signs are disregarded

(c) the ranks are shared for any scores which are tied.

(See Appendix 2 on p. 929 for how to rank data.)

4 Calculate the sum of the ranks which correspond to:

(a) the differences with the + sign; and

(b) the differences with the − sign.

Call the smaller of these values T. In the example below:

Sum of the ranks which correspond to the differences with the + sign

$$= 2.5 + 1 = 3.5$$

Sum of the ranks which correspond to the differences with the − sign

$$= 4 + 2.5 + 9 + 6 + 6 + 8 + 6 = 41.5$$

The smallest sum of ranks is T.

Therefore, the observed value of $T = 3.5$.

5 Consult the table in Appendix 5 to obtain the critical values of T (a critical value is the maximum value of T that is significant at a given level of probability). (Statistical significance is discussed earlier in this unit on p. 916.)

In order to obtain the critical value of T, you need to know:

(a) the value of N (the number of pairs of scores). (Note that pairs of scores with a difference of zero are not included.) In this example, the number of pairs of scores = 9.

(b) whether a one-tailed or two-tailed test is required. In this example, let us assume a two-tailed test.

(The concept of directional and non-directional hypotheses is discussed in Unit 7.)

If the observed value of T is equal to or less than the critical value for a given level of significance, the null hypothesis can be rejected. (Null and alternative hypotheses are discussed in Unit 7.)

Participant no.	No. of words recalled (control condition)	No. of words recalled (experimental condition)	Difference	Rank order
1	17	20	−3	4
2	12	14	−2	2.5
3	16	14	+2	2.5
4	12	19	−7	9
5	16	15	+1	1
6	14	19	−5	6
7	13	13	0	(omitted)
8	11	16	−5	6
9	13	19	−6	8
10	11	16	−5	6

A minimum significance level of $p \leq 0.05$ will be assumed in this case. From Appendix 5, the critical value of T for $N = 9$ for a two-tailed test at $p = 0.05$ is 5. As the observed value of T (3.5) is less than the critical value (5), the likelihood of the results occurring through chance is less than 5% ($p < 0.05$).

In this case, the null hypothesis could be rejected in favour of the alternative hypothesis.

Note: If the observed value had been greater than the critical value, then the likelihood of results such as these occurring through chance would have been greater than 5%. In this case, the null hypothesis would not have been rejected.

THE SIGN TEST

The Sign Test is a test of difference that is suitable for use with data gathered from a repeated measures design that are at a nominal level of measurement. The test examines the direction of any difference between pairs of scores.

1 The example that follows uses data obtained from an investigation which set out to discover whether the perceptions of psychology held by students changed after completing a GCSE psychology course. Place the data to be analysed into the appropriate columns of a table drawn up in a similar way to that in the table shown below.

   Note: It is also possible to derive the direction of difference from numerical values (e.g. if actual ratings had been used in the example table, before and after taking a GCSE psychology course).

Participant no.	Attitude	Direction of difference
1	More favourable	+
2	More favourable	+
3	No change	omitted
4	Less favourable	–
5	More favourable	+
6	More favourable	+
7	More favourable	+
8	No change	omitted
9	More favourable	+
10	More favourable	+

Formula for large observations

The formula for the calculation of the Wilcoxon Matched Pairs Signed Ranks Test when there are more than 25 pairs of scores is given below:

$$z = \frac{N(N + 1) - 4T}{\sqrt{\left(\dfrac{2N(N + 1)(2N + 1)}{3}\right)}}$$

This formula provides the researcher with a z score (see Appendix 1).

2 Enter a plus sign or a minus sign to indicate the direction of difference for each participant (see direction of difference column in the table below).

3 Add the number of times the less frequent sign occurs, and call this s. In the example given, the less frequent sign is the minus sign, which occurs once. Therefore the observed value of $s = 1$.

4 Consult the table in Appendix 6 to obtain the critical values of s. A critical value is the maximum value of s that is significant at a given level of probability. In order to obtain this, you need to know:

   (a) The value of N (the number of pairs of scores).
       Note that pairs of scores with no + or – sign are not included. In this case, the number of pairs of scores = 8.

   (b) Whether a one-tailed or two-tailed test is required (in this case, let us assume two-tailed). (The concept of directional and non-directional hypotheses is discussed in Unit 7.)

If the observed value of s is equal to or less than the critical value for a given level of significance, the null hypothesis can be rejected. (Null and alternative hypotheses are discussed in Unit 7.)

A minimum significance level of $p \leq 0.05$ will be assumed in this case. From Appendix 6, the critical value of s for $N = 8$ for a two-tailed hypothesis at $p = 0.05$ is 0. As the observed value of s (1) is greater than the critical value (0), the probability of results such as these occurring through chance is greater than 5%. In this case, the null hypothesis cannot be rejected.

Note: If the observed value had been less than or equal to the critical value, then the likelihood of results such as these occurring through chance would have been less than 5%. In this case, the null hypothesis would have been rejected.

SPEARMAN'S RANK ORDER CORRELATION COEFFICIENT (r_s)

Spearman's Rank Order Correlation Coefficient (r_s) is a test of correlation suitable for use with pairs of scores. It can be used when data are at least at an ordinal level of measurement. It can therefore be used with data on an interval or ratio level of measurement that are converted to an ordinal level for the purposes of the test.

Specimen calculation

The example below uses data obtained from a study to investigate the possible correlation between psychology test scores and biology test scores from a group of participants studying both subjects.

1 Draw a scattergraph of the data sets that you wish to correlate. This is important as this technique measures only straight-line relationships, and drawing a scattergraph can help you to decide if this is the case (see p. 241).

2 Place the data to be analysed into the appropriate columns of a table drawn up in a similar way to that in the table below.

Participant no.	Psychology test score	Rank order	Biology test score	Rank order	d	d^2
1	95	10	92	9	1	1
2	27	2	36	2	0	0
3	47	4	40	3	1	1
4	68	7	57	5	2	4
5	50	5	61	6	−1	1
6	94	9	91	8	1	1
7	33	3	41	4	−1	1
8	26	1	35	1	0	0
9	93	8	93	10	−2	4
10	59	6	70	7	−1	1
						$\Sigma d^2 = 14$

3 Rank each set of scores separately, giving the lowest score rank 1 and the highest score rank N.

Note: Accuracy is diminished if this test is used when ranks are shared for any scores that are tied. In such cases, the appropriate procedure is to carry out the calculation for Pearson's Product-moment Correlation Coefficient on the two sets of ranks. This test is covered in more advanced texts such as Coolican (1999) and Dyer (1995). However, unless there are large numbers of ties, the effects on the outcome are likely to be very small.

(If the test is carried out where ranks are tied, see Appendix 2 for how to rank your data.)

4 Find the difference (d) between each pair of rank order scores (see d column in above table).

5 Square each of the d values (see d^2 column in above table).

6 Calculate the sum of the d^2 values. This is the value described as Σd^2 in the table above.

7 Substitute in the following formula:

$$r_s = 1 - \left(\frac{6\Sigma d^2}{N(N^2 - 1)} \right)$$

Here:

r_s = the observed (i.e. calculated) value of Spearman's correlation coefficient

Σd^2 = the sum of the squared differences

N = the number of pairs of scores being correlated.

Here:

$$r_s = 1 - \left(\frac{84}{10(100 - 1)} \right)$$

$$= 1 - \left(\frac{84}{10 \times 99} \right)$$

$$= 1 - \frac{84}{990}$$

$$= 1 - 0.0848$$

$$= 0.9152$$

This is the observed value of r_s.

8 Consult the table in Appendix 7 to obtain the critical values of r_s (a critical value is the minimum value of r_s that is significant at a given level of probability). In order to obtain this you need to know:

(a) the value of N (the number of pairs of scores)

(b) whether a one-tailed or two-tailed test is required (in this case, let us assume one-tailed).

If the observed value of r_s is equal to or greater than the critical value for a given level of significance, the null hypothesis can be rejected. (Null and alternative hypotheses are discussed in Unit 7.)

A minimum significance level of $p \leq 0.05$ will be assumed in this case. From Appendix 7, when $N = 10$, the critical value of r_s for a one-tailed

hypothesis at $p = 0.05$ is 0.564. As the observed value of r_s (0.9152) is greater than the critical value (0.564), the likelihood of results such as these occurring through chance is less than 5%. In this case, the null hypothesis can be rejected.

Note: If the observed value had been less than the critical value, then the likelihood of results such as these occurring through chance would have been greater than 5%. In this case, the null hypothesis would not have been rejected.

✓ CHECK YOUR UNDERSTANDING

Check your understanding of inferential statistics by answering these questions from memory. Check your answers by looking back through Topic 2.

1 What does the use of inferential statistical techniques enable a researcher to do that descriptive statistics do not?

2 Is the following hypothesis a null or an alternative hypothesis?
'There is no difference in boys' and girls' grades in their mock A-level exams.'

3 'A statistically significant result is one which is highly likely to have occurred through chance.' Is this statement TRUE or FALSE?

4 Describe what is meant by the term 'level of significance'.

5 Is a significance level of $p < 0.001$ more or less stringent than a significance level of $p < 0.05$? When might a researcher choose to use more stringent levels of statistical significance?

6 Describe what is meant by a Type I and a Type II error.

7 What type of error would you be more likely to make if you were using the following levels of significance instead of the 5% level ($p < 0.05$):
(a) a 10% level of significance ($p < 0.1$)
(b) a 1% level of significance ($p < 0.01$)?

8 A researcher has collected nominal data and is interested in whether any association exists. Which statistical test should be used to analyse these data?

9 A researcher is interested in whether ordinal data collected from two independent groups are different. Which statistical test should be used to analyse these data?

10 When is it appropriate to use a one-tailed test and when should a two-tailed test be used?

REVISION SUMMARY

Having covered this topic you should be able to:

✓ outline how inferential statistical techniques can be used to support or reject a null hypothesis

✓ describe the concept of: (a) probability, (b) statistical significance and (c) level of significance

✓ explain the difference between a Type I and a Type II error

✓ discuss when more or less stringent levels of significance might be used

✓ decide which test should be used with which level of data and experimental design

✓ follow the step-by-step guides to calculate:

    (a) the Mann-Whitney U Test   (d) the Sign Test

    (b) the Chi-squared Test for Independent Samples   (e) Spearman's Rank Order Correlation Coefficient

    (c) the Wilcoxon Matched Pairs Signed Ranks Test

✓ interpret the observed value for a particular inferential statistic and decide whether the null hypothesis should be retained or rejected.

Topic 1: Calculating the standard deviation

- The **standard deviation** is a measure of dispersion suitable for use with normally distributed data that are at an ordinal or ratio level of measurement. Calculation allows us to make statements of the variability of scores within a particular data set and to make statements about how likely or unlikely a given value is to occur.

Topic 2: Inferential statistics

- **Inferential statistical tests** can be used to calculate the **probability level** of the obtained results occurring by chance. Tests may measure **differences**, **associations** or **correlations** between sets of data.

- **Inferential statistical techniques** enable researchers to draw conclusions about the **populations** from which their samples have been drawn. By using these techniques, the researcher may reach reasoned conclusions concerning whether to retain or reject the **null hypothesis**. Reaching this conclusion is based on the probability of such results occurring through chance.

- The decision concerning which inferential statistical test to use is based on factors which include the **level of measurement** of the data, the **design of the study** and whether the researcher seeks to establish a **difference**, **correlation** or an **association**.

- **The significance level** is used as a criterion for ascertaining whether a particular set of data differs from what would be expected if chance factors operated.

Coolican, H. (1999) *Research Methods and Statistics in Psychology*, London: Hodder & Stoughton.

A clearly written text that covers all the inferential statistical techniques that you are likely to encounter.

Coolican, H. (1996) *Introduction to Research Methods and Statistics in Psychology*, London: Hodder & Stoughton.

A condensed version of the Coolican text above.

Dyer, C. (1995) *Beginning Research in Psychology: A Practical Guide to Research Methods and Statistics*, Oxford: Blackwell.

A detailed text that covers the statistical tests included in this unit; good use of examples.

Foster, J.F. and Parker, I. (1995) *Carrying Out Investigations in Psychology: Methods and Statistics*, Leicester: BPS & Blackwell.

A detailed and advanced text that could be useful for reference purposes.

Haslam, S.A. and McGarty, C. (1998) *Doing Psychology: An Introduction to Research Methodology and Statistics*, London: Sage.

A clear introduction to the main research methods and statistical techniques used by psychologists, including step-by-step guides to statistical procedures.

Malim, T. and Birch, A. (1997) *Research Methods and Statistics*, Basingstoke: Macmillan.

This text is aimed at A-level students and includes self-assessment questions, making it ideal for self-study.

Searle, A. (1999) *Introducing Research and Data in Psychology: A Guide to Methods and Analysis*, London: Routledge.

Provides a user-friendly introduction to statistical methods that is particularly suitable for those who find statistics daunting.

The table provided below gives the area beneath the normal distribution curve between the mean and any given standard score (i.e. *z* score). These values are therefore also the probabilities of finding a value within the area concerned.

- Column A gives the positive *z* score.
- Column B gives the area between the mean and *z* (see diagram below left). Since the curve is symmetrical, areas for negative *z* scores are the same as for positive ones.
- Column C gives the area that is beyond *z* (see diagram below right).

To find the proportion of individuals between a given standard score and the mean:

1 Calculate the mean and the standard deviation for the sample concerned.

2 Calculate the standard score (or *z* score, i.e. the number of standard deviations a given score is away from its mean). For example, if a sample of test scores has a mean of 100 and a standard deviation of 10, then a test score of 80 would have a standard score of 2 (two standard deviations below the mean). Similarly, a test score of 107 would have a standard score of 0.7 (and so on).

3 Look up this standard score in the left-hand column of the table (Column A) and read off the corresponding value in Column B. This is the probability of a score occurring between the mean and the standard score.

4 If a percentage is required, the value obtained should be multiplied by 100. If a probability is required for a score occurring between the same number of standard scores either side of the mean, then the value obtained should be doubled.

| A | B | C | A | B | C | A | B | C |
z	Area between mean and *z*	Area beyond *z*	*z*	Area between mean and *z*	Area beyond *z*	*z*	Area between mean and *z*	Area beyond *z*
0.00	.0000	.5000	0.20	.0793	.4207	0.40	.1554	.3446
0.01	.0040	.4960	0.21	.0832	.4168	0.41	.1591	.3409
0.02	.0080	.4920	0.22	.0871	.4129	0.42	.1628	.3372
0.03	.0120	.4880	0.23	.0910	.4090	0.43	.1664	.3336
0.04	.0160	.4840	0.24	.0948	.4052	0.44	.1700	.3300
0.05	.0199	.4801	0.25	.0987	.4013	0.45	.1736	.3264
0.06	.0239	.4761	0.26	.1026	.3974	0.46	.1772	.3228
0.07	.0279	.4721	0.27	.1064	.3936	0.47	.1808	.3192
0.08	.0319	.4681	0.28	.1103	.3897	0.48	.1844	.3156
0.09	.0359	.4641	0.29	.1141	.3859	0.49	.1879	.3121
0.10	.0398	.4602	0.30	.1179	.3821	0.50	.1915	.3085
0.11	.0438	.4562	0.31	.1217	.3783	0.51	.1950	.3050
0.12	.0478	.4522	0.32	.1255	.3745	0.52	.1985	.3015
0.13	.0517	.4483	0.33	.1293	.3707	0.53	.2019	.2981
0.14	.0557	.4443	0.34	.1331	.3669	0.54	.2054	.2946
0.15	.0596	.4404	0.35	.1368	.3632	0.55	.2088	.2912
0.16	.0636	.4364	0.36	.1406	.3594	0.56	.2123	.2877
0.17	.0675	.4325	0.37	.1443	.3557	0.57	.2157	.2843
0.18	.0714	.4286	0.38	.1480	.3520	0.58	.2190	.2810
0.19	.0753	.4247	0.39	.1517	.3483	0.59	.2224	.2776

A z	B Area between mean and z	C Area beyond z	A z	B Area between mean and z	C Area beyond z	A z	B Area between mean and z	C Area beyond z
0.60	.2257	.2743	1.05	.3531	.1469	1.50	.4332	.0668
0.61	.2291	.2709	1.06	.3554	.1446	1.51	.4345	.0655
0.62	.2324	.2676	1.07	.3577	.1423	1.52	.4357	.0643
0.63	.2357	.2643	1.08	.3599	.1401	1.53	.4370	.0630
0.64	.2389	.2611	1.09	.3621	.1379	1.54	.4372	.0618
0.65	.2422	.2578	1.10	.3643	.1357	1.55	.4394	.0606
0.66	.2454	.2546	1.11	.3665	.1335	1.56	.4406	.0594
0.67	.2486	.2514	1.12	.3686	.1314	1.57	.4418	.0582
0.68	.2517	.2483	1.13	.3708	.1292	1.58	.4429	.0571
0.69	.2549	.2451	1.14	.3729	.1271	1.59	.4441	.0559
0.70	.2580	.2420	1.15	.3749	.1251	1.60	.4452	.0548
0.71	.2611	.2389	1.16	.3770	.1230	1.61	.4463	.0537
0.72	.2642	.2358	1.17	.3790	.1210	1.62	.4474	.0526
0.73	.2673	.2327	1.18	.3810	.1190	1.63	.4484	.0516
0.74	.2704	.2296	1.19	.3830	.1170	1.64	.4495	.0505
0.75	.2734	.2266	1.20	.3849	.1151	1.65	.4505	.0495
0.76	.2764	.2236	1.21	.3869	.1131	1.66	.4515	.0485
0.77	.2794	.2206	1.22	.3888	.1112	1.67	.4525	.0475
0.78	.2823	.2177	1.23	.3907	.1093	1.68	.4535	.0465
0.79	.2852	.2148	1.24	.3925	.1075	1.69	.4545	.0455
0.80	.2881	.2119	1.25	.3944	.1056	1.70	.4554	.0446
0.81	.2910	.2090	1.26	.3962	.1038	1.71	.4564	.0436
0.82	.2939	.2061	1.27	.3980	.1020	1.72	.4573	.0427
0.83	.2967	.2033	1.28	.3997	.1003	1.73	.4582	.0418
0.84	.2995	.2005	1.29	.4015	.0985	1.74	.4591	.0409
0.85	.3023	.1977	1.30	.4032	.0968	1.75	.4599	.0401
0.86	.3051	.1949	1.31	.4049	.0951	1.76	.4608	.0392
0.87	.3078	.1922	1.32	.4066	.0934	1.77	.4616	.0384
0.88	.3106	.1894	1.33	.4082	.0918	1.78	.4625	.0375
0.89	.3133	.1867	1.34	.4099	.0901	1.79	.4633	.0367
0.90	.3159	.1841	1.35	.4115	.0885	1.80	.4641	.0359
0.91	.3186	.1814	1.36	.4131	.0869	1.81	.4649	.0351
0.92	.3212	.1788	1.37	.4147	.0853	1.82	.4656	.0344
0.93	.3238	.1762	1.38	.4162	.0838	1.83	.4664	.0336
0.94	.3264	.1736	1.39	.4177	.0823	1.84	.4671	.0329
0.95	.3289	.1711	1.40	.4192	.0808	1.85	.4678	.0322
0.96	.3315	.1685	1.41	.4207	.0793	1.86	.4686	.0314
0.97	.3340	.1660	1.42	.4222	.0778	1.87	.4693	.0307
0.98	.3365	.1635	1.43	.4236	.0764	1.88	.4699	.0301
0.99	.3389	.1611	1.44	.4251	.0749	1.89	.4706	.0294
1.00	.3413	.1587	1.45	.4265	.0735	1.90	.4713	.0287
1.01	.3438	.1562	1.46	.4279	.0721	1.91	.4719	.0281
1.02	.3461	.1539	1.47	.4292	.0708	1.92	.4726	.0274
1.03	.3485	.1515	1.48	.4306	.0694	1.93	.4732	.0268
1.04	.3508	.1492	1.49	.4319	.0681	1.94	.4738	.0262

A z	B Area between mean and z	C Area beyond z	A z	B Area between mean and z	C Area beyond z	A z	B Area between mean and z	C Area beyond z
1.95	.4744	.0256	2.40	.4918	.0082	2.85	.4978	.0022
1.96	.4750	.0250	2.41	.4920	.0080	2.86	.4979	.0021
1.97	.4756	.0244	2.42	.4922	.0078	2.87	.4979	.0021
1.98	.4761	.0239	2.43	.4925	.0075	2.88	.4980	.0020
1.99	.4767	.0233	2.44	.4927	.0073	2.89	.4981	.0019
2.00	.4772	.0228	2.45	.4929	.0071	2.90	.4981	.0019
2.01	.4778	.0222	2.46	.4931	.0069	2.91	.4982	.0018
2.02	.4783	.0217	2.47	.4932	.0068	2.92	.4982	.0018
2.03	.4788	.0212	2.48	.4934	.0066	2.93	.4983	.0017
2.04	.4793	.0207	2.49	.4936	.0064	2.94	.4984	.0016
2.05	.4798	.0202	2.50	.4938	.0062	2.95	.4984	.0016
2.06	.4803	.0197	2.51	.4940	.0060	2.96	.4985	.0015
2.07	.4808	.0192	2.52	.4941	.0059	2.97	.4985	.0015
2.08	.4812	.0188	2.53	.4943	.0057	2.98	.4986	.0014
2.09	.4817	.0183	2.54	.4945	.0055	2.99	.4986	.0014
2.10	.4821	.0179	2.55	.4946	.0054	3.00	.4987	.0013
2.11	.4826	.0174	2.56	.4948	.0052	3.01	.4987	.0013
2.12	.4830	.0170	2.57	.4949	.0051	3.02	.4987	.0013
2.13	.4834	.0166	2.58	.4951	.0049	3.03	.4988	.0012
2.14	.4838	.0162	2.59	.4952	.0048	3.04	.4988	.0012
2.15	.4842	.0158	2.60	.4953	.0047	3.05	.4989	.0011
2.16	.4846	.0154	2.61	.4955	.0045	3.06	.4989	.0011
2.17	.4850	.0150	2.62	.4956	.0044	3.07	.4989	.0011
2.18	.4854	.0146	2.63	.4957	.0043	3.08	.4990	.0010
2.19	.4857	.0143	2.64	.4959	.0041	3.09	.4990	.0010
2.20	.4861	.0139	2.65	.4960	.0040	3.10	.4990	.0010
2.21	.4864	.0136	2.66	.4961	.0039	3.11	.4991	.0009
2.22	.4868	.0132	2.67	.4962	.0038	3.12	.4991	.0009
2.23	.4871	.0129	2.68	.4963	.0037	3.13	.4991	.0009
2.24	.4875	.0125	2.69	.4964	.0036	3.14	.4992	.0008
2.25	.4878	.0122	2.70	.4965	.0035	3.15	.4992	.0008
2.26	.4881	.0119	2.71	.4966	.0034	3.16	.4992	.0008
2.27	.4884	.0116	2.72	.4967	.0033	3.17	.4992	.0008
2.28	.4887	.0113	2.73	.4968	.0032	3.18	.4993	.0007
2.29	.4890	.0110	2.74	.4969	.0031	3.19	.4993	.0007
2.30	.4893	.0107	2.75	.4970	.0030	3.20	.4993	.0007
2.31	.4896	.0104	2.76	.4971	.0029	3.21	.4993	.0007
2.32	.4898	.0102	2.77	.4972	.0028	3.22	.4994	.0006
2.33	.4901	.0099	2.78	.4973	.0027	3.23	.4994	.0006
2.34	.4904	.0096	2.79	.4974	.0026	3.24	.4994	.0006
2.35	.4906	.0094	2.80	.4974	.0026	3.30	.4995	.0005
2.36	.4909	.0091	2.81	.4975	.0025	3.40	.4997	.0003
2.37	.4911	.0089	2.82	.4976	.0024	3.50	.4998	.0002
2.38	.4913	.0087	2.83	.4977	.0023	3.60	.4998	.0002
2.39	.4916	.0084	2.84	.4977	.0023	3.70	.4999	.0001

Appendix 2 >> Method for ranking data in statistical tests

1 Organize data into ascending order of values (see specimen data below).
2 Allocate rank 1 to the lowest value.
3 Allocate ranks to the remaining values, averaging the ranks for any tied scores (see below).

Scores	Rank	Notes
10	1	
12	2.5	Both scores of 12 are given the average
12	2.5	rank of positions 2 and 3. Note that the
15	4	next score is rank 4, not 3.
17	5	
18	7	
18	7	Three scores of 18 are given the average
18	7	rank of positions 6, 7 and 8. Note that the
20	9	next score is rank 9, not 8.
25	10	

Appendix 3 >> The critical values of U

Table 1: Critical values of U for a one-tailed test at $p = 0.005$;
two-tailed test at $p = 0.01$ * (Mann-Whitney)

N_1

N_2	1	2	3	4	5	6	7	8	9	10	11	12	13	14	15	16	17	18	19	20
1	–	–	–	–	–	–	–	–	–	–	–	–	–	–	–	–	–	–	–	–
2	–	–	–	–	–	–	–	–	–	–	–	–	–	–	–	–	–	–	0	0
3	–	–	–	–	–	–	–	–	0	0	0	1	1	1	2	2	2	2	3	3
4	–	–	–	–	–	0	0	1	1	2	2	3	3	4	5	5	6	6	7	8
5	–	–	–	–	0	1	1	2	3	4	5	6	7	7	8	9	10	11	12	13
6	–	–	–	0	1	2	3	4	5	6	7	9	10	11	12	13	15	16	17	18
7	–	–	–	0	1	3	4	6	7	9	10	12	13	15	16	18	19	21	22	24
8	–	–	–	1	2	4	6	7	9	11	13	15	17	18	20	22	24	26	28	30
9	–	–	0	1	3	5	7	9	11	13	16	18	20	22	24	27	29	31	33	36
10	–	–	0	2	4	6	9	11	13	16	18	21	24	26	29	31	34	37	39	42
11	–	–	0	2	5	7	10	13	16	18	21	24	27	30	33	36	39	42	45	48
12	–	–	1	3	6	9	12	15	18	21	24	27	31	34	37	41	44	47	51	54
13	–	–	1	3	7	10	13	17	20	24	27	31	34	38	42	45	49	53	56	60
14	–	–	1	4	7	11	15	18	22	26	30	34	38	42	46	50	54	58	63	67
15	–	–	2	5	8	12	16	20	24	29	33	37	42	46	51	55	60	64	69	73
16	–	–	2	5	9	13	18	22	27	31	36	41	45	50	55	60	65	70	74	79
17	–	–	2	6	10	15	19	24	29	34	39	44	49	54	60	65	70	75	81	86
18	–	–	2	6	11	16	21	26	31	37	42	47	53	58	64	70	75	81	87	92
19	–	0	3	7	12	17	22	28	33	39	45	51	56	63	69	74	81	87	93	99
20	–	0	3	8	13	18	24	30	36	42	48	54	60	67	73	79	86	92	99	105

*Dashes in the body of the table indicate that no decision is possible at the stated level of significance. For any N_1 and N_2, the observed value of U is significant at a given level of significance if it is equal to or less than the critical values shown.

Table 2: Critical values of U for a one-tailed test at $p = 0.01$; two-tailed test at $p = 0.02$* (Mann-Whitney)

N_1

N_2	1	2	3	4	5	6	7	8	9	10	11	12	13	14	15	16	17	18	19	20
1	–	–	–	–	–	–	–	–	–	–	–	–	–	–	–	–	–	–	–	–
2	–	–	–	–	–	–	–	–	–	–	–	0	0	0	0	0	0	0	1	1
3	–	–	–	–	–	–	0	0	1	1	1	2	2	2	3	3	4	4	4	5
4	–	–	–	–	0	1	1	2	3	3	4	5	5	6	7	7	8	9	9	10
5	–	–	–	0	1	2	3	4	5	6	7	8	9	10	11	12	13	14	15	16
6	–	–	–	1	2	3	4	6	7	8	9	11	12	13	15	16	18	19	20	22
7	–	–	0	1	3	4	6	7	9	11	12	14	16	17	19	21	23	24	26	28
8	–	–	0	2	4	6	7	9	11	13	15	17	20	22	24	26	28	30	32	34
9	–	–	1	3	5	7	9	11	14	16	18	21	23	26	28	31	33	36	38	40
10	–	–	1	3	6	8	11	13	16	19	22	24	27	30	33	36	38	41	44	47
11	–	–	1	4	7	9	12	15	18	22	25	28	31	34	37	41	44	47	50	53
12	–	–	2	5	8	11	14	17	21	24	28	31	35	38	42	46	49	53	56	60
13	–	0	2	5	9	12	16	20	23	27	31	35	39	43	47	51	55	59	63	67
14	–	0	2	6	10	13	17	22	26	30	34	38	43	47	51	56	60	65	69	73
15	–	0	3	7	11	15	19	24	28	33	37	42	47	51	56	61	66	70	75	80
16	–	0	3	7	12	16	21	26	31	36	41	46	51	56	61	66	71	76	82	87
17	–	0	4	8	13	18	23	28	33	38	44	49	55	60	66	71	77	82	88	93
18	–	0	4	9	14	19	24	30	36	41	47	53	59	65	70	76	82	88	94	100
19	–	1	4	9	15	20	26	32	38	44	50	56	63	69	75	82	88	94	101	107
20	–	1	5	10	16	22	28	34	40	47	53	60	67	73	80	87	93	100	107	114

Table 3: Critical values of U for a one-tailed test at $p = 0.025$; two-tailed test at $p = 0.05$* (Mann-Whitney)

N_1

N_2	1	2	3	4	5	6	7	8	9	10	11	12	13	14	15	16	17	18	19	20
1	–	–	–	–	–	–	–	–	–	–	–	–	–	–	–	–	–	–	–	–
2	–	–	–	–	–	–	–	0	0	0	0	1	1	1	1	1	2	2	2	2
3	–	–	–	–	0	1	1	2	2	3	3	4	4	5	5	6	6	7	7	8
4	–	–	–	0	1	2	3	4	4	5	6	7	8	9	10	11	11	12	13	13
5	–	–	0	1	2	3	5	6	7	8	9	11	12	13	14	15	17	18	19	20
6	–	–	1	2	3	5	6	8	10	11	13	14	16	17	19	21	22	24	25	27
7	–	–	1	3	5	6	8	10	12	14	16	18	20	22	24	26	28	30	32	34
8	–	0	2	4	6	8	10	13	15	17	19	22	24	26	29	31	34	36	38	41
9	–	0	2	4	7	10	12	15	17	20	23	26	28	31	34	37	39	42	45	48
10	–	0	3	5	8	11	14	17	20	23	26	29	33	36	39	42	45	48	52	55
11	–	0	3	6	9	13	16	19	23	26	30	33	37	40	44	47	51	55	58	62
12	–	1	4	7	11	14	18	22	26	29	33	37	41	45	49	53	57	61	65	69
13	–	1	4	8	12	16	20	24	28	33	37	41	45	50	54	59	63	67	72	76
14	–	1	5	9	13	17	22	26	31	36	40	45	50	55	59	64	67	74	78	83
15	–	1	5	10	14	19	24	29	34	39	44	49	54	59	64	70	75	80	85	90
16	–	1	6	11	15	21	26	31	37	42	47	53	59	64	70	75	81	86	92	98
17	–	2	6	11	17	22	28	34	39	45	51	57	63	67	75	81	87	93	99	105
18	–	2	7	12	18	24	30	36	42	48	55	61	67	74	80	86	93	99	106	112
19	–	2	7	13	19	25	32	38	45	52	58	65	72	78	85	92	99	106	113	119
20	–	2	8	13	20	27	34	41	48	55	62	69	76	83	90	98	105	112	119	127

Table 4: Critical values of U for a one-tailed test at $p = 0.05$; two-tailed test at $p = 0.10$* (Mann-Whitney)

N_1

N_2	1	2	3	4	5	6	7	8	9	10	11	12	13	14	15	16	17	18	19	20
1	–	–	–	–	–	–	–	–	–	–	–	–	–	–	–	–	–	–	0	0
2	–	–	–	–	0	0	0	1	1	1	1	2	2	2	3	3	3	4	4	4
3	–	–	0	0	1	2	2	3	3	4	5	5	6	7	7	8	9	9	10	11
4	–	–	0	1	2	3	4	5	6	7	8	9	10	11	12	14	15	16	17	18
5	–	0	1	2	4	5	6	8	9	11	12	13	15	16	18	19	20	22	23	25
6	–	0	2	3	5	7	8	10	12	14	16	17	19	21	23	25	26	28	30	32
7	–	0	2	4	6	8	11	13	15	17	19	21	24	26	28	30	33	35	37	39
8	–	1	3	5	8	10	13	15	18	20	23	26	28	31	33	36	39	41	44	47
9	–	1	3	6	9	12	15	18	21	24	27	30	33	36	39	42	45	48	51	54
10	–	1	4	7	11	14	17	20	24	27	31	34	37	41	44	48	51	55	58	62
11	–	1	5	8	12	16	19	23	27	31	34	38	42	46	50	54	57	61	65	69
12	–	2	5	9	13	17	21	26	30	34	38	42	47	51	55	60	64	68	72	77
13	–	2	6	10	15	19	24	28	33	37	42	47	51	56	61	65	70	75	80	84
14	–	2	7	11	16	21	26	31	36	41	46	51	56	61	66	71	77	82	87	92
15	–	3	7	12	18	23	28	33	39	44	50	55	61	66	72	77	83	88	94	100
16	–	3	8	14	19	25	30	36	42	48	54	60	65	71	77	83	89	95	101	107
17	–	3	9	15	20	26	33	39	45	51	57	64	70	77	83	89	96	102	109	115
18	–	4	9	16	22	28	35	41	48	55	61	68	75	82	88	95	102	109	116	123
19	–	4	10	17	23	30	37	44	51	58	65	72	80	87	94	101	109	116	123	130
20	–	4	11	18	25	32	39	47	54	62	69	77	84	92	100	107	115	123	130	138

*Dashes in the body of the table indicate that no decision is possible at the stated level of significance. For any N_1 and N_2, the observed value of U is significant at a given level of significance if it is equal to or less than the critical values shown.

Source: Runyon and Haber (1976)

Appendix 4 >> Critical values of χ^2

Level of significance for a one-tailed test

df	0.10	0.05	0.025	0.01	0.005	0.0005
1	1.64	2.71	3.84	5.41	6.64	10.83

Level of significance for a two-tailed test

df	0.20	0.10	0.05	0.02	0.01	0.001
1	1.64	2.71	3.84	5.41	6.64	10.83
2	3.22	4.60	5.99	7.82	9.21	13.82
3	4.64	6.25	7.82	9.84	11.34	16.27
4	5.99	7.78	9.49	11.67	13.28	18.46
5	7.29	9.24	11.07	13.39	15.09	20.52
6	8.56	10.64	12.59	15.03	16.81	22.46
7	9.80	12.02	14.07	16.62	18.48	24.32
8	11.03	13.36	15.51	18.17	20.09	26.12
9	12.24	14.68	16.92	19.68	21.67	27.88
10	13.44	15.99	18.31	21.16	23.21	29.59
11	14.63	17.28	19.68	22.62	24.72	31.26
12	15.81	18.55	21.03	24.05	26.22	32.91
13	16.98	19.81	22.36	25.47	27.69	34.53
14	18.15	21.06	23.68	26.87	29.14	36.12
15	19.31	22.31	25.00	28.26	30.58	37.70
16	20.46	23.54	26.30	29.63	32.00	39.29
17	21.62	24.77	27.59	31.00	33.41	40.75
18	22.76	25.99	28.87	32.35	34.80	42.31
19	23.90	27.20	30.14	33.69	36.19	43.82
20	25.04	28.41	31.41	35.02	37.57	45.32
21	26.17	29.62	32.67	36.34	38.93	46.80
22	27.30	30.81	33.92	37.66	40.29	48.27
23	28.43	32.01	35.17	38.97	41.64	49.73
24	29.55	33.20	36.42	40.27	42.98	51.18
25	30.68	34.38	37.65	41.57	44.31	52.62
26	31.80	35.56	38.88	42.86	45.64	54.05
27	32.91	36.74	40.11	44.14	46.96	55.48
28	34.03	37.92	41.34	45.42	48.28	56.89
29	35.14	39.09	42.69	46.69	49.59	58.30
30	36.25	40.26	43.77	47.96	50.89	59.70
32	38.47	42.59	46.19	50.49	53.49	62.49
34	40.68	44.90	48.60	53.00	56.06	65.25
36	42.88	47.21	51.00	55.49	58.62	67.99
38	45.08	49.51	53.38	57.97	61.16	70.70
40	47.27	51.81	55.76	60.44	63.69	73.40
44	51.64	56.37	60.48	65.48	68.71	78.75
48	55.99	60.91	65.17	70.20	73.68	84.04
52	60.33	65.42	69.83	75.02	78.62	89.27
56	64.66	69.92	74.47	79.82	83.51	94.46
60	68.97	74.40	79.08	84.58	88.38	99.61

Calculated value of χ^2 must equal or exceed the table (critical) values for significance at the level shown.

Source: abridged from Fisher and Yates (1974)

The critical values of *T* for the Wilcoxon Matched Pairs Signed Ranks Test

Level of significance for a two-tailed test

	0.10	0.05	0.02	0.01

Level of significance for one-tailed test

N	0.05	0.025	0.01	0.005
5	0			
6	2	0		
7	3	2	0	
8	5	3	1	0
9	8	5	3	1
10	10	8	5	3
11	13	10	7	5
12	17	13	9	7
13	21	17	12	9
14	25	21	15	12
15	30	25	19	15
16	35	29	23	19
17	41	34	27	23
18	47	40	32	27
19	53	46	37	32
20	60	52	43	37
21	67	58	49	42
22	75	65	55	48
23	83	73	62	54
24	91	81	69	61
25	100	89	76	68

Values of *T* that are equal to or less than the tabled value are significant at or beyond the level indicated.

Source: taken from Table 1 of McCormack (1965)
With permission of the publishers.

The critical values of *s* in the Sign Test

Level of significance for one-tailed test

	0.05	0.025	0.01	0.005	0.0005

Level of significance for two-tailed test

N	0.10	0.05	0.02	0.01	0.001
5	0	–	–	–	–
6	0	0	–	–	–
7	0	0	0	–	–
8	1	0	0	0	–
9	1	1	0	0	–
10	1	1	0	0	–
11	2	1	1	0	0
12	2	2	1	1	0
13	3	2	1	1	0
14	3	2	2	1	0
15	3	3	2	2	1
16	4	3	2	2	1
17	4	4	3	2	1
18	5	4	3	3	1
19	5	4	4	3	2
20	5	5	4	3	2
25	7	7	6	5	4
30	10	9	8	7	5

Critical values of Spearman's Rank Order Correlation Coefficient (r_S)

Level of significance for a two-tailed test

	0.10	0.05	0.02	0.01

Level of significance for one-tailed test

N	0.05	0.025	0.01	0.005
4	1.000			
5	.900	1.000	1.000	
6	.829	.886	.943	1.000
7	.714	.786	.893	.929
8	.643	.738	.833	.881
9	.600	.700	.783	.833
10	.564	.648	.745	.794
11	.536	.618	.709	.755
12	.503	.587	.671	.727
13	.484	.560	.648	.703
14	.464	.538	.622	.675
15	.443	.521	.604	.654
16	.429	.503	.582	.635
17	.414	.485	.566	.615
18	.401	.472	.550	.600
19	.391	.460	.535	.584
20	.380	.447	.520	.570
21	.370	.435	.508	.556
22	.361	.425	.496	.544
23	.353	.415	.486	.532
24	.344	.406	.476	.521
25	.337	.398	.466	.511
26	.331	.390	.457	.501
27	.324	.382	.448	.491
28	.317	.375	.440	.483
29	.312	.368	.433	.475
30	.306	.362	.425	.467

Values of r_s that equal or exceed the tabled value are significant at or below the level indicated.

Source: Zar (1972)
With permission of the author and publisher.

32 UNIT

PREPARING FOR THE
A2 Examination

PREVIEW

In this unit we shall be looking at the following aspects of the exam process:

>> examination preparation

>> examination performance

>> examination marking.

INTRODUCTION

Examinations are generally among the most feared times in our lives. The stress of the lead-up period, the pressure to do well, the impenetrable questions and those awful two months when we fear that examiners are doing all they can to undo our best efforts. However, it doesn't have to be that way. Like an athlete training for the Olympics, a student training for an A-level exam simply needs to know how to harness all their talent and energy in the most cost-effective way possible. The pressure? Well, much of that is self-imposed – and perhaps we all need to be reminded that in the great scheme of things, exam success is relatively unimportant compared to some of the more significant aspects of our lives. Unlike some things, you can always take your exam again.

The exam process is no longer a closely guarded secret; questions and marking schemes for previous exams are readily available from AQA. Everything else is as predictable as a wet day at Wimbledon. And what does happen to your exam paper after you emerge from the exam hall, your job done with the long wait for the results about to begin? This unit takes you through the A2 examination process, and should ensure that all the good psychology from the rest of this book doesn't get wasted because of poor preparation or inadequate exam technique.

Read on ...

Mike
Cardwell

REVISION STRATEGIES

'How do I revise for the exam?' This is probably one of the questions most often asked by students coming up to this or any exam. In this first section, we focus on important points that have specific relevance to the A2 exam.

1 Revise carefully

The number of hours spent staring at a book is not directly proportional to exam success. There are, however, a number of useful things you can do with your time. Take a look at the AQA psychology specification. The specification is split into a number of options (*Social, Developmental, Individual Differences*, etc.). You will also see that each of these options is split into a number of sub-sections (represented by the units in this book). The Assessment and Qualifications Alliance (your exam board) guarantee one question from each of these sub-sections. When planning what to revise, you should take this into account.

A word of warning though. If you do decide to concentrate your revision on certain sub-sections of the specification, make sure you cover *everything* in that sub-section rather than just concentrating on the bits you like. This book has been constructed with this type of approach in mind. Each unit should stand alone for revision purposes. In other words, if you read and absorb Unit 9, you should be able to answer any question set on the 'Social cognition' sub-section of the *Social Psychology* part of the specification.

The other important aspect of careful revision is to check what you are revising against the requirements of the specification. Can you do what the specification asks you to do? If you can, then there should be no problem.

2 Revise actively

Merely reading material in textbooks is not necessarily the most productive way of using your time. In the A2 exam, you will be given a specific set of instructions which tell you what you should write about and also which specific skills you should demonstrate in your answer. Students often do far worse than they deserve to do in exams because they do not address the second of these points. They can often describe theories in great detail, but cannot provide any evaluative commentary. It is a fact in A2-level psychology, that you will always be asked to provide narrative content (description, explanation, etc.) and commentary (evaluation, analysis, etc.) *in equal measures*. In your revision notes, highlight those points that are part of

the narrative (i.e. your AO1 material) and those that are part of your commentary (i.e. your AO2 material). In the sections that follow, you should become more familiar with how to play this 'skills' game more successfully.

3 Organizing your revision

As the exams get closer, your precious time seems to become scarcer than ever. It is never too early to plan your revision.

Decide (realistically) just how much of the specification you are going to revise and make a plan of what you are going to revise and when. Read the A2 Introduction again (at the start of the book) and you will become familiar with the specification and with what you are expected to do in your revision. It is certainly permissible (perhaps even advisable) to concentrate on certain areas of the specification at this stage. If you find you are spending hours and hours on one particular sub-section of the specification, then it might be worth dumping it in favour of a sub-section where you feel more confident of doing well. When you plan your revision, remember to allocate your time profitably. You might divide your revision time for the 'perception' sub-section as shown in Fig 32.1 overleaf.

Above all, remember you are studying psychology! Try to use your knowledge of psychology to help you make this a profitable time. For example, don't cram too much into one session ('maximum span of attention'), nor expect to remember everything perfectly immediately after the revision session ('the reminiscence effect'). Reward yourself when you have had a productive session ('positive reinforcement'), and don't spend time worrying about what you should be doing – just do it and congratulate yourself on a job well done ('positive feedback').

4 Don't get taken by surprise

Many of the questions you will come across in your A2 exam will require you to focus on more than one theory, therapy or explanation. This means dividing your time, but not in a random way. Take a look at Piaget's theory of cognitive development in Unit 18 (pp. 552–7). Would you be able to outline this theory effectively in just 150 words? The skill of précis is well worth acquiring *before* you go into the exam room. Have a go at the activity overleaf, and repeat this with as many theories/therapies/explanations as you like until you feel confident you can repeat this skill in an exam.

Writing précis

Look back over the units you have covered in this book. In the example exam questions at the end of each topic, you will see that some of these ask you to 'outline and evaluate' **two** theories.

1 Construct a 300-word description (for each theory) of two appropriate theories and then précis each description down into just 150 words.

2 Now do the same for the evaluation of each theory and then précis these down to 150 words as well.

Figure 32.1 ➤➤ *Revision timetable for 'Perception' subsection*

AO1 AND AO2

The AQA examination tests your ability in two main skill areas. These are known as AO1 and AO2. Every exam question tests both of these skills and they are equally weighted in the marking schemes. You will already have met these terms at AS-level, and so you are familiar with them in practice, but what do we mean by AO1 and AO2 in the context of an A2 exam?

The best way of thinking about them is to see AO1 as a *narrative* (i.e. giving information and showing understanding) and AO2 as a *commentary* (i.e. offering some comments about the narrative, such as evaluating the points made or showing how they fit into a wider body of knowledge). Each question might ask you to offer a slightly different form of AO1 and AO2, depending on the requirements of the question.

The 'instructions' on how to answer questions are contained in the terms used in the question wording itself, which are published by the AQA in the document *Terms Used in A2 Examinations*. A simplified version of this document is presented in Table 32.1.

It is well worth your while learning the differences between the different terms, particularly which are AO1 terms, which are AO2, and which require a mixture of AO1 + AO2.

Let's take a look at this in the context of a specific exam question:

● Discuss **one** theory of moral understanding.

(24 marks)

The 'instruction' in this question is 'discuss', which we can translate as requiring a *description* (the AO1 requirement) and an *evaluation* (the AO2 requirement) of one theory of moral development. This would mean that you must describe *and* evaluate to gain maximum marks. The AQA document, *Terms Used in A2 Examinations*, also offers a translation of these terms (see Table 32.1) so that you can be quite sure what an exam question is asking you to do. As we shall see later, all A2 questions (with the exception of questions

AO1 terms

>> *Describe, outline, explain, define* – these terms require evidence of **AO1**

In addition:

Outline requires a summary description only (more breadth than detail/depth).

Define requires a statement of what is meant by a particular term.

AO2 Terms

>> *Evaluate, assess, analyse, to what extent* – these terms require evidence of **AO2**.

AO1 and AO2 terms

>> *Discuss, critically consider, compare and contrast* – require evidence of **AO1** *and* **AO2**.

In addition:

Compare and contrast – requires a demonstration of knowledge and understanding of the stipulated topic areas (**AO1**), as well as similarities (compare) *and* differences (contrast) between the stipulated topic areas (**AO2**). Alternatively, you can address the **AO1** and **AO2** requirements of such questions by *describing* similarities and differences (**AO1**), and then analysing/evaluating these similarities and differences (**AO2**).

Qualifiers

>> *One or more, two or more* – It is acceptable to focus on one or two theories in depth, or an increasing number in less detail. Bear in mind that a superficial review of many might mean that you don't do adequate justice to any of them (see 'Specific demands within questions' on p. 944).

Other terms

>> *Evidence* – Material from studies or theories that may be used to support or contradict an argument or theory

>> *Findings* – The outcome or product of research

>> *Research* – The process of gaining knowledge through the examination of data derived empirically (i.e. through studies) or theoretically (i.e. through theories, explanations or models)

>> *Study* – An investigation providing *evidence* which may be empirical or non-empirical (such as meta-analysis)

>> *Theory* – A complex set of interrelated ideas/assumptions/principles intended to explain or account for certain observed phenomena

>> *Model* – An explanation which is less complex/elaborate than a theory

>> *Applications* – Actual or possible ways of using psychological knowledge in an applied/practical setting.

---

set in AQA Module 5) require answers to be written in 30 minutes.

An alternative version of the question set above might be the following:

● Outline and evaluate **two** theories of moral understanding. *(24 marks)*

The major difference between these two questions is that the second requires coverage of *two* theories, although in less depth. For example, in responding to the first question, you might well be able to sustain a discussion of Kohlberg's theory, but in what way would your account of this theory be different if you were responding to the second question? As we have seen, the skill of précis is a skill worth developing, and the A2 exam will give you plenty of opportunity to put this skill into practice.

Innovative and effective AO2

For many students, AO2 amounts to nothing more than 'slagging off' whatever psychological theory or finding

they have previously been describing. Psychology would be a pretty pointless discipline if all its theories and findings were as flawed as students like to believe when answering exam questions.

There are many valid opportunities for 'commentary' (a generic term for analysis and evaluation) when addressing the AO2 component of both AS and A2 questions. There are two important points to remember when constructing your AO2 material:

1 Good commentary should be *plentiful* rather than restricted to one or two throwaway points.

2 Good commentary means *effective* commentary – something that is often overlooked.

Innovative AO2

AO2 skills come in many different forms. These broaden the possibilities for you to maximize your marks for this assessment objective. The following examples are placed in the context of social psychology, but can be used usefully whatever the context. Remember, in order to make AO2 obvious, it is always useful to employ a little lead-in phrase as below.

- **'So we can see ...'** – 'So we can see that none of the theories of altruism suggest that helping behaviour is entirely without selfish motive, but rather that the relationship between giver and receiver may in some way mediate this process.'

- **'This would imply ...'** – 'This would imply that human nature is fundamentally selfish, and that what appears to be altruistic behaviour is actually selfish behaviour in disguise.'

- **'One consequence of this would be ...'** – 'One consequence of this would be that people begin to discriminate against members of the out-group because they are evaluated more negatively compared to members of the in-group.'

- **'This is supported by ...'** – 'This is supported by evidence from Mann (1981) who analysed incidents of suicides reported in American newspapers in the 1960s and 1970s, and found that factors such as size of crowd, darkness and distance from the "jumper" tended to produce a state of deindividuation in individual members of the crowd, making them more prone to "baiting".'

- **'This is challenged by ...'** – 'This is challenged by Mandel (1998), who found, in his studies of real-life events during the Holocaust, little evidence of the types of "blind obedience" proposed by Milgram.'

- **'Not everyone reacts in the same way – for example ...'** – 'Not everyone reacts in the same way – for example, Wood and Duck (1995) point out that we know very little about relationships between lesbian gay, disabled or other marginalized groups in society.'

- **'There may be cultural variations ...'** – 'There may be cultural variations in this behaviour, and so many of these explanations may not be applicable or relevant to Western cultures. They represent a more narrow view of human behaviour, which is, in turn, the product of researchers whose own views are inevitably shaped by the same cultural experience.'

- **'This has been applied to ... situation'** – 'This theory has been applied to collective dilemmas (such as saving water during a drought), where a person's primary identity (either personal or collective) defines the likelihood of them behaving altruistically in such situations.'

Each of the examples given above demonstrates a different form of commentary on the material. Some of these ('So we can see ...', 'This would imply ...') are nothing more than pointing out what may seem obvious to you, but they indicate to the examiner that you understand the *conclusions* that could be drawn, as well as the *implications* of a particular study or point of view. Others ('This is supported by ...', 'This is challenged by ...') demonstrate that you appreciate the degree to which a study or theory has been backed up by actual research evidence. Note that when choosing your commentary, you still have to represent it in an

AO2 form rather than simply adding more descriptive material. If you look back at the example concerning cultural variations, you will see that this does more than simply identify cultural variations, but indicates *why* these variations are problematic for the explanation in question. This is our next problem. How do we ensure that whatever points of analysis or evaluation we make, we make *effectively*?

Effective AO2

We have covered quite a few of the different forms of 'commentary' appropriate for the AO2 component of your answer. One thing should be clear from this: effective commentary is more than just identifying a point of evaluation. To give your commentary real impact, you should first identify and then develop a point. Having identified a point of commentary, you need to ensure that:

- it is **appropriate** to the material being 'evaluated' – 'Is it relevant?'

- it is **justified** – 'How do I know that?'

- it is **elaborated** – 'So why exactly is this a problem?'

For example:

- **'This study lacked ecological validity...'** – 'This study lacks ecological validity because (**identification**) ... attempts to replicate the findings in other situations have been largely unsuccessful (**justification**) ... This therefore means that the results of this study cannot be generalized beyond this situation (**elaboration**)'

- **'This study only used students ...'** – 'This study only used student (**identification**) ... There is evidence (Sears 1986) that students react differently to other sections of the population when participating in psychological research (**appropriateness**). In laboratory studies of altruism, for example, they are more likely to see tasks as a challenge to be overcome individually, and are therefore less likely to ask others for help (**justification**). This may, therefore, limit the validity of Western models of altruism, based largely on such laboratory studies, particularly when these models are used to contrast with research in non-Western cultures, which generally show a greater willingness to seek and give help (**elaboration**)'

- **'The study was unethical ...'** – 'The study was unethical in that Zimbardo, by allowing the "guards" to engage in anti-social behaviour against the "prisoners", effectively gave the pursuit of scientific knowledge priority over the welfare of his participants. A consequence of this decision has been a tightening of ethical guidelines to give other psychologists shared responsibility for the research behaviour of their colleagues.'

Of course, the expansion necessary to really give your commentary clout means that you have to be a bit more selective about the *number* of AO2 points you are going to make. You should always aim for a balance between *how many* points you make, and how much you elaborate them. Examiners must use both criteria when awarding marks, so a few points coherently elaborated will always get more marks than a long list of evaluative points with little elaboration. So, analysis and evaluation may seem pretty challenging, but with a bit of creativity and some careful thought, anything is possible.

ACTIVITY

Test your knowledge of exam terms

Knowing your AO1 instructions from your AO2 instructions is a vital part of exam success. Many students come unstuck simply because they respond inappropriately to the words in a question. The list below comprises a number of these terms. Some are AO1 terms, some AO2 and some AO1+AO2. These are mixed in with some bogus terms that are not in the AQA document *Terms Used in A2 Examinations*. Which are which, and which are bogus?

Admire	Analyse	Appraise	Assess
Compare and contrast	Critically consider	Debate	Define
Describe	Discuss	Evaluate	Explain
Inspect	Outline	Slag off	To what extent

QUESTION-SETTING

When Principal Examiners sit down to write an examination paper, they have to follow a number of basic rules and guidelines. The main guidelines are as follows:

● All questions must be drawn from the specification, with similar wording wherever possible.

● One question is set on each sub-section of the specification (i.e. three from *Social Psychology,* three from *Cognitive Psychology,* and so on).

● All questions (except those in *Approaches*) have an equal weighting of AO1 (12 marks for Module 4 and 15 for Module 5) and AO2 (also 12 and 15). No matter how many parts there are to a question, the same number of marks will always be given for AO1 as for AO2.

● Specification content which is preceded by the words 'should include' or 'including' can be specified in an exam question. Content which is preceded by the words 'for example' cannot be specified in a question, but *may* appear as an example to help jog your memory concerning suitable material.

● There are no rules regarding repetition of questions. The fact that a topic area is examined one year does not mean it will not be examined the next. Similarly, the fact that a particular topic hasn't been examined for a year or two doesn't mean that it will automatically be examined soon.

When exam questions are set, the AQA employ a 'Reviser' whose job is to check that the questions are appropriate in terms of standard and complexity, and could be answered within the time given. The Reviser must also check that the 'rules' outlined above are adhered to. For example, a question such as the following would be rejected by the Reviser:

● Describe and evaluate Freud's explanation of personality development.   *(24 marks)*

This would not be appropriate because, although Freud's name appears under the second sub-section of the *Developmental Psychology* specification (Personality development), it is included merely as an *example* of a psychodynamic explanation that might be considered. In other words, you don't have to study Freud and so questions cannot be asked specifically about him.

SYNOPTIC ASSESSMENT

Your A2 exam includes a synoptic component, which will test your understanding of the subject as a whole. This will always take place at the end of your course, and accounts for 20 per cent of the total marks awarded for this A-level. By placing this part of the assessment at the end of the examination process, it gives you a chance to develop an *overview* of the subject that would be impossible earlier in the course. In the AQA examinations, most of the synoptic assessment comes in AQA Module 5, *Individual Differences,* and *Perspectives*. Because of this extra requirement, questions in this AQA Module are answered in 40 minutes, unlike questions in AQA Module 4, which are answered in 30 minutes. This extra time allowance is reflected in the extra marks available for this part of the exam. Each question in AQA Module 5 is worth 30 marks (15 marks for AO1 and 15 marks for AO2).

What counts as synoptic assessment?

The AQA requirement is that you gain an understanding and critical appreciation of the 'breadth of theoretical and methodological approaches, issues and debates in psychology'. This can be demonstrated in a variety of ways, including the following:

- *different explanations* or *perspectives* relating to the topic area – for example, schizophrenia can be explained from many different perspectives; different perspectives also have different positions in the nature–nurture and free-will-versus-determinism debates
- *different methods* used to study the topic area – for example, the origins of psychopathological conditions might be studied using twin studies, cross-cultural studies, and so on
- *overarching issues* relating to the topic area – for example, the use of biological therapies might be discussed in terms of the issue of reductionism, nature–nurture, or ethics
- *links with other areas* of the specification – for example, depression might be seen as having an adaptive role within human evolution; Freud's views of personality development might demonstrate a gender bias
- *psychology-wide concerns* and *issues* such as reliability and validity, cultural variation and aspects of investigative design (such as demand characteristics and participant reactivity).

How is synopticity assessed?

All sections of AQA Module 5 credit synopticity. However, all the questions set in this Module are by their very nature 'synoptic', so you are addressing the synoptic requirement of a question simply by answering it in the format required. For example, a question in *Individual Differences* would not ask you to discuss *one* therapy, as this would not be synoptic (i.e. it could be answered without resorting to any of the different types of synoptic content given above). On the other hand, if you were asked to discuss *two* therapies, then this *would* be synoptic (as it covers more than one explanation/perspective).

This means that you could concentrate on the questions set without worrying about any extra requirements, but synoptic content does offer you an additional route to high marks. It is perfectly possible to get maximum marks just answering the question set and not worrying about doing anything else. However, few people manage to get maximum marks on exam questions because they run out of relevant (and worthwhile) things to write about, and so the inclusion of some synoptic material may just nudge your answer into the next mark band.

The clue's in the question ...

There is always some clue as to the synoptic route through a particular question. For example, you may be required to cover more than one of something (theories, therapies, etc.) or to discuss more than one *issue* when responding to a 'quote/discuss' question. Such questions give you a quotation first:

- 'Scientists have made considerable advances in their understanding of human behaviour through the study of non-human animals. This alone would appear sufficient to make scientific and ethical objections to their use inappropriate.'

  With reference to issues raised in the quotation, discuss the use of non-human animals in psychological research.   *(30 marks)*

The question then invites you to discuss something (cultural bias, ethics, etc.) either with reference 'to *issues raised* in the quotation' or 'to issues *such as those* raised in the question'. There is a subtle but important difference in the requirements of these two questions, with the former more prescriptive than the latter. Either way, the synoptic requirement is to cover more than one issue (i.e. different methods used to arrive at these conclusions, different explanations, etc.).

Approaches in psychology

In this section of the exam, you will be required to apply your knowledge of any two theoretical approaches in psychology to a situation given within the stimulus material. You should try to develop a good working knowledge of the methods, strengths and limitations of the different approaches in psychology and those areas of behaviour where you feel they offer a plausible explanation. An example of a 'spider diagram' for evolutionary explanations of behaviour is shown in Fig. 32.2. You might like to elaborate on this by considering each of its points (see Units 23 and 27), and then repeating the exercise for as many other approaches as you are able.

Approaches questions

The questions will not specify which approaches you should use, so this is your opportunity to be creative. Although this sounds quite daunting, the friendly part of these questions is the fact that the questions themselves will always be the same, only the stimulus material and its associated topic area will change.

Questions will ask you to do the following:

(a) Describe how **two** different approaches might try to explain ... *(the subject outlined in the stimulus material).*   *(12 marks)*

(b) Assess one of these explanations of ... *(the subject outlined in the stimulus material)* in terms of its strengths and limitations.   *(6 marks)*

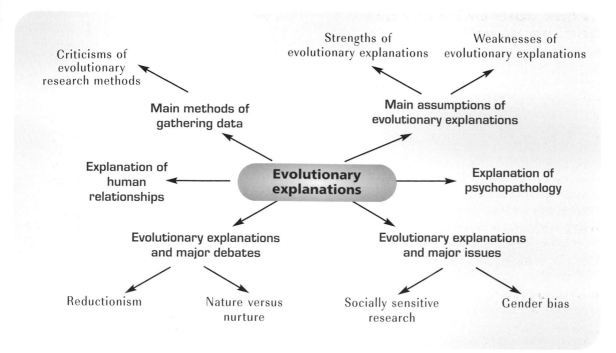

Figure 32.2 >> *Spider diagram of 'evolutionary explanations'*

(c) How might ... *(the subject outlined in the stimulus material)* be investigated by **one** of these approaches? *(6 marks)*

(d) Evaluate the use of this method for investigating ... *(the subject outlined in the stimulus material).* *(6 marks)*

The stimulus material for these questions may be drawn from almost any area of human functioning, so it does not give anyone an advantage to have studied one area of psychology rather than another. Unit 29 deals with the specific skills and techniques that will help you deal with the Approaches question, and an example of this type of question can be seen in the panel below.

Answering an approaches question

This question about childhood experience and later adult offending can be answered in a number of ways. For part (a), you may choose to explain this relationship from the viewpoint of one of the major *perspectives* in psychology. For example, the behavioural perspective might explain this relationship in terms of juvenile crime being rewarding for children (status, access to resources, etc.). Alternatively, the psychodynamic perspective might explain this relationship in terms of a deficient superego (and hence a less well-developed sense of guilt or shame).

However, you are not restricted to using the major perspectives identified in the specification. You might,

---

An example of an 'Approaches' question

The findings of research into childhood predictors of adult offending suggest that a range of adverse features in early life are associated with social difficulties and the onset of antisocial behaviour and later criminal behaviour. The intensity and severity of such disadvantage appear to be predictive of chronic offending in later life.

(a) Describe how two different approaches might explain this relationship between childhood experience and later adult offending. *(12 marks)*

(b) Assess the strengths and limitations of one of these explanations. *(6 marks)*

(c) Analyse how the relationship between childhood experience and later adult offending might be investigated by one of these explanations. *(6 marks)*

(d) Evaluate the use of this method for investigating the relationship between childhood experiences and later adult offending. *(6 marks)* for example, explain the relationship in terms of children's exposure to the 'discourses' of a deviant sub-culture, which helps to construct a pattern of deviant behaviour in adulthood that they see as normal (a social constructionist perspective). Note that this last explanation may appear more sociological than psychological. This does not matter, as students are encouraged to explore insights into human behaviour that can be derived from other disciplines such as sociology and philosophy.

Once you have picked your two approaches and have constructed how you think they might explain this novel situation, you can then move on to the other questions. Bear in mind that you should *focus your responses on the subject matter of the stimulus material* at all times, rather than slipping into a more general account of the approach in question or its methods of investigation.

It is important (and comforting) to remember that you are not meant to *know* how each of these approaches explains the phenomenon in the stimulus material (it may never have been studied by that perspective), but simply to be able to *speculate* how your knowledge of these approaches might be applied in its explanation. It is worth practising doing just that, explaining every novel behaviour you read about from as many different psychological viewpoints as possible (you will soon become a liability to your friends ...).

The same advice applies to part (c) of the question. You are not meant to know how these approaches *have* investigated that particular behaviour, merely how they *might* investigate it. It is important to be plausible in your descriptions, so don't describe totally implausible or overly ambitious scenarios that would be virtually impossible in real life. These issues are covered in more detail in Unit 29.

Topic 2 >> Examination performance

READING QUESTIONS

A vital skill in tackling examinations is interpreting what is actually required from a particular question. This should not be as difficult as it might appear, given what you now know about the way that questions are actually set. We have included examples of exam questions in each unit ('Eye on the Exam'), together with an interpretation and suggested route through the answer. There is no substitute for practice in this respect, so get hold of as many past papers as possible and

'deconstruct' the questions into their constituent skills and parts. Try the following activity.

When you are skilled at working out exactly what is required in each question, you are ready to move on to the next stage – planning an effective response. Although this *seems* a fairly straightforward process, things can go wrong when you least expect them. This next section looks at some of the typical errors that can creep in at this stage.

ACTIVITY

What do exam questions actually require?

What specific skills are required in each of the following questions?

1 (a) Outline **one** theory of cognitive development. *(6 marks)*

(b) Discuss applications of this theory (e.g. to education). *(18 marks)*

2 Compare and contrast biological and behavioural therapies. *(30 marks)*

3 'There have been many instances of psychological research that have shown gender biases (such as alpha bias, beta bias and androcentrism). These biases may distort the value of such research.'

With reference to issues such as those raised by the quotation above, discuss gender bias in psychology. *(30 marks)*

ANSWERING QUESTIONS

What can go wrong?

When answering exam questions, many students wander off the point, use the wrong sort of information or the right bit in the wrong place. The problem is largely due to their not *thinking* enough about a

question before they answer it and while they are answering it. Try the activity on p. 943. The response to the question given reads quite well, but there are a number of reasons why it is not effective.

'What did I do wrong?'

On the right is a question that could be set about pro- and anti-social behaviour. An example answer is given below. Using the marking allocations for AQA Module 4 in Table 32.2 on p. 947, give this answer a mark for each part of the question.

(a) Outline **two** social psychological theories of aggression. *(12 marks)*

(b) Evaluate each of the theories you outlined in part (a) in terms of relevant research studies. *(12 marks)*

(a) In this essay I intend to first say what is meant by aggression, and look at different types of aggression. Then I will move on to describe different social-psychological theories of aggression. These will be social learning theory and deindividuation theory. In the second part of the question I will evaluate my theories of aggression by looking at research evidence. I will look at the strengths and weaknesses of each theory as part of my evaluation.

Aggression is usually thought to be anti-social, including any behaviour that is intended to inflict harm on another person. However, some aggression can be pro-social such as when police shoot a terrorist who has murdered hostages and is threatening others. Other types of aggression are sanctioned by society, such as in cases of self-defence, e.g. when a woman injures a rapist while defending herself.

The social learning theory of aggression is demonstrated in Bandura's study with the Bobo doll (Bandura et al. 1961). This involved children observing aggressive and non-aggressive adult models and then being tested to see if they imitated any of the behaviours modelled by the adult. Children who watched an adult behaving aggressively showed a good deal of physical and verbal aggression when given the opportunity to interact with the Bobo doll. Children who had seen a model behaving non-aggressively towards the Bobo doll, later showed virtually no aggressive behaviour in their own interactions with the doll.

My second theory is deindividuation theory (Zimbardo 1969). Deindividuation is a process whereby the normal constraints on behaviour are weakened as people lose their sense of individuality. People are likely to become deindividuated when they join a crowd or a large group. Factors that contribute to deindividuation include anonymity (for example, if people wear a uniform) and altered states of consciousness due to drugs or alcohol. Deindividuated people tend to behave aggressively because the loss of individuality leads to reduced self-restraint. This leads to impulsive behaviour and reduced attention to how our behaviour might be evaluated by others. When we are in a crowd, being anonymous has the consequence of

reducing inner restraints and increasing those behaviours (such as aggression) that are usually inhibited. In large groups or in crowds, people have greater anonymity and therefore a reduced fear of negative evaluation of their actions and of feelings of guilt for any deviant behaviour.

Another theory of aggression is relative deprivation theory, where people may feel frustrated because they do not feel that they have what they deserve (e.g. decent jobs and living conditions, freedom from harassment by police). This can produce feelings of anger and may be responsible for many of the riots (e.g. Toxteth and St. Pauls) that have happened over the last 20 years.

(b) In the Bobo doll studies, children between 3 and 5 years were used. Half of these were exposed to aggressive models and half were exposed to non-aggressive models. These models displayed some distinctive physically aggressive acts (such as hitting the doll with a mallet) accompanied by verbal aggression. Children were then frustrated by being shown attractive toys and not being allowed to play with them. As I stated earlier, children in the aggressive condition (who had seen a model acting aggressively towards the Bobo doll) reproduced a lot of the aggressive behaviour (both physical and verbal) they had seen from the model.

A strength of social learning theory is that this can explain differences between individuals (who may or may not have been exposed to aggressive models) and within individuals. People may behave differently in different situations because they have observed different consequences for aggressive behaviour in those situations.

Zimbardo carried out a study on deindividuation in his prison study. He took normal students and divided them into prisoners and guards in a mock prison. He found that the guards bullied the prisoners and that the prisoners became very upset. He had to stop the study before the end. This study has been criticized because of the ethics of exposing people to such stress. Critics have said that Zimbardo lost sight of what the study was really about, and let his participants suffer far too much before ending the study.

What *did* go wrong?

This essay shows a lot of good knowledge. It is all accurate, but how well does it fit with the question?

Part (a)

- The first paragraph is totally wasted. Don't waste time saying what you are going to do, just get straight on and do it.

- The second paragraph is interesting but not necessary. There is no requirement to define terms in this way as the question has already made very specific demands. Students often feel obliged to include this sort of information, as if they will be penalized for leaving it out. This is not the case.

- The third paragraph is not outlining the *theory* but a *study* related to social learning theory. An examiner would be able to pick a couple of implicit points out of this, but far better that the assumptions of the theory had been made explicit in the first place.

- The deindividuation paragraph is excellent, and at 155 words is the ideal length for an outline (you could even lose the first sentence which again is stating the obvious).

- The last paragraph of part (a) is another wasted one, as this is a *third* theory when the question asked for only two. An examiner might even choose this as being better than SLT, except it hasn't been addressed in part (b).

Part (b)

- The first paragraph is simply a *description* of a study that might be relevant, but it is not used in an *evaluative* way (i.e. do the results *support* or *challenge* the assumptions of the theory?). Having already described this study in part (a), our confused student is struggling to find any more to say.

- The second paragraph will not gain any marks as it is general evaluation, rather than evaluation in terms of 'relevant research studies'.

- This final paragraph *does* refer to a relevant study, but it again only *describes* the study, and also fails to include *any* reference to deindividuation at all.

What does this tell us?

This essay is hugely imbalanced, at over 450 words for part (a) and under 250 words for part (b). This student has not divided their time appropriately, hence part (b) is rushed and therefore short (despite also being worth 12 marks). There is a lot of irrelevant information throughout the essay, showing that they have not thought about what might be relevant to the question and, perhaps more importantly, what might get them marks. Examiners must abide by the instructions of their mark scheme, which means they can only give marks for material that is answering the question set. It doesn't matter how interesting or insightful something is, it can only get marks if it maps onto the mark

scheme. In this case, part (a) would get **9** marks (nearly all for deindividuation), and part (b) a far less impressive **2** marks, for a total of **11** marks. Next time you sit down to answer an exam question, take a little time to think about how best to fit what you know to the *specific* demands of the question.

Specific demands within questions

One, two or more

One of the features of AQA A2 questions is that they frequently invite you to write about either 'one or more' or 'two or more' of something. Although you may think that you would get more marks for including more theories, studies or whatever, this is not necessarily the case. What it tells you is that if you don't have enough material to just write about *one* theory, then you can write about more than one (or if you don't have enough for two, you can write about more than two). There is no hidden agenda here: it really is up to you which route you take. When making your decision, be careful to consider *depth* (if you use more than the minimum, might your discussion become superficial?) and *breadth* (if you restrict yourself to the minimum, might your discussion lacks breadth of coverage of the topic?). The very best marks are awarded for a balance of depth *and* breadth, and that can be achieved by either route.

When is evaluation not evaluation?

The answer to this riddle is – when it is just more description. This is most common when introducing alternative theories or studies that may (or may not) support the conclusions of the material in question. For example, in the question 'Discuss one theory of moral understanding', you may choose to introduce other theories that offer a different perspective to the one you have chosen for your AO1. Likewise, you may introduce studies that support (or challenge) your theory. The trick is to actually *use* this material to construct an evaluative argument that is focused on your chosen theory. This may involve pointing out how the weak points of your chosen theory are overcome in the alternative theory, or how your chosen theory is superior to the alternative on some appropriate criterion. The same applies to research studies. These may either support or challenge the conclusions of your AO1 material, but it is up to you to make this clear, rather than leaving it to the examiner to make links on your behalf. The section on 'Innovative and effective AO2' on p. 937 gives you some ideas on how to do this.

Parted questions

Some questions are divided into two parts and (very occasionally) three. The spilt between AO1 and AO2 is the same in both variations, but split questions do require careful planning to ensure you don't slip up in your response. The two parts of the question may or may not be tied together (e.g. 'in this theory ...' is definitely tied, whereas 'in *such* theories ...' is not) or the second part of the question may make quite specific demands in terms of the AO2 component of your answer. For example:

(a) Outline two theories of the attribution of causality. *(12 marks)*

(b) Evaluate the two theories of the attribution of causality that you outlined in part (a) in terms of relevant research studies. *(12 marks)*

In the above example, you are asked to evaluate 'in terms of relevant research studies'. In such a question, more general evaluation that is not in the form of research studies would not receive credit.

Alternatively, you may be asked to 'assess the cultural differences ...' in some behaviour in part (b) of a question. For example:

(a) Describe **one or more** explanations of human altruism. *(12 marks)*

(b) To what extent are there cultural differences in pro-social behaviour? *(12 marks)*

Here, the *only* form of AO2 that would receive credit would be an assessment of cultural variations in that behaviour. You should also remember the advice of the previous point, that what would be required would be more than just a *description* of any such variations, but an *assessment* of such variations (e.g. the implications of such variation for an understanding of the behaviour in question, research support for such claims of variations, and so on).

What happens if you put the right material in the wrong part? Do you simply lose it? No, the examination system is a lot fairer than that and the examiner will, up to a point, 'export' relevant material to its right home within the question as a whole. The rule for this 'import-export' procedure is as follows:

>> If a candidate includes material that is *clearly relevant* and would earn marks in one part of a question, it should remain (when determining marks) *regardless* of whether it might earn more marks elsewhere. If the material is only *peripherally relevant* or *irrelevant* to one part of the question and would earn marks in the other part, then it should be "exported" (when determining marks) to that part. >>

Arguments for and against

Some areas of the specification (in AQA Module 5) require knowledge of arguments *for* and *against* some particular point of view. For example, in the topic '*the use of non-human animals*', arguments for and against their use have to be studied. Questions might be set on arguments for *and* arguments against, or they might be set only on arguments for *or* arguments against. Whatever the question, it is necessary to provide AO2 material as commentary on your description of these arguments (which would count as AO1).

Confused? There is no need to be. This simply means that *whatever* the AO1 material, it must also be accompanied by some AO2 commentary. To make this easier for you, questions in this area tend to focus on *either* arguments for *or* arguments against. As a result, you can use your arguments for (if that is the question) as AO1 and your arguments against as AO2. Alternatively, if the question specifies arguments *against*, then you can use your arguments *for* as AO2. This is all very friendly, but there is a proviso – the AO2 arguments must be linked to the AO1 arguments, rather than a totally separate set of considerations. For example, an argument *for* the use of animals in research is that they have given us invaluable insights into the effects of stress. A linked argument *against* the use of animals is that such insights have often been achieved at the expense of considerable suffering for the animals concerned.

TIME MANAGEMENT

Having unravelled the requirements of the questions, the next hurdle is for you to manage your time effectively in the exam. This involves both time management *between* questions and *within* questions.

Between questions

This really should present no problems to the well-prepared student. Each question in AQA Module 4 requires a 30-minute response (in Module 5, the questions are allocated 40 minutes each). If you extend the time you give to one question, you are effectively stealing it from another. You should also remember that this 30 minutes includes thinking time. This means that, in reality, you tend only to have around 25 or so minutes of writing time for each question. Imagine the following two scenarios involving AQA Module 4. Two students spend different amounts of time on their three essays and receive the marks shown:

Student A		Student B	
Time (mins) per essay	*Mark*	*Time (mins) per essay*	*Mark*
40	18	30	16
40	18	30	16
10	6	30	16
Total:	**42**	**Total:**	**48**

It is much easier to push a mark up from 10 to 16, than it is to push it from 16 to 20, as Student A has found to their cost. It is rarely cost-effective to extend any one individual essay beyond the 30 minutes allocated to it, within the confines of a one-and-a-half-hour exam.

Within questions

The second problem is to manage your time within a question, so that all the different aspects and requirements of the question are covered. Let us take a typical question as an example:

- Describe and evaluate research (explanations and/or studies) into the influence of the media on antisocial behaviour. *(24 marks)*

With only 30 minutes to answer this question, you may be tempted to start writing straight away and run the risk of only getting half or two-thirds through the whole question when the 30 minutes is up. To perform effectively and maximize your marks for any particular question, you need a strategy. There are many such strategies, but a particularly effective one is as follows:

- Decide *exactly* what is required in each question, or part of a question.
- Calculate how much time should be allocated to each aspect of the question.

- Divide the answer into about six paragraphs, about 100 words, or 5 minutes per paragraph.
- Plan what will go into each paragraph.
- Finally, stick to that plan, and don't go over the allocated time span.

This strategic method has a number of advantages. First, it makes sure that you are answering all parts of the question (provided your planning is appropriate). Second, it ensures that you do not get caught short of time before you have made significant progress into the question. Finally, it makes the whole process of writing an essay less daunting. Writing a series of pre-planned 100-word chunks is much easier than writing one 600-word essay. If the thought of writing 100 words worries you, you may be interested to know that there are exactly 100 words in this paragraph!

Topic 3 >> Examination marking

MARKING SCHEMES

This part of the exam process may not appear to be something you can actively take part in, but knowing how papers are marked can certainly help you in your quest for the highest marks. The AQA uses a separate marking grid for AO1 and AO2, but they work in the same way. A simplified version of these marking grids can be seen in Table 32.2. and Table 32.3 (adapted from AQA marking guidelines).

There is a separate set of marking allocations for the AQA Module 5 *Approaches* questions, shown in Table 32.4. When answering questions in this section, remember the need to engage with the stimulus material at all times – don't just write a general response that details a psychological perspective and its associated methodologies (see Unit 29).

Table 32.2 >> Marking allocations for AQA Module 4 questions

AQA Module 4 – AO1

Marks	Content	Detail and accuracy	Organization and structure	Breadth and depth
12–11	Substantial	Accurate and well-detailed	Coherent	Substantial evidence of both and balance achieved
10–9	Slightly limited	Accurate and reasonably detailed	Coherent	Evidence of both but imbalanced
8–7	Limited	Generally accurate and reasonably detailed	Reasonably constructed	Increasing evidence of breadth and/or depth
6–5	Basic	Generally accurate, lacks detail	Reasonably constructed	Some evidence of breadth and/or depth
4–3	Rudimentary	Sometimes flawed	Sometimes focused	
2–0	Just discernible	Weak/muddled/inaccurate	Wholly/mainly irrelevant	

AQA Module 4 – AO2

Marks	Evaluation is	Selection and elaboration	Use of material
12–11	Thorough	Appropriate selection and coherent elaboration	Highly effective
10–9	Slightly limited	Appropriate selection and elaboration	Effective
8–7	Limited	Reasonable elaboration	Reasonably effective
6–5	Basic	Some evidence of elaboration	Restricted
4–3	Superficial and rudimentary	No evidence of elaboration	Not effective
2–0	Muddled and incomplete	Wholly or mainly irrelevant	

Table 32.3 >> Marking allocations for AQA Module 5 questions

AQA Module 5 – AO1

Marks	Content	Detail and accuracy	Organization and structure	Breadth and depth
15–13	Substantial	Accurate and well-detailed	Coherent	Substantial evidence of both
12–10	Slightly limited	Accurate and reasonably detailed	Coherent	Evidence of both
9–7	Limited	Generally accurate and reasonably detailed	Reasonably constructed	Some evidence of both
6–4	Basic	Lacking detail	Sometimes focused	Little evidence
3–0	Just discernible	Weak/muddled/inaccurate	Wholly/mainly irrelevant	Little or no evidence

AQA Module 5 – AO2

Marks	Evaluation is	Selection and elaboration	Use of material synoptic possibilities
15–13	Thorough	Appropriate selection and coherent elaboration	Highly effective
12–10	Slightly limited	Appropriate selection and elaboration	Effective
9–7	Limited	Reasonable elaboration	Reasonably effective
6–4	Basic	Some evidence of elaboration	Restricted
3–0	Weak, muddled and incomplete	Wholly/mainly irrelevant	Not effective

Table 32.4 >> AQA Module 5: the Approaches question

Part (a)

Marks	Content	Accuracy	Engagement
6–5	Reasonably thorough	Accurate	Coherent
4–3	Limited	Generally accurate	Reasonable
2–0	Basic	Sometimes flawed/inaccurate	Muddled

Part (b) and Part (d)

Marks	Commentary	Use of material	Engagement
6–5	Reasonably thorough	Effective	Coherent
4–3	Limited	Reasonably effective	Reasonable
2–0	Basic	Restricted	Muddled

Part (c)

Marks	Commentary	Plausibility	Engagement
6–5	Reasonably thorough	Appropriate	Coherent
4–3	Limited	Reasonably appropriate	Reasonable
2–0	Basic	Largely inappropriate	Muddled

HOW EXAMINERS APPROACH MARKING

Contrary to popular opinion, examiners are not in the business of trying to find ways to award the lowest marks possible, but neither can they award 'sympathy' marks for essays that are good psychology yet not particularly relevant to the question set. There is a lot involved in examining at this level, but some of the basic rules are as follows:

- **Examiners are realistic** – All answers are marked at the level of a notional 18-year-old who is writing for 30 minutes (or 40 minutes if AQA Module 5) under exam conditions. What this means in practice is that examiners do not look for the 'perfect' answer and are realistic in what they can expect a student to write in 30 (or 40) minutes.

- **Positive marking** – Examiners engage in a process known as 'positive marking'. This means that they do not look for opportunities to take marks off (because of errors), but rather for opportunities to add marks on (for correct and appropriate material). If you write something that is wrong, the examiner effectively ignores it, and looks for content that can be credited under the terms of the question.

- **No prescribed single right answer** – One of the features of this subject is that there are many ways to approach questions and many different perspectives to take in answering them. Students often worry that they might be answering a question in the 'wrong' way. Provided that their answer is relevant to the question, it will be credited by the examiner. Examiners often learn things from students, so it is gratifying to know that your work is being marked by an appreciative audience.

- **Marking guidelines** – Examiners do not mark with ideas of pass and fail in their mind, nor of the grades they think an answer might be worth. Examiners will award marks according to the marking guidelines illustrated in Table 32.2 and 32.3, together with any special requirements of the question (for example, have the candidates included two theories if asked to do so?). You may be surprised (and relieved) to know that in 2003, it was possible to get a Grade A with just two-thirds of the marks available!

- **Names and dates** – These are not as important as you might imagine. Students often spend a great deal of their time revising as many names and dates as they can, perhaps under the impression that it is the weight of such detail that gets the high marks. This impression is bolstered when you read learned academic journals, which appear to be brimming over with research names and dates. There they do serve an important function, but they are less important in A-level exams. Including a researcher's name or the date of the research certainly helps to place the research in context, but as long as a piece of research is recognizable and is described in a way that is both accurate and relevant to the question, it will gain as many marks as if it were anchored to a name and date.

- **Quality of written communication** – Each exam script is assessed as a whole, and up to four marks awarded for the quality of written communication used. This involves the accurate expression of ideas, the precise use of specialist terms, and good grammar, punctuation and spelling.

Topic 1: Examination revision

● **Effective revision** is more than good intentions and lots of time. The important thing is to be aware of the skills and topics of the specification, and to structure your revision in a way that is most likely to bring maximum rewards. This means knowing *what* to revise, *how* to revise and *when* to revise. Given that exams are both predictable and fair, poor performance is often due to poor preparation.

Topic 2: Examination

● It is important to read the questions properly, looking in particular for the 'instructions' contained in the *Terms Used in A2 Examinations* document such as 'Describe', 'Assess' and 'Critically consider'. It is also important to respond to instructions about the type of material required (e.g. theories, research findings) and the number of theories, research findings, etc.

● The exam, in AQA Module 5, also assesses candidates in terms of synopticity – an understanding and critical appreciation of the breadth of theoretical and methodological approaches in psychology. This might be achieved by showing your understanding of:
   – different explanations or perspectives relating to the topic area
   – different methods used to study the topic area
   – overarching issues relating to the topic area
   – links with other areas of the specification.

Topic 3: Examination marking

● Examiners are guided by a set of guidelines that underlie all A-level exam marking. There are no prescriptive answers, nor do examiners mark in terms of pass or fail.

● Examiners engage in positive marking, looking for opportunities to give marks for appropriate material, rather than knocking them off for material that is wrong or inappropriate.

ANSWERS TO ACTIVITIES

Test your knowledge of exam terms, p. 939

AO1 terms	*AO2 terms*
Define	Analyse
Describe	Assess
Explain	Evaluate
Outline	To what extent

AO1 + AO2 terms	*Bogus terms*
Compare and contrast	Admire
Critically consider	Appraise
Discuss	Debate
	Inspect
	Slag off

What do exam questions actually require? p. 942

1 (a) AO1 – Give a summary description (i.e. a précis) of one theory of cognitive development (6 marks)

(b) AO1 – Give a summary description of at least two applications of this theory (6 marks).
AO2 – Evaluate these applications (12 marks)

2 AO1 – A description of one or more biological therapies and one or more behavioural therapies.

AO2 – Consideration of the similarities and the differences between biological and behavioural therapies.

Alternatively:

AO1 – A description of the similarities and the differences between biological and behavioural therapies.

AO2 – Commentary (analysis and/or evaluation) of the similarities and the differences between biological and behavioural therapies.

3 AO1 – Description of examples of gender bias in psychology, and one or more issues that arise from such gender bias.

AO2 – Commentary (analysis and/or evaluation) on these issues, in terms of the consequences suggested by the quotation, or other related implications/consequences/counterarguments.

Glossary

Ablation: surgical removal of brain tissue.

Abnormality: *see Psychological abnormality*.

Accommodation: the process of changing existing schemas when new information cannot be assimilated.

Action slip: a form of absent-mindedness where a person performs an action that was not intended; caused by not paying attention to what is going on.

Activity theory: proposition that individuals prefer to remain active and productive in later life, even resisting disengagement from society – contrasts with social disengagement theory.

Actor/observer biases (in attribution): these refer to the tendency for (a) actors to explain their own behaviour in situational terms and (b) observers to explain the behaviour of others in dispositional (person) terms.

Adaptation: a feature of an organism that has been shaped by natural selection so that it enhances the fitness of its possessor.

Adolescence: a transitional period of development between puberty and adulthood. The concept of a distinct developmental period of adolescence has often been seen as a Westernized phenomenon, with progression from childhood to adulthood in other cultures being more abrupt and marked by rituals and 'rites of passage'.

Adoption studies: investigations that compare correlations, e.g. of children's IQ scores with both their biological and adoptive parents.

Adulthood: the period when one has matured or grown to full size and strength. May be arbitrarily defined in the UK as the period between 16 or 18 years, and death.

Aggression: an action or a series of actions where the aim is to cause harm to another person or object.

Aim: the intended purpose of an investigation, i.e. what the research investigation is actually trying to discover.

Alpha bias: refers to theories and research which assume real and enduring differences between men and women. Sometimes alpha bias theories heighten the value of women, and sometimes they are used to devalue women (*see also Beta bias*).

Alternative hypothesis (may be referred to as the **experimental hypothesis** in an experiment): predicts that something other than chance alone has produced the results obtained; in a well-designed experiment this should be the effects of the independent variable.

Altruism (animal): an animal is said to be engaging in altruistic behaviour when by so doing it increases the survival chances of another animal whilst decreasing its own. The term 'apparent altruism' refers to the fact that such behaviours are frequently selfish when viewed from another level.

Altruism (human): helping behaviour that is voluntary, costly to the altruist and motivated by something other than the expectation of material or social reward.

Anal stage: the second stage of psychosexual development (according to psychoanalytic theory) when the child's main source of pleasure is the anus and the expelling or withholding of faeces.

Analyse: show understanding by examining the different components of a topic area (in the exam, requires an AO2 response).

Androcentrism: refers to the tendency of some theories to offer an interpretation of women based on an understanding of the lives of men (*see also Alpha bias and Beta bias*).

Animal language: as an area of research, this refers to either (a) attempts to teach non-human animals to speak, or (b) studies of animals'

'natural' language in their own natural environment.

Anorexia nervosa: (literally, a nervous loss of appetite) a disorder characterized by the pursuit of extreme thinness and by an extreme loss of weight.

Anti-social behaviour: this is a general term used to refer to any behaviour that harms or offends another person. Common examples are aggression and discrimination.

Anxiety disorders: the most common of adult mental disorders, characterized by severe anxiety. Phobias are probably the most familiar of these disorders.

AO1 (Assessment Objective 1): the demonstration of knowledge and understanding through clear and effective communication. Questions that require an AO1 response use terms such as 'outline', 'give a brief account of', 'describe', 'explain', 'give', 'what is meant by'.

AO2 (Assessment Objective 2): analysis and evaluation of specification content. Questions that require an AO2 response use terms such as 'evaluate'. Some questions embed the AO2 requirement within more general instructions such as 'consider' and 'to what extent'.

AO3 (Assessment Objective 3): design, conduct and report.

APFCC studies: (at AS-level) (a) *Aims* – What was the purpose of carrying out a particular study? What were the researchers trying to find out? (b) *Procedures* – How did the researchers carry out the study? What did they do to whom? (c) *Findings* – What did they discover? For example, saying that "Milgram discovered that 65 per cent of participants delivered the full 450 volts" is a *finding*.

(d) *Conclusions* – What did researchers learn about the behaviour in question as a result of carrying out a study? A statement that "Milgram found that ordinary men and women will go against their conscience and blindly follow instructions from an authority figure" is a *conclusion*.

(e) *Criticisms* – often seen as equivalent to listing what is bad about something, criticisms can also be *positive*, in that you can detail what is *good* about a theory, study or whatever.

Apparent altruism: *see* **Altruism (animal)**.

Applications: actual or possible ways of using psychological knowledge in an applied or practical setting.

Approaches: the term 'approach' in psychology refers to what was once called a 'school of thought' – a group of psychologists who share a common way of thinking about things and share characteristic methods for studying phenomena.

Arousal: refers to the body's level of alertness and activation as reflected in certain physiological responses such as heart rate or muscle tension.

Assess: a considered appraisal of an area through a review of the strengths and weaknesses of the information presented (in the exam, requires an AO2 response).

Association cortex: areas of cerebral cortex not directly involved with sensory input or motor control, but with higher cognitive functions, such as language or problem-solving.

Attachment: this refers to the result of a bonding process between two individuals (usually the mother and her offspring), characterized by mutual involvement and the desire to remain close to each other.

Attention: a focused concentration of mental activity (*see also* **Focused attention** and **Divided attention**).

Attenuator theory of attention: Treisman's proposal that, instead of selecting one channel and blocking the others, the filtering mechanism (a) selects one channel and passes it on for semantic analysis, and (b) allows the unattended channels through for processing but in weakened (attenuated) form.

Attribution (of causality): the way in which we infer the causes of our own or another person's behaviour according to a set of cognitive rules and biases. As a result of these strategies we decide whether a person's behaviour is caused by their own stable characteristics, or whether it is a result of situational influences.

Attributional biases: the tendency to depart from the normal rules of attribution and make biased attributions about the behaviour of others or ourselves.

Authoritarian personality: personality style strongly associated with prejudiced attitudes, where the person is intolerant of ambiguity or uncertainty, submissive to those in authority and dismissive or arrogant towards those perceived to be of lower social status.

Autokinetic effect: an optical illusion experienced when a person in a totally dark room sees a stationary spot of light appearing to move.

Automatic processing: a type of mental operation that is normally rapid; does not require conscious awareness; does not interfere with other mental activities; is usually a result of prolonged practice.

Autonomic nervous system (ANS): part of the nervous system that maintains the normal functioning of the body's inner environment. The ANS has two sub-divisions: (a) the sympathetic division whose activity mobilizes energy resources and prepares the body for action, and (b) the parasympathetic division

whose activity tends to conserve the body's energy resources and restore inner calm.

Availability heuristic: a rule of thumb used to make decisions about frequencies of events based on how easily relevant examples can be remembered – a cognitive short cut.

Aversion therapy: a behavioural treatment that aims to rid the individual of an undesirable habit (e.g. smoking) by pairing the habit with unpleasant (aversive) consequences.

Bar chart: a series of vertical bars of equal width used to illustrate the frequencies of a non-continuous variable displayed on the x-axis. It is superficially similar to a histogram.

Behavioural approach: the view that one need go no further than what is observable when trying to explain behaviour and that all behaviour can be explained in terms of learning and the environment (i.e. nurture rather than nature).

Behavioural model of abnormality: the view that abnormal behaviours are maladaptive learned responses to the environment which can be replaced by more adaptive behaviours.

Behavioural therapies: therapeutic techniques of changing behaviour that are based on the principles of classical conditioning. The term 'behaviour modification' is more usually used for techniques derived from operant conditioning.

Behaviourism: one of the major orientations in psychology that concentrates on overt (observable) events rather than covert (unobservable) mental processing. Behaviours are seen as being acquired through the processes of learning.

Beta bias: The tendency of some theories to ignore or minimize differences between men and women. They have done this either by ignoring

questions about the lives of women or by assuming that findings from studies of men apply equally well to women (*see also* **Alpha bias**).

Bias: a leaning in a particular direction, a systematic distortion in one's attitudes and beliefs based on prejudices or pre-existing ideas.

Biological approach: the view that behaviour can be explained in terms of physical factors, either physiological, genetic or evolutionary.

Biological psychology: the study of the relationship between the physiological systems in the body and behaviour.

Biological rhythms: cycles of activity that occur with some regularity in an organism. Infradian rhythms occur less than once a day (e.g. human menstrual cycle), circadian rhythms repeat themselves every 24 hours (e.g. sleep/waking cycle), and ultradian rhythms more than once a day (e.g. stages of sleep during one night).

Biological (somatic) therapies: an approach to the treatment of mental disorders that relies on the use of physical or chemical methods.

Bipolar depression/disorder (manic-depressive disorder): a mood disorder characterized by extremes of mania and depression.

Black English Vernacular (BEV): an English dialect spoken by Black people in both America and the UK, commonly referred to as 'Black English'.

Bottom-up processing: processing of information (stimulus) that is determined solely by aspects of the stimulus (*see also* **Top-down processing**).

Broca's area: the area of the inferior pre-frontal cortex of the left hemisphere of the brain, hypothesized by Broca to be the centre of speech production.

Bulimia nervosa: characterized by secret binge eating followed by vomiting, misuse of laxatives, diuretics, excessive exercise, etc., in order to lose weight.

Bystander behaviour: the behaviour shown by those who witness an emergency. This is often referred to as 'bystander apathy' because of the tendency of bystanders to ignore the emergency when in the company of others.

Capacity: the amount of information that can be stored in memory at any particular time.

Capacity models/resource allocation models (of divided attention): those models proposing that we have a pool of processing resources that we can allocate according to the demands of the task and environmental factors.

Cardiovascular disorder: any disorder of the cardiovascular system, e.g. high blood pressure, coronary heart disease (heart attack) or stroke. (The cardiovascular system consists of the heart and the blood vessels. It is responsible for distributing oxygen and nutrients to the body's organs.)

CAT (computed axial tomography) scans: see **CT scans**.

Categorization: a short cut used when processing information. A category is a set of items perceived to have at least one feature in common. In interpersonal perception, categories such as young–old and male–female are used.

Cerebral cortex: an area of the brain resembling a folded sheet of grey tissue that covers the rest of the brain. It is associated with 'higher functions', such as language and reasoning.

Chemotherapy: treatment by using drugs.

Chi-square Test: an inferential test of association for independent data at a nominal level.

Chunking: combining individual letters or numbers into larger meaningful units.

Circadian rhythms: see **Biological rhythms.**

Classical conditioning: a form of learning where a neutral stimulus is paired with a stimulus that already produces a response, such that over time, the neutral stimulus also produces that response.

Cocktail party phenomenon: refers to (a) a person's ability to concentrate on just one conversation although others are going on all around and (b) the way a person engaged in (attending to) one conversation will nevertheless hear their own name if it is mentioned in a nearby conversation.

Cognitive approach: cognitive psychologists are interested in how mental processes affect behaviour, likening the mind to an information processing machine.

Cognitive–behavioural therapies: techniques that involve helping clients to identify their negative, irrational thoughts and to replace these with more positive, rational ways of thinking.

Cognitive development: the growth of cognitive (thinking) abilities. This may be studied by examining changes in the form and structure of children's thinking as they get older, or by looking at individual differences in the power of children's thinking as measured, e.g. by IQ tests.

Cognitive labelling: Schachter and Singer's theory that emotional states involve a combination of non-specific bodily arousal, and cognitive appraisal of the situation that labels the arousal as a particular emotion, e.g. anger, euphoria, fear.

Cognitive model of abnormality: the view that stresses the role of cognitive problems (such as illogical thought processes) in abnormal functioning.

Cognitive psychology: research field in psychology that focuses on mental processes used to acquire, store, retrieve and use knowledge.

Cohort: a group of individuals who were born during the same time interval, i.e. a 'generation'.

Collectivist cultures: cultures that value group loyalty, prefer group to individual decisions and where the needs of the group outweigh the concerns of the individual.

Colour processing/vision: refers to the ability to see chromatic colours (hues) such as yellow, green and blue. Two theories have been proposed – trichromatic and opponent-process – but no satisfactory complete explanation exists.

Commentary: a generic AO2 term used by examiners to describe any material used by a candidate to 'comment on' rather than 'describe' psychological material. Analysis and evaluation count as commentary, as does any other material that is *about* the material being described rather than a further description of it.

Communication: occurs when one animal (the signaller) performs an action that in turn causes some voluntary change of behaviour in another animal (the receiver) as a result of their perception of that signal.

Companionate love: the emotional state that combines feelings of affection and attachment characterized by mutual concern for each other – less intense than romantic love.

Compare and contrast: consider both the similarities and the differences between two topic areas (in the exam, requires an AO1+AO2 response).

Computer-mediated communication (CMC): interpersonal interactions over the Internet, e.g. via e-mails and chat rooms.

Concept(s): an idea or group of ideas that might be used as the basis for a psychological theory.

Conditioning: see **Classical conditioning; Operant conditioning.**

Confidentiality: the ethical concern that information gathered during psychological research or therapy should not be divulged to others unless otherwise agreed in advance or unless there is a legal requirement to disclose it.

Conformity/majority influence: a form of social influence where people adopt the behaviours, attitudes and values of other members of a reference group.

Consent: see **Informed consent**

Consider/Critically consider: show knowledge and understanding of the topic area, as well as the strengths and limitations of the material presented (in the exam, requires an AO1+AO2 response).

Constructivist theories (of perception): top-down (or concept-driven) theories that emphasize the need for several sources of information in order to construct our perception of the world. In addition to information available in the sensory stimulus, we need to use higher cognitive processes, according to this theory, to interpret the information appropriately.

Contact hypothesis: suggestion that prejudice can be reduced if members of different groups are brought into contact with each other.

Contrast processing: term used in the study of visual perception to describe the ability to differentiate between brightness levels in adjoining areas.

Control group: in an experimental design, the group used as a baseline against which to compare the performance of the experimental group.

Controlled (attentional) processing: a mental operation that is conscious, relatively slow and easily interrupted.

Control (psychological): the sense that we can anticipate events that occur in our environment – a feeling that we can accomplish things and are not at the mercy of forces beyond our control.

Correlation: the degree of relatedness between sets of scores – that is, the extent to which different variables co-vary.

Correlation coefficient: a statistic that expresses the strength of a correlation. The closer the coefficient is to +1 or −1 the stronger the correlation (relationship).

Correlational analysis: a type of analysis used to measure the extent of relationship between variables that are thought likely to co-vary.

Cortical activity: neural activity in the cortex of the brain.

Co-variation model of attribution: Kelley's theory that people decide on the cause of a behaviour by weighing up how consistent and distinctive the behaviour is and how much consensus there is about it.

Crisis: a psychological conflict which needs to be resolved if the individual is to move on to the next stage of development.

Criticize: evaluate a topic area in terms of its strengths and weaknesses.

Cross-cultural variation: variations between people of different cultures.

Crowding: the feeling that is induced if our expectations about the use of space are violated by the presence of others.

Crystallized intelligence: the ability to store and manipulate learned information.

CT (computed tomography) scans: a non-invasive,

multiple X-ray procedure for creating images of the brain.

Cultural bias: a tendency in psychological theory and research to ignore the differences between cultures and impose understanding based on the study of one culture alone.

Cultural identity: the influence of one's culture on the development of identity. Individualist cultures stress the importance of personal achievement and independence, while collectivist cultures stress the importance of collective achievement and dependence.

Cultural relativism: the idea that judgements about definitions of human behaviour (e.g. abnormal behaviour) cannot be made in absolute terms but only within the context of a given culture.

Culture: the enduring rules, customs, morals, ways of interacting, child-rearing practices and so on shared by a group of people. Such attitudes and practices bind the group of people together. They are learned through the process of socialization.

Culture-bound syndromes: according to DSM-IV-TR, these are recurrent, locality-specific patterns of aberrant behaviour and troubling experience – many are considered to be 'illnesses' and most have local names.

Day care: a form of care for infants and children, offered by someone other than close family, taking place outside the home, but returning home at night.

Debate: a discussion where two (or more) contrasting points of view are presented, a formalized system of logical argument.

Decay: the memory trace fades away with time so that the memory is no longer available.

Deception: withholding information or misleading research participants.

Decision-making: kind of reasoning that involves

making choices and sometimes taking risks.

Defence mechanism: according to psychoanalytic theory, an unconscious strategy used to protect the ego from anxiety by falsifying, distorting or denying reality.

Define: explain what is meant by a particular term (in the exam, requires an AO1 response).

Deindividuation: process that occurs when one loses one's sense of individual identity so that social, moral and societal constraints on behaviour are loosened.

Demand characteristics: the tendency for experimental participants to adjust their behaviour according to their own interpretation of the aims of the experiment.

Depth/distance (visual) perception: the ability to experience the world in three dimensions by using monocular and binocular cues to assess depth and distance between objects.

Depression (unipolar disorder): a type of mood disorder where the person experiences feelings of great sadness, worthlessness and guilt, and finds the challenges of life overwhelming.

Deprivation: to have something taken away, such as food or warmth, i.e. a loss. In the context of attachment, deprivation refers to the loss of emotional care that results in the breaking of emotional bonds.

Describe: show knowledge of a topic area (in the exam, requires an AO1 response).

Descriptive statistics: techniques used to describe or characterize obtained data.

Determinism: the philosophical doctrine that an individual's behaviour is shaped or controlled by internal or external forces rather than an individual's will to do something (*see also Free will*).

Deviation from ideal mental health: behaviour that does not meet the six criteria

relating to mental health or optimal living first proposed by Jahoda (1958).

Deviation from social norms: behaviour that violates the implicit and explicit rules and moral standards of a given society.

Diagnostic and Statistical Manual (DSM) of Mental Disorders: a classification, definition and description of over 200 mental health disorders which groups disorders in terms of their common features. The latest version is DSM-IV-TR published in 2000.

Diathesis-stress model (of mental disorders): general model of disorders postulating that people develop mental disorders when they possess both a constitutional vulnerability (diathesis) and are exposed to stressful events.

Diffusion of responsibility: a decrease in an individual's sense of responsibility for helping in an emergency because other bystanders are present.

Direct theories of perception: bottom-up (or data-driven) theories proposing that there is sufficient information in the sensory stimulus to allow us to make sense of our environment without the involvement of stored knowledge or problem-solving skills.

Directional hypothesis: an alternative hypothesis which predicts the direction in which any differences (or any correlation in an investigation using correlational analysis) in the results of an investigation are expected to occur.

Discrimination: a way of behaving towards members of a categorized group such that all members of that group are treated in the same (usually unfair) way, i.e. the behavioural expression of prejudice.

Discuss: describe and evaluate a topic area (in the exam, requires an AO1+AO2 response).

Displacement: items currently in STM are pushed out to make room for incoming new ones.

Dispositional attribution: inferring that the reason for a person's behaviour is something about themselves such as their personality.

Dissociative disorders: disorders that involve changes in memory for personal events.

Dissociative Identity Disorder (also known as **Multiple-Personality Disorder**): a disorder where a disruption in memory causes a separation of one part of a person's identity from another.

Dissolution of relationships: refers to the study of how and why relationships break down.

Distributed functions: the principle that specific functions involve combined activity across many regions of the cortex. For example, visual perception depends upon processing distributed across several brain regions.

Divided attention: the ability to divide our attentional processing between more than one task.

Dizygotic (fraternal) twins: twins that develop from different zygotes (eggs) and are no more likely to be similar than any pair of siblings.

Dreaming: a stage of sleep characterized by the experience of visual imagery and rapid eye movements (REM).

Drive reduction theory (of motivation): Hull's thesis that all behaviour is motivated and that all motivation originates in the satisfaction of homeostatic drives such as hunger and thirst. The stimuli that reduce the drives (e.g. food and water) serve to reinforce the behaviour that led to them.

DSM: see **Diagnostic and Statistical Manual.**

Duration: the length of time that information can be kept in memory.

Early-selection theories (of attention): those theories (e.g. Broadbent's) which place the filtering mechanism that selects some inputs and rejects others early on in the attentional process, before analysis for meaning occurs (*see also* **Late-selection theories**).

Eating disorder: a serious disruption of healthy eating habits or appetite.

Ecological theory of sleep: theories of the function of sleep that emphasize evolutionary and ecological aspects of animal behaviour. The simplest version proposes that sleep keeps an animal safe from predators at times when normal activities like feeding are impossible.

Ecological validity: the degree to which the findings from a study can be generalized beyond the context of the investigation.

EEA (Environment of Evolutionary Adaptiveness): the environment to which a species is adapted and the set of selection pressures that operated at that time, generally regarded as a period between 10,000 and 5 million years ago.

EEG: electroencephalogram, a non-invasive recording of the electrical activity of the brain, using electrodes fixed to the scalp.

Ego: according to psycho-analytic theory, the part of the personality responsible for decision-making and dealing with reality.

Egocentrism: a feature of thinking in the young child, characterized by an inability to take the perspective of another person.

Egoism: the tendency to act out of self-interest.

Elaborated code: speech that is not context bound; it uses more complex grammatical structures and more abstract vocabulary than restricted code.

Electrical self-stimulation of the brain (ESB): the technique used by Olds and Milner of implanting an electrode in the hypothalamus (area of the brain) of a living animal, so that when the animal performs a specified task it receives stimulation there.

Electroconvulsive therapy (ECT): a treatment involving passing an electrical current through the brain by the application of between 70 and 130 volts which induces a convulsion or epileptic seizure.

Emotion: a complex pattern of events, involving perception of a situation, appraisal of the situation as threatening or harmless, feeling towards the situation, and expression of emotion in terms of behavioural and physiological changes.

Empathy: feeling an emotional response that is consistent with another's emotional state or condition (i.e. feeling sad when we meet someone who is sad).

Empathy-altruism hypothesis: altruistic behaviour is explained as a consequence of empathy, i.e. being able to imagine how the person who needs help feels.

Encoding: changing sensory input into a form or code to be processed by the memory system.

Endogenous depression: thought to arise from within the person, independent of external events.

Endogenous pacemakers (biological clocks): internal timing mechanisms that enable biological rhythms to continue in the absence of obvious external cues. The best example is the suprachiasmatic nucleus in the hypothalamus (*see also* **Exogenous zeitgebers** and **Biological rhythms**).

Enrichment: attempts either to accelerate early learning ('hothousing') or to overcome early deprivation through the provision of compensatory education programmes.

Environmental stressors: aspects of the physical environment (such as noise or crowding) that may contribute to aggression.

Equity theory: proposition that people stay in relationships as long as they perceive them to be fair. Equity is not the same as equality. If one partner gives more in a relationship but also benefits more than the other person does, then the relationship may still be equitable.

Ethical guidelines: prescriptive guidance on the conduct of psychologists in research and practice. These represent the key issues that face psychologists in their work with humans and animals and are regularly updated by the organizations that issue them.

Ethical issue: arises in research where there is a conflict between the rights and dignity of participants and the goals and outcomes of research.

Ethics: that which is deemed right or wrong in terms of human behaviour. Ethics are the moral principles used by a group of professionals, such as doctors, solicitors or psychologists.

Ethnocentrism: the term used to describe the belief in the superiority of one's own ethnic and cultural group.

Evaluate: make an informed judgement as to the value of an argument, theory or piece of research (in the exam, requires an AO2 response).

Evidence: material that might be drawn from theories or investigations and is used to support or contradict an argument or theory.

Evolution: the change over successive generations in the genetic make-up of a particular group or species. The dominant force in this change is natural selection.

Evolutionary approach: the view that behaviours can be explained in terms of the principles of natural selection, i.e. any behaviour that is adaptive is more likely to be perpetuated in future generations. Selection is made at the level of the genes.

Exogenous zeitgebers ('time givers'): external events that play a role in rhythmic activities (*see also* **Endogenous pacemakers** and **Biological rhythms**).

Expectancy/incentive: refers to the ability of rewarding stimuli to 'pull' or 'elicit' behaviour on the basis of previous experience, and contrasts with the drive approach that sees motivated behaviour as 'pushed' by internal drives.

Experiment: an investigative technique which involves the manipulation of an independent variable in order to see its effect on a dependent variable.

Experimental (internal) validity: a measure of whether the experimental procedures actually worked and the effects observed were genuine (i.e. caused by the experimental manipulation). The conclusions of a study are justified when there is a high level of experimental validity.

Explain: show understanding of a topic through coherent and intelligible explanation (in the exam, requires an AO1 response).

Extent: see **To what extent**

External validity: is concerned with the extent to which results can be generalized to other settings beyond that of the study concerned.

Extinction: the procedure, after classical or operant conditioning, of repeatedly presenting the conditioned stimulus without any reinforcement until the conditioned response ceases to be produced.

Eyewitness testimony: an area of memory research that investigates the accuracy of memory following an accident, crime or other significant event, and the types of errors that are commonly made in such situations.

Failure to function adequately: an assessment of an individual whose disability prevents them from pursuing normal activities and goals (e.g. alcohol addiction preventing normal performance at work or interfering with social activities).

Feature detection theory: an explanation for pattern recognition; the proposal that we process images in terms of their constituent parts and then match the features of a pattern to those features stored in memory.

Feature processing: term used in the study of visual perception to describe the ability to detect contours, essential for the recognition of objects.

Field experiment: an experimental manipulation of an independent variable that takes place in a natural setting rather than in the more artificial setting of the laboratory.

Findings: the outcome of a research investigation.

Fitness: a measurement of the number of offspring left behind by an individual compared to the number of offspring left behind by other members of the same species.

Flashbulb memory: a vivid, long-lasting memory of a highly significant event accompanied by recollection of details such as where we heard the news and what we were doing at the time.

Flooding: a behavioural technique used to treat phobias. The phobic person is exposed to the feared situation for an extended period with no opportunity to escape.

Fluid intelligence: a general, problem-solving ability that we bring to bear on novel or unfamiliar problems.

fMRI (functional magnetic resonance imaging): a form of magnetic resonance imaging of the brain that registers blood flow to functioning areas of the brain (*see also* **Imaging techniques** and **MRI**)

Focal theory (of adolescence): the argument that adolescents deal with changes that occur by focusing on different issues at different times. Consequently, they are likely to experience little stress. This theory contrasts with the view of adolescence as inevitably a period of 'storm and stress'.

Focused attention: the ability to focus on one thing at a time to the exclusion of other competing stimuli.

Foraging: the different ways that animals are able to satisfy their nutritional requirements (e.g. grazing, predation, scavenging).

Forgetting: the loss of the ability to recall or recognize something previously learned.

Free will: the philosophical doctrine that individuals are capable of making their own choices, i.e. can be self-determining and free from coercion (*see also* **Determinism**).

Frequency polygon: a form of graphical representation used to present data on interval or ratio levels of measurement. It consists of a line linking points that represent the frequencies of the variable placed on the x-axis.

Fundamental attribution error: a tendency to see the behaviour of others as being due to their stable personality characteristics rather than the influence of situational factors.

Gender: the psychological element of a person's sex; masculinity and femininity as distinct from the biological category of male and female.

Gender bias: the treatment of men and women in psychological research and/or theory in a way which offers a view of behaviour and experience that might not fully represent the characteristics of both genders.

Gender role: a set of expectations that describe how males and females should think, act and feel.

Gender schema theory: the cognitive-developmental approach that claims children develop gender schema (concept clusters such as stereotypes) as soon as they recognize that there is a difference between men and women.

General Adaptation Syndrome (GAS): a model, described by Hans Selye, of how the body reacts during stressful situations. There are three stages:
(a) *alarm stage* when an arousal response is activated
(b) *resistance stage* when the body is apparently coping with the stressor
(c) *exhaustion stage* – if stress continues for too long, it can lead to physical symptoms such as a stomach ulcer or heart attack.

Generalizability: the ability of researchers to offer a justifiable extension of their findings beyond the actual sample of participants used to a wider population of people.

Genetics: the part of biological science concerned with the study of heredity and the role of genes throughout one's life.

Genital stage: the final stage of psychosexual development (according to psychoanalytic theory) when the main source of pleasure is the genitals.

Gestalt approach: in problem-solving this refers to the need for structural understanding, i.e. the ability to understand how all parts of the problem fit together to meet the goal.

Helping: a general term for giving assistance to another person.

Hemisphere asymmetries: refers to the fact that some functions of the cortex are located in one hemisphere only, rather than being symmetrically organized across both hemispheres.

Heritability: refers to the proportion of the total variation in a given characteristic, in a given population, that can be attributed to genetic differences between members of that population.

Heuristic: a problem-solving strategy that involves taking the most likely option – a rule of thumb – a cognitive short cut.

Histogram: a form of graphical representation used to present data on interval or ratio levels of measurement. It consist of a series of vertical bars of equal width, which represent the frequencies of the variable placed on the *x*-axis.

Homeostasis: the stability of an organism's internal environment.

Homeostatic drive: motivated behaviour aimed at satisfying a physiological drive, such as hunger or thirst, and so maintaining homeostasis.

Homing: the ability of animals to navigate towards a target that is usually their home range.

Hormones: chemicals released by the endocrine system into general circulation.

Humanistic model of abnormality: abnormality seen in terms of blocks and frustrations to an individual's self-growth and development.

Humanistic psychology: a view of human beings that sees every person as unique and possessing an innate potential for positive growth.

Humanistic therapy: a treatment where the therapist tries to see the world through the client's eyes and endeavours to encourage the client to exercise free will and decide on their own life course.

Hypothalamus: area of brain located just below the thalamus (the large, two-lobed structure at the top of the brain stem). It plays an important role in the regulation of some motivated behaviours (*see also* **Limbic system**).

Hypothesis: a specific, testable statement that enables a researcher to predict the results of a study.

Iatrogenic disorder: a disorder unintentionally induced by therapeutic practice.

ICD-10: *see International Classification of Disorders*.

Id: according to psychoanalytic theory, the part of the personality present at birth, the mental representation of biological drives.

Identification: (a) in the area of social influence, this refers to the process of adopting the views of a group because one wants to be with or be liked by the group. Such views may not be maintained if the group is no longer present; (b) in Freud's theory of psychosexual development, the process when the child incorporates the qualities and ideas of the parent of the same sex.

Identity formation: the process, according to Erikson, whereby a person achieves a sense of integrity and continuity. Failure to achieve a sense of identity may result in role confusion. Marcia named four stages in this process: identity confusion, identity foreclosure, identity moratorium and identity achievement.

Illusions: perceptual experiences that are not true representations of the physical event that is experienced through the senses. A visual illusion is an image that 'tricks' the perceptual system so that one 'sees' things the way they aren't.

Illusory correlations: relationships that appear to exist between two events where, in fact, none exist.

Imaging techniques: *see CAT, fMRI, MEG, MRI* and *PET scans*.

Imitation: copying another person's behaviour.

Immune system: the system that protects the body against infection; a network of cells and chemicals that seek out and destroy invading particles.

Imposed etic: term that refers to the assumption that research questions or procedures used in one culture will have the same meaning for participants when applied in another culture and that consequently their responses will mean the same in the new culture.

Incentive: a stimulus that elicits goal-directed behaviour.

Inclusive fitness: a measurement of an individual's own fitness, plus their effect on the reproductive success of genetic relatives.

Independent groups design: an experimental design which involves using different participants in each condition of the experiment.

Individualistic cultures: cultures where self-interest and individual rights are promoted, rather than the needs and interests of others.

Individuation: refers to the desire to be distinguished from others.

Inferential statistics: the techniques (tests) used to analyse the data from samples to enable us to infer or draw conclusions about the population from which the sample is drawn. Such tests include Chi-square, Binomial Sign, Wilcoxon Matched Pairs, Mann-Whitney U, and Spearman's Rho.

Information-processing approach: a reference to the belief that the processing of sensory information takes place in a series of stages. In developmental psychology, this approach assumes that if adults think more successfully than children do, it is because they can process more information than children can.

Informed consent: an ethical requirement that participants or clients should have sufficient information about an experiment or therapeutic intervention to enable them to make an informed judgement about whether or not to take part.

Infradian rhythms: *see Biological rhythms*.

In-group: a group of which one perceives oneself a member (in contrast to the out-group).

Insecure attachment: a less optimal form of attachment, at least in Western culture. Insecurely attached children show disturbed behaviour during separation and reunion.

Insights: perceptions from theories or investigations that enable us to understand or appraise a topic area.

Intelligence: an underlying ability which enables an individual to adapt to and function effectively within a given environment.

Intelligence test: a type of assessment that purports to measure intelligence.

Interference: memory traces are disrupted or obscured by other information.

Internal validity: is concerned with the extent to which we can be sure that research findings are due to the mechanisms suggested, such as manipulation of the independent variable in an experiment, and not to the action of some other unwanted variable, such as individual differences or the effects of practice.

International Classification of Disorders (ICD): a classification of physical and psychological disorders published and regularly updated by the World Health Organization. The current edition is ICD-10, published in 1992.

Interval level data: *see Levels of measurement*.

Interview: any face-to-face situation where one person (the interviewer) asks a series of questions of another person (the respondent). These questions may be structured, semi-structured or unstructured.

Invasive methods: techniques for investigating the brain that involve penetrating through the skull into brain tissue. Examples include electrical stimulation and lesions.

Investigator effects: result from the effects of a researcher's behaviour and characteristics on an investigation.

IQ (Intelligence quotient): see **Measured intelligence**.

James-Lange theory of emotion: the idea that the perception of an emotion-arousing stimulus leads to a behavioural response. This response involves changes in the body's physiology which are detected by the brain and interpreted as an emotion.

Kin selection: animals are more likely to show cooperation and altruism towards close genetic relations. The closer the genetic relationship, the greater the likelihood of help, and therefore the greater the likelihood of these relatives surviving and reproducing.

Kinship (family) studies: investigations which look at the correlation in some characteristic or quality (e.g. intelligence) between pairs of individuals who are genetically related to varying degrees.

Laboratory experiment: an investigative technique where the experimental manipulation of the independent variable takes place within such conditions that careful control of extraneous variables is possible.

Language: an agreed set of symbols and rules that enable us to convey meaning and converse with others who share the same language.

Language acquisition: the processes by which children acquire or develop human language.

Language Acquisition Device (LAD): an innate mechanism that is programmed to recognize grammatical structure and therefore makes it easy for children to acquire language.

Late-selection theories (of attention): those theories (e.g. Deutsch and Deutsch's) claiming that both attended and unattended inputs are analysed for meaning before one input is selected and reaches consciousness (see also **Early-selection theories**).

Lateralization of function: an aspect of the organization of the human brain in that functions are primarily controlled by one hemisphere or the other. An example is the left hemisphere control of language and the right hemisphere specialization for visuo-spatial functions. Also referred to as functional asymmetries.

Law of effect: Thorndike's theory that reinforced behaviour is more likely to be repeated and unreinforced behaviour is likely to die out.

Learned helplessness: a psychological state produced as a result of being exposed to uncontrollable events. Observed in people who give up trying to cope because previous attempts have been frustrated and led to failure.

Lesioning: injuring brain tissue, e.g. by heating the tip of an implanted electrode so that a small area of tissue is destroyed.

Level of significance: the cut-off point (e.g. 5% or 1%) used by researchers to determine whether a particular set of data differs from that which would be expected if only chance factors were operating.

Levels of measurement: types of data. Four levels (scales) of data are commonly met in psychology. (a) The **nominal level** is the weakest level and deals with frequency count data, e.g. the number of students who gained grade A in their History exam.

(b) **Ordinal level** data can be placed in rank order, i.e. from the highest to the lowest value, e.g. names and positions of top five contestants in a general knowledge competition. (c) **Interval level data** has all the properties of the ordinal scale but it also has equal intervals between adjacent units on the scale, e.g. the Celsius temperature scale. (d) The highest level of measurement is called a **ratio scale**. It has the properties of an interval scale but also has an absolute zero point, e.g. the Kelvin temperature scale where 0 degree is the complete absence of heat.

Levels of processing: a theory of memory put forward by Craik and Lockhart, that the amount of information retained in LTM depends on how deeply it is processed during learning.

Life changes: major life events, such as marriage, divorce, moving house and having a baby, that are scored according to their psychological impact within the *Social Readjustment Rating Scale (SRRS)* and used to investigate the relationship between life changes and stress-related health breakdown.

Limbic system: collections of nuclei and tracts in the brain that border the thalamus; plays a role in emotion (see also **Hypothalamus**).

Linguistic relativity hypothesis: theory that the language we use is responsible for shaping our thoughts about the world. The weak version states that language influences thinking, whereas the strong version states that language determines the way we think.

Localization of function: the principle that specific functions are localized to specific areas of cortex, such as the role of Wernicke's area in understanding speech.

Long-term memory (LTM): an unlimited capacity system for storing information for long periods.

Longitudinal study: an investigation where participants are studied over an extended period of time.

Maintaining relationships: refers to the study of the strategies people use to prevent relationships breaking down.

Mann-Whitney U Test: an inferential test of difference for independent groups when at least ordinal level data have been obtained.

Matched participants design: an experimental design which involves matching each participant in one of the experimental conditions as closely as possible with another participant in the second condition on variables considered to be relevant to the experiment in question.

Matching hypothesis: proposal that people tend to select partners who are alike in terms of physical attractiveness, background, etc.

Mean: the arithmetic average of a set of scores, calculated by adding all the scores together and dividing by the number of scores.

Means-end analysis: a problem-solving strategy that involves breaking problems down into their constituent parts, which are then solved in turn until the solution (goal) is reached.

Means of representation: in problem-solving this refers to the way in which we construe and approach a problem.

Measured intelligence: refers to the score achieved on taking an intelligence test. This is sometimes called an intelligence quotient (IQ).

Measures of central tendency: a descriptive statistic that provides a single value which is representative of a set of numbers by indicating the most typical (average) value. The mode, median and mean are measures of central tendency.

Measures of dispersion: descriptive statistics that enable us to examine the variability within sets of data; they help us to understand whether scores in a given set of data are similar to, or very different from, each other. The range and standard deviation are measures of dispersion.

Media influences: the way in which the media (e.g. television, Internet) might cause changes in behaviour in those who are exposed to it. Much of the debate concerning media influences has focused on its effects on aggressive behaviour.

Median: the middle value of a set of scores arranged in ascending or descending order.

Medical model of abnormality: a view of abnormality that sees mental disorders as being caused by abnormal physiological processes such as genetic and biochemical factors. Abnormality, according to this model, is seen as an illness or disease.

MEG (magneto-encephalography): non-invasive technique for visualizing (imaging) the brain by recording tiny magnetic fields produced by active neurons.

Memory: the mental processes involved in registering, storing and retrieving information.

Mental disorder: see **Psychological disorder.**

Methodology: a way of conducting research in order to verify theories and explanations.

Methods: the different ways that research investigations can be carried out.

Migration: term usually used to describe the mass movement of members of a species from one location to another (e.g. seasonal migrations of birds).

Mind–body problem: the problem of determining the relationship between the physical realm (the body) and the mental realm (the mind).

Minority influence: a form of social influence where a persuasive minority exerts pressure to change the attitudes, beliefs or behaviours of the majority. Minorities are most influential when they appear consistent and principled.

Mode: the most frequently occurring value in a data sequence.

Model: a term that is used synonymously with 'theory', although it may refer to something that is less elaborate or complex.

Modelling: the term used by Bandura to describe observational learning.

Modular theories (of divided attention): propose that humans possess several different processing mechanisms (modules) of attention that specialize in handling particular tasks.

Monozygotic (identical) twins: twins that develop from the same zygote (egg) and are therefore genetically identical.

Moral development: the process by which children come to internalize standards of right and wrong, and ultimately make their own decisions concerning moral issues.

Motivation: literally, why organisms act in the way that they do, i.e. the study of what arouses and directs behaviour.

Motor cortex: areas of the cerebral cortex specialized for controlling movement of the body muscles. Motor cortex occupies the pre-central gyrus.

Movement perception: refers to our ability to perceive accurately the movement of people and objects.

MRI (magnetic resonance imaging): a non-invasive technique for picturing (imaging) the brain (or other soft tissue of the body) by subjecting it to a sequence of pulsed radio waves while the head (or other body part) is held in a powerful magnetic field.

Multiple-Personality Disorder (now more commonly known as **Dissociative Identity Disorder**): a disorder where a disruption in memory causes a separation of one part of a person's identity from another.

Multi-store model of memory: an explanation of memory as a flow of information through a series of stages in a fixed sequence. The best-known model of this type was proposed by Atkinson and Shiffrin.

Nativist theory: in the area of language development, the proposition that children are biologically equipped to acquire language (see also **Language Acquisition Device**).

Natural animal language: characteristics of animal communication patterns that satisfy at least some of the criteria for human language.

Natural experiment: an example of a 'quasi-experiment' where the allocation of participants to the different experimental conditions is outside the control of the investigator, but rather is manipulated fortuitously by some outside agency.

Natural selection: the part of Darwin's theory that states that those animals that are well adapted to their environment will leave behind more offspring than those animals who are less well adapted.

Naturalistic observation: an observational technique where behaviour is observed in its natural context without intrusion by the person who is doing the observing.

Nature–nurture debate: the controversy about the relative contributions of genetic factors (nature) versus environmental factors (nurture) in determining a person's characteristics and abilities, e.g. their level of intelligence.

Navigation: true navigation is the ability to reach a goal regardless of starting point. This is contrasted with simple compass orientation, which involves always heading in one specific compass direction regardless of the 'correct' direction.

Needs: Maslow's term for human motives, ranging from basic physiological needs to aesthetic needs and self-actualization.

Negative correlation: a measurement of the extent to which high values on one variable are associated with low values on another. A negative correlation is indicated by a correlation coefficient between zero and −1.

Negative reinforcement: see **Reinforcement.**

Negative-state relief model: theory that we help others in order to feel better ourselves, e.g. to improve our mood.

Neonate research: investigations carried out using newborn infants.

Nominal level data: see **Levels of measurement.**

Non-directional hypothesis: an alternative hypothesis which does not predict the direction in which any differences (or any correlation in an investigation using correlational analysis) in the results of an investigation are expected to occur.

Non-homeostatic drive: behaviour that is aroused and directed, but does not appear to be associated with homeostatic drives. Examples in animals include curiosity and manipulation, and a range of complex human behaviours such as studying for A-levels.

Non-invasive methods: techniques for investigating the brain that do not penetrate the skull. Examples include the electro-encephalograph (EEG) and modern brain scanners.

Normal distribution: a bell-shaped, continuous distribution, symmetrical about its midpoint.

NREM sleep: stages of sleep where no rapid eye movements are found.

Null hypothesis: predicts no differences between the results from the different conditions of an experiment (it predicts no correlation in an investigation using correlational analysis). Under the null hypothesis, any difference (or correlation) found is due to chance alone.

Nurture: aspects of behaviour that are acquired through experience, i.e. learned from interactions with the physical and social environment.

Obedience to authority: an outcome of social influence where an individual acts according to the orders of some authority figure. It is assumed that without such an order the person would not have acted in this way.

Object permanence: the knowledge that things that are out of sight actually still exist.

Obsessive–compulsive disorder: an anxiety disorder in which the individual is plagued with uncontrollable thoughts (obsessions) and performs seemingly senseless rituals (compulsive behaviours).

Operant conditioning: an explanation of learning that sees the consequences of a behaviour as being of vital importance to the future appearance of that behaviour. If a behaviour is followed by a desirable consequence, it becomes more frequent; if it is followed by an undesirable consequence, it becomes less frequent.

Operation Head Start: an enrichment intervention programme set up for pre-school children in the USA in the 1960s. It was designed to reverse the effects of social disadvantage.

Operationalization: the process whereby a variable is defined in terms of the steps or behaviours necessary to measure it. For example, using the behaviour 'laughing' as a measure of 'happiness' or the maximum number of

digits a person can recall immediately after learning as a measure of short-term memory capacity.

Opportunity sample: a type of sample where the researcher selects anyone who is available to take part from a given population.

Optimal arousal: the term refers to the claim that a major motivation for animals is to maintain an optimal level of alertness and activation (arousal) that is neither too high nor too low.

Oral stage: the first stage of psychosexual development (according to psychoanalytic theory) when the infant's main source of pleasure is the mouth.

Ordinal level data: *see* **Levels of measurement**.

Out-group: a group of which one is not a member (in contrast to the in-group).

Outline: offer a summary description of the topic area (in the exam, requires an AO1 response).

Parental investment: actions that increase the survival chances of one set of offspring but at the expense of the parent procuring more offspring.

Participants: those people who are studied and contribute data in a research investigation.

Pattern recognition: the process by which we transform and organize the raw information provided by our sensory receptors into a meaningful whole.

Perception: the process by which we transform sensory information from the environment into the experience of objects, sounds, movement, etc.

Perceptual constancies: the tendency for objects to provide the same perceptual experience despite changes in the viewing conditions.

Perceptual development: the systematic change of perceptual abilities and processes that develop as a

result of maturation and experience.

Perceptual organization: the ability of an organism to organize the information that arrives via the senses into some meaningful perceptual experience.

Personality: a relatively stable, characteristic set of behaviours, attitudes, interests and capabilities, sometimes used as a means of distinguishing between people – an individual difference.

PET (positron emission tomography) scans: a non-invasive technique for visualizing (imaging) the activity in the brain by measuring the accumulation of a radioactive substance in various regions of the brain. A battery of detectors scans the brain after the radioactive substance has been injected into the bloodstream.

Phallic stage: the third stage of psychosexual development (according to psychoanalytic theory) when the child focuses on the genitals and initially on the opposite gender parent. Crisis at this stage is resolved by identifying with the same gender parent.

Phobic disorder: a type of anxiety disorder where there is a persistent and unreasonable fear of an object or situation.

Physiological approach: explaining behaviour in terms of the body systems, such as nerves and hormones.

Piaget, Jean: a Swiss psychologist whose major contribution to psychology was the theory that intelligence was the product of a natural and inevitable sequence of developmental stages and processes.

Pilot study: a small-scale prototype of a research investigation, carried out on a small number of participants in order to find out whether there are any problems with any aspect of the proposed study.

Pluralistic ignorance: the phenomenon where bystanders to an emergency define the situation wrongly as one that does not require intervention because other bystanders do not seem concerned.

Positive correlation: a measurement of the extent to which high values on one variable are associated with high values on another. A positive correlation is indicated by a correlation coefficient between zero and +1.

Post-traumatic stress disorder: a type of anxiety disorder that arises as a result of some traumatic event. The symptoms begin shortly after the event and may last for years.

Prejudice: pre-judging individuals on the basis of their membership of a particular category or group.

Preparedness: species-specific, biological predisposition to fear certain potentially dangerous stimuli, dating back to our ancestors.

Primary motor area: area of the cortex, in the frontal lobe, where sensorimotor signals converge and depart.

Privation: a lack of the necessities of life. In the context of attachment, privation refers to a complete lack of emotional care, especially during the first few years of life. Such a lack of emotional care results in no attachments being formed. It has been proposed that this lack of early attachment results in permanent harm to emotional and social development.

Probability: a numerical measure of the chance that something will happen.

Problem-solving: a complex skill used whenever we need to reach a goal that is not readily available.

Pro-social behaviour: an act that benefits others but may appear to have no direct benefit for the person performing it.

Pro-social reasoning: the area of thinking concerned with helping or comforting others, possibly at a personal cost.

Protection of participants: an ethical requirement that researchers have a duty of care towards their participants. Normally, the risk of harm to participants should be no greater than they would expect to meet in ordinary life.

Prototype theory: an explanation for pattern recognition; the proposal that we match incoming information against an abstract model in long-term memory that embodies the most typical features of an object or pattern.

Psychoanalysis: therapeutic method in which a person is given insights into the unconscious psychological conflicts that are seen as the cause of their symptoms.

Psychodrama: therapeutic technique in which clients work in groups to gain insight into their problems by 'acting out' chosen scenarios from problem areas in their lives.

Psychodynamic approach: any approach that emphasizes the dynamics of behaviour, i.e. the forces that motivate it. This approach is associated with psychoanalytic theories.

Psychodynamic models of abnormality: models that view abnormal behaviour as being caused by underlying psychological forces of which the individual is probably unaware.

Psychodynamic theories: theories that emphasize change and development in the individual and where 'drive' is a central concept in the process of development.

Psychodynamic therapies: treatments that help clients to uncover past traumatic events and the conflicts that have resulted from them. These conflicts can then be resolved so that the client is able to restore an adaptive level of functioning.

Psychological abnormality: behaviour and psychological functioning that is considered different from the 'normal'. Usually called 'mental disorder'.

Psychological disorder: a term used synonymously with 'mental disorder', it refers to a level of functioning that is harmful or distressing to the individual or to those around them. Psychological disorders are usually defined and described according to some current classification system such as DSM-IV-TR.

Psychology as science: the use of scientific methods to establish a body of psychological knowledge that is considered trustworthy and verifiable.

Psychopathology: the study of the origins and course of psychological disorders such as schizophrenia and depression.

Psychopathology thesis: in social influence research the suggestion that people who commit atrocities are psychologically impaired and different to most people (in contrast to Milgram's 'normality thesis').

Psychosocial theory: the view that personality continues to develop throughout adulthood, with an emphasis on social forces as important in shaping personality.

Psychosomatic illness: an illness with physical symptoms but thought to be caused by the continual mobilization of the autonomic nervous system (ANS) under stress.

Psychosurgery: cutting brain tissue in order to alleviate the symptoms of severe psychological disorder.

Punishment: that which decreases the probability of the response that preceded it, the opposite of reinforcement.

Qualitative data: information in non-numerical, narrative form, e.g. speech, written words, pictures.

Quantitative data: information collected in the course of a research study that is in a quantified (numerical) form (e.g. speed of response in milliseconds).

Questionnaire survey: a technique, using a structured set of questions, for asking a large sample of people about their views and behaviours, etc. Questionnaire surveys may be conducted in person, by telephone, by post, via the Internet, etc.

Random sample: a subset of a target population in which every person or item stands an equal chance of being selected for inclusion. This requires the researcher to be able to identify every person or item in the target population before selection of a sample takes place. The selection process therefore takes place in a completely unbiased way.

Range: the difference between the highest and lowest scores in a given set of data.

Ratio scale: see **Levels of measurement.**

Rational-emotive behaviour therapy: a form of psychotherapy, based on the work of Ellis, where the therapist actively confronts clients about their irrational thinking.

Reactive depression: a reaction to stressful events outside ourselves, such as the death of someone close, redundancy or failing exams.

Realistic conflict theory: an explanation for prejudice and discrimination proposing that inter-group hostility develops when groups are competing for scarce resources.

Recognition-by-components theory (RBC): proposition that an object can be recognized when we have identified its constituent geons (basic three-dimensional shapes) and how these are spatially related.

Reconstructive memory: a term usually associated with Bartlett which refers to a memory distorted by the individual's prior knowledge and expectations.

Reductionism: the act of breaking complex phenomena into simpler components. A belief in reductionism implies that this is preferable because complex phenomena are best understood in terms of a simpler level of explanation.

Reinforcement: the process by which a response is strengthened. This can be positive, when a response produces a pleasant outcome or negative when the response leads to the removal of something unpleasant. Each outcome strengthens the response it follows.

Reinforcement-affect model: the theory that we find people attractive (a) because they were around when positive things happened and so we associate them with feeling good, or (b) because they are themselves reinforcing, e.g. by being helpful and friendly.

Relative deprivation: the state that people experience when they perceive a gap between what others have and what they have themselves, i.e. others are seen as relatively better off.

Reliability: the degree to which a description or score is consistent over time or across different observers. If the findings of research are consistently replicable then they can be called reliable.

REM (rapid eye movement) sleep: sometimes called paradoxical sleep; the stage of sleep characterized by rapid eye movements, loss of muscle tone and a waking EEG pattern. The stage of sleep strongly associated with dreaming.

Repeated measures design: an experimental design which involves exposing every participant to each of the experimental conditions, so, in effect, participants are used as their own controls.

Repression: (a) defence mechanism (unconscious process) in which a distressing memory or impulse is excluded from conscious awareness; (b) a theory of forgetting.

Research: the process of gaining knowledge, either by an examination of appropriate theories or through empirical data collection.

Resource allocation models (of attention): see *Capacity models*.

Restoration (recuperation) theory of sleep: the hypothesis that the purpose of sleep is to restore the body to its full waking capacity. Therefore, sleep acts to repair the damage inflicted by wakefulness.

Restricted code: a pattern of speech that uses fairly basic vocabulary, contains mainly concrete description and can usually only be understood when set in context (*see also Elaborated code*).

Retina: the light sensitive part of the eye, where light is changed into a neural response to be passed to the brain via the optic nerve. It consists of three layers of neural tissue including a layer of photoreceptors called rods and cones.

Retrieval failure: items stored in LTM cannot be accessed because no suitable retrieval cues are available.

Rewards-cost model: theory by Piliavin that bystanders decide whether or not to help a victim in distress by weighing up the rewards and costs of helping and not helping.

Romantic (passionate) love: an intensely emotional state characterized by physical longing when object of passion is absent, joy when relationship is going well and anguish when it goes wrong.

Sample: a subset of a target population which shares the characteristics of the population despite its smaller size.

Scaffolding: a term coined by Wood *et al.* to explain how a tutor can advance a child's thinking by providing a framework within which the child can develop.

Scattergraph (or scattergram): a graphical technique used to illustrate sets of data that are being correlated with each other. Data from one of the variables being correlated are presented on the x-axis, and data from the same individual for the second variable on the *y*-axis.

Schema: a cluster of inter-related concepts that tell us about how things function in the world – a schema about television would include our knowledge about how they work and what sort of programmes they are likely to display.

Schizophrenia: a serious mental disorder that is characterized by severe disruptions in psychological functioning and a loss of contact with reality.

Science: a body of knowledge, or a method of study devoted to developing this body of knowledge, gained through systematized observation and experimentation.

Seasonal affective disorder (SAD): a mood disorder related to changes in season. A period of depression in winter is the most common.

Secure attachment: the optimal form of attachment, associated with healthy emotional and social development. Securely attached infants feel content to explore a strange environment using their caregiver as a safe base.

Selection: the differential survival of organisms or genes in a population as a result of some selective force.

Selective attention: the ability to focus on one thing at a time to the exclusion of other competing stimuli.

Selectivity theory: proposition that focuses on the way in which social relationships, and the needs they fulfil, change with age.

Self-recognition: the ability to look in a mirror and recognize the image as belonging to oneself.

Self-serving bias: a type of attributional bias where people attribute failure to factors outside their control and success to their own ability or effort.

Sensory adaptation: the ability of the sensory systems to adapt to a change in the environment.

Sensory and motor processes: those physiological or psychological processes which relate to the senses (sensory) or to the actions (motor) of an organism.

Sensory cortex: areas of the cerebral cortex specialized for processing sensory input such as vision and hearing.

Separation: to be physically set apart from something – in the context of attachment, to be physically apart from one's caregiver, especially one's mother figure. Separation does not inevitably result in deprivation. Substitute emotional care can be provided to avoid the disruption of emotional bonds.

Sexual selection: the observation that individuals possess features that make them attractive to members of the opposite sex (intersexual selection), or help them to compete with members of the same sex for access to mates (intrasexual selection).

Shadowing: in studies of focused attention, this refers to repeating back a message that is heard in one ear.

Short-term memory (STM): a limited capacity system for storing information for short periods.

Sign (Binomial sign) Test: an inferential test of difference for use with related data, measured at a nominal level.

Signalling: term refers to what happens when one animal indirectly causes another animal to change its behaviour because it perceived the signal through its sense organs. Examples of signalling systems include bird song and the release of pheromones (smell signals) by moths and ants.

Similarity or representative heuristic: rule of thumb that a particular instance will be similar to its prototype or stereotype.

Situational attribution: inferring that a person's behaviour is caused by something about the situation they are in.

Sleep: a loss of consciousness which is characterized by specific behavioural and physiological effects. Sleep can be non-REM (*NREM*) or *REM* which is associated with dreaming.

Sociability: a child's willingness to interact with others and to seek their attention or approval.

Social class: term used to describe the broad variations in economic and social positions within a society.

Social cognition: the area of social psychology concerned with how people think about other individuals or other groups of people.

Social constructionism: theory that knowledge is relative, socially constructed and 'facts' are not permanent realities.

Social development: acquiring social behaviours, i.e. any behaviours that assist relationships with other members of one's species. This includes the abilities to form relationships, to cooperate with others and to conform, and also involves the process of socialization.

Social disengagement theory: proposition that healthy ageing is a gradual and mutual process of separation between individuals and their social roles and interests (*see also Activity theory*).

Social exchange theory: an explanation of why some relationships continue while others end, based on the notion that people remain in relationships as long as the rewards of staying outweigh the costs.

Social identity theory: proposition that human beings categorize themselves and others into in-groups and out-groups. Because of the need to maintain a positive social identity, unfavourable comparisons are made between the two and competition and discrimination develop.

Social influence: the process by which a person's attitudes, beliefs or behaviours are modified by the presence or actions of others. There are two types of social influence that lead people to conform: *normative social influence* (based on our desire to be liked) and *informational social influence* (based on our desire to be right).

Social learning theory: an explanation of the way in which people learn by observing and imitating the behaviour of others.

Social norms: the rules for behaviour established by a society.

Social perception: how we come to form impressions and make inferences about others.

Social Readjustment Rating Scale (SRRS): a rating scale, devised by Holmes and Rahe, that scores major life events and life changes according to their psychological impact, proposing that higher scores on the SRRS increase the chances of stress-related health breakdown.

Social relationship: an encounter with another person (or people) that endures through time.

Social representations: the common-sense explanations that are shared by and shape the understanding of members of a particular group or culture.

Social-selection theory: the argument that people who suffer from schizophrenia become or remain poor because they are unable to function effectively.

Socialization: the process by which an individual acquires the attitudes, beliefs,

values, social skills and so on that enable them to become a part of a particular social group.

Socially sensitive research: any research that may have direct social consequences for those taking part in the study or the class of people who are represented.

Sociobiological theory: the explanation of social behaviour in evolutionary terms, e.g. that males place a high value on female physical attractiveness because youth and health indicate someone likely to produce healthy babies and so pass on the father's genes.

Sociogenic hypothesis: the argument that poorer people in society are placed under the greatest stress and that this, in turn, makes mental illness more likely.

Somatic therapies: *see Biological therapies*.

Spatial memory: the ability of an animal to form a mental image or 'map' of a familiar area or home range.

Spearman's Rank Order Correlation Coefficient (Rho): an inferential test of correlation suitable for use with pairs of scores when at least ordinal levels of measurement have been obtained.

Species: a set of organisms that possess similar inherited characteristics and have the potential to interbreed to produce fertile offspring.

Split brain: the cutting of the corpus callosum resulting in the effective separation of the two hemispheres of the brain.

Spontaneous disorder: a disorder that is 'real' as opposed to being induced by a therapist.

Spontaneous recovery: the phenomenon in classical conditioning observed by Pavlov: when the process of extinction is completed and the animal is later replaced in the experimental situation, it may well spontaneously produce the previously conditioned behaviour. This finding demonstrates that

extinction is not the same as forgetting, but rather is a process of inhibition.

Stage theory: a theory that describes development in terms of an invariant sequence of separate ability levels. At each stage, a child can do or think in a progressively more sophisticated (adult-like) way. This applies, for example, to cognitive or moral development. It is presumed that development from one stage to the next is related to biological maturation.

Stages of sleep: sleep can be divided into slow wave sleep (SWS) and REM (or dreaming) sleep. SWS can be divided into four stages, each with characteristic EEG activity. REM sleep combines an EEG characteristic of waking behaviour with deep sleep, and can therefore be referred to as paradoxical sleep.

Standard deviation: a statistical measure of the variation from the mean in a set of scores.

Statistical infrequency: in psychopathology, this term is used for behaviour that occurs rarely within the general population.

Statistical significance: a conclusion drawn from the data collected in a research study that the results are unlikely to have been caused by chance, and can therefore be attributed to the particular relationship under study.

Stereotyping: generalizing about a group of people so that the same characteristics (often unflattering) are assigned to all members of the group regardless of individual variations between members. Stereotyping may underlie prejudice and discrimination.

Stimulus discrimination: in classical conditioning, this refers to the situation where one conditioned stimulus (CS) is paired with an unconditioned stimulus while another conditioned stimulus is left unpaired. In this case, only the paired CS

will evoke the conditioned response (CR).

Stimulus generalization: in conditioning, this refers to the finding that once a response to a given stimulus has been learned, the response may also be evoked by other similar stimuli.

Strange situation: a laboratory-based structured observation method of assessing how securely or insecurely attached an infant is to its caregiver.

Stress: three ways of defining stress: (a) as a response or reaction to something in the environment; (b) as a stimulus or stressor – a feature of the environment that produces a 'stress' response; (c) as a lack of fit between the perceived demands of the environment and the perceived ability to cope with those demands. This transactional model of stress is the most popular among psychologists.

Stress-inoculation training: a cognitive–behavioural strategy used in stress management. It has three phases: Conceptualization – client relives stressful event and analyses its features to achieve a more realistic understanding of the demand being made; Skills training and practice – to help overcome key elements causing stress; Real-life application – put training to test in real-life situations.

Stress management: methods of managing the negative effects of stress. These include: (a) the use of drugs and biofeedback (b) the use of relaxation and meditation (c) cognitive and behavioural training (d) the use of exercise and social support networks.

Stress reduction: techniques used by an individual to cope with stress and reduce its adverse effects.

Stressor: any stimulus in the environment that produces the stress-response, as described by Selye – for example, life events (such as dealing with death and bereavement or the breakdown of a long-term relationship) or events associated with the workplace (such as workload, conflict between home and work, keeping up with changes or lack of career prospects).

Stroop effect: refers to how colour name words have an interfering effect on the time taken to name the ink colours of non-matching colours.

Studies: usually these refer to empirical investigations, although in a general sense they refer to any attempt to study a person or persons (or any other organism) in order to find out something about them.

Sub-cultural differences: those differences found within a particular culture, society or country, e.g. differences between social classes, or between men and women.

Superego: according to psychoanalytic theory, the part of the personality that acts as the conscience.

Synoptic assessment: in psychology this term applies to the assessment of the candidate's understanding and appreciation of the breadth of theoretical and methodological approaches, issues and debates in psychology (AQA).

Systematic desensitization: a behavioural therapy used to treat phobias and anxieties. After being trained in relaxation techniques, the phobic person is gradually exposed to situations that are more and more anxiety provoking until the fear response is replaced by one of relaxation.

Target population: a group of people that share a given set of characteristics, about which a researcher wishes to draw conclusions.

Temperament: refers to a person's typical energy level or characteristic mood. Temperament is usually viewed as a genetic predisposition because of the wide differences seen in newborns in terms of their reactivity to stimulation and general mood.

Template theory: an explanation for pattern recognition; the proposal that we match incoming information against miniature copies (templates) of patterns that we have stored in long-term memory.

Terminal drop: the notion that there is little decline in intellectual functioning until about the last five years of life.

Theory: a set of interrelated ideas or principles that can be used to explain observed phenomena.

Theory of mind: the ability to understand that someone may have different thoughts from one's own.

Therapy: a systematic intervention to help people overcome their psychological difficulties.

To what extent: an instruction to consider arguments surrounding a particular point of view (e.g. "To what extent can anorexia nervosa be explained from a biological perspective?"). It is not necessary to reach a conclusion based on this information, although by balancing different points of view against each other, this should be possible.

Token economies: a behaviour modification programme where a person receives rewards in the form of tokens for desirable behaviour. Tokens can be exchanged later for goods or privileges.

Top-down processing: processing that is guided by expectations, stored knowledge and context (*see also* **Bottom-up processing**).

Transference: a process that occurs during psychoanalysis when a client redirects feelings towards the therapist that are unconsciously directed towards a significant person in their life.

Type I error: the error that occurs when a null hypothesis is wrongly rejected.

Type II error: the error that occurs when a null hypothesis is retained when it is in fact false.

Ultradian rhythms: see **Biological rhythms**.

Understudied relationships: refers to those relationships that have, until recently, received little attention by researchers, e.g. gay relationships, relationships formed via the Internet.

Unipolar depression /disorder: see **Depression**.

Validity: the degree to which a test, measurement or experimental manipulation is doing the job it has been designed to do.

Variable: something that alters or can be changed.

Variation: term used to describe the differences found among individuals of sexually reproducing species (because offspring do not exactly resemble either parent).

Visual information processing: the transformation of a visual input into a meaningful perceptual experience.

Visual pathways: refers to the routes by which nerve impulses pass from the retina to the visual areas of the brain. The most studied pathway is the retina-geniculate-striate pathway that conducts signals to the primary visual cortex via the lateral geniculate nuclei of the thalamus.

Visual perception: the process by which we transform sensory information from the eyes to produce an experience of depth, distance, colour, etc.

Voluntary and involuntary relationships: voluntary relationships are those entered into freely, while involuntary relationships are those where the partners (or participants) have no choice (e.g. some arranged marriages).

Vygotsky, Lev: a Russian psychologist who believed that cognitive development was founded on social interaction, with a child's understanding of the world being derived from collaboration with others.

Wernicke's area: area of left temporal cortex hypothesized by Wernicke to be the centre where language is comprehended.

Wilcoxon Matched Pairs Signed Ranks Test: an inferential test of difference suitable for use with related data when at least ordinal level data have been obtained.

Withdrawal from investigation: an ethical requirement of psychological research that participants have the right to withdraw at any time from the investigation.

Working memory: a model of memory formulated by Baddeley and Hitch to replace the concept of short-term memory. It proposes a multi-component, flexible system concerned with active processing and storage of short-term information.

Workplace stressor: any stimulus in the workplace environment that produces the stress-response, such as work overload or role ambiguity.

Yerkes-Dodson law: performance increases along with arousal up to an optimum point, after which further increases in arousal are associated with decrements in performance.

Zeitgeber: means 'time giver', and refers to external stimuli that help in synchronizing biological rhythms to the outside world. The most important one is light.

Zone of proximal development (ZPD): the distance between a child's current abilities (when working unassisted) and their potential abilities or what they can do under expert guidance.

References

Abed, R.T. (2000) 'Psychiatry and Darwinism: time to reconsider?', *British Journal of Psychiatry*, 177, pp.1-3.

Abed, R.T. and de Pauw, K.W. (1999) 'An evolutionary hypothesis for obsessive-compulsive disorder: a psychological immune system?', *Behavioural Neurology*, 11, pp.245-50.

Abèles, R.D. (1976) 'Relative deprivation, rising expectations, and black militancy', *Journal of Social Issues*, 32, pp.119-37.

Abraham, U., Gwinner, E. and Van't Hof, T.J. (2000) 'Exogenous melatonin reduces the resynchronization time after phase shifts of a nonphotic zeitgeber in the house sparrow (Passer domesticus)', *Journal of Biological Rhythms*, 15, pp.48-56.

Abramson, L.Y., Metalsky, G.I. and Alloy, L.B. (1989) 'Hopelessness depression: a theory-based subtype of depression', *Psychological Review*, 96, pp.358-72.

Abramson, L.Y., Seligman, M.E.P. and Teasdale, J.D. (1978) 'Learned helplessness in humans: critique and reformulation', *Journal of Abnormal Psychology*, 87, pp.49-74.

Ackermann, R. and DeRubeis, R.J. (1991) 'Is depressive realism real?', *Clinical Psychology Review*, 10, pp.565-84.

Adey, P. and Shayer, M. (1993) 'An exploration of long-term far-transfer effects following an extended intervention program in the high school science curriculum', *Cognition and Instruction*, 11(1), pp.1- 29.

Adorno, T.W., Frenkey-Brunswick, E., Levinson, D.J. and Sanford, R.N. (1950) *The Authoritarian Personality*, New York: Harper & Row.

Ainsworth, M.D.S. (1967) *Infancy in Uganda: Child Care and the Growth of Love*, Baltimore: John Hopkins University Press.

Ainsworth, M.D.S. and Bell, S.M. (1970) 'Attachment, exploration, and separation: illustrated by the behavior of one-year-olds in a Strange Situation', *Child Development*, 41, pp.49–65.

Ainsworth, M.D.S., Bell, S.M. and Stayton, D.J. (1974) 'Infant/mother attachment and social development as a product of reciprocal responsiveness to signals', in M.P.M. Richards (ed.) *The Integration of the Child into a Social World*, Cambridge: Cambridge Univ. Press.

Akiyama, M.M. (1984) 'Are language acquisition strategies universal?', *Developmental Psychology*, 20, pp.219-28.

Allen, J.G. (1995) *Coping with trauma: A guide to self-understanding*, Washington, DC: American Psychiatric Press.

Allman, J. (2000) *Evolving Brains*, New York: Freeman

Alloy, L.B. and Tabachnik, N. (1984) 'Assessment of covariation by humans and animals: the joint influence of prior expectations and current situational information', *Psychological Review*, 91, pp.112-49.

Allport, D.A. (1980) 'Attention and performance', in G. Claxton (ed.) *Cognitive Psychology: New Directions*, London: Routledge and Kegan Paul.

Allport, D.A., Antonis, B. and Reynolds, P. (1972) 'On the division of attention: a disproof of the single channel hypothesis', *Quarterly Journal of Experimental Psychology*, 24, pp.225-35.

Allport, F.H. (1955) *Theories of Perception and the Concepts of Structure*, New York: John Wiley & Sons.

Allport, G. (1954) *The Nature of Prejudice*, New York: Double-Day Anchor.

American Psychiatric Association (1994) *Diagnostic and Statistical Manual of Mental Disorders* (4th edn), Washington, DC: American Psychiatric Association.

American Psychiatric Association (1997) 'Practice guidelines for the treatment of patients with schizophrenia', *The American Journal of Psychiatry*, 154(4), Supplement, pp.1-63.

American Psychiatric Association (2000) *DSM-IV-TR: Diagnostic and Statistical Manual of Mental Disorders* (4th edn), Washington, DC: American Psychiatric Association.

Anand, B.K. and Brobeck, J.R. (1951) 'Hypothalamic control of food intake in rats and cats', *Yale Journal of Biological Medicine*, 24, pp.123-40.

Anderson, C.A. (1989) 'Temperature and aggression: the ubiquitous effects of heat on the occurrence of human violence', *Psychological Bulletin*, 106, pp.74-96.

Anderson, K.G., Kaplan, H. and Lancaster, J.B. (1999) 'Paternal care by genetic fathers and stepfathers I: reports from Albuquerque men', *Evolution and Human Behavior*, 20, pp.405-31.

Andersson, B.-E. (1992) 'Effects of daycare on cognitive and socio-emotional competence of 13-year-old Swedish schoolchildren', *Child Development*, 63, pp.20–36.

Andersson, M. (1982) 'Female choice for extreme tail length in widow bird', *Nature*, 299, pp.818–19.

Andrade, M. (1996) 'Sexual selection for male sacrifice in the Australian Redback Spider', *Science*, 271, pp.70-72.

Andrews, B., Morton, J., Bekerian, D.A., Brewin, C.R., Davies, G.M. and Mollon, P. (1995) 'The recovery of memories in clinical practice', *The Psychologist*, 8 (5), pp.209-14.

Andrews, G. and Peters, L. (1997) 'The CIDI-Auto: A computerised diagnostic interview for psychiatry', http://www.unsw.edu.au/clients/crufad/cidi/discuss.htm

Andrews, G., Slade, T. and Peters, L. (1999) 'Classification in psychiatry: ICD-10 versus DSM-IV-TR', *British Journal of Psychiatry*, 174, pp.3-5.

Angst, J. (1992) 'Epidemiology of depression', *Psychopharmacol*, 102, pp.71–74.

Animals (Scientific procedures) Act (1986) *Halsbury's statutes* (4th edn) *Current statutes service*, Issue 9, Vol. 2, London: Butterworth.

Ankney, C.D. (1992) 'Sex differences in relative brain size: the mismeasure of woman, too?' *Intelligence*, 16, pp.329-36.

Ankney, C.D. (1995) 'Sex differences in brain size and mental abilities: comments on R. Lynn and D. Kimura', *Personality and Individual Differences*, 18, pp.423-4.

Antin, J., Gibbs, J. and Smith, G.P. (1978) 'Intestinal satiety requires pregastric food stimulation', *Physiology and Behavior*, 20, pp.67-70.

Antin, J., Gibbs, J., Holt, Young, R.C. and Smith, G.P. (1975) 'Cholecystokinin elicits the complete behavioral sequence of satiety in rats', *Journal of Comparative and Physiological Psychology*, 89, pp.784-90.

Apter, T. (1990) *Altered Loves: Mothers and Daughters during Adolescence*, New York: St. Martin's Press.

Archer, J. (1989) 'Childhood gender roles: structure and development', *The Psychologist*, 12, pp.367-70.

Archer, S.L. (1982) 'The lower age boundaries of identity development', *Child Development*, 53, pp.1551-6.

Archer, S.L. and Waterman, A.S. (1994) 'Adolescent identity development: Contextual perspectives', in C.B. Fisher & R.M. Lerner (eds) *Applied developmental psychology*, New York: McGraw-Hill

Arendt, H. (1963) 'Eichmann in Jerusalem: a report on the banality of evil', New York: Viking Press, cited in A.G. Miller (1986) *The Obedience*

Experiments, New York: Praeger Publishers.

Argyle, M. (1988) 'Social relationships', in M. Hewstone, W. Stroebe, J.P. Codol and G.M. Stephenson (eds) *Introduction to Social Psychology*, Oxford: Blackwell.

Argyle, M. (1992) *The Social Psychology of Everyday Life*, London: Routledge.

Argyle, M. (1994) *The Psychology of Interpersonal Behaviour*, Harmondsworth: Penguin.

Argyle, M. and Henderson, M. (1985) *The Anatomy of Relationships*, London: Penguin.

Arieti, S. and Meth, J. (1959) 'Rare, unclassifiable, collective, exotic syndromes', in S. Arieti (ed.) *American Handbook of Psychiatry* (Vol. 1), New York: Basic Books, pp.546-63.

Armsby, R.E. (1971) 'A re-examination of the development of moral judgement in children', *Child Development*, 42, pp.1241-8.

Armsden, G. and Greenberg, M.T. (1984) *The inventory of parent and peer attachment: Individual differences and their relationship to psychological well-being in adolescence*, unpublished manuscript, University of Washington.

Arnold, M. (1960) 'Emotion and Personality', Vol. I, *Psychological Aspects,* New York: Columbia University Press.

Aronson, E. (1984/4th edn, 1988/5th edn, 1995/7th edn, 1999/8th edn) *The Social Animal*, New York: W.H. Freeman.

Asch, S.E. (1951) 'Effects of group pressure upon the modification and distortion of judgements', in H. Guetzkow (ed.) *Groups, Leadership and Men*, Pittsburg: Carnegie Press.

Asch, S.E. (1956) 'Studies of independence and conformity: a minority of one against a unanimous majority', *Psychological Monographs*, 70 (9).

Aserinsky, E. and Kleitman, N. (1953) 'Regularly occurring periods of eye mobility and concomitant phenomena during sleep', *Science*, 118, p.273.

Association for the Teaching of Psychology (1992) *Ethics in Psychological Research: Guidelines for Students at Pre-degree Level*, Leicester: Association for the Teaching of Psychology.

Atchley, R.C. (1982) 'Retirement as a social institution', *Annual Review of Sociology*. 8, 263-287.

Atchley, R.C. (1988) *Social Forces and Aging*, Belmont, CA: Wadsworth.

Atkin, C.K., Greenberg, B.S., Korzenny, F. and McDermott, S.

(1979) 'Selective exposure to televised violence', *Journal of Broadcasting*, 23, pp.5-13

Atkinson, R.C. and Shiffrin, R.M. (1968) 'Human memory: a proposed system and its control processes', in K.W. Spence and J.T. Spence (eds) *The Psychology of Learning and Motivation*, Vol. 2, London: Academic Press.

Attanasio, V., Andrasik, F., Burke, E.J., Blake, D.D., Kabela, E. and McCarran, M.S. (1985) 'Clinical issues in utilising biofeedback with children', *Clinical Biofeedback and Health*, 8, pp.134–41.

Au, T.K. (1983) 'Chinese and English counterfactuals: the Sapir-Whorf hypothesis revisited', *Cognition*, 15, pp.155-87.

Augoustinos, M. and Walker, I. (1995) *Social Cognition: An Integrated Introduction*, London: Sage.

Averill, J.R. and Boothroyd, P. (1977) 'On falling in love in conformance with the romantic ideal', *Motivation and Emotion*, 1, pp.235-47.

Axelrod, R. and Hamilton, W.D. (1981) 'The evolution of cooperation', *Science*, 211, pp.1390-6.

Ayala, F.J. (1995) 'The myth of Eve: molecular biology and human origins', *Science*, 270, pp.1930-6.

Ayres, J. (1983) 'Strategies to maintain relationships: their identification and usage', *Communication Quarterly*, 31, pp.207-25.

Azar, B. (1997) 'Nature, nurture: not mutually exclusive', *APA Monitor* at www.apa.org/monitor/may97/twinstud.html

Baddeley, A.D. (1966) 'Short-term memory for word sequences as a function of acoustic, semantic and formal similarity', *Quarterly Journal of Experimental Psychology*, 18, pp.362–5.

Baddeley, A.D. (1986) *Working Memory*, Oxford: Clarendon Press.

Baddeley, A.D. (1988) 'But what the hell is it for?', in M.M. Gruneberg, P.E. Morris and R.N. Sykes (eds) *Practical Aspects of Memory: Current Research and Issues*, Vol. 1, Chichester: John Wiley & Sons.

Baddeley, A.D. (1997) *Human Memory: Theory and Practice* (revised edn), Hove: Psychology Press.

Baddeley, A.D. (1999) *Essentials of Human Memory*, Hove: Psychology Press.

Baddeley, A.D. and Hitch, G. (1974) 'Working memory', in G.H. Bower (ed.) *The Psychology of Learning and Motivation*, Vol. 8, London: Academic Press.

Baddeley, A.D. and Hitch, G.J. (1977) 'Recency re-examined', in

S. Dornic (ed.) *Attention and Performance*, New Jersey: Erlbaum.

Baddeley, A.D., Grant, S., Wight, E. and Thomson, N. (1973) 'Imagery and visual working', in P.M.A. Rabbitt and S. Dornic (eds) *Attention and Performance V*, London: Academic Press.

Baddeley, A.D., Thomson, N. and Buchanan, M. (1975) 'Word length and the structure of short-term memory', *Journal of Verbal Learning and Verbal Behaviour*, 14, pp.575–89.

Baerends, G.P. (1941) 'Fortpflanzungsverhalten und Orientierung der Grabwaspe *Ammophila campestris*', *Jur. Tijdscher. Ent. Deel*, 84, pp.268-75.

Bahrick, H.P. (1984) 'Memory for people', in J.E. Harris and P.E. Morris (eds) *Everyday Memory, Actions and Absentmindedness*, London: Academic Press.

Bahrick, H.P. and Hall, L.K. (1991) 'Lifetime maintenance of high school mathematics content', *Journal of Experimental Psychology: General*, 120, pp.20–33.

Bahrick, H.P. and Phelps, E. (1987) 'Retention of Spanish vocabulary over eight years', *Journal of Experimental Psychology: Learning, Memory and Cognition*, 13, pp.344–9.

Bahrick, H.P., Bahrick, P.O. and Wittlinger R.P. (1975) 'Fifty years of memory for names and faces: a cross sectional approach', *Journal of Experimental Psychology: General*, 104, pp.54–75.

Baker, R.R. and Bellis, M.A. (1995) *Human Sperm Competition*, London: Chapman & Hall.

Balda, R.P. and Kamil, A.C. (1992) 'Long-term spatial memory in Clark's nutcracker *Nucifraga columbiana*', *Animal Behaviour*, 44, pp.761-9

Bales, R.F. (1970) *Personality and Social Behaviour*, New York: Holt, Rinehart & Winston.

Baltes, P.B. and Baltes, M.M. (eds) (1990) *Successful Aging: Perspectives from the Behavioural Sciences*, Cambridge: Cambridge University Press.

Bandura, A. (1965) 'Influence of a model's reinforcement contingencies on the acquisition of imitative responses', *Journal of Personality and Social Psychology*, 1, pp.589-95.

Bandura, A. (1969) *Principles of Behaviour Modification,* New York: Holt, Rinehart & Winston.

Bandura, A. (1973) *Aggression: A Social Learning Analysis*, London: Prentice Hall.

Bandura, A. (1977) 'Self-efficacy: toward a unifying theory of behaviour change', *Psychological Review*, 84, pp.191-215.

Bandura, A. (1986) *Social Foundations of Thought and Action: A Social Cognitive Theory*, Englewood Cliffs, NJ: Prentice Hall.

Bandura, A. and Menlove, F.L. (1968) 'Factors determining vicarious extinction of avoidance behaviour through symbolic modelling', *Journal of Personality and Social Psychology*, 8, pp.99-108.

Bandura, A. and Walters, R.H. (1963) *Social Learning and Personality Development*, New York: Holt, Rinehart & Winston.

Bandura, A., Blanchard, E.B. and Ritter, B. (1969) 'Relative efficacy of desensitization and modelling approaches for inducing behavioural, affective and attitudinal changes', *Journal of Personality and Social Psychology*, 13, pp.173-99.

Bandura, A., Ross, D. and Ross, S. (1963) 'Imitation of film-mediated aggressive models', *Journal of Abnormal and Social Psychology*, 66, pp.3-11.

Bandura, A., Ross, D. and Ross, S.A. (1961) 'Transmission of aggression through imitation of aggressive models', *Journal of Abnormal and Social Psychology*, 63, pp.575–82.

Banister, P., Burman, E., Parker, I., Taylor M. and Tindall, C. (1994) *Qualitative Methods in Psychology: A Research Guide*, Buckingham: Open University Press.

Banyard, P. and Hunt, N. (2000) 'Reporting research: something missing?', *The Psychologist*, 13, pp.68-71.

Barlow, D.H. and Lehman, C.L. (1996) 'Advances in the psychosocial treatment of anxiety disorders', *Archives of General Psychiatry*, 53, pp.727-35.

Barnes, P. E. (1995) *Personal, Social and Emotional Development of Children*, Oxford: Blackwell.

Barnier, A.J. (2002) 'Posthypnotic amnesia for autobiographical episodes: a laboratory model of functional amnesia?', *Psychological Science*, 13, pp.232-7.

Baron, R.A. and Byrne, D. (1997) *Social Psychology* (8th edn), London: Allyn & Bacon.

Bartholomew, R. (1994) 'The illusion of science in psychiatry', *Skeptic*, 2, pp.77-85.

Bartlett, F.C. (1932) *Remembering*, Cambridge: Cambridge University Press.

Basso, K. (1979) *Portraits of 'The Whiteman'*, Cambridge University Press.

Bates, E., O'Connell, B. and Shore, C. (1987) 'Language and communication in infancy', in J.D. Osofsky (ed.) *Handbook of Infant Development* (2nd edn), New York: Wiley.

Bates, E., Thal, D. and Janowsky, J.S. (1992) Early language development and its neural correlates', in I. Rapin and S. Segalowitz (eds) *Handbook of Neuropsychology*, Vol. 6, Amsterdam: Elsevier.

Bateson, G., Jackson, D.D., Haley, J. and Weakland, J. (1956) 'Toward a theory of schizophrenia', *Behavioural Science*, 1, pp.251-64.

Bateson, P. (1986) 'When to experiment on animals', *New Scientist*, 109, pp.30-2.

Batson, C. (1991) *The altruism question: Towards a social-psychological answer*, Hillsdale, NJ: Lawrence Erlbaum Associates.

Batson, C.D., Duncan, B.D., Ackerman, P., Buckley, T. and Birch, K. (1981) 'Is empathic emotion a source of altruistic motivation?', *Journal of Personality and Social Psychology*, 40, pp.290-302.

Baumrind, D. (1964) 'Some thoughts on ethics of research after reading Milgram's "Behavioural study of obedience"', *American Psychologist*, 19, pp.421-3.

Baumrind, D. (1985) 'Research using intentional deception: ethical issues revisited', *American Psychologist*, 40, pp.165-74.

Baumrind, D. (1991) 'Effective parenting during early adolescent transition', in P.A. Cowan & E.M. Hetherington (eds) *Advances in family research* (Vol. 2), Hillsdale, NJ: Erlbaum.

Baxter, L.R., Schwartz, J.M., and Bergman, K.S. (1992) 'Caudate glucose metabolic rate changes with both drug and behaviour therapy for obsessive-compulsive disorder', *Archives of General Psychiatry*, 49, p. 681.

Beach, F.A. (1974) 'Effects of gonadal hormones on urinary behaviour in dogs', *Physiology and Behaviour*, 12, pp.1005-13.

Beall, A.E. and Sternberg, R.J. (1995) *The Psychology of Gender*, New York: Guilford Press.

Beals, K.L., Smith, C.L. and Dodd, S.M. (1984) 'Brain size, cranial morphology, climate and time machines', *Current Anthropology*, 25, pp.301-30.

Beck, A.T. (1963) 'Thinking and depression', *Archives of General Psychiatry*, 9, pp.324-33.

Beck, A.T. (1976) *Cognitive Therapy and the Emotional Disorders*, New York: Penguin Books.

Beck, A.T. (1991) 'Cognitive therapy: a 30-year retrospective', *American Psychologist*, 46(4), pp.368-75.

Beck, A.T. and Cowley, G. (1990) 'Beyond lobotomies', *Newsweek*, 26 March 1990, p.44.

Beck, A.T., Emery, G. and Greenberg, R.L. (1985) *Anxiety Disorders and Phobias: A Cognitive Perspective*, New York: Basic Books.

Beck, A.T., Freeman, A. and Associates (1990) *Cognitive Therapy of Personality Disorders*, New York: Guilford Press.

Beck, A.T., Ward, C.H., Mendelson, M., Mock, J. and Erlbaugh, J. (1961) 'An inventory for measuring depression', *Archives of General Psychiatry*, 4, pp.561-71.

Beck, A.T., Weissman, A., Lester, D. and Trexler, L. (1974) 'The measurement of pessimism: the hopelessness scale', *Journal of Consulting and Clinical Psychology*, 42 (6), pp.861-5.

Bee, H. (1994) *Lifespan Development*, New York: Harper Collins.

Bee, H. (1995) *The Developing Child* (7th edn), London: HarperCollins.

Bee, H. (1998) *Lifespan Development* (2nd edn), New York: Longman.

Bee, H. (1999) *The Developing Child* (9th edn), Boston: Allyn & Bacon.

Bee, H. and Boyd, D. (2003) *Lifespan Development*: Study edition. London: Allyn & Bacon.

Bee, H. and Mitchell, S. K. (1984) *The Developing Person: A Life-Span Approach* (2nd edn), New York: Harper & Row.

Bekerian, D.A. and Bowers, J.M. (1983) 'Eye-witness testimony: were we misled?', *Journal of Experimental Psychology: Learning, Memory and Cognition*, 9, pp.139–45.

Bekerian, D.A. and Dennett, J.L. (1993) 'The cognitive interview: reviving the issues', *Applied Cognitive Psychology*, 7, pp.275–97.

Bell, B. (1999) 'The Folk Illness Glossary (FIG)', http://ihs2.unn. ac.uk:8080/figtab.htm

Belsky, J. and Rovine, M.J. (1987) 'Temperament and attachment security in the Strange Situation: A rapprochement', *Child Development*, 58, pp.787–95.

Belsky, J. and Rovine, M.J. (1988) 'Non-maternal care in the first year of life and the security of parent–infant attachment', *Child Development*, 59, pp.157–167.

Belson, W. (1978) *Television Violence and the Adolescent Boy*, Franborough: Teakfield.

Belyaev, D.K. (1979) 'Destabilizing selection as a factor in domestication', *The Journal of Heredity*, 70 (5), pp.301-8.

Bem, S.L. (1974) 'The measurement of psychological androgyny', *Journal of Consulting and Clinical Psychology*, 42, pp.155-62.

Bem, S.L. (1976) 'Probing the promise of androgyny', in A.G. Kaplan and J.P. Bean (eds) *Beyond sex-role stereotypes: Readings toward a psychology of androgyny* (pp.48-62), Boston: Little, Brown.

Bem, S.L. (1989) 'Genital knowledge and gender constancy in pre-school children', *Child Development*, 60, pp.649-62.

Bemis-Vitousek, K. and Orimoto, L. (1993) 'Cognitive-behavioural models of anorexia nervosa, bulimia nervosa and obesity', in K.S. Dobson and P.C. Kendall (eds) *Psychopathology and Cognition*, San Diego: Academic Press.

Benhamou, S. (1996) 'No evidence for cognitive mapping in rats', *Animal Behaviour*, 52, pp.201-12.

Benin, M. (1997, August) *A longitudinal study of marital satisfaction*, a paper presented at the meeting of the American Sociological Association, Toronto.

Bennett, M. (1995) 'Why don't men come to counselling? Some speculative theories', *Counselling*, 6(4), pp.310–13.

Bennett, N. and Dunne, E. (1991) 'The nature and quality of talk in co-operative classroom groups', *Learning and Instruction*, 1(2), pp.103-18.

Benton, D. and Cook, R. (1991) 'Vitamin and mineral supplements improve intelligence scores and concentration', *Personality and Individual Differences*, 12(11), pp.1151-8.

Berbaum, K. and Lenel, J.C. (1983) 'Objects in the path of apparent motion', *American Journal of Psychology*, 96, pp.491-501.

Bergin, A.E. (1971) 'The evaluation of therapeutic outcomes', in A.E. Bergin and S.L. Garfield (eds) *Handbook of Psychotherapy and Behaviour Change: An Empirical Analysis*, New York: Wiley.

Bergin, A.E. and Lambert, M.J. (1978) 'The evaluation of therapeutic outcomes', in S.A. Garfield and A.E.Bergin (eds), *Handbook of Psychotherapy and Behaviour Change*, NY: Wiley.

Berglas, S. and Jones, E.E. (1978) 'Drug choice as an externalization strategy in response to non-contingent success', *Journal of Personality and Social Psychology*, 36, pp.405-17.

Berk, L.E. (1998) *Development through the Lifespan*, London: Allyn & Bacon.

Berk, L.E. and Garvin, R.A. (1984) 'Development of private speech among low-income Appalachian children', *Developmental Psychology*, 20 (2), pp.271-86.

Berk, L.E. (1994) 'Why children talk to themselves', *Scientific American*, November, pp.78-83.

Berkowitz, L. (1970) 'The contagion of violence: an S-R meditational analysis of observed aggression' in W.J. Arnold and M.M. Page (eds) *Nebraska Symposium on Motivation*, 18, Lincoln: Univ. of Nebraska Press.

Berkowitz, L. (1972) 'Frustrations, comparisons, and other sources of emotional arousal as contributors to social unrest', *Journal of Social Issues*, 28, pp.77-91.

Berkowitz, L. (1984) 'Some effects of thoughts on anti- and pro-social influences of media events: a cognitive neoassociation analysis', *Psychological Bulletin*, 95, pp.410-27.

Berkowitz, L. (1989) 'Frustration-aggression hypothesis: examination and reformulation', *Psychological Bulletin*, 106, pp.59-73.

Berkowitz, M.W. and Gibbs, J.C. (1983) 'Measuring the developmental features of moral discussion', *Merill-Palmer Quarterly*, 29, pp.299-410.

Berlin, B. and Kay, P. (1969) *Basic Colour Terms: Their Universality and Evolution*, Berkeley & Los Angeles: University of California Press.

Bernard, C. (1856) 'Leçons de physiologie expérimentale appliquée à la médecine', *Cours du Semestre d'Eté*, 1855, 2, pp.49-52.

Berndt, T.J. (1979) 'Developmental changes in conformity to peers and parents', *Developmental Psychology*, 15, pp.608-16.

Bernstein, B. (1971) *Classes, Codes and Control*, Vol. 1, London: Routledge & Kegan Paul.

Berry, J. (1969) 'On cross-cultural comparability', *International Journal of Psychology*, 4, pp.119-28.

Berry, J. (1971) 'Müller-Lyer susceptibility: culture, ecology, or race?', *International Journal of Psychology*, 6, pp.193-7.

Berry, J. W. (1997) 'Individual and group relations in plural societies', in C. Granrose and S. Oskamp (eds) *Cross-Cultural Workgroups* (pp.17-35), Thousand Oaks: Sage.

Berry, J.W., Poortinga, Y.H., Segall, M.H. and Dasen, P.R. (1992) *Cross Cultural Psychology: Research and Applications*, Cambridge, MA: Cambridge University Press.

Best, B.J. (1973) *Classificatory Development in Deaf Children: Research on Language and Cognitive Development*, Occasional Paper No. 15, Research Development and Demonstration Center in

Education of Handicapped Children, University of Minnesota.

Bettencourt, B.A., Brewer, M.B., Croak, M.R. and Miller, N. (1992) 'Co-operation and the reduction of intergroup bias: the role of reward structure and social orientation', *Journal of Experimental Social Psychology*, 28, pp.301-9.

Betzig, L.L. (1996) *Human Nature: A Critical Reader*, Oxford: Oxford University Press.

Beurs, E., van Balkom, A.J.L.M., Lange, A., Keole, P. and van Dyck, R. (1995) 'Treatment of panic disorder with agoraphobia', *American Journal of Psychiatry*, 152, pp.683-91.

Bhavnani, K.K. and Phoenix, A. (1994) *Shifting Identities, Shifting Racism: A Feminism and Psychology Reader*, London: Sage.

Bickerton, D. (1984) 'The language bioprogram hypothesis', *Behavioural and Brain Sciences*, 7, pp.173-221.

Bickerton, D. (1990) *Language and Species*, Chicago: University of Chicago Press.

Bickman, L. (1972) 'Social influence and diffusion of responsibility in an emergency', *Journal of Experimental Social Psychology*, 8, pp.438-45.

Bickman, L. (1974) 'The social power of a uniform', *Journal of Applied Social Psychology*, 4, pp.47–61.

Bieling, P.J. and Alden, L.E. (1997) 'The consequences of perfectionism for patients with social phobia', *British Journal of Clinical Psychology*, 36, pp.589-97.

Bierbrauer, G. (1979) 'Why did he do it? Attribution of obedience and the phenomenon of dispositional bias', *European Journal of Social Psychology*, 9, pp.67-84.

Bierhoff, H.W., Klein, R. and Kramp, P. (1991) 'Evidence for the altruistic personality from data on accident research', *Journal of Personality*, 59, pp.263-80.

Bierut, L.J., Heath, A.C., Bucholz, K.K., Dinwiddie, S.H., Madden, P.A.F., Statham, D.J., Dunne, M.P. and Martin, N.G. (1999) 'Major depressive disorder in a community-based twin sample', *Archives of General Psychiatry*, 56, pp.557-63.

Billig, M. (1985) 'Prejudice, categorisation and particularisation: from a perceptual to a rhetorical approach', *European Journal of Social Psychology*, 15, pp.79-104.

Binkley, S. (1979) 'A timekeeping enzyme in the pineal gland', *Scientific American*, 240, pp.66-71.

Bisagni, G. M. and Eckenrode, J. (1995) 'The role of work identity in women's adjustment to divorce'. *American Journal of Orthopsychiatry*. 65(4), 574-583.

Blakemore, C. and Cooper, G.F. (1970) 'Development of the brain depends on the visual environment', *Nature*, 228, pp.477–8.

Blau, P.M. (1964) *Exchange and Power in Social Life*, New York: Wiley.

Blaye, A., Light, P., Joiner, R. and Sheldon, S. (1991) 'Collaboration as a facilitor of planning and problem solving on a computer based task', *British Journal of Educational Psychology*, 61, pp.471-83.

Blehar, M.C. and Rosenthal, N.E. (1989) 'Seasonal affective disorders and phototherapy. Report of a National Institute of Mental Health-sponsored workshop', *Archives of General Psychiatry*, 46, pp.469-74.

Bloom, A.H. (1981) *The Linguistic Shaping of Thought: A Study on the Impact of Language on Thinking in China and the West*, Hillsdale, NJ: Erlbaum.

Bloom, L. (1993) *The Transition from Infancy to Language: Acquiring the Power of Expression*, Cambridge: Cambridge University Press.

Blos, P. (1967) 'The second individuation process of adolescence', *Psychoanalytic Study of the Child*, 22, pp.162-86.

Blos, P. (1967) *On Adolescence: A Psychoanalytic Interpretation*, New York: Free Press.

Boesch, C. (1991) 'Teaching among wild chimpanzees', *Animal Behaviour*, 41A, pp.530-2.

Boesch, C., Hohmann, G. and Marchant, L.F. (2002) *Behavioural Diversity in Chimpanzees and Bonobos*, Cambridge: Cambridge University Press.

Bohannon, P. (1970) *Divorce and After*, New York: Doubleday.

Boker, W. (1992) 'A call for partnership between schizophrenic patients, relatives and professionals', *British Journal of Psychiatry*, 161 (Supplement 18), pp.10-12.

Boles, L.C. and Lohmann, K.J. (2003) 'True navigation and magnetic maps in spiny lobsters', *Nature*. 421, pp.60-3.

Bolger, T. (1989) 'Research and evaluation in counselling', in W. Dryden, D. Charles-Edwards and R. Woolfe (eds) *Handbook of Counselling in Britain*, London: Routledge.

Bolles, R.C. (1967) *Theory of Motivation*, New York: Harper & Row.

Bolton, P. (1984) 'Management of compulsorily admitted patients to a high security unit', *International Journal of Social Psychiatry*, 30, pp.77-84.

Bond, J, Coleman, P. and Peace, S. (eds) (1993) *Ageing in Society: An introduction to social gerontology*. London: Sage.

Bond, M.H. (1988) 'Finding universal dimensions of individual variation in multicultural studies of values', *Journal of Personality and Social Psychology*, 55, pp.1009-15.

Bornstein, M.H., Tamis-LeMonda, C.S., Tal, J., Ludermann, P., Toda, S., Rahn, C.W., Pecheux, M., Azuma, H. and Vardi, D. (1992) 'Maternal responsiveness to infants in three societies: the United States, France and Japan', *Child Development*, 63, pp.808-21.

Bouchard, T.J. and McGue, M. (1981) 'Familial studies of intelligence: a review', *Science*, 22, pp.1055-9.

Bower, G. (1990) 'Awareness, the unconscious and repression: an experimental psychologist's perspective', in J. Singer (ed.) *Repression and Dissociation*, Chicago: University of Chicago Press, pp.209-32.

Bower, G.H. and Winzenz, D. (1969) 'Groups structure, coding and memory for digit series', *Journal of Experimental Psychology*, Monograph 80 (No. 2, Pt 2), pp.1–17.

Bower, T.G.R. (1965) 'Stimulus variables determining space perception in infants', *Science*, 149, pp.88-9.

Bower, T.G.R. (1966) 'The visual world of infants', *Scientific American*, 215, pp.80-92.

Bower, T.G.R. (1981) 'Cognitive development' in M. Roberts and J. Tamburrini (eds) *Child Development 0-5*, Edinburgh: Holmes McDougall.

Bower, T.G.R., Broughton, J.M. and Moore, M.K. (1970) 'Infant responses to approaching objects: an indicator of response to distal variables', *Perception and Psychophysics*, 9, pp.193-6.

Bowlby, J. (1944) 'Forty-four juvenile thieves: their characters and home lives', *International Journal of Psychoanalysis*, 25, pp.107–27.

Bowlby, J. (1953; 2nd edn 1965) *Child Care and the Growth of Love*, Harmondsworth: Penguin.

Bowlby, J. (1969) 'Attachment and Loss', Vol. 1, *Attachment*, London: Hogarth Press.

Bowlby, J. (1973) Attachment and Loss, Vol. 2, *Separation, Anxiety and Anger*, New York, Basic Books.

Bowlby, J. (1981) 'Psychoanalysis as a natural science', *International Review of Psychoanalysis*, 8(3), pp.243–56.

Bowlby, J., Ainsworth, M., Boston, M. and Rosenbluth, D. (1956) 'The effects of mother–child separation: a follow-up study', *British Journal of Medical Psychology*, 29, pp.211–47.

Boyden, T., Carroll, J.S. and Maier, R.A. (1984) 'Similarity and attraction in homosexual males: the effects of age and masculinity-feminity', *Sex Roles*, 10, pp.939-48.

Boyse, E.A., Beauchamp, G.K., Yamazaki, K. and Bard. J. (1991) 'Genetic components of kin recognition in mammals', in P.G. Hepper (ed.), *Kin Recognition*, Cambridge: Cambridge University Press.

Bradbury, T.N. and Miller, G.A. (1985) 'Season of birth in schizophrenia: a review of evidence, methodology and etiology', *Psychological Bulletin*, 98, pp.569-94.

Bradley, B.P. and Baddeley, A.D. (1990) 'Emotional factors in forgetting', *Psychological Medicine*, 20, pp.351–5.

Bradley, R.H. and Caldwell, B.M. (1984) '174 Children: a study of the relationships between the home environment and cognitive development during the first five years', in A.W. Gottfried (ed.) *Home Environment and Early Cognitive Development: Longitudinal Research*, New York: Academic Press.

Bradshaw, J.L. (1997) *Human Evolution: A Neuropsychological Perspective*, Hove: Psychology Press.

Bradshaw, J.L. and Sherlock, D. (1982) 'Bugs and faces in the two visual fields: the analytic/holistic processing dichotomy and task sequencing', *Cortex*, 18, pp.211-226.

Bradshaw, J.L. and Wallace, G. (1971) 'Models for the processing and identification of faces', *Perception and Psychophysics*, 9, pp.443-8.

Brady, J.V., Porter, R.W., Conrad, D.G. and Mason, J.W. (1958) 'Avoidance behavior and the development of gastroduodenal ulcers', *Journal of the Experimental Analysis of Behavior*, 1, pp.69–72.

Braine, M.D.S. (1971) 'On two types of models of the internalisation of grammars', in D.L. Slobin (ed.) *The Ontogenesis of Grammar*, New York: Academic Press.

Brandimonte, M.A., Hitch, G.J. and Bishop, D.V.M. (1992) 'Influence of short-term memory codes on visual image processing: evidence from image transformation tasks', *Journal of Experimental Psychology: Learning, Memory and Cognition*, 18, pp.157–65.

Bransford, J.D. and Johnson, M.K. (1972) 'Contextual prerequisites for understanding: some investigations of comprehension and recall', *Journal of Verbal Learning and Verbal Behaviour*, 11, pp.717–26.

Brearley, H.C. (1932) *Homicide in the United States*, Montclair, NJ: Patterson-Smith.

Breland, K. and Breland, M. (1951) 'A field of applied animal psychology', *American Psychologist*, 6, pp.202-4.

Breland, K. and Breland, M. (1961) 'The misbehaviour of organisms', *American Psychologist*, 16, pp.681-4.

Brent, D.A., Holder, D., Kolko, D., Birmaher, B., Baugher, M., Roth, C., Iyengar, S. and Johnson, B.A. (1997) 'Clinical psychotherapy trial for adolescent depression comparing cognitive, family and supportive therapy', *Archives of General Psychiatry*, 54, pp.877-85.

Brewer, M.B. and Campbell, D.T. (1976) *Ethnocentrism and Intergroup Attitudes: East African Evidence*, New York: Sage.

Brewer, M.B. and Miller, N. (1984) 'Beyond the contact hypothesis: theoretical perspectives on desegregation', in N. Miller and M.B. Brewer (eds) *Groups in Contact: The Psychology of Desegregation*, New York: Academic Press.

Brewer, W.F. and Treyens, J.C. (1981) 'Role of schemata in memory for places', *Cognitive Psychology*, 13, pp.207–30.

Brewerton, T. (1994) 'Hyper-religiosity in psychotic disorders', *Journal of Nervous and Mental Disease*, 182, pp.302-4.

Bristowe, W.S. (1945) 'Spider superstitions and folklore', *Transactions of the Connecticut Academy for Arts and Science*, 36, pp.53-90.

Bristowe, W.S. (1958) *The World of Spiders*, London: Collins.

British Association for the Advancement of Science (1990) *Animals and the Advancement of Science*, London.

British Psychological Society (1993) *Code of Conduct, Ethical Principles and Guidelines*, Leicester: BPS.

British Psychological Society (2000) *Code of Conduct, Ethical Principles and Guidelines*, Leicester: BPS.

British Union for the Abolition of Vivisection (BUAV) (2003) www.buav.org/f_infocentre.html

Broadbent, D.E. (1954) 'The role of auditory localization in attention and memory span', *Journal of Experimental Psychology*, 47, pp.191-6.

Broadbent, D.E. (1958) *Perception and Communication*, Oxford: Pergamon.

Broca, P. (1861) 'Remarques sur le siège de la faculté du langage articulé, suivées d'une observation d'aphémie', *Bulletin de la Société Anatomique* (Paris), 6, pp.330-57.

Brodbar-Nemzer, J.Y. (1986) 'Divorce and group commitment: the case of the Jews', *Journal of Marriage and the Family*, 48, pp.329-40.

Bromley, D.B. (1988) *Human Ageing: An introduction to Gerontology* (3rd edn), Harmondsworth: Penguin.

Bronfenbrenner, U. (1974) 'The origins of alienation', *Scientific American*, 231, pp.53-61.

Brooks-Gunn, J., Klebanov, P. and Duncan, G.J. (1996) 'Ethnic differences in children's intelligence test scores: Role of economic deprivation, home environment and maternal characteristics', *Child Development*, 67(2), pp.396-408.

Broverman, I.K., Broverman D.M., Clarkson, F.E., Rosencrantz, P.S. and Vogel, S.R. (1981) 'Sex role stereotypes and clinical judgements of mental health', in E. Howell and M. Bayes (eds) *Women and Mental Health*, New York: Basic Books.

Brown, A.S. (1991) 'A review of the tip-of-the-tongue experience', *Psychological Bulletin*, 109, pp.204–33.

Brown, B.B. and Lohr, M.J. (1987) 'Peer-group affiliation and adolescent self-esteem: An integration of ego-identity and symbolic-integration theories', *Journal of Personality and Social Psychology*, 52, pp.47-55.

Brown, G.W. (1972) 'Influence of family life on the course of schizophrenic disorders: a replication', *British Journal of Psychiatry*, 121, pp.241-8.

Brown, G.W. and Harris, T.O. (1978) *The Social Origins of Depression*, London: Tavistock.

Brown, G.W., Harris, T.O. and Hepworth, C. (1995)' Loss, humiliation and entrapment among women developing depression: a patient and non-patient comparison', *Psychological Medicine*, 25, pp.7-21.

Brown, R. (1958) *Words and Things*, New York: Free Press.

Brown, R. (1965) *Social Psychology*, London: Collier McMillan.

Brown, R. (1973) *A First Language: The Early Stages*, Cambridge, MA: Harvard University Press.

Brown, R. (1995) *Prejudice: Its Social Psychology*, Oxford: Blackwell.

Brown, R. and Hanlon, C. (1970) 'Derivational complexity and order of acquisition in child speech', in J.R. Hayes (ed.) *Cognition and the Development of Language*, New York: John Wiley & Sons.

Brown, R. and Kulik, J. (1977) 'Flashbulb memories', *Cognition*, 5, pp.73–99.

Brown, R. and Lenneberg, E.H. (1954) 'A study in language and cognition', *Journal of Abnormal and Social Psychology*, 49, pp.454-62.

Brown, R., Colter, N. and Corsellis, J.A.N. (1986) 'Post-mortem evidence of structural brain changes in schizophrenia: differences in brain weight, temporal brain area, and parahippocampal gyrus compared with affective disorder', *Archives of General Psychiatry*, 43, pp.36-42.

Brown, T.A., DiNardo, P.A., Lehman, C.L., and Campbell, L.A. (2001) *'Reliability of DSM-IV anxiety and mood disorders: implications for the classification of emotional disorders', Journal of Abnormal Psychology*, 110, pp.49-58.

Browne, K. (1998) *Divided Labours: An Evolutionary View of Women at Work*, New Haven: Yale University Press.

Bruce, V. (1995) 'Perceiving and recognising faces', in I. Roth and V. Bruce (eds) *Perception and Representation: Current Issues* (2nd edn), Buckingham: Open University Press.

Bruce, V. and Green, P.R. (1990) *Visual Perception: Physiology, Psychology and Ecology* (2nd edn), Hove: Lawrence Erlbaum.

Bruce, V. and Young, A.W. (1986) 'Understanding face recognition', *British Journal of Psychology*, 77, pp.305-27.

Bruce, V., Burton, A.M., Hanna, E., Healey, P., Mason, O., Coombes, A., Fright, R. and Linney, A. (1993) 'Sex discrimination: how do we tell the difference between male and female faces', *Perception*, 22, pp.131-52.

Bruch, H. (1979) *The Golden Cage*, New York: Vintage Books.

Bruner, J.S. (1983) *Child's Talk: Learning to Use Language*, New York: Norton.

Bryan, J.H. and Bryan, N.H. (1970) 'Preaching and practising self-sacrifice: children's actions and reactions', *Child Development*, 41, pp.329-53.

Bryan, J.H. and Test, M.A. (1967) 'Models and helping: naturalistic studies in aiding behavior', *Journal of Personality and Social Psychology*, 6, pp.400-7.

Bryant, B., Harris, M. and Newton, D. (1980) *Children and Minders*, London: Grant McIntyre.

Bryant, P.E. and Trabasso, T. (1971) 'Transitive inferences and memory in young children', *Nature*, 232, pp.456-8.

Buchsbaum, M.S. (1990) 'The frontal lobes, basal ganglia, and temporal lobes as sites for schizophrenia', *Schizophrenia Bulletin*, 16, pp.379-89.

Buckingham, D. (1996) *Moving Images: Understanding Children's Emotional Responses to Television*, Manchester: Manchester University Press.

Bugnyar, T. and Huber, L. (1997) 'Push or pull: an experimental study on imitation in marmosets', *Animal Behaviour*, 54, pp.817-31.

Burke, D. and Fulham, B. J. (2003) 'An evolved spatial memory bias in a nectar-feeding bird?', *Animal Behaviour*. 66(4), pp.695–701

Burke, M., Drummond, L.M. and Johnston, D.W. (1997) 'Treatment choice for agoraphobic women: exposure or cognitive-behavioural therapy?', *British Journal of Clinical Psychology*, 36, pp.409-19.

Burling, R. (1973) *English in Black and White*, New York: Holt, Rinehart & Winston.

Burton, A.M. and Bruce, V. (1993) 'Naming faces and naming names', *Memory*, 1, pp.457-80.

Burton, A.M., Bruce, V. and Johnston, R.A. (1990) 'Understanding face recognition with an interactive activation model', *British Journal of Psychology*, 81, pp.361-80.

Bushnell, I.W.R., Sai, F. and Mullin, J.Y. (1989) 'Neonatal recognition of the mother's face', *British Journal of Developmental Psychology*, 7, pp.3–15.

Buss, A.H. (1989) Personality as traits. *American Psychologist*, *44(11)*, pp.1378-88.

Buss, D. (1989) 'Sex differences in human mate preferences', *Behavioural and Brain Sciences*, 12, pp.1-49.

Buss, D. (1995) 'Evolutionary psychology: a new paradigm for psychological science', *Psychological Inquiry*, 6, pp.1-30.

Buss, D. (1999) *Evolutionary Psychology*, Boston: Allyn & Bacon.

Buss, D., Larsen, R.J., Westen, D. and Semmelroth, J. (1992) 'Sex differences in jealousy: evolution, physiology and psychology', *Psychological Science*, 3, pp.251-5.

Bussey, K. and Bandura, A. (1992) 'Self-regulatory mechanisms governing gender-development', *Child Development*, 63, pp.1236-50.

Button, E.J., Sonuga-Barke, E.J.S., Davies, J. and Thompson, M. (1996) 'A prospective study of self-esteem in the prediction of eating problems in adolescent schoolgirls: Questionnaire findings', *British Journal of Clinical Psychology*, 35, pp.193–203.

Byrne, R. (1995) *The Thinking Ape: Evolutionary Origins of*

Intelligence, Oxford: Oxford University Press.

Byrne, R. and Whiten, A. (1985) 'Tactical deception of familiar individuals in baboons', *Animal Behaviour*, 33, pp.669-73.

Byrne, R. and Whiten, A. (1988) *Machiavellian Intelligence: Social Expertise and the Evolution of Intellect in Monkeys, Apes and Humans*, Oxford: Oxford University Press.

Caldwell, B.M. and Bradley, R.M. (1978) *Home Observation for Measurement of the Environment*, Little Rock: University of Arkansas.

Cameron, C., Oskamp, S. and Sparks, W. (1977) 'Courtship American style: newspaper ads', *Family Coordinator*, 26, pp.27-30.

Campbell, F.A., Pungello, E.P., Miller-Johnson, S., Burchinal, M. and Ramey, C.T. (2001) 'The development of cognitive and academic abilities: Growth curves from an early childhood experiment', *Developmental Psychology*, 37(2).

Campbell, S.S. and Murphy, P.J. (1998) 'Extraocular circadian phototransduction in humans', *Science*, 279, pp.396-9.

Campos, J.J., Langer, A. and Krowitz, A. (1970) 'Cardiac response on the cliff in pre-locomotor human infants', *Science*, 170, pp.196-7.

Camras, L.A., Malatesta, C. and Izard, C. (1991) 'The development of facial expression in infancy', in R. Feldman and B. Rime (eds) *Fundamentals of Non-verbal Behavior*, Cambridge: Cambridge University Press.

Cannon, T.D., Zorrilla, L.E., Shtasel, D., Gur, R.E., Gur, R.C., Marco, E.J., Moberg, P. and Price, R.A. (1994b) 'Neuropsychological functioning in siblings discordant for schizophrenia and healthy volunteers', *Archives of General Psychiatry*, 51, pp.651-61.

Cannon, W.B. (1914) 'The interrelations of emotions as suggested by recent physiological researches', *American Journal of Psychology*, 25, pp.256-63.

Cannon, W.B. (1927) 'The James-Lange theory of emotions: A critical examination and an alternative', *American Journal of Psychology*, 39, pp.106-124.

Cannon, W.B. (1929) *Bodily Changes in Pain, Hunger, Fear and Rage*, New York: Appleton-Century-Crofts.

Cannon, W.B. (1931) 'Again the James-Lange and the thalamic theories of emotions', *Psychological Review*, 38, pp.281-95.

Cannon, W.B. (1932) *The Wisdom of the Body*, New York: Norton.

Cannon, W.B. and Washburn, A.L. (1912) 'An explanation of hunger', *American Journal of Physiology*, 29, pp.441-54.

Caplan, M.Z. and Hay, D.F. (1989) 'Preschoolers' responses to peer distress and beliefs about bystander intervention', *Journal of Child Psychology and Psychiatry*, 30, pp.231-42.

Caplan, P.J. (1995) *They Say You're Crazy: How the World's Most Powerful Psychiatrists Decide Who's Normal*, Reading, MA: Addison-Wesley.

Caraco, T. and Wolf, L.L. (1975) 'Ecological determinants of group size of foraging lions', *American Naturalist*, 109, pp.343-52.

Cardno, A.G., Marshall, E.J., Coid, B., Macdonald, A.M., Ribchester, T.R., Davies, N.J., Venturi, P., Jones, L.A., Lewis, S.W., Sham, P.C., Gottesman I.I., Farmer, A.E., McGuffin, P., Reveley, A.M. and Murray R.M. (1999) 'Heritability estimates for psychotic disorders', *Archives of General Psychiatry*, 56 (4), pp.162-8.

Cardwell, M.C. (1996) *The Complete A-Z of Psychology Handbook*, London: Hodder & Stoughton.

Cardwell, M.C. (2000) *The Complete A–Z of Psychology Handbook* (2nd edn), London: Hodder & Stoughton.

Carey, G. and Gottesman, I. (1981) 'Twin and family studies of anxiety, phobic, and obsessive disorders', in D. Klein and J. Rabkin (eds) *Anxiety: New Research and Changing Concepts*, New York: Raven Press.

Carlat, D.J., Carlos, M.D., Camargo Jr, A. and Herzog, D.B. (1997) 'Eating disorders in males: a report on 135 patients', *American Journal of Psychiatry*, 154, pp.1127–32.

Carlson, N.R. (1994) *Physiology of Behavior* (5th edn), Boston: Allyn & Bacon.

Carlson, N.R., Buskit, W. and Martin, G.N. (2000) *Psychology: The Science of Behaviour*, Harlow: Allyn and Bacon.

Carmichael, L., Hogan, H.P. and Walter, A.A. (1932) 'An experimental study of the effect of language on the reproduction of visually presented forms', *Journal of Experimental Psychology*, 15, pp.73-86.

Caro, T.M. and Hauser, M.D. (1992) 'Is there teaching in non-human animals?', *Quarterly Review of Biology*, 67, pp.151-74.

Carpenter, L. and Brockington, I.F. (1980) 'A study of mental illness in Asians, West Indians and Africans living in Manchester', *British Journal of Psychiatry*, 137, pp.201-5.

Carroll, B.J. (1982) 'The dexamethasone suppression test for melancholia', *British Journal of Psychiatry*, 140, pp.292-304.

Carroll, J.B. and Casagrande, J.B. (1958) 'The function of language classifications in behaviour', in E.E. Maccoby, T.M. Newcombe and E.L. Hartley (eds) *Readings in Social Psychology* (3rd edn), New York: Holt, Rinehart & Winston.

Cartwright, J. (2000) *Evolution and Human Behaviour*, London: Macmillan.

Cartwright, R. (1984) 'Broken dreams: a study of the effects of divorce and separation on dream content', *Journal for the Study of Interpersonal Processes*, 47, pp.251-9.

Casey, P. (2001) 'Multiple personality disorder', *Primary Care Psychiatry*, 7 (1), pp.7-11.

Caspi, A. and Herbener, E.S. (1990) 'Continuity and change: assortative marriage and the consistency of personality in adulthood', *Journal of Personality and Social Psychology*, 58, pp.250-8.

Castner, S.A., Algan, O., Findlay, H.A., Rakic, P. and Goldman-Rakic, P.S. (1998) 'Fetal Xirradiation in monkeys impairs working memory after but not prior to puberty', *Society of Neuroscience*, 24, Part 1, p.225.

Cha, J.-H. (1994) 'Aspects of individualism and collectivism in Korea', in U. Kim, H.C. Triadis, C. Kagiticibasi, S.-C. Choi and G. Yoon (eds) *Individualism and Collectivism: Theory, Method and Applications*, Newbury Park: Sage.

Chaiken, M. (1990) 'The ontogeny of antiphonal calling in European starlings', *Developmental Psychobiology*, 23, pp.233-46.

Chandler, M.J., Greenspan, S. and Barenboim, C. (1973) 'Judgements of intentionality in response to videotaped and verbally presented moral dilemmas: the medium is the message', *Child Development*, 44, pp.315-320.

Chapman, G.B. and Johnson, E.J. (1994) 'The limits of anchoring', *Journal of Behavioural Decision Making*, 7, pp.223-42.

Chen, H., Yates, B.T. and McGinnies, E. (1988) 'Effects of involvement on observers' estimates of consensus, distinctiveness, and consistency', *Personality and Social Psychology Bulletin*, 14, pp.468-78.

Cheney, D. and Seyfarth, R. (1990) *How Monkeys See the World*, Chicago: University of Chicago Press.

Cheng, P.W. (1985) 'Restructuring versus automaticity: alternative accounts of skills acquisition', *Psychological Review*, 92, pp.414-23.

Cherny, L. (1998) Paper submitted to the SIGGRAPH 1998 committee.

Cherry, E.C. (1953) 'Some experiments on the recognition of speech with one and two ears', *Journal of the Acoustical Society of America*, 25, pp.975-9.

Chisholm, L. and Hurrelmann, K. (1995) 'Adolescents in modern Europe: pluralized transition patterns and their implications for personal and social risks', *Journal of Adolescence*, 18, pp.129-158.

Chodorow, N. (1978) *The Reproduction of Mothering*, Berkeley: University of California Press.

Chomsky, N. (1957) *Syntactic Structures*, The Hague: Mouton.

Chomsky, N. (1968) *Language and Mind*, New York: Harcourt Brace.

Chomsky, N. (1981) *Lectures on Government and Binding*, Dordrecht: Foris.

Chorney, M.J., Chorney, K., Seese, N., Owen, M.J., Daniels, J., McGuffin, P., Thompson, L.A., Detterman, D.K., Benbow, C.P., Lubinski, D., Eley, T.C. and Plomin, R. (1998) 'A quantitative trait locus (QTL) associated with cognitive ability in children', *Psychological Science*, 9, pp.159-66.

Christianson, S.A. and Hubinette, B. (1993) 'Hands up! A study of witnesses' emotional reactions and memories associated with bank robberies', *Applied Cognitive Psychology*, 7, pp.365–79.

Christie, D.F. and Ellis, H.D. (1981) 'Photofit constructions versus verbal descriptions of faces', *Journal of Applied Psychology*, 66, pp.358–63.

Cialdini, R.B., Borden, R.J., Thorne, A., Walker, M.R., Freeman, S. and Sloan, L.R. (1976) 'Basking in reflected glory: three (football) field studies', *Journal of Personality and Social Psychology*, 34, pp.366-374.

Cialdini, R.B., Kenrick, D.T. and Bauman, D.J. (1982) 'Effects of mood on pro-social behaviour in children and adults', in N. Eisenberg-Berg (ed.) *Development of Prosocial Behaviour*, New York: Academic Press.

Cialdini, R.B., Schaller, M., Honlainhan, D., Arps, H., Fultz, J. and Beaman, A.L. (1987) 'Empathy-based helping: is it selflessly or selfishly motivated?', *Journal of Personality and Social Psychology*, 52, pp.749-58.

Claes, M. (1998) 'Adolescents' closeness with parents, siblings and friends in three countries: Canada, Belgium and Italy', *Journal of Youth and Adolescence*, 27, pp.165-84.

Clare, A.W. (1985) 'Hormones, behaviour and the menstrual cycle', *Journal of Psychosomatic Research*, 29, pp.225-33.

Clark, D.M. and Teasdale, J.D. (1982) 'Diurnal variatons in clinical depression and accessibility of memories of positive and negative experiences', *Journal of Abnormal Psychology*, 91, pp.87–95.

Clark, E.V. (1993) *The Lexicon in Acquisition*, Cambridge: Cambridge University Press.

Clark, H.H. (1991) 'Words, the world and their possibilities', in G.R. Lockhead and J.R. Pomerantz (eds) *The Perception of Structure*, Washington, DC: American Psychological Association.

Clark, M.S. and Mills, J. (1979) 'Interpersonal attraction and communal relationships', *Journal of Personality and Social Psychology*, 37, pp.12-24.

Clark, R.D. and Word, L.E. (1974) 'Where is the apathetic bystander? Situational characteristics of the emergency', *Journal of Personality and Social Psychology*, 29, pp.279-87.

Clark, R.D. III. (1994) 'A few parallels between group polarization and minority influence', in S. Moscovici, A. Mucchi-Faina and A. Maass (eds) *Minority Influence*, Chicago: Nelson Hall.

Clarke, A.D.B. and Clarke, A.M. (1979) 'Early experience: Its limited effect upon later development', in D. Shaffer and J. Dunn (eds) *The First Year of Life*, Chichester: John Wiley.

Clarke-Stewart, K.A., Gruber, C.P. and Fitzgerald, L.M. (1994) *Children at Home and in Day Care*, Hillsdale, NJ: Erlbaum.

Clayton, C. and Krebs, J.R. (1995) 'Memory in food-storing birds: from behaviour to brain', *Current Opinion in Neurobiology*, 5 (2), pp.149-54.

Cloward, R.D. (1967) 'Studies in tutoring', *The Journal of Experimental Education*, 36, pp.14-25.

Clutton-Brock, T.H. and Albon, S.D. (1979) 'The roaring of red deer and the evolution of honest advertisement', *Behaviour*, 69, pp.145-70.

Clutton-Brock, T.H. and Vincent, A.C.J. (1991) 'Sexual selection and the potential reproductive rates of males and females', *Nature*, 351, pp.58-60.

Cochrane, R. (1977) 'Mental illness in immigrants to England and Wales: an analysis of mental hospital admissions', 1971, *Social Psychiatry*, 12, pp.25-35.

Cochrane, R. (1983) *The Social Creation of Mental Illness*, London: Longman.

Cochrane, R. (1995a) 'Mental illness and the built environment', *Psychology Review*, 1(4), pp.12–15.

Cochrane, R. (1995b) 'Women and depression', *Psychology Review*, 2(1), pp.20–4.

Cochrane, R. and Sashidharan, S.P. (1995) 'Mental health and ethnic minorities: a review of the literature and implications for services', Paper presented to the Birmingham and Northern Birmingham Health Trust.

Cochrane, R. and Stopes-Roe, M. (1980) 'Factors affecting the distribution of psychological symptoms in urban areas of England', *Acta Psychiatrica Scandinavica*, 61, pp.445–60.

Cohen, C. (1981) 'Person categories and social perception: testing some boundaries of the processing effects of prior knowledge', *Journal of Personality and Social Psychology*, 40, pp.441-52.

Cohen, D. (1988) *Forgotten Millions: The Treatment of the Mentally Ill – A Global Perspective*, London: Paladin.

Cohen, D. (1995) 'Now we are one, two, or three', *New Scientist*, 146, pp.14-5.

Cohen, G. (1993) 'Everyday memory', in G. Cohen, G. Kiss and M. LeVoi, *Memory: Current Issues* (2nd edn) Buckingham: Open University Press.

Cohen, G. (1996) *Memory in the Real World* (2nd edn), Hove: Psychology Press.

Cohen, J.E. (1995) 'The uniqueness of present human population growth', in J. Brockman and K. Matson (eds) *How Things Are: A Science Tool-Kit for the Mind*, London: Weidenfeld and Nicolson.

Cohen, S., Tyrrell, D.A.J. and Smith, A.P. (1993) 'Negative life events, perceived stress, negative affect, and susceptibility to the common cold', *Journal of Personality and Social Psychology*, 64, pp.131–40.

Colby, A. and Kohlberg, L. (1987) *The Measurement of Moral Judgement*, Cambridge: Cambridge University Press.

Colby, A., Kohlberg, L., Gibbs, J. and Liebermann, M. (1983) 'A longitudinal study of moral development', *Monographs of the Society for Research in Child Development*, 48(1-2), No. 200.

Coleman, J.C. (1961) *The adolescent society*, London: Methuen.

Coleman, J.C. (1974) *Relationships in Adolescence*, London: Routledge & Kegan Paul.

Coleman, J.C. and Hendry, L. (1990) *The Nature of Adolescence*, London: Routledge.

Collett, P. and O'Shea, G. (1976) 'Pointing the way to a fictional place, a study of direction giving in England and Iran', *European Journal of Social Psychology*, 6, pp.447-58.

Comer, R.J. (1995/2nd edn, 1999/3rd edn, 2000/4th edn, 2004/5th edn) *Abnormal Psychology*, New York: W.H. Freeman.

Compton, W.M., Helzer, J.E., Hwu, H.G., Yeh, E.K., McEnvoy, L., Topp, J.E. and Spitznagel, E.L. (1991) 'New methods in cross-cultural psychiatry in Taiwan and the United States', *American Journal of Psychiatry*, 148, pp.1697-704.

Comstock, G. (1989) *The Evolution of American Television*, Newbury Park: Sage.

Condor, S. (1991) 'Sexism in psychological research: A brief note', in *Feminism and Psychology*, 1, pp.430–4.

Conel, J.L. (1951) *The Postnatal Development of the Cerebral Cortex* (Vol. 3), Cambridge: Harvard University Press.

Connell, C.M. and Gibson, G.D. (1997) 'Racial, ethnic, and cultural differences in dementia caregiving: Review and analysis', *Gerontologist*, 37, pp.355–64.

Conrad, R. (1964) 'Acoustic confusions in immediate memory', *British Journal of Psychology*, 55, pp.75–84.

Constable, J.F. and Russell, D.W. (1986) 'The effect of social support and the work environment upon burnout among nurses,' *Journal of Human Stress*, 12, pp.20–6.

Conway, M.A. (1995) *Flashbulb Memories*, Hove: Erlbaum.

Conway, M.A., Anderson, S.J., Larsen, S.F., Donnelly, C.M., McDaniel, M.A., McClelland, A.G.R. and Rawles, R.E. (1994) 'The formation of flashbulb memories', *Memory and Cognition*, 22, pp.326-43.

Cook, M. and Mineka, S. (1989) 'Observational conditioning of fear to fear-relevant versus fear-irrelevant stimuli in rhesus monkeys', *Journal of Abnormal Psychology*, 98, pp.448-59.

Cooley, C.H. (1902) *Human Nature and the Social Order*, New York: Scribner.

Coolican, H. (1995) *Introduction to Research Methods and Statistics in Psychology*, London: Hodder & Stoughton.

Coolican, H. (1999) *Research Methods and Statistics in Psychology* (3nd edn), London: Hodder & Stoughton.

Coons, P. (1989) 'Iatrogenic factors in the misdiagnosis of multiple personality disorder', *Dissociation*, 2, pp.70-6.

Cooper P.J. (1988) 'Non-psychotic psychiatric disorder after childbirth: a prospective study of prevalence, incidence course and nature', *British Journal of Psychiatry*, 152, pp.799-806.

Cooper, M.L., Shaver, P.R. and Collins, N.L. (1998) 'Attachment styles, emotional regulation and adjustment in adolescences', *Journal of Personality and Social Psychology*, 74, pp.1380-97.

Cooper, R.P. and Aslin, R.N. (1994) 'Developmental differences in infant attention to the spectral properties of infant directed speech', *Child Development*, 65, pp.1663-77.

Coren, S. (1996) *Sleep Thieves*, New York: Free Press.

Coren, S., Ward, L.M. and Enns, J.T. (1999) *Sensation and Perception* (5th edn), Orlando: Harcourt Brace.

Corey, G. (1995) *Theory and Practice of Group Counselling*, California: Brookes/Cole.

Corrigan, R. (1978) 'Language development as related to stage 6 object permanence development', *Journal of Child Language*, 5, pp.173-89.

Corsini, R.J. and Wedding, D. (1995) *Current Psychotherapies* (5th edn), IL: F.E. Peacock Publishers.

Corteen, R.S. and Dunn, D. (1973) 'Shock associated words in a non-attended message: a test for momentary awareness', *Journal of Experimental Psychology*, 102, pp.1143-4.

Corteen, R.S. and Wood, B. (1972) 'Autonomous response to shock associated words in an unattended channel', *Journal of Experimental Psychology*, 94, pp.308-13.

Cosmides, L. and Tooby, J. (1987) 'From evolution to behavior: Evolutionary psychology as the missing link', in J. Dupre (ed.) *The Latest on the Best: Essays on evolution and optimality*, Cambridge, MA: The MIT Press.

Courage, M.L. and Adams, J. (1996) 'Infant peripheral vision: the development of monocular visual acuity in the first three months of postnatal life', *Vision Research*, 36, pp.1207-15.

Cowlishaw, G. (1992) 'Song function in gibbons', *Behaviour*, 121, pp.131-53.

Crabb, P.B. and Bielawski, D. (1994) 'The social representation of material culture in children's books', *Sex Roles*, 30 (1/2), pp.69-79.

Craik, F.I.M. and Lockhart, R.S. (1972) 'Levels of processing: a framework for memory research', *Journal of Verbal Learning and Verbal Behaviour*, 11, pp.671–84.

Craik, F.I.M. and Lockhart, R.S. (1986) 'CHARM is not enough: comments on Eich's model of cued recall', *Psychological Review*, 93, pp.360–4.

Craske, M.G. and Barlow, D.H. (1993) 'Panic disorder and

agoraphobia', in D.H. Barlow (ed.) *Clinical Handbook of Psychological Disorders: A Step-by-Step Treatment Manual* (2nd edn), New York: Guilford.

Cray, E. (1995) 'Teaching about racism', *Psychology Teaching*, 4, Association for the Teaching of Psychology, Leicester: British Psychological Society.

Crick, F. and Mitchison, G. (1983) 'The function of dream sleep', *Nature*, 304, pp.111-14.

Crocker, J. and Major, B. (1989) 'Social stigma and self-esteem: the self-protective properties of stigma', *Psychological Review*, 96, pp.608-30.

Crow, T.J. (2000) 'Schizophrenia as the price that Homo sapiens pay for language: a resolution of the central paradox in the origin of the species', *Brain Research Review* 31, pp.118-29.

Crutchfield, R.S. (1955) 'Conformity and character', *American Psychologist*, 10, pp.191–8.

Csikszentmihalyi, M. and Larson, R. (1984) *Being Adolescent: Conflict and Growth in the Teenage Years*, New York: Basic Books.

Cumming, E., and Henry, W. (1961) *Growing old*, New York: Basic Books.

Cunningham, M.R. (1988) 'Does happiness mean friendliness? Induced mood and heterosexual disclosure', *Personality and Social Psychology Bulletin*, 14, pp.283-97.

Curtiss, S. (1977) *Genie: A Psycholinguistic Study of a Modern-day 'Wild Child'*, London: Academic Press.

Cuthill, I. (1991) 'Field experiments in animal behaviour', *Animal Behaviour*, 42, pp.1007-14.

Czeisler, C.A., Moore-Ede, M.C. and Coleman, R.M. (1982) 'Rotating shift work schedules that disrupt sleep are improved by applying circadian principles', *Science*, 217, pp.460-3.

Dalman, C., Allebeck, P., Cullberg, J., Grunewald, C. and Koster, M. (1999) 'Obstetric complications and the risk of schizophrenia: a longitudinal study of a national birth cohort', *Archives of General Psychiatry*, 56 (3), pp.234-40.

Dalton, K. (1964) *The Premenstrual Syndrome*, London: Heinemann.

Daly, M. and Wilson, M. (1988) *Homicide*, Belmont: Wadsworth.

Daly, M. and Wilson, M.I. (1978) *Sex, Evolution and Behavior: Adaptations for Reproduction*, North Scituate, MA: Duxbury Press.

Daly, M. and Wilson, M.I. (1988) 'Evolutionary social psychology and family homicide', *Science*, 242, pp.519-24.

Dana, C.L. (1921) 'The anatomic seat of the emotions: a discussion of the James-Lange Theory', *Archives of Neurology and Psychiatry* (Chicago), 6, pp.634-9.

Danner, F.W. and Day, M.C. (1977) 'Eliciting formal operations', *Child Development*, 48, pp.1600-6.

Darley, J. and Latané, B. (1968) 'Bystander intervention in emergencies', *Journal of Personality and Social Psychology*, 8, pp.377-83.

Darley, J.M. (1992) 'Social organization for the production of evil', *Psychological Inquiry*, 3 (2), pp.199-218.

Darwin, C. (1859) *On the Origin of Species by Means of Natural Selection*, London: John Murray.

Darwin, C. (1869) *The Autobiography of Charles Darwin*, New York: Norton.

Darwin, C. (1871) *The Descent of Man and Selection in relation to Sex*, London: John Murray. For a general source book of Darwin's original writings, see Porter, D.M. and Graham, P.W. (eds) (1993) *The Portable Darwin*, Harmondsworth: Penguin Books.

Dasen, B. (1994) 'Culture and cognitive development from a Piagetian perspective', in Lonner and Malpass (eds) *Psychology and Culture*, Boston: Allyn & Bacon.

Davey, G. (1994) 'The "disgusting" spider: the role of disease and illness in the perpetuation of fear of spiders', *Society and Animals*, 2 (1), pp.17-25.

Davies, G. (1994) 'Ethical considerations', *Psychology Review*, 1(1), pp.13-15.

Davies, M.H. (1993) 'Psychodrama group therapy', in M. Aveline and W. Dryden (eds) *Group Therapy in Britain*, Milton Keynes: Open University Press.

Davies, N.B., Brooke, M. de L. and Kacelnik, A. (1996) 'Recognition errors and probability ability of parasitism determine whether reed warblers should accept or reject mimetic cuckoo eggs', *Proceedings of the Royal Society of London B*, 263, pp.925-31.

Davis, J.D., Kane, J.M., Marder, S.R., Brauzer, B., Gierl, B., Schooler, N., Casey, D.E. and Hassan, M. (1993) 'Dose response of prophylatic antipsychotics', *Journal of Clinical Psychiatry*, 54 (3), pp.24-30.

Davison, G.C. and Neale, J.M. (1997) *Abnormal Psychology* (7th edn), New York: John Wiley & Sons.

Davison, G.C., Neale, J.M. and Kring, A.M. (2004) *Abnormal Psychology* (9th edn), Chichester: Wiley.

Dawkins, M.S. (1985) 'The scientific basis for assessing suffering in animals', in P. Singer *Defence of Animals*, Oxford: Blackwell.

Dawkins, R. (1976) *The Selfish Gene*, Oxford: Oxford University Press.

Dawkins, R. (1981) 'Communication', in D. McFarland (ed.) *The Oxford Companion to Animal Behaviour*, Oxford: Oxford University Press, pp.78-91.

Day, R.H. (1990) 'The Bourdon illusion in haptic space', *Perception and Psychophysics*, 47, pp.400-4.

Dayton, T. (1994) *The Drama Within*, Florida: Health Communications Inc.

Deacon, T.W. (1997) *The Symbolic Species: The Co-evolution of Language and Human Brain*, London: Penguin.

Dean, G., Walsh, D., Downing, H. and Shelley, E. (1981) 'First admissions of native-born and immigrants to psychiatric hospitals in South-East England, 1970', *British Journal of Psychiatry*, 139, pp.506-12.

Deaux, K. (1976) *The Behaviour of Women and Men*, Monterey, CA: Brooks/Cole.

Deaux, K., Dane, F.C. and Wrightsman, L.S. (1993) *Social Psychology in the '90s* (6th edn), Pacific Grove, CA: Brooks/Cole.

De Boer, M.F., Ryckman, R.M., Pruyn, J.F.A. and Van den Borne, H.W. (1999) 'Psychosocial correlates of cancer relapse and survival: a literature review', *Patient Education and Counseling*, 37, pp.215–30.

DeLongis, A., Coyne, J.C., Dakof, G., Folkman, S. and Lazarus, R.S. (1982) 'Relationship of daily hassles, uplifts, and major life events to health status', *Health Psychology*, 1, pp.119–36.

DeLucia, P. and Hochberg, J. (1991) 'Geometrical illusions in solid objects under ordinary viewing conditions', *Perception and Psychophysics*, 50, pp.547-54 .

Dement, W. and Kleitman, N. (1957) 'Cyclic variations in EEG during sleep and their relation to eye movements, body motility and dreaming', *Electroencephalography and Clinical Neurophysiology*, 9, pp.673-90.

Dement, W.C. (1978) *Some Must Watch While Some Must Sleep*, New York: Norton.

Dennett, D. (2003) *Freedom evolves*, London, Allen Lane.

Dennis. W. (1960) 'Causes of retardation among institutional children: Iran', *Journal of Genetic Psychology*, 96, pp.47-59.

Deregowski, J. (1972) 'Pictorial perception and culture', *Scientific American*, 227, pp.82-8.

Deregowski, J. (1980) 'Illusions, patterns and pictures: a cross-cultural perspective', London: Academic Press.

Deutsch, J.A. and Deutsch, D. (1963) 'Attention, some theoretical considerations', *Psychological review*, 70, pp.80-90.

Deutsch, J.A., Young, G.W. and Kalogeris, T.J. (1978) 'The stomach signals satiety', *Science*, 201, pp.165-7.

Deutsch, M. and Collins, M.E. (1951) *Interracial Housing: A Psychological Evaluation of a Social Experiment*, Minneapolis: University of Minneapolis Press.

Deutsch, M. and Gerard, H.B. (1955) 'A study of normative and informational influence upon individual judgement', *Journal of Abnormal and Social Psychology*, 51, pp.629–36.

DeValois, R.L. and DeValois, K.K. (1980) 'Spatial vision', *Annual Review of Psychology*, 31, pp.309-41.

Devanand, D.P., Dwork, A.J., Hutchinson, E.R., Bolwig, T.G. and Sackeim, H.A. (1994) 'Does ECT alter brain structure?', *American Journal of Psychiatry*, 151, pp.957-70.

DeVellis, B.M. and Blalock, S.J. (1992) 'Illness attributions and hopeless depression: the role of hopelessness expectancy', *Journal of Abnormal Psychology*, 101, pp.257-64.

de Villiers, P.A. and de Villiers, J.G. (1992) 'Language development', in M.H. Bornstein and M.E. Lamb (eds) *Developmental Psychology: An Advanced Textbook* (3rd edn), Hillsdale, NJ: Erlbaum.

de Waal, F.B.M. (1999) 'The end of nature versus nurture', *Scientific American*, 281, 6, pp.56-61.

Dewe, P.J. (1992) 'Applying the concept of appraisal to work stressors: some exploratory analysis', *Human Relations*, 45, pp.143–64.

Diamond, J.M. (1991) *The Rise and Fall of the Third Chimpanzee*, London: Radius.

Dickersin, K. (1990) 'The existence of publication bias and risk factors for its occurrence', *JAMA*, 263(10), pp.1385-9.

Dien, D. (1983) 'Big me and little me: A Chinese perspective on self', *Psychiatry*, 46, pp.281-6.

Diener, E. (1980) 'Deindividuation: the absence of self-awareness and self-regulation in group members', in P. Paulus (ed.) *The Psychology of Group Influence*, Hillsdale, NJ: Lawrence Erlbaum.

Dindia, K. and Baxter, L.A. (1987) 'Maintenance and repair strategies in marital relationships', *Journal of Social and Personal Relationships*, 4, pp.143-58.

Dohrenwend, B.P., Levav, P.E., Schwartz, S., Naveh, G., Link, B.G., Skodol, A.E. and Stueve, A. (1992) 'Socio-economic status and psychiatric disorders: the causation-selection issue', *Science*, 255, pp.946-52.

Doi, T. (1973) *The anatomy of dependence*, New York: Norton.

Dollard, J. and Miller, N.E. (1950) *Personality and Psychotherapy: An Analysis in terms of Learning, Thinking and Culture*, New York: McGraw-Hill.

Donaldson, M. (1978) *Children's Minds*, London: Fontana.

Dooling, R.J., Soli, S.D., Kline, R.M., Park, T.J., Hue, C. and Bunnell, T. (1987) 'Perception of synthetic speech sounds by the budgerigar (*Melopsittacus undulatus*)', *Bulletin of the Psychonomic Society*, 25, pp.139-42.

Drubach, D. (2000) *The Brain Explained*, Upper Saddle River, NJ: Prentice-Hall.

Duck, S. (1981) 'Toward a research map for the study of relationship breakdown', in S. Duck and R. Gilmour (eds) *Personal Relationships*, Vol. 3, *Personal Relationships in Disorder*, London: Academic Press.

Duck, S. (1988) *Relating to Others*, Milton Keynes: Open University Press.

Duck, S. (1999a) *Relating to Others* (2nd edn), Buckingham: Open University Press.

Dunbar, R.I.M. (1993) 'Coevolution of neocortical size, group size and language in humans', *Behavioural and Brain Sciences*, 16, pp.681-735.

Dunbar, R.I.M. (1995) 'Are you lonesome tonight?', *New Scientist*, 11 February, pp.26-31.

Dunbar, R.I.M. (1992) 'Neocortex size as a constraint on group size in primates', *Journal of Human Evolution*, 20, pp.469-93.

Duncan, H.F., Gourlay, N. and Hudson, W. (1973) 'A study of pictorial representation among the Bantu and white primary school children in South Africa', Johannesburg: Witwatersrand University Press.

Duncker, K. (1945/35) 'On problem solving', *Psychological Monographs*, 58, pp.1-113 (originally published in German in 1935).

Durkheim, E. (1898) 'Representations individuelles et representations collectives', *Revue de Metaphysique*, 6, pp.274-302 (in D.F. Pocock (trans.) *Sociology and Philosophy*, New York: Free Press, 1953).

Durkin, K. (1995) *Developmental Social Psychology*, Oxford: Blackwell.

Dutton, D.C. and Aron, A.P. (1974) 'Some evidence for heightened sexual attraction under conditions of high anxiety', *Journal of Personality and Social Psychology*, 30, pp.510-17.

Dyer, C. (1995) *Beginning Research in Psychology: A Practical Guide to Research Methods and Statistics*, Oxford: Blackwell.

Dyer, F.C. (1996) 'Spatial memory and navigation by honeybees on the scale of the foraging range', *The Journal of Experimental Biology*, 199, pp.147-54.

Dyer, F.C. and Dickinson, J.A. (1994) 'Development of sun compensation by honey bees: how partially experienced bees estimate the sun's course', *Proceedings of the National Academy of Sciences USA*, 91, pp.4471-4.

Eagley, A.H. and Crowley, M. (1986) 'Gender and helping behaviour: a meta-analytic review of the social psychological literature', *Psychological Review*, 100, pp.283-308.

Eagly, A.H. and Carli, L. (1981) 'Sex of researchers and sex-typed communications as determinants of sex differences in influenceability: A meta-analysis of social influence studies', *Psychological Bulletin*, 90, pp.1-20.

Eaton, S.B. and Konner, M. (1985) 'Paleolithic nutrition. A consideration of its nature and current implications', *New England Journal of Medicine*, 312, pp.283-9.

Eaton, W.W., Dryman, A. and Weissman, M.M. (1991) 'Panic and phobia', in L.N. Robins and D.A. Reiger (eds) *Psychiatric Disorders in America*, New York: The Free Press.

Eccles, J.S., Midgley, C., Wigfield, A. and Buchanan, C.M. (1993) 'Development during adolescence: the impact of stage-environment fit on young adolescents' experiences in schools and in families', *American Psychologist*, 48, pp.90-101.

Eckensberger, L.H. (1983) 'Research on moral development', *German Journal of Psychology*, 7(3), pp.195-244.

Egeland, B. and Hiester, M. (1995) 'The long-term consequences of infant day-care and mother-infant attachment', *Child Development*, 66, pp.474-85.

Egrise, D., Rubinstein, M., Schoutens, A., Cantraine, F. and Mendlewicz, J. (1986) 'Seasonal variation of platelet serotonin uptake and 3H-imipramine binding in normal and depressed subjects', *Biological Psychiatry*, 21, pp.283-92.

Eich, J.E. (1980) 'The cue-dependent nature of state-dependent retrieval', *Memory and Cognition*, 8, pp.157-73.

Eisenberg, N. and Lennon, R. (1983) 'Sex differences in empathy and related capacities', *Psychological Bulletin*, 94(1), pp.100-31.

Eisenberg, N. and Mussen, P.H. (1989) *The Roots of Pro-social Behaviour in Children*, Cambridge: Cambridge University Press.

Eisenberg, N., Guthrie, I.K., Murphy, B.C., Shepard, S.A. Cumberland, A. & Carlo, G. (1999) 'Consistency and development of pro-social dispositions: A longitudinal study', *Child Development*, 70(6), pp.1360-72.

Eisenberg, N., Lennon, R. and Roth, K. (1983) 'Pro-social development: a longitudinal study', *Developmental Psychology*, 19, pp.846-55.

Eisenberg, N., Miller, P.A., Shell, R., McNalley, S. and Shea, C. (1991) 'Pro-social development in adolescence: a longitudinal study', *Developmental Psychology*, 27, pp.849-57.

Eisenberg, N., Shell, R., Paternak, J., Lennon, R., Beller, R. and Mathy, R.M. (1987) 'Pro-social development in middle childhood: a longitudinal study', *Developmental Psychology*, 23, pp.712-718.

Eisenberg-Berg, N. and Hand, M. (1979) 'The relationship of preschoolers' reasoning about pro-social moral conflicts to prosocial behaviour', *Child Development*, 50, pp.356-63.

Elliott, J. (1977) 'The power and pathology of prejudice', in P.G. Zimbardo and F.L. Ruch, *Psychology and Life* (9th edn), Diamond Printing, Glenview, IL: Scott, Foresman.

Elliott, J. (1990) in *Discovering Psychology*, Program 20 [PBS video series], Washington DC: Annenberg/CPB Program.

Ellis, A. (1962) *Reason and Emotion in Psychotherapy*, New York: Citadel.

Ellis, A. (1980) 'Discomfort anxiety: a new cognitive-behavioural construct. Part 2', *Rational Living*, 15 (1), pp.25-30.

Ellis, A. (1991) 'The revised ABCs of rational-emotive therapy', *Journal of Rational-Emotive and Cognitive-Behaviour Therapy*, 9, pp.139-92.

Ellis, H.D. (1986) 'Processes underlying face recognition', in R. Bruyer (ed.) *The Neuropsychology of Face Perception and Facial Expression*, Hove: Laurence Elbaum Associates.

Elms, A.C. (1972) *Social psychology and social relevance*, Boston: Little, Brown.

Emmelkamp, P.M. (1994) 'Behaviour therapy with adults', in A.E. Bergin and S.L. Garfield (eds) *Handbook of Psychotherapy and Behaviour Change* (4th edn), New York: Wiley.

Emmelkamp, P.M., Visser, S. and Hoekstra, R.J. (1988) 'Cognitive therapy vs exposure in the treatment of obsessive compulsives', *Cognitive Therapy Research*, 12 (1), pp.103-14.

Emmerlich, W., Goldmann, K., Kirsh, K. and Sharabany, R. (1977) 'Evidence for a transitional phase in the development of gender constancy', *Child Development*, 48, pp.930-6.

Engel, M., Nechglin, H. and Arkin, A.M. (1975) 'Aspects of mothering: correlates of the cognitive development of black male infants in the second year of life', in A. Davids (ed.) *Child Personality and Psychopathology: Current Topics*, Vol. 2, New York: Wiley.

Engels, G.I., Garnefski, N. and Diekstra, R.F.W. (1993) 'Efficacy of rational-emotive therapy: a quantitative analysis', *Journal of Consulting and Clinical Psychology*, 61(6), pp.1083-90.

Epstein, A.N., Fitzsimons, J.T. and Rolls, B.J. (1970) 'Drinking induced by injection of angiotensin into the brain of the rat', *Journal of Physiology* (London), 210, pp.457-74.

Epstein, L.C. and Lasagna, L. (1969) 'Obtaining informed consent', *Archives of Internal Medicine*, 123, pp.682-8.

Epstein, R., Lanza, R.P. and Skinner, B.F. (1981) '"Self-awareness" in the pigeon', *Science*, 212, pp.695-6.

Epstein, S. (1979) 'The stability of behavior: I. on predicting most of the people much of the time', *Journal of Personality and Social Psychology*, 37(7), pp.1097-1126.

Erikson, E.H. (1968) *Identity: Youth and Crisis*, London: Faber.

Erikson, E.H. (1980) *Identity and the Life Cycle*, New York: Norton.

Eron, L. (1992) 'The impact of televised violence', Testimony on behalf of the American Psychological Association before the Senate Committee on Governmental Affairs, June 18.

Ervin-Tripp, S. (1964) 'An analysis of the interaction of language, topic and listener' *American Anthropologist*, 66, pp.94-100.

Ervin-Tripp, S., Guo, J. and Lampert, M. (1990) 'Politeness and persuasion in children's control acts', *Journal of Pragmatics*, 14, pp.307-31.

Evans, C.S. and Marler, P. (1995) 'Language and animal communication: Parallels and contrasts', in H.L. Roitblat and J.-

A. Meyer (eds) *Comparative Approaches to Cognitive Science*, Cambridge, MA: MIT Press.

Evans, G., Bullinger, M. and Hygger, S. (1998) 'The effects of chronic exposure to aircraft noise', *Psychological Science*, 9, pp.75–7.

Evans, M.D., Hollon, S.D., DeRubeis, R.J. and Associates (1992) 'Differential relapse following cognitive therapy and pharmacotherapy for depression', *Archives of General Psychiatry*, 49, pp.802-8.

Evans, P.D. (1990) 'Type A behaviour and coronary heart disease: when will the jury return?', *British Journal of Psychology*, 81, pp.147–57.

Everson, C.A., Bergmann, B.M. and Rechstaffen, A. (1989) 'Sleep deprivation in the rat: III. Total sleep deprivation', *Sleep*, 12, pp.13-21.

Eysenck, H.J. (1952) 'The effects of psychotherapy: an evaluation', *Journal of Consulting Psychology*, 16, pp.319-24.

Eysenck, H.J. (1953) *The Structure of Human Personality* (3rd edn), London: Methuen.

Eysenck, H.J. (1963) 'Biological basis of personality', *Nature*, 199, pp.1031-4.

Eysenck, H.J. (1967) *The Biological Basis of Personality*, Springfield, IL: Charles C. Thomas.

Eysenck, M.W. and Keane, M.T. (1995) *Cognitive Psychology: A Student's Handbook* (3rd edn), Hove: Lawrence Erlbaum Associates.

Fagot, B.I. (1985) 'Beyond the reinforcement principle: another step toward understanding sex role development', *Developmental Psychology*, 21, pp.1097-1104.

Fairburn, C.G., Cooper, Z., Doll, II.A. and Welch, S.L. (1999) 'Risk factors for anorexia nervosa', *Archives of General Psychiatry*, 56, pp.468–76.

Falkai, P., Bogerts, B., and Rozumek, M. (1988) 'Limbic pathology in schizophrenia', *Proceedings of the National Academy of Science, USA*, 2, pp.560-3.

Fantz, R.L. (1961) 'The origin of form perception', *Scientific American*, 204 (5), pp.66-72.

Faraone, S.V., Seidman, L.J., Kremen, W.S., Toomey, R. and Pepple, J.R. (1999) 'Neuropsychological functioning among the nonpsychotic relatives of schizophrenic patients: a four-year follow-up study', *Journal of Abnormal Psychology*, 108, pp.176-81.

Farr, R. (1977) 'Heider, Harré and Herzlich on health and illness: some observations on the structure of 'représentations collectives', *European Journal of*

Social Psychology, 7, pp.491-504.

Farrell, M. P. and Rosenberg, S.D. (1981) *Men at Midlife*, Boston: Auburn House.

Feldman, N.S., Klosson, E.C., Parsons, J.E., Knoles, W.S. and Ruble, D.N. (1976) 'Order of information presentation and children's moral judgements', *Child Development*, 47, pp.556-9.

Feltham, C. (1996) 'Psychotherapy's staunchest critic: an interview with Hans Eysenck', *British Journal of Guidance and Counselling*, 24, pp.423-35.

Feltz, D.L. (1982) 'Oath analysis of the causal elements in Bandura's theory of self-efficacy and an anxiety-based model of avoidance behaviour', *Journal of Personality and Social Psychology*, 42, pp.764-81.

Fenson, L., Dale, P.S., Resnick, J.S., Bates, E., Thal, D.J. and Pethick, S.J. (1994) 'Variability in early communicative development', *Monographs of the Society for Research in Child development*, 59 (5, Serial No. 242).

Fernando, S. (1988) *Race and Culture in Psychiatry*, London: Croom Helm.

Fernando, S. (1991) *Mental Health, Race and Culture*, London: Macmillan/Mind.

Festinger, L., Schachter, S. and Back, K.W. (1950) *Social Pressures in Informal Groups*, New York: Harper.

Fiedler, K. (1982) 'Causal schemata: review and criticism of research on a popular construct', *Journal of Personality and Social Psychology*, 42, pp.1001-13.

Field, D. and Minkler, (1988) 'Continuity and change in social support between young-old, old-old and very old adults', *Journal of Gerontology*, 43, pp.100-6.

Fine, M. and Gordon, S.M. (1989) 'Feminist transformations of/despite psychology' in M. Crawford and M. Gentry (eds) *Gender and Thought: Psychological Perspectives*, New York: Springer-Verlag.

Fischer, M. (1971) 'Psychosis in the offspring of schizophrenic monozygotic twins and their normal co-twins', *British Journal of Psychiatry*, 118, pp.43-52.

Fishbein, M. and Ajzen, L. (1975) *Belief, Attitude, Intention and Behaviour: An Introduction to Theory and Research*, Reading, MA: Addison-Wesley.

Fisher, A.E. and Coury, J.N. (1962) 'Cholinergic tracing of a central neural circuit underlying the thirst drive', *Science*, 138, pp.691-3.

Fisher, H. (1992) *Anatomy of Love*, New York: Norton & Company.

Fisher, R.A. and Yates, F. (1974) *Statistical Tables for Biological, Agricultural and Medical Research* (6th edn), Harlow: Longman Group Ltd.

Fisher, R.P., Geiselman, R.E. and Amador, M. (1989) 'Field test of the cognitive interview: enhancing the recollection of actual victims and witnesses of crime', *Journal of Applied Psychology*, 74, pp.722–7.

Fiske, S.T. (1989) 'Interdependence and stereotyping: from the laboratory to the Supreme Court (and back)', Invited address, American Psychological Association: New Orleans.

Fiske, S.T. and Neuberg, S.L. (1990) 'A continuum model of impression formation, from category based to individuating processes: influence of information and motivation on attention and interpretation', in M.P. Zanna (ed.) *Advances in Experimental Social Psychology*, Vol. 23, New York: Academic Press.

Fitzgibbon, C.D. and Fanshawe, J.H. (1988) 'Stotting in Thompson's gazelles: an honest signal of condition', *Behavioural Ecology and Sociobiology*, 23, pp.69-74.

Flanagan, C. (1996) *Applying Psychology to Early Child Development*, London: Hodder & Stoughton.

Flanagan, C. (1999) *Early Socialisation*, London: Routledge.

Flanagan, C. (2000) 'New insights into aggression', *Psychology Review*, 6, (3), pp.12-13.

Flaum, M., Swayze II, V.W., O'Leary, D.S., Yuh, W.T.C., Ehrhardt, J.C., Arndt, S.V. and Andreasen, N.C. (1995) 'Effects of diagnosis, laterality and gender on brain morphology in schizophrenia', *American Journal of Psychiatry*, 152 (2), pp.704-14.

Flavell, J.H. (1985) *Cognitive Development* (2nd edn), Englewood Cliffs, NJ: Prentice-Hall.

Fleeson, F. (2001) 'Toward a Structure- and Process-Integrated View of Personality Traits as Density Distributions of States', *Journal of Personality and Social Psychology*, 80(6), pp.1011-27.

Floody, O.R. (1968) 'Hormones and aggression in female animals', in B.B. Suare (ed.) *Hormones and Aggressive Behaviour*, New York: Plenum Press.

Flynn, J. R. (1994) 'IQ gains over time', in R. J. Sternberg (ed.) *Encyclopedia of Human Intelligence* (pp.617-23). New York: Macmillan.

Flynn, J.P. (1976) 'Neural basis of threat and attack', in R.G.

Grenell and S. Gabay (eds) *Biological Foundations of Psychiatry*, New York: Raven Press.

Fong, G.T., Krantz, D.H. and Nisbett, R.E. (1986) 'The effects of statistical training on thinking about everyday problems', *Cognitive Psychology*, 18, pp.253-92.

Ford, C. and Neale, J.M. (1985) 'Effects of a helplessness induction on judgements of control', *Journal of Personality and Social Psychology*, 49, pp.1330-6.

Foster, J.J. and Parker, I. (1995) *Carrying out Investigations in Psychology: Methods and Statistics*, Leicester: BPS Books.

Foster, R.A., Libkuman, T.M., Schooler, J.W. and Loftus, E.F. (1994) 'Consequentiality and eyewitness person identification', *Applied Cognitive Psychology*, 8, pp.107–21.

Fowler, H. (1965) *Curiosity and Exploratory Behaviour*, New York: Macmillan.

Fox, N. (1977) 'Attachment of Kibbutz infants to mother and metapelet', *Child Development*, 48, pp.1228–39.

Francks, C., DeLisi, L.E., Shaw, S.H., Fisher, S.E., Richardson, A.J., Stein, J.F. and Monaco, A.P. (2003) 'Parent-of-origin effects on handedness and schizophrenia susceptibility on chromosome 2p12-q11', *Human Molecular Genetics*, 12, pp.3225-30.

Frankenhaeuser, M., Dunne, E. and Lundberg, U. (1976) 'Sex differences in sympathetic adrenal medullary reactions induced by different stressors,' *Psychopharmacology*, 47, pp.1–5.

Freeman, D. (1983) *Margaret Mead and Samoa: The Making and Unmaking of an Anthropological Myth*, Cambridge, MA: Harvard University Press.

French, C.C. and Richards, A. (1993) 'Clock this! An everyday example of a schema-driven error in memory', *British Journal of Psychology*, 84, pp.249-53.

Freud, A. (1936) *The Ego and the Mechanisms of Defence*, London: Chatto and Windus.

Freud, S. (1901) *Psychopathology of Everyday Life*, London: Hogarth Press. Republished 1976 Harmondsworth, Middlesex: Penguin.

Freud, S. (1910) 'The origin and development of psychoanalysis', *American Journal of Psychology*, 21, pp.181-218.

Freud, S. (1915–18) *Introductory Lectures on Psychoanalysis*, London: Hogarth Press.

Freud, S. (1920) *A General Introduction to Psychoanalysis*, New York: Washington Square Press.

Freud, S. (1955) *The Interpretation of Dreams*, New York: Basic Books.

Freud, S. (1990, original work published in 1909) 'Case study of Little Hans' in *Sigmund Freud 8, Case Histories I*, London: Penguin Books.

Frey, C.U. and Rothlisberger, C. (1996) 'Social support in healthy adolescents', *Journal of Youth and Adolescence*, 25 (1), pp.17-31.

Friedman, M. and Rosenman, R.H. (1959) 'Association of specific overt behaviour pattern with blood and cardiovascular findings', *Journal of the American Medical Association*, 169, pp.1286-96.

Friedman, M. and Rosenman, R.H. (1974) *Type A Behavior and Your Heart*, New York: Knopf.

Friedman, S.L. and Stevenson, M. (1980) 'Perception of movements in pictures', in M. Hagen (ed.) *Perception of Pictures*, Vol. 1, *Albert's Model: The Projective Model of Pictorial Information*, New York: Academic Press.

Friedrich-Cofer, L.K., Huston-Stein, A., Kipnis, D.M., Susman, E.J. and Clewett, A.S. (1979) 'Environmental enhancement of prosocial television content: effects on interpersonal behavior, imaginative play and self-regulation in a neutral setting', *Developmental Psychology*, 15, pp.637-746.

Fromm-Reichmann, F. (1948) 'Notes on the development of treatment of schizophrenics by psychoanalytic psychotherapy', *Psychiatry*, 11, pp.263-73.

Fuld, K.,Wooten, B.R. and Whalen, J.J. (1981) 'The elemental hues of short-wave and extra-spectral lights', *Perception and Psychophysics*, 29, pp.317-22.

Fuligni, A.J. and Eccles, J.S. (1993) 'Perceived parent-child relationships and early adolecsents' orientation towards peers', *Developmental Psychology*, 29, pp.622-32.

Fulton, R. (1970) 'Death, grief and social recuperation', *Omega: Journal of Death and Dying*, 1, pp.23-8.

Fultz, J., Batson, C.D., Fortenbach, V.A., McCarthy, P.M. and Varney, L.L. (1986) 'Social evaluation and the empathy-altruism hypothesis', *Journal of Personality and Social Psychology*, 50, pp.761-9.

Furlow, B. (2000) 'The uses of crying and begging', *Natural History*, 10, pp.62-7.

Furman, C.E. and Duke, R.A. (1988) 'Effect of majority consensus on preferences for recorded orchestral and popular music', *Journal of Research in Music Education*, 36(4), pp.220–31.

Fyer, A., Leibowitz, M., Gorman, J., Compeas, R., Levin, A., Davies, S., Goetz, D. and Klein, D. (1987) 'Discontinuation of alprazolam treatment in panic patients', *American Journal of Psychiatry*, 144, pp.303-8.

Fyer, A.J., Mannuzza, S., Gallops, M.S., Martin, L.Y., Aaronson, C., Gorman, J.M., Liebowitz, M.R. and Klein, D.F. (1990) 'Familial transmission of simple fears and phobias', *Archives of General Psychiatry*, 40, pp.1061-4.

Gaertner, S.L. and Dovidio, J.F. (1977) 'The subtlety of white racism, arousal and helping behaviour', *Journal of Personality and Social Psychology*, 35, pp.691-707.

Gaertner, S.L., Dovidio, J.F., Anastasio, P.A., Bachevan, B.A. and Rust, M.C. (1993) 'The common ingroup identity model: recategorization and the reduction of intergroup bias', in W. Stroebe and M. Hewstone (eds) *European Review of Social Psychology*, 4, Chichester: John Wiley.

Gaertner, S.L., Mann, J., Murrell, A.J. and Pomere, M. (1990) 'How does co-operation reduce intergroup bias?', *Journal of Personality and Social Psychology*, 59, pp.692-704.

Gale, A. (1995) 'Ethical issues in psychological research', in A.M. Colman (ed.), *Psychological Research Methods and Statistics*, London: Longman Essential Psychology.

Galef, B.G. Jr and Wigmore, S.W. (1983) 'Transfer of information concerning distant foods: a laboratory investigation of the "Information-centre" hypothesis', *Animal Behaviour*, 31, pp.748-58.

Gallo, P.S., Smith, S. and Mumford, S. (1973) 'Effects of deceiving subjects upon experimental results', *Journal of Social Psychology*, 89, pp.99–107.

Gallup, G.G. (1970) 'Chimpanzees: self-recognition', *Science*, 167, pp.86-7.

Gallup, G.G. (1983) 'Toward a comparative psychology of mind', in R.E. Mellgren, *Animal Cognition and Behaviour*, New York: Elsevier.

Galton, F. (1874) *English men of science: Their nature and nurture*, London: Macmillan & Co.

Galton, F. (1888) 'Co-relations and their measurement, chiefly from anthropometric data', *Proceedings of the Royal Society of London*, 45, pp.135-45.

Gamson, W.B., Fireman, B. and Rytina, S. (1982) *Encounters with Unjust Authority*, Homewood, IL: Dorsey Press.

Gannon, K.M., Skowronski, J.J. and Betz, A.L. (1994) 'Depressive diligence in social information

processing: implications for order effects in impressions and for social memory', *Social Cognition*, 12, pp.263-80.

Garcia, J. and Koelling, R.A. (1966) 'Relation of cue to consequence in avoidance learning', *Psychonomic Science*, 4, pp.123-4.

Garcia, J., Rusiniak, K.W. and Brett, L.P. (1977) 'Conditioning food-illness in wild animals: *Caveant canonici*', in H. Davis and H.M.B. Hurwitz (eds), *Operant-Pavlovian Interactions*, Hillsdale, NJ: Lawrence Erlbaum Associates pp.273-316.

Gardner, B.T. and Gardner, R.A. (1969) 'Teaching sign language to a chimpanzee', *Science*, 165, pp.664-72.

Garland, H.A., Hardy, A. and Stephenson, L. (1975) 'Information search as affected by attribution type and response category', *Personality and Social Psychology Bulletin*, 1, pp.612-15.

Garmon, L.C., Basinger, K.S., Gregg, V.R. and Gibbs, J.C. (1996) 'Gender differences in stage and expression of moral judgment', *Merrill-Palmer Quarterly*, 42(3), pp.418-37.

Garner, D.M., Garfinkel, P.E., Rockert, W. and Olmsted, M.P. (1987) 'A prospective study of eating disturbances in the ballet', *Psychotherapy and Psychosomatics*, 48, pp.170–5.

Garner, W.R. (1979) 'Letter discrimination and identification', in A.D. Pick (ed.) *Perception and Its Development: A Tribute to Eleanor Gibson*, Hillsdale, NJ: Erlbaum.

Garnets, L. and Kimmel, D. (1991) 'Lesbian and gay male dimensions in the psychological study of human diversity', in J. Goodchilds (ed.) *Psychological Perspectives on Human Diversity in America: Master Lectures*, Washington DC: American Psychological Association.

Gaskin, D.E. (1982) *The Ecology of Whales and Dolphins*, London: Honeymoon.

Gauld, A. and Stephenson, G.M. (1967) 'Some experiments relating to Bartlett's theory of remembering', *British Journal of Psychology*, 58, pp.39–50.

Gauntlett, D. (1998) 'Ten things wrong with the 'effects model', in R. Dickinson, R. Harindranath and O. Linné (eds) *Approaches to Audiences – A Reader*, London: Arnold.

Gauze, C.M. (1994, February) 'Talking to Mom about friendship: What do mothers know?', paper presented at the meeting of the Society for Research on Adolescence, San Diego.

Gee, S. and Baillie, J. (1999) 'Happily ever after? An

exploration of retirement expectations', *Educational Gerontology*, 25 (2), pp.109-28.

Geen, R.G. (1990) *Human Aggression*, Milton Keynes: Open University Press.

Geiselman, R. (1988) 'Improving eyewitness testimony through mental reinstatement of context', in G.M. Davies and D.M. Thomson (eds) *Memory in Context: Context in Memory*, Chichester: Wiley.

Geiselman, R.E., Fisher, R., Mackinnon, D. and Holland, H.L. (1985) 'Enhancement of eyewitness testimony with the cognitive interview', *American Journal of Psychology*, 99, pp.385–401.

Gelder, M., Gath, D., Mayou, R. and Cowen, P. (1998) *Oxford Textbook of Psychiatry* (3rd edn), Oxford: Oxford Medical Publications/Oxford University Press.

Gelernter, C.S., Uhde, T.W. and Cimbolic, P. (1991) 'Cognitive-behavioural and pharmacological treatments of social phobia – a controlled study', *Archives of General Psychiatry*, 49, p. 938.

Gelfand, D.M., Hartmann, D.P., Walder, P. and Page, B. (1973) 'Who reports shoplifters? A field-experimental study', *Journal of Personality and Social Psychology*, 25, pp.276-85.

Gergen, K.J., Morse, S.J. and Gergen, M.M. (1980) 'Behavior exchange in cross-cultural perspective', in H.C. Triandis and R.W. Brislin (eds) *Handbook of Cross-cultural Psychology: Social Psychology*, Boston, MA: Allyn & Bacon.

Gerkema, M.P. and Dann, S. (1985) 'Ultradian rhythms in behavior: the case of the common vole (microtus arvalis)', in H. Schulz and P.Lavie (eds), *Ultradian Rhythms in Physiology and Behavior*, Berlin: Springer-Verlag.

Gibons, A. (1998) 'Solving the brain's energy crisis', *Science*, 280, pp.1345-7.

Gibson, E.J. (1969) *Principles of Perceptual Learning and Development*, New York: Prentice-Hall.

Gibson, E.J. and Walk P.D. (1960) 'The visual cliff', *Scientific American*, 202, pp.64-71.

Gibson. J.J. (1979) *The Ecological Approach to Visual Perception*, Boston: Houghton Mifflin.

Gigerenzer, G. (1991) 'How to make cognitive illusions disappear: beyond heuristics and biases', in W. Stroebe and M. Hewstone (eds) *European review of Social psychology* (Vol. 2, pp 83-115), Chichester: Wiley

Gilani, N. (1995) 'A study of mother-daughter relationships in two cultures'. Unpublished PhD dissertation. University of Sussex.

Gilligan, C. (1982) *In a Different Voice: Psychological Theory and Women's Development*, Cambridge, MA: Harvard University Press.

Gilligan, C. and Attanucci, J. (1988) 'Two moral orientations: gender differences and similarities', *Merrill-Plamer Quarterly*, 34, pp.223-37.

Gilligan, C., Lyons, N.P. and Hanmer, T.J. (eds) (1990) *Making Connections: The relational worlds of adolescent girls at Emma Willard School*. Cambridge: Harvard University Press, 1990.

Gillin, J.C., Sitaram, N., Janowsky, D., Risch, C., Huey, L. and Storch, F. (1985) 'Cholinergic mechanisms in REM sleep', in A. Wauquier, J.M. Gaillard, J. Monti and M. Radulovacki (eds) *Sleep: Neurotransmitters and Neuromodulators*, New York: Raven Press.

Gitlin, M.J., Swendsen, J., Heller, T.L. and Hammen, C. (1995) 'Relapse and impairment in bipolar disorder', *American Journal of Psychiatry*, 152, pp.1635-40.

Glanzer, M. and Cunitz, A.R. (1966) 'Two storage mechanisms in free recall', *Journal of Verbal Learning and Verbal Behaviour*, 5, pp.351–60.

Glass, D. and Singer, J. (1972) *Urban Stress: Experiments on Noise and Social Stressors*, New York: Academic Press.

Glassman, N. (1999) 'All things being equal: the two roads of Piaget and Vygotsky', in P. Lloyd and C. Fernyhough (eds), *Lev Vygotsky: Critical Assessments: Vygotsky's Theory*, Vol. I (pp.282-310), New York, NY: Routledge.

Gleason, J.B. and Ratner, N.B. (1993) Language development in children', in J.B. Gleason and N.B. Ratner (eds) *Psycholinguistics*, Fort Worth, TX: Harcourt Brace Jovanovich.

Gleaves, D. (1996) 'The socio-cognitive model of dissociative identity disorder: a re-examination of the evidence', *Psychological Bulletin*, 120, pp.42-59.

Gleitman, H. (1991) *Psychology* (3rd edn), London: W.W. Norton & Co.

Godden, D. and Baddeley, A. (1975) 'Context-dependent memory in two natural environments: on land and under water', *British Journal of Psychology*, 66, pp.325–31.

Goldstein, E.B. (1999) *Sensation and Perception* (5th edn), Pacific Grove: Brooks/Cole Publishing.

Goldstein, M.J. (1988) 'The family and psychotherapy', *Annual*

Review of Psychiatry, 39, pp.283-99.

Gombrich, E.H. (1972) 'The mask and the face. The perception of physiognomic likeness in life and in art', in E.H. Gombrich, J. Hochberg and M. Black (eds) *Art, Perception and Reality*, Baltimore: Johns Hopkins Press.

Goodwin, D.W., Powell, B., Bremer, D., Hoine, H. and Stern, J. (1969) 'Alcohol and recall: state dependent effects in man', *Science*, 163, p.1358.

Goodwin, R. (1999) *Personal Relationships Across Cultures*, London: Routledge.

Goodwin, R., Adatia, K., Sinhal, H., Cramer, D. and Ellis, P. (1997) *Social Support and Marital Well-being in an Asian Community*, York: Joseph Rowntree Foundation.

Gopnik, M. and Crago, M.B. (1991) 'Familial aggregation of a developmental language disorder', *Cognition*, 29, pp.1-50.

Gordon, J.C.B. (1981) *Verbal Deficit: A Critique*, London: Croom Helm.

Gotlib, I.H. and Macleod, C. (1997) 'Information processing in anxiety and depression: a cognitive-developmental perspective', in J. Burack and J. Enns (eds), *Attention, Development and Psychopathology*, New York: Guilford Press.

Gottesman, I.I. (1963) 'Heritability of personality: a demonstration', *Psychological Monographs*, 77 (Whole no. 572).

Gottesman, I.I. and Shields, J. (1982) *Schizophrenia: The Epigenetic Puzzle*, Cambridge: Cambridge University Press

Gottman, J.M. (1998) 'Psychology and the study of marital processes', *Annual Review of Psychology*. 49, pp.169-97.

Gould, J.L. (1986) 'The locale map of honey bees: do insects have cognitive maps?' *Science*, 207, pp.545-7.

Gould, J.L. (1992) 'Honey bee cognition', in C.R. Gallistel (ed.) *Animal Cognition*, Cambridge, MA: MIT Press.

Gould, R.L. (1978) *Transformations: Growth and change in adult life*. New York: Simon and Schuster.

Gould, R.L. (1980) 'Transformation tasks in adulthood', in *The Course of Life*, Vol. 3, *Adulthood and Aging Processes*, Bethesda MD: National Institute of Mental Health.

Gould, S.J. (1984) 'Only his wings remained', *Natural History*, 93, pp.10-18.

Gould, S.J. (1987) *An Urchin in the Storm*, New York: W.W. Norton.

Grafen, A. (1982) 'How not to measure inclusive fitness', *Nature*, 298, pp.425-6.

Grafen, A. (1990) 'Do animals really recognize kin?', *Animal Behaviour*, 2, pp.42-54.

Grammer, K. and Thornhill, R. (1994) 'Human (Homo Sapiens) facial attractiveness and sexual selection: the role of symmetry and averageness', *Journal of Comparative Psychology*, 108, pp.233-42.

Granrud, C.E. and Yonas, A. (1985) 'Infants' sensitivity to the depth cue of shading', *Perception and Psychophysics*, 37, pp.415-19.

Gray, J.A. and Wedderburn, A.A. (1960) 'Grouping strategies with simultaneous stimuli', *Quarterly Journal of Experimental Psychology*, 12, pp.180-4.

Gredler, M. (1992) *Learning and Instruction Theory into Practice*, New York: Macmillan Publishing Company.

Green, S. (1994) *Principles of Biopsychology*, Hove: Erlbaum.

Greene, B. (1994) 'Lesbian and gay sexual orientations', in B. Greene and G.M. Herek (eds), *Lesbian and Gay Psychology: Theory, Research and Clinical Applications*, London: Sage.

Greeno, J.G. (1994) 'Gibson's affordances', *Psychological Review*, 101, pp.336-42.

Greenough, W.T., Black, J.E., and Wallace, C.S. (1987) 'Experience and brain development', *Child Development*, 58, pp.539–59.

Gregory, R.L. (1966, 1973/2nd edn, 1978/3rd edn, 1990/4th edn) *Eye and Brain*, New York: McGraw Hill.

Grier, J.W and Burk, T. (1992) *Biology of Animal Behaviour*, St Louis: Mosby.

Griest, J.H., Klein, M.H., Erdman, H.P., Bires, J.K., Bass, S.M., Machtinger, P.E. and Kresge, D.G. (1987) 'Comparison of computer- and interviewer-administered versions of the Diagnostic Interview Schedule', *Hospital and Community Psychiatry*, 38, pp.1304-11.

Griffin, D.R. (1984) *Animal Thinking*, Cambridge, MA: Harvard University Press.

Griffin, D.R. (1991) *Animal Minds*, Chicago: Chicago University Press.

Griffiths, M. (1998) 'Violent video games – are they harmful?', *Psychology Review*, 4:4, pp.28-9.

Gross, R.D. (1996) *Psychology: The Science of Mind and Behaviour* (3rd edn) (2001/4th edn), London: Hodder & Stoughton.

Gross, R.D. (2003) *Themes, Issues and Debates in Psychology* (2nd edn), London: Hodder & Stoughton.

Grossmann, K.E. and Grossmann, K. (1991) 'Attachment quality as an organizer of emotional and behavioural responses in a longitudinal perspective', in

C.M. Parkes, J. Stevenson-Hinde and P. Marris (eds), *Attachment across the Life Cycle*, London: Tavistock/Routledge.

Grudin, J.T. (1983) 'Error patterns in novice and skilled transcription typing', in W.E. Cooper (ed.) *Cognitive Aspects of Skilled Typewriting*, New York: Springer.

Gualtieri, C. (1991) *Neuropsychiatry and Behavioural Pharmacology*, New York: Springer-Verlag.

Guarnaccia, P.J., Good, B.J. and Kleinman, A. (1990) 'A critical review of epidemiological studies of Puerto Rican mental health', *American Journal of Psychiatry*, 147, pp.1449–56.

Gull, W.W. (1874) 'Anorexia nervosa', *Transactions of the Clinical Society of London*, 7, pp.22–8.

Gunter, B. and McAleer, J. (1997) *Children and Television*, London: Routledge.

Gustafson, R. (1992) 'The relationship between perceived parents' child-rearing practices, own later rationality, and own later depression', *Journal of Rational-Emotive and Cognitive Behaviour Therapy*, 10(4), pp.253–8.

Gyger, M., Karakashian, S., and Marler, P. (1986) 'Avian alarm calling: Is there an audience effect?', *Animal Behaviour*, 34, pp.1570-2.

Haaga, D.A. and Davison, G.C. (1989) 'Outcome studies of rational-emotive therapy', in M.E. Bernard and R.D. DiGiuseppe (eds) *Inside Rational-Emotive Therapy*, San Diego, CA: Academic Press.

Haaga, D.A. and Davison, G.C. (1993) 'An appraisal of Rational-Emotive Therapy', *Journal of Consulting and Clinical Psychology*, 61 (2), pp.215-20.

Haeger, G. (1993) 'Social and temporal comparisons in a European context', Unpublished MSc thesis: University of Kent.

Hagell, A. and Newburn, T. (1994) *Young Offenders and the Media: Viewing Habits and Preferences*, London: Policy Studies Institute.

Hagen, M. and Jones, R. (1978) 'Cultural effects on pictorial perception: how many words is one picture really worth?', in R. Walk and H. Pick (eds) *Perception and Experience*, New York: Plenum Press.

Haier, R.J., Siegel, B.V. Jr., Nuechterlein, A. and Soderling, E. (1992) 'Regional glucose metabolic changes after learning a complex visuospatial/motor task: a positron emission tomographic study', *Brain Research*, 570, pp.134-43.

Haith, M.M. (1990) *Rules that Babies Look By*, Hillsdale, NJ: Erlbaum.

Halaas, J.J., Gajiwala, K.S., Maffei, M., Cohen, S.L., Chait, B.T., Rabinowitz, D., Lallone, R.L., Burley, S.K. and Friedman, J.M. (1995) 'Weight-reducing effects of the plasma protein encoded by the obese gene', *Science*, 269, pp.543-6.

Hall, C.S. and Lindzey, G. (1970) *Theories of Personality*, London: Wiley.

Hall, G.S. (1904) *Adolescence*, New York: Appleton-Century-Crofts.

Hall, T.M. (1998a) 'Culture-bound syndromes', http://weber.ucsd.edu~thall/cbs_intro.html

Hall, T.M. (1998b) 'Glossary of culture-bound syndromes', http://weber.ucsd.edu~thall/cbs_glos.html

Hall, T.M. (1998c) 'Index of culture-bound syndromes by symptoms', http://weber.ucsd.edu~thall/cbs_sxs.html

Hall, T.M. (1998d) 'Index of culture-bound syndromes by culture', http://weber.ucsd.edu~thall/cbs_cul.html

Hall, T.M. (1999) Personal communication, 10 December 1999.

Hallak, J.E.C., Crippas, J.A.S. and Zuardi, A.W. (2000) 'Treatment of koro with citalopram', *Journal of Clinical Psychology*, 61, pp.951-2.

Halpern, D. (1995) *More than Bricks and Mortar? Mental Health and the Built Environment*, London: Taylor & Francis.

Hamilton, D.L. and Gifford, R.K. (1976) 'Illusory correlation in interpersonal perception: a cognitive basis of stereotypic judgements', *Journal of Experimental Social Psychology*, 12, pp.392-407.

Hamilton, D.L. and Sherman, J.W. (1994) 'Stereotypes', in R.S. Wyer and T.K. Srull (eds) *Handbook of Social Cognition* (2nd edn), Vol. 2, Hillsdale, NJ: Lawrence Erlbaum.

Hamilton, M. (1960) 'A rating scale for depression', *Journal of Neurology, Neurosurgery and Psychiatry*, 23, pp.56-62.

Hamilton, S., Rothbart, M. and Dawes, R.M. (1986) 'Sex bias, diagnosis, and DSM-III', *Sex Roles*, 15, pp.269-74.

Hamilton, W.D. (1963) 'The evolution of altruistic behaviour', *The American Naturalist*, 97, pp.354-6.

Hamilton, W.D. (1964) 'The genetic evolution of social behaviour I and II', *Journal of Theoretical Biology*, 7, pp.1-52.

Hampson, P.J. and Morris, P.E. (1996) *Understanding Cognition*, Oxford: Blackwell.

Harcourt, A.H. (1992) 'Coalitions and alliances: are primates more complex than non-primates?', in A.H. Harcourt and F.de Waal (eds) *Coalitions and Alliances in Humans and Other Animals*, Oxford: Oxford University Press, pp.445-72.

Harcourt, A.H., Harvey, P.H., Larson, S.G. and Short, R.V. (1981) 'Testis weight, body weight and breeding system in primates', *Nature*, 293, pp.55-7.

Harden-Jones, F.R. (1968) *Fish Migration*, Edward Arnold: London.

Hare-Mustin, R.T. and Marecek, J. (1988) 'The meaning of difference: gender theory, post-modernism, and psychology', *American Psychologist*, 43, pp.455-64.

Harley, T.A. (1995) *The Psychology of Language: from Data to Theory*, Hove: Erlbaum (UK), Taylor & Francis.

Harlow, H.F. and Harlow, M.K. (1962) 'Social deprivation in monkeys', *Scientific American*, 207(5), pp.136-146.

Harlow, H.F. and Zimmerman, R.R. (1959) 'Affectional responses in the infant monkey', *Science*, 130, pp.421-32.

Harris, C.R. (2003) 'Factors associated with jealousy over real and imagined infidelity: an examination of the social-cognitive and evolutionary psychology perspectives', *Psychology of Women Quarterly*, 27, pp.319-329.

Harris, M.J., Milich, R., Corbitt, E.M., Hoover, D.W. and Brady, M. (1992) 'Self-fulfilling effects of stigmatising information on children's social interactions', *Journal of Personality and Social Psychology*, 63, pp.41-50.

Harrison, A.A. and Saeed, L. (1977) 'Let's make a deal: an analysis of revelations and stipulations in lonely hearts advertisements', *Journal of Personality and Social Psychology*, 35, pp.257-64.

Harrison, G, Ineichen, B., Smith, J. and Morgan, H.G. (1984) 'Psychiatric hospital admissions in Bristol. 2. Social and clinical aspects of compulsory admission', *British Journal of Psychiatry*, 145, pp.605-11.

Hart, B. and Risley, T. (1995) *Meaningful Differences in the Everyday Experiences of Young American Children*, Baltimore: Paul Brooks Publishing Company.

Hartlage, S., Alloy, L.B., Vazquez, C. and Dykman, B. (1993) 'Automatic and effortful processing in depression', *Psychological Bulletin*, 113 (2), pp.247-78.

Hartline, H.K., Wagner, H.G. and Ratliff, F. (1956) 'Inhibition in the eye of Limulus', *Journal of General Physiology*, 39, pp.651-73.

Hartshorne, H. and May, M.S. (1928) *Moral Studies in the Nature of Character: Studies in the Nature of Character*, New York: Macmillan.

Hartup, W.W. (1983) 'Peer relations', in P.H. Mussen (ed.) *Handbook of Child Psychology*. Vol. 4: *Socialisation, personality and social development*, New York: Wiley.

Harvey, E. (1999) 'Short-term and long-term effects of early parental employment on children of the National Longitudinal Survey of Youth', *Developmental Psychology*, 35(2), pp.445-59.

Harvey, P.H. and Harcourt, A.H. (1984) 'Sperm competition, testes size, and breeding systems in primates', in Smith, R.L.(ed.) *Sperm Competition and the Evolution of Animal Breeding Systems*. Academic Press: New York), pp.589-600

Harvey, P.H. and May, R.M. (1989) 'Gathering and the Hominid Adaption', in L. Tiger and H.T. Fowler (eds) *Female Hierarchies*. Chicago: Beresford Book Service.

Harvey, P.H., Martin, R.D. and Clutton-Brock, T.H. (1987) 'Life histories in comparative perspective', in B.B. Smuts, D.L. Cheney, R.M. Seyfarth, T.T. Struhsaker and R.W. Wrangham (eds) *Primate Societies*, Chicago: University of Chicago Press, pp.181-96.

Hatfield, E. (1987) 'Love' in R.J. Corsini (ed.), *Concise Encyclopaedia of Psychology*, New York: Wiley.

Hatfield, E. and Walster, G.W. (1981) *A New Look at Love*, Reading, MA: Addison-Wesley.

Hatfield, E., Utne, M.K. and Traupmann, J. (1979) 'Equity theory and intimate relationships', in R.L. Burgess and T.L. Huston (eds) *Exchange Theory in Developing Relationships*, New York: Academic Press.

Havighurst, R.J., Neugarten, B.L. and Tobin, S.S. (1968) 'Disengagement and patterns of aging', in B.L. Neugarten (ed.), *Middle Age and Aging*, Chicago: University of Chicago Press.

Hawkins, P.R. (1973) 'Social class, the nominal group and reference', in B. Bernstein (ed.) *Class, Codes and Control*, Vol. 2, London: Routledge & Kegan Paul.

Hawton, K. and Fagg, J. (1992) 'Trends in deliberate self-poisoning and self-injury in Oxford 1976-1990', *British Medical Journal*, 304, pp.1409-11

Hay, D.C. and Young, A.W. (1982) 'The human face', in A.W. Ellis (ed.) *Normality and Pathology in Cognitive Functions*, London: Academic Press.

Hayes, N. (1993) *Principles of Social Psychology*, Hove: Erlbaum.

Hays, R.B. (1985) 'A longitudinal study of friendship development', *Journal of Personality and Social Psychology*, 48, pp.909-24.

Hazan, C. and Shaver, P.R. (1987) 'Romantic love conceptualised as an attachment process', *Journal of Personality and Social Psychology*, 52, pp.511-24.

Hazen, N.L. and Durrett, M.E. (1982) 'Relationship of security of attachment to exploration and cognitive mapping abilities in 2-year-olds', *Developmental Psychology*, 18, pp.751-9.

Healy, A.F. (1976) 'Detection errors on the word "the": evidence for reading units larger than letters', *Journal of Experimental Psychology: Human Perception and Performance*, 2 (2), pp.235-42.

Healy, S.D., Gwinner, E., and Krebs, J.R. (1996) 'Hippocampal volume in migratory and non-migratory warblers: effects of age and experience', *Behavioural Brain Research 81* (1-2), 61-68.

Hearold, S. (1986) 'A synthesis of 1,043 effects of television on social behaviour', in G. Comstock (ed.) *Public Communications and Behaviour*, Vol. I, New York: Academic Press.

Heather, N. (1976) *Radical perspectives in psychology*, London: Methuen.

Hebb, D.O. (1949) *Organisation of Behaviour*, New York: Wiley.

Hebb, D.O. (1958) *A Textbook of Psychology*, Philadelphia: W.B. Saunders.

Hedge, A. and Yousif, Y.H. (1992) 'The effect of urban size, cost and urgency on helpfulness: a cross-cultural comparison between the United Kingdom and the Sudan', *Journal of Cross-Cultural Psychology*, 23, pp.107-15.

Heider, K.G. (1976) 'Dani sexuality: a low energy system', *Man*, 11, pp.188-201.

Heisenberg, W. (1927) 'Uber den anschlauchichen Inhalt der quantentheoretischen Kinetik und Mechanik'. *Zeitschrift für Physik*, 43, pp.172-98.

Helmholtz, H.L.F. von (1896) *Vorträge und Reden*, Braunschweig: Vieweg und Sohn.

Hendrick, C. and Hendrick, S. (1986) 'A theory and method of love', *Journal of Personality and Social Psychology*, 50, pp.392-402.

Hendrick, S.S. and Hendrick, C. (1992) *Liking, Loving and Relating* (2nd edn), Pacific Grove, CA: Brooks/Cole.

Herek, G.M. (1989) 'Gay and lesbian youth', *Journal of Homosexuality*, 17, pp.1-4.

Hering, E. (1964) *Outlines of a Theory of the Light Sense* (trans. L. Hurvich and D. Jameson) Cambridge, MA: Harvard University Press (original work published in 1878).

Herrnstein, R.J. and Murray, C. (1994) *The Bell Curve: Intelligence and Class Structure in American Life*, New York: The Free Press.

Herzlich, C. (1973) *Health and Illness: A Social Psychological Analysis*, London: Academic Press.

Hewstone, M., Stroebe, W., Codol, J.P. and Stephenson, G.M. (1988) *Introduction to Social Psychology: A European perspective*, Oxford: Blackwell.

Heyes, C.M. (1995) 'Self-recognition in primates: further reflections create a hall of mirrors', *Animal Behaviour*, 50, pp.1533-42.

Heyes, C.M. (1998) 'Theory of mind in nonhuman primates', *Behavioural and Brain Sciences*, 21 (1), pp.101-34.

Hilgard, E.R., Irvine, R.P. and Whipple, J.E. (1953) 'Rote memorization, understanding and transfer: an extension of Katona's card trick experiment', *Journal of Experimental Psychology*, 46, pp.288-92.

Hill, E. and Williamson, J. (1998) 'Choose six numbers, any numbers', *The Psychologist*, 11, pp.17-21.

Hill, K. and Kaplan, H. (1988) 'Tradeoffs in male and female reproductive strategies among the Ache: Part 1', in L. Betzig, M. Borgerhoff Mulder and P. Turke (eds) *Human Reproductive Behaviour: A Darwinian perspective*, Cambridge: Cambridge University Press, pp.277-89.

Hill, R. (1970) *Family Development in Three Generations*, Cambridge, MA: Schenkman.

Hilton, D.J. and Slugoski, B.R. (1986) 'Knowledge-based causal attribution: the abnormal conditions focus model', *Psychological Review*, 93, pp.75-88.

Hinde, R.A. (1977) 'Mother–infant separation and the nature of inter-individual relationships: experiments with rhesus monkeys', *Proceedings of the Royal Society of London* (B), 196, pp.29-50.

Hinde, R.A. and Fisher, J. (1951) 'Further observations on the opening of milk bottles by birds', *British Birds*, 44, pp.392-96.

Hiroto, D.S. and Seligman, M.E.P. (1975) 'Generality of learnt helplessness in man', *Journal of Personality and Social Psychology*, 31, pp.311–27.

Hladik, E.G. and Edwards, H.T. (1984) 'A comparative analysis of mother-father speech in the naturalistic home environment', *Journal of Psycholinguistic Research*, 13, pp.321-32.

Hoaker, P. and Schnurr, R. (1980) 'Genetic factors in obsessive-compulsive neurosis', *Canadian Journal of Psychiatry*, 25, pp.167-72.

Hobson, J.A. (1988) *The Dreaming Brain*, New York: Basic Books.

Hochberg, J. and Brooks, V. (1962) 'Pictorial recognition as an unlearned ability. A study of one child's performance', *American Journal of Psychology*, 75, pp.624-8.

Hockett, C.F. (1959) 'Animal "languages" and human language', *Human Biology*, 31, pp.32-9.

Hockett, C.F. (1960) 'Logical considerations in the study of animal communication', in W.E. Lanyon and W.N. Tavolga (eds) *Animal Sounds and Communication*, Washington, DC: American Institute of Biological Sciences.

Hodges, J. and Tizard, B. (1989) 'Social and family relationships of ex-institutional adolescents', *Journal of Child Psychology and Psychiatry*, 30(1), pp.77–97.

Hoffman, C., Lau, I. and Johnson, D.R. (1986) 'The linguistic relativity of person cognition', *Journal of Personality and Social Psychology*, 51, pp.1097-1105.

Hofling, C.K., Brotzman, E., Dalrymple, S., Graves, N. and Pierce, C.M. (1966) 'An experimental study in nurse-physician relationships', *Journal of Nervous and Mental Disease*, 143, pp.171-80.

Hofstede, G. (1980) *Culture's Consequences: International Differences in Work related Values*, Beverley Hills, CA: Sage.

Hofstede, G. (1994) *Cultures and Organizations: Software of the Mind*, London: Harper-Collins.

Hoge, S.K., Appelbaum, P.S., Lawler, T., Beck, J.C., Litman, R., Greer, A., Gutheil, T.G. and Kaplan, E. (1990) 'A prospective, multicenter study of patient's refusal of antipsychotic medication', *Archives of General Psychiatry*, 47, pp.949-56.

Hogg, M.A. and Vaughan, G.M. (1995, 1998/2nd edn) *Social Psychology*, Hemel Hempstead: Prentice Hall/Harvester Wheatsheaf.

Hohmann, G.W. (1966) 'Some effects of spinal cord lesions on experimental emotional feelings', *Psychophysiology*, 3, pp.143-56.

Holden, C. (1997) 'National Institute of Health to explore St John's Wort', *Science*, 278, p. 391.

Hole, R.W., Rush, A.J. and Beck, A.T. (1979) 'A cognitive investigation of schizophrenic delusions', *Psychiatry*, 42, pp.312-19.

Holland, A.J., Hall, D.J., Murrey, R., Russell, G.F.M. and Crisp, A.H. (1984) 'Anorexia Nervosa: A study of 34 twin pairs and one set of triplets', *British Journal of Psychiatry*, 145, pp.414–18.

Hölldobler, B. (1971) 'Communication between ants and their guests', *Scientific American*, 224, pp.86-93.

Hollis, K.L. (1984) 'The biological function of Pavlovian conditioning: the best offence is a good defence', *Journal of Experimental Psychology: Animal Behaviour Processes*, 10, pp.413-25.

Hollis, K.L. (1990) 'The role of Pavlovian conditioning in territorial aggression and reproduction', in D.A. Dewsbury (ed.) *Contemporary Issues in Comparative Psychology*, Sunderland, MA: Sinaur Associates.

Hollis, K.L., Pharr, V.L., Dumas, M.J., Britton, G.B. and Field, J. (1997) 'Classical conditioning provides paternity advantage for territorial male blue gouramis (*Trichogaster trichopterous*)', *Journal of Comparative Psychology*, 111, pp.219-25.

Hollon, S.D., DeRubeis, R.J., Evans, M.D., Wiemer, M.J., Garvey, M.J., Grove, W.M. and Tuason, V.B. (1992) 'Cognitive therapy and pharmacotherapy for depression: singly and in combination', *Archives of General Psychiatry*, 49, pp.774-809.

Holmes, D.S. (1990) 'The evidence for repression: an examination of sixty years of research', in J. Singer (ed.) *Repression and Dissociation: Implications for Personality Theory, Psychopathology and Health*, Chicago: University of Chicago Press.

Holmes, D.S. (1993) 'Aerobic fitness and the response to psychological stress' in P. Seraganian (ed.) *Exercise Psychology: The Influence of Physical Exercise on Psychological Processes*, New York: Wiley.

Holmes, J. (1993) *John Bowlby and Attachment Theory*, London: Routledge.

Holmes, T.H. and Rahe, R.H. (1967) 'The social readjustment rating scale', *Journal of Psychosomatic Research*, 11, pp.213-18.

Holmes, W.G. and Sherman, P.W. (1982) 'The ontogeny of kin recognition in two species of ground squirrels', *Animal Behaviour*, 34, pp.38-47.

Holtgrave, D.R., Tinsley, B.J. and Kay, L.S. (1994) 'Heuristics, biases and environmental health risk analysis', in L. Heath, R.S. Tindale, J. Edwards, E.J. Posovac, F.B. Bryant, E. Henderson-King, Y. Suarez-Balcazar and J. Myers (eds) *Applications of Heuristics and Biases to Social Issues*, New York: Plenum.

Homan, R. (1991) *Ethics of Social Research*, Harlow: Longman.

Home Office (2003) www.homeoffice.gov.uk/docs2/reg toxicologydraftrevision4_03.html

Hope-Simpson, R.E. (1981) 'The role of season in the epidemiology of schizophrenia', *Journal of Hygiene*, 86, pp.35-47.

Horn, J.L. (1994) 'Crowding', in R. Corsini (ed.) *Encyclopedia of Psychology*, Vol. 1 (2nd edn), New York: John Wiley.

Horn, J.M. (1983) 'The Texas Adoption Project: adopted children and their intellectual resemblance to biological and adoptive parents', *Child Development*, 54, pp.266-75.

Horne, J. (1978) 'A review of the biological effects of total sleep deprivation in man', *Biological Psychology*, 7, pp.55-102.

Horne, J. (1988) *Why We Sleep*, Oxford: Oxford University Press.

Horowitz, F.D. (1993) 'The need for a comprehensive new environmentalism', in R. Plomin and G.E. McClearn (1993) (eds) *Nature, Nurture and Psychology*, Washington, DC: American Psychological Association.

Horowitz, M.J. (1975) 'Intrusive and repetitive thoughts after experimental stress', *Archives of General Psychiatry*, 32, pp.223-8.

Horrobin, D.F. (1998) 'Schizophrenia: the illness that made us human', *Medical Hypotheses*, 50, pp.269-88.

Howell, E. (1981) 'The influence of gender on diagnosis and psychopathology', in E. Howell and M. Bayes (eds) *Women and Mental Health*, New York: Basic Books.

Howell, N. (1979) *Demography of the Dobe !Kung*, New York: Academic Press.

Howes, C., Galinsky, E. and Kontos, S. (1998) 'Caregiver sensitivity and attachment', *Social Development*, 7(1), pp.25–36.

Howitt, D. and Owusu-Bempah, J. (1994) *The racism of Psychology: Time for change*, Hemel Hempstead: Harvester.

Hsu, I.K.G. (1990) *Eating Disorders*, New York: Guildford Press.

Hubel, D.H. and Wiesel, T.N. (1959) 'Receptive fields of single neurons in the cat's visual cortex', *Journal of Physiology*, 148, pp.574-91.

Hubel, D.H. and Wiesel, T.N. (1962) 'Receptive fields, binocular interaction and functional architecture in the cat's visual cortex', *Journal of Physiology*, 160, pp.106-54.

Hubel, D.H. and Wiesel, T.N. (1979) 'Brain mechanisms of vision', *Scientific American*, 82, pp.84-97.

Hudson, W. (1960) 'Pictorial depth perception in sub-cultural groups in Africa', *Journal of Social Psychology*, 52, pp.183-208.

Hudson, W. (1962) 'Pictorial perception and educational adaptation in Africa', *Psychologica Africana*, 9, pp.226-39.

Huesmann, L.R. (1982) 'Television and aggressive behaviour', in D. Pearl, L. Bouthilet and J. Lazar (eds) *Television and Behaviour: Ten Years of Scientific Progress and Implications for the Eighties*. Vol. 2: *Technical Reviews*, Rockville, MD: National Institute of Mental Health.

Huesmann, L.R. (1988) 'An information processing model for the development of aggression', *Aggressive Behaviour*, 14, pp.13-24.

Hugh, M. (1998) *Counselling Skills and Theory*, London: Hodder & Stoughton.

Hughes, M. (1975) 'Egocentrism in preschool children', Unpublished PhD thesis, University of Edinburgh, UK.

Hull, C.L. (1943) *Principles of Behavior*, New York: Appleton-Century-Crofts.

Humphreys, P.W. (1997) 'Social, cultural and subcultural differences in the determination of (ab)normality', *Psychology Review*, 3 (4), pp.10-15.

Humphreys, P.W. (1999) 'Culture-bound syndromes', *Psychology Review*, 6 February, pp.14-18.

Hunt, E. and Agnoli, F. (1991) 'The Whorfian hypothesis: a cognitive psychological perspective', *Psychological Review*, 98, pp.377-89.

Hunt, H. (1989) *The Multiplicity of Dreams: Memory, Imagination, and Consciousness*, New Haven, CT: Yale University press.

Hunt, R.R. and Elliott, J.M. (1980) 'The role of non-semantic information in memory: orthographic distinctiveness on retention', *Journal of Experimental Psychology: General*, 109, pp.49–74.

Hunter, M., Philips, C. and Rachman, S. (1979) 'Memory for pain', *Pain*, 6, pp.35–46.

Hurvich, L. and Jameson, D. (1957) 'An opponent-process theory of colour vision', *Psychological Review*, 64, pp.384-404.

Hyde, T.S. and Jenkins, J.J. (1973) 'Recall for words as a function of semantic, graphic and syntactic orienting tasks', *Journal of Verbal Learning and Verbal Behaviour*, 12, pp.471–80.

Ineichen, B., Harrison, G. and Morgan, H.G. (1984) 'Psychiatric hospital admissions in Bristol: 1. Geographical and ethnic factors', *British Journal of Psychiatry*, 145, pp.600-4.

Ingoldsby, B.B. (1995) 'Mate selection and marriage', in B.B. Ingoldsby and S. Smith (eds) *Families in Multicultural Perspective*, New York: Guilford.

Inoue-Nakamura, N. and Matsuzawa, T. (1997) 'Development of stone tool use by wild chimpanzees (*Pan troglodytes*)', *Journal of Comparative Psychology*, 111, pp.159-73.

Insko, C.A., Drenan, S., Soloman, M.R., Smith, R. and Wade, T.J. (1983) 'Conformity as a function of the consistency of positive self-evaluation and being liked and being right', *Journal of Experimental Social Psychology*, 19, pp.341–58.

Isabella, R.A., Belsky, J. and Von Eye, A. (1989) 'Origins of infant–mother attachment: an examination of interactional synchrony during the infant's first year', *Developmental Psychology*, 25, pp.12–21.

Isack, H.A. and Reyer, H.U. (1989) 'Honeyguides and honey gatherers: interspecific communication in a symbiotic relationship', *Science*, 243, pp.1343-6.

Isen, A.M. (1984) 'Toward understanding the role of affect in cognition', in R.S. Wyer and T.K. Krull (eds) *Handbook of Social Cognition*, Hillsdale, NJ: Erlbaum.

Islam, M.R. and Hewstone, M. (1993) 'Dimensions of contact as predictors of intergroup anxiety, perceived outgroup variability and outgroup attitude: an integrative model', *Personality and Social Psychology Bulletin*, 19, pp.700-10.

Jacklin, C.N. and Maccoby, E.E. (1978) 'Social behaviour at 33 months in same-sex and mixed-sex dyads', *Child Development*, 49, pp.557-69.

Jacobsen, E. (1932) 'The electrophysiology of mental activities', *American Journal of Psychology*, 44, pp.677-94.

Jahoda, G. (1971) 'Retinal pigmentation, illusion perceptibility and space perception', *International Journal of Psychology*, 6, pp.199-208.

Jahoda, M. (1958) *Current Concepts of Positive Mental Health*, New York: Basic Books.

James, W. (1884) 'What is an emotion?', *Mind*, 19, pp.188-205.

James, W. (1890) cited in Thigpen, C. and Cleckey, H. (1954) 'A case of multiple personality disorder', *Journal of Abnormal and Social Psychology*, 49, pp.135-51.

Jarrett, R.B., Schaffer, M., McIntire, D., Witt-Browder, A., Kraft, D. and Risser, R.C. (1999) 'Treatment of atypical depression with cognitive therapy or phenalzine: a double-blind placebo-controlled trial', *Archives of General Psychiatry*, 56, pp.431-7.

Jarvis, M. (2000) *Theoretical approaches in Psychology*, London: Routledge.

Jennings, G., Nelson, L., Nestel, P., Esler, M., Korner, P., Burton, D. and Bazelmans, J. (1986) 'The effects of changes in physical activity on major cardiovascular risk factors, hemodynamics, sympathetic function, and glucose utilization in man: a controlled study of four levels of activity', *Circulation*, 73, pp.30–40.

Jensen, A.J. (1999) 'Adolescent storm and stress, reconsidered', *American Psychologist*, 54 (5), pp.317-26.

Jensen, A.R. (1969) 'How much can we boost IQ and scholastic achievement?', *Harvard Educational Review*, 39, pp.1-123.

Jerison, H.J. (1973) *Evolution of the Brain and Intelligence*, New York: Academic Press.

Jimerson, D.C., Wolfe, B.E., Metzger, E.D., Finkelstein, D.M., Cooper, T.B. and Levine, J.M. (1997) 'Decreased seratonin function in bulimia nervosa', *Archives of General Psychiatry*, 54. pp.529–33.

Jobanputra, J. (1995) 'Psychology and racism: views from the inside', *Psychology Teaching*, 4, Association of Teachers in Psychology, Leicester: British Psychological Society.

Johansson, G. (1975) 'Visual motion perception', *Scientific American*, 232, pp.76-89.

Johansson, G., Aronsson, G. and Linstrom, B.O. (1978) 'Social psychological and neuroendocrine stress reactions in highly mechanised work', *Ergonomics*, 21, pp.583–99.

Johnson, H., Olafsson, K., Anderson, J. and Pledge, P. (1989) 'Lithium every second day', *American Journal of Psychiatry*, 146, p. 557.

Johnson, J.R. and Ramsted, V. (1983) 'Cognitive development in preadolescent language impaired children', *British Journal of Disorders of Communication*, 18, pp.49-55.

Johnson, R.D. (1987) 'Making judgements when information is missing: inferences, biases and framing effects', *Acta Psychologica*, 66, pp.69-72.

Johnson, T.J., Feigenbaum, R. and Weiby, C.R. (1964) 'Some determinants and consequences of the teacher's perception of causality', *Journal of Educational Psychology*, 55, pp.237-46.

Johnston, A., DeLuca, D., Murtaugh, K. and Diener, E. (1977) 'Validation of a laboratory play measure of child aggression', *Child Development*, 48, pp.324-7.

Johnston, W.A. and Heinz, S.P. (1978) 'Flexibility and capacity demands of attention', *Journal of Experimental Psychology: General*, 107, pp.420-35.

Johnston, W.A. and Heinz, S.P. (1979) 'Depth of non-target processing in an attention task', *Journal of Experimental Psychology*, 5, pp.168-175.

Johnstone, L. (1989) *Users and Abusers of Psychiatry: A Critical Look at Traditional Psychiatric Practice*, London: Routledge.

Joiner, T.E. Jr, Heatherton, T.F. and Keel, P.K. (1997) 'Ten-year stability and predictive validity of five bulimia-related indicators', *American Journal of Psychiatry*, 154, pp.1133–8.

Jolicoeur, P. and Landau, M.J. (1984) 'Effects of orientation on the identification of simple visual patterns', *Canadian Journal of Psychology*, 38, pp.80-93.

Jones, D. and Elcock, J. (2001) *History and theories of Psychology: A critical perspective*, London: Hodder.

Jones, D.N., Pickett, J., Oates, M.R. and Barbor, P. (1987) *Understanding Child Abuse* (2nd edn), London: Macmillan.

Jones, E.E. and Nisbett, R.E. (1971) *The Actor and the Observer; Divergent Perceptions of the Causes of Behaviour*. Morristown, NJ: General Learning Press.

Jones, J. (1999) *On the Distinction between Ethics and Morality*, Department of Philosophy, Raritan Valley Community College.

Kaffman, M. (1993) 'Divorce in the Kibbutz: lessons to be drawn', *Family Process*, 32 (1), pp.117-33.

Kagan, J. (1982) *Psychology Research on the Human Infant: An Evaluative Summary*, New York: W.T. Grant Foundation.

Kagawa, Y. (1978) 'Impact of westernization on the nutrition of Japanese: changes in physique, cancer, longevity and centenarians', *Preventive Medicine*, 7, pp.205-217.

Kahn, R.L. and Antonucci T.C. (1980) 'Convoys over the life course: Attachments, roles and social support', in P.B. Baltes and O.G. Brim, Jr (eds) *Life-span Development and Behaviour* (Vol. 3), New York: Academic Press.

Kahneman, D. (1973) *Attention and Effort*, Englewood Cliffs, NJ: Prentice Hall.

Kahneman, D. and Tversky, A. (1972) 'Subjective probability: a judgement of representativeness', *Cognitive Psychology*, 3, pp.430-54.

Kahneman, D. and Tversky, A. (1973) 'On the psychology of prediction', *Psychological Review*, 80 (4), pp.237-51.

Kalven, H. Jr, and Zeisel, H. (1966) *The American Jury*, Chicago: University of Chicago Press.

Kamarck, T.W., Peterman, A.H. and Raynor, D.A. (1998) 'The effects of the social environment on stress-related cardiovascular activation: current findings, prospects, and implications', *Annals of Behavioral Medicine*, 20, pp.247–56.

Kamen, L.P. and Seligman, M.E.P. (1989) 'Explanatory style and health', in M. Johnston and T. Martineau (eds) *Applications in Health Psychology*, New Brunswick: Transaction.

Kamin, L.J. (1977) *The Science and Politics of IQ*, Harmondsworth, Middlesex: Penguin.

Kamo, Y. (1993) 'Determinants of marital satisfaction. – A comparison of the United States and Japan', *Journal of Social and Personal Relationships*. 10(4), pp.551-68.

Kandel, ER (1979) *Behavioural biology of Aplysia*, San Francisco: W.H.Freeman & Co.

Kanner, A.D., Coyne, J.C., Schaefer, C. and Lazarus, R.S. (1981) 'Comparison of two modes of stress measurement: daily hassles and uplifts versus major life events', *Journal of Behavioural Measurement*, 4, pp.1–39.

Karni, A., Tanne, D., Rubinstein, B.S., Askenasy, J.J. and Sagi, D. (1994) 'Dependence on REM sleep of overnight improvement of a perceptual skill', *Science*, 265, pp.679-82.

Karp, M. (1995) 'An introduction to psychodrama counselling', *Journal of the British Association of Counselling*, 6(4), pp.294-8.

Katz, D. and Braly, K.W. (1933) 'Racial stereotypes of 100 college students', *Journal of Abnormal and Social Psychology*, 28, pp.280-90.

Katz, P.A. (1987) 'Variations in family constellation: effects on gender schemata', in L.S. Liben and M.L. Signorella (eds) *Studies in mother-infant interaction*, London: Academic Press.

Kaufman, M. (1993) 'Divorce in the Kibbutz: Lessons to be drawn', *Family Process*. 32(1), pp.117-33.

Kawai, M. (1965) 'Newly-acquired pre-cultural behavior of the natural troop of Japanese Monkeys on Koshima Islet', *Primates*, 6(1), pp.1-30.

Kaya, N. and Erkíp, F. (1999) 'Invasion of personal space under the condition of short-term crowding: a case study on an automatic teller machine', *Journal of Environmental Psychology*, 19, pp.183-9.

Kaye, K.L. and Bower, T.G.R. (1994) 'Learning and intermodal transfer of information in new-borns', *Psychological Science*, 5, pp.286-88.

Keesey, R.E. and Corbett, S.W. (1983) 'Metabolic defence of the body weight set-point', in A.J. Stunkard and E. Stellar (eds) *Eating and Its Disorders*, New York: Raven Press.

Keeton, W.T. (1971) 'Magnets interfere with pigeon homing', *Proceedings of the National Academy of Sciences*, 68 (1), pp.102-6.

Keith, S.J., Regier, D.A. and Rae, D.S. (1991) 'Schizophrenic disorders', in L.N. Robins and D.S. Regier (eds) *Psychiatric Disorders in America: The Epidemiological Catchment Area Study*, New York: Free Press.

Kelley, H.H. (1967) 'Attribution theory in social psychology', in D. Levine (ed.) *Nebraska Symposium on Motivation*, Vol. 15, Lincoln, NE: Nebraska University Press.

Kelley, H.H. (1972) 'Causal schemata and the attribution process', in E.E. Jones *et al.* (eds) *Attribution: Perceiving the Causes of Behaviour*, Morristown, NJ: General Learning Press.

Kelley, H.H., Berscheid, E., Christensen, A., Harvey, J.H., Huston, T.L., Levinger, G., McClintock, E., Pellau, L.A. and Peterson, D.R. (1983) *Close Relationships*, New York: W.H. Freeman.

Kelly-Radford, L. (1999) 'Diversity', Paper presented at the National Institute for Occupational Safety and Health/American Psychological Association Conference on Work Stress and Health, March 1999.

Kelman, H.C. (1958) 'Compliance, identification and internalisation: three processes of attitude change', *Journal of Conflict Resolution*, 2, pp.51–60.

Kendler, K.S. Masterson, C.C. and Davis, K.L. (1985) 'Psychiatric illness in first degree relatives of patients with paranoid psychosis, schizophrenia and medical controls', *British Journal of Psychiatry*, 147, pp.524-31.

Kendler, K.S., McLean, C., Neale, M., Kessler, R., Heath, A. and Eaves, L. (1991) 'The genetic epidemiology of bulimia nervosa', *American Journal of Psychiatry*, 148, pp.1627–37.

Kendler, K.S., Neale, M.C., Kessler, R.C., Heath, A.C. and Eaves, L.J. (1992a) 'Major depression and generalized anxiety disorder', *Archives of General Psychiatry*, 49, pp.716-22.

Kenrick, D.T. and MacFarlane, S.W. (1986) 'Ambient temperature and horn honking: a field study of the heat/aggression relationship', *Environment and Behaviour*, 18, pp.179-91.

Kerckhoff, A.C. and Davis, K.E. (1962) 'Value consensus and need complementarity in mate selection', *American Sociological Review*, 27, pp.250-95.

Kerr, P. (1982, Sept 16) 'Now, computerized bulletin boards', *New York Times*, pp.Cl, C7.

Kessler, R.C., McGonagle, K.A., Zhao, S., Nelson, C.B., Highes, M., Eshleman, S., Wittchen, H.U. and Kendler, K.S. (1994) 'Lifetime and 12-month prevalence of DSM-III-R psychiatric disorders in the United States', *Archives of General Psychiatry*, 51, pp.8-19.

Kettlewell, H.B.D. (1955) 'Selection experiments on industrial melanism in the Lepidoptera', *Heredity*, 9, pp.323–42.

Kety, S.S., Wender, P.H., Jacobsen, B., Ingraham, L.J., Jansson, L., Faber, B. and Kinney, D.K. (1994) 'Mental illness in the biological and adoptive relatives of schizophrenia adoptees', *Archives of General Psychiatry*, 51, pp.442-55.

Khan, A. and Khan, S. (2000) 'Are placebo controls ethical in antidepressant clinical trials?', *Psychiatric Times*, 17 (4).

Kiecolt-Glaser, J.K., Dura, J.R., Speicher, C.E., Trask, O.J. and Glaser, R. (1991) 'Spousal caregivers of dementia victims: longitudinal changes in immunity and health', *Psychosomatic Medicine*, 53, pp.345–62.

Kiecolt-Glaser, J.K., Fisher, L.D., Ogrocki, P., Stout, J.C., Speicher, C.E. and Glaser, R. (1987) 'Marital quality, marital disruption, and immune function', *Psychosomatic Medicine*, 49, pp.13–34.

Kiecolt-Glaser, J.K., Garner, W., Speicher, C., Penn, G.M., Holliday, J. and Glaser, R. (1984) 'Psychosocial modifiers of immunocompetence in medical students', *Psychosomatic Medicine*, 46, pp.7–14.

Kiecolt-Glaser, J.K., Glaser, R., Cacioppo, J.T. and Malarkey, W.B. (1998) 'Marital stress: immunologic, neuroendocrine, and autonomic correlates', *Annals of the New York Academy of Sciences*, 840, pp.656–63.

Kilham, W. and Mann, L. (1974) 'Level of destructive obedience as a function of transmitter and executant roles in the Milgram obedience paradigm', *Journal of Personality and Social Psychology*, 29, pp.696-702.

Kiloh, L.G., Gye, R.S., Rushworth, R.G., Bell, D.S. and White, R.T. (1974) 'Stereotactic amygdaloidotomy for aggressive behavior', *Journal of Neurology, Neurosurgery, and Psychiatry*, 37, pp.437-44.

Kim, H.K. and McKenry, P.C. (1998) 'Social networks and support: A comparison of African Americans, Asian Americans, Caucasians, and Hispanics', *Journal of Comparative Family Studies*, 29, pp.313–36.

Kim, U. and Berry, J.W. (1993) *Indigenous Psychologies: Research and Experience in Cultural Context (Cross-Cultural Research and Methodology*, Vol. 17), London: Sage.

Kimmel, A.J. (1996) *Ethical Issues in Behavioural Research: A Survey*, Cambridge, MA: Blackwell.

Kimura, D. (1992) 'Sex differences in the brain', *Scientific American*, 10, pp.26-31

Kingdon, D.G. and Turkington, D. (1994) *Cognitive-Behavioural Therapy of Schizophrenia*, Hove: Erlbaum.

Kirchler, E., Pombeni, M.L. and Palmonari, A. (1991) 'Sweet sixteen ... Adolescents' problems and the peer group as a source of support', *European Journal of Psychology and Education*, 6, pp.393-410.

Kirchner, W.H. and Towne, W.F. (1994) 'The sensory basis of the honey bee's dance language', *Scientific American*, (June) 270, pp.52-9.

Kirsch, I., Moore, T.J., Scoboria, A. and Nicholls, S.S. (2002) 'The emperor's new drugs: an analysis of antidepressant medication data submitted to the U.S. Food and Drug Administration. Prevention and Treatment 5:Article 23', available at:journals.apa.org/prevention/volume5/pre0050023a.html.

Kitzinger, C., and Coyle, A. (1995) 'Lesbian and gay couples: Speaking of difference', *The Psychologist*, 8, pp.64–9.

Klaus, M.H. and Kennell, J.H. (1976) *Parent–Infant Bonding*, St Louis: Mosby.

Kleiner, L. and Marshall, W.L. (1987) 'Interpersonal problems and agoraphobia', *Journal of Anxiety Disorders*, 1, pp.313-23.

Kleinginna, P.R.Jr. and Kleinginna, A.M. (1981) 'A categorised list of emotional definitions, with suggestions for a consensual definition', *Motivation and Emotion*, 5, pp.345-79.

Kleitman, N. (1963) *Sleep and Wakefulness* (2nd edn), Chicago: Chicago University Press.

Klerman, G.L. (1988) 'Depression and related disorders of mood (affective disorders)', in A.M. Nicholi Jr (ed.) *The New Harvard Guide to Psychiatry,* Cambridge, Massachussets: Harvard University Press.

Kline, P. (1988) *Psychology Exposed, or, The Emperor's New Clothes,* London: Routledge.

Klinowska, M. (1994) 'Brains, behaviour and intelligence in cetaceans', *11 Essays on Whales and Man* (2nd edn), High North Alliance.

Kluft, R.P. (1984) 'Introduction to multiple personality disorder', *Psychiatric Annals,* 14, pp.19-24.

Kluver, H. and Bucy, P. (1939) 'Preliminary analysis of functions of the temporal lobes in monkeys', *Archives of Neurology and Psychiatry,* 42, pp.979-1000.

Knapp, R. (1997) 'Stuttering', www.rogerknapp.com/medical/stutter.htm. Accessed December 2003.

Knight, R. and Knight, M. (1959) *A Modern Introduction to Psychology,* London: University Tutorial Press.

Kobasa, S.C. (1979) 'Stressful life events, personality, and health: an enquiry into hardiness', *Journal of Personality and Social Psychology,* 37, pp.1-11.

Kobasa, S.C. and Maddi, S.R. (1977) 'Existential personality theory', in R. Corsini (ed.) *Current Personality Theories,* Itasca: Peacock.

Kobasa, S.C., Maddi, S.R., Puccetti, M.C. and Zola, M.A. (1985) 'Effectiveness of hardiness, exercise and social support as resources against illness', *Journal of Psychosomatic Research,* 29, pp.525–33.

Koestner, R. and Wheeler, L. (1988) 'Self presentation in personal advertisements: the influence of implicit notions of attraction and role expectations', *Journal of Social and Personality Psychology,* 5, pp.149-60.

Kohlberg, L. (1966) 'A cognitive-developmental analysis of children's sex-role concepts and attitudes', in E.E. Maccoby (ed.), *The Development of Sex Differences,* Stanford, CA: Stanford University Press.

Kohlberg, L. (1969) 'Stage and sequence: the cognitive-developmental approach to socialization', in D.A. Goslin (ed.), *Handbook of Socialization Theory and Research,* Chicago: Rand McNally.

Kohlberg, L. (1969) *Stages in the Development of Moral Thought and Action,* New York: Holt.

Kohlberg, L. (1973) 'Continuities in childhood and adult moral development revisited', in P.B. Baltes and K.E. Schaie, *Lifespan Development Psychology* (2nd edn), New York: Academic Press.

Kohlberg, L. (1976) 'Moral stages and moralization', in T. Likona (ed.), *Moral Development and Behaviour,* New York: Holt, Rinehart & Winston.

Kohler, W. (1925) *The Mentality of Apes,* New York: Harcourt Brace Jovanovich.

Kohn, A. (1993) *Punished by Rewards,* Boston: Houghton Mifflin.

Kolota, G. (1987) 'Associations or rules in learning languages?', *Science,* 237, pp.113-14.

Koluchová, J. (1976) 'A report on the further development of twins after severe and prolonged deprivation', in A.M. Clarke and A.D.B. Clarke (eds) *Early Experience Myth and Evidence,* London: Open Books.

Koriat, A. and Goldsmith, M. (1996) 'Memory metaphors and the real life/laboratory controversy: correspondence versus storehouse conceptions of memory', *Behavioural and Brain Sciences,* 19, pp.167–228.

Korte, C. and Kerr, N. (1975) 'Response to altruistic opportunities in urban and nonurban settings', *Journal of Social Psychology,* 95, pp.183-4.

Korte, C. and Ayvalioglu, N. (1981) 'Helpfulness in Turkey: Cities, towns, and urban villages', *Journal of Cross-Cultural Psychology,* 12, pp.123-41.

Kramer, G. (1952) 'Experiments on bird orientation', *Ibis,* 94, pp.265-85.

Krantz, S.E. and Rude, S. (1984) 'Depressive attributions: selection of difference causes or assignment of different meanings?', *Journal of Personality and Social Psychology,* 47, pp.103-203.

Krebs, J.R., Sherry, D.F., Healy, S.D., Perry, V.H. and Vaccarino, A.L. (1989) 'Hippocampal specialisation of food-storing birds', *Proceedings of the National Academy of Sciences USA,* 86, pp.1388-92.

Kreithen, M.L. (1975) 'Effects of magnetism, barometric pressure and polarized light on the homing pigeon', Thesis: Cornell University.

Kroger, J. (1996) *Identity in Adolescence: The balance between self and other* (2nd edn), London: Routledge.

Kruger, A.C. (1992) 'The effect of peer and adult-child transactive discussions on moral reasoning', *Merill-Palmer Quarterly,* 38, pp.191-211.

Kübler-Ross, E. (1969) *On Death and Dying,* New York: Macmillan.

Kuczaj, S.A. (1977) 'The acquisition of regular and irregular past tense forms', *Journal of Verbal Learning and Verbal Behaviour,* 16, pp.589-600.

Kuhl, P. (1981) 'Discrimination of speech by nonhuman animals: basic auditory sensitivities conducive to the perception of speech-sound categories', *Journal of the Acoustical Society of America,* 70, pp.340-9.

Kuhn, T.S. (1962) *The Structure of Scientific Revolutions,* Chicago: University of Chicago Press.

Kulik, J.A. and Mahler, H.I.M. (1989) 'Social support and recovery from surgery', *Health Psychology,* 8, pp.221–38.

Kunda, Z. and Nisbett, R.E. (1986) 'The psychometrics of everyday life', *Cognitive Psychology,* 18, pp.195-224.

Kupersmidt, J.B. and Coie, J.D. (1990) 'Pre-adolescent peer status, aggression, and school adjustment andd predictors of externalizing problems in adolescence', *Child Development,* 53, pp.1350-63.

LaBerge, S. (1985) *Lucid Dreaming,* Los Angeles: Jeremy Tarcher.

Labov, W. (1970) 'The logic of non-standard English', in J.E. Alatis (ed.) *20th Annual Round Table,* Washington, DC: Georgetown University Press.

Labov, W. (1972) *Language in the Inner City: Studies in the Black English Vernacular,* Philadelphia: University of Pennsylvania Press.

Lacan, J. (1966) 'Function et champ de la parole et du language en psychoanalyse', *Ecrits,* Paris: Seuil.

Lakatos, I. (1970) 'Falsification and the methodology of scientific research programmes', in I. Lakatos and A. Musgrave (eds) *Criticism and the growth of knowledge,* Cambridge: Cambridge University Press.

Lam, R.W., Zis, A.P., Grewal, A., Delgado, P.L., Charney, D.S. and Krystal, J.H. (1996) 'Effects of rapid tryptophan depletion in patients with seasonal affective disorder in remission after light therapy', *Archives of General Psychiatry,* 53, pp.41-4.

Lamb, M.E. (1977) 'The development of mother–infant and father–infant attachments in the second year of life', *Developmental Psychology,* 13, pp.637–48.

Lamb, M.E. and Roopnarine, J.L. (1979) 'Peer influences on sex-role development in preschoolers', *Child Development,* 50, pp.1219-22.

Lambe, E.K., Katzman, D.K., Mikulis, D.J., Kennedy, S.H. and Zipursky, R.B. (1997) 'Cerebral gray matter volume deficits after weight recovery from anorexia nervosa', *Archives of General Psychiatry,* 54, pp.537–42.

Lang, F.R. and Carstensen, L.L. (1994) 'Close emotional relationships in later life: Further support for proactive aging in the social domain', *Psychology and Aging,* 9, pp. 315-24.

Lange, C.G. (1885) *The Emotions* (English translation 1922), Baltimore: Williams & Wilkins.

Langer, E.J. and Rodin, J. (1976) 'The effects of choice and enhanced personal responsibility for the aged', *Journal of Personality and Social Psychology,* 34, pp.191–8.

Langer, E.J., Bashner, R.S. and Chanowitz, B. (1985) 'Decreasing prejudice by increasing discrimination', *Journal of Personality and Social Psychology,* 49, pp.113-20.

Langlois, J.H., Roggman, L.A., Casey, R.J., Ritter, J.M., Riser-Danner, L.A. and Jenkins, V.Y. (1987) 'Infant preferences for attractive faces: rudiments of a stereotype?', *Developmental Psychology,* 23 (3), pp.363-9.

Lantz, D. and Stefflre, V. (1964) 'Language and cognition revisited', *Journal of Abnormal Psychology,* 69, pp.472-81.

Larson, R. (1999, September) Unpublished review of J.W. Santrock's *Adolescence* (8th edn), New York: McGraw Hill.

Latané, B. and Darley, J.M. (1970) *The Unresponsive Bystander: Why Doesn't He Help?',* New York: Appleton Century Crofts.

Latané, B. and Nida, S. (1981) 'Ten years of research on group size and helping', *Psychological Bulletin,* 89, pp.308-24.

Latané, B., Williams, K. and Hawkins, S. (1979) 'Many hands make light work: the causes and consequences of social loafing', *Journal of Personality and Social Psychology,* 37, pp.822-32.

Lattal, K.A. and Gleeson, S. (1990) 'Response acquisition with delayed reinforcement', *Journal of Experimental Psychology: Animal Behaviour Processes,* 16, pp.27-39.

Laursen, B. (1995) 'Conflict and social interaction in adolescent relationships', *Journal of Research on Adolescence,* 5, pp.55-70.

Laursen, P. (1997) 'The impact of aging on cognitive functioning: an 11 year follow-up study of four age cohorts', *Acta Neurologica Scandinavica,* 96, No. S172.

Laws, G., Davies, L. and Andrews, C. (1995) 'Linguistic structure and non-linguistic cognition: English and Russian blues compared', *Language and Cognitive Processes,* 10, pp.59-94.

Lazar, I. and Darlington, R. (1982) 'Lasting effects of early education: a report from the Consortium of Longitudinal Studies', *Monographs of the Society for Research in Child Development,* 47(2-3), Serial No. 195.

Lazarus, R.S. (1984) 'On the primacy of cognition', *American Psychologist*, 39, pp.124-9.

Lea, M. and Duck, S. (1982) 'A model for the role of similarity of values in friendship development', *British Journal of Social Psychology*, 21, pp.301-10.

Leary, M.A., Greer, D. and Huston, A.C. (1982) 'The relation between TV viewing and gender roles', Paper presented at the Southwestern Society for Research in Human Development, Galveston, Texas.

LeBon, G. (1947, first published 1895) *The Crowd: A Study of the Popular Mind,* London: Ernest Benn.

Lecrubier, Y., Baker, A., and Dunbar, G. (1997) 'Long term evaluation of paroxetine, clomiphramine and placebo in panic disorder', *Acta Psychiatrica Scandinavica*, 95, pp.153-60.

Lee, V.E., Brookes-Gunn, J., Schnur, E. and Liaw, F. (1990) 'Are Head Start effects sustained? A longitudinal follow-up comparison of disadvantaged children attending Head Start, no preschool, and other preschool programs', *Child Development*, 61, pp.495-507.

LeMagnen, J. (1981) 'The metabolic basis of dual periodicity of feeding in rats', *The Behavioral and Brain Sciences*, 4, pp.561-607.

Leng, G.A. (1985) 'Koro – a cultural disease', in R.C. Simons and C.C. Hughes (eds) *The Culture-Bound Syndromes: Folk Illnesses of Psychiatric and Anthropological Interest*, Dordrecht, The Netherlands: D. Reidel Publishing Company.

Lenneberg, E.H. and Roberts, J.M. (1956) *The Language of Experience*, Memoir 13, Indiana University Publications in Anthropology and Linguistics.

Levine, J (1976) 'Real kids versus the average family', *Psychology Today*, June, 14-15.

Levine, R., Sato, S., Hashimoto, T. and Verma, J. (1995) 'Love and Marriage in 11 cultures', *Journal of Cross-Cultural Psychology*. 26(5), pp.554-71.

Levinger, G. and Clark, J. (1961) 'Emotional factors in the forgetting of word associations', *Journal of Abnormal and Social Psychology*, 62, pp.99–105.

Levinson, D.J. (1978) *The Seasons of a Man's Life*, New York: Knopf.

Levy, B. and Langer, E. (1994) 'Aging free from negative stereotypes: successful memory in China and among the American deaf', *Journal of Personality and Social Psychology*, 66, pp.989-97.

Lewinsohn, P.M. (1974) 'A behavioural approach to depression', in R.J. Friedman and M.M. Katz (eds) *The Psychology of Depression: Contemporary Theory and Research*, Washington, DC: Winston Wiley.

Lewinsohn, P.M., Mischel, W., Chaplin, W. and Barton, R. (1980) 'Social competence and depression: the role of illusory self-perceptions', *Journal of Abnormal Psychology*, 89, pp.203-12.

Lewis, J.L. (1970) 'Semantic processing of unattended messages using dichotic listening', *Journal of Experimental Psychology*, 85, pp.225-8.

Lewis, R. A. and Spanier, G. B. (1979) 'Theorising about the quality and stability of marriage', in W. Burr, R. Hill and I. L. Reiss (eds) *Contemporary Theories about the Family* (Vol.1), New York: Free Press.

Liben, L.S. and Signorella, M.L. (1993) 'Gender-schematic processing in children: the role of initial interpretations of stimuli', *Developmental Psychology*, 29, pp.141-9.

Libow, J. (1985) 'Gender and sex role issues as family secrets', *Journal of Strategic and Systematic Therapies*, 4(2), pp.32-41.

Lichstein, K.L. (1988) *Clinical Relaxation Strategies*, New York: Wiley.

Liebert, R.M. and Baron, R.A. (1972) 'Short term effects of television aggression on children's aggressive behaviour', in J.P. Murray, E.A. Rubenstein, and G.A. Comstock (eds) *Television and Social Behaviour*, Vol. 2, Television and Social Learning, Washington, DC: United States Government Printing Office.

Liebowitz, M. (1983) *The Chemistry of Love*, New York: Berkley Books.

Lieven, E.V.M. (1994) 'Crosslinguistic and crosscultural aspects of language addressed to children', in C. Gallaway and B.J. Richards (eds) *Input and Interaction in Language Acquisition*, Cambridge: Cambridge University Press.

Lifton, R.J. (1986) *The Nazi Doctors: Medical Killing and the Psychology of Genocide*, New York: Basic.

Lilienfield, S., Lyn, S., Kirsch, T., Chaves, J., Sarbin, T., Gammaway, G. and Powell, R. (1999) 'Dissociative identity disorder and the sociocognitive model: recalling the lessons of the past', *Psychological Bulletin*, 125 (5), pp.507-23.

Linaza, J. (1984) 'Piaget's marbles: The study of children's games and their knowledge of rules', *Oxford Review of Education*, 10, pp.271-4.

Lindauer, M. (1955) cited in D.R. Griffin (1992) *Animal Minds,* Chicago: Chicago University Press.

Lindstrøm, T. C. (1999) 'Coping with bereavement in relation to different feminine gender roles', *Scandinavian Journal of Psychology*, 40(1), pp.33-41.

Lippmann, W. (1922) *Public Opinion*, New York: Harcourt, Brace & World.

Liss, M.B. and Reinhardt, L.C. (1979) 'Behavioral and attitudinal responses to pro-social programs', Paper presented at the meeting of the Society for Research in Child Development, San Francisco, CA.

List, J.A. (1986) 'Age and schematic differences in reliability of eyewitness testimony', *Developmental Psychology*, 22, pp.50–57.

Little, A.C. and Hancock, P.J. (2002) 'The role of masculinity and distinctiveness on the perception of attractiveness in human male faces', *British Journal of Psychology*, 93, pp.451-64.

Littlewood, J. (1992) *Aspects of Grief: Bereavement in Adult Life*, London: Tavistock/Routledge.

Litton, I. and Potter, J. (1985) 'Social representations in the ordinary explanation of a 'riot', *European Journal of Social Psychology*, 15, pp.371-88.

Liu, L.G. (1985) 'Reasoning counterfactually in Chinese: are there any obstacles?', *Cognition*, 21, pp.239-70.

Lock, A.J. (1980) *The Guided Reinvention Of Language*, London: Academic Press.

Loehlin, J.C., Horn, J.M., & Willerman, L. (1989) 'Modelling IQ change: Evidence from the Texas Adoption Project', *Child Development*, 60, pp.893–904.

Loftus, E.F. (1975) 'Leading questions and the eyewitness report', *Cognitive Psychology*, 7, pp.560–72.

Loftus, E.F. (1979) 'Reactions to blatantly contradictory information', *Memory and Cognition*, 7, pp.368–74.

Loftus, E.F. (1997) 'Creating false memories', *Scientific American*, September, pp.50–5.

Loftus, E.F. and Ketcham, K. (1991) *Witness for the Defence*, New York: St Martin's Press.

Loftus, E.F. and Loftus, G.R. (1980) 'On the permanence of stored information in the human brain', *American Psychologist*, 35, pp.409–20.

Loftus, E.F. and Palmer, J.C. (1974) 'Reconstruction of automobile destruction: an example of the interaction between language and memory', *Journal of Verbal Learning and Verbal Behaviour*, 13, pp.585–9.

Loftus, E.F., Miller, D.G. and Burns, H.J. (1978) 'Semantic integration of verbal information into a visual memory', *Journal of Experimental Psychology: Human Learning and Memory*, 4, pp.19–31.

Logothetis, N.K. and Pauls, J. (1995) 'Psychophysical and physiological evidence for viewer-centred object representaions in the primate', *Cerebral Cortex*, 5, pp.270-88.

Lohmann, K.J. and Lohmann, C.M.F. (1996) 'Orientation and open-sea navigation in sea turtles', *Journal of Experimental Biology*, 199, 73-81.

Lombroso, C. (1911) *Crime: Its Causes and Remedies*, Boston: Little, Brown.

Lord, C.G. (1997) *Social Psychology*, Fort Worth: Harcourt Brace College.

Lorenz, K.Z. (1937) 'The companion in the bird's world', *Auk*, 54, pp.245–73.

Lorenz, K.Z. (1952) *King Solomon's Ring: New light on animal ways*, London: Methuen & Co.

Lotem, A. (1993) 'Learning to recognise nestlings is maladaptive for cuckoo (*Cuculus canorus*) hosts', *Nature*, 362, pp.743-5.

Lott, B.E. (1994) *Women's Lives: Themes and Variations in Gender Learning*, Pacific Grove, CA: Brooks Cole.

Lovelace, V. and Huston, H.C. (1983) 'Can television teach pro-social behaviour?', *Prevention in Human Services*, 2, pp.93-106.

Lucas, K. and Lloyd, B. (1999) 'Starting smoking: girls' explanations of the influence of peers', *Journal of Adolescence*, 22, pp.647-55

Luchins, A.S. (1942) 'Mechanization in problem-solving', *Psychological Monographs*, 54 (6), Whole No. 248.

Lugo, J. O. and Hershey, G. L. (1979) *Lifespan Development*, (2nd ed.) London: Macmillan.

Lujansky, H. and Mikula, G. (1983) 'Can equity theory explain the quality and stability of romantic relationships?', *British Journal of Social Psychology*, 22, pp.101-12.

Lukes, S. (1975) *Emile Durkheim, His Life and Work: A Historical and Critical Study*, Harmondsworth: Penguin.

Lydiard, R.B., Brawman-Mintzer, O. and Ballenger, J.C. (1996) 'Recent developments in the psychopharmacology of anxiety disorders', *Journal of Consulting and Clinical Psychology*, 64, pp.660-8.

Lynch, K. (1960) *The Image of the City*, Cambridge, MA: MIT Press.

Lynch, P. (1994) 'Type A behaviour, hostility, and cardiovascular function at rest after playing video games in teenagers', *Psychosomatic Medicine*, 56, p.152.

McArthur, L.Z. and Post, D.L. (1977) 'Figural emphasis and person perception', *Journal of Experimental Social Psychology*, 13, pp.520-35.

McCarthy, G. (1999) 'Attachment style and adult love relationships and friendships: A study of a group of women at risk of experiencing relationship difficulties', *British Journal of Medical Psychology*, 72, pp.305–21.

McCarty, J.P. (1996) 'The energetic cost of begging in nestling passerines', *Auk*, 113, pp.178-88.

McClelland, D.C. (1961) *The Achieving Society*, Princeton, New Jersey: Van Nostrand.

McCloskey, M., Wible, C.G. and Cohen, N.J. (1988) 'Is there a special flashbulb memory mechanism?', *Journal of Experimental Psychology: General*, 117, pp.171–81.

Maccoby, E.E. (1980) *Social Development: Psychological Growth and the Parent–child Relationship*, San Diego: Harcourt Brace Jovanovich.

Maccoby, E.E. and Jacklin, C.N. (1974) *The Psychology of Sex Difference*, Stanford, CA: Stanford University Press.

McCormack, R.L. (1965) 'Extended tables of the Wilcoxon matched pair signed rank statistic', *Journal of the American Statistical Association*, 60, pp.864-71.

McDermott, M. (1993) 'On cruelty, ethics and experimentation: profile of Philip G. Zimbardo', *The Psychologist*, 6(10), pp.456–9.

McDougall, W. (1908) *Introduction to Social Psychology*, cited by Thigpen, C. and Cleckey, H. (1954) 'A case of multiple personality disorder', *Journal of Abnormal and Social Psychology*, 49, pp.135-51.

Macedonia, J.M. (1990) 'What is communicated in the anti-predator calls of lemurs: evidence from anti-predator call playbacks to ring-tailed and ruffed lemurs', *Ethology*, 86, pp.177-90.

McFarland, D. (1993) *Animal Behaviour* (2nd edn), Harlow: Addison Wesley Longman.

McGarrigle, J. and Donaldson, M. (1974) 'Conservation accidents', *Cognition*, 3, pp.341-50.

McGeoch, J.A. and MacDonald, W.T. (1931) 'Meaningful relation and retroactive inhibition', *American Journal of Psychology*, 43, pp.579–88.

McGinnies, E. (1949) 'Emotionality and perceptual defence', *Psychological Review*, 56, pp.244-51.

McGovern, D. and Cope, R. (1987) 'The compulsory detention of males of different ethnic groups, with special reference to offender patients', *British Journal of Psychiatry*, 150, pp.505-12.

McGrath, T., Tsui, E., Humphries, S. and Yule, W. (1990) 'Successful treatment of a noise phobia in a nine-year-old girl with systematic desensitization *in vivo*', *Educational Psychology*, 10(1), pp.79-83.

McGregor, P.K., Dabelsteen, T., Shepherd, M. and Pedersen, S.B. (1992) 'The signal value of matched singing in great tits: evidence from interactive playback experiments', *Animal Behaviour*, 43, pp.987-98.

McGuffin, P., Katz, R., Watkins, S. and Rutherford, J. (1996) 'A hospital-based twin register of the heritability of DSM-IV unipolar depression', *Archives of General Psychiatry*, 53, pp.129-36.

McHugh, P.R. and Moran, T.H. (1985) 'The stomach: a conception of its dynamic role in satiety', *Progress in Psychobiology and Physiological Psychology*, 11, pp.197-232.

McKenna, S.P. and Glendon, A.I. (1985) 'Occupational first aid training: decay in cardiopulmonary resuscitation (CPR) skills', *Journal of Occupational Psychology*, 58, pp.109–17.

McKenry, P.C. and Price, S.J. (1995) 'Divorce: a comparative perspective', in B.B. Ingoldsby and S. Smith (eds) *Families in Multicultural Perspective*, New York: Guilford Press.

Mackintosh, N.J. (1981) 'Learning', in D. McFarland (ed.) *The Oxford Companion to Animal Behaviour*. Oxford: Oxford University Press.

MacLean, P.D. (1949) 'Psychosomatic disease and the "visceral brain": Recent developments bearing on the Papez theory of emotion', *Psychosomatic Medicine*, 11, pp.338-53.

McLelland, L., Mynors-Wallis, L. and Treasure, J. (1991) 'Sexual abuse, disordered personality and eating', *British Journal of Psychiatry*, 158, pp.63–8.

MacLeod, C. and Campbell, L. (1992) 'Memory accessibility and probability judgements: an experimental evaluation of the availability heuristic', *Journal of Personality and Social Psychology*, 63, pp.890-902.

McNally, R.J. and Steketee, G.S. (1985) 'The etiology and maintenance of severe animal phobias', *Behaviour Research and Therapy*, 23(4), pp.431-5.

McNaughton, S. and Leyland, J. (1990) 'Maternal regulation of children's problem-solving behaviour and its impact on children's performance, *Child Development*, 61, pp.113-126.

McNeil, B.J., Pauker, S.G., Sox, H.C. and Tversky, A. (1982) 'On the elicitation of preferences for alternative therapies', *New England Journal of Medicine*, 306, pp.1259-62.

McNeil, J.D. (1966) *The ABC Learning Activity: Language of Instruction*, New York: American Book.

McNeil, J.D., Pauker, S.G. and Tversky, A. (1988) 'On the framing of medical decisions', in D.E. Bell, H. Raiffa and A. Tversky (eds) *Decision Making: Descriptive, Normative and Prescriptive Interactions*, New York: Cambridge University Press.

McTear, M.F. (1985) *Children's Conversations*, Oxford: Ellis Horwood.

Madden, P.A.F., Heath, A., Rosenthal, N.E. and Martin, N.E. (1996) 'Seasonal changes in mood and behaviour', *Archives of General Psychiatry*, 53, pp.47-55.

Magee, W.J., Eaton, W., Wittchen, H.U., McGonagle, K.A. and Kessler, R.C. (1996) 'Agoraphobia, simple phobia and social phobia in the national comorbidity survey', *Archives of General Psychiatry*, 53 (2), pp.159-68.

Magnusson, A. and Stefansson, J.G. (1993) 'Prevalence of seasonal affective disorder in Iceland', *Archives of General Psychiatry*, 50, pp.941-6.

Maguire, E.A., Gadian, D.G., Johnsrude, I.S., Good, C.D., Ashburner, J. Frackowiak, R.S. and Frith, C.D. (2000) 'Navigation-related structural change in the hippocampi of taxi drivers', *Proceedings of the National Academy of Science*, 97(8), pp.4398-403.

Maier, S.J. and Seligman, M.E.P. (1976) 'Learned helplessness: theory and evidence', *Journal of Experimental Psychology: General*, 105, pp.2-46.

Main, M. and Cassidy, J. (1988) 'Categories of response to reunion with the parent at age six: predicted from infant attachment classifications and stable over a one-month period', *Developmental Psychology*, 24, pp.415–26.

Malamuth, N.M. and Check, J.V.P. (1981) 'The effects of mass media exposure on acceptance of violence against women: a field experiment', *Journal of Research in Personality*, 15, pp.436-46.

Malotki, E. (1983) *Hopi Time: A Linguistic Analysis of Temporal Concepts in the Hopi Language*, Berlin: Mouton.

Mandel, D.R. (1998) 'The obedience alibi: Milgram's account of the Holocaust reconsidered', *Analyse und Kritik: Zeitschrift für Sozialwissenschaften*, 20, pp.74–94.

Mann, J.J., Malone, K.M., Diehl, D.J., Perel, J., Cooper, T.B. and Mintun, M.A. (1996) 'Demonstration in vivo of reduced serotonin responsivity in the brain of untreated depressed patients', *American Journal of Psychiatry*, 153, pp.174-82.

Mann, L. (1981) 'The baiting crowd in episodes of threatened suicide', *Journal of Personality and Social Psychology*, 41, pp.703-9.

Manning, A. and Dawkins, M.S. (1998) *A Introduction to Animal Behaviour*, Cambridge: Cambridge University Press.

Manstead, A.S.R. and Hewstone, M. (1995) *The Blackwell Encyclopaedia of Social Psychology.*, Oxford: Blackwell.

Mantell, D.M. (1971) 'The potential for violence in Germany', *Journal of Social Issues*, 27, pp.101–12.

Maranon, G. (1924) 'Contribution à l'étude de l'action émotive de l'adrénaline', *Revue Française d'Endocrinologie*, 2, pp.301-25.

Marcia, J. (1966) 'Development and validation of ego identity status', *Journal of Personality and Social Psychology*, 3, pp.551-8.

Marcia, J. (1980) 'Identity in adolescence', in J. Adelson (ed.) *Handbook of Adolescent Psychology*, New York: Wiley.

Marcus, J., Hans, S.L., Nagier, S., Auerbach, J.G., Mirsky, A.F. and Aubrey, A. (1987) 'Review of the NIMH Israeli Kibbutz-City and the Jerusalem infant development study', *Schizophrenia Bulletin*, 13, pp.425-38.

Margulis, L. and Sagan, D. (1991) *Mystery Dance: On the Evolution of Human Sexuality*, New York: Summit Books.

Marie-Claire (1993) 'Hi-tech sex', *Marie-Claire* (London edn), May, pp.22-5.

Markowitz, L.M. (1991) 'Homosexuality: are we still in the dark?', *The Family Therapy Networker*, January pp.26-9; February pp.31-5.

Marks, I.M. (1981) 'Review of behavioural psychotherapy: obsessive-compulsive disorders', *American Journal of Psychiatry*, 138, pp.584-92.

Markus, H. and Kitayama, S. (1991) 'Culture and the self: Implications for cognition, emotion and motivation',

Psychological Review, 98, pp.224-53.

Marler, P. (1991) 'Song-learning behaviour: the interface with neuroethology', *Trends in Neurosciences*, 14, pp.199-206.

Marmot, M.G., Smith, G.M., Stansfield, S., Patel, C., North, F., Head, J., White, I., Brunner, E. and Feeney, A. (1991) 'Health inequalities among British Civil Servants: the Whitehall II study', *The Lancet*, 337, pp.1387–93.

Marsh, P., Rosser, E. and Harre, R. (1978) *The Rules of Disorder*, London: Routledge.

Marshall, G.D. and Zimbardo, P.G. (1979) 'Affective consequences of inadequately explained physiological arousal', *Journal of Personality and Social Psychology*, 37, pp.970-88.

Martin, C. and Halverson, C. (1983) 'Gender constancy: a methodological and theoretical analysis', *Sex Roles*, 9, pp.775-90.

Martin, C.L. and Little, J.K. (1990) 'The relation of gender understanding to children's sex-typed preferences and gender stereotypes', *Child Development*, 61, pp.1427-39.

Martin, C.L., Eisenbud, L. and Rose, H. (1995) 'Children's gender-based reasoning about toys', *Child Development*, 66, pp.1453-71.

Maruyama, G., Fraser, S.C. and Miller, N. (1982) 'Personal responsibility and altruism in children', *Journal of Personality and Social Psychology*, 42 (4), pp.658-64.

Maslach, C. (1979) 'Negative emotional biasing of unexplained arousal', *Journal of Personality and Social Psychology*, 37, pp.953-69.

Maslow, A.H. (1954) *Motivation and Personality*, (1987, 3rd edn) New York: Harper & Row.

Maslow, A.H. (1968) *Towards a Psychology of Being* (2nd edn), Princeton, NJ: Van Nostrand Reinhold.

Masters, J.C., Burish, T.G., Hollon, S.D. and Rimm, D.C. (1987) *Behavior Therapy: Techniques and Empirical Findings* (3rd edn), San Diego: Harcourt Brace Jovanovich.

Matlin, M.W. (1998) *Cognition* (4th edn), Orlando: Harcourt Brace College Publishers.

Matthews, K. and Haynes, S. (1986) 'Type A behavior pattern and coronary disease risk', *American Journal of Epidemiology*, 123, pp.923–7.

Maurer, D. and Maurer, C. (1989) *The World of the Newborn*, London: Viking.

May, J.L. and Hamilton, P.A. (1980) 'Effects of musically evoked affect on women's interpersonal attraction and perceptual

judgements of physical attractiveness of men', *Motivation and Emotion*, 4, pp.217-28.

Mead, M. (1928) *Coming of Age in Samoa*, New York: Morrow.

Meddis, R. (1979) 'The evolution and function of sleep', in D.A. Oakley and H.C. Plotkin (eds) *Brain, Behaviour and Evolution*, London: Methuen.

Mednick, S.A., Machon, R.A., Huttunen, M.O. and Bonett, D. (1988) 'Adult schizophrenia following prenatal exposure to an influenza epidemic', *Archives of General Psychiatry*, 45 (2), pp.189-92.

Meeus, W.H.J. and Raaijmakers, Q.A.W. (1986) 'Administrative obedience: carrying out orders to use psychological-administrative violence', *European Journal of Social Psychology*, 16, pp.311-24.

Meichenbaum, D.H. (1972) 'Cognitive modification of test anxious college students', *Journal of Consulting and Clinical Psychology*, 39 (3), pp.370-80.

Meichenbaum, D.H. (1975) 'Self-instructional methods', in F.H. Kanfer and A.P. Goldstein (eds) *Helping People Change: A Textbook of Methods*, New York: Pergamon.

Meichenbaum, D.H. and Cameron, R. (1973) 'Training schizo-phrenics to talk to themselves: a means of developing attentional controls', *Behaviour Therapy*, 4, pp.515-34.

Meichenbaum, D.H. and Cameron, R. (1983) 'Stress inoculation training: toward a general paradigm for training coping skills', in D. Meichenbaum and M.E. Jarenko (eds) *Stress Reduction and Prevention*, New York: Plenum.

Meichenbaum, D.H. and Turk, D. (1982) 'Stress, coping, and disease: a cognitive-behavioral perspective', in R.W.J. Neufield (ed.) *Psychological Stress and Psychopathology*, New York: McGraw-Hill.

Meilman, P.W. (1979) 'Cross-sectional age changes in ego identity status during adolescence', *Developmental Psychology*, 15, pp.230-1.

Melhuish, E.C. (1993) 'Behaviour measures: a measure of love? An overview of the assessment of attachment', *ACPP Review and Newsletter*, 15 (6), pp.269–75.

Meloen, J.D., Hagendoorn, L., Raaijmakers, Q. and Visser, L. (1988) 'Authoritarianism and the revival of political racism: reassessments in the Netherlands of the reliability and validity of the concepts of authoritarianism used by Adorno et al.', *Political Psychology*, 9, pp.413-29.

Menzies, R.G. and Clarke, J.C. (1993) 'A comparison of *in vivo* and vicarious exposure in the treatment of childhood water phobia', *Behavioural Research Therapy*, 31 (1), pp.9-15.

Mersky, H. (1992) 'The manufacture of multiple personality disorder', *British Journal of Psychiatry*, 160, pp.327-40.

Messer, D. (1999) 'The development of communication and language', in D. Messer and S. Millar (eds) *Exploring Developmental Psychology*, London: Arnold.

Mettke-Hofmann, C. and Gwinner, E. (2003) 'Long-term memory for a life on the move', *Proceedings of the National Academy of Sciences of the United States of America*, 100(10), pp.58-63

Miale, F.R. and Selzer, M. (1975) *The Nuremberg Mind: The Psychology of the Nazi Leaders*, New York: Quadrangle.

Middlemist, R.D., Knowles, E.S. and Matter, C.F. (1976) 'Personal space invasions in the lavatory: Suggestive evidence for arousal', *Journal of Personality and Social Psychology*, 33, pp.541-6.

Milavsky, J.R., Kessler, R.C., Stipp, H.H. and Rubens, W.S. (1982) *Television and Aggression: A Panel Study*, New York: Academic Press.

Milgram, S. (1963) 'Behavioural study of obedience', *Journal of Abnormal and Social Psychology*, 67, pp.371-8

Milgram, S. (1964) 'Issues in the study of obedience: a reply to Baumrind', *American Psychologist*, 19, pp.848–52.

Milgram, S. (1965) 'Some conditions of obedience and disobedience to authority', *Human Relations*, 18, pp.57-76.

Milgram, S. (1970) 'The experience of living in cities', *Science*, 167, pp.1461-8.

Milgram, S. (1974) *Obedience to Authority*, New York: Harper & Row.

Miller, D.T. and Ross, M. (1975) 'Self-serving biases in the attribution of causality: fact or fiction?', *Psychological Bulletin*, 82, pp.213-25.

Miller, G.A. (1956) 'The magical number seven, plus or minus two: some limits on our capacity for processing information', *Psychological Review*, 63, pp.81–97.

Miller, G.F. (1994) 'Exploiting mate choice in evolutionary computation: sexual selection as a process of search, optimization, and diversification', in T.C. Fogarty (ed.) *Evolutionary Computing: Proceedings of the 1994 Artificial Intelligence and Simulation of Behavior (AISB)*

Society Workshop, New York: Springer-Verlag, pp.65-79.

Miller, G.F. (1996) 'Sexual selection in human evolution', in C. Crawford and D.L. Krebs (eds) *Evolution and Human Behaviour*, Mahwah: Lawrence Erlbaum.

Miller, G.F. (1998) 'How mate choice shaped human nature: A review of sexual selection and human evolution', in C. Crawford and D. Krebs (eds) *Handbook of Evolutionary Psychology: Ideas, Issues and Applications*, Mahwah, New Jersey: Lawrence Erlbaum, pp.87-129.

Miller, J.G. (1984) 'Culture and the development of everyday social explanation', *Journal of Personality and Social Psychology*, 46, pp.961-78.

Miller, J.G. and Bersoff, D.M. (1992) 'Culture and moral judgment: How are conflicts between justice and interpersonal responsibilities resolved', *Journal of Personality and Social Psychology*, 26, pp.541-54.

Miller, J.G. and Bersoff, D.M. (1998) 'The role of liking in perceptions of the moral responsibility to help: a cultural perspective', *Journal of Experimental Social Psychology*, 34, pp.443-69.

Miller, L. (1994) www.radix.net/ ~reimann/enet/VC94/Msg/msg3 4.html. Referenced March 2003.

Miller, L.C., Lechner, R.E. and Rugs, D. (1985) 'Development of conversational responsiveness: preschoolers' use of responsive listener cues and relevant comments', *Developmental Psychology*, 21, pp.473-80.

Millward, L. (1998) 'Social Psychology', in M. Eysenck (ed.) *Psychology: An Integrated Approach*, Harlow: Longman.

Milner, B. (1966) 'Amnesia following operation on the temporal lobes', in C.W.M. Whitty and O.L. Zangwill (eds) *Amnesia*, London: Butterworth.

Milner, P. (1970) *Physiological Psychology*, London: Holt, Rhinehart & Winston.

Milton, K. (1993) 'Diet and primate evolution', *Scientific American*, 269, pp.70-7.

Minai, N. (1981) *Women in Islam: Tradition and Transition in the Middle East*, New York: Seaview Books.

Mineka, S., Davidson, M., Cook, M. and Keir, R. (1984) 'Observational conditioning of snake fear in rhesus monkeys', *Journal of Abnormal Psychology*, 93, pp.355–72.

Minuchin, S. (1974) *Families and family therapy*, Cambridge, MA: Harvard University Press.

Minuchin, S., Rosman, B.L. and Baker, L. (1978) *Psychosomatic Families: Anorexia Nervosa in Context*, Cambridge, MA: Harvard Univ. Press.

Mischel, W. and Shoda, Y. (1998) 'Reconciling processing dynamics and personality dispositions', *Annual Review of Psychology*, 49, 229-58. Palo Alto, CA: Annual Reviews Inc.

Mischel, W. (1968) *Personality and Assessment*, New York: Wiley.

Mischel, W. (1973) 'Toward a cognitive social learning reconceptualization of personality', *Psychological Review*, 80, pp.252-83.

Mischel, W. and Peake, P.K. (1982) 'Beyond déja vu in the search for cross-situational consistency', *Psychological Review*, 89, pp.730-55.

Mitchell, D. and Blair, J. (2000) 'State of the art: psychopathy', *The Psychologist*, 13, pp.356-60.

Mixon, D. (1972) 'Instead of deception', *Journal of the Theory of Social Behaviour*, 2, pp.139–77.

Modgil, S., Modgil, M. and Brown, G. (1983) *Jean Piaget: An interdisciplinary critique*. London: Routledge.

Moffitt, A., Kramer, M. and Hoffman, R. (1993) *The Function of Dreams*, New York: State University of New York Press.

Moghaddam, F.M. (1998) Social Psychology: Exploring Universals across Cultures, New York: W.H. Freeman.

Moghaddam, F.M., Taylor, D.M. and Wright, S.C. (1993) *Social Psychology in Cross-Cultural Perspective*, New York: W.H. Freeman.

Moksnes, A. and Røskaft, E. (1995) 'Egg-morphs and host preferences in the common cuckoo (*Cuculus canorus*): an analysis of cuckoo and host eggs from European museums', *Journal of Zoology*, 236, pp.625-46.

Money, J. and Ehrhardt, A.A. (1972) *Man and Woman, Boy and Girl*, Baltimore: John's Hopkins University Press.

Montemayor, R. (1982) 'The relationship between parent-adolescent conflict and the amount of time adolescents spend with parents, peers and alone', *Child Development*, 53, pp.1512-19.

Montemayor, R., McHenry, C. and Julian, P. (1993) 'Men in midlife and the quality of father-adolescent communication', *New Directions in Child Development*, 62, pp.59-72.

Montessori, M. (1912) *The Montessori Method: A Scientific Pedagogy as Applied to Child Education in the 'Children's Houses'*, translated from the Italian by A.E. George, New York: Frederick A. Stokes Co.

Moore, C. and Frye, D. (1986) 'The effect of the experimenter's intention on the child's understanding of conservation', *Cognition*, 22, pp.283-98.

Moos, R.H. and Swindle, R.W. Jr (1990) 'Stressful life circumstances: concepts and measures', *Stress Medicine*, 6, pp.171–8.

Moos, R.H., McCoy, L. and Moos, B.S. (2000) 'Global Assessment of Functioning (GAF) ratings: determinants and roles as predictors of one-year treatment outcomes', *Journal of Clinical Psychology*, 56, pp.449-61.

Moray, N. (1959) 'Attention in dichotic listening: affective cues and the influence of instructions', *Quarterly Journal of Experimental Psychology*, 11, pp.56-60.

Moreno, J.L. (1965) 'Psychodynamic rules, techniques and adjunctive methods', *Group Psychotherapy*, Vol. 23, Washington, DC: Heldref Publications.

Moreno, J.L. (1970) *Psychodrama I, II, III*, Boston, MA: Beacon Press.

Morris, J.S., Frith, C.D., Perrett, D.I., Rowland, D., Young, A.W., Calder, A.J. and Dolan, R.J. (1996) 'A differential neural response in the human amygdala to fearful and happy facial expressions', *Nature*, 383, pp.812-5.

Moscovici, S. (1961) *La Psychoanalyse, Son Image et Son Public*, Paris: Presses Universitaires de France.

Moscovici, S. (1980) 'Towards a theory of conversion behaviour', in L. Berkowitz (ed.) *Advances in Experimental Social Psychology*, London: Academic Press.

Moscovici, S. (1981) 'On social representations', in J.P. Forgas (ed.) *Social Cognition: Perspectives in Everyday Understanding*, London: Academic Press.

Moscovici, S. (1985) 'Social influence and conformity', in G. Lindzey and E. Aronson (eds) *Handbook of Social Psychology* (3rd edn), New York: Random House.

Moscovici, S. (1985) 'The myth of the lonely paradigm: a rejoinder', *Social Research*, 51, pp.939-67.

Moscovici, S., Lage, E. and Naffrechoux, M. (1969) 'Influence of a consistent minority on the responses of a majority in a colour perception task', *Sociometry*, 32, pp.365–80.

Mouritsen, H. and Frost, B.J. (2002) 'Virtual migration in tethered flying monarch butterflies reveals orientation mechanisms', *Proceedings of the National Academy of Science of the United States of America*, 99, pp.10,162-6.

Mufson, L., Weissman, M.M., Moreau, D. and Garfinkel, R. (1999) 'Efficacy of interpersonal psychotherapy for depressed adolescents', *Archives of General Psychiatry*, 56, pp.573-9.

Mugny, G. and Perez, J. (1991) *The Social Psychology of Minority Influence*, Cambridge: Cambridge University Press.

Mukhametov, L.M. (1984) 'Sleep in marine mammals', in A.Borbely and J-L. Valatax (eds) *Sleep Mechanisms. Experimental Brain Research*, Suppl. 8, Berlin: Springer-Verlag, pp.227-37.

Mukherjee, S., Sackeim, H.A. and Schnur, D.B. (1994) 'Electroconvulsive therapy of acute manic episodes: a review of fifty years experience', *American Journal of Psychiatry*, 151, pp.169-76.

Mumford, D.B., Whitehouse, A.M. and Plattes, M. (1991) 'Sociocultural correlates of eating disorders among Asian schoolgirls in Bradford', *British Journal of Psychiatry*, 158, pp.222–8.

Munjack, D.J. (1984) 'The onset of driving phobias', *Journal of Behaviour Therapy and Experimental Psychiatry*, 15, pp.305-8.

Munk, J.P. and Mortensen, P.B. (1992) 'Social outcome in schizophrenia: a 13-year follow-up', Social Psychiatry and Psychiatric Epidemiology, 27(3), pp.129-34.

Munroe, R.H., Shimmin, H.S. and Munroe, R.L. (1984) 'Gender understanding and sex role preference in four cultures', *Developmental Psychology*, 20, pp.673-82.

Murdock, B.B. (1961) 'The retention of individual items', *Journal of Experimental Psychology*, 62, pp.618–25.

Murray, H.A. (ed.) (1938) *Explorations in Personality*, New York: Oxford University Press.

Murray-Parkes, C. (1972) *Bereavement: Studies of Grief in Adult Life*, New York: International Universities Press.

Murstein, B.I. (1972) 'Physical attractiveness and marital choice', *Journal of Personality and Social Psychology*, 22 (1), pp.8-12.

Myers, D.G. (1999) *Social Psychology* (6th edn), Boston: McGraw-Hill College.

Myers, L.B. and Brewin, C.R. (1994) 'Recall of early experiences and the repressive coping style', *Journal of Abnormal Psychology*, 103, pp.288-92.

Nadler, A. (1986) 'Help seeking as a cultural phenomenon: differences between city and kibbutz dwellers', *Journal of Personality and Social Psychology*, 51, pp.976-82.

Nadler, A. (1993) Personal communication, in R.A. Baron and D. Byrne (1994) *Social Psychology: Understanding Human Interaction* (7th edn), Boston, MA: Allyn & Bacon.

Nagell, K., Olguin, R.S. and Tomasello, M. (1993) 'Processes of social learning in the tool use of chimpanzees (*Pan troglodytes*) and human children (*Homo sapiens*)', *Journal of Comparative Psychology*, 107, pp.174-86.

Nasser, M. (1986) 'Comparative study of the prevalence of abnormal eating attitudes among Arab female students of both London and Cairo universities', *Psychological Medicine*, 16, pp.621–7.

Naveh-Benjamin, M. and Ayres, T.J. (1986) 'Digit span, reading rate, and linguistic relativity', *Quarterly Journal of Experimental Psychology*, 38, pp.739–51.

Neff, N. (undated.) 'Folk medicine in Hispanics in the Southwestern United States', accessed at: www-sbp.bcm.tmc.edu/Hispanic Health/Courses/mod7/amod7_ html

Neisser, U. (1964) 'Visual search', *Scientific American*, 210, pp.94-102.

Neisser, U. (1967) *Cognitive Psychology*, New York: Appleton-Century-Crofts.

Neisser, U. (1976) *Cognition and Reality*, San Francisco: W.H. Freeman.

Neisser, U. (1978) 'Memory: what are the important questions?', in M.M. Gruneberg, P.E. Morris and R.N. Sykes (eds) *Practical Aspects of Memory*, London: Academic Press.

Neisser, U. (1982) *Memory Observed*, San Francisco: W.H. Freeman.

Nemeroff, C.B., Krishnan, R.R., Reed, D., Leder, R., Beam, C. and Dunnick, N.R. (1992) 'Adrenal gland enlargement in major depression', *Archives of General Psychiatry*, 49, pp.384-7.

Nemeth, C. (1986) 'The differential contributions of majority and minority influence', *Psychological Review*, 93, pp.23–32.

Nesse, R.M. (1999) 'Testing evolutionary hypotheses about mental disorders', in S.C. Stearns (ed.) *Evolution in Health and Disease*, New York: Oxford University Press, pp.260-6

Nesse, R.M. (2000) 'Is depression an adaptation?', *Archives of General Psychiatry*, 57, pp.14-20.

Nesse, R.M. and Williams, G.C. (1994) *Why We Get Sick: The New Science of Darwinian Medicine*, New York: Times Books.

Neugarten, B.L. (1968) *Personality in Middle and Late Life* (2nd edn), New York: Atherton Press.

Neugarten, B.L. (1980) 'Act your age: must everything be a midlife crisis?', in *Annual Editions: Human Development, 1980/1981*, Guilford, CT: Dushkin Publishers, pp.289-90.

Newcomb, T.M. (1961) *The Acquaintance Process*, New York: Holt, Rinehart & Winston.

Newell, A. and Simon, H.A. (1972) *Human Problem-solving*, Englewood Cliffs, NJ: Prentice-Hall.

Newell, A., Shaw, J.C. and Simon, H.A. (1958) 'Elements of a theory of general problem-solving', *Psychological Review*, 65, pp.151-66.

NICHD Early Child Care Research Network (1997) 'The effects of infant child care on infant–mother attachment security: Results of the NICHD study of early child care', *Child Development*, 68(5), pp.860–79.

NICHD Early Child Care Research Network (2001) 'Further explorations of the detected effects of quantity of early child care on socio-emotional development', Paper presented at the Biennial Meeting of the Society for Research in Child Development, Minneapolis, MN.

Nicholson, N., Cole, S.G. and Rocklin, T. (1985) 'Conformity in the Asch situation: a comparison between contemporary British and US university students', *British Journal of Social Psychology*, 24, pp.59–63.

Nickel, H., Quaiserpohl, C., Rollett, B., Vetter, J. and Werneck, H. (1995) 'Changing marital satisfaction during the transition to parenthood: cross cultural studies in four countries', *Psychologie in Erziehung und Unterricht*, 42 (1), pp.40-53.

Nicolson, P. (1999) 'Evolutionary psychology is not the answer to everything', *Proceedings of the British Psychological Society Annual Conference*.

Nisbett, R.E. (1972) 'Hunger, obesity and the ventro-medial hypothalamus', *Psychological Review*, 79, pp.433-53.

Nisbett, R.E. and Ross, L. (1980) *Human Inference Strategies and Shortcomings of Social Judgement*, Englewood Cliffs, NJ: Prentice Hall.

Nishida, T., Hasegawa, T., Hayaki, H., Takahata, Y. and Uehara, S. (1992) 'Meat-sharing as a coalition strategy by an alpha male chimpanzee?', in T. Nishida, W.C. McGrew, P. Marler, M. Pickford and F.B.M. de Waal (eds) *Topics in Primatology, Vol. I: Human Origins*, Tokyo: University of Tokyo Press. pp.159-174.

Nolen-Hoeksema, S. (1995) 'Gender differences in coping with depression across the lifespan', *Depression*, 3, pp.81-90.

Nolen-Hoeksema, S. (2002) 'Gender differences in depression', in I.H. Gotlib and C.L. Hammen (eds) *Handbook of Depression*, New York: Guilford, pp.492-509.

Nolen-Hoeeksema, S., Girgus, S., and Seligman, M.E.P. (1992) 'Predictors and consequences of childhood depressive symptoms: a five-year longitudinal study', *Journal of Abnormal Psychology*, 101, pp.405-22.

Noller, P. and Callan, V. (1991) *The Adolescent in the Family*, London: Routledge.

Norman, D.A. (1981) 'Categorization of action slips', *Psychological Review*, 88, pp.1-15.

Northcraft, G.B and Neale, M.A. (1987) 'Experts, amateurs and real estate: an anchoring-and-adjustment perspective on property pricing decisions', *Organizational Behavior and Human Decision Processes*, 39 (1), pp.84-97.

Novick, L.R. (1988) 'Analogical transfer, problem similarity and expertise', *Journal of Experimental Psychology*, 14, pp.510-20.

Novick, L.R. and Holyoak, K.J. (1991) 'Mathematical problem-solving by analogy', *Journal of Experimental Psychology: Learning, Memory and Cognition*, 17, pp.398-415.

Nowakowski, R.S. (1987) 'Basic concepts of CNS development', *Child Development*, 58, pp.568-95.

Noyes, R., Crowe, R.R., Harris, E.L., Hamra, B.J., McChesney, C.M. and Chaudhry, D.R. (1986) 'Relationship between panic disorder and agoraphobia: a family study', *Archives of General Psychiatry*, 43, pp.227-32.

O'Connor, D.J. (1971) *Free will*, New York: Doubleday.

Office for National Statistics (Great Britain) (1999) *Social Trends 29*, J. Matheson and J. Pullinger (eds), London: The Stationery Office.

O'Keefe, J. and Nadel, L. (1978) *The Hippocampus as a Cognitive Map*, Oxford: Clarendon Press.

Olds, J. and Milner, P. (1954) 'Positive reinforcement produced by electrical stimulation of the septal area and other regions of the rat brain', *Journal of Comparative and Physiological Psychology*, 47, pp.419-27.

Olson, S.L., Bayles, K. and Bates, J.E. (1986) 'Mother-child interaction and children's speech progress: a longitudinal study of

the first two years', *Merrill-Palmer Quarterly*, 32, pp.1-20.

Oltmanns, T.F. and Emery, R.E. (2004) *Abnormal Psychology* (4th edn), New Jersey: Pearson.

Olton, D.S. (1976) 'Spatial memory', *Scientific American*, 236, pp.82-98.

Orlans, B. (1997) 'Ethical decision making about animal experiments', in K.D. Pimple, F.B. Orlans and J.P. Gluck (1997) 'Ethical issues in the use of animals in research', *Ethics and Behaviour*, 7 (2).

Orne, M.T. (1962) 'On the social psychology of the psychology experiment with particular reference to demand characteristics and their implications', *American Psychologist*, 16, pp.776–83.

Orne, M.T. and Holland, C.C. (1968) 'On the ecological validity of laboratory deceptions', *International Journal of Psychiatry*, 6 (4), pp.282-93.

Osborn, I. (1998) *Tormenting Thoughts and Secret Rituals: The Hidden Epidemic of OCD*, New York: Pantheon Books.

Osborne, L. (2001) 'Regional disturbances', *The New York Times*, 6 May, p.A17.

Ost, L.G., Salkovskis, P.M. and Hellstrom, K. (1991) 'One-session therapist-directed exposure vs self-exposure in the treatment of spider phobia', *Behavior Therapy*, 22, pp.407-22.

Oswald, I. (1980) *Sleep* (4th edn), Harmondsworth: Penguin Books.

Owen, F., Cross, A.J., Crow, T.J. and Poulter, M. (1978) 'Increased dopamine receptor sensitivity in schizophrenia', *Lancet*, 2, pp.223-6.

Pagel, M. and Bodmer, W. (2003) 'A naked ape would have fewer parasites', *Proceedings of the Royal Society*, London, 270, pp.117-9.

Palmer, S.E. (1975) 'The effects of contextual scenes on the identification of objects', *Memory and Cognition*, 3, pp.519-26.

Papez, J.W. (1937) 'A proposed mechanism of emotion', *Archives of Neurology and Psychiatry (Chicago)*, 38, pp.725-43.

Park, S., Holtzman, P.S. and Goldman-Rakic, P.S. (1995) 'Spatial working memory deficits in the relatives of schizophrenic patients', *Archives of General Psychiatry*, 52, pp.821-8.

Parke, R.D. (1981) *Fathers*, Cambridge, MA: Harvard University Press.

Parke, R.D., Berkowitz, L., Leyens, J.P., West, S. and Sebastian, R.J. (1977) 'Some effects of violent and nonviolent movies on the behaviour of juvenile delinquents', in L. Berkowitz

(ed.) *Advances in Experimental Psychology*, 10, New York: Academic Press.

Parker, G. (1979) 'Reported parental characteristics of agoraphobics and social phobics', *British Journal of Psychiatry*, 135, pp.555-60.

Parker, G., Gladstone, G., Roussos, J., Wilhelm, K., Mitchell, P., Hadzi-Pavlovic, D., Austin, M.P. and Hickie, I. (1998) 'Qualitative and quantitative analyses of a "lock and key" hypothesis of depression', *Psychological Medicine*, 28, pp.1263-73.

Parker, I. (1987) 'Social representations: social psychology's (mis)use of sociology', *Journal for the Theory of Social Behaviour*, 17, pp.447-69.

Parker, K.C. and Forrest, D. (1993) 'Attachment disorder: An emerging concern for school counselors', *Elementary School Guidance and Counseling*, 27(3), pp.209–15.

Parker, S.T. and Gibson, K.R. (1979) 'A developmental model for the evolution of language and intelligence in early hominids', *The Behavioural and Brain Sciences*, 2, pp.367-408.

Patterson, F. (1978) 'The gestures of a gorilla: sign language acquisition in another pongid species', *Brain and Language*, 5, pp.72-97.

Paulson, F.L. (1974) 'Teaching co-operation on television: an evaluation of Sesame Street social goals programs', *Audio-Visual Communication Review*, 22, pp.229-46.

Paulus, P.B. (1977) *Crowding in the Laboratory and its Relation to Social Facilitation*, Paper presented at the meeting of the Midwestern Psychological Association, Chicago.

Pavlov, I.P. (1927) *Conditioned Reflexes*, Oxford: Oxford University Press.

Paykel, E.S. (1981) 'Have multivariate statistics contributed to classification?', *British Journal of Psychiatry*, 139, pp.357-62.

Pearce, J.M. (1997) *Animal Learning and Cognition* (2nd edn), Hove: Psychology Press.

Pearson, G. (1984) *Hooligan: A History of Respectable Fears*, London: Macmillan.

Pederson, N.L., Plomin, R., Nesselroade, J.R. and McClearn, G.E. (1992) 'A quantitative genetic analysis of cognitive abilities during the second half of the life span', *Psychological Science*, 3(6), pp.346-53.

Penfield, W. (1958) 'Functional localization in temporal and deep Sylvian areas', *Research Publications of the Association for Research into Nervous and Mental Disease*, 36, pp.210-26.

Penn, J.V., March, J. and Leonard, H.L. (1997) 'Obsessive-compulsive disorder in children and adolescents', in L.J. Dickstein, M.B. Riba and J.M. Oldham (eds) *Review of Psychiatry, 16, Section III*, Washington DC: American Psychiatric Press, pp.III 7–III 28.

Pennebaker, J.W., Hendler, C.S., Durett, M.E. and Richards, P. (1981) 'Social factors influencing absenteeism due to illness in nursery school children', *Child Development*, 52, pp.692–700.

Pennington, D.C., Gillen, K. and Hill, P. (1999) *Social Psychology*, London: Arnold.

Penrod, S. (1983) *Social Psychology*, Englewood Cliffs, NJ: Prentice-Hall.

Penton-Voak, I.S., Perrett, D.I., Castles, D.L., Kobayashi, T., Burt, D.M., Murray, L.K. and Minamisawa, R. (1999) 'Female preference for male faces changes cyclically', *Nature*, 399, pp.741-2.

Peplau, L.A. (1991) 'Lesbian and gay relationships', in J. Gonsiorek and J. Weinrich (eds), *Homosexuality: Research Implications for Public Policy*, Newbury Park: Sage.

Pepperberg, I.M., Garcia, S.E., Jackson. E.C. and Marconi, S. (1995) 'Mirror-use by African Grey parrots (*Psittacus erithacus*)', *Journal of Comparative Psychology*, 109, pp.182-95.

Perrett, D.I., May, K.A. and Yoshikawa, S. (1994) 'Facial shape and judgements of female attractiveness', *Nature*, 368, pp.239-42

Perrin, S. and Spencer, C. (1980) 'The Asch effect – a child of its time', *Bulletin of the British Psychological Society*, 33, pp.405–6.

Perrin, S. and Spencer, C. (1981) 'Independence or conformity in the Asch experiment as a reflection of cultural and situational factors', *British Journal of Social Psychology*, 20, pp.205–9.

Peterson, L.R. and Peterson, M. (1959) 'Short-term retention of individual verbal items', *Journal of Experimental Psychology*, 58, pp.193–8.

Petrie, M. (1992) 'Peacocks with low mating success are more likely to suffer predation', *Animal Behavior*, 44, pp.585-6.

Petrie, M., Halliday, T. and Sanders, C. (1991) 'Peahens prefer peacocks with elaborate trains', *Animal Behavior*, 41, pp.323-31.

Pettigrew, T.F. (1959) 'Regional differences in anti-negro practice', *Journal of Abnormal and Social Psychology*, 59, pp.28-56.

Pettigrew, T.F. (1979) 'The ultimate attribution error: extending Allport's cognitive analysis of prejudice', *Personality and Social Psychology Bulletin*, 5, pp.461-76.

Pfeiffer, W.M. (1982) 'Culture-Bound Syndromes', in I. Al-Issa (ed.) *Culture and Psychopathology*, Baltimore, Maryland: University Park Press.

Phinney, J.S. (1996) 'When we talk about American ethnic groups, what do we mean? *American Psychologist*, 51, pp.918-27.

Phinney, J.S. and Alipuria, L.L. (1990) 'Ethnic identity in college students from four ethnic groups, *Journal of Adolesecnece*, 13, pp.171-83.

Piaget, J. (1926) *The Language and Thought of the Child*, New York: Harcourt Brace Jovanovich.

Piaget, J. (1932) *The Moral Judgement of the Child*, Harmondsworth: Penguin.

Piaget, J. (1954) *The Construction of Reality in the Child*, New York: Basic Books.

Piaget, J. (1960) *Psychology of Intelligence*, Paterson, NJ: Littlefield, Adams.

Piaget, J. and Inhelder, B. (1956) *The Child's Conception of Space*, London: Routledge & Kegan Paul.

Pick, H.L. (1987) 'Information and the effects of early perceptual experience', in N. Eisenberg (ed.) *Contemporary Topics in Developmental Psychology*, New York: Wiley.

Pike, K.L. (1967) *Language in relation to a unified theory of the structure of human behaviour*, The Hague: Mouton.

Pike, K.M. and Rodin, J. (1991) 'Mothers, daughters and disordered eating', *Journal of Abnormal Psychology*, 100(2), pp.198–204.

Pilcher, J.J. and Huffcutt, A.I. (1996) 'Effects of sleep deprivation on performance: A meta-analysis', *Sleep*, 19, pp.318-326.

Pilgrim, D. and Rogers, A. (1993) *A Sociology of Mental Illness*, Buckingham: Open University Press.

Piliavin, I., Rodin, J. and Piliavin, J. (1969) 'Good Samaritanism: an underground phenomenon?', *Journal of Personality and Social Psychology*, 13, pp.289-99.

Piliavin, J.A., Dovidio, J.F., Gaertner, S.L. and Clark, R.D. (1981) *Emergency Intervention*, New York: Academic Press.

Pilleri, G. (1979) 'The blind Indus dolphin', *Platanista indi. Endeavour*, 3, pp.48-56.

Pinker, S. (1989) *Learnability and Cognition*, Cambridge, MA: MIT Press.

Pinker, S. (1990) 'Language Acquisition', in D.N. Osherson and H. Lasnik (eds) *Language: An Invitation to Cognitive Science*, Vol. 1, Cambridge, MA: MIT Press.

Pinker, S. (1994) *The Language Instinct*, Harmondsworth: Allen Lane.

Pirchio, M., Spinelli, D., Fiorentini, A. and Maffei, L. (1978) 'Infant contrast sensitivity evaluated by evoked potentials', *Brain Research*, 141, pp.179-84.

Pi-Sunyer, X., Kissileff, H.R., Thornton, J. and Smith, G.P. (1982) 'C-terminal octapeptide of cholecystokinin decreases food intake in obese men', *Physiology and Behavior*, 29, pp.627-30.

Pitz, G.F. and Sachs, N.J. (1984) 'Judgement and decision: theory and application', *Annual Review of Psychology*, 35, pp.139-63.

Plomin, R. (1994) *Genetics and Experience: The Interplay between Nature and Nurture*, Thousand Oaks, CA: Sage.

Plomin, R., DeFries, J.C. and Fulker, D.W. (1988) *Nature and Nurture during Infancy and Early Childhood*, New York: Academic Press.

Polimeni, J. and Reiss, J. (2002) 'How shamanism and group selection may reveal the origins of schizophrenia', *Medical Hypotheses*, 58 (3), pp.244-8.

Polimeni, J. and Reiss, J. (2003) 'Evolutionary perspectives on schizophrenia', *Canadian Journal of Psychiatry*, 48, pp.34-9.

Pollack, R.H. (1963) 'Contour detectability thresholds as a function of chronological age', *Perceptual and Motor Skills*, 17, pp.411-17.

Pollack, R.H. and Silvar, S.D. (1967) 'Magnitude of the Müller-Lyer illusion in children as a function of pigmentation of the Fundus oculi', *Psychonomic Science*, 8, pp.83-4.

Poltrock, S.E., Lansman, M. and Hunt, E. (1982) 'Automatic and controlled attention processes in auditory target detection', *Journal of Experimental Psychology: Human Perception and Performance*, 8, pp.37-45.

Pomerantz, J.R. (1981) 'Perceptual organisation in information processing', in M. Kubovy and J.R. Pomerantz (eds) *Perceptual Organisation*, Hillsdale, NJ: Erlbaum.

Popper, K. (1959) *The Logic of Scientific Discovery*, New York: Basic Books.

Posner, M. and Keele, S.W. (1968) 'On the genesis of abstract ideas', *Journal of Experimental Psychology*, 77, pp.353-63.

Potter, J. and Litton, I. (1985) 'Some problems underlying the theory of social representations', *British Journal of Social Psychology*, 24, pp.81-90.

Povinelli, D.J. (1989) 'Failure to find self-recognition in Asian elephants (*Elephas maximusi*) in contrast to their use of mirror cues to discover hidden food', *Journal of Comparative Psychology*, 103, 122-31.

Povinelli, D.J., Nelson, K.E. and Boyson, S.T. (1990) 'Inferences about guessing and knowing by chimpanzees (*Pan troglodytes*)', *Journal of Comparative Psychology*, 104, pp.203-10.

Povinelli, D.J., Rulf, A.B., Landau, K.R. and Bierschwale, D.T. (1993) 'Self-recognition in chimpanzees: distribution, ontogeny and patterns of emergence', *Journal of Comparative Psychology*, 107, pp.347-72.

Premack, D. and Woodruff, G. (1978) 'Does the chimpanzee have a theory of mind?', *Behavioural and Brain Sciences*, 4, pp.515-26.

Prentice-Dunn, S. and Rogers, R.W. (1989) 'Deindividuation and the self-regulation of behaviour', in P. Paulus (ed.) *The Psychology of Group Influence*, Hillsdale, NJ: Lawrence Erlbaum.

Price, J.S., Sloman, L., Gardner, R. and Rohde, P. (1994) 'The social competition hypothesis of depression', *British Journal of Psychiatry*, 164, pp.309-15.

Prien, R.F. (1988) 'Somatic treatment of unipolar depressive disorder', in A.J. Frances and R.E. Hales (eds) *Review of Psychiatry*, Washington, DC: American Psychiatric Press.

Prince, M. (1906) *The Dissociation of a Personality: A Biographical Study in Abnormal Psychology*, New York: Longmans, Green.

Procopio, M. and Marriott, P.K. (1998) 'Is the decline in diagnosis of schizophrenia caused by the disappearance of a seasonal aetiological agent? An epidemiological study in England and Wales', *Psychological Medicine*, 28, pp.367-73.

Quinn, W.G., Sziber, P.P. and Booker, R. (1979) 'The *Drosophila* memory mutant amnesiac', *Nature*, 77, pp.212-4.

Quinton, D., Rutter, M. and Liddle, C. (1985) 'Institutional rearing, parenting difficulties and marital support', *Annual Progress in Child Psychiatry and Child Development*, pp.173–206.

Rack, P. (1982) *Race, Culture and Mental Disorder*, London: Routledge.

Rahe, R.H., Mahan, J. and Arthur, R. (1970) 'Prediction of near-future health-change from subjects' preceding life changes', *Journal of Psychosomatic Research*, 14, pp.401–6.

Ramachandran, V.S. (1992) 'Blind spots', *Scientific American*, pp.102-9.

Ramachandran, V.S. and Blakeslee, S. (1999) *Phantoms in the Brain*, London: Fourth Estate.

Randrup, A. and Munkvad, I. (1966) 'On the role of dopamine in the amphetamine excitatory response', *Nature*, 211, p.540.

Rank, S.G. and Jacobson, C.K. (1977) 'Hospital nurses' compliance with medication overdose orders: a failure to replicate', *Journal of Health and Social Behaviour*, 18, pp.188–93.

Raphael, K.G., Cloitre, M. and Dohrenwend, B.P. (1991) 'Problems of recall and misclassification with checklist methods of measuring stressful life events', *Health Psychology*, 10, pp.62–74.

Rapoport, J.L. (1989) 'The biology of obsessions and compulsions', *Scientific American*, 260, pp.83-9.

Rapoport, J.L. and Fiske, A. (1998) 'The new biology of obsessive-compulsive disorder: implications for evolutionary psychology', *Perspectives in Biology and Medicine*, 41 (2), pp.159-71.

Ratcliffe-Crain, J. and Baum, A. (1990) 'Individual differences and health: Gender, coping, and stress', in H.S. Friedman (ed.) *Personality and Disease*, New York: Wiley.

Rattner, A. (1988) 'Convicted but innocent: wrongful conviction and the criminal justice system', *Law and Human Behaviour*, 2, pp.283–93.

Reader, S.M. and Laland, K.N. (2002) 'Social intelligence, innovation and enhanced brain size in primates', *Proceedings of the National Academy of Science, USA*, 99 (7), pp.4436-41.

Reason, J. (1979) 'Actions not as planned: the price of automatization', in G. Underwood and R. Stephens (eds) *Aspects of Consciousness* (Vol.1), London: Academic Press.

Reason, J. (1992) 'Cognitive underspecification: its variety and consequences', in B.J. Baars (ed.) *Experimental Slips and Human Error: Exploring the Architecture of Volition*, New York: Plenum Press.

Reber, A.S. (1995) *Penguin Dictionary of Psychology* (2nd edn), London: Penguin.

Reed, S. (1972) 'Pattern recognition and categorisation', *Cognitive Psychology*, 3, pp.382-407.

Reed, T.E. and Jensen, A.R. (1993) 'Cranial capacity: new Caucasian data and comments on Rushton's claimed Mongoloid–Caucasoid brain-size differences', *Intelligence*, 17, pp.423-31.

Regan, T. (1983) *The Case for Animal Rights*: University of California Press.

Regan, T. and Singer, P. (eds) (1976) *Animal Rights and Human Obligations*, Englewood Cliffs, NJ: Prentice-Hall.

Reich, J. and Yates, W. (1988) 'Family history of psychiatric disorders in social phobia', *Comprehensive Psychiatry*, 29, pp.72-5.

Reicher, S.D. (1984) 'The St Paul's riot: an explanation of the limits of crowd action in terms of a social identity model', *European Journal of Social Psychology*, 14, pp.1–21.

Reicher, S.D. and Potter, J. (1985) 'Psychological theory as intergroup perspective: a comparative analysis of "scientific" and "lay" accounts of crowd events', *Human Relations*, 38, pp.167–89.

Reid, E. (1998) 'The Self and the Internet: variations on the illusion of one self', in J. Gackenbach (ed.) *Psychology and the Internet*, San Diego: Academic Press.

Reik, W., Romer, I., Barton, S.C, Surani, M.A., Howlett, S.K. and Klose, J. (1993) 'Adult phenotype in the mouse can be affected by epigenetic events in the early embryo', *Development*, 119, pp.933-42.

Reitman, J.S. (1974) 'Without surreptitious rehearsal, information in short-term memory decays', *Journal of Verbal Learning and Verbal Behaviour*, 13, pp.365–77.

Renner, F. (1990) *Spinnen: Ungeheuer Sympathisch*, Kaiserslautern: Verlag.

Rescorla, R.A. (1980) *Pavlovian Second-order Conditioning*, Hillsdale, NJ: Lawrence Erlbaum Associates.

Revelle, W. (1993) 'Individual differences in personality and motivation: "Non-cognitive" determinants of cognitive performance', in A.D. Baddeley and I. Weiskrantz (eds) *Attention: Awareness, Selection and Control*, Oxford: Oxford University Press.

Reynolds, P.C. (1981) *On the Evolution of Human Behaviour*, Berkeley and Los Angeles: University of California Press.

Rholes, W.S. and Pryor, J.B. (1982) 'Cognitive accessibility and causal attributions', *Personality and Social Psychology Bulletin*, 8, pp.719-27.

Richardson, J.T.E. (1984) 'Developing the theory of working memory', *Memory and Cognition*, 12, pp.71–83.

Ridley, M. (1995) *Animal Behaviour* (2nd edn), Oxford: Blackwell.

Ridley, M. (2003) *Nature via Nurture*, London: Fourth Estate.

Roberts P. and Newton, P M. (1987) 'Levinsonian studies of women's adult development', *Psychology and Aging*, 2, pp.154-63.

Robertson, J. and Robertson, J. (1971) 'Young child in brief separation', *Psychoanalytic Study of the Child*, 26, pp.264–315.

Robinson, J.O., Rosen, M., Revill, S.L., David, H. and Rus, G.A.D. (1980) 'Self-administered intravenous and intramuscular pethidine', *Anaesthesia*, 35, pp.763–70.

Rock, I. (1983) *The Logic of Perception*, Cambridge, MA: MIT Press.

Rock, I. (1995) *Perception*, New York: Scientific American Library.

Rockman, S. (1980) *On the Level: Final Report on Formative Evaluation*, Bloomington, in: Agency for Instructional Television.

Rogers, C.R. (1974) 'In retrospect: forty-six years', *American Psychologist*, 29, pp.115-23.

Rogers, J. (1993) 'The phylogenetic relationships among Homo, Pan and Gorilla', *Journal of Human Evolution*, 25:, pp.201-15.

Rokeach, M. (1956) 'Political and religious dogmatism: an alternate to the authoritarian personality', *Psychological Monographs*, 70, No. 18.

Rolls, B.J., Rowe, E.A. and Rolls, E.T. (1982) 'How sensory properties of food affect human feeding behavior', *Physiology and Behavior*, 29, pp.409-17.

Romaine, S. (1984) *The Language of Children and Adolescents: The Acquisition of Communicative Competence*, Oxford: Basil Blackwell.

Rose, S. (1997) *Lifelines: Biology, Freedom, Determinism*, London: Penguin.

Rose, S.A. and Blank, M. (1974) 'The potency of context in children's cognition: an illustration through conservation', *Child Development*, 45, pp.499-502.

Rosenblatt, P.C. and Anderson, R.M. (1981) 'Human sexuality in cross-cultural perspective', in M. Cook (ed.) *The Bases of Human Sexual Attraction*, London: Academic Press.

Rosenhan, D.L. (1973) 'On being sane in insane places', *Science*, 179, pp.250-8.

Rosenhan, D.L. and Seligman, M.E.P. (1984) *Abnormal Psychology*, New York: W.W. Norton

Rosenhan, D.L. and Seligman, M.E.P. (1995) *Abnormal Psychology* (3rd edn), New York: Norton.

Rosenthal, R. (1966) *Experimenter effects in behavioural research*, New York: Appleton-Century-Crofts.

Rosenwasser, A.M., Boulos, Z. and Ternan, M. (1981) 'Circadian organisation of food intake and meal patterns in the rat', *Physiology and Behavior*, 27, pp.33-39.

Rosenzweig, M.R., Leiman, A.L. and Breedlove, S.M. (1999) *Biological Psychology* (2nd edn), Sunderland, MA: Sinauer Associates, Inc.

Ross, L.D. (1977) 'The intuitive psychologist and his shortcomings: distortions in the attribution process', in L. Berkowitz (ed.) *Advances in Experimental Social Psychology*, Vol. 10, New York: Academic Press.

Ross, L.D., Amabile, T.M. and Steinmetz, J.L. (1977) 'Social roles, social control, and biases in social perception: biased attributional processes in the debriefing paradigm', *Journal of Personality and Social Psychology*, 35, pp.485-94.

Rotter, J.B. (1966) 'Generalised expectancies for internal versus external control of reinforcement', *Psychological Monographs*, 80, pp.1–28.

Rubin, Z. (1973) *Liking and Loving: An Invitation to Social Psychology*, New York: Holt, Rinehart & Winston.

Rubin, Z., Hill, C.T., Peplau, L.A. and Dunkel-Schetter, C. (1980) 'Self-disclosure in dating couples: Sex roles and the ethic of openness', *Journal of Marriage and the Family*, 42, pp.305-17.

Ruhm, C.J. (2000) *Parental Employment and Child Cognitive Development*, National Bureau of Economic Research, NBER Working Paper No. 7666.

Rumbaugh, D.M., Savage-Rumbaugh, E.S. and Sevcik, R.A. (1994) 'Biobehavioural roots of language: a comparative perspective of chimpanzee, child and culture', in R.W. Wrangham, W.C. McGrew, F.B.M. de Waal, P.G. Heltne and L.A. Marquardt (eds) *Chimpanzee Cultures*, Cambridge, MA: Harvard University Press, pp.319-34.

Runciman, W.G. (1966) *Relative Deprivation and Social Justice*, London: Routledge & Kegan Paul.

Runyon, R. and Haber, A. (1976) *Fundamentals of Behavioural Statistics* (3rd edn), Reading, MA: McGraw Hill.

Rusak, B. and Zucker, I. (1975) 'Biological rhythms and animal behavior', *Annual Review of Psychology*, 26, pp.137-71.

Rusbult, C.E. (1983) 'A longitudinal study of the investment model: the development and deterioration of satisfaction and commitment in heterosexual involvements', *Journal of Personality and Social Psychology*, 45, pp.101-17.

Rusbult, C.E. and Martz, J.M. (1995) 'Remaining in an abusive relationship: an investment model analysis of nonvoluntary dependence', *Personality and Social Psychology Bulletin*, 21, pp.558-71.

Rushton, J.P. (1995) *Race, Evolution and Behavior: A Life-history Perspective*, New Brunswick, NJ: Transaction.

Rushton, J.P. and Owen, D. (1975) 'Immediate and delayed effects of TV modelling and preaching on children's generosity', *British Journal of Social and Clinical Psychology*, 14, pp.309-10.

Russek, M. (1982) 'Effects of hepatic denervation on the anorexic response to epinephrine, amphetamine, and lithium chloride: a behavioral identification of glucostatic afferents', *Journal of Comparative and Physiological Psychology*, 96, pp.361-75.

Russell, C.M. (1999) 'A meta-analysis of published research on the effects of non-maternal care on child development', *Dissertations Abstracts International, A (Humanities and Social Sciences)*, 59(9-A), p.3362.

Russell, M.J., Switz, G.M., and Thompson, K. (1980) 'Olfactory influences on the human menstrual cycle', *Pharmacology, Biochemistry and Behaviour*, 13, pp.737-8.

Russell, W.M.S. and Birch, R. (1959) *The Principles of Humane Experimental Technique*, Methuen, London.

Russon, A.E. and Galdikas, B.M.F. (1995) 'Constraints on great apes' imitation: model and action selectivity in rehabilitant orangutan (*Pongo pygmaeus*) imitation', *Journal of Comparative Psychology*, 109, pp.5-17.

Rutter, M. (1976) 'Parent–child separation: psychological effects on the child', in A.M. Clarke and A.D.B. Clarke (eds) *Early Experience: Myth and Evidence*, London: Open Books.

Rutter, M. (1981) *Maternal Deprivation Reassessed* (2nd edn), Harmondsworth: Penguin.

Rutter, M., Anderson-Wood, L., Beckett, C., Bredenkamp, D., Castle, J., Dunn, J., Ehrich, K., Groothues, C., Harborne, A., Hay, D., Jewett, J., Keaveney, L., Kreppner, J., Messer, J., O'Connor, T., Quinton, D. and White, A. (1998) 'Developmental catch-up and deficit, following adoption after severe global early privation', *Journal of Child Psychology and Psychiatry*, 39, pp.465–76.

Rutter, M., Graham, P., Chadwock, O. and Yule, W. (1976) 'Adolescent turmoil: fact or fiction?', *Journal of Child Psychology and Psychiatry*, 7, pp.35-56.

Ryan, R.M. and Lynch, J.H. (1989) 'Emotional autonomy versus detachment: revisiting the vicissitudes of adolescence and young adulthood', *Child Development*, 60, pp.34-64.

Ryle, G. (1949) *The Concept of Mind*, New York: Barnes & Noble.

Rymer, R. (1993) *Genie: Escape from a Silent Childhood*, London: Michael Joseph.

Sachs, J., Bard, B. and Johnson, M.L. (1981) 'Language with restricted input: case studies of two hearing children of deaf parents', *Applied Psycholinguistics*, 2, pp.33-54.

Sackeim, H.A. (1988) 'The efficacy of electroconvulsive therapy', *Ann. NY Academic Science*, 462, pp.70-5.

Sackeim, H.A., Nordlie, J.W. and Gur, R.C. (1993) 'Effects of stimulus intensity and electrode replacement on the efficacy of the effects of electroconvulsive therapy', *New England Journal of Medicine*, 328, pp.839-46.

Sackeim, H.A., Prudic, J. and Devanand, D.P. (1990) 'The impact of medication resistance and continuation of pharmacotherapy following response to electroconvulsive therapy in major depression', *Journal of Clinical Pharmacology*, 10, pp.96-104.

Saegert, S., Swap, W. and Zajonc, R.B. (1973) 'Exposure, contact and interpersonal attraction', *Journal of Personality and Social Psychology*, 25, pp.234-42.

Sameroff, A., Seifer, R., Baldwin, A. and Baldwin C. (1993) 'Stability of intelligence from preschool to adolescence: the influence of social and family risk factors', *Child Development*, 64, pp.80-97.

Santrock, J.W. (2001) *Adolescence* (8th edn), Boston: McGraw Hill.

Sapir, E. (1921) *Language*, New York: Harcourt, Brace & World.

Sapolsky, R.M. (1994) *Why Zebras Don't Get Ulcers*, New York: Freeman.

Sarason, I.G., Johnson, J.H. and Siegel, J.M. (1978) 'Assessing the impact of life changes: development of the Life Experiences Survey', *Journal of Consulting and Clinical Psychology*, 46, pp.932–46.

Savage-Rumbaugh, E.S. (1986) *Ape Language from Conditioned Response to Symbol*, New York: Columbia University Press.

Savage-Rumbaugh, E.S. (1988) 'A new look at ape language: comprehension of vocal speech and syntax', *Nebraska Symposium on Motivation*, 35, pp.201-55.

Savage-Rumbaugh, E.S. (1991) 'Language learning in the bonobo: How and why they learn', in N.A. Krasnegor, D.M. Rumbaugh, R.L. Schiefelbusch and M. Studdert-Kennedy (eds) *Biological and behavioural determinants of language development*. Hillsdale, NJ: Lawrence Erlbaum Associates Inc.

Savage-Rumbaugh, E.S. and Fields, W.M. (2000) 'Linguistic, cultural and cognitive capacities of bonobos (*Pan paniscus*)', *Culture and Psychology*, 6, pp.131-53.

Savage-Rumbaugh, E.S. and Lewin, R. (1994) *Kanzi: The Ape at the Brink of the Human Mind*, London: Doubleday.

Savin, H.B. (1973) 'Professors and psychological researchers: conflicting values in conflicting roles', *Cognition*, 2(1), pp.147–9.

Scarr, S. and Carter-Salzmann, L. (1979) 'Twin method: Defense of a critical assumption', *Behavior Genetics*, 9, pp.527-42.

Scarr, S. and Weinberg, R.A. (1976) 'IQ test performance of black children adopted by white families', *American Psychologist*, 31, pp.726-39.

Schachter, S. and Singer, J.E. (1962) 'Cognitive, social, and physiological determinants of emotional state', *Psychological Review*, 69, pp.379-99.

Schaffer, H.R. (1998) *Making Decisions about Children*, Oxford: Blackwell.

Schaffer, H.R. and Emerson, P.E. (1964) *The Development of Social Attachments in Infancy*, Monographs of the Society for Research in Child Development, 29(3), Serial No. 94.

Schaie, K.W. and Hertzog, C. (1983) 'Fourteen-year cohort-sequential analysis of adult intellecual development', *Developmental Psychology*, 19, pp.531-43.

Schaie, K.W. and Willis, S.L. (1991) *Adult Development and Aging*, New York: Harper Collins.

Schettino, A.P. and Borden, R.J. (1975) 'Group size versus group density: where is the affect?', *Personality and Social Psychology Bulletin*, 2, pp.67-70.

Schneider, B.H., Smith, A., Poisson, S.E. and Kwan, A.B. (1997) 'Cultural dimensions of children's peer relations', in S. Duck (ed.) *Handbook of Personal Relationships: Theory, Research and Interventions* (2nd edn), Chichester: John Wiley.

Schoenthaler, S.J., Bier, I.D., Young, K., Nichols, D. & Jansenns, S. (2000) 'The effect of vitamin-mineral supplementation on the intelligence of American schoolchildren: a randomized, double-blind placebo-controlled trial', *Journal of Alternative and Complementary Medicine*, 6(1), pp.19-29.

Schreiber, F.R. (1973) *Sybil*, New York: Warner.

Schuler, H. (1982) *Ethical Problems in Psychological Research*, New York: Academic Press.

Schumm, W.R., Webb, F.J. and Bullman, S.R. (1998) 'Gender and marital satisfaction: Data from a national survey of families and households', *Psychological Reports*, 83(1) 319-327.

Schunk, D.H. (1983) 'Reward contingencies and the development of children's skills and self-efficacy', *Journal of Educational Psychology*, 75, pp.511-18.

Schuster, B., Fosterling, F. and Weiner, B. (1989) 'Perceiving the causes of success and failure: a cross-cultural examination of attributional concepts', *Journal of Cross-Cultural Psychology*, 20, pp.191-213.

Schwartz, J.J. (1991) 'Why stop calling? A study of unison bout singing in a neotropical treefrog', *Animal Behaviour*, 42, pp.565-77.

Schwartz, J.M., Stoessel, P.W., Baxter, L.R., Martin, K.M. and Phelps, M.E. (1996) 'Systematic changes in cerebral glucose metabolic rate after successful behaviour modification treatment of obsessive-compulsive disorder', *Archives of General Psychiatry*, 53, pp.109-13.

Schwartz, S. (1997) 'Values and Culture', in D. Munro, S. Carr and J. Schumaker (eds) *Motivation and Culture*, New York: Routledge.

Schwartz, S.H. (1971) 'Modes of representation and problem solving: well evolved is half solved', *Journal of Experimental Psychology*, 91, pp.347-50.

Schweickert, R. and Boruff, B. (1986) 'Short-term memory capacity: magic number or magic spell?', *Journal of Experimental Psychology: Learning, Memory and Cognition*, 12, pp.419–45.

Schweinhart, L.J., Barnes, H.V. and Weikart, D.P. (1993) 'Significant Benefits: The High/Scope Perry Preschool Study through Age 27', *Monographs of the High/Scope Educational Research Foundation*, 10, Ypsilanti, MI: High/Scope Press.

Scroppo, J., Weinberger, J., Drob, S. and Eagle, P. (1998) 'Identifying dissociative identity disorder: a self-report and projective study', *Journal of Abnormal Psychology*, 92, pp.272-84.

Searle, J. (1980) 'Minds, brains and programs', *The Behavioural and Brain Sciences*, 3, pp.417-57.

Sears, D.O. (1986) 'College sophomores in the laboratory: Influences of a narrow data base on psychology's view of human nature', *Journal of Personality and Social Psychology*, 51, pp.513-30.

Sebrechts, M.M., Marsh, R.L. and Seamon, J.G. (1989) 'Secondary memory and very rapid forgetting', *Memory and Cognition*, 17, pp.693–700.

Segal, S.J. and Fusella, V. (1970) 'Influence of imaged pictures and sounds on the detection of visual and auditory signals', *Journal of Experimental Psychology*, 83, pp.458-64.

Segall, M.H., Campbell, D.T. and Herskovits, M.J. (1963) 'Cultural differences in the perception of geometric illusions', *Science*, 193, pp.769-71.

Segall, M.H., Campbell, D.T. and Herskovits, M.J. (1966) *The Influence of Culture on Visual Perception*, Indianapolis: Bobbs-Merrill.

Segall, M.H., Dasen, P.R., Berry, J.W. and Poortinga, Y.H. (1990) *Human Behaviour in Global Perspective: An Introduction to Cross-cultural Psychology*, New York: Pergamon Press.

Selfridge, O.G. (1959) 'Pandemonium: a paradigm for learning', in *Symposium on the Mechanisation of Thought Processes*, London: HMSO.

Seligman, M.E.P. (1970) 'On the generality of the laws of learning', *Psychological Review*, 77, pp.406-18.

Seligman, M.E.P. (1971) 'Phobias and preparedness', *Behaviour Therapy*, 2, pp.307-20.

Seligman, M.E.P. (1974) 'Depression and learned helplessness', in R.J. Friedman and M.M. Katz (eds) *The Psychology of Depression: Contemporary Theory and Research*, Washington, DC: Winston Wiley.

Seligman, M.E.P. (1975) *Helplessness: On Depression, Development and Death*, London: W.H. Freeman.

Seligman, M.E.P., Abramson, L.Y., Semmell, A. and von Baeyer, C. (1979) 'Depression and attributional style', *Journal of Abnormal Psychology*, 88, pp.242-7.

Selye, H. (1956) *The Stress of Life*, New York: McGraw-Hill.

Senra, C. and Polaino, A. (1998) 'Assessment of treatment outcome in depressed patients: concordance of methods', *British Journal of Clinical Psychology*, 37, pp.217-27.

Sergent, J. (1984) 'An investigation into component and configural processes underlying face recognition', *British Journal of Psychology*, 75, pp.221-42.

Sergent, J. and Signoret, J.L. (1992) 'Functional and anatomical decomposition of face processing: evidence from prosopagnosia and PET study of normal subjects', in V. Bruce, A. Cowey, A.W. Ellis and D.I. Perrett (eds) *Processing the Facial Image*, Oxford: Clarendon Press.

Seyfarth, R.M. and Cheney, D.L. (1980) 'The ontogeny of vervet monkey calling: a preliminary report', *Zeitschrift für Tierpsychologie*, 54, pp.37-56.

Seyfarth, R.M. and Cheney, D.L. (1992) 'Meaning and mind in monkeys', *Scientific American*, 267, pp.122-8.

Shaffer, D.R. (1993) *Developmental Psychology: Childhood and Adolescence* (3rd edn), Pacific Grove, CA: Brooks/Cole.

Shaffer, D.R. (2002) *Developmental Psychology* (6th edn), Belmont, CA: Thomson Learning.

Shaffer, L.H. (1975) 'Multiple attention in continuous verbal tasks', in P.M.A. Rabbitt and S. Dornic (eds) *Attention and Performance*, London: Academic Press.

Shallice, T. (1967) Paper presented at NATO symposium on short-term memory, Cambridge, England.

Shanab, M.E. and Yahya, K.A. (1977) 'A behavioural study of obedience in children', *Journal of Personality and Social Psychology*, 35, pp.530–6.

Shapley, R. and Lennie, P. (1985) 'Spatial frequency analysis in the visual system', *Annual Review of Neuroscience*, 8, pp.547-83.

Sharkey, K.M. (2001) 'Melatonin administration to phase shift circadian rhythms and promote sleep in human models of night shift work', *Dissertation Abstracts International: Section B – The Sciences and Engineering*, 61, pp.51-78.

Sharpley, C.F. and Layton, R. (1998) 'Effects of age of retirement, reason for retirement, and pre-retirement training on psychological and physical health during retirement', *Australian Psychologist*, 33 (2), pp.119-24.

Shatz, M. and Gelman, R. (1973) 'The development of common skills: modifications in the speech of young children as a function of the listener', *Monograph of the Society for Research in Child Development*, 152.

Shaw, D.F. (1997) 'Gay men and computer communication: a discourse of sex and identity in cyberspace', in S.G. Jones (ed.) *Virtual Culture: Identity and Communication in Cybersociety*, Thousand Islands: Sage.

Sheehy, G. (1996) *New Passages*, New York: Harper Collins.

Shekelle, R.B., Hulley, S.B., Neaton, J.D., Billings, J.H., Borhani, N.O., Gerace, T.A., Jacobs, D.R., Lasser, N.L., Mittelmark, M.B. and Stamler, J. (1985) 'The MRFIT Behavior Pattern Study: II. Type A behavior and incidence of coronary heart disease', *American Journal of Epidemiology*, 122, pp.559–70.

Shephard, R.N. and Zare, S.L. (1983) 'Path-guided apparent motion', *Science*, 220, pp.632-4.

Sherif, M. (1966) *Group Conflict and Co-operation: Their Social Psychology*, London: Routledge & Kegan Paul.

Sherif, M. and Sherif, C.W. (1953) *Groups in Harmony and Tension: An Integration of Studies on Intergroup Relations*, New York: Octagon.

Sherif, M., Harvey, O.J., White, B.J., Hood, W.R. and Sherif, C.W. (1961) *Intergroup Conflict and Cooperation: The Robber's Cave Experiment*, Norman, Oklahoma: University of Oklahoma.

Sherman, P.W. (1981) 'Kinship, demography and Belding's ground squirrel nepotism', *Behavioral Ecology and Sociobiology*, 8, pp.251-9.

Sherry, D. F. and Galef, B.G. Jr. (1990) 'Social learning without imitation: more about milk bottle opening by birds', *Animal Behaviour*, 40, pp.987-9.

Sherry, D., Jacobs, L.F. and Gaulin, S.J.C. (1992) 'Spatial memory and adaptive specialisation of the hippocampus', *Trends in Neurosciences*, 15, pp.298-303.

Shettleworth, S.J. (1995) 'Comparative studies of memory in food storing birds: From the field to the Skinner box', in E. Alleva, A. Fasolo, H.P. Lipp, L. Nadel, and L. Ricceri (eds) *Behavioural Brain Research in Naturalistic and Semi-Naturalistic Settings*, Dordrecht: Kluwer Academic Press.

Shettleworth, S.J. (1998) *Cognition, Evolution and Behavior*, New York: Oxford University Press.

Shields, J. (1962) *Monozygotic Twins Brought Up Apart and Brought up Together*, London: Oxford University Press.

Shiffrin, R.M. and Schneider, W. (1977) 'Controlled and automatic human information processing: perceptual learning, automatic attending and a general theory', *Psychological Review*, 84, pp.127-90.

Shiloh, S. (1994) 'Heuristics and biases in health decision making: their expression in genetic counselling', in L. Heath, R.S. Tindale, J. Edwards, E.J. Posavac, F.B. Bryant, E. Henderson-King, Y. Suarez-Balcazar and J. Myers (eds) *Applications of Heuristics and Biases to Social Issues*, New York: Plenum.

Shweder, R.A., Mahapatra, M. and Miller, J.G. (1987) 'Culture and moral development', in J. Kagan and S. Lamb (eds) *The emergence of morality in young children*, (pp.1-83), Chicago: University of Chicago Press.

Sieber, J.E. and Stanley, B. (1988) 'Ethical and professional dimensions of socially sensitive research', *American Psychologist*, 43 (1), pp.49-55.

Simpson, J.A., Campbell, B. and Berscheid, E. (1986) 'The association between romantic love and marriage: Kephart (1967) twice revisited', *Personality and Social Psychology Bulletin*, 12, pp.363-72.

Sinclair-de-Zwart, H. (1969) 'Developmental psycholinguistics', in D. Elkind and J.H. Flavell (eds) *Studies in Cognitive Development*, Oxford: Oxford University Press.

Singer, P. (1975) *Animal Liberation*, New York: Avon.

Skeels, H. (1966) 'Adult status of children with contrasting early life experiences: A follow-up study', *Monographs of Society for Research of Child Development*, 31(3), whole issue.

Skeels, H. and Dye, H.B. (1939) 'A study of the effects of differential stimulation on mentally retarded children', *Proceedings and Addresses of the American Association on Mental Deficiency*, 44, 114–36.

Skinner, B.F. (1938) *The Behavior of Organisms*, New York: Appleton-Century-Crofts.

Skinner, B.F. (1953) *Science and Human Behavior*, New York: Macmillan.

Skinner, B.F. (1957) *Verbal Behaviour*, New York: Appleton-Century-Crofts.

Skinner, B.F. (1971, 1973) *Beyond Freedom and Dignity*, New York: Knopf.

Skinner, B.F. (1974) *About Behaviourism*, New York: Knopf.

Skinner, B.F. (1981) 'Selection by consequences', *Science*, 213, pp.501-4.

Skinner, B.F. (1987) 'What is wrong with daily life in the Western world?', in B.F. Skinner *Upon Further Reflection*, Englewood Cliffs, NJ: Prentice-Hall.

Skodak, M. and Skeels, H. (1949) 'A final follow-up study of 100 adopted children', *Journal of Genetic Psychology*, 75, pp.85–125.

Slaby, R.G. and Frey, K.G. (1975) 'Development of gender constancy and selective attention to same-sex models', *Child Development*, 46, pp.849-56.

Slater, A. and Morrison, V. (1985) 'Shape constancy and slant perception at birth', *Perception*, 14, pp.337-44.

Slater, E. and Sheilds, J. (1969) 'Genetic aspects of anxiety', *British Journal of Psychiatry*, 3, pp.62-71.

Slife, B.D. and Williams, R.N. (1995) *What's behind the Research? Discovering Hidden Assumptions in the Behavioural Sciences*, Thousand Oaks: Sage.

Slobin, D.I. (1985) 'Crosslinguistic evidence for the language-making capacity', in D.I. Slobin (ed.), *The Crosslinguistic Study of Language Acquisition*, Vol. 2, *Theoretical Issues*, Hillsdale, NJ: Erlbaum.

Slugoski, B. (1998) *Social Cognition*, Leicester: BPS Books.

Small, M.F. (1993) *Female Choices: Sexual Behavior in Female Primates*, Ithaca: Cornell University Press.

Smith, C. (1999) Quoted in 'Perchance to learn', *New Scientist*, 2205, pp.26-30.

Smith, C. and Lloyd, B. (1978) 'Maternal behaviour and perceived sex of infant: revisited', *Child Development*, 49, pp.1263-5.

Smith, E. and Mackie, D. (2000) *Social Psychology*, Philadelphia, PA: Psychology Press.

Smith, J.F. and Kida, T. (1991) 'Heuristics and biases: expertise and task realism in auditing', *Psychological Bulletin*, 109, pp.472-89.

Smith, K. and Crawford, S. (1986) 'Suicidal behavior among "normal" high school students', *Suicide and Life Threatening Behavior*, 16, pp.313-25.

Smith, P. and Bond, M.H. (1993, 1998/2nd edn) *Social Psychology Across Cultures: Analysis and Perspectives*, Harvester Wheatsheaf: New York.

Smith, P.K. (1979) 'The ontogeny of fear in children', in W. Sluckin (ed.) *Fear in Animals and Man*, London: Van Nostrand.

Smith, P.K. and Daglish, L. (1977) 'Sex differences in parent and infant behaviour in the home', *Child Development*, 48, pp.1250-4.

Smith, P.K., Cowie, H. and Blades, M. (1998) *Understanding Children's Development* (3nd edn), Oxford: Blackwell.

Smith, S.M. (1979) 'Remembering in and out of context', *Journal of Experimental Psychology: Human Learning and Memory*, 5, pp.460–71.

Smith, S.M., Brown, H.O., Thomas, J.E.P. and Goodman, L.S. (1947) 'The lack of cerebral effects of d-tubocurarine', *Anesthesiology*, 8, pp.1-14.

Snarey, J.R. and Keljo, K. (1991) 'In a gemeinschaft voice: The cross-cultural expansion of moral development theory', in W.M. Kurtines and J.L. Gewitz (eds) *Handbook of moral behaviour and development* (Vol. 1), Hillsdale, NJ: Erlbaum.

Snarey, J.R., Reimer, J. and Kohlberg, L. (1985) 'Development of social-moral reasoning among kibbutz adolescents: a longitudinal cross-cultural study', *Developmental Psychology*, 21, pp.3-17.

Sneddon, L.U., Braithwaite, V.A., Gentle, M.J., Broughton, B. and Knight, P. (2003) 'Trout trauma puts anglers on the hook', *Proceedings from the Royal Society*, April 30.

Snedecor, G.W. (1956) *Statistical Methods*, Iowa State University Press.

Snow, C.E. (1994) 'Beginning from baby talk: twenty years of research on input and interaction', in C. Gallaway and B. Richards (eds) *Input and Interaction in Language Acquisition*, Cambridge: Cambridge University Press.

Snyder, S.H. (1984) 'Drug and neurotransmitter receptors in the brain', *Science*, 224, pp.22-31.

Solso, R. and McCarthy, J.E. (1981) 'Prototype formation of faces: a case for pseudomemory', *British Journal of Psychology*, 72, pp.499-503.

Solyom, L., Beck, P., Solyom, C. and Hugel, R. (1974) 'Some etiological factors in phobic neurosis', *Canadian Psychiatric Association Journal*, 21, pp.109-13.

Sommers, C.H. (2000) The war against boys. *The Atlantic Monthly*, May, www.theatlantic.com/issues/2000/05/sommers.htm

Spanos, N. (1994) 'Multiple identity enactments and multiple personality disorder: a socio-cognitive perspective', *Psychological Bulletin*, 116, pp.143-65.

Spanos, N., Weekes, J. and Bertrand, L. (1985) 'Multiple personality: a social psychological perspective,' *Journal of Abnormal Psychology*, 94, pp.362-376.

Spelke, E.S., Hirst W. and Neisser, U. (1976) 'Skills of divided attention', *Cognition*, 4, pp.215-30.

Sperry, R.W. (1982) 'Some effects of disconnecting the cerebral hemispheres', *Science*, 217, pp.1223-6.

Sperry, R.W. (1985) 'Consciousness, personal identity, and the divided brain', in D.F. Benson & E. Zaidel (eds), *The dual brain: Hemispheric specialisation in humans*. New York: Guilford Press.

Spiegel, R. (1989) *Psychopharmacology* (2nd edn), New York: Wiley.

Spiegel, T.A. (1973) 'Caloric regulation of food intake in man', *Journal of Comparative and Physiological Psychology*, 84, pp.24-37.

Spitz, R.A. and Wolf, K.M. (1946) 'Anaclitic depression', *Psychoanalytic Study of the Child*, 2, pp.313–42.

Spitzer, R.L. and Williams, J.B.W. (1985) 'Classification in psychiatry', in H.I. Kaplan and B.J. Sadock (eds) *Comprehensive Textbook of Psychiatry* (4th edn), Baltimore: Williams and Wilkins.

Sprafkin, J.N., Liebert, R.M. and Poulos, R.W. (1975) 'Effects of a prosocial televised example on children's helping', *Journal of Experimental Child Psychology*, 20, pp.119-26.

Springer, S.P. and Deutsch, G. (1997) *Left Brain, Right Brain* (5th edn), New York: Freeman.

Squire, L.R., Ojemann, J.G., Miezin, F.M., Petersen, S.E., Videen, T.O., and Raichle, M.E. (1992) 'Activation of the hippocampus in normal humans: A functional anatomical study of memory', *Proceedings of the National Academy of Science, USA*, 89, pp.1837–41.

Srole, L., Langner, T.S., Michael, S.T. and Opler, M.K. (1961) *Mental Health in the Metropolis*, New York: McGraw-Hill.

Sroufe, L.A., Carlson, E.A., Levy, A.K., and Egeland, B. (1999) 'Implications of attachment theory for developmental psychopathology', *Development and Psychopathology*, 11, pp.1–13.

Stanford, C.B. (1999) *The Hunting Apes*, Princeton: Princeton University Press.

Stangor, C. and Ruble, D. N. (1989) 'Differential influences of gender schemata and gender constancy on children's information processing and behavior', *Social Cognition*, 7, pp.353-72.

State University of New York at Buffalo (1999) *Abnormal Psychology*, Lecture 2, accessed at: http://ub-counseling.buffalo.edu/Abpsy/lecture2.html

Steele, C.M. and Southwick, L. (1985) 'Alcohol and social behaviour I. The psychology of drunken excess', *Journal of Personality and Social Psychology*, 48, pp.18-34.

Steinberg, L. and Morris, A.S. (2001) 'Adolescent development', *Annual Review of Psychology*, 52, pp.83-110.

Steinberg, L. and Silverberg, S.B. (1986) 'The vicissitudes of autonomy in early adolescence', *Child Development*, 57, pp.84-51.

Steiner, W. (1991) 'Fluoxetine-induced mania in a patient with obsessive-compulsive disorder', *American Journal of Psychiatry*, 148, pp.1403-4.

Stephens, W. (1963) *The Family in Cross-cultural Perspective*, New York: Holt, Rhinehart & Winston.

Stern, W.C. and Morgane, P.J. (1974) 'Theoretical view of REM sleep: maintenance of catecholamine systems in the central nervous system', *Behavioral Biology*, 11, pp.1-32.

Sternberg, R.J. (1986) 'A triangular theory of love', *Psychological Review*, 93, pp.119-35.

Sternberg, R.J. (1988) *The Triangle of Love*, New York: Basic Books.

Stevens, A. and Price, J. (2000) *Evolutionary Psychiatry: A New Beginning* (2nd edn), London: Routledge.

Stewart, V.M. (1973) 'Tests of the "carpentered world" hypothesis by race and environment in America and Zambia', *International Journal of Psychology*, 8, pp.83-94.

Stickgold, R. (1998) 'Sleep: Offline memory reprocessing', *Trends in Cognitive Sciences*, 2, pp.484-7.

Stokols, D. (1976) 'The experience of crowding in primary and secondary environments', *Environment and Behaviour*, 8, pp.49-86.

Stokols, D., Rall, M., Pinner, B. and Schopler, J. (1973) 'Physical, social and personal determinants of the perception of crowding', *Environment and Behaviour*, 5, pp.87-117.

Stoney, C.M., Mathews, K.A., McDonald, R.H. and Johnson, C.A. (1990) 'Sex differences in acute stress response: lipid, lipoprotein, cardiovascular and neuroendocrine adjustments', *Psychophysiology*, 12, pp.52–61.

Storr, A. (1989) *Freud*. Oxford: Oxford University Press.

Stouffer, S.A., Suchman, E.A., DeVinney, L.C., Star, S.A. and Williams, R.M. Jr. (1949) *The American Soldier*: Vol. 1, *Adjustment During Army Life*, Princeton, NJ: Princeton University Press.

Stringer, C.B. and Andrews, P. (1988) 'Genetic and fossil evidence for the origin of modern humans', *Science*, 11, 239 (4845), pp.1263-8.

Stroebe, W. and Stroebe, M. S. (1987) *Bereavement and Health*, Cambridge: Cambridge University Press.

Stroebe, W., Stroebe, M.S. and Abakoumkin, G. (1999) 'Does differential social support cause sex differences in bereavement outcome?', *Journal of Community and Applied Social Psychology*, 9, pp.1–12.

Strongman, K.T. (1987) *The Psychology of Emotion* (3rd edn), Chichester: Wiley.

Stroop, J.R. (1935) 'Studies of interference in serial verbal reactions', *Journal of Experimental Psychology*, 18, pp.643–62.

Stuart, R.J. (1991) 'Kin recognition as a functional concept', *Animal Behaviour*, 41, pp.1093-4.

Stuart-Hamilton, I (2000) 'Ageing and intelligence', *Psychology Review*, Vol. 6(4) (in press).

Styles, E.A. (1997) *The Psychology of Attention*, Hove: Psychology Press.

Sue, D.W. and Sue, D. (1999) *Counselling the Culturally Different* (3rd edn), New York: Wiley.

Suggs, R.C. (1966) *Marquesan Sexual Behavior*, New York: Harcourt, Brace & World.

Suppes, T., Baldessarini, R.J. and Faedda, G.L. (1991) 'Risk of recurrence following discontinuation of lithium treatment in bipolar disorder', *Archives of General Psychiatry*, 48, pp.1082-7.

Susser, E., Neugebauer, R., Hoek, H. W., Brown, A. S., Lin, S. and others (1996) 'Schizophrenia after prenatal famine: further evidence', *Archives of General Psychiatry*, 53, pp.25-31.

Szasz, T. (1972) *The Manufacture of Madness,* London: Routledge and Kegan Paul.

Tajfel, H. (1970) 'Experiments in intergroup discrimination', *Scientific American*, 223, pp.96-102.

Tajfel, H. (1981) *Human Groups and Social Categories,* Cambridge: Cambridge University Press.

Tajfel, H. (ed.) (1978) *Differentiation between Social Groups: Studies in the Social Psychology of Intergroup Relations*, London: Academic Press.

Tajfel, H., Flament, C., Billig, M.G. and Bundy, R.P. (1971) 'Social categorisation and intergroup behaviour', *European Journal of Social Psychology*, 1, pp.149-78.

Takahashi, K. (1990) 'Are the key assumptions of the "strange situation" universal?', *Human Development*, 33, pp.23-30.

Takahashi, T., Sasaki, M., Itoh, H., Yamadera, W., Ozone, M., Obuchi, K., Hayashida, K., Matsanuga, N. and Sano, H. (2002) 'Melatonin alleviates jet lag symptoms caused by an 11-hour eastward flight', *Psychiatry and Clinical Neurosciences*, 56, pp.301-2.

Tanaka, J.W. and Farah, M.J. (1993) 'Parts and wholes in face recognition', *Quarterly Journal of Experimental Psychology*, 46A, pp.225-45.

Tanford, S. and Penrod, S. (1986) 'Jury deliberations: Discussion content and influence processes in jury decision making', *Journal of Applied Social Psychology*, 16, pp.322–47.

Tannen, D. (1990) *You Just Don't Understand: Women and Men in Conversation*, New York: William Morrow, Ballantine.

Tannen, D. (1993) *Framing in Discourse*, Oxford: Oxford University Press.

Tannen, D. (1995) *Talking from 9 to 5,* London: Virago Press.

Tanner, N. and Zihlman, A (1976) 'Gathering and the Hominid Adaption', in L. Tiger and H.T. Fowler (eds) *Female Hierarchies*, Chicago: Beresford Book Service.

Tapp, J.T. (1969) 'Activity, reactivity and the behaviour-directing properties of stimuli', in J.T. Tapp (ed.) *Reinforcement and Behavior*, New York: Academic Press.

Tavris, C. (1993) 'The mis-measure of women', *Feminism and Psychology*, 3(2), pp.149-68.

Tavris, C. and Wade, C. (1995) *Psychology in Perspective*, New York: HarperCollins.

Taylor, S.E., Fiske, S.T., Etcoff, N.I. and Ruderman, A.J. (1978) 'Categorical and contextual bases of person memory and stereotyping', *Journal of Personality and Social Psychology*, 36, pp.778-93.

Taylor, S.E., Klein, L.C., Lewis, B.P., Grunewald, T.L., Gurung, R.A.R. and Updegraff, J.A. (2000) 'Biobehavioural responses in stress in females: tend-and-befriend, not fight-or-flight', *Psychological Review*, 107, p.3.

Terrace, H.S., Petitto, L.A., Sanders, R.J. and Bever, T.G. (1979) 'Can an ape create a sentence?', *Science*, 206, pp.891-902.

Terry, D.J., McHugh, T.A. and Noller, P. (1991) 'Role dissatisfaction and the decline of marital quality across the transition to parenthood', *Australian Journal of Psychology*, 43(3), pp.129-32.

Tesser, A. and Paulhus, D.L. (1976) 'Toward a casual model of love', *Journal of Personality and Social Psychology*, 34, pp.1095-l05.

Thase, M.E., Frank, E. and Kupfer, D.J. (1991) 'Biological processes in major depression', in E.E. Beckham and W.R. Leber (eds) *Handbook of Depression*, Homewood, IL: Dorsey Press.

Thase, M.E., Greenhouse, J.B., Frank, E., Reynolds, C.F., Pilconis, P.A., Hurley, K., Grochocinski, V. and Kupfer, D.J. (1997) 'Treatment of major depression with psychotherapy or psychotherapy-pharmacotherapy combinations', *Archives of General Psychiatry*, 54, pp.1009-15.

Thibaut, J.W. and Kelley, H.H. (1959) *The Social Psychology of Groups*, New York: Wiley.

Thigpen, C. and Cleckey, H. (1954) 'A case of multiple personality disorder', *Journal of Abnormal and Social Psychology*, 49, pp.135-51.

Thigpen, C. and Cleckey, H. (1957) *The Three Faces of Eve*, New York: McGraw Hill.

Thomas, A. and Chess, S. (1977) *Temperament and Development*, New York: Brunner-Mazel.

Thomas, A. and Chess, S. (1980) *The Dynamics of Psychological Development*, New York: Brunner-Mazel.

Thomas, J.C. (1974) 'An analysis of behaviour in the hobbits-orcs problem', *Cognitive Psychology*, 6, pp.257-69.

Thomas, L.K. (1998) 'Multicultural aspects of attachment', www.bereavement.demon.co.uk/lbn/attachment/lennox.html. *See also* Thomas, L.K. (1995) 'Psychotherapy in the context of race and culture', in S. Fernando (ed.) *Mental Health in a Multi-ethnic Society*, London: Routledge.

Thorndike, E.L. (1911) *Animal Intelligence: Experimental Studies*, New York: Macmillan.

Thornhill, R. and Gangestad, S. (1993) 'Human facial beauty: averageness, symmetry and parasite resistance', *Human Nature*, 4, pp.237-69.

Thornhill, R. and Gangestad, S. (1999) 'Facial attractiveness', *Trends in Cognitive Sciences*, 3, pp.452-60.

Thorpe, S.J. and Salkovskis, P.M. (1997) 'The effect of one-session treatment for spider phobia on attentional bias and beliefs', *British Journal of Clinical Psychology*, 36, pp.225-41.

Tienari, P., Sorri, A., Lahti, I. and Naarala, M. (1987) 'Genetic and psychosocial factors in schizophrenia: The Finnish adoptive family study', *Schizophrenia Bulletin*, 13, pp.477-84.

Tinbergen, N. and Kruyt (1938) cited in Tinbergen N. (1951) *The Study of Instinct*, Oxford: Oxford University Press.

Tinbergen, N. and Perdeck, A.C. (1950) 'On the stimulus situation releasing the begging response in the newly hatched herring gull chick', *Behaviour*, 3, pp.1-38.

Tizard, B. (1979) 'Language at home and at school', in C.B. Cazden and D. Harvey (eds), *Language in Early Childhood Education*, Washington, DC: National Association for the Education of Young Children.

Tizard, B. and Hughes, M. (1984) *Young Children Learning*, London: Fontana.

Tolman, E.C. (1948) 'Cognitive maps in rats and men', *Psychological Review*, 55, pp.189-208.

Tomasello, M. and Mannle, S. (1985) 'Pragmatics of sibling speech to one-year-olds', *Child Development*, 56, pp.911-17.

Toon, F., Fraise, J., McFetridge, M. and Alwin, N. (1996) 'Memory or mirage? The FMS debate', *The Psychologist*, 9 (2), pp.73-77.

Tordoff, M.G., Novin, D. and Russek, M. (1982) 'Effects of hepatic denervation on the anorexic response to epinephrine, amphetamine and lithium chloride: a behavioral identification of glucostatic afferents', *Journal of Comparative and Physiological Psychology*, 96, pp.361-75.

Torgersen, S. (1983) 'Genetic factors in anxiety disorders', *Archives of General Psychiatry*, 40, pp.1085-9.

Torrey, E.F. (1987) 'Psychiatric survivors and non-survivors', *Psychiatric Services*, 48, p.143.

Torrey, E.F., Bowler, A.E., Taylor, E.H. and Gottesman, I.I. (1994) *Schizophrenia and Manic-depressive Disorder: The Biological Roots of Mental Illness as Revealed by the Landmark Study of Identical Twins*, New York: Basic Books.

Torrey, E.F., Rawlings, R. and Waldman, I.N. (1988) 'Schizophrenia births and viral diseases in two states', *Schizophrenia Research*, 1, pp.73-7.

Torrey, E.F., Rawlings, R.R., Ennnis, J.M., Merrill, D.D. and Flores, D.S. (1996) 'Birth seasonality in bipolar disorder, schizophrenia, schizoaffective disorder and stillbirths', *Schizophrenia Research*, 21 (3), pp.141-9.

Tovee, M.J., Rolls, E.T. and Azzopardi, P. (1994) 'Translation invariance in the responses to faces of single neurons in the temporal visual cortex areas of the alert macaque', *Journal of Neurophysiology*, 72, pp.1049-60.

Tower, R.K., Kelly, C. and Richards, A. (1997) 'Individualism, collectivism and reward allocation: a cross-cultural study in Russia and Britain', *British Journal of Social Psychology*, 36, pp.331-45.

Treisman, A.M. (1960) 'Contextual cues in selective listening', *Quarterly Journal of Experimental Psychology*, 12, pp.242-8.

Treisman, A.M. (1964) 'Verbal cues, language and meaning in selective attention', *American Journal of Psychology*, 77, pp.206-19.

Treisman, A.M. and Geffen, G. (1967) 'Selective attention: perception or response?', *Quarterly Journal of Experimental Psychology*, 19, pp.1-18.

Triseliotis, J. (1984) 'Identity and security in adoption and long-term fostering', *Early Child Development & Care*, 15(2-3), pp.149-70.

Trivers, R. (1971) 'The evolution of reciprocal altruism', *Quarterly Review of Biology*, 46, pp.35-57.

Trivers, R. (1972) 'Parental investment and sexual selection', in B. Campbell (ed.) *Sexual Selection and the Descent of Man*, Chicago: Aldine de Gruyter.

Trivers, R.L. (1974) 'Parent–offspring conflict', *American Zoologist*, 14, pp.249-64.

Tronick, E.Z., Morelli, G.A. and Ivey, P.K. (1992) 'The Efe forager infant and toddler's pattern of social relationships: Multiple and simultaneous', *Developmental Psychology*, 28, pp.568-77.

Trut, L.N. (1999) 'Early canid domestication: the farm-fox experiment', *American Scientist*, 87, pp.160-9.

Tulving, E. (1966) 'Subjective organisation and effects of repetition in multi-trial free-recall learning', *Journal of Verbal Learning and Verbal Behaviour*, 5, pp.193-7.

Tulving, E. (1983) *Elements of Episodic Memory*, Oxford: OUP.

Tulving, E. and Osler, S. (1968) 'Effectiveness of retrieval cues in memory for words', *Journal of Verbal Learning and Verbal Behaviour*, 5, pp.381-91.

Tupuola, A.M. (1993) 'Critical analysis of adolescent development – a Samoan woman's perspective', unpublished master's thesis, Victoria University of Wellington, New Zealand.

Turiel, E. (1983) *The Development of Social Knowledge: Morality and Social Convention*, Cambridge: Cambridge University Press.

Turing, A.M. (1950) 'Computing machinery and intelligence', *Mind*, 59, pp.433-60.

Turkheimer, E., Haley, A., Waldron, M. D'Onofrio, B. & Gottesman, I.I. (2003) 'Socioeconomic status modifies heritability of IQ in young children', *Psychological Science*, 14(5), pp.623-8.

Turkington, C. and Harris, J.R. (2001) *The Encyclopedia of Memory and Memory Disorders* (2nd edn), New York: Facts on File.

Turnbull, C. (1961) 'Some observations regarding the experiences and behaviour of the Bambuti', *American Journal of Psychology*, 74, pp.153-63.

Turner, J. (1991) *Social Influence*, Milton Keynes: Open University Press.

Turner, J. S. and Helms, D. B. (1983) *Lifespan Development*, New York: Holt Rinehart and Winston.

Turner, J.C. (1982) 'Towards a cognitive redefinition of the social group', in H. Tajfel (ed.) *Social Identity and Intergroup Relations*, Cambridge: Cambridge University Press.

Tversky, A. and Kahneman, D. (1974) 'Judgement under uncertainty: heuristics and biases', *Science*, 815, pp.1124-31.

Tversky, A. and Kahneman, D. (1982) 'Judgement under uncertainty: heuristics and biases', in D. Kahneman, P. Slovic and A. Tversky (eds) *Judgement under Uncertainty: Heuristics and Biases*, New York: Cambridge University Press.

Tversky, A. and Kahneman, D. (1987) 'Rational choice and the framing of decisions', in R. Hogarth and M. Reder (eds) *Rational Choice: The Contrast between Economics and Psychology*, Chicago: University of Chicago Press.

Tyerman, A. and Spencer, C. (1983) 'A critical test of the Sherifs' robbers cave experiments: intergroup competition and co-operation between groups of well acquainted individuals', *Small Group Behaviour*, 14, pp.515-31.

Tyler, C.W. (1997) 'Analysis of human receptor density', in V. Lakshminarayanan (ed.) *Basic and Clinical Applications of Vision Science*, Norwell, MA: Kluwer Academic.

Tyler, L.E. (1965) *The Psychology of Human Differences* (3rd edn), New York: Appleton-Century-Crofts.

Tyler, S.W., Hertel, P.T., McCallum, M.C. and Ellis, H.C. (1979) 'Cognitive effort and memory', *Journal of Experimental Psychology: Human Learning and Memory*, 5(6), pp.607-17.

Ucros, C.G. (1989) 'Mood-state dependent memory: a meta-analysis', *Cognition and Emotion*, 3, pp.139-67.

Ulusahin, A., Basoglu, M. and Paykel, E.S. (1994) 'A cross-cultural comparative study of depressive symptoms in British and Turkish clinical samples', *Social Psychiatry and Psychiatric Epidemiology*, 29, pp.31-9.

Umbenhauer, S.L. and DeWitte, L.L. (1978) 'Patient race and social class: attitudes and decisions among three groups of mental health professionals', *Comprehensive Psychiatry*, 19 (6), pp.509-15.

Umbricht, D. and Kane, J.M. (1996) 'Medical complications of new antipsychotic drugs', *Schizophrenia Bulletin*, 22, pp.475-83.

Underwood, B.J. (1957) 'Interference and forgetting', *Psychological Review*, 64, pp.49-60.

Underwood, G. (1974) 'Moray vs. the rest: the effects of extended shadowing practice', *Quarterly Journal of Experimental Psychology*, 26, pp.368-72.

Ussher, J. (1992) *Women's Madness: Misogyny or Mental Illness?*, Hemel Hempstead: Harvester Wheatsheaf.

Vaillant, C.O. and Vaillant, G.E. (1993) 'Is the U-curve of marital satisfaction an illusion? A 40-year study of marriage', *Journal of Marriage and the Family*, 55(1), pp.230-9.

Valenstein, E.S. (1967) 'Selection of nutritive and non-nutritive solutions under different conditions of need', *Journal of Comparative and Physiological Psychology*, 63, pp.429-33.

Valentine, E.R. (1992) *Conceptual issues in psychology* (2nd edn), London: Routledge.

Van Avermaet, E. (1996) 'Social influence in small groups', in M. Hewstone, W. Stroebe, G.M. Stevenson (eds), *Introduction to Social Psychology*, Oxford: Blackwell.

Van de Castle, R. (1994) *Our Dreaming Mind*, New York: Ballantine.

Van der Doef, M. and Maes, S. (1998) 'The job demand-control (-support) model and physical outcomes: a review of the strain and buffer hypotheses', *Psychology and Health*, 13, pp.909-36.

Van Dusen, K.T., Mednick, S.A., Gabrielli, W.F. and Hutchings, B. (1983) 'Social class and crime in an adoption cohort', *Journal of Criminal Law and Criminology*, 74, pp.249-69.

Van Gelder, L. (1985) 'The strange case of the electronic lover', *Ms.*, October, pp.94-124.

Van IJzendoorn, M.H. and Kroonenberg, P.M. (1988) 'Cross-cultural patterns of attachment: A meta-analysis of the Strange Situation', *Child Development*, 59, pp.147–56.

Van IJzendoorn, M.H., Sagi, A. and Lambermon, M.W.E. (1992) 'The multiple caretaker paradox: Data from Holland and Israel', in R.C. Pianta (ed.) *Beyond the Parent: The Role of Other Adults in Children's Lives*, San Francisco, CA: Jossey-Bass Publishers.

Van Yperen, N.W. and Buunck, B.P. (1990) 'A longitudinal study of equity and satisfaction in intimate relationships', *European Journal of Social Psychology*, 20, pp.287-310.

Vaughn, C.E. and Leff, J.P. (1976) 'The influence of family and social factors on the course of psychiatric illness. A comparison of schizophrenia and depressed neurotic patients', *British Journal of Psychiatry*, 129, pp.125-37.

Veijola, J., Puukka, P., Lehtinen, V., Moring, J., Lindholm, T. and Vaisanen, E. (1998) 'Sex differences in the association between childhood experiences and adult depression', *Psychological Medicine*, 28, pp.21-7.

Vivian, J. and Brown, R. (1995) 'Prejudice and intergroup conflict', in M. Argyle and A. Colman (eds) *Social Psychology*, Harlow: Longman.

Vogele, C., Jarvis, A. and Cheeseman, K. (1997) 'Anger suppression, reactivity, and hypertension risk: Gender makes a difference', *Annals of Behavioral Medicine*, 19, pp.61–9.

Volkow, N. D. et al. (1997) 'Relationship between subjective effects of cocaine and dopamine transporter occupancy', *Nature*, 24 April, Vol. 386, p. 827.

von Frisch, K. (1967) *The Dance Language and Orientation of Bees*, Cambridge, MA: Harvard University Press.

Von-Neumann, J. and Morgenstern, O. (1947) *Theory of Games and Economic Behavior* (2nd edn), Princeton: Princeton University Press.

Vygotsky, L.S. (1987) 'The development of scientific concepts in childhood', in R.W. Rieber and A.S. Carton (eds) *The Collected Works of L.S. Vygotsky*, Vol. 1, New York: Plenum Press.

Wade, T., Martin, N.G. and Tiggemann, M. (1998) 'Genetic and environmental risk factors for the weight and shape concerns characteristic of bulimia nervosa', *Psychological Medicine*, 28, pp.761–72.

Wadeley, A., Birch, A. and Malim, T. (1997) *Perspectives in Psychology* (2nd edn), London: Macmillan.

Walker, I. and Mann, L. (1987) 'Unemployment, relative deprivation, and social protest', *Personality and Social Psychology Bulletin*, 13, pp.275-83.

Walker, L. (1984) 'Sex differences in the development of moral reasoning: a critical review', *Child Development*, 55, pp.677-91.

Walker, L.J., deVries, B. and Trevethan, S.D. (1987) 'Moral stages and moral orientations in real-life and hypothetical dilemmas', *Child Development*, 58, pp.842-58.

Walker, M.M., Dennis, T.E., Kirschvink, J.L. (2002) 'The

magnetic sense and its use in long-distance navigation by animals', *Current Opinion in Neurobiology*, 12, pp.735-44.

Walker, W.D., Rowe, R.C. and Quinsey, V.L. (1993) 'Authoritarianism and sexual aggression', *Journal of Personality and Social Psychology*, 65, pp.1036-45.

Wallraff, H.G. (1990) 'Navigation by homing pigeons', *Ethology, Ecology and Evolution*, 2, pp.81-115.

Walster, E. and Piliavin, J.A. (1972) 'Equity and the innocent bystander', *Journal of Social Issues*, 28(3), pp.165-89.

Walster, E.H. and Walster, G.W. (1969) 'The matching hypothesis', *Journal of Personality and Social Psychology*, 6, pp.248-53.

Walster, E.H., Aronson, E., Abrahams, D. and Rottman, L. (1966) 'Importance of physical attractiveness in dating behavior', *Journal of Personality and Social Psychology*, 4, pp.325-42.

Walster, E.H., Walster, G.W. and Berscheid, E. (1978) *Equity Theory and Research*, Boston, MA: Allyn & Bacon.

Walters, R.H. and Thomas, L. (1963) 'Enhancement of punitiveness by visual and audiovisual displays', *Canadian Journal of Psychology*, 16, pp.244-55.

Walton. G.E., Bower, N.J.A. and Bower, T.G.R. (1992) 'Recognition of familiar faces by newborns', *Infant Behaviour and Development*, 15, pp.265-9.

Wark, G. and Krebs, D.L (1996) 'Gender and dilemma differences in real-life moral judgment', *Developmental Psychology*, 32, pp.220-30.

Warr, P.B. (1965) 'Proximity as a determinant of positive and negative sociometric choice', *British Journal of Social and Clinical Psychology*, 4, pp.104-9.

Wartner, U.G., Grossman, K., Fremner-Bombik, I. and Guess, G.L. (1994) 'Attachment patterns in south Germany', *Child Development*, 65, pp.1014-27.

Washburn, L. and Lancaster, C.S. (1968) 'The evolution of hunting', in R.B. Lee and I. DeVore (eds) *Man the Hunter*, Chicago, Ill.: Aldine, pp.293-303.

Wason, P.C. and Shapiro, D. (1971) 'Natural and contrived experience in reasoning problems', *Quarterly Journal of Experimental Psychology*, 23, pp.63-71.

Waterman, A.S. (1982) 'Identity development from adolescence to adulthood: an extension of theory and a review of research', *Developmental Psychology*, 18, pp.341-58.

Waterman, A.S. (1985) 'Identity in the context of adolescent psychology', *New Directions for Child Development*, 30, pp.5-24.

Waterman, C.K. and Waterman, A.S. (1975) 'Fathers and sons: a study of ego-identity across two generations', *Journal of Youth and Adolescence*, 4, pp.331-8.

Waterman, T.H. (1989) *Animal Navigation*, New York: Scientific American Library.

Watson, J.B. (1913) 'Psychology as the behaviourist views it', *Psychological Review*, 20, pp.158-77.

Watson, J.B. and Rayner, R. (1920) 'Conditioned emotional reactions', *Journal of Experimental Psychology*, 3, pp.1-14.

Watson, P.J. and Andrews, P.W. (2002) 'Toward a revised evolutionary adaptationist analysis of depression: the social navigation hypothesis', *Journal of Affective Disorders*, 72, pp.1-14.

Watson, S.L., Shively, C.A., Kaplan, J.R. and Line, S.W. (1998) 'Effects of chronic social separation on cardiovascular disease risk factors in female cynomolgus monkeys', *Atherosclerosis*, 137, pp.259-66.

Waugh, N.C. and Norman, D.A. (1965) 'Primary memory', *Psychological Review*, 72, pp.89-104.

Weaver, C.A. (1993) 'Do you need a "flash" to form a flashbulb memory?', *Journal of Experimental Psychology: General*, 122(1), pp.39-46.

Weber, E.U., Bockenholt, U., Hilton, D.J. and Wallace, B. (1993) 'Determinants of diagnostic hypothesis generation: effects of information, base rates and experience', *Journal of Experimental Psychology: Learning, Memory and Cognition*, 19, pp.1131-64.

Weg, R.B. (1983) 'Changing physiology of aging', in D.S. Woodruff and J.E. Birren (eds), *Ageing: Scientific Perspectives and Social Issues,* (2nd edn), Monterey: Brooks/Cole.

Wehren, A. and DeLisi, R. (1983) 'The development of gender understanding: judgements and explanations', *Child Development*, 54, pp.1568-78.

Weinberg, R. A., Scarr, S. and Waldman, I. D. (1992) 'The Minnesota Transracial Adoption Study: A follow-up of IQ test performance at adolescence', *Intelligence*, 16, pp.117-35.

Weinberger, D.R. (1988) 'Premorbid neuropathology in schizophrenia', *Lancet*, 2, pp.959-60.

Weindruch., Walford, R.L., Fligiel, S. and Guthrie, D. (1986) 'The retardation of aging in mice by dietary restriction: Longevity, cancer, immunity, and lifetime energy intake', *Journal of Nutrition*, 116, pp.641-54.

Weiner, B. (1979) 'A theory of motivation for some classroom experiences', *Journal of Educational Psychology*, 71, pp.3-25.

Weiner, B. (1986) *An Attributional Theory of Motivation and Emotion*, New York: Springer-Verlag.

Weinstein, B.A. (2002) 'Gender differences in the moderating effects of social support on college student stress: a prospective study', *Dissertation Abstracts International: Section B:- The Sciences and Engineering*, 62, pp.543-5.

Weisman, A.D. (1972) *On Dying and Denying: A psychiatric study of terminality*, New York: Behavioural Publications.

Weiss, J.M. (1972) 'Influence of psychological variables on stress-induced pathology', in J. Knight and R. Porter (eds), *Physiology, Emotion and Psychosomatic Illness*, Amsterdam: Elsevier.

Weissman, M.M., Bland, R.C. and Canino, G.J. (1994) 'The cross national epidemiology of obsessive compulsive disorder: the Cross National Collaborative Group', *Journal of Clinical Psychiatry*, 55, pp.5-10

Wells, G. (1985) 'Preschool literacy-related activities and success in school', in D.R. Olson, N. Torrance and A. Hildyard (eds) *Literacy, Language and Learning,* Cambridge: Cambridge University Press, pp.229-55.

Wernicke, C. (1874) *Der Aphasische Symptomenkomplex*, Breslau: Cohn & Weigert.

Wertheimer, M. (1945) *Productive Thinking*, New York: Harper & Row.

Wertsch, J.V. (1985) 'Adult-child interaction as a source of self-regulation in children', in S.R. Yussen (ed.) *The growth of reflection in children* (pp.69-97).

West, M.J. and King, A.P. (1988) 'Female visual displays affect the development of male song in the cowbird', *Nature*, 334, pp.244-6.

Wetherell, M. and Potter, J. (1992) *Mapping the Language of Racism: Discourse and the Legitimation of Exploitation*, London and New York: Harvester Wheatsheaf and Columbia University Press.

White, C. and Burke, O. (1987) 'Ethnic role identity among black and white college students: An interactionist approach', *Sociological Perspectives*, 30, pp.310-31.

Whiten, A. and Byrne, R. (1988) 'Tactical deception in primates', *Behavioural and Brain Sciences*, 11, pp.233-44.

Whiting, B. and Edwards, C. (1988) *Children of Different Worlds: The Formation of Social Behaviour*, Cambridge, MA: Harvard University Press.

Whiting, B. and Whiting, J.W.M. (1975) *Children of Six Cultures*, Cambridge, MA: Harvard University Press.

Whiting, J.W. (1966) *Six Cultures Series 1: Field Guide for a Study of Socialization*, New York: Wiley.

Whorf, B.L. (1956) *Language, Thought and Reality*, Cambridge, MA: MIT Press.

Wickens, A. (2000) *Foundations of Biopsychology*, London: Prentice-Hall.

Wickens, D.D. (1970) 'Encoding categories of words: an empirical approach to meaning', *Psychological Review*, 77, pp.1–15.

Wickler, W. (1968) *Mimicry in Plants and Animals*, New York: McGraw-Hill.

Wilkins, H. (1991) 'Computer talk: long distance conversations by computer', *Written Communcation*, 8, pp.56-78.

Wilkinson, G.S. (1984) 'Reciprocal food sharing in the vampire bat', *Nature*, 308, pp.181-4.

Willerman, L., Schultz, R., Rutledge, J.N. and Bigler, E.D. (1992) 'Hemispheric size asymmetry predicts relative verbal and nonverbal intelligence differently in the sexes: an MRI study of structure-function relations', *Intelligence*, 16, pp.315-28.

Williams, J.H. (1987) *Psychology of Women* (3rd edn), London: W.W. Norton & Co.

Williams, L.M. (1992) 'Adult memories of childhood abuse: preliminary findings from a longitudinal study', *The Advisor*, 5, pp.19–20.

Williams, R.L. (1972) *The BITCH Test (Black Intelligence Test of Cultural Homogeneity)*, St. Louis: Washington University.

Williams, S.L., Kinney, P.J., Harap, S.T. and Liebmann, M. (1997) 'Thoughts of agoraphobic people during scary tasks', *Journal of Abnormal Psychology*, 106, pp.511-20.

Williams, T.M. (1985) 'Implications of a natural experiment in the developed world for research on television in the developing world. Special issue: Television in the developing world', *Journal of Cross Cultural Psychology*, 16 (3), pp.263-287.

Williams, T.M. (1986) *The Impact of Television: A Natural Experiment in Three Communities*, New York: Academic Press.

Willis, L., Thomas, P., Garry, P.J. and Goodwin, J.S. (1987) 'A prospective study of response to stressful life events in initially healthy elders', *Journal of Gerontology*, 42, pp.627–30.

Wills, C. (1999) *Children of Prometheus*, Perseus Publishing.

Wills, T.A. (1992) 'The helping process in the context of personal relationships', in S. Spacaman and S. Oskamp (eds) *Helping and Being Helped: Naturalistic Studies*, Newbury Park, CA: Sage.

Wilson, E.O. (1975) *Sociobiology, The New Synthesis*, Cambridge, MA: Harvard University Press.

Wilson, E.O. (1978) *On Human Nature*, Cambridge, MA: Harvard University Press.

Wilson, E.O. (1992) *The Diversity of Life*, Harmondsworth: Penguin.

Wilson, J.W. (1987), *The truly disadvantaged: The inner city, the underclass, and public policy*, Chicago: University of Chicago Press.

Winson, J. (1997) 'The meaning of dreams', *Scientific American*, Special Issue, 7, pp.58-67.

Wispe, L.G. (1972) 'Positive forms of social behaviour: an overview', *Journal of Social Issues*, 28 (3), pp.1-19.

Wolf, A.P. (1995) *A Chinese Brief for Edward Westermarck*, Stanford: Stanford University Press.

Wolpe, J. (1958) *Psychotherapy by Reciprocal Inhibition*, Stanford, CA: Stanford University Press.

Wonderlich, S.A., Crosby, R.D., Mitchell, J.E., Roberts, J.A., Haseltine, B., DeMuth, G. and Thompson, K.M. (2000) 'Relationship of childhood sexual abuse and eating disorders in children', *Journal of the Academy of Child and Adolescent Psychiatry*, 39, pp.1277–83.

Wonderlich, S.A., Wilsnach, R.W., Wilsnach, S.C. and Harris, T.R. (1996) 'Childhood sexual abuse and bulimic behaviour in a nationally representative sample', *American Journal of Public Health*, 86, pp.1082–6.

Wong, D.F., Wagner, H.N., Tune, L.E., Dannals, R.F., Pearlson, G.D. and Links, J.M. (1986) 'Positron emission tomography reveals elevated D2 dopamine receptors in drug-naive schizophrenics', *Science*, 234, pp.1558-62.

Wood, D.J., Bruner, J.S. and Ross, G. (1976) 'The role of tutoring in problem-solving', *Journal of Child Psychology and Psychiatry*, 17, pp.89-100.

Wood, N. and Cowan, N. (1995) 'The cocktail party phenomenon revisited: how frequent are attention shifts to one's name in an irrelevant auditory channel?', *Journal of Experimental*

Psychology: Human Perception and Performance, 16, pp.135-49.

Woodruff, G. and Premack, D. (1979) 'Intentional communication in the chimpanzee: the development of deception', *Cognition, 7*, pp.333-62.

Woodruff, P.W.R., Wright, I.C., Shuriquie, N., Russouw, H., Rushe, T., Howard, R.J., Graves, M., Bullmore, E.T. and Murray, R.M. (1997) 'Structural brain abnormalities in male schizophrenics reflect fronto-temporal dissociation', *Psychological Medicine*, 27, pp.1257-66.

Worell, J. and Remer, P. (1992) *Feminist Perspectives in Therapy*, Chichester: Wiley.

Workman, L. and Reader, W. (2004) *Evolutionary Psychology*, Cambridge: Cambridge University Press.

World Health Organization (1992/3) *The ICD-10 Classification of Mental and Behavioural Disorders: Diagnostic Criteria for Research*, Geneva: WHO.

Wortman, C.B. and Brehm, J.W. (1975) 'Responses to uncontrollable outcomes: an integration of the reactance theory and the learned helplessness model', in L. Berkowitz (ed.) *Advances in Social Psychology*, New York: Academic Press.

Wrangham, R.W. (1975) *The Behavioural Ecology of Chimpanzees in Gombe National Park, Tanzania*, Unpublished PhD thesis, Cambridge University.

Yamada, J.E. (1990) *Laura: A Case for the Modularity of Language*, Cambridge, MA: MIT Press.

Yang, M.M. (1994) *Gifts, Favors, and Banquets: The Art of Social Relationships in China*, Ithaca, NY: Sage.

Yap, P.-M. (1974) *Comparative Psychiatry: A Theoretical Framework*, Toronto: University of Toronto Press.

Yarkin, K.L., Town, J.P. and Wallston, B.S. (1982) 'Blacks and women must try harder: stimulus person's race and sex attributions of causality', *Personality and Social Psychology Bulletin*, 8, pp.21-24.

Yerkes, R.M. and Dodson, J.D. (1908) 'The relation of strength of stimuli to rapidity of habit-formation', *Journal of Comparative Neurology and Psychology*, 18, pp.459-82.

Yin, R.K. (1969) 'Looking at upside-down faces', *Journal of Experimental Psychology*, 81, pp.141-5.

Yonas, A. (1981) 'Infants' responses to optical information for collision', in R.N. Aslin, J.R. Alberts and M.R. Peterson (eds) *Development of Perception:*

Psychobiological Perspectives, Vol. 2, *The Visual System*, New York: Academic Press.

Yonas, A. and Owsley, C. (1987) 'Development of visual space perception', in P. Salapatek and L. Cohen (eds) *Handbook of Infant Perception*, Vol. 2, *From Perception to Cognition*, Orlando: Academic Press.

Young, A.W., Newcombe, F., deHaan, E.H.F., Small, M. and Hau, D.C. (1993) 'Face perception after brain injury', *Brain*, 116, pp.941-59.

Young, J.E. (1994) *Cognitive Therapy for Personality Disorders: A Schema Based Approach* (2nd edn), Sarasota, FL: Professional Resource Press.

Young, W.C., Goy, R.W. and Phoenix, C.H. (1964) 'Hormones and sexual behaviour', *Science*, 143, pp.212-8.

Zahavi, A. (1979) 'Ritualisation and the evolution of movement signals', *Behaviour*, 72, pp.77-81.

Zahavi, A. (1991) 'On the definition of sexual selection, Fisher's model and the evolution of waste and of signals in general', *Animal Behaviour*, 42 (3), pp.501-3.

Zaidel, D.W. (1999) 'Regional differentiation of neuron morphology in human left and right hippocampus: comparing normal to schizophrenia', *International Journal of Psychophysiology*, 34 (3), pp.187-96.

Zajonc, R.B. (1984) 'On the primacy of affect', *American Psychologist*, 39, pp.117-23.

Zar, J.H. (1972) 'Significance testing of the Spearman Rank Correlation Coefficient', *Journal of the American Statistical Association*, 67, pp.578-80.

Zhang, Y., Proenca, R., Maffei, M., Barone, M., Leopold, L. and Friedman, J.M. (1994) 'Positional cloning of the mouse gene and its human homologue', *Nature*, 372, pp.425-32.

Zihl, J., von Cramon, D. and Mai, N. (1983) 'Selective disturbance of movement vision after bilateral posterior damage', *Brain*, 106, pp.313-40.

Zimbardo, P.G. (1969/1970) 'The human choice: individuation, reason and order versus deindividuation, impulse and chaos', in W.J. Arnold and D. Levine (eds) *Nebraska Symposium on Motivation*, Vol. 17, Lincoln, Nebraska: University of Nebraska Press.

Zimbardo, P.G., Banks, P.G., Haney, C. and Jaffe, D. (1973) 'Pirandellian prison: the mind is a formidable jailor', *New York Times Magazine*, 8 April, pp.38–60.

Zimbardo, P.G., McDermott, M., Janz, J. and Metaal, N. (1995) *Psychology: A European Text*, London: HarperCollins.

Zohar, J., Judge, R. and the OCD paroxetine study investigators (1996) 'Paroxetine vs. clomipremine in the treatment of obsessive-compulsive disorder', *British Journal of Psychiatry*, 169, pp.468-74.

Zucker, I., Boshes, M. and Dark, J.S. (1983) 'Suprachiasmatic nuclei influence circannual and circadian rhythms of ground squirrels', *American Journal of Physiology*, 244, pp.R472-80.

Zuckerman, M. (1994) *Behavioral Expressions and Biosocial Bases of Sensation Seeking*, Cambridge: Cambridge University Press.

Zuckerman, M., Ulrich, R.S. and McLaughlin, J. (1993) 'Sensation seeking and reactions to nature paintings', *Personality and Individual Differences*, 15, pp.563-76.

Zung, W.W.K. (1965) 'A self-rating depression scale', *Archives of General Psychiatry*, 12, pp.63-70.

Hopi, ideas of time 521
horizon ratio 497
horizontal cells 489
hormone release 405, 410
hormone replacement therapy 768
hormones 414, 879
  abnormality 128
  and gender 603, 816
  role in depression 768, 769
  stress 79, 83
Horne, Jim 413–14, 415, 416
hostility 96
Howell, E. 706, 710
Hubel, D.H. 477, 478, 493–4, 870
Huesmann, L.R. 340, 368, 369, 371
Hughes, 527, 554, 555
Hull, C.L. 442–3, 854, 855
human rights 801
humanistic approach 858–9
  cultural bias 856
  free will and determinism in 855–6
Humphreys, Paul 304, 726, 744, 746
hunger 430–2, 438–9
Hunt, 418, 523–4, 896
hunter-gatherers 706, 720, 722
hunting 658–9
Huntington's chorea 783
Huntington's disease 709
Huston, T.L. 364, 365, 366, 834
hydrophobia 777
hyperactivity 299, 793, 794
hypercomplex cells 478, 494
hyperglycaemic coma 431
hypericum 792
hypertension 82
hypnosis 740, 741
hypnotic regression 808
hypothalamic-autonomic nervous system-adrenal medulla pathway 79
hypothalamic-pituitary-adrenal cortex (HPAC) 9, 768
hypothalamus 79, 144–5, 380, 384, 405, 406, 435, 878
  and feeding centres 430–4, 439
  role in emotional expression 445–6
hypotheses 215, 216–17, 905–6
hypothesis testing 479, 499, 863, 892, 895
hypovolemic thirst 433–4

I

iatrogenic disorders 726, 727, 737, 740–1
ICD (International Classification of Diseases) 727, 728, 823
  ICD-10 729, 730, 754
iconic memory 5

id 130, 588, 589, 590, 886, 887
ideal mental health 119
identification 156, 589
identity,
  development in adolescence 606–8, 610, 611–12, 613
  formation and roles 823
  homosexual 329
  negative 606
  versus intimacy 627
identity confusion 606, 608, 610, 621
identity statuses 607–10
illusions, visual 498, 499, 501, 502–4, 511–12
illusory correlations 288
imitation 525, 532, 592, 665
immediate digit span 5
immigrants, and stress 823
immune system 77, 82–3, 85–6, 415, 704
immunosuppression 83
implosion therapy 799
imposed etic 824, 885
impression management 280, 332
imprinting 54
impulses, obsessional 783
inclusive fitness 651, 701, 713, 883
independence 156, 358, 581
  in adolescence 605, 610, 611, 612, 613
independent groups design 215, 219–20, 221
independent variable 196
indigenous psychology 328, 744, 824
indirect reinforcement 597–8, 869, 891
individual differences 326
  in achievement attribution 277
  in adaptation to retirement 638
  attachment 46–51
  biological rhythms 407, 408
  in brain lateralization 397
  in cognitive development 562
  conformity 161
  ethical issues in 832
  in learning 560, 564
  locus of control 108–9
  and mental disorders 788–813
  obedience to authority 180
  personality 588
  stress response 95–9
individualistic cultures 163, 278, 280, 315, 318, 319, 325, 327, 560
  adolescents in 613–14
  bias to 821
  and free will 851, 856
  love in 630
  and moral development 576, 581

and pro-social behaviour 353, 358–9
individuation 605, 610
induced altruism 653, 654
infanticide 712
infants,
  defensive responses 832
  face recognition 552
  perceptual development 506–11
  pleasure principle 588
  Strange Situation 824
  vision 506–11
  see also neonates
infection 128
inferential statistics 912, 916–24
inferiority 807
informational social influence 154, 157, 355
information overload hypothesis (Milgram) 360, 361
information-processing,
  bottom-up/top-down 478, 487, 495, 496
  in dreams 402
  models 894
  schemas in 472
  stereotyping and social 289
  visual 487, 490–4
information-processing approach 519
  to attention 457–8
  to perception 495–500
  to problem-solving 540–1, 542
informed consent 181, 182, 730–1, 797, 827–8, 829–30, 902
infradian rhythms 404–5, 406, 879
in-group 166
  favouritism 294, 295, 333, 361
  schemas 601
in-group out-group behaviour 278, 283, 343
  realistic conflict theory 293–4
inheritance 646, 650
inhibition 354, 657
innate factors, and environmental factors see nature–nurture debate
inner speech 525, 559, 560, 804
insight 538, 539, 540, 542, 794, 808, 830
insight therapies 806
insomnia, fatal familial 415
instinct, and learning 868–70
instinctive drift 663
institutional care 62–3
institutional review boards (IRBs) 829
institutionalization 314
insulin 430, 431, 880
integration 580, 613
intellect, structure of the 552–3, 557

intelligence 550, 566, 639, 647, 701
  in animals 646, 667–70
  and brain size 717–20, 864
  crystallized 619, 639
  cultural factors in 569–71
  development of measured 566–72
  ecological theories 720–1
  evolution of 570, 700, 717–22
  fluid 619, 639
  (IGF2R) gene 568
  nature–nurture debate 567–72, 870
  polygenic 568
  practical 559
  and race 833, 834
  social theories 721–2
intelligence quotient see IQ
intelligence tests see IQ tests
intelligent perception 486, 499, 894
intention 574, 575, 850
interactionist theories 535–6
interactions,
  frequency of 309, 311
  transactive 577
interdependence 280, 353, 358, 581, 613
interference 20, 22–3
intergroup bias 293–4
intergroup comparison 296
intergroup conflict 270, 293–4
internal validity 170, 175, 216, 227, 830, 864, 893
internal working model 51
internalization 156, 157
International Classification of Diseases (ICD) 727, 728, 823
  ICD-10 729, 730, 754
Internet relationships 330–4
interpersonal attraction 306, 309–11
  economic theories 823
interquartile range 238, 912
inter-rater reliability 729
interval scales 913
interviewer bias 885
interviews 202, 209–11, 888, 889
  data analysis 234
  design 223–4
intimacy 321, 322, 330, 606, 622, 627
  versus isolation 621, 630
introvert/extrovert 593
invariant information (perception) 497–8
invasive methods of brain study 375, 378–80, 880–1
investigator effects 216, 229
investment model of relationships 314
in vitro techniques 299, 800
in vivo techniques 799, 800
involuntary relationships 326–7, 328